A Global History of Architecture

# A Global History of Architecture™

Francis D. K. Ching
Mark M. Jarzombek
Vikramaditya Prakash

BICENTENNIAL 1807 WILEY 2007 BICENTENNIAL
John Wiley & Sons, Inc.

This book is printed on acid-free paper. ♾



Published by John Wiley & Sons, Inc., Hoboken, New Jersey
Published simultaneously in Canada



Library of Congress Cataloging-in-Publication Data:

Ching, Frank, 1943-
A global history of architecture / Francis D. K. Ching, Mark Jarzombek, Vikramaditya Prakash.
p. cm.
Includes bibliographical references and index.
ISBN 13: 978-0-471-26892-5
ISBN 10: 0-471-26892-5 (cloth)
1. Architecture--History. I. Jarzombek, Mark. II. Prakash, Vikramaditya. III. Title.
NA200.C493 2006
720.9--dc22

2005034527

Printed in the United States of America

10 9 8 7 6 5 4 3 2 1

# Contents

## CONTENTS

**CONTENTS**

## CONTENTS

# Preface

What is a global history of architecture? There is, of course, no single answer, just as there is no single way to define words like "global," "history," and "architecture." Nonetheless, these words are not completely openended, and they serve here as the vectors that have helped us construct the narratives of this book. In the end, with this book, we hope to provoke discussion about these terms and, at the same time, furnish a framework a student can use to begin discussion in the classroom.

Geographically, this book is global in that it aspires to represent the history of the whole globe, and not just a part of it. Whereas any book like this must inevitably be selective about what it can and cannot include, we have attempted to represent a wide swath of the globe, in all its diversity. At the same time, for us, the global is not just a geographic construct that can be simply contrasted with the regional or local. The global is also a function of the human imagination, and one of the things we are very interested in is the manner in which local histories imagine the world. This book, however, is not about the sum of all local histories. Its mission is bound to the discipline of architecture, which requires us to see connections, tensions, and associations that transcend so-called local perspectives. Needless to say, our narrative is only one of many possible narratives in that respect.

For us, synchrony has served as a powerful frame for our discussion. Thus, for instance, as much as Seoul's Kyongbokgung Palace is today heralded in Korea as an example of traditional Korean architecture, we note that it also belongs to a Eurasian building campaign that stretched from Japan (Katsura Imperial Villa), through China (Beijing and the Ming Tombs), to Persia (Isfahan), India (Taj Mahal), Turkey (Suleymaniye Complex), Italy (St. Peter's Basilica and Villa Rotonda), Spain (Escorial), France (Chambord), and Russia (Cathedral of the Intercession of the Virgin on a Moat). The synchrony of these buildings opens up for us questions such as: What did one person know about the other? How did information travel? How did architectural culture move or become, one can say, translated? Some of these questions, we have addressed directly, others we have raised and left unanswered. But to call Kyongbokgung Palace "traditional" is to overlook the extraordinary modernity of all the buildings listed above.

This is not to say that our story is only the story of influence and connection. There are numerous examples of architectural production where the specific circumstances of their making were overwhelmingly singular and unique to their own immediate context. Indeed, we have tried to be faithful to the specificities of each individual building as far as possible. At the same time, it has been important for us to remember that every specific architectural project is always embedded in a larger world that affects it directly or indirectly. These effects could be a consequence of the forces of economy, trade, and syncretism; of war, conquest, and colonization; or the exchange of knowledge, whether forced, borrowed, or bought.

Our post-19th century penchant to see history through the lense of the nation-state often makes it difficult to decipher such global pictures. Furthermore, in the face of today's increasingly hegemonic global economy, the tendency by historians, and often enough by architects, to nationalize, localize, regionalize, and even microregionalize history—perhaps as meaningful acts of resistance—can blind us to the historical interconnectivity of global realities. What would the Turks be today had they stayed in east Asia? The movement of people, ideas, and wealth has bound us to each other since the beginning of history. And so, without denying the reality of nation-states and their claims to unique histories and identities, we have resisted the temptation to streamline our narratives to fit nationalistic guidelines. Indian architecture, for instance, may have some recognizable traits from the beginning to the present day, but there is less certainty about what those traits might be than one may think. The flow of Indian Buddhism to China, the settling of Mongolians in the north, the influx of Islam from the east, and the colonization by the English from the coast, not to mention India's then current economic expansion, are just some of the more obvious links that bind India, for better or worse, to global events. It is as much these links, and the resultant architecture, as the Indianness of Indian architecture that interests us in this book. Furthermore, it is important to remember that India has historically been divided into numerous kingdoms that, like Europe, could easily have, and in some cases have, evolved into their own nations. The 10th-century Chola Dynasty of peninsular India, for example, was not only an empire but it possessed a unique world view of its own. In writing their history, we have attempted to preserve their distinct identity, while marking the ways in which they map their own global imagination.

## PREFACE

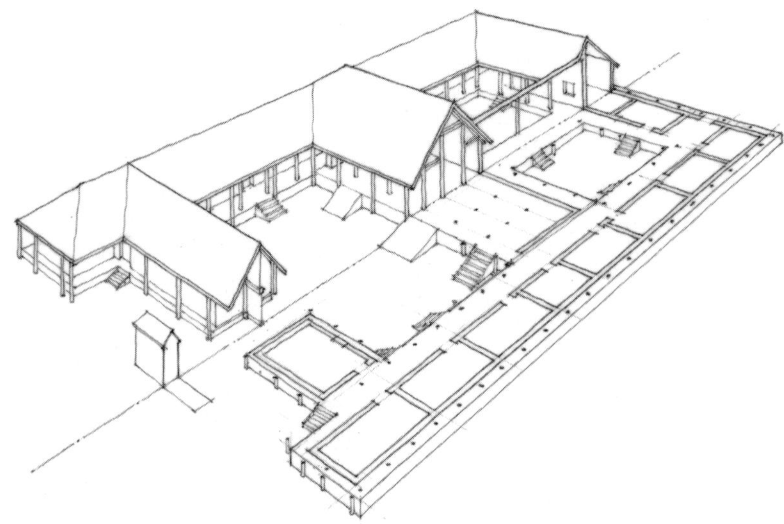

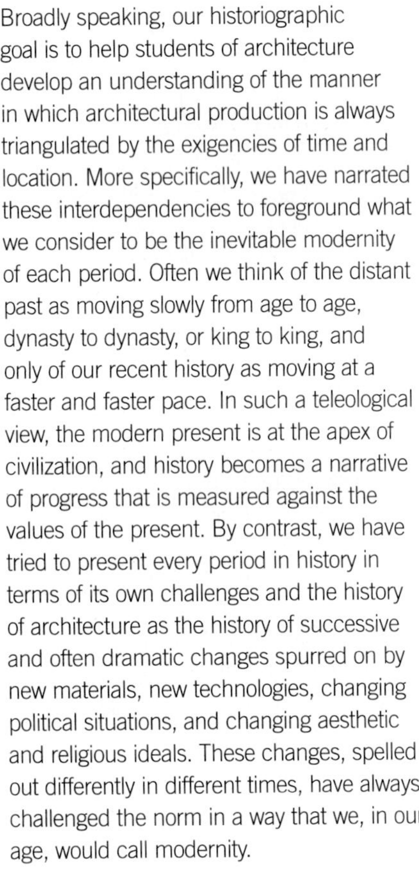

Broadly speaking, our historiographic goal is to help students of architecture develop an understanding of the manner in which architectural production is always triangulated by the exigencies of time and location. More specifically, we have narrated these interdependencies to foreground what we consider to be the inevitable modernity of each period. Often we think of the distant past as moving slowly from age to age, dynasty to dynasty, or king to king, and only of our recent history as moving at a faster and faster pace. In such a teleological view, the modern present is at the apex of civilization, and history becomes a narrative of progress that is measured against the values of the present. By contrast, we have tried to present every period in history in terms of its own challenges and the history of architecture as the history of successive and often dramatic changes spurred on by new materials, new technologies, changing political situations, and changing aesthetic and religious ideals. These changes, spelled out differently in different times, have always challenged the norm in a way that we, in our age, would call modernity.

The Sumerian urbanization of the Euphrates delta made the earlier village-centered economy of the Zargos Mountains obsolete. The introduction of iron in the 9th century BCE spelled the demise of the Egyptians and allowed societies, such as the Dorians, Etruscans, and Nubians, who were once relatively marginal in the global perspective, to suddenly dominate the cultural and architectural landscape. The Mongolian invasion of the 13th century may have destroyed much, but in its wake came unprecedented developments. By concentrating on the modernity of each historical example, we have, to put it in different terms, used the global perspective to foreground the drama of historical change rather than see architecture as driven by traditions and essences.

Turning now to the term "architecture," few would probably have any difficulty in differentiating it from the other arts, like painting and sculpture, but what architecture itself constitutes is always the subject of great debate, particularly among architects, architectural historians, and critics. Some have argued that architecture arises out of an urge to protect oneself from the elements, others that it is an expression of symbolic desires, or that it is at its best only when it is embedded in local traditions. In this book, without foreclosing the discussion, we hope that the reader begins to see architecture as a type of cultural production.

We have emphasized issues of patronage, use, meaning, and symbolism, where appropriate, and have attempted to paint a broad civilizational picture of the time and context while, at the same time, making sure we have covered the salient formal features of a structure.

Of course, words like culture and civilization are, like the word architecture, open to contestation and will have different meanings in different contexts. And yet, despite this ambiguity, we believe that civilization is unthinkable without those buildings that are given special status, whether for purposes of religion, governance, industry, or living. Just like the processes of agricultural and animal domestication, architecture emerged in our prehistory and will remain an integral part of human expression to the very end.

We should also note that by and large we have only dealt with large or significant symbolic monuments, the traditional objects of academic scrutiny. We have not, in other words, painted a picture of the historical development of vernacular and other nonmonumental architecture, such as the domestic space. This is not because we do not recognize the importance of the latter but simply because we have used the category of monumental architecture as one of the constraints by which we have delimited the boundaries of this book.

| |
|---|
| **3500 BCE** |
| **2500 BCE** |
| **1500 BCE** |
| **800 BCE** |
| **400 BCE** |
| **0** |
| **200 CE** |
| **400 CE** |
| **600 CE** |
| **800 CE** |
| **1000** |
| **1200** |
| **1400** |
| **1600** |
| **1700** |
| **1800** |
| **1900** |
| **1950** |



**Organization of the Book**

Rather than preparing chapters on individual countries or regions, such as India, Japan, or France, we have organized the book by timecuts. Eighteen chronological timecuts, beginning with 3500 BCE and ending with 1950 CE, comprise the armature of the book. Each timecut marks not the beginning of a time period but roughly the middle of the period with which each chapter is concerned. The 800 CE timecut, for instance, covers the period 700 CE to 900 CE. Yet we have not been strict about the scope of a particular timecut. Whenever necessary, for purposes of coherence, we have not hesitated to include material before and after the prescribed limits of a timecut. Each timecut should, therefore, be seen more as a marker amidst the complexity of the flowing river of history rather than a strict chronological measuring rod.

800 CE

**Introduction Page**

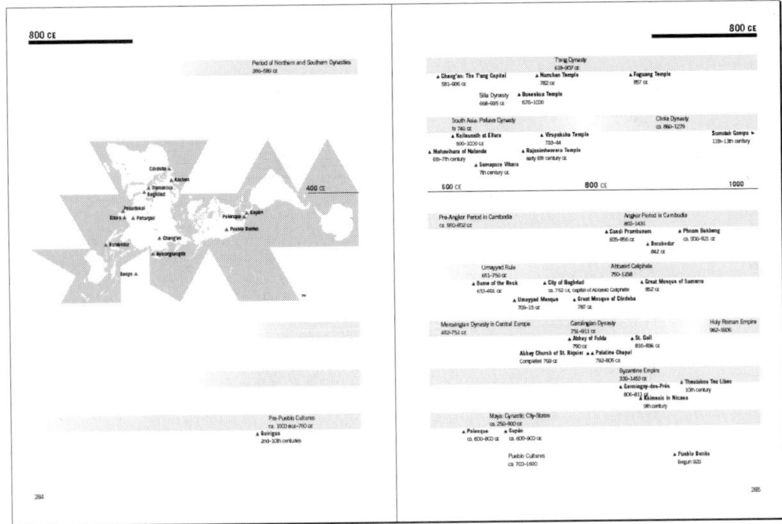


**Map / Timeline Spread**

We have begun each timecut with a one-page summary of the historical forces graphing that timecut, followed by a map and a timeline locating all of the major buildings we discuss. After that, the discussions of individual buildings and groups of buildings are in a series of small subsections marked by relevant subcontinental location, that is, east Asia, Southeast Asia, south Asia, west Asia, Europe, Africa, North America, Central America, or South America. Rather than arrange all the subsections in the same order, every timecut is organized according to its own internal order. Despite the difficulties that this may pose for ease of reading, we have chosen this strategy, at one level, to remind readers that the globe does not really begin in the east or the west but can indeed be started and ended anywhere. On the other hand, we have arranged the sequence of the subsubsections, as it makes sense to maintain continuity in the narrative of a particular chapter. Often this continuity is provided simply by geographical adjacency. At other times, however, we have linked subsections to make a point about historiographical issues, such as the influence and movement of ideas or contrasts between kingdoms.

The individual subsections, which can be just a single page or four or five pages in length, are conceived as mini case studies, coherent in themselves. These can be prescribed as independent readings. Besides ensuring that the relevant facts and descriptions of each significant project we address are adequately covered, we have emphasized the cultural and global investments of their creators. For instance a discussion of the Italian High Renaissance consists of pages on the Campidoglio, il Gesù, Villa Farnese, il Redentore, Palladian villas, and the Uffizi. The number of case studies accompanying each civilizational discussion is not uniform. Sometimes there could be six, at other times, just two or three, or even just one. The differences are largely a measure of our judgment of the importance of the material and the availability of literature on a topic.

One has to remember that there exists a great disparity of information. While we know very much about the early civilizations of Mesopotamia, what we know of Pre-Columbian civilization is startlingly little. An archaeologist that we spoke with estimated that only 15 percent of the sites have been excavated. And if we look around the world we find that there are many sites in war-torn countries, and as well there are even sites that cannot be excavated because they are seen as irrelevant to national interests. All this means that a global picture is still a dream that we can aspire to but are far from possessing.

The drawings that are on all the pages are intended to be integral to the narrative of the book. They are there not only to illustrate the text but also as entities that tell a story of their own. Not everything in the text is illustrated by drawings, just as the drawings can be used to communicate things that are not referenced in the text. We have tried to make a virtue out of this fact by roughly sharing the physical and epistemological space on a page as evenly as we could between text and image. The drawings also speak to the diminishing art of drawing in an age of photography and computationally-enhanced plans.

By its format, the book suggests that a lecture course that uses this book should be organized according to the timecuts. Since most survey courses are usually taught chronologically, this format should not pose many difficulties. Individual faculty, however, may want to emphasize certain case studies more and others less. Since all the case studies are complete miniessays, they can be prescribed as readings by themselves.

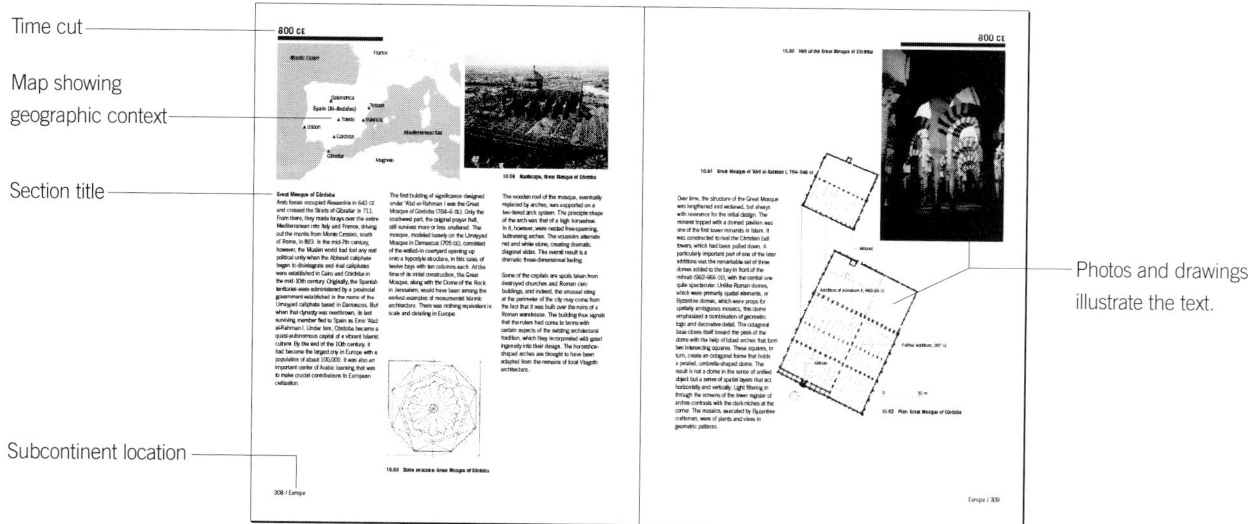


**Typical Section Spread**

Other faculty may, of course, not want to organize their syllabi by the timecuts, in which case they may find it useful to cut-and-paste selectively chosen subsections together to suit their own historical narrative. Such selections could be made geographically or by other means. Once again, the fact that the subsections are conceived as individual case studies allow them to be read coherently even out of their timecuts.

A book like this faces almost insurmountable problems in trying to establish a single standard for use of terms and spellings, particularly those of nonwestern origin. Sometimes a particular mosque, for instance, can have different English, Arabic, Persian, and Hindu names. Which one does one pick? And, then, should one say Nijo-jo or Nijo Castle (the suffix *jo* in Japanese means castle)? Should one call a pagoda a *ta*, as it is called in Chinese, or should we persist with its conventional English name? Generally speaking, we have tried to use the names that are most commonly used in current scholarship in English.

It would be foolish to dispense with the Greek word for those Egyptian buildings that we call pyramids, named after the Greek bread called *pyramidos*, but we would like to suggest that Angkor Wat be called by its real name Vrah Vishnulok, to cite one example. Once we have made a choice regarding the spelling of a particular proper noun, we have tried to remain consistent in our use of it. However, at several places, we have intentionally used non-English terms, even when the word is in common English usage. This we have done whenever we have felt that the English translation is misleading (the English pagoda, for instance, has nothing to do with the *ta*) or when a local linguistic discussion helps make an illuminating etymological explanation. Our aspiration is to make some small beginning toward forming a more diverse and appropriate vocabulary for the world's architecture. Language, like architecture, is a living thing with distinct yet blurry edges. It is, as such, a fascinating but somewhat messy and open-ended reminder of architecture's status as a multifaceted cultural signifier. We hope that the reader will get a sense of, and enjoy, the complex multilingual reality of architecture.

In conclusion, we would like to admit that in preparing and writing this book, a process that we have enjoyed at every turn, we were continually reminded of our ignorance on many matters. Conversations with colleagues were particularly valuable, as were the trips to some of the sites we covered; but, in the end, a work like this can only be the beginning of a long process of refinement. And so we ask all readers who wish to do so to contact us, to point out inaccuracies, to tell us about things that should be included in subsequent editions, or to open a conversation, even at the most fundamental level, about history, the world, and our place within it.

## ACKNOWLEDGEMENTS

A work on this scale could not have been done without the help, support, and good will of a very large number of people. Many students and colleagues worked on elements of the text and are to be especially noted: Jeremy Gates and Tim Morshead (1200); Fabia Cigni, Tom Dietz, and Svea Heinemann (1950); Nikki Moore (Buckminster Fuller); Mechtild Widrich (Gothic architecture); Tijana Vujosevic (Russian architecture); Luis Berrios-Negron (Caribbean modernism); Shuishan Yu and Ying Zhou (Chinese architecture); Diana Kurkovsky and Ashish Nangia (Le Corbusier); Michelangelo Sabatino (Italian Fascism); Alexander Tulinsky (Japanese architecture); M. Ijlal Muzaffar (Modernism); Robert Cowherd (Colonial Indonesia); Lenore Hietkamp (Khmer architecture); Kokila Lochan (Indian architecture); Alona Nitzan-Shiftan (Israeli modernism); Cynthia Bogel (Japanese architecture); and Kang Young Hwan (Korean architecture). Additionally, Alexander Tulinsky, Kokila Lochan, Jan Haag, Ashish Nangia, Kim Bahnsen, and Paula Patterson helped with the research and editing of various sections of the text. Innumerable students at MIT and University of Washington suffered through lectures and seminars on topics in global history and offered their sage advice and student papers in help.

Profound gratitude is due to our friends and colleagues who gave us valuable advice and wise counsel and corrected many of our mistakes. Many prompted us to rethink our positions. These include: Nasser Rabbat, Erika Naginski, Stanford Anderson, David Friedman, Anthony Vidler, Arindam Dutta, Gail Fenske, Maha Yahya, Sibel Bozdogan, Alfred B. Hwangbo, Jonghun Kim, Hadas Steiner, Annie Pedret, Jorge Otero-Pailos, Reinhold Martin, Franz Oswald, Brian McLaren, Kyoko Tokuno, Patricia Ebrey, Vince Rafael, Kent Guy, Clark Sorensen, Rick Meyer, Michael Duckworth, Jeffrey Ochsner, Trina Deines, Ken Tadashi Oshima, Kathryn Merlino, Sergio Palleroni, and Alex Anderson.

A long list of colleagues contributed images to this text and are acknowledged on page 779. Of these, some were generous enough to contribute multiple images: Stanford Anderson, David Friedman, Maha Yaha, John Lopez, Larry Vail, Nasser Rabbat, Eric Jenkins, Sibel Bozdogan, Walter Denny, David Aasen Sandved, Kang Young Hwan, Jerry Finrow, Bonnie MacDougall, Norman Johnston, Jeff Cohen, and Mark Brack. Generous image contributions to the text were made by the College of Architecture and Urban Planning's Visual Resources Collection at the University of Washington; the Rotch Slide Library and the Aga Khan Program for Islamic Architecture at MIT; and the R. D. MacDougall Collection in the Knight Visual Resources Facility at Cornell University.

Special thanks are due to Anne Deveau and Melissa Bachman, who served as administrative assistants in the History, Theory and Criticism section at MIT, as well as the librarians, Merrill Smith and Michael Leininger, at MIT's Rotch Library of Architecture and Planning. At the University of Washington, Y. Nancy Shoji, Karen Helland, Diane Stuart, Caroline Orr, Rachel Ward, Eric Gould, and Shanna Sukol provided excellent staff support, and Heather Seneff, Director of CAUP's Visual Resources Collection, made available the slides in her collection. Support of various kinds was kindly provided by Dean Adèle Naudé Santos at MIT, Stanford Anderson, former chair of the Department of Architecture at MIT, and Dean Robert Mugerauer and Associate Dean Doug Zuberbuhler at the University of Washington.

We would like to especially extend our appreciation to the Graham Foundation for Advanced Studies in the Fine Arts for their financial support of this project.

For their review of early drafts of the text, we would like to thank: Richard Cleary, University of Texas at Austin; Dr. Roger T. Dunn, Bridgewater State College; Clifton Ellis, Texas Tech University; Mark Gelernter, University of Colorado at Denver; William J. Glover, University of Michigan; Kathleen James-Chakraborty, University of California at Berkeley; Edward D. Levinson, Miami-Dade Community College; Taisto Makela, University of Colorado at Denver; Anne Marshall, University of Idaho; Gerald Walker, Clemson University; and Janet White, University of Nevada at Las Vegas.

We would like to thank our publisher, John Wiley and Sons, Inc., and in particular, Amanda Miller, Paul Drougas, Lauren LaFrance, and David Sassian, who worked tirelessly with the itinerant authors.

Finally, we would like to thank our families, Nancy, Andreas, and Elias, and Henry and Marianne Jarzombek; Leah, Saher, and Savitri and Aditya Prakash; and Debra, Emily, and Andrew, for simply bearing with us.

**C1 Temple of Luxor, Karnak, Egypt, began 1400 BCE**

C2 The Parthenon, Athens, Greece, 447–438 BCE

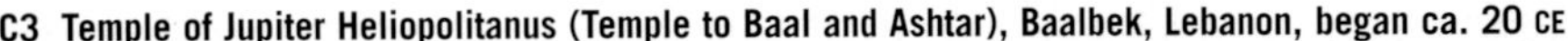

C3 Temple of Jupiter Heliopolitanus (Temple to Baal and Ashtar), Baalbek, Lebanon, began ca. 20 CE

C4 Teotihuacán, near Mexico City, Mexico 150 BCE–150 CE

C5 Alahan Monastery, Alahan, Turkey, 5th and 6th century CE

C6 Hagia Sofia, Istanbul, Turkey, 532–537 CE; Anthemius of Tralles and Isidore of Miletus

C7 Dome of the Rock, Jerusalem, completed 692 CE

**C8 Khandariya Mahadeva Temple, Khajuraho, India, 1000–25 CE**

**C9 Gloucester Cathedral, Gloucester, England, 1089–1100 CE**

C10 Vishnulok (Angkor Wat), Siem Reap, Cambodia, 12th century CE

C11 Chichén Itzá, Yucatan Peninsula, Mexico, 7th–13th century CE

C12 Notre Dame de Paris (Church of Our Lady of Paris), Paris, France, 1163–1285 CE

C13 Kinkakuji (Golden Pavilion), Kyoto, Japan, 1394 CE (rebuilt 1955 CE)

C14 Hall of Prayer for a Prosperous Year, Temple of Heaven complex, Beijing, China, 1420s CE

C15 Cathedral of Florence (Il Duomo), Florence, Italy, 1294–1436 CE, Arnolfo di Cambio; Dome, 1420–1434 CE, Filippo Brunelleschi; Lantern, 1446–1461 CE, Filippo Brunelleschi

C16 Machu Picchu, Peru, 1460–1470 CE

C17 Diwan-i-Khas, Fatehpur Sikri, India, 1571–1575 CE

C18 Himeji Castle, Himeji, Japan, originally built 1346 CE, redesigned 1581 CE, rebuilt and enlarged in 1601–1609 CE

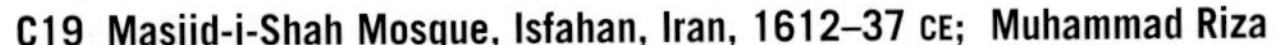

C19 Masjid-i-Shah Mosque, Isfahan, Iran, 1612–37 CE; Muhammad Riza

C20 Rauza-I-Munavvara (Taj Mahal), Agra, India, 1630 to 1653 CE

C21 Sant'Andrea al Quirinale, Rome, Italy, 1658–1665 CE; Giovanni Lorenzo Bernini

C22 Neresheim Abbey, Neresheim, Germany, 1747–1792 CE; Balthasar Neumann

C23 Grand Palace, Bangkok, Thailand, began 1782 CE

C24 Royal Pavilion, Brighton, England,1818–1822 CE; John Nash

C25 Oxford University Museum of Natural History, Oxford, England, 1853 CE; Benjamin Woodward

C26 German Pavilion, Barcelona, Spain, 1928–1929 CE (rebuilt 1986 CE); Mies van Der Rohe

C27 Fallingwater, Ohiopyle (Bear Run), Pennsylvania, USA, 1936–1939 CE; Frank Lloyd Wright

C28 Assembly Building, Chandigarh, India, 1953–1963 CE; Le Corbusier

C29 Centre Pompidou, Paris, France, 1972–1976 CE; Richard Rogers and Renzo Piano

C30 Walt Disney Concert Hall, Los Angeles, California, USA, 1999–2004 CE; Frank Gehry

C31 Terminal 4, Madrid Barajas Airport, Madrid, Spain, 2006 CE; Richard Rogers Partnership

# Early Cultures

In a slow but relentless process, humans by 12,000 BCE had distributed themselves over much of the globe, from Africa, Spain, West Asia, to the southern tip of South America. What one would have found, generally, was a society of hamlets with settlements near caves or along shores and streams, allowing for a combination of farming and hunting. The domestication of animals and plants, a slow and gradual process, required not only an understanding of the seasons but also ways to hand down that knowledge generation to generation. And it is in that same spirit that the building arts and its more specialized uses for religious and communal purposes began to develop and to play an increasingly important role. Whether it was using mud for bricks, reeds for thatch, bitumen as a coating, stone as foundations, or wood as post and beams, specialized tools and social specialization were essential. But the results were by no means uniform. Some societies were more pragmatic than others, some more symbolic. Some emphasized granaries, others temples. For some, the specialized crafts associated with building were controlled by the elite. In other places, the building arts found more common expression. It is thus a mistake to divide the history of architecture into prehistory and history, with writing serving as the traditional dividing point in that distinction. It is wrong to see the Stone Age as primitive or as a unified historical moment. Architecture, like civilization itself, was born in our prehistory, much as the other arts, and was plural from the beginning.

Paleolithic humans create animal paintings on the walls and ceilings of numerous cave sites, such as at Lascaux and Chauvet, in present-day southwestern France and northern Spain. 30,000–10,000 BCE

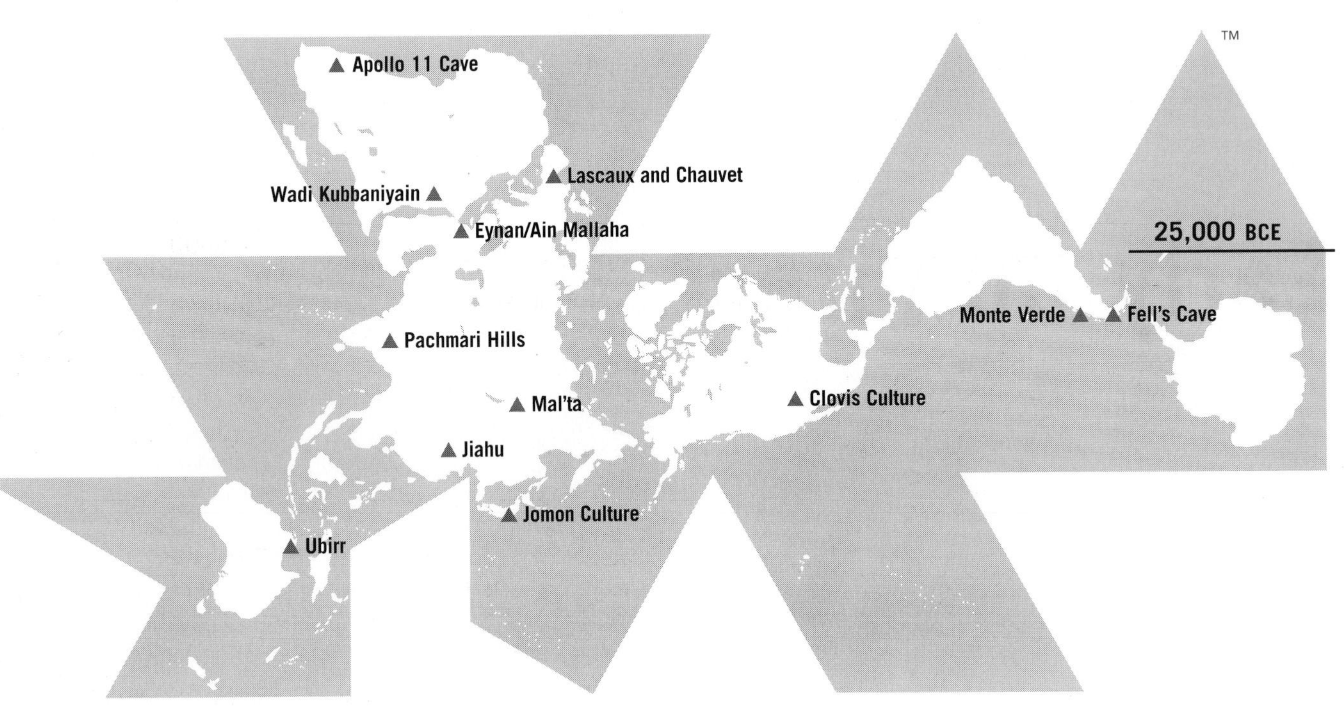


Aboriginal rock painting represents the longest continuously practiced artistic tradition in the world. The rock faces at Ubirr have been painted and repainted for millennia. ca. 40,000 BCE–present

Apollo 11 cavestones are among the oldest known artwork in the African continent. 25,500–23,500 BCE

Mal'ta cultural tradition thrives in north and central Asia. Sites consist of a series of subterranean houses containing carved bone, ivory, and antler objects. ca. 20,000 BCE

Late paleolithic camps are established at Wadi Kubbaniyain, in what is now upper Egypt. Sites show evidence of tools for hunting, fishing, and collecting and processing plants. ca. 17,000–15,000 BCE

First permanent settlements in the Near East cultivate cereals. Rich artistic tradition exists in Eynan and Ain Mallaha in the Levant. ca. 10,000–8200 BCE

▲ Walled town of Jericho is founded. ca. 8300 BCE

Pottery and woolen textiles are made in Catal Hüyük. ca. 6000 BCE

Experimentation with copper ores begins in Anatolia. ca. 7000 BCE

**15,000 BCE** — **5000 BCE**

**Peak of Last Ice Age**
ca. 22,000 BCE

**Ice Age declines**
ca. 14,000 BCE

**Early Neolithic Period**
ca. 10,000–5000 BCE

Farming occurs in Greece and the Aegean ca. 7000 BCE, reaching Iberia and Britain ca. 5000 BCE and Scandinavia ca. 4000 BCE.

Jomon Culture in Japan produces examples of the earliest known pottery. ca. 10,500–8000 BCE

Sandstone rock shelters are decorated with ceiling and wall paintings in the Pachmari Hills in present-day central India. ca. 9000–3000 BCE

Jiahu is a flourishing and complex society in central China, where the earliest examples of flutes have been found. Evidence of rice cultivation also exists. ca. 7000–5700 BCE

First humans migrate to the Americas. ca. 13,000 BCE

The Clovis Culture are Paleo-Indians in Central and North America who use flint spearpoints to hunt big game. ca. 10,000–9000 BCE

Corn (maize) is cultivated in Central America. ca. 5000 BCE

The lower Pacific coast region of South America evidences human inhabitation at Monte Verde and Fell's Cave in Patagonia, a rock shelter occupied by hunters who used stone tools and spearpoints. ca. 10,500–9500 BCE

# 3500 BCE

No single narrative fits over the whole age. In some places, especially around the Mediterranean, the Stone Age mother goddess still reigned supreme; in others, as in Mesopotamia, she was beginning to be replaced by complex pantheons suitable to a more industrialized economy. In Egypt, which had to accommodate itself to rapid growth from the beginning, the mother goddess never developed as an autonomous entity at all, whereas in China, with its spread-out network of villages, the goddess cult would remain central for a long time to come. Similarly architecture was not a univalent force. Though clearly within the purview of the governing elites, some buildings were built for the dead, others for the living; some were temples, others granaries. And so, while there are many parallels between the different regions, in actuality each developed along its own pathways and with different factors determining growth and development. In this section we will discuss the primary sites in the world where, around 3500 BCE, these developments were beginning to take place.

Egyptian culture, unified around 3200 BCE and densely populated along the Nile River, developing a highly vertical social structure very early on. In the third millennium BCE, the ruling elite were able to expand their control while defining religious practices around the theme of the afterlife of the ruler. The Mesopotamian highlands, allowing agriculture in the valleys and hunting and grazing in the hills and mountains, became the site of a vast network of interconnected villages and social groups that traded with each other over large stretches of territory. Tombs and palaces were still quite rare. Instead, the villages in the Zagros Mountains, Anatolian highlands and in Lebanon became part of an interconnected society oriented to the great rivers of the Euphrates and Tigris as well as to the metal-producing regions in the mountains. Here, grain, most famously, became the principal commodity. The situation in South Asia was similar. A series of settlements developed in the hills of Baluchistan, far West of the Indus, the largest of which were located around Mehrgarh, which, however, possessed no major religious sites. China, despite the presence of equally imposing river valleys, was the least dense of these early civilizations. Its rivers did not become flashpoints for urban civilizations until the first millennium BCE. Instead, a series of villages spread across a vast tract of land were connected together by shared mortuary and goddess ritual centers that the residents traveled long distances to participate in. The Yangshao and Hongshan cultures in the north, Dawenkou and Longshan on the east coast, and Liangzhu in the south were all disaggregated but shared temples and altars.

In the Americas, the Asian people who crossed the Bering Strait into North America had found shelter in caves or temporary structures made of wood. They began placing significant burials beneath earth-and-stone mounds. Near the Great Lakes, people of the Old Copper Culture begin using copper for tools. Of all these emerging protocivilizations, the peoples along the Peruvian Pacific coast in South America seemed to thrive the most, drawing their economy directly from the sea. In the past this has been used to explain the slower development of South American cultures, but it has recently been proven that even along the coast of Peru the shift from agricultural production to sociopolitical architectural production took place on a par with Eurasia around 2500 BCE.

Europe was a loose fabric of villages and clan-dominated areas. Grain, which had been domesticated and harvested in great quantities in Mesopotamia and Egypt, did not make it to England until about 3500 BCE. European cultures also had to pay careful attention to the planting seasons, which were much shorter than in Mesopotamia and thus more precious as a commodity. Nonetheless, the relatively warmer weather than what one finds today facilitated the development of village life. The areas to the west and north of the Black Sea were known for their pottery and mining, and they were certainly trading with Mesopotamia. Though most structures in Europe were of wood, the coastal areas along the Atlantic belonged to a megalithic culture that, as in most parts of Asia, built large stone tombs. In Britain these cultures built thousands of stone circles that were used as religious sites and as places of trading.

## 3500 BCE

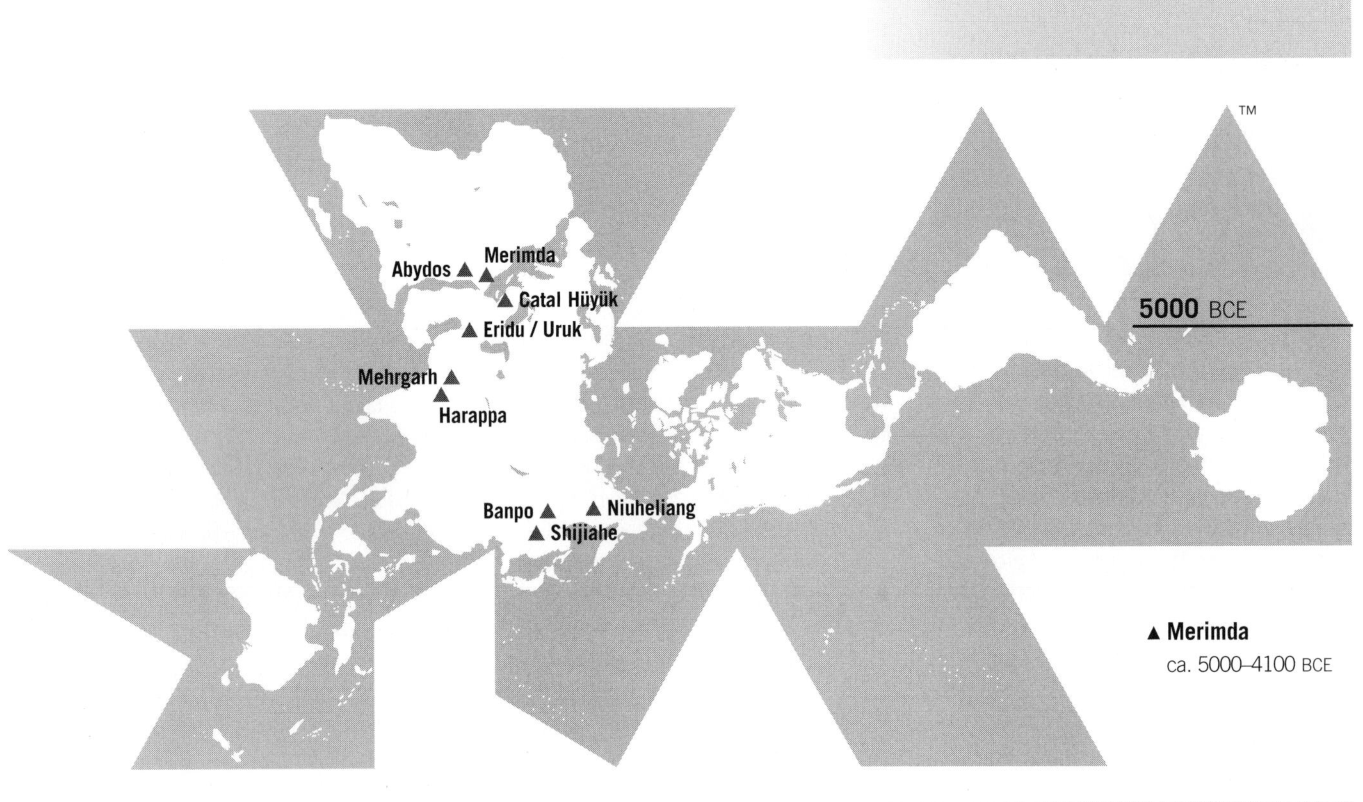


**▲ Merimda**
ca. 5000–4100 BCE

Mesopotamia: Ubaid Period
ca. 5500–4000 BCE

**▲ Eridu settled**
ca. 5000 BCE

**▲ Neolithic Village of Catal Hüyük**
flourishes ca. 6900–5400 BCE

China: Yangshao Culture
ca. 5000–1500 BCE

▲ **Banpo**
ca. 4500–3750 BCE

▲ **Niuheliang Ritual Center**
ca. 3500 BCE

▲ **Yaoshan Ritual Altar**
ca. 3300–2000 BCE

▲ **Shijiahe**
ca. 2800–2000 BCE

Indus Valley: Early Harappan Period
ca. 5000–2600 BCE

▲ **Mehrgarh**
ca. 6500–2800 BCE

**4500** BCE — **3500** BCE — **2500** BCE

**Late Neolithic Period**
ca. 5000–2000 BCE

**Early Bronze Age**
ca. 3000–2000 BCE

Egypt: Predynastic Period
ca. 4500–3100 BCE

Early Dynastic Period
ca. 3100–2649 BCE

▲ **Abydos**
ca. 4000 BCE–641 CE

▲ **Tomb of Hor Aba**
ca. 3100 BCE

▲ **Mastaba K1 at Bet Challaf**
ca. 2600 BCE

Uruk Period
ca. 4000–3100 BCE

▲ **Uruk settled**
ca. 4000 BCE

▲ **Tell es-Sawwan**
ca. 3500 BCE

▲ **Temple at Uruk**
ca. 3000 BCE

▲ **Temple at Eridu**
ca. 3000 BCE

⦿ Invention of the wheel
ca. 3600 BCE

⦿ Earliest readable documents in Mesopotamia
ca. 3200 BCE

⦿ Bronze casting begins in the Near East.
ca. 3600 BCE

Europe: Passage Tombs and Dolmens of Megaliths
ca. 3500–2500 BCE

Neolithic China centered around the fertile plains of the Yellow and Yangtze Rivers.

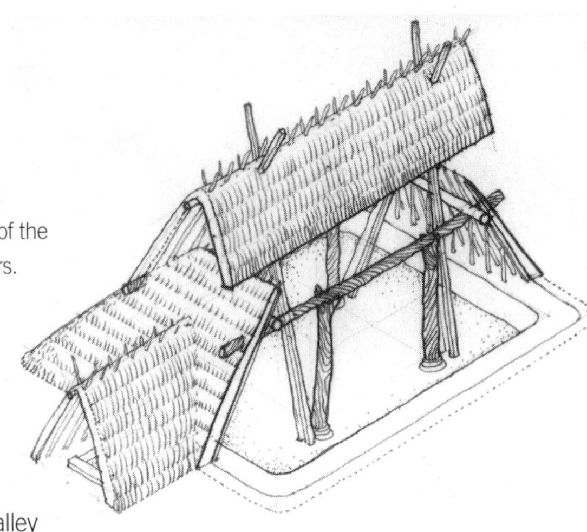

Cutaway view

**BEGINNINGS OF CHINA'S CIVILIZATIONS**

A broad outline of Chinese architectural history, compiled by Nancy Steinhardt, notes that by the 4th millennium BCE, a continuous fabric of settlements had developed from the Inner Mongolian plains in the north of China, along the Yellow River valley, down to Hangzhou Bay in the south. This more of less corresponds to the present-day provinces of Shanxi and Henan. Agriculture within and between the river valleys easily supported large populations. But because there were no compact cities, what one sees at this early phase in Chinese history is a disaggregated civilization with small towns spread over a large area. These dispersed settlements often shared a common ritual center that linked the communities by means of a shared symbolic order. Whether the religious geography coincided with the political one has not yet been clearly established, but what is known is that the right to rule was based on ancestral lineage.

Banpo, located in the Yellow River Valley (near the modern-day city of Xian) and dating from about 4500 BCE, was just one of several large, well-organized settlements. Discovered only in 1953, it was spread out over a large area of about sixty square kilometers, of which only five percent has been excavated so far. It was surrounded by a ditch or moat, five to six meters wide, probably for drainage and defense. The homes were circular mud and wood structures, with overhanging thatched roofs, all raised on shallow foundations with fire pits at the center. Entrances were ramps that sloped down into the dwelling. The dead were buried either in the back of caves, or, in the matrilineal clans, outside the village in simple pits in a communal burial area. Children, it seems, were interred in urns, just outside their homes.

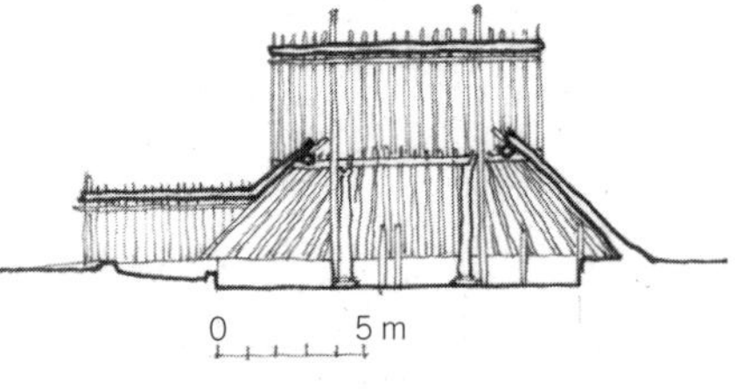


Longitudinal section

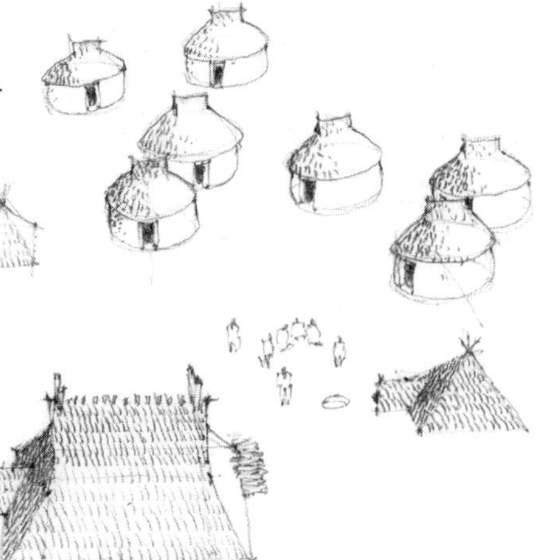

**1.1 Reconstruction of housing cluster of Banpo, Yangshao Culture**

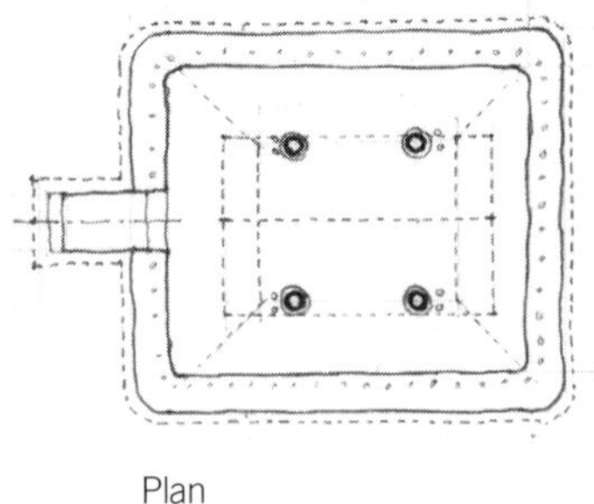

Plan

**1.2 Banpo: Reconstruction of meeting hall**

1.3 Ritual altar at Yaoshan

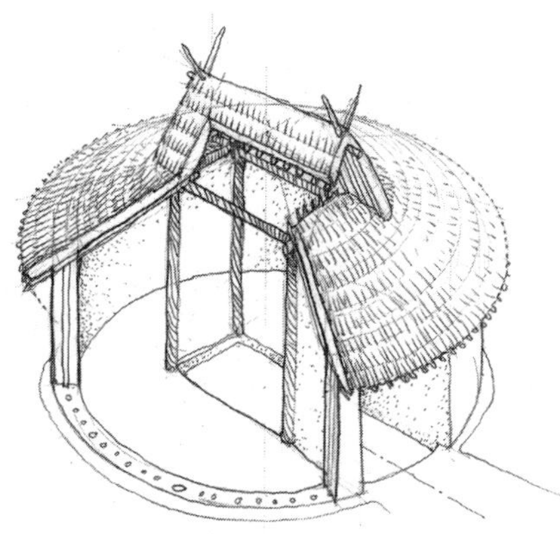

Cutaway view

On the civic scale, we find structures with large open plazas and storage holes, which are indicative of civic hierarchy and organization. One area of the village was dedicated to the production of pottery, indicating the emergence of protoindustrial specialization. One of the oldest kilns in the world can be found here.

A ritual altar at Yaoshan (ca. 3300–2000 BCE) in Zhejiang gives us some indication of religious edifices of the time. A ditch defines a sacred precinct 25 meters square, at the center of which is a platform measuring 6 by 7 meters and constructed of rammed red earth. Archaeologists found 12 graves arranged in two rows under the floor of the altar, which are presumed to have belonged to priests. We are still unsure how this platform was used, although it might have involved ancestral worship.

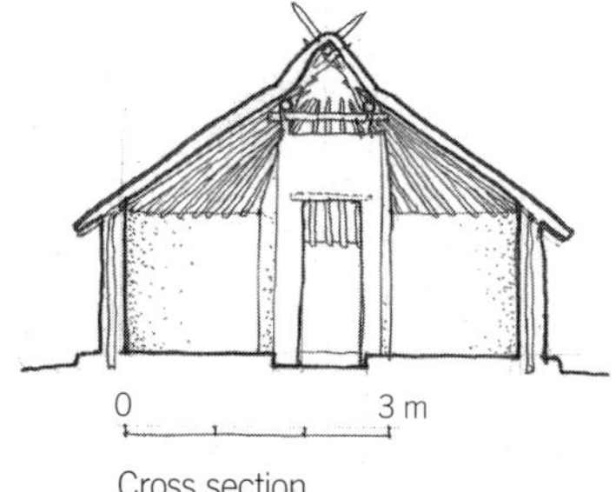


Cross section

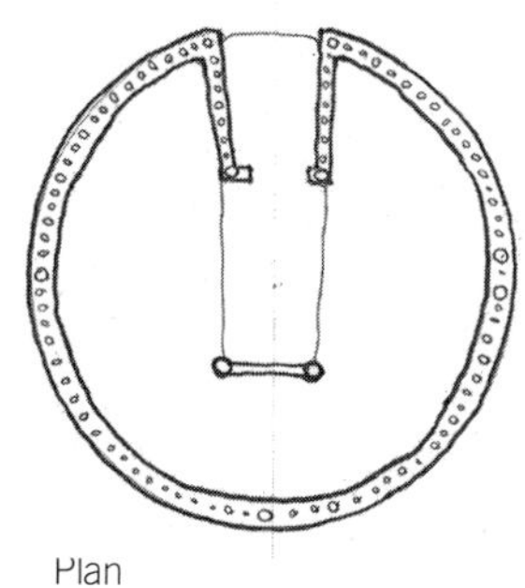

Plan

1.4 Banpo: Reconstruction of circular dwelling

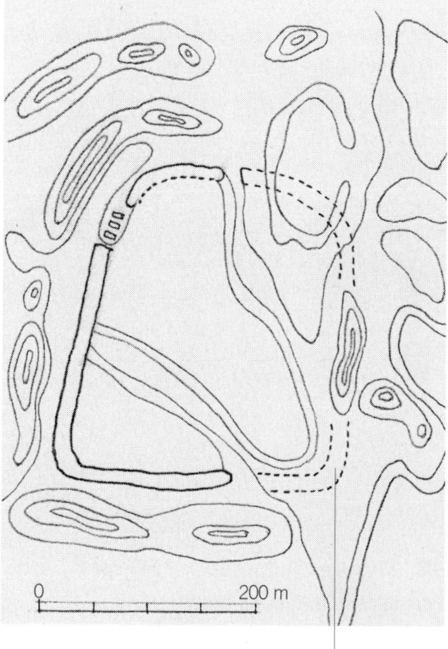


1.5 Walled city of Shijiahe

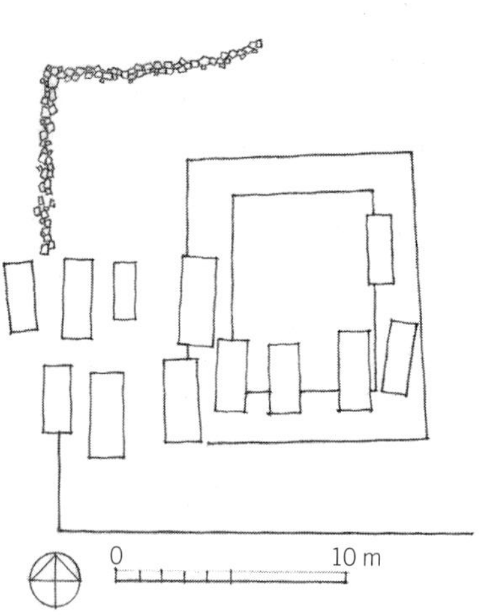


1.6 Plan: Ritual altar at Yaoshan

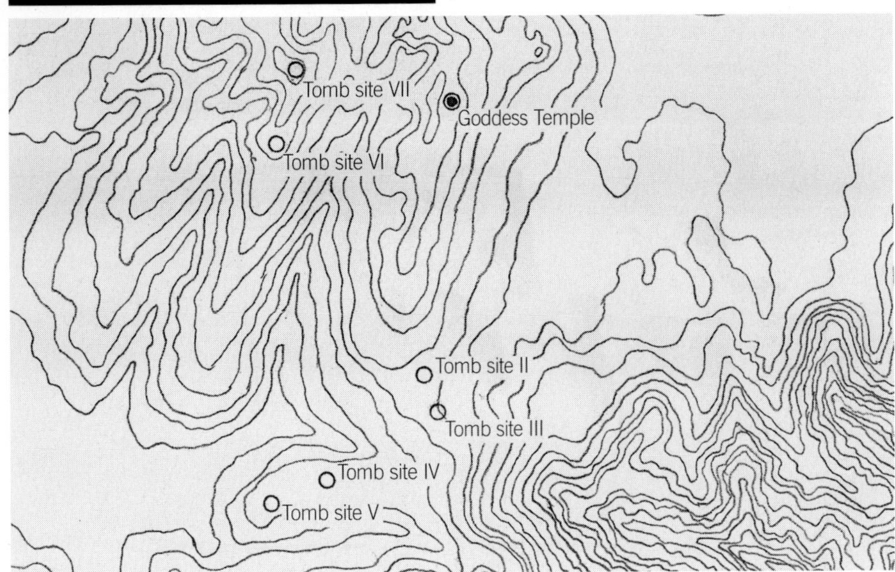


**1.7 Site of Niuheliang Ritual Center, Inner Mongolia, China**

### Niuheliang Ritual Center

Among the recent finds pertaining to early Chinese civilization are those of the Hongshan Culture of Inner Mongolia, located along the middle and upper reaches of the Laoha River and along the Yingjin River valley. Dating from around 3500 BCE, the Niuheliang Ritual Center is a large burial and ritual area consisting of 16 sites located on top of hills scattered over 50 square kilometers. More or less at the center of this area is a 40 by 60-meter loam platform on which rested a temple structure that is presumed to have been a Goddess Temple. A north-south axis connects the ritual center complex with the central peak of Zhushan, or "Pig Mountain," further to the south. The temple consisted of eight interconnected subterranean chambers and was constructed in an asymmetrical lobed shape, 25 meters from south to north and two to nine meters wide. Its footings contain elaborate geometric designs made with clay in high relief and painted yellow, red, and white. On its northern end it had a single detached room where excavations have uncovered clay body parts, including a head, torso, and arms, perhaps belonging to a goddess, from which the site got its name. There is no evidence of village settlements near Niuheliang, and yet its size is immense, much larger than one clan or village could support, suggesting that it served as a ritual center for the whole region.

One of the tombs contained high-quality jade objects and was surrounded by smaller graves that are differentiated—so it seems—by rank. All in all, this ritual center already seems to have contained some of the essential elements that would characterize later Chinese ancestor worship—burial cairns, platforms, and a ritual temple—as evidenced, for example, by the Ming tombs, built five thousand years later.

A tomb dated to about 4000 BCE was recently found in Xishuipo, Henan province. It contains a human skeleton, flanked by the outline of a dragon on one side and a tiger on the other, both painstakingly and beautifully made out of hundreds of shells. Dragons and tigers, still central to Chinese Confucian symbolism, are considered to be prospectors, both in life and death. Hill ranges, especially those with prominent peaks, are considered to be dragons. Burials, in particular imperial tombs, were placed at the base of major peaks.

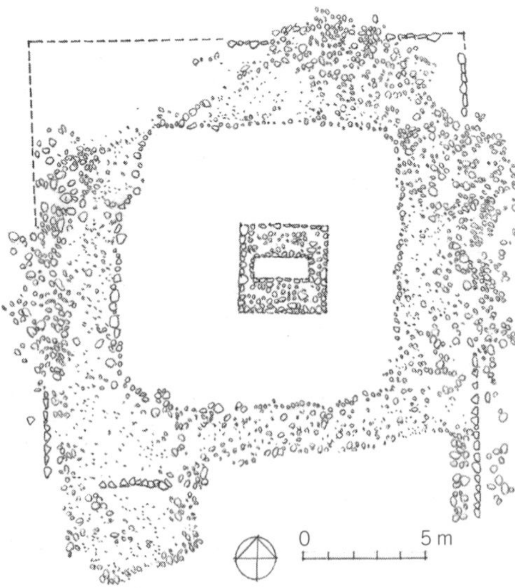


**1.8 Niuheliang Ritual Center, Tomb site II: Plan of cairn with stone tomb**

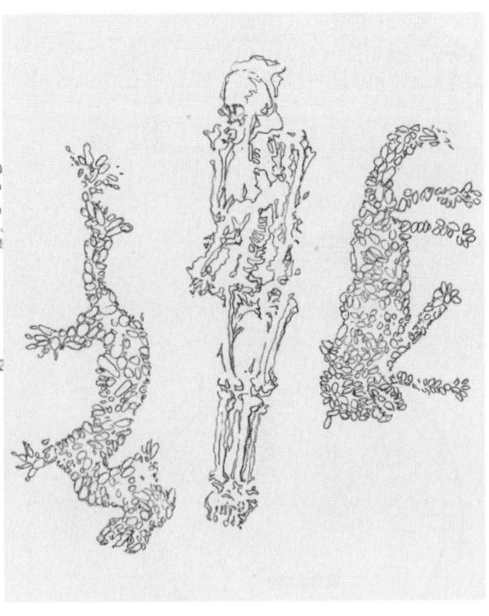

**1.9 Dragon, human, and tiger figures found in tomb at Xishuipo, Henan province**

**Location of the Indus civilizations of Mehrgarh and Harappa**

This period is characterized by the elaboration of ceramics, the beginning of copper metallurgy, stone-bead making, and seal bone carving. The beginning of writing is seen in the form of graffiti on pottery from ca. 3500 BCE.

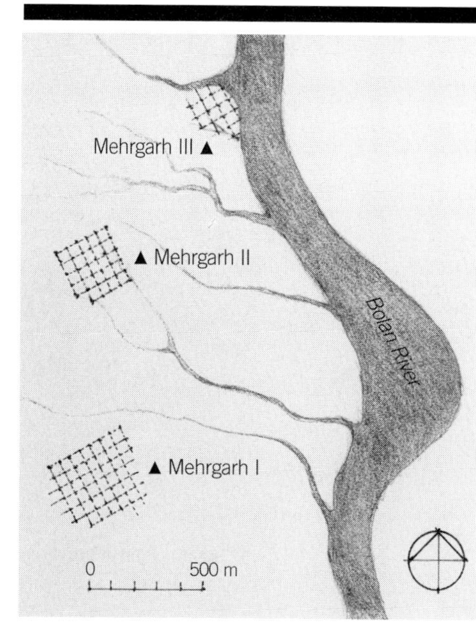


**1.10 Site plan of Mehrgarh, Pakistan**

## EARLY INDUS SETTLEMENTS

Though evidence of the Neolithic occupation of India dates back to 10,000 BCE, settled cultures begin to emerge around 7000 BCE in the eastern hills of the Baluchistan Mountains in today's Pakistan. It was a typical agropastoral environment for the age, allowing farming in the flat lands of the Indus River valley and herding and hunting in the hills and mountains. Though such a topography was similar to that in China and Mesopotamia, the differences in architectural response are pronounced. The Baluchistan cultures did not develop ritual sites, nor did they practice ancestral burial cults. This is perhaps explained by the fact that the people of the Indus Valley were among the first to develop concentrated protourban environments in which one's identity derived more from social structure and craft and less from family lineage or affiliation to a particular god or deity.

Of the numerous sites still being excavated, as Raymond Allchin has shown, the ones around contemporary Mehrgarh have emerged as the most important. This area was strategically located overlooking the Kachi Plain southeast of modern Quetta near the Bolan Pass, an important gateway connecting South Asia to the rest of the continent. One can trace its 5000-year history from a village to an important regional trading center, covering, at the peak of its development, an area of 200 hectares.

By 3500 BCE, the occupants had not only mastered extensive cultivation of grain but made it the center of their culture. Dominating the urban landscape were large mud-brick "box buildings," presumed to be granaries designed as multiroomed, rectangular structures with a long narrow corridor running more or less down the center. The absence of doors suggests that grain was fed from the top, as it would be into a silo.

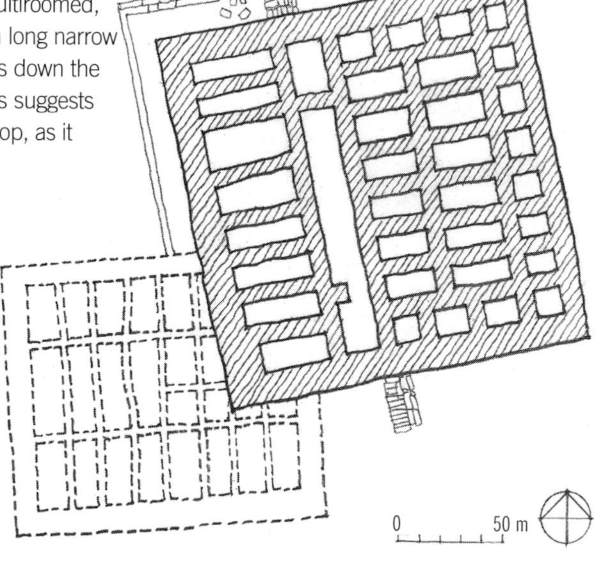


**1.11 Mehrgarh II: Plan of mud-brick granaries**

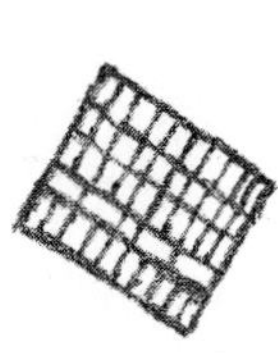

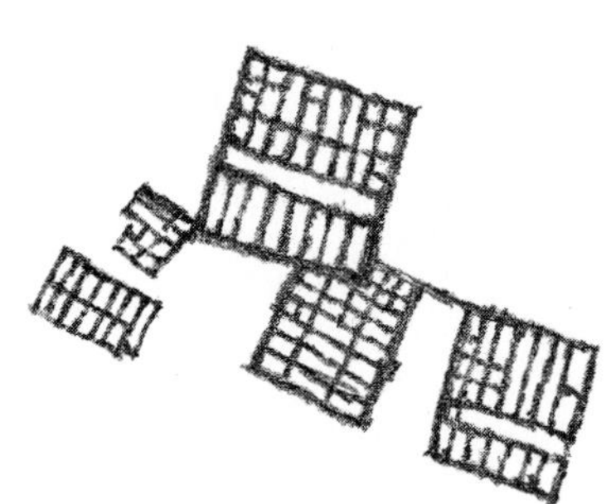

1.12 Mehrgarh: Typical arrangement of granaries

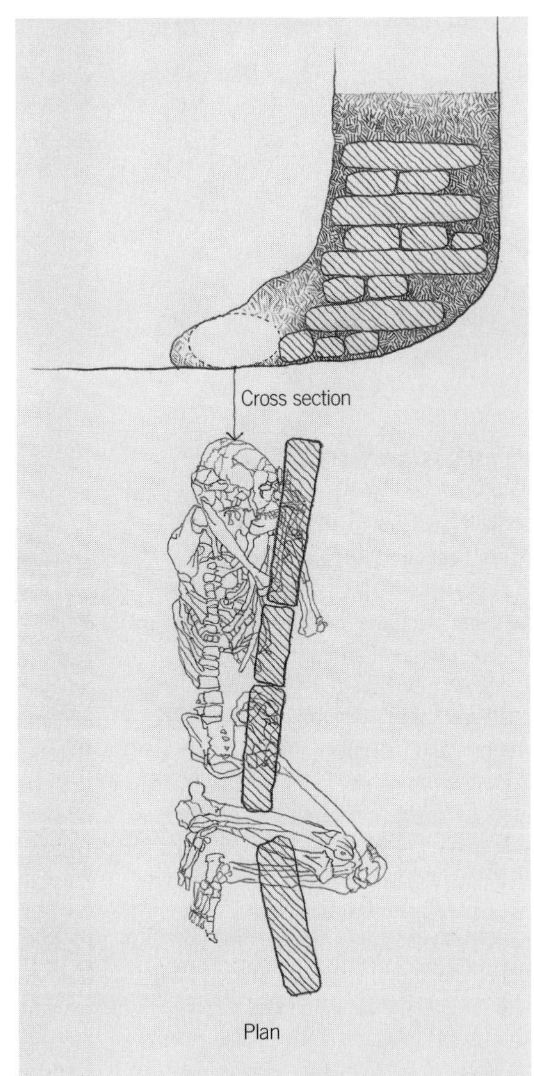


1.13 Sidewall grave at Mehrgarh

Though the presence of these granaries suggests a centralized social organization, there is no evidence of dominant temples or ritual structures. Nor are the granaries aligned with adjoining structures. And yet it is clear that the granaries were the center of social life. Outside one such granary, along its western wall, a large hearth has been found, complete with several hundred charred grains. Along the southern wall archaeologists found the remains of the stone tools and drills of a steatite- or soapstone-cutter's workshop. On the eastern side, there were heaps of animal bones mixed with ashes, indicating the presence of intense butchering activity. Life, in other words, was organized around the granaries. The granaries were also the center of ritual mortuary practices, given that human bones, presumably of priests, were found buried in its corridors and intermediary spaces.

1.14 Mehrgarh I: Reconstruction of House E

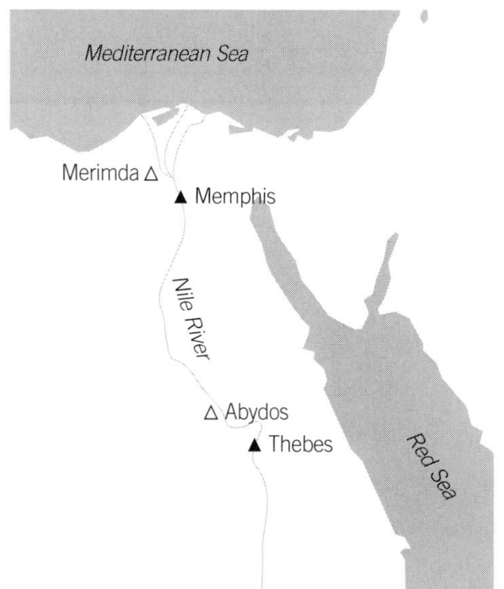


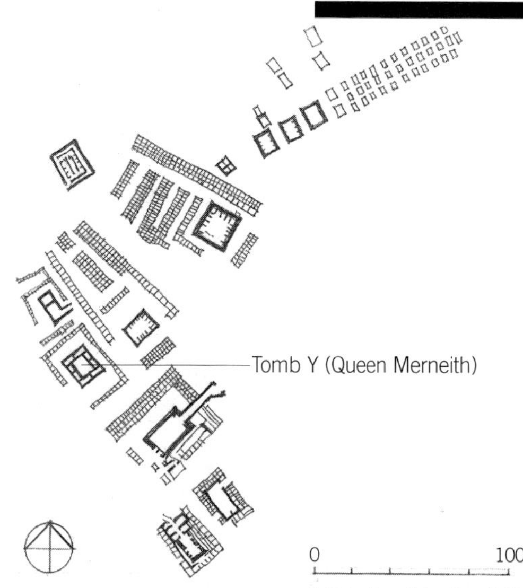


**1.15 Royal tombs at Umm el-Qaab, Abydos, Egypt**

**PREDYNASTIC EGYPT**

North Africa was once a vast, fertile area of forests and pasture lands populated by humans at an early date. But in the sixth millennium BCE, a dramatic warming that affected the whole globe changed North Africa, bit by bit, into the endless stretches of sand that we now call the Sahara Desert. The populations moved either westward to Morocco, Spain, and beyond, or eastward to the banks of the Nile. The result was that in an astonishingly short period of time, in Egypt by the fourth millennium BCE, villages had grown to towns, and trade was being pursued along the Nile and throughout the Aegean islands.

The density of the Nile River population was unlike anything one would have seen anywhere else in the world at that time; that it did not overwhelm the social system was predicated on several conditions, one being that the local elites quickly learned to define themselves as divine, assuring the mechanism by which to protect and isolate their power. This meant that Egyptian religion never went through a chthonic phase based on the mother goddesses and caves that were common in many places in Eurasia and the Mediterranean.

Egyptian religion was, at its start, a religion for the elite alone. There were no epic tales of communal destiny but rather myths of heroic actions of kings who passed the torch of succession down to the next generation. This explains why a complex pantheon of gods, stretching from the bovine Hathor to the more abstract-like Ptah and Amun, could develop so quickly. It was only during the New Kingdom (1540–1069 BCE) that the features of this religion began to have a broader role in society. Another factor that stabilized Egypt's existing social order was the fact that the Nile flooded after the harvest in the middle of October; this meant that the more people were working the fields, the more food was produced. But in contradistinction to the celebration of water and food, there was for the Egyptians the fearsome entombing power of the earth. Life and death, the river, and the mountains of sand became intimately and naturally connected to each other around the all-encompassing mythology of divine rulership.

One of the oldest Egyptian sites, belonging to the Predynastic period, is Merimda, 50 kilometers northwest of Cairo and at the western base of the Nile Delta. It dates back to the sixth millennium BCE and consists of a collection of oval huts with grain silos sunk into the ground.

The dead lay in shallow pits in burial grounds outside of the town. They were wrapped in matting and accompanied by goods such as clay vessels and shells. Idols, vessels (some used for the preparation of cosmetics), and wall paintings all point to an aesthetic that was to become characteristically Egyptian: smooth surfaces, abstract forms, and heroic actions.

A tomb from around 3200 BCE, located at Abydos, which was an important early city 100 kilometers upstream from Thebes, shows the emerging notion of a burial site as an entombed house. It consists of a rectangular pit roughly ten meters long, five meters wide and one-and-a-half meters deep. It would have been covered by timbers, mud, and sand to form a low hill. The rooms were linked to each other by narrow slits thought to simulate doors. Some of the chambers contained masonry jars and others were for the grave gods. In one of the tombs, the walls were painted with scenes depicting ships, hunting, and fishing. A hunter is seen on one of them swinging his mace at two approaching lions.

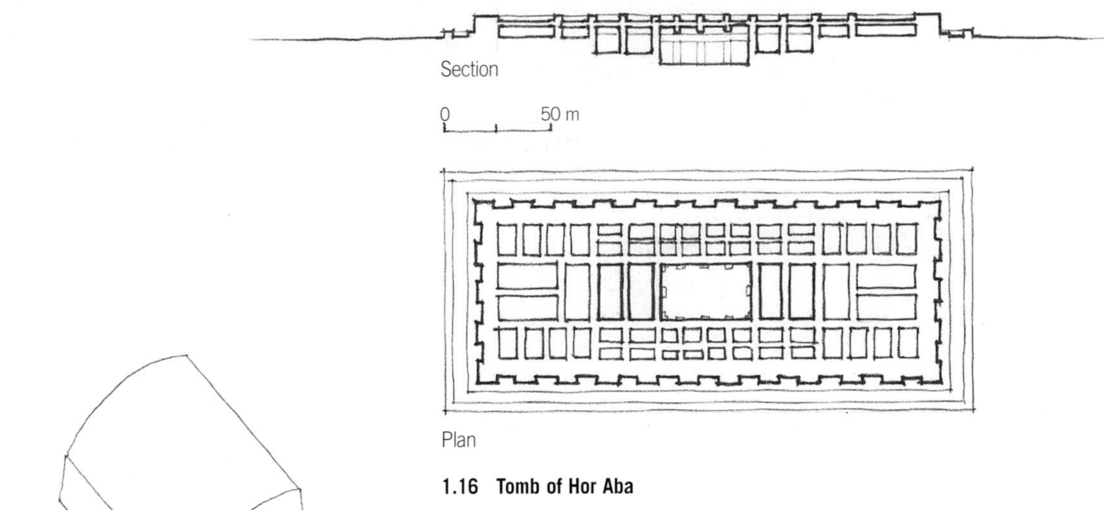


**1.16 Tomb of Hor Aba**

**1.17 Tomb Y (Queen Merneith) at Abydos**

The design and the decoration of these tombs clearly anticipates the development of the mastaba (from the Arabic word for "bank"). The grandest was the Tomb of Hor Aba, from 3100 BCE at Saqqra, just outside of Memphis. Some argue that the complex niche pattern in the walls represented wooden or reed walls; others have suggested an influence from Mesopotamia or the Near East. Only the five central chambers, dug into the earth, constitute the tomb. A mastaba, built in the third dynasty, Bet Challaf, north of Abydos, measured an impressive 45 by 85 meters and was eight meters high. The tomb was laid out as a multiroomed house embedded in the ground and reached by steps and a long corridor.

In this early stage of Egyptian culture, there was no temple architecture as one might find in China where religious practices unified broad swaths of society. Instead, architecture played the role of defining the interface between life and death for the members of that elite. Its place in society was thus more limited than in China and India, but its purpose could not be more dramatic. Death for the Chinese involved the handing down of family memories and could be articulated spatially with house shrines and fragile wooden temples on earthen mounds. In Egypt, death—in religious terms—was only allowed for the ruler, with his and sometimes her spirit rising majestically over the trivialities of domesticity and family in a specially constructed, simulated house with all the accoutrements of a comfortable life. What went on in that house, and how the spirit moved about, ate and drank, was a matter of great concern, since it was thought to determine the flow of history in the present and beyond. But the "house" was only half of the equation. Death in Egypt had an inside and an outside shape. Entombing the "house" at the scale of the landscape was the structure's outside shape. Eighty percent of Queen Merneith's mastaba was nothing more than a dark mass of walls and spaces that link these two scales. The architect's job, in essence, was to bring the inner and outer manifestations of the ruler's death into unity.

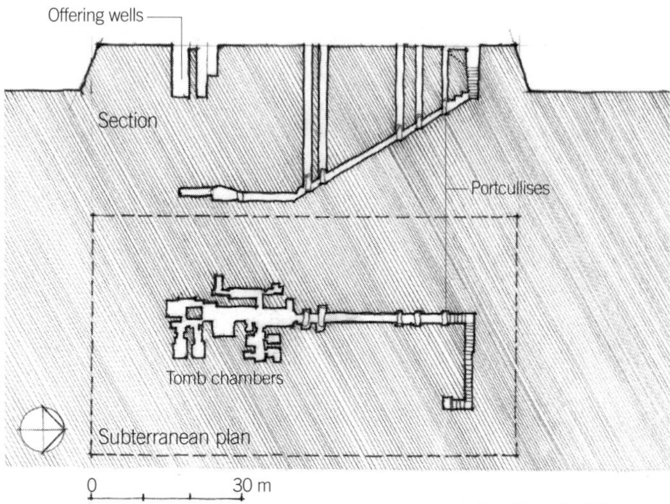


**1.18 Mastaba K1 at Bet Challaf**

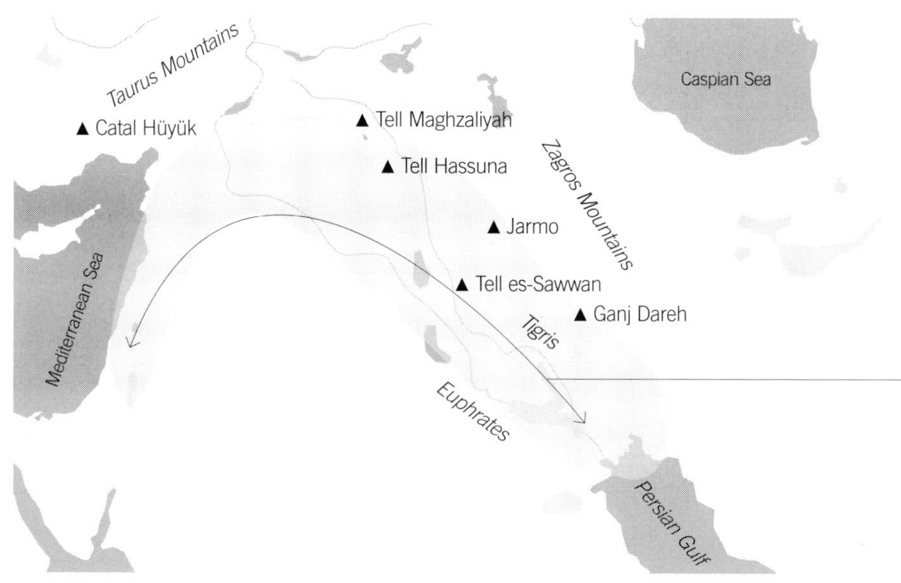


Mesopotamia comes from the Greek words *mesos* and *potamas*, meaning "middle river," and refers to the fertile plain between the Tigris and Euphrates rivers.

The Fertile Crescent is an agricultural region that runs along the foot of the Taurus and Zagros Mountains in a broad arc from the eastern shores of the Mediterranean to present-day Iraq.

**MESOPOTAMIA**

The cultures we have discussed so far, the Chinese, the Indus, and the Egyptian, had geographies large enough for their diverse needs, and therein lay their strength. The Chinese were not dependent on salt or metal imported from across the Himalayas. The Indus River valley system was also relatively self-contained. The Egyptians were somewhat more dependent on trade, importing metal from the Aegean Islands or from Nubia to the south. They were able, nevertheless, to protect themselves for millennia from heavy foreign influence or invasion.

A different situation developed in the areas of the Tigris and Euphrates rivers, where, by 4000 BCE, a vast network of villages had formed in the highlands. The inhabitants had already spent several millennia transforming the valleys into one of the most productive grain-bearing regions of the world. These areas are now divided by the borders of Iran, Iraq, Syria, Turkey, Lebanon, and Jordan.

The climate was also cooler, meaning that the verdant valleys of the Tigris and Euphrates rivers were far different from the deserts of today; in the highlands there were bands of forest interspersed with steppes and savannas rich in flora and abounding with goats, boars, deer, and fox. Farmers worked in the valley, but the community lived in the more easily fortifiable hills. But unlike in China and India, these villagers had two economic orientations, downhill to the fields of grain and uphill into the mountains of Anatolia with their rich mines of gold and copper. Mesopotamian cultures were thus continually in a state of flux, which had its own advantages and difficulties.

**1.19**
*Tell*, an Arabic word for a hillock, is often used to describe the enormous mounds accumulated from the remains of mud-brick houses and generations of rubbish, such as this site of Ganj Dareh.

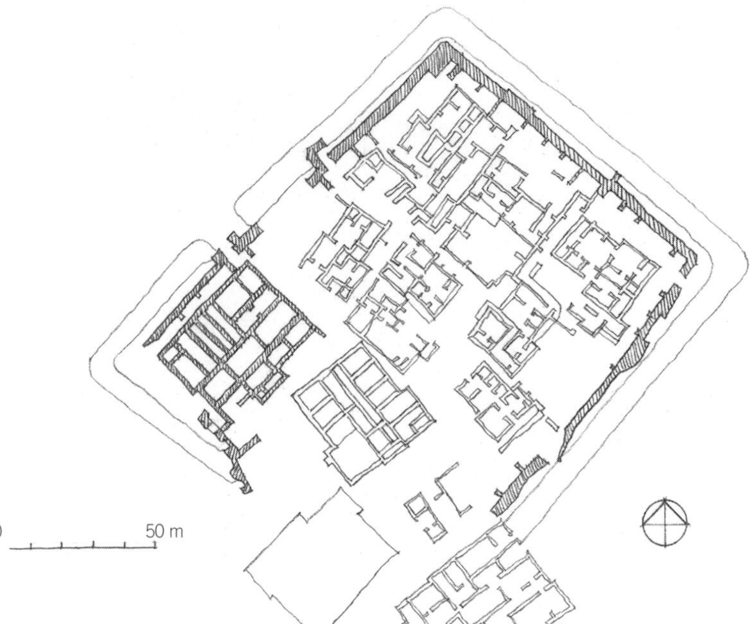


**1.20 Housing pattern at Tell es-Sawwan, Iraq**

One of the most important groupings of villages dating from this period (6000–2500 BCE) were located just to the east of a rain-fed agricultural zone that arches northeastward from the northern tip of the Persian Gulf along the flanks of the Zagros Mountains. Among these settlements were Tell Hassuna, today in western Iraq south of Mosul, in the hills above the Tigris River; Tell Maghzaliyah, 150 kilometers to the northwest; Tell es-Sawwan on the left bank of the Tigris near Samarra; and Jarmo and Ganj Dareh in Iran.

Initially, these settlements started as fortified villages of about 200 people, growing over time into substantial communities. The basic building material was mud and timber, with the mud mixed with reeds and applied in horizontal courses to form walls of various heights. The walls of the houses were laid out in a honeycomb pattern to add to their durability, which meant that houses were composed of rectilinear rooms, measuring on average about one-and-a-half by two meters. At Ganj Dareh, archaeologists found house shrines with wild sheep skulls attached to a plastered niche, recalling similar shrines at Catal Hüyük in Anatolia. The horizontal roofs consisted of adjoining beams of oak, on which were placed a layer of branches and reeds that were sealed with mud, bitumen, and gypsum.

The houses were more than mere shelters. Some of the interior wall surfaces were decorated with gypsum plaster, which was to remain a central part of building construction in the entire area and which had been developed as early as 7000 BCE. From the extensive outcrops of rock gypsum in northern Iraq and Syria, stone blocks were mined, stacked, and burnt to form an easily transportable white powder. This building material was not only used locally but also exported as a trade commodity. The development of trade in craft goods, pottery, building materials, and metal objects stimulated the economies of the region and played a central part in its drift toward craft specialization and urbanization. The Hassuna culture had abundant grain, of course, which was exported to surrounding regions.

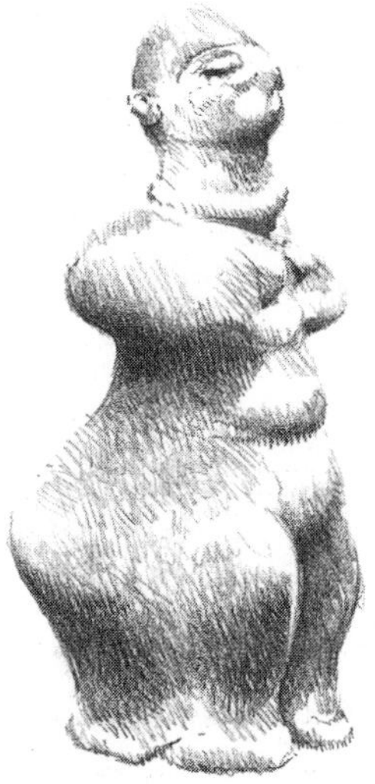

**1.21 Hassuna culture figurine, ca. 6000 BCE**

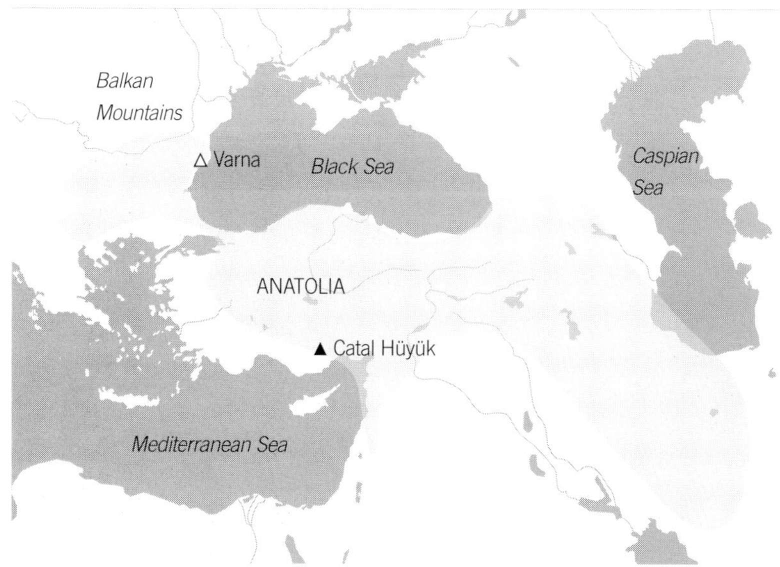


**Catal Hüyük**

The principal copper-producing area of Eurasia stretched from the Caspian Sea through Anatolia and around the Black Sea into the Balkans. Mines in these areas came into operation around 7000 BCE. A set of graves found in Varna on the Black Sea and dating from around 4500 BCE gives clear evidence of the wealth that metals brought to the villages. The graves yielded finely crafted beads, jewelry, objects made of shell and copper, as well as an ornament in the shape of horned bulls, which are certainly not native to the region, made of hammered sheet gold. Another commodity from the north was salt, which was mined early on in Austria and elsewhere. One need only think of the salt mines around Salzburg (literally, "Salt Mountain"), which became the source of wealth of the later Halstadt Culture. Nor should one forget that some of the oldest fired-clay figurines ever found came from sites in the former Czechoslovakia and date from 25,000 BCE, while early baskets appeared there around 10,000 BCE.

The area from the former Czechoslovakia to the Caspian Sea is thus a "crescent" all its own, a Metal Crescent, composed mainly of a hamlet culture that survived by trading minerals, ores, and the craft objects associated with them. It is a good reminder that even though we often think of the Tigris and Euphrates region as the birthplace of urban civilization, the truth is that civilization— if we can use that complex and awkward word, at least in this area—was the product of a combined culture in which some built cities, while others built mines. The raising of grain and the production of metals were mutually reinforcing activities.

At the center of the metal trade was the city of Catal Hüyük in central Anatolia near the modern city of Konya. With a population estimated to have been around 3,000, it was one of the largest cities of the time in that area and dates as far back as 7400 BCE. Metal objects found there are among the oldest known examples in the Near East. Other local commodities were traded, in particular volcanic glass, which was used for decoration and as barter.

**1.22 Housing pattern at Catal Hüyük, near Konya, Turkey**

0 15 m

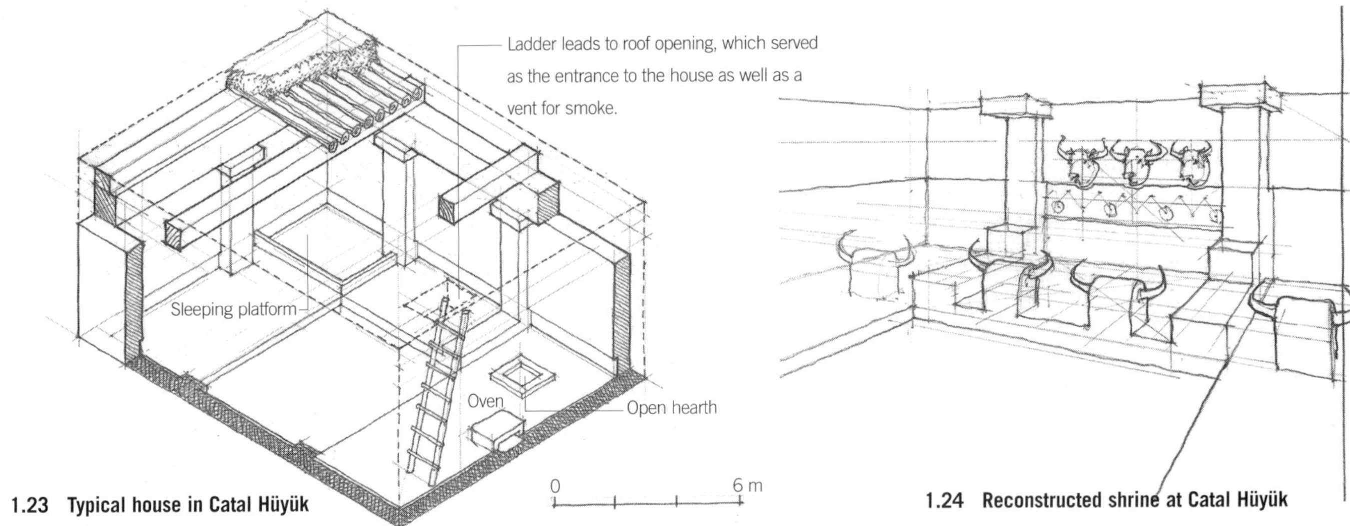


1.23 **Typical house in Catal Hüyük**

1.24 **Reconstructed shrine at Catal Hüyük**

The city consisted of rectangular flat-roofed houses packed together into a single architectural mass with no streets or passageways. Inhabitants moved across rooftops and descended into their homes through the roofs via ladders. Walls were made of mud bricks reinforced by massive oak posts. Light came from small windows high in the walls. If a family died out, their house was abandoned for a period of time, leaving gaps in the urban fabric, until eventually the space was reclaimed. The typical residence contained one large room connected to smaller storage rooms. The main room was equipped with benches, ovens, and bins. The average size of the room was a generous 5 by 6 meters. Walls were plastered and many were decorated with spectacular hunting scenes, textile patterns, or landscapes. There were raised benches on three sides of the room for sleeping and other activities.

A great deal of space was devoted to family rites. There was no central or communal sacred space. Each house had its own shrine consisting of a wall decorated with bulls or horns. In some cases pairs of horns were set in clay at the edge of platforms or embedded in benches. The dead of the family were buried in this room and their bones incorporated into the shrine. (Bodies were first left outside until only the bones remained.)

Stone and clay female statues that were found at the site were certainly deities, though the nature of the belief system practiced here is much debated. One statue, remarkable for its bold three-dimensional design, is of a voluminous seated woman giving birth. The chair on which she sits has armrests in the shape of lions. The figurine represented fecundity and regeneration and was part of the widespread mother-goddess worship typical of European and Mediterranean late-Stone Age and early-Bronze Age societies.

1.25 **Terra-cotta figurine of seated woman from Catal Hüyük**

1.26 **Bull design on a shrine wall at Catal Hüyük**

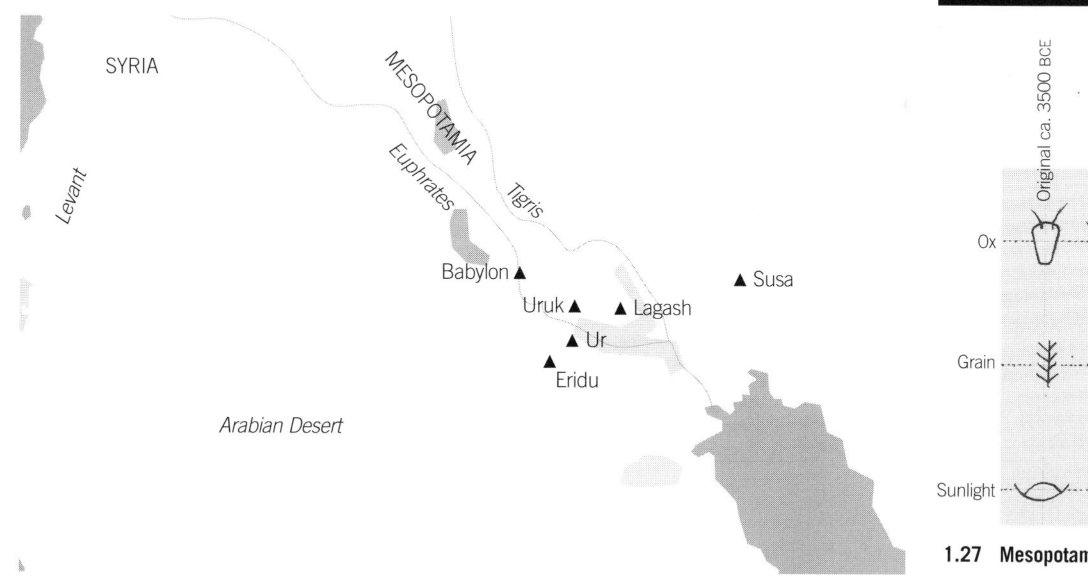


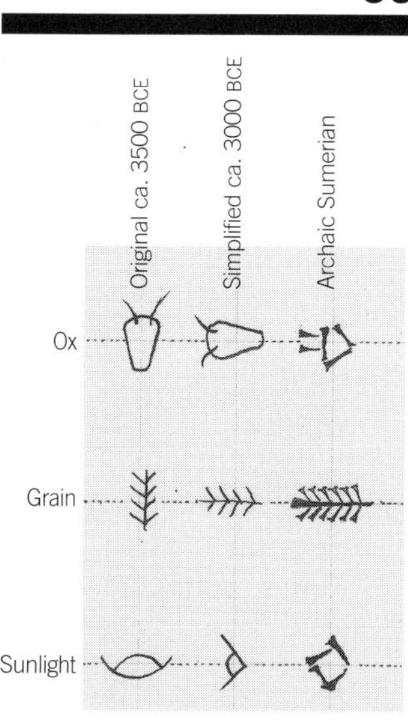


**1.27 Mesopotamian pictographs and cuneiform**

### Eridu and Uruk

The identifying elements of the protocivilizations discussed so far are the presence of ritual centers, agro-industrial specialization, a military or religious elite, and urban density. These elements did not develop simultaneously. In China, we find ritual centers and agro-industrial production. But life still went on at the scale of the village. In the Indus River Valley and at Catal Hüyük, cities emerged as sites where production could be centralized and coordinated, but we do not find large-scale ritual centers. Religion was limited to the family and clan and, in Anatolia and Mesopotamia, to the mother-goddess cults. In South Asia, however, the absence of communal religious sites, despite agricultural specialization, is particularly intriguing and was to remain a characteristic of its urban culture through the next millennium. Where we first find a coming together of ritual centers, urban density, and agro-industrial production on a par with Egypt and the Indus Valley was in the lower Mesopotamian region of present-day southern Iraq and Iran. It has been suggested that the move into the marshes was predicated by the same changes in global climate that had created the Sahara Desert. In fact, research has shown that as the mountains became drier, tribes had to move to the plains in search of better soil. But whether by necessity or by desire, the system of mountain villages that given Eurasia its bounty of domesticated animals and grain was now being replaced by a more thoroughly industrialized river-based culture. There might have been other factors, but the move was, in the time frames of these early cultures, quite sudden. Societies gave up their partial dependency on an integrated farming-hunting lifestyle and concentrated on farming alone, which meant that they were vulnerable to the uncertainties associated with weather, rivers, and trade. The move into the marshes of the river delta went hand in hand with improved technical advances. The Tigris and Euphrates, unlike the Nile, flooded before the harvest, namely in April and May, and this had made lower-lying reaches unusable for agriculture. But sedimentation brought by the rivers tended to build up natural levees that farmers reinforced. The bottom of the river bed became somewhat higher than the surrounding countryside, allowing for openings in the levees to be made for irrigation channels. Aerial photography has recently proven the extensive nature of these ancient canals and dikes, some more than 100 kilometers in length.

The new relationship with the rivers was a delicate and dangerous one. The system was vulnerable to flood, war, and neglect. Records from Ur talk repeatedly of repair work. But the investment was worth the effort and in a few centuries the area became an economic engine unparalleled anywhere in the world except in Egypt, and it would remain so until about 800 CE, when the development of iron tools made the growing and harvesting of grain more widespread, with a negative impact on Mesopotamia.

The wheel came into use to haul loads, and standardized weights were invented. The need for accurate record keeping among the merchants led to another civilizational achievement—writing, which was put to use to record matters of trade. Concomitant with this was the development of a legal and archival system. Evidence of the impact this made can be found even today in vestigial remnants of words deeply embedded in our present-day language. In Ur, the ancient title designating "king" is *lugal*, which is probably the origin of the Latin *lex* and the English word *law*. And another ancient Mesopotamian word, *pala*, referring to the garment of kingship, constitutes the root of our word "palace."

We see the emergence of not only elaborate urban defensive wall systems but also a complex religious world in tune with the equally complex life of urban civilization. The mother goddess, who had ruled in many places throughout Eurasia, now had to compete with an expanding list of divine presences—including powerful male gods to tie society firmly into a network of obligations. Concomitant with the shift was the emergence of a priestly class responsible for all aspects of society, from religion to administration and to technology. Significantly, the mother goddess, Apsi, who controls the oceans, is "killed" by her son Ea, earth, who divides her unruly waters into chambers.

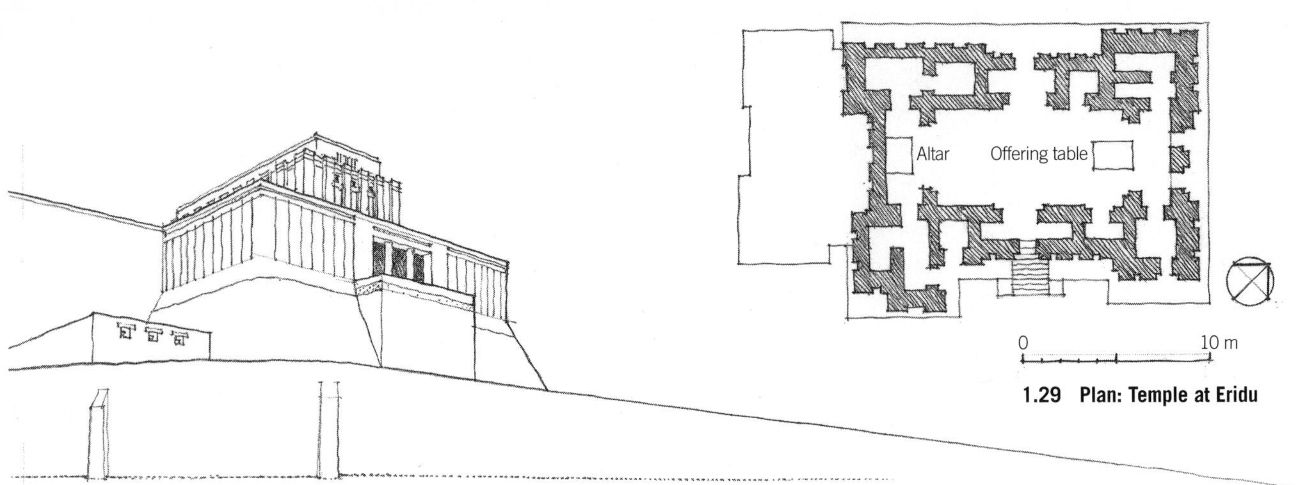


1.29 **Plan: Temple at Eridu**

1.28 **Temple atop the stone-faced platform at Eridu, near Abu Shahrain, Iraq**

The culture that first began to master the Tigris and Euphrates rivers as early as 5000 BCE was known as the Ubaid. Around 3000 BCE, they were superseded by the Sumerians, who were to no small degree the first modernizers, replacing old and well-established traditions with new ones. In comparison to their new cities of Uruk, Eridu, and the Elamite city of Susa, Hassuna was now a backward village. Eridu was located on the banks of the Euphrates in the delta, which has since silted up so that its ancient site is now located 90 kilometers inland. The Temple at Eridu was positioned on an enormous plinth of clay bricks and was visible for miles around. It had a form defined by rhythmically spaced buttresses, and though roughly rectangular in shape, it had an irregular perimeter. A flight of steps at the center of the broader side led up to the entrance where a shallow vestibule gave access to a large lengthwise-placed central room. Ancillary spaces, probably used as reliquaries, were located at the corners.

That the Temple at Eridu came to be viewed by later Mesopotamians as an important prototype is confirmed by the fact that a statue made about a thousand years later in 2150 BCE shows the plan of a temple with similar attributes. It is placed on the lap of King Gudea of Lagash and, in its accuracy and precision, leaves no doubt as to the planning that went into these early temple designs. Its position on the king's lap also proves that the plan as such was more than just a convenience of the builders. It was an expression of the claim to legitimacy of the monarch and his sacrosanct function.

Archaeologists surmise that the chief deity of the city was Ea. This god, son of the mother god Apsu, was not only an earth god but also manifest in "sweet waters." He was seen as crafty, for he "avoids rather than surmounts obstacles, goes round and yet gets to his goal." Ea, who in some accounts made human beings by mixing his own essence with that of his brother, Enlil (the earth and storm god), was also worshipped as the god of wisdom and as a friend to humankind. Images of Ea show him wearing a cloak of fish scales, which coincides with the discovery of fish bones near the offering table at Eridu. A text written somewhat later states that:

> When Ea rose, the fishes rose and adored him,
> He stood, a marvel unto the deep...
> To the sea it seemed that awe was upon him;
> To the Great River terror seemed to hover around him
> While the south wind stirred the depth of the Euphrates.
>
> (After Thorkild Jacobsen, *Journal of Near Eastern Studies,* 5:140, 1946.)

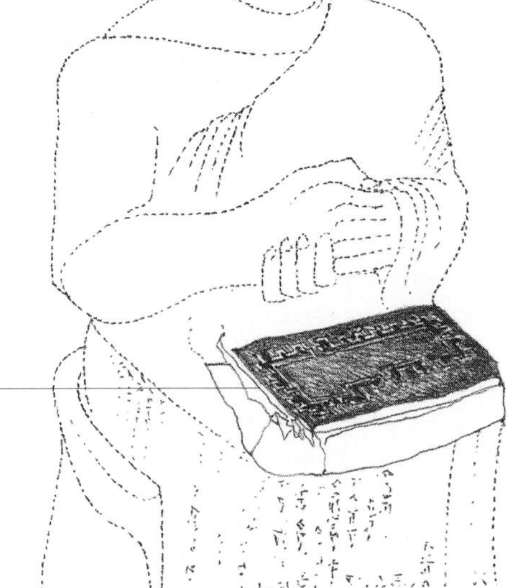

1.30 **Statue of King Gudea with a temple plan carved on a lap tablet**

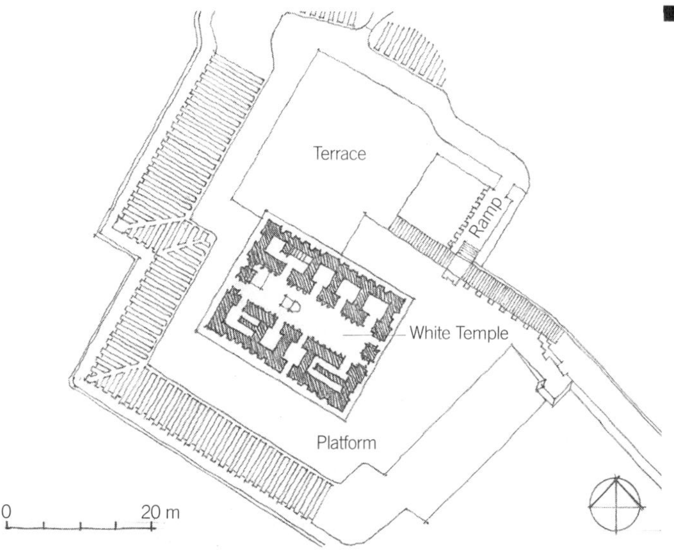


**1.31 Plan: White Temple at Uruk, near Samawa, Iraq**

The other early city of Sumer, Uruk, was probably dedicated to the god Anu, a sky god, and an important and newly emerging deity linked to the number "one" and thus to mathematics and trade. His temple, the so-called White Temple, rested on a broad terrace on top of a tall artificial mountain, irregular in outline and rising 13 meters above the plain with its vast expanse of fields and marshes. Access was by a stairway on the northeastern face. The overall shape, in comparison with Eridu, is much simplified, but as at Eridu, one passed through a shallow vestibule into a great hall. Here, however, there was in one corner a platform or altar with a flight of narrow steps leading up to it. Toward the middle of the space was an offering table with a low semicircular hearth built up against it.

During this time, Mesopotamian builders discovered how to use the kiln to harden bricks, roof tiles, and drainage tubes. The Mesopotamians may have acquired this skill on their own but more likely learned it from the Indus Valley civilization, with which they most certainly were in contact. They had developed brick very early on. As wood for kilns was scarce in the Mesopotamian marshes, bricks were a luxury item and were mainly used for palaces, temples, and gates, the Gate of Ishtar at Babylon being the most famous of these. The kilns devoured enormous amounts of wood, depleting wood resources and contributing, so it is now thought, to the growth of the desert that is now pervasive in these parts.

The use of brick in the foundation of Uruk was an indication of the status of the building. It was seen even by Mesopotamians as one of its wondrous aspects. Near the beginning of the epic of *Gilgamesh*, composed in the later third millennium BCE, we read:

> Look at its wall which gleams like copper,
> inspect its inner wall, the likes of which no one can equal!
> Take hold of the threshold stone—it dates from ancient times!
> Go close to the Eanna Temple, the residence of Ishtar,
> such as no later king or man ever equaled!
> Go up on the wall of Uruk and walk around,
> examine its foundation, inspect its brickwork thoroughly.
> Is not (even the core of) the brick structure made of kiln-fired brick,
> and did not the Seven Sages themselves lay out its plans?

*The Epic of Gilgamesh*, Translated by Maureen Gallery Kovacs (Stanford: Stanford University Press, 1985) p. 3.

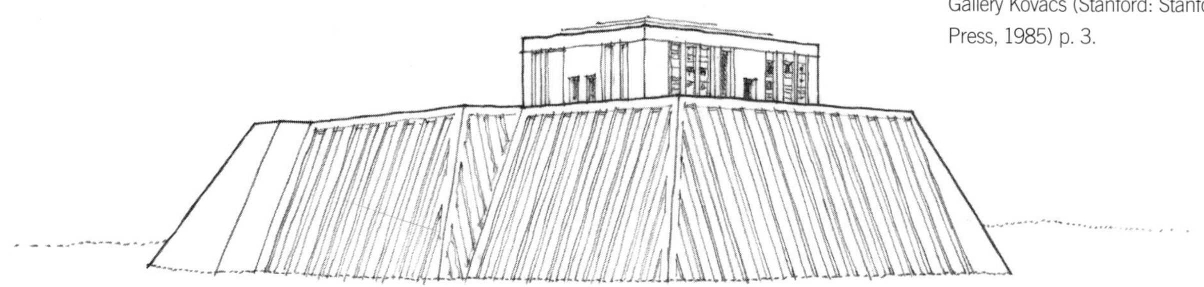

**1.32 White Temple at Uruk**

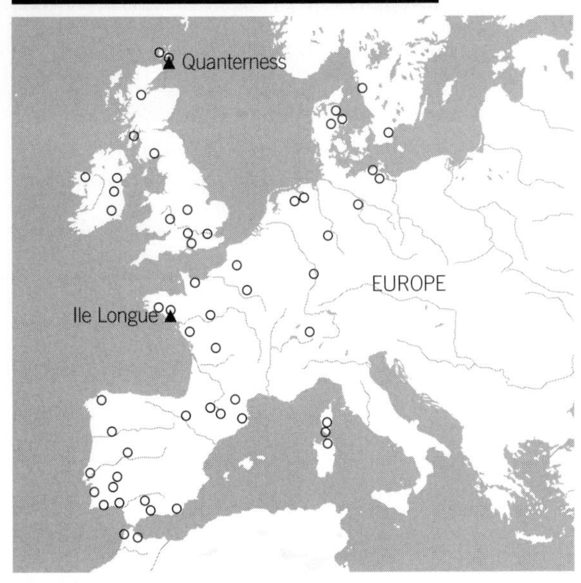


1.33 Sites of European megalithic chamber tombs, ca. 3000 BCE

1.34 Plans of Portuguese passage graves

## EUROPEAN MEGALITHIC TOMBS

Europe's complex geography of shorelines, rivers, and mountain ranges meant that a single civilizational unit was unlikely to develop as it did in Egypt, China, and India. Furthermore, Europe, because of difficulties of transplanting grain northward, as opposed to east and west, was only fully settled around 3500 BCE. Because European cultures developed without the "history" of agricultural domestication in their background, their focus was not on family matriarchal histories wherein such knowledge, by necessity, was handed down, but on the clans that could pull communities together to overcome obstacles and define their relationships to the outside world. This explains why the Europeans did not develop a temple culture or, for that matter, a more complex priestly culture until much later. The first architectural expressions were tombs, which preserved the memories of clan lineages and served as places for gathering, trade, and ritual. Examples can be found throughout Europe, in Portugal, France, England, even as far north as Norway, as well as in Morocco and Sardinia.

The Portuguese tombs, which are among the oldest, consist of a chamber built of stone slabs approached through a narrow passageway. For this reason, these tombs are often referred to as either "chamber tombs" or "passage graves." They were covered by an artificial mound of earth or stone called a barrow—thus also the name "barrow tomb"—and were sometimes fortified by retaining walls.

The ceilings of some of the chambers were corbeled with stones placed further and further toward the center of the space till they meet at the top. An example of this can be found in the passage grave on Ile Longue, South Brittany, France. At Quanterness, in the Orkney Islands of Great Britain, the central chamber is surrounded by six side chambers, all with corbeled roofs. Used for over 500 years, it accumulated the remains of about four hundred people.

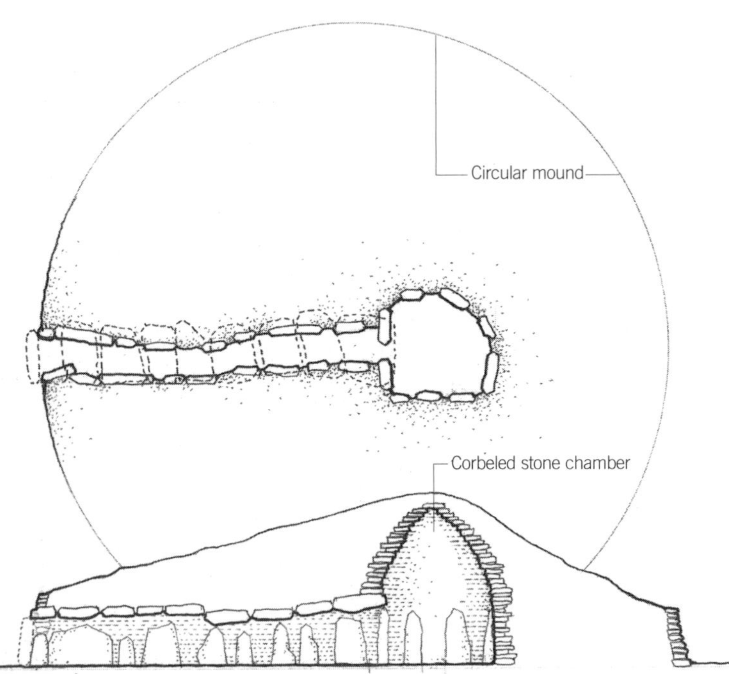


1.35 Passage grave on Ile Longue, South Brittany, France, ca. 4100 BCE

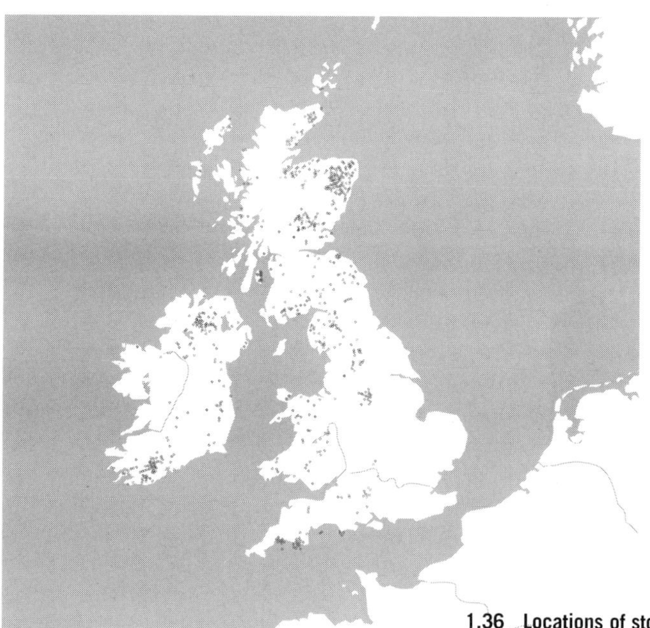

1.36 Locations of stone circles discovered in England

**Stone Circles**

In England, toward the end of the fourth millennium BCE, land overuse, famine, or plague put a dent in the development toward more complex social organizations. Tombs were blocked up and abandoned. A natural disaster may have been at the heart of this calamity. In Greenland there is evidence that acid rain from volcanic eruptions in Iceland, dating from 3250 BCE, created clouds so dense that they blocked the sunlight. Vast tracks of land were rendered uninhabitable. The effects were disastrous but short-lived. The weather rebounded and so too, according to Burl Aubrey, one of the leading researcher of English stone circles, did the human spirit. In fact, during the late Stone Age and early Bronze Age, the climate in England would have been warmer than today, and thus farming was possible in more places in 2000 BCE than in 2000 CE. A new generation of tomb structures, called "coves," appeared that consisted of three upright slabs set in the configuration of a "U" facing east, open to the sky, and often surrounded by circular embankments and stone circles.

The most important expression of that time, was, however, not the tombs but stone circles. How widespread they were has only been understood since the second half of the twentieth century, when aerial photography revealed additional locations. It is estimated that at one time there might have been as many as 4000 of them, of which two-thirds were erected in the major building phase between 3000 and 1300 BCE.

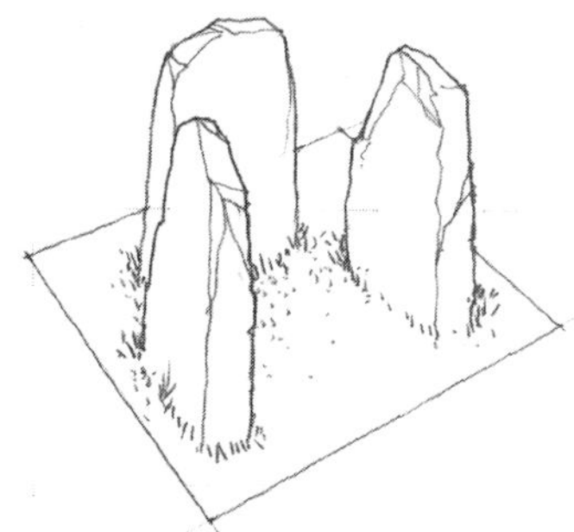

Cove: Three standing stones, two on the sides and one at the back.

Trilithon: A structure consisting of two upright stones supporting a horizontal lintel.

Dolmen: A burial tomb consisting of three or more upright stones and one or more capstones.

1.37 Types of early megalithic tomb structures

1.38 **Stone Circle at Avebury, England**

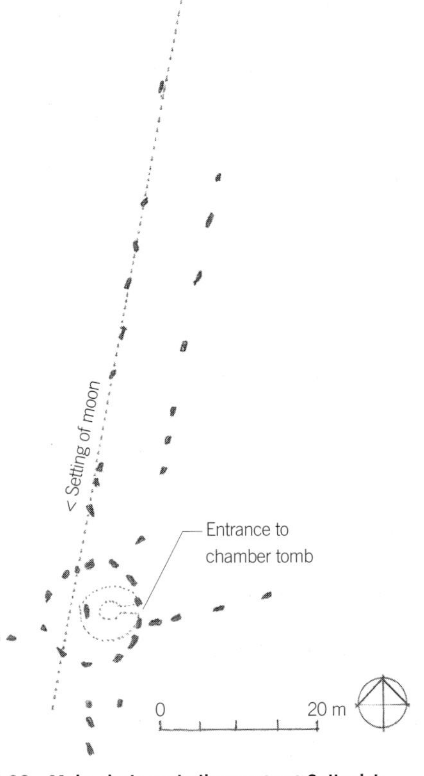


1.39 **Main circle and alignments at Callanish, Scotland**

The earliest circles ranged in size from 18 to 30 meters in diameter, with the stones standing shoulder to shoulder. For the most part they were near a village or clan compound and were built with local stones. The architectural expression of the circles is, however, not uniform. They could be round or oval, they could have concentric embankments of stone circles, and many had approach avenues. Some were associated with burials, others with cremation. In some locations, such as Loanhead of Daviot, the stones were not upright but lay flat on the ground, distinguished by glittering bright quartz fragments and concentrated in positions associated with the setting moon. At the center of that site, archaeologists found the remnants of a fire pit with cremated human bones. Other structures had burrows. Many had a central stone.

A cluster of early Bronze Age sites exists across the English Channel, on the southern coast of Brittany at the base of the peninsula, but circular structures, though not unknown in Europe, were uncommon. At the village of Menec, north of the town of Carnac, is a large cromlech of closely placed stones. Leading to this stone circle is an impressive ritual road, 100 meters wide and 1165 meters long, running southwest to northeast and formed of almost 1100 standing stones or menhirs in 11 rows. How these stone circles worked as celestial observatories is much debated, but there is agreement that they were meant to follow the movements of the moon and stars (and not the sun), as would have been typical for early agrarian-based societies.

Cromlech: A circular arrangement of monoliths enclosing a dolmen or burial mound.

1.40 **Cromlech and alignments of standing stones near Carnac, France**

0 100 m

# 2500 BCE

By the beginning of the third millennium BCE the various river-oriented civilizations were primed for rapid cultural development. But the history of their development is not simply the history of urbanism, nor are the terms of "civilization" spelled out equally. In China, the first recorded dynasty, the Xia dynasty, emerged around 2100 BCE. Nonetheless, we still find a horizontal civilization of villages and towns unified around common ritual centers. In Mesopotamia, by contrast, the divergent cultural elements and the need to establish trade networks over large geographical areas made it difficult for one stable, central power to emerge. Nevertheless, the area created its own economic dynamic by an enriching interaction of divergent population groups that led to important trading cities. Irrigation canals placed a great deal of wealth in the hands of the new generation of rulers who operated in close alliance with a priestly class ruling out of temples that were built as artificial mountains rising in colorful terraces above the plains.

The Egyptians rivaled Mesopotamia in wealth only because they were able to protect themselves from invaders and harness large numbers of laborers. Pharaoh Zoser built a temple complex at an unprecedented scale; it was one of the first monumental stone buildings in the world. It was also a building of great complexity answering to the intricate cosmology used by the Egyptian ruling elite. From that point of view, the Egyptians had been the first to modernize cosmology to fit the complex needs of their culture and economy. The Mesopotamians, developing their own complex political and social structures, were joining them in this respect, by replacing the older female gods with more dominant male deities.

In South Asia, along the Indus and Ghaggar-Hakra river systems, one finds cities segmented by class and organized around well-thought out drainage systems that controlled the seasonal flow of river water. But instead of a ziggurat or pyramid at the center of the town, there were huge public baths, such as the one at Mohenjo-Daro. Trade among the cities, and with Mesopotamia, up the Persian Gulf was the basis of their civilization. Indeed the entire area from Mesopotamia to the Indus and from the Caspian Sea to Arabia was what archaeologists are now calling a zone of interconnection. Not only did the people themselves travel and trade, but the civilizations of this zone also had continuities in their culture and language as far back as the third millennium BCE.

In Europe the somewhat mysterious Beaker People, known for their advanced metal-working skill, left their traces in various locations, yet their origin is unknown and much debated. Eventually they arrived in England where they encountered such sites as Stonehenge, which they took over and redesigned, orienting it to the sun rather than to the moon. While physically this was largely a matter of "fine-tuning," the cultural implications this reorientation presupposes are imponderable.

In the Americas, the Andean population inhabited a thin sliver of a coastline between the Pacific Ocean and a desert. Though these communities could easily have become a forgotten niche culture, the currents of the Pacific Ocean, with their rich bounty of marine life, helped sustain settled life until the inhabitants learned to tame the rivers descending from the Andes mountains by canalization and terracing. Very recently, archaeologists have dated a large ceremonial complex above the Supe Valley in the Peruvian Andes to about 2750 BCE. This discovery has overturned Andean chronology, dating large-scale ceremonial architecture at a much earlier time than previously thought. Large tracts of Andean sites have still not been explored and carbon-dated so their stories remain to be told.

Indus Valley: Early Harappan Period
5000–2600 BCE

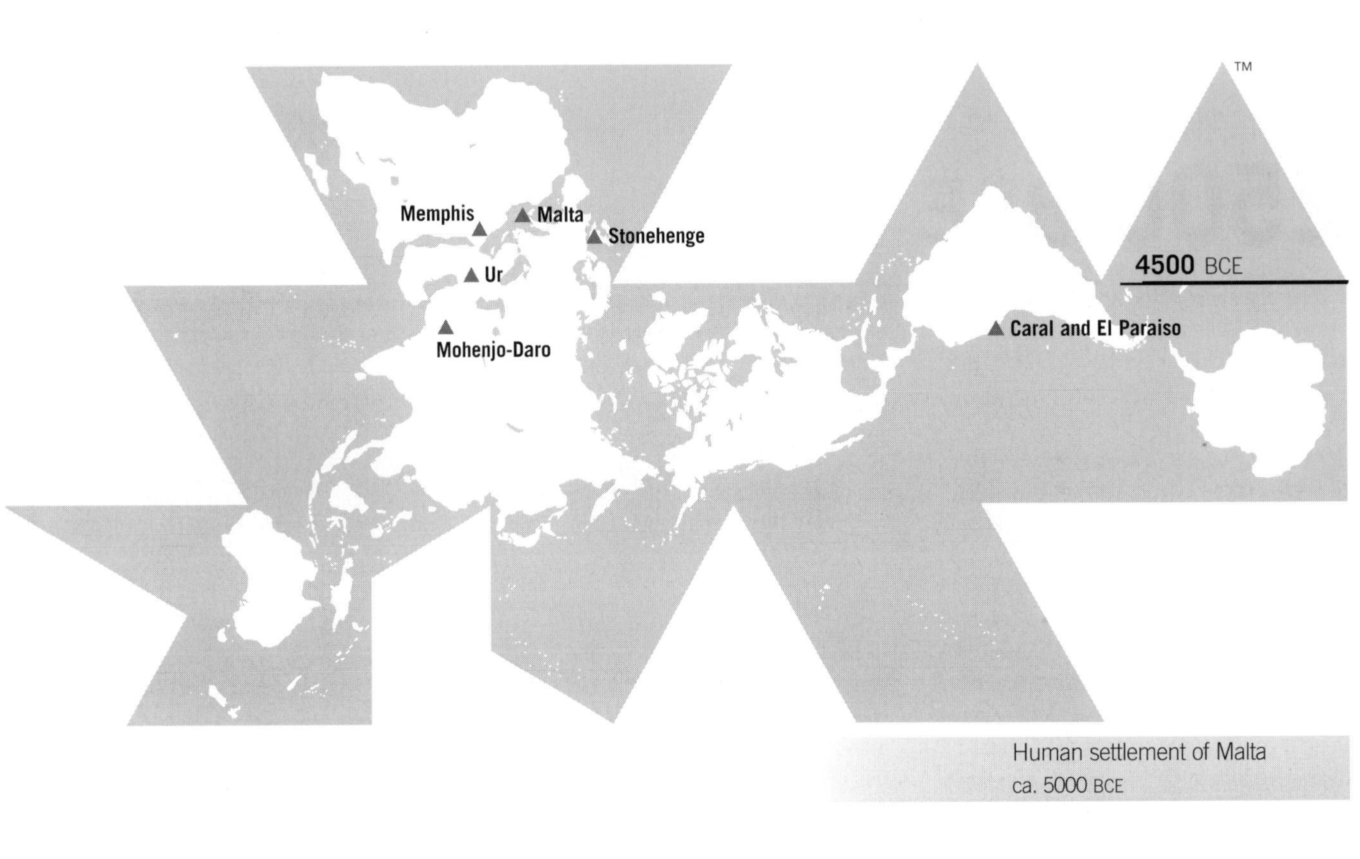


Human settlement of Malta
ca. 5000 BCE

Ghaggar-Hakra Civilization
2600–1800 BCE

▲ **Dholavira**
ca. 3000–2000 BCE

▲ **Mohenjo-Daro and Harappa prosper**
ca. 2600–1900 BCE

Mesopotamia: Early Dynastic Period
ca. 2900–2350 BCE

Akkadian Dynasty
ca. 2350–2150 BCE

ca. 2000–1600 BCE

Third Dynasty of Ur
ca. 2100–2000 BCE

▲ **Ziggurat at Ur**
ca. 2100 BCE

**3500** BCE — **2500** BCE — **1500** BCE

**Late Neolithic Period**
ca. 5000–2500 BCE

**Early Bronze Age**
ca. 3000–2000 BCE

Egypt: First Intermediate Period
ca. 2150–2030 BCE

Egypt: Old Kingdom
ca. 2649–2150 BCE

Middle Kingdom
ca. 2030–1640 BCE

▲ **Step Pyramid of Zoser**
ca. 2750 BCE

Second Intermediate Period
ca. 1640–1550 BCE

▲ **Bent Pyramid**
ca. 2600 BCE

▲ **Great Pyramid of Khufu**
ca. 2590 BCE

Building of megalithic temples
ca. 3500–2500 BCE

Brittany and British Isles: Megalithic Building Cultures
ca. 4200–2000 BCE

Beaker Culture
ca. 2800–1800 BCE

▲ **Stonehenge**
Begun ca. 3000 BCE

⦿ 3100 BCE
Mythic base date of the
Maya Long Count Calendar

North and Central Andes: Early Ceramic Cultures
ca. 4000–1800 BCE

▲ **Caral**
ca. 2627–2000 BCE

▲ **El Paraiso**
ca. 1800 BCE

### INDUS GHAGGAR-HAKRA CIVILIZATION

Around 2500 BCE, the Mehrgarh people moved down from the Baluchistan hills and settled in the river valleys that define the eastern edge of the South Asian subcontinent—those of the Indus and the Ghaggar-Hakra. The Indus is one of the defining rivers of South Asia. In ancient Sanskrit the Indus was known as the "Sindhu." In Central Asian languages, Sindhu became "Hindhu," which then became the "Indus" among the Greeks. The term was soon applied to all the people living in the subcontinent.

**2.1 Example of the intricately carved seals of the Indus civilization that were probably used in trade.**

The inhabitants of the Indus Valley seemed to have called themselves something akin to the "Meluhha." That, at least, is what the contemporary Mesopotamians, with whom they traded extensively both by northern land routes and by ship through the Arabian gulf, called them. Thousands of terra-cotta seals with a wide range of human, animal, and mythical forms on them, each with distinctive markings that are presumably letters of an alphabet, have been found distributed throughout the civilization. Excavations have yielded several tablets that specifically mention the presence of ships from Dilmun, the Arabian Sea, and Meluhha as part of their trade network. Ships carried bricks, beads, lumber, metals, and lapis lazuli, a semiprecious stone mined in Afghanistan, up the Persian Gulf to the cities of Mesopotamia. We are not sure what they carried back since few Mesopotamian objects have been found at the Indus. Nonetheless, the entire area covering Mesopotamia, central Asia, eastern India, and both coasts of the Arabian sea was closely interconnected. Archaeologists are still in the process of working out the full cultural and historical implications of this zone of interconnection.

Besides those cities along the Indus, archeologists have also discovered hundreds of small towns densely clustered around the inland delta of a lost river known in latter-day Sanskrit texts as the Saraswati (or the Ghaggar in India and Hakra in Pakistan). Cultivation in the rich alluvium deposited by the inland delta of the Ghaggar-Hakra allowed for intense agricultural production. When the Ghaggar-Hakra gradually dried up over two or three centuries around 1500 BCE, it was an ecological disaster of unprecedented proportions and spelled the end of the entire civilization. Where the people went is still something of a mystery. The majority probably dispersed eastward to the plains of the Ganges River, but others went westward and relocated as far away as Assyria, causing a ripple effect of disruptions that were felt all the way to Egypt.

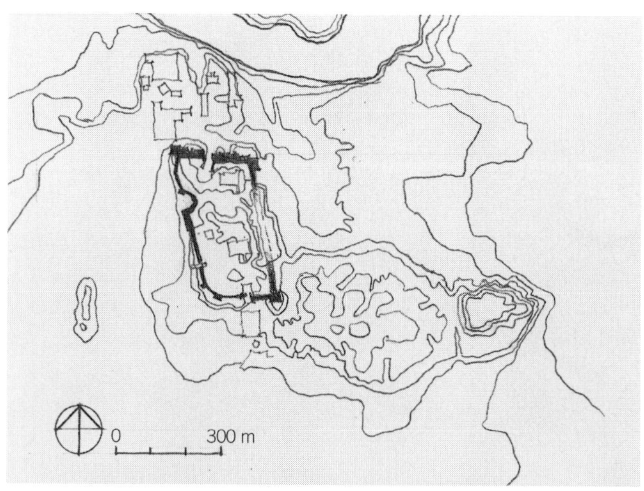


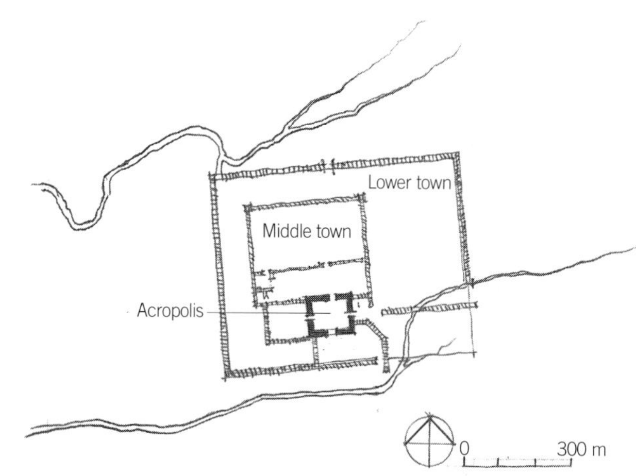


**2.2 Site plans of three cities of the Indus Ghaggar-Hakra Civilization, drawn to the same scale: left, Harappa; right, Dholavira; below, Mohenjo-Daro**

The Indus Ghaggar-Hakra was the first urban civilization in the true sense of the term. Over a thousand cities and towns have been discovered spread over a quarter of a million square miles, an area roughly equivalent to modern-day France. Five of the largest cities were: Mohenjo-Daro and Harappa on the Indus, Ganeriwala and Rakhigarhi on the Ghaggar-Hakra systems, and Dholavira, on an island in the vast delta of the Rann of Kutch. Though these cities were distant from each other, they communicated with the same language and shared a standardized system of weights and measures. Their economy was supported by agricultural surpluses, advanced crafts such as bead making, and by internal and external trade. It does not seem that the cities functioned like competitive "city-states" as in Mesopotamia, for none have anything more than the most rudimentary defense systems.

Although they clearly had a social hierarchy with a strong elite and with cities divided into sections with larger and smaller houses, there is little evidence of a centralized kingship, like the kind found in contemporary Egypt, Mesopotamia, and China. No large castles or palaces have been found, nor do the thousands of terra-cotta seals that have been discovered throughout the civilization clearly depict royal personages.

In the same vein, tabulating the civilization's famous "have nots," they did not build any large temples or pyramids. Their terra-cotta seals show that they certainly had a mythological system. Supernatural animals, in particular unicorns, abound, and there is the recurrent depiction of a proto-Shivalike person, who is sometimes shown sitting in the yoga lotus position, wearing bull horns on his head, and worshipped by animals of all sorts. There is a proliferation of sculptural figures dedicated to fertility and procreation. But there are no centralized religious structures. How the Indus people managed to build a hugely successful polity without a central authority legitimized by overarching religious ideology, remains an open question.

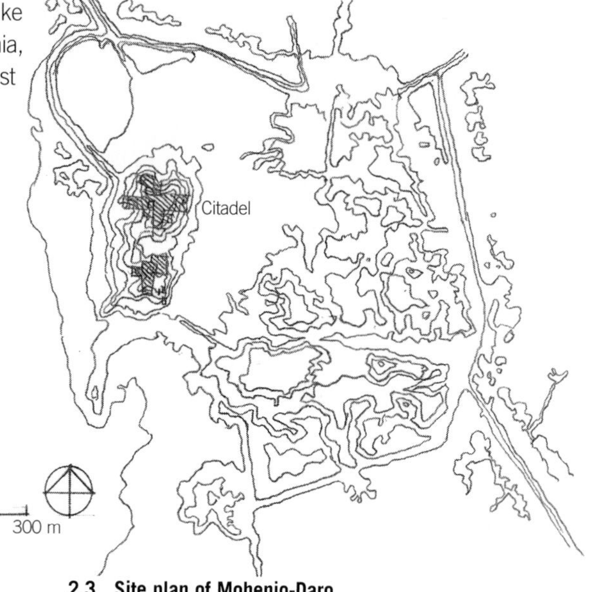


**2.3 Site plan of Mohenjo-Daro**

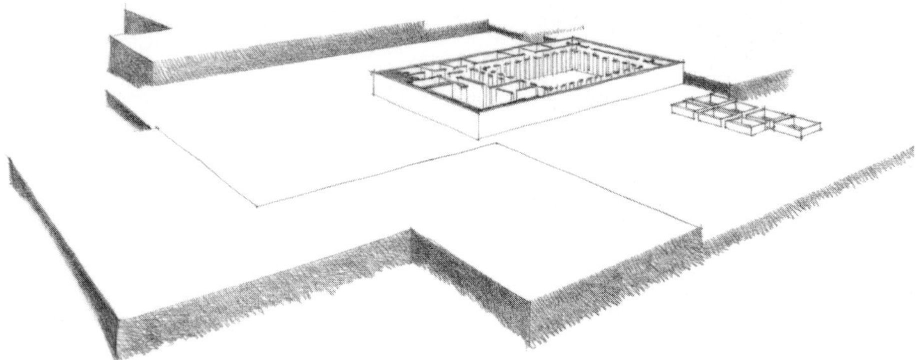

**2.4 Reconstruction of the foundation platform of the citadel of Mohenjo-Daro**

### Mohenjo-Daro

The two main elements of the Indus Ghaggar-Hakra's social organization were town planning and hydro-engineering. Mohenjo-Daro, the largest known city, was constructed on vast platforms made from millions of burnt bricks, built together with a complex subterranean drainage system that drained everything from a large public bath to the smallest drain of a lavatory in a house. The very act of building Mohenjo-Daro a few hundred feet west of the Indus was an act of defiant engineering. The Indus originates in the high Himalayas, which means that it is frequently subject to ice and landslide dams that can hold back the water for a while, but eventually they give way, resulting in sudden huge flash floods. To guard against these, the two largest building areas of Mohenjo-Daro were raised high on a platform of bricks, and in the event of flooding the drainage was designed to disperse large amounts of water quickly through oversized culverts (The site of Mohenjo-Daro itself receives very little rain). The main streets had drains running below them, to periodic settling tanks which could be accessed and cleaned.

Hydro-engineering at Dholavira was of a completely different order. Since it sits in the middle of a vast delta in a very dry area, the problem at Dholavira was not to keep water out in the time of flooding, but to ensure that enough water was trapped to maintain an adequate supply in the long dry months. The ingenious solution was to construct a series of strategically located dams on the streams to drive water into vast holding tanks but which would also allow excess water to escape during a flood. In Lothal, a port city, water was let through a sluice into a vast rectangular tank that some speculate functioned as a dry-dock for the seafaring vessels.

The Indus valley neighborhoods were inward looking. The main streets looked onto blank walls, and even the secondary streets usually did not have any major houses opening directly onto them. Accessible by inner alleys only, the houses were usually constructed around open courtyards with the larger ones usually two stories, with the upper built of wood. Access was controlled by an entrance vestibule that protected the houses' privacy via a spatial knuckle, such as an L-turn. The number of rooms in the houses varied from two to more than twenty. A good number of the rooms contained wells, and the larger ones had bathing rooms and toilets.

**2.5 Great Bath on the Citadel of Mohenjo-Daro**

**2.6 First Street in the lower town of Mohenjo-Daro**

Located at the intersection of the major north-south and east-west streets, the Great Bath of Mohenjo-Daro was the social center of the city. Its 12 by 7-meter pool, 3 meters deep, was accessed by symmetrical stairs on the north and south. The bath is surrounded by a narrow deep-water channel, and an outlet from one corner of the bath leads to a high-corbeled drain that eventually empties out into the surrounding lowlands. Burnt bricks lined the pool while a layer of bitumen waterproofed it. It was surrounded by a brick colonnade, behind which were a series of rooms of various sizes (one of these with a well). The whole structure had a wooden second story, although the central pool courtyard was probably open to the sky. Access was carefully controlled, with only one opening from the south. Ritual urns with ashes of presumably important people, were found close to the entrance. One can only guess at the social practices that took place there, but the very presence of the Great Bath indicates the dominance of water and bathing in their ideology.

To the west of the bath, connected and built at the same time, is a group of 27 blocks of brickwork, crisscrossed by narrow ventilation channels, all of which come together to form a large high platform. Archaeologists originally assumed this was a huge granary, but more recent evidence suggests that it may have been a general-purpose warehouse. The largest stair, going down from the mound to the lowlands, is found just to the south of this structure on the west.

With the drying up of the rivers, the cities were slowly abandoned. The process of decay was, however, gradual. The Great Bath, for instance, was first converted into a workshop, and then eventually abandoned. The smaller cities in the south, around Kutch, actually grew as the big cities of the Indus decayed, but these too were eventually abandoned. The work of establishing what really did happen to the Indus people that caused them to abandon their cities is still to be done.

0 100 m

**2.7 Plan of the Citadel of Mohenjo-Daro**

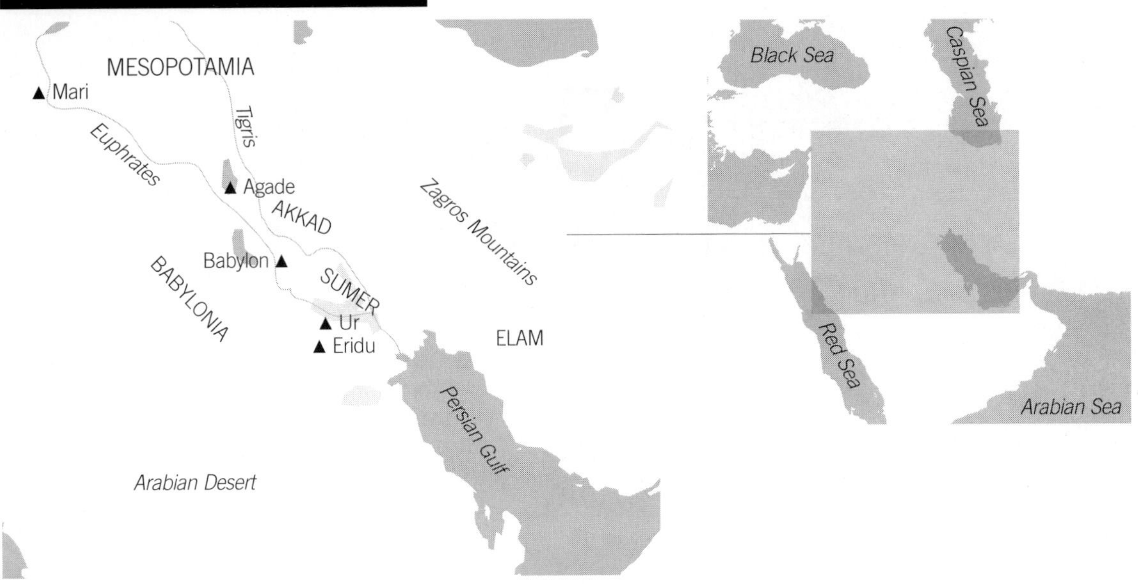


**EARLY EMPIRES OF MESOPOTAMIA**

Though settlements in the upper reaches of the Euphrates region date from very early on, large-scale urbanization of the lower Euphrates would have been impossible without a social system sufficiently complex and centralized to produce an economic surplus to develop and pay for the technology of irrigation. The Ubaids and Sumerians were the first to make that leap, but they were soon joined in their efforts and then rivaled by the Akkadians to the north. No one knows when the Akkadians first began to infiltrate into central Mesopotamia nor what their origins were, but by 2300 BCE they were predominant in the vicinity of modern Baghdad and further north along the rivers.

**2.8 Statue of the head of an Akkadian ruler**

The Sumerians and the Akkadians were not related. The Sumerian language was agglutinative whereas the Akkadian was Semitic and inflective. Of the two, it was initially the Akkadians who came to dominate Mesopotamia with the ascendancy of Sargon, the ruler of Umma, who reigned ca. 2334–2279 BCE. His was the first known successful centralization of power in the Mesopotamian region. His capital city, Agade, was located on the Euphrates about 30 kilometers south of modern Baghdad. Sargon's notion of kingship had lasting impact in Mesopotamian culture. The idea of village-based civic loyalty, so important to early Sumerians, was replaced by the concept of loyalty to the ruler, with Sargon taking measures that deliberately diminished the power of local chieftains. This new concept of kingship is expressed in the statue of a head representing an Akkadian ruler, found in the city of Nineveh. It is notable for its bold features, braided beard, and majesty of bearing. The mouth, from which the pronouncements of law and rule came, figures just as strongly as the eyes, which were once inlaid with stone, resulting in an active image in marked contrast to the quiet, open-eyed, and contemplativeness of the Sumerian figures.

Around 2000 BCE, the Akkadian dynasty was overthrown by tribes from the mountainous northeast who descended to the plains, contributing nothing to the civilization they ransacked. The survival of Mesopotamia was now suddenly dependent on kingdoms in the Sumerian south. They took up the challenge, drove the mountain people back and reunited the realm under the kings of Ur. These kings, part of the Third Dynasty (2112–2004 BCE), accepted many of the innovations that had been created under Sargon. The Akkadian language, for example, remained the official tongue even though it was written in the cuneiform first developed by the Sumerians. To the east around the bend of the Persian Gulf there was a parallel kingdom, the Elamites, working the fertile lowlands of the rivers descending from the Zagros mountains. Known for their metalworking skills, they developed urban and religious practices similar to those of the Sumerians. At first the two regions were more or less equal, but the Sumerians had a huge and simple advantage in the size of the river wetlands between the Tigris and Euphrates.

**2.9 Group of statues from the Abu Temple, Tell Asmar**

### Ur

The rulers of Ur defined kingship as a privilege that descended from heaven and was bestowed upon one city at a time, but only for a limited period. There was no notion of a single political entity comprising a nation in the modern sense. Rulers were, in essence, stewards of the gods who gave them protection and guidance. The temples—or the gods as the usage of the time expressed it—were also the principal landowners, which, to all practical effects, meant that the priests controlled and organized the labor needed to build and maintain the canals and ditches. They were, in essence, the managers of the city's economy and infrastructure. The political structure was thus a type of theocratic socialism in which all the citizens worked in their various capacities in the service of the city-state.

The god of the heavens who reigned supreme was Anu. Below him was Enlil, the earth or storm god, and Ea, the water god whom we encountered in Eridu. Nanna, the moon god who ruled supreme in Ur, was among a group of gods at a slightly lower level. He measured time and provided fertility. Senior members of the pantheon served as patron deities of individual cities, while deities of lesser rank were associated with smaller urban centers. Scientific and religious texts reveal that there were over 3000 other gods and demons, governing even things like pickaxes and brick molds. The flexibility with which the minor gods and goddesses came and went and syncretically changed their names makes it difficult to speak about a specific Mesopotamian pantheon. Some of these deities were shared across various regions; some were part of local cults. This divine population was thought to meet regularly in an assembly and to arrive at agreements that bound all deities to the more senior deities. The temple was the domicile of the god rather than merely a place for making contact with the divine powers, with one of the principal jobs of the priests being the interpretation of the omens, which had a powerful influence on every sphere of activity in Sumerian society.

**2.10**

Example of a boundary post, or *kudurru*, containing a record of lands that had been gifted and placed under the protection of the greatest possible number of gods, usually represented in their symbolic form and arranged according to the hierarchy of the pantheon. At the top is the supreme triad of Anu (sky), Enlil (earth) symbolized by horned crowns, and Ea (water) symbolized by a scepter carried by a goat-fish.

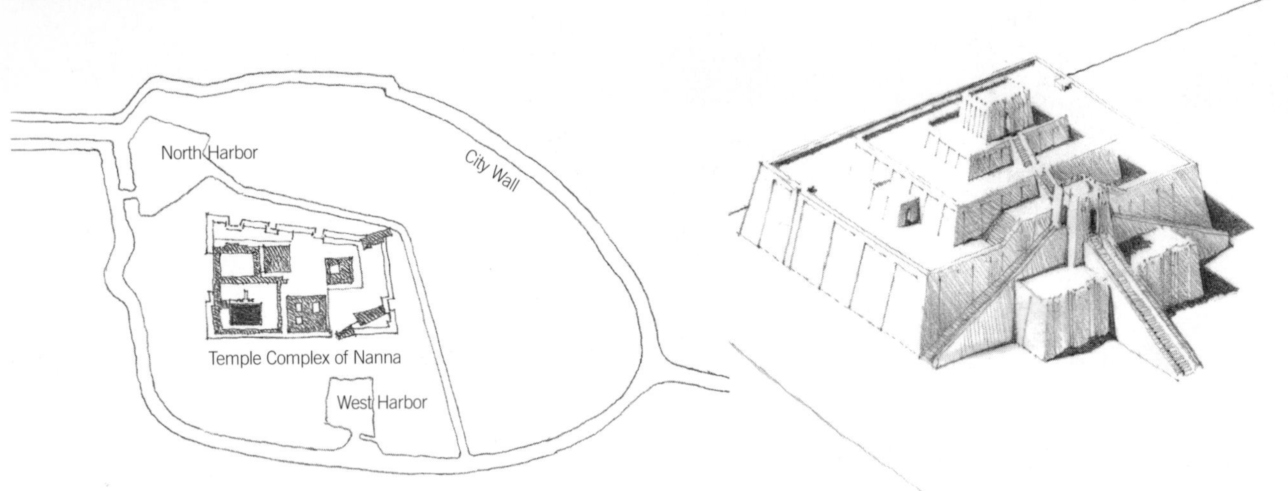


**2.11 Plan of Ur, near Nasiriyah, Iraq**

**2.12 Massing of the Ziggurat at Ur**

**Ziggurat at Ur**

Mesopotamian religion was heavy in superstitions and subscriptive behavior, with life after death portrayed as a sad and pitiable state with the dead potentially hostile toward the living. Thus, apart from rituals to appease the dead, burial architecture was rare. This meant that one's association with the gods was based very much in the hear-and-now and on a principle of constant vigilance. For the manufacture of cult statues, for example, a text, slightly modified here, reads:

> When you make the statues of cornel wood in the morning at sunrise you shall go to the wood. You shall take a golden axe and a silver saw, and with censor, torch and holy water you shall consecrate the tree ... You shall sweep the ground, sprinkle clear water, set up a folding table, sacrifice a sheep and offer the shoulder and fatty tissue and the roast, scatter dates and fine meal, set out a cake made with syrup and butter, pour out beer, kneel down, and stand up in front of the cornel tree and recite the incantation: 'Evil is the broad steppe.' With golden axe and the silver saw you shall touch the cornel tree and cut it down with a hatchet; you shall damp it with water, then remove the set-out material, kneel down and break the cornel tree into pieces.
>
> (Frans A. M. Wiggermann, *Mesopotamian Protective Spirits: The Ritual Texts* [Groningen: Styx Publications, 1992], condensed from pages 7-9)

The person then carves the statues as if "clad in their own garment, holding in their right hand a cornel-stick charred at both ends and with their left clasping their breasts." After writing his name on the statues, the person was asked to bring the statues he had made to his house for the purification ritual, placing them "on a pedestal in a walking pose so as to repel the evil ones." He was then asked to touch various parts of the house while reciting incantations and performing other proscribed rituals. Statues such as these were set up in temples, creating a charged ocular environment, with the eyes of the supplicant seeking to establish an unblinking connection between the profane and the sacred. Coming back from the other direction were the silent commands of the gods, translated into words by the priests. This exchange played itself out most grandly in the ziggurats.

That ziggurats also served as conjugal sites is proven at Ur where the ziggurat was linked by a watercourse to a small temple four miles west of the city dedicated to the mother goddess, Ninkhursag. She was represented by the cow, whereas Nanna, the moon god who ruled over Ur, was sometimes referred to as a bull.

Once a year, Ninkhursag, who was referred to as the Lady of the Mountain, whether embodied in statues or by a priestess herself, would have been brought to the city in a procession and led up to the shrine on top of the ziggurat to consummate her marriage while sacrifices and chants proceeded outside. Similar notions existed in Hinduism and in ancient Greece with the celebration of the mystic marriage, the Hierogamos (*hiero*, sacred; *gamos*, marriage). Ninkhursag thus represented the older goddess tradition that had been preserved and incorporated into the more complex mythologies needed after the move into the Mesopotamian marshes.

The Ziggurat at Ur was one of the most impressive structures of the times and remains of it are still extant at Tall al Muqayyar in Iraq, about 42 kilometers south of Babylon. Some reconstruction drawings show it as a freestanding object similar to an Egyptian pyramid; it was in actuality surrounded by precinct walls and connected to a large square-shaped sacristy dedicated to Nanna's divine wife, Ningal. The whole was part of a larger terraced temple-complex enclosed by defensive walls. The palace for Nanna stood just in front of the ziggurat and in front of that was a combination shrine, gatehouse, and law court; it appears from inscriptions that judges sat there to pass sentence.

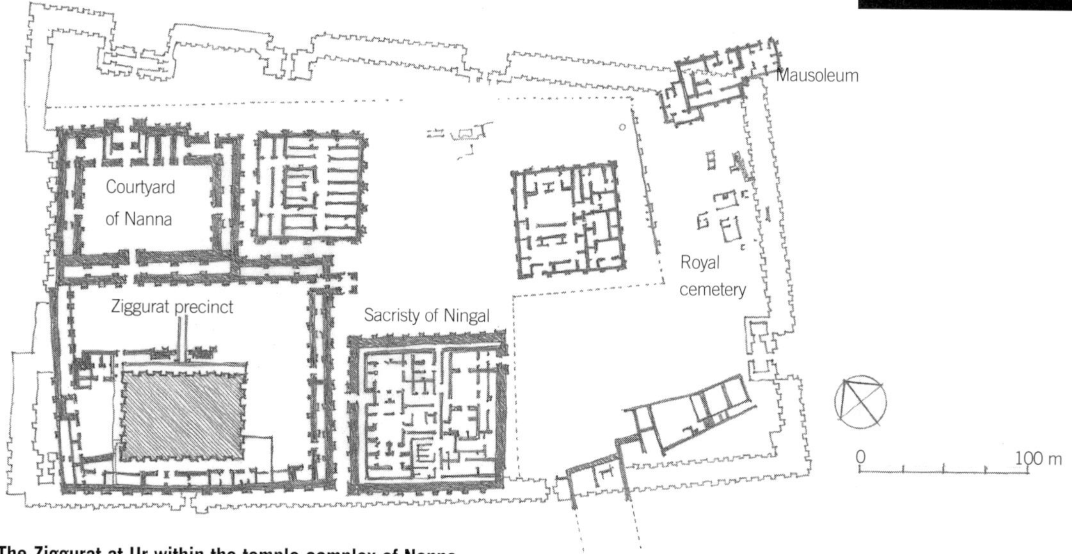


**2.13 The Ziggurat at Ur within the temple complex of Nanna**

The start of a construction of such a scale was accompanied by elaborate rituals in which the king fashioned the first brick and carried up the first basket of earth. This act of dedication was commemorated by the burial of peg-shaped copper figurines in the foundation. The hard work was done by slaves taken from conquered lands, a common practice that was to be used for millennia. The structure was made of square flat bricks mortared with bitumen. Reed matting soaked with bitumen was inserted horizontally at various layers to add cohesion and protect against vertical shear forces. The bricks were stamped with an inscription reading "Ur-Nammu, king of Ur, who built the temple of Nanna."

The ziggurat, which measured 65 meters by 100 meters at its base, was 21 meters high and consisted of three terraces with the sacred shrine on the highest one. Though the ornamentation of the ziggurat cannot be confirmed, the building was not the volumetric heap of bricks that we see today in the 20th-century reconstruction. The sides would have been plastered smooth and painted to serve as a visual key to a cosmological narrative, the principal character of which was Apsu, god of the primeval waters who fathered heaven and earth. Despite his importance, he was defeated and killed by Ea, who transformed Apsu into still or stagnant subterranean waters. The lowest terrace of the ziggurat, representing Apsu, was painted white. The next terrace, probably black, represented Ea floating on and dominating the water. The top level would have been red, representing the sun-kindled air. The blue tiles that were found on the site are thought to have come from the temple at the top since it would have represented the blue heaven upon the earth.

What made this structure so innovative from an architectural point of view is that the elements—the stairs, the platforms, and the temple itself—were no longer arranged as a geographical mass, as at Uruk, but brought into the embrace of a unified and dramatic design. Geographical simulation had been replaced by an architectural abstraction. Three monumental staircases rose up the northeast flank of the ziggurat, converging at a canopied vestibule at the top of the first platform, 20 meters up from the ground. From there, the central stair continued on to the next stage and then to the third. Though highly axial, the axis did not carry through to the surrounding architecture. Access to the court was not from the front but diagonally from a gate at one of its corners.

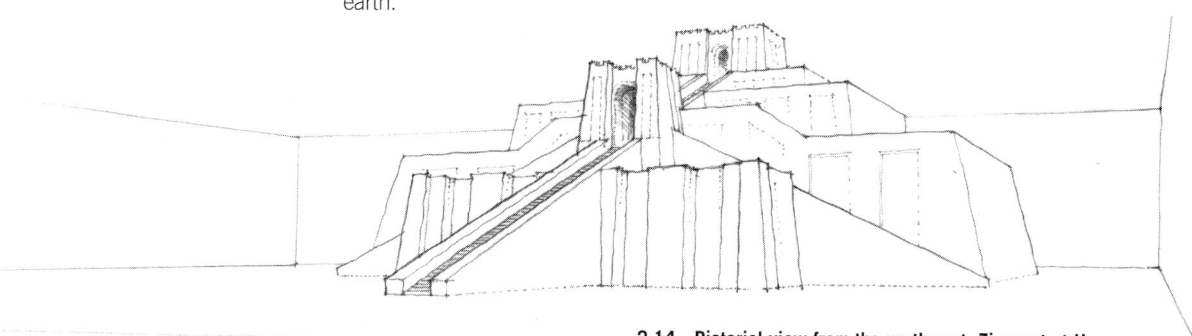

**2.14 Pictorial view from the northwest: Ziggurat at Ur**

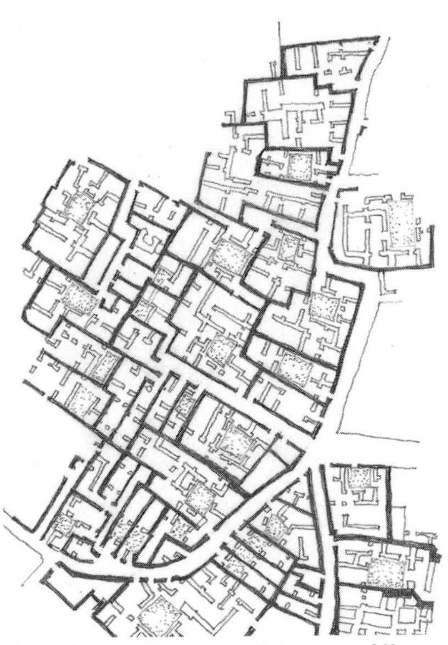


2.15 **Portion of a residential quarter of Ur**

The houses of Ur, of varying quality depending on the wealth of the occupant, were organized around small courtyards as is typical even today. Some of the better ones had baked-brick foundation walls. The side opposite the entrance was generally the location of the principal room. Long and shallow, it was used for meals and receptions. A baked-clay model of such a house, dating from 2400 BCE, was found in an Ishtar temple in the city of Ashur; it shows a two-level house with the upper level recessed and an elegantly perforated wall covering the front. Rather than facing the street directly, the house would have fronted onto its courtyard.

2.16 **Clay model of Mesopotamian house**

The city of Ur was almost oval in shape with the Euphrates River coursing around its sides. There were harbors on its north and west side, with the temple complex clamped between them. The surrounding walls, as is the case in all Mesopotamian cities, were intended just as much to impress as to protect. From their ramparts one would have seen the vast stretches of cultivated fields in all directions as well as the villages of farm laborers tending them. The presence of gardens and orchards near the walls was also common.

Much effort was made in the design and outfitting of the gates, which were flanked by towers decorated on top with bands of shields. The visitor, upon entering through the gates, would immediately confront the densely built-up jumble of the city. There was, however, little evidence of organized city planning. Royal roads would be designed only later. Streets varied from narrow lanes to routes two to three meters wide and served not only as passageways but as a convenient place in which to dump garbage, a practice that one encountered even in medieval Europe. Because windows were rare, the narrow lanes formed curving chutes punctuated only by doors or enlivened by lean-tos where goods or food was sold.

Much of the city was built of sun-baked mud brick, making destruction by acts of war easy and common. Sargon, in a text repeated again and again by later rulers, writes: "Their twelve strong and walled cities ... I captured. I destroyed their walls, I set fire to the houses inside them, I destroyed them like a flood, I turned them into mounds of ruins." Such destructions helped empty the countryside while consolidating the power of the victorious. Cities were, however, also relatively easily rebuilt. Though Ur was destroyed in various battles around 2000 BCE, it was rebuilt and remained important mainly for its religious shrines. Life continued, though at a slower pace, under the tutelage of various rulers until the city was abandoned around 400 BCE, by which time the Persian Gulf was many miles away due to the silting of the delta.

Domestic dwellings were generally organized around small courtyards. Some of the better ones had baked-brick foundations. The side opposite the entrance was generally the location of the principal room. Long and shallow, it was used for meals and receptions. A baked clay model of such a house dating from 2400 BCE and found in an Ishtar temple in the city of Ashur shows a two-level house with the upper level recessed and an elegant perforated wall covering the front. The house would face the courtyard rather than the street.

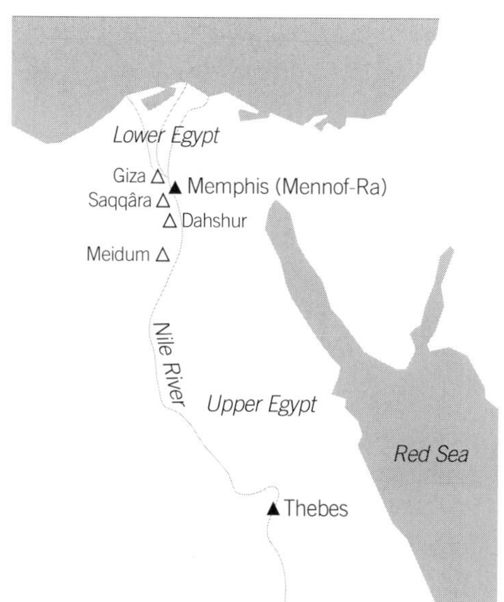

**2.17 Mortuary complex of Zoser, Saqqâra, Egypt**

**EGYPT: THE OLD KINGDOM**

Though later Egyptians describe their early history as emerging after the unification of the Upper and Lower Egypts, archaeological evidence suggests that unification was a protracted process that took place over several centuries. Out of this unification there emerged what later Egyptians would themselves call the "Old Kingdom," with its capital in Memphis. This new political unity, combined with the rapid development of a hieroglyphic script and a powerful bureaucracy, was the final stage of Egypt's transformation from a jungle-filled, swampy valley into a complex and vertically structured society with a population of several million.

Unlike Mesopotamia and China, Egypt was organized around an efficient and vast workforce that had little contact with the religious practices of the ruling elite. It has been estimated that already by the third millennium BCE, the Nile Valley produced three times its own domestic requirements. From very early on, plenty of labor was available, above and beyond the stage of self-sufficiency, to work in the crafts and building arts.

Soon, huge workforces of slaves, laborers, technicians, bureaucrats, and cooks were employed solely for royal projects. And there was no shortage of building material. Stone was abundant all up and down the Nile: the colorful red granite of Aswan, the white marble of Gebel Rokham, the black basalt from Faiyum, not to mention the various types of soft sandstone brought downriver from Nubia. One tremendous obelisk of red granite 41 meters long still lies on its side in the quarry near Aswan.

By the third dynasty of the Old Kingdom, the political stability of Egypt was secure, with Zoser (2686–2613 BCE) creating building projects against which later rulers would measure their accomplishments. The Mortuary Complex of Zoser, located west of Memphis and just to the north of Saqqâra, was enclosed by a 277 by 544 meter wall, laid out in precise orientation to the four cardinal points. The walls were of white stone and an impressive 10.5 meters high. They served more symbolic and aesthetic purposes than defensive ones, meant to protect the mortuary complex from the "chaos" of the unordered world outside. There were fifteen gateways, yet only one was a functionable entrance. The structure was so impressive that Egyptian historians for centuries would continue to praise and honor it.

The Ptah temple in that city was called "Mansion of the Ptah," which in ancient Egyptian was pronounced *haykuptah*; it was from this that the Greeks later derived the word *Aiguptos*, or Egypt.

**2.18 King Zoser**

2.19 Entrance Hall to the mortuary complex of Zoser

One entered the complex from the southern end of the eastern wall. The visitor passed through a one-meter wide hallway into a narrow corridor defined by two rows of columns attached to wall fins that projected into the space and supported a massive stone ceiling. These columns are probably the earliest monumental stone columns in the history of architecture. They are fluted and simulate a bundle of reeds. It was an ancient practice in Egypt to decorate wooden columns with a skirt of reeds as a representation of the mother goddess. But these columns were gigantic and meant to impose on the visitor the difference of scale that separates the divine from the mortal world.

The shadowy entranceway led to the south court in front of the step pyramid. This was the Sed festival court where ceremonial races were enacted. In the centuries before the Old Kingdom, the King had to prove that he was strong and capable of ruling by running a course for each of the provinces he governed. If he failed he would be sacrificed in a religious ritual. From this derives the name Sed, or "slaughter festival." By the time of the Old Kingdom this practice died out, but it remained an important element in the symbolic attributes of kingship and in architecture itself. Zoser conceived the complex as a review stand for this event, which lasted five days, ending with a final ceremonial sprint. Originally it was to be held for every king in the thirtieth year of his reign, but that was not always the case. Ramses II celebrated his Sed in grand style by inviting foreign dignitaries.

Since Zoser did not live long enough to perform this ritual, the court was designed so that he could perform it in death. This is confirmed by the fact that the complex contained two mastabas—one on the south side, next to the wall, a type of fake mastaba and the other, belonging to Zoser, to the north. The two structures have almost identical tomb designs, a room at the bottom of a 28-meter-deep shaft sealed by a three-ton granite plug. In the southern mastaba, archaeologists found the wall decorated with small blue tiles with a glaze just as brilliant today as it was four thousand years ago. They represent a reed matting set in stone posts designed to imitate the appearance of wood, the whole thing creating the illusion of an outdoor, canopied room. Between the tile sections is a large stone relief of Zoser "running" the ceremonial race.

2.20 Mortuary Complex of Zoser: Section through Entrance Hall

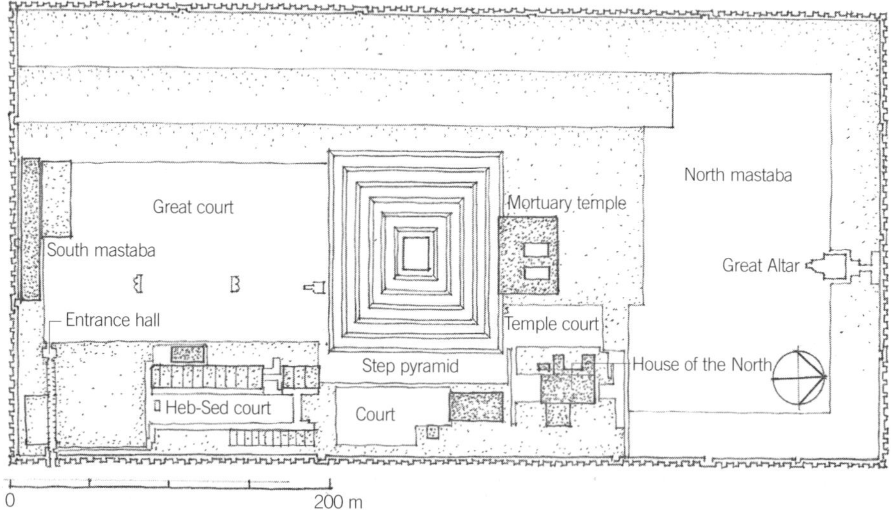


2.21 **Plan of the mortuary complex of Zoser**

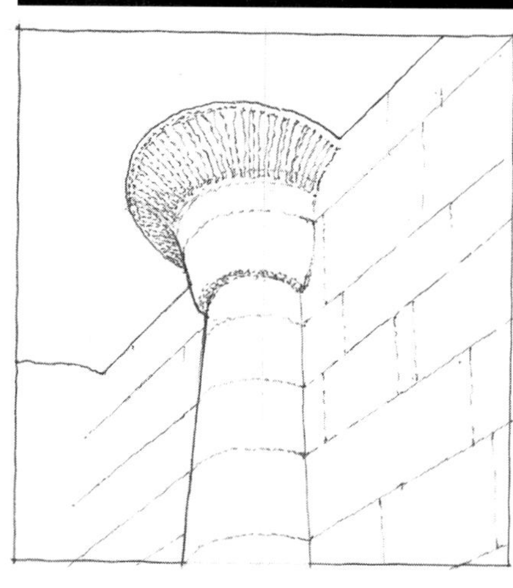

2.22 **Engaged column with papyrus capital**

Originally, the north mastaba was similar to the southern one as both were low, flat-topped structures. But that design was changed in a dramatic way during the course of construction when the northern mastaba was covered with a stone superstructure with four gently sloping steps. No sooner was that built than it was decided to expand yet again. It was transformed into a 60-meter high, six-tiered structure by adding material in the northerly direction. The first mortuary temple behind this step pyramid was also rebuilt and expanded.

To the east there was another court lined on both sides with chapels, one for each of the Egyptian provinces. Behind them rose the facades of ten tall dummy buildings, replicating government buildings or more probably granaries. Slender columns, drawing on the imagery of reed bundles, ornamented their surfaces. On their other side we see engaged columns with smooth-angled shafts holding bell-shaped capitals modeled on the shape of the papyrus flower. Like the reed-shaped columns, the papyrus also had symbolic value. It was used to decorate the Djed pillar that was thought to represent Hathor pregnant with Osiris in the Egyptian mystery play of the death and resurrection of the god. The raising of the pillar represented the resurrection of the dead Pharaoh. As part of the temple's stone architecture they guaranteed his eternal life.

The north part of the complex was dominated by a monumental altar on which offerings were brought each day, standing metaphorically for the offering place of the northern heaven. In a small chapel positioned against the north side of the pyramid was a life-size statue of Zoser, showing him wearing a priest's Sed festival cloak, a ceremonial beard, and a ritual headdress. Sitting in the dark chamber, he could gaze through two small holes in the wall placed at the statue's eye level, through which he could watch the ceremonies taking place in the court.

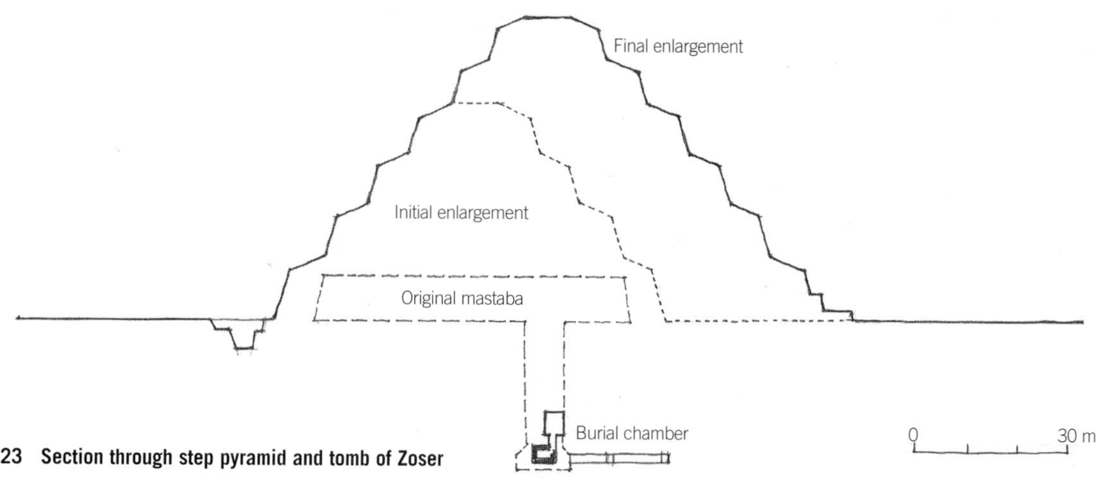


2.23 **Section through step pyramid and tomb of Zoser**

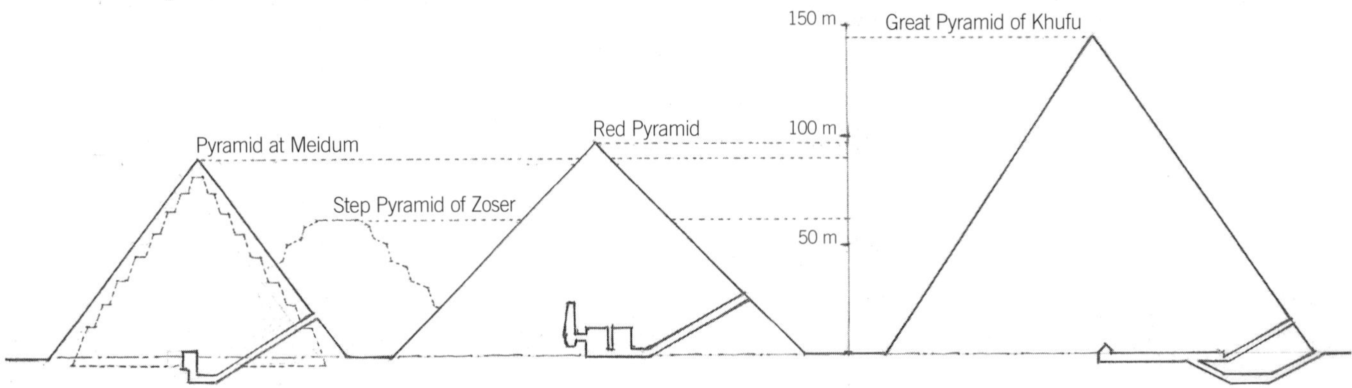


**2.24 A scalar comparison of Egyptian Pyramids**

After Zoser the pharaonic institution began to assert its cosmological narrative with ever-greater force and precision. One of the places where this becomes manifest is in a cult center for the falcon-god Menthu not far from Medamud, a provincial town lying 5 kilometers northeast of Karnak at Thebes. The original sanctuary, which dates from about 2500 BCE, consisted of a roughly lozenge-shaped enclosure 83 meters at its widest, surrounded by a 1.75-meter high wall with a gate to the east; in essence it was a three-sided courtyard embedded into the shape of the enclosure. The interior contains a grove of trees and two burial mounds. A thick pylonlike gate leads to the inner court or vestibule from which two winding paths lead into the center of some earth mounds. It is possible to interpret this in terms of the unifying theology of later times, which took the concept of the primeval mound, which had first appeared above the waters of chaos as a symbol of regenerative power, presaging new life beyond the grave. This cult site contains features that would continue to be part of later temple architecture. The mounds become pyramids, the enclosing wall becomes a square, and the entrance courtyard becomes the pyramid temple.

With Snefru (2613–2589 BCE), who ruled during the Fourth Dynasty, one sees the rapid maturity of the Medamud prototype. But it took Snefru several tries. His first project was the steep-faced Pyramid at Meidum. Innovative was the location of the tomb chambers. The two chambers, separated horizontally in the Zoser temple complex, are here placed one on top of the other, the lower one representing the chthonic aspect of the Egyptian religion. Snefru abandoned the building after 15 years of work and started another, larger pyramid complex 50 kilometers north, near Dahshur. Originally planned to be a towering 150 meters high, it was too bold and the ground gave way under part of it. In an effort to save the building, the designers added a kink or bend to reduce the weight and angle of the slope, which is why today it is called the Bent Pyramid.

The failure forced Snefru to ask his builders to return to the Step-Pyramid of Meidum. They added a layer that transformed it into a true pyramid, but this time, only after careful preparation of the ground. (In Roman times, the stone facing was removed to be made into stucco. Hence it is possible to see the original form.) However, for Snefru that was not enough. He constructed a third pyramid two miles north of the Bent Pyramid. Not as steep as the earlier ones, it is called the Red Pyramid because of the reddish cast of the stone, and this is where Snefru was actually buried. It is the first true pyramid. The harmonious proportions of the form and the perfection of the system of tomb chambers made it the model for subsequent tombs. Construction was so well thought out that despite the weight of the two million tons of stones on the roofs of the chambers, cracks have yet to appear.

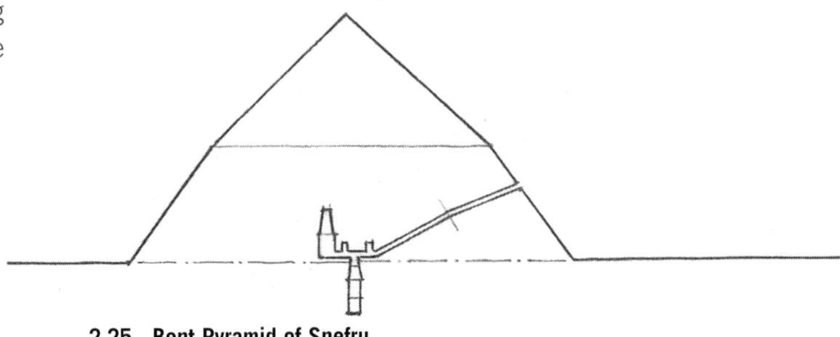

**2.25 Bent Pyramid of Snefru**

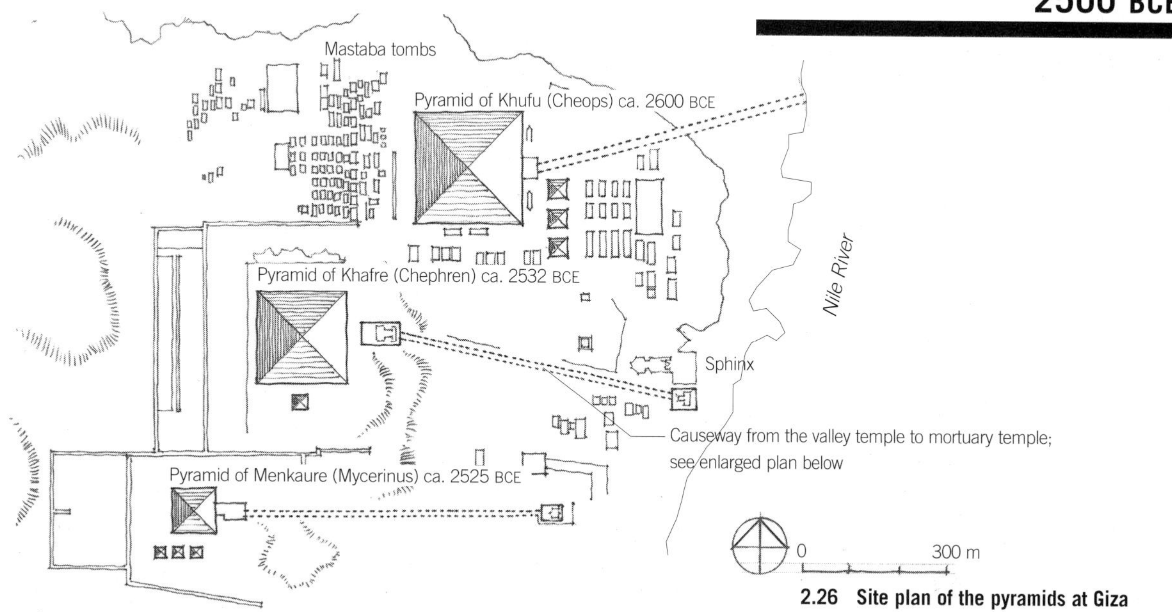


**2.26 Site plan of the pyramids at Giza**

**Pyramids at Giza**

Though the pyramids today are seen as freestanding, they were actually surrounded by a wall that defined the sacred precinct. An altar stood on the base of the pyramid on the eastern side and a mortuary temple on the western side. At the ceremonial center of the temple complex was the Ka statue that embodied the still living spirit of the king. The statue had to be tended to and provided with food and drink. Though a Ka statue might have been placed near the altar, others were placed in the mortuary temple. If anything were to happen to the Ka statue, the spirit of the deceased would never gain entrance into the heavenly realm.

The mortuary temple was connected to a so-called Valley Temple placed along the Nile River. The pharaoh's body would be brought there on a funerary ship. Once the body had been properly prepared, the coffin was sledded or dragged up to the mortuary temple where other rituals would take place, including daily prayers, incantations, and offerings.The mummy, then enclosed in its case and attended by a lavish funerary cortege, was brought into the pyramid and placed in the stone sarcophagus that was built into the burial chamber of the pyramid. Once the pharaoh and the Canopic jars that contained his entrails, along with various assorted possessions, were placed in the tomb chamber and offerings made, the funerary party exited the pyramid and the entrance was sealed so well that the last casing stone was indistinguishable from the thousands of other stones.

At the cosmological center of this system was the belief in the sun god Re, creator of all things. In some legends, he creates himself out of a mound that emerged from the primeval ocean. The sun god legitimized the divinity of the King. Snefru's son Khufu (Cheops) identified himself in his pyramid complex with the sun god to such an extent that his successors referred to themselves by the new royal title, "Son of Re."

At Giza, the only preserved valley temple is that associated with the Pyramid of Khafre (Chephren), the second pyramid complex to get built after that of Khufu. Khafre's mortuary temple consisted of an intricate though largely symmetrical combination of galleries and courts, at the center of which was a monumental courtyard with 12 colossal statues in niches along its perimeter. Behind the courtyard was a row of five chapels that held the sacred barges that had brought the sarcophagus and other objects down the Nile from Memphis. The plain square piers support red granite lintels that, in their stark simplicity, show the supreme confidence of the architect.

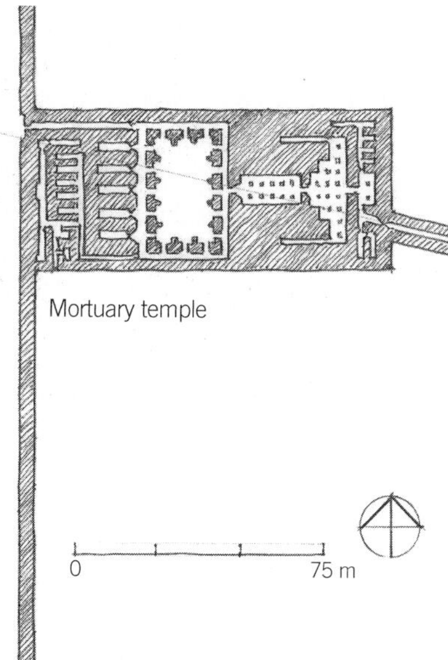


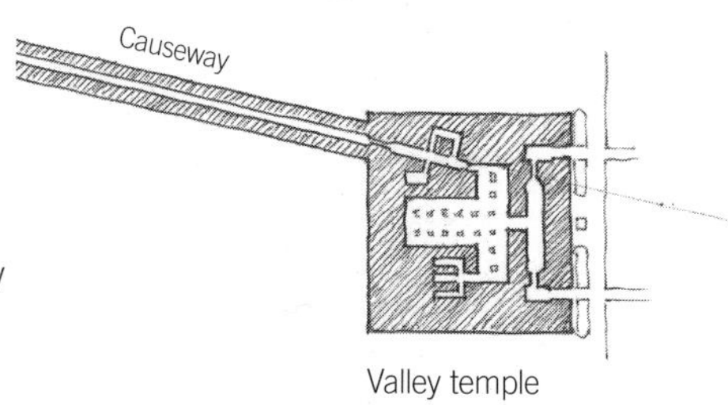


**2.27 Plan of the mortuary and valley temples of Khafre at Giza**

**2.28 Pyramids of Menkaure, Khafre, and Khufu at Giza**

When engineers set about to build the Great Pyramid of Khufu (Cheops), they took no chances and chose a solid rock foundation on the ridge above what is now Giza. It is oriented so close to true north that the question of how the ancient Egyptians achieved such accuracy has been widely debated. Six million tons of solid masonry, consisting of 2,300,000 individual stones, rested on that rock foundation. The core was mostly of yellow limestone quarried from the immediate area, while the stones of the casing are of a white unblemished limestone from quarries at Tura and Masara on the east bank of the Nile on the outskirts of Cairo. The outer casing was fitted together with such precision that the sides would have been seen as a smooth sheet glistening in the sun. The architects, for reasons unknown, did not design a true pyramid with flat sides. Instead the pyramid is an eight-sided figure, concave in the middle of the sides. The deviation is so slight that it escaped attention until 1940.

The Egyptians were the most highly proficient mathematicians of the world at the time, but which mathematical and associated astronomical system was used in the design is a much debated topic. Furthermore, exterior measurements of the pyramid are uncertain, because the outer surface has been removed over the years. Generally, however, it is agreed that the sides of the pyramid are about 440 Egyptian royal cubits and that its height would have been about 280 royal cubits. The face of the triangle intersects the ground at an angle a little less than 51.5 degrees. This means that the height of the triangle along the surface to the top is phi (the golden section or ratio, 1.61803399) and that the vertical height of the pyramid at its center is the square root of phi. The angles of the internal passages, as well as the location of the various chambers, are also thought to have been defined mathematically. There is also solid evidence that the layout of the three pyramids is not haphazard but that it too conforms to a unifying geometric plan.

**2.29 Great Pyramid of Khufu: Section**

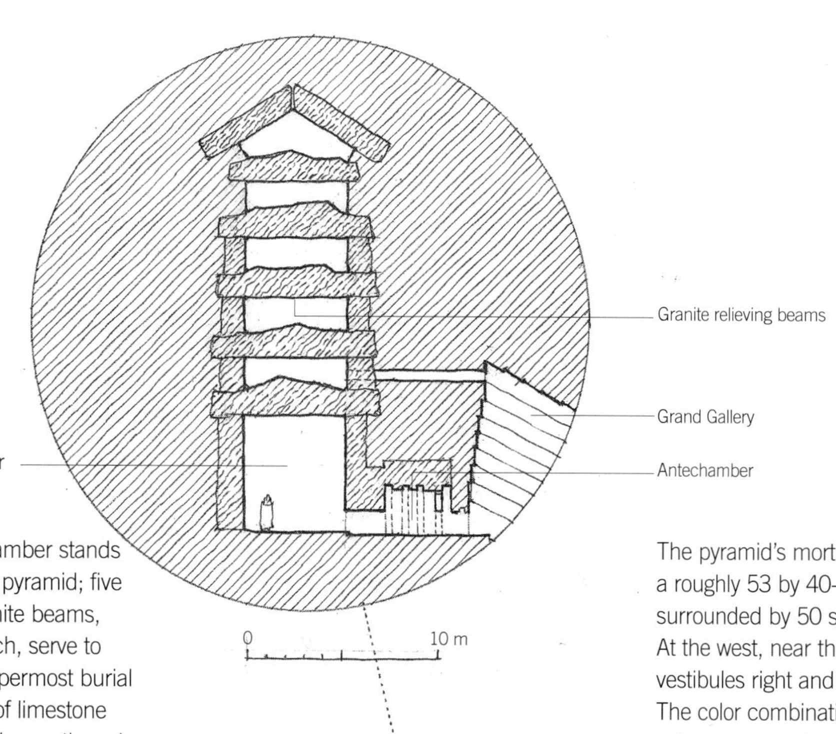


**2.30 Great Pyramid of Khufu**
Section through King's Chamber

The upper granite burial chamber stands isolated in the interior of the pyramid; five "upper chambers" with granite beams, weighing up to forty tons each, serve to relieve the pressure. The uppermost burial chamber has a gabled roof of limestone blocks. From the middle of the south and north walls of the burial chamber narrow mock corridors point toward the southern and northern skies to provide a direct route to heaven for the deceased's soul. The northern one, so it is thought, symbolically also allows the regenerative north wind to flow down to meet the body of the king. The room below the burial chamber was meant to house the Ka statue of Khufu. Though the statue has been lost, early accounts describe it as a statue of a man of green stone, standing inside the niche. This room has been misnamed the Queen's Chamber by early explorers, but it cannot have served as a tomb since it was not provided with a stone sarcophagus and was not sealed by a portcullis (stone plug). A unique aspect of the pyramid is a subterranean chamber that was cut out of the solid bedrock. But unlike the precision of the structure above, it was designed with a rough and disorderly look. It is clearly cultish in nature, but its purpose remains unknown.

The pyramid's mortuary temple was a roughly 53 by 40-meter courtyard surrounded by 50 square granite columns. At the west, near the pyramid, were two large vestibules right and left of the sanctuary. The color combination was impressive. The columns were of rose granite, the walls were of white limestone, and the floor of black basalt.

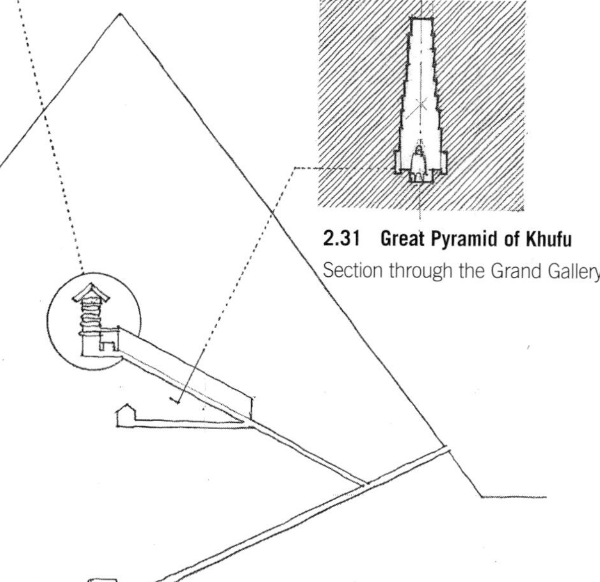

**2.31 Great Pyramid of Khufu**
Section through the Grand Gallery

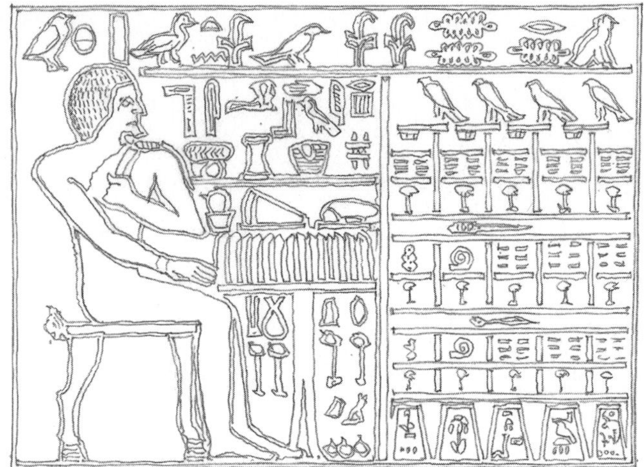

**2.32**
A slab stela shows a royal personage at a funerary repast sitting next to an offering table covered with the loaves of bread that have been brought to him. Next to him on the floor on small platforms are containers holding incense and ointments, figs, and wine.

### Architecture and Food

For both Mesopotamian and Egyptian societies, food was not only the sustenance of humans but also of the gods. The offerings were laid out in front of the Ka statue in its niche to provide for the difficult journey ahead. They consisted of meat, roasted fowl, bread, fruit, vegetables, beer, and wine, all delivered out of the temple district's own gardens. The slaughter of the animals, out of sight of the god, was supervised by the priests. From an anthropological perspective, one can say that this equation was necessary for social and political cohesion. There is also evidence that the ziggurat was itself an elevated feasting platform. A text states that "In the first night watch, on the roof of the high temple of the ziggurat…when (the star of) the great Anu of heaven comes out," the feast was to be laid out upon a golden table for Anu and his wife Antum as well as for the seven planets. The most exact instructions were given for the nourishment and entertainment of the god. The flesh of the cattle, sheep, and birds, and beer of first quality along with wine "poured from a golden ewer."

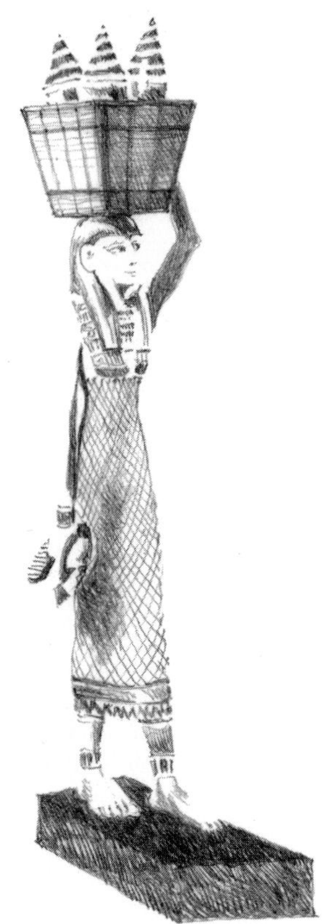

**2.33 Statuette of a woman bearing offerings**

Though both Mesopotamian and Egyptian food sacrifices emphasized breads, drinks, and the bounty of the land, the Mesopotamians rarely sacrificed animals as they were not naturally plentiful in the alluvial plain. For the Egyptians, animal sacrifices were not uncommon, with offerings coming mainly from hunting, especially of gazelles and antelope, geese, ducks, and pigeons. The meat was offered in either boiled or roasted form. The shank and the heart were thought to have a particularly reviving effect for the Ka. Unlike the Greeks, the Egyptians did not perform the actual killing and bloodletting in "sight" of the gods, but the meat arrived fully cooked. The difference is telling. The Ka is visualized as alive and sensitive or at least as coaxed back to life by tasty morsels. The Greeks, as will be discussed later, saw the sacrifice very differently.

It was only at the time of the New Kingdom, the Mycenaeans, and later the Dorians that one finds the multiple slaughter of large animals such as bulls. Furthermore, for the Greeks, the sacrificial animals could only be taken from domesticated herds, such as cattle and sheep. Sacrifice would remain important but mainly in a symbolic sense in Judaism and Christianity. Hinduism is one of the few modern religions that still preserves ritual food offerings to the gods, though meat sacrifices are forbidden.

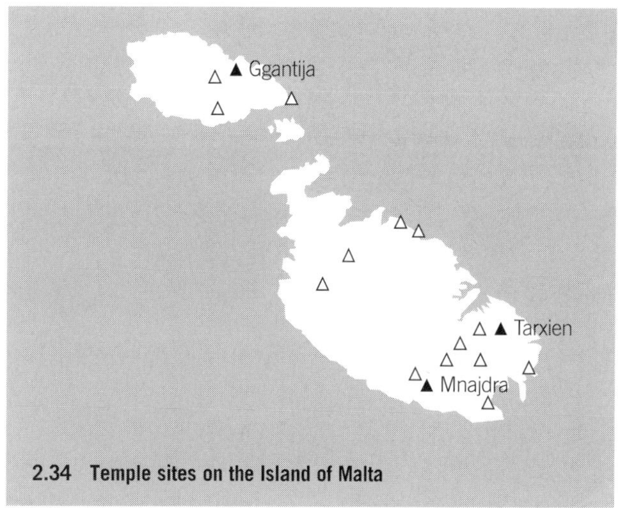


2.34 Temple sites on the Island of Malta

## MEGALITHIC TEMPLES OF MALTA

Around 4000 BCE, settlers arrived at the Maltese archipelago, a string of rocky islands between Sicily and the North African coast. There they set up farms and traded with Sicily and Sardinia for flint, obsidian, and other nonnative tools and materials. It is difficult to know the climatic and geographic conditions of the islands at the time. Today, without modern technology, the island would be relatively inhospitable given that there are few trees and no natural water sources. But in ancient times there must have been natural springs and an environment suitable for agriculture, for the Maltese flourished for a thousand years between 3500 and 2500 BCE, more or less contemporaneously with the Old Kingdom in Egypt.

Unlike in Egypt, which saw a rapid shift to a complex cosmology controlled by the elite, in Malta, religion revolved only around the ancient mother-goddess cult. We should, however, not see Malta as more primitive but rather as a place where the goddess cult survived in comparison with more industrialized areas such as Egypt and Mesopotamia. It is also unlikely that Malta was completely isolated. In fact, their drive for monumental expression conforms to parallel drives in Egypt.

The temples that have been unearthed both inland and along the coast share common characteristics. The outer walls were made of raw, undressed megalithic stones set vertically in the ground forming an oval. How the massive multiton stones were brought to the sites is a mystery. Archaeologists have found parallel ruts along which the stones might have been pulled, possibly on round stones used as rollers; but these ruts do not lead to the temple in efficient lines. Instead they zigzag through the landscape, nor are they always parallel.

In the interior space of the temples, the stones were meticulously dressed and set out in such a way that they created lobed chambers, the surfaces of which were sometimes finished with plaster. The space between the outer and inner walls was filled with dirt and rubble, and on the outside the whole was mounded over to form an artificial hill. How the spaces were roofed is still debated. Corbeled neolithic tombs can be found in Spain and Portugal; but given the absence of such stones, it seems likely that the roofs were supported by timber beams not unlike early tomb structures in Egypt. A model of a tomb, made by the ancient builders themselves, shows that these buildings were not arbitrarily formed but conformed to a prototype of planned symbolic spaces.

2.35 Interior of Hal Saflieni Hypogeum, Malta

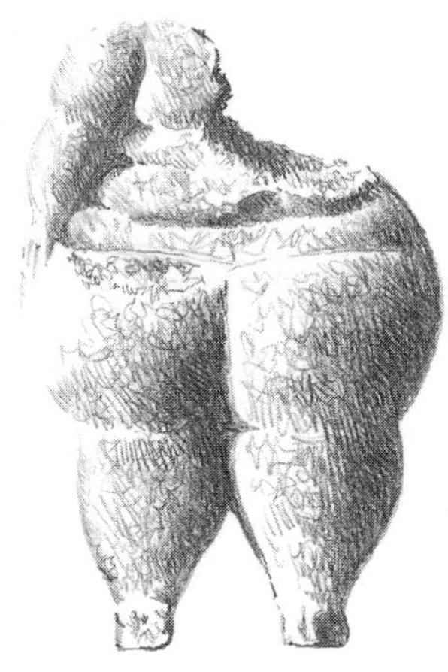

2.36 Figure of the Earth goddess

# 2500 BCE

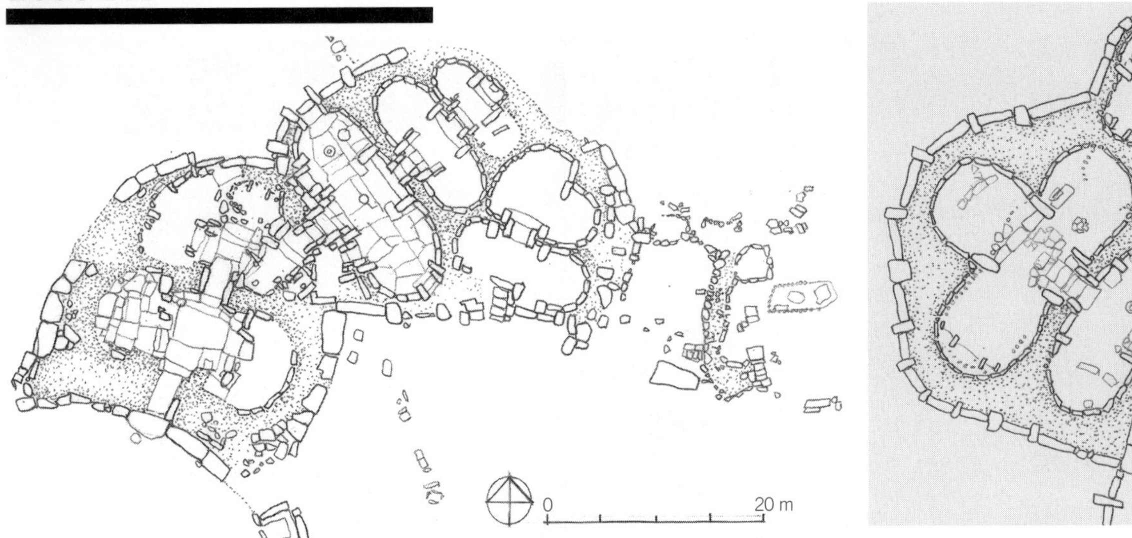


**2.37 Plans of temple complexes on Malta drawn at the same scale and orientation: Ggantija (upper left), Tarxien (above right) and Mnajdra (below).**

The nature of the rituals for which these structures were built has been lost to history. But statuettes of heavyset earth goddesses found on the sites are evidence of a cult dedicated to fertility, death, and renewal. The deities, some sitting upright, others lying asleep, look not unlike the temples themselves—a squat rounded figure harboring a mysterious, bodily inner world. Animal bones and statuettes testify to the ritual offerings and sacrifices that were likely associated with the cult. Many temples contained carved or freestanding stone altars, and most had libation stones with wells for liquid offerings to the earth. The later temples have a type of plaza in front and were equipped with stone benches indicating that the temples were used in communal gatherings.

The earliest and best preserved temple on Malta is Ggantija, part of a cluster of temples situated on the island of Gozo. This temple was used continuously for hundreds of years, with the earliest material possibly dating to around 3500 BCE. Ggantija was a double temple, nearly 30 meters long. It had a floor of crushed limestone slurry that formed a hard concretelike surface. The portals from chamber to chamber were huge post-and-lintel configurations of megalithic stones. The exterior was monumental and simple. The core cloverleaf configuration to the west was built first. Two more lobed chambers were then added along its entry passage. Later a second temple was built adjacent to the first and enclosed within the original mound. Perhaps the local population expanded and exceeded the original temple's capacity. Perhaps a plentiful harvest year prompted the farmers to renew their thanks to the earth goddess. The reasons are unclear. But over the generations, the Maltese regularized and expanded the design, testing, refining, and reproducing the archetypal shape at different scales, with different orientations, and with varying numbers of chambers.

The temple at Tarxien, built around 2500 BCE, is the most complex of the surviving temples. The imposing concave facade of the main temple was composed of finely coursed stone, larger blocks at the base and smaller blocks at the roof, which corbel outward to form a small cornice. Within, pairs of symmetrical chambers were built successively deeper over the centuries, one connected to the next by dual *trilithon* portals and connecting passageways.

At nearby Mnajdra is a complex of three temples of the same period overlooking an oval court. The southern temple is aligned such that at sunrise on the equinox, the sun's beam enters the temple and illuminates its main axis.

**2.38 Plan: Temple complex at Mnajdra**

**2.39 Temple complex at Mnajdra**

2.40 **Stonehenge as it stands today, near Salisbury, England**

Earth bank
Ditch
0 50 m

2.41 **Plan of Stonehenge, ca. 3000 BCE**

## STONEHENGE

Among Bronze Age sites in Europe, Stonehenge is preeminent. Wrecked by the Romans, who were trying to suppress local religions, chipped by tourists, threatened with demolition in 1914, sold at auction in 1915 for £6,600, and finally, its value as an irreplaceable relic of England's past understood, given to the nation in 1918. Today, this structure is one of the most important tourist attractions of England. It is natural to compare Stonehenge with the megalithic temples in Malta, and in its early formation, there might have been some general connective thread. But the Maltese temples only underwent a process of refinement and enlargement, as one might expect from a rather static society, whereas Stonehenge underwent several revisions that significantly and purposefully altered its use and meaning. The structure as we see it today is in fact a combination of the last two phases and dates from between 2500 and 1800 BCE, making it more or less contemporary with Ur in Mesopotamia and the end of the age of pyramids in Egypt. This should be borne in mind because there is a tendency to over-state the primitivism of Stonehenge, when in actuality it was a relatively advanced Bronze Age structure. Today, because Stonehenge is isolated in the landscape, it is difficult to remember that originally the area was densely settled. In the immediate landscape of Stonehenge one would have seen hundreds of burial mounds, some dating back to the fourth millennium BCE.

The first version of Stonehenge, dating to about 3000 BCE, was consistent with the circular henges of that age, except that this one was an impressive 100 meters across with two or perhaps three spaces left open for access to the inside of the circle. At the center, archaeologists speculate, was a circular timber building about 30 meters across. A long avenue marked by stones ran up to the trench and alongside a single 4.9-meters-high stone just outside the circle. It has a pointed top and is known as the Heel Stone. Two alignments were built into it, one astronomical at the northeast entrance toward the northernmost rising of the moon, the other to the cardinal point to the south at the other causeway.

Around 2500 BCE, the structure was transformed by the Beaker People, so named because of the fine beaker vessels that they produced and that were found in their villages and tombs. Having beliefs different from those who originally built Stonehenge, they changed the earthwork structure, and indeed the symbolic landscape associated with it, from a lunar to a solar monument. The origin of the Beaker People is much debated, but the argument in favor of them coming from eastern Europe is strengthened by the fact that they were experts in the mining and trading of gold and copper. Metal ores had been discovered, perhaps by the Beaker People themselves, at several places in Ireland, as well as at Great Orme's Head on the north coast of Wales facing into the Irish Sea.

The Beaker People integrated the geographically disparate technologies of mining, smelting, metal production, and trade into a single economic system, and they transformed Stonehenge from a local temple to a focal point for a larger civilizational entity. They filled the area for miles around with their circular burial mounds and founded a new city to the northeast of Stonehenge, now called Durrington Walls, which was defended by circular defensive walls 480 meters across. Their wealth shows in their graves. In one archaeologists found gold ornaments as well as bronze pins from Bohemia, blue faience beads from Egypt, and amber beads from central Europe.

At the center of their cosmology was a connection between the smelting of ore and the sun. For this reason they had to redesign Stonehenge, transforming its orientation from the moon to the sun. To do this they rotated the axis an almost imperceptible 3 degrees eastward to coincide with the rising midsummer sun, this according to the research of Gerald S. Hawkins in collaboration with John B. White. The Beaker People also imposed a rectangular shape measuring 33 by 80 meters onto the circle by adding four large stones that point to summer and winter risings and settings. Though the precise nature of how the stones worked is in dispute, Stonehenge's latitude as it turns out is the only one in Europe where this combination is even possible.

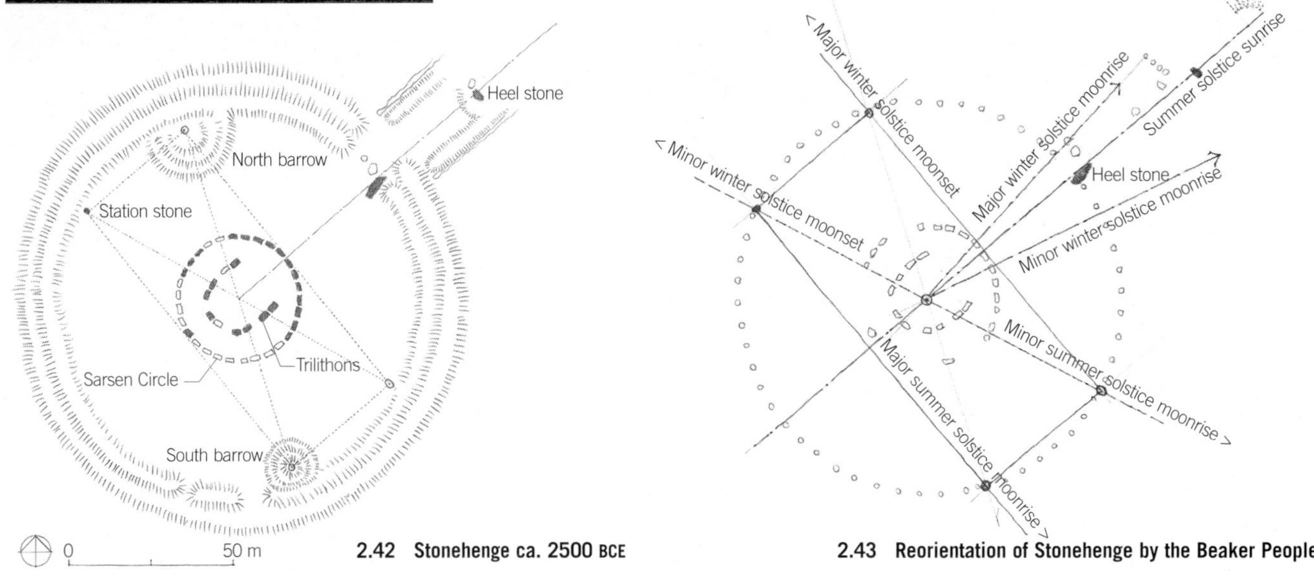


2.42 Stonehenge ca. 2500 BCE

2.43 Reorientation of Stonehenge by the Beaker People

The most significant change attributed to the Beaker People was the addition of a ring of 60 large "bluestones" to the interior. They also constructed, about a kilometer north of Stonehenge, a *cursus*, as archaeologists call it—a 3-kilometer-long and 100-meter-wide rectangular form, slightly beveled toward the ends. Created by incising a ditch into the landscape, it lies in an east-west orientation. Though simply built, it is laid out with great precision. Its purpose is unknown, even though there are other *cursi* scattered across the region, some predating the arrival of the Beaker People. It certainly was not a running track as the name implies. One can surmise that since the eastern sector was associated with the sunrise and the western side with the sunset, the cursus played an important part in the ritual expressions of life and death. Was it a pathway for the soul?

No sooner had the Beaker People completed their work in or around 2300 BCE, than Stonehenge underwent yet another and even more impressive transformation. The new designers no longer belonged to the Beaker culture. They were now working at the behest of a culture represented by chieftains whose numerous cemeteries were added to the landscape around Stonehenge. Their origin is even more mysterious than that of the Beaker People. The new overlords removed the bluestones that had been put there by the Beaker People and added the now famous Sarsen Ring of *trilithons*, Sarsen being the name of the local sandstone boulders. The ring, 33 meters across, was composed of 30 enormous stones with an average weight of 26 tons. The transportation of the blocks from a site 30 kilometers away would have been a feat in itself.

Particularly noteworthy was the effort made in the preparation of the stones. Moving in unison and using stone mauls swung on ropes, workers pummeled the surface of the boulders to pulverize protrusions, first with large mauls the size of pumpkins and then moving down in size to mauls the size of tennis balls. When the surfaces were finally flat, other teams were set to work rubbing the surfaces with large flat stones, back and forth like a woodworker with sandpaper. When they were done, the posts measured 4.1 meters high, 2.1 meters wide, and 1.1 meters thick. They were surmounted by 30 six- to seven-ton lintels that formed a continuous circle around the top.

2.44 Aerial view of Stonehenge

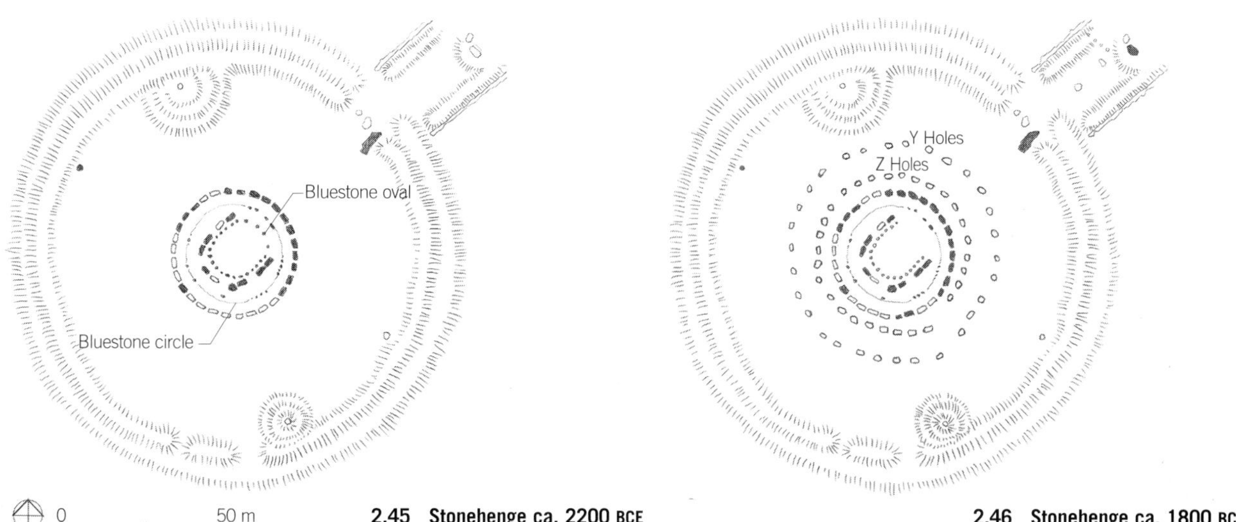


**2.45 Stonehenge ca. 2200 BCE**

**2.46 Stonehenge ca. 1800 BCE**

The precision was remarkable. The tops of the lintels, once they were in place, never varied more than ten centimeters from the horizontal. Such carefully worked stone is not typical of other English henges where the stones were not only brought from closer in but were left natural, perhaps because they were seen as possessing a magical, chthonic presence. The Sarsen Ring was architecture of a particular type, for it was in reality something akin to carpentry in stone.

The sanding of the surfaces, and the way in which the stones were fitted together, all seem to imply a direct application of the techniques of carpentry to stone. Possibly the designers were replicating in stone a wooden prototype, or perhaps they were seeking to enhance the power of the stone structure by embodying in it the more familiar techniques of woodworking.

Stonehenge went through yet another transformation. In this final phase some of the bluestones that had been removed were brought back to the site with some being erected within the Sarsen Ring and others placed in a horseshoe configuration. Such a horseshoe was uncommon in England but occurred more frequently across the channel in Brittany. The implications of this have yielded much speculation, but it is almost certain that southern England and French Brittany in this phase were part of a single cultural province. As a result, so it is thought, of climatic cooling, the society that built Stonehenge devolved into a hamlet society with little capacity to continue the great architectural accomplishments of its predecessors. In the shadowy remnants, a druid culture emerged that contributed practically nothing to the architectural legacy of England.

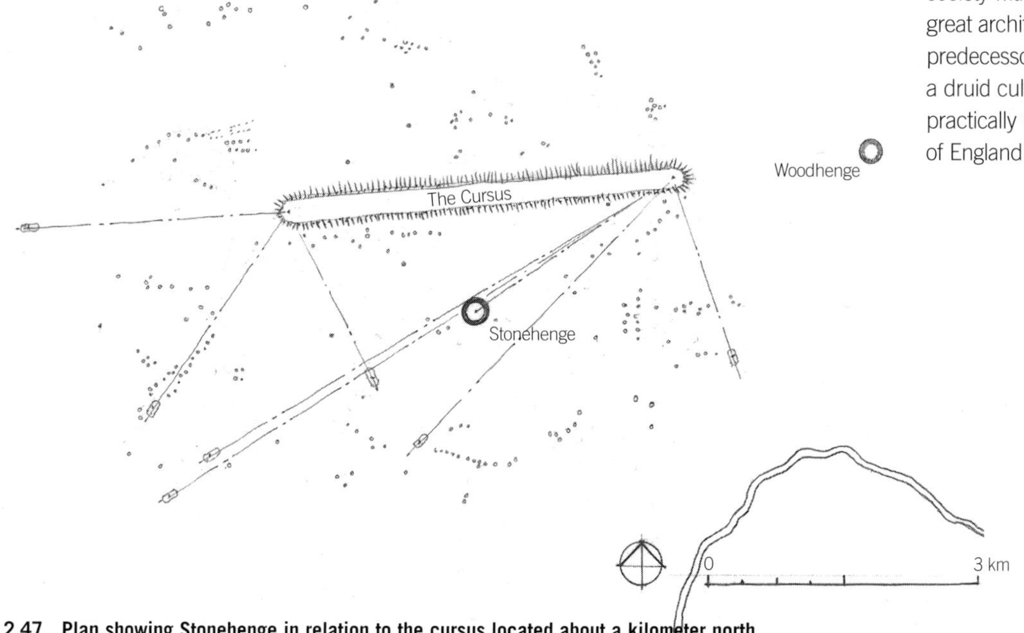


**2.47 Plan showing Stonehenge in relation to the cursus located about a kilometer north**

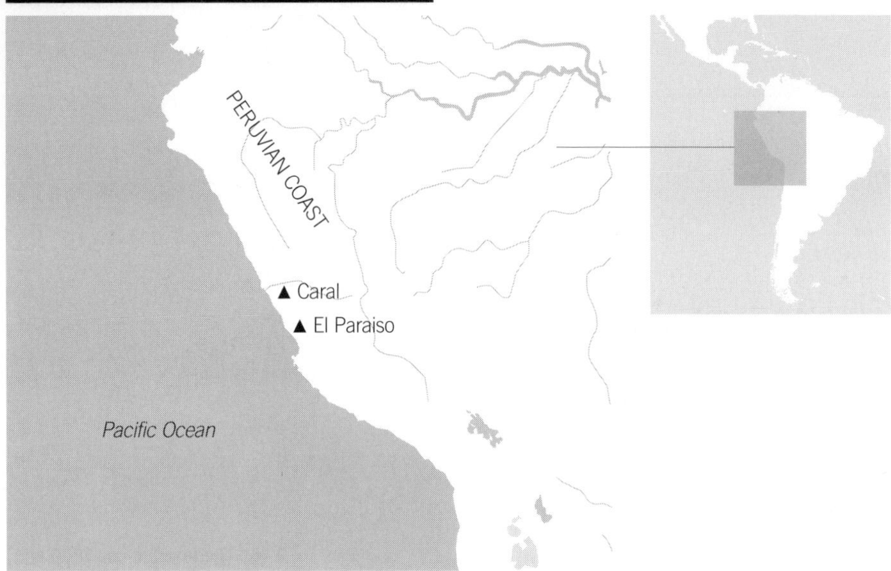


**FIRST CIVILIZATIONS OF THE AMERICAS**
During the Ice Age, between 30,000 and 10,000 BCE, nomadic populations from China and Mongolia crossed the Bering Straits land bridge, moving first into the great plains of North America and then south along the shore of the Pacific Ocean. By 10,000 BCE they had reached the southern tip of South America. (Recently it has also been proposed that another stream of people may have come westward from Europe, following the edge of the Atlantic ice shelf. This is based on the similarities of arrow-heads in both locations.) Throughout the Americas, the social structure of the native Americans remained that of hunter-gatherers until between 5000 and 3400 BCE when, in Central America, archaeologists find the first attempts to make permanent settlements and cultivate crops such as corn, avocados, chili peppers, amaranth, squash, and beans. By 2500 BCE, villages appear with shelters made of wattle and daub, and by 1500 BCE we see the first examples of pottery.

The indigenous people of the Americas are generally called "Pre-Columbians," a term that marks the arrival of Christopher Columbus in 1492. In this text we will generally refer to them all as "native Americans" to recognize the ancient continuities between the civilizations of North, Central, and South America.

The thin sliver of the Andean coastline, sandwiched between the Pacific and the rising peaks of the Andes, turned out to be particularly suitable for the development of the earliest advanced native American settlements. It was home to a wide array of ecological life zones, ranging from the tundra of the upper valleys, the grasslands of the middle altitudes, and the deserts of the northern coast. There, once domestication of plants and the llama had taken place, one sees the rapid growth of settlements into medium-sized villages with populations of up to 3000 people.

There were, however, drawbacks to the natural landscape. The Andean coast did not have the advantage of gigantic river-valley systems. In fact, because of the direction of the prevailing winds and temperature inversions, the central Andean coast was a desert. Other than during periods of El Niño, moisture-laden winds skip over the coast until they hit the high peaks of the Andes, from where small rivers flow swiftly toward the ocean. These conditions would have the makings of an extremely inhospitable environment were it not for the warm Pacific Ocean coastal currents that supported a rich marine life. Thus the earliest Andean settlers lived principally off the ocean, the only civilization of this age to do so.

The ocean alone, however, was not likely to have been enough to support the large, concentrated populations that would have been required for building and maintaining the hundreds of huge ceremonial complexes that dot the high river valleys of Peru. These date to later times, when the native Americans learned to canalize water and cultivate the lower reaches of the narrow valleys. Later still technology developed to enable cultivation of upper valleys. Ten to fifteen kilometers upstream irrigation canals could be fewer in number, require less labor and maintenance, and could irrigate a much larger area. The cultivation of cotton, beans, potatoes, peanuts, and avocados flourished. At the same time, aided by the versatile llamas, travel along the coast became easier and more frequent.

This irrigated agricultural phase is usually dated to about 1500 BCE. However, most of the coastal Andean complexes are still unexcavated. In 2001 archaeologists found that the carbon dating of organic fragments from the Rio Supe Valley of Peru dated to 2620 BCE. Since this discovery, the chronology of civilizational development in South America has been keenly debated and is presently undergoing significant revisions.

2.48 Aerial view of the Caral, Rio Supe valley, Peru

Pyramid Major was constructed in two major phases. First, the mound walls were built by filling in open-mesh reed bags with cut stones. The outer surface of the mound was then covered with multiple layers of colored plaster.

### Caral

Caral's location on a natural terrace 25 meters above the Rio Supe flood plain and its size, 65 hectares, point to a large powerful aristocracy with extensive constructional resources. A huge central plaza, roughly 500 meters by 175 meters, is surrounded by an extensive array of buildings that include six large platform mounds, a range of smaller mounds, two major sunken circular plazas, an array of residential structures, and various complexes of platforms and buildings, whose purposes are not yet known. Each of the mounds is associated with formally arranged residential complexes.

Although the ceremonial structures of the early Andean civilizations have the outline of a pyramid and are usually called "pyramids," it is more accurate to refer to them as "platform mounds." This is because they were conceptually conceived as a series of platforms, of which the earth was first, rather than as pyramids with an implied internal volume. The word "pyramid," one must remember, is from a Greek word to describe Egyptian structures. What the native Americans called their structures is unknown. We will use the word "pyramid," however, in cases where convention has already established it as part of the name.

Pyramid Major, Caral's dominant platform mound (160 by 150 meters and 18 meters high) is perched on the northern end of the site, at the very edge of the terrace from where it overlooks the valley. Five other platform mounds join with it to form a C-shaped plaza, facing south. Just beyond its open mouth, at the center of a low mound, is a sunken circular plaza, 50 meters in diameter and almost directly on axis with a small platform mound. If the main plaza, surrounded by mounds high above the valley floor, creates the impression of a vast bounded space reminiscent of a high valley plateau, then the circular sunken plaza, reminiscent of the later kivas of North America, repeats that space on a smaller scale.

Caral is still being excavated (most recently by Ruth Shady), but we can anticipate that the site was laid out facing toward the mountains, celestial bodies, and other celestial events, such as the rising sun, the planets, and various stars. If the main plaza seems to be identified with human life on earth, the circular spaces below grade may have functioned as gathering spaces corresponding to the lower elements of life with the upper platforms presumably accessed only by the priests.

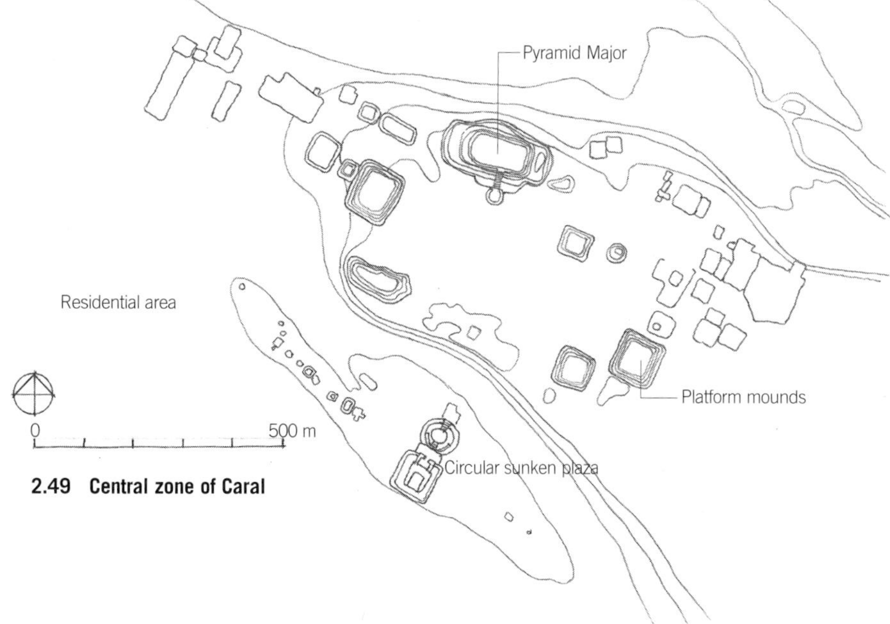


2.49 Central zone of Caral

**2.50 View of El Paraiso, Rio Chillon, Peru**

## El Paraiso

El Paraiso, spread out over about 50 hectares, is on the southern bank of the Rio Chillon, about three kilometers inland from the coast in an agricultural valley. Its construction, dating to about 2000 BCE, involved the quarrying, transportation, and assembly of some hundred thousand tons of rock. The two largest mounds run parallel to each other, with a scattering of smaller mounds to the southwest forming a U with a central plaza that is roughly 50 meters wide and 150 meters long. The plaza opens toward the river, toward the northeast and to a distant mountain peak. The mounds associated with the plaza are made of interconnected rectangular courts, rooms, and passages. The walls are 1.5 to 2.5 meters high and one meter thick and are made of stone blocks set in mortar and then covered by mud plaster that shows traces of red and white pigment. The plaza, therefore, would have been brightly colored in its own time.

The spatial themes one finds in Caral and El Paraiso, sacred mounds, plazas, and observatories, became the main characteristics of subsequent Andean and Mesoamerican architecture. One of the smaller mounds of El Paraiso has been reconstructed. It is a residential structure, probably for the aristocracy, consisting of a complex maze of interconnected rooms that were added to over time by building new structures to the side or by filling in older rooms to enable rooms to be built at a higher level. The interior as a consequence is somewhat haphazard.

A sense of the ceremonial, however, is preserved in the staging of the entrance sequence. A narrow flight of stairs cuts through a small opening in the center of a large portal and lands in a wide and narrow antechamber that opens into a large square hall with four hearths and a square sunken floor in the middle. It is surrounded by a complex maze of interconnected rooms.

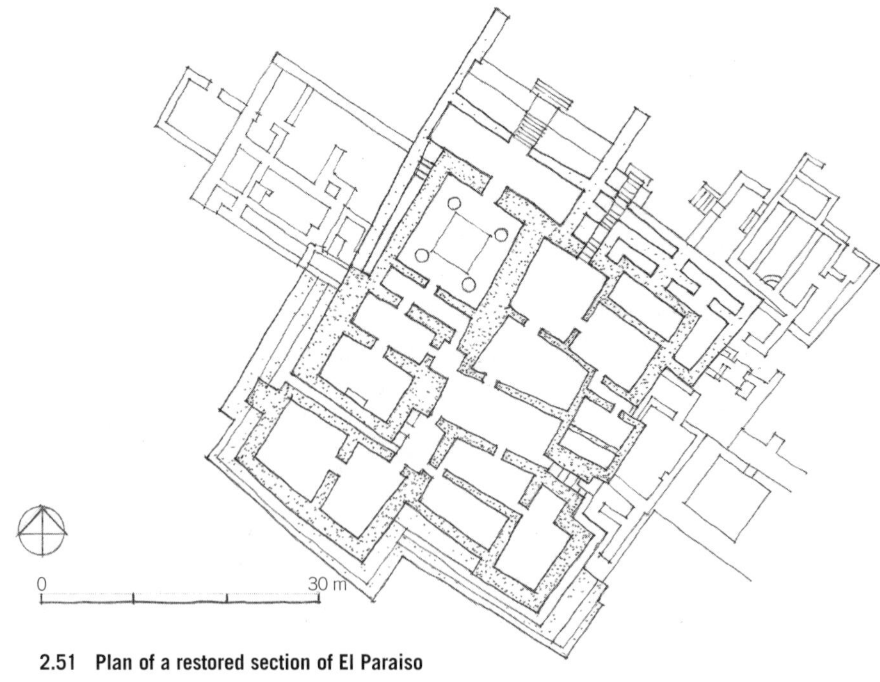


**2.51 Plan of a restored section of El Paraiso**

# 1500 BCE

Central and West Asia were in a state of flux and insecurity. Assyria, Babylon, and other Mesopotamian cities were overrun by hordes of invaders of unknown provenance. The Mitanni and Kassites, about whom we know little, moved in from the north and the east. The incursions of the so-called Sea-People, who came eastward along the coast of the Mediterranean, complicated the picture further. Though the reasons for this mass movement of peoples remains unknown, the collapse of the Indus Ghagger-Hakra civilization in or around 1700 BCE certainly played a part.

Among the newcomers were the Hittites who settled in Anatolia and who founded a new capital with numerous temples. They also recognized and reaped the benefits of the camel that was domesticated during the middle centuries of the second millennium BCE. Camel and donkey caravans, with some composed of as many as 600 animals, were making new trade routes across the desert plains. Eventually the Hittites and the Egyptians were the dominant land powers, with Egypt embarking on a remarkable period of temple architecture epitomized by the constructions in Luxor.

The turmoil in the Mesopotamian heartland enabled the eastern Mediterranean cultures to rise in importance in the global economy. This was especially true for the Minoans on Crete and later the Mycenaeans in Greece and on the Peloponnese. They became wealthy not because of grains or minerals, but almost solely as merchant mediators. This was a new and modern source of wealth that was to play an increasingly important role in the world economy.

In South Asia, the demise of the Indus Ghagger-Hakra civilization created a political vacuum that set the preconditions for the emergence of the so-called Aryans, who conquered the region and imposed themselves onto it as an elite. Lately, questions as to the correctness of this theory have been raised, but the fact remains that during the middle of the second millennium BCE large groups of people moved across the steppes into northern India, bringing with them a culture far different from that of the Ghagger-Hakra civilization. They built cities out of wood rather than brick, which is why very little has survived. Most importantly, unlike the Indus Ghagger-Hakra people, the Indo-Aryans were decidedly warlike.
In China, the bronze-age Shang Dynasty in 1650 BCE came to control a large area in northeast and north-central China, with large cities now being designed, such as Zhengzhou and Anyang, the former, roughly one-and-a-half by two kilometers, and one of the largest planned cities in the world at that time. Major sites include Zhengzhou, a regional cult center with numerous temples and burials. This period is noted for its extraordinary bronze vessels used to hold wine and food in rituals linking rulers and their ancestors. They are cast using multiple ceramic molds, a technology that has no parallel elsewhere in the ancient world.

Along the Gulf Coast of North America, with corn having been developed as the principal staple, the region in coastal Louisiana now called Poverty Point emerged as the center of an important chiefdom. In the Andes, improvements in irrigation technology enabled farmers to move upstream, away from the ocean, expand their economies, and build large sites such as Cardal in present-day Peru. These involved enormous U-shaped ceremonial complexes, built at huge human expenditure and social organization, given that the Andeans had neither the wheel nor beasts-of-burden. Many sites remain inaccessible and unexcavated to this day, and how they were used remains unknown.

# 1500 BCE

Egypt: Early Dynastic Period
ca. 3100–2649 BCE

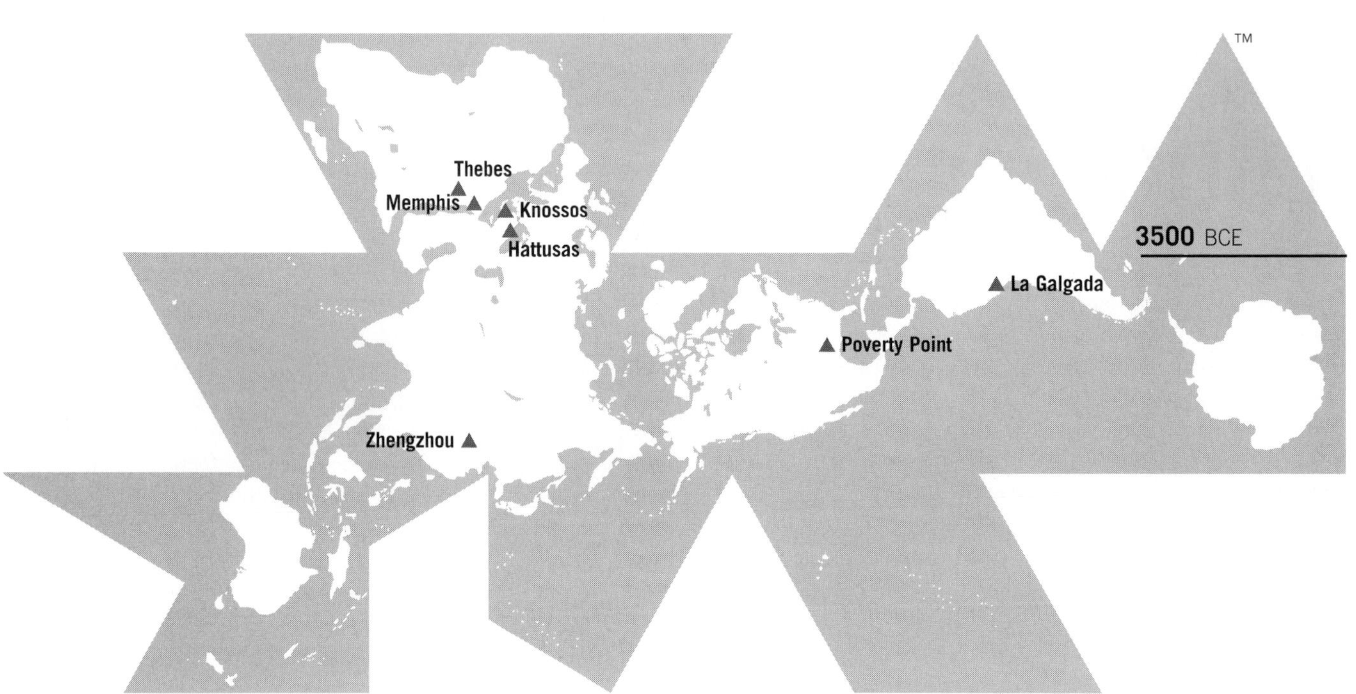


North and Central Andes: Valdivia Cultures
3300–1500 BCE

China: Yangshao Culture
5000–1500 BCE

Egypt: First Intermediate Period
ca. 2150–2030 BCE

Second Intermediate Period
ca. 1640–1550 BCE

Old Kingdom
ca. 2649–2150 BCE

Middle Kingdom
ca. 2030–1640 BCE

New Kingdom
ca. 1550–1070 BCE

Third Intermediate Period
ca. 1070–712 BCE

Late Period
ca. 712–332 BCE

▲ **Temple of Amun: Karnak**
ca. 1500–323 BCE

▲ **Temple of Queen Hatshepsut**
ca. 1520 BCE

▲ **Temple at Luxor**
ca. 1400–1300 BCE

▲ **Abu Simbel**
ca. 1300 BCE

▲ **Hattusas**
ca. 1800 BCE

**2500** BCE — **1500** BCE — **500** BCE

**Middle Bronze Age**
ca. 2000–1600 BCE

**Late Bronze Age**
ca. 1600–1200 BCE

**Iron Age**
ca. 1200 BCE

Minoan Culture
ca. 3000–1200 BCE

▲ **Knossos**
ca. 3000–1400 BCE

Mycenaean Culture
ca. 1600–1100 BCE

▲ **Treasure of Atreus**
ca. 1250 BCE

Nuraghic Civilization
ca. 1600–750 BCE

Machalilla Culture
1500–1100 BCE

▲ **La Galgada**
ca. 2600–1400 BCE

▲ **Huaricoto**
2200–2000 BCE

▲ **Salinas de Chao**
ca. 1610–1300 BCE

▲ **Cardal**
ca. 1465–975 BCE

▲ **Poverty Point**
ca. 1700–700 BCE

Xia Dynasty
ca. 2100–1600 BCE

Shang Dynasty
ca. 1600–1050 BCE

Western Zhou Dynasty
ca. 1046–771 BCE

▲ **Zhengzhou**
ca. 1700–1400 BCE

▲ **Shang tombs at Anyang**
ca. 1400–1100 BCE

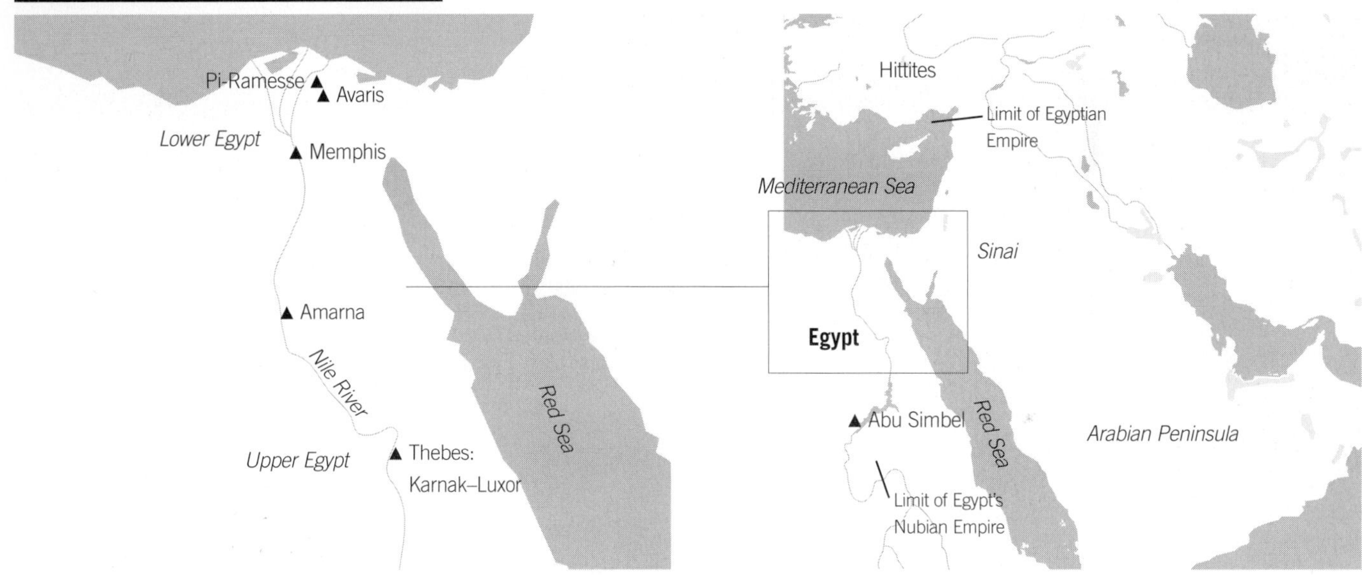


## EGYPT: THE NEW KINGDOM

Around 1720 BCE, Lower Egypt was invaded and occupied by the Hyksos, who ruled Lower Egypt from their capital Avaris until driven out by Ahmose I of Thebes in 1567 BCE. The origin of the Hyksos, and even their name, is the subject of scholarly debate. Some hold them to have been from Asia, others tend to the hypothesis that they were of Semitic origin. Though they contributed little to the art and architecture of Egypt, they introduced a number of practical inventions, such as the composite bow and arrow, which could shoot 180 meters farther than the Egyptian bows. They also introduced to Egypt the lyre, the vertical loom, as well as the horse and the horse-and-chariot combination. Once introduced, the Egyptians made particularly good use of the martial possibilities of the horse and chariot and subsequently made it the centerpiece of their military machine. In 1550 BCE, Ahmose I, founder of the 18th Dynasty and of what is called the New Kingdom—a rule of dynasties lasting until 1069 BCE—was able to throw off the Hyksos and regain control over the country. Seeking to guarantee the borders against the all-too-volatile political environment of the Near East, the Egyptians marched into Syria and besieged Nineveh and Babylon. No longer isolationists, as they had been in the Old Kingdom, they now had become colonizers.

The return to stability meant that the vigorous trade in goods on which so many Near Eastern societies depended could recommence. Ekron, and other cities controlled by the Philistines, traded in pottery and metals. The turquoise mines in the Sinai were reopened. The Egyptians also tightened their control over Nubia, an important supplier of gold, moving southward, step by step. An important change with the re-establishment of unity was that religion was no longer only the purview of the elite, and now involved larger sections of society. Festivals, processions, and celebrations were introduced that could draw thousands of participants.

**3.1 Amun-Re**

### Karnak

The most important of these processions were staged at Karnak, near the city of Thebes, as the family that had thrown out the Hyksos came from Thebes, and thus elevated the Theban ram-god Amun-Re to the status of a national deity. Ramses I leveled the old city that had grown up there over time to create room for the city-temple complex that is now called Karnak. Without replacing the other gods, Amun-Re took on their essences, thereby becoming the all-encompassing god of creation, the god of the sun and the heaven, and the omnipresent Father of the Kings who guaranteed the world order.

The temple complex consisted of three districts. In the center stood the establishments of Amun-Re (begun in 1505 BCE), in the south, those of Mut, the mother goddess, and in the north those of Montu, the god of warfare, strength, and masculine virility. To the north of the enclosure was a small sanctuary to Ptah, who was sometimes seen as an abstract form of the Self-Created One. He was intimately connected with the plastic arts and especially with the mysteries of architecture and stone masonry. A critical element was a shrine, open at both ends, that contained the specially designed portable bark by which the image of Amun could be carried outside the temple—borne on poles carried on the shoulders of priests—for important festivals.

**3.2 Temple at Luxor, Egypt**

Obelisks of Ramses II
Entrance pylon of Ramses II
Court of Ramses II
0
100 m
Colonnade with scenes of Opet Festival
Court of Amenophis III
Bark sanctuary of Amenophis III

**3.3 Plan: Temple at Luxor**

Egyptian temples, unlike Mesopotamian temples, or even later Greek and Roman temples, were not conceived as finalities. Instead they could grow, be changed, get rebuilt, and even be allowed to decay over time. In the case of Luxor, rulers added courts and hypostyle halls as indications of their support and patronage. The Amun-Re temple, for example, grew steadily toward the Nile, with new gateways added and others redesigned. The place where the divine family triad—Amun, his spouse Mut, the mother of gods, and their son, the moon god Khonsu—"gathered" was the Temple at Luxor.

The procession to bring them there, in which ordinary citizens as well as musicians, dancers, and the kingdom's entire nobility participated, took place in the month of Akhat, our October, during the second month of the flood. The procession was called *opet*, which means "secret chamber." At a particular moment during the events, the deity "spoke," that is, affirmed the legitimacy of the king and thence was of prime importance for the Pharaoh. The celebration lasted for 27 days.

The building is not axially aligned but follows the gentle easterly bend of the processional route, as it was extended in later building campaigns further and further toward the north. One enters through a rhomboid-shaped courtyard, built later by Ramses II, that leads to a passageway of two rows of seven impressively scaled columns, 21 meters high. That space opens to a court and a hypostyle hall and finally the sanctuary itself. A series of successively smaller telescoping rooms then leads to the sanctuary where the bark was stored. From a door to the left one gained access to the hall placed at right angles to the axis, which was defined as the mythical place of the path of the sun. Three doors opened to rooms, one for each of the cult images of the divine triad.

In another processional ritual, Amun's cult image traveled every ten days from the temple of Luxor on the east bank to the shrine of Medinet Habu on the west bank. Countless priests and officials were responsible for participating in these activities. Since the king, obviously, could no longer be present everywhere, the priests came to play increasingly important roles, which in turn gained them more and more influence over internal politics.

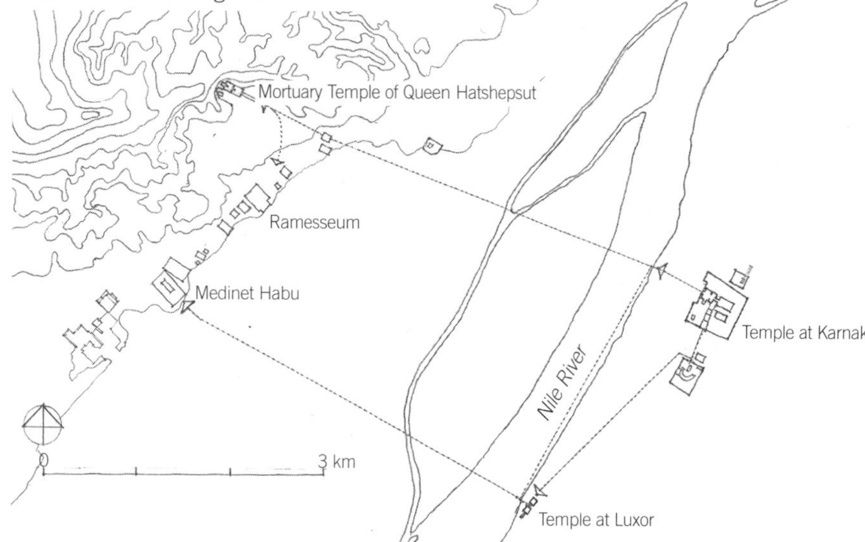


**3.4 Map of Thebes in the New Kingdom, showing the principal temples and processional routes**

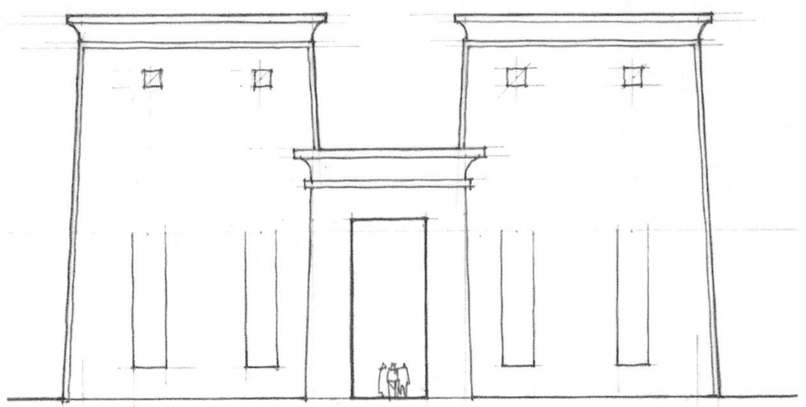

3.5 Entrance pylon to the Temple of Khonsu

3.6 Detail: Seventh Pylon of Karnak

The Temple Complex at Karnak has two entrances, one for those arriving from the direction of the Nile to accommodate the bark procession, the other from Luxor. Both were defined by a series of majestic pylons. A *pylon* ( a Greek word for "gate") is a high, inclined, and slightly trapezoidally shaped wall with a large, central entrance guarding a sacred precinct. It was often accented by tall flag poles and obelisks with their tops sheathed in gold plating.

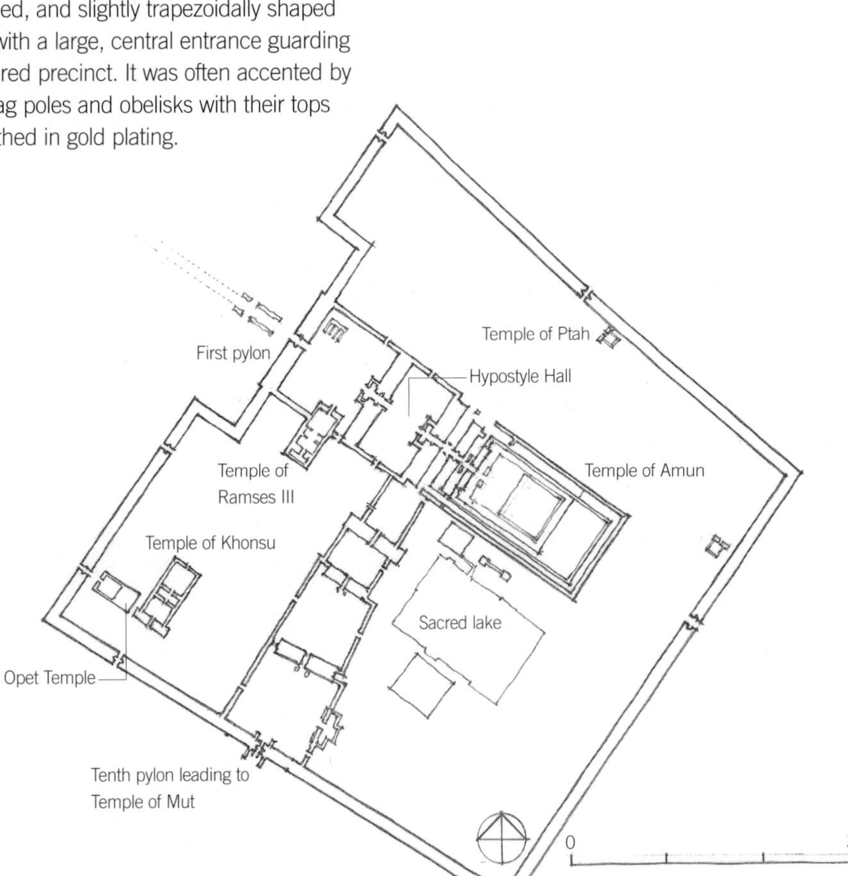


3.7 Plan of the Temple Complex at Karnak, dedicated to the divine triad: Amun, Mut, and Khonsu

The two flanks of the pylon, formal and imposing, symbolized the mountain ranges that hem in the Nile. Their form was a purely symbolic expression of Egyptian power. Though all architectural forms of the period— such as the ziggurat in Mesopotamia, the *megaron* in Greece, and the processional paths in Egypt—had symbolic value, the Pylon Gates were among the earliest architectural forms that condensed wall, gate, and cosmology into a single declaration of power. Like huge billboards, they proclaimed in image and text the great deeds of the pharaoh. On one, the Seventh Pylon of Karnak, a huge Thutmosis III is shown holding a club and taking a swing at a cluster of enemy soldiers—depicted smaller—whom he seemed to seize by the hair. Beneath his feet, in three rows, are the names of the conquered cities and peoples, also listed in three rows. The conquest of the Lybians, Hittites, and Bedouins are particularly and vigorously portrayed. The pylons were most often covered with a fine layer of stucco and painted white, while the figures and other pictorial elements were rendered in vivid colors.

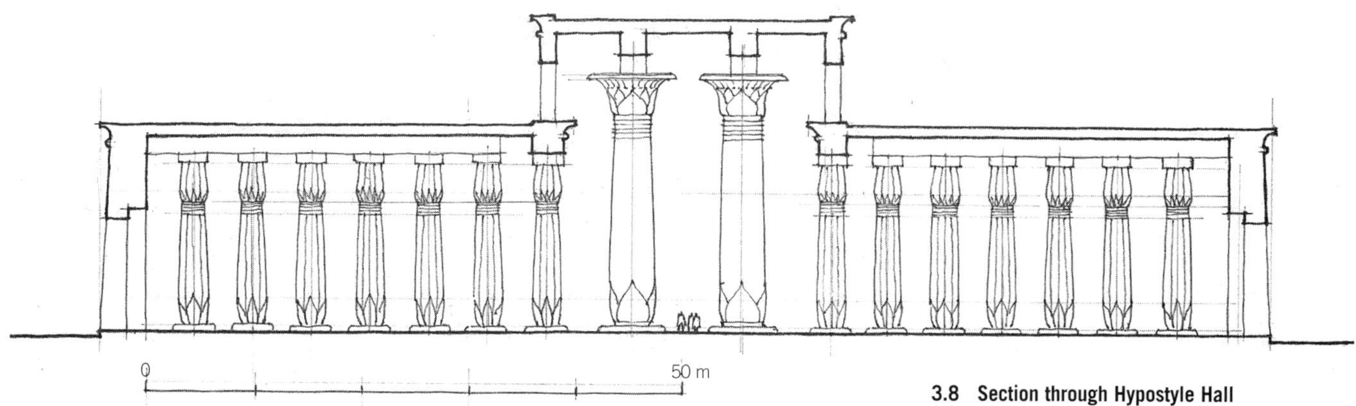


3.8 Section through Hypostyle Hall

Like at Luxor, the temple at Karnak received a series of additions that extended its reach westward as time went on. The first interior space of the Temple of Amun, located behind the second Pylon, was the so-called Hypostyle Hall, or "hall with many columns." The intervals between the enormous columns are proportionately small, dwarfing the visitor who feels as if walking among colossal giants. The columns, 24 meters high, are more than just structural support for the roof; they serve as superdimensional history books, with the scenes painted on them referring to the religious practices and great achievements of the king. At the bottom they are decorated with images of papyrus and at the top with offering scenes. These details were not meant to be literally read by visitors, as the screened light coming from the clerestory windows high up under the roof would have created a shadowy and half-dark environment with the bulk of the columns rising majestically into darkness.

Nested within the innermost sanctum of the building was the Ka chamber. The *Ka* is the spirit or soul that leaves a person at death, but it can be embodied in the form of a statue. In front of the Ka figure of the pharaoh, the priest would set out the sacrifices, while incense burned in a small pot. While the Ka statue was believed to be absorbing these offerings, musicians, singers, and dancers entertained him.

At the eastern end of the building was a Festival Hall, the exact purpose of which is open to interpretation. Most likely it served as a place for jubilee festivals as well as a type of hall of fame glorifying the deeds of the royal conqueror. On its walls are scenes of gardens and animals. Close to the south entrance there was a space into which the sacred boat could be brought and turned to appear poised to go down the central isle.

3.9 Columns of the Hypostyle Hall

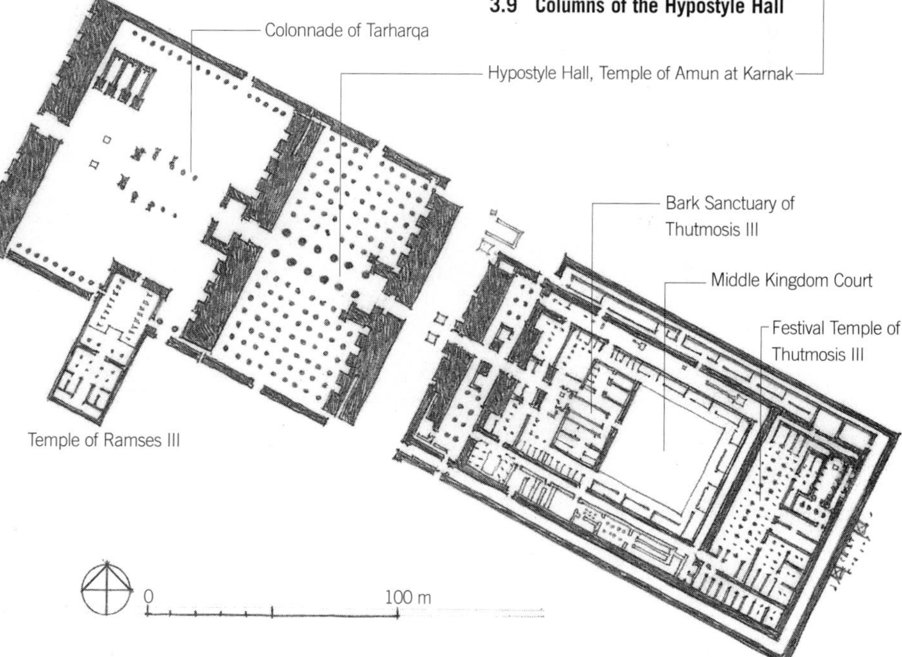


3.10 Plan of the Temple of Amun at Karnak

3.11 Mortuary Temple of Queen Hatshepsut, near Karnak, Egypt

Hatshepsut, daughter of Thutmosis I, was a charismatic and controversial figure, given her position as a female monarch. She ruled for twenty years during a particularly strong moment in the Egyptian economy. After her death, it is presumed that Thutmosis III, her stepson, ordered the systematic erasure of her name from any monument she had built, including her temple at Deir-el-Bahri. Some of her monuments were destroyed outright. Such destructions were not uncommon in Egyptian history. The architect of the Mortuary Temple was a man known as Senmut.

**Mortuary Temple of Queen Hatshepsut**

Ramses' temples set up the prototype of sanctuaries enclosed by high walls and connected by means of ritual celebrations and processions. There were, however, several notable exceptions, such as the Mortuary Temple of Queen Hatshepsut (re. 1503 to 1480 BCE). It is located across the river from Karnak, at a placed called Djeseret, or "Holy Place," that was dedicated to Hathor, a mother goddess as well as the goddess of love and beauty.

Finished in or around 1470 BCE, it combines mortuary temple, processional way, rock-cut tomb, and ancillary chapels into one synthetic unity with no parallel in Egyptian architecture. Particularly innovative was the use of terraces that reach out into the valley floor, prompting speculation about outside influences. The design consists of three of these terraces leading upward to an imposing cliff face. An axis defined by flanking rows of sphinxes runs through the entire scheme with ramps connecting the various courts. From the second level, a ramp connects to a chapel of Hathor.

On the opposite side is a chapel to Anubis, the jackal-headed god of the dead. The axis leads through a Hypostyle Hall to the last courtyard, with the rock wall rising impressively above it. To the left there is a faux palace for Hatshepsut's ancestors, and to the right an open-air sanctuary dedicated to Re-Horakhty. (Re, the sun god, went through a daily cycle of death and rebirth, dying at the end of each day and being reborn in the morning as Re-Horakhty.) The rooms for the bark sanctuary, which terminate the axis, together with the room for the cult image, were carved right out of the rock itself. The plan displays a brilliant use of symmetry and asymmetry based on the integration of different elements. Particularly noteworthy are the columns along the front of the temple. They lack the bombastic excesses of Karnak and seem to be part of a wall and pier system that foreshadows later development.

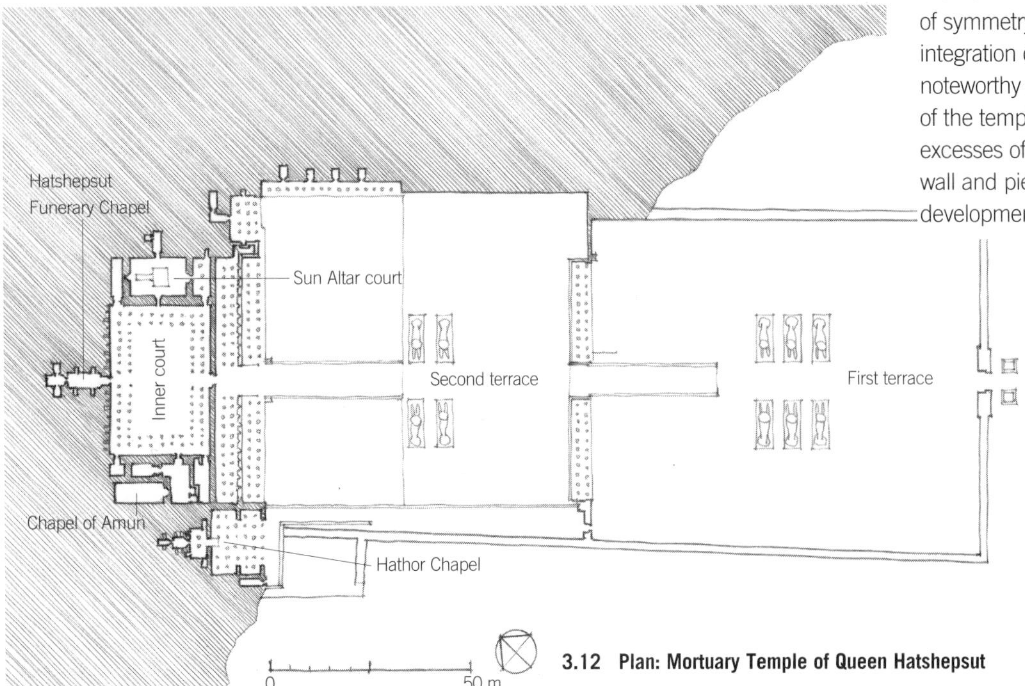


3.12 Plan: Mortuary Temple of Queen Hatshepsut

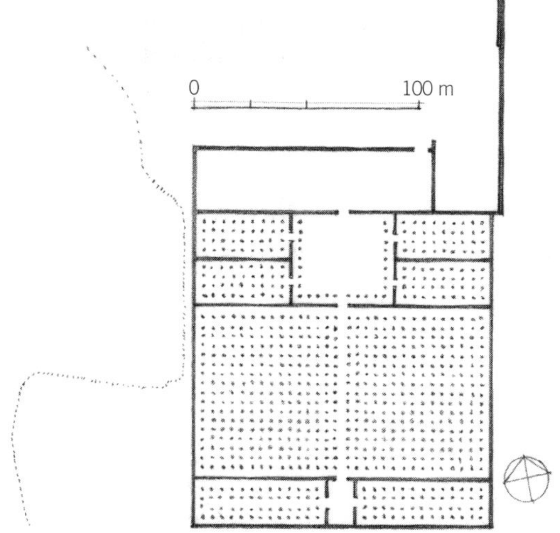


**3.13 Plan: Storehouse with 544 columns**

### Sun Temple at Amarna

Amenhotep IV, who ruled from 1352 to 1336 BCE and renamed himself Akhenaten, the Glory of Aten, introduced significant changes in the cultic practices of Egypt, replacing the cult of Amun and its polytheistic pantheon with the cult of Aten, a single sun god. To this deity he built the unusual Temple at Amarna (ca. 1345 BCE) halfway between Karnak and the Nile delta; there he also established a new capital called Akhetaten, or Horizon of the Sun (now Tell el-Amarna). While traditional temples wrapped the image of god in darkness and secreted it inside windowless inner sanctums, Amenhotep's temple was open to the sky where the god could be seen directly. Lack of background information prevents us from knowing if this novel cult was representative of a more widespread intellectual ferment possibly spreading through the ancient Middle East or, as some have speculated, was an early attempt in the direction of monotheism. It was, however, not monotheism as defined by the Jews, as it was not linked to moral teaching. The sun god Re, as explained by the Egyptologist, Barry Kemp, was a cosmic force, unconcerned with man's destiny; nor was he perceived as invisible, since he was the actual sun in the sky. Possibly un-Egyptian influences played into this. Akhenaten was well aware of the Mitanni who had established bonds of marriage with Egyptian royalty.

Measuring 210 meters in length but only 32 meters in width, and surrounded by a vast rectangular enclosure containing gardens, the temple was in essence roofless. One entered by way of pylons and a vestibule. But on the inside, the temple consisted of a series of spaces connected by an aisle running down the middle, with each space getting more intimate and containing hundreds of offering altars. Presumably it would have involved a mass ritual involving all members of the court.

The palace was located to the south, along a Royal Road that ran parallel to the Nile and also connected to the North Palace. The road was a processional route linked to other sun-god related rituals. At the southern terminus was an extraordinary building containing only brick columns, 544 in all, possibly a royal store house.

North Riverside Palace
North Palace
Nile River
Royal Road
Great Aten Temple
Great Palace
King's House
Storehouse with 544 columns
(See plan above)
Smaller Aten Temple
0
1 km

**3.14 Area plan of Amarna, near al-Minya, Egypt**

3.15 Temple at Abu Simbel, near Philae, Egypt

3.16 Temple at Abu Simbel: view looking toward the sanctuary

### Abu Simbel

Under Ramses II (1290–1224 BCE), Egyptian architecture began to resume some of its former theatrics. Ramses II was a pragmatic as well as a capable ruler. He married a Hittite princess to form an alliance, and to deal with the problem of the Sea People, he accepted them as soldiers in his army. The sphere of Egyptian influence now extended from the upper valleys of the Euphrates to the fourth cataract of the Nile. Nubian gold from the mines of Wabi el-Allaqui swelled his coffers. To protect the trade routes, he built a series of temple outposts that also served to spread the Egyptian cosmological beliefs. His wealth enabled him to carry out numerous large-scale building campaigns, the most ambitious of which was the founding of the city of Ramses (Pi-Ramesse). Close to the old Hyksos capital, Pi-Ramesse stood at the departure point of the increasingly important and well-fortified road to Palestine. The city was sprawling, crowded with temples to state gods, palaces, and military installations (including stables and weapons factories). Copper, the all-important raw material, was delivered here from the newly opened mines at Timma in Israel.

Ramses II's Temple at Abu Simbel (1260 BCE) represents the pinnacle of Egyptian rock temples. Here, the pharaoh reestablished conventional Egyptian practices after the "interruption" by the heretical Akhenaten. One of ten temples Ramses II built south of Aswan was located along the Nile close to the second cataract and elaborated on the tradition of Nubian rock tombs. The facade carved into the high sandstone cliff takes the form of a pylon; it is dominated by four colossal seated figures, 22 meters tall, all portrayals of Ramses. On either side of the statues and between the legs of each are figures of Queen Nefertari and some of the royal children.

Above the temples, Ramses is shown sacrificing to the lord of the temple, Re. This is, however, no longer Re Aten, but now the previous Re Amun. The cornice is decorated with a row of baboons, their arms raised in worship of the rising sun. On the interior, the temple contains two pillared halls, storage rooms, and a sanctuary deep in the rock. The 10-meter high walls are mainly covered with scenes and inscriptions relating to the king's military exploits against the Hittites and against the Kushites in Nubia. The axis ends in the sanctuary on the west wall with a row of four seated statues of Ptah, Amen, Ramses, and Re-Harmachis. The small altar in front of them is the place where sacrifices were made when the light of the rising sun illuminated the sanctuary at dawn.

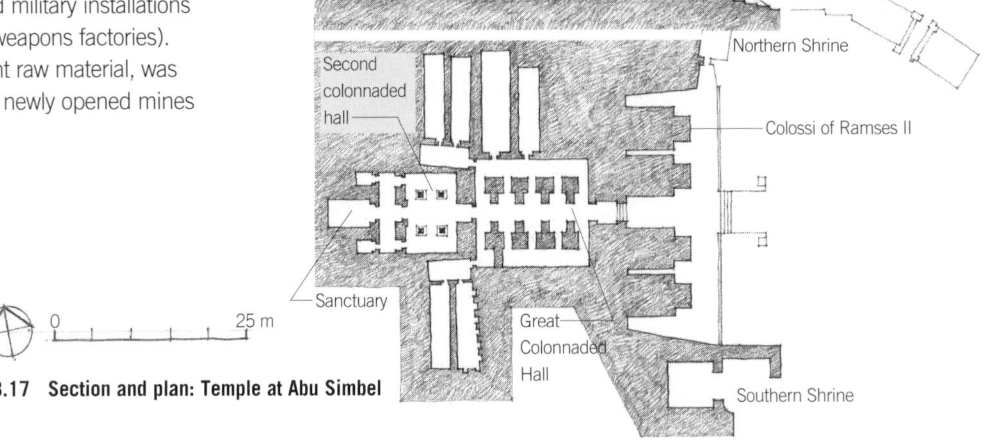


3.17 Section and plan: Temple at Abu Simbel

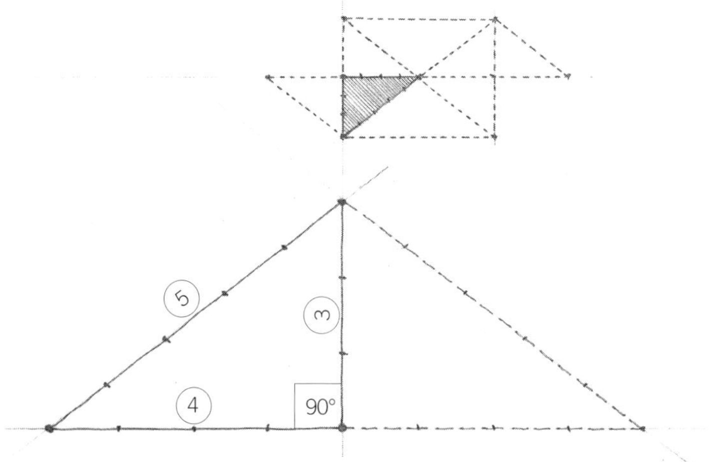


3.18 **Laying out construction with knotted cords and pegs**

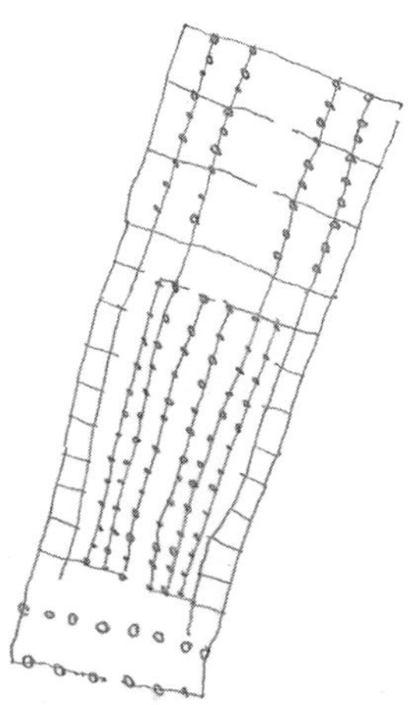

3.19 **Low relief of a pylon: an early example of an architectural design**

**Egyptian Design Methods**

Architecture, given its permanence, cost, and prestige, was an important subject in the discourse of the time. Texts relating to architecture, surveying, and town planning make it obvious that it had risen to the level of a distinct craft. Beside the title of "royal architects," "builder," or "overseer of works," there were also priest-architects who had access to "secret books" that had plans and specifications of buildings and statues.There was even a goddess of architecture and reckoning, Seshat, who begins to appear in Egyptian records beginning about 2500 BCE. She is depicted as bearing a seven-pointed star or rosette on her head, sometimes above a wand. She was also the goddess of the art of writing.

The king himself played an important part in the planning and the symbolic execution of a structure. In one mural, Thutmosis II is shown performing the ceremony of staking out the ground plan of a temple using a special "plan net," a netlike webbing of rope with knots in it to mark off locations. The procedure consisted in stretching a net along the axis and then spreading it out to determine the basic points of the construction.

To form a right angle, for example, the Egyptians used a cord with 12 intervals that was wound around three stakes at units of 3, 4, and 5. For construction, plans were certainly produced. Sketches have even been found on the walls of a quarry. On the pylon of the temple of Khonsu at Karnak is a low relief of a pylon that could very well have been one of the first architectural design projects ever.

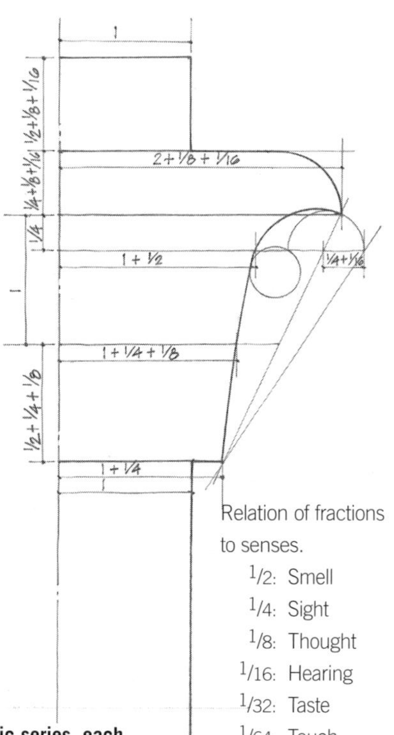


3.20 **Design of a column capital based on a geometric series, each fraction of which symbolizes a different part of the eye of Horus.**

Drawings from the roof of the hypostyle hall of Edfu and elsewhere give us some indication of how columns were designed using a complex ordering of ratios in which a cubit was used in conjunction with a geometrical series of fractions. For example, to a column 9 cubits high, the architect would add 1/4 + 1/8 + 1/16, with each fraction symbolizing a different part of the eye of Horus. Unlike later Greek and Hellenistic assumptions, which positioned mathematics in relationship to cosmological spheres, Egyptian mathematics was connected to the physiology of the body. The eye was seen as one unit with each of the parts measuring a fraction. This "unit" was named after Hequat, who was a goddess represented by a frog; she was also the sign of fertility. The name is fitting since Egyptian mathematics involves a system of leapfrogging over various fractions to achieve the desired answer. The carving of a column and capital was thus a shortcut for these operations.

Though we do not know for certain the geometry of the pyramids, it has been ascertained with a fair amount of probability that the height-to-width was determined through the ratio of 4:1 pi or sometimes 3:1 pi. All in all Egyptian mathematics, as discussed by Corinna Rossi in her book on the subject, was the most advanced in the world at the time. By 1700 BCE, the date of various papyrus scrolls dealing with mathematical topics, various complex mathematical systems were being devised.

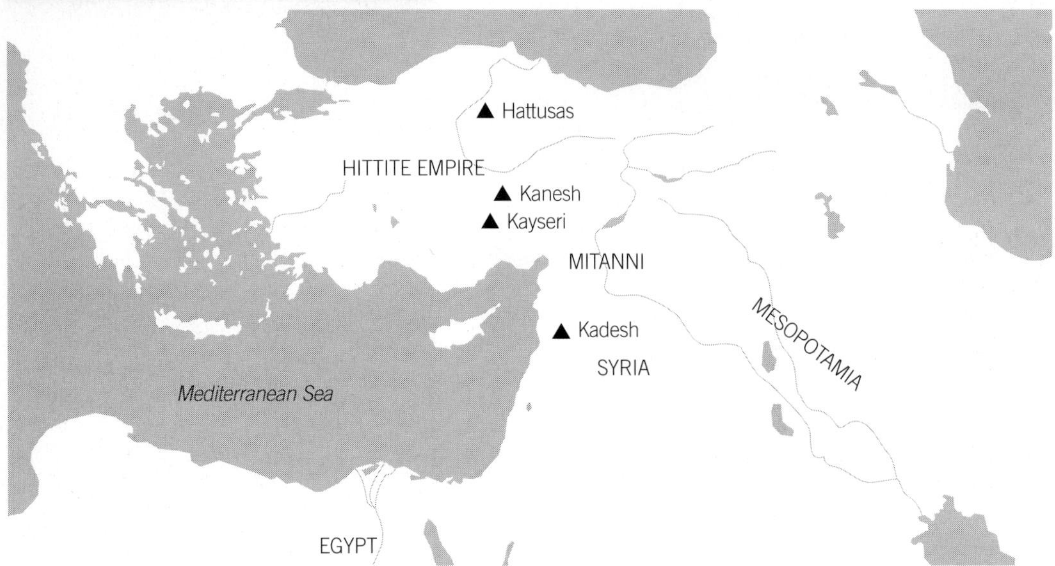


### HITTITE EMPIRE

The Hittites, who settled in Anatolia around 1600 BCE and who were revealed to the amazement of scholars as Indo-Aryan once their language was deciphered, must have chosen the site of their capital Hattusas with an eye to dominate the intersection of two important trading routes that ran from the Aegean coast, from a harbor later to become Ephesus, to the Black Sea. The other route ran southward from the Black Sea port of Amisus (Samsum) to the headwaters of the Euphrates. To further stimulate trade, the Hittites permitted Assyrians to set up posts for their donkey and camel caravans in eastern Anatolia such as the one at Kanesh, 20 km northeast of Kayseri and only 100 km southwest of Hattusas. At its height, the Hittite Empire stretched into the Levant, leading to conflict with the Egyptians and to the famous battle for Kadesh (1275 BCE) in northern Syria. After the battle, which was a draw, the two parties wrote up a treaty that guaranteed peace and security throughout the area, allowing the cities along the Syrian coast to grow in importance. A cuneiform version of this treaty, found at Hattusas, hangs today in an enlarged copy at the United Nations Building to demonstrate the age-old importance of international treaties.

Though the Hittite economy was basically agricultural, the Hittites conducted a lively export in copper, bronze, and later, most prized of all, iron. Many of the mines were in the vicinity of Bokar-Maden in the Taurus mountains. The main military strength of the Hittites lay in the intensive development of new weapons, such as the light, horse-drawn chariot with its six-spoked wheels. It contributed greatly to speed and mobility in battle. The Sumerians had already had chariots pulled by wild asses, but the wheels were made of solid wood. Egyptian chariots held only two men while the Hittite's held three, the driver, and two soldiers, one each for attack and defense.

The Hittites, similar to the Mesopotamians, had a vast pantheon of intermarried gods and goddesses, in the center of which was the male weather god, symbolized by a bull. His consort controlled the rivers and the sea but was also sometimes known as a sun goddess. Even though temples were important for the Hittites, they also had outdoor sanctuaries. In this they were much more like the Minoans than either the Egyptians or the Mesopotamians. One such sanctuary is Yazilikaya, a little over a kilometer to the northeast of Hattusas, to which it was connected by a processional way. It had a pantheon of gods chiselled on the face of the cliff, perhaps arriving to the house of the weather god for the spring festival.

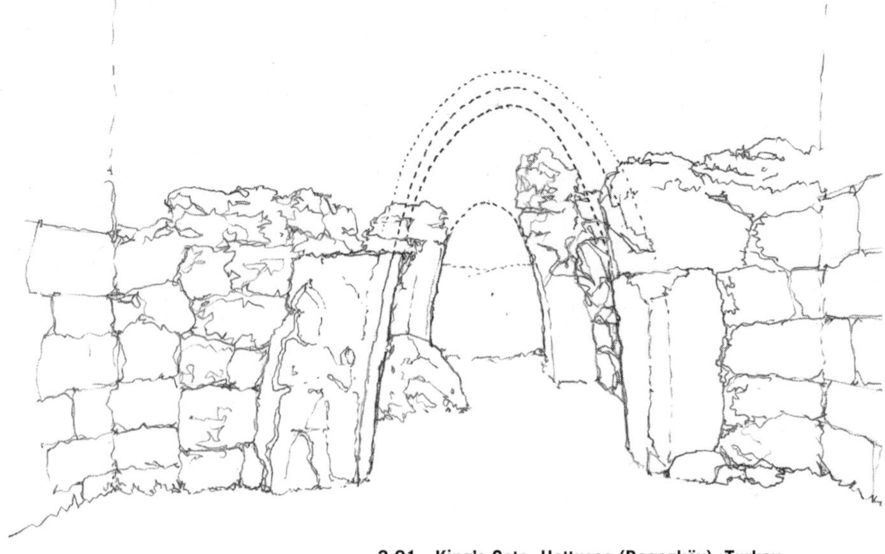

**3.21 King's Gate, Hattusas (Bogazköy), Turkey**

**3.22 Relief from a rock-cut shrine at Yazilikaya, near Bogazköy**

### Hattusas

Hattusas (modern Bogazköy), situated at the juncture of two ancient trade routes in north central Turkey, lies on the northern slope of a ridge where a high plateau begins to slope down toward the valley. Of the many temples in the city, the most notable was the so-called Temple I, squarish in plan with an annex in the back. It took up an irregularly-shaped city block and was composed principally of storage cells for sanctuary treasure and food. Archaeologists found jars of Cretan and Mycenaean provenance. The storage room walls were very thick, suggesting that the building was two or three stories high. The entire complex, including the storerooms, measures 160 by 135 meters. The temple was built of limestone, whereas the annex that contained the sacred statues was built of granite, indicating its special status. The courtyard in front of it was entered through a symmetrically laid out gate, square in plan, and divided into nine spaces. In the rest of the plan there was an attempt to balance the right and left sides of the courtyard. In the northeast corner was a wash-house while a portico at the far end gave access to the sacred rooms in the annex, consisting of two large rooms and several smaller ones. The cult statues were in the larger of the two rooms to the northwest and was dedicated to the sun goddess, while the other room was dedicated to the weather god. All in all, the building appears as an aggregation of different elements, the gate, the court, and the annex.

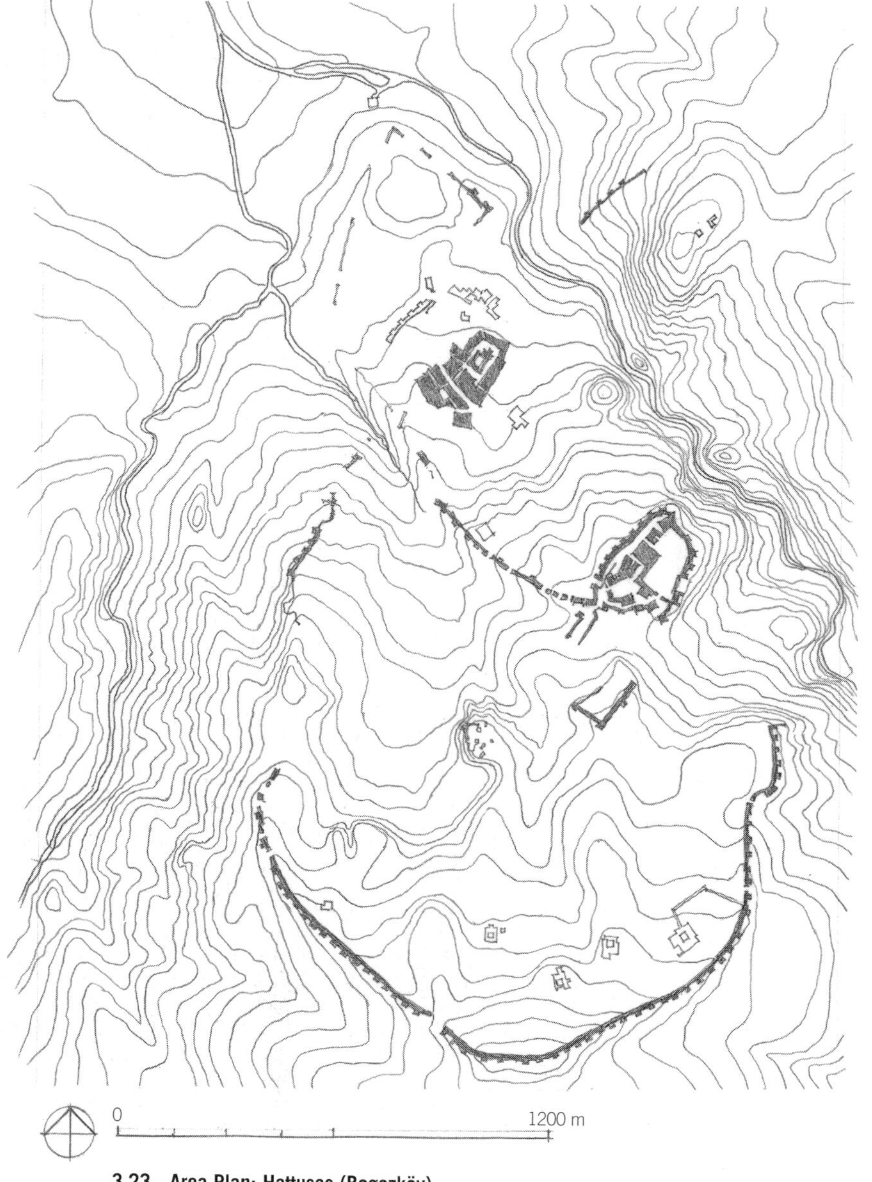


**3.23 Area Plan: Hattusas (Bogazköy)**

3.24 **Plan: Temple I, Hattusas**

3.25 **Propylaeum to Temple I, Hattusas**

How the temple service was conducted has been partially clarified from various found texts. The most important event was a springtime festival at which the combat of the weather god and a dragon was acted out or recited. During the festival, the king and queen accompanied by jesters and musicians, would enter through the ceremonial gate on the eastern wall and proceed to a stone basin where the king would perform a ritual handwashing, using a jar made of gold. From there he would enter the temple courtyard through the monumental gate. A master of ceremonies then prepared the king and the assembled dignitaries for a feast, perhaps in the colonnade of the courtyard or in the throne room itself.

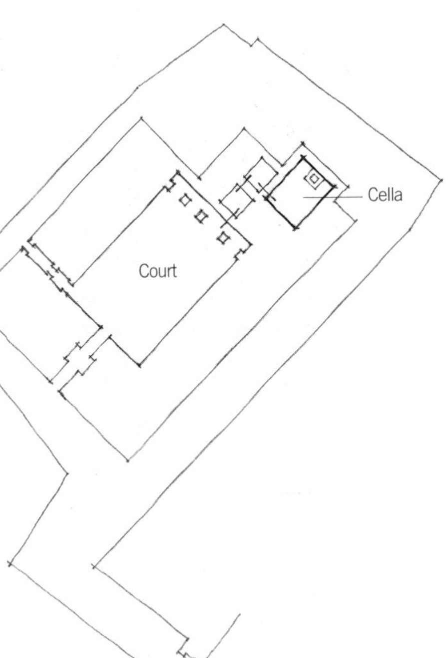


3.26 **Diagram of indirect access to cella characteristic of Hittite temples.**

The Hittites, like the Mesopotamians, employed no columns or capitals in their architecture. Instead, they grouped rooms around paved courts. Both also saw the temple as an administrative entity. But that is where the similarity ends. The *cella* of the Babylonian temple communicated with the court through an intervening antechamber or antechapel, so that the congregation in the court would have a clear view of the god's statue in its niche. In the Hittite temples, the entrance to the cella was not in the wall opposite the cult-statue but in one of the adjacent sides. The cult room was approached indirectly, through side rooms, meaning that the statue would not have been visible from the court. This has led archaeologists to conclude that the cella was reserved for the priests or a corresponding elite who alone were admitted to the sanctum. In contrast to Sumerian temples, in which rooms received daylight from windows high up in the walls, resulting in dark and mysterious interiors, the Hittite architects employed tall windows starting close to floor level. Such windows were placed on both sides of the cult statue and would have bathed it in brilliant light. The Hittites also employed colonnades in a type of wall-and-pier system that considerably enriched their spatial vocabulary. And finally Hittite architects strove for a deliberate tension between symmetry and asymmetry that has parallels as we shall see with Minoan architecture.

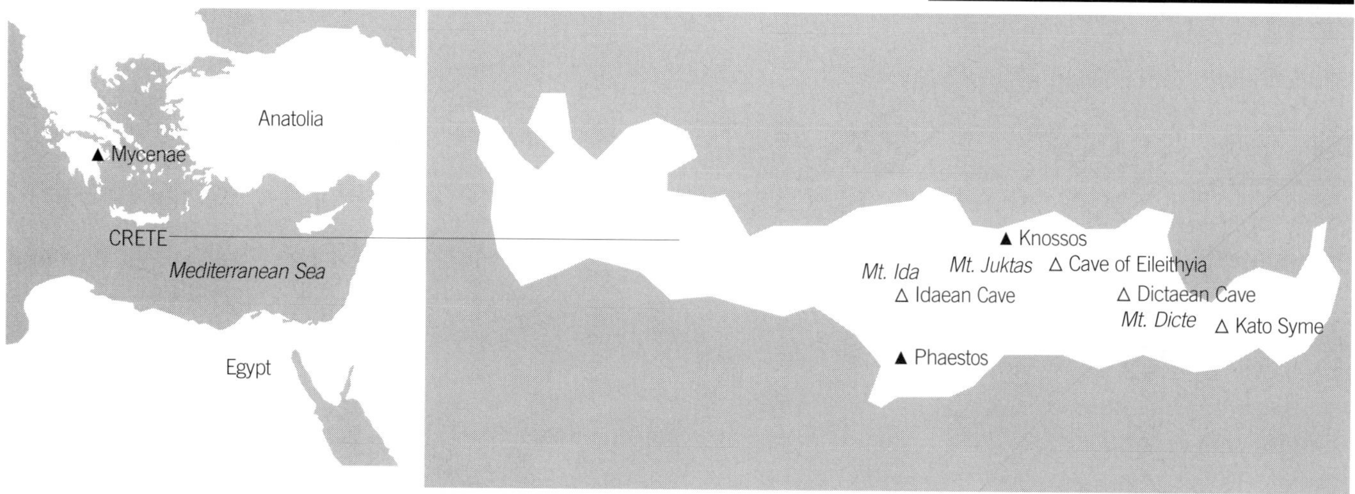


**MINOAN CIVILIZATION**

The rise of the Minoans has to be seen in relationship to the difficulties that the Mesopotamians were facing, first from the invasions by the Mitannians and other invaders and as a buffer between the Hittites and the Egyptians. This allowed the eastern Mediterranean to become an economic engine all its own. The Minoans on the island of Crete were the first to take advantage of this phenomenon by developing into a trading sea power. The origin of the Minoans has not yet been determined, although scholars of late weigh the possibility that the culture was an indigenous development. Evidence points to Neolithic settlements going back to 6000 BCE.

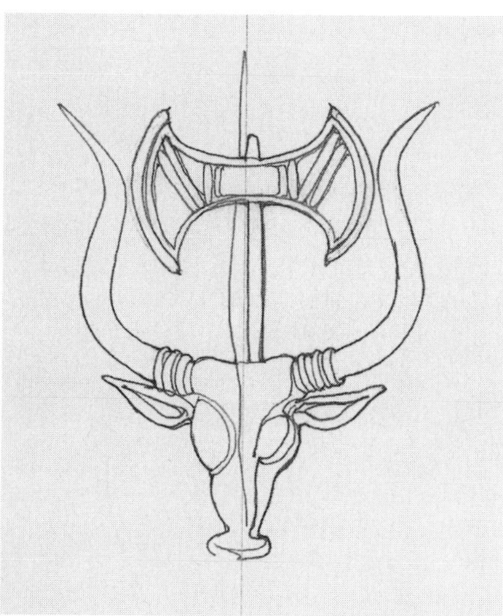

**3.27 The Double Axe or *Lavrys*, principal symbol of the Minoan-Mycenaean religion, standing erect on a bull's head**

Because the Minoans, unlike the Egyptians and Mesopotamians, never came under the same type of economic and political stresses that necessitated complex cosmologies, they emerge on the scene still clothed in chthonic religious practices. The Cretan's relationship to the divine was thus significantly more intimate and less formal than worship in Egypt and Mesopotamia. They saw no need to recreate a cosmological landscape with the help of architecture since, in their view, divinity was everywhere they looked and lived, with the landscape serving as the prop for the stories. The principal characteristic of Cretan religion was the cave cult.

Of the Cretan caves, three were particularly important: the Dictaean Cave on Mount Dicte near the village Psychro, the Idaean Cave on Mount Ida near Anogheia, and the Cave of Eileithyia, dedicated to the birth goddess. The Dictaean Cave, cold and moist even in the heat of summer, with a pool of water surrounded by stalactites, was the site of rituals dating back to the earliest time of Cretan habitation. The Cave of Eileithyia is now a Christian site and is still visited by Cretan women.

Associated with the cave cult was the mother goddess, her symbol a double–sided axe. Initially a weapon or harvesting tool, this particular type of axe was associated with Demeter, the grain goddess. The axe is never found in the hands of a male god. The mother goddess also existed as a goddess of the moon and fertility, and later, under the Dorians, she came to be known as Demeter, the goddess of grain.

One cave sanctuary to the mother goddess was located on Mt. Juktas. Processions led up to the peak of the mountain, to a special sanctuary where offerings were "fed" into a cleft in the rocks. Still today an annual procession makes its way up to the top of the mountain for the feast of Afendis Christos—an instance where Christianity tried to nullify "heathen" cults by appropriating ancient rituals and customs. Another landscape ritual site was known as Kato Syme, located in southeastern Crete on the slopes of Mount Dicte, overlooking the coast from a height of 1130 meters. The cave most intimately connected with the Cretan creation myth is the cave on Mount Ida where the earth mother Rhea gave birth to Zeus. Myth describes him as tended by nymphs and protected by youths against his father, the legendary Chronos. Zeus then fathered Minos, who became King of Knossos and of Crete.

3.28 The Minoan bull-god

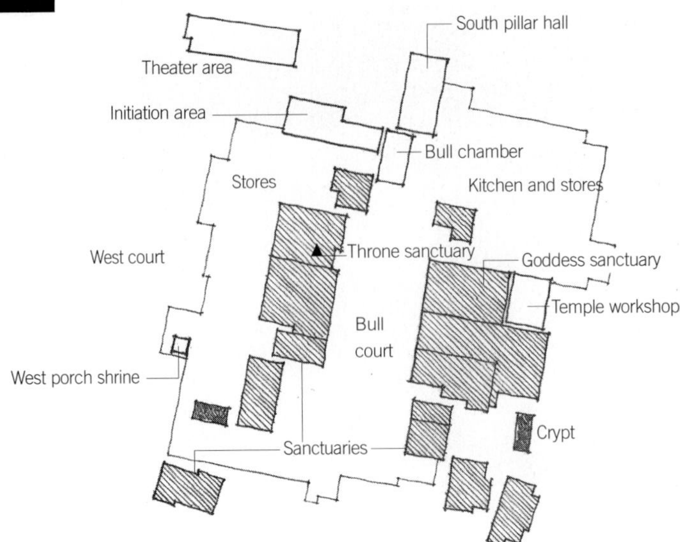


3.29 Schematic plan: Palace at Knossos, Island of Crete, Greece

**Knossos**

During the Bronze Age, Cretan religion began to become more complex; some see, for example, the emergence of strong male gods and, in particular, of the Cretan Zeus, a fertility god who, despite his name, was close in spirit to Dionysus as he died annually and was reborn in a sacred festival. In religious terms, the element of continuity was present in the fertility cycle and the female element, whereas the male god stood for discontinuity and symbolized the cycle of birth, death, and resurrection. The Cretan Zeus took the form of a bull, which was central to a festival known as the Thiodaisia, during which the cities renewed their oaths of alliance to each other. These rites included large-scale drinking and feasting and were staged in the open landscape or in front of the major palaces in special theaterlike places. The events seem to have involved a dance in which performers somersaulted over a charging bull, as represented vividly on the walls of the palace. Men and women are both portrayed as performing the jump, the man in one case in midair, waiting to be caught in the open arms of a woman. Despite these changes, given that the entire landscape was sacred, the Minoans did not build temples but rather palaces, the largest of which was at Knossos, built in 1900 BCE on top of a prior neolithic settlement. It was rebuilt and enlarged in 1700 BCE after a large earthquake, and rebuilt again in 1500 BCE after a fire had destroyed it.

The palace contained residences, kitchens, storage rooms, bathrooms, ceremonial rooms, workshops, and sanctuaries. There were sophisticated infrastructural installations, ventilation systems, and ground water conduits. In storage basements, archaeologists have found elephant tusks from Syria and copper ingots from Cyprus. The palace, lying south of the modern city of Iraklio on the northern shore of the island, faced south toward the double-horned profile of Mt. Juktas, which forms a natural proscenium to an outdoor performance area.

Though we do not know what role the priest-king who ruled there assumed, it is clear that the palace with its many different kinds and sizes of interior spaces, terraces, courtyards, and platforms contained a mosaic of interwoven activities. It was part palace, part warehouse, part factory, part religious center. At the center of the palace and of its communal life was a large rectangular courtyard laid out on an almost perfect north-south axis, with several entrances converging onto it. The courtyard was surrounded by verandas at the upper levels allowing views into its space. Because of the verandas, windows, porches, steps, and doors that folded open into the sides of the walls, the visual interrelationship between inner and outer space is particularly intricate, more so than in any other palace architecture of this period.

3.30 View from Knossos toward Mt. Juktas

3.31 **Throne Room, Palace at Knossos**

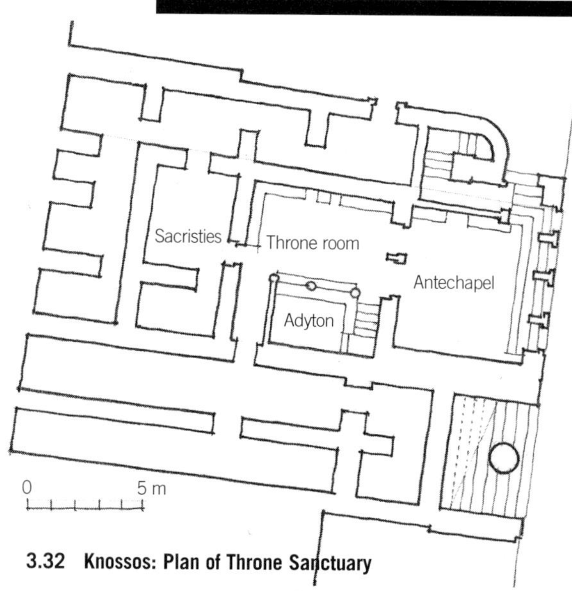


3.32 **Knossos: Plan of Throne Sanctuary**

Flanking the courtyard was the Throne Room, which had gypsum benches on the north and south walls with a place for the insertion of a wooden throne to be replaced with a gypsum one later. The red stucco walls are covered with images of griffins, legendary animals with the head and wings of an eagle and the body of a lion that are thought to have symbolized strength and vigilance.

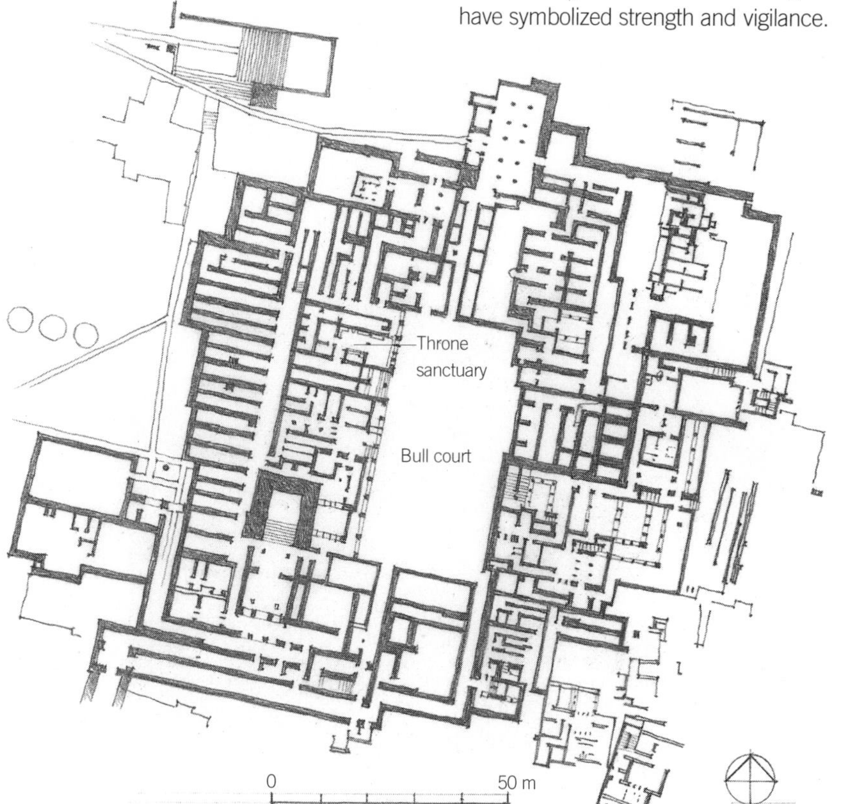


3.33 **Court-level plan: Palace at Knossos**

The floor seems also to have been stained red. The benches, though at seat height, were probably used to hold votive offerings. Opposite the throne was a lustral basin to which steps descended and which may have served for initiation rites. The room, kept dark and low, was meant, according to scholars like Rodney Castleden, to possibly simulate a sacred cave. Around the room were the various storage rooms mentioned above, some of which were repositories for precious objects used in the ceremonies. The whole complex of chambers, sixteen in all, was designed as a self-contained unit that had a public entrance from the courtyard but that also had a private staircase connecting to the floor above.

Well-squared limestone was used for column bases, doors, and other supportive elements. The wooden columns, tapered toward the bottom, were painted blue; the capitals, painted red, had the profile of cushions. The stone rubble walls finished with a fine layer of plaster were, in the principal rooms, painted in a frescolike technique, depicting scenes of animals and plant forms and of nautical life of remarkable vibrancy and beauty. Minoan art was among the first to represent human movement. The main colors used were black (carbonaceous shale), white, (hydrate of lime), red (hematite), yellow (ochre), blue (silicate of copper), and green (blue and yellow mixed).

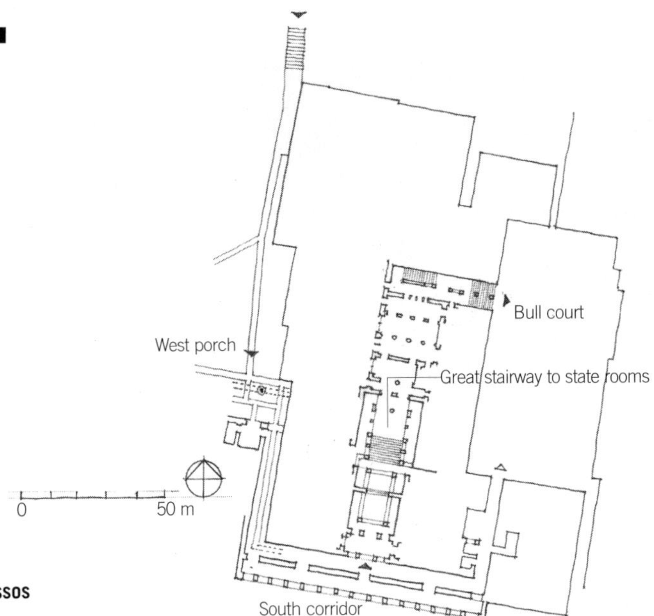


**3.34 Diagram of entry sequence: Palace at Knossos**

Though palaces, almost by definition, require controlled access, usually leading to the throne room, entry into the Palace at Knossos was more than a sequence of gates and antechambers; it was an extended theatrical space. The starting point was the west porch that consisted of a single column standing between walls, an iconic representation of the mother goddess. From that point one walked south to a terrace that offered a broad vista to Mount Juktas. No visitor would have missed the reference to the Cretan Zeus here. Through an opening midway down the terrace, one entered a series of state rooms that led to a great columnar hall illuminated by clerestory windows designed as a box within a box. It, in turn, opened up to a flight of steps flanked by a colonnaded veranda for spectators. At the top of the stairs was a lobby with two ceremonial doors right and left of the axis leading to another hall. At the back of this hall a door led to a staircase that descended at right angles in the direction of the processional way down to the central courtyard.

Descending the stairs, the visitor faced across the court to a goddess sanctuary, an imposing structure with a wide ceremonial staircase leading up through a colonnade to a landing in front of a pier-and-door partition. Inside was a spacious room 18.5 by 15 meters, with eight tapering pillars around a central square that was probably open from above. A statue was placed against the back wall, with the walls themselves richly decorated with scenes of boxing and bull-grappling and more griffins.

It is possible to imagine the central court as a plateau, positioned at the intersection of sunken throne room on one side and elevated skylight cult space on the other.

In the middle of the courtyard was a small altar for burnt offerings and, off to one corner, a large circular stone with concavities in it, probably also for offerings. It was perhaps in this space that the bull ceremony was performed with the spectators viewing it from the numerous balconies and verandas.

**3.35 One of the grand stairways at the Palace at Knossos**

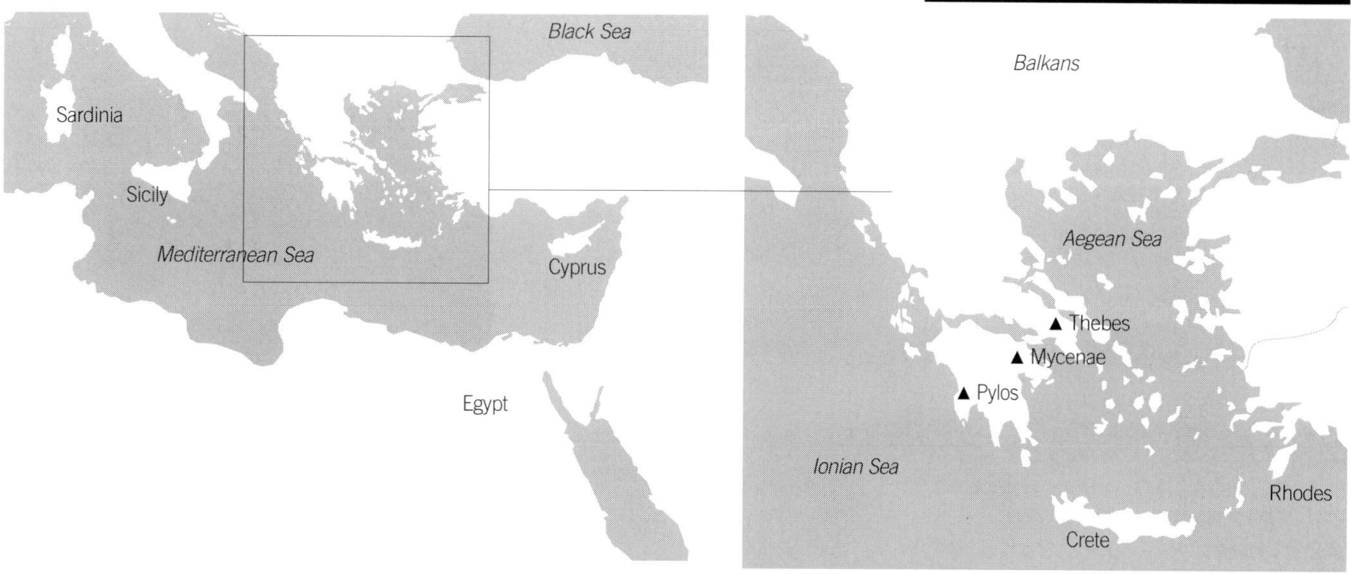


**MYCENAEAN CIVILIZATION**

The Mycenaeans, from parts unknown, settled in Greece around 2000 BCE where, like the Hittites, they quickly developed into a unified Bronze Age social order. The numerous harbors and islands of the Peloponnesus lent themselves to a system of regional chieftains or kings operating under the umbrella of the lord of Mycenae, to whom they were connected by ties of blood or tribal loyalties. The lord of Mycenae commanded a powerful fleet and so could ensure that city-state's foremost position. With the decline and eventual demise of the Minoans, the reach of Mycenae extended to all the Aegean islands, including Rhodes and Cyprus and beyond to the western Mediterranean. Their form of power was a novelty in world history. They were not centralized and had no land-based army. But it was precisely this that propelled them into world events. Tribal affiliations created small but loyal fighters, and not having large or specialized industrial capacities, meant that they had little on the home land that neighbors would want.

Their power was thus almost completely based on trade with Sicily, Southern Italy, Egypt, the Black Sea, and Sardinia. The Mycenaeans, however, did develop their own export commodities. Their carpenters, for example, used ivory from Syria with great skill for the adornment of furniture. Their metallurgical work was also legendary. There were obviously interactions with the Minoans, from whose long culture the Mycenaeans borrowed elements of wall decorations and building techniques. Mycenaean architectural sensibilities were, however, their own.

**3.36 Plan: Palace Complex at Pylos**

Nestor's Palace Complex at Pylos, built between 1300–1200 BCE, for example, is not built around an open courtyard but rather around a *megaron*, or "great hall." We encounter it here as a square room with four fluted columns and an elevated hearth four meters in diameter in the center; it was vented by a clerestory type ceiling. The floor was plastered and decorated with a grid the fields of which were painted with nonfigural patterns. The reason for the slight slant of the grid remains a mystery. One field in front of the throne (to-no in Mycenaean Greek, from whence comes the word "throne"), along the east wall was filled with the drawing of an octopus, which must have had a special meaning. Did the slippery, multiarmed organism resemble the adept multizoned Mycenaean social structure? The throne was made of wood, plated in gold and ebony. The walls were covered with an elaborate series of frescos showing animals, musicians, and individuals carrying offerings and a bull sacrifice. Behind the room were two storage rooms containing large pots for the storage of oil. The residential quarters were in a discrete block at the eastern corner. There was even a room with a bath of terra-cotta. The whole palace is quite small and could almost fit into the central court of the palace of Knossos.

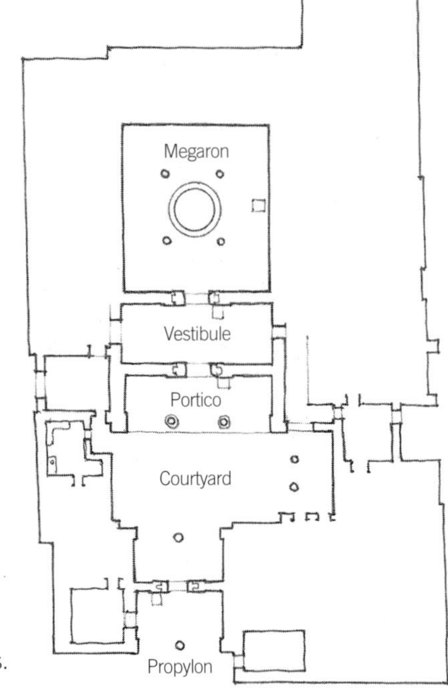


3.37 Plan of courtyard and *megaron* at Pylos, Greece

3.38 Lion Gate, Citadel of Mycenae, Greece

Access to the *megaron* was more direct than the labyrinthine approach at Knossos. From the outside one entered through an H-shaped *propylon* (the word means literally "before the gate") with a single column dividing the path into two, much as one would have found in Crete. It did not lead to a hall or corridor but into a courtyard where a porch of columns and a set of doorways formed the entrance into the *megaron*. On the right was the guard room, and on the left of the entrance, the palace archives and records of trade transactions. A visitor, before entering the *megaron*, would first have been led to a room on the left side of the courtyard, which was a place for ritual preparation.

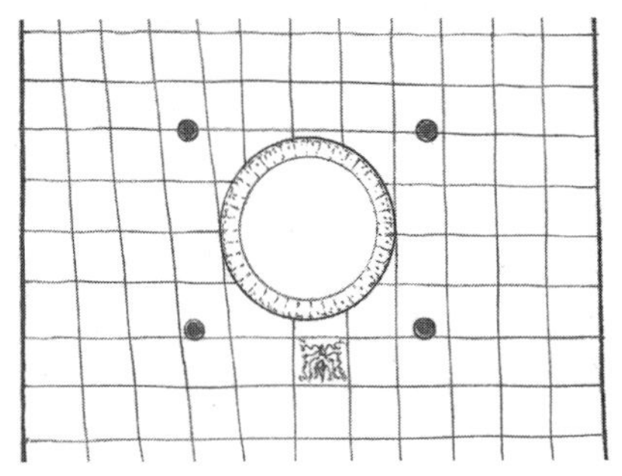

3.39 Floor grid of *megaron* at Pylos

Mycenae was defended by thick ring walls, built around 1450 BCE. Part of the wall was built in a so-called Cyclopean Style, named for the seemingly human strength-defying boulders of which they are composed. In other parts one finds regular rows of blocks of stone fitted without mortar. One enters the citadel through the Lion Gate, which might imply a connection to Hattusas. Just to its right is a circular burial *tholos*, which archaeologists found almost intact, with six chambered tombs containing gold, silver and bronze burial treasures. Entrance to this circle was restricted to the elite. Unlike the Egyptian pharaohs who were placed in pyramids and later in secret caves, the Mycenaean dead were displayed within the city at a place where memory and narrative were most likely to converge. Later Greeks would call the gathering of people in commemorating places a *choros*. Indeed, Homer would emerge, long after the Mycenaean Age had waned, recounting the tales of Mycenaean heroes, among them Agamemnon.

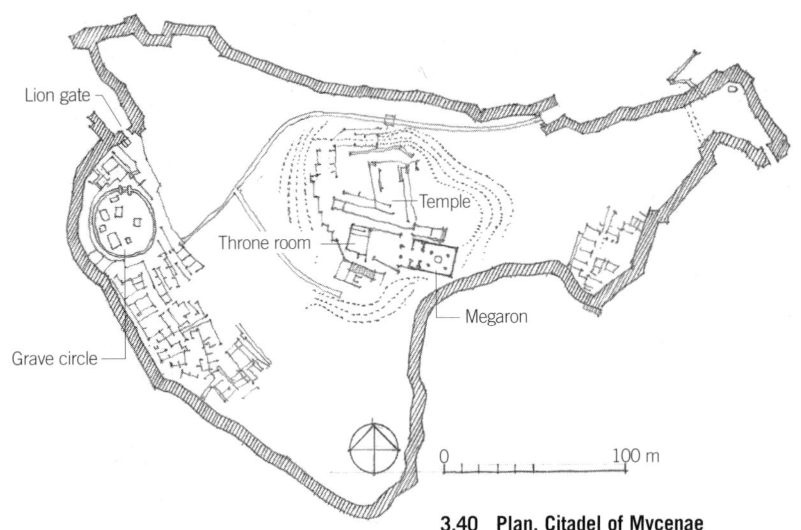


3.40 Plan, Citadel of Mycenae

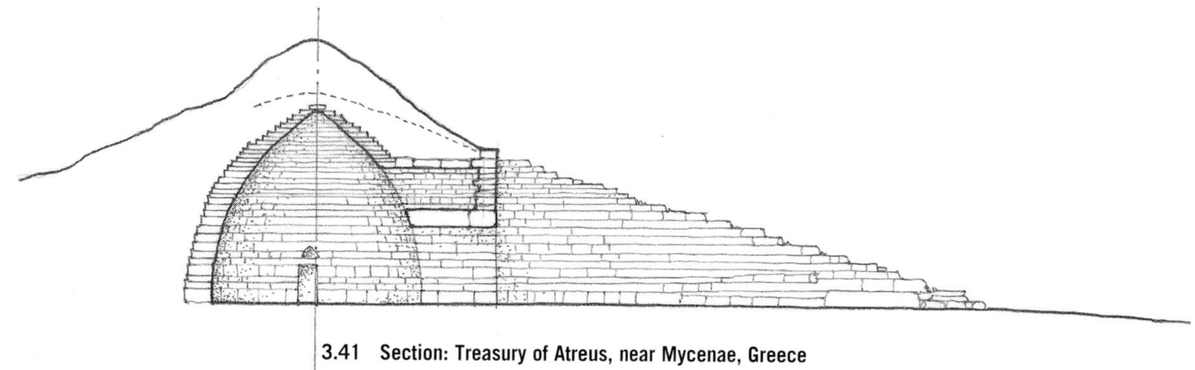

3.41 Section: Treasury of Atreus, near Mycenae, Greece

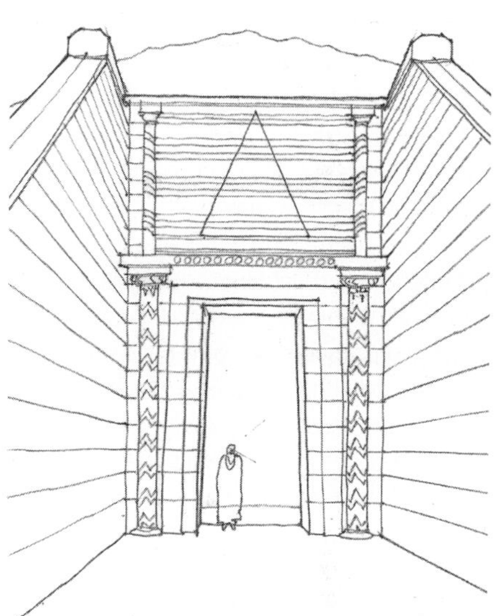

3.42 Entrance facade, Treasury of Atreus

**Treasury of Atreus**

Beginning in the late Bronze Age, the kings were buried outside the city to the west in great beehive or *tholos* tombs, monumental symbols of wealth and power. The most famous and most finely built is the so-called Treasury of Atreus. It consists of a great circular chamber cut into the hillside, some 15 meters in both diameter and height and entered by a corridor (*dromos*) about 36 meters long and 6 meters wide. The tomb was roofed by a corbeled dome made of finely cut ashlar blocks. A rectangular room, the burial chamber proper, was tucked in next to the central one. The whole was covered with earth to form a conical hill. The high façade at the entrance was flanked by two half-columns of green porphyr—a stone native to Egypt—carved with chevrons and spirals. Though fitted with Minoan-style capitals, their bulbous proportions foreshadowed the transformation the capitals would undergo subsequently after the Dorian invasion. The stone lintel above the door was also elaborately decorated with running spirals and other patterns.

By the end of the twelfth century, the Mediterranean was in disarray largely due to the incursions of the so-called Sea People. Though no one knows who they were or where they came from, it was clear they were not just warriors but entire communities on the move. Presumably they were a mix or coalition of different population groups. The Egyptians were able to repulse them only after several major battles, forcing them into the Levant. Simultaneously, the Dorians swept down from the north destroying everything before them. The great citadels of Mycenae were set upon and suffered disastrous fires. The generally accepted date for the demise of the Mycenaean culture is 1120 BCE. For several centuries, with Egypt weakened by its struggle against the Sea People and the invading Dorians bent on destruction rather than building, the eastern Mediterranean on which so much had depended for so long vanished as an economic entity and a Dark Age prevailed.

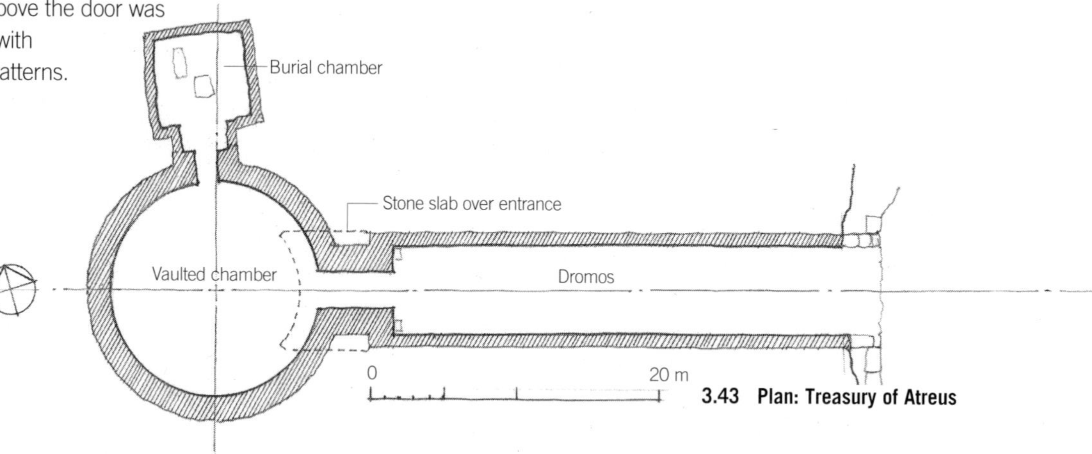


3.43 Plan: Treasury of Atreus

# 1500 BCE

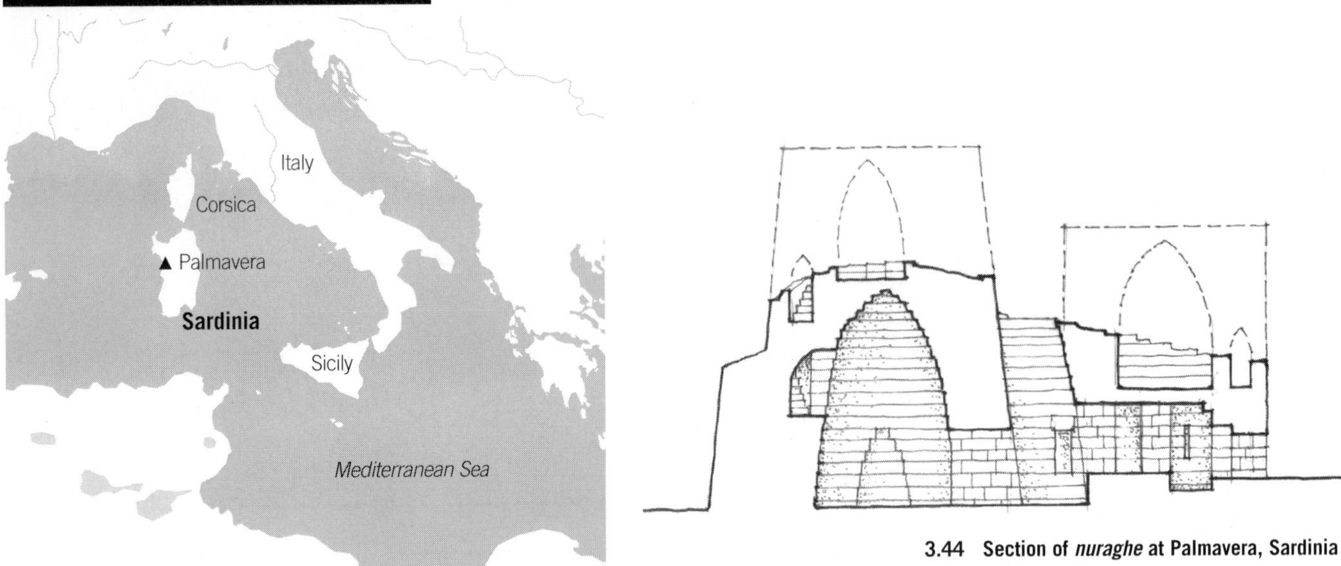


3.44 **Section of *nuraghe* at Palmavera, Sardinia**

### Sardinia

The period of turmoil in Mesopotamia and in the Eastern Mediterranean is linked to the appearance, around 1500 BCE, of a group of settlers who arrived in Sardinia from parts unknown. They were unlike other invaders into the Mediterranean who came from the north and brought with them for the most part only rudimentary building skills. These people possessed advanced building techniques and beautiful Hellenic-styled pottery. But whether they were colonists from Mycenae or had been driven out of their previous location because of natural disaster or warfare is anybody's guess. Called the Nuraghic People, their famous small bronze figurines are unique for this time period in their sparse expressive power. They built roughly 30,000 circular fortified dwellings, located on hills above the plains, many in sight of each other obviously representing a carefully planned system of defense. Today, 7000 of these sites are known.

The word *nuraghe* is a Sardinian word that archaeologists adopted to identify this culture. Its root is *nur,* which means "hollow heap." Despite this characterization the buildings that the Nuraghe built are not haphazard heaps of stone. The work is excellent and, indeed, remarkably skilled. They are also clearly well engineered.

One of the best preserved is near Palmavera, a few miles inland from the shore on the northwest side of the island. It consists of two conical-shaped towers and a courtyard. The towers, each 20 meters in height, contain corbeled vaulted inner spaces, not unlike the tholos tombs of Mycenae, with a staircase leading to the roof. Each one of these citadels appears to have protected a village. While all these fortified dwellings conform to certain conventions, each one differs in some aspects. Some are solitary, others are surrounded by a wall within which can be several towers.

For the Nuraghic People, water was held in veneration, as one might expect in an island with few streams. Archaeologists have uncovered at least 50 sacred wells, the construction of which followed a relatively uniform plan. From a courtyard, often lined with small stone benches to place votive gifts and ritual vases, a corridor sloped down to the underground site of the spring.

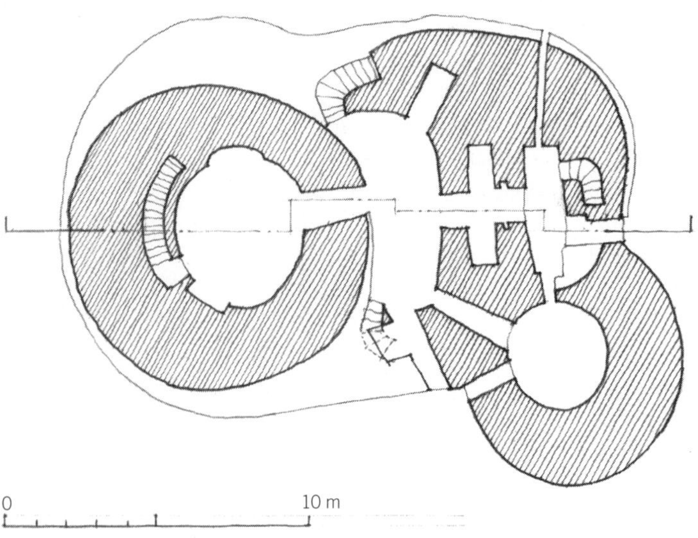


3.45 **Plan of *nuraghe* at Palmavera**

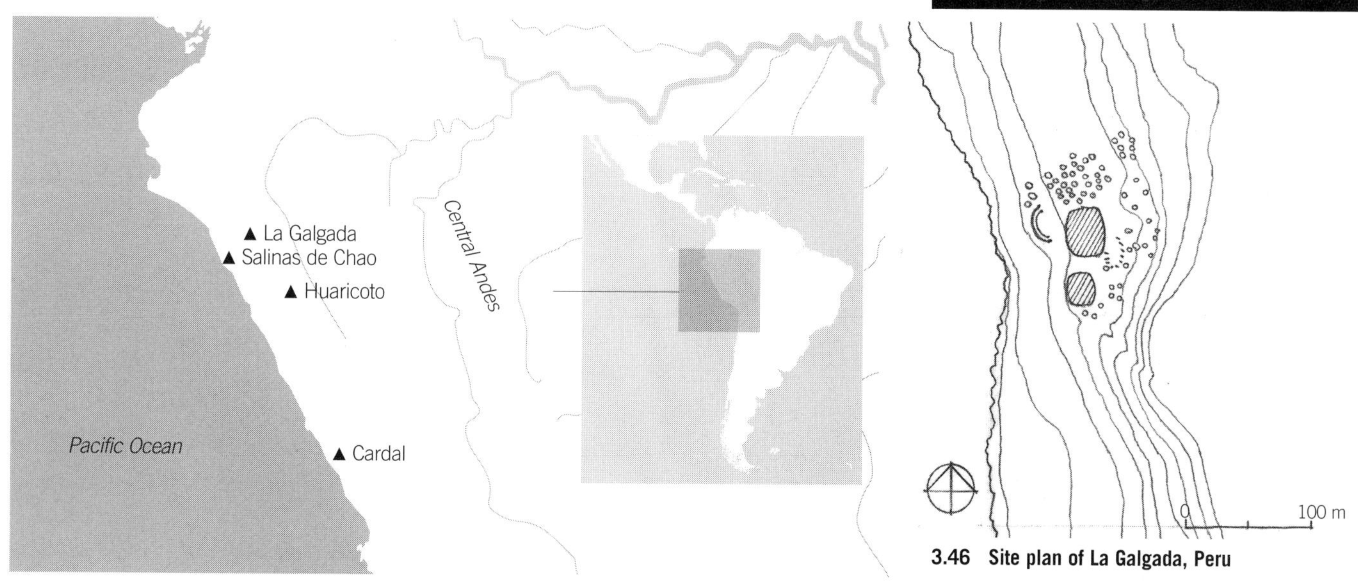


3.46 **Site plan of La Galgada, Peru**

## CIVILIZATION OF THE HIGH ANDES

By 1500 BCE, the Andean cultures had moved into the higher valleys of the Peruvian mountains, from where trade routes, moving north and south, were much easier to establish than along the coast. Aided by the versatile llama, the burgeoning trade enabled the development of a series of interconnected highland centers, such as Cajamarca and Ancash and in the river valleys of the Moche, Casma, Chillon, Rimac, and Lurin. Each had large storage structures to accumulate agricultural produce. As large, centralized surpluses of wealth were generated, competition amongst the elites of the various centers pushed the development of ritual complexes into ever larger sizes and increasing complexity. In the period 2000–1000 BCE, relatively simple and approachable ceremonial structures such as at La Galgada were replaced by a string of enormous U-shaped complexes, amongst the largest of which was at Salinas de Chao.

At Huaricoto, ca. 2200–2000 BCE, there are 13 superimposed, deeply buried ritual structures. Relatively intimate in size, they were used by small groups for fire sacrifices, which were performed by themselves rather than by a priestly class. Each ritual structure, after being used for a while, became a burial site—presumably for the family or clan to which it belonged—and was then filled in to form the base of the next generation's ritual structure. By this time, the sacrifice of living human beings and children had become a part of Andean social practices.

Located a thousand meters above the Tablachaca River, La Galgada (2600–1400 BCE) consists of two mounds, a ring platform, and a low circular wall forming a plaza. Just like at Huaricoto, one finds here small circular masonry ritual chambers, but more formalized, complete with plastered interiors, niches, benches, and a central hearth with built-in ventilator shafts. The older chambers are scattered around the site. The mounds may also contain superimposed layers of ritual structures, but those have not yet been excavated. The latest chambers, however, are located on the north mound, organized in a loose U-shaped arrangement within a walled enclosure and accessed from a small plaza on the west by long, steeply pitched stairs.

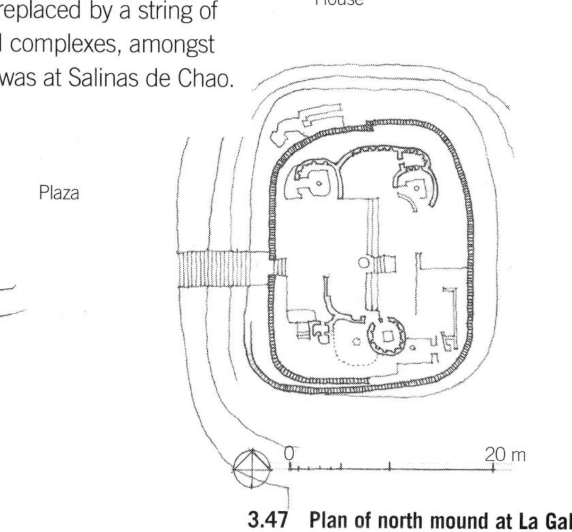


3.47 **Plan of north mound at La Galgada**

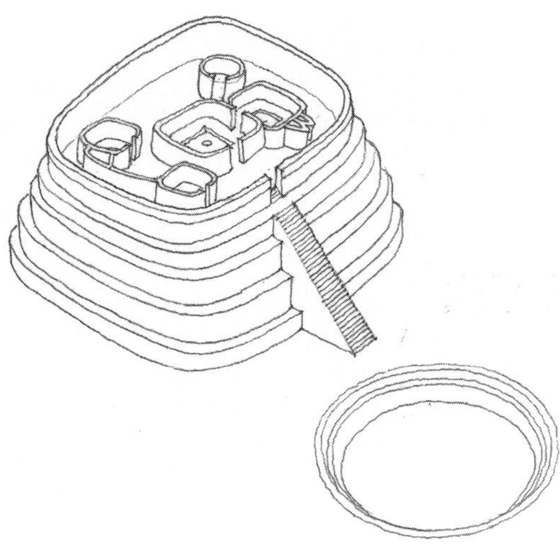

3.48 **Pictorial view of north mound at La Galgada**

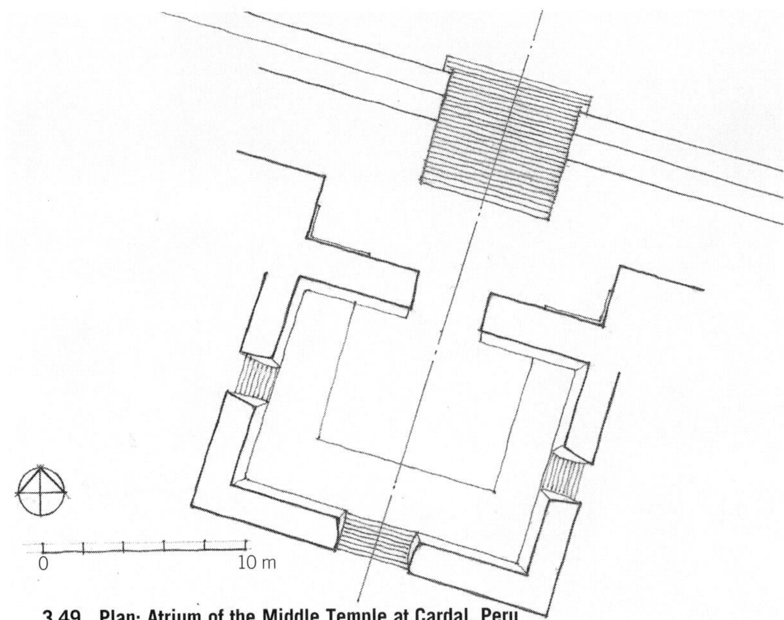


3.49 Plan: Atrium of the Middle Temple at Cardal, Peru

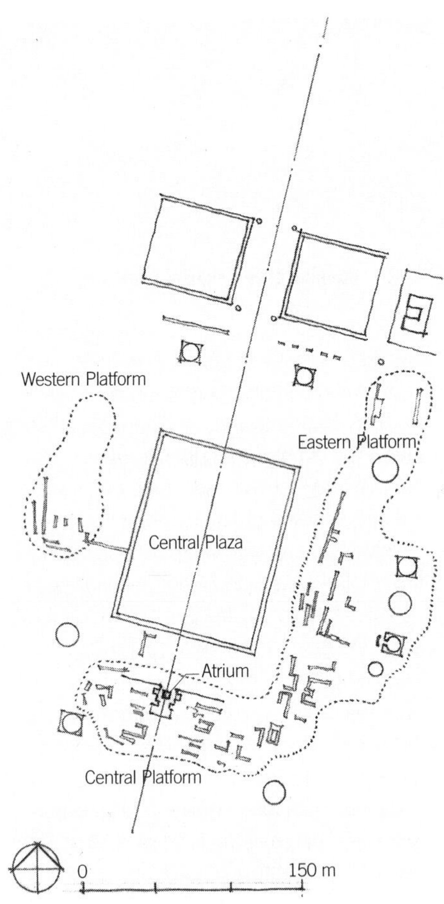


3.50 Site plan of Cardal

Cardal (1465–975 BCE) located 14 kilometers upstream on the Lurin River, consists of three large platform mounds, made from irregular, quarried stone set into clay mortar and arranged in a monumental U-shape open to the north. The main platform mound, dominating the site is 145 by 60 meters and 17 meters high. A steep 6.5-meter-wide stairway leads up to the focal structure, an atrium, atop this mound. There are 3 subsidiary plazas to the North. Eleven circular sunken platforms are scattered across the entire site, some on top of the mounds, others around the plaza. Outlines of residential structures for about 300 inhabitants are also visible at the site.

Cardal was most likely a major regional hub that functioned somewhat like a modern convention center with multiple places designed to accommodate public gatherings of different sizes and composition. The small circular courts dispersed across the site probably functioned both individually for small sacrificial events and collectively as part of larger, orchestrated events.

The two circular courts in the north were probably connected to two smaller plazas at the northern end. For the largest rituals the central plaza served as the main gathering space of the complex, with the atrium atop the largest platform mound forming the focus of the gathering. Rituals performed in the sacred atrium would have been clearly visible in the plaza and, given the steepness of the slope, the position of the spectators, and size of the mound, would have appeared monumental and impressive.

Besides Cardal, massive U-shaped ceremonial complexes were constructed in the Andean highlands at places such as Las Aldas (1600–1100 BCE), Sechin Alto (1800–1700 BCE), and Moxeke (1500–1300 BCE). Sechin Alto was the largest of these, with its largest 300 by 250-meter platform mound rising an imposing 44 meters above the surrounding plain. Not built upon a preexisting hill, this mound contained 2 million cubic feet of fill, masonry, and conical mud bricks, making it one of the largest prehistoric constructions in the new world at that time. Three large circular sunken platforms, positioned right in the middle on axis, dominate the top two and fourth terraces.

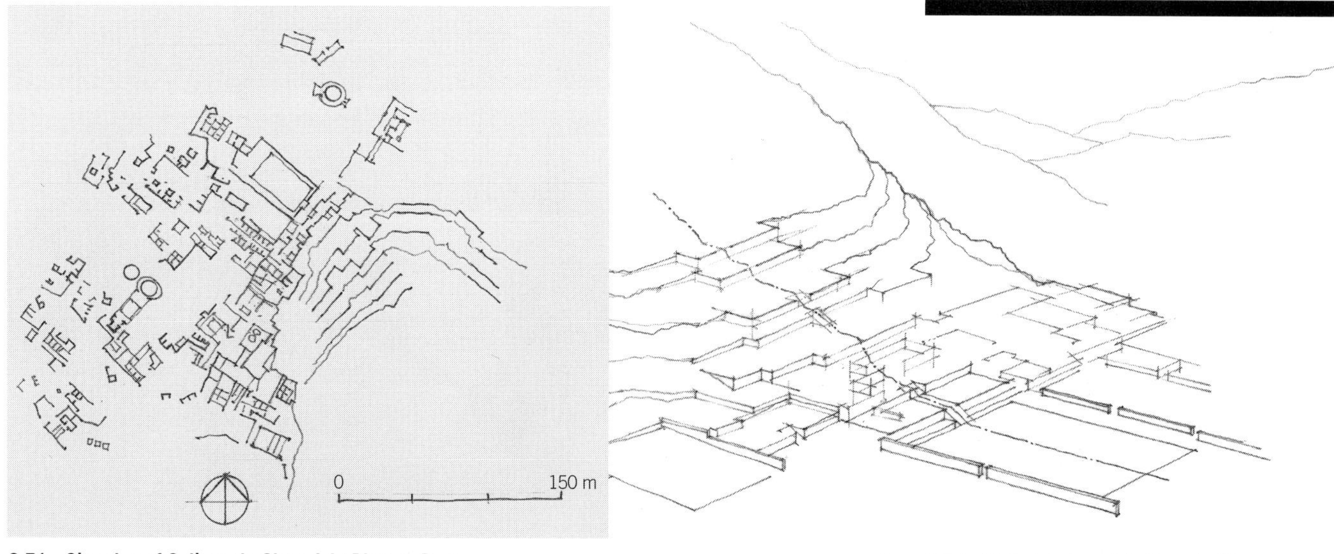


**3.51 Site plan of Salinas de Chao, Isla Blanca, Peru**

**3.52 Pictorial view of Salinas de Chao**

### Salinas de Chao

Salinas de Chao (1610–1300 BCE), located 8 kilometers inland from the Pacific Ocean, shows the ritual complexes integrated within an urban fabric. A haphazard residential order is punctuated by numerous ritual centers. Two of these dominate. The smaller one, 8 meters by 30 meters, consists of a temple, a circular sunken court, and a large rectangular plaza. Unlike Cardal, the longitudinal axis is elongated and knitted together by sidewalls into a single unit, terminating in the circular court. Entered from two opposing stairs on the diagonal axis, the circular court appears as a large open courtyard and terrace. The ritual structure is raised on three levels, exploiting the natural slope of the land. A series of symmetrical platforms and terraces and a central stair further magnify the central presence and the upward monumentalizing thrust of the focal structure, telescoping its presence into the plaza, in contrast with the enveloping negative space of the sunken court.

Although the larger complex is built around the longitudinal axis and exploits the natural elevation of the hillside, its architectural expression points to a more monumental, processional order. The composition emphasizes the length of the longitudinal axis that ends in the mountain itself (although there may have been a focal temple there at one time.) When the complex was expanded in the 14th century BCE, the hillside was carved to create three new terraces on axis with the older ones, only much higher.

The creation of U-shaped ritual complexes in the highland Andes inaugurated a new kind of ritual space that became the staple center of South American architecture until the arrival of the Spanish in the 15th century. While older Andean ritual structures were intimate and focused on ritual theater to be witnessed by those below, the U-shaped complexes were much too large for bounded ceremonies. They would have required impossibly large populations to fill them, and furthermore the rituals on their mounds would not have been visible from even an average distance. One can imagine that many smaller ceremonies could have been carried out simultaneously in them. One possibility is that their lengths and sequences may have been designed to stage elaborate processions from one court to another, stringing them together in time. Yet their size also suggests that these complexes may have been conceived as embodiments of larger cosmic orders, of value simply in their creation.

As Jerry Moore has noted, there is an element of mimicry of the natural environment at Salinas de Chao. The U-shaped spatial composition echoes the character of the river valleys in which it is located. Peru is an earthquake-prone zone. El Niño effects, flash floods, and landslides were periodic occurrences beyond human control. Propitiating the gods of nature and carefully practicing a life in harmony with temporal rhythms, both agricultural and astronomical, was the keystone of not only early Andean beliefs but of most subsequent Southern and Mesoamerican cultures. While archaeologists still debate the exact nature of their rituals, they seem to agree that they have been organized around the necessity of cyclical sacrifice and ritual repetition of natural rhythms. Processional architecture would have facilitated a ritualistic repetition of units of time. These complexes are not sacred structures per se. They are not houses of God. Nor are they landscaped gestures raised skyward. Rather, they are ritual theaters.

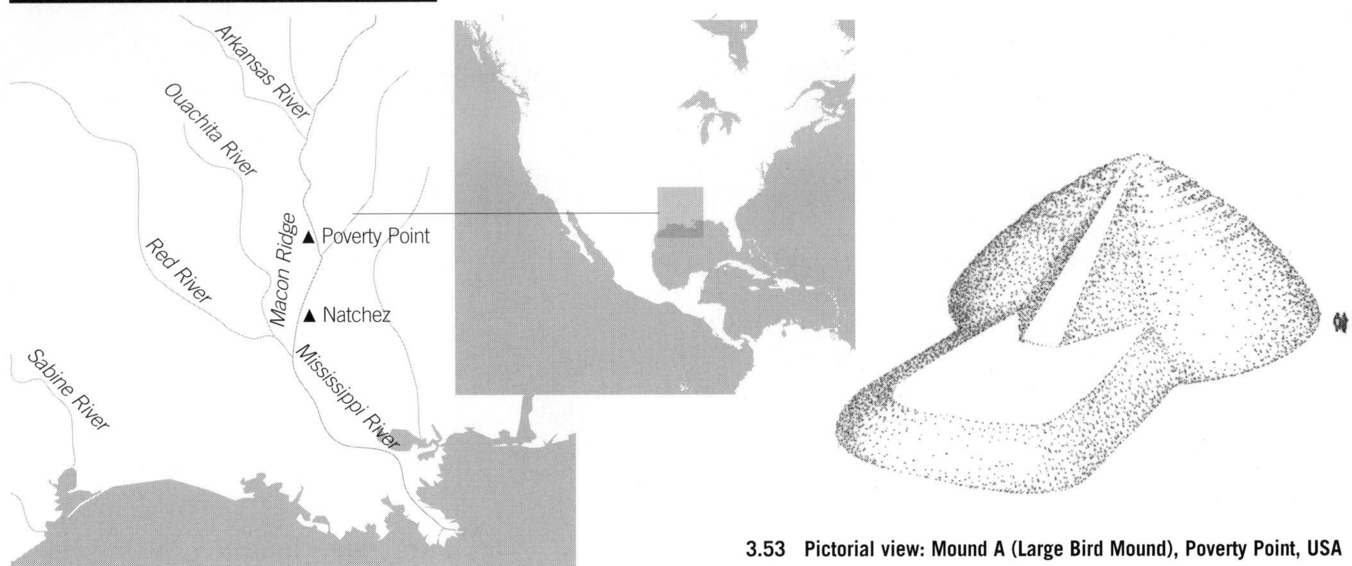


3.53 Pictorial view: Mound A (Large Bird Mound), Poverty Point, USA

## POVERTY POINT

First reported in 1873, the semielliptical ridges of Poverty Point were thought to be natural formations. It was only in the 1950s, when the site was viewed from the air, that archaeologists realized they were artificial constructions. Located in the lower Mississippi valley of Parish County, Louisiana, near both the Gulf Coast and the confluence of six major rivers, Poverty Point is not a unique construction. Huge earth mounds have been found all over North America, particularly along the Mississippi and the coastal regions, some of them dating as far back as 3000 BCE. However, the complexity of Poverty Point, and the huge amount of sacred and secular objects found there clearly indicate that it was a center of both sacred and secular significance.

First settled around 1500 BCE, the Poverty Point area extended throughout the lower Mississippi valley, from New Orleans to the southern tip of Illinois, a distance of about 800 kilometers.The people that lived near Poverty Point chose their locations carefully, linking the sites to the waterways of the Mississippi and allowing for easy trade and communication. Objects excavated at Poverty Point and related sites were often made of materials that originated in distant places—implying viable trade networks—and include chipped-stone projectile points and tools, ground-stone plummets, and shell and stone beads.

Poverty Point's first earthen structures were completed around 1350 BCE. The six concentric semielliptical rings abut a bluff over the Bayou Macon, a short distance from the Mississippi, and enclose an open plaza covering an area of about 34 acres. Aisle-like openings run between the concentric rings, dividing them into six sections, which are thought to have stood over two meters high. In and around the complex are six to eight constructed earthen mounds, also connected to the complex. Besides providing protection from flooding, the rings may have functioned, at least partially, as living areas, since domestic objects have been found in the excavation. At the same time, nonsecular objects have also been found at the site, indicating that the complex must have had a sacred ritualistic function as well.

The main plaza faces east, and every morning the rising sun viewed from the top of the mound overlooking the surrounding forest would have formed a spectacular event. In addition, a person looking along the aisles from the center outward would be looking toward the winter solstice in one direction and the summer solstice in the other direction. The ceremonial center functioned as a cosmic instrument, but exactly how is still not known for sure. It may also have served as a "protective" enclosure, keeping out evil spirits.

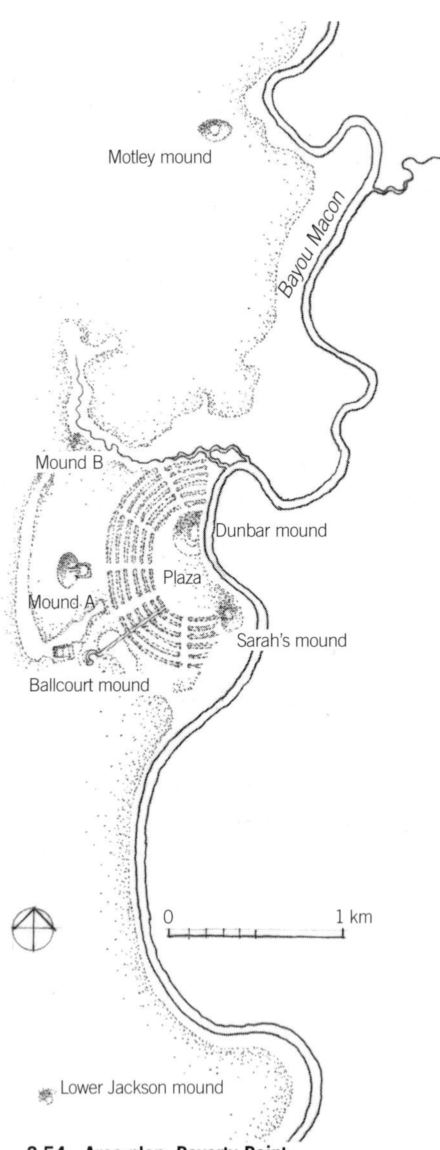


3.54 Area plan: Poverty Point

**SHANG DYNASTY CHINA**

China's earliest dynasties, the Xia (2000–1600 BCE) and the Shang (1600–11 BCE) developed at this time. Kingship and divine power, first fused at this time, have a particularly strong symbolic bond in Chinese history, codified later by Confucius. Because of this bond, kings and dynastic periods dominate Chinese chronology. All the calendars (throughout East Asia in fact) are tied to dynastic periods, with each new dynasty inaugurating a new calendar. Managing time became a central responsibility of kingship. And every dynasty also built a distinctive new walled capital city to be identified with its reign.

Zhengzhou, about three square kilometers in area and the first of many Chinese capitals, was situated along the Yellow River, in the heart of the Shang territories. The most important discovery at Zhengzhou is that of the Hangtu Enclosure, which is of immense size. The east wall is approximately 1700 meters long, the west wall 1870 meters and the south and north walls about 1700 meters. In the northwestern corner of the city platforms of different sizes have been found that once were the bases of large buildings, presumably palaces and temples. The largest is 60 by 13 meters and oriented to the cardinal points. Along the southern and northern edges of the top of the platform there are two rows of rectangular pits that held pillars that supported some form of superstructure.

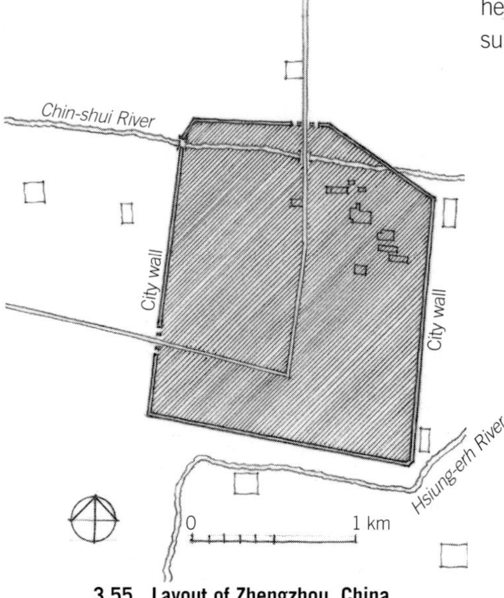


**3.55 Layout of Zhengzhou, China**

**3.56 Reconstruction of Shang dynasty palace**

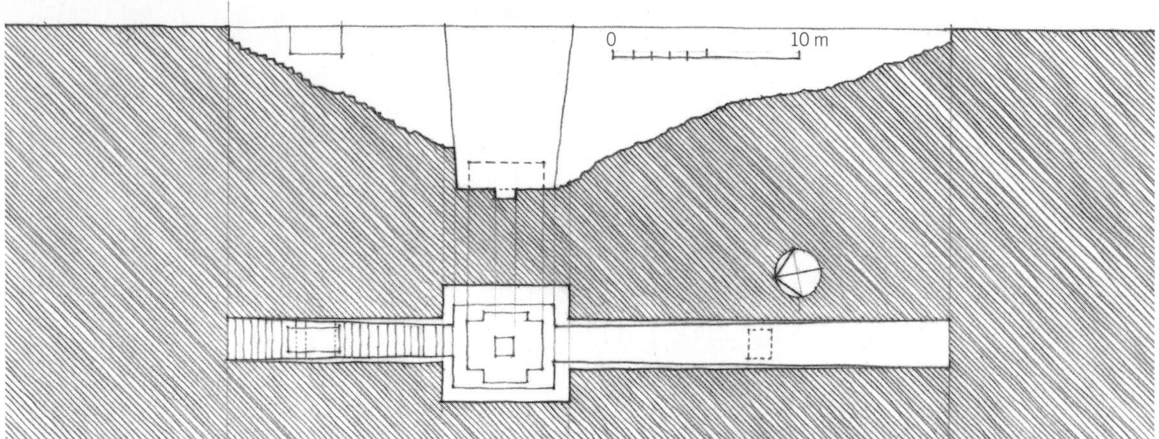


**3.57 Plan and section: Tomb of Fu Hao, near Yin, China**

A large number of tombs have been found near Yin, Anyang county, the last Shang capital. Only the tomb of one of the Shang kings' consorts, Fu Hao, was found intact. Dated around 1250 BCE, it consists of a single large pit, 5.6 meters by 4 meters at the mouth. The opening at the top of the tomb was covered by a rammed earth foundation, possibly the base of a sacrificial altar. Although most of the other tombs of the time had ramps leading down to them, her tomb did not. The floor level housed the royal corpse and most of the utensils and implements buried with her. Below the corpse was a small pit holding the remains of six dogs, and along the perimeters lay the skeletons of 16 humans. Inside the pit was a wooden chamber 5 meters long, 3.5 meters wide, and 1.3 meters high. Within the chamber was a lacquered coffin that has since rotted away. There also seems to have once been a structure built over the tomb for holding memorial ceremonies.

**3.58 Inscriptions on an oracle bone from the Anyang site**

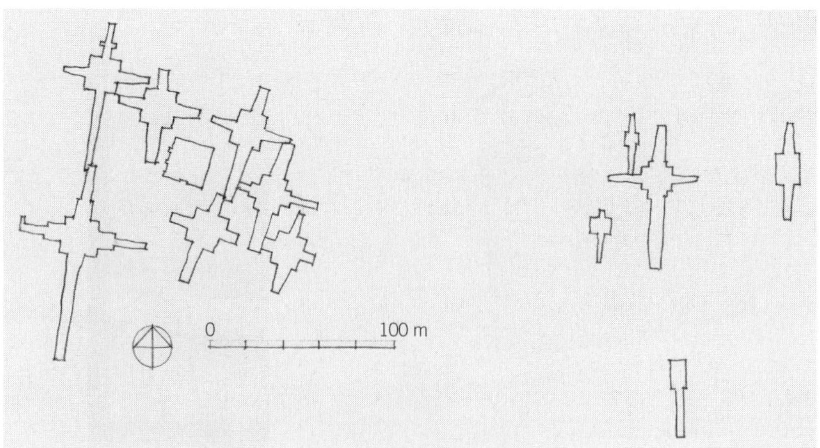


**3.59 Layout of Shang tombs near Yin, Anyang county**

# 800 BCE

By 1000 BCE, the coastal communities of South America moved into the highlands from whence they were able to better control trade. Ritual centers, such as Chavín de Huántar, were located at the intersections of these trade routes. In Central America meanwhile, the Olmecs were able to drain the marshy lands of Veracruz and convert them into thriving agricultural fields. This enabled them to develop a prosperous local trading economy that was the basis of the first major ritual centers of Central America at places such as San Lorenzo and La Venta in modern-day Mexico.

Whereas Mesoamerica had just entered the Bronze Age, the Eurasian world was entering the Iron Age. Iron also reshaped the political and the architectural geography of Eurasia and West Asia in particular. Egypt, which had been the dominant power but which had no way of producing iron on a large scale, was now defeated by the Assyrians in 700 BCE. The political vacuum that this created resulted in the emergence of several Iron-Age centers. In north Italy, we find the Etruscans; in Greece, the Dorians and along the coast of Turkey, the Ionians; in Armenia, the Urartu; and in southern Egypt, the Nubians. Metal was their leverage in overcoming their geographic remoteness. Along the eastern Mediterranean coast, cities like Biblos, Sidon flourished, as did the Israelite kingdom centered in Jerusalem.

It was within this context that the Dorians who invaded and subsumed the Mycenaean world, established their hold on the Mediterranean ports and extended their power toward the west by founding colonies in Sicily and Italy to secure their hold on these newly developed grain-producing regions. Magna Graecia, as it was called, was so strong that by the year 500 BCE, one has to view it as a single economic and cultural continuity. It was thus in Sicily and Italy that one finds some of the most developed early Greek experiments in stone architecture.

Initially, after the conquest of the Egyptians, the Assyrians and Babylonians could reestablish themselves in Mesopotamia, but though their empires were extensive and their new cities famous, their inability to establish coherent financial and trade environment policies made their dominions vulnerable. The fall of the Babylonian Empire to Persia in 539 BCE marked the beginning of the end of a Mesopotamia-centered culture that had, for over two millennia, been one of the dominating regenerating forces, both culturally, economically, and politically, in Eurasia. With the collapse of the Mesopotamian cultures, and the power shift to the Iranians, one could argue that it is here that the east and west begin to develop a growing distance in outlook and philosophy.

Further to the east, in India, the Vedic Indo-Aryan elite who had invaded from the north in previous centuries had by this time occupied large sections of the Indo-Gangetic Plain, where they established 16 *mahajanapadas*. Initially the state of Kashi, with its capital at Varanasi, gained supremacy, but it was subsumed by Koshala. Varanasi, however, remained as an important center of learning and became home to scholars from all the mahajanapadas.

The Western Zhou civilization of China was also turbulent, and yet it was during this time that two of China's four great cities arose, Xian and Luoyang, establishing important models for subsequent urban planning. But because the Chinese, like the south Asians, were building in wood, little has survived. The Zhou Dynasty began a process of cleansing society of unwanted barbarians. All those who did not conform to its language of customs were killed or exiled, mainly to the south, becoming the ancestors of the Thai, Burmese, and Vietnamese. The result was the construction of the largest unified cultural system in the world, all under the control of dynastic kings who claimed to rule as intermediary between heaven and earth. Large bureaucracies with strict adherence to rules and rituals were set up to regulate and govern this vast dominion.

# 800 BCE

▲ **San Lorenzo**
1500–900 BCE

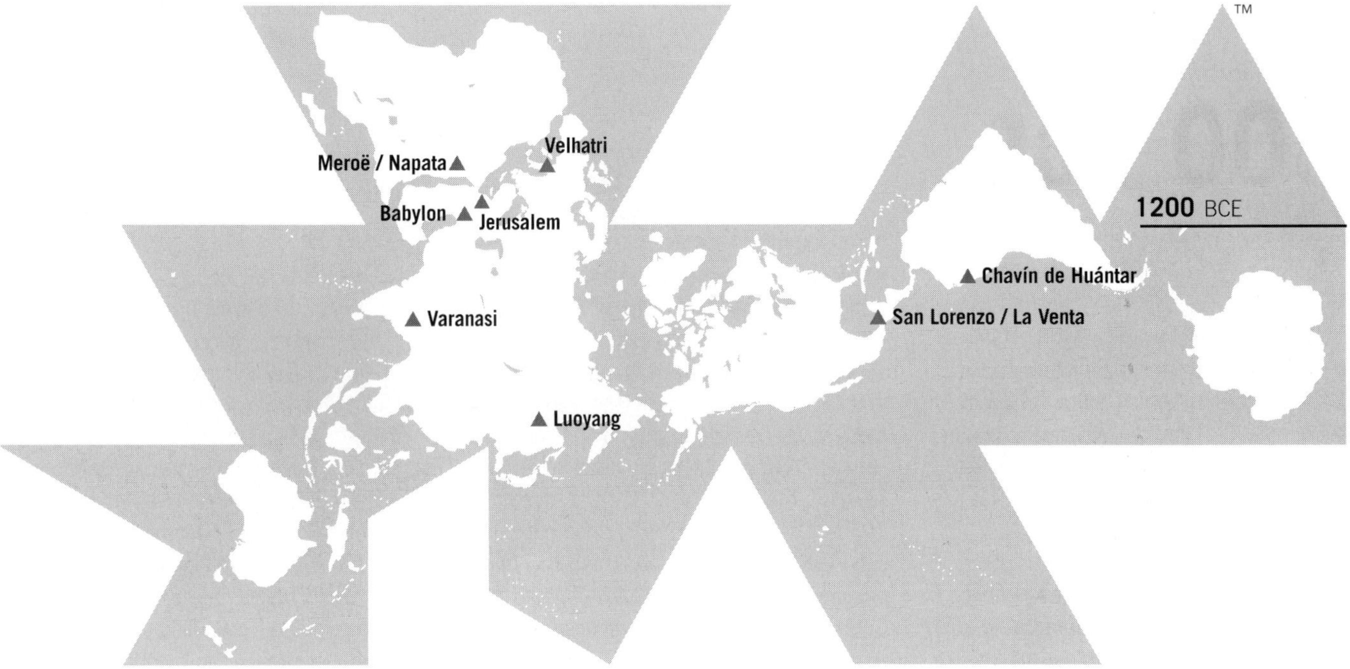

™

Meroë / Napata ▲
Velhatri ▲
Babylon ▲
▲ Jerusalem
▲ Varanasi
▲ Luoyang
▲ Chavín de Huántar
▲ San Lorenzo / La Venta

**1200** BCE

Balkan Peninsula: Mycenaean Era
ca. 1600–1100 BCE

Middle Assyrian Period
ca. 1350–1100 BCE

Olmec Cultures
ca. 1500–400 BCE

▲ **La Venta**
1000–600 BCE

Chavín Culture
ca. 1000–400 BCE

▲ **Chavín de Huántar**
ca. 900 BCE

Western Zhou Dynasty
ca. 1046–771 BCE

Eastern Zhou Dynasty
771–256 BCE

▲ **Ritual Complex at Fengchu**
ca. 1000 BCE

**1000** BCE — **800** BCE — **600** BCE

**Iron Age II**
ca. 1000–586 BCE

▲ **Holy City of Varanasi**
ca. 0–present

▲ **Temple of Solomon**
953–586 BCE

Etruscan Culture
ca. 750–90 BCE

▲ **Banditaccia**
8th–3rd centuries BCE

▲ **Volterra**
5th–4th centuries BCE

Greece: Geometric Period
ca. 900–700 BCE

Greece: Archaic Period
ca. 700–480 BCE

▲ **Temple of Hera at Samos**
8th century BCE

▲ **Temple of Apollo at Thermun**
630 BCE

▲ **Temple of Poseidon at Isthmia**
7th century BCE

⦿ ca. 776 BCE
Olympic games founded

Kingdom of Kush
ca. 760 BCE–350 CE

**Meroë** ▲
ca. 590 BCE

Neo-Assyrian Empire
ca. 911–612 BCE

▲ **Dur-Sharrukin**
717–705 BCE

▲ **Babylon**
Rebuilt 605 BCE

▲ **Nineveh**
705–612 BCE

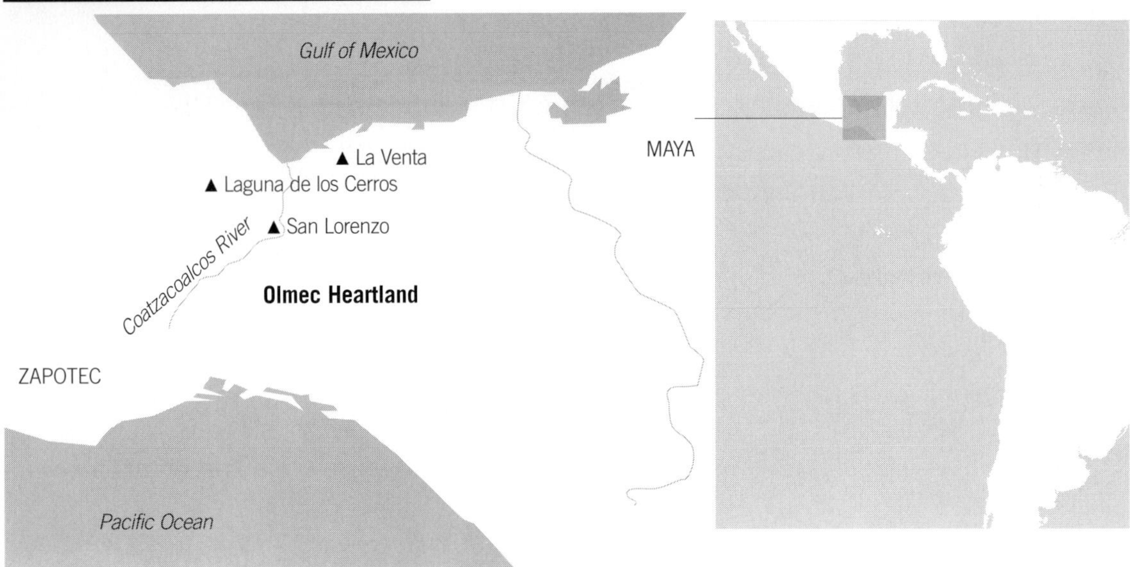


## OLMECS

The first culture in Central America to produce a formal architectural vocabulary out of permanent material was the Olmecs (1500–400 BCE), with their heartland extending in an arc of about 200 kilometers along the southern shore of the Gulf of Mexico on the coastal plains of Veracruz and Tabasco. The Olmec converted a swampy land to their advantage. They first cultivated on the natural levees that rose above the land. Eventually, by dredging and piling up earth to heighten and extend these levees, they could not only create cultivable land but also harvest fish, clams, and turtles from the waterways. It was around this time that we see the emergence of a permanent population of elites, who of course lived on the highest land created by extensive modification of the earth. By 1000 BCE San Lorenzo had substantial reservoirs and drainage systems, integrated into a palatial complex with causeways, plazas, and platform mounds. After San Lorenzo, the Olmecs developed centers at La Venta, Tenochtitlán, and Laguna de los Cerros. The establishment of centers became an impetus for trade, not only amongst themselves but throughout Central America. Their jade for instance came from Guatemala.

The emergence of the Olmec culture coincided with the development of a high-yielding maize, that with beans and squash, all very suited to swampy environments, formed the basis of the economy. It has been suggested that the sudden emergence of an organized and cohesive culture was also due to a lively trade in salt and the discovery of methods to process salt for medicinal, religious, and culinary purposes. Salt was eventually used for money by the Mayans.

**4.1 Characteristic motif of Olmec art was the were-jaguar, a human face with the mouth of a jaguar.**

In addition to agricultural rituals, the religious life of the Olmecs centered on active natural formations, such as caves, springs, and volcanoes.The volcano, which figured strongly in the art of these centers, was associated with the world being born from below and was also the home of the storm clouds, lightning, and rain. One encounters it in Olmec art as a dragon with its gaping mouth representing the portal to the underworld. The sky was ruled by a bird monster or sun god whose energy powered the cosmos and made the plants grow. Underneath the dragon the Olmecs visualized a watery void out of which the world was formed. The main deity in the Olmec mythology was the rain god depicted as a jaguar, a shamanistic symbol of transformation. This were-jaguar, much like the werewolf, could assume other forms, even human forms. The sexual union of a woman and a jaguar gave birth to a special class of gods that were represented in sculpture as having a snarling mouths, toothless gums, fangs, and a cleft head. The Olmecs learned to drag and float stones and columns of up to 40 tons over a distance of 160 kilometers. Most were made into jaguars and human heads by Olmec sculptors. Unlike the angular and sharp features of later civilizations, the Olmec heads were round and soft, and very lifelike.

4.2 Colossal monolithic head uncovered at San Lorenzo

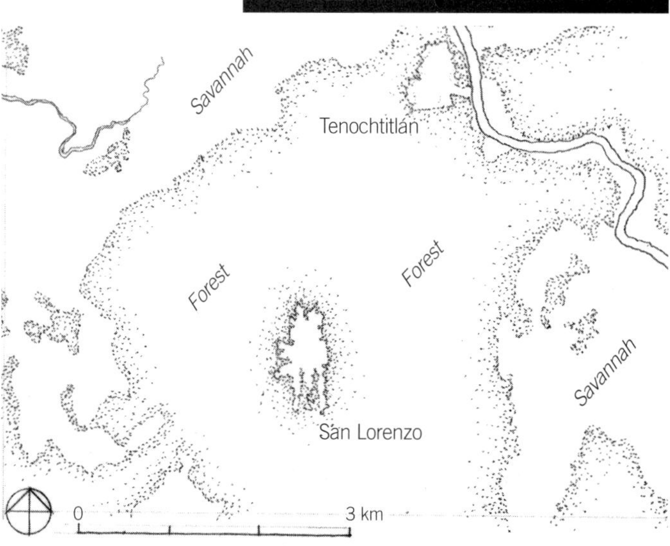

4.3 Area plan of San Lorenzo, Mexico

**San Lorenzo**

Olmec ceremonial structures were located on islands or on elevated lands that remained dry during the rainy season.This was true for one of their principal sites, San Lorenzo (1500–900 BCE), named after a nearby modern village, and located in the lower reaches of the Coatzacoalcos River, some 60 kilometers to the southeast of the majestic volcanic mountains of Santa Marta and San Martín. The Coatzacoalcos River is the only tropical river system in central America, which means that in the dry season the water flows mainly in the river channels, but in the wet season, the river expands to form a vast fluvial network.

Although now dry, San Lorenzo was, in 1000 BCE, basically an island hill that had been dramatically modified—filled in here and cut away there—all done without the aid of beasts of burden or wheels. The final shape, covering an area of about 7 square kilometers, resembled that of a bird.

Though the wooden architecture has long since disappeared, the use of a scarce basaltic stone, brought from the distant Tuxtla Mountains, for steps, columns, and aqueducts gives us vivid indication of the scale and grandeur of Olmec architecture. The main ceremonial complex consisted of a series of modified earth platform mounds arranged north-south in a series of courts. Huge monolithic heads, most likely representations of the rulers, stood in the middle of the courts. Cut-stone cisterns collected water for the dry season. Drainage was through a network of canals built of large basalt blocks.

From the central court, six long artificial ridges projected outward on the north, south, and western sides of the mound. The only one that has been excavated so far reveals that the Olmecs had to have transported 67,000 cubic meters of soil to create a platform about 200 meters long, 50 meters wide, and 6.5 meters high. While the exact purpose of these ridges is still in dispute, the current thesis is that these ridges may have been the sites of palace complexes, as evidenced by their sheer size and the basalt thrones that were found there, and the 200-meter-long drainage system. The Olmec sculptures were not idols to be worshipped but, so it seems, representations used to reenact mythological or historical events.

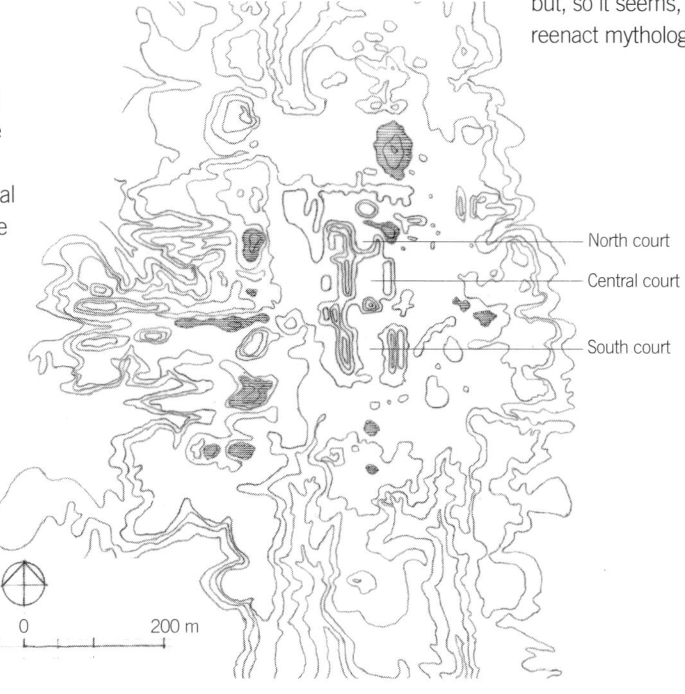

4.4 Site plan of San Lorenzo

**4.5 Tomb found at La Venta**

## La Venta

Unique amongst Central American constructions is the conical pyramid at the Olmec site, La Venta (1200–400 BCE), 80 kilometers northeast of San Lorenzo, closer to the shore of the Gulf of Mexico. Beneath the mounds and plazas, archaeologists have found sculptures and ritual objects, often of a particular type of blue-green jade, the source of which has recently been determined to be located in Guatemala. One extraordinary tomb created for two infants is constructed from large basalt columns that form a type of subterranean log house. It is evident that La Venta was not an isolated ritual site, but the center of a large and thriving urban center that, at its height, was estimated to have supported up to 18,000 people. La Venta was destroyed around 300 BCE and its sculptured monuments apparently intentionally defaced by the inhabitants for reasons not yet fully understood.

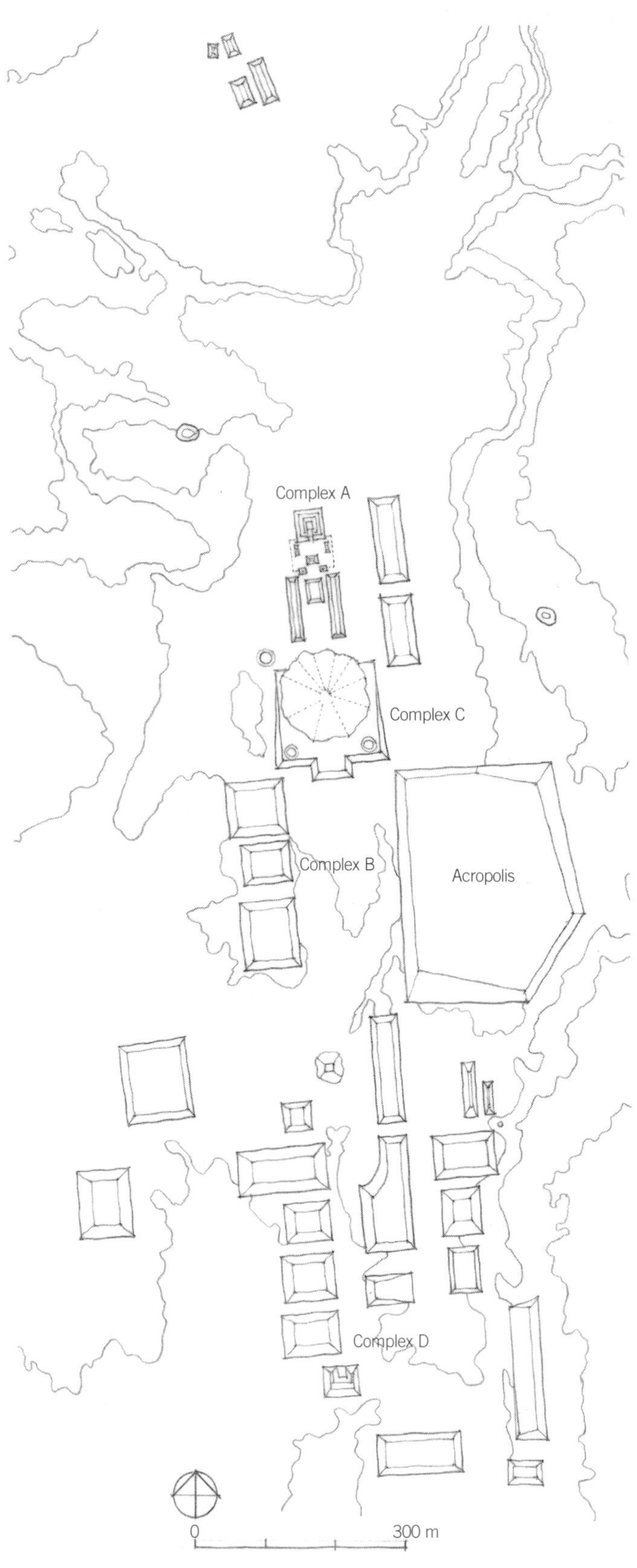


**4.6 Site plan of La Venta**

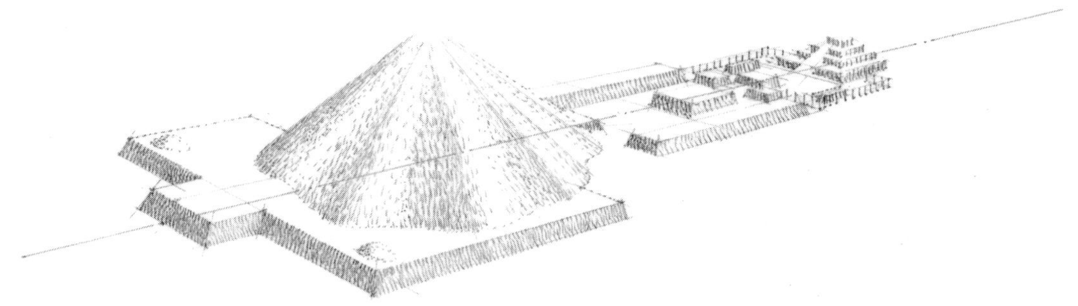

4.7 Aerial view of the ceremonial center at La Venta

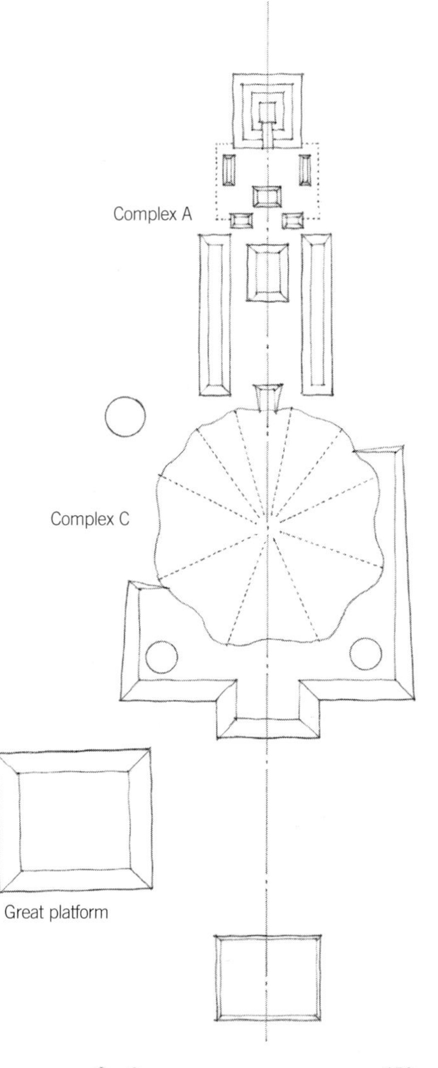


4.8 Plan of the ceremonial center at La Venta

The La Venta pyramid, about 30 meters high and 150 meters in diameter, is the largest of the Olmec pyramids. It was constructed from 130,000 cubic feet of beaten earth and clay to form a conical shape rising from a rectangular base; a series of unique "flutings" or depressions and protrusions make up its surface. No other structure built by native Americans is known to have these "flutings," the meaning and purpose of which are unknown. The pyramid was part of a ceremonial complex arranged along a north-south axis. The court at the northern end was originally surrounded by an enclosure of prismatic basalt columns. Recent archaeological evidence suggests that the fluted pyramid may have been the terminus of the structures not to its north, as it might at first appear, but to a larger group of platform mounds to the south, which are presently under excavation. As at San Lorenzo, excavations at the so-called Acropolis (which may have been the base of a palace complex) show a complex drainage system with stone troughs and collecting basins.

Excavation crews at El Manati, a boggy site at the base of a hill 32 kilometers from San Lorenzo, have recently uncovered at least 40 life-size, carved, wooden human heads. One of these has been carbon dated to 1200 BCE. Unlike San Lorenzo and La Venta, this site was not a populated settlement but an isolated ritual center, where the heads were part of ritual sacrifices performed to water gods. Skeletons of sacrificed children, as well as seven rubber balls, have also been found there.

## 800 BCE

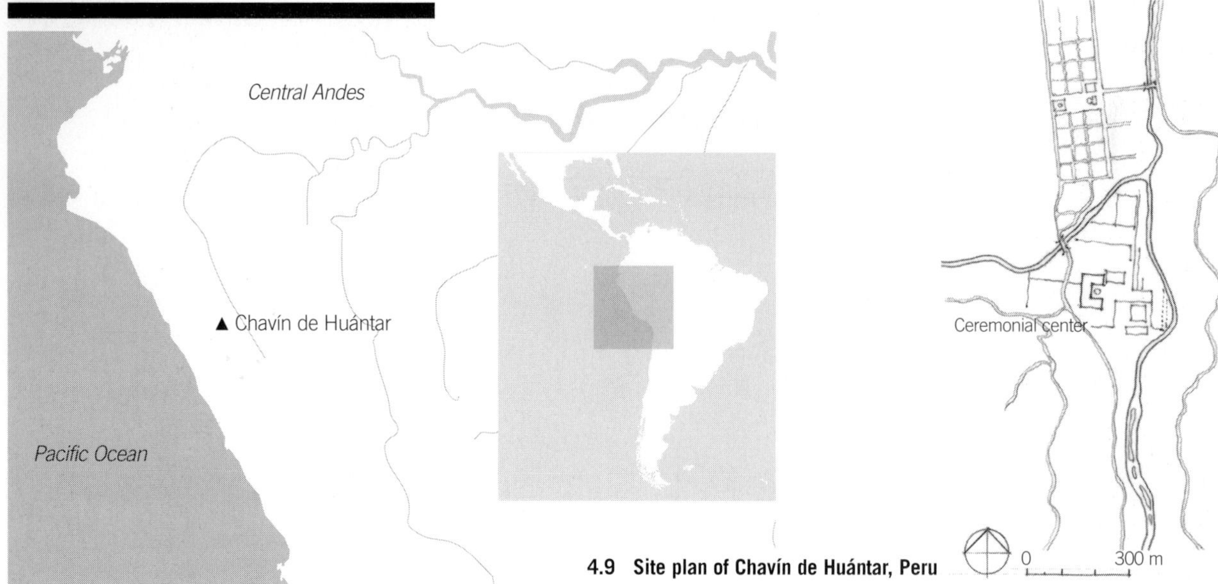


**4.9 Site plan of Chavín de Huántar, Peru**

### CHAVÍN DE HUÁNTAR

By 800 BCE, Andean civilization had developed further into the highlands of the Andes, building new towns and ritual centers much higher than before. One of these, Chavín de Huántar, appears to have been founded around 900 BCE. It is located at a place where the Mosna River narrows into the precipitous gorges of the Cordillera Blanca in northwest Peru. The city was a trading center, relying on exchange of meat from the highland people with seafood from the coast. Though seemingly remote, it was only about a six-day walk to the Pacific Ocean to the west and to the tropical forests to the east. The first ceremonial structure that was built there was a U-shaped pyramidal platform mound called the Old Temple, facing east, at the center of which was a large circular sunken plaza, with the customary dual stairs on axis and a centralized main staircase leading to the raised terrace.

The central section of this platform attains a height of 11 meters, the northern wing 14 meters, and the southern wing, the highest, 16 meters. The walls of this freestanding structure, 200 meters in length, are slightly slanted, rising dramatically above the observer on the ground or in the sunken circular plaza. The walls are adorned with gigantic grotesque heads, carved in the round and supported by tenons inserted in the massive masonry.

The plaza, sunk 2.5 meters below the surface of the court and with a diameter of 21 meters, could have held about 500 people at one time. Two thin horizontal slabs, alternating with single rows of large rectangular slabs, all precisely cut, line the wall-edge of the plaza. The lower of these slabs depict seven jaguars, with the corresponding upper slabs displaying matching pairs of mythical figures, all of which seem to be marching toward the main staircase leading to the platform mound. The walls of the court bring the steep slopes of the surrounding mountains directly into the space of the visual temple.

Remarkably, the platform mound of the Old Temple is honeycombed by a windowless labyrinth of corridors, staircases, and air ducts so complex that no adequate plan has yet been published. The passageways, no more than a meter wide and varying in height, are large enough for a single person to walk through and were used undoubtedly for ceremonial purposes. Some of these galleries span several floor levels and are connected by stairways. The most significant one is located on axis with the central staircase. It leads through a long narrow passage to a cruciform chamber in the middle of which is a 4.5-meter-tall carved shaft of white granite on which is a carved image of a fanged anthropomorphic deity, clearly the central deity of the complex. Known today as the Lanzón, it is carved in a way that follows the undulating surface of the stone. Set in the dark passage, it still has an awe-inspiring presence. Its top is fitted into a space in the gallery ceiling. In the chamber's walls are niches that could have served the purpose of storing objects.

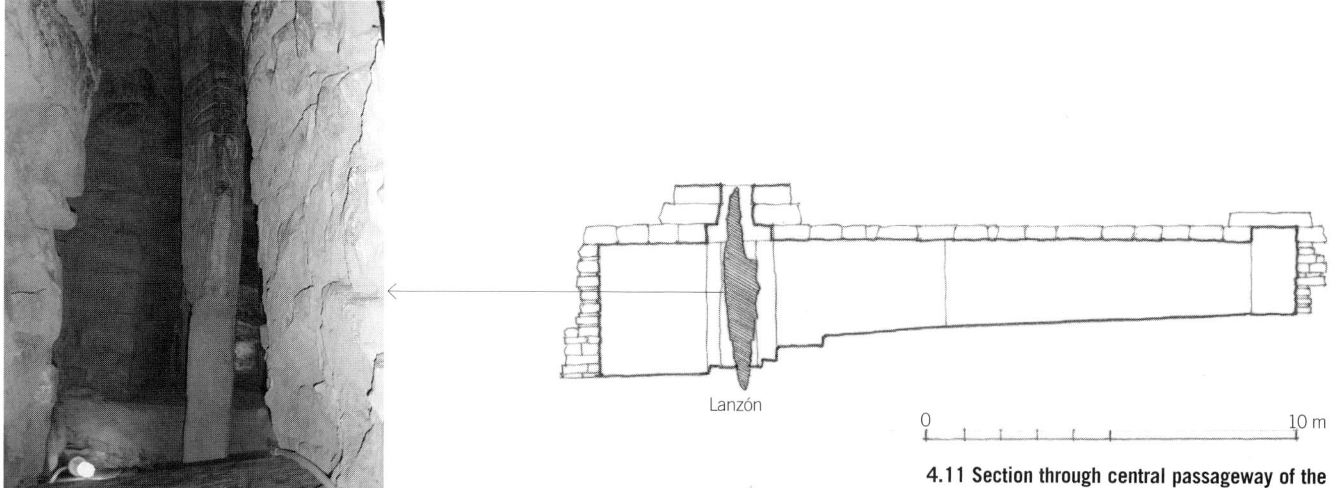


4.10 **Lanzón, a large stone idol representing the supreme deity of Chavín de Huántar**

4.11 **Section through central passageway of the Old Temple: leading to the Lanzón at Chavín de Huántar**

Between 900–500 BCE, a New Temple was built, for which the southern platform was extended and doubled in area. The two temple buildings of cut-and-dressed stone, which were placed on the platform would have been visible far into the distance. The long maze of galleries from the Old Temple was extended into the platform. There does not seem to be a new central gallery room, however, indicating the continued reign of the old deity in the cruciform chamber. Unlike the Old Temple, however, there is no direct external staircase leading to the roof platform of the New Temple. Two openings in the platform floor lead up to the platform so that a priest would appear to observers below to be emerging magically on the platform.

To the east, on axis with the New Temple, is a square semisubterranean ritual court about 20 meters wide with shallow stairs in the middle of all its sides. The court is flanked on the north and south by two additional platform mounds, completing the complex. Construction in and around these complexes came to an end around 700–500 BCE. The reasons are unclear, as is so much about early Peruvian civilization.

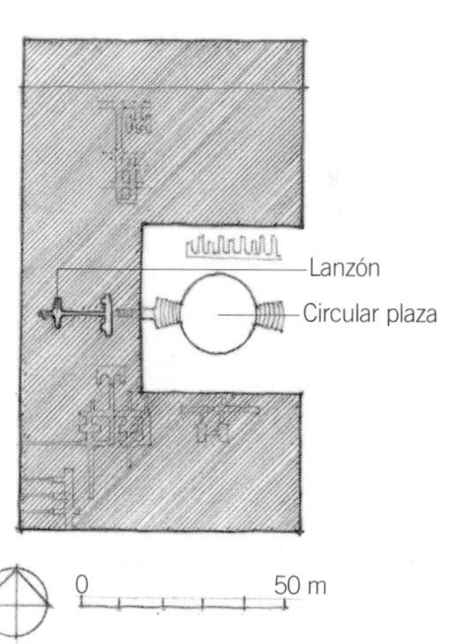


4.12 **Plan of Old Temple: Chavín de Huántar**

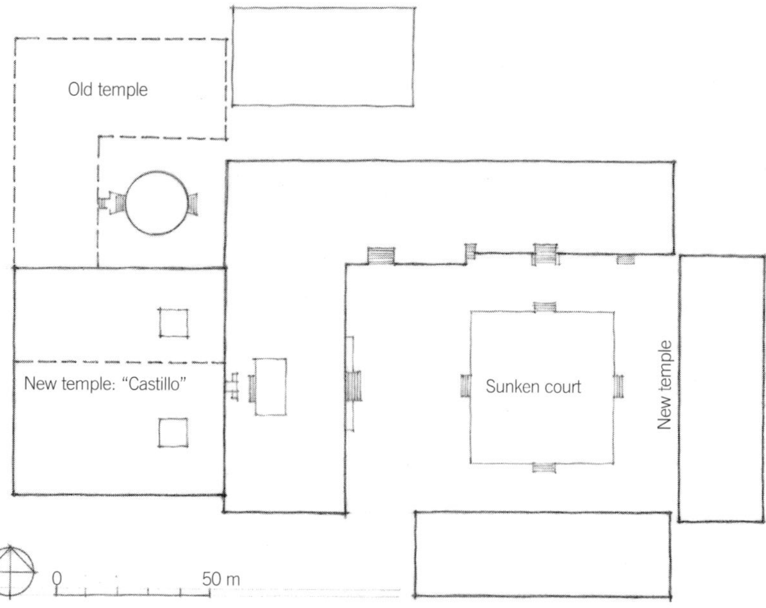


4.13 **Plan of New Temple: Chavín de Huántar**

**4.14 Confucius (K'ung-fu-tzu)**

## ZHOU DYNASTY CHINA

Though it might seem that China had been "Chinese" from early on, prior to the Zhou Dynasty, which began in 1046 BCE, there were several regional and linguistic groups (somewhat similar to what one might have found in South Asia), where by 800 BCE, there were already at least 40 different languages. The Zhou, however, in their conquests enforced the use of the Chinese language, seeing this as part of a civilizing agenda. Non-Chinese speaking peoples were defined as "barbarians" and were depicted with unkempt hair and tattoos, sounding much like remnant populations of Polynesian islanders. Those who did not want to succumb to this modernization, moved southward, displacing or integrating into local populations to become the ancestors of modern Thai, Laotians, and Burmese. Because the Zhou Dynasty lasted longer than any other previous dynasty, the result was the largest unified linguistic geographical group in the world. Still today one can go from Manchuria in the north to the Gulf of Tonkin in the south and remain within land occupied by speakers of Mandarin and its dialects.

The Zhou were most likely tribes from northwestern China who adopted modern Shang weaponry, in particular the bow and arrow and the chariot, to conquer the Shang. They also adopted Shang culture and values, before overthrowing them and establishing their own dynasties. The Zhou Dynasty is divided into two periods, the Western Zhou (1046–771 BCE) and the Eastern Zhou (771–256 BCE). The Western and Eastern periods are separated by the movement of the capital city from Hao (near the present city of Xian) in the west to Luoyang in Henan province. The move was apparently prompted by the need to stabilize the eastern provinces. Though they were initially successful, the Zhou soon entered into a period of internal strife, known as the Warring States Period (475–221 BCE). Despite this, the Zhou made the transition to iron, developing cast-iron production (as opposed to forged iron in the West) around 500 BCE and establishing the first imperial cities, two of which—Xian and Luoyang—are today still major urban centers.

The names of Chinese dynasties are not always related to family or clan names. They are quite often one-word themes that, like a sound bite, define the principle of the dynasty. *Zhou*, for example, means "state" or "country." *Ming*, the name of the most famous Chinese dynasty, means "bright."

During the Zhou Dynasty many of the cultural and political ideals that were to pervade Chinese imperial society were established. Rites of worship, an ideology of "harmony," and the offering of sacrifices to ancestral deities were all central in the effort to link political and religious authority. Philosophers began to articulate this as the "Mandate of Heaven" (*tianming*). Many of the social principles developed during the Western Zhou period were actually codified in the later Eastern Zhou period by K'ung-fu-tzu, known to the West as Confucius (551–479 BCE). The Eastern Zhou reign was politically a very unstable time. It was in this context that Confucius articulated an essentially conservative philosophy that was based on the principles of proper conduct. The ideal Confucian man had to earn the right to authority by strict adherence to hierarchical rules and the proper observance of ancestral rituals; the cultivation of music and the arts were also important. The Zhou rulers began to incorporate some of Confucius' ideas into state religious practices, using ritual (*li*) as a sign of aristocratic behavior. Several Zhou period texts, *Zhou li* (Rituals of Zhou), *Yi li* (Ceremonial and Ritual), and *Li ji* (Record of Ritual), detail the organization at the early Zhou court and the duties that governed every rank and office.

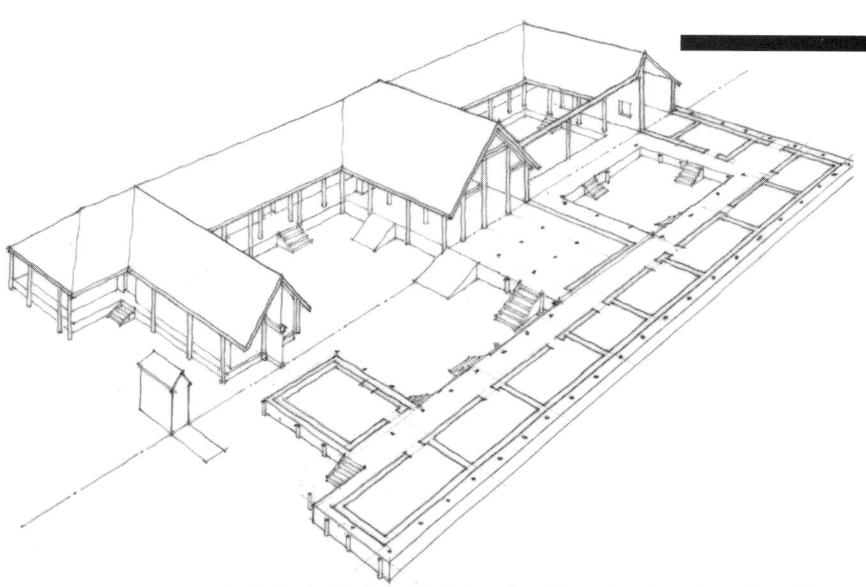

4.15 **Pictorial view: Ritual Complex at Fengchu, Shaanxi Province, China**

**Ritual Complex at Fengchu**

Under the Zhou, the ancestral temple became the site for rituals celebrating the authority of the state. Its components were a gatehouse, a large central court, a major hall, and flanking halls. The overall plan was governed by a strict adherence to geometry and was designed so that the position and role of each participant was exactly spelled out.

A proposed reconstruction of the Zhou Ritual Complex at Fengchu (1100–1000 BCE) shows a rigidly axial and symmetrically arranged series of buildings and courtyards framed on three sides by a walled enclosure. The entrance was defined by a gate that had in front of it a freestanding wall, which, as in later Chinese structures, served to ward off unwanted spirits and prevent them from entering the complex. Behind the gate there was a large courtyard, framing the main hall, elevated on a platform and accessible by three flights of stairs. Excavations beneath some of the rooms to the rear have uncovered inscribed tortoise shells and oracle bones, whence the presumption that this was a ceremonial complex. The main construction was of wood, with bronze used to bind and reinforce structural elements at the joints.

The Zhou crafted special ceremonial objects for every phase of the rituals performed in the building. Bronze chimes, for example were used to mark noble rank. One chime of 65 bells, which would have required six musicians standing and kneeling at both sides, was recovered intact in the tomb of the Marquis Yi of Zeng

4.16 **Ritual wine container, late Western Zhou dynasty**

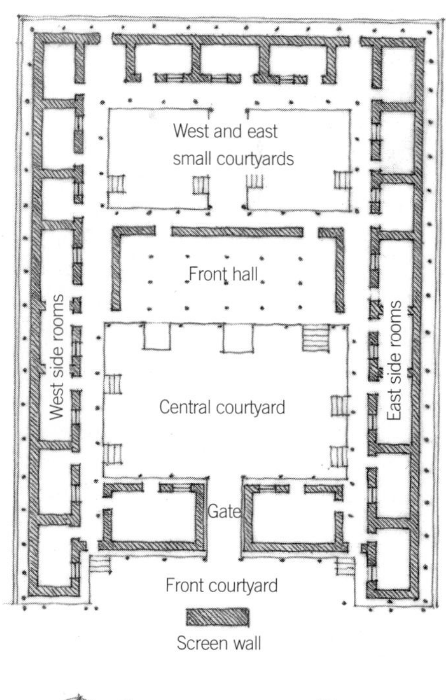


4.17 **Plan: Ritual Complex at Fengchu**

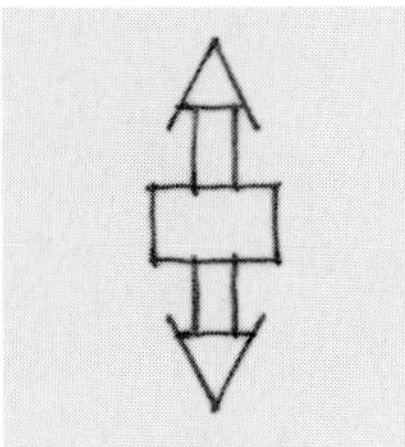

4.18 Chinese pictograph for "walled city"

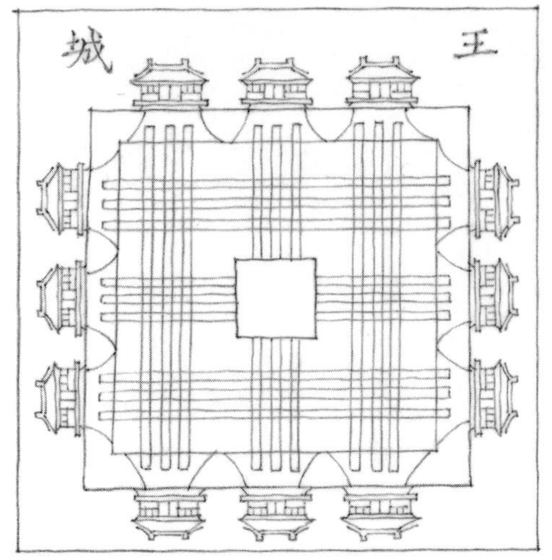


4.19 Idealized Plan of Wangcheng

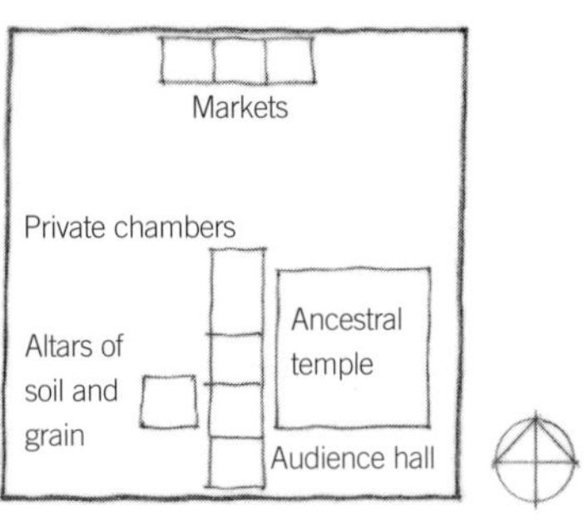


4.20 Inner City of Wangcheng

### Wangcheng Plan

To protect themselves from invaders from the north, the Zhou began to erect large walls, which later, in the following short-lived Qin Dynasty, were combined to form the basis of the 4800-kilometer-long Great Wall. The base of some parts of the wall was nearly 7 meters wide. On the large stones that were its foundations, earth was rammed layer upon layer. Traces of wood, possibly the remains of posts used to hold the wall in place, have also been discovered.

Walls were not only defensive but also a symbol of a ruler's power and nobility. The city was, in fact, defined as "a wall." The three words *cheng, du,* and *jing* are each commonly translated into English as "city," but *cheng*, as a verb, meant "walling a city." Later, in imperial China, *cheng* referred to a walled administrative city. Even in common parlance today, *cheng* is translated as "city wall" or simply "wall."

Although the only physical evidence of Zhou cities are earth foundations, there is an important description of an ideal city, accompanied by an illustration, in the *Rituals of Zhou.* The description is presumed to be of Luoyang, capital of the Eastern Zhou Dynasty, but is better known as Wangcheng, or "Ruler's City":

> The jiangren, or master-craftsman, builds the state, leveling the ground with the water by using a plumb-line. He lays out posts, taking the plumb-line (to ensure the posts' verticality), and using their shadows as the determinators of a mid-point. He examines the shadows of the rising and setting sun and makes a circle which includes the mid-points of the two shadows.
>
> The master craftsman constructs the state capital. He makes a square nine li of each side; each side has three gates. Within the capital are nine north-south and nine east-west streets. The north-south streets are nine carriage tracks in width. On the left (as one faces south, or to the east) is the Ancestral Temple, and to the right (west) are the Altars of Soil and Grain. In the front is the Hall of Audience and behind, the markets.
>
> (Nancy Shatzman Steinhardt, *Chinese Imperial City Planning* [Honolulu: University of Hawaii Press, 1990] Pg. 33)

15th- and 17th-century drawings of Luoyang illustrate the salient features of the description, with the addition of the inner city walls. Not far from the temple one finds soil and grain altars, the private or sleeping chambers (*qin*) and the markets. Although no single Chinese city of later date seems to actually have been built according to the Wangcheng plan, it can be argued that most subsequent major Chinese cities developed along its basic principles. In particular, Wangcheng embodies spatially the idea that the Chinese emperor is at the center of the world, facing south; in addition, the number nine was associated with the emperor and held supreme.

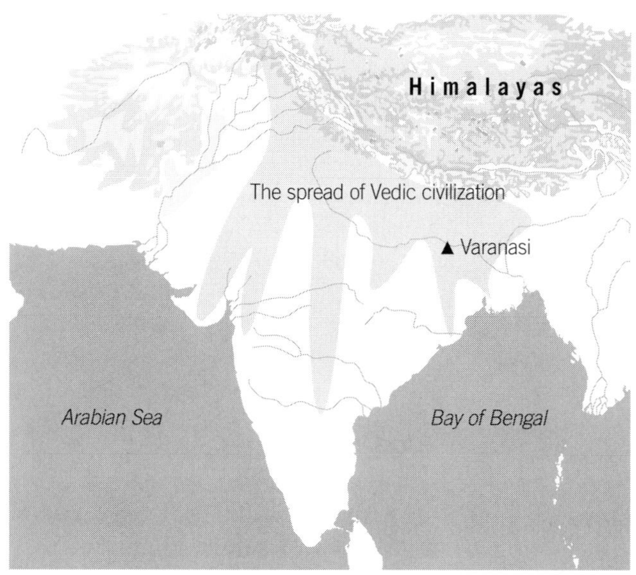


**VARANASI: THE ARYAN CONQUEST**

The thousand years spanning 1500–500 BCE on the South Asian subcontinent are, architecturally speaking, shrouded in mystery. What is known is that after the cities of the Indus-Ghaggar-Hakra civilization had withered away, a group of invaders, who called themselves Aryans, made their appearance, first settling south of the Thar Desert around 1500 BCE, and then moving along the Ganges River around 1200 BCE, pushing the local inhabitants of the time to the south. The Indus-Ghaggar-Hakra people—whose cities we know well but whose language and cultural values we know very little— were supplanted by a people from whom we have inherited vast and extensive literature and philosophical texts but who left no physical evidence of their settlements. By the year 1000 BCE, the Indo-Aryans had created 16 kingdoms, known as *mahajanapadas*, spread across the Gangetic plain. Roughly from West to East, these mahajanapadas were Kamboja, Gandhara, Kuru, Surasena, Matsya, Avanti, Assaka, Panchala, Chedi, Vatsa, Kosala, Kasi, Malla, Vajji, Magadha, and Anga. Although most were monarchies, a few, like Vajji, were republics. Warfare amongst the mahajanapadas was constant with victors absorbing vanquished, resulting in gradual consolidation of territories. By 500 BCE, four mahajanapadas dominated the Gangetic plains: Magadha, Kosala, Kasi and Vajji.

Amongst the Aryans, the basic expectation of the caste responsibility of the kings and their warrior-kshatriya caste was to confirm their valor and worth by waging war. Nevertheless, the mahajanapadas were closely related. Intermarriage amongst their royalty was a routine occurrence. Like their contemporary Mitannians in West Asia (to whom they had to have been somehow connected) and the Zhou in China, the two-wheeled horse drawn chariot was their choice instrument of war. Displays of prowess with the bow and iron-tipped arrow, particularly from the moving chariot, was a matter of pride and honor. The sacred philosophical dialogue between Krishan and Arjuna, known as the Gita, is between a warrior and his charioteer.

The Ganges was at the center of Vedic mythology. At Varanasi, on the Ganges, even today vestiges of Vedic rituals continue. Varanasi was founded as the capital of the Kashi mahajanapada but lost its political importance after being conquered by Kosala and then Magadha around 600 BCE. It developed, however, into a leading religious site. A wide spectrum of contemporary Hindu philosophical thought can be traced back to this period. When the Shakyamuni Buddha gained enlightenment in the 6th century BCE, his first stop was Varanasi. Mahavira and Shankara came to Varanasi to learn and teach, their philosophical treatises setting the foundations of Hinduism.

Vedic rituals did not require temples or even the creation of statues. They were based on fire sacrifices of various kinds that need only brick platforms. Fire was the agent that enabled the transformation of the sacrificial food (matter) into smoke and air (energy). Though no early Vedic altars have survived, the legacy of their rituals is still alive at Varanasi and in Hinduism in general. At dawn every morning thousands of Hindus gather on all the steps leading down to the shore (known as ghats) to face the sun that rises across the broad expanse of the Ganges and that is reflected in its waters. Half immersed in the river, they greet the sun by cupping a little of the Ganges into their palms and pouring it back into the river with arms extended. This is followed by a slow turn of 360 degrees on the spot, a miniature act of circumambulation. A quick dip in the river completes the ritual. This ritual can be repeated many times over or be performed with greater elaboration, including long chants and sequences of yogic postures.

4.21 View of Varanasi, Indian, 1922

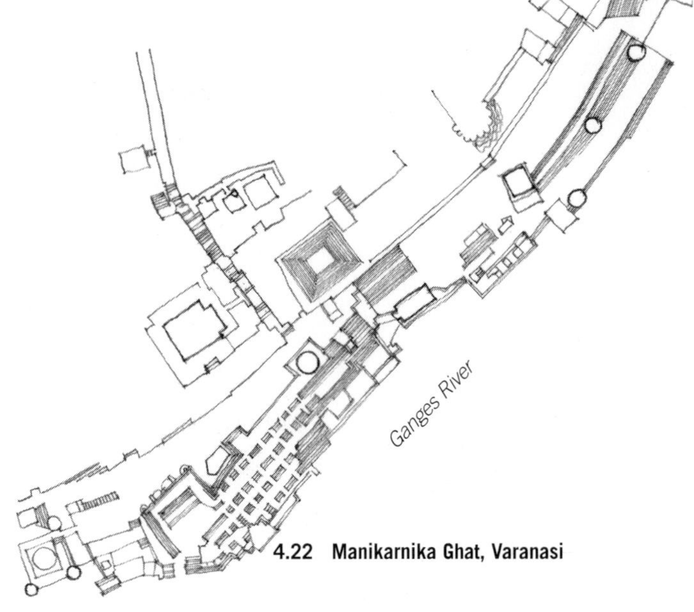


4.22 Manikarnika Ghat, Varanasi

Unlike Buddhism, which developed later, the religions practiced in Varanasi were never formalized, even during the time in which Hinduism and Buddhism were competing reilgious ideologies. With the development of the Hindu pantheon, Varanasi was designated as the city chosen by Shiva to be his permanent dwelling on earth. With that Varanasi assumed the status as the primary pilgrimage site of the Hindu world. It was, in the Hindu religion, the site where the male and female principles embodied by Shiva and Shakti (as Ganges) are conjoined in conjugal harmony. This coming together of Shiva and Shakti is recreated in every Shiva temple.

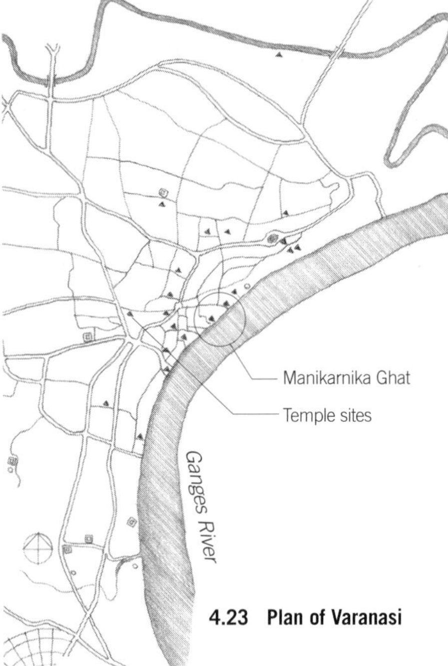


4.23 Plan of Varanasi

As Diana Eck notes, the city is built on a natural high berm, located on the northwestern banks of the Ganges at a point where the river makes a sharp right turn, flowing north and then west. The high berm (built up with cankar or lime concretion) not only ensures that the city enjoys a dramatic prospect, some 15 meters above the normal level of the water; it also ensures that the city is protected from the river's floods, the impact of which is borne by the opposite shore. Because of its geography, Varanasi has been situated at the very same spot for 3000 years, unmoved by the Ganges, yet in constant engagement with its rising and falling waters. Behind the berm, in a semicircular arch, lies the dense fabric of the medieval city, with twisting narrow streets and a multitude of temples, water tanks, and street shrines. Although the whole city is sacred, it is Varanasi's berm, where Shiva's city meets the divine Ganges, that constitutes the most sacred geography of the city.

From more than 50 locations along the berm, long flights of stairs reach down to the riverlike roots. These stairs, interspersed with a complex array of platforms and temples, embody the essential spiritual character of Varanasi. They are known as ghats (literally, landings or banks). Along the ghats, one can see rituals pertaining to almost every aspect of human life, such as the shaving of a newborn's head, the first blessing after a marriage, or the penances of old age. Most importantly, however, there are two ghats, known as the Manikaran and Harishchandra Ghats, that are dedicated only to the ritual of cremations; from these ghats ashes can be immersed directly into the Ganges River. To be born and, more importantly, to die and be cremated at Varanasi on the bank of the Ganges and to have one's ashes immersed in its waters is to attain the highest aspiration of Hindu practice, that is, *moksha* or nirvana, freedom from the cycle of birth and death.

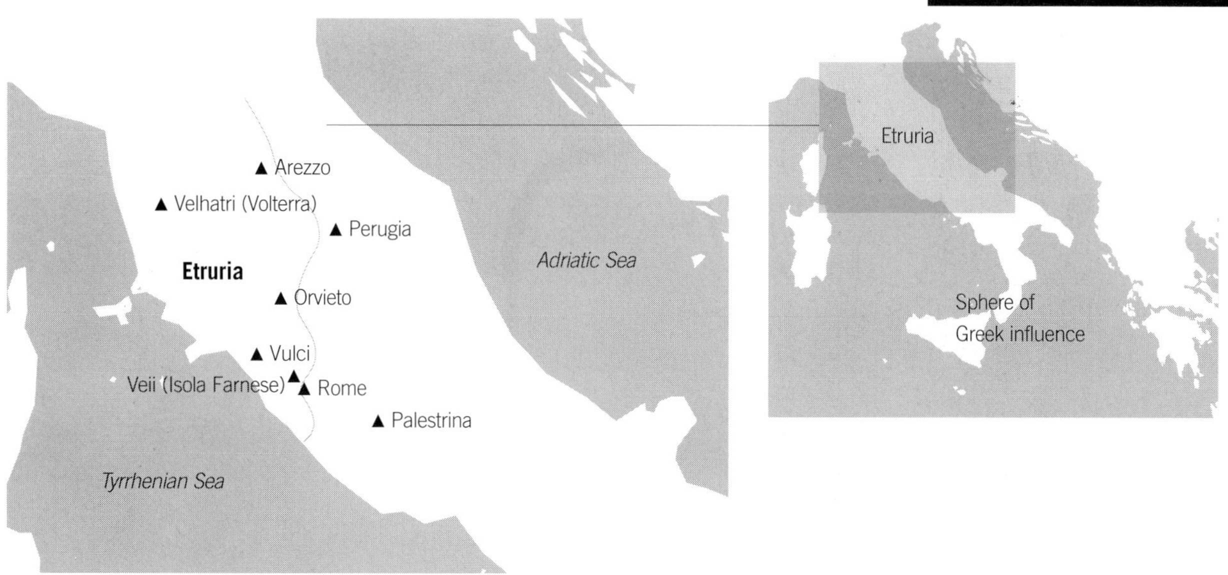


## ETRUSCAN CIVILIZATION

Scholars generally think that forging techniques had been developed by the Hittites, who kept it as a trade secret. Its development had taken thousands of years of familiarity with kilns, metals, and extraction methods before high-temperature smelting could be mastered. But after the downfall of the Hittites in 1200 BCE, the art of forging spread rapidly westward to the Dorians and Etruscans by 800 BCE, and eastward reaching China around 600 BCE. Iron had a particularly important impact on the development of agriculture in sub-Saharan Africa, where for the first time, large scale agriculture and land clearing could be undertaken. Besides weapons, iron was effective for making agricultural implements like plows and wheels, and the new plows meant that the plains of Sicily, the north coast of Africa, and even the high plains in Eastern Anatolia could become major grain-producing regions, significantly weakening the need for grain from Mesopotamia and Egypt.

Among the principal and newly emerging metal-oriented societies, the Urartu in Armenia, the Nubians in the Sudan, and the Etruscans in Italy, only the Etruscans produced an architecture that had profound consequences for future development. Little is left of Urartu architecture, most of it torn down in centuries of warfare. The Nubians, though producing extensive architectural works, continued the Egyptian traditions. The Etruscans, however, created a highly refined civic-legal description of the divine that was to impact European architecture for centuries, insofar as many Etruscan concepts were taken over by the Romans.

The principal source of the Etruscans' wealth was abundant metal ore—copper, iron, lead, and silver mined in the various hills of the region. Volterra, for example, was close to Colline Metallifere (Metalliferous Hills). The Etruscans were noted for their superb skills in metal crafting. Their jewelry has turned up in locations around the Mediterranean and even further afield. The Etruscan city of Vulci was especially noted for its bronze work production. It was not just their economic might that propelled them into the annals of cultural and architectural history but also their religious-political world view.

Etruscan society began to take shape in the 7th century BCE in Etruria (modern Tuscany). The Etruscans were more or less contemporaneous with the ascendancy of the Dorians and Ionians in Greece and Turkey but, by comparison, they were still rather primitive in their aesthetic and architectural expressions. The three groups—the Dorians, Ionians, and Etruscans—however, have to be seen together, especially since they all played an important part in restoring the Mediterranean to economic and cultural prominence following the disruptions of the preceding centuries. The Etruscans are the most mysterious of the group, their origin a hotly debated issue.

4.24 Example of an Etruscan arch

By the 7th century BCE the Etruscans exercised political authority over most of the northern half of the Italian peninsula. Despite the encroachment of the Greeks in the south of Italy, they were able to maintain their hold, reaching a peak in the 6th century BCE, until they were assimilated into the Roman empire. Many of the cities, like Veii, north of Rome, were in their heydays as big as Athens, with a population estimated to have been as high as 100,000 inhabitants. Though the physical fabric of Etruscan cities has largely been lost, we still find many walls and gateways in Rome, Perugia, Cortona, and other places. At Velhatri (today's Volterra) the wall enclosure, built during the 5th and 4th centuries BCE, was 7 kilometers long.

The city gate of Perugia exhibited bold use of the arch, a building element that, along with the vault, was introduced by the Etruscans and became one of their main contributions to Roman architecture. In Rome itself, several famous structures, including the Circus Maximus and the Cloaca Maxima, the Roman sewage system still in use today, were built by Etruscan masons. The deft and totally secure use of arches that emerged in Etruria was to have a tremendous impact on architecture henceforth.

4.25 Etruscan tomb, Tarquinia, Italy

**4.26 Etruscan sarcophagus from Cerveteri, late 6th century BCE**

**4.27 Bronze Etruscan model of liver, 3rd century BCE**

### Etruscan Religion

The outward aspect of Etruscan religion was its scrupulous adherence to ritualistic formulae. And yet, through Etruscan art and painting, one senses an appreciation of individuality. This vibrancy came at the expense of stylistic unity, but on the positive side one senses an unmistakable, and in some sense unusual, receptivity toward outside influences. Elements of Corinthian, Ionian, and Attic art are all in evidence. This manifests itself also in their religion, so much so that their own deities came to be fused with and coalesced around Greek ones, paving the way for the later Roman assimilation of Greek culture. Unlike the Greeks, however, the Etruscan pantheon included supernatural and chthonic beings whose number and nature are still unknown to us. The Etruscans also had a complex system of augury—the prediction of events by examining the entrails, especially the liver of sacrificial animals, or by interpreting natural phenomena, such as comets or the flight paths of birds (*auspicium*, or divination).

A 3rd-century BCE bronze model of a liver (found near Piacenza, Italy) has been recovered that was perhaps used to train Etruscan priests (haruspices) in the art of interpretation. The upper surface is divided into 40 sections, corresponding to the celestial zones of the Etruscan pantheon; these have the names of gods, including many with whom we are unfamiliar, engraved on it. The particularities of the animal's liver told the priest which deity to invoke. It was probably meant to be aligned north-south.

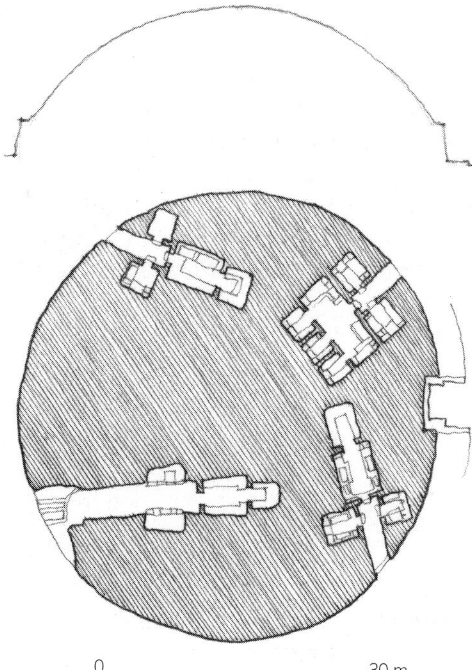


**4.28 Tumulus mound, Etruscan necropolis of Banditaccia at Cerveteri, 7th–5th centuries BCE**

One of the words used to describe this liver was *templum*, which could refer to the sky, to a consecrated area on earth, or to a much smaller surface, such as the liver of an animal used in divination, as long as the orientation and partition of the area followed the celestial model. A *templum* could thus be a physical space, in which case it would be marked or enclosed, but it could also be an area of the sky, in which the birds would be observed. A *templum*, in other words, was a space where humans, represented by priests (augurs), can interact with the gods. In all ancient Mediterranean and Mesopotamian cultures, nature was associated with divine presences, but for the Etruscans, the gods spoke through signs. This was not the case in Mesopotamian religions, where gods spoke more directly through the priests. For the Minoans, religion centered on nature's life cycles, with the gods representing the stories associated with those cycles. For the Etruscans, religion was a practice of translation. Unlike the more fearsome and arbitrary gods of the Mesopotamians, Etruscan gods readily "communicated" their intentions. Disaster could come about just as much from the actions of the gods as from misunderstanding their messages.

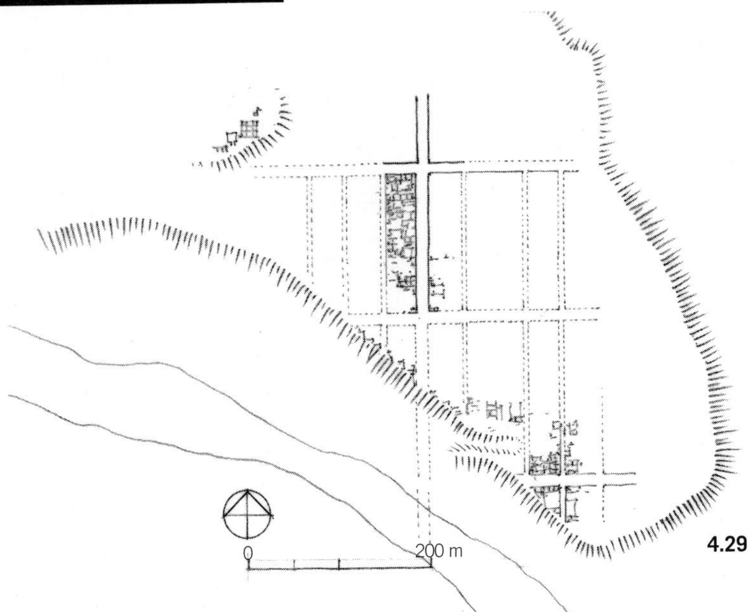


4.29 **Site plan of Marzabotto, Italy, 5th century BCE**

The orientation of Etruscan temples was of critical importance and was determined by the intersection of two axes, one north-south called *cardo*, and the other east-west, called *decumanus*. The idea was employed later by the Romans in setting up military camps according to strictly standardized rules and subsequently became fundamental to Roman town planning. Apparently these orthogonal lines were closely connected to the Etrusco-Italic religious iconography. The observer's place was at the cross-point of the two lines, with his back to the north; the eastern sector to his left (*pars sinistra*) was of good omen and superior gods. To the right, the western sector, was of ill omen (*pars dextra*) and for the infernal deities. The vault of heaven, thus quartered and oriented, was further subdivided into 16 minor sections in which were placed the habitations of many divinities. This plan corresponds to the outer ring of 16 compartments of the Piacenza liver.

N
Cardo
W
Decumanus
E
*pars dextra*
*pars sinistra*
S

4.30 **Diagram of cardo and decumanus**

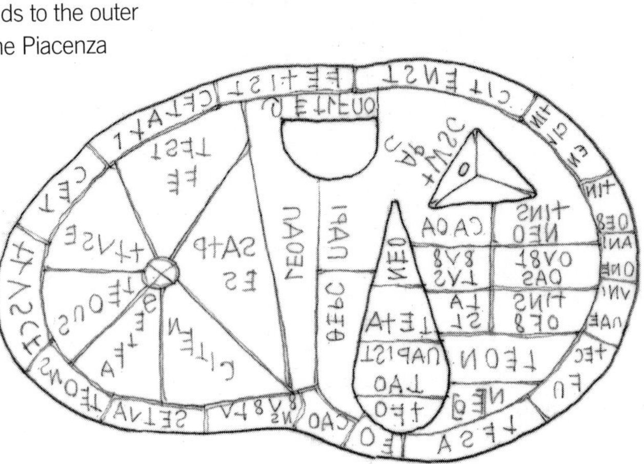

4.31 **Diagram of the Piacenza liver**

The position of signs manifested in the sky, thunderbolts, flights of birds, and other portents, as studied by the augur, would indicate which god was responsible for a particular message and whether it was a good or a bad omen. This process was called *auspicium*, a word that was formed of avis (bird) and specio (to see). The priest and soothsayer watched the flight and feeding of birds, listened to their cries, and even examined their entrails. From this came words like *contemplatio*, meaning literally "with a template." There was also the distinction between whether the message was an order or a friendly reminder. All in all, the *templum* (as a type of three-dimensional template) stood between the ephemeral and the real, linking the invisible absolute realities of the divine with the real needs of the supplicants. The consecrated ground on which this took place was expressed in Etruscan language by the word *sacni* (becoming the Latin *sancti*). When the temple was finished, the opening was presided over by the augur in a ceremony called *inauguratio*.

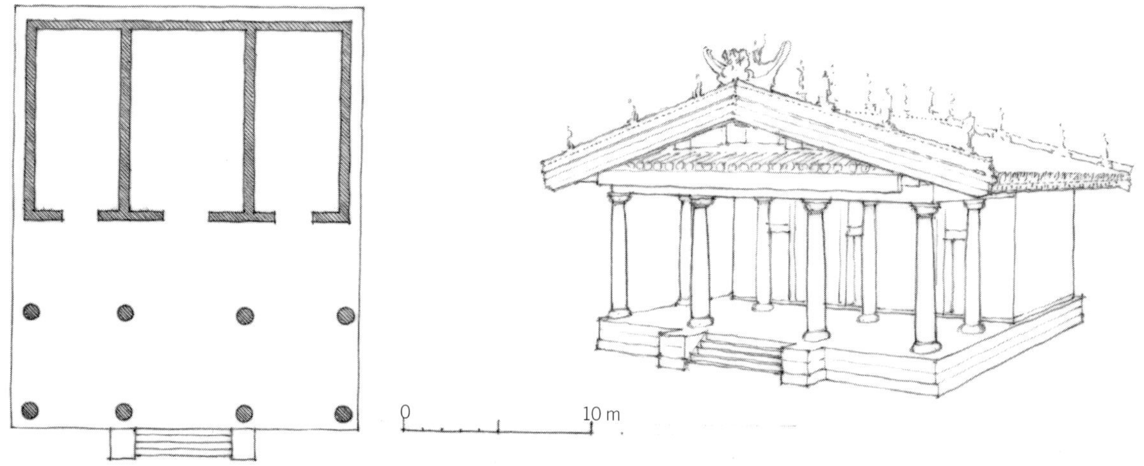


**4.32 Plan and pictorial view of an Etruscan temple, based on descriptions by Vitruvius**

### Etruscan Temples

The form of Etruscan temples paralleled certain aspects of Greek temples, but there are several important differences. The Etruscans never made the leap to stone. Except at a very late period, the Etruscan temple was not thought of as requiring permanence. The podium that raised the temple above the surrounding ground level, however, was often of stone, with stairs or ramps leading to the top. The temple proper was built of mud, brick, and timber. Though similar to Greek temples in that respect, Etruscan temples were meant to be viewed only from the front and sides, rather than stand as an object in the landscape. They have no rear façade. The pitch of the roof was relatively low, and they had overhanging eaves. The pediment was originally open so that the roof timbers could be seen.

Also distinctive was the roomy colonnaded porch, known as the *pronaos* (meaning literally, "in front of the *naos*"), in front of the *cella*. Etruscans often organized gods into a *trivium*, meaning that many temples had three *cellae* and the overall shape was a rectangle tending toward the square. Etruscan temples introduced the principal of an axial connection between temple and altar, which the Greeks eschewed until very late, and probably then under Italian influence. Characteristic also was the striking use of color for the various elements and the way the mass was broken up by antefixae, acroteria, and sculptural groups.

As for columns, the Etruscans experimented with a range of options including the Ionic until, by the 5th century BCE, they developed the Tuscan column, as it was later called by Vitruvius. It was a smooth wooden column with diminution at the top and a capital akin to the Doric, consisting of a round cushion (echinus) and a square abacus. The bases, however, were inspired by the Ionic order (Doric columns had no bases). Because these structures were of wood, Etruscan temples had wide intercolumniations.

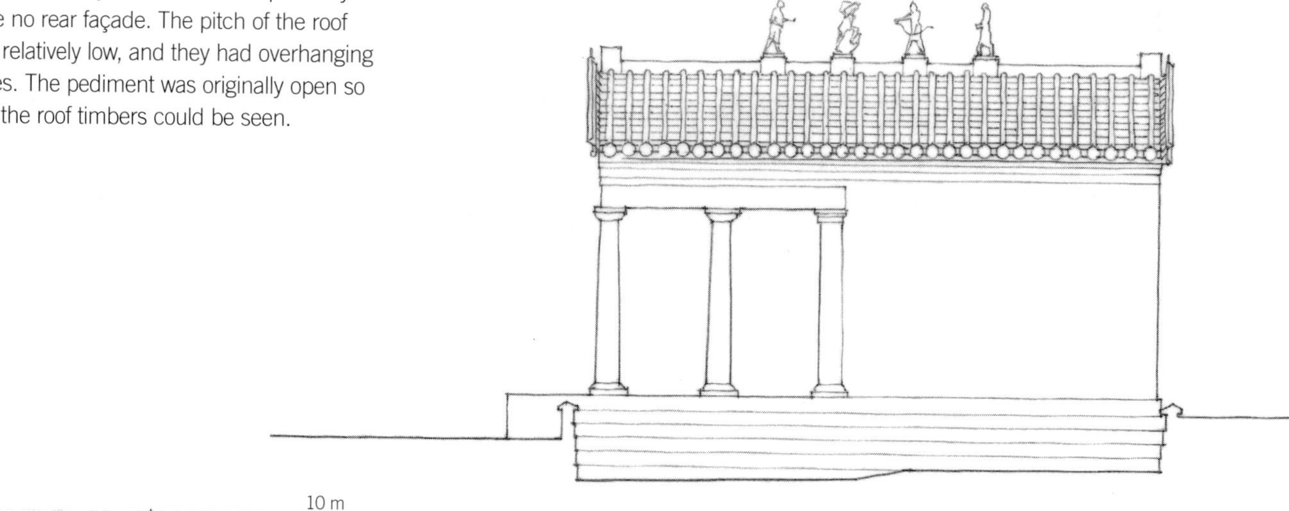


**4.33 Side elevation: Portonaccio Temple at Veii, Italy, 515–490 BCE**

The habit of ornamenting the temple with decorative terra-cotta elements may have been taken over from the Greeks but was implemented by the Etruscans with particular showmanship.

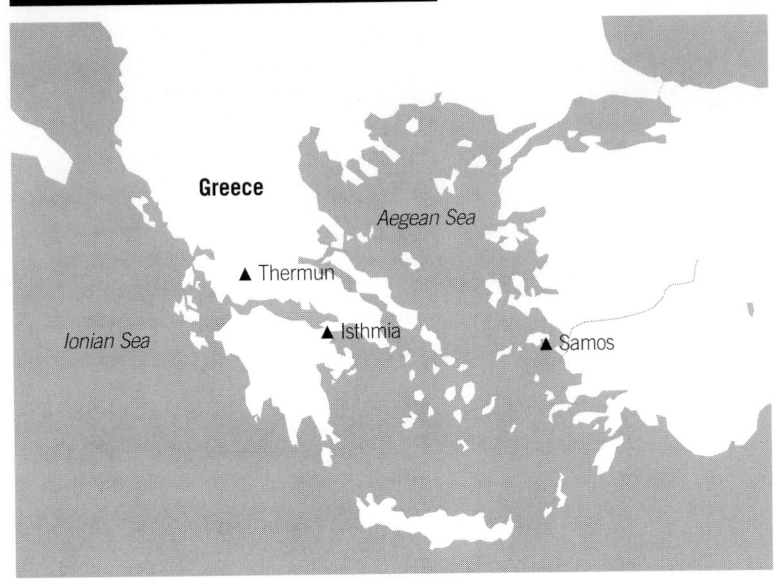

**4.34 Geometric period Greek vase, typically serving as a monumental grave marker**

**GREECE: GEOMETRIC PERIOD**

Post-Mycenaean Greece was a period of migrations, confusion, and poverty. But over time, the Dorians in Greece and the Ionians along the Turkish coast came to develop common cultural practices that fused elements unique to them with residues of the Minoan and Mycenaean cultures. This explains some of the differences in their development from the Etruscans. The Minoans and Mycenaeans, having had no temples in the technical sense, held caves and mountains sacred, with worship augmented by shrines. Homer represents the gods not as having temples but as being highly mobile creatures constantly visiting each other in their palaces. The early Dorian religious practices also took place outside, which made it easy to incorporate some of the features and even locations of Minoan religion into their own.

These rites, as described by George Hersey, also often involved trees, or groves of trees, that were fenced off and decorated with materials used in sacrifices—bones, horns, urns, lamps, weapons, fruits, and vegetables. Trees held a special place in Greek culture and almost every god was associated with one. Athena was, for example, associated with the olive tree. The altar dedicated to a god was set out in front of his or her particular tree or grove.

The participants would bathe and dress themselves in special clothes and go, singing in a procession, accompanied by flutists, to the place of sacrifice. They were led by a girl carrying a basket of grain on her head. Under the grain and concealed from view was the slaughtering knife. The sacrificial animal, decorated with wreaths on his horns, was then led up to the altar with a fire already burning on it. The participants, gathered around in a circle, would then wash their hands from a jug of water, with the water also sprinkled on the animal. The barley grains from the girl's basket would be flung over the animal, altar, and earth. Once the knife was revealed, the priest would step forward, take it, and prepare for the sacrifice.

**4.35 Statue of a calf-bearer**

For the Greeks, the beast must be willing to engage in the sacrifice. To achieve this, the priest placed a bowl of milk at the base of the altar. As the animal stepped forward, it would bow its head to drink. The act of lowering its head was then interpreted as a sign of submission. Another form of assent was the animal shivering in the sight of the god, a process helped by the liberal use of cold water. The Greeks saw the blood as precious and drained it through the altar into conduits and pits beneath. The animal was then carved up, with special meaning given to various parts, with the liver being, of course, particularly important for the augur. Some parts were chopped up and wrapped in fat to form a type of reconstituted body. Sometimes, the skull was placed on a stake near the altar and draped in an animal skin. These types of representations of the sacrifice extended to trophies and spoils taken from battle, even from the conquered, to assuage the spirit of the dead. After the carving of the animal, the flesh was roasted and eaten. The communality of the meal was meant to bind together social units, from the family to the city. The gods received the act of devotion and the smoke rising up from the altar that, though immaterial, was a sign of human reverence. In exchange for this act of devotion, the humans could then "read" the message of the gods embedded in the physical shape of the liver.

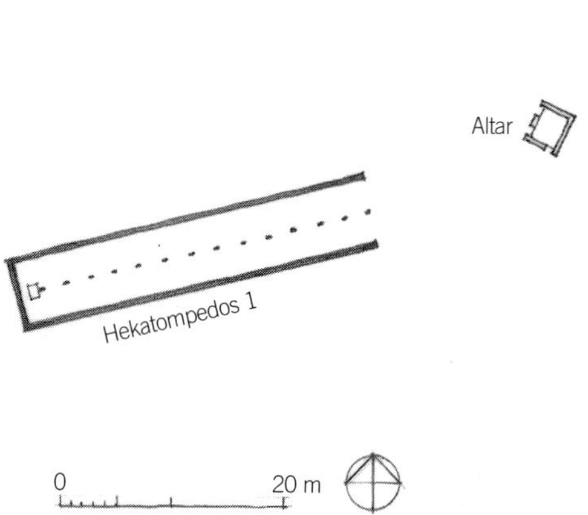


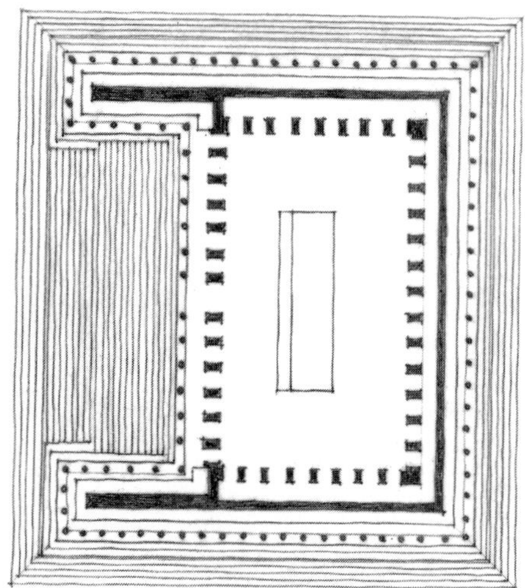

**4.36 Plans of the Sanctuary at Samos, Greece (above) and the Altar of Zeus at Pergamon (upper right), drawn at the same scale and orientation**

This exchange lies at the heart of the arrangement, as explained by the Greeks in the myth of Prometheus. He had stolen fire from the gods, and in so doing allowed humankind to civilize itself. The gods did not take the fire back but punished Prometheus by chaining him to a cliff and having an eagle eat out his liver. The liver would grow back every day only to be eaten again. The sacrifice was thus part of the ritual remembrance of humankind's emergence into civilization and of their dependence on the gods in the regulation of their lives. But the sacrifice also marked the difference between humankind and gods, for unlike the gods who existed in an ethereal form, humankind had to work to keep the communication active. A skinny bull or decrepit goat would not do. It had to be the best of the lot.

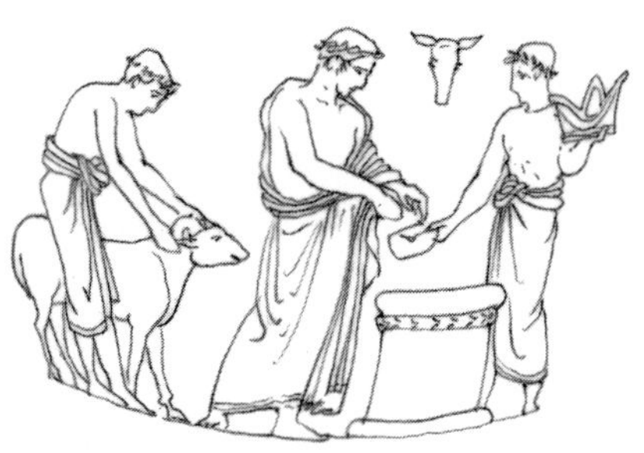

**4.37 Scene depicting early Greek sacrificial rites**

The difference between the Dorians and the Minoans, and even the Etruscans, lay in the philosophical importance placed on sacrifice. Etruscan sacrifice seems more technical and Minoan sacrifice more intimate than that of the Greeks. In comparison too with Egyptians, Greek sacrifice was connected to the principles of farming and herding rather than to the palace garden. Bread and meat were at the center of Greek sacrifice rather than the celebratory feast of the Egyptians. The Greek attitude toward sacrifice needs to be understood because so many of their altars were removed by Christians that one might easily forget their importance. In fact, in the early days of Greek religion, there were no temples, only altars in the open. The Sanctuary of Hera at Samos, ca. 950 BCE, consisted of no more than a low enclosure of flat stones forming a rectangle about 2 by 3.5 meters. The altars became larger as time progressed; the one on the Acropolis at Athens, for example, held a dozen bulls at one time. The Altar of Zeus at Pergamon, now in the Pergamon Museum in Berlin, was the most spectacular of all. Built in 197–159 BCE, it featured a flight of steps on its west side and flanking Ionic colonnades. It stands on a five-stepped, almost square plinth. The altar proper was inside the court. The altars were not necessarily aligned symmetrically on axis with the temple, especially during the Archaic Period. At Samos, the altar with its sacred tree, stood at first at an oblique angle, referring perhaps to a different celestial moment than that of the temple.

The emergence of the altar plus temple form coincided with the personification of gods in statues and, once again, seems to be part of the learning curve that the Dorians made when coming into contact with older Mediterranean practices. Early Greek representations of their gods show influences from both the Mesopotamian and the Egyptian cultures. But Greek representations were rarely as diminutive as the Mesopotamian and Minoan statues could be, nor as large as the Egyptians often were. And perhaps therein lies the origin of the Greek advancement of the depiction of the human figure. The earliest three-dimensional representations of divinities known as kore (draped female statue) were carved from wooden columns or planks at a scale that were roughly life-size. The Greeks called such statues *kolossos*, which had nothing to do with their size, but denoted an image that was shaped like a pillar or column. Furthermore, Greek statues gradually came to show the gods in a more relaxed stance, one foot forward with the weight of the body balanced naturalistically on the real leg.

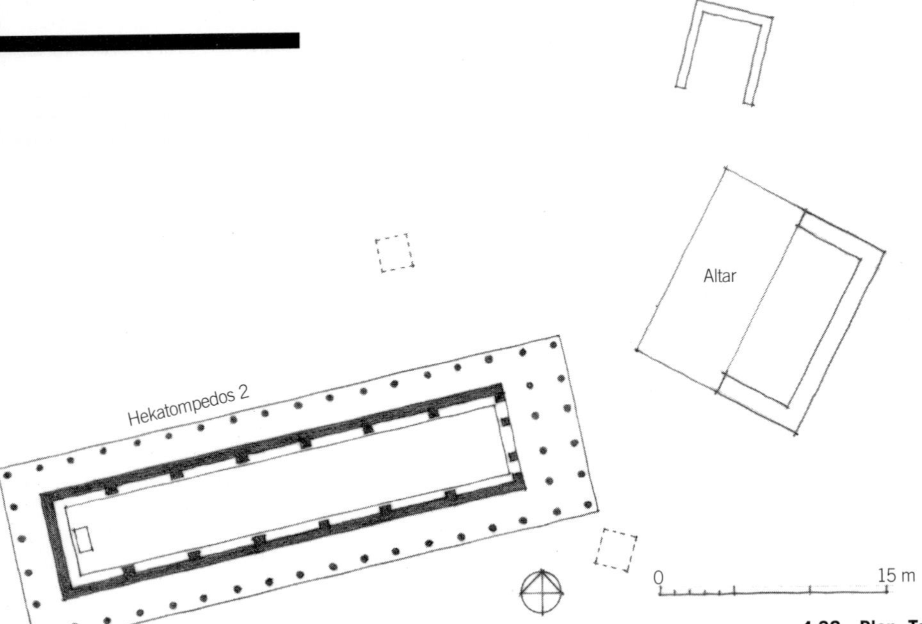


**4.38 Plan: Temple of Hera at Samos, Greece**

**Emergence of the Greek Temple Form**

The shift from open-air altars to altar plus temple took place around 700 BCE. The earliest temples, built of mud bricks and thatch roofs, were modeled, presumably, on chieftains' houses and consisted of a single elongated windowless room—a *naos* or cella (from which the word cellar comes)—that was eventually divided into a *pronaos* and *naos*. There were no side chambers, ancillary spaces, or storage rooms. Soon a continuous porch was added around the body of the building to form an oblong shape, which over time became regularized and systemized. The Greek sanctuary, however, was far from being a detached and spiritual sphere, Symbolically, it was representative of the political, economic and military life and the well-being of the city and the region. Many temples served as war museums, holding the spoils of conquest as well as serving as armories.

At the Temple of Apollo at Thermum (630 BCE) in the area of Aetolia in western Greece, we see the development from a cella surrounded by columns in an oblong shape to the regularized form of later temples. The Temple of Hera at Samos (675–625 BCE), on the Turkish coast, is similar to the Temple of Apollo at Thermum, having an elongated form with proportions of almost 5 to 1.

Though Greek temples can be found facing the various directions of the compass, more than 80 percent of them were laid out to face sunrise, and most more specifically toward the sunrise on the actual day of their founding, which in turn coincided with the festival day of the respective divinity to which it was dedicated. From this custom arises the term "orientation," primarily applied to the direction of the axis of a temple. Temples, however, were also sometimes oriented to elements in the landscape, to a solitary peak that represented the presence of Zeus or to double peaks, remindful of a bull's horn as held sacred in the Minoan-influenced districts.

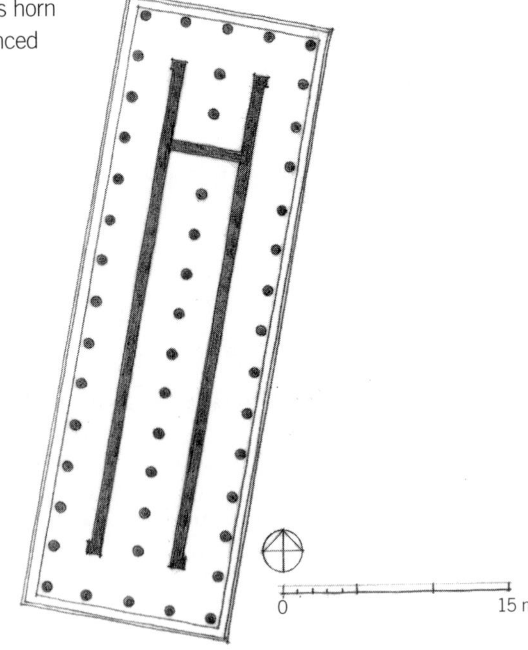


**4.39 Plan: Temple of Apollo at Thermum, Greece**

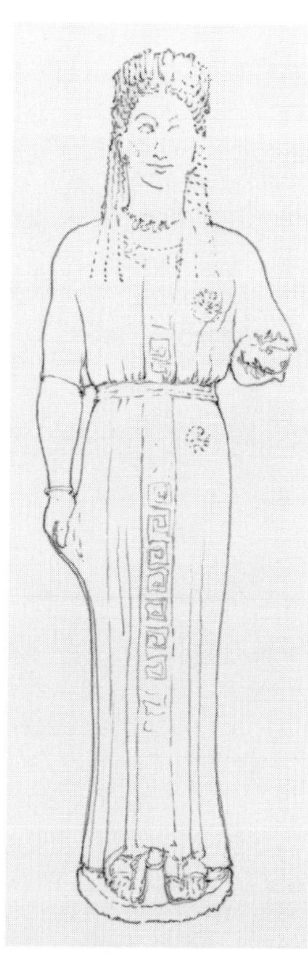

4.41 **Slightly over life-sized female figure, mid-6th century BCE**

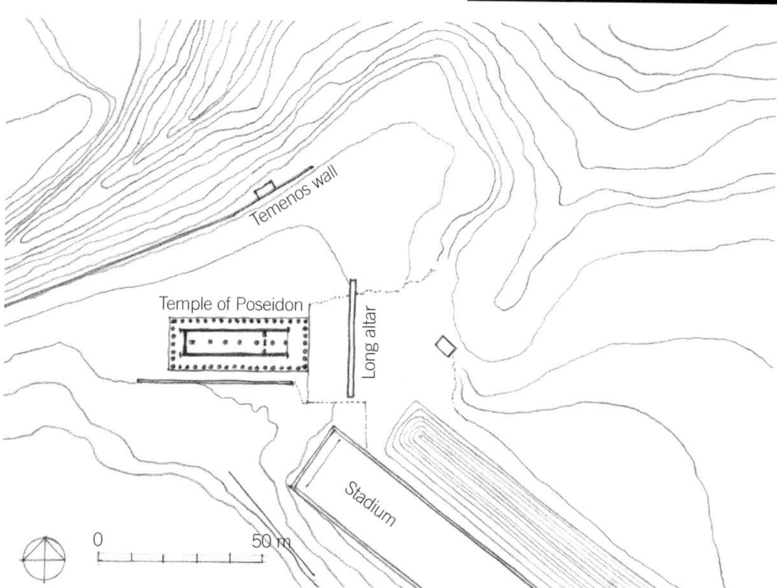


**4.40 Plan: Sanctuary at Isthmia, Greece**

The Temple of Poseidon at Isthmia (ca. 700 BCE), not far from Corinth, is among the earliest known Greek temples. Its podium measures 14 by 40 meters with a central row of five columns within the cella and two in the pronaos. Seven columns stood on each end, and 18 stood on each flank. The cella was of stone, but the columns and entablature were of wood, and the roof was low-pitched and covered in fired terra-cotta tiles—a Greek invention.

The site was fortified in about 1200 BCE and ritual festivities were performed from the middle of the 11th century BCE onward. The first temple of Poseidon was built there in the 7th century BCE. The Sanctuary of Poseidon was eventually to be the site of the Panhellenic Games, called "the Isthmia," which took place every two years in honor of Melicertes-Palaemon or Poseidon. The altar was a long 30-meter structure in front of the temple, with the sports field and stadium just to the south.

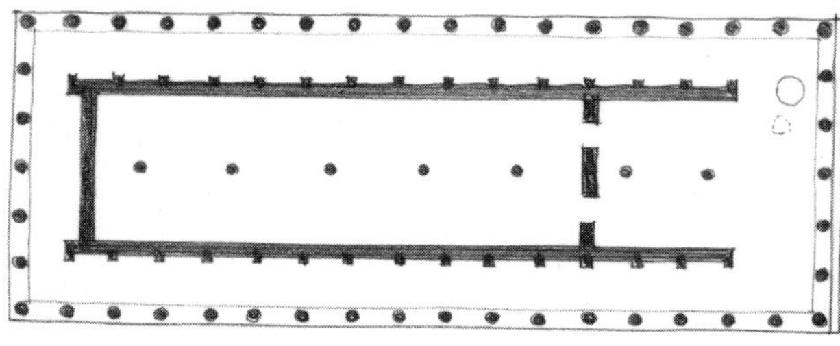

**4.42 Plan: Temple of Poseidon at Isthmia**

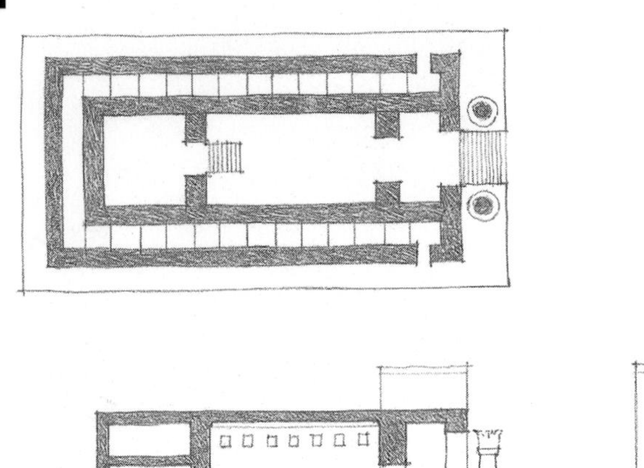

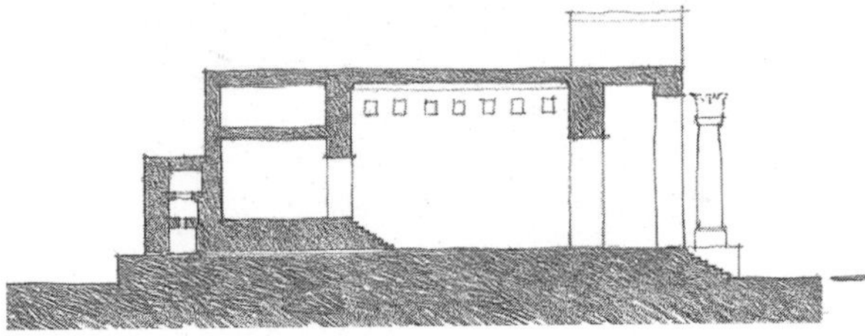

**4.43 Conjectural plan, elevation and section: Temple of Solomon, Jerusalem**

## TEMPLE OF SOLOMON

With the Egyptian kingdom in decline and the revival of Mediterranean trade, Western Asia and the Levant in particular experienced a moment of semiautonomy. The Israelite kingdom, which had been established in the late 13th century BCE, following exodus of the Jews from Egypt, rose as an important regional power. One of Judaism's great contributions lies in its concept of ethical Monotheism, which is the base of both Christianity and Islam. But though these religions played major roles in the history of architecture, the development of Judaism's own architecture was cut short by the destruction of the Second Temple and the forced diaspora of Jews by Emperor Titus in 70 CE. Without a land of their own, and facing restrictions on their life and customs throughout Europe into the 19th century, Jewish architecture had little opportunity to develop.

The Jewish conception of religious space is a complex one. The Jahweh of the Israelites is an invisible, unrepresentable entity, a purely ethical force, that is not even permitted to be called by name. Furthermore, due to the nomadic origin of the ancient Hebrews, the mental image of the Israelites' self-identification was that of a desert tribe living in tents in which permanent buildings played no role. Indeed, it has been held by some scholars that Moses refused to bring his charges across the Jordan into Canaan for fear that they would settle and became slaves to property and agriculture.

After Moses's death, the Israelites entered the Promised Land and founded Jerusalem as their capital. A threshing floor was brought from the Jebusite "Zion" on Mt. Moriah as a place for the carrying out of the traditional sacrifices and as a place to display the Ark. As described in the Bible, the Ark was a gold-plated, portable chest containing the two stone tablets of Moses with the Ten Commandments. On top of it sat the images of two winged cherubim facing each other, the only kind of bodily representation permitted. Their outspread wings formed the throne of God, while the Ark itself was his footstool. Wherever the Israelites went, the Ark was carried in front of them by priests, especially in wars where its leading presence was viewed as a blessing for the enterprise. It was veiled in badgers' skin and blue cloth so that even the Levites, who were the only ones allowed to handle it, could not see it. As a more symbolic statement of permanence, Solomon, King David's son, built the First Temple for the Ark (dedicated in 953 BCE). It was built with substantial help from Hiram of Tyre, who not only delivered the famous Cedars of Lebanon used in its construction, but also, so it is suggested by specialists, his favorite architect Chiram Abiff.

Because Solomon married the daughter of Amenhotep III one could also expect a certain amount of Egyptian influence in the artistic tastes of the Solomonic court. Even though the temple had an altar in front of it for animal sacrifices, the temple was not the residence of a god but the elaborate container for the Ark in the windowless Holy of Holies (*Kodesh Kodashim*). This room, which also served as a type of ear of the god, contained no furniture, but had, guarding the Ark, two tall statues representing cherubim with their outspread wings meeting in the center of the room. Over the centuries, many attempts at a reconstruction have been made from the sketchy details given in the Bible. Details as to the temple's features are given in 1 Kings 6:19 and 8:6.

The temple was destroyed in 586 BCE by the Babylonians when the population was taken into the Babylonian Exile (597–537 BCE). Today's Wailing Wall is a remnant of the foundations of the Second Temple (515 BCE), built by the Israelites after their return from enforced exile to Babylon. It was that temple that was destroyed, in 70 CE, by the Romans. Hadrian built a temple to Jupiter on the site.

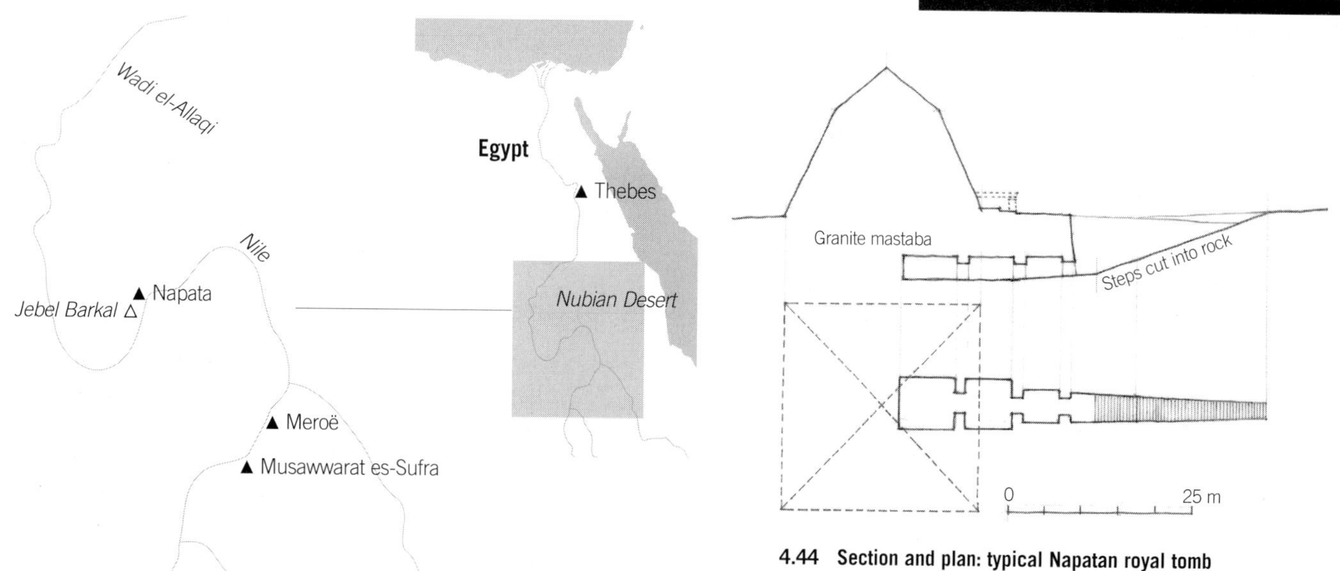


**4.44 Section and plan: typical Napatan royal tomb**

## KINGDOM OF KUSH

The imperial expansion of the New Kingdom dynasties of Egypt into Nubia, Libya, and Syria meant that the subjugated peoples often adopted Egyptian religion, culture, and weapons of war. The Nubians, for example, who served as valued mercenaries in the Egyptian army, worshipped Egyptian gods, and built pyramids to entomb their rulers. Nubia was rich in natural resources, notably gold, with mines numbering in the hundreds scattered over the desert. The New Kingdom pharaohs asserted strong control over Nubia to guarantee the flow of gold to support their imperial ambitions in Asia. To extract the metal from the veins of the quartz rock, the rock was first cracked by means of fire, then crushed into a powder by mills, and finally washed to separate the ore, which was melted into small ingots. The system was hugely labor intensive but yielded, by one estimation, 40,000 kilograms of gold a year, an amount that would not be exceeded again until the 19th century CE.

With the demise of the New Kingdom, Nubia, also known as Kush, was free to assert itself and during the reign of Piye (747–716 BCE) conquered Egypt and ruled there as the 25th Dynasty. Iron played an important role in this, for the Kushites had learned the techniques of iron-working from their Assyrian enemies. Though the Kushites had iron, they did not have the fuel to smelt it. For that they had to turn southward to the area around the city of Meroë, where the ancient, largely unexcavated slag heaps are still visible today.

The Kushite pharaohs promoted the Egyptian religion and embarked on programs of temple restoration. At first, the center of the Kushite state was at Napata, lying just above the fourth cataract in the Nile River. Its focal point was the sacred flat-topped mountain of Jebel Barkal, which stands like a natural altar in the landscape a few kilometers from the northern bank of the Nile. In its shadow, Ramses II had already built several temples, one of which was the rather substantial Temple of Amun. The tombs at Napata are sited on both sides of the Nile and are all that is left of the Nubian capital. The early tombs were round mastabas. These gave way to pyramids mounted on high bases with distinctive porches. During the last phase, at the height of Kushite control over Egypt, the rulers simplified the form to a pyramid and porch.

**4.45 Plan: Temple of Amun at Jebel Barkal, Sudan**

4.46 **Remains of the Great Enclosure at Musawwarat es-Sufra, Sudan**

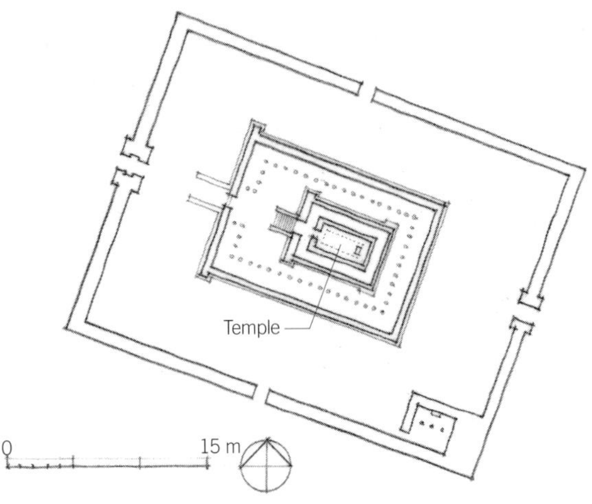


4.47 **Plan: Sun Temple at Meroë, Sudan**

### Sun Temple at Meroë

Because of trouble with the Assyrians, the Kushite rulers moved south to Meroë, on an overland trade route that links with the Nile, leaving Napata as the religious capital of the kingdom. Given the numerous slag heaps in the area, it is clear that the iron industry was the foundation of Meroitic prosperity. It has been described as the Birmingham of ancient Africa. Equipped with the iron spear and iron hoe, the Kushites were able to trade and conquer far and wide in the Sudanic belt of Africa. By the year 300 BCE, they were trading with Alexandria and Persia. The sculpted relief of a king of Kush seated on an Indian elephant suggests contact even with India. Their wealth not only derived from gold and iron but also from the export of slaves, ivory, and rare animal skins.

Though the ruins of Meroë are still largely unexcavated, a few monumental buildings have been studied, including a Sun Temple just outside the city. It is surrounded by a *temenos* wall with a stone-faced doorway. A ramp leads to a platform with the colonnade enclosing the sanctuary. The sanctuary is approached by a flight of steps and its floor and walls are covered in blue glazed tiles.

Fifty kilometers southwest is the city of Musawwarat es-Sufra, of which little remains except for a structure called "The Great Enclosure." It consists of a labyrinthine cluster of open plazas, corridors, and chambers that have no parallel in Nubian or Egyptian architecture. Recent excavations have done much to clarify the plan but have shed no light on its origin or purpose. The acres of bare, beautifully smooth sandstone walls are entirely devoid of reliefs or inscriptions The temple is a rectangle with four columns surrounded by a colonnade. It is accessed by various corridors and surrounded by variously shaded polygonal enclosures. The date given for the building is 220 BCE.

4.48 **Plan: Great Enclosure at Musawwarat es-Sufra**

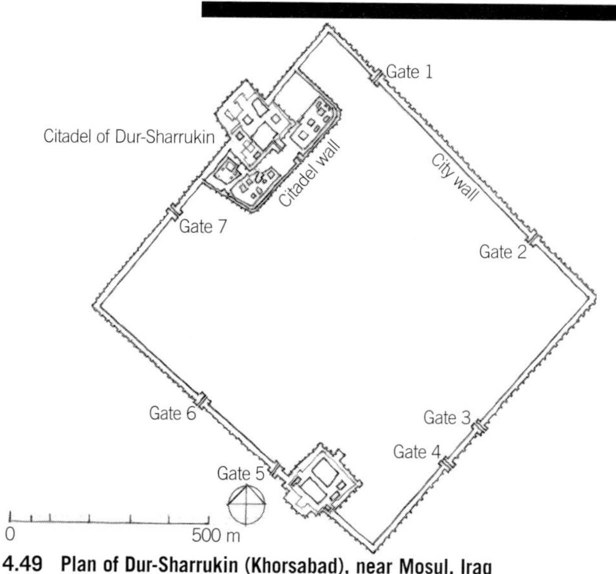


**4.49 Plan of Dur-Sharrukin (Khorsabad), near Mosul, Iraq**

**NEO-ASSYRIAN EMPIRE**

The open terrain of the Mesopotamian heartland exposed the Assyrians, who controlled the northern river regions, to the semi-nomadic intrusions of the Kassites, the Hurrians, and then by the Mitannians, whose kingdom extended its sway over all of northern Mesopotamia. Assyria remained under Mitannian rule until early in the 14th century BCE, with only the core of its kingdom more or less intact, a narrow strip of land 150 kilometers long and only 40 kilometers wide along the western bank of the Tigris. But when Mitanni suffered a serious defeat at the hands of the Hittites, the Assyrians began to reassert themselves, with King Ashur-Uballit I freeing Assyria from Mitanni, and with Assur-Nasir-Pal II (884–859 BCE) invading Syria and compelling cities of the Mediterranean coast like Tyre, Sidon, Bylos, and Arvad to pay tribute. In 663 BCE, the Assyrians sacked the Egyptian city of Thebes. The Assyrians were able to accomplish this because they were the first to create a truly iron-age army. Though linked to Mesopotamian divine practices, the Neo-Assyrians, with the god Assur at the top of their pantheon, imposed a particularly strict rule of divine-sanctioned warfare. Their engineers built bridges, tunnels, moats, and weapons of various sorts. By the year 668 BCE, the Assyrians had control of Egypt and the Nile valley as well.

The Assyrian's first capital was Ashur, on the west bank of the Tigris, but since it lay open to the western steppe, Assur-Nasir-Pal II moved the capital to old Kalakh, now Nimrud, 64 kilometers to the north. But shortly after he came to the throne in 721 BCE, Sargon II designed a new city, the remarkable Dur-Sharrukin, on whose ruins the modern Iraqi village of Khorsabad was built. Located 24 kilometers to the northeast of Nineveh (20 kilometers northwest of Mosul in Iraq), it was not finished when Sargon died in 705 BCE. It commanded the main pass from the mountains to the north and probably was intended to fend off any threat of invasion by the northern tribes.

In plan, the city was a squarish parallelogram with the palace, temples, and government buildings all compressed into an autonomous unit straddling the walls. In all, it covered 741 acres of ground. On the northwest side, half within and half without the circuit of the walls, protruding into the plain like a great bastion, stood the royal enclave. It rested on a 16-meter-high, 25-acre platform overlooking the city wall and comprised more than 200 rooms and 30 courtyards. In the center was the palace, which opened around a large inner court.

In the palace were the public reception rooms, elaborately decorated with sculptures and historical inscriptions, representing scenes of hunting, worship, feasts, and battles. The harem, with separate provisions for four wives, occupied the south corner. The stables, kitchen, bakery, and wine cellar were located at the east corner. In the west corner stood the temple with a multistage ziggurat, its seven floor levels painted in different colors and connected by ramps. Below this enclave, on the inner side, was a zone with its own walls that held the administrative heart of the city and the sumptuous houses of high-ranking officials.

The Assyrians, though possessing a formidable military machine, were unable to translate their success into economic longevity. This was largely because, in their effort to thwart rebellion, they relocated vast numbers of people, estimated to be around 6 million! Not only were the resettled peoples unfamiliar with their new land, but many of their skills were no longer appropriate. In essence, the Assyrians obliterated their own tax base and quickly ran out of money.

**4.50 Ishtar Gate leading into Babylon from the north**

### Babylon

By the year 560 BCE, Babylon was certainly the most spectacular city in all of Western Asia. The Babylonians, defeating the Assyrians, marched into Egypt and began amassing huge wealth. This New Babylonian Empire (to differentiate it from Hammurabi's Babylonian Empire (ca. 1750 BCE) reached its zenith under Nebuchadnezzar (ca. 605–562 BCE). During his reign, the city became one of the largest—if not the largest—city in West Asia. By way of comparison it defined an area some fifteen times that of Ur.

Babylon was the last great Mesopotamian city-empire of the ancient age. The forced resettlement of conquered populations, the Israelites among them, left large territories untended or improperly governed. As with the Assyrians, slaves were often used as farmers. Furthermore, the fact that the Greeks no longer needed Mesopotamian grain, having developed Sicily for that purpose, combined with the distance to metal-producing regions, all led to an untenable economic situation. Eventually, the Persians to the east, with a more coherent sociopolitical system and better suited to control the emerging trade routes between east and west, become the dominant regional player. Babylonia was folded into the Persian Empire in 539 BCE.

The city that spanned the Euphrates had two principal residential districts with the palace and ziggurat compounds located along the shore. The palace had a garden on a high terrace some 18 meters over the river. It came to be known already in ancient time as the "Hanging Gardens." A pump brought water up from the river. One can get a sense of the splendor of the city at the Ishtar Gate, which was lined with colorful glazed brick. It was the terminus of a processional way that led from the palace to the temple of Ishtar of Agade (Bit Akitu) that was used during the New Year festival. The Ishtar Gate was brilliantly decorated with animals in glazed brick with the background color in vivid blue, the animals appearing in yellow and white.

Northern fortress
Outer wall
Ishtar gate
Palace
Canal
Temple of Marduk
Euphrates River
Nebuchadnezzar's outer wall
0
1 km

**4.51 Plan of Babylon, near Al Hillah, Iraq**

# 400 BCE

This is the age in which an ethical and civic imagination begins to take root in many parts of Eurasia. In China, for example, a debate emerged between the new followers of Confucius who argued for an envisioned world governed by reason and social ritual and the followers of Daoism who felt that the self was essentially a mystical entity that should not be actively manipulated. In India, Buddha and Mahavira challenged Vedic orthodoxy in preference of a religious practice that emphasized individual action. *Arthashastra*, a textbook on polity ascribed to Kautilya, a Brahman, was composed in the 4th century BCE. In Western and Central Asia, Zoroastrianism, with its sharp contrast between good and evil, was beginning to spread. In Greece, there were vigorous debates about democracy, law, and social philosophy by Socrates, Plato, Aristotle, and others. All in all, this is an age in which discussions about religion and social thinking break with millennium-old traditions that had presumed that power was something either imposed from above or suffered from below, but not practiced from a theorized point of view. Important to note is that the elite were part of the discussion. Spurred on by the collapse of the Egyptian, Assyrian, and Babylonian empires, leaders searched for a more politically stable notion of the relationship between religion and power based not only on military might and arbitrary signs from the heavens but also on the ideal of social cohesion. Athens, with its experiment in democracy, was Europe's leading city in this respect, spreading Hellenized ideas to West Asia.

From a political point of view the collapse of the Egyptian, Assyrian, and Babylonian empires allowed Persia to extend its reach from northern India to Greece, which it unsuccessfully attempted to conquer. The Persians created new architectural forms in their expansive capitals of Pasargadae and Persepolis. When western and central Asia were conquered by Alexander of Macedonia (356–323 BCE) it seemed that the Greek Empire would stretch to the Indus. Instead, something unexpected emerged. A series of quasi-independent states and regional power centers, though lacking cohesion, became an interconnected economic system linked by large trading companies, state-supported banks, and a newly vibrant Egyptian economy. Alexandria in Egypt, Pergamon in Anatolia, and even the small island trading-city of Delos emerged as the principal cosmopolitan centers of the world. A Hellenistic aesthetic with sensibilities tending to realism, delicacy, and emotion impacted art and architecture from Greece to India.

In the 6th century, a man was born who came to be known as Buddha and whose quest to find a more personalized path to happiness found numerous converts in the ritualistic ranks of Vedic followers. Buddhism might have remained tangential to history had it not been made into a state religion by Asoka, the creator of the first empire of South Asia. In this sense, Asoka (304–232 BCE) was to Buddhism what Constantine would later be to Christianity. Since Buddhism at the time was largely an ascetic practice, Asoka did not order the construction of large temples, but the erection of pillars with the teachings of the Buddha etched onto them.

In China, the Zhou period remained politically unstable, with the warring entities vying with each other in the construction of large palaces, introducing the imperial tomb as a sign of prestige and power. By the 3rd century BCE, the various factions consolidated themselves into states that finally, in 221 BCE were unified by the Qin (Ch'in) Dynasty, which gave China its name.

In North America, the first complex cultures developed in the eastern woodlands along the Ohio River and its tributaries. The ground was fertile, fish and game abounded, and the waterways facilitated trade. In this environment, the people known as Mound Builders emerged. In South America, the most important cultural developments were well-organized societies that emerged in the Peruvian lowlands among the Moche to the north and the Nazca to the south. The Olmecs, who had been the most influential culture in Mesoamerica for some time, were in decline by 400 BCE, but they were replaced by the Maya and Zapotec peoples, who were making the transition from chiefdoms to small states.

## 400 BCE

Neo-Assyrian Empire
ca. 911–612 BCE

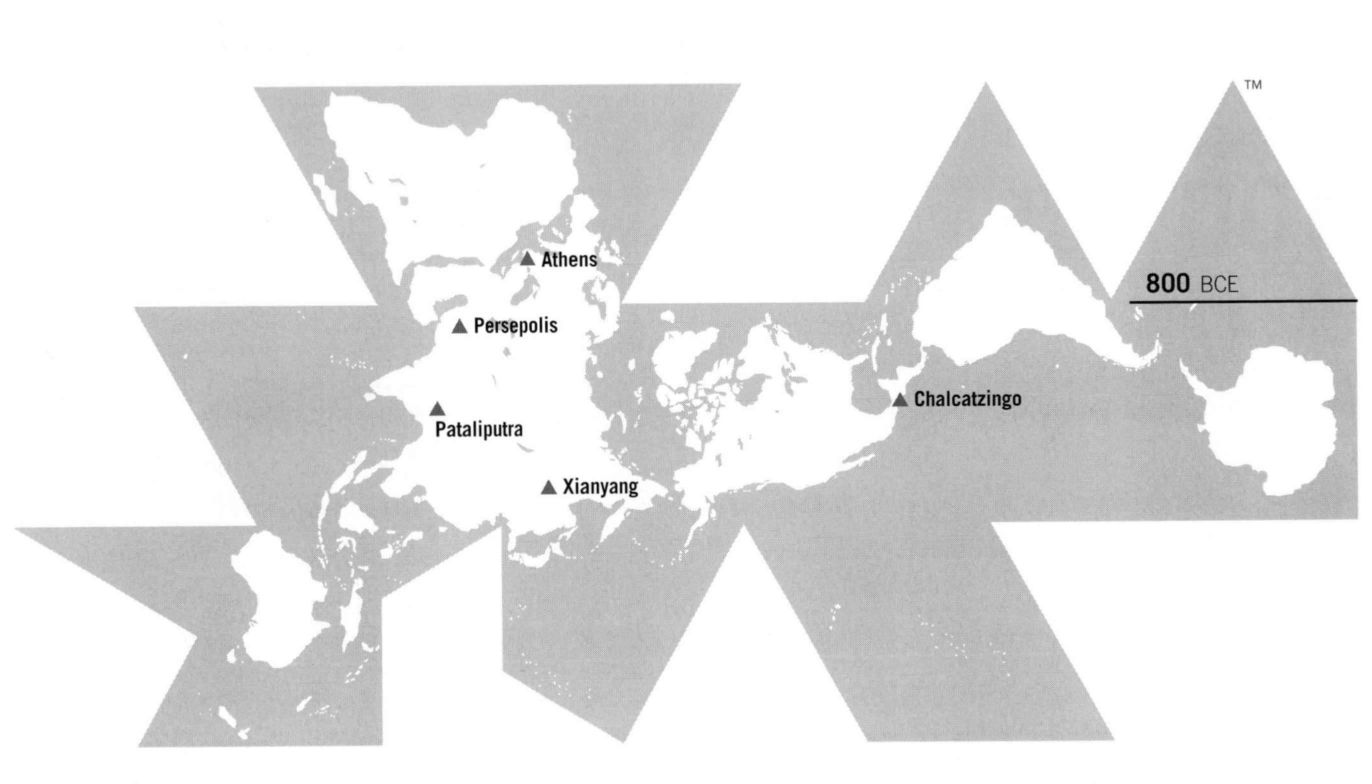


Olmec Cultures
ca. 1500–400 BCE

Achaemenid Dynasty
ca. 559–330 BCE

▲ Pasargadae
ca. 546 BCE

▲ Persepolis
ca. 518 BCE

Alexandrian Empire
334–ca. 301 BCE

Seleucid Period
ca. 305–247 BCE

Greece: Archaic Period
ca. 700–480 BCE

▲ **Temple of Poseidon at Isthmia**
ca. 600 BCE

▲ **Temple of Artemis at Corfu**
ca. 580 BCE

▲ **Miletus**
Founded ca. 500 BCE

Classical Period
ca. 480–323 BCE

▲ **Parthenon**
ca. 447–432 BCE

▲ **Erechtheum**
ca. 421–405 BCE

▲ **Temple of Athena Nike**
ca. 425 BCE

Hellenistic Period
ca. 323–31 BCE

▲ **Athena Polias at Priene**
334 BCE

▲ **Temple of Apollo at Didyma**
ca. 313 BCE–41 CE

**Sanctuary of Athena at Lindos** ▲
ca. 190 BCE

▲ **Priene**
Founded 334 BCE

▲ **Dura-Europos**
Founded ca. 300 BCE

**600** BCE — **400** BCE — **200** BCE

Egypt: Ptolemaic Dynasty
323–40 BCE

▲ **Temple of Horus**
Begun 237 BCE

⦿ Gautama Buddha
Born 566 BCE

Rise of Great States in South Asia
8th–6th Centuries BCE

Mauryan Empire
ca. 323–185 BCE

▲ **Lomas Rsi Cave**
ca. 300 BCE

China: Eastern Zhou Dynasty
771–256 BCE

▲ **Tomb of Zeng Hou Yi**
ca. 433 BCE

▲ **Xianyang Palace**
4th century BCE

Preclassic Maya Culture
ca. 1000 BCE–250 CE

▲ **Chalcatzingo**
ca. 400 BCE

▲ **Teopantecuanitlán**
ca. 400 BCE

▲ **Kaminaljuyu**
ca. 400 BCE

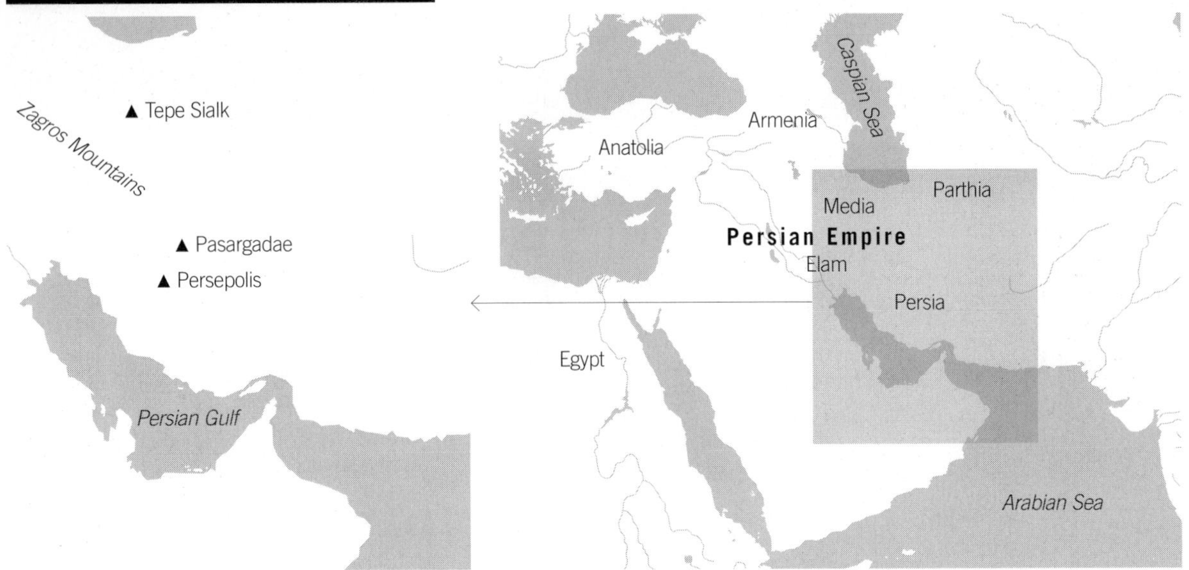


**ACHAEMENID DYNASTY**

Settlers arrived on the Iranian plateau sometime before or during the fifth millennium BCE, with one of the their ancient cities, Tepe Sialk (in Central Iran near the present-day city of Kashan) surviving various occupations until about 800 BCE. By that time, the area had become known as Mede, with powerful kings spreading their control southward over the Elamite civilization located in the plains around Susa. With the weakening of the Assyrians to the east, one of the Median kings, Cyaxares (625–585 BCE), was able to invade and destroy its capital, Nineveh, marching all the way to the gates of Sardis, but turned back when a solar eclipse, interpreted as a bad omen, occurred.

The capital of the Median kingdom was at Hagmatana (The Place of Assembly), a city dating back millennia and located under the modern city of Hamadan, 200 kilometers west of Tepe Sialk. The Median kingdom, however, underwent an inner transformation when the Persians, a branch of the Medians, took control. One of the Persian rulers, Cyrus the Great (559–530 BCE) picked up where Cyaxares left off and began to put pressure on the Babylonian empire and, with its collapse, inherited its mantel, in effect uniting the Elamite, Median, and Babylonian realms into a region that extended from Anatolia to the Persian Gulf.

Cyrus was succeeded by Darius (522–486 BCE), who extended the boundaries of the empire even further into the heart of Egypt. Though the famous military campaigns by both Cyrus and Darius against the Greeks were unsuccessful, the Persians, in alliance with the Phoenicians, who contributed substantially to their fleet, brought prosperity to the Levant and its cities along the eastern Mediterranean coast. Temples were restored and monumental buildings in the Persian style were built. Phoenician cities like Byblos and Sidon experienced something of a renaissance. The Israelites were allowed to rebuild their temple.

**5.1 Relief of Cyrus the Great**

The Persians, seeing for the first time the great buildings of Egypt and Western Asia, were eager to match these accomplishments. From the Ionians, the Persians not only collected taxes, but took their famously skilled craftsmen. An inscription of Darius relates that the stonecutters who worked on his palaces were from Ionia and the wood craftsmen were brought in from Lebanon, along with large loads of lumber.

Cyrus initiated the first major building effort of the Persians when he established Pasargadae as his capital in 546 BCE. It was located at one of the beginning points for the caravan route northward across the Great Salt Desert. What is remarkable about the planning of the city's administrative core is its spaciousness. The palace, audience hall, altars, and pavilions were distant from one another, but integrated into a parklike setting with shady trees and gardens. Watercourses also ran through the site. At the far north there was a sacred enclosure that consisted of a walled precinct with a set of flat terraces supporting an open altar. Though little of the city remains, fragments indicate a style of building that incorporated decoration based partly on Urartian and partly on older Assyrian and Babylonian art, as Cyrus wished his empire to appear as the rightful heir of Urartu, Ashur, and Babylon. The climate, not as harsh as is today, supported the extensive gardens of the palace.

**5.2 Tomb of Cyrus the Great at Pasargadae, Iran**

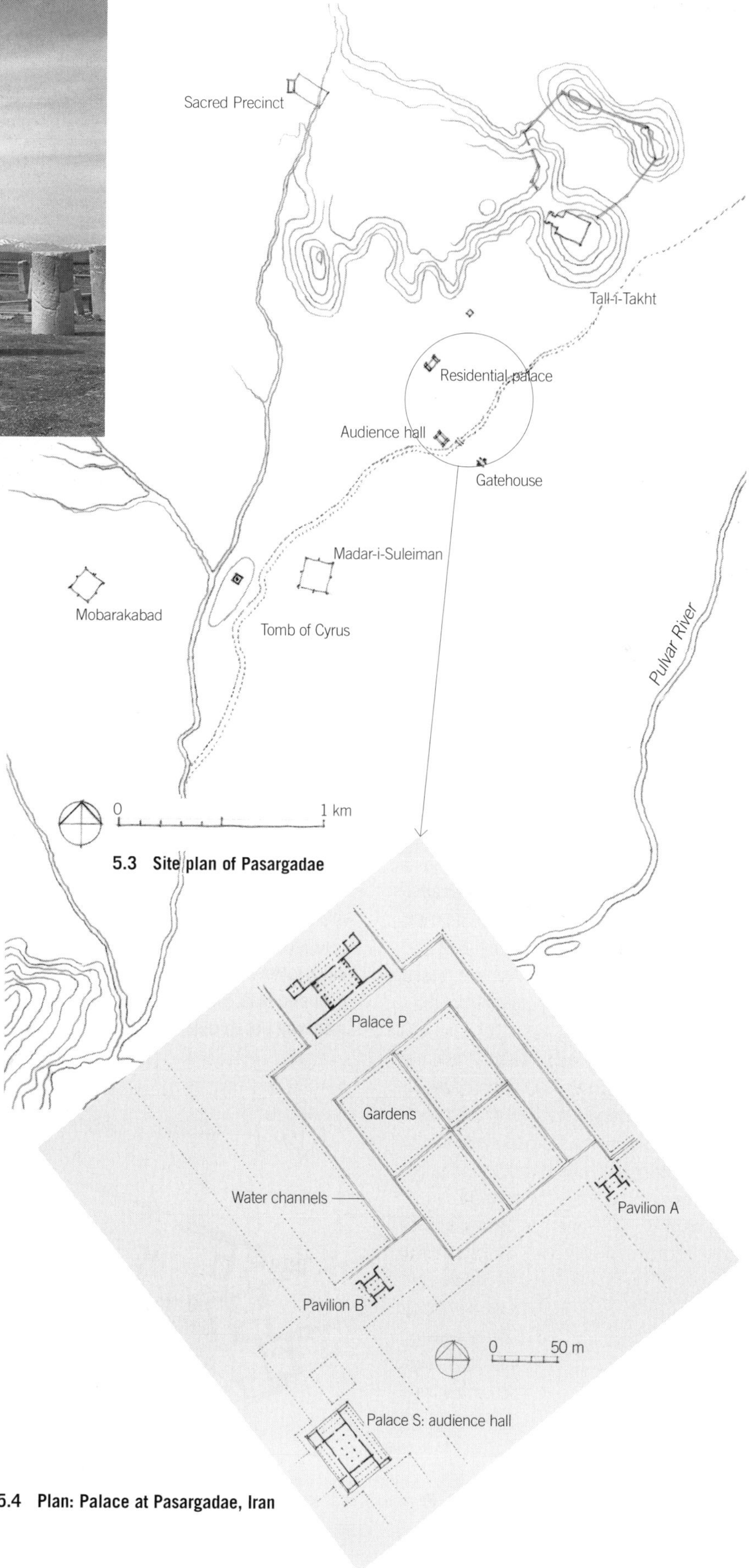

Not far from Pasargadae is the Tomb of Cyrus. Its cella is 6 meters high and rests on a six-level stepped plinth that measures 13.5 by 12.2 meters at the base. The entire 13-meter-high edifice is of white limestone. Five huge stones, slanted to shed heavy rains, make up the roof. The monument, sitting boldly in the landscape, is an elegant combination of sepulcher box and sanctuary. Though one can only speculate, it recalls similarly designed, though more modest, Greek Ionian tombs. The cyma moulding that runs around the top of the walls is also a Greek feature. The building was probably enclosed in a courtyard.

Sacred Precinct
Tall-i-Takht
Residential palace
Audience hall
Gatehouse
Madar-i-Suleiman
Mobarakabad
Tomb of Cyrus
Pulvar River
0
1 km

**5.3 Site plan of Pasargadae**

Palace P
Gardens
Water channels
Pavilion A
Pavilion B
0
50 m
Palace S: audience hall

**5.4 Plan: Palace at Pasargadae, Iran**

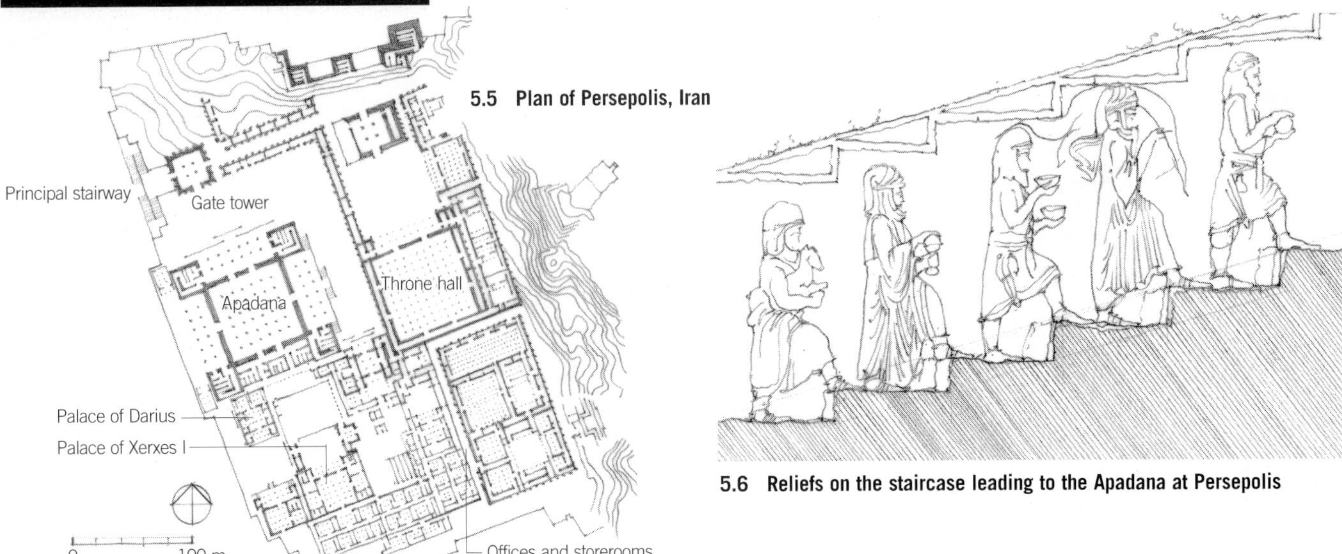


5.5 Plan of Persepolis, Iran

5.6 Reliefs on the staircase leading to the Apadana at Persepolis

### Persepolis

Pasargadae as a capital was relatively short-lived, for the new Persian king, Darius, designed his own capital city, Pars, or Persepolis, "The city of the Persians," as the Greeks called it, 10 kilometers to the southwest of Pasargadae and about 50 kilometers northeast of Shiraz in the province of Pars, closer to the fertile lands along the coast. It is a dramatic site at the edge of a large bare plain, the Marv Dasht basin, surrounded by cliffs. The palace is located directly under the west-facing slope of one of those cliffs. Construction went through several phases between 515 and 330 BCE, with the first one involving cutting into the irregular and rocky mountainside to level a large platform 10 to 20 meters above the ground and measuring about 300 meters in length and 450 meters in width. A complex system of drainage and water channels was cut into the foundations. Of the buildings themselves, however, little is left standing since most of the walls were of mud brick. What we see today are the remnants that were built in stone, the columns, foundations, and carvings.

Access to the terrace was provided by a double staircase carved with reliefs that show tribute-bearers from all corners of the Persian Empire. The steps were flat and deep enough so that important guests were able to ride up on their horses. At the head of the staircase was a gate, its sockets still visible, guarded by a pair of large bulls in the west and bulls with the heads of bearded men in the east. Black marble benches line the wall. The largest building, the Apadana, or main reception hall of the king, had 72 slender, 20-meter-high, fluted, and tapered limestone columns surmounted by bull- or lion-shaped capitals. The ceiling beams of cedar, ebony, and teak were gold-plated and inlaid with ivory and precious metals. The general concept of a columnar hall dates to early Median architecture. An 8th century BCE palace-citadel in Gobin Tepe had one with 30 columns, as did Cyrus' palace in Pasargadae.

The reliefs on the staircases leading to the Apadana represent rows upon rows of subjects, emissaries, soldiers, and chariot drivers. It is a virtual film strip showing us how the peoples of the vast empire dressed and what kind of ornaments, weapons, and hairstyles were in vogue. These and other sculptural elements and reliefs that have been preserved emphasize the formal and the grand in contrast to the lively movement and zest of the Assyrian and neo-Babylonian art. This formalizing style influenced the early art of India.

5.7 Persepolis as it stands today

**5.8 Aerial view of Persepolis**

The northern part of the terrace, which included the Throne Hall (known also as the Hall of a Hundred Columns), measured 70 by 70 meters and represented the official section of the complex that was accessible only to a restricted few. The southern section contained the palaces of Darius I and Xerxes, the Harem, a Council Hall, and storerooms. The storerooms also held the booty of the conquered tribes and states as well as the annual tribute sent by the king's subjects. Records that were found show that in the year 467 BCE, no less than 1,348 people were employed in the treasury.

Persepolis was not only a grand palace but also a dynastic center and a burial place. On the hillside above the palaces are tombs ascribed to the last Persian kings, Artaxerxes II and III, and Darius III. The whole scheme reflects, however, only the secular power of the empire, for as yet no shrine or temple has been identified. The question as to where the court lived is still being debated. Some argue that there was a royal palace somewhere in the plan. Others argue that Persepolis was only a temporary residence for kings who had their major seat of power elsewhere and that when in use, the court and the army camped in tents around the palace.

The splendor of Persepolis was short-lived. It was looted and burned by Alexander the Great in 331–330 BCE, whose army took revenge on it for the destruction of Athens by the Persians in 480 BCE.

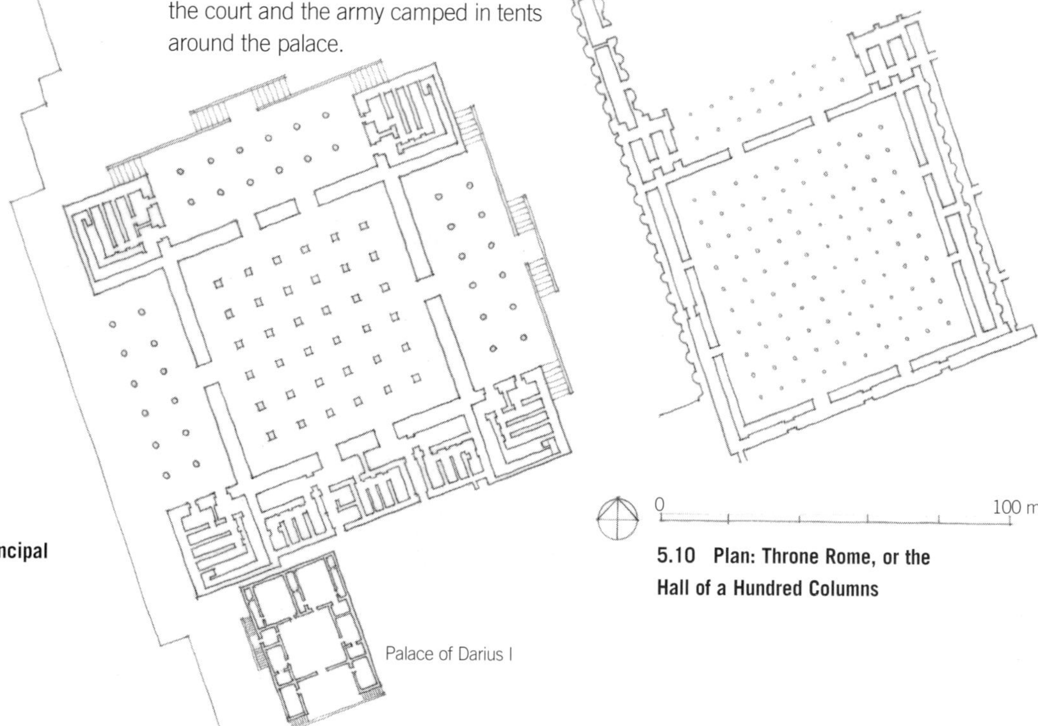


**5.9 Plan: Apadana, the principal audience hall of Darius I**

**5.10 Plan: Throne Rome, or the Hall of a Hundred Columns**

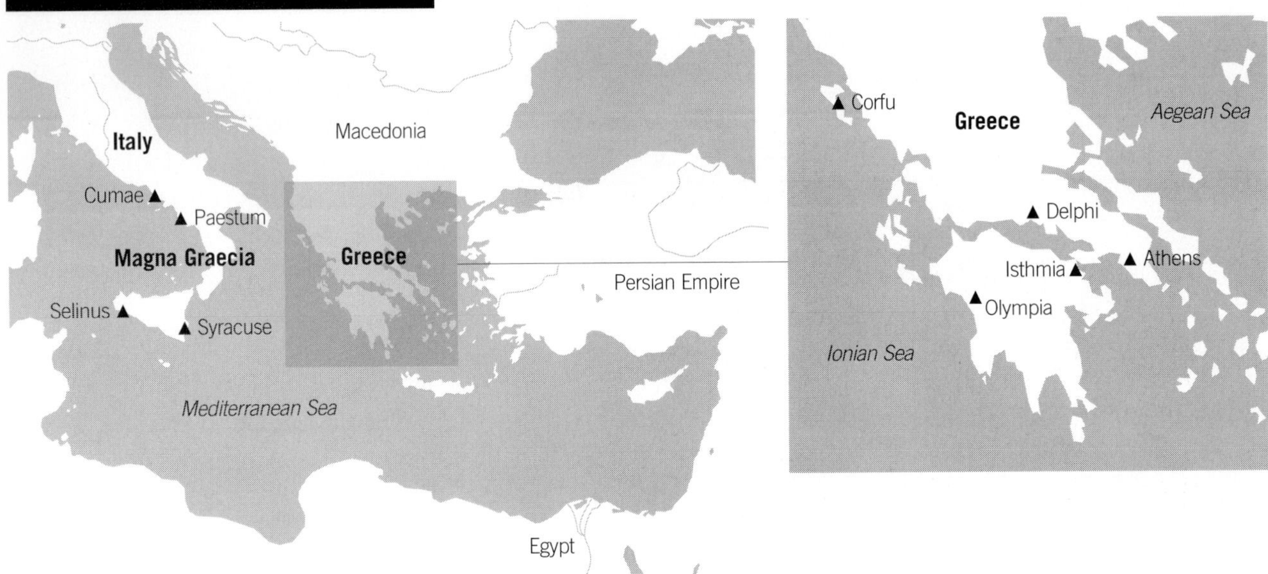


## CLASSICAL GREECE

Greek temple design changed considerably in the middle of the 6th century BCE and in particular because wood was abandoned for stone. This was partially due to a desire for permanence, but it was also a result of the Greeks having first-hand observation of Egyptian architecture. At the time, the northern part of Egypt had been divided among a dozen vassals of the Assyrian Empire. Around 664 BCE, an Egyptian prince named Psamtik was banished to the marshes. Plotting his return, he allowed the Dorians around 620 BCE to settle in Naucratis, on the western edge of the Nile delta, on the promise that they help with his military ambitions, which were indeed successful. He was able to defeat his rivals, break with Assyria, and reunify Egypt. This opened up a series of mercantile exchanges between Egypt and Greece that was profitable to both. Naucratis became a type of duty-free zone, with the Greeks setting up factories to produce pottery and ornaments in an Egyptian style for the Egyptian market. They also imported silver, which was still rare in Egypt, and in return they appeared to have received Egyptian grain.

When the Greeks first saw the Egyptian stone temples and pyramids, they certainly must have been astonished. But for Egyptian architecture to have had an impact on Greek building, the Greeks would have had to study Egyptian construction techniques and building management, which indeed they appeared to have done. They certainly had plenty of opportunity because Psamtik had embarked on an extensive building campaign, which gave the Greeks ample opportunity to observe Psamtik's workers quarrying, transporting, positioning, clamping, and dressing the stones, which were much harder than the porous limestone available in Corinth and Isthmia.

The impact of this lesson must have been immediate for there is very little evidence that the Doric order existed before the Greek experience in Egypt. One has to, therefore, differentiate the early Doric temples from the Doric order as it began to take shape in some of the first stone temples, like the Temple of Hera at Olympia. Initially, like the Temple of Poseidon at Isthmia, its columns and entablature were entirely of wood and the *cella* walls of mud brick. But already by the time of its completion around 600 BCE, the oak columns were replaced by an assortment of stone columns. A Roman visitor in 176 CE reports that one oak column was still standing. Being transitional, some of these stone columns were huge monoliths, others had drums of varying heights and diameters. The earliest known Doric temple completely of stone was the large Temple of Artemis at Corfu (580 BCE) also known as the Gorgon Temple, named after the mythical figure portrayed with her offspring Pegasus and Chrysoar on the tympanum.

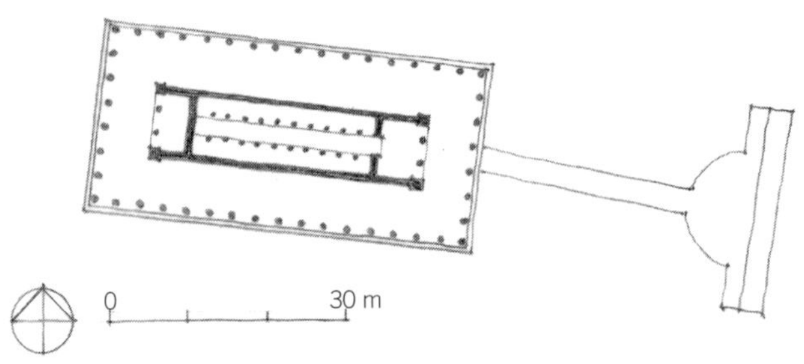


**5.11 Plan: Temple of Artemis at Corfu (Kerkira), Greece**

5.12 Temple of Segesta, Sicily, Italy

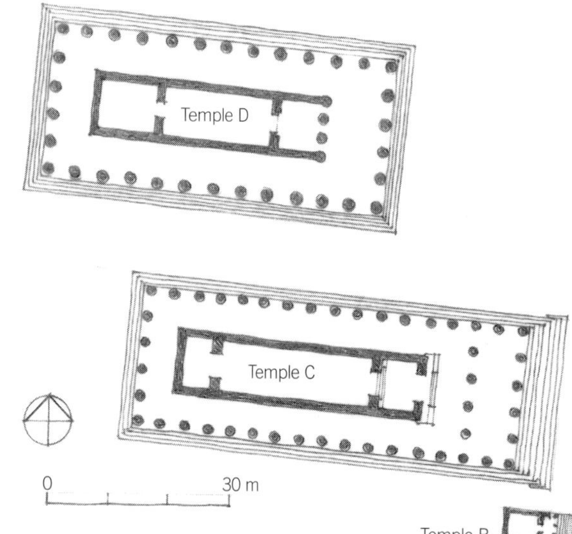


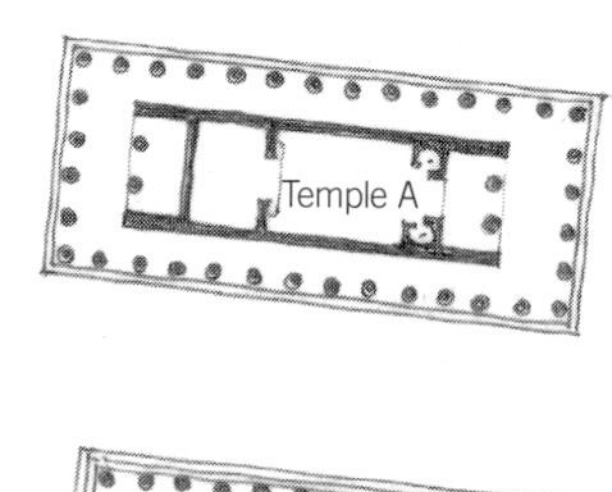


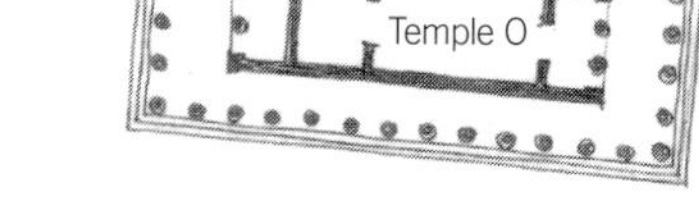


5.13 Plan: Temples at Selinus, Sicily, Italy

## Magna Graecia Temples

In the 6th century BCE the city-states began to compete more vigorously for markets, and many even began to mint their own coins. Greek cities also began to lay claim to particular mythical heroes or episodes. This helped escalate the competition for artists and, ultimately, so it seems, for temples with ever greater refinements. This was particularly true in the cities in Sicily and southern Italy, which became the center of Greek grain production, important since it reduced the Greek dependency on Egypt and Mesopotamia.

The first Greek colonies were created around 770 BCE by the Euboeans (Pithekoussai and Cumae in central Italy and Naxos and Leotini in eastern Sicily). The Achaeans, around 710 BCE, founded Sybaris and Croton in southern Italy. The Spartans founded Tarentum around 650 BCE. Syracuse was founded by the Dorians in 743 BCE. All in all, in a span of one hundred years, some thirty colonies had been founded. The settlers maintained close relationships to their mother city and often appealed to them in times of war. But the colonies also began to flex their own military muscle. In 480 BCE, Syracuse defeated Carthage and in 413 BCE defeated an Athenian fleet.

At Selinus, the temples, seven in all, were lined up on the acropolis and a nearby ridge. Distinguished by letters, as their dedications are still under discussion, they are: Temple C, 570 BCE; Temple D, 560 BCE; Temple F, 550 BCE; Temples A and O, 490 BCE; Temple E, 460 BCE; and Temple G, unfinished at 409 BCE. At Paestum in Italy there is the Basilica, 550 BCE; the Temple of Demeter, 520 BCE; and the Temple of Poseidon, 460 BCE. The differences between the early Temple C at Selinus and the later Temple of Poseidon in Paestum show the development toward opening up the inner *cella* by means of an inner colonnade as well as a tighter fit that the architects attempt to achieve between the body of the temple and the *pteron*, or columnar surround.

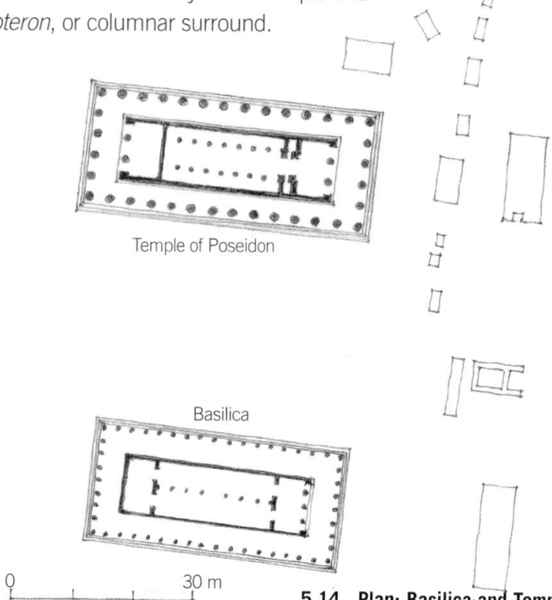


5.14 Plan: Basilica and Temple of Poseidon at Paestum, Italy

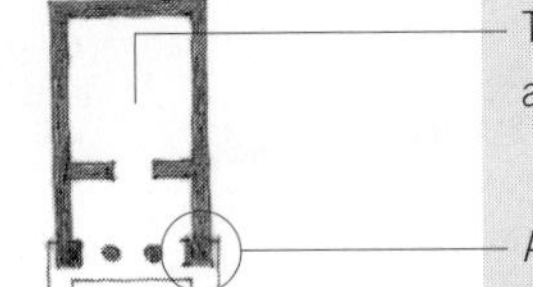

The *cella* ends with either columns in antis or a *prostyle* portico.

Anta refers to the thickening of the projecting end of one of the lateral walls. If columns are set between them, then the columns are said to be in antis.

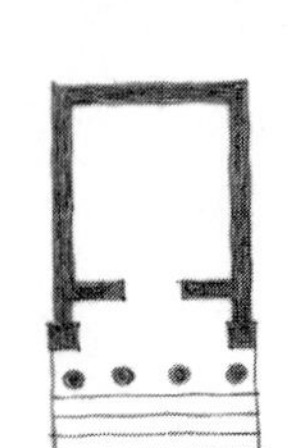

A *prostyle* portico has columns running across the entire front.

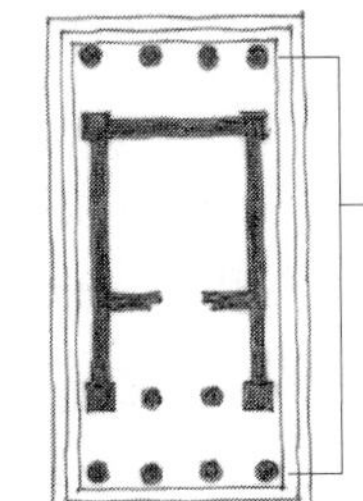

An *amphiprostyle* temple has *prostyle* porticoes at both ends.

**Greek Architecture and Language**

Greek and Roman temples are described according to the number of columns on the entrance front, type of colonnade, and type of portico. The Parthenon, for example, is an *octastyle peripteral* temple with *hexastyle* porticoes at both ends. The temple of Zeus at Olympia is a *hexastyle peripteral* with *distyle* in-antis porches at both ends. The Basilica in Paestum is a rare *enneastyle pseudodipteral* temple with a *tristyle* in-antis portico.

Almost all surfaces of the temple—the steps, columns, capitals, walls, even the figures on the pediment—were painted in bright reds, blues, blacks, and yellows. What we know about the colors used for the temples comes from both archaeological and literary sources. The pigments were made from minerals, soot, ground stones, vegetables, and animal stuff. The purple dye, for example, came from shellfish; the yellowish color that was applied to columns and beams came from saffron. The colors were applied sometimes with wax but usually on stucco.

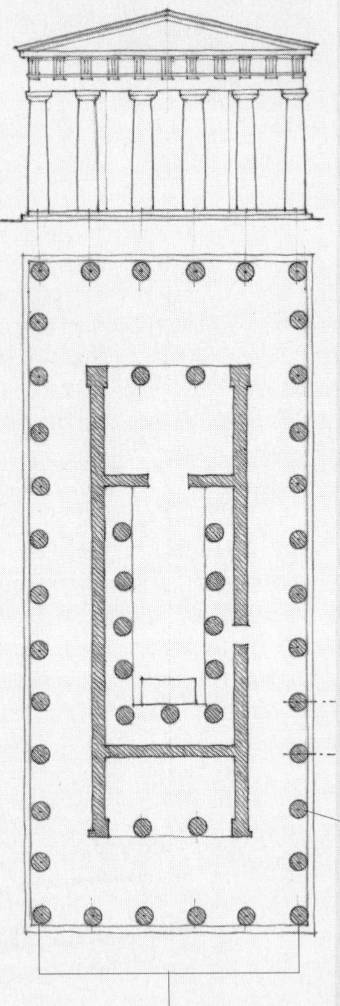

The most basic element of the temple was the colonnade. Though so common today that many might see it as a natural architectural form, one has to remember that it was a unique innovation of the Greeks. It was called a *pteron* and was a sacred form always reserved for temples. *Pteron* means wing or fin, but also oar and sail. It perhaps refers to early awnings placed against buildings. But it also indicates that the Greeks saw the building as a dynamic place, as something that literally catches the wind and thus the voices of the gods. The *pteron* also evoked the idea of a grove of trees, especially if one recalls that the columns were originally made of wooden trunks. The *pteron* has also been associated with stout soldiers forming a phalanx—a rectangular military formation—protecting the statue within the *cella*.

The following terms describe the type of colonnade surrounding the *naos* of a Greek temple:

- *Peripteral*: one row of columns
- *Dipteral*: two rows of columns
- *Tripteral*: three rows of columns
- *Pseudodipteral*: suggesting a dipteral colonnade but without the inner colonnade

The following terms refer to the number of columns on the entrance front of a Greek temple:

- *Henostyle*: one column
- *Distyle*: two columns
- *Tristyle*: three columns
- *Tetrastyle*: four columns
- *Pentastyle*: five columns
- *Hexastyle*: six columns
- *Heptastyle*: seven columns
- *Octastyle*: eight columns
- *Enneastyle*: nine columns
- *Decastyle*: ten columns

**5.15 Greek Temple Terminology**

Corona refers to the projection at the top of a cornice and was a word associated with the forehead and with controlling things from above. It was also associated with the eagle, the bird of omen, and Zeus's favorite bird. For these reasons it was the appropriate topping-off element of the temple.



On the abacus of a capital rests the architrave, the main stone or marble beam running from column to column. Above the architrave comes the frieze, which consists of alternating *triglyphs* and metopes. Beneath each *triglyph*, on the face of the architrave, is a smooth band, the *regula*, on the underside of which hang six stone pegs or guttae. There is normally one *triglyph* to each column and one to each intercolumniation. The metopes were often decorated with paintings or relief sculpture, depicting individual episodes from the myths associated with the god to whom the temple was dedicated or to the local hero.

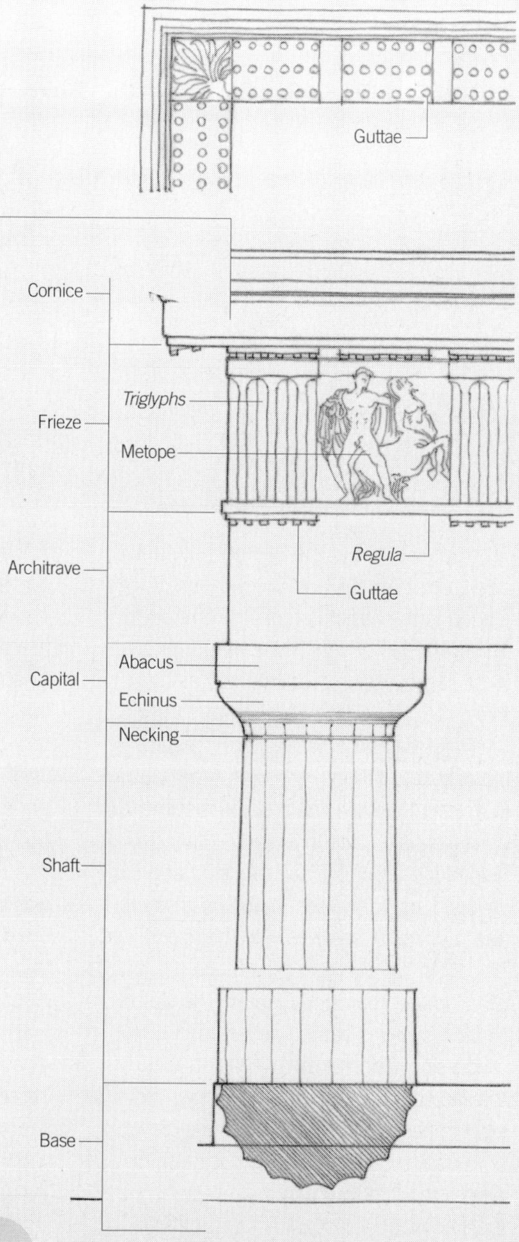

- *Pycnostyle*: 1.5 diameters
- *Systyle*: 2 diameters
- *Eustyle*: 2.25 diameters
- *Diastyle*: 3 diameters
- *Araeostyle*: 3.5 diameters

Intercolumniation refers to the space between columns, expressed in column diameters. This systematization applies mainly to Hellenistic and Roman temples.

**5.16 Elements of the Doric Order**

The temple rested on a *crepis*, which means a base of a building but also a shoe or sandal—a footing, in other words, proper to the divine presence. This foundation was constructed from roughly dressed masonry that was not concealed below the ground but was designed to appear as steps leading up to the platform on which the temple columns rested.

The capital, which derives its name from the Latin word *caput* (head), was in Greek terminology the *kranion*, which refers to the top of the head or skull. The Doric capital, carved out of a single stone block, consists of a spreading convex molding, the echinus, a word that was applied to almost any kind of curved and spiny thing in nature, and a low square block, the abacus.

The column shaft tapers from the bottom upward in the form of a delicate curve called an entasis or swelling. The shaft of a Doric column almost always stands directly on the floor without a base. Early columns of the 6th century BCE are often monolithic, but later the shaft came to be composed of superimposed drums, which were rounded by turning them on a lathe. The drums were dowelled together with wooden or sometimes bronze spikes enclosed in concavities at the center. The shafts were fluted after the columns were in place. There are usually 20 broad and shallow flutes, which meet to form sharp edges or arrises. The joints between the columns would have been concealed by marble stucco.

The steps were often too tall to ascend with comfort, so a flight of stairs or a ramp was provided at the entrance. This shows that the steps had nothing to do with the necessities of construction, for they could easily have been designed with more risers. Instead the steps fulfill the need for the Greeks to have the temple appear as if rising on a natural outcropping, cleaned and smoothed in preparation for the building.

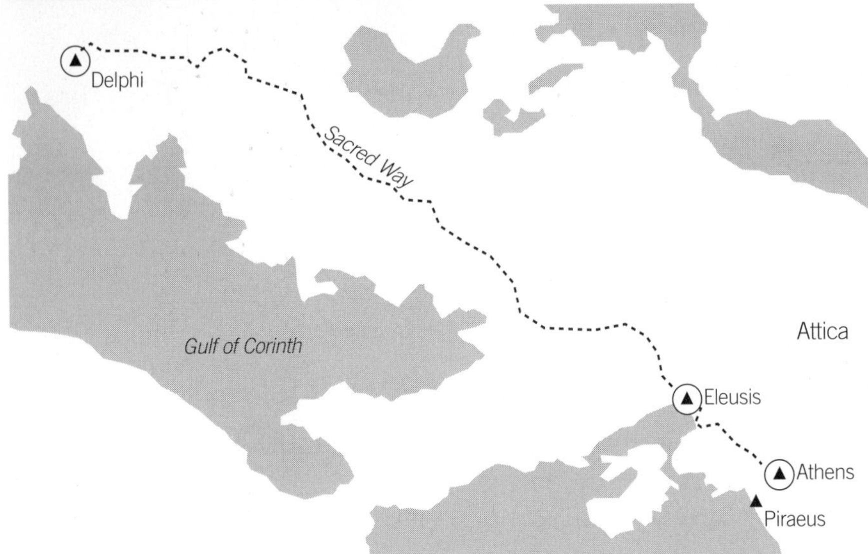


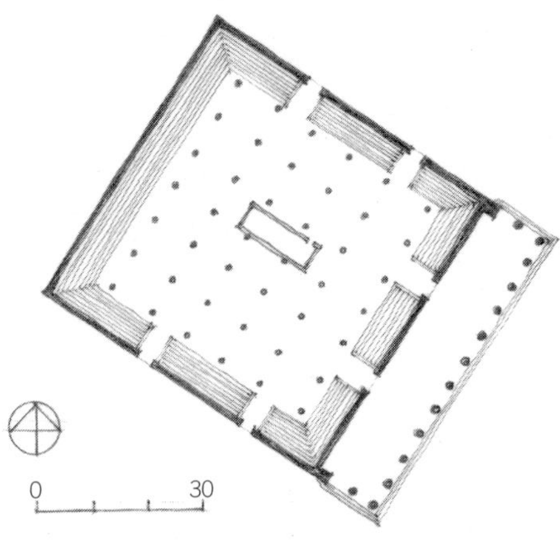


5.17 Plan: Telesterion at Eleusis, Greece

**Telesterion at Eleusis**

Festivals were an important part of Greek political and religious life. In this there is some similarity with Middle Kingdom practices in Egypt, except that Greek festivals were often considerably more populist in nature. Nonetheless, they were not profane celebrations but events deeply rooted in cultic practices unique to each site. The Poseidon temple at Isthmia, for example, was the center of a festival that involved a major athletic contest. In Athens, festivals accentuated the flow of the year and in fact filled 120 days, or one-third of the calendar year.

One of the oldest of these festivals was the Thesmophoria, a harvest festival that centered on the Sanctuary of Demeter at Eleusis where the Great Mysteries took place. Dating back to Mycenaean times, it became part of Athenian state festivals in the 6th century BCE. It was a seven-day celebration in September (officially the 15th day of the Greek month of Boedromion). This particular festival, unlike others, was open to both free people and slaves, men and women. The procession followed the road from Athens to Delphi, which was sacred because, according to legend, this was where Apollo had traveled on his mission to civilize humankind. The festival remained in operation until the Christianization of the Roman Empire.

The route started at the Sacred Gate in the city walls of Athens and proceeded through Eleusis to the Sanctuary of Demeter on the Thriasian Plain. Every September a great torch-lit procession made its way along this route. Two days before it was to begin, the *hiera* (sacred objects) were brought in baskets to Athens by young Athenians in military training. The initiates met their *mystagogus* (a person already initiated who helped them through the process) and took piglets down to the sea, bathed with them, and purified themselves with their sacrificed blood. On the fifth day, they made the long 25-kilometer march to Eleusis. The statue of Dionysus was carried at the head of the procession. Then came the priests with the sacred objects of the cult hidden from sight in baskets, and finally a huge crowd of *mystai* (initiates). The high point of the procession took place in the Telesterion, a square, windowless building arranged in its final configuration with tiers of seats on either side to accommodate some 3,000 people.

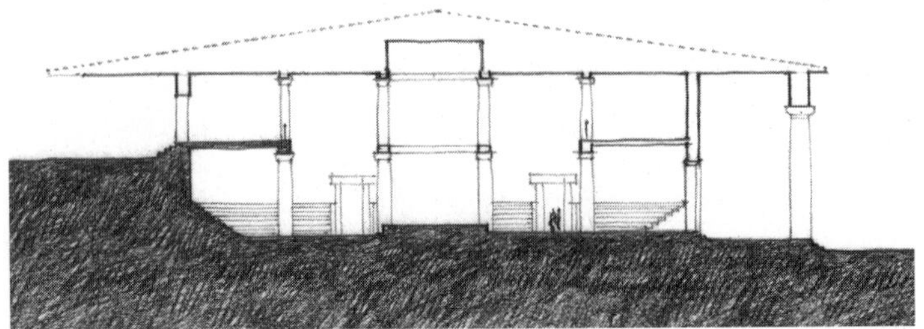

5.18 Section: Telesterion at Eleusis

The interior room housed the *hiera* and was known as the Anaktoron (Palace). Though a small and windowless box, it was precious not only in its meaning but also in its antiquity. The renovations and additions that were made to the Telesterion changed only the space around it, not the Anaktoron itself. Significant expansions took place under the Athenian rulers Peisistratos, ca. 550–510 BCE, and Kimon, ca. 479–461 BCE. The building in its final form (ca. 435 BCE) was designed by the architect Koroibos. In the 4th century BCE, a colonnaded porch known as the Stoa of Philon was added to the southeastern side of the building.

Though the songs and offerings could be seen by everyone, the experiences of the *mystai* in the sanctuary during the initiation were secret. Despite more than one thousand years of use, very little is known for certain about the rituals that took place in this building. We can only speculate that the viewers were privileged to a dramatic nighttime representation of the union of Zeus and Demeter.

Though we may perceive Greek temples today as isolated objects, they were actually framed in the landscape by a *temenos*, or sacred precinct, which could consist of something as simple as a row of stones but could also be a built-up wall. The *temenos* was the territory of the deity and had to be approached in a prescribed manner and entered only at special place defined by a *propylon* (*pro-pylon*, or "before the gate").

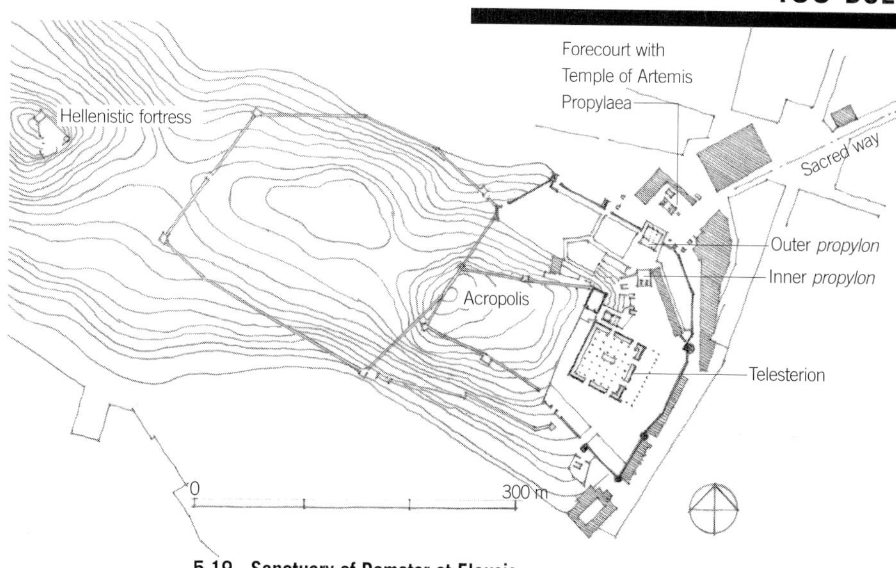


**5.19 Sanctuary of Demeter at Eleusis**

### Delphi

Delphi was without doubt the most sacred of the religious sites in Greece and came with its own festivals and celebrations. One approached it from Eleusis on the sacred route that crosses the Boeotian Plains, passes the city of Thebes, and courses its way through increasingly rugged and remote territory filled with history and myth. Finally, the dramatic scenery of the limestone cliffs, from which gushes the Castalian Spring with its great cleft, comes into view, the buildings of the sanctuary rising up against the very base of the cliff.

**5.20 Plan of *temenos* at Delphi, Greece**

The early history of Delphi is the story of a struggle between different types of religious practices. Initially, the site was dedicated to the great mother goddess in the Minoan tradition. With the arrival of the Dorians, we see the maternalistic element superseded by the paternalistic world concept of the Dorians. Nonetheless, despite the seizure of the shrine by the followers of Apollo the new religion did not obliterate the old, but metamorphosed it into its own mythologies. The mother goddess was transformed into the serpent Pytho who is said to be buried there. Furthermore, the earth goddess, Gaia, as she came to be called by the Greeks, retained her ancient *temenos* close to the Temple of Apollo, near the rock of the Sybil. The temple foundations come close to her spot, but do not obliterate it. This indicates that to win acceptance, the Apollo cult was forced to compromise with these older deities.

5.21 **Treasury of Athens, Delphi**

5.22 **Pediment: Temple of Apollo at Delphi**

**Temple of Apollo at Delphi**

The figure of Dionysus, with whom Apollo shares this sanctuary, also takes up some of the chthonic elements of the previous cult. In fact, he takes over the shrine for three months of the year to celebrate the return of his wife, Persephone, from the underworld. Out of the dances and choruses of Dionysus, the Greek drama was born, and at Delphi, above the great Temple of Apollo, there lies on cross-axis to the temple and facing straight down the slope a brilliant example of such a theater. Filling and defining a natural concavity at the base of the cliff, the natural and man-made merge into one majestic swath, one great hymn, one could almost say, to the creation cycle of life.

From just inside the wall of the *temenos*, the viewer would see the silhouette of the Temple of Apollo floating against the backdrop of the cliff. The path to the temple was not a direct one but rather snaked its way upward past the various treasuries of often distant colonies, to emerge just below the broad terrace built up against the slope. A supplicant, guided by an assistant to the Delphian cult, would have been led to the temple terrace to await his turn with the oracle. He would have had the opportunity to look straight down into the ancient precinct of Gaia. He might have spent some time regarding the temple itself.

What we see today is the last temple built on the same location as a 7th-century BCE temple that burned in 548 BCE and was replaced by a larger structure in 525 BCE, which in turn was destroyed again in 373 BCE.

On the east pediment facing the altar in front of the temple, sculptures portrayed the "arrival" of Apollo at Delphi, shown with his mother, Leto; his sister, Artemis; and his companions, the Muses. At the other pediment, Dionysus, Apollo's brother, occupied the center, establishing a principle of balance between these two gods. The Dionysian and the Apollonian were represented as counterpoles, not only of nature but also of one's psychic well-being. Below the east pediment were hung the golden shields, a gift to the temple by the Athenians from the spoils of the Persian War.

The most important festival associated with Delphi was the change of rule that took place between Apollo and Dionysus. It was enacted in the great open-air theater above the temple with its thronelike view of the sanctuary and the surrounding landscape. The sports events that accompanied these festivals took place in the heights above the *temenos*.

Once inside the temple, the supplicant would smell the meat burning on the hearth and see the smoke rising toward the opening in the roof where shafts of sunlight penetrated down into the gloom. Visitors also mentioned a perfumed smell. Against the walls, supplicants would also have seen tripods, statues, pieces of armor, even entire racing chariots, brought to the temple as donations from the entire world of Magna Graecia and often from foreign countries.

After depositing his own offering, the supplicant would have been led toward the far end of the chamber where steps led down to a sunken area a meter below the level of the floor. From there he made his way into the *adyton* at the back wall on which there was a bench where he sat. On the other side of a curtain sat the prophetess on a tripod, which was positioned over a crack in the rocks, close to the branches of a laurel tree as well as a golden statue of Apollo. An attendant would draw back the curtain, and would relay the question of the petitioner. From the chthonic depth, she received and relayed the encoded messages from the god. Whatever the response—and often it made a large allowance for interpretation—it probably involved the requirement for further sacrifices.

5.23 Ionic capital from temple at Neandris

5.24 Bronze female figure with headdress

5.25 Temple of Athena Nike

**Ionic Order**

Though discussed usually after the Doric, the Ionic should not on that account be regarded as later. The development of the Ionic and the Doric orders paralleled each other, but there are notable differences. First, the columns rested upon molded bases that stand on square plinths. These moldings consist of combinations of torus, scotia, and rondelles, often in pairs. The capital has different front and side views and is meant to be seen chiefly from the front and back. Its design begins with a flat-topped molding with a profile like that of the Doric echinus, but it is usually carved with egg-and-dart moldings. Above this lies the volute with its loose ends wound up in dropping spirals on each side of the shaft, ending in buttonlike oculi (eyes). As for the entablature, it usually consists of three bands of fasciae of unequal height, each projecting a little beyond the one below it. Above it runs a band of egg-and-dart decorations, on top of that a row of dentils, and on top of that a projecting cornice often decorated with lion faces and plant motifs. The Ionic capital came into its own during the 7th century BCE. Unlike the Doric, the Ionic did not derive from a structural system but perhaps from symbolic headdresses or from poles with leaves bundled around them marking sacred areas. An early example of the latter was found at a site about 35 kilometers south of Troy.

The capital consisted of two large spirals that spring upward and outward from the shaft, as if a pliant stick were split at the ends and each half curved outward to form a spiral. The space between the spirals was decorated with a fanlike pattern. Capitals of similar form were found on the island of Lesbos.

As they developed, the volutes were tautened and formed an actual capital articulated as a cushion laid upon the shaft. To construct the volutes, craftsmen devised a system of gridded holes in which pegs were inserted and around which a cord was wound and then, with a stylus attached, unwound. In essence, the spiral was a series of interconnected quarter-circles and semicircles. One of the most elegant Ionic temples is undoubtedly the small Temple of Athena Nike (425 BCE) at the Acropolis in Athens.

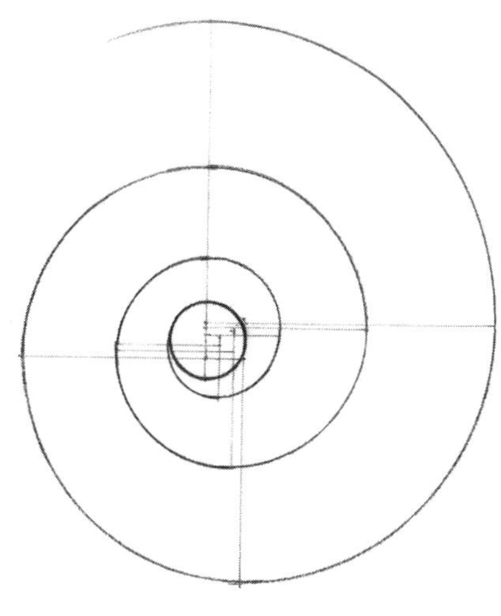

5.26 Development of the Ionic spiral

5.27 Temple of Athena Nike, Acropolis, Athens

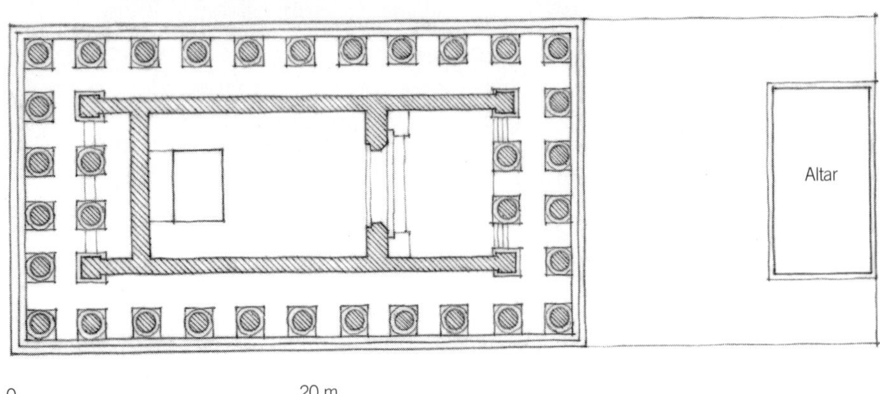


**5.28 Plan: Temple of Athena Polias at Priene, Turkey**

Though proportional systems were most certainly in play in the designing of the Doric order, formalizing the system began with the Ionic. Pythius, the architect for Athena Polias at Priene (334 BCE; an example of the Ionic at its most classic), wrote a book explaining the proportions of this temple. The larger proportions were worked out in similar ratios of 1:2.

The overall dimensions of the *stylobate* measured 19.5 by 37.2 meters for a ratio of 11:21. The axial spacing between the columns was twice the width of the square plinths. The antae of the porch and the *opisthodomos* stood opposite the penultimate columns of the ends and sides and enclosed a rectangle measuring 12 by 30 meters for a ratio of 1:2.5. The days when architects manipulated the form to adjust for optical illusion were replaced by geometric precision.

The Ionic was codified further around 150 BCE by the architect Hermogenes of Priene. He worked out a series of ideal proportions that influenced the writings of Vitruvius a century later. According to this system, the height of the column varied inversely according to the axial spacing, so that the sum of axial spacings and height was always 12.5 column diameters.

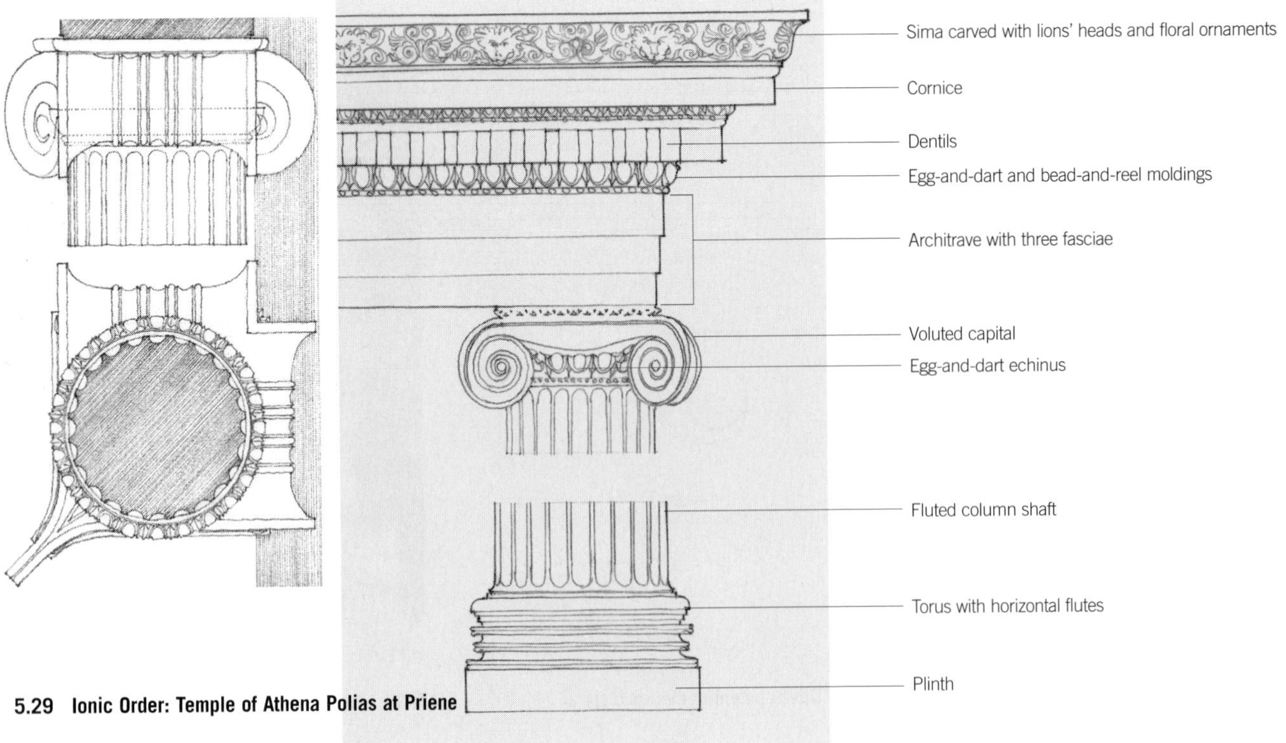


**5.29 Ionic Order: Temple of Athena Polias at Priene**

The *propylon* that defined the entrance to a *temenos* was more important for its symbolism than for protection. Its design is unmistakably reminiscent of Minoan and Mycenaean architecture, and there can be no doubt that it was incorporated into the Greek architectural language for its legitimizing allusions to an age that the Dorians themselves perceived as heroic.

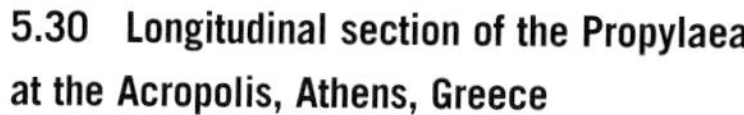

**5.30 Longitudinal section of the Propylaea at the Acropolis, Athens, Greece**

## Athenian Propylaea

Though the temple was at the center of our understanding of Greek architecture, it would be wrong to assume that Greek architects were unable to think beyond its regulatory confines. The Propylaea and the Erechtheum on the Athenian acropolis are examples of complex design thinking where the architect had to solve multiple programmatic and sacred purposes. The Propylaea is approached by a massive ramp 20 meters wide and 80 meters long. It enters into a U-shaped structure with a Doric facade. The road continues through the building and is flanked by slender Ionic columns. Though the central parts are symmetrical, the outlying spaces are different. To the left was a ceremonial banquet hall, or *pinacotheca*, that reached to the very edge of the acropolis wall. In it were spaces for 17 couches. It is known to have contained paintings on the walls.

The area to the south led to the Temple of Athena Nike (410 BCE), the first temple on the Acropolis to be built in the Ionic style, the first construction on the Acropolis following the devastation of the Acropolis by the Persian invasion, and the first temple to be built entirely of Pentelic marble. Nike was a goddess who personified triumph and victory. There was also in this area a statue to Hermes, a god traditionally associated with boundaries.

Remarkable is the intricate play of solid and void spaces. The building itself is like a bracket yielding to the thrust of the ramp. The Ionic columns on the interior are much more slender than their Doric counterparts and impart a lightness to the shadowy interior that contrasts with the sturdy exterior and the brightness in front and back. Cross views were also important. From the door of the *pinacotheca*, for example, the view falls directly across the front of the main colonnade positioning a viewer both inside and outside at the same time.

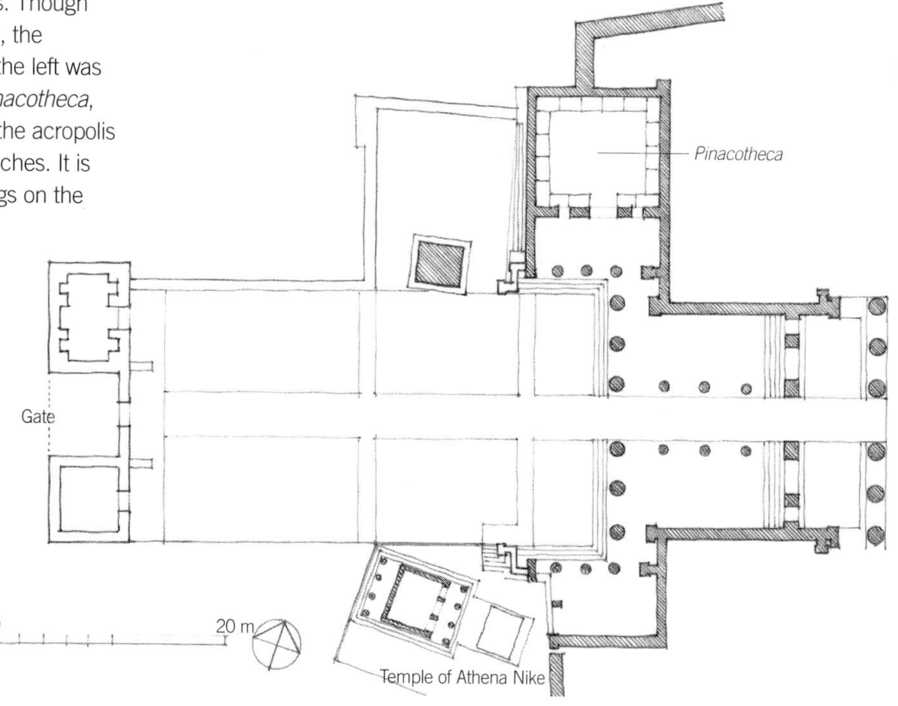


**5.31 Plan of the Propylaea**

5.32 Caryatid Porch, Erectheum, Acropolis, Athens, Greece

5.33 Elevation: Caryatid Porch, Erectheum

**Erectheum**

When one exits from the Propylaea, one is presented with a sweeping view of the buildings on the acropolis. Straight ahead, one sees Mt. Hymettos with its mythical allusions to Zeus, presiding just over the massive altar of Athena (of which hardly a trace exists today). To the right is the Parthenon. To the left is the Erechtheum (421–405 BCE), a complex building that, like the Propylaea, wraps up different mythical narratives into a single composition. The Erechtheum was built on two levels; it has three porticoes of different design and four entrances, not to speak of a subterranean entrance under the north porch. This irregularity was due to the necessity of designing a building around the spots that were essential to the narrative of the founding of Athens.

Erectheus, after whom the Erechtheum is named, is reputedly the mythical founder of Attica and the "earth-born king of Athens." At that time, gods challenged one another to be honored by cities. Unfortunately, both Poseidon and Athena aspired to control Athens, so Erectheus set up a contest in which each had to give a gift to the city. Poseidon drew saltwater by striking the ground on the acropolis with his trident while Athena grew the first olive tree on its slopes. Erechtheus judged Athena's gift to be the most useful to the people of Athens and the city was named in her honor.

The central elements of the drama can be read by entering first through the north porch dedicated to Poseidon. Its expansive design takes in the grand vista and can be seen from the agora below. On the floor, to the left of the door, a type of window looks down at the bedrock where one can see the indentations of Poseidon's trident. An opening in the roof above defines the space through which the trident was thought to have flown. The great door leads to a narrow room that contained a shrine to Erechtheus. Under the floor was a cistern containing the saltwater of Poseidon. A door to the right leads to the sacred court containing Athena's olive tree. Continuing on the axis made by the porch of Poseidon, one goes up the flight of stairs to the Caryatid porch, which today sits isolated in the field of ruins.

The plan of the building may thus seem chaotic, but it makes sense as a three-dimensional celebration of the founding myth of Athens.

The north porch is the largest and projects forward two intercolumniations, and the height of its roof is almost level with the eaves of the central block. The south porch is less than half as high, but it is raised upon a terrace, and instead of columns there are caryatids, or statues of women, carrying the load of the entablature on their heads. The east porch consists of six Ionic columns. The central block that holds all this together has two levels corresponding to the north and east porches. Three doors lead into it, the great door of the north porch, a plain opening at the bottom of the west wall, and a small door on the south side to which a staircase leads down from the interior of the Caryatid Porch.

5.34 Erectheum from the south, as it stands today

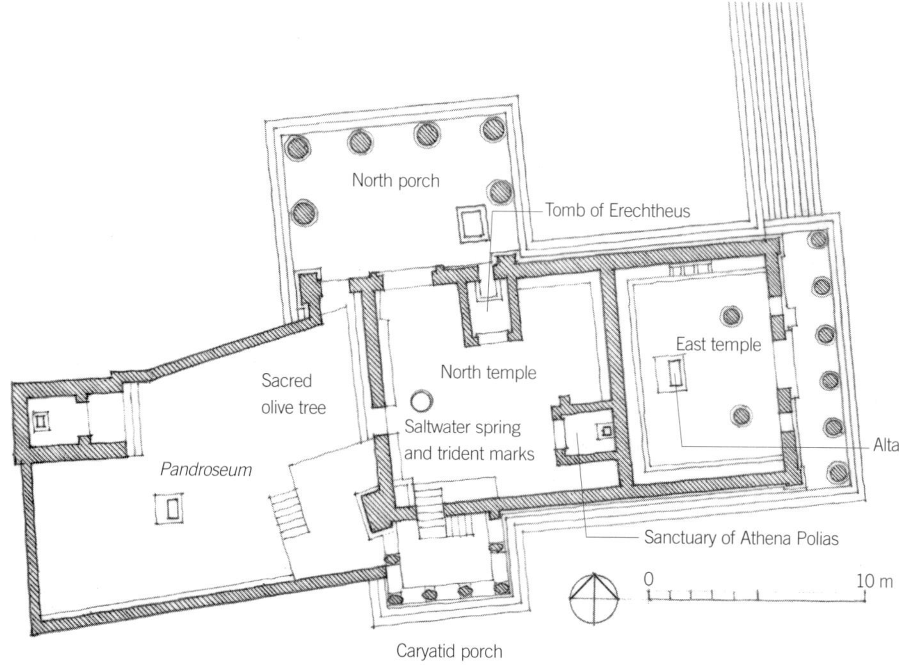


Plan

East elevation

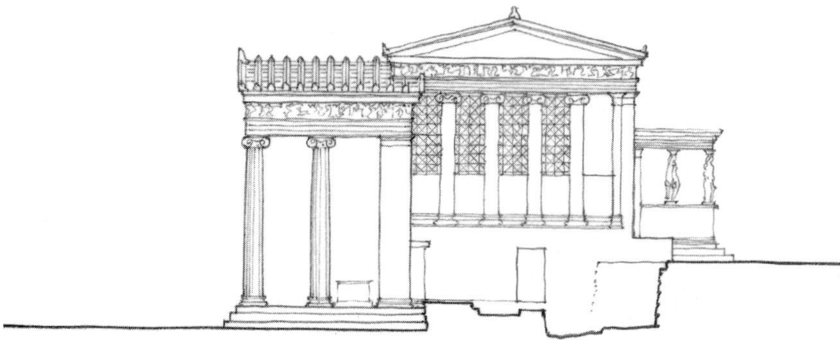

Section

**5.35 Erectheum, Acropolis, Athens**

Rising up over the entire story and at a 90 degree cross-axis is the edifice of the victor, Athena, facing east. At the diagonal, when one descends the external stairs on the northern side and before one enters the north porch, was an area dedicated to Zeus, the ultimate arbiter over the contest. His position seems to address the dynamic northeasterly pull of conical Mt. Lykabettos, for it too plays into the story. According to legend, Athena was absent from her city to retrieve a mountain to use on the Acropolis. Her sisters were curious about the chest in which Athena was protecting the young Erechtheus and opened it, contrary to Athena's orders. She became so angry that she dropped the mountain. How this plays out in the design is unknown, but from the agora below the acropolis, the mountain and the Erechtheum are clearly in dialogue.

Because of the constant warfare in ancient Greece, almost every city was divided into a lower town and an acropolis, a word that literally means a "city on the height." The Acropolis of Athens was no exception. It sits on a great isolated slab of limestone, tilted toward the west side from which it had to be approached. Already fortified with a wall by the Mycenaeans, it was held to be invested with divine presences from ancient times. A spring on its southern flank is still today considered to give forth healing waters.

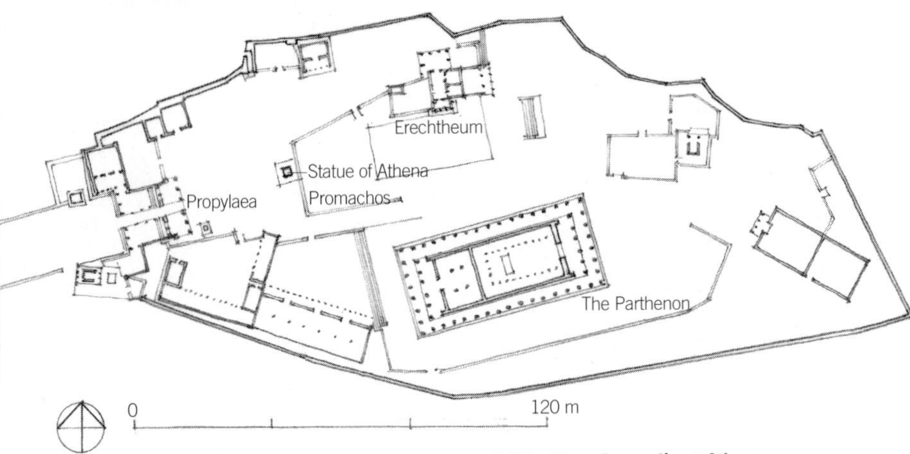


**5.36 Plan: Acropolis at Athens**

**Parthenon**

Over the course of two generations, beginning in 550 BCE, the people of Athens would establish democracy (510 BCE), win the battle of Marathon (490 BCE) over the Persians, and build an economic and political empire within mainland Greece. The preeminent political figure of the time was Pericles, who was responsible for rebuilding the Parthenon as a panhellenic sanctuary clad in white marble from nearby Mt. Pentelikon. An earlier temple had been destroyed by the Persians in 180–79 BCE. The new Parthenon, designed by Ictinus (with advice from Callicrates and Phidias) and built in less than ten years, between 447 and 438 BCE, was perched at the prow of the ancient hilltop of the gods, facing Mt. Hymettos to the east and the Bay of Salamis to the west. It stood as a grand monument and votive to Athena, the city's patron deity. The Parthenon was bigger than any temple ever before built on the Greek mainland, its *stylobate* measuring 30.9 by 69.5 meters. Early accounts of the temple call it Hekatompedos, or "Hundred Footer," referring either to its overall width or the length of the large eastern room of its *cella*, also know as the *hekatompedos*.

Size was not its only unusual feature. The east and west facades were lined with eight towering Doric columns, making the Parthenon the only *octastyle, peripteral* temple built in ancient Greece.

The interior of the *naos* has been variously reconstructed, some with a standard roof and others with an opening. The columns in the *naos* supported a second tier of columns, and there was a shallow rectangle in front of the statue, used possibly as a reflecting pool. The complexity and elegance of its construction was also unusual in its time and have remained a benchmark to the present day.

Underlying the construction is a system of precise refinements that control the delicate curvature of horizontal lines, the elegant convergence of vertical lines, and the nuanced size and spacing of the fluted marble columns. In no other temple was this visual tension as refined as in the Parthenon.

The *stylobate* was not a flat plane but rather like a section of a very large sphere; it curves upward toward the middle, rising 41 millimeters (1.6 inches) on its short sides and 102 millimeters (4 inches) on its long flanks. This curvature was carried upward through the entire structure, imparting a subtle upward curvature on the architrave, the cornice, and nearly every "horizontal" line of stone. Every column demonstrated entasis, or the slight bulging of the column's middle.

Entasis is a countermeasure to undo the optical illusion created by numerous parallel vertical lines that appear slightly concave.The entasis here measured only 20 millimeters of deviation from a straight line, much more subtle and restrained than the entasis of earlier temples. Moreover, each of the 46 perimeter columns was tilted slightly inward with the corner column tilting on a diagonal. If the columns of the short sides were to be extended upward, they would meet around 4.8 kilometers above the roof.

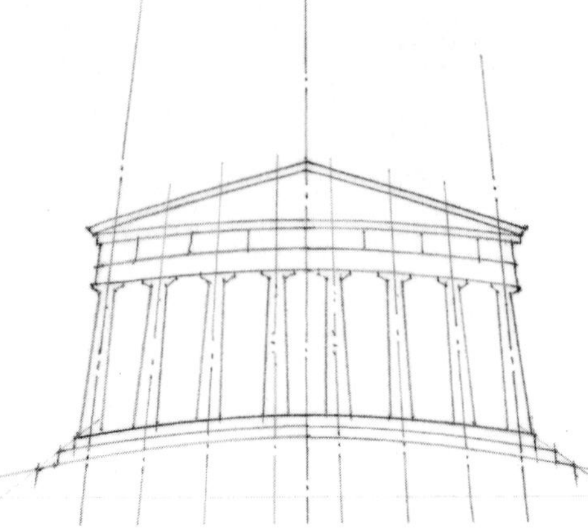

**5.37 Diagram of the curved stylobate and inclined vertical axes of the perimeter columns of the Parthenon.**

**5.38 Approach to the Parthenon from the Propylaea**

**5.39 Detail of the pediment of the Parthenon**

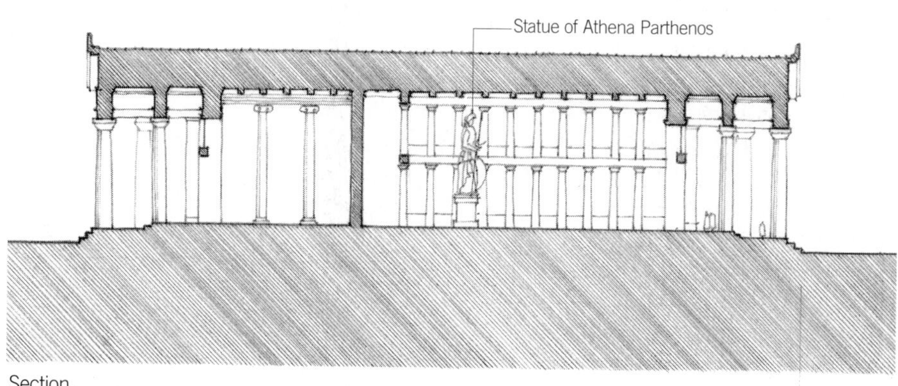


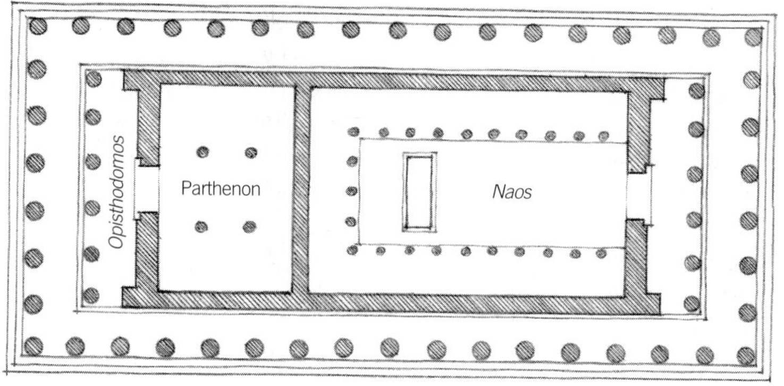

**5.40 The Parthenon, Athens**

While each of these refinements have functional advantages—the curvature to shed water, the angling to increase lateral structural support during earthquakes, and the corner adjustments to maintain proper column alignments with the metopes above, scholars, beginning with the Roman architect and historian Vitruvius, have argued that the refinements were mostly for aesthetic effect. The plastic quality of the architecture befits a building so rich in sculptural detailing. The artisans behind the Parthenon's sculptural program are not known. It is generally assumed that Phidias led a large team of sculptors who carved the pediments, metopes, and frieze. Much of the sculpture has been lost due to looting, defacement by Christians, and the explosion that nearly destroyed the Parthenon in 1687. But the drawings of French architecture student Jacques Carrey made in 1669 have been invaluable in reconstructing the form and meaning of the original sculpture. Thomas Bruce, the 7th Earl of Elgin, dismantled about two-thirds of Phidias' frieze and had it shipped to England (1801–6) where the so-called Elgin Marbles are in the British Museum, to the outrage of many.

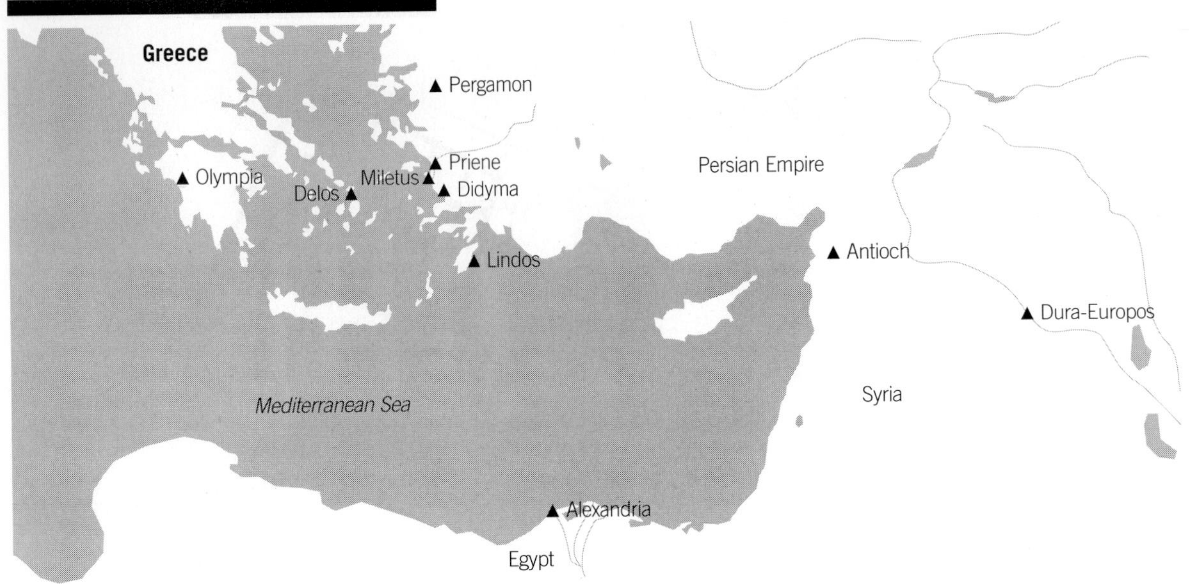


## EARLY HELLENIC AGE

Though the tendency in the narrative of the history of western architecture is to go from the classical Greeks to the Romans, one should not overlook the enormous impact Hellenism and the rule of the Ptolemies had in effecting that transition. Roughly, the period of transition corresponds to the death of Alexander in 323 BCE and the death of Augustus in 14 CE. While Alexander's empire collapsed soon after his death, it brought new life to the cities of Asia Minor, which began to cohere into a series of small but powerful quasi-autonomous states like Pergamon, Miletus, and the island of Delos. In Syria one saw the brief flourishing of the Seleucid Empire. It had been formed by one of Alexander's captains, who founded Antioch, Apamea, Laodicea, Seleucia Pieria, and, on the shores of the Euphrates, Dura-Europos, bringing in Greek settlers to farm the land. Dura-Europos, until it was captured by the Persians in 135 CE, was not only a military outpost but an important link in the attempt to reestablish trade routes to the east.

The monuments of this era show a loosening up of the conventions that governed Greek architecture, blending native elements with those of Greece (and vice versa), and showing above all a great deal of experimentation. Lateral and rear entrances in the *cella* ceased to be rare features, and wall surfaces were decoratively modeled. The time-honored system of having two metopes over each intercolumniation began to give way to three.

Hellenistic art is marked not only by technical virtuosity but also by a heightened sensitivity to emotional content that had never been attempted before. There was also a great deal of experimentation with new cults and religious practices, many centered on healing and bathing, Among those new religions were the followers of Christ.

Old cities like Athens, which became for a while part of the Kingdom of Antigonus, were given new buildings. Some were paid for locally; some came from foreign investments. The enormous Olympian Temple to Zeus in Athens, begun in 170 BCE, was paid for by Antiochus IV (d. 164 BCE) of the Seleucids on northern Syria. A new harbor, council hall, and residential quarter were added to Miletus. Assos redesigned its central agora with a long two-story high stoa. New cities were laid out, some as far away as Ai Khanum on the Afghan bank of the Oxus River.

Though planned cities go back millennia, the architecture of cities and the architecture of palaces or temples were generally speaking quite distinct. In Hellenistic cities, urbanism and architecture begin to overlap for the first time. Theaters, temples, villas, palaces, libraries, stadia, and streets are all equally important in Hellenistic cities. Though many Hellenistic cities would flourish only later during Roman times, the principal ones were Priene, Pergamon, and Dura-Europos. Rhodes was so wealthy that, when an earthquake destroyed the city in 225 BCE, citizens were able to rebuild speedily.

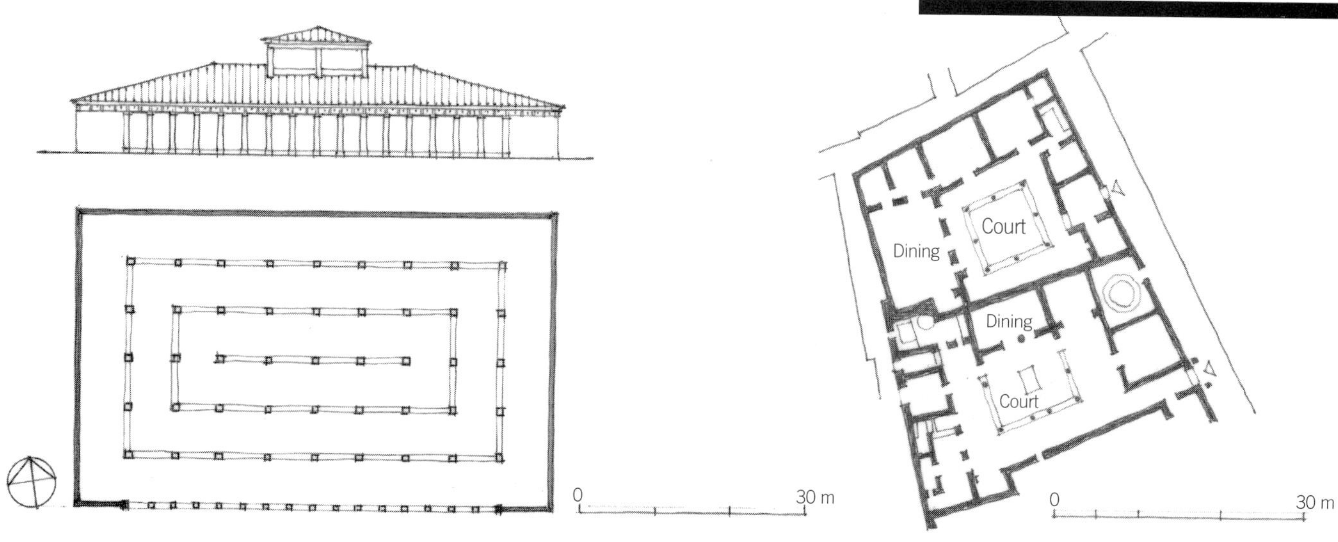


**5.41 Mercantile Hall, Delos, Greece**

**5.42 Plans of two houses, Delos**

### Delos

The economic engine that drove this tremendous expansion was not Athens but Egypt. After the breakup of Alexander's Empire, Egypt was claimed by a Macedonian king named Lagus who proclaimed himself Ptolemy I (d. 284 BCE). Once he had consolidated his power, his son, Ptolemy II (r. 285–246 BCE), began a series of financial and infrastructural reforms that made Egypt the economic marvel of the Mediterranean. By the time of Ptolemy III (245–221 BCE), Egyptian fleets controlled most of the shipping lanes of the eastern Mediterranean. Building on the old pharaonic tradition of state control, the Ptolemaic kings updated technologies and production systems, transforming the country with its population of seven million into a grain-producing machine of unprecedented proportions. The Ptolemaic rulers introduced the water screw of Archimedes and built machines with drums or wheels driven by humans for raising water and pushing back the desert. Salt production was escalated. Mines and quarries, as well as the development of a state-run bank, were integrated into the system. It was in some respects one of the first examples of state-supported modernization.

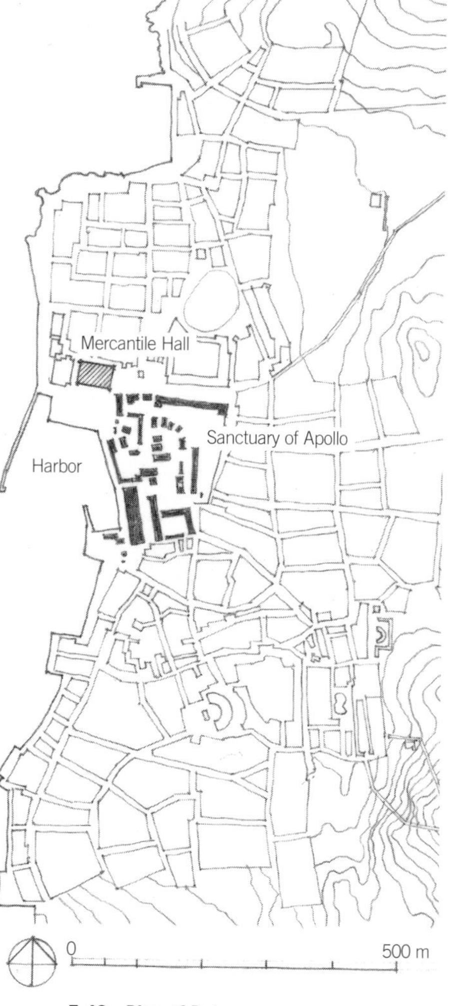


**5.43 Plan of Delos**

One of the places that most quickly adapted to the new world order was Delos. Though the island was small, one of the smallest in the Aegean, and though it had no local economy to speak of, it was almost equidistant from the various ports in the Aegean Sea. It entered into economic relations with Egypt and Macedonia to become the leading Mediterranean trading station. The tradition that had begun with the Minoans was perfected by the rulers of Delos. Money was made in the transfer of goods rather than in their manufacture and sale.

On one side of its harbor was a special landing place for the pilgrims visiting the sacred sites, on the other side, the large and new mercantile harbor fringed with storage houses, wharves, and commercial buildings. The Egyptians, bringing their grain for redistribution, were building shrines to their gods; Phoenicians were coming to sell ivory; Jews built for themselves a synagogue; and the Italians were on the scene as well, building an agora all of their own. Everything could be exchanged there, including slaves and spices. A Mercantile Hall measuring about 60 by 35 meters was built in 210 BCE, with houses for the merchants laid out with unprecedented richness.

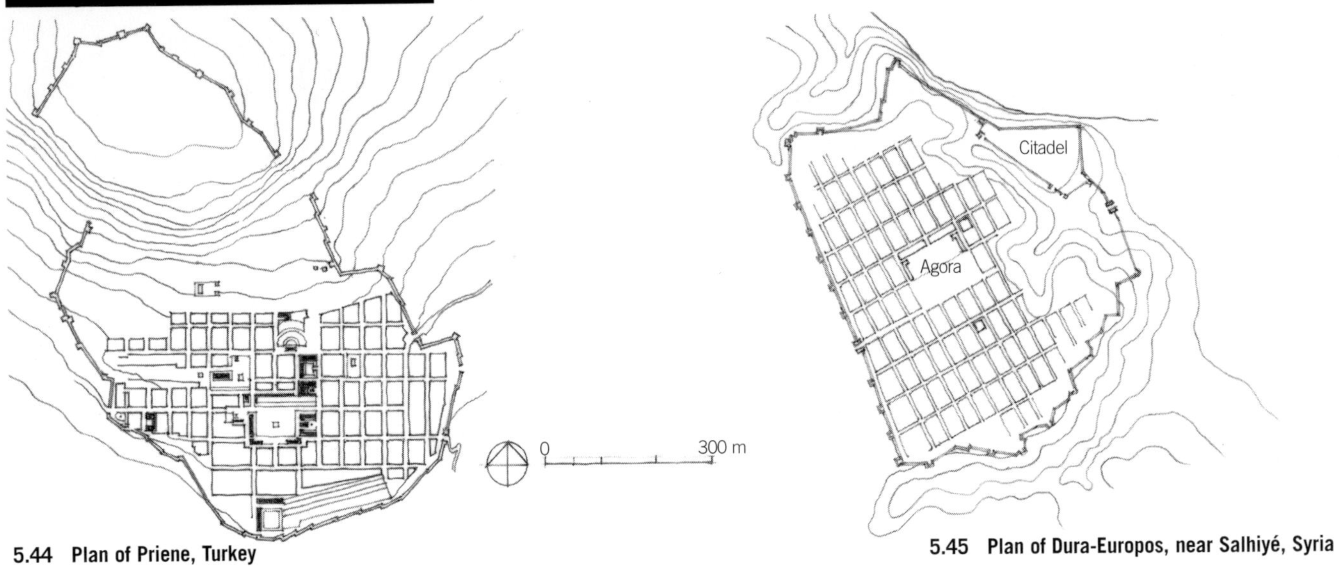


5.44 Plan of Priene, Turkey

5.45 Plan of Dura-Europos, near Salhiyé, Syria

### Priene

The city Priene was founded in 334 BCE to tap into the escalating trade between Anatolia, Turkey, and Egypt. It occupies a sloping ground beneath an almost inaccessible acropolis 300 meters high. The streets run east-west along level ground and are about 4.5 meters across. From south to north, with the ground rising steeply, the streets are mostly narrower. The principal civic elements of the city are embedded in the structure of this grid and yet in dynamic resistance to it. The agora, for example, juts out from the grid to the south and does not align with the side streets. Across from it is a three-block-long stoa. Up the hill a few blocks to the west is the platform with the temple of Athena, and a block higher yet but to the east was a theater with spectacular views into the valley below and the mountains across. Further northward yet, where the city ends and the steep slope of the acropolis begins, is a sanctuary dedicated to Demeter. A stadium and gymnasium define the lower edge. The city, because of its composite character, could easily appear to have been built up over time, but it is in actuality a skillful play of solids and voids, and of private and public zones, spread out over a difficult terrain.

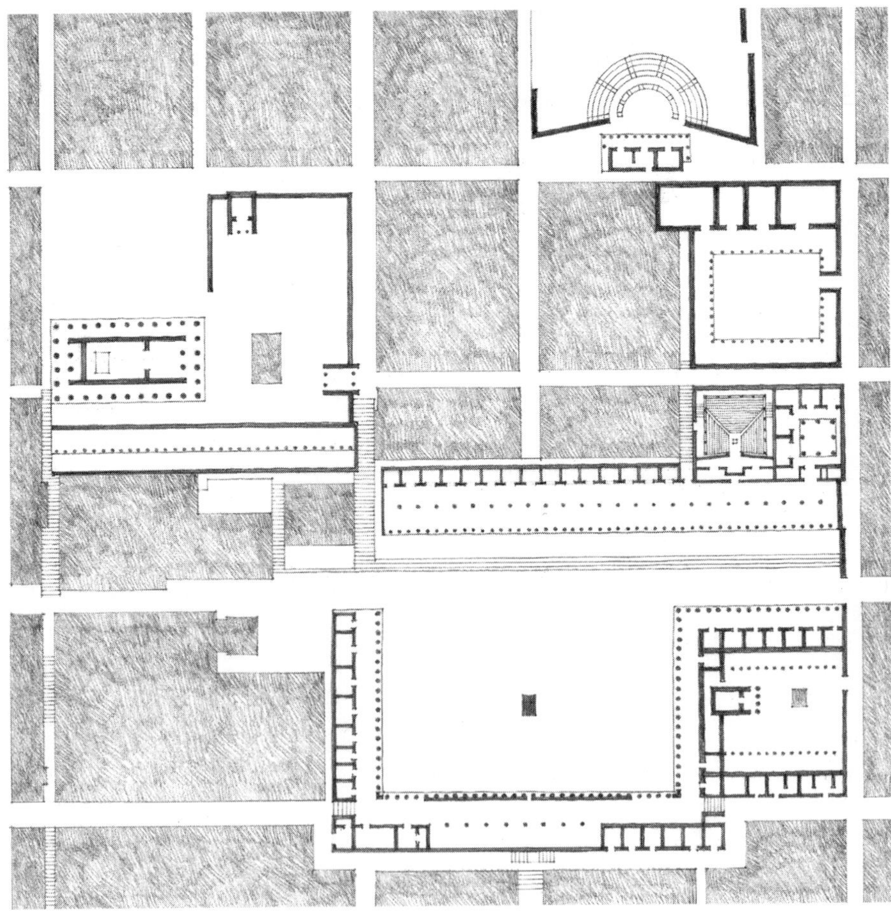

5.46 Plan: Agora at Priene

5.47 Temple of Apollo, Didyma, Turkey

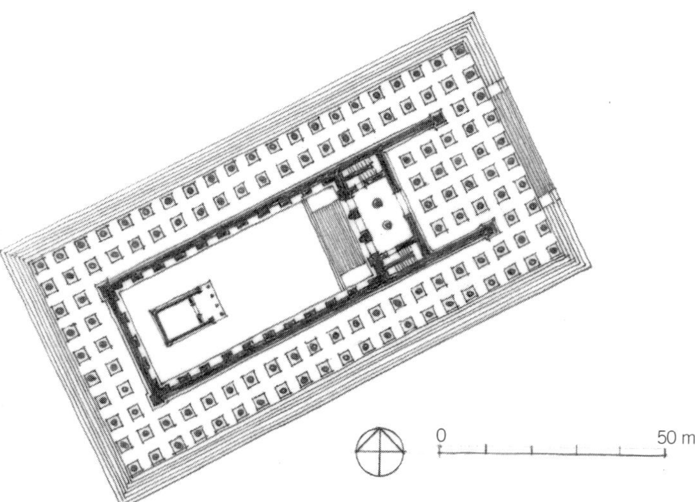


5.48 Plan: Temple of Apollo, Didyma

**Temple of Apollo at Didyma**

It is difficult to speak of a "Hellenistic temple" as a single aesthetic form. In the cosmopolitan environment of Western Asia, one sees different tastes in different places as well as variable influences. In Egypt, buildings of the Hellenistic era were designed in an Egyptian revival style. Such neoarchaisms were not outside the aesthetic interests of the Greeks. The Hellenistic aesthetic did, however, draw on centuries of experience in creating complex, composite relationships between space, landscape, and mythical narration—in fact, organizing it, as we have seen at Priene—into single aesthetic wholes.

One of the most spectacular Hellenistic temples in this respect is the unfinished Temple of Apollo at Didyma, south of Miletus. Sitting on a gentle hill, exposed on all sides, it contained the unusual feature of an open court, planted with bay trees, among which stood a shrinelike Ionic temple. Though several Greek temples, possibly even the Parthenon, had open interiors, this was something altogether different. The architects are said to have been Paeonius and Demetrios of Ephesus. Though much of the plan may have been laid out by them around 313 BCE, the work took well over 300 years to complete and was abandoned in 41 CE.

The temple's Ionic double *pteron* stands on a stylobate accessed by seven huge steps. Upon going up the steps, one enters into the deep porch of the *pronaos*, behind which is an antechamber. The antechamber is actually higher than the *pronaos*, with the door serving as a window from which the oracles were delivered. Standing among the *pronaos'* treelike columns, the tallest of any Greek temple, the windows would have appeared to be the mouth of a cave. Access to the inner courtyard was by way of small doorways on either side of the window, through sloping, dark tunnels roofed with barrel vaults. Penetrating through the dark grotto, so to speak, one enters into the sacred grove. But this "inside" was in fact an "outside." The artificial grove of trees, which is what the temple would have looked like from the outside, gave way to real trees on the inside. Furthermore, within that grove was another temple with its axis oriented toward the entry, for the small Ionic temple at the far end of the open *cella* faced a grand staircase leading back up to the antechamber from which the priests could officiate. It was a consummate example of Hellenistic brilliance, folding one temple compound into another.

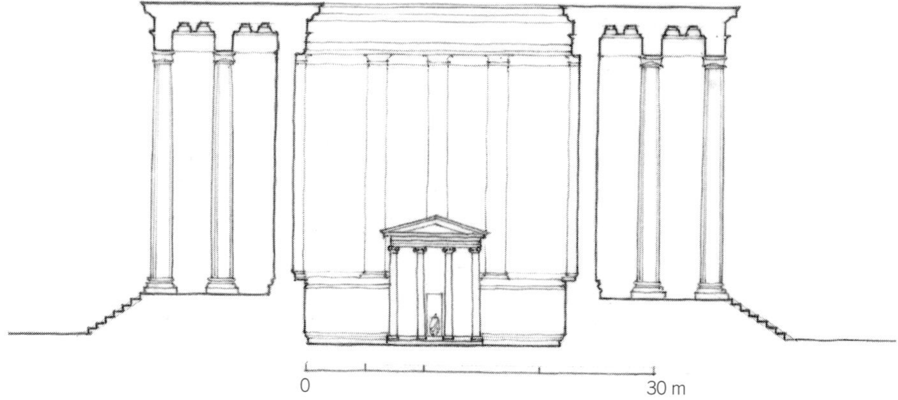


5.49 Section: Temple of Apollo, Didyma

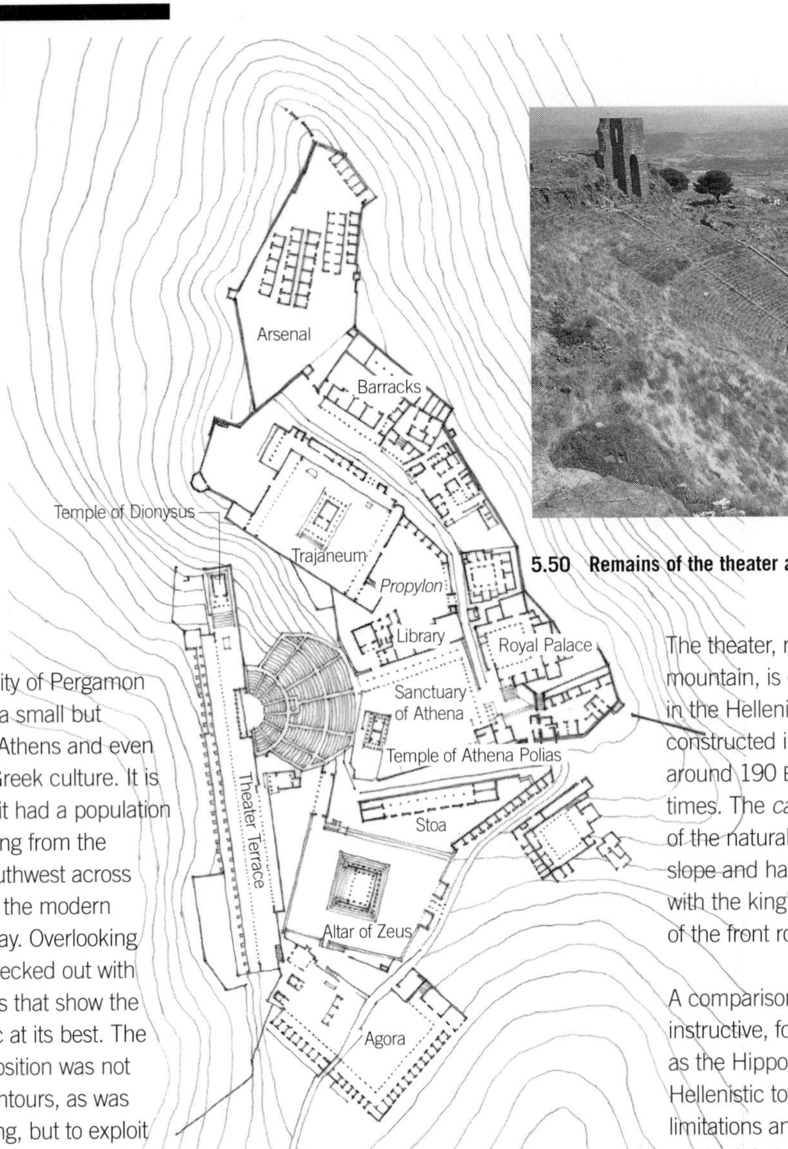


**5.50 Remains of the theater at Pergamon, near Bergama, Turkey**

**5.51 Plan of Pergamon**

### Pergamon

By the year 281 BCE, the city of Pergamon had become the center of a small but powerful city-state rivaling Athens and even Alexandria as a center of Greek culture. It is estimated that at its peak, it had a population of 300,000 people spreading from the mountaintop site to the southwest across the Caicus Plain, much as the modern town of Bergama does today. Overlooking the city was an acropolis decked out with an assortment of structures that show the Hellenistic spatial aesthetic at its best. The object of the overall composition was not simply to work with the contours, as was traditional in Greek planning, but to exploit them for their inherent sculptural qualities. At the heart of the acropolis stood a temple to Athena, the protectress of the city, dating from the beginning of the third century BCE and most likely the oldest structure on the acropolis. It is one of the very rare Doric temples in Asia Minor and was no doubt built as an homage to the Parthenon. It was enclosed in a *temenos* with stoas on three sides that clamp it into the hill. Just behind the stoa was the palace of Eumenes II. Behind another wing of the stoa but at a higher level was the famous library built around 190 BCE, which held up to 200,000 volumes. Further up is the military zone of the acropolis with its storehouses, officers' housing, barracks, and arsenal.

The theater, resting against the slope of the mountain, is one of the most spectacular in the Hellenic world. It was originally constructed in the third century BCE, rebuilt around 190 BCE, and refurbished in Roman times. The *cavea*, or auditorium, forms part of the natural contour of the west-facing slope and has room for 10,000 spectators, with the king's marble box just at the center of the front row.

A comparison of Pergamon with Priene is instructive, for it shows that, as important as the Hippodamian city grid-plan was, Hellenistic town planners also saw its limitations and, as at Pergamon, adopted a method that followed the lay of the land and indeed exploited it with great skill. At Priene the grid marches directly across and down the hill with no attempt to benefit from the almost precipitous site, whereas at Pergamon it is quite obvious that the planners considered the potential of the site from the very beginning.

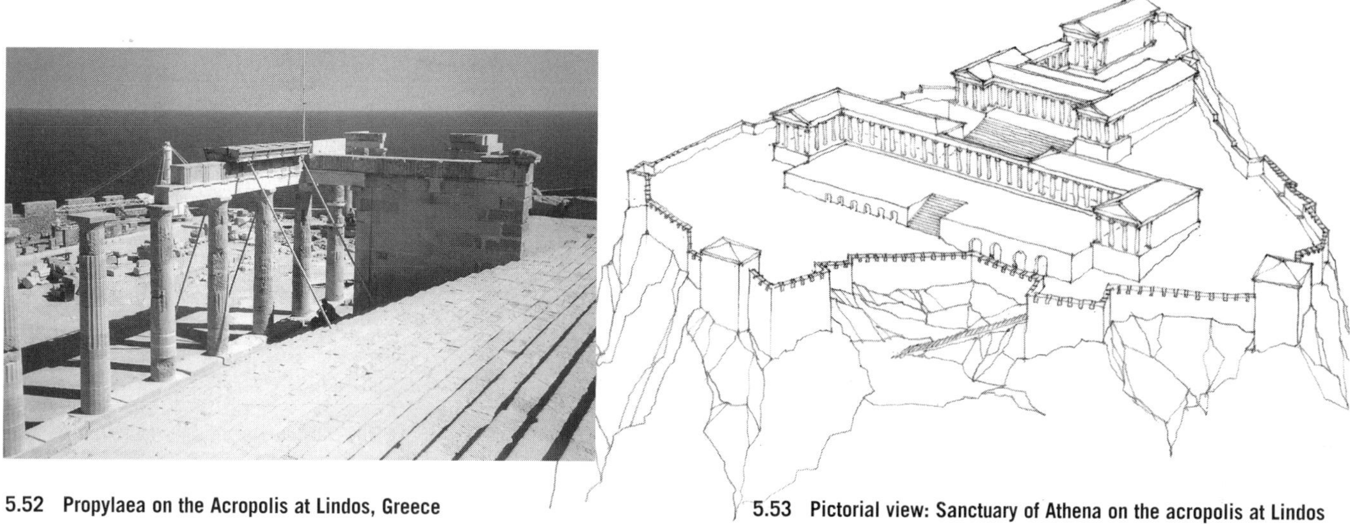

5.52 **Propylaea on the Acropolis at Lindos, Greece**

5.53 **Pictorial view: Sanctuary of Athena on the acropolis at Lindos**

Toward the south at the edge of the acropolis and on a terrace 25 meters below the Athena temple is the Altar of Zeus, built for Eumenes II soon after his victory over the Gauls in 190 BCE. The Gauls had been sweeping southward from western Europe, and even though they would continue to harass the northern borders of Mediterranean countries for centuries, Eumenes had managed to hold them at bay, at least for a while. The altar can be described as a U-shaped, Ionic, stoalike structure perched on top of a high socle with a vast flight of stairs leading up its west side to the level of the colonnade. On its enormous socle level was a frieze representing the mythical battle between the Olympian gods and the ancient Giants, symbolizing the triumphs of the Pergamon kingdom over the Gauls.

The altar stands in a courtyard atop an almost square plinth. It was surrounded by a colonnade that sheltered a wall on which there was another frieze celebrating the legitimacy of the Pergamon kings. This altar was not only the traditional end point of the sacrificial procession but also a political monument and even a war memorial. These are roles that had been in earlier days connected with the temple, the Parthenon being an excellent example. But here the altar reverted to an autonomous cultural object.

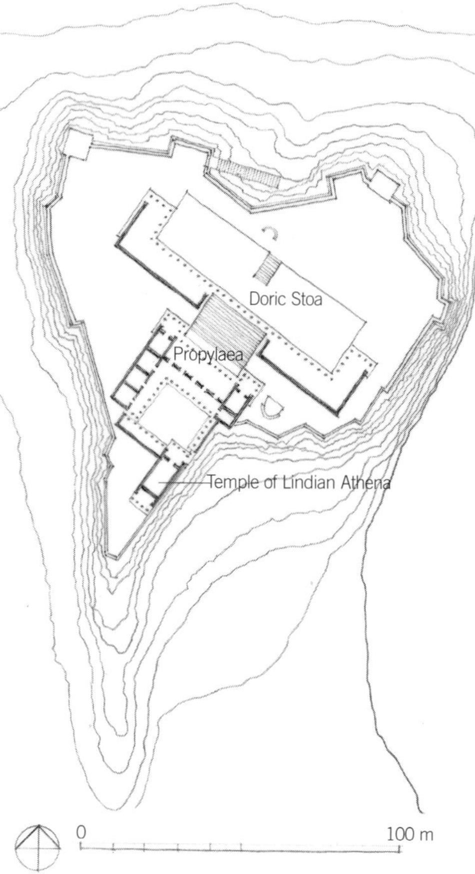


5.54 **Plan: Sanctuary of Athena on the acropolis at Lindos**

### Sanctuary of Athena at Lindos

Though Pergamon is a masterpiece of adaptation to the landscape, resulting in a multifaceted architectural environment, it went against the trend that favored symmetry and mastery over the landscape. For an example one can turn to the acropolis of Lindos on the island of Rhodes. The old temple, sited spectacularly on the edge of a cliff around which this sanctuary was built, becomes almost a cleverly concealed element in a grand and dramatic axial scheme. Nonetheless, and typically Hellenistic, when the old meets the new, the new adjusts and gives up the symmetry to create a dynamic tension between the two. At Pergamon, the structure barely fits the top of the acropolis. The first terrace is framed out over the landscape by an outward facing winged stoa, opened at the center by a broad flight of stairs. The stoa's front row of columns still manages to hold its edge to form a screenlike passage across the front of the steps. The steps lead to the top level and to a broad porch that opens into a courtyard with an altar in the middle. But the columns of the courtyard purposefully do not align with the front of the temple, which is allowed to intrude at the corner into the space of the courtyard.

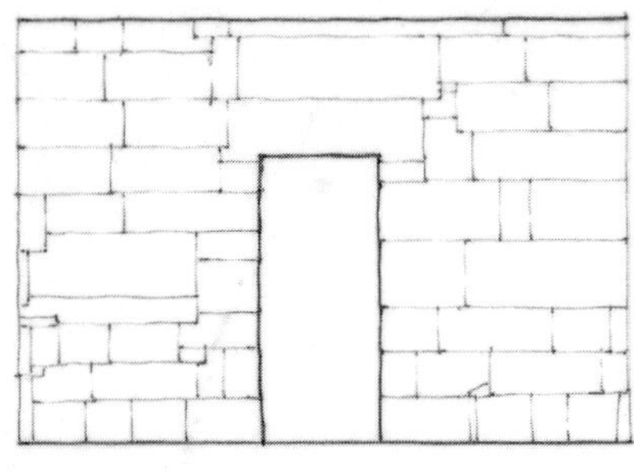

**5.55 Comparison between Middle and New Kingdom walls and Ptolemaic walls**

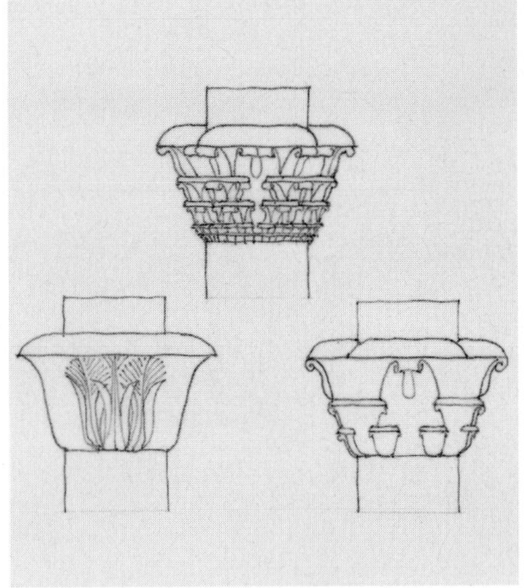

**5.56 Examples of Ptolemaic capitals**

### Ptolemies

The center of the Hellenistic world was Alexandria. Situated on the western extremity of the Nile River delta, the city was founded in 332 BCE by Alexander to serve as a regional capital. It soon became the largest city in the Mediterranean basin, and it was unlike any other, with libraries, museums, and a rich cosmopolitan culture. Though little is left of the city, the Ptolemaic period left a vibrant record of its art and architecture in many parts of Egypt, with the construction of about 50 medium-sized and large temple complexes, not to mention smaller architectural works. The Ptolemies and their queens had little problem following Egyptian tradition in positioning their statues as cult images.

The Greek architects made significant changes not only in spatial arrangements but in construction as well. In older times, a wall was fitted together from stones of different shapes, with the surface treatment unifying the appearance. The Hellenistic architects cut stones in regular courses, creating a clarity and precision, or, depending on one's taste, monotony and rigidity. But true to the Hellenistic desire for complexity, the new temples introduced a feature rarely explored in older Egyptian architecture, the section.

Middle and New Kingdom buildings were relatively flat volumes on the outside. Very little was learned about the interior arrangement of the temples from the perspective of an outside observer. Ptolemaic buildings emphasized the play of volumes and the contrast between the towering pylon, the surrounding walls, and the *hypostyle* hall peaking over the top of the wall. To add to the idea of contrast, Ptolemaic architects did not place windows at the top of the walls, as the earlier Egyptians had done; their *hypostyle* halls are pitch black if one closes the doors; Ptolemaic architects, also added ambulatories around the temple, making it an autonomous object within the confines of the outer walls.

Much innovation was devoted to elaborations of columns and their capitals. The capital could be round or single stemmed, quatrefoil or even eight stemmed. The plant motifs are palm, papyrus, lotus, and lily, even though the lily was not a native Egyptian species. The leaves of these plants could then come in different stacked variations, from two to five. The richness of form was augmented by lively coloring.

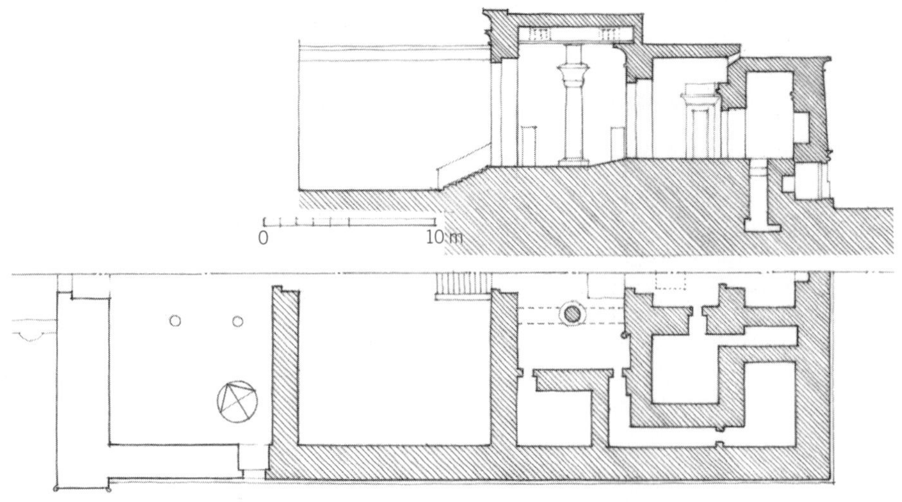


**5.57 Half-plan and section: Temple of Ptolemy III at Karnak, Egypt**

5.58 *Pronaos* at the Temple of Horus, Edfu, Egypt

5.59 Hypostyle Hall, Temple of Horus

## Temple of Horus

The Temple of Horus (begun in 237 BCE) is an excellent example of these tendencies. The building had not only to reflect the needs of the cult of Horus but also to serve as a pantheon for all cumulative aspects of Egyptian religion. The entrance is marked by a grand pylon 62.6 meters across and 30.5 meters high, leading to a court that has colonnades on three sides, a very un-Egyptian motif. The colonnade frames the entrance of the temple. But it is also a type of extended porch, framed by the perimeter walls to form a passageway. That passageway in turn connects to the ambulatory between the temple and its enclosing wall. What is Hellenistic in this design is that nearly every surface of the temple is covered by carvings and hieroglyphics, some of which were defaced by early Christians, who considered the images to be pagan. There were two *hypostyle* halls. The second one had rooms on the sides, a place for the preparation of sacred ointments to the west and a treasury for cult implements and clothes to the east. Once past the two *hypostyle* halls, one comes to an inner court in the center of which is the freestanding sanctuary of Horus. The court also gives access to 13 small chapels for the pantheon, all windowless and completely dark except for tiny slit entries. There was great care to align the pylon to the sun at noon on the midsummer solstice. At that particular moment, the pylon does not cast a shadow.

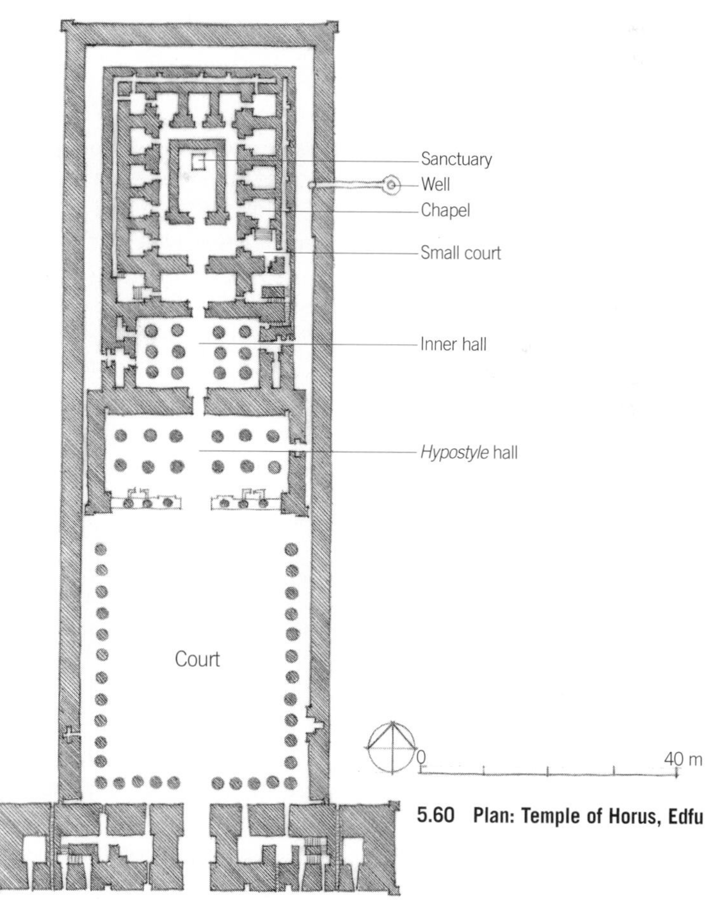


5.60 Plan: Temple of Horus, Edfu

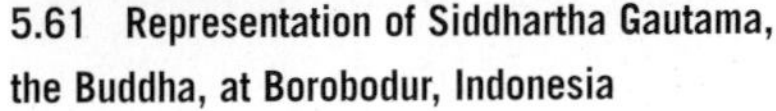

5.61 **Representation of Siddhartha Gautama, the Buddha, at Borobodur, Indonesia**

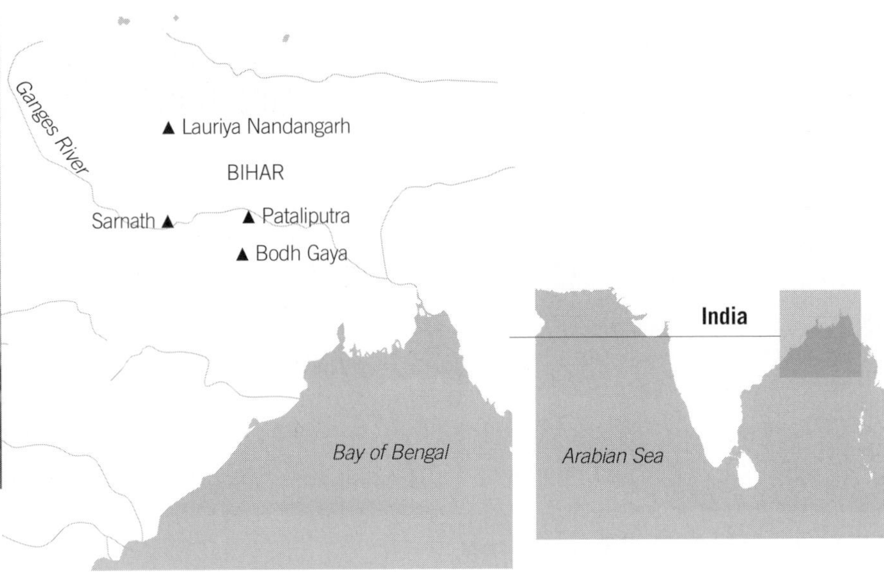


### ADVENT OF BUDDHISM

Judging by their extensive and colorful literature, the sixteen Vedic Indo-Aryan *mahajanapadas* (kingdoms) of South Asia must have been places of cultural ferment and economic prosperity, and yet they were known for incessant warfare, with armies provoking challenges and contending for supremacy. As cities were built and burnt, legends and heros were created, all interwoven into the epic literature of the time.

According to Romila Thapar, it was perhaps in response to the constant warfare that in the 6th century BCE two men, Siddhartha Gautama (the Buddha, or "enlightened one") and Mahavira Jain, rejected the elaborate Vedic ritual in favor of quiet meditation and the renunciation of violence. Gautama and Jain also rejected the significance of high birth and conceived of nirvana as accessible to all. For more on this, refer to Romila Thapar's *Early India: From the Origins to AD 1300*, which remains one of the basic texts on the early history of India.

Buddhism might have remained just another intellectual stream had it not been for Chandragupta Maurya, who conquered all the *mahajanapadas* and established the Mauryan Empire, the first major empire of South Asia. His timing may have been just right, and he may perhaps have been inspired by the suprahistorical figure of Alexander the Great, who had reached the borders of South Asia in 327 BCE. One way or another, by 323 BCE Chandragupta Maurya had established a kingdom that extended from the Hindu Kush mountains in the west to modern Myanmar in the east. Chandragupta's capital, Pataliputra, was located at the confluence of the Ganges and one of its tributaries, the Gandak. Not much has been recovered of this city, but an account by Megasthenes, the Greek ambassador in Chandragupta's court, describes it as about 15 kilometers long and 2.5 kilometers wide; girded with a wooden wall with 64 gates and some 570 towers, all pierced with holes for the discharge of arrows; fronted by a 200-meter-wide moat for the defense of the city and for receipt of the sewage of the city. Megasthenes also describes the city as having had gilded pillars, large artificial ponds stocked with fish, and extensive grounds with innumerable peacocks.

Excavations at the site have so far uncovered only what appears to be a large audience hall of a grand scale, as indicated by the surviving bases of 80 highly polished stone pillars set about 5 meters apart, whose original height is estimated to have been 10 meters. In form, the hall appears reminiscent of contemporary Achaemenid and Egyptian halls, clearly suggesting a lively east-west contact (although evidence of the exact mechanism and direction of this contact is debated). The strongest evidence of contact is given by the discovery of a pillar capital found at Bulandibagh, a subsidiary site of Pataliputra, whose composition and decorative motifs are visibly Eurasian and even Hellenic.

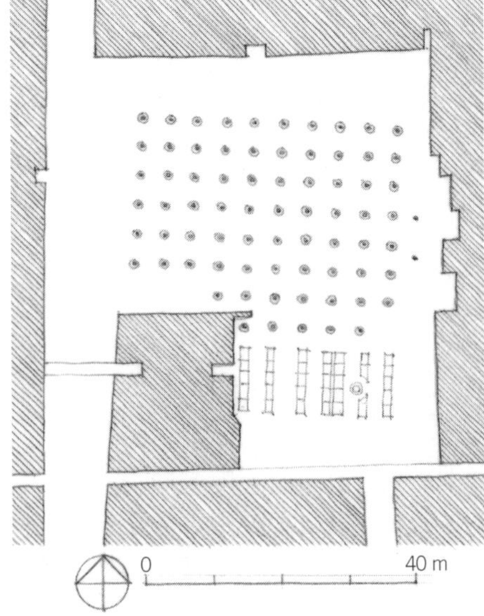


5.62 **Plan: Audience hall at Palaliputra, India**

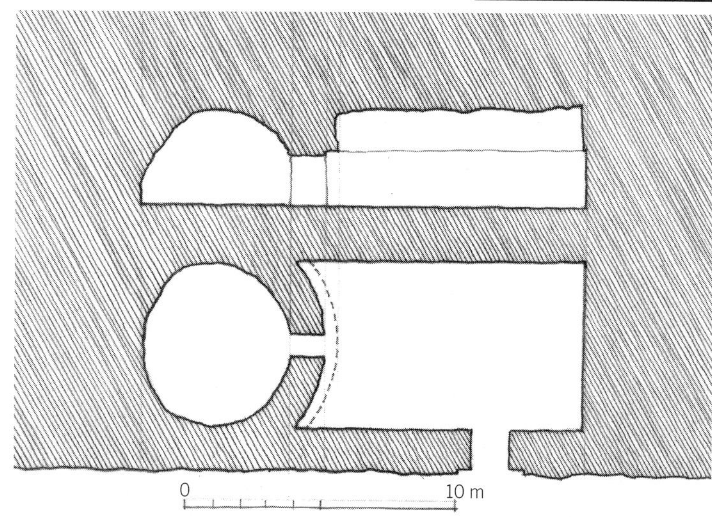


5.63 **Plan and section: Lomas Rsi Cave, near Bodh Gaya, India**

### Asokan Pillars

The most famous of the Mauryan kings was Chandragupta's grandson, Asoka (r. 272–231 BCE). After a particularly brutal battle, he is said to have converted to Buddhism, thus establishing it as the state religion. Making it his mission to spread the Buddha's teachings to the furthest corners of his empire, he relied not on the force of armies but on the words of the Buddha, to be transmitted orally by travelling emissaries and by edicts etched in stone. Carved in caves, rocks, and pillars, in the vernacular language of his kingdom, these edicts in many ways reflect the ideas of Asoka himself, who is referred to in them as Priyadarsin, or Beloved of the Gods.

5.64 **A pillar of Asoka**

Of the forty or so Asokan Pillars or Pillars of Law (*dhamma-thambani*) that are mentioned in the literature, about 20 have survived, though not all may be original to Asoka. One, still standing in Lauriya Nandangarh, Bihar, made from a single piece of polished sandstone, rises 12 meters above the ground and extends 3 meters into the earth. Though it is surmounted by an ornate capital, it is the shaft with the inscribed edicts that is of primary significance, identifying Asoka with the symbolic vertical axis that was supposed to have been erected by the god Indra to separate the earth from the sky.

The capitals of the Asokan pillars consist of a stylized lotus base that supports an ornamental drum on which there are sculptures of animals, ranging from the bull to the lion, signifying royal authority. The most famous of these is the capital of the pillar found at Sarnath, the site of the Buddha's first sermon, whose lotus base and drum is surmounted by a capital of four lions. Surmounting all this, at least originally, was the Buddhist wheel of law, which has, in turn, been adopted as the symbol of the modern Indian nation-state.

### Lomas Rsi Cave

In the mid-3rd century BCE, we find the earliest known rock-cut Buddhist caves, the Lomas Rsi Cave, in the Barabar Hills of Bihar. They were used by the Buddhist mendicants, or itinerant travellers, during the monsoon season, when roads and paths were unusable. The Lomas Rsi cave represents the first attempt to make a cave into a permanent dwelling. In the centuries to come this simple beginning was to flower into a tradition of rock-cut buildings that spread throughout South Asia and China. The interior of Lomas Rsi is unadorned—a rectangular hall with a circular room carved out to suggest the form of a thatched hut. Its entrance is carved to mimic the outline of a hutlike structure, complete with a bent-wood roof, supporting columns, and an ornamental elephant frieze.

5.65 **Entrance, Lomas Rsi Cave**

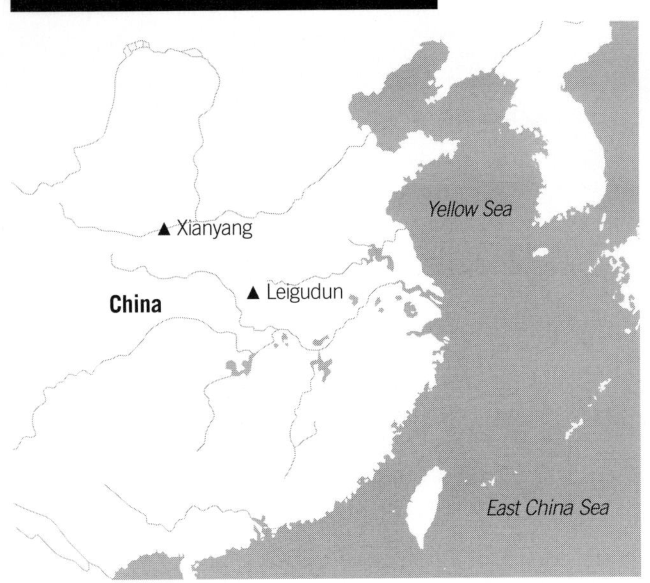


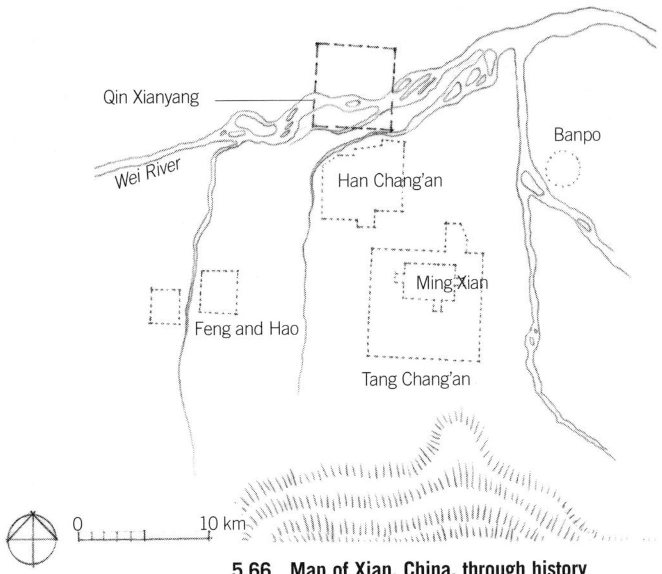


**5.66 Map of Xian, China, through history**

## CHINA: THE WARRING STATES PERIOD

In the Warring States Period (481–221 BCE), the old league of cities ruled by the Zhou nobility was replaced by a system of territorial states (seven major and about seven minor ones) under the command of monarchs who seemed to have engaged in feverish construction activity. They fortified existing city walls, multiplied enclosures and barricades, and established satellite towns, all primarily for the purpose of defense. An important transformation had occurred though; the monarchs no longer built ritual complexes, as the older Zhou had done, but elaborate palaces, organized axially and raised on high *tai* platforms. Furthermore, instead of building multistory wood and stone buildings, the architects placed their buildings on high foundation platforms. Unlike the enclosed and understated ritual complexes, these palaces projected themselves into space as imposing three-dimensional objects, visible from the distance. In general, the higher the *tai*, the stronger the claim to power by the ruler who commissioned it. In a time when there were numerous competing monarchic interests, and rulers and states were constantly being overthrown, theatrically establishing the authority of a ruler was critical to the image of authority. For instance, a Chu king constructed an imposing platform at the site of his meeting with other lords. History reveals that his guests, struck with awe at the sight of this platform, agreed to join the Chu alliance.

Ritual canons compiled during this period make a distinction between *jili*, auspicious rituals performed within the city in ancestral temples, and *xiongli*, inauspicious rituals performed outside the city at graveyards. Correspondingly, the vessels used in ancestral temples were called *jiqi* (sacrificial vessels) and those furnishing a burial were called *mingqi* (spirit vessels) or *guiqi* (vessels for ghosts). The architecture of tombs and graveyards became increasingly important at that time.

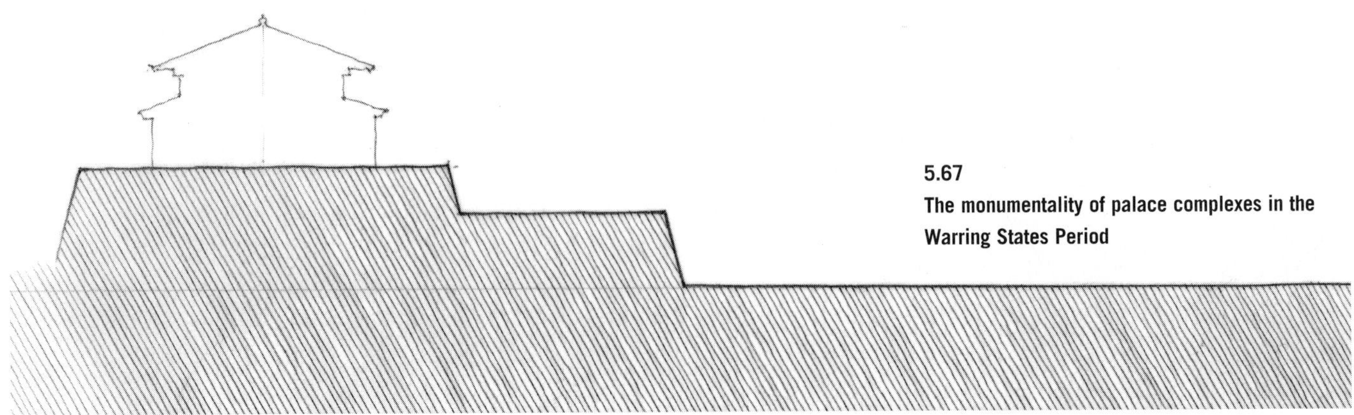

**5.67**
**The monumentality of palace complexes in the Warring States Period**

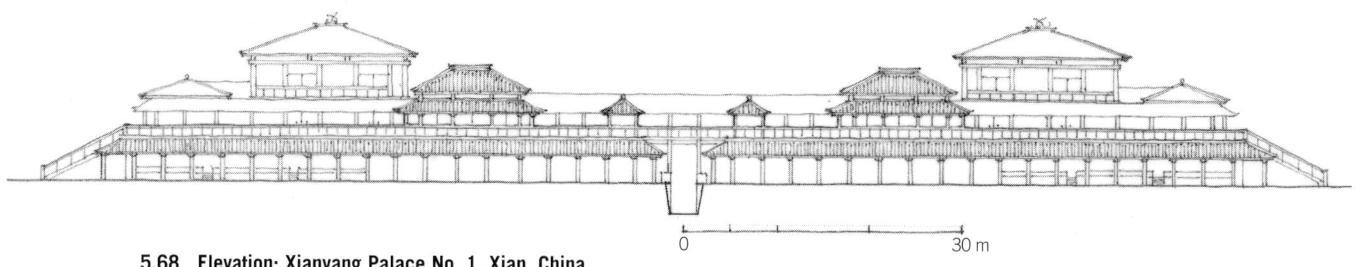


**5.68 Elevation: Xianyang Palace No. 1, Xian, China**

**Xianyang Palace**

A dramatic terrace pavilion, the Xianyang Palace No. 1 consisted of a series of rooms and corridors, built one on top of the other around an earthen core, giving the impression of a multilevel structure of great volume and height. While this structure has been identified with the Xianyang Palace of Qin Shi Huangdi, First Emperor of Qin, recent evidence suggests that it was first built during the Warring States Period and subsequently integrated into Shi Huangdi's palatial complex.

Located north of the Wei River, the palace's foundations are 60 meters long east to west, 45 meters wide, and about 6 meters high. The reconstruction suggests that the palace superstructure was symmetrical with two wings. The earthen core was surrounded by bays on all sides, creating the image of a three-story building of immense size. A drainage system guided water into underground pipes. The chambers were connected by intricate passages, and balconies were decorated with elaborate bronze accessories and colorful murals.

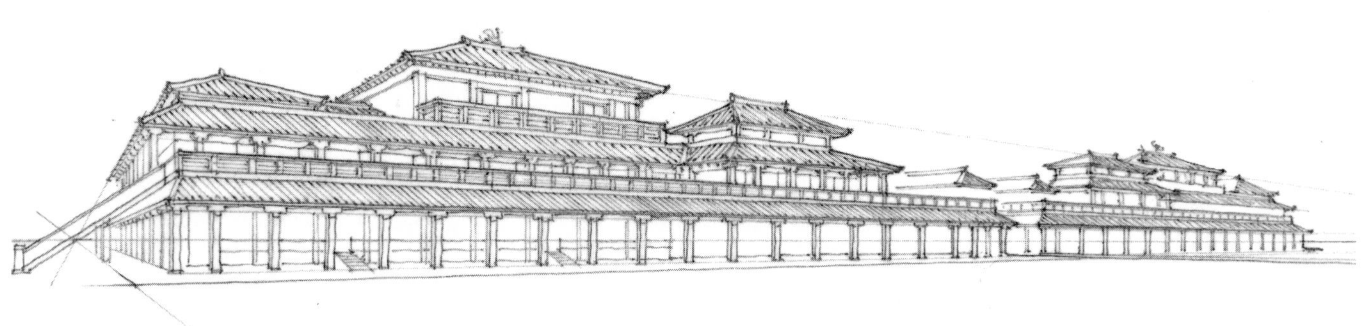

**5.69 Pictorial view: Xianyang Palace No. 1**

5.70 Tomb of Zeng Hou Yi as excavated

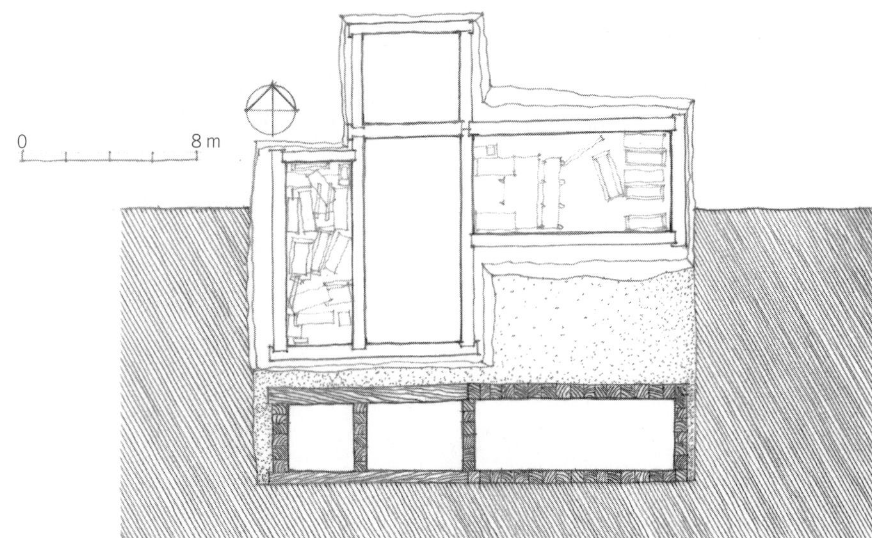


5.71 Plan and section: Tomb of Zeng Hou Yi, Sui Zhou, China

**Tomb of Zeng Hou Yi**

More than 6,000 large and small Eastern Zhou tombs have been discovered. The Tomb of Zeng Hou Yi ( Marquis Yi of Zeng) attracted international attention when a large collection of bronze objects was found there, including a set of 65 bells weighing a total of 2,500 kilograms, that have become world famous. The tomb consisted of an irregularly shaped vertical pit, 13 meters deep, and more than 200 square meters in area. It was divided by wooden planks into four chambers, with the principal chamber, on the east, containing the marquis' body. The body was placed in multiple coffins, and the space between the outer coffin and the chamber walls filled in with charcoal, clay, and earth to seal it as completely as possible. The eastern chamber had coffins of eight women, who may have been the musicians, sacrificed at the time of the burial (although human sacrificial internment was almost over by this time in Chinese history). The western chamber held skeletons of 13 young women, who may have been the ruler's concubines. The remaining two chambers were filled with ritual objects and weapons made of bronze, gold, copper, lacquer, wood, jade, and other materials.

A curious aspect of this tomb is that small windowlike openings connect all of the four chambers. Even the Marquis's outer coffin bears a rectangular hole, and his inner coffin is painted with doors and windows having lattice patterns. Similar openings have been found in several other Chu tombs. According to Chinese Daoism, when a person dies, his *hun* (the spiritual soul) would leave, but his *p'o* (the earthly soul) would remain attached to his body. The series of doorways in this tomb might be there to facilitate the movement of *p'o* in its underground "palace."

5.72 Coffins with window- and doorlike openings found in the Tomb of Zeng Hou Yi

5.73 Bianzhong bells found in the Tomb of Zeng Hou Yi along with a 125-piece orchestra and 25 musicians

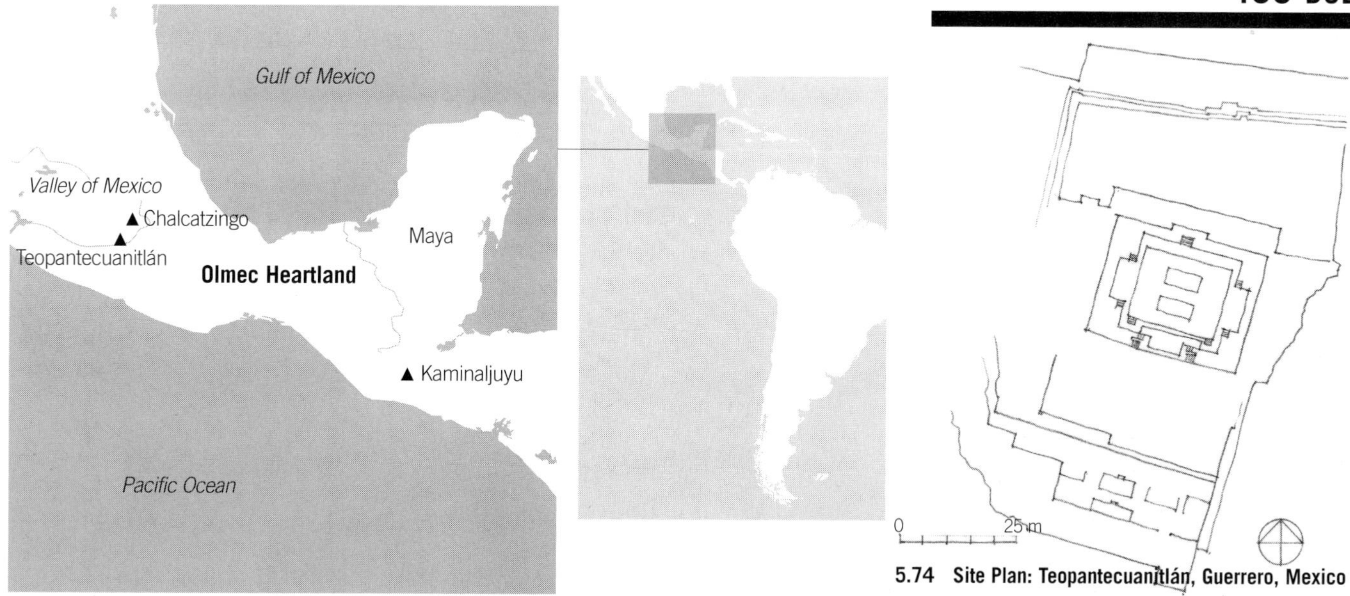


5.74 Site Plan: Teopantecuanitlán, Guerrero, Mexico

### LATE OLMEC CENTERS

In the central Mexican highlands, in the Amatzinac Valley about 65 kilometers southeast of Cuernevaca, lies Chalcatzingo, situated dramatically at the foot of one of three 300-meter-high volcanic cones that were considered sacred by the Aztecs, and probably also by the Olmecs. The area holds remnants of various cultures from 3000 BCE to the present, with the settlement reaching its peak of cultural development between 700–500 BCE, during the Middle Formative Period of central Mexico. Olmec traders of ceramics, agricultural goods, and raw materials are thought to have used the settlement as an outpost and trading center.

The site consists of platform mounds and terraces, but most notable are a series of bas-reliefs on several large boulders and on the cliff face depicting mythical and religious themes associated with agriculture, rain, and fertility. Some were portraits of members of the elite class. The similarities in style and symbology of these carvings to monuments on the Gulf Coast suggest a relationship between Chalcatzingo and the Olmec. Some have suggested that they established the iconographic foundation for all subsequent Mesoamerican mythology.

One of the carvings depicts a woman ruler enthroned in a stylized cave with clouds floating out of it. Like the special reverence reserved for caves as places of origin in Hindu culture and the architecture of South Asia, caves associated with female deities were especially revered in early Olmec culture and remained a force until much later in Mesoamerican civilization. One example of their abiding importance is the extraordinary clover-leaf-shaped volcanic tube cave that lies on axis beneath the base of the Pyramid of the Moon at Teotihuacán.

Teopantecuanitlán (The Place of the Temple of the Jaguar-God), one of the oldest Olmec sites to be discovered, lies in a remote area of western Mexico, about 160 kilometers south of Cuernevaca, at the confluence of the Amacuzac and Balsas rivers. It had two ball courts, a stone-lined aqueduct, and a large stone pyramid. The corbel vaulting in the pyramid dates to 600 BCE. The site occupies about 90 square kilometers and shows three phases of occupation. In the period 1400–1200 BCE, earliest construction was with clay walls in the ceremonial center with carved clay masks. Then from 1200 to 800 BCE, an irrigation system was put in place with fitted stone walls, aqueducts, and a stone-lined sunken court with drains. Four inverted T-shaped monumental sculptures bearing Olmec-style zoomorphic representations have also been found from this period. Finally, from the 800–600 BCE period, there are six structures built in a semicircle.

5.75 Bas relief from Chalcatzingo, Morelos, Mexico

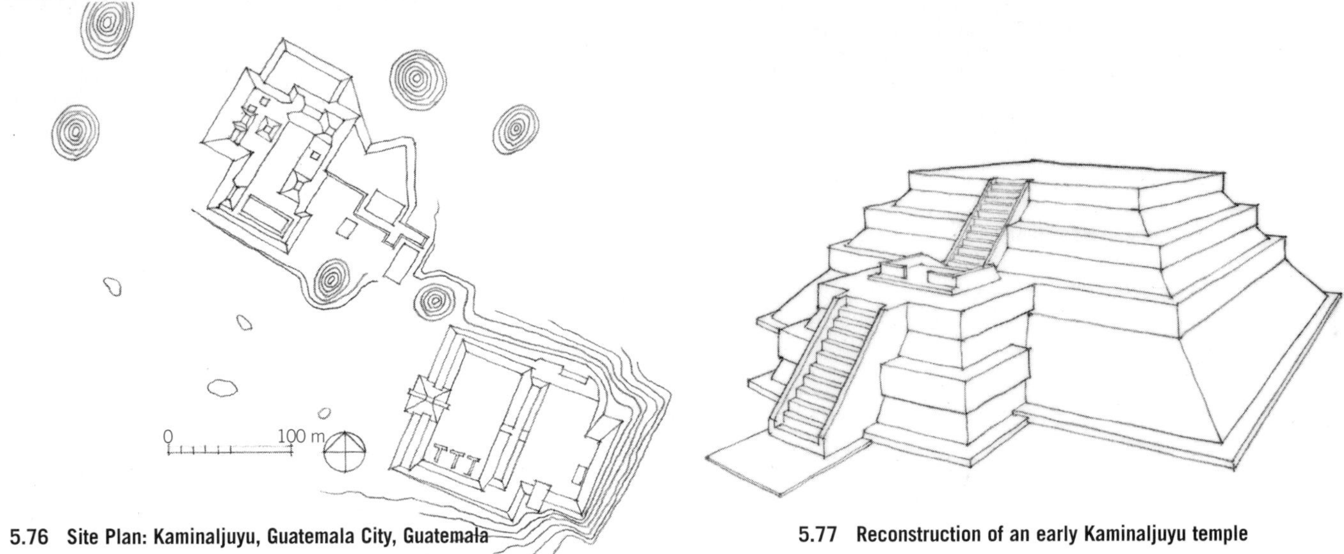


5.76 Site Plan: Kaminaljuyu, Guatemala City, Guatemala

5.77 Reconstruction of an early Kaminaljuyu temple

**Kaminaljuyu**

The earliest Mayan settlements arose in today's Guatemala, in the middle of the Yucatan rainforest, in an area where seasonal marshes enabled intensive agriculture. The Maya had inhabited the Peninsula since 1500 BCE, and by 1200 BCE, extensive trade networks were in place. Each village was linked to the next by causeways, which were paved with white stones, thus their Mayan name, sacbe or "white way." The roads formed a network that extended hundreds of kilometers. Cities exchanged salt for maize, obsidian for food stuff. Oyster shells were prized and stingray spines, shark teeth, conch shells, and turtle shells were all in demand for rituals. By 1000 BCE, the Maya elite were beginning to live in separate compounds and develop a highly esoteric religious philosophy.

The early Maya archaeological site, Kaminaljuyu, is situated just outside Guatemala City. Dating back to the Pre-classic period (800 BCE–300 CE), the site originally consisted of more than 100 platforms and mounds, distributed over an area of 5 square kilometers, organized around plazas that opened off wide avenues. Kaminaljuyu had its largest population and dominated the highlands of Guatemala between 300 BCE and 150 CE. Its people were early practitioners of irrigation agriculture, using aqueducts to distribute water. Around 400 CE, Kaminaljuyu came under Teotihuacán influence. This is when the largest mound found on the site was built (Mound E-III-3). It contained the tombs of two successive members of the elite.

5.78 Kaminaljuyu Stela 2

# 0

Eurasia was dominated by two great political units, China and the Roman Empire. Though the governments were different—Rome changing from a republic to an empire and China becoming highly centralized and bureaucratized—both were able to bring large territories into their sway. The power and size of these realms began to set in play a desire for trade between east and west that was to draw the two worlds and everything in between into increasingly close contact. But the time was not quite ripe for a continuous flow of goods. The Persians were sliding into decline, and in India, Asoka's empire was breaking into small kingdoms. But because transcontinental trade routes were now important economic engines, two formerly peripheral cultures emerged as powerful intermediaries, the Gandharan in Afghanistan and the Nabataeans in Jordan. Both were sites not only of vibrant cultural intermixings but also of architecturally important experimentations. The rock-cut tombs of the Nabataeans brought Hellenized animation to the still stiff forms of Roman architecture.

Initially, the ascendancy of Rome, in economic terms, cast a pall over the Eastern Mediterranean, where very little of consequence was built during the 1st century BCE. But with the change from a republic to an empire, Rome not only had centralized wealth to spend but also an interest in the cohesion of its expanding world. Building resumed in the east. The emperors from Augustus to Trajan changed the architectural face of the Roman world, building impressive temples, forums, and villas. In fact, what we today call classical architecture was the result of Rome spreading its vocabulary across the large geographical area of Europe, North Africa, and the Levant. Never had such a vast region been brought under the sway of such a unified architectural vocabulary.

In China, the Qin dynasty rose to power through the ruthless extermination of opposition and the establishment of a centralized government bureaucracy and a uniform currency. For this achievement the Qin emperor, Shi Huangdi is known as the First Emperor. It is from the name Qin (Ch'in) comes the name China. Shi Huangdi's rule was controversial and his methods ruthless. After his death his dynasty quickly collapsed and was replaced by the Han dynasty (202 BCE–220 ce), which, by way of contrast, is known for a long period of peace and is traditionally deemed China's imperial age. The Han maintained the Qin's unified and centralized empire, but it made the court more accountable and transparent. Thus although Shi Huangdi is known as the First Emperor, the mainland Chinese people are still known as "Han-Chinese." At the turn of the millennium, the Han dynasty ruled an area larger than the Roman Empire. Han architecture set the stage for subsequent dynasties. Although little remains of their actual palaces, cities, and monumental stone sculptures, clay models and literary references contain vivid descriptions. By the 1st century CE, "spirit roads" with stone monuments and figures lining the approach to an imperial tomb, replaced the terra-cotta armies of the Qin.

In South Asia, because of the disintegration of the Mauryan empire around 200 BCE, the nomadic Yueh-chi from Mongolia established the Kushan Empire (1st century BCE– 3rd century CE) that stretched from parts of Afghanistan and Iran to Pataliputra in the central Gangetic Plains in the east, and down to Sanchi in the south. Due to its unique location, the Kushan Empire served as a melting pot for people and ideas from India, Persia, China, and even the Roman Empire.

Teotihuacán in the Valley of Mexico and Monte Albán in the Valley of Oaxaca rapidly rose to power in Mesoamerica. An interconnected network of villages in the Yucatan Peninsula had evolved into the distinctive culture of the Maya. A strong trading network connected by causeways ensured that the Maya would evolve into a new Central American power in the coming millennium. On the Pacific Coast, in the area around central Jalisco, shaft tombs reveal a new culture of death. Built into the heart of the settlements, these tombs were intended to integrate the dead into the activities of feasting and everyday life.

0

Roman Republic
509–27 BCE

◄ **Pompeii**
From 6th century BCE

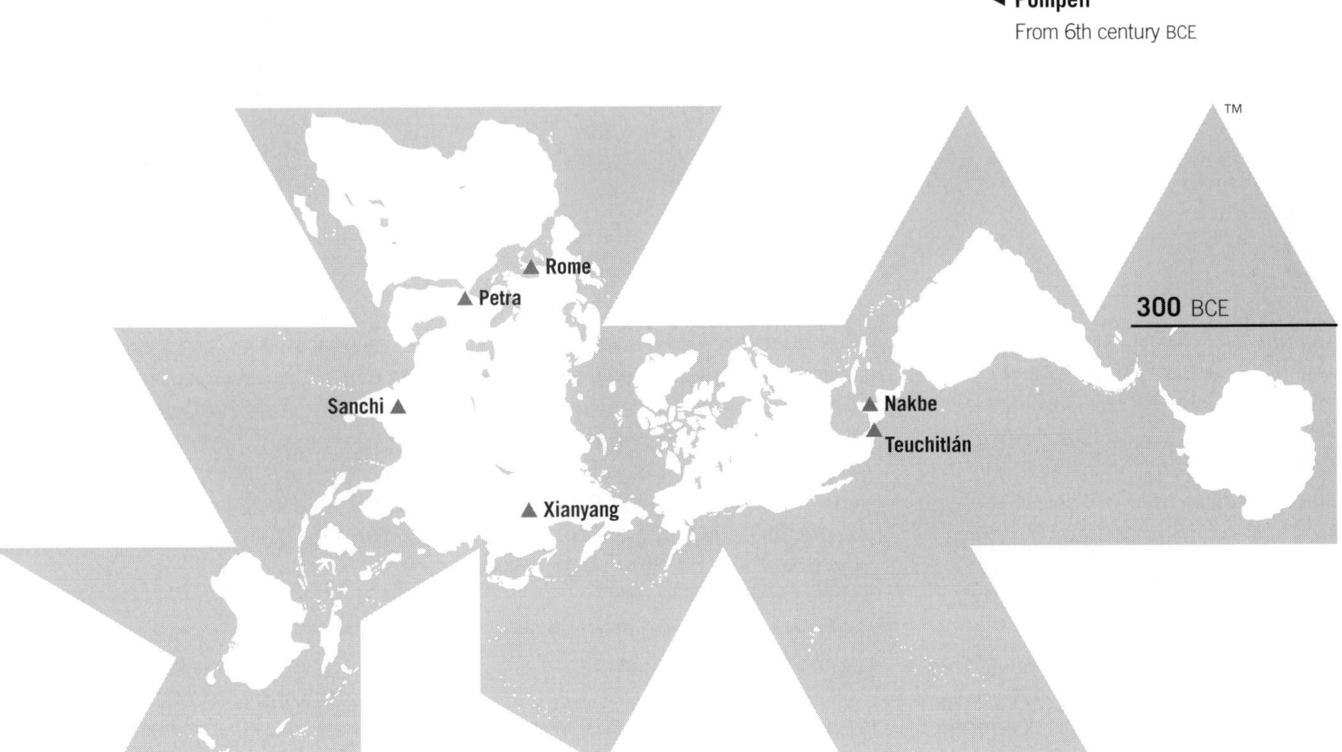


Eastern Zhou Dynasty
771–256 BCE

Qin Dynasty
221–206 BCE

◄ **Xianyang Palace**
4th–3rd century BCE

▲ **Nakbe**
350 BCE–250 CE

Roman Empire
27 BCE–393 CE

▲ **Temple of Zeus Olympius**
Begun 170 BCE

▲ **Colosseum**
72–80 CE

▲ **Pantheon**
125 CE

▲ **The Imperial Forums**
48 BCE–112 CE

▲ **Domus Aurea**
ca. 65 CE

▲ **Pergamon**
From 3rd century BCE

▲ **Temple of Fortuna at Praeneste**
40 BCE

▲ **Palace of Domitian**
92 CE

▲ **Hadrian's Villa**
118–134 CE

▲ **Petra Rock-Cut Tombs**
312 BCE–106 CE

**200** BCE — **1** CE — **200** CE

4239: Egyptian calendar
3763: Jewish calendar
756: Roman calendar
752: Babylonian calendar
547: Buddhist calendar
1 of the Yuanshi era of the Han Dynasty: Chinese calendar

▲ **Taxila**
150 BCE–100 CE

Mauryan Empire
ca. 323–185 BCE

Kushan Empire
2nd century BCE–3rd century CE

▲ **Stupa Complex at Sanchi**
ca. 100 BCE

▲ **Rock-Cut Caves at Junnar**
100–25 BCE

Wang Mang Interregnum
9–25 CE

Western Han Dynasty
206 BCE–9 CE

Eastern Han Dynasty
25–220 CE

▲ **First Emperor's Tomb**
246–210 BCE

▲ **Mingtang-Biyong Ritual Complex**
141–86 BCE

Teuchitlán Tradition
ca. 300 BCE–900 CE

▲ **El Openo**
300 BCE–200 CE

Preclassic Maya Culture
ca. 1000 BCE–250 CE

▲ **El Mirador**
150 BCE–150 CE

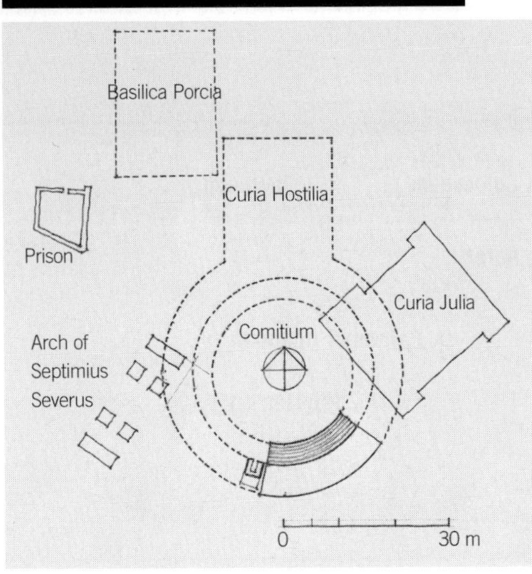


**6.1 Plan: Forum Romanum, Rome, Italy**

**6.2 Plan: Cosa, near Orbetello, Italy**

## REPUBLICAN ROME

The origins of Rome remain shrouded in myth. According to Virgil, it was Aeneas, fleeing from Troy, who founded the city. According to local lore, it was founded by Romulus. Archaeological evidence points to settlements dating back to Etruscan times, which may or may not have been taken over by newcomers. What is clear, however, is that during the 4th century BCE, Rome became conquest-oriented and that one by one, the neighboring cities fell to them until by the 3rd century BCE, Rome was in control of most of Italy. When the Greek city Tarentum in Sicily fell in 272 BCE, Rome emptied the city and enslaved all of its citizens. The fall of Syracuse followed in 212 BCE. The sack of Corinth in 146 BCE brought Greece itself under Roman control.

In the same year, following a century of conflict with the Carthaginians, Rome took Carthage, razed it, and sowed its ground with salt, taking uncontested control over the Mediterranean basin. A new class of entrepreneurs arose, the Equites, who played an influential role in the century before their power was suppressed by Augustus. The religious life of the Romans was centered around the Temple to Saturn (498 BCE) and the Temple to Concord (336 BCE) on the Capitoline Hill.

At the city's civic heart was the Comitium, a meeting place for the people (from whence comes the word "committee"), on the forum just below the Capitoline Hill. It had a speaker's platform, the Rostra, named after the ships' prows that were hung there following the Battle of Antium in 338 BCE. Its exact shape is in dispute, but it was a shallow circular amphitheater in front of the council chamber, or curia. Though not a building, it was a *templum* or sacred space unto its own and was laid out on a north-south axis.

To cement its control of its territories, Rome built garrisons, fortifications, and even cities, like Cosa, which was laid out in 273 BCE. It occupies a rocky site on the coast of Etruria, 100 kilometers north of Rome. Its eastern gate led to a road down an incline to the harbor. Roughly trapezoidal in plan, it contained at its highest point a Capitolium (built 175–150 BCE) as well as a long rectangular forum, located not at the center but on flatter ground in the northeastern corner of the city but connected axially to a principal street. It was in essence an enclosed outdoor urban space, accessed by gates and containing the religious, mercantile, and governmental core of the city. The Comitium, with its circular steps and a curia behind it, was on the longer northeastern side. Near the Comitium was a basilica.

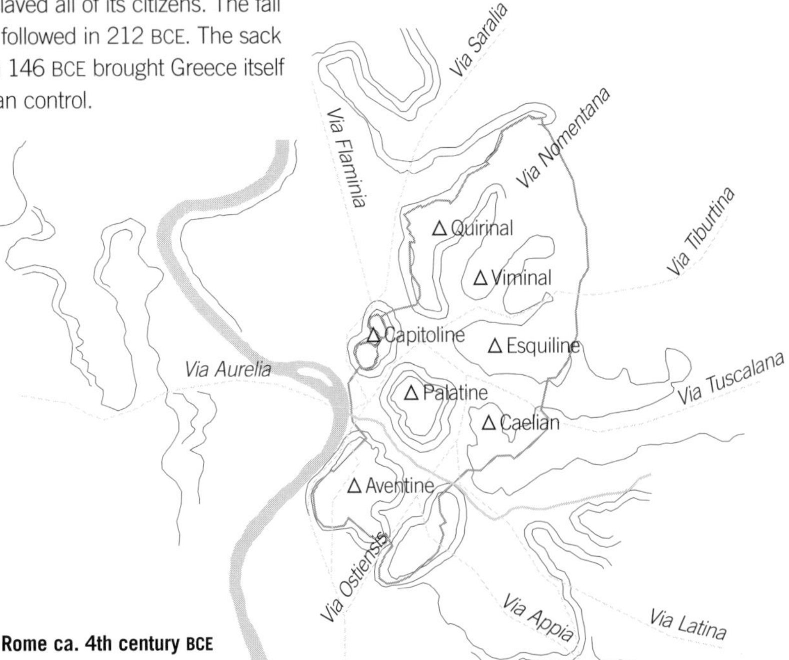


**6.3 Map of Rome ca. 4th century BCE**

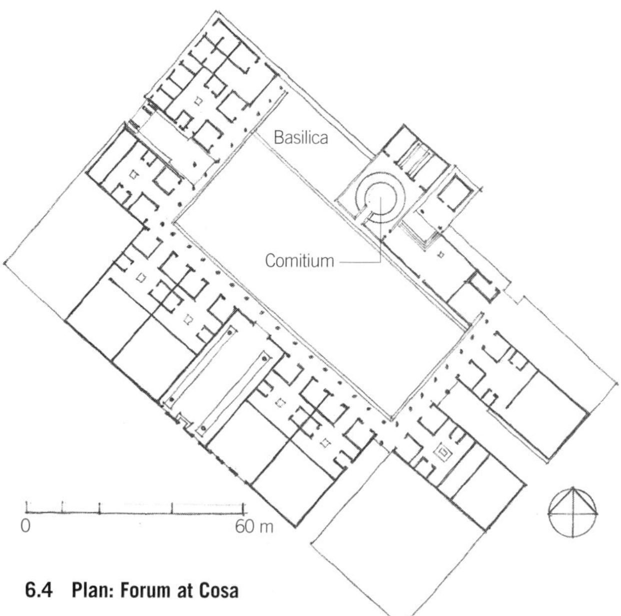


**6.4 Plan: Forum at Cosa**

**6.5 Forum and basilica of Pompeii, Italy**

**Pompeii**

Originally a Greek settlement, Pompeii was an old and flourishing town long before the arrival of the Romans, who transformed it into a bustling port and resort. Because of its destruction during the eruption of Vesuvius in 79 CE, it is today a sort of museum where one can study the daily life of a Roman town as it was 2000 years ago with its houses, big and small, and its gardens, restaurants, forum, and civic buildings. When the Romans took control in 80 BCE, all they had to do was make improvements to the forum to make it conform to their image. On the western side was the older Temple to Apollo, built around 130 BCE, and next to it a basilica from the same period. At the narrow southern end of the forum was a trio of municipal offices, including the senate house, and to the east, around the corner, a squarish unroofed building with its own *temenos*, used as a law court. Built around 100 BCE, it was unroofed so as not to violate the religious dictates that trials be held in the open air. The Romans added the Temple of Jupiter (80 BCE), rising high on a podium with two equestrian statues flanking the steps and an altar in front. Seen from the southern end of the forum, it closes the sweep of the open forum, drawing a direct connection to the mass of Vesuvius rising behind it.

They also reworked the eastern flank of the forum, adding a vegetable market and shops, the *macellum* (provision market), and a Sanctuary of the City Lares (guardian deities), built after an earthquake in 62 CE. Next to it is a small Temple of the Genius Augusti, flanking the Porticus Eumachiae. Tying everything together was a two-story colonnaded portico.

**6.6 Plan: Forum of Pompeii**

The origins of the building type known as a basilica are obscure; it has no clear precursors from the eastern Mediterranean, where its Greek name would seem to locate it. It thus appears to be a Roman invention. Whatever its history, it spread rapidly and had a clearly identifiable form—a central axis leading to an altar along the back wall and a raised roof over the central aisle, with light coming in through clerestory windows. Basilicas could be used for various purposes, but the ones in the forum were used as law courts. Curtained partitions isolated parts of the building. The basilica was to remain an architectural type into modern times. In Roman times the basilica corresponded to the Greek stoa except that the Roman version is a true interior space. It thus quickly served as a frame for activities and rituals, the giving of judgments, and the veneration of the imperial family.

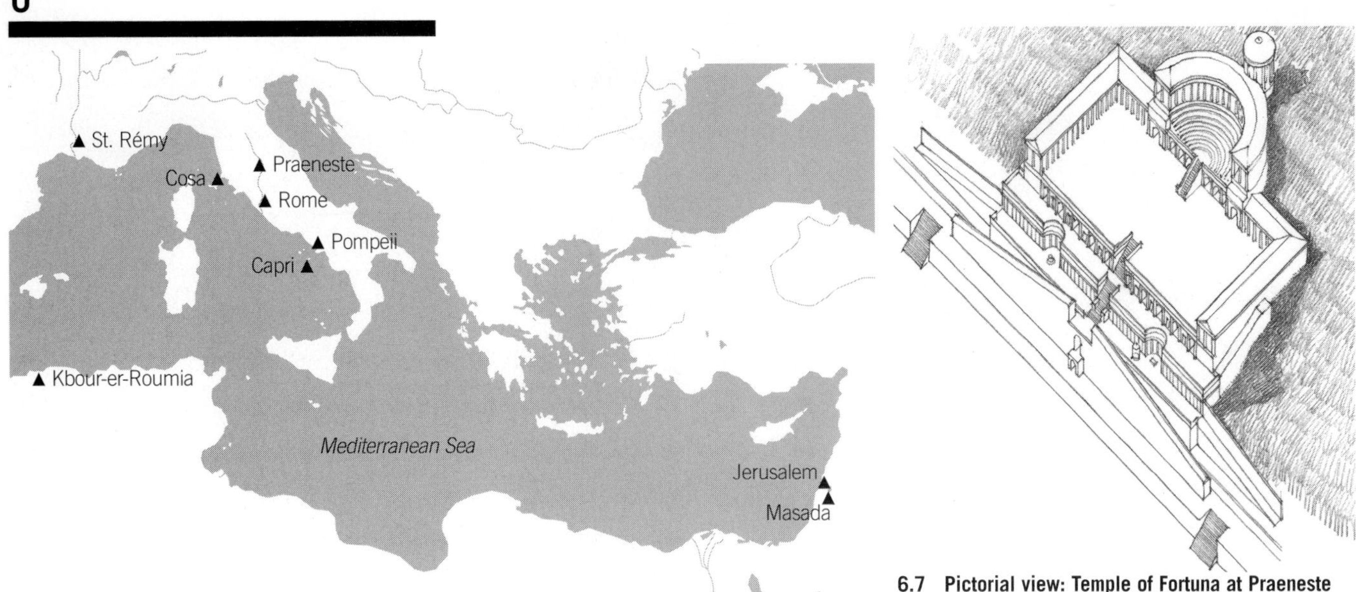


**6.7 Pictorial view: Temple of Fortuna at Praeneste**

**Temple of Fortuna at Praeneste**

Impressive is the adept use of concrete by Roman architects, its earliest use going back to 190 BCE, which contributed much to the longevity of Roman structures. By the time of Emperor Augustus (63 BCE–14 CE), they had developed a superior cement by the addition of pozzolana, a reddish volcanic ash named after its place of origin, Pozzuoli, near Naples. While the Roman architects might not have known the chemistry behind the bonding of concrete, they were well aware of its properties, one of which was that it set under water, which came in handy in the design of ports and harbors.

Though the famous Roman architectural theorist, Vitruvius, ever conservative, was still highly suspicious of the material when he was writing his treatise in 40 BCE, the architects of the Temple of Fortuna at Praeneste (Palestrina) showed no lack of confidence in their use of it. The temple (ca. 82 BCE) consisted of seven concrete terraces, accessed by ramps and stairs. The symmetrical arrangement, inspired by Hellenistic design notions, rises up the side of a hill 60 meters from the bottom. The uppermost terrace was framed by a Corinthian colonnade , double L-shaped, around a semicircular theater that was itself surmounted by a colonnade. Behind the composition, on the central axis, stood a small round temple or *tholos*, cut partially out of the rock, indicative of a particular sacred site. Except for the columns and other architectural elements, the structure was built entirely of concrete, including the support vaults.

Exploiting the potential of the new material, several kinds of vaults were used, including ramping and annular forms. That the facade of the upper level rested on a vault below rather than the wall beneath it was unthinkable in the days before concrete. There are also several innovations in the designing of the spaces. The two semicircular indentations in the façade of the lower zone, opening out to nothing more than the landscape, introduce design possibilities that would be expanded upon later by Roman architects.

How the temple was exactly used is still uncertain, but Fortuna refers to the goddess of luck. Also the site was associated with an oracle—a small gifted boy who randomly chose from among oak sticks inscribed with oracular pronouncements. The upper terrace and the theater were used for festivals, dances, and rituals.

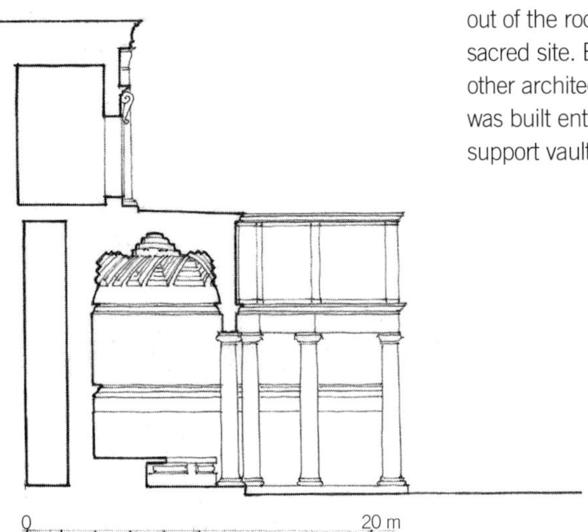


**6.8 Section of *hemicycle*: Temple of Fortuna at Praeneste**

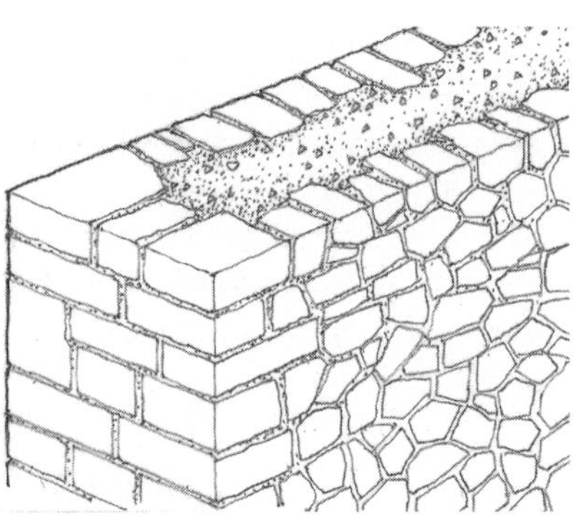

**6.9 *Opus incertum***

6.10 Residential fabric of Pompeii

**Roman Urban Villa**

Until the 2nd century BCE, Roman houses had followed the old Mediterranean plan with rooms grouped around the tall, rather dark atrium. But during the last decades of the Republic (which ended with the establishment of the Empire in 44 BCE), with the continued influx of wealth, the design of private houses became ever more splendid. Depending on the owner's wealth, a colonnaded garden inspired by Egyptian architecture was added behind the house. Exedras and libraries were installed, as well as fountains, summer dining rooms, and even private baths. Windows became bigger and walls were ornamented with illusionistic pictures. Upstairs dining rooms with views to the street were also added.

A remnant of urban fabric of Pompeii, destroyed in 79 CE, shows how densely packed the houses became as they expanded into the urban block. Clearly some families had bought out their neighbors and attempted to define an orderly progression of spaces out of the chaotic jumble. One can compare this with Sirkap, in present-day Pakistan, founded by the Greeks around 190 BCE. It shows a dense fabric of houses with little differentiation in scale. A single urban villa in Pompeii could be as large as an entire city block in Sirkap.

Rome's wealthy class, building on Etruscan traditions, placed great value on the importance of feasting. Meals had become elaborate affairs, prepared by professional cooks, served on silver plates, with occasional drinking bouts. In 182 BCE, the Senate passed a law regulating the size of parties, but it did little to stem the tide. Villas grew to enormous scale and can be found in the hills or by the coast. They were embellished with dining pavilions, towers, colonnades, fish ponds, and formal parks.

During that time, wealthy Romans began sending their sons to Greece to learn rhetoric, which could come in handy for a future career in law or politics. The Romans also admired Greek art and architecture, but they had little interest in Greek literature, music, or science. The Romans brought a sundial from Greece, but it took them a hundred years to learn that by having moved the sundial they had to adjust it for the change in latitude.

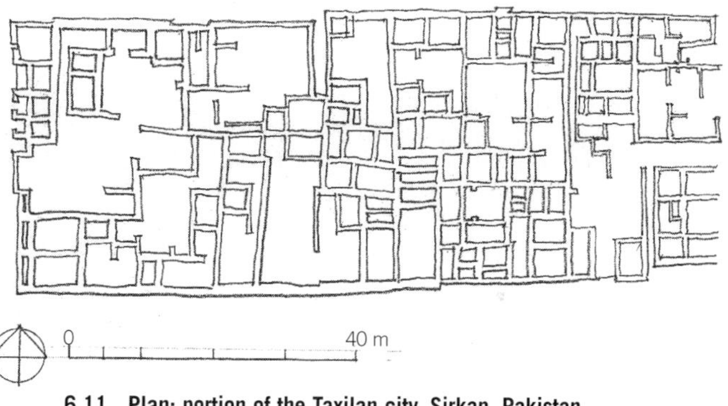


6.11 Plan: portion of the Taxilan city, Sirkap, Pakistan

6.12 Tomb of Marcus Vergilius Eurysaces, Rome

6.13 Monument of the Julii, St. Rémy, France

## Republican Tombs

Death, prior to Hellenism, was either a rather ignoble affair or ritualized only for the kings. But with the rise of a wealthy merchant class and Hellenistic emotionalism, we see the emergence of a funerary architecture for the wealthy class that became an autonomous form of architectural expression. Although this can easily be dismissed as a minor architectural typology, it played a key role in setting up a field of experimentation in which architects worked out complex matters of siting, proportion, and program. The tomb of Marcus Vergilius Eurysaces (30 BCE) is a case in point. A wealthy Roman baker, he asked the architect to design something on the theme of a *panarium* (receptacle for storing bread). By necessity of its location, it is trapezoidal in plan. The exterior is decorated with large rows of vertical tubes that hold the *panarium* framed by pilasters at the corners. The top has been lost, but it was most likely a pyramid. The Monument of the Julii in St. Rémy, France is more sedate. It consists of three zones: a socle or foundation zone, a four-sided arch, and a delicate round *tempietto* on top.

In Dugga in Tunisia, one finds a 21-meter-tall tomb monument built by Nubian masons for a Carthaginian or Numidian prince. Inscriptions list the architect as a certain Ateban. The lowest story rests like a vast exposed foundation for a *crepis* and a temple on top with four attached columns on the side that, in turn, becomes the base for a tower.

The so-called Tomb of Absalom in Jerusalem is a mixed construction with the lower part carved out of the bedrock while the remainder is constructed of ashlar. In the lower part, a socle supports a cubic box, the faces of which are decorated with Ionic half-columns. Though the bases are Ionic, the entablature is Doric. On this rests a plain and unornamented attic element that is the base for the drum and a concave conical roof. The whole is 20 meters high.

6.14 Tomb of Absalom, Jerusalem

6.15 Tomb of the Christian woman (Kbour-er-Roumia), Algiers, Algeria

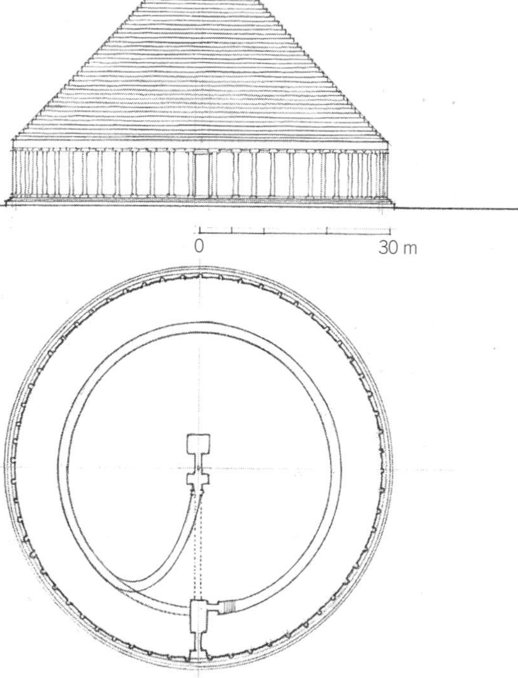


6.16 Plan and elevation: Kbour-er-Roumia

## Tholoi Tombs

In Algiers, one finds several tumulus tombs that obviously harken to ancient traditions. Such tombs had proliferated in the age of the Etruscans some 400 years earlier. Particularly impressive is the Tomb of the Christian woman (Kbour-er-Roumia), located in Algiers, west of Tipsa. It has a diameter of 60 meters and rests on a low square base. A three-stepped *crepis* supports a ring of sixty slender Ionic half-columns that decorate a drum from which rises a stepped conical hill, terminating in a circular platform 32 meters above the ground. The crowning sculptural elements have been removed. To reach the tomb, one traveled along a spiral corridor. It is dated to around 19 BCE. Though such a tomb might strike one as alien to the classical sensibility, these types of tombs were the model for the Mausoleum of Augustus in Rome, built in 28 BCE. It has a circular base 87 meters in diameter and is composed of five spiral rings with radial walls creating the structure. The outside was covered with travertine and had a Doric frieze. Flanking the entrance of the building were two Egyptian obelisks. One of the obelisks is now in the Esquiline square and the other in the Quirinale. Flanking the door of the grave were bronze tablets summarizing the emperor's achievements. On top of the base of the monument, surmounted by a tumulus planted with cypress trees, stood another cylinder on which was a shallow mound with a bronze statue of the emperor at the peak.

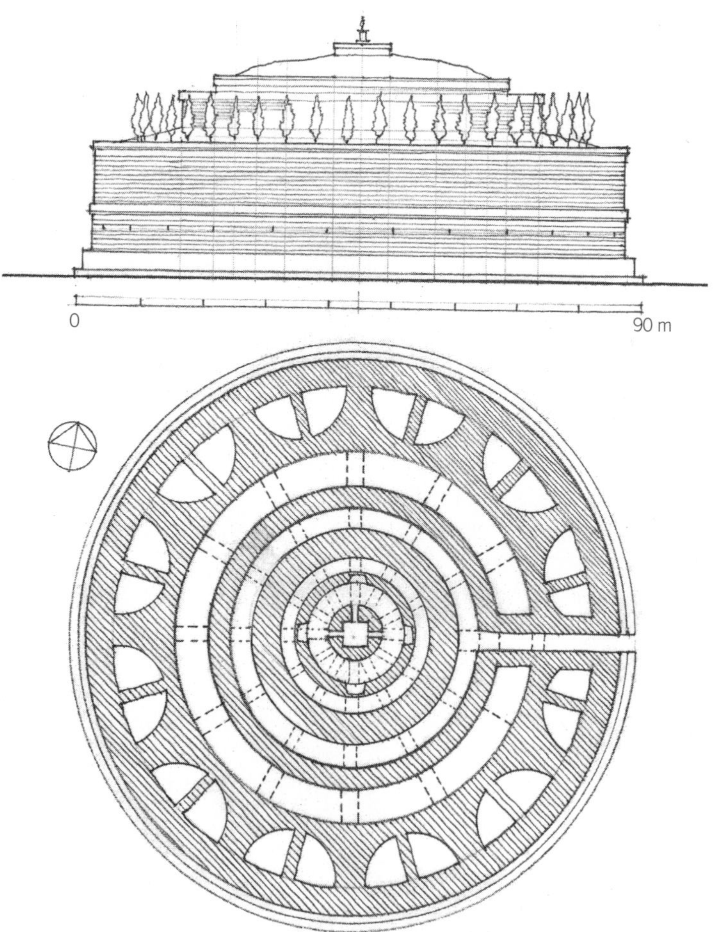


6.17 Plan and elevation: Mausoleum of Augustus, Rome

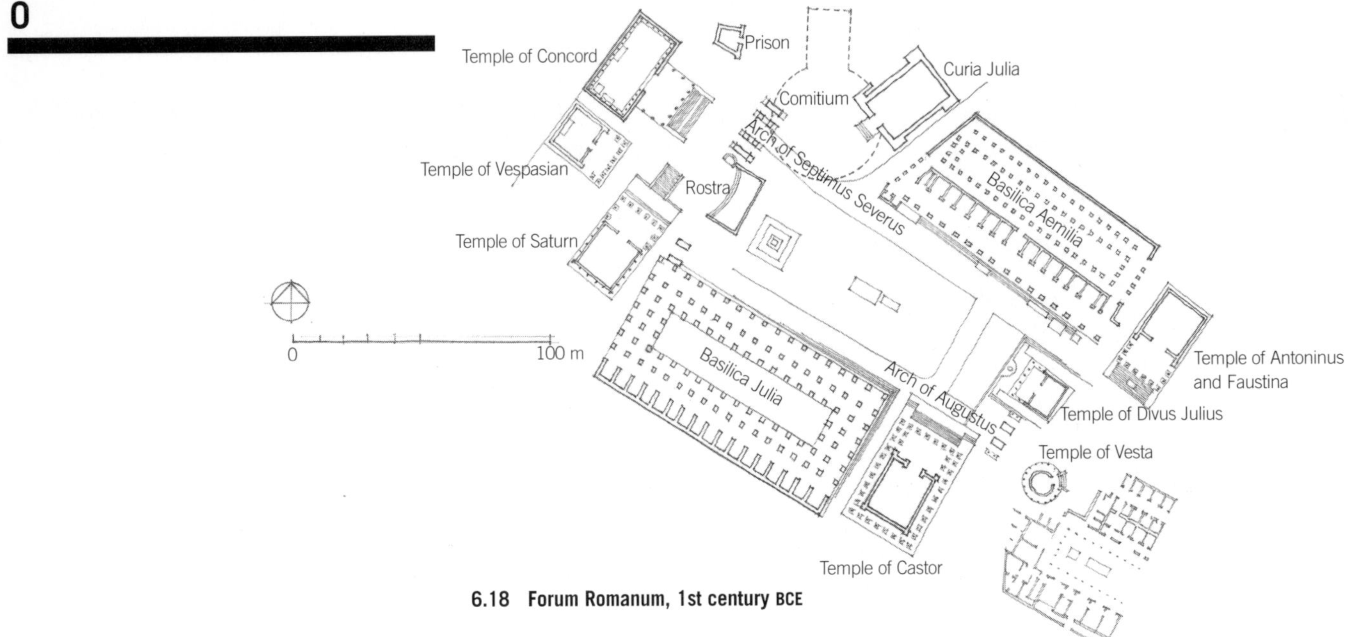


6.18 Forum Romanum, 1st century BCE

## AUGUSTAN ROME

The shift from Republic to Empire fell in line with the larger Hellenistic trend toward the deification of rulers. But it was backed up with unimaginable power and wealth, much of which Augustus put to architectural use. When he began his rule in 27 BCE, it is said that he found Rome a city of brick, but when he died, he left it a city of marble. This is not far from the truth, for in the 40 years of his reign, Augustus practically rebuilt the entire city, enlarging roads and redesigning infrastructure, but more than anything, he entirely remodeled the Roman Forum.To understand the magnitude of Augustus' efforts we have to remember that before Augustus' long tenure (27 BCE–14 CE), Rome was an unattractive and even an unsafe city. It was inhabited by a population of one million, and though the government attempted to maintain control, corruption, speculation, and mismanagement meant that temples were neglected and public structures crumbling. Many parts of the city were slums. Fires broke out continuously in 16, 14, 12, and 7 BCE. Floods ravaged low-lying areas.

The shift from Republic to dictatorship under Sulla and then under Caesar, meant greater control could be imposed. Caesar had begun several projects to upgrade the city. He even planned to straighten the Tiber. His assassination in 44 BCE brought these plans to a halt, but his ambition was passed on to Augustus who instituted an imperial system that allowed him to gain control over all aspects of Roman life. Among his efforts was an attempt to bring order to the core of the city. After a major storm, he asked for a study of roof tiles. He also created a new water system, restored 82 temples, increased spending on building and street repairs, and even established a fire brigade of 600 slaves.

6.19 Basilica Julia, Rome

One of Augustus' first acts to bring monumental architecture to the city was to finish the Forum of Caesar, which was begun by his predecessor. It was rectangular in shape, roughly similar in scale to the old forum but enlarged to the north and connected to it by a portal. The temple of white marble sat on a high podium, dominating one of the narrow ends. The building had columns on only three sides, giving the appearance of the *pteron* and the *cella* having been snapped into each other. The fundamental idea was once again Hellenic, but the simplicity and orderliness set it up as a prototype. The new forum encroached, however, upon the old Comitium, which had to be moved further to the south. The Senate House, where Caesar was murdered, also had to be rebuilt. It was placed so that it fit neatly along the Forum's perimeter at the southern corner. These transformations were only the beginning. Early in Augustus' reign, he completed the Basilica Julia, which served as a courthouse for the 180 members who sat in four panels and dealt with wills and inheritance matters. The building is 101 meters long and 49 meters wide, with its long side defining the edge of the forum. Lightweight partitions were used to accommodate different needs. Opposite the Basilica Julia was the Basilica Aemilia. It had been restored by Julius Caesar but was rebuilt by Augustus. It had a 16-bay, two-story façade, richly articulated with columns and marbles, and it was considered one of the most beautiful buildings in Rome.

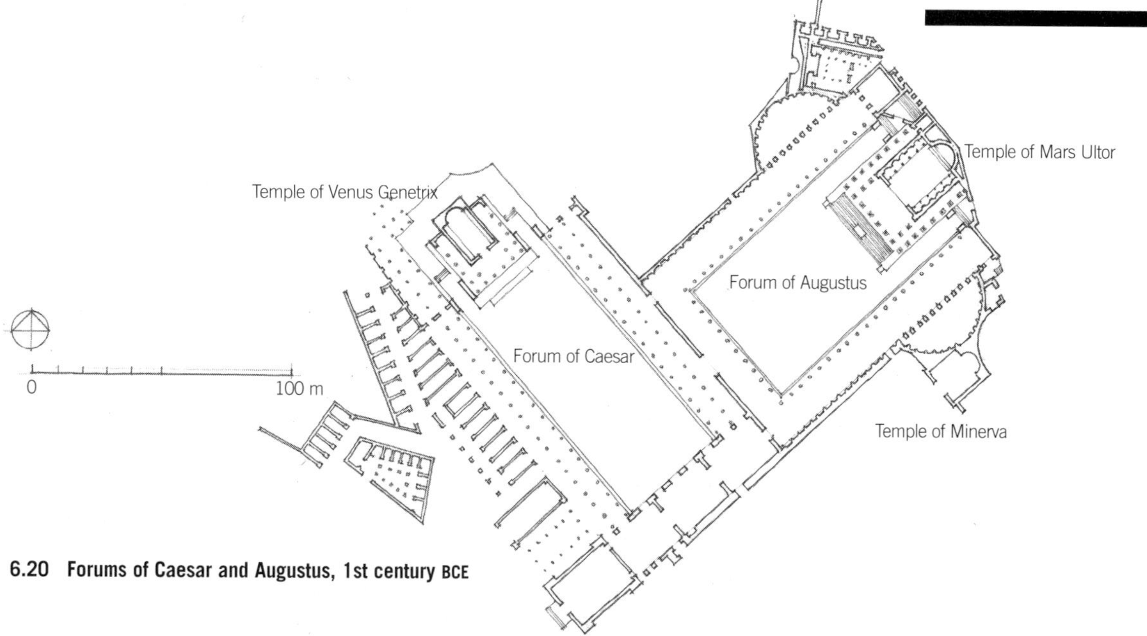


**6.20 Forums of Caesar and Augustus, 1st century BCE**

### Forum of Augustus

Augustus also laid out a forum of his own (Forum Augustum, 10–2 BCE), turned 90 degrees to the Forum of Caesar and along the city wall to the west. Since it was in a thickly settled area, houses had to be purchased at great expense and cleared away. One entered the Forum from the south side, on axis with the temple, which was placed at the far end of the forum. It seems that Augustus was not able to purchase all the land he needed for the plan even though the area behind the Forum was one of the poorer sections of town. A large wall was erected behind the building as a firewall and to shield against the squalor. To resolve the irregularity of the site, the architect added porticoes to conceal back entrances to the right and left of the temple. The northern portico ends in a square room that contained a colossal statue of Augustus.

The temple was dedicated to Mars the Avenger (Mars Ultor) in accordance with a vow made by Augustus before the Battle of Philippi (42 BCE) in which Brutus and Cassius, the assassins of Julius Caesar, were killed. There are eight Corinthian columns in front and along the flanks. The plan is nearly square, measuring 38 by 40 meters. By omitting two rows of columns, space was created for a spacious entrance. Inside the temple, in the apse, elevated five steps above the floor, were statues of Mars, Venus, and the deified Julius Caesar.

Forming a cross-axis are two large exedrae. Their purpose was to hold statues that tell the story of the great men of Rome's founding, Romulus featured in one and Aeneas in the other. The Augustan empire was to be seen as the culmination of this history, with Augustus himself presiding over this portrait gallery in the form of a bronze statue on a pedestal in the middle of the Forum. Quite apart form the religious ceremonies that took place here, the Forum became the starting point for magistrates departing for the provinces and the repository of the triumphal banners. It was also used for Senate meetings when reports of military successes were to be expected.

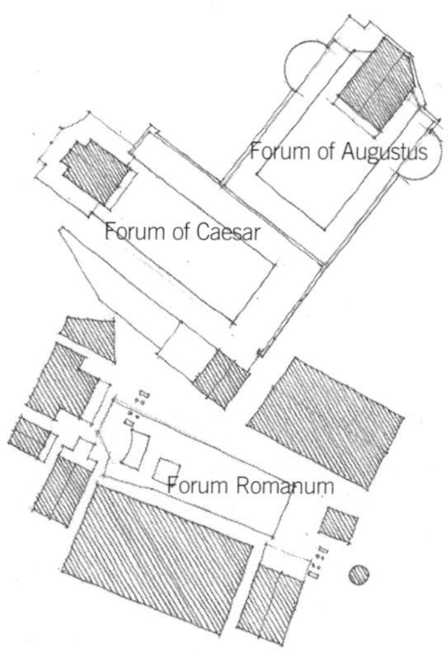


**6.21 Relationship of the Forum Romanum to the Forums of Caesar and Augustus**

### Vitruvius

The Augustinian age was a boon for architects, leading Marcus Vitruvius Pollio (ca. 70–25 BCE) to compose a treatise entitled *De Architectura* (On Architecture) and known today as the *Ten Books on Architecture*. Though the book contains a vast amount of useful information on construction materials, choice of site, and even the education of an architect, Vitruvius, in general, was critical of the architectural developments of his age. He was hesitant to accept concrete and felt that many of the new buildings commissioned by Augustus were built without guiding principles. In attempting to reestablish these principles, he argued that the three orders, Doric, Ionic, and Corinthian, should be governed by proportions unique to each. Vitruvius also differentiated between *firmitas, utilitas,* and *venustas* (durability, usefulness, and beauty). Each building, he argued, needed to be designed with these criteria in mind. A warehouse, for example, should be built with usefulness in mind, but not be unpleasant to look at, whereas a palace should be built with beauty in mind, but designed nonetheless to last the ages. The impact of Vitruvius on Roman architecture was minimal but when a copy of his treatise was rediscovered in 1414 in the monastic library of St. Gallen in Switzerland, it became the foundation of architectural theory in Europe for the next three centuries.

6.22 Corinthian capitals: Temple of Mars the Avenger

6.23 Temple of Athena, Tegea

6.24 Temple of Castor

### Corinthian Capitals

Among the major orders, the Corinthian capital was a latecomer. Its first appearance in architecture, so it is now thought, was at the Temple of Apollo at Bassae (420–400 BCE), where it stands framed at the end of the *cella*. It appears on the exterior only at the Temple of Zeus Olympius (begun 170 BCE), a huge Hellenistic-era temple in Athens. The use of the Corinthian remained intermittent until the age of Augustus, at which time it became synonymous with the young empire.

The conceptual origins of the Corinthian capital are obscure, but Vitruvius tells the story of a Corinthian girl who died. Her nurse put various pots and cups into a basket and placed it on her tomb. The following spring an acanthus root that had been under the tomb begun to send sprouts through the basket. The architect Callimachus just happened to pass by and decided to model a capital on the arrangement. There is no way of knowing if this is accurate, but the themes of purity and death were certainly important attributes of the column, and the acanthus had long been associated with immortality.

6.25 Capital: Temple of Apollo, Didyma

Unlike the Doric and Ionic, which could be transformed only in subtle ways, the Corinthian capital tolerated numerous variations that are usually described by noting how many rings of acanthus leaves there are (typically two). From behind these rise the stalks, usually springing in pairs at the corners and curving into volutes (literally turns) under the abacus. At the center of the abacus, one often finds a blossom. The Corinthian capital of the Temple of Athena in Tegea (350 BCE) is shorter and has stalks with greater definition than Augustinian era Corinthians (as at the Temple of Castor from 6 CE), which emphasize the leaves. Sometimes an Ionic capital is added to the Corinthian to make what is known as a composite capital. At the temple of Apollo at Didyma, the architect added a palmette between the stalks.

6.26 Capital: Temple of Zeus Olympius, Athens

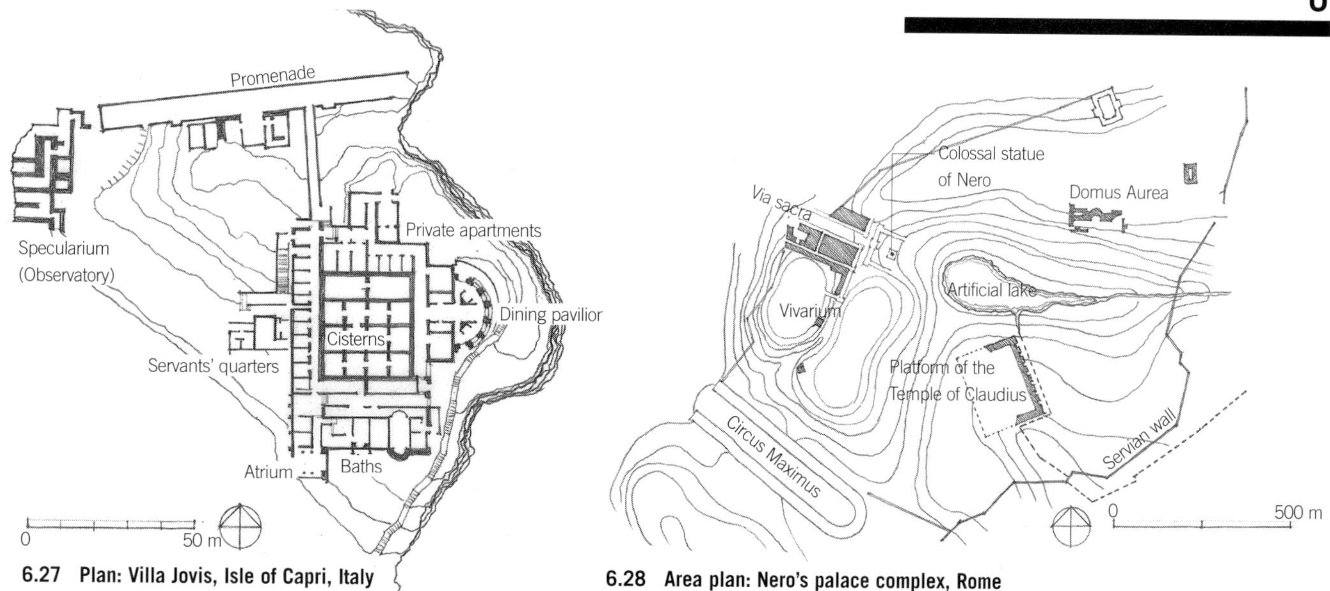


6.27 Plan: Villa Jovis, Isle of Capri, Italy

6.28 Area plan: Nero's palace complex, Rome

### POST-AUGUSTAN ROME

After the death of Augustus in 14 CE, there was less emphasis on grand public monuments and more on lavish residences, picking up on the trend established in the closing century of the Republic. Emperor Tiberius' main residence, for example, was the Villa Jovis (Villa of Jupiter) at Capri, perched on top of a sheer cliff at one end of the island. It was built around 30 CE on an enormous vaulted concrete undercroft that served as a cistern to catch rainwater, the only source of water for the villa. A semicircular hall and dining pavilion looked out eastward, directly over the cliff's edge. A loggia was to the north of the courtyard, the baths to the south, and service rooms and kitchen were in the wing to the west. It was from this grand perch that Tiberius ruled the far-flung empire.

6.29 Villa Jovis, Isle of Capri

The great fire of 64 CE completely destroyed more than four of Rome's 14 regions, clearing large areas of land in the city center. Nero, who was always rumored to have set the fire, immediately cleared a place for his new residence, a type of villa grafted into the urban landscape and the stage for complex rituals and ceremonies involving the imperial person. The grounds filled the valley between the Esquiline, Caelian, and Palatine hills. There was an artificial lake in the middle where the Colosseum now stands. Suetonius' description of Nero's palace complex gives some impression of the splendor.

> It had a vestibule, in which stood a colossal statue of him [40 meters high]; the area it covered was so great that it had a triple portico a mile long; it also had a pool which looked like a sea, surrounded by buildings which gave the impression of cities; besides this there were rural areas with ploughed fields, vineyards, pastures and woodlands and filled with all types of domestic animals and wild beasts. Everything in the other parts of the palace was inlaid with gold and highlighted with gems and mother-of-pearl. There were dining rooms whose ceilings had rotating ivory panels to sprinkle flowers and pipes to sprinkle perfumes on those below.

Only one wing of the palace complex remains, the Domus Aurea (Golden House) and it rests against the side of the Esquiline Hill and is in itself a remarkable piece of architectural ingenuity. A large-scale form is attacked, if you will, by smaller-scale tactically applied axial elements. To the east there is an octagonal room and associated chambers woven into a register of rooms to the rear. The vault of the octagonal room was so designed that light could filter in behind the shell of the vault, which is supported by eight brick-faced concrete piers originally adorned with marble and stucco. Though it begins as an octagon, the vault blends into a sphere at the top, where a wide oculus, 6 meters across, brings light into the room. Based on iconographic and literary evidence, some scholars have suggested that the oculus was covered by a lantern dome. Equally ingenious is the waterfall room on the room's northern axis.

Further to the east, a large, open pentagonal court intrudes into the building from the south and pushes the rooms once again against the service rooms to the back. On axis is a vaulted room flanked by a suite of supporting rooms. The western wing contains a particularly elegant sequence of spaces that, like pistons, connect the front with a courtyard to the rear ending in a fountained chamber. The long axis of the courtyard ends in a large vaulted dining room that also seems to back its way into the side of the hill.

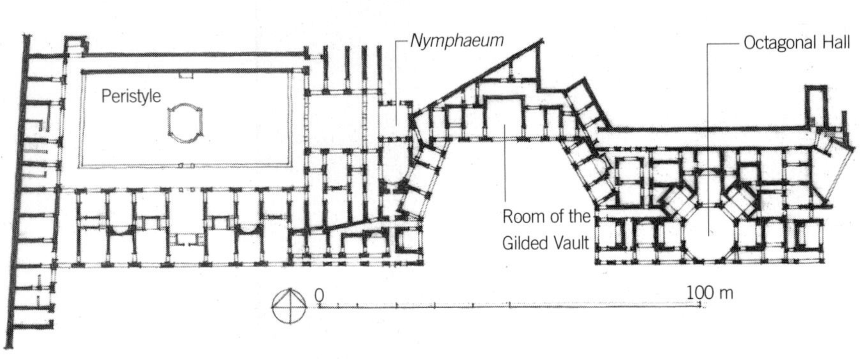


**6.30 Plan: Esquiline wing of the Domus Aurea**

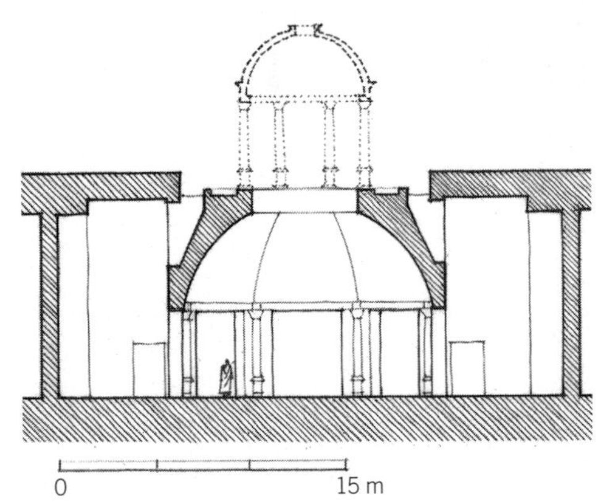


**6.31 Section of the Octagonal Hall: Domus Aurea**

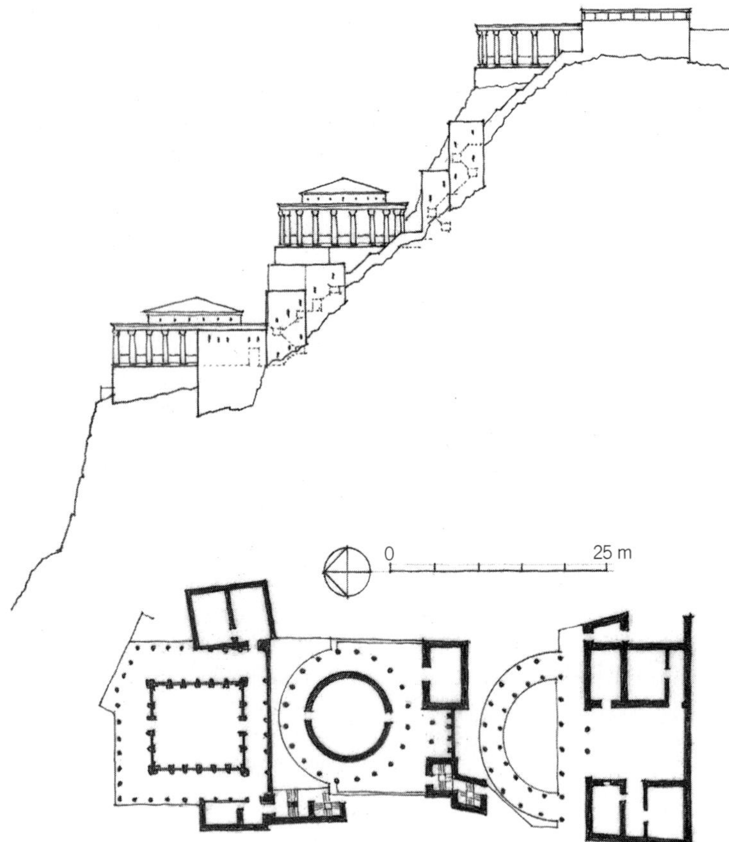


**6.32 Plan and elevation: Northern Palace at Masada, Israel**

### Northern Palace at Masada

Another striking example of Roman-styled palace architecture is Herod's Palace at Masada, a mountaintop fortress city rising above the shores of the Dead Sea in the Judaean desert, 20 kilometers southeast of Jerusalem. It demonstrates in particular the synthesis of Roman and Hellenistic architecture. Called the Northern Palace and recently dated to 30–20 BCE, it begins at the apex of the habitable acropolis and descends down the steep northern slope of the cliff in a tour de force encounter between architecture and nature. The upper terrace had rooms placed around a large hall and was used as a dwelling. The hall opened onto a large semicircular pavilion or balcony, offering a fine view over the almost vertical drop of the cliff. Steps lead down to the middle terrace dominated by a rotunda, used perhaps as a dining room. Behind it, carved out of the cliff face, was a library and an enclosed room, perhaps a treasury. Below that was another terrace, a *hypostyle* hall, and bath complex. Herod built several other spectacular structures. The so-called Herodion, south of Jerusalem, built ca. 24 BCE as both a palace and a fortress, lies atop an 80-meter-high semiartificial hill; and it is defined by two concentric walls that contained the palace. The garden was to the east and the rooms of the palace to the west.

**6.33 Water garden, Palace of Domitian, Palatine Hill, Rome**

**6.34 View into court, Palace of Domitian**

**Palace of Domitian**

Following a period of violence and anarchy after the death of Nero, stability was returned with Vespasian (r. 69–79 CE) and a century-long sequence of rulers whose policies, broadly considered, brought peace and unity to the ancient Mediterranean world. Peace for Romans, of course, came at a price for others. In 70 CE, Vespasian destroyed the second temple of the Jews in Jerusalem and forced the Jews into slavery. About 10,000 Jews were transported to Rome to be used as workers to help build the Colosseum. In the wake of these and other victories, Vespasian's son Domitian (r. 81–96 CE) began a new imperial palace (also known as the Flavian Palace or Domus Augustana), which, on the eastern ridge of the Palatine Hill, was to become the permanent residence of the emperors. It was still in use when Narses, the conqueror of the Goths, died there in 571. Domitian imposed his absolutist tendencies upon society and the state to a degree previously unknown. Under his rule, the lingering pragmatism of Roman culture became increasingly infused with an ideology of Near-Eastern flavor, with its implications of the quasi-divine nature of the ruler. The new palace had to be not only sumptuous but reflect power and majesty. The tight, almost chaotic jumble of conflicting axial realities that made Nero's palace so startling gave way to more controlled expressions.

Domitian's architect, Rabirius, cut a great step into the hillside to create a split-level palace. The residence was in the lower part. Though there was a great deal of spatial innovation, everything was thought through. There were no awkward or surprising collisions of space, as one finds in Nero's palace. The entrance was on an axis that led through two *peristyle* courts and into a structure that is at first symmetrical but, at its right and left perimeters, connects fluidly into other spatial geometries.

Helping to negotiate the spatial transitions is the ingenious use of curved and rectilinear geometries. The entrance, for example, is marked by a curved vestibule that leads through a series of spaces that expand and contract, playing on the theme of the vaults above and on openings of different sizes and qualities that lead to side rooms.

The more one studies the plan, the more combinations one can make of these spaces, depending on what one wants to read as recessive or dominant. At the far end of the axis were two summer houses, located at the top of the large curve of the Circus Maximus, with views down into it. On the east side of the palace there was another register of spaces dominated by a hippodrome, the floor of which is some 10 meters lower. A viewing box forms the terminus of a cross-axis connecting the garden fountain and the *peristyle* court. The *Aula Regia*, or audience hall, overlooked the forum.

A staircase leads to the lower level, where the residence of the emperor was located, just at the seam between the two swaths of buildings. Roman stairs were never very elaborate, and this is no exception. The principal rooms are arranged around the court with its fountain, and the emperor's private chambers are on the northwest. The central room projected out into the space of the courtyard's ambulatory. To the right and left were fountain rooms. The entire suite was separated from the retaining wall by a service corridor. To the northern side three remarkable rooms with niches, *aediculae*, and complex vaulting formed another unit. The whole was a palace within a palace.

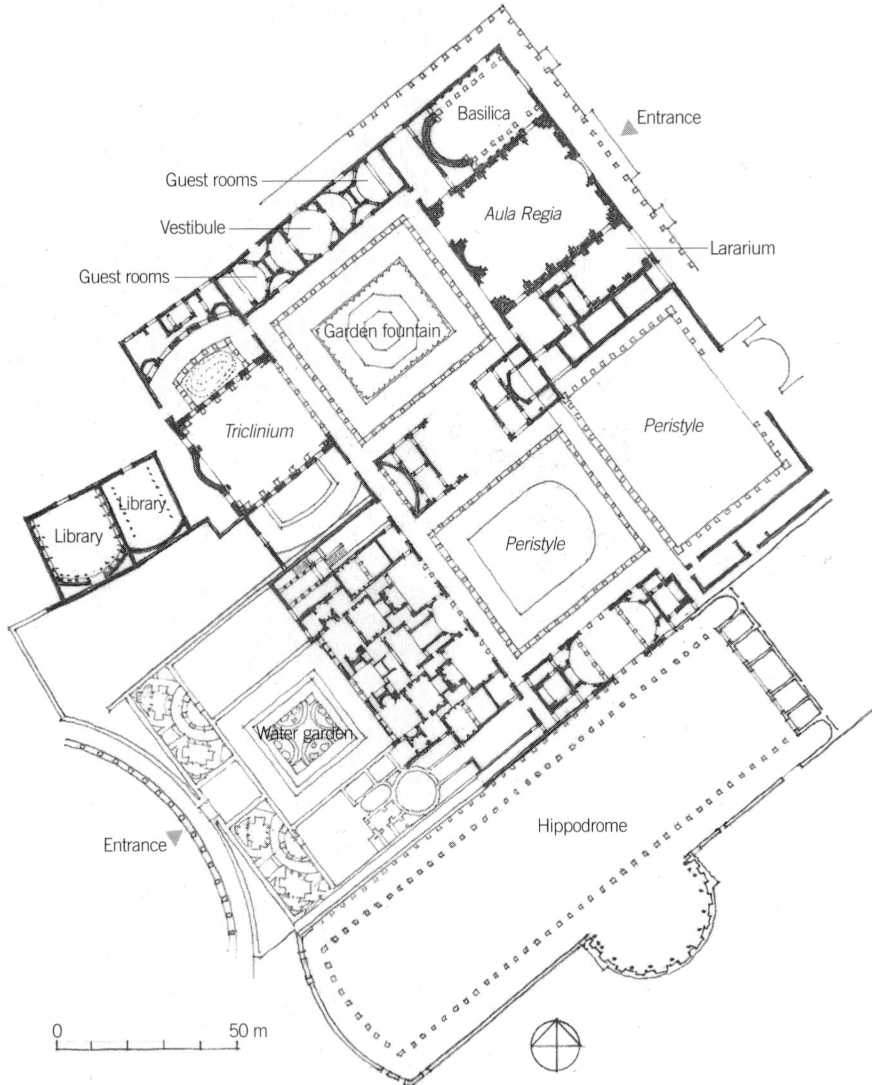


**6.35 Plan: Palace of Domitian, Palatine Hill, Rome**

To the west is another axis, but one that is enclosed. This is the part dedicated to the imperial state and is conventionally called Domus Flavia. One gets to it through a gate that leads to a *peristyle* court. On the northern side are three state chambers, the basilica, the *Aula Regia* (audience hall), and the *lararium*, or palace chapel. The basilica has attracted considerable attention since it seems to prefigure the form of the Early Christian basilica. Though there are many potential sources for this kind of space, there is no doubt that its long architectural life as a proper setting for a supposedly all-powerful figure or godhead was guaranteed by its presence in this palace. Next to it was the *Aula Regia*, where embassies and audiences were held in a space calculated to dramatize Rome's claim to majesty and unity. It was a spectacular room, with surfaces covered in marble. Ornamental columns attached to spur walls projected into the space. Between the columns were alternating round and square niches, each with an *aedicula* inside, another feature that would become a trademark of Roman wall articulation.

Opposite the court was a large *triclinium*, or dining hall. Doors in the side walls led out onto gardens with an ingenious display of fountains in the shape of an elliptical island rising from a pool.

6.36 **The Colosseum, Rome**

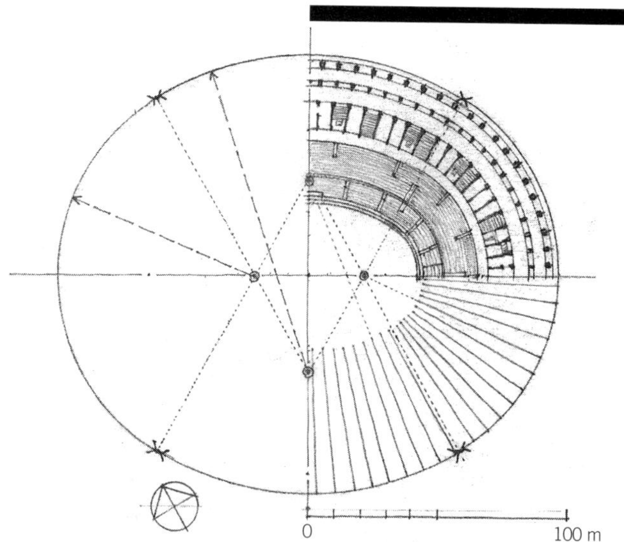


6.37 **Possible method for laying out the Colosseum**

**Colosseum**

The Colosseum (72–80 BCE), much like the Temple of Fortuna, derives its structural strength from its concrete vaults. If the building, after earthquakes, fires, and lootings, today still conveys its one-time grandeur and even up to a point its usability for certain open-air functions, we have to thank the ancients for the bold use of that material. Though theaters were a common element in Greek and Roman cities, this was the first that was designed as a freestanding object. An earlier design dating from 80 BCE in Pompeii and another from 56 BCE in Lepcis Magna in North Africa were similar in plan, but both were partially carved down into the rock. The Colosseum sits in a shallow valley between three hills, making it visible from all directions and giving it the status of a landmark from the very beginning.

It is elliptical in plan and could hold 50,000 spectators with boxes for the emperor and the dignitaries at the centers of the longer sides. Gladiatorial combats and the exhibition of wild beasts did not stop with the Christianization of Rome. Romans remained Romans. While gladiatorial combats were abolished in 404 CE, games came to an end only in the middle of the 6th century. It remained a place of public punishment well into the 8th century. The masses of stone that came down in an earthquake in 1231 and 1349 provided Rome with building material for more than four centuries.

If the undercroft shows once again the skill of the engineers in designing and organizing a building on this scale, its façade shows the confidence of the architects in their use of the orders in relationship to the solids and voids of the building. Though ornamentation is at a minimum, the system of attached columns and arched openings allows a balanced interpretation of structure and mass. The 53-meter-high wall was divided into Doric, Ionic, and Corinthian layers. The fourth story had no openings, but brackets in the cornice allowed large masts to be clamped against the building to support awnings.

The capitals were stripped to their elemental form. While this may have been for economy, it also keeps the columns from becoming just ornaments. Instead, they seem to be infused with the same purposefulness, as the vaults, even though they belong to a different structural system. Furthermore, the arches have an architectural profile created by the way a molding separates each arch from its supporting pier at the impost blocks and lightens the appearance of each arch from the heavy voussoirs of which it is composed. In essence, the columns look more structural than they are and the arches less so. A less skilled hand could easily have tipped the balance one way or the other.

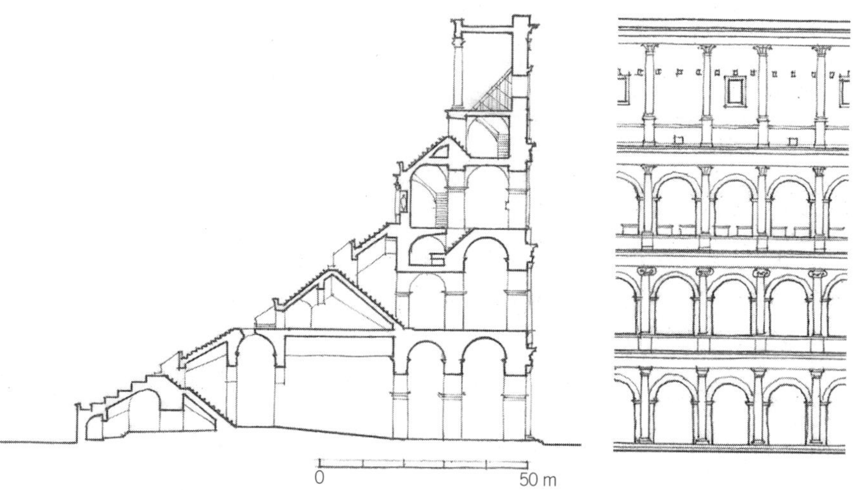


6.38 **Partial section: The Colosseum**

6.39 **Partial elevation: The Colosseum**

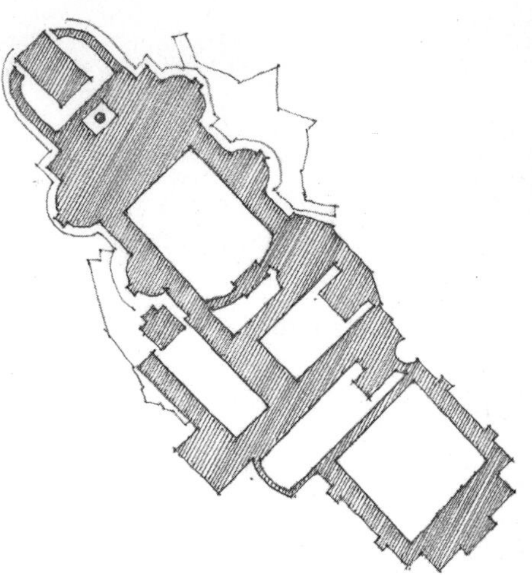

6.40 **Figure-ground: Imperial forums**

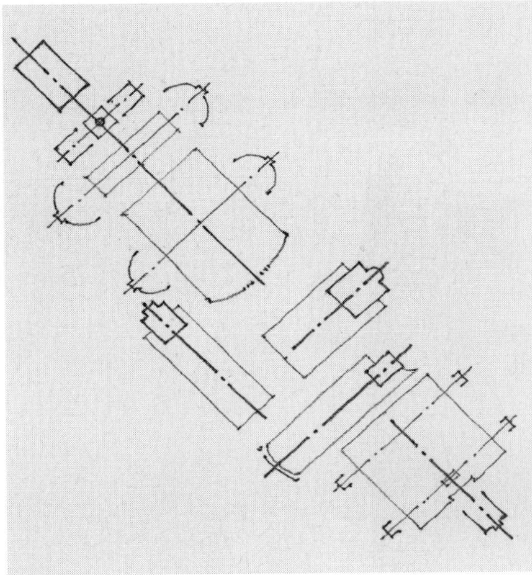

6.41 **Axial Relationships: Imperial forums**

## IMPERIAL ROME

At the beginning of the 2nd century CE, under Trajan (r. 98–117 CE) and then Hadrian (r. 117–138 CE), Rome was at the height of its power. Trajan defeated the Dacians in Romania (101–106 CE) to dispossess them of their plentiful gold mines. Other campaigns led into Armenia and Mesopotamia. The wealth that flowed back into the capital restored the public treasury and insured vigorous implementation of architectural programs. And the rulers set a vigorous pace. Trajan had Ostia, Rome's harbor rebuilt, a new public bath established and existing streets repaired or extended. Above all, he ordered a new forum to be built. Attributed to the architect Apollodoro of Damascus, it was a complex larger than any of the other forums. Three-hundred meters long, it covered more than three times the area of the Forum of Augustus. To prepare the site, the engineers had to chop away a section of a hill that connected the Quirinale to the Campidoglio.

The Forum was entered through a gateway located in a gently bulging wall. At the far end was the sideways-oriented Basilica Ulpia (107–113 CE), with apses on both its ends echoing the ones built into the colonnade of the forum that, in turn, emulated the ones in the Forum of Augustus. Apart from the size of the basilica, it was designed in a traditional manner. Two rows of gray granite columns defined the aisles with light filtering down, as usual, from the roof that covered the central space. The roofs of the side aisles were covered by concrete vaults rising directly from the architraves, while the roof over the central aisle was probably spanned with wooden timbers. Sculptures and relief panels show the campaigns and triumphs of the emperor. On the main axis just behind the basilica, stands Trajan's Column with a spiral sculptural relief, reading from the bottom to the top and showing the various important events of the Trajan campaign in Dacia. At the top was a bronze statue of Trajan himself. The freestanding column, an unusual feature in its own right, was also unusual for Roman architecture insofar as it interrupted the axial flow to the temple. But it also highlights the central role of the Forum as a war memorial. The column is flanked by libraries, one for Greek scrolls, the other for Latin. The whole complex ends with the temple to Trajan himself. It was enormous with columns measuring two meters across. It has been suggested that the unusual design of the Forum comes from the fact that it emulates the central administrative area of a military camp. Trajan's Column and flanking libraries seem similar to the location of the general's standard and military archives, which were set up behind the basilica. Trajan was born in Spain and was raised as a soldier, and it was thus a piece of his military iconography that has been translated into a civic monument.

| | |
|---|---|
| 48 BCE | Forum of Caesar |
| 2 BCE | Forum of Augustus |
| 1 CE | Forum of Nerva, dedicated to Minerva |
| 71–75 CE | Forum of Vespasian, or "Templum Pace" (Temple of Peace), erected after the bloody taking of Jerusalem and the ending of the Jewish War. |
| 112 CE | Forum of Trajan |

6.42 **Development of the imperial forums**

6.43 **Interior hall, Markets of Trajan**

Taken as a whole, the imperial forums constitute a remarkable urban composition. There are no streets and no spatial or axial connections between the spaces. The axis between the Temple of Trajan and the Temple of Peace (though not exactly axial) is purely planimetric. The elements are simply bonded to each other to create a sequence of open, colonnaded, and enclosed spaces. The words that come to mind when looking at this are graft, montage, or assemblage.

The Forum of Nerva, sometimes called the *Transitorium* (place of crossing), was the principal connection between the hill and the old forum. A road led to a semicircular piazza on the eastern side, the only place where the outside world infringes into the space of the forums. But even that receptacle forced the foot traffic to the left and around the side of the Temple of Minerva. Traffic, moving then diagonally through the space, exited at the other end at the right, to the street that ran along the curia wall. There was no attempt to make this forum into a street.

6.44 **Plan: The imperial forums**

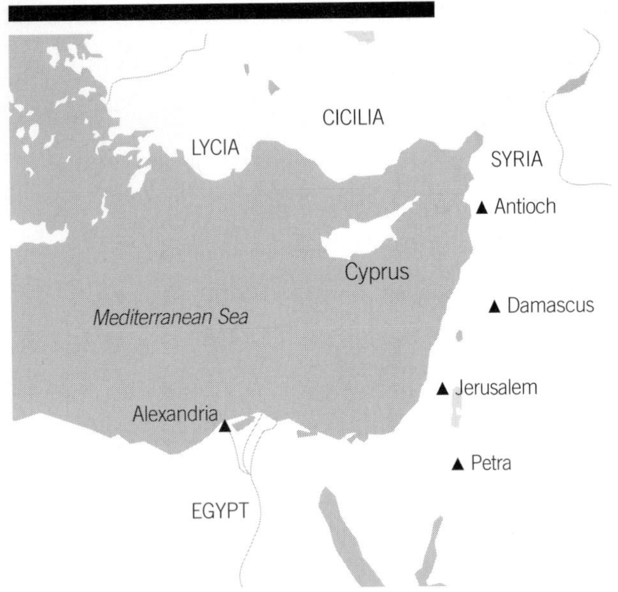


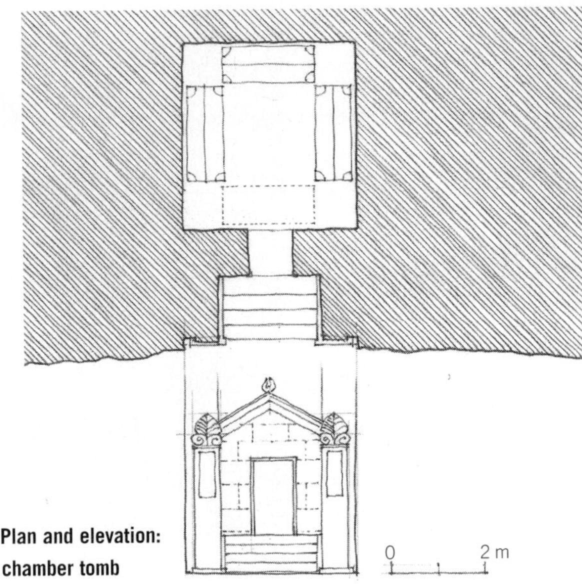


**6.45 Plan and elevation: Lycian chamber tomb**

### ROCK-CUT TOMBS

Though the use of rock-cut tombs was restricted to regions with appropriate geological formations, the idea was an ancient one. Hittite rock-cut sanctuaries date back to 1250 BCE. The so-called Midas Monument (ca. 700 BCE) near Eskisehir in west-central Turkey and the monumental Phrygian rock facades are other links in the history of rock-cut tombs. The Modan Monument contained, however, only a small recessed niche for the cult statue. In the west, the Etruscans also built elaborate rock-cut tombs from the 6th century BCE onward. How the skills needed to create rock-cut architecture found such wide distribution is not known. The tombs were never as popular or as elaborate as they became when the custom was revived by Darius I (521–486 BCE), whose own tomb was carved out of the cliffs of Pars.The rock-cut tombs in Lycia on the southern coast of Turkey date from the 4th century BCE, with many having temple facades in miniature as their fronts.

Some of the main sites of rock-cut architecture by date:

| | | |
|---|---|---|
| 1450 BCE | Tombs | Thebes, Egypt |
| 700 BCE | Tombs | Lycia and Cyprus |
| 500 BCE | Tombs | Etruria, Italy |
| 480 BCE | Tomb of Darius | Persepolis |
| 250 BCE | Buddhist caityas | Eastern India |
| 100 BCE | Buddhist caityas | Western Ghats, India |
| 100 CE | Tombs | Petra, Jordan |
| 100 CE | Buddhist caityas | Northwestern India |
| 100 CE | Houses | Tiermes, Spain |
| 400 CE | Buddhist caves | Dunhuang, China |
| 480 CE | Buddhist caves | Ajanta, India |
| 600 CE | Hindu temples | Elephanta, India |
| 650–750 CE | Hindu temples | Southern India |
| 700–900 CE | Hindu, Buddhist, and Jain caves | Ellora, India |
| 900 CE | Churches | Cappadocia, Turkey |
| 1000 CE | Churches | Lalibela, Ethiopia |

**6.46 Rock of Naqsh-i-Rustam, near Persepolis, Iran**

**6.47 El-Deir, Petra, Jordan**

**6.48 Temple facades of Lycian chamber tombs at Kaunos**

**Petra**

The Nabataeans, whose fame spread as far as the Han dynasty in China, where Petra was known as Likan, created an independent, cosmopolitan culture in south Jordan for 400 years. They were of Arab descent, but little is known of the exact origin of these people or the reason why they migrated north into the Levant, the highly contested area of land on the eastern Mediterranean that includes present-day Israel, Syria, Lebanon, and Jordan. Their architectural legacy is best preserved in the isolated city of Petra, meaning "rock" in Greek. On this site, temples, theaters, and hundreds of tombs—all cut into the living rock of the steep mountains that surround the Petra Valley—still stand in testament to this largely forgotten culture. It is located in the area of Jordan called Edom, meaning red, from the color of the Shara Mountains that ring the Petra Valley, which is only accessible through the 1.6-kilometer-long canyon, or *Siq*.

Their well-developed systems of water control and storage, including rock-cut cisterns and ceramic pipes, have led some to believe that their original homeland was in the bone-dry southern part of the Arabian peninsula. At any rate, their geographic position—between the Hellenistic empires of Ptolemy to the south and the Seleucid to the north, and between Arabia to the east and the busy Mediterranean port of Gaza to the west—facilitated the transition of the Nabataeans from shepherding to trading. They became middlemen in the trade of luxury items, including frankincense, myrrh, gold, and camels, which they bred extensively. They moved in caravans and maintained a cultural tradition that forbade building permanent houses. Only the dead were afforded the luxury of permanence.

The smaller and most abundant of these tombs are called Hegr Tombs and date from the early decades of the 1st century CE. The facades reveal the highly eclectic architectural preferences of the Petran populace and the range of cultural influence at play in the city. Some tombs are framed by pilasters and topped with stepping "crow's feet" ornamentation, a motif of Assyrian and Babylonian origin. Still others are massive, largely unadorned facades with small, clearly delineated entrances recalling an Egyptian pylon. An unfinished tomb façade in Petra reveals the method of their construction. These facades, carved from solid rock, simulate in low relief the freestanding architectural form of monuments built stone by stone from the ground up. Ironically, Nabataean stonecutters worked from the top down.

**6.49 Rock-cut tombs at Petra**

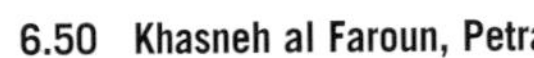

6.50 **Khasneh al Faroun, Petra**

6.51 **Plan and facade: Khasneh al Faroun, Petra**

The early tombs in Petra match the ones in Lycia in scale and size, but at a certain moment they far exceed these earlier ones. Two in particular, on the outskirts of the city, are in an excellent state of preservation. Though built within 50 years of each other, their ornamental programs are studies in contrast. Outside the valley, before the entrance to the *Siq*, stands the Obelisk Tomb, so called because above the portal, four large engaged obelisks taper toward the sky. Each is thought to represent a different deity.

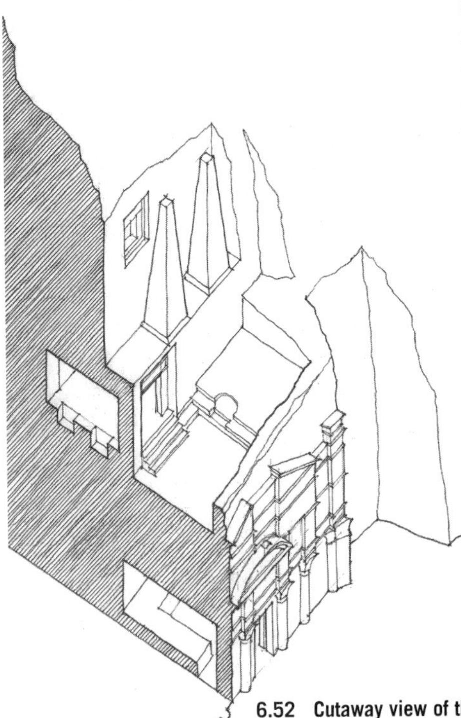

6.52 **Cutaway view of the Obelisk Tomb, Petra**

At the other end of the *Siq*, one encounters the beautifully preserved deep-pinkish façade of the Khasneh al Faroun. The dating is unknown and much debated. Some suggest that it was built for King Aretas III (87–65 BCE), which would make it a truly revolutionary structure. Others place it in the 2nd century CE, while others place it in the 1st century CE, which seems the most plausible. The inside has three large, unadorned chambers. But the highly articulated façade, standing 30 meters high, recalls the massing and intercolumniation of some Hellenistic temples. Twelve columns, six on the lower level and six above, are capped with rich Corinthianesque capitals and highly ornamented moldings and friezes. The upper columns are shorter than the lower, but from the perspective of the viewer from the ground, they seem well proportioned. The spaces between the attached columns contain high-reliefs depicting Nabataean deities and animals. The griffins that decorate the frieze are clearly rooted in Mesopotamian lore. The façade with its temple front is surmounted by a round *tholos*, standing largely free and framed by broken pediments. The upper and lower stories are ingeniously balanced. Neither overpowers the other.

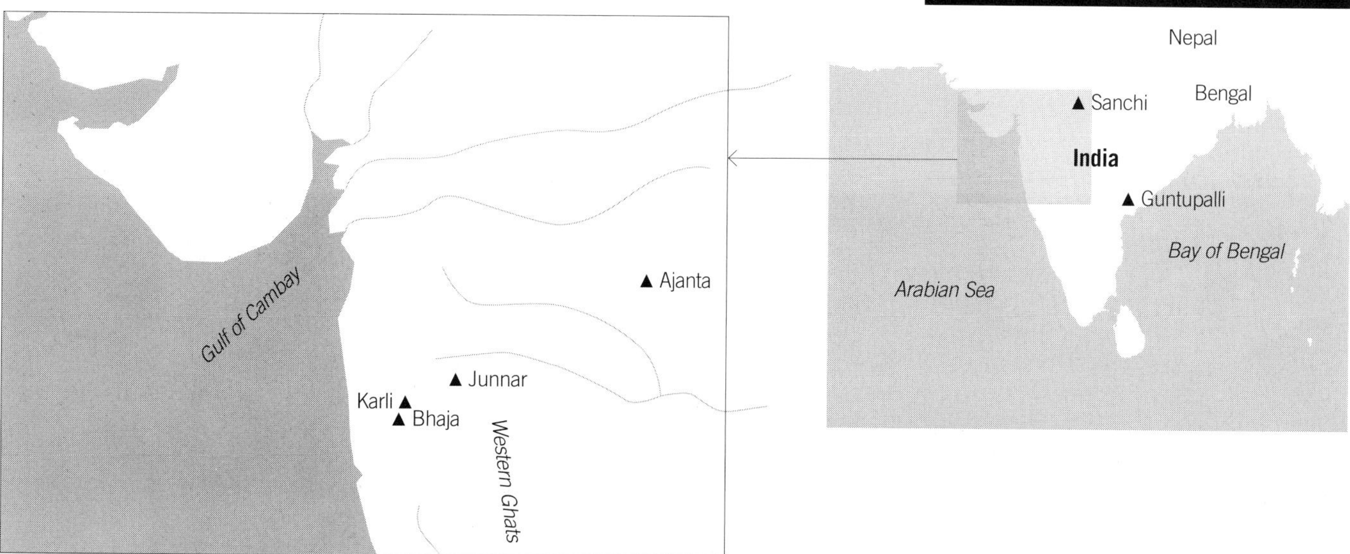


**DEVELOPMENT OF MAHAYANA BUDDHISM**

Late in the 2nd century BCE, Asoka's Mauryan Empire began to disintegrate, resulting in the formation of a series of smaller kingdoms and dynasties: the Sunga Dynasty (180–72 BCE) in the west, the Satavahanas (235 BCE–225 CE) to the south, and in the north, the Shakas. This transformation paralleled an equally important transformation within Buddhism with important implications in the field of architecture. As originally conceived, the Buddhist monkhood (*sangha*) was strictly mendicant. Its members lived itinerantly in poverty and survived by begging; as well, they were not to erect shrines, acquire property, or deify the Buddha. Mendicant Buddhism was subsequently referred to as Hinayana (or the "Lesser Vehicle"). In time, as Buddhism began to receive royal patronage and its practitioners became more diverse, a more monastic and populist form of Buddhism, known as Mahayana (or the "Greater Vehicle") emerged, one that required the establishment of institutions and places where Buddhist monks could live, study, and learn.

Buddhism's transformation from mendicancy to monasticism can be tracked through the Four Great Buddhist Councils called to reconcile differences of interpretation. King Ajatsatru convened the 1st Buddhist Council in the 5th century BCE, soon after the Buddha's death (*parinirvana*) to record the extant sayings of the Buddha (Sutra) and to codify the mendicant rules (Vinaya).

Continuing conflicts between the Hinayana and Mahayana schools of Buddhism prompted the convening of the 2nd Buddhist Council convened by King Kalasoka in 383 BCE at Vaisali. That council ended with the victory of the mendicants. But by the time Asoka convened the 3rd Great Buddhist Council in 250 BCE at Pataliputra, the tide was beginning to turn. In anticipation of extensive royal patronage, the council prepared the definitive treatises of Buddhism, in particular the Tripitaka (the "Three Baskets"), the three texts considered to be directly transmitted from the Buddha. The Tripitaka consisted of the core doctrine (the Sutra Pitaka), the doctrines associated with mendicant discipline (Vinaya Pitaka), and a new body of philosophical texts (the Abhidharma Pitaka).

The 4th Council was convened by the Kushan emperor, Kanishka, around 100 CE in Kashmir. At this Council, 300,000 verses and over 9,000,000 statements were compiled by 500 Buddhists over 12 years, written in Sanskrit. These became the basis of Mahayana Buddhism, which now began to flourish and spread into Central Asia, China, Korea, and Japan. Today there are at least 13 distinct variations on Buddhism in the world.

Significant parts of the Mahayana credo were articulated by Nagarjuna, the 2nd century Indian philosopher and the most influential Buddhist thinker after the Buddha himself. Nagarjuna promoted what is known as Madhayamika, or the Middle Path, as a compromise between the ascetic and worldly sects of Buddhism. He argued that Asoka, as the virtuous Buddhist king, was a *cakravartin*, and should thus be considered to have direct access to nirvana or Buddhahood. Nagarjuna's definition of kingship served as a model for generations of rulers throughout Asia, including the 18th century Qin Dynasty Emperor Qianlong.

6.53 **Stupa II at Sanchi. near Bhopal, India**

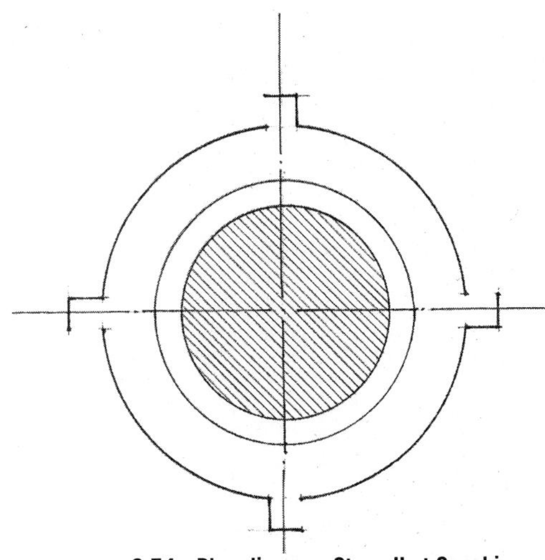

6.54 **Plan diagram: Stupa II at Sanchi**

### Sanchi Complex

The most important of the remaining Sunga-period Buddhist complexes is Sanchi, which was founded by Asoka and flourished for 13 centuries. The complex is located near the ancient town of Vidisa, along the southern trade route (or *dakshinapatha*) in the midst of a series of fertile river valleys. It is located on a hill that rises sharply above a valley, making its three stupas distinctly visible from afar. The surrounding hills are also surmounted by stupas, all of which establish the area as a sacred landscape. Originally Sanchi's stupas were plastered and painted, and on festival days were gaily decorated with flowers and other ritual offerings. Large groups of visiting monks and laity alike came to Sanchi in processions.

Stupas started out as reliquary mounds or *caityas*, denoting any sacred place, usually marked off by a wooden railing, where a funeral pyre or consecration had occurred. Asoka had the Buddha's bodily remains divided into eight parts and distributed throughout his empire as relics, with their location marked by ceremonial mounds. Stupa means "piled up."

Built by the thousands and becoming the dominant symbol of Buddhism, stupas came to embody many meanings, some standing in for the body of the Buddha, others for his enlightenment, and yet others serving as a cosmic diagram.

Conceptually a stupa is a cosmological diagram linking the body of the Buddha to the cosmos. The fundamental elements of a stupa are present in the oldest of Sanchi's stupas, the so-called Stupa II (100 BCE). The central mass consists of an earthen, hemispherical mound, faced with fired bricks, with a shallow berm (or *medhi*) ringing its base. This round structure is then surrounded by a stone balustrade (or *vedika*) that replicates a construction out of wood. Both the interior and exterior surface of the *vedika* are carved with shallow reliefs and medallions depicting scenes and events of Buddhist significance. The *vedika* has openings on four sides aligned to the cardinal directions. These are accessed, however, not on axis but at right angles, through bent entrances, all of which open in a counterclockwise direction. The cross-axis of the cardinal directions, coupled with the directional openings, together form a space-time cosmological diagram or mandala in the form of a *svastika* (or swastika). The directions represent space, and the bent entrances, replicating the movement of the stars, represent time.

The purpose of the *vedika* is to give spatial definition to the ritual counterclockwise circumambulation of *parikrama*. A Buddhist monk, or a pilgrim, in performing the *parikrama* engages in a haptic reenactment of the fundamental order of space and time, and in the process, brings his or her body into harmony with that larger order. In Buddhism, as in Hinduism, *parikrama*, along with the mandala and the *svastika* (totally unrelated to its Nazi appropriation), are still fundamental to architectural expression.

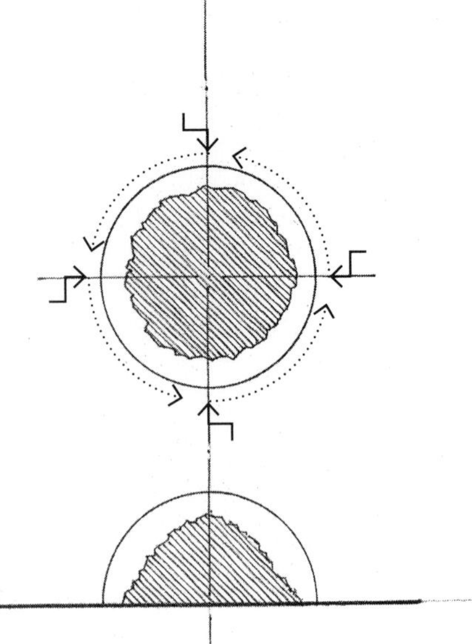

6.55 **The idea of the stupa**

**6.56** ***Hamika*** **and** ***chattri*****: Great Stupa at Sanchi**

Stupa I is the largest stupa at Sanchi; it is also known as the Mahastupa or the Great Stupa. Begun by Asoka, it was enlarged to its present diameter of 36 meters late in the Sunga period. It is a solid mass built up in the form of hundreds of stone rings that were surfaced with plaster and painted. (This outer surface has eroded away and has not been replaced.) The significance of the Mahastupa is highlighted by the rare presence of one of Asoka's pillars at the southern entrance. The Mahastupa is essentially a magnification of Stupa II in plan, with the addition of another *vedika* around the inner berm, or *medhi*, which is also accessible by stairs on the south, making it possible to conduct a double *parikrama* around the stupa.

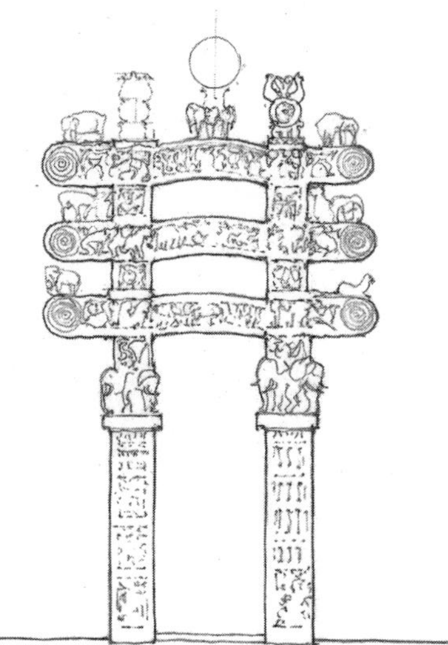

**6.58 East** ***torana*****: Great Stupa at Sanchi**

At the top of the stupa is another *vedika*, one that is inaccessible and serves only symbolic purposes, called the *harmika*. In the middle of the *harmika* is a finial, with three stone discs, called *chattris*, of diminishing size balanced on a columnar support. The *harmika* and the *chattris* collectively denote the stupa's vertical axis, echoing Asoka's pillar and completing the cosmic connections of the stupa. The other innovation at the Mahastupa is the monumental stone gateways called *toranas*. The *toranas*, imitating wooden construction, consist of two vertical pillars supporting three horizontal bars that are slightly bent at their center and that project well beyond the posts. The beams end in volutes that connote the sacred scrolls, the treasured objects of the Buddhist *sanghas*. The Chinese rulers would later send their emissaries to India to obtain these scrolls, which they would then have copied and preserved. Like the *vedikas*, the surface of the *torana* is elaborately decorated, depicting Buddhist themes and events, and completes the classic stupa as we know it.

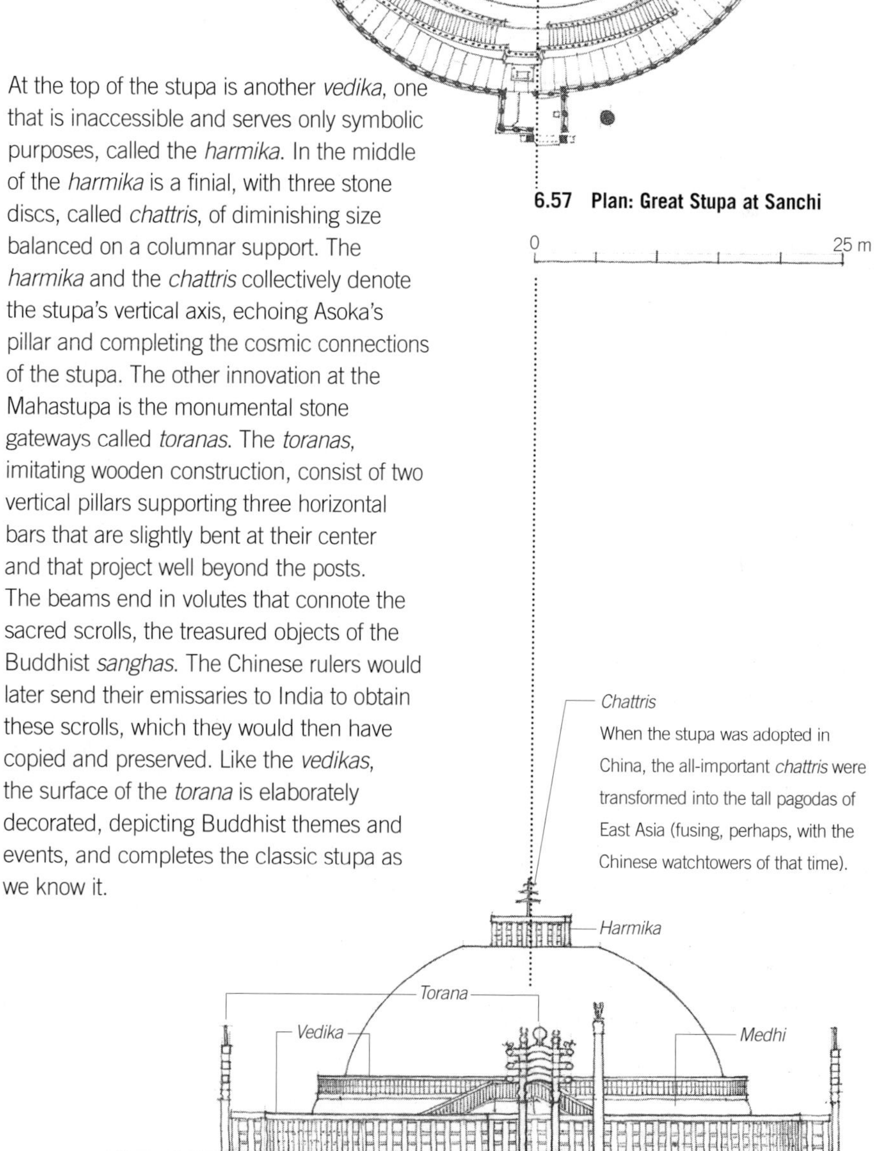


**6.57 Plan: Great Stupa at Sanchi**

**6.59 Elevation: Great Stupa at Sanchi**

6.60 **Great Stupa at Sanchi**

Sanchi enjoyed extensive patronage and grew into a large monastic complex of Buddhist learning and worship, including subsidiary structures where the monks lived. Over time a number of small stupas were added in the complex. The more important the person whose relics were contained in these stupas, the closer their stupa was to the Mahastupa. (During excavation In the mid-19th century, most of these were unfortunately removed.) The Hindus also recognized this site as important and one of the oldest Hindu stone temples from the 4th century is to be found there, close to the southern entrance of the Mahastupa. Large groups of pilgrims regularly visited Sanchi. A relief on the northern *torana* of the Mahastupa depicts a large ceremonial procession, complete with musical instruments and offerings and led by elephants, on its way to the Mahastupa. The relief also shows that the stupa would have been extensively decorated with garlands and flowers in its time. One has to imagine Sanchi thus, not as a remote monastery populated by mendicant Buddhist monks totally disassociated from ordinary life but as a bustling center of religious activity, where the monks and their patrons enjoyed extensive contact and communication.

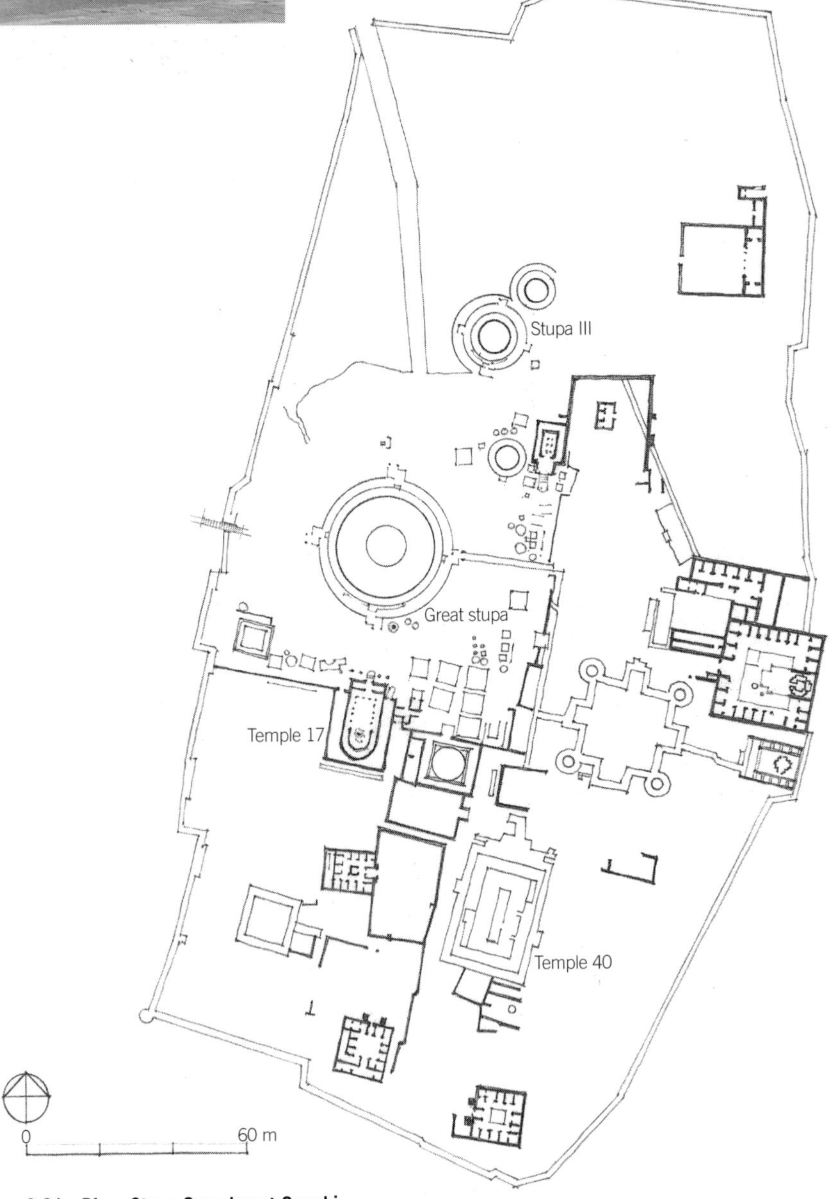


6.61 **Plan: Stupa Complex at Sanchi**

**6.62 View of Junnar Caves, near Nanghat, India**

**6.63 Entrance to Bhuta Lena cave (No. 26), Junnar**

### Junnar Caves

Seven sets of early Buddhist caves in the outer reaches of the Satavahana Kingdom are all that remain of the early Hinayana phase of Buddhism. Dating from the 1st century BCE to the 1st century CE, they are close to Nanaghat, a remote place at the head of a mountain pass linking the Satavahana capital, Paithan, to the port of Kalyan. It is still today barely inhabited, but it was once important because of the sea trade routes. One of the caves contains an inscription from about 100 BCE, listing all the major rulers of the Satavahanas and is considered to be the definitive record of their lineage.

The Tulija Lena (100–25 BCE), is significant because its *caitya* hall is completely round in plan, as if the *parikrama* plan of the stupa chamber at Kondivte had, for a brief moment, become the complete *caitya* itself. By way of comparison, a similar circular *caitya*, but without the parikrama pillars, was also excavated at Guntupalli, in the Krishna river basin of Central India. These two caves define the brief moment when Buddhists considered adopting an alternate expression of their main worship space, exploring the possibilities of the circular spaces excavated in the earliest *caityas*.

**6.64 Plans of *caitya* halls: Lenyadri**

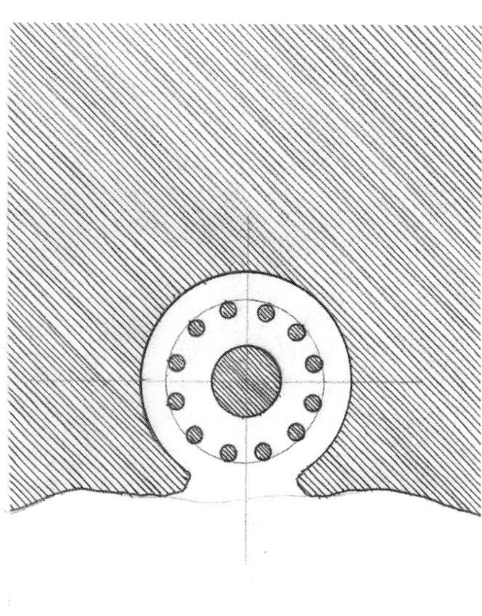

**Tulija Lena**

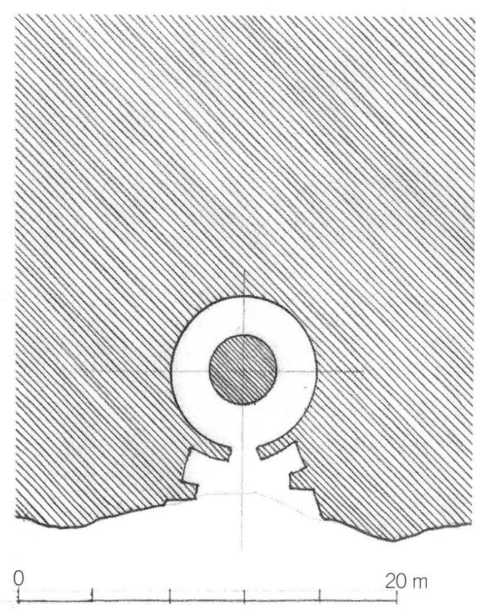


**Guntupalli**

**6.65 Plan: Caitya Hall at Kondivte, India**

**6.66 Entrance to the Caitya Hall at Kondivte**

### Caitya Hall at Kondivte

In the 2nd and 1st centuries BCE, rock-cut Buddhist architecture became highly elaborate in concept and execution. Caves were carved all over South Asia, but in particular in the Western Ghats, a mountain chain in western India running some 45 to 90 kilometers inland from the Arabian Sea. The largest concentrations of rock-cut architecture are in Bhaja and Pitalkhora. These were of two types: a *caitya*, or meditation hall, consisting of an apsidal hall focused on a stupa, and a *vihara*, or living quarter, consisting of a number of cells organized around a rectilinear, columnar court.

**6.67 Interior: Caitya Hall at Bhaja, near Lonavla, India**

The Caitya Hall at Kondivte, Maharashtra, (100 BCE) marks an important moment of transition. Like the Lomas Rsi Caves, the stupa is contained in a circular enclosure, leaving barely enough room for one person to perform *parikrama* around it. Unlike Lomas Rsi, however, this *caitya* hall is entered on axis, rather than from the side. All subsequent rock-cut *caitya* halls are entered on axis.

The final *caitya* form is found in the Caitya Hall at Bhaja, Maharashtra (100–70 BCE). Besides being much larger in size than the rest, the Caitya Hall at Bhaja dissolves the distinction between the stupa chamber with its *parikrama* path and the antechamber. Rather, it fuses them into one large space while maintaining the distinctive presence of the *parikrama* path by creating a long U-shaped colonnade that extends the entire length of the hall. The consequence is a simple and elegant building that has the effect of separating an independent three-dimensional form from within the larger excavation. A distinct colonnaded hall, in other words, appears to emerge out of the more amorphous space of the cave. The presence of this contained hall is projected at the entrance in the form of a large opening with a horseshoe-shaped top, reflecting the vaulted ceiling of the hall.

As is the case with all Buddhist rock-cut architecture, the Caitya Hall at Bhaja is carved out to faithfully imitate wood construction, complete with ribs, inward leaning columns, and traces of joinery. Those features certainly serve no structural purpose. Rather, it seems that the wooden architecture is present for representational purposes, as part of a mise-en-scène or stageset intended to evoke the scenario of a sacred place, such as, one presumes, might have been created out of wood. That the intent is representative rather than deceptive is evidenced by the fact that the exterior façade carved into the stone around the central opening is designed as a stage set, consisting of a number of miniaturized faux building façades, complete with carved human figures leaning over railings.

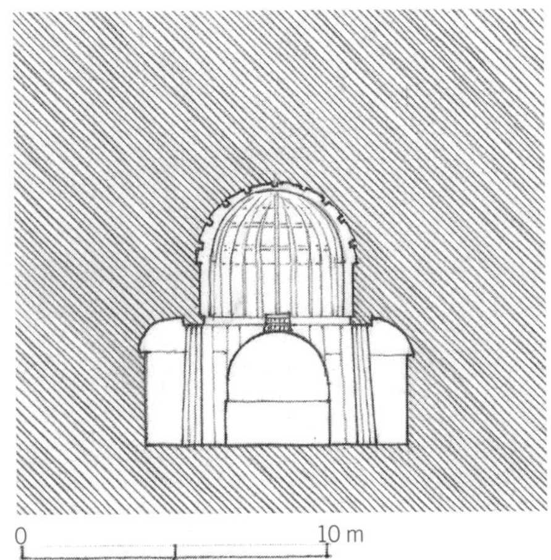


**6.68 Cross section: Caitya Hall at Bhaja**

6.69 **Dharmarajika Stupa, Taxila**

**TAXILA: THE GANDHARAN COSMOPOLIS**

In the period from 150 BCE to 100 CE, the Gandharan region was ruled by the Shakas from Sogdiana and the Parthians, who took over this region from Alexander's governors. The Shakas and the Parthians both adopted Buddhism, cultivated Hellenistic workers, and brought some of their own Persian and Central Asian backgrounds to the mix, creating an architecture that was an international synthesis of varying tendencies. Located on a major tributary of the Indus River, the Gandharan capital city, Taxila, was positioned at the meeting point of three trade routes, one extending east to the Indian heartland, a second west to Bactria and Persia, and a third to Central Asia and the northern path of the Silk Route. Taxila was rebuilt several times until an earthquake in the 1st century CE prompted a complete rebuilding.

The urban layout of Taxila is rigidly rectilinear in plan and bound by a high wall, betraying its Hellenic roots. Dense courtyard housing of various sizes is organized in blocks around a main street. A number of religions seem to have commingled in Taxila. The ancient Buddhist texts, the Jatakas, refer to Taxila as a university center where students could gain an education in numerous areas of study. One of the city blocks was given over to what is known as the Apsidal Temple, which is like a *caitya* hall of the type extensively built in South Asia at the time but built here as a freestanding object. Sitting in the middle of an open courtyard, measuring about 40 by 75 meters, the Apsidal Temple is raised on a high plinth and accessed by a large axial stair, with a stupa at the other end. The stair is flanked by two stupas on square bases. Further away, on another plateau, is the large Dharmarajika Stupa. The mound on which it sits is surrounded by a multitude of monks' cells.

North of the city, on a high rocky outcrop, is a Jandial Temple, a Greek peristyle temple complete with a *pronaos, naos,* and *opisthodomos*. The base of this temple, however, is thicker than structurally necessary, promoting speculation that there may have been another superstructure above the main walls, which might suggest that the temple may have been a fire temple of the Zoroastrians.

6.70 **Plan: Dharmarajika Monastery, Taxila, Pakistan**

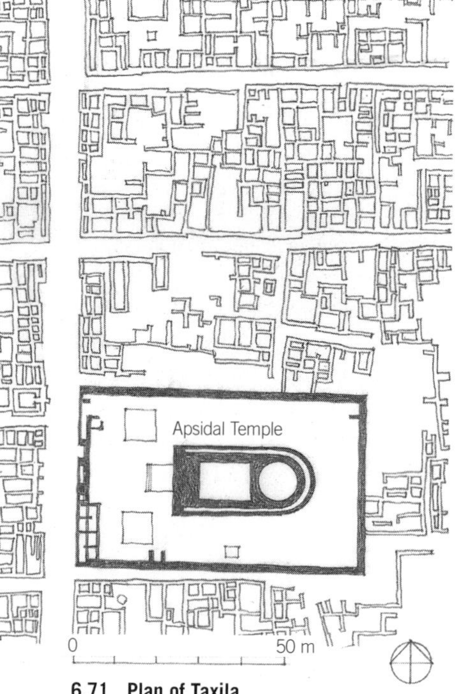


6.71 **Plan of Taxila**

0

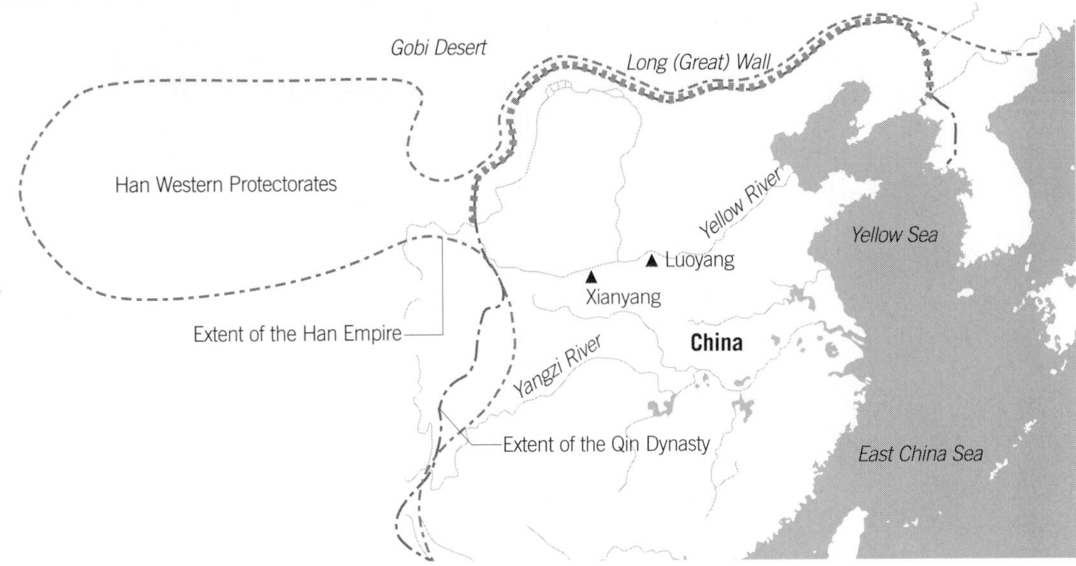


**QIN DYNASTY CHINA**

After almost 200 years of warring factions, China came to be unified under the short-lived but supremely despotic Qin Dynasty (221–206 BCE). Qin means "to catch" or "to seize." The first ruler of the dynasty, Ying Zheng, renamed himself Shi Huangdi (meaning First Emperor) and validated his rule by claiming divine mandate. He put in place a centralized bureaucracy and administration that could account for the diverse sections of the Empire. Under the direction of the bureaucracy, the individual commanderies and prefectures were administered jointly by civil and military officials. The system of writing was standardized as was the language. A single currency was introduced, a copper coin with a hole in the middle so it could be strung on a string. Shi Huangdi also connected the existing defensive fortifications in the north of China to form the first Great Wall to fend off invading "barbarians" from the north. Despite these accomplishments, in his time Shi Huangdi was unpopular; he raised taxes, deprived the nobility of power, was ruthlessly intolerant of those who opposed him and suppressed the writings of alternative philosophers.

Although Shi Huangdi's short-lived dynasty was controversial, Qin (pronounced chin) is the origin of the Western name China. The Chinese themselves called their land the Middle Kingdom.

The ideal of a unified China, which was to remain persistent throughout Chinese history, can be contrasted with the histories of South Asia and Europe, where even though emperors were periodically able to conquer large territories, the idea of a single unified empire was always keenly contested. It was only a function of European colonialism in the 18th and 19th centuries that India, for example, became a single nation.

**6.72 Qin dynasty coin**

After Shi Huangdi's death, rebellion ensued, resulting in the establishment of the Han Dynasty (206 BCE–220 CE). The Han Dynasty abandoned Shi Huangdi's absolutism for a more balanced philosophy of governance, but they held on to the Qin idea of a unified and centralized China. By the turn of the millennium, the Han ruled an area larger than the Roman Empire. Other than a short period of rebellion from 9 to 23 CE, the Han ruled continuously for just over 400 years. The Han Emperor Wudi (141–86 BCE), established new commanderies in Korea, and his conquest of Ferghana and neighboring regions in 101 BCE gave China control of the trade routes running north and south of the Taklamakan Desert, its gateway to the west. In return for its silk and gold, China received wine, spices, woolen fabrics, grapes, pomegranates, sesame, broad beans, and alfalfa. Under the Han, poetry, literature, and philosophy prospered, and the voluminous *Shiji* (Historical Records), written by Sima Qian (145–80 BCE), set the standard for later government-sponsored histories.

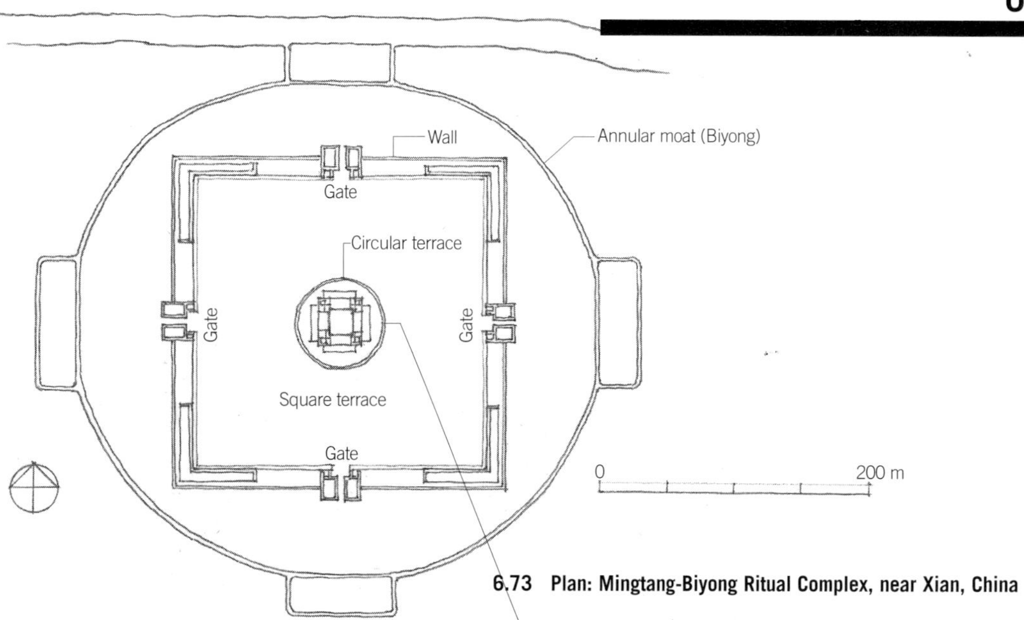


**6.73 Plan: Mingtang-Biyong Ritual Complex, near Xian, China**

**Mingtang-Biyong Ritual Complex**

According to the *Shiji*, the Qin sacrificial rituals, known as *zhi*, were meant to be performed on high grounds in forested areas, where offerings were made to the four deities of the directions, represented by the colors white, azure, yellow, and red. Sacrifices to the dynastic ancestors were also performed in the ancestral temple of the Han dynasty capital, Chang'an. The Han multiplied the Qin rituals and offered sacrifices to the gods of heaven and earth, mountains and rivers, the sun and moon, and the stars and planets, but they built artificial replicas of natural altars. These ritual structures, known as the Mingtang (Bright Hall) and Biyong (Jade Ring Moat) and built during the reign of Han Wudi (141–86 BCE) near Chang'an, were designated as the intersection of heaven (circle) and earth (square), oriented around the four cardinal directions. The circular moat (Biyong) that defines its outer perimeter is bridged by paths coming in from the cardinal directions and heading into a square enclosure, in the center of which, on a round terrace, there was the main bilevel sacred hall (Mingtang). The walls of the four outer chambers were painted with colors associated with each direction: east, green; south, red; west, white; and north, black.

Han writers understood the human realm as a land mass surrounded by water, with the empire in the center, and with peripheral territories occupied by marginal, barbaric people at the edges. At the conceptual center of it all was the emperor, who ruled by divine mandate, and was the Son of Heaven. From this spot, the calendar was regulated and its knowledge disseminated. This was also where young emperors were educated.

Sacred Hall (Mingtang)

0 30 m

**6.74 Plan and elevation: Central structure of Mingtang-Biyong Ritual Complex**

**0**

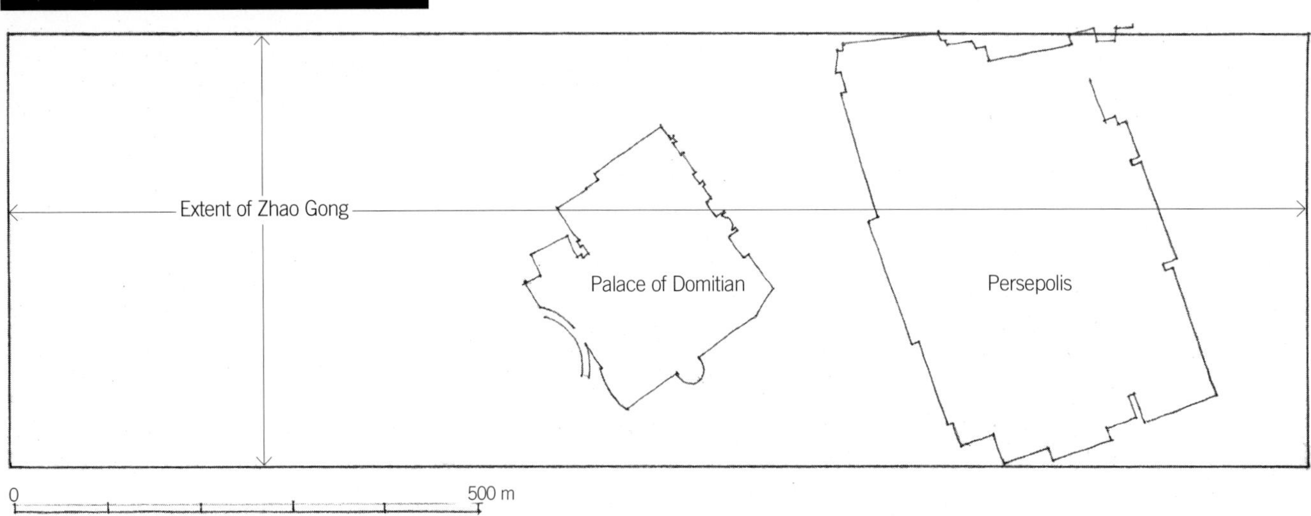


**6.75 A size comparison of the First Emperor of Qin's palatial complex, Zhao Gong, with contemporary palace complexes**

### Zhao Gong

Though the Qin and Han palaces were destroyed in dynastic wars, they are extensively described in the literature, and excavations in the late 1970's have discovered that these palaces are quite similar to these descriptions. One of the most impressive was, of course, the palace of Qin Shi Huangdi himself. It was located at his capital, Xianyang, about 28 kilometers west of present-day Xian. In an attempt to symbolize the centralization of power, the palace was actually a series of buildings designed to imitate the palatial buildings of each of the six warring states conquered by the Qin. Each time a kingdom was conquered, a replica of its palace would be built in Xianyang.

Three large groups of palatial foundations have been discovered in Xianyang. The oldest (Palace No. 1) is a two-level structure, with the upper level imposingly raised six meters above the lower. The upper level is L-shaped and extended 60 meters east to west and 45 meters north to south. At its center is the principal hall, with a large pillar right at its center. A smaller hall to the southeast is thought to be the emperor's residence. The L-shape suggests that another similar complex was to be symmetrically placed to the east.

In 212 BCE, Shi Huangdi commissioned the construction of an enormous palatial complex, Zhao Gong (Shining Lord), on the south side of the Wei River. The foundations show that the entire complex measured about 1400 meters by 450 meters and was built on a rammed-earth foundation 7 to 8 meters high. According to the *Shiji*:

> Then he had palaces constructed in the Shanglin gardens, south of the Wei River. The front palace, Epang, was built first ... The terraces above could seat 10,000 and below there was room for banners [20 meters] in height. One causeway round the palace led to the South Hill at the top of which a gateway was erected. A second led across the Wei River to [the capital] ...
>
> (Sima Qian, *Selections from Records of the Historian*, English translation by Yang Hsien-yi and Gladys Yang [Peking: Foreign Languages Press, 1979], pg.179)

When Shi Huangdi died, construction was delayed to build his tomb. Later it was resumed, but the palace was never completed, due to the overthrowing of the Qin Dynasty by the Han.

6.76 **Remains of the Qin Great Wall, Ningxia, China**

6.77 **Clay model of a Han beacon tower**

**Great Wall of China**

The empire created by Shi Huangdi had few serious enemies to its south, and to the west, the enormous Taklamakan Desert served as an impediment to all but the heartiest of traders. But to the north, the nomadic Mongol tribes were such a threat that they embodied for the Qin and Han dynasties the quintessential "barbarians." The Mongols' skill with horses gave them a military advantage that would, under Chengiz (Ghengis) Khan, not only yield China to them but indeed take them to the very doors of Europe. The Chinese response to the Mongol threat was to reach for a radical option that could only be mounted by a highly organized empire—the creation of a vast defensive wall, the *wanli qangqeng* (10,000-*li*-long wall), popularly called the Great Wall since colonial times. Small segments of earthen ramparts had been constructed along the northern frontier in the Warring States Period under the Zhou. Shi Huangdi conceived the idea of connecting and extending these segments and it was realized by the Han emperors. The resulting fortification is not a single continuous structure but rather a network of walls and towers. Whenever possible, it was backed into mountains or otherwise located to take advantage of naturally occurring defensive formations.

To maintain its integrity, the Great Wall was constantly patrolled, and signal systems were set up to transmit messages from one watchtower to another. As the counterpart to the unified Empire, designating the barbarians beyond, the Great Wall is *the* symbol of the Middle Kingdom. In spite of being expanded and reinforced repeatedly, the Great Wall was repeatedly breached by northern nomadic civilizations, many of which went on to establish successful ruling dynasties in China, such as the Jin, the Liao, the Yuan, and the Qing. These supposedly "barbarian" dynasties, of course, had less interest in reinforcing the wall.

Extending from contemporary North Korea all the way to the Jade Gate in Gansu Province, the Great Wall had several architectural components:

- Border towns: Of varying shapes and sizes, these towns were small and defensible, complete with moats, walls, streets, dwellings, and watchtowers;
- Fortifications: Small forts, 50–150 square kilometers in area and protected by moats and high walls, served as military stations;
- Check points: Two- to three-story watchtowers were built everywhere the wall encountered intersections or was open to movement;
- Beacon towers: Watchtowers on platforms were located about 130 meters apart, from where lookouts could spot approaching enemies and alert adjacent towers by smoke signals.

Most of the Qin and Han sections of the Great Wall were made of pounded earth and paved with stones. Some parts, however, were made of Chinese tamarisk and reeds that were arranged in a checkerboard pattern and then filled in with sand and stone. While much of the ancient wall of Shi Huangdi has disappeared, most of what was built in the Ming Dynasty (1368–1644), following a route different from that of Shi Huangdi's fortifications, survives today.

6.78 **View of the Great Wall**

6.79 **Terra-cotta warriors in the Tomb of the First Qin Emperor**

6.80 **The First Emperor of Qin, Shi Huangdi**

**Tomb of the First Emperor**

The Tomb of the First Emperor, one of the most celebrated archaeological finds in China, is located in Lishan, just south of Xian. Its outer perimeter wall, 6 meters thick and constructed of rammed earth, encloses an area of approximately 2 square kilometers. The main entrance is on the east. Within the perimeter there was a second walled enclosure with four more gates, one on each of the four sides.

Outside the eastern entrance, archaeologists have uncovered more than 8000 life-size terra-cotta figures, grouped in battle order, rank by rank, some mounted on horse-drawn chariots, others in infantry groups armed with spears, swords, and crossbows (although the spear shafts, bows and other wooden objects have decayed away).

Vault no. 1 is the largest, measuring 60 by 210 meters. In 11 parallel trenches there are over 3000 terra-cotta foot soldiers arranged as an infantry regiment, facing away from the emperor's tomb. They wear no helmets since only officers wore them during the Qin dynasty, but they all have harnesses.

In the eastern gallery are bowmen and crossbowmen in a formation of three rows, making a total of almost 200 sharpshooters. Most were armed with actual crossbows with a range of 200 meters. Archaeologists once believed that each warrior had individual traits—that they were portraits of the emperor's guard-of-honor—but it now seems that there are about 100 different types of faces.

Vault no. 2 contains a formation of chariots and cavalry with supporting troops, all turned toward the east. There are 1430 warriors and horses divided into four groups. Vault no. 3 seems to be the headquarters of the terra-cotta army, with a commander along with 68 officers. The 4th vault is empty and may never have been used.

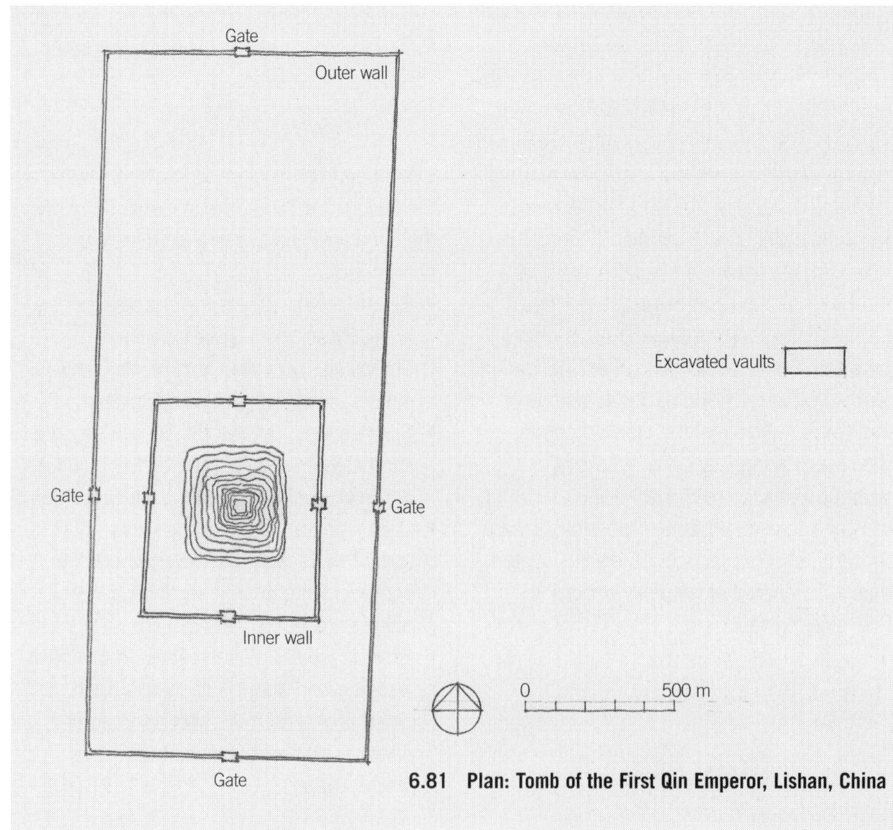


6.81 **Plan: Tomb of the First Qin Emperor, Lishan, China**

**6.82 Partial section: Vault no. 1 of the Tomb of the First Qin Emperor**

The mound beneath which the First Emperor is buried is 350 meters square, and 76 meters high. It remains unexcavated. But the Shiji contains a fabulous description of the burial itself, which still awaits confirmation:

> As soon as the First Emperor became king of Qin, excavations and building had been started at Mount Li, while after he won the empire, more than 700,000 conscripts from all parts of the country worked there. They dug through three subterranean streams and poured molten copper for the outer coffin, and the tomb was filled with models of palaces, pavilions, and offices as well as fine vessels, precious stones, and rarities. Artisans were ordered to fix up crossbows so that any thief breaking in would be shot. All the country's streams, the Yellow River, and the Yangzi were reproduced in quicksilver and by some mechanical means made to flow into a miniature ocean. The heavenly constellations were above and the regions of the earth below. The candles were made of whale oil to insure the burning for the longest possible time.
>
> (Sima Qian, *Selections from Records of the Historian*, English translation by Yang Hsien-yi and Gladys Yang [Peking: Foreign Languages Press, 1979], pg.186)

The excavation of the First Emperor's tomb, if it has not already been looted, may yield untold riches.

The use of smaller terra-cotta armies to guard the perimeters of imperial tombs continued for at least a century. One spectacular group of more than 40,000 such figures, about one-third life-size, was excavated in 1990 outside the joint tomb of Emperor Jingdi (r. 157–141 BCE) and his wife, Empress Wang.

**6.83 Terra-cotta cavalryman and saddle horse: Tomb of the First Qin Emperor**

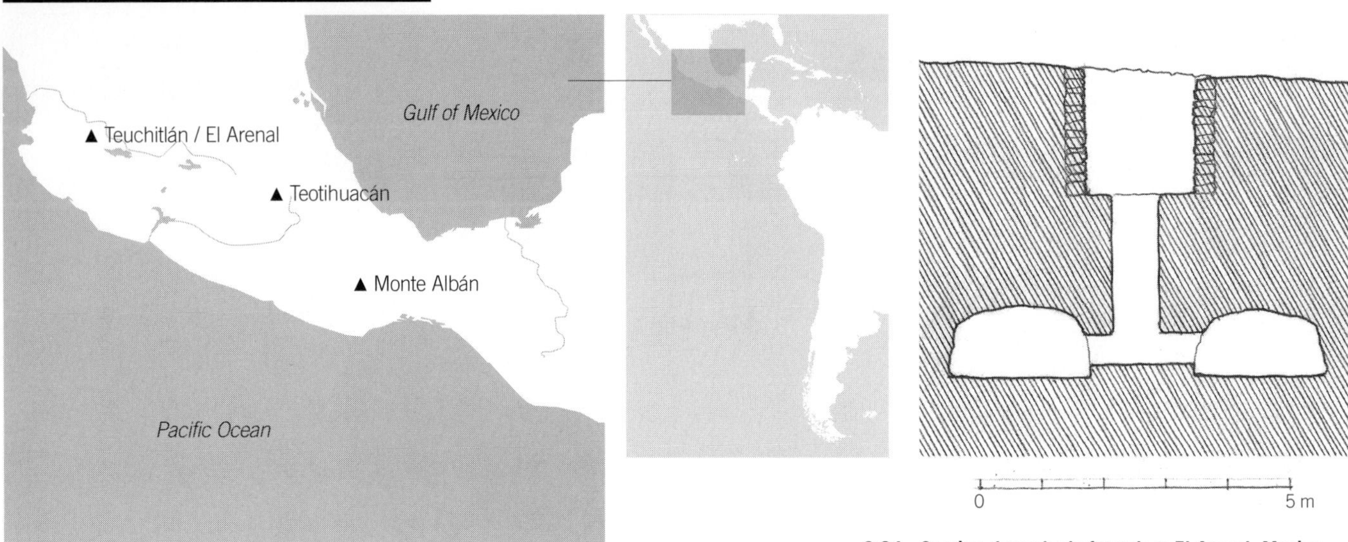


**6.84 Section through shaft tomb at El Arenal, Mexico**

## SHAFT TOMBS OF TEUCHITLÁN

At the turn of the millennium, Central America was dominated by the Zapotecs, with their elaborate capital in the Oaxaca valley. The Zapotecs eventually replaced the Olmecs, who were by now in serious decline. In the Yucatan Peninsula, the Mayan culture had begun to take firm root with the development of the earliest stages of the monumental platform-and-pyramid complexes in the El Mirador basin and Tikal. At the edges of these great civilizations, in the high lake valleys of western Mexico, we find a relatively minor but fascinating civilization in particular at Teuchitlán, around the slopes of the extinct volcano Tequila. The remains today consist essentially of funerary shaft tombs, accompanied by corresponding surface level ritual architecture, created as integral parts of small chieftain settlements, the largest of which probably had about 20,000 to 30,000 inhabitants. Though burial chambers were a constant in Western Mexico, significant here is that no pyramids or images of the usual deities have been found. The origin of this particular culture and the reasons for their autonomous architectural development are not well understood. *Ancient West Mexico* (edited by Richard Townsend) contains some of the more recent studies.

For the residents of Teuchitlán, funerary tombs were a critical part in establishing the connection between the living and their ancestors. They were used by hereditary chieftains and their families and became the symbolic center of the society's communal life. The earliest type of tombs (1500–800 BCE) consisted of a round opening surrounded by a low platform, from which a short, stepped passage led into the mortuary chamber. Such small tombs from all periods are found everywhere in Western Mexico. Little is known of the tombs from the period between 800 and 300 BCE, since none have been scientifically excavated, although tombs are found throughout the lake-basin district. In the period 300 BCE–200 CE, the shaft tombs, used by hereditary chieftains and their families, became the symbolic center of the society.

Carved into volcanic tuff, the tombs are generally boot- or bottle-shaped, with vertical shafts cut anywhere from 1 to 21 meters below the surface before opening into one or more side chambers in which the dead were interred, along with a large offering of hollow ceramic figures, shell jewelry, obsidian jewelry, ground stone, and other items. There is evidence that the tombs held burials from different times and were therefore reopened as necessary.

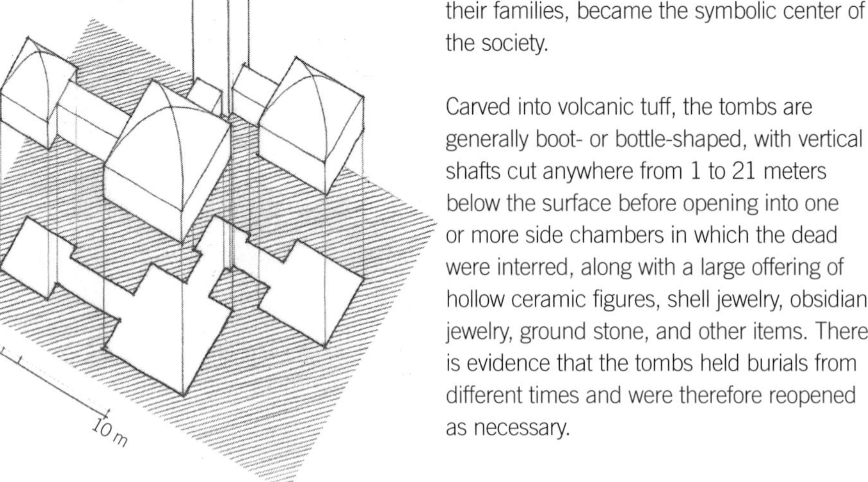


**6.85 Plan and pictorial view of shaft tomb at El Arenal**

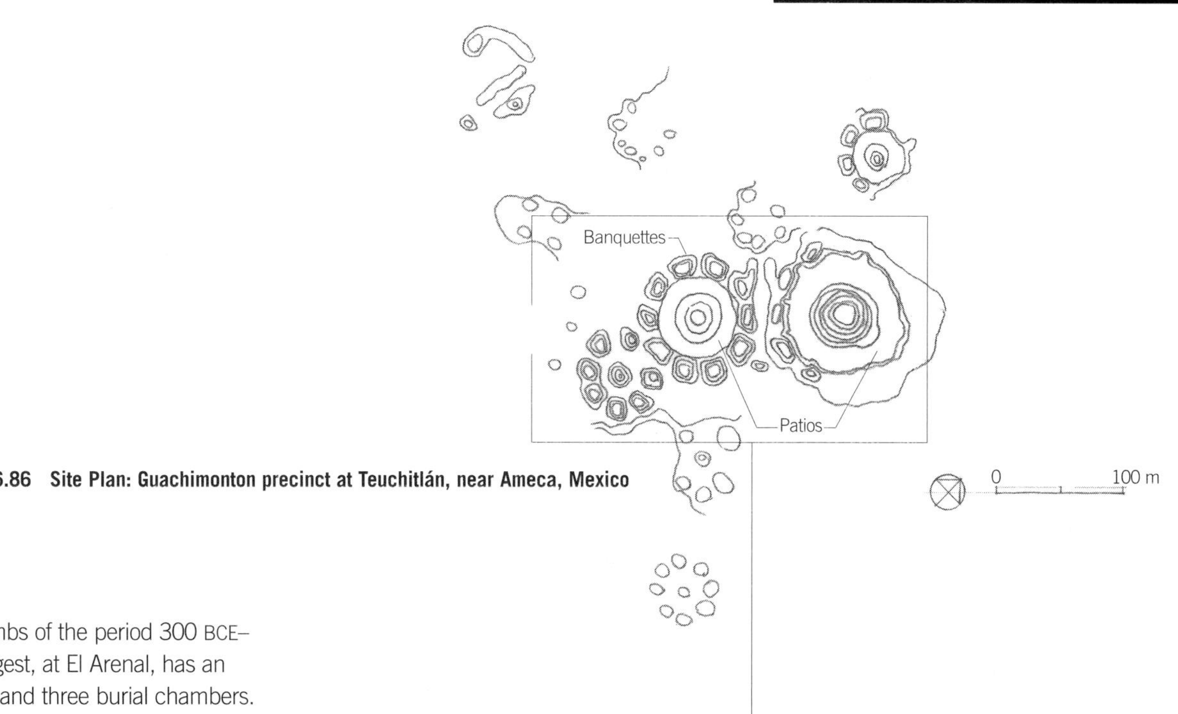


**6.86 Site Plan: Guachimonton precinct at Teuchitlán, near Ameca, Mexico**

Of the shaft tombs of the period 300 BCE–200 CE, the largest, at El Arenal, has an 18-meter shaft and three burial chambers. Two other shaft tombs are located within the same ceremonial area. On the surface, the shaft emerged at the center of a circular stepped mound that was surrounded by an elevated circular patio, at the edge of which were 8 to 12 evenly spaced rectangular platforms. Made of rubble and packed earth, the larger complexes of the later phase (300–800 CE) range from 28 meters at Portrero de las Chivas to well over 100 meters at Guachimonton, the largest of the Teuchitlán ritual sites. The circles were often found in groups of two and three, with some of the circles overlapping. Ball courts are also found in association with these circles.

Later, in the period 300 to 800 CE, shaft tombs became less important and huge surface circles, along with ball courts, came to dominate the construction to the point that their burial chambers are as yet undiscovered.

**6.87 Plan and section: Central circular structures of the Guachimonton complex at Teuchitlán**

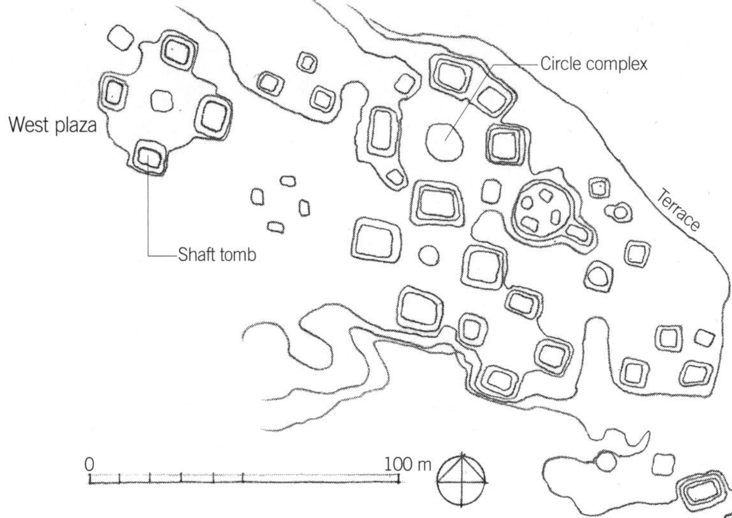


6.88 Site plan of Huitzilapa, near Guadalajara, Mexico

The graves of El Arenal, like most shaft tombs, have been looted or destroyed. One that has been excavated intact at Huitzilapa is a shaft tomb 8 meters deep, with two burial chambers, several burials, and about 60,000 artifacts. The tomb sits at the western end of the 50 by 200-meter settlement. At the eastern end is a large, elongated ball court. The center of the settlement is dominated by a religious complex consisting of eight platform mounds surrounding a circular pyramid. This complex abuts another, smaller circular complex to its west, consisting of four platform mounds fronting onto a square court with a small circular pyramid in the middle. The shaft tomb is located in one of the mounds. Low abutments indicate that the four platforms were linked together in a ring at their base. The shaft tapers about one-third of its way down and then opens into two domical chambers, oriented north-south, which are entered through narrow openings and stairs. Within, six skeletons, one of whom is clearly the chieftain, are laid out with their heads toward the entrance, surrounded by offerings.

Clay models found with the offerings testify to the self-consciousness of the designs, linking community festivals to the order of the cosmos, the rhythms of the seasons, and the cycles of life and death. The circle replicates the encompassing ring of the horizon; cardinal and intercardinal orientations are established by pyramid stairways along axes related to the path of the sun. The models show a tall mast rising from the central pyramid, which in mystical parlance would be the axis mundi, connecting the apex of the sky to the central point of the earth's surface and to the underworld nadir. These sites were also the location of observations and rites on the day of the summer solstice, the annual time of the sun's zenith passage, the beginnings of the rains, and the renewal of the earth's fertility.

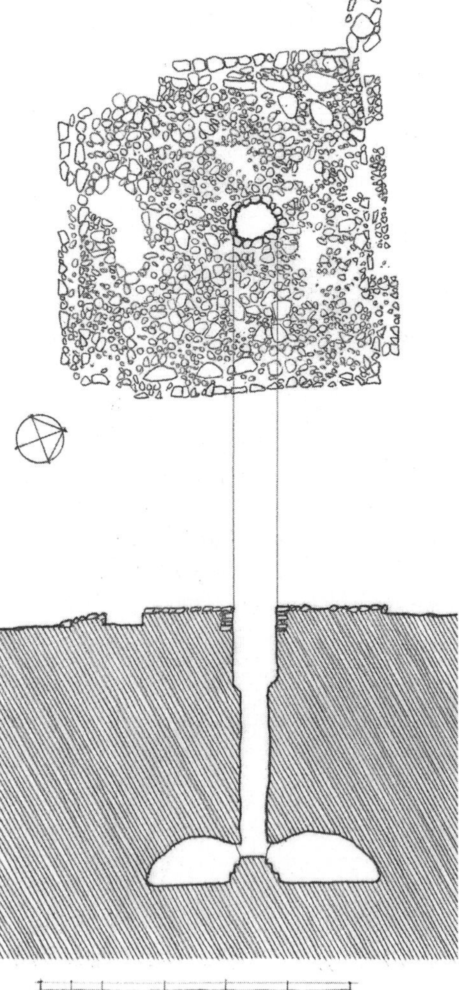


6.89 Plan and section: Two-chambered shaft tomb at Huitzilapa

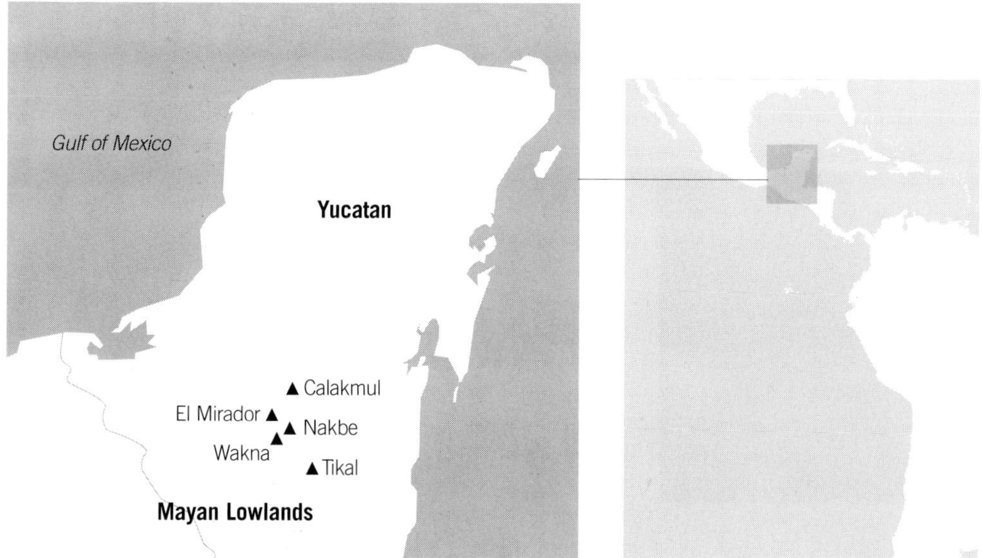


## Nakbe

In the Mayan heartland, a religious philosophy, devised by a professional priesthood and built around the importance of astronomical manifestations, gradually took shape. It involved the eternal struggle between the powers of good and evil over the destiny of mankind. The benevolent gods bring thunder, lightning, rain, and insure plenty, whereas the malevolent ones bring death, destruction, hurricanes, and war. The religion developed into a worship of time in its various manifestations; it was highly esoteric in nature, requiring priests, mathematicians, prophets, and ritualists. Dancing was an important aspect of the religious ceremonies, as was the giving of sacrifices. These ranged from food offerings to ornaments, like feathers and shells, to the general practice of human sacrifice.

No doubt maize production played an important role for the Maya, but the land is not particularly suitable for agriculture. It seems that trees were cut down for rubber and for resin. The copal tree produced a specially prized, sweet-smelling resin that was used in religious ceremonies. It has also been suggested that different urban settlements specialized in different types of resins. Trade in such valuable commodities within the Mayan civilization and to outsiders would have allowed them to purchase maize from others.

This specialized production and dependency on foreign trade might have been the reason for both the success and the eventual demise of the Maya. Trees were also felled to fuel the kilns where limestone was burned to make lime. Deforestation, it has been suggested, led to a gradual erosion of both land and wealth.

By 350 BCE, a centralized elite was able to control large labor populations whose rapid rate of production was aided by the development of standardized construction modules and faster stone-cutting techniques. In this period, we witness the emergence of monumental Mayan architecture in the Yucatan Peninsula at a scale not seen before. An abundance of massive architectural assemblages, ranging from 40 to 72 meters high, are found in the Mirador Basin. Since they are located in marshes, all the major building groups were raised on large platforms that were then connected by elevated causeways.

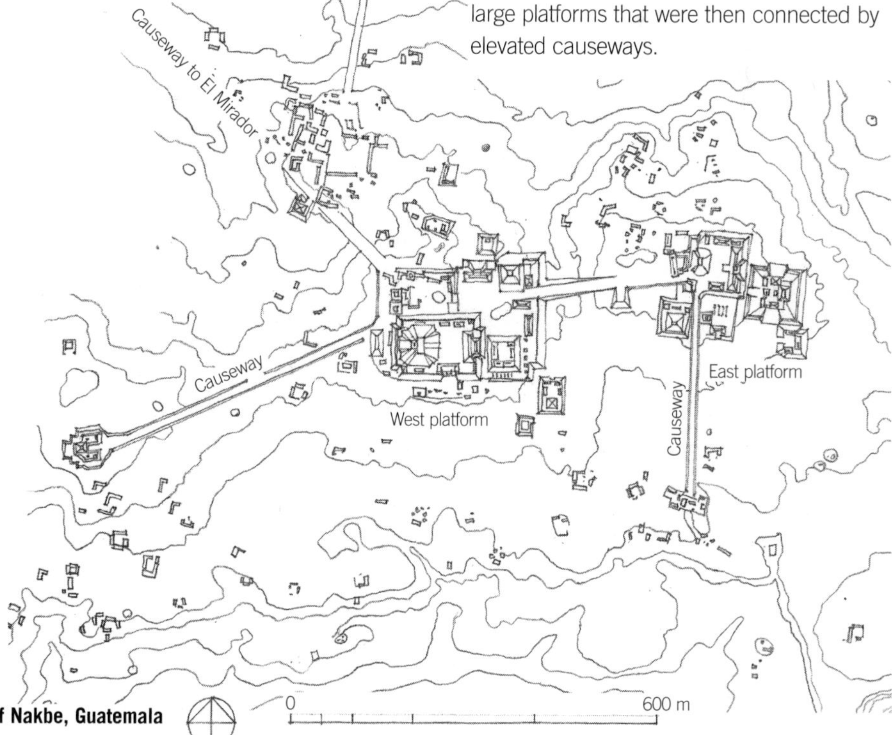


**6.90 Site plan of Nakbe, Guatemala**

6.91 Roof comb of El Mirador

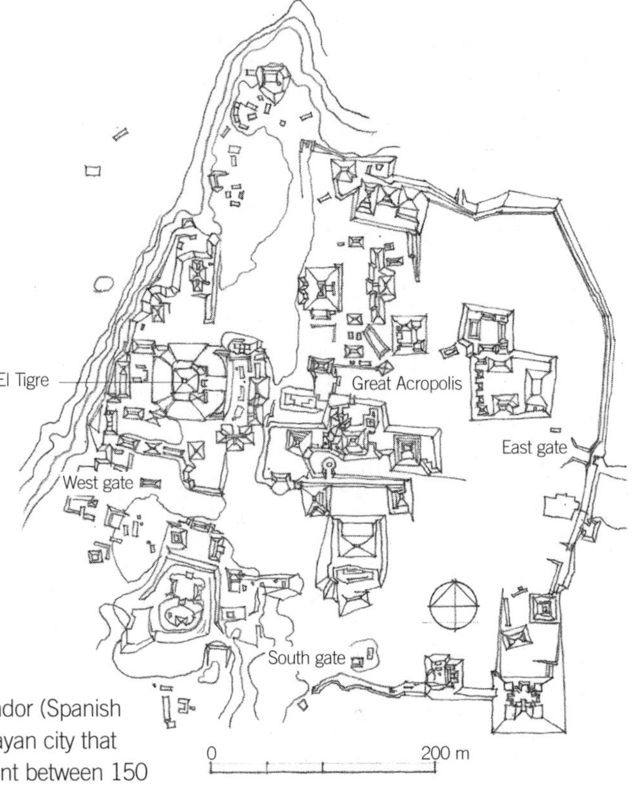


6.92 Site plan of the West Group at El Mirador, Guatemala

In general, the organization of early Maya ceremonial complexes was devoted to creating distinct visual hierarchies by means of a system of interconnected raised platform terraces surmounted by temples. The central ceremonial complex at Nakbe consists of two major, connected, built-up platforms (the eastern 32 meters high and the western 45 meters high), on top of which the principal structures are clustered.

The eastern platform has two parts. One is a cluster of low-platform structures on a terrace creating a court that is anchored on its west side by a large freestanding pyramid. The other part has a larger pyramid, which is visible from the court, but with access restricted to priestly use. Thus a complex ceremonial whole was formed with multiple hierarchically organized centers, both spatial and visual, that was used for multiple ceremonial functions.

Across the causeway is the western platform, which consists of three terraced courtyards, the highest of which supports the large pyramid, access to which, as with the others, is restricted through the small courtyard in front of it. Since the function of Mayan pyramids was to support the temple, they were always flat-topped. The pyramid itself consisted of tightly compressed layers of stones and clay sealed by a brick casing.

**El Mirador**

Just north of Nakbe, El Mirador (Spanish for lookout) was an early Mayan city that reached its cultural high point between 150 BCE and 150 CE. Though the city was spread out over an area of 16 square kilometers, the center was a crowded constellation of sacred and secular buildings. Here the platforms have been built up successively over time, comprising the largest set of platforms found anywhere in the Mayan world. The entire site was dominated by the so-called El Tigre, a gigantic building complex covering 5.6 hectares. We can see here the emerging Mayan typology of the triple summit structures, consisting generally of a central dominant structure with two smaller buildings, facing each other in front of it. Archaeologists believed that this arrangement represented the three stars in the constellation of Orion—known as Alnitak, Saiph, and Ligel—within which was supposed to burn the fire of creation.

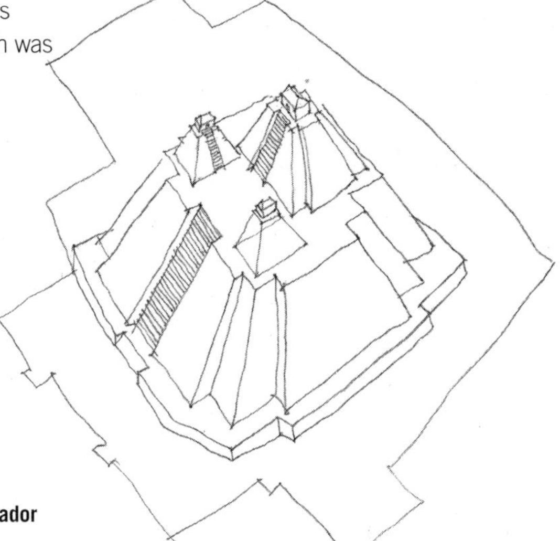

6.93 Reconstruction of El Tigre, El Mirador

# 200 CE

In the year 200 CE, Rome, Chang'an, and Teotihuacán were the megacities of the world; all three centers of vast empires and benchmarks against which subsequent kingdoms would measure themselves. Imperial Rome, with more than a million, had the most inhabitants. At 20 square kilometers, Teotihuacán was the largest. In 500 CE, Teotihuacán at its height had 200,000 inhabitants. In 200 CE Han Dynasty Chang'an covered only 4.5 square kilometers, with anywhere between 250,000 to 500,000 inhabitants. But by the 8th century Chang'an covered 86 square kilometers and had a population of a million; it was the largest city in the world. By then Teotihuacán had been torched and abandoned, and Rome was a shadow of its imperial self.

During the two hundred years of Pax Roma, wealth was lavished not only on temples and palaces but also on baths, viaducts, libraries, courts, streets, theaters, and amphitheaters. As a result, the architectural history of this period, from England to North Africa and from Spain to the Levant is categorized under the term "Roman architectural history." The broad scope of Roman architecture would have tremendous impact on subsequent developments throughout Europe.

The Han Dynasty transformed the vision of a centralized state developed by the Qin into a model of governance based on Confucian principles. The emperors built cities, palaces, and tombs on an unprecedented scale, while also making remarkable advances in technology and mining. Trade with the west was so important that the Chinese founded their western capital, Chang'an, as the starting point for caravans heading westward over the Taklamakan Desert.

Between these two great powers, China and Rome, both of which had at their core relatively static religious practices, we see ferment in matters of religion from the Levant in west Asia to northern India. These new religious ideas would eventually have a profound impact on world history and architecture. Generally, these religions offered practices that were more personal and mystical in nature, such as that offered by the cult of Isiris in Egypt, the cult of Baal in the Levant and the Mithraism practiced increasingly in many places in the Roman Empire. Christianity was also developing, as were different Jewish sects. The dominant religion in West Asia was, however, Zoroastrianism, which was elevated to a state religion by the Parthians. With the fall of the Parthians to Islam, Zoroastrianism was systematically suppressed and driven underground, surviving today mainly in India.

Buddhism established an architectural presence in South Asia with monastic universities located along trade routes. Buddhist monasteries were patronized mostly by merchants who were traveling along trade routes, conducting their business not only within South Asia but also with China, Central Asia, and the Roman Empire by both land and sea. And along these routes Buddhism made its way to China, particularly along the southern Silk Route.

In the global encounter between east and west, one has to mention the Kushans, a Chinese people who had been pushed out of China into present-day Afghanistan, supplanting the Gandharan empire. Living at the crossroads of the region, between the Persians, Indians, and Chinese, they produced stupa complexes that were Hellenic in articulation and Indian in form, with Zoroastrian influences mixed in as well.

In the Pampas region of the Peruvian coast of South America, the Nazca civilization created large pilgrimage centers, such as those in Cahuachi, and later created mysterious patterns on the ground, celebrated today as the Nazca Lines. These elaborate designs, which can only be seen from the air, remain unresolved, as do the questions about the nature of the Nazca's geographical and religious practices. But the superpower of the region unquestionably was based in Teotihuacán, the capital of an empire that encompassed most of Central America and the center of a trading network that extended from the Mississippi Delta to the Peruvian coast. Teotihuacán was the largest and most influential city of precolonial America. All subsequent architecture in Central America was influenced by the Teotihuacán legacy. Much further north, the Hopewell cultures of the Mississippi river built preliminary mound cultures, a distant echo of Teotihuacán.

Roman Republic
509–27 BCE

▲ Miletus
470 BCE–250 CE

▲ Ephesus
100 BCE–420 CE

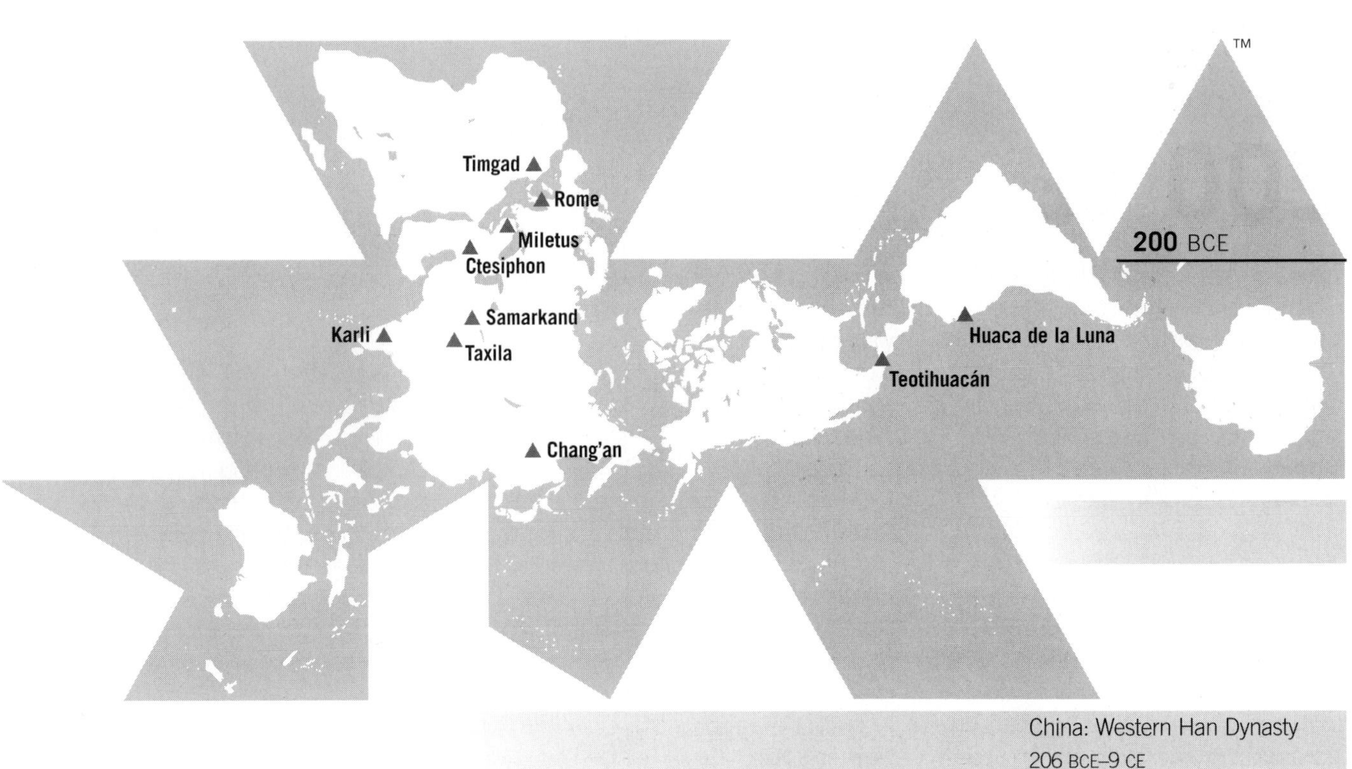


China: Western Han Dynasty
206 BCE–9 CE

Roman Empire
27 BCE–393 CE

▲ **Hadrian's Villa**
118–134 CE

▲ **Bath of Caracalla**
212–216 CE

▲ **Temple of Jupiter at Baalbek**
Begun ca. 10 CE

▲ **Pantheon**
125 CE

▲ **Baths of Diocletian**
298–306 CE

▲ **Library of Celsus at Ephesus**
110 CE

▲ **Diocletian's Palace**
300 CE

Parthian Empire
247 BCE–224 CE

Sassanian Empire
224–651 CE

▲ **Takht-i-Suleiman**
ca. 300 BCE–110 CE

▲ **Palace of Ardashir**
ca. 224 CE

**0** — **200** CE — **400** CE

Satavahana and Ikshvaku Dynasties
2nd century BCE–4th century CE

◄ **Amaravati Stupa**
ca. 3rd century BCE

▲ **Caitya Hall at Karli**
ca. 2nd century CE

Kushan Empire
2nd century BCE–3rd century CE

▲ **Kushan temple at Mat**
1st century CE

▲ **Takht-i-Bahi**
2nd century CE

Wang Mang Interregnum
9–25 CE

Eastern Han Dynasty
25–220 CE

Sixteen Kingdoms Period: North China
25–220 CE

▲ **Han Tombs**
3rd century BCE–3rd century CE

The Nazca
300 BCE–200 CE

Moche Cultures
ca. 200 BCE–700 CE

▲ **Huaca del Sol and Huaca de la Luna**
ca. 100 CE

Teotihuacán Culture
ca. 150 BCE–650 CE

▲ **Pyramid of the Sun**
ca. 200 CE

▲ **Pyramid of the Moon**
ca. 250 CE

Hopewell Culture
200 BCE–500 CE

# 200 CE

## ROMAN EMPIRE

The Romanization of Europe and the Mediterranean basin was most strongly felt in the creating, rebuilding, and expanding of cities. The list includes Aosta, Bordeaux, Florence, London, Mainz, Mantua, Paris, Silchester (Hampshire, England), Trier, Turin, Verona, and Vienna, to name only a few. Many cities, like Florence, Milan, Paris, and Trier, still carry the imprint of the Roman grid. Though the paradigm for the city was the *castrum*, or military camp, which was divided by two main streets, the *cardo* and *decumanus*, in reality, Roman urbanism was more flexible and less stereotyped than one might assume. The *castrum* model was used mainly in the initial phases of colonization in Europe and North Africa, but it was rarely used in the East where cities were already well established or in second phases of urban expansion.

North Africa is an excellent place to study Roman urbanism. North Africa became particularly important for Rome, as it supplied the capital with staple crops and luxury goods. Lex Hadriana offered free, stable tenancy and a period of tax exemption to anyone who would reside permanently upon marginal land and put it under cultivation. It was a successful policy that transformed many agricultural towns into urban environments in their own right, particularly in North Africa. In some places a new town was founded like Timgad, a gridded city roughly the size of Florence, where, as at Lepcis Magna (east of Tripoli), the planners adopted a flexible and additive approach.

Thus, instead of fixating on the Roman penchant for order, one should focus instead on one of the principal contributions of Roman urbanism and a feature that distinguishes it from that of the Greeks—namely, the urban armature around which the residential quarters are packed. These armatures, as described by the noted classicist, William Lloyd MacDonald, are typical of the second phase of Roman urbanism and consisted of main streets, squares, fountains, gates, honorific columns, and the essential public buildings, all organized into a flowing system that marks Rome's imperial presence.

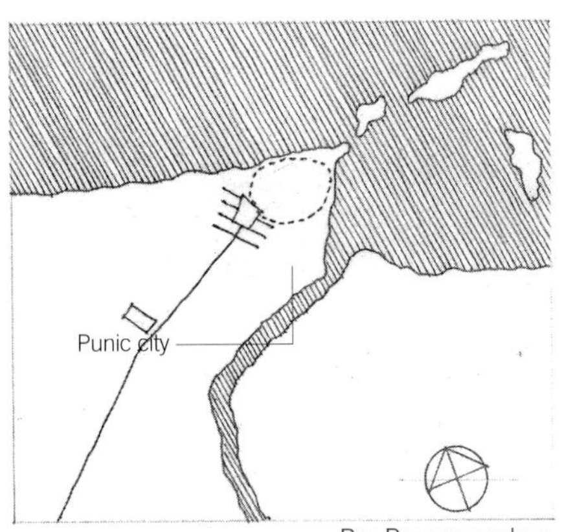


Pre-Roman nucleus

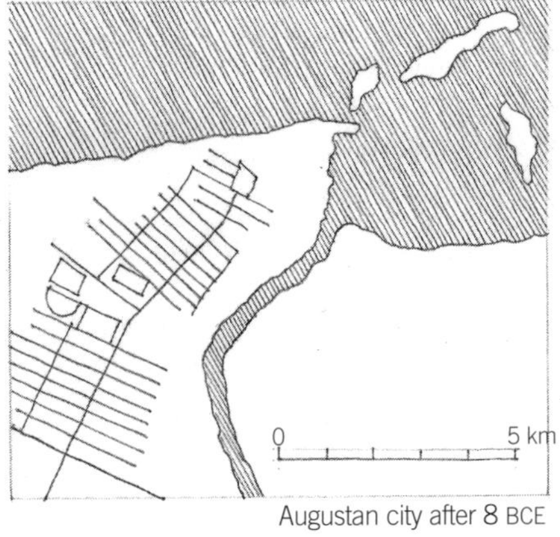


Augustan city after 8 BCE

Severan city in the 3rd century CE

**7.1 Development of Lepcis Magna**

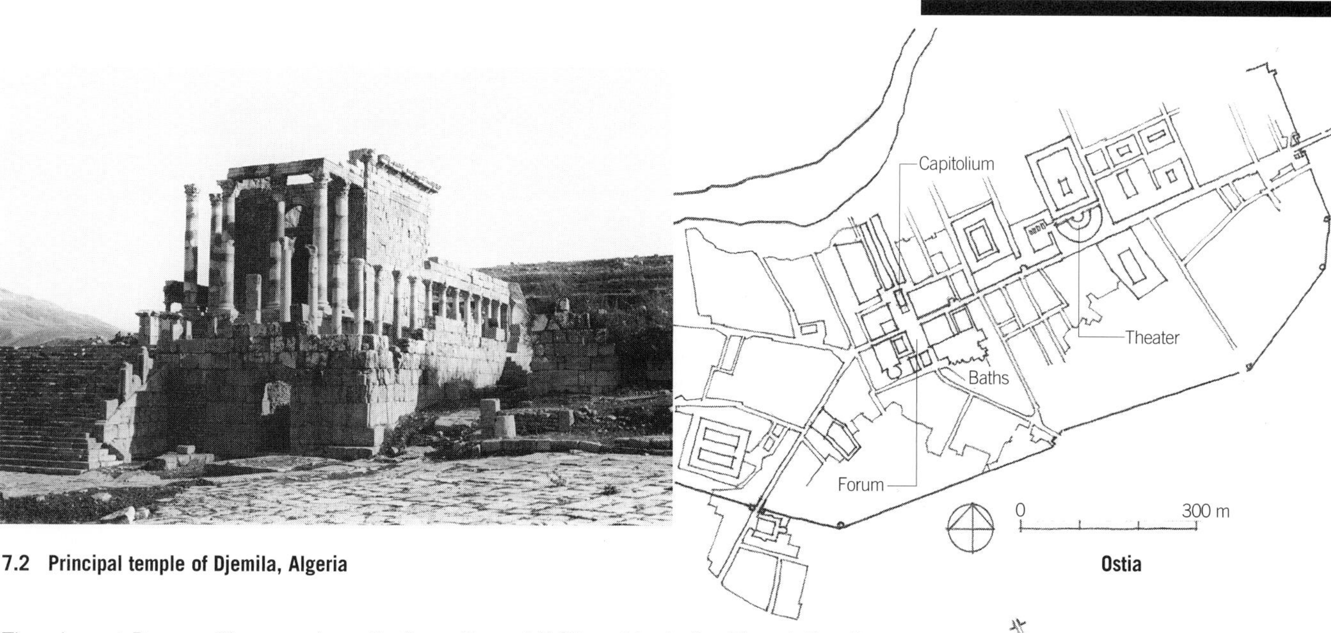


7.2 **Principal temple of Djemila, Algeria**

Though most Roman cities are schematically analogous, they differ from place to place, especially since these armatures are also organic—growing over time—and are rarely set out all at once. Orthogonality, though admired, was not imposed wholesale as one is often led to believe. Some Greek cities were expanded in this way (Athens, for example, with its much rebuilt agora) but others, like Priene, were not, as Priene by that time was in decline and apparently of so little importance in Roman times that its Hellenistic plan and housing survived more or less intact.

At Palmyra and Ostia we can see the attempt to graft the armature onto places that had been founded at an earlier date when they were more towns than cities. Djemila (96 CE), a town in western Numidia (Algeria), is typical—its elongated shape is a result of the terrain. The first part of the city to the north shows a relatively systematized layout with the agora at the center of the town along the main road. But when that proved inadequate, a new forum, temple, and theater were built in a southward extension that followed the curves of an existing road.

Timgad (100 BCE) is similar. Though the city is often given as a typical example of the rigorous application of the grid, the original town soon outgrew its borders. In fact, the elements of the armature that were originally left out of the town—the baths, gates, even a capitolium—had to be grafted into it or placed outside of the original design. A new arch, the Lambaesis Gate, demarcates the extent of the new extension. So even though the initial plan shows a great deal of control, the later extensions show a willing negotiation with the landscape and existent roads.

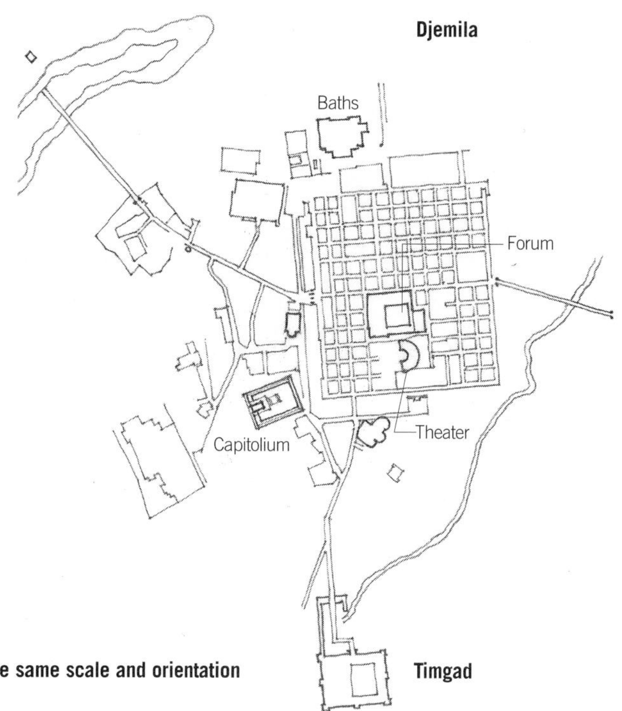


7.3 **Plans of three Roman towns drawn at the same scale and orientation**

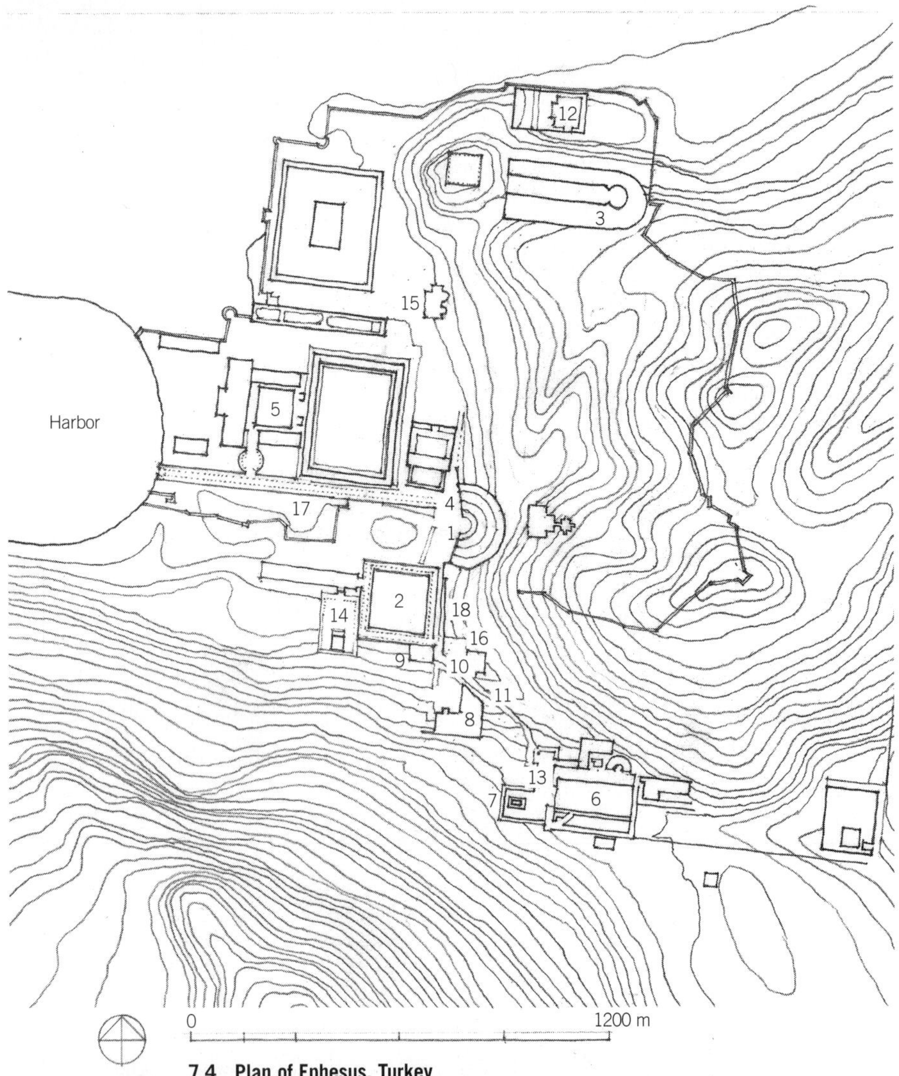


7.4 Plan of Ephesus, Turkey

7.5 Theater at Ephesus

In many places, the Romans were more than willing to work within the Hellenistic design mold, leaving the imprint of their urban structures in Athens and Pergamon, though the most spectacular examples are at Ephesus and Miletus. Ephesus had its origins as a small town and religious center on the Turkish coast. Around 100 CE it was developed into an increasingly important port. It was designed not from the top down but horizontally, in a protected valley and along the curving slopes of the flanking hills that open in dramatic fashion onto a harbor. By the end of the 5th century the port silted up and the city fell into disuse.

| | | |
|---|---|---|
| 1 | Theater | 100 BCE |
| 2 | Agora | 4 CE |
| 3 | Stadium | 54 CE |
| 4 | Fountain | 86 CE |
| 5 | Gymnasium | 90 CE |
| 6 | State Agora and Odeum | 100 CE |
| 7 | Temple of Domitian | 96 CE |
| 8 | Nymphaeum | 102 CE |
| 9 | Library of Celsus | 110 CE |
| 10 | Temple of Hadrian | 120 CE |
| 11 | Gates of Heracles | 150 CE |
| 12 | Gymnasium of Vedius | 150 CE |
| 13 | Pollio Fountain | 150 CE |
| 14 | Temple of Serapis | 170 CE |
| 15 | Palace of the Proconsul | 300 CE |
| 16 | Baths of Scholastica | 370 CE |
| 17 | Arcadiane | 395 CE |
| 18 | Marble Way | 420 CE |

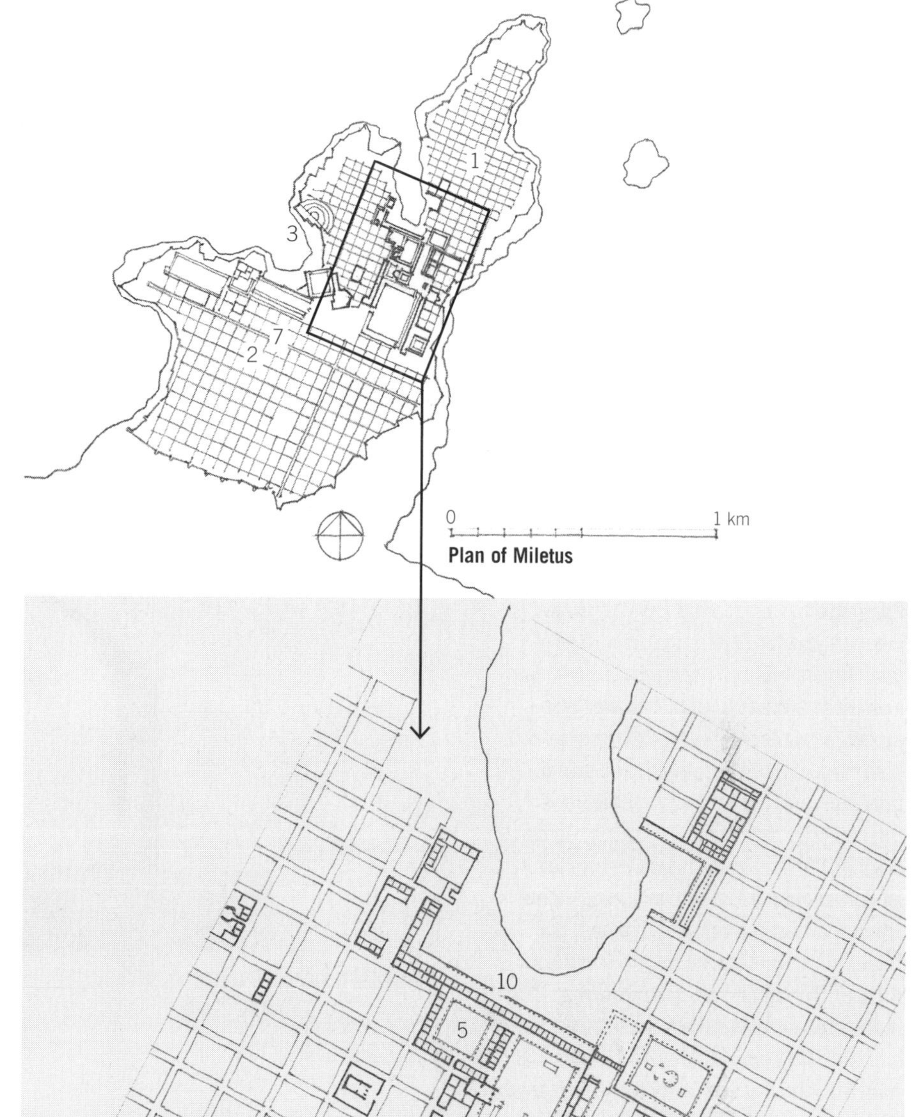


Plan of Miletus

Miletus went through three distinct phases. As a Greek colony, as a quasi-independent city-state, prospering during Hellenistic times, and then as part of the Roman Empire. In that later phase, the designers—working sometimes with and sometimes against the grain of the grid, while preserving some of the older buildings like the Bouleuterion (175–164 BCE) and destroying others—designed an intricate web of public buildings, streets, gates, and spaces that linked the old harbor with the new extension to the south. The dates show the pace of construction.

| | | |
|---|---|---|
| | Miletus destroyed | 479 BCE |
| | *First Phase* | |
| 1 | Northern street grid | 470 BCE |
| 2 | Temple of Athena | 450 BCE |
| 3 | Theater | 450 BCE |
| | *Rise to Prominence* | |
| 4 | Bouleuterion | 175 BCE |
| 5 | North Agora | 170 BCE |
| 6 | Gymnasium | 150 BCE |
| 7 | Stadium | 150 BCE |
| 8 | South Agora | 150 BCE |
| | *Imperial Era* | |
| 9 | Baths of Capito | 50 CE |
| 10 | Harbor Stoa, redesigned | 50 CE |
| 11 | Processional Way | 150 CE |
| 12 | *Nymphaeum* | 150 CE |
| 13 | Baths of Faustina | 170 CE |
| 14 | Temple of Serapis | 250 CE |

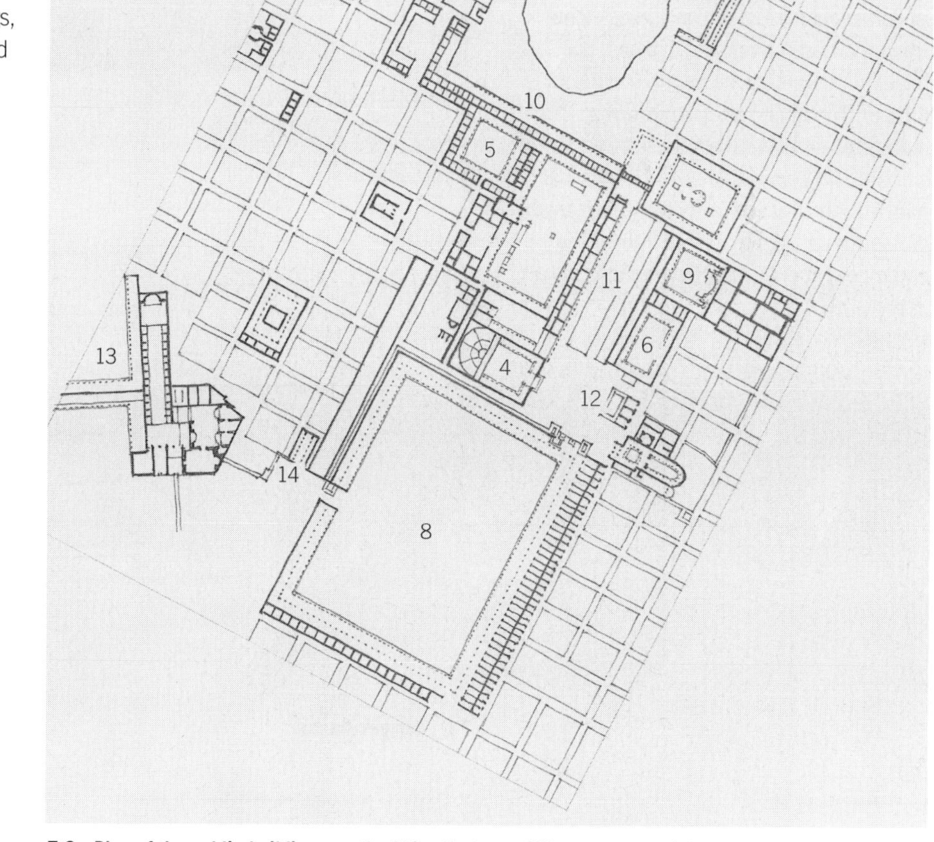


**7.6 Plan of the public buildings south of Lion Harbor at Miletus, near Yenihisar, Turkey**

7.7 **The Pantheon, Rome**

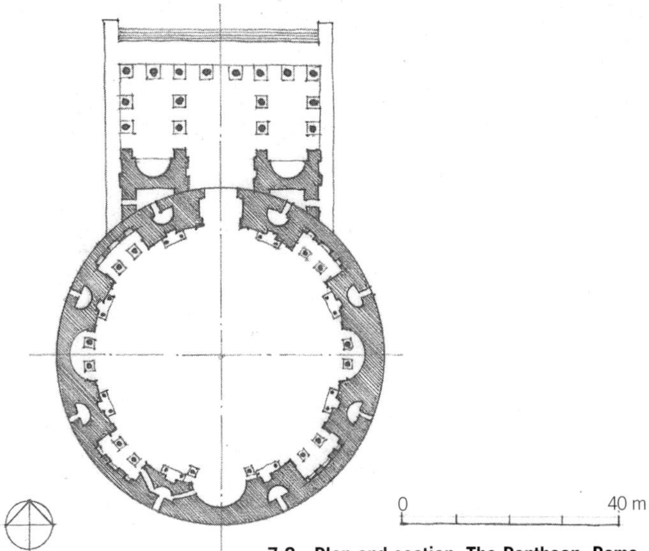

0 40 m

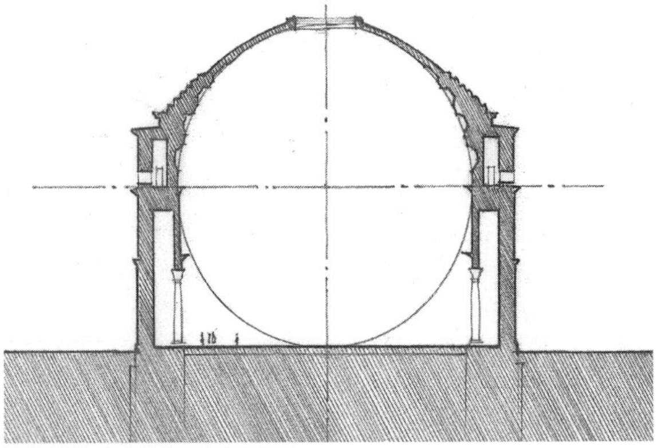

7.8 **Plan and section: The Pantheon, Rome**

## Pantheon

Hadrian was far different in character than Trajan. He had the deepest personal interest in architecture, but he was also a poet, a painter, as well as a competent commander. His reign in general was a peaceful one, but the revolt of the Jews in the east was repressed with savage ferocity. Hadrian's effect on architecture was felt in all corners of the Empire, including Rome, where he built numerous buildings, but none more significant than the Pantheon (25 CE). Though it has been repaired many times, the Pantheon has served as a church for centuries, has lost its original marble cladding, and lacks the impressively dimensioned court that once framed the entrance of the facade. However, it is still an impressive building.

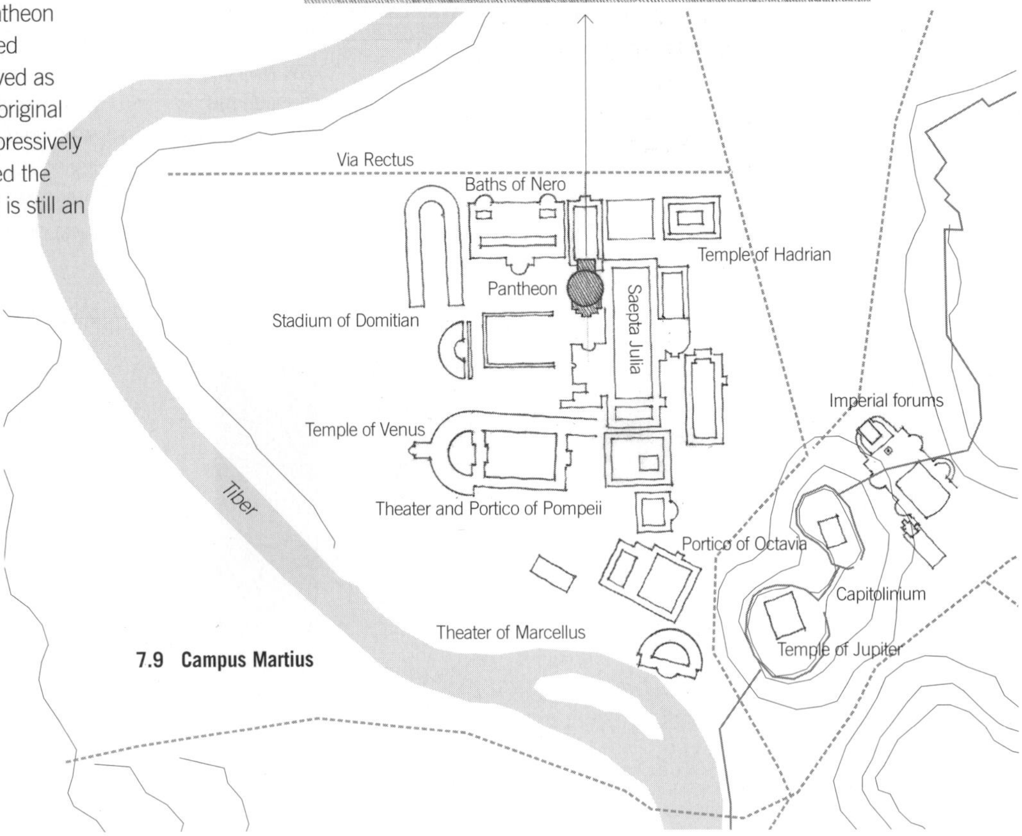

Via Rectus
Baths of Nero
Temple of Hadrian
Pantheon
Saepta Julia
Stadium of Domitian
Imperial forums
Temple of Venus
Tiber
Theater and Portico of Pompeii
Portico of Octavia
Capitolinium
Theater of Marcellus
Temple of Jupiter

7.9 **Campus Martius**

7.10 Oculus of the Pantheon

7.11 Interior of the Pantheon

Though much of the Pantheon's bulk is overdimensioned, one cannot fault its architects for wanting a building that would last through the ages. Its bold interior space was, even for the Romans, an innovation. Though domed spaces were not uncommon, none compared to this one. It derives conceptually from Greek and Egyptian mathematical interest in spatial geometry, which was brought in essence to Rome by Hadrian, who had spent time in Alexandria. It was the Greek, Archimedes, who had solved the problem of measuring the volume of the sphere and cylinder in relation to each other. Romans contributed practically nothing to analytical geometry. In that sense, the building is relatively un-Roman. Against the vertical alignment of the half-spherical dome, one has to add the startling dynamic of the sun's rays as they move slowly through the space like a searchlight, slowly illuminating elements of the architectural interior—sometimes the floor with its pattern of orange, red, and white marbles brought in from all over the Empire, sometimes the orange marble columns, sometimes the coffering of the dome itself.

The classical *cella* had always been a dark and mysterious place oriented horizontally to the rising sun. This building, almost inexplicably, rejects that old model. Jupiter is represented not by a statue but, so it seems, by the abstraction of light itself. It was a remarkable anomaly in Roman thinking, for while smaller domed oculus structures had been built earlier, they were for bathhouses, like the one that still stands at Baia, on the north shore of the Bay of Naples. These places might have been a good place to work out technical issues, but they were certainly not models in the symbolic sense. The octagonal room in Nero's palace brings us closer in that it ended in an oculus and descriptions emphasize its symbolic purpose. Perhaps 75 years later, with Hadrian, Roman architects had an emperor who, like Nero, had a verve for architectural experimentation and an interest in the Hellenistic east, where more dynamic, personal, and experimental religious forms were being developed. Unfortunately, no Roman text has been found yet that explains the inner arrangement of the divine statues, the ritual practices undertaken in the building, or even the symbolism of the oculus. But it is safe to argue that the building represents the unity of the divine and imperial realms. Apart from sun temples that were beginning to be built in Syria (Hadrian was the governor of Syria for a while), there are mystery cults that emphasized light and darkness, like the Eleusinian Mysteries practiced in Greece, into which Hadrian was initiated.

Originally a flight of five steps as wide as the entrance portico led to the floor level of the interior. The monolithic shafts of the facade are gray Egyptian granite. The four inner columns are reddish Egyptian granite and the capitals, Pentelic marble. The porch leads to a barrel-vaulted entranceway, flanked by niches. Between the porch and the rotunda are areas for stairways to reach the spaces that honeycomb the cylindrical structure. The threshold is defined by a huge block of Portasanta marble. The walls, carved out by alternating square and round niches, form four axial connections through the space.

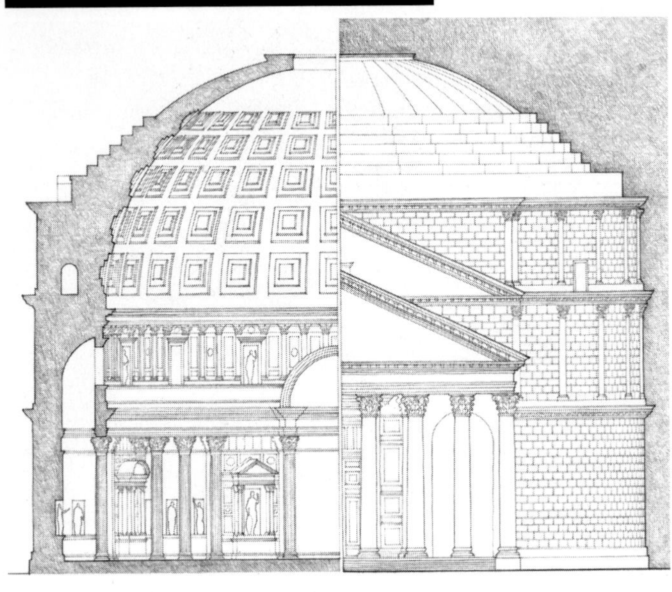

7.12 Section-elevation: The Pantheon

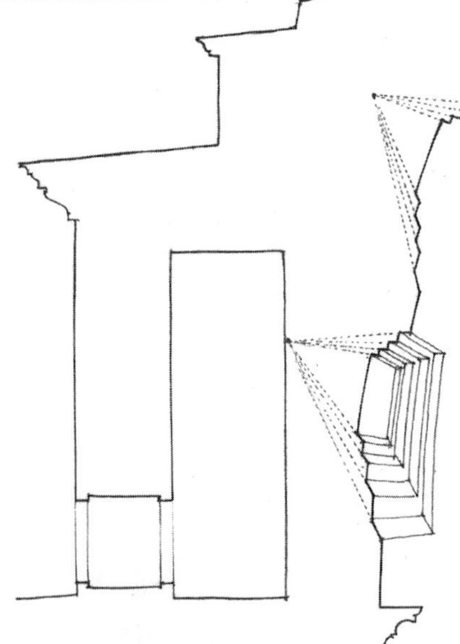

7.13 Dome detail: The Pantheon

The niches are screened by columns and flanked by pilasters of yellow-orange marble, under a continuous entablature. The apse alone is marked by freestanding columns that interrupt the entablature running along the back of the niche.The dome consists of rings of coffering that diminish in size and depth as they near the oculus. They end, however, not at the mouth of the oculus but well short of it, leaving a smooth platelike area around the opening. Given the change of material and the nature of the coffering (28 coffers in each ring), the dome seems to float effortlessly on the architecture below it, but that is a modern experience, for we have no way of knowing how it was finished in Roman times. The edges of the oculus, and perhaps the coffering as well, were probably gilded, with rosettes filling the centers of the coffers and creating in its overall impression a much more ephemeral and less "structural" effect than today. One should observe in this respect that only the upper half of the dome is identical with the structure itself. The lower half of the coffering bears no relationship whatsoever to the structure behind it. In that sense, the architects were willing to work with the illusion of structure or at least wanted to separate the visual vocabulary of a dome's "structure" from the hard reality of the structural support. We should, therefore, not see the coffering as a three-dimensional concrete space frame in the modern sense.

Though the Romans are often praised for structural innovation, they could easily make structure subservient to the architectural vision. Even the coffering was designed from an optical point of view. The steps are shallower on their lower edge and steeper on the higher, so as to appear even when viewed from the center of the floor.

The lower part of the structure is brick-faced concrete with voids serving to reduce the overall weight. Massive curving vaults direct the forces to the ground. For the dome, only concrete was used. The pour, made against a temporary wooden formwork, had to be seamless, meaning that it had to be placed bottom to top without pause so as to guarantee the cohesion of the whole. Organizing the production of the concrete, its immediate transport to the level of the dome, and its distribution to the right places by men carrying small batches was a feat in itself. The width of the dome at the bottom is 6.15 meters. It thins to only 1.5 meters at the level of the oculus, which is 8.3 meters across, and it is open to the air and weather.

Despite the powerful evocations of the building, Hadrian's experiment would not get repeated or at least not in a way that can be confirmed. Though Roman architects continued to work with domed spaces, as in the Baths of Caracalla, the dome-and-oculus combination remained rare.

Orvieto
Tivoli
Rome
Ostia
Velletri
Tyrrhenian Sea


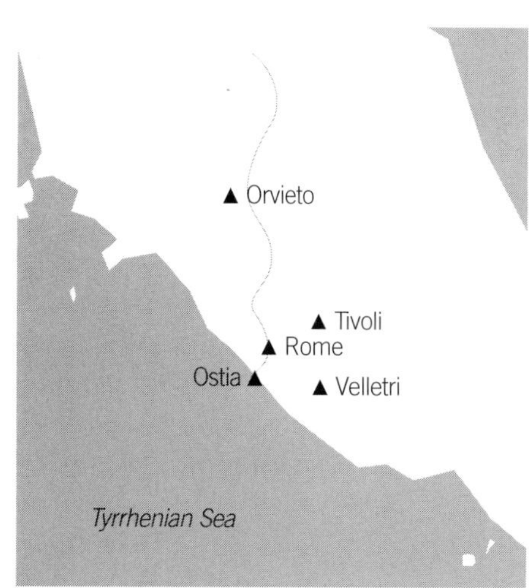

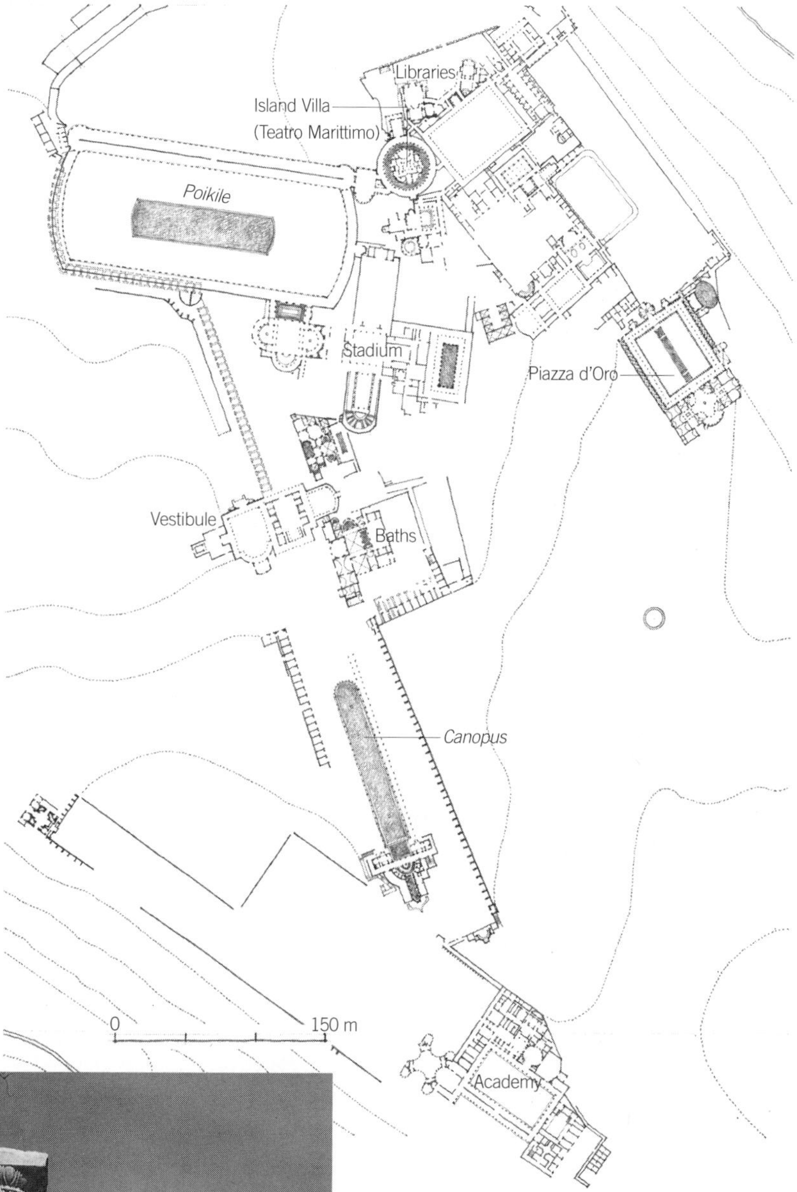

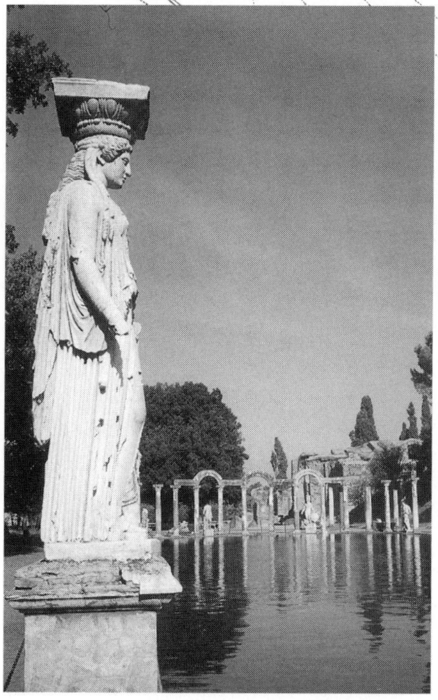

Libraries
Island Villa
(Teatro Marittimo)
Poikile
Stadium
Piazza d'Oro
Vestibule
Baths
Canopus
0
150 m
Academy


7.14 **Plan: Hadrian's Villa, Tivoli, Italy**

### Hadrian's Villa

Combining the numerous traditions and technologies available to him, Hadrian built for himself an extravagant villa (118–134 CE) near the modern town of Tivoli. It lies on flat land at the top of a hill, allowing for broad eastward vistas to Rome. Built in several phases, its buildings constitute a type of vast experimentation on the subject of architecture, landscape, ritual, marble, water, and memory. Unlike Domitian's Palace with its compressed orderliness, this villa returns to the more freewheeling texture of Nero's palace. There are dozens of distinct elements separated from each other in the landscape yet linked to each other in purposefully surprising ways—often one could say hinged to each other so that the whole design seems to unfold itself in relationship to program and site. The residential parts were to the north. More to the south was the stadium followed by a series of baths ending in a spectacular *canopus*, lined with copies of the caryatids of the Erechteum. The whole was meant to evoke the international and particularly Greek flavor of Hadrian's trips. In that sense the villa was also a collection of memories and allusions.

7.15 **Canopus, Hadrian's Villa**

7.16 Island Villa, Hadrian's Villa

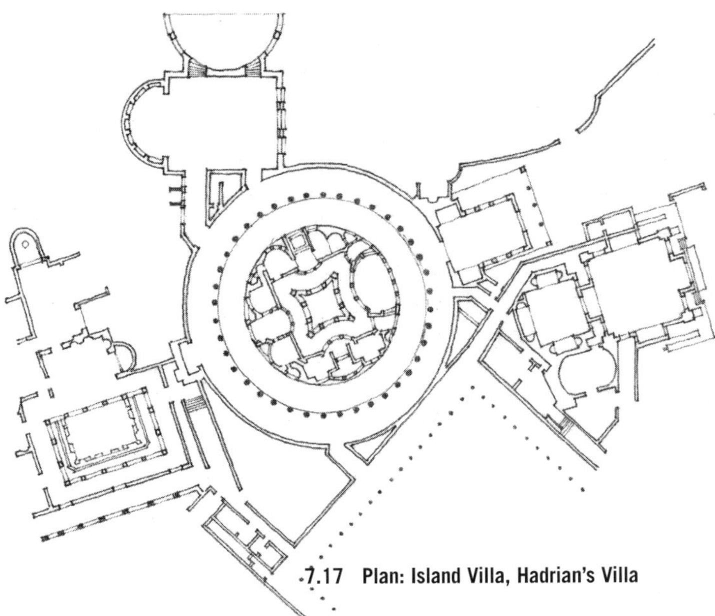

7.17 Plan: Island Villa, Hadrian's Villa

Among the numerous astonishing elements of the villa is the so-called Island Villa. It is surrounded by a moat and a colonnade. Access across bridges leads into an architectural composition of concave and convex curves. The seeming symmetry at the center, as is typical of the spatial imagination of Roman architects, feathers out toward the perimeter as if the architect has less and less control over the volumes, in a sense a metaphor for the Roman Empire itself. At any rate, the two bedroom suites were on the east side. The dining room was on the south. The western side was taken up by a small bathing suite. At the center of the compressed peristyle court was a fountain, its sound filtering its way through the rooms.

To the east one finds the Piazza d'Oro. It consists of a large peristyle court, almost square, with a pool in the center. At the far end is a pavilion or *nymphaeum*. The main room is composed of rounded walls turned concave and then convex to form a flowing four-armed space. These were not walls in the strict sense but curved colonnades. It was open to the sky. The four ancillary spaces at the corners are all identical. The concave side leads to rooms with fountains in the floors whereas the one on the principal axis leads to a curving space, the back wall of which is lined with fountains.

The *canopus* is a long lake decorated along its edges with columns supporting alternating arches and lintels. The Serapeum on the southern end is built against the steeply sloping hillside to give the impression of a grotto or miniature gorge with a waterfall at the back. With water from an aqueduct above flowing through the gorge, and around the crescent-shaped masonry couch toward the long riverlike pool, diners reclining on the curved bench seats would have had a cool and enjoyable meal, even in the heat of summer. A small semicircular pool where food could be floated back and forth added even more charm. The surfaces of the vaults were covered with blue and green mosaics. And the walls of the exedra were decorated with semicircular niches that held statues.

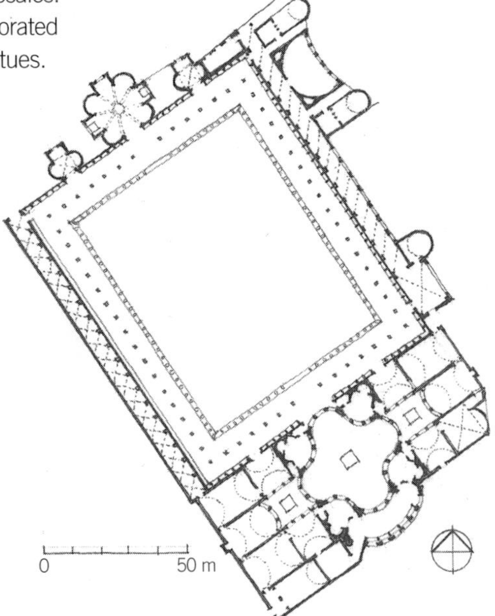


7.18 Plan: Piazza d'Oro, Hadrian's Villa

7.19 **Fornix system of the Tabularium**

7.20 **Arch of Septimus Severus, Rome**

### Roman Vertical Surface

Since the Egyptians covered their temple walls with images or historical reliefs, there was no opportunity for architects to think of the wall as anything other than a space definer. In Greek architecture, walls were often hidden behind columns and even though the Greeks invented the pilaster in the form of columns in antis, and sometimes came to articulate walls with shallow panel recesses, they never saw the wall as anything other than a wall. But, by the time of the Colosseum, Roman architects were experimenting with complex articulations of the vertical surface. For the first time, the wall becomes architecture itself. The technique of framing arches within engaged half-columns supporting an entablature, called the fornix system of ornamentation (fornix means vault or arched room), dates back to about 150 BCE. The fornix system came into its own at the Tabularium (ca. 78 BCE) and then became a paradigm with the Augustan Theatre of Marcellus.

For most of the 1st century CE this was the principal model for arches and applied columns. The amphitheater of Nîmes, late in the century, recapitulates the theme as do numerous triumphal arches, such as the Arch of Titus (81 CE). But designing with *aediculae* and niches, as one can see in that arch, was not yet part of the architectural vocabulary. Much more interesting is the so-called Arch of Trajan at Timgad (100 CE), a path-breaking design. The central arch is flanked by smaller arches surmounted by *aediculae* flanked by their own columns. The two sides are then organized by enormous columns that reach to the top of the *aedicule* and that, with the help of imposts, rise to a level where the arches can spring over them. The two side elements are then united by an entablature that is reduced to a thin projection. It is perhaps a bit awkward, but certainly kinetic.

7.21 **Arch of Trajan at Timgad**

Few vertical surfaces of the Roman palaces exist, most having been stripped of their columns and marbles in the Middle Ages for other buildings. As a result, it is easy to equate Roman architecture with the columnar temple front, when in reality, by the early part of the century, architects were getting increasingly bolder in their compositions. To get a sense of this we turn once again to the rock-cut tombs of Petra in southern Jordan. The so-called Palace Tomb, which has been variously dated to the second half of the 1st century CE or early 2nd century, for example, shows a stratified design, with the lower register of four doors framed by roundheaded and pedimented *aediculae* with unusual abstracted capitals. The whole is tied together by an unbroken entablature on which rests a row of half columns, the last ones being pilasters, and above that, an accordion-style entablature with the pilaster order shadowing its way through to the top. The Tomb of Sextius Florentinus is particularly refined. Above the lower register is a pilaster order and a second set of capitals. This interpenetration of horizontals and verticals show a capacity to see in the x- and y-directions simultaneously. It would be a complexity that would return only with the Italian Renaissance.

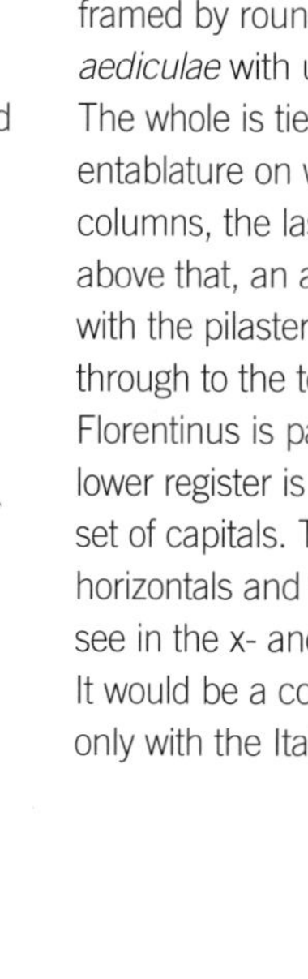

7.22 South Market Gate, Miletus, Turkey

7.23 Library of Celsus, Ephesus, Turkey

These experimentations became particularly vibrant in the 2nd century CE. Richly elaborated architectural fronts that had once been associated with prosceniums of theaters come out into public space. This is certainly true with the facade of the Library of Celsus at Ephesus (110 CE). It stands on the western end of a marble courtyard, and it is approached by a flight of nine steps. The three entrances, with large windows above them, are flanked by four niches that contain statues personifying the virtues of Celsus, who had been Roman senator and Proconsul of Asia. In front of the facade there are four double-story pairs of columns. The lower capitals are Corinthian but with Ionic tops. In a display of further design skill, the architect changed the pairing between top and bottom. At the top the columns are brought together with pedimental and rounded arches spanning the gaps. The end columns stand almost free against the facade. These displays of columns were more than just architectural excess. They conformed to the Hellenistic desire for immediacy that permeated even religion. The columns are thus meant to emphasize the qualities and generosity of the patron.

At the *Nymphaeum* at Nîmes the columnar elements form an exoskeleton against which the mass of the walls behind presses. The walls conform to the exoskeleton, with the usual niche between the columns. The multiplication of units, assemblies, and diverse formations reaches its peak at the stage for the South Theater in Gerasa. Though the first floor has been reconstructed, it shows a row of paired columns on dados forming a screen in front of pedimented doorways with *aediculae* between them, the base of the *aedicula* lifted up on the top of the dado.

A similarly well thought-out scheme can be found at the court of the Temple of Zeus at Baalbek. Two Corinthian columns in antis work with two pilasters to create the semblance of a screen unit. The *aediculae*, roundheaded at the bottom and pedimented at the top, are squeezed in between the pilasters, leaving practically nothing visible of the wall surface. The theme continues in the large niche behind the columns. The whole is tied together by a single unbroken entablature.

7.24 Facade detail: Court of the Temple of Zeus, Baalbek, Lebanon

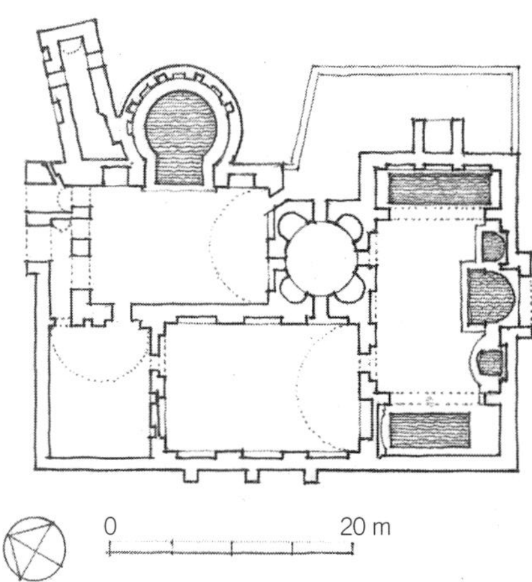

**7.25 Plan of Agora Baths at Ephesus, Turkey**

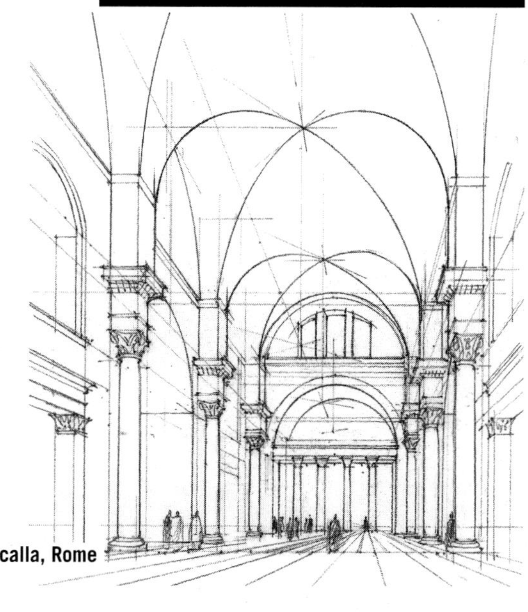

**7.26 Interior scale: Baths of Caracalla, Rome**

**Roman Baths**

Although wealthy Romans had baths in their townhouses and country villas, heating a series of rooms or even a separate building especially for this purpose, they would frequent the numerous public bathhouses in the cities and towns throughout the empire. These baths, called *thermae*, were owned by the state and often covered several city blocks. Entrance fees were quite reasonable and within the budget of most free Roman males. The area in these baths that was covered in water was, however, relatively small, for the bulk of the structure was filled by exercise spaces, lounges, and places to stroll. Since the Roman workday began at sunrise, work was usually over at a little after noon. About 2 to 3 PM, men would go to the baths and plan to stay for several hours of sport, bathing, and conversation, after which they would be ready for a relaxing dinner. Republican bathhouses often had separate bathing facilities for women and men; but by the time of the empire, the custom was to open the baths to women during the early part of the day and reserve it for men from 2 PM until closing at sundown.

The baths were, if you will, secular spaces. They were not associated with altars or divine patronage. Some of the thermal or mineral baths, however, might be associated with local river nymphs or the gods of medicine. Baths offered an environment that was both sensual and social. Some baths even had lecture halls and libraries. The origin of these institutions goes back to the beginning of classical culture and the emphasis placed by the Greeks on physical fitness and prowess. The Greeks viewed bathing as a part of the hygienic rituals associated with sports. Their gymnasiums, in which sports and education were combined, were reserved primarily for the sons of citizens and a place for military training. Under Alexander, however, the baths of the gymnasium become a more social environment, and with the Roman bath, even more so. In fact, few citizens were so poor that they could not afford the entrance fee. Aware of the beneficial role these institutions played in the health, education, and entertainment of the people, the Roman state placed the building and maintenance of these baths at the top of the list of its responsibilities. The larger buildings were also the perfect vehicle for state propaganda. Their lavish interiors were decorated with trophies, inscriptions, and sculptures reflecting the reach and power of the emperor.

The Baths of Caracalla (212–216 CE) are recognized as the best developed example of the Roman public bath. The main building (200 by 114 meters) was set in an enclosure (328 by 400 meters) that contained cisterns, running tracks, gardens, libraries, and shops. The facade is relatively austere and has only a few doors, but in contrast, the back facade is open and sunny. The play of light and shade was an important feature of these structures. The first pool was the *natatio*, or swimming pool. Though it had no roof, the towering walls on all sides would have meant that by the afternoon, most of it would have been in the cool shade. The *frigidarium* was at the center of the composition. It was covered by three cross-vaults that soared above the level of the surrounding rooms. Clerestory light would have filtered down into the space. The right and left rooms led to the *palaestrae*, the exercise courts. Then came the *tepidarium*, with small plunge baths of warm water on both sides. The climax is a circular *caldarium* 35 meters across, with large windows in the walls. Heat was supplied by a furnace from below (the hypocaust).

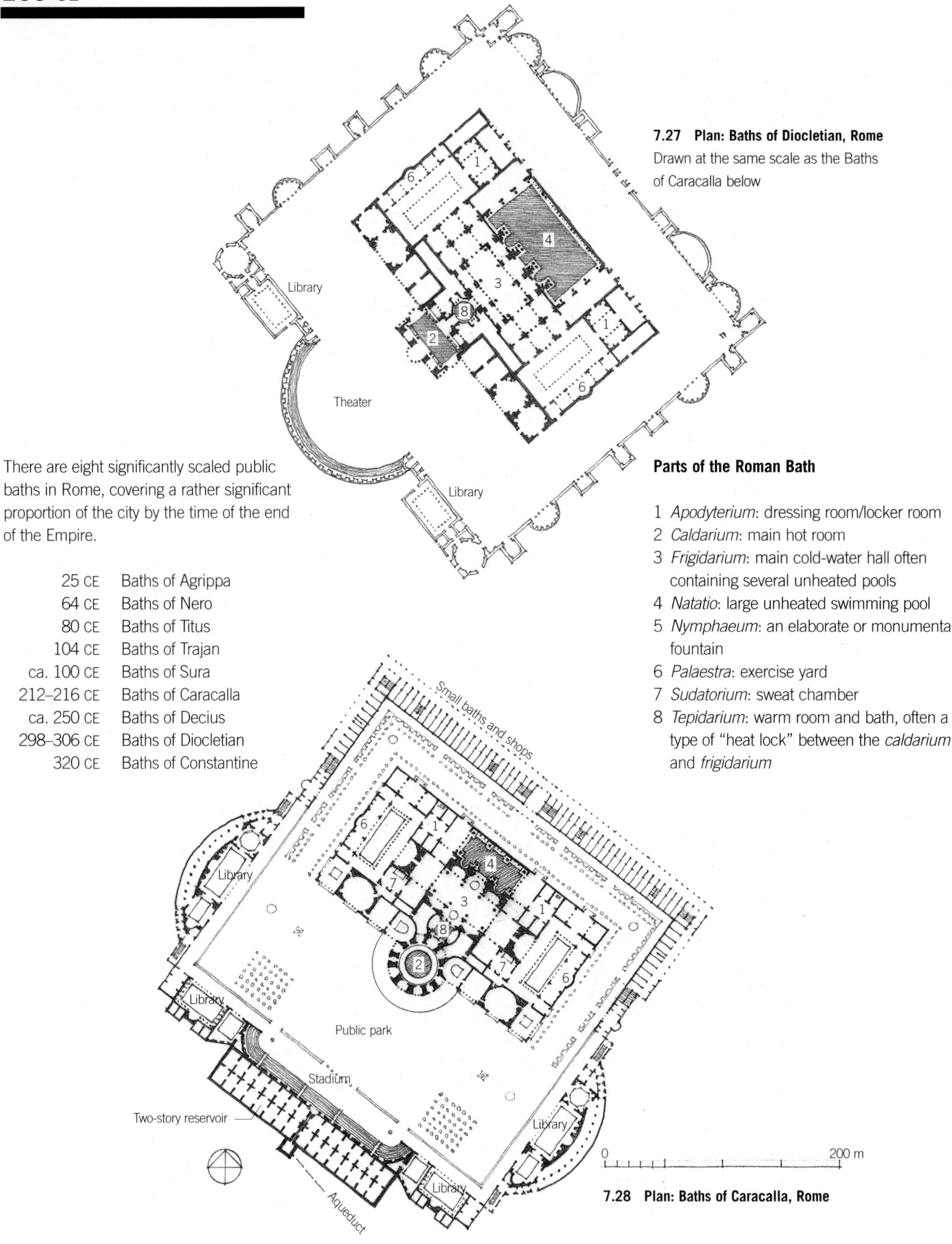


**7.27 Plan: Baths of Diocletian, Rome**
Drawn at the same scale as the Baths of Caracalla below

There are eight significantly scaled public baths in Rome, covering a rather significant proportion of the city by the time of the end of the Empire.

| | |
|---|---|
| 25 CE | Baths of Agrippa |
| 64 CE | Baths of Nero |
| 80 CE | Baths of Titus |
| 104 CE | Baths of Trajan |
| ca. 100 CE | Baths of Sura |
| 212–216 CE | Baths of Caracalla |
| ca. 250 CE | Baths of Decius |
| 298–306 CE | Baths of Diocletian |
| 320 CE | Baths of Constantine |

**Parts of the Roman Bath**

1 *Apodyterium*: dressing room/locker room
2 *Caldarium*: main hot room
3 *Frigidarium*: main cold-water hall often containing several unheated pools
4 *Natatio*: large unheated swimming pool
5 *Nymphaeum*: an elaborate or monumental fountain
6 *Palaestra*: exercise yard
7 *Sudatorium*: sweat chamber
8 *Tepidarium*: warm room and bath, often a type of "heat lock" between the *caldarium* and *frigidarium*

**7.28 Plan: Baths of Caracalla, Rome**

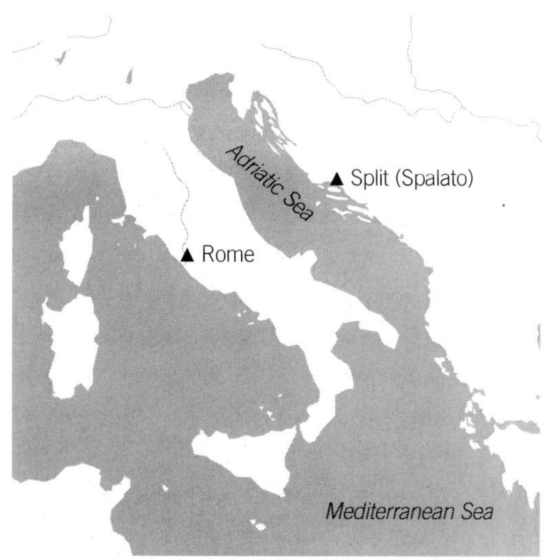


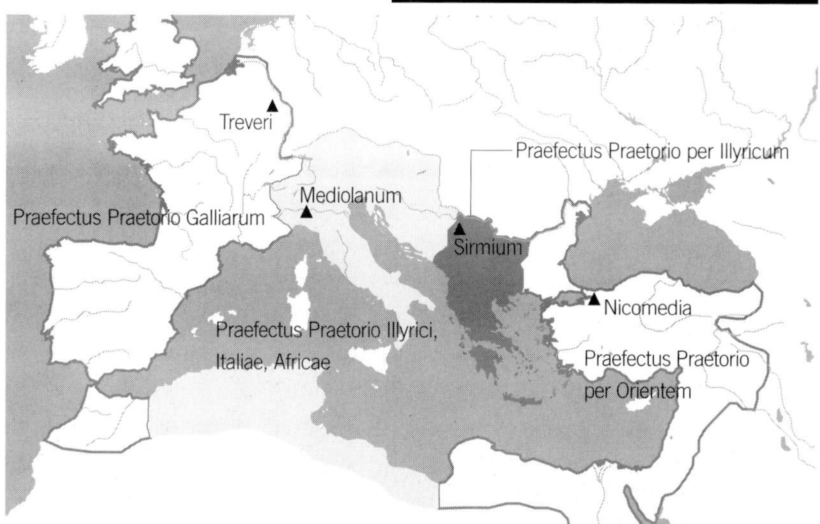


**7.29 Reorganization of the Roman Empire into four Praetorian Prefects ca. 405 CE**

### Diocletian's Palace

By the beginning of the 3rd century CE, the Empire was under attack from all directions. In 166 CE, Germanic tribes breached Rome's defenses along the upper Danube frontier, and in 172 CE the Moors from northern Africa invaded Spain. In 253 CE, the Franks from the middle- and lower-Rhine regions began to launch intermittent attacks on northern Spain. In 257 CE, the Goths raided Greece and Asia Minor. In 267 CE, they sacked Athens, Corinth, and Sparta. With the empire suddenly under siege, the Romans, in 273 CE, under the emperor Aurelius, built a massive fortification wall around the city. A good part of the problem, however, was with Rome itself. In the decades before Diocletian became emperor (r. 284–316 CE), there were no less than 20 emperors proclaimed by the Senate and at least as many usurpers and pretenders. To restore order in Gaul and to prevent usurpation of the throne, Diocletian fundamentally changed the empire with implications for the rest of Europe. He split the empire into two, and then into two again, with his friend Maximian serving as coregent in the western part of the empire.

The four rulers had their respective capitals at Nicomedia, Mediolanum (modern Milan), Treveri (modern Trier), and Sirmium. Diocletian governed the Asiatic part of the empire and Egypt from Nicomedia, using the Persian model of rulership, implementing other territorial partitionings of the empire, and separating military from civilian administration. Initially these efforts were successful. In 296 CE, Britain was restored to the empire; in 298 CE, the Persians were subjugated and the Germans were expelled. Although initially tolerant of Christianity, which was growing in momentum, in 303 CE, Diocletian issued an edict in Nicomedia in which he prohibited it. This brought about numerous executions, the confiscation of property, and the destruction of churches. On May 1, 305 CE, he abdicated and retired to the palace he had prepared for his retirement in Split (Spalato), on the Bay of Aspalathos on the coast.

Diocletian and Maximian both built sumptuous palaces. The Piazza Armerina, by Maximian is located in Sicily and follows some of the conventions of Hadrian's Villa, though with less overall compositional quality. The elements, in comparison, for example, with Flavian's palace in Rome, seem to be stuck relatively arbitrarily together around the large open courtyard. Nonetheless, the composition is not without order. From a curved entrance courtyard, the visitor turns right into a series of slightly disjointed spaces leading up to the audience hall at the east. The composition is tied together by a type of "street" running north and south that links the principal elements of the program.

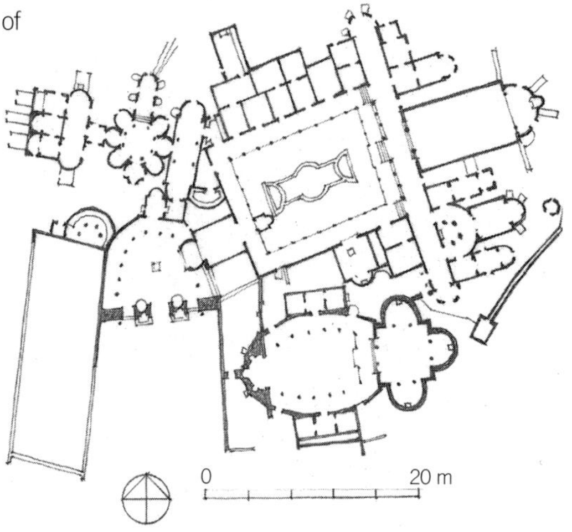


**7.30 Plan: Piazza Armerina, Sicily, Italy**

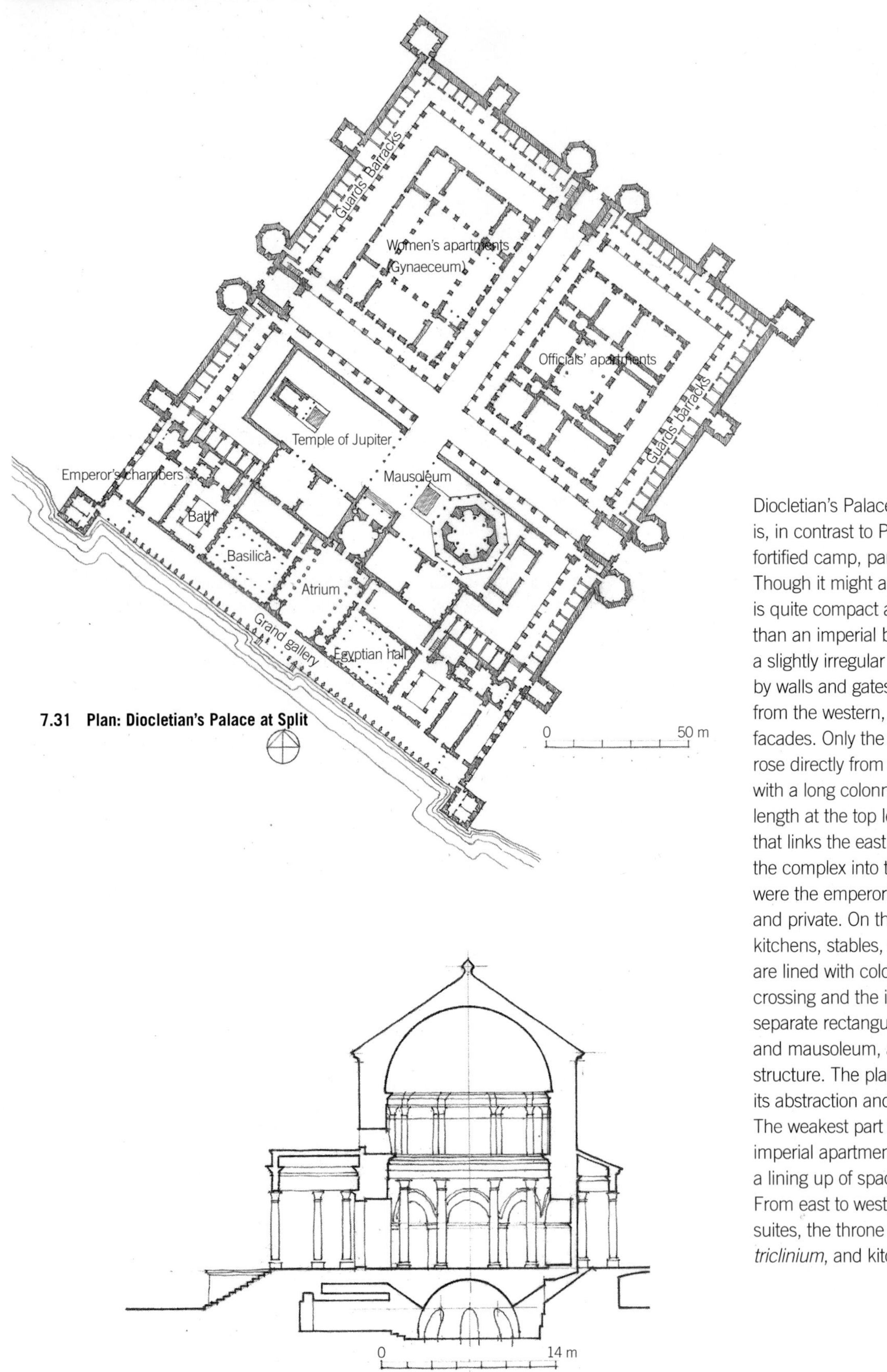


**7.31 Plan: Diocletian's Palace at Split**

**7.32 Section through the Mausoleum at Diocletian's Palace**

Diocletian's Palace (175 by 216 meters) is, in contrast to Piazza Armerina, part fortified camp, part city, and part villa. Though it might appear large, its footprint is quite compact and not much bigger than an imperial bath. It is in the form of a slightly irregular rectangle, protected by walls and gates with towers projecting from the western, northern, and eastern facades. Only the southern facade, which rose directly from the sea, was unfortified with a long colonnade running the whole length at the top level. The *decumanus* that links the east and west gates divides the complex into two halves. On the south were the emperor's quarters, both public and private. On the other half, one finds kitchens, stables, and storage. The streets are lined with colonnades. Between the main crossing and the imperial apartments is a separate rectangular zone for the temple and mausoleum, an octagonal, domed structure. The plan of the villa is powerful in its abstraction and in its zoning of functions. The weakest part is probably the area of the imperial apartments, which are reduced to a lining up of spaces on the great terrace. From east to west, there are the private suites, the throne room, reception hall and *triclinium,* and kitchen and service rooms.

7.33 **Cella of the Temple of Bacchus, Baalbek**

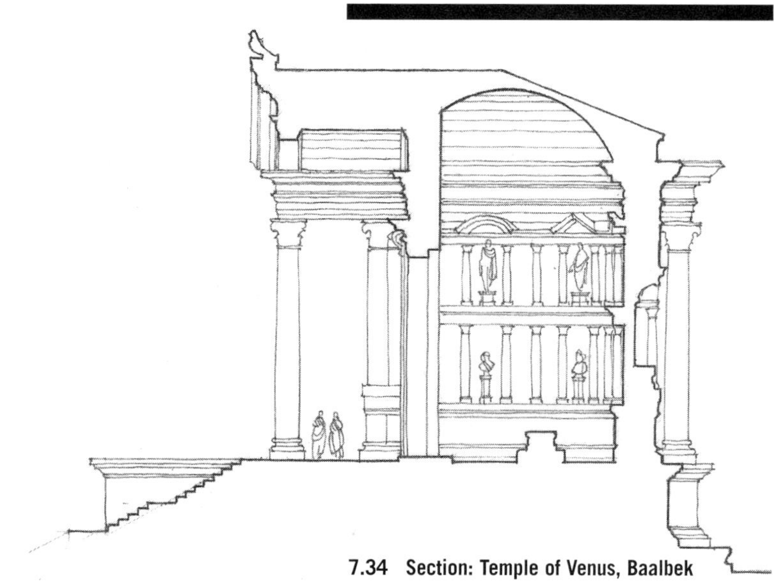

7.34 **Section: Temple of Venus, Baalbek**

**Baalbek**

The supreme god of the Canaanites was El, the sun god who also carried the bull as an attribute. He represented the agricultural basis of society. The fertility goddess, Ashera, was his companion. Worshippers were not allowed to pray directly to the couple but could use the mediating influence of their son, Baal, the master of rain, tempest, and thunder. This was typical of Hellenistic religions, which saw the emergence of several sons of deities. The principal site of the worship of Baal was at Baalbek, near a natural rock fissure some 15 meters deep, at the bottom of which was a small rock-cut altar. Since the altar was hardly accessible, a larger altar was constructed on the hill. This was then formalized with protective gates and towers. Eventually a temple was added on a high undercroft so as to be at the height of the upper altar. This was then expanded again during republican times.

Trajan visited the shrine around 115 CE to consult the oracle before his Parthian campaign, and it may even have influenced him in the design of his forum. Hadrian visited it too in 130 CE. In the following years the Levant prospered and the pace of building accelerated. A new temple was now begun, dedicated to Bacchus. In 195 CE, Septimus Severus (r. 193–211 CE) bestowed upon Baalbek the title, *jus italicum*, moving it up into the most prominent class of Roman cities. Construction was now at its peak and continued during the rule of Caracalla (211–117 CE), a member of the Syrian dynasty of emperors. Building activity was still taking place until Emperor Constantine in 330 CE declared Christianity the official religion of the Roman state, putting an end to one of the largest and longest building projects in the Levant.

The Temple of Jupiter was begun during the reign of Augustus (27 BCE–14 CE). It was constructed on a scale unknown in Rome at that time. Some of the foundation stones weighed 800 tons. Nonetheless, it was not as big as some of the enormous Hellenistic temples, such as the one at Didyma. It was set on a podium 17 meters high, with columns reaching another 22 meters. The entrance was demarcated by two buildings, the Propyleum (3rd century CE) and a Hexagonal Court (2nd century CE). The latter opens onto the principal open court, which is surrounded by porticoes and rooms serving various functions. The creative combinations of columns, attached columns, arches, and *aediculae*, with round or pedimental tops, would all be rediscovered only in the age of the Baroque.

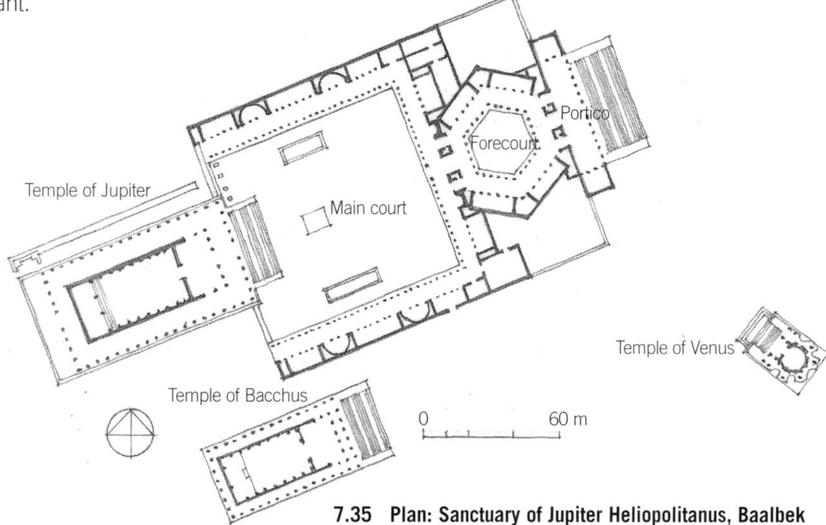


7.35 **Plan: Sanctuary of Jupiter Heliopolitanus, Baalbek**

# 200 CE

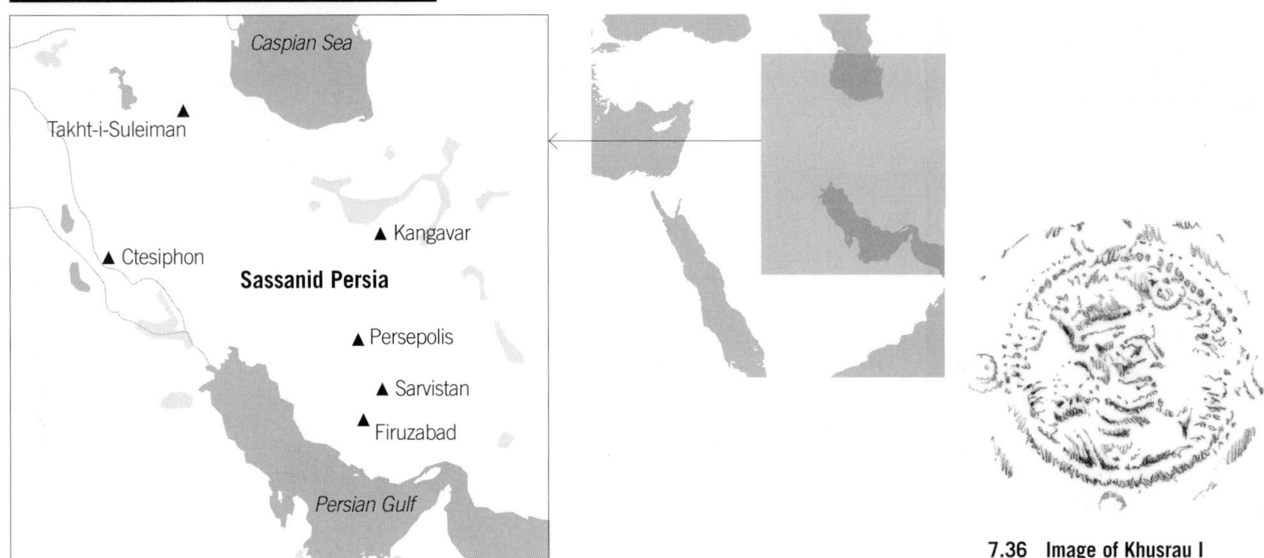


**7.36 Image of Khusrau I**

### Ctesiphon

The desolate area of present-day Ctesiphon today gives little indication of its once lush orchards and rose gardens. The city lies on the east bank of the Tigris River at its confluence with the Diyala River, 32 kilometers south of Baghdad, and was situated on the so-called Royal Road, which connected Susa with the Assyrian heartland. The road, begun by the Assyrians, was set up with guard posts and stables to facilitate fast communication. When the Parthians created Ctesiphon as their western capital, they used it mainly as the winter residence of their kings after 129 BCE. It is not clear when Ctesiphon became important, but it seems that the spoils of a large campaign against the Roman empire in 41 BCE were invested in the new capital, making it one of the great cities in the ancient world. The Romans sought to take the city and did so in 116, 165, and 198 CE, but in 224 CE, Ardashir, king of Persis, overthrew the Parthian monarchy and established the Sassanian empire with Ctesiphon as his capital. It fell into disuse and ruin when the Arabs assaulted the Sassanid Empire between 636 and 642 CE.

Little remains of the city itself, since everything was built in mudbrick. However, the central vault of the palace entrance remains. It spans 28 meters and is possibly the largest vault in ancient history. It is thought that the arch was built without wooden supports during the building phases. The thin, unfired mudbrick is laid on a slant, its weight transferred to the side walls. Architecturally, the arch is a pointed ovoid, an arch peculiar to Mesopotamia.

Visitors to the throne hall of Khusrau I (r. 531–579 CE) tell that the vast floor was covered in a splendid "Winter Carpet" of heavy woven silk and joined with gold and jewels. Its pattern was supposed to represent a beautiful pleasure garden with running brooks and interlaced paths. Though never equaled, it became the model for garden carpets. The carpet was confiscated when the Arabs took Ctesiphon in 638 CE. Scornful of the display of royal luxury, they cut it up and divided it among their warriors, and yet, the idea of a carpeted floor was soon to become a permanent fixture of Islamic mosques.

**7.37 The capture of Ctesiphon by the Romans as depicted on the Arch of Septimus Severus.**

7.38 Palace of Shapur I at Ctesiphon

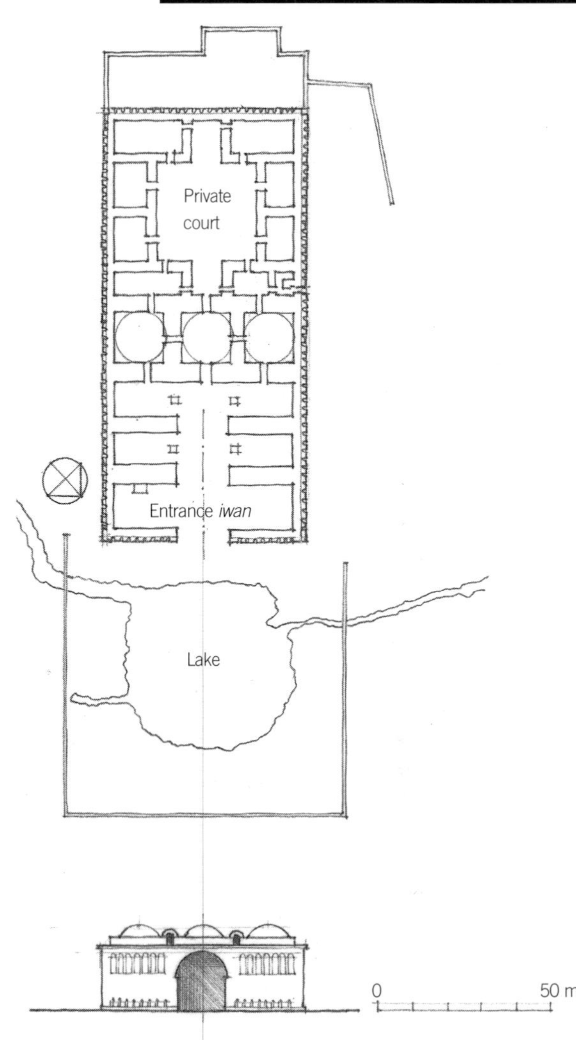


7.39 Plan and front elevation: Palace of Ardashir

At the front and center of Ardashir's palace, one of the most important in Persian architectural history, was a great open, arched throne room, or *iwan*, flanked by side chambers. To the rear were three domed rooms and behind that a courtyard and garden. Most of the structure was mudbrick dressed with stucco and stone elements. The *iwan*, or arched entry, was a building innovation of the later Parthian era that is found predominately in Sassanian palaces and buildings of importance. The palace lay to the south of Ardashir's planned circular city, over two kilometers in diameter. At the center was a large tower that, so it is thought, served as a Zoroastrian fire temple.

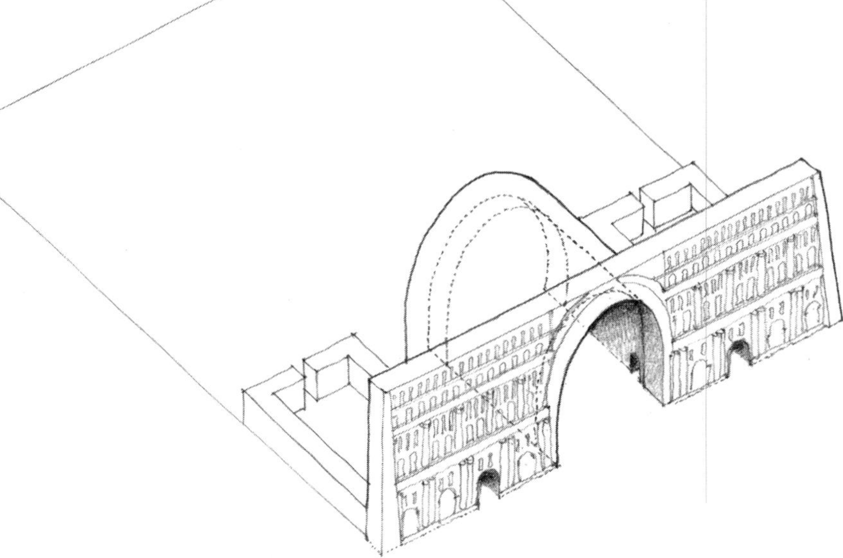

7.40 Pictorial view of *iwan*: Palace of Khusrau I

7.41 **Fire temple in modern-day Iran**

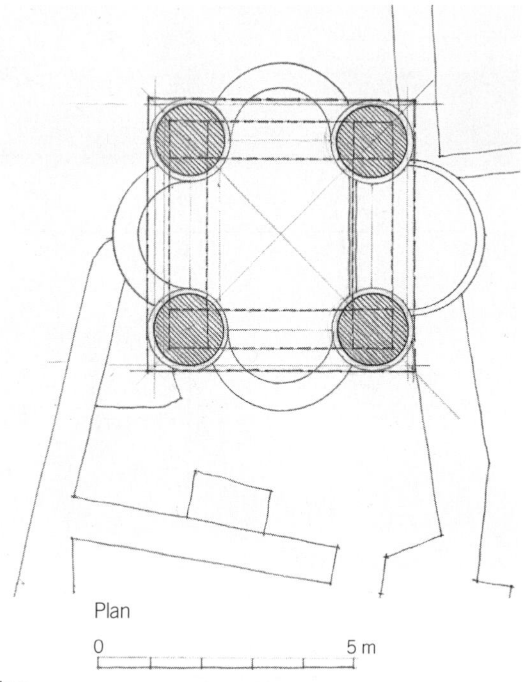


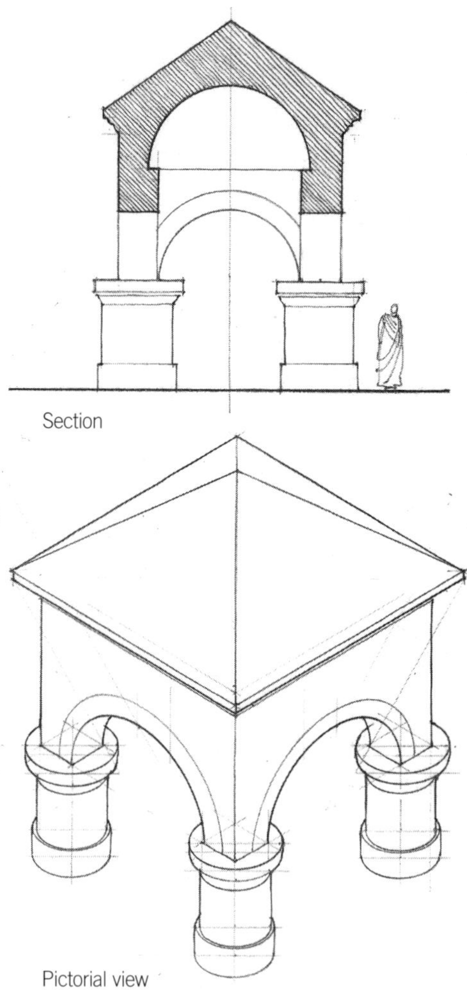


7.42 **Possible Fire Temple at Ani, Armenia**

## ZOROASTRIAN FIRE TEMPLES

It is presumed that Zoroaster (Zarathustra) lived around 600 BCE, but no one knows exactly when or where he lived or died; there are only traditions. And there is just as much ambiguity about the fire temples that were built for the faith that he developed. Fire was ranked according to its uses, from the lesser fires of potters and goldsmiths, through cooking-fires and hearth-fires, up to the three great symbolically perceived eternal fires of the farmers, warriors, and priests.

Zoroastrianism was opposed to the use of images, and during the Sassanian period cult statues were removed. The use of images was also forbidden, even though anthropomorphized divinities remained. Zoroastrian fire rites were performed in the open, on hilltops and platforms, or in enclosed temples. As the rituals and practices became canonized, the religious architecture also became standardized, but the most interesting feature of the religion was that it existed not as one fire but as a complex network of temples. Though each king had his own royal fire, there were also fires corresponding to the three prescribed classes of society: rulers, warriors, and farmers.

There was a prescribed ritual for renewing the home fire from the city fire and the city fire from the royal fire. Rituals together with the rites of purification were all in essence part of the state bureaucracy. Some have drawn parallels to the Hindu caste society and to Mandarin China.

It is difficult to construct a clear architectural history of the fire temples since only about 60 ruinous examples remain for the entire 1200-year period from 550 BCE to 650 CE. At their peak, fire temples ranged from Azerbaijan to Osh, Kyrgystan, on the border with China, where pockets of Zoroastrian beliefs still linger on, to Stakhra, 20 kilometers south of Persepolis and even further at Taxila in Pakistan. Some of the fire-temple ruins belong to the Sassanian era (224–642 CE), during which Zoroastrianism flourished as the official religion, but others date to the earlier Achaemenian, Seleucid, and Parthian periods. Many fire temples were built in the vicinity of geothermal springs. This is certainly the case in Azerbaijan where burning eruptions of gas from the numerous mud volcanoes light up the sky still today and are linked to the fire temples at Nush-Dzhan-Tepe, Adurgushnaep, Surakhany, Pirallahi, Hovsany, Shakhdag, and elsewhere.

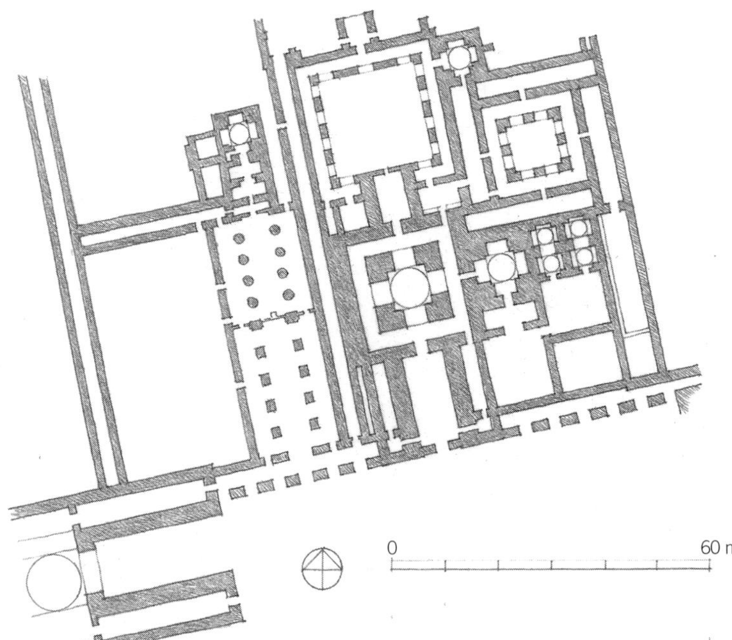


**7.43 Plan: Fire Temple at Takht-i-Suleiman, Iran**

An important fire-temple site is Takht-i-Suleiman (the Throne of Solomon), near Mt. Zindan in southern Azerbaijan. Tradition has it that it was the birthplace of Zoroaster. It is a spectacular site, consisting of the much worn crater of a former volcano that still spews out blasts of sulfuric air. Though little remains today, we know from descriptions that the temple was in use for several hundred years.

The southern facade of the temple fronted onto a sacred lake. The *iwan* led through a hallway to a space called the *adurian* (also the *atashgah*), which housed the purified fire that was fed by priests five times a day. This fire was an eternal one and never allowed to go out. It was not seen by the congregation. Another interpretation holds that the fire was next door to the right and brought for display to the faithful. It seems that the central domed space was, however, used for the complicated Haoma ceremony, which involves the ritual preparation of vegetable substances, including the Haoma plant and the recitation of texts. The fire used here is kindled specifically for the ceremony and later extinguished. Behind the *adurian*, a small doorway led to a small room that exits onto a courtyard. To the west is another tract, presumably an earlier temple, which contains a colonnaded hall, ending in a small domed room.

The demise of Zoroastrianism was sudden. To the west, Christianity vigorously suppressed it. Islam effectively chased it from the realm, destroying the temples and dispersing the congregations. Today, most believers live in Hindu areas in India, with a large community, for example, living in Bombay.

**7.44 Remains of a fire altar in modern-day Iran**

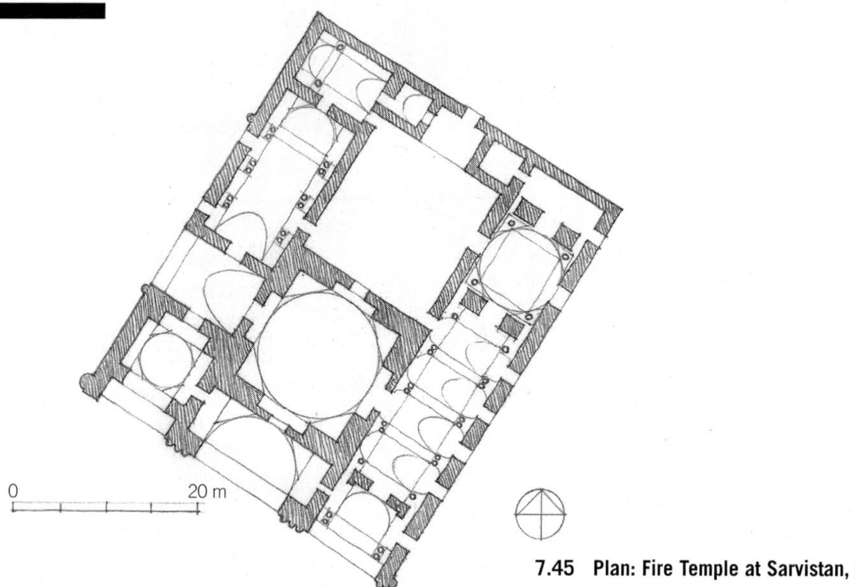


**7.45 Plan: Fire Temple at Sarvistan, Iran**

A building thought to be a fire temple lies at Sarvistan, 100 kilometers south of Persepolis. It is now a sparsely populated high plain, but it once possessed a pleasant climate, produced fruits in both warm and cold regions, and was filled with *sarv* (cypress) trees, which were still in demand until the middle ages. The *sarv* tree, after which Sarvistan was named, was sacred to Zoroaster. The area's canals were abandoned, however, with deforestation, and the region slowly gave way to scrubland and desert. The date of the building is unknown, and estimates place it between the end of the Sassanian Empire (420 CE) and the early 8th century, when Islam had already spread to the area. Though the Islamic chalifs exerted a strong anti-Zoroastrian campaign, certain congregations were at first allowed to practice on the payment of money.

The fire-temple plan is a simple rectangle measuring 45 by 37 meters, with the main facade facing southwest. Despite the tripartite division of the rectangle into two lateral segments of equal width, the internal arrangement is asymmetrical with each longitudinal section laid out independently. The central track consists of a shallow *iwan* preceding a large domed hall with a square open court behind it. The eastern tract contains a small entrance *iwan,* a columned hall, and a tall domed room. On the west, there is also a columned hall, but it is set behind an antechamber. No two rooms are alike. The *adurian* is thought to have been located in the room at the northwestern corner, even though other fire ceremonies were performed in the larger and smaller domed chambers.

There was a temple, not seemingly a fire temple but a Zoroastrian temple nonetheless, dedicated to the goddess Anahita at Kangavar, a small town lying directly on the route between Bisitun and Hamada. Here, too, little remains, but it was mentioned by the Greek geographer Isidor of Charax in the 1st century CE as well as by the Arab geographer Yakut. It seems that the temple was both vast and sumptuous, its cedar columns covered with silver and gold. It was plundered by Alexander in 335 BCE, then further stripped during the reigns of Antigonus (325–301 BCE) and Seleucus Nicator (312–280 BCE).

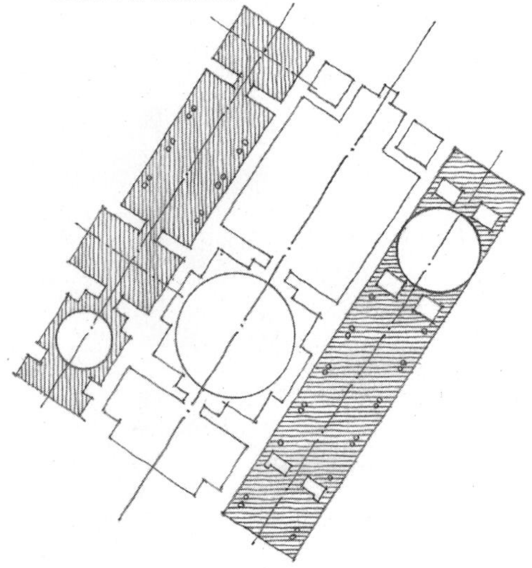

**7.46 Plan diagram: Fire Temple at Sarvistan**

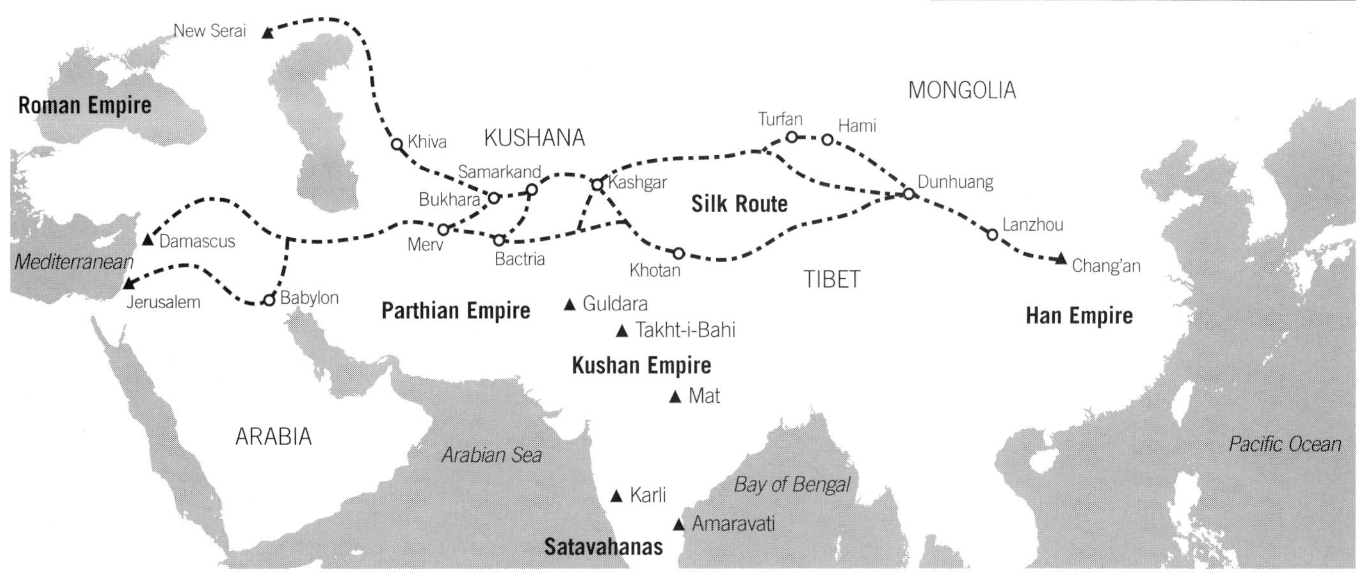


**BUDDHISM OF THE SATAVAHANAS**

In the 2nd and 3rd centuries CE, South Asia was dominated by two major dynasties, the Satavahanas, who control central and southern India, and the Kushan who, although having recently migrated to the region, end up ruling a vast area stretching from Central Asia to northern India. Both enjoyed great prosperity, thanks in great measure to the development of extensive trading networks. Both were predominantly Buddhist, although the Satavahanas were already witness to a reemergent Hinduism, and the Kushans continued to practice aspects of their older beliefs.

Outstanding traders, the Satavahanas called themselves the *dakshinapath-pati*, i.e., the rulers of the southern trade route that linked Egypt, controlled by the Romans, with the Han rulers of China. Under the Satavahanas, port cities flourished on both the east and west coasts of peninsular India. Buddhist monasteries were catalysts of this mercantile development as they were often located along trade routes, serving as resting places and transition points for the traders. Since the Buddhists did not discriminate on the basis of caste, their support became more reliable and universal. Thus, although initially established by royal support, these monasteries flourished in large part due to patronage of merchants who paid for the help they received in their transit.

The most famous of the Satavahana merchant constructions, the Amaravati Stupa (3rd century BCE), was dismantled in the 19th century and distributed in the museums of Europe. Like the earlier ones at Sanchi and Bharut, the Amaravati Stupa probably began as a simple mound under the Mauryas, but it was significantly enlarged and adorned under the patronage of the merchants. Not much remains on-site, but the elaborately carved railings and gateways preserved in museums depict vivid scenes from a bustling urban cityscape. Turban-wearing people fill every panel; musicians play for well-endowed dancers; richly adorned women lean from barrel-vaulted balconies; horses, bullocks, and elephants crowd the streets along with oxcarts. In the distance, large ships with open sails are ready to take to the sea.

**7.47 Carved slabs from the Amaravati Stupa, near Guntur, India**

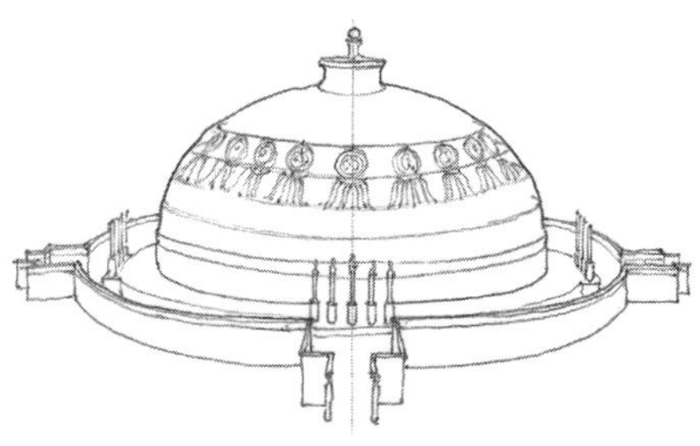

**7.48 Pictorial view: Amaravati Stupa**

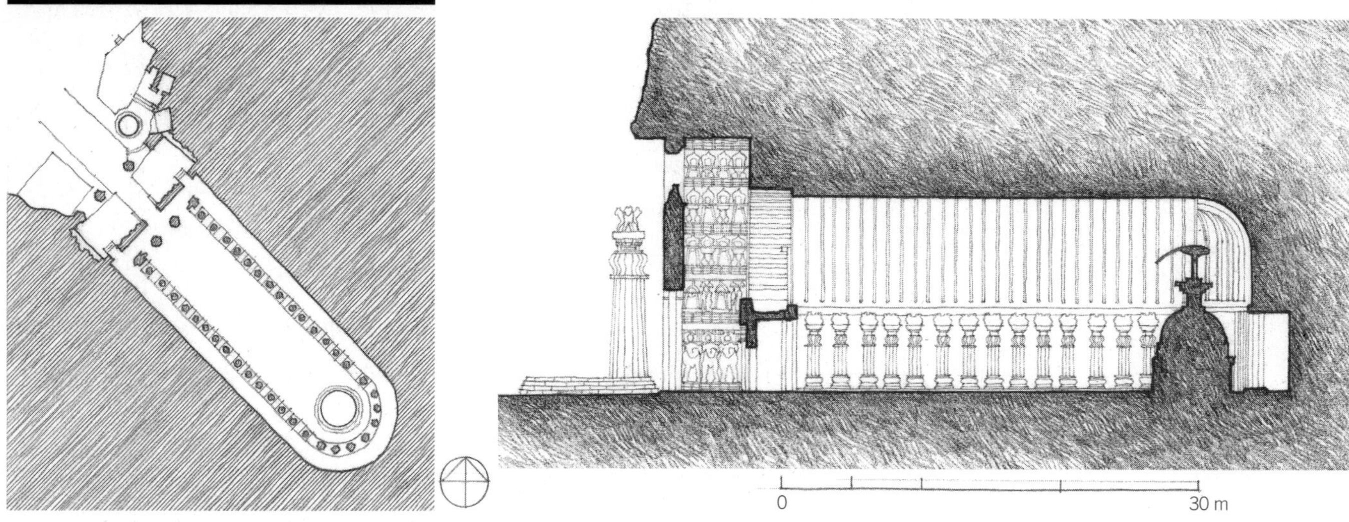


7.49 Plan: Caitya Hall at Karli, Maharashtra, India

7.50 Longitudinal section: Caitya Hall at Karli

## Caitya Hall at Karli

In 120 CE, at Karli on the western Deccan plateau, one of the largest and most impressive of the Buddhist *caityas* was built. About 40 meters deep and 12 meters wide, the Karli cave is fronted by a recessed entrance of stone screens, which has holes in it, indicating that originally a larger wooden construction was added to complete the building. Just beyond the screen, on the left, is a large pillar carved from the same matrix as the rest of the cave. The end wall of the entrance portico displays a stamped-out, repeated set of horse-shoe-arched building motifs that sit atop a plinth composed of life-size elephants, as if they were supporting the weight of the superstructure (as at Pithalkhora). The central panel of the cave entrance is dominated by several panels of male-female couples, known as Mithuna couples, holding each other affectionately with a distinctive touch of sensuality. According to one source, Mithuna couples represent "the notion of the individual's reintegration with the Universal principle, expressed through their affectionate gestures and implicit sexuality." (The entrance panels also contain bodhisattvas, but these were carved in the late 5th century CE, when the iconography was "modernized.")

Karli is famous for its interior, in part due to its sheer size, but more so because of the balanced and measured nature of the overall composition of its elements. Karli brings the *caitya* vocabulary to one of its finest resolutions. Compared to earlier *caitya* caves, the width of Karli's central space is much more generous in relation to its height and depth. The Karli stupa is no longer the incidental center of a crowded array of elements but the focus of a hierarchical composition. The stupa itself is relatively simple in form. An unadorned, simple hemisphere sits atop a slightly tapered base, ornamented with carved *vedikas*. At the same time, it is much bolder than most earlier stupas, as its *chattra* rises simply from a rectangular base, or *harmika*, which expands into mushrooming tiers of horizontal bands. But, then, it suddenly projects into space on a high vertical *stambha*, upon which sits the final *chattra*, which becomes the focus of the entire composition. The *chattra* catches the light in the dark surroundings, and thereby appears as a horizontal flash in the vertical composition. (The *chattra* denotes the umbrella of the Buddhist ideal under which the monk finds shelter and faith.)

7.51 Interior of the Karli Cave

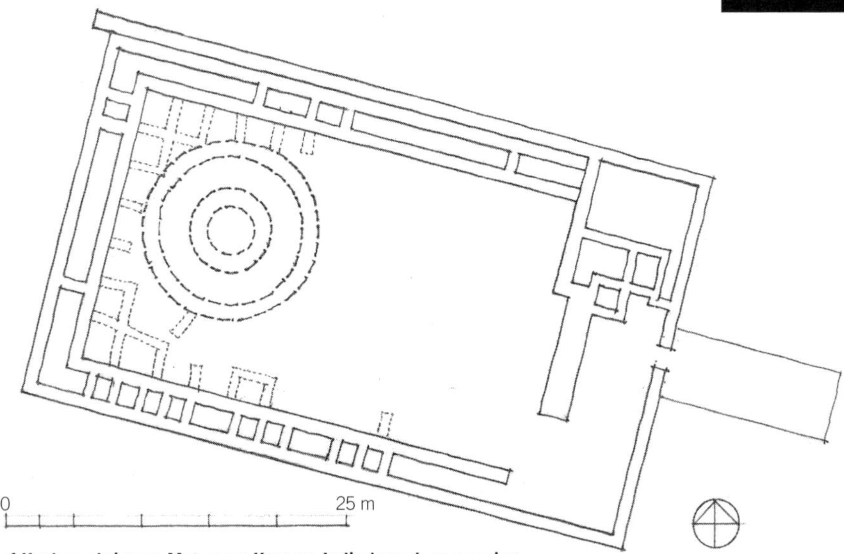


**7.52 Schematic plan of Kushan shrine at Mat, near Kanpur, India,based on remains**

## KUSHAN

The Chinese historical records known as the Shiji refer to the Kushan as a barbarian people; they lived in northwestern China until they were driven west by another group, the Xiongnu, in 176–160 BCE. The Kushan ruled from two capitals: Purushapura (now Peshawar) near the Khyber Pass, and Mathura in northern India. Like the Satavahanas, the Kushan were traders, participating in the sea trade with the West as well as in the silk trade with China. They enjoyed a flourishing urban life. They adopted Buddhist thought and culture as their core belief system, although they added their own distinctive elements to it.

Under the Kushan, the Gandhara region continued to be home to a multiethnic society tolerant of religious differences. A distinctive aspect of Kushan art and architecture was the emphasis on the emperor as a divine person, an idea whose roots could have been Indic as well as Chinese and Parthian (and even Egyptian).

At Mat, just north of their Southern capital in Mathura, there are the ruins of one of the few Kushan temples (1st century CE) to have survived. It is a large rectangular structure, oriented eastward, and built on a high plinth. One entered on axis but had to maneuver around a baffle before coming into the main courtyard with the shrine at the far end. It was defined by two concentric round walls. A large statue of Kanishka, more than 2 meters high, was found at this site; it probably stood at the center of the concentric walls.

**7.53 Stupa at Guldara, near Kabul, Afghanistan**

In the Afghan region to the north, the Kushan constructed large numbers of stupas and Buddhist monasteries, only a few of which survive. A stupa at Guldara (2nd century CE), near present-day Kabul in Afghanistan, has survived largely intact. Oriented to the east and accessed by a large stairway, the round stupa is raised on a very high rectangular base, unlike the stupas further south, so that the emphasis on the base becomes equivalent to the stupa itself. The cardinal directions are marked by deep niches with rounded arches, which are further embellished by ogee-shaped arches and pilasters. The entire base and stupa is divided into panels by pilasters of distant Hellenistic derivation. The diaper-masonry technique of construction is of Parthian origin. It consists of flat slabs of sedimentary rock, piled in even, horizontal rows, with the decorative elements, such as the pilasters and their capitals, formed by protruding, carefully orchestrated rocks beyond the main surface. Each rock that was used in the construction was carefully preconceived to go into the right place, creating the general impression of a mosaic. The interior, however, was primarily filled with rubble.

7.54 **Aerial view of Takht-i-Bahi, near Peshawar, Pakistan**

**Takht-i-Bahi**

Just northwest of Peshawar, Pakistan, on the critical trade route over the Khyber Pass, on the spur of a hill overlooking the route, lie the ruins of the Kushan monastic complex Takht-i-Bahi (2nd century CE). Built on levels, Takht-i-Bahi commands a dramatic view of the valley below. The main complex consists of the south stupa court, which faces, on axis, a *vihara* cloister, also clustered around a courtyard. The stupa is at the highest level and is enclosed on three sides by alternating large and small niches. The fourth side, where the main entrance is located, is plain. The stupa and *vihara* courts are connected by flights of stairs to a central intermediate court which splays out in an east-west direction and is mostly covered by a series of platforms of various sizes that originally would have held small stupas and shrines. The edges of this intermediate court are defined by niches of various sizes that may have originally held statues or may have functioned as small shops or storage compartments. All that remains of the stupa at Takht-i-Bahi is its rectangular platform and the stairs leading up to it.

One can imagine what the stupa might have looked like by studying the small votive stupas found in the region. One example, preserved in the Calcutta museum, consists of a square base, upon which the hemispherical stupa rises in several stepped levels, each level adorned with a different iconographic program. The *harmika* has five stages, each slightly larger than the previous; from the middle of the *harmika* rises the central pillar, which carries a seven-stage *chattra*, diminishing in diameter. Somewhat between the stupas of central India—which are dominated by the girth and body of the main stupa and are surmounted by a small symbolic *harmika* and *chattra*—and the Chinese pagoda—which are almost entirely composed out of the *chattra* conceived on a grand scale—the Kushan stupas of the Gandhara region faithfully reflect their location as the halfway house, the intermediate space through which diverse ideas passed and were in the process transformed and renewed.

7.55 **Plan: Monastic complex of Takht-i-Bahi**

7.56 Pottery model of a multistory watchtower

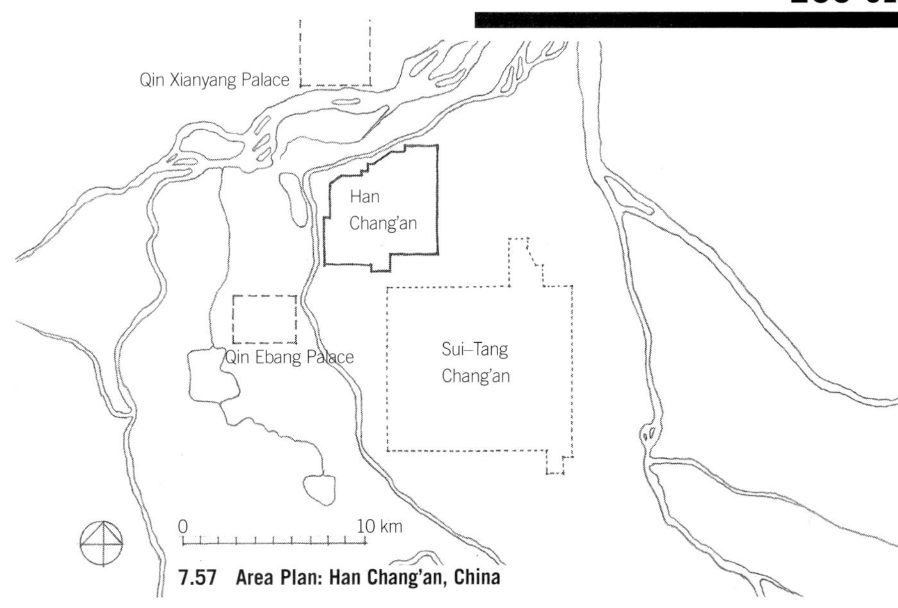


7.57 Area Plan: Han Chang'an, China

## HAN CHINA

The Han dynasty is generally divided into two major periods: the Western or Early Han (206 BCE–9 CE) and the Eastern or Later Han (25–220 CE). Under the Han, by 100 CE, trade along the Silk Route began to flourish, with caravans reaching Luoyang almost every month. International diplomatic exchanges became common, including those with Emperor Andun (the Chinese name for the Roman emperor Marcus Aurelius Antoninus) in 166 CE. By the 3rd century CE, paper was widely used in China, replacing bamboo, wood, and silk slips. Paper was exported to Korea and Japan in the 7th century, and then to Europe, most likely through Central Asia and Arab intermediaries, in the 12th century. The existence of water clocks, sundials, astronomical instruments, and even a seismograph in 132 CE attest to the Han's technological and scientific sophistication.

Very little survives of the vast wooden constructions of the Han. However, funerary objects placed in royal tombs often contained models of structures for use in the afterlife. These models show multistory timber-frame watchtowers with corner piers and with the upper levels generally smaller than the lower levels, resulting in tapered profiles. At each level, widely overhanging roofs and balconies were supported by elaborate bracket sets and braces.

The Western Han occupied the Wei river valley of the Zhou and built their new capital south of the river at Chang'an. Since the Wei has changed course many times since, always shifting toward the north, the old Qin capital has been drastically eroded. The Han planners sited their new city around the remains of an old Qin palace and renamed it the Changle Palace. To its west, the new Weiyang Palace was constructed with an audience hall. Later in 190 CE, walls were built defining the outline of an irregular city, edged by the river to the north and the palaces to the south. One can still see the classic arrangement of three gates opening into each side of the city. At the time of the first census in 2 CE, Chang'an's population was somewhere between a quarter and a half million.

Like the Qin palaces, the gigantic Han palaces were built of wood around a solid earthen core. The grandest Han structure at Chang'an was the Eternal Palace, which measured about 350 meters by 150 meters. It rose in three steps to 15 meters. The Han also constructed a major palace complex west of the city at Shanglin Park, along with an artificial lake, the Kunming Chi.

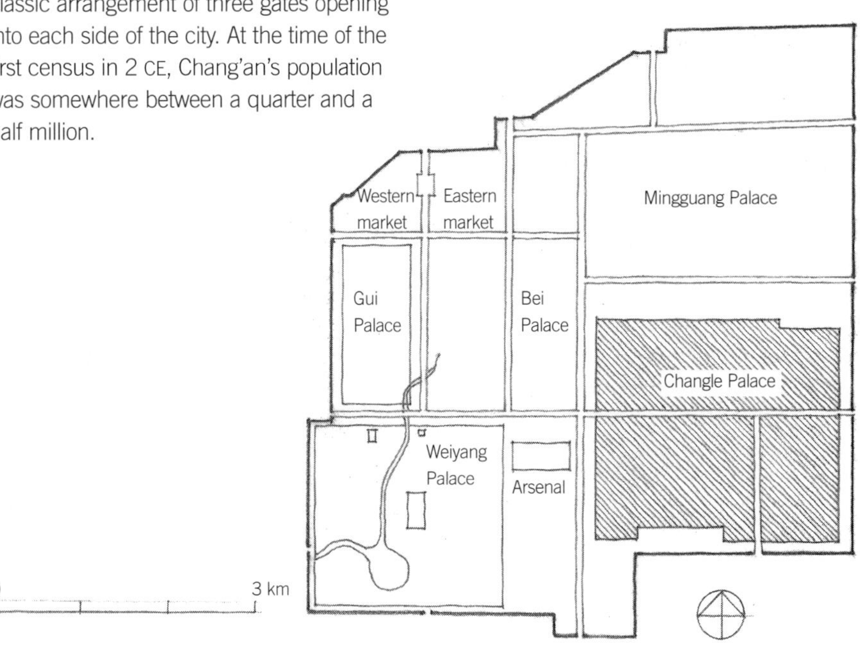


7.58 Plan of Han Chang'an

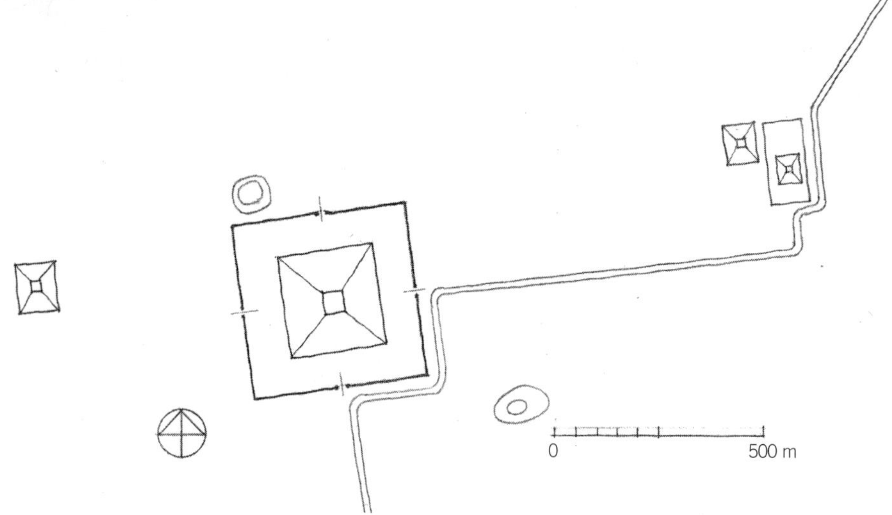


7.59 Maoling Mausoleum: Tomb of Emperor Wudi

### Han Tombs

Like the Qin before them, the Han emperors, both at Chang'an and Luoyang, allocated significant wealth, perhaps up to one-third of their revenues, for tombs for themselves and, unlike the Qin, for their empresses as well (usually in a smaller tomb nearby). The tombs of nine of the eleven emperors of the Western Han are spread along the north bank of the Wei River. (The other two were built southeast of the capital.) The tombs, though all different, had square-shaped mounds enclosed by four-sided walls. For instance, Lu Bang and his wife, Empress Lu, are buried under two truncated pyramids separated from each other by 280 meters. Lu Bang's mound was 55 by 35 meters and rose 32.8 meters, and the Empress Lu's was slightly smaller. Each was enclosed by its own wall, and both were enclosed by a common wall encompassing roughly 780 meters square. These Han funerary complexes were associated with their own cities as, for instance, the funerary city of emperor Wudi is said to have had about 300,000 residents. (The funerary tombs of the Eastern Han have been so completely destroyed that little is known about them.)

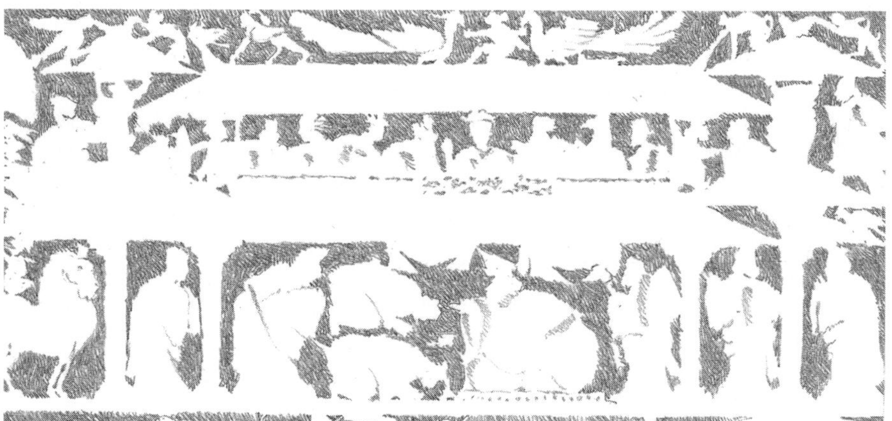

7.60 Rubbing of a palace scene on a sepulchral stone from the Wu family cemetery

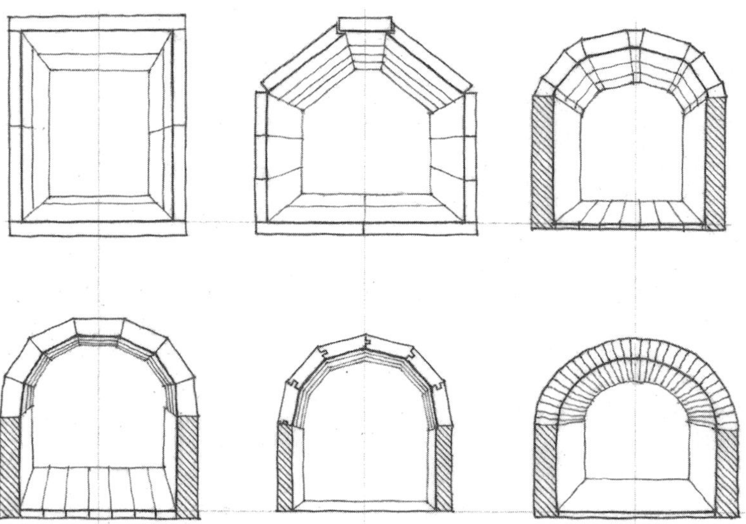

7.61 Forms of vaulting used in Han Dynasty tombs

**MOCHE AND NAZCA CIVILIZATIONS**

Two South American civilizations rose simultaneously in Peru during this time: the Moche on the north coast and the Nazca in the south. (They are known by the current names of the rivers in whose valleys their ruins are located.) Very little is known about their political and social organization. The Moche were, however, outstanding metal workers, and both the Moche and the Nazca were potters and weavers.

The Moche valley on the northern Peruvian coast had been occupied for a long time. The largest of the pre-Moche settlements were made by the Salinar (450–200 BCE). The period was one of turmoil, and it was for that reason that one sees the development of large protected cities, one of which, known as Cerro Arena, sprawls for two kilometers along a ridge on the south side of the Moche valley, overlooking a trade route. Its 200 structures made of quarried granite range from small one-room residences to elaborate 20-room structures. Strangely, the Salinar seem not to have built any ceremonial structures.

About 100 CE, construction began on the ceremonial complexes of Huaca del Sol and, 500 meters away, the Huaca de la Luna, in the center of the Moche Valley. About 10,000 people are believed to have lived in the neighborhood of these two huge platform mounds. As was the tradition in Mayan structures, Huaca del Sol was successively expanded; it was rebuilt in eight stages, the last in 450 CE. Little remains of their gigantic (345 by 160 by 40 meters) pyramid because most of it was carried away by 17th century looters. But an analysis of the adobe bricks shows that each brick had a mark on it, generally believed to be that of the builders and suppliers of the bricks. This indicates the presence of a complex, highly organized building guild or similar social organization.

**7.62 Aerial view of Huaca del Sol, near Trujillo, Peru**

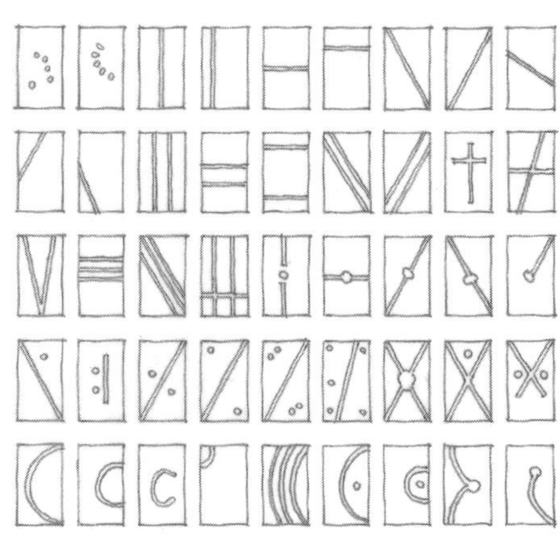

**7.63 Maker's marks impressed on adobe bricks at Huaca del Sol**

7.64 Massive remains of Huaca del Sol

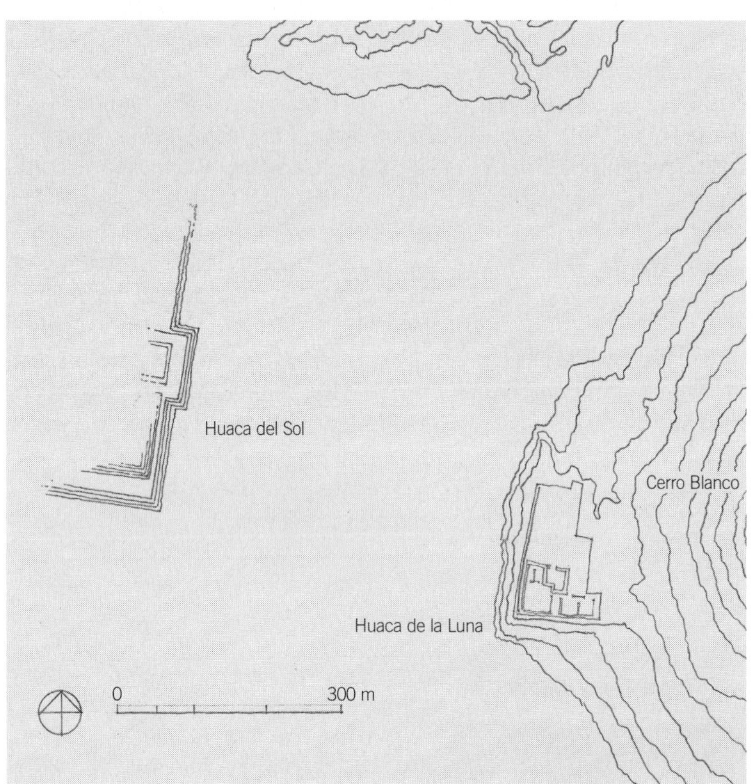


7.65 Area plan of the Moche pyramids, Huaca del Sol and Huaca de la Luna

Huaca del Sol is believed to have served an administrative function, while Huaca de la Luna was clearly a ceremonial structure. Built in six stages (290 by 210 by 22 meters) and consisting of three platforms and four plazas, Huaca de la Luna was the region's paramount shrine for human sacrificial ceremonies. In an enclosure at its back, archaeologists have found the remains of more than 40 men, ranging from 15 to 30 years old, buried in thick layers of sediment, indicating that they had all been sacrificed during the unusual heavy rains that occur during El Niño periods.

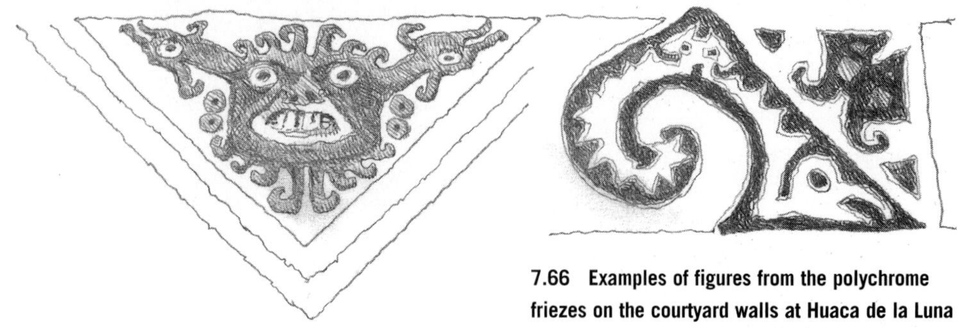

7.66 Examples of figures from the polychrome friezes on the courtyard walls at Huaca de la Luna

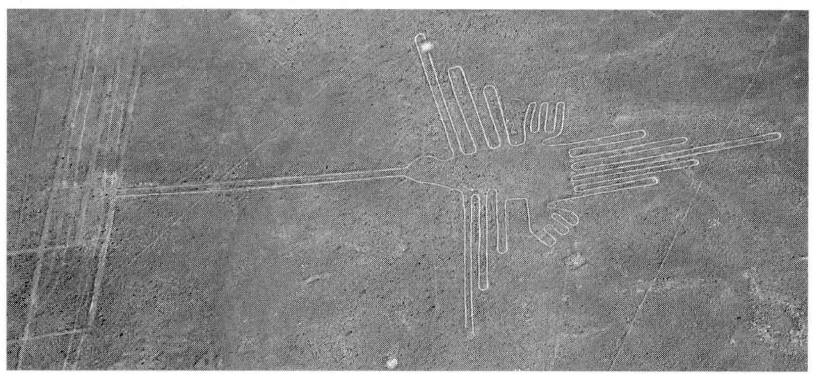

**7.67 Aerial view of a Nazca ground drawing, Peru**

### Nazca Lines

The Nazca, unlike the large centralized societies of the north, consisted of a loose federation of allied communities on the Pracas peninsula from ca. 300 BCE to 200 CE. Religious life centered around pilgrimage centers such as Cahuachi.

Cahuachi's significance was due to its geographical location: the Nazca river, because of its geological path, goes underground midvalley and emerges at a point just below Cahuachi. In a water-scarce region, the reappearance of the river would have been viewed as miraculous. Cahuachi's adobe platform mounds are much smaller than those of their Moche neighbors, and they cap some forty low-lying hills overlooking the Nazca river.

In time, Cahuachi was abandoned and the Nazca people moved north to the pampas, where they etched gigantic patterns in the ground. In this extremely dry region, over the millennia, manganese and iron oxide deposits covered the stony desert surface with a thin patina. The Nazca created their markings by removing this darker surface to expose the lighter soil beneath and, then, enhancing the outline by laying the cleared stones along the edges. These large-scale drawings, which are in fact visible only from the air, are of animals such as birds, a spider, a monkey, as well as straight lines and geometric shapes.

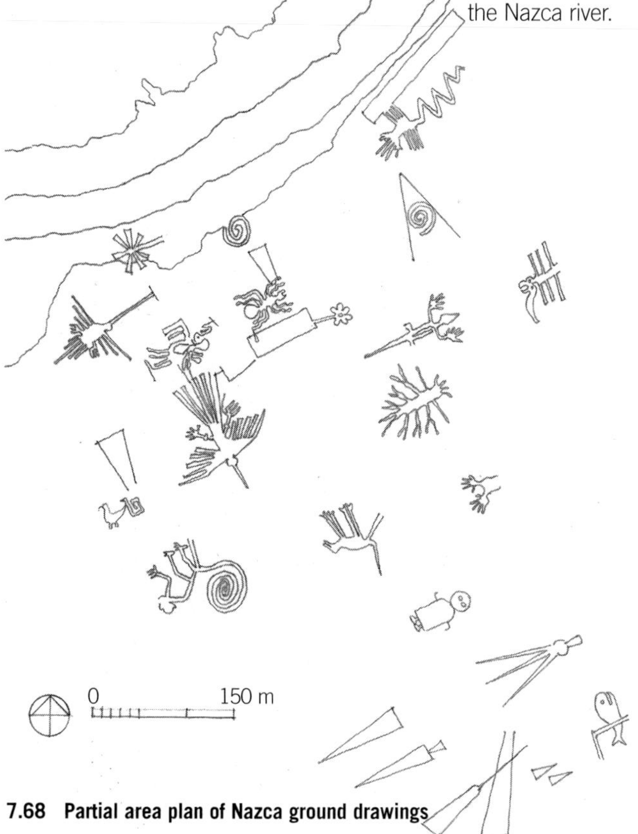


**7.68 Partial area plan of Nazca ground drawings**

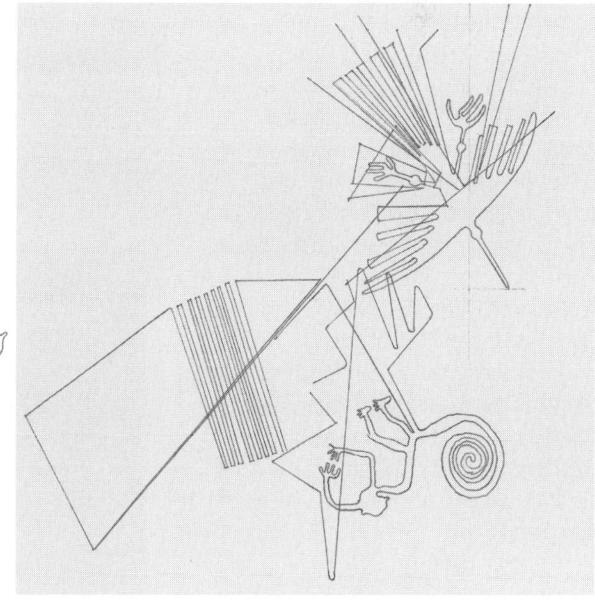

**7.69 Nazca bird and monkey drawings**

**7.70 Teotihuacán, near Mexico City: View down the Avenue of the Dead**

## TEOTIHUACÁN

Teotihuacán was the largest and most impressive of America's cities until modern times. Located in the highlands of central Mexico, Teotihuacán existed for a period of 900 years, growing from a large village of about 6,000 people into a metropolis of 150,000 to 200,000 inhabitants around 600 CE, with an urban core extending across 20 square kilometers. It was the center of an empire that dominated the culture and politics of even the furthest Mayan city-states and kingdoms. 3rd-century inscriptions on stelae at Tikal and Copán record that Teotihuacán controlled their dynasties. They may have also influenced the mound cultures of the Mississippi.

In spite of its size and magnificence, little is known of Teotihuacán's multiethnic inhabitants. Evidence of a writing system is only just coming to light, most of it seemingly destroyed when the city fell. The contemporary Maya called the city Puh (Place of the Reeds), but its name Teotihuacán, "The Place where Men become Gods," was given to it later by the Aztecs, who built their own capital, Tenochtitlán, further to the south a millennium later. The original name is not known, but it is clear that already by the time of the Aztecs, Teotihuacán was already a place of legend and mystery.

Archaeologists believe that a four-chambered cave, discovered by local residents in the early years of the 1st century BCE, marks the beginning of Teotihuacán's rapid growth. Caves played an integral role in the Mesoamerican religion; they were considered places connected with the origin of the gods and ancestors, as well as portals to the underworld, the world of demons, and other potent beings. The Teotihuacán lava cave may have held particular significance as its four lobes could represent the four parts of the Mesoamerican cosmos. It was a focal point of fire and water rituals. In the 2nd century CE, Teotihuacán's largest pyramid, the Pyramid of the Sun, was built directly over the cave.

**7.71 The Citadel of Teotihuacán**

The city, most of it laid out between 150 BCE–150 CE, was organized into quadrants, with one avenue running east-west and the other, more important one, running north-south. The latter, called by the Aztecs the Avenue of the Dead, was aligned with the sacred mountain, Cerro Gordo, and pointed approximately 15 degrees east of north. The width of the avenue varied, ranging from 40 to 95 meters. A large, long channel under the floor of the avenue gathered rain water from neighboring architectural units and drained it into the Rio San Juan. The Pyramid of the Moon, facing south, defined the northern end of the avenue, along with the Pyramid of the Sun, facing west, about a kilometer down the avenue. The east-west street was not exactly 90 degrees to the north-south avenue, but lay 16 degrees, 30 minutes north of west, once again for reasons having to do with astronomy. Further south there was a great sunken plaza, known as Ciudadela.

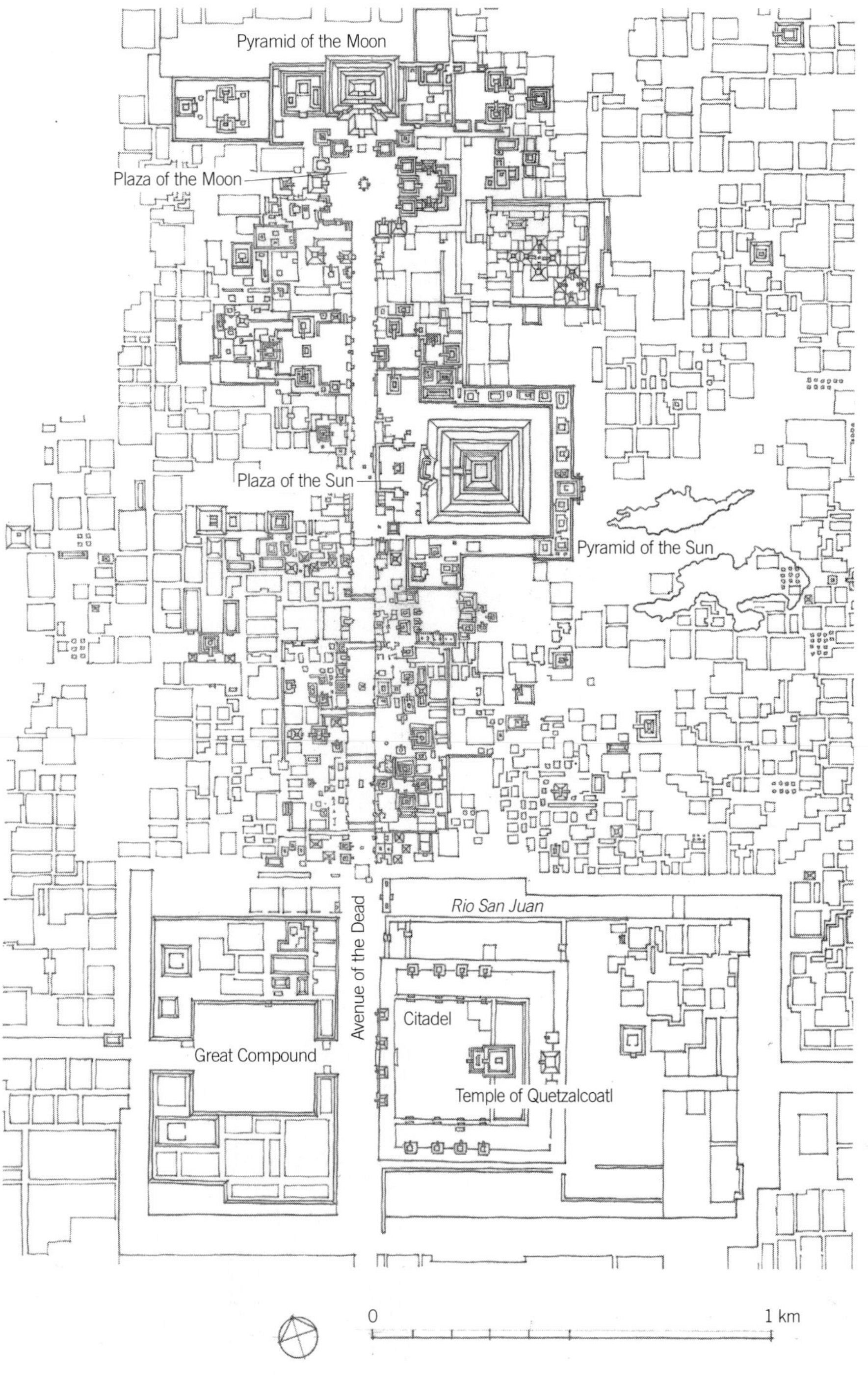


**7.72 Plan: Central zone of Teotihuacán**

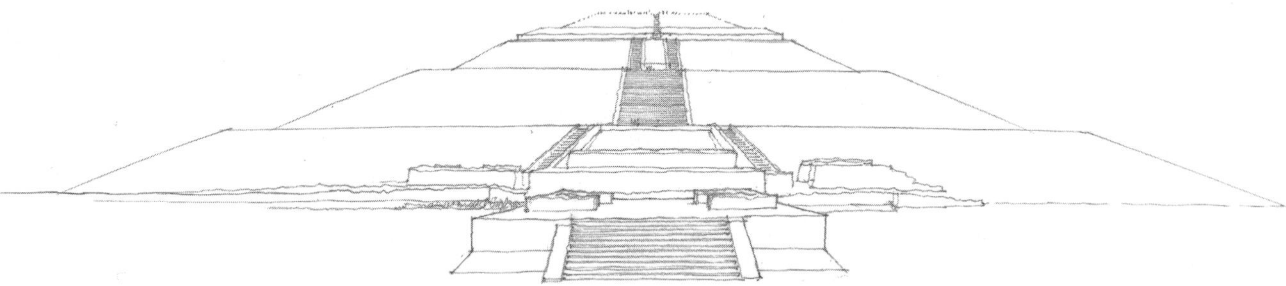

7.73 Pyramid of the Sun, Teotihuacán

The Pyramids of the Sun and the Moon, echoing the shapes of the mountains surrounding the valley, were constructed by hauling millions of cubic yards of sun-dried bricks, and all without the help of wheels and beasts of burden. Beneath the pyramids are earlier structures, perhaps even tombs of Teotihuacán rulers. The first to be built was the Pyramid of the Sun, completed around 200 CE. One of the largest structures built in the ancient Americas, it was 215 meters square and some 63 meters tall. The profile as it exists today is misleading and a product of the imagination of its reconstructors in the early part of the 20th century. The pyramid originally consisted of four stepped platforms, surmounted by a temple and an Adosada platform, which was built over what was originally the principal facade of the pyramid. Originally its exterior was covered with a thick layer of smooth plaster and was probably painted red.

The Pyramid of the Moon at the northern end of the Street of the Dead was completed around 250 CE. Recent excavations near the base of the pyramid staircase have uncovered the tomb of a male with numerous grave goods of obsidian and greenstone, as well as sacrificial animals. One of the most significant tombs yet discovered at Teotihuacán, it might indicate that even more important tombs lie buried at the heart of the pyramid. At the foot of the Pyramid of the Moon, there is a plaza (204 by 123 meters) surrounded by platforms that in ancient times were stuccoed, painted, and topped with temples. A low platform at the center of the plaza and visible from all the surrounding platforms served as an important ritual site.

7.74 Pyramid of the Moon, Teotihuacán

7.75 **The Feathered Serpent god (Quetzalcoatl), Teotihuacán**

**Temple of the Feathered Serpent**

After the Pyramid of the Sun and the Pyramid of the Moon were completed, construction shifted to the south where a large ritual complex and palace compound called the Ciudadela—a sunken plaza large enough to hold most of the city's inhabitants—was centered on the Temple of the Feathered Serpent (Quetzalcoatl). Completed in the early 3rd century CE, the temple is flanked by two apartment compounds where the city's rulers may have lived, and 15 smaller stepped pyramids, three at its back on the west, and four each on the other three sides.

The initial construction phase of the Temple of the Feathered Serpent appears to have been marked by several mass burials of people who were apparently sacrificed, their hands tied behind their backs, during the construction of the pyramid. They appear to have been killed as part of a warfare cult that, according to archaeoastronomers, was regulated by the position of the planet Venus in the heavens during its 584-day celestial cycle.

The Temple of the Feathered Serpent may have marked the first use of the distinctive Teotihuacán architectural profile known as *talud-tablero*, in which a rectangular panel (the *tablero*) sitting atop a sloping panel (the *talud*). The surfaces were usually decorated with murals. All the platforms at Teotihuacán have this profile, and its presence at other sites is generally an indicator of Teotihuacán influence throughout Mesoamerica. The balustrade and *tableros* of the Temple of the Feathered Serpent featured large, tenoned serpent heads with low-relief bodies, upon which elaborate mosaic headdresses appear at intervals. The headdresses, with their prominent eyes and fangs, were integral to the military iconography at Teotihuacán and were used throughout Mesoamerica.

By 200 CE, all major construction at the site had been completed, and the Puh Empire attended to building and improving the city's residential areas. Teotihuacán's complex urban grid was filled with single- and multifloor apartment compounds. This grid, the only one known in Mesoamerica before the 14th-century Aztec capital, Tenochtitlán, implies a high degree of social control.

From 200 to 600 CE, Teotihuacán continued to flourish, with long-distance trade becoming an important factor in its prosperity. But its success did not last. Around 750 CE the city burned to the ground, possibly torched by invaders from the city of Cacaxtla, 210 kilometers to the east.

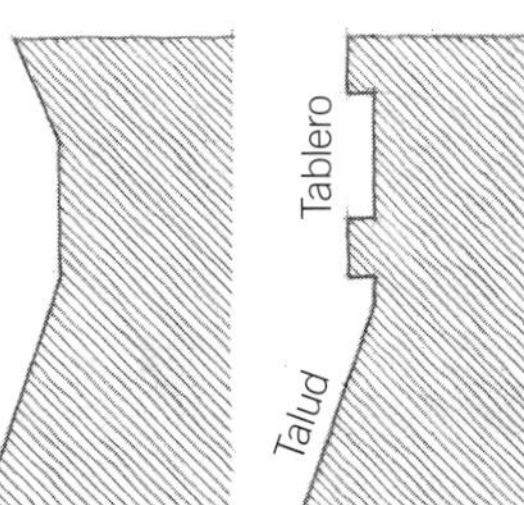

7.76 **Sectional profiles of the *talud-tablero* motif and an example at the Temple of Quetzalcoatl, Teotihuacán**

**7.77 Copper falcon and mica hand: Hopewell Mound Group**

**OHIO'S HOPEWELL MOUNDS**

Located on the north fork of Park Creek in Ross County, Ohio, the Hopewell Mound Group was first mapped in the mid-19th century when its ancient construction was still visible. The main feature of the site is the rectangular earthwork, known as the Great Enclosure, that covered about 99 acres and followed the terraces of the North Fork. Structures within the enclosure include a D-shaped containment for several mounds. Mound 25, the largest of these, consisted of three parts that covered earlier constructions. Burials containing elaborate grave goods were found in the mound.

Another Hopewell site, known as Mound City, is near Chillicothe, Ohio, and it has a particularly high concentration of burial mounds, leading to the supposition that it was primarily a funerary site used by local tribes. An extensive trade with exotic materials existed during this period, consisting of enormous quantities of precious objects available for use by, and burial with, the powerful people of the communities.

Burials in the so-called Mound of Pipes at Mound City contained more than 200 smoking pipes made of stone and depicting animals and birds in well-realized three-dimensional form. Copper from the Great Lakes area and mica from the southern Appalachians were used to create elaborate plaques, ornaments, and profile cutout images. The copper ornaments included necklaces, bracelets, breastplates, and ear spools. A sophisticated ceramic tradition produced many short, round jars that have been found in burial sites throughout the Hopewellian trading area.

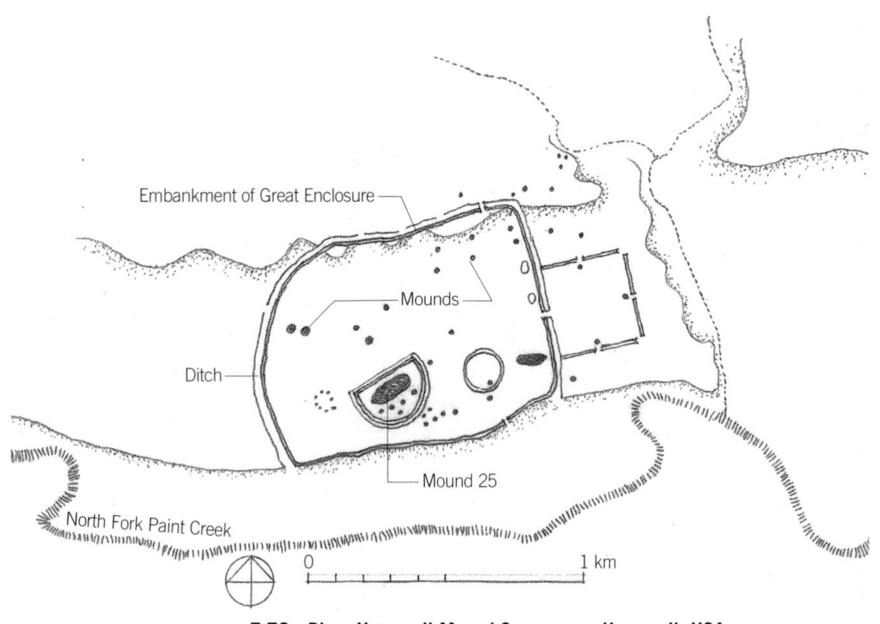

**7.78 Plan: Hopewell Mound Group, near Hopewell, USA**

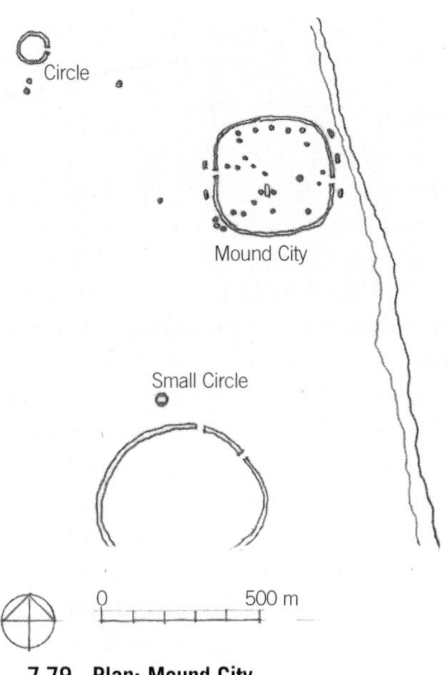


**7.79 Plan: Mound City**

# 400 CE

400 CE finds Eurasian architecture in a moment of adjustment with the South Asian, Chinese, and Roman worlds being transformed by new religions. South Asia experienced the rebirth of Hinduism, China came under the sway of Buddhism, and the Roman world began the process of converting to Christianity. In Central America, as the Zapotecs built a new capital in the valley of Oaxaca at Monte Albán, the Japanese had its first encounter with centralized government following the ascent of the Yamato clan.

In South Asia, as the Kushans went into decline early in the 3rd century CE, their empire was divided into the eastern and western halves in 225 CE. The western half was taken over by the Sassanians around 240 CE, and by 270 CE the eastern half, in the Gangetic heartland of India, fell to Sri Gupta, the king of Magadha. The Gupta rulers were able to quickly leverage their capture of Kushan territories to build an empire that controlled all of North India by 400 CE. The Gupta mission was to revive Hinduism in northern India, but they did so in a manner that not only accepted Buddhist practitioners but also adapted their practices and institutions to Hindu ends. The Hindu "renaissance" under the Gupta, therefore, was simultaneous with a flourishing Buddhist practice along the trade routes in places such as Ajanta and Nalanda. Alongside the Gupta's first brick Hindu temples, the oldest Buddhist brick temple was also constructed at Bodh-Gaya, the place of the Buddha's enlightenment. Mahayana Buddhism continued to flourish in the eastern half of the erstwhile Kushan empire with Bamiyan in Afghanistan, located at the intersection of the Eurasian trade routes, colossal rock-cut Buddha figures were built that were to have a profound influence on the development of Chinese, Korean, and Japanese Buddhism.

In China, the collapse of the Han Dynasty gave way to Sixteen Kingdoms, with the Chinese religious world impacted by the arrival of Buddhism, brought in by traders and monks from India. Dunhuang, located at the western end of the Great Wall where the Silk Route split into its northern and southern arms that go around the Taklamakan Desert, the Buddhist monks built one of the largest cave complexes in the world. Hundreds of caves, carved out of the sheer cliff face, functioned as a publishing house, where thousands of copies were made of the sutras from India for distribution throughout China.

But just as Buddhism moved into China along trade routes, Christianity was moving eastward along the Persian Royal Road. The most impressive buildings at the time were made by the Parthians and Sassanians in Iraq and Iran, where Zoroastrianism still reigned supreme. Little remains of these buildings, however, creating a gap in how we understand the history of architectural development of that time.

In Rome, Constantine stopped the repression of Christianity, but more for practical than religious reasons, founding a new city, Constantinople, that used a hybrid of Christian and pagan motifs. Soon after his death, the Christianization of the Empire began in earnest as "heathen" altars and temples were destroyed, and new forms of architecture, suitable for the religious needs of Christianity, were established. The architecture now centered on the great martyry cities like Rome and Jerusalem. At the same time invasions from the Russian steppes were taking their toll on the unity of the Empire, which was now split into different jurisdictions. Cities in the eastern provinces, like Antioch and Constantinople, with their strong Hellenistic traditions, remained, however, relatively wealthy and would become for a while the key to the survival of European learning.

Climate is known to have played an important role in developments in this period. The volcanic eruption of Krakatau in 416 CE created years of famine and disruption around the globe.

Kushan Empire
2nd century BCE–3rd century CE

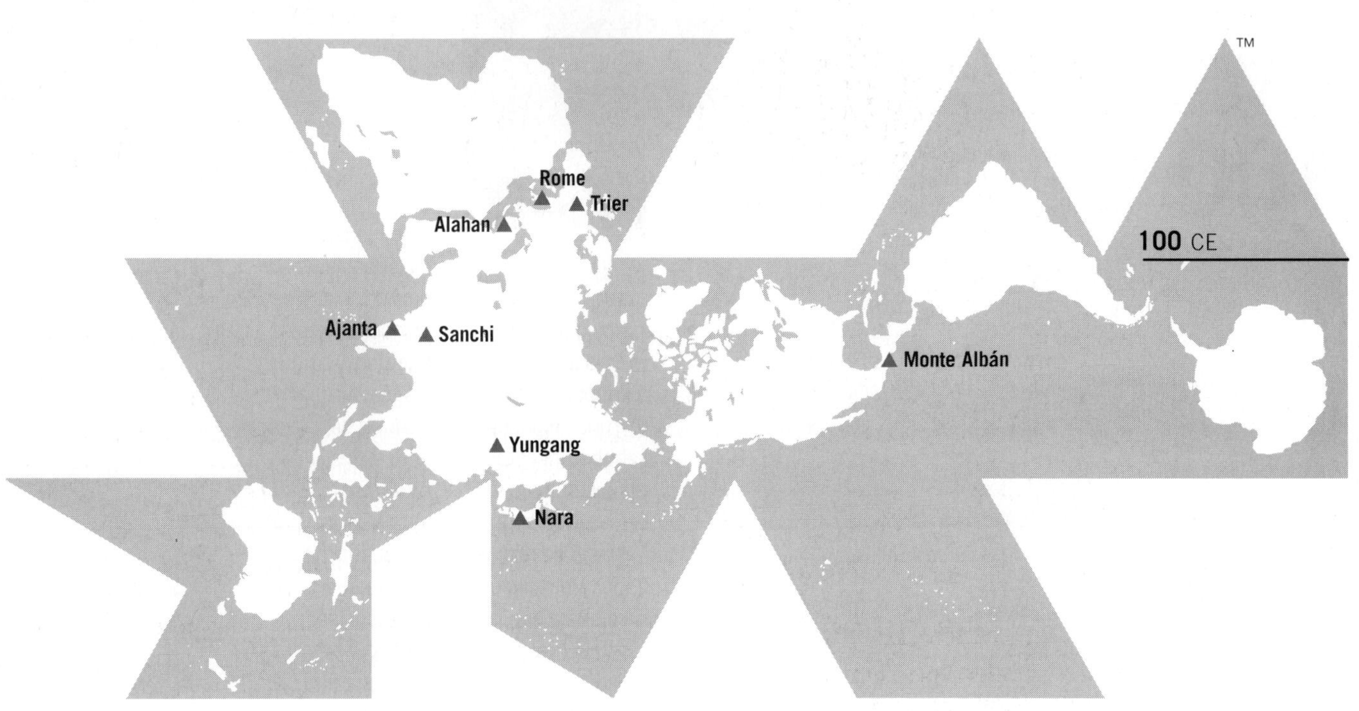

Gupta Empire
ca. 321–500 CE

▲ **Temple at Bhitargaon**
400–450 CE

▲ **Mahabodhi Temple**
Late-Gupta Period

▲ **Gupta Caves at Udayagiri**
Early-5th century

▲ **Ajanta Caves**
Mid-5th to late-6th centuries

China: Eastern Han Dynasty
25–220 CE

Sixteen Kingdoms Period
304–439 CE

Period of Northern and Southern Dynasties
386–589 CE

▲ **Mogao Caves**
4th to 14th centuries CE

▲ **Yungang Caves**
Mid-5th to late-6th centuries CE

**200** CE — **400** CE — **600** CE

Roman Empire
27 BCE–393 CE

Western Roman Empire
393–476 CE

Merovingian Dynasty in Central Europe
482–751 CE

▲ **Basilica at Trier**
ca. 310 CE

▲ **Basilica of St. Peter**
ca. 330 CE

▲ **St. John Lateran**
ca. 330 CE

▲ **St. Sabina**
425–432 CE

▲ **St. Maria Maggiore**
432 CE

▲ **St. Stefano Rotondo**
468–483 CE

Byzantine Empire
330–1453 CE

▲ **Church of the Prophets**
465 CE

▲ **Qualb Louzeh**
500 CE

▲ **Qalat Siman**
470 CE

▲ **Church of Acheiropoeitos**
470 CE

▲ **Tomb of King Theodoric**
ca. 520 CE

▲ **Alahan Monastery**
5th century CE

Monte Albán Culture
ca. 500 BCE–900 CE

Japan: Kofun Culture
ca. 3rd century–538 CE

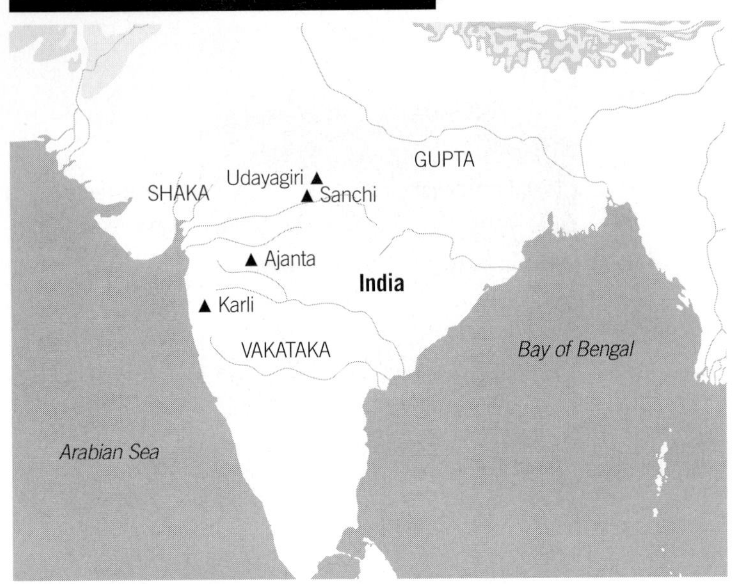


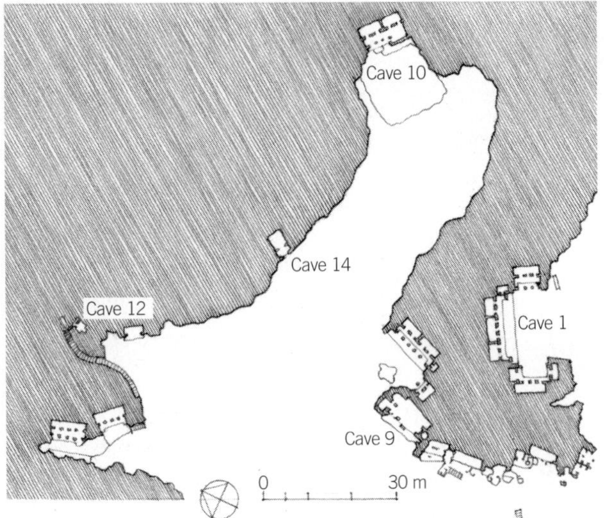


**8.1 Location of Caves 1, 9, 10, 12, and 14 at Udayagiri, India**

## HINDU RENAISSANCE

At the very time Buddhism was becoming dominant across East Asia, in India it was gradually disappearing. This transition took place during the time of the Gupta Empire, who began to fuse Buddhist practices with the surviving Vedic practices of pre-Buddhist times to create a new and well-organized religion that we now call Hinduism. Beginning as rulers of Magadha, one of the smaller kingdoms of the Gangetic Plain, the Gupta took advantage of the breakup of the Buddhist Kushan empire to conquer its eastern half in 270 CE. By 330 CE, Chandragupta expanded the kingdom across the entire Gangetic Plain. By 400 CE, under Vikramaditya, the empire stretched from Afghanistan to Burma, from the Himalayas to the Deccan plateau.

The Gupta revival of a transformed Vedic Hinduism was a skillful exercise in adaptation and invention. Unlike the Mauryas and the Han Chinese, the Gupta maintained subject kings as vassals and did not consolidate every kingdom into a single administrative unit. This enabled them not only to maintain and profit from the trade routes that were still controlled by the Buddhists, but also to exploit Buddhist institutions for Hindu purposes. Buddhist practices were not prohibited, and in fact were encouraged, and their institutions continued to thrive.

The interblending of Buddhist and Vedic cultures was described by Fa Hein, the famous Chinese pilgrim to the Gupta state from 399 to 414 CE. He talks of a magnificent procession of about 20 wheeled stupas, with figures of seated Buddhas attended by standing bodhisattvas, coming to the Gupta capital of Pataliputra, where it was received by the Hindu Brahmins and ushered into the city with great ceremony. The Buddhists by this time were themselves routinely making stone images of the Buddha. In some instances, a Buddhist *caitya* hall would be reused for Hindu gods. And in something of a stroke of genius, the Buddha himself was deified as another manifestation of Vishnu from the Hindu pantheon. The Hinduism of the Guptas thus was not a simple revival of pre-Buddhist Vedic practices, focused on fire sacrifices. Rather it was a process of assimilation that modernized through Mahayana Buddhism. So complete was this cohabitation that, by the 12th century, Buddhism had completely disappeared as an autonomous religion in India.

To understand the significance of this peaceful transmutation, one could imagine a counterfactual situation where, say, centuries after Constantine had accepted Christianity, Charlemagne would decide to revive the Roman pagan gods and their temples and absorb Jesus and his disciples into that pantheon as full-fledged members and bring about a "renaissance" through entirely peaceful means.

It is important to note that the new Hindu pantheon with its rituals was not invented out of the blue. The earliest intact Hindu architecture, the Gupta Caves at Udayagiri (early 5th century) already display a full array of Hindu deities, including Shiva, Vishnu, and Durga. Part excavated, part structural, these rudimentary caves show the essential attributes of a Hindu temple—that is, an unadorned inner womb-chamber or *garbh-griha*, which was the resident deities' home, preceded by an antechamber or *mulaprasada*, the place for the worshipper.

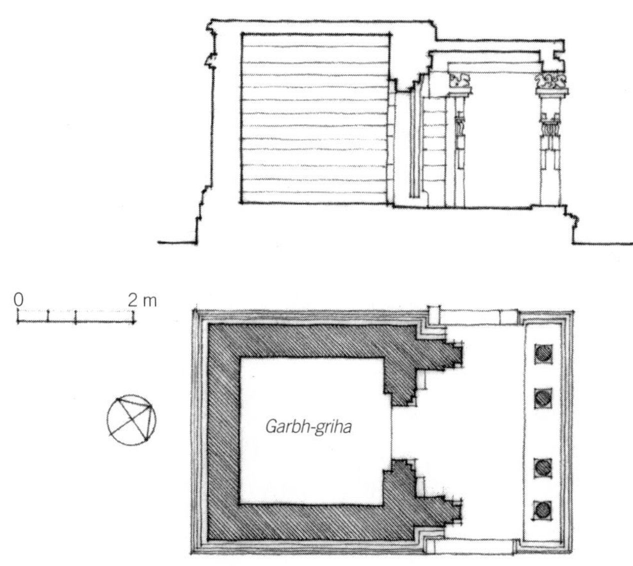


8.2 **Section and plan: Temple 17, Sanchi, near Bhopal, India**

8.3 **Temple 17, Sanchi**

**Gupta Period Temples**

In Hindu worship, the *antarala* (doorway or threshold) between the *garbh-griha* (literally "womb chamber," the innermost sanctum) and a *mulaprasada* or *mandapa* (a prechamber for rituals) marks the all-important moment of transition, at which the worshipper and the deity come into direct visual contact and enact the critical transaction called *darsana* (beholding of an auspicious deity). Indeed, the whole temple can be considered a two-way portal between the worlds of the worshipper and the deity. The deity, in essence, descends into the idol while the worshipper ascends to the sacred threshold. The deity is considered to be a guest in the world of the worshipper. In a ritual called *atithi-seva*, the worshipper offers the deity food (and, at times, such gifts as clothing and ornaments) on a tray. The *pandit*, or priest, who stands at the threshold and mediates the ritual, takes the food from the tray and touches it to the mouth of the deity. He keeps a portion for the temple, returning the rest with some additional special food from the temple, called *prasada*, for the worshipper.

The deity's home, the *garbh-griha*, is derived from the Buddhist *caitya* caves, now morphed into a conceptual "womb." This chamber, the receptacle of the occasional presence of the deity, is considered to be without form and perfect. The human world, by contrast, is the world of form (*maya*). The *garbh-griha* is thus solid and unadorned, and it has no other openings except the one to the *mulaprasada*. The *mulaprasada*, by contrast, is an open portico held up by lavishly decorated columns.

This basic configuration can be seen at the so-called "Temple 17" at Sanchi and the Kankali Devi at Tigawa, both from the early 5th century CE. Both consist of a flat-roofed *garbh-griha* and *mulaprasada*, linked together by a simple stepped stylobate and architrave. An example of a full-fledged Hindu temple is the brick-and-mud mortar Temple at Bhitargaon (400–450 CE). Here the *garbh-griha* is surmounted by a large tapering superstructure, called the *shikhara*. The *shikhara* marks the vertical axis in the form of the cosmic mountain. Its purpose is to enable the worshipper to visualize the order of the complete universe as described by Hindu cosmogony. A *shikhara*, therefore, is a three-dimensional model of the Hindu cosmos. All temples culminate in a finial, the conceptual center of the structure. From there, the "cosmos" splays outward, cascading down the building, so to speak, along radial lines. The actual geometries of the *shikhara* are determined by its mandala or astrological diagram. *Shikharas* are conceived of as solid and for the most part are, even though for structural reasons, some may have internal hollows.

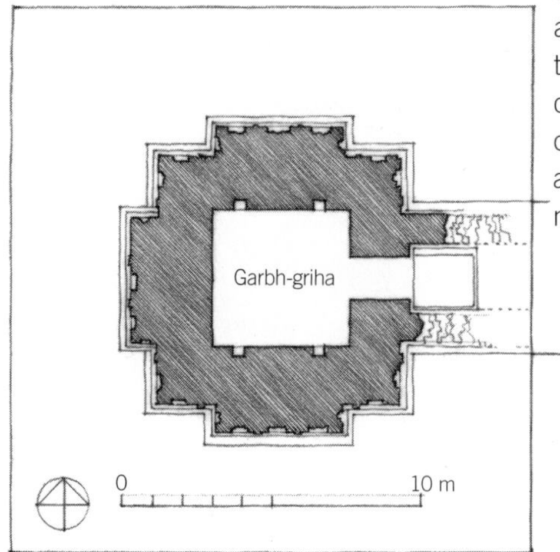


8.4 **Temple at Bhitargaon, near Kanpur, India**

8.5 Ghandaran Buddha

8.6 View of Ajanta Caves from Cave 26

**Ajanta Caves**

In 390 CE the Gupta king Vikramaditya arranged the marriage of his daughter Prabhavatigupta to Rudrasena II, the prince of the vassal state of Vakataka, through which *dakshinapatha*, the southern trade route, went. The Vakatakas' gratitude for their status as guardians of *dakshinapatha* is recorded in their lavish patronage of Ajanta, the largest assemblage of Buddhist rock-cut *caityas* and *viharas* found anywhere in South Asia. Like the Sunga period Sanchi complex, Ajanta was likely a kind of college monastery. At its prime it would have afforded accommodations for up to several hundred teachers and pupils. Chinese pilgrim and scribe Hsuan Tsang (Xuanzang) notes that Dinnaga, a celebrated Buddhist author of books on logic, resided there. Though the books are lost, the Ajanta caves have survived with even their paintings relatively intact. Though somewhat difficult to access, their location along the *dakshinapatha* meant that they could effectively cater to the needs of both the monastic Mahayana Buddhists and their patrons; the names of many of the latter are inscribed within the caves.

As Mahayana practitioners, Ajanta's monks were allowed and encouraged to create Buddha figures and thus to propagate the concept that many had attained nirvana even before and after the historical Buddha. Since virtuous worldly acts were also a way of attaining nirvana or Buddhahood in Mahayana Buddhism, the laity's patronage of the Ajanta monks helped them in their own quest for nirvana.

The Ajanta caves are located along the sheer rock wall of a dramatic C-shaped chasm carved by the Waghora River. The Waghora, a mountain stream, forces its way into the valley and forms in its descent a series of waterfalls, 60 meters high, which must have certainly been audible to the monks in the caves. The thirty odd caves vary from 10 to 33 meters in elevation above the river.

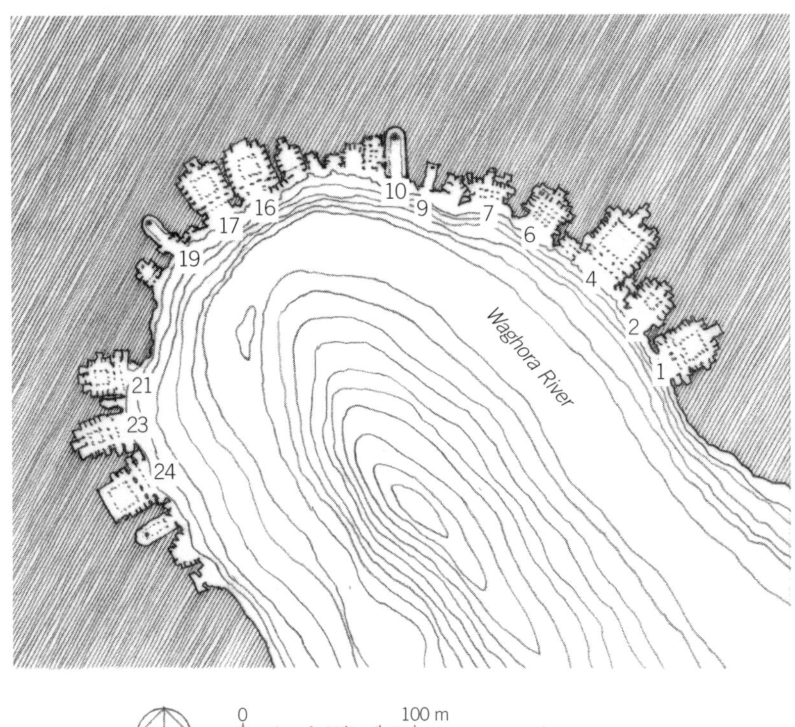


8.7 Plan of cave complex at Ajanta, near Aurangabad, India

8.8 Entrance to a vihara at Ajanta

8.9 Interior of Cave 9 at Ajanta

The oldest pre-Vakataka *caityas* (Caves 9 and 10, located almost in the middle) were relatively simple, with an apsidal colonnade marking the circumambulatory route around a largely unadorned stupa at the end. However, *caityas* 19 (450 CE) and 26 (490 CE), from the reign of Harisena, take on strong Mahayana overtones. Both have an elaborate forecourt open to the sky, with side chambers hewn directly out of the rock. Unlike the great *caitya* at Karli, whose entrance replicates a wooden assemblage of *caityas*, these are covered by large and small Buddha figurines and stupas. No longer imitation-wood stage sets, they are symbolic entities in themselves. Their *caitya* window, originally an imitation horseshoe-shaped wooden window, has now been transformed into an abstract representation of the Buddha, with a prominent topknot and elongated side "ears," reminiscent literally of the ears of the Buddha in the statues. Similarly, the columns are richly sculptured with floral and figural representations symbolic of the gardens where the Buddha preached and gained enlightenment. The column capitals and bases bulge like the folds of the corpulent Buddha. The stupas are also richly ornamented with Buddha statues attached directly to their surfaces, presaging the eclipsing of the stupa as the primary representational element of the ceremonial Buddha statue, in particular in China and Southeast Asia.

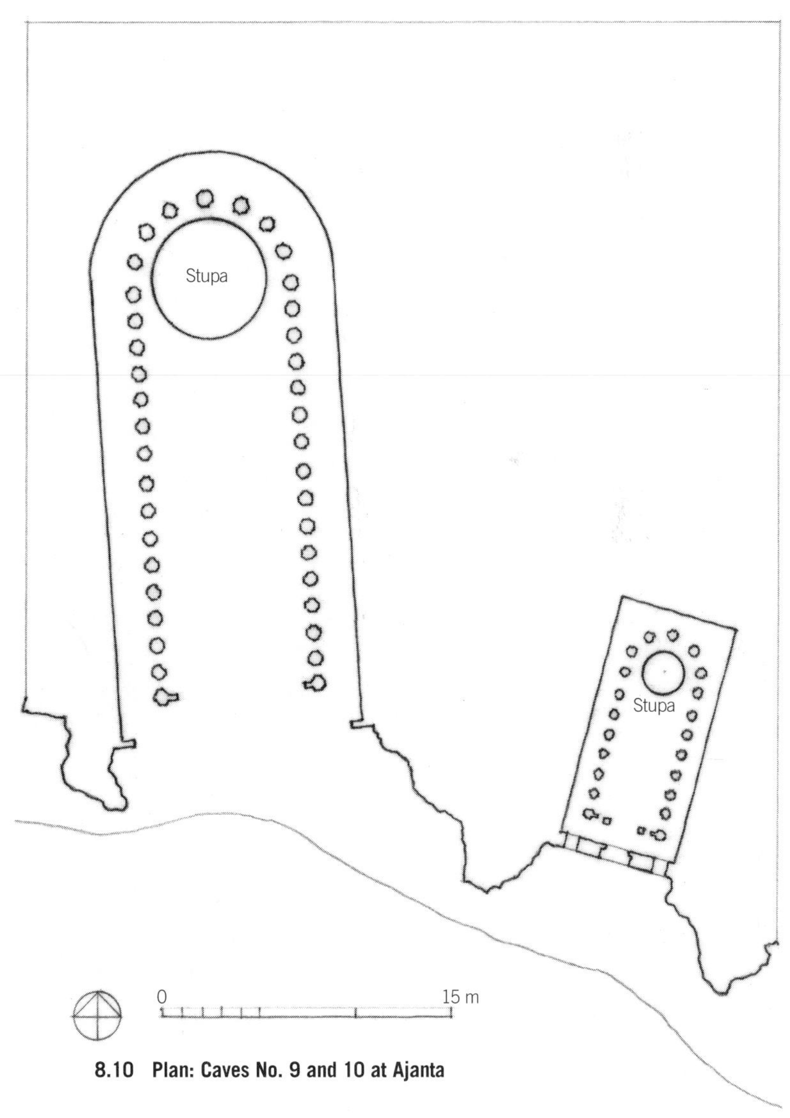


8.10 Plan: Caves No. 9 and 10 at Ajanta

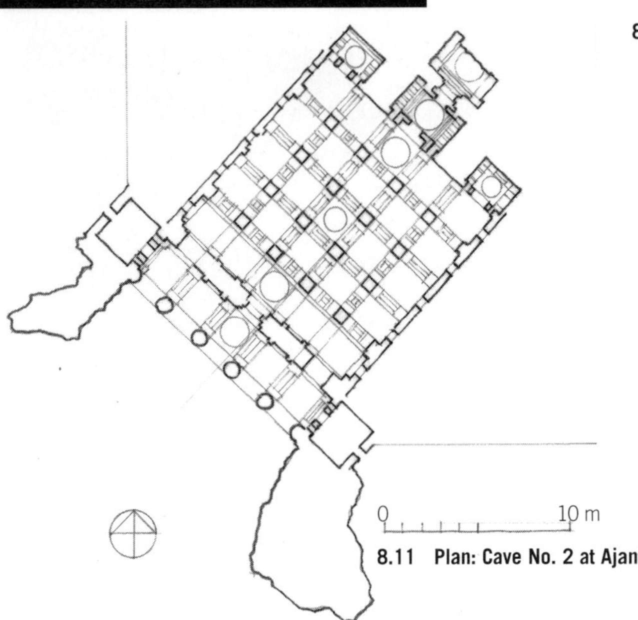


8.11 Plan: Cave No. 2 at Ajanta

8.12 Entrance to Cave No. 2 at Ajanta

As Mahayana Buddhism became ever more popular, it developed a more elaborate liturgical practice that supported a richer artistic program. Evidence of this can be seen in Ajanta's *viharas*, which served as the residences of the monks. Over time, the *viharas* at Ajanta changed from being simple dwellings for the monks to full-fledged ceremonial spaces. The basic form, a rectangular colonnaded hall, preceded by a portico and surrounded by cells, still persists. The Ajanta *viharas* have a broad verandah; its roof is supported by pillars that open into a central pillared hall averaging in size about 6 by 10 meters. The cells open to this hall. The number of the cells vary according to the size and importance of the *vihara*.

8.13 Interior of Cave No. 19 at Ajanta

Some of the cells, associated perhaps with particularly significant monks, were transformed into shrines with votive Buddha statues (like at Caves 17, 2, and 6). The later *viharas* also acquired multiple stories (Cave 6) and circumambulatory routes (usually defined by a colonnaded passage) and, as they became used more for ceremonies, they also became more ornamental and decorative with images depicting scenes from the life of the Buddha and from Buddhist treatises painted onto the walls.

A certain nonmonastic sensuousness pervades the images, which are not confined to designated panels. Despite the dim light, every surface of the *viharas* was painted over. Art, sculpture, and architecture, in other words, commingle to create a seamless, sensory experience. Structural expression is denied. Like the imitation-wood construction present in the older *caityas*, the essential symbolic message of the Ajanta *viharas* was to display the profound beauty of the life and world of the Buddha and, at the same time, underline its character as an illusion, or *maya*—a fundamental doctrine of Mahayana Buddhist practice on the path to nirvana.

8.14 **Mahabodhi Temple, Gaya, India**

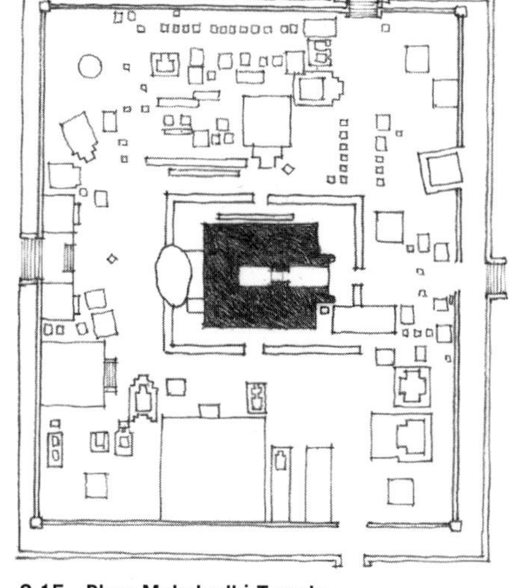

8.15 **Plan: Mahabodhi Temple**

**Mahabodhi Temple**

Bodh Gaya, the garden in Gaya near Patna, where the Buddha is said to have attained enlightenment while sitting under a *peepal* tree, is one of the most venerated pilgrimage destinations of the entire Buddhist world. The Mahabodhi (literally "Great Buddha") Temple at this site was begun by Asoka who ordered the construction of a simple stone platform, known as the *Vajrasana* or Diamond-Throne, to mark the spot where the Buddha supposedly sat. In accordance with the nonrepresentational requirements of Hinayana Buddhism, Asoka had no other representation or temple built at the site. The tree itself is said to have been cut down by zealots first in the 4th century BCE and then again in the 7th century CE. But a sapling from the original tree, taken to Sri Lanka by Asoka's daughter in the 4th century BCE, still thrives, and it is the longest continuously documented tree in the world. In the late Gupta period, the Mahabodhi Temple was constructed next to the tree (late 5th or 6th century).

The temple as it stands today, however, has been renovated repeatedly over time, and it is difficult to be absolutely certain what is original to the Gupta period. Nonetheless, its contours today are not that different from its description by Hsuan Tsang (Xuanzang) from 637 CE.

Hsuan Tsang recorded that the Bodhi Tree was enclosed by a strong, high brick wall (originally built by Asoka) 500 paces in circumference. Rare trees offered shade with fine grasses, flowers, and strange plants covering the ground. The main gate opened east toward the Niranjana River, while the south gate connected to a large lotus tank, the sacred tank where it is believed that Buddha had spent a week. The north gate opened into the grounds of a large monastery. Inside there were innumerable stupas and shrines, built as memorials by sovereigns and high officials. In the center of the Bodhi Tree enclosure—defined by a stone *vedika* or fence like the one around the Sanchi stupa—was the *Vajrasana*, sandwiched between the Bodhi Tree to its west and the Mahabodhi Temple, 48 meters high with a width of twenty paces, to its east.

The temple was made of bricks and coated with lime. It had tiers of niches with gold images; its four walls were adorned with exquisite carvings of pearls; and at its top, there was a gilt-copper stupa. Hsuan Tsang separately also recorded that south of the Bodhi Tree was an Asokan pillar more than 30 meters high.

The Mahabodhi Temple today is clearly similar to this description. It is surrounded by four subsidiary shrines at the corners that were added in the 19th century. The central chamber houses the image of the enthroned Buddha of the temple. The brick *shikhara* contains another *cella* at the upper level with a secondary image of the Buddha.

Along with the Bhitargaon Temple, the Mahabodhi Temple is among the oldest multistory brick temples of South Asia. Although they went out of fashion in India once stone temples were begun, it is also possible that the development of the Buddhist pagodas in China may have in part been inspired by Hsuan Tsang's description of this temple, which was widely circulated.

8.16 View of Bamiyan, Afghanistan

## KUSHANS OF BAMIYAN

Bamiyan was at the center of the 5th-century Eurasian world. Trade routes from China, India, and West Asia came together in this valley, located in the middle of contemporary Afghanistan. The site was protected by a large Buddhist monastery, with more than a hundred caves of various sizes carved out of the sheer cliff face of the nearby mountains. In their midst, separated by about 1 kilometer, the Kushan emperor, Kanishka, initiated the construction of two gigantic Buddha statues, known as the Bamiyan Buddhas. They were completed in the 4th and 5th centuries, under the Sassanians. Colossal Buddhas, never built in India, were a Kushan invention that was subsequently widely imitated throughout China, Korea, and Japan for centuries to come. Although the Bamiyan Buddhas were among the first of their kind, in March 2001 they were destroyed by the Taliban government of Afghanistan as idols.

The Bamiyan cliff rises sharply at the northwestern edge of its wide and expansive valley. To the north toward China and to the east toward India, the valleys coming to Bamiyan are narrow and sharp. The traders coming upon Bamiyan would have encountered a dramatic change in landscape. The traders' attention, however, would have been focused on the imposing sandstone cliff that rises sharply at the northwestern edge of a wide valley. As seen from across the valley, the 1.6-kilometer-long cliff, pockmarked by the caves, rises to a peak in the middle. Behind it, one after another, are visible the silhouettes of successive layers of the Himalayas, with the most distant ranges perpetually clad in snow. Even from this distance, the Bamiyan statues would have been clearly visible and would have in that sense measured up against the distant Himalayan peaks.

The bodies of two Bamiyans were first cut directly from the stone and then molded with a mixture of mud and straw to create the folds of the robes, the hands and the details of the face. The drapery was made by suspending ropes from the stone surface of the upper body. At the base the ropes were held in place by wooden pegs and then covered over with mud plaster. The entire surface was originally painted in gold and other bright colors. The outward expression of the statues, in particular the folds of the garments, has a Hellenic character. Most of the smaller caves at Bamiyan were covered with paintings, very similar in style to the one found at Ajanta. But the origin of the idea of building colossal statues is as yet unknown. The only known precedents of this type are from pharaonic Egypt.

8.17 Bamiyan Buddha

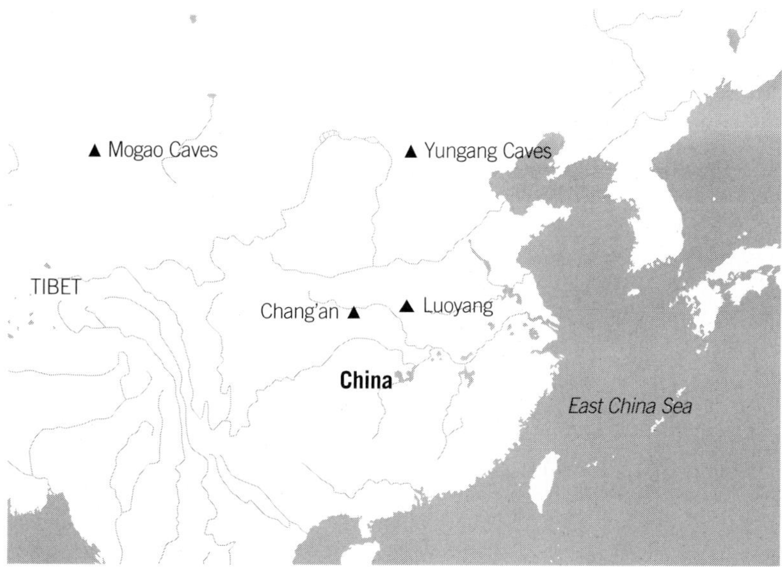


**ESTABLISHMENT OF CHINESE BUDDHISM**

By the 6th century CE, Mahayana Buddhism had settled into China, made its way into Korea, and from there crossed into Japan. Never accompanied by the sword, Buddhism was spread by the trade routes, benefiting from the symbiotic relationship between monastic monks and itinerant traders. Traffic between China and South Asia in the 7th century was heavy. Though the Silk Route extended to Rome, South Asia was in fact China's largest trading partner at the time. In Chinese literature, India is referred to as "The Western Kingdom" (not Europe). Besides silk, which was the prime luxury commodity, South Asian kingdoms imported camphor, fennel, vermilion, fine leather, pear, and peach from China. The Chinese, much more self-sufficient, seemed to be interested mostly in Buddhism. The Han emperor Ming-di was the first to officially invite Indian Buddhist monks to China to translate Buddhist sutras into Chinese. In 64 CE, after the long and arduous journey, Dharmaratna and Kasyapa Matanga, arrived in Luoyang, the new Han capital, with a white horse laden with sutras. The Han emperor built a monastery for them called the Baima-si (or the White Horse Monastery). Although the current structure dates mostly from the 14th century, Baima-si is by reference the oldest surviving temple of China. After Dharmaratna and Matanga, over the next millennium, hundreds of Indian monks came to live in China. Not as many Chinese travelers came to India, although the ones that did were very well known, even in their own times, because they kept extensive records of their travels and actively interpreted Buddhism for the Chinese. These include Faxian in the 5th century and Hsuan Tsang (Xuanzang) and Yi Jing in the 7th century, all of whom made the long and arduous journey to South Asia and back. Although Buddhism travelled rapidly across East Asia, its translation into relevant Chinese concepts took time.

Buddhism, however, was only one amongst many competitive intellectual traditions current in China at the time. Not everyone was convinced that Buddhism was an improvement on local Confucian and Daoist principles. Confucianists, for instance, challenged Buddhism's inability to set out principles of an organized social and political order, which was of course Confucianism's strength. Competition between these two philosophical traditions was to remain a hallmark of Chinese history for the next 2000 years. There were several attempts at mediation between them, most famously the Qing emperor Qianlong's creation of a Tibetan Buddhist model of governance, with the role of the emperor central to it, in the 18th century. In general, though Buddhism governed the temples and monasteries, the court still operated on Confucian principles. Buddhism, in other words, had to prove its way into China. In that process it was translated into Chinese both literally and conceptually. The stupa for instance became contracted to the *ta*. Thus East Asian Buddhism has a distinct flavor, different from that of South Asia and even Southeast Asia. With that, esoteric Chinese schools of Buddhism, such as Pure Land Buddhism, founded in the 3rd century CE, began to develop. It was Chinese Buddhism that was exported to Korea and Japan, where it also took on a local flavor, but remained based largely on the Chinese mold as distinct from that of the South Asian mold.

8.18 View of some of the more than 500 Mogao Caves at Dunhuang, China

**Mogao Caves**

Carved out of the cliffs on the western bank of the Dunhuang river, the 500 or so Mogao caves document the first millennium of Buddhism in China, from roughly 300 to 1350 CE. As one would expect the caves are located at an important junction of the Silk Route, right at the western end of the Great Wall. Surrounded by desert, at Dunhuang the Silk Route breaks into its northern and southern paths. West of Dunhuang begins, or ends, one of the most arduous parts of the journey through the arduous Lopnar and Taklamakan deserts. Abandoned in the 14th century, the Mogao caves were rediscovered in the early 1900s to the acclaim of a spectacular find of 50,000 manuscripts found sealed in one of the caves. Intentionally sealed in the 11th century, this cache held thousands of copies of sutras, letters, contracts, poems, prayer sheets, and various official documents. In some cases, there were multiple copies of the best-known sutras, handwritten with brushes dipped in lustrous black ink on paper, establishing the fact that Mogao was a critical center for the dissemination of Buddhist knowledge. Large quantities of these manuscripts were distributed to Japanese and European museums before the Chinese government intervened and took the rest to the national museum in Beijing. The work of properly translating and understanding the significance of these manuscripts is still ongoing.

Like Bamiyan, the architectural significance of the Mogao caves lies as much in their individual characteristics as in their collective presence as a marvelous city of caves. Visible from the distance in the arid landscape, three to five tiers of caves are carved into a long cliff face, fairly close to one another. Some are small niches with room enough for a single monk to sit in meditation, whereas others have lofty ceilings and are large enough for a procession of a hundred or so worshippers. Changes in dynasties marked new beginnings in different parts of the Dunhuang cliff. The earliest caves were simple chambers with niches and sculptures of the Buddha.

8.19 Fresco depicting Emperor Wudi worshipping statues of Buddha at the Mogao Caves

**8.20 Mogao Caves: West wall of Cave 285**

By the Northern Dynasties period, the caves became more complex and took the form of short corridors leading from the entrance hall to a transverse chamber with a simulated gabled roof. Opposite the entrance, the principal Buddha image was placed against a central pillar, allowing the worshippers, as at Ajanta, to perform *parikrama* or circumambulation around the central image. Cave 285 (539 CE) has its side walls lined with niches for monks to sit and meditate. Cave 428, the bequest of the Governor of Dunhuang, Prince Jian Ping, (565–576 CE), is one of the fanciest of this period, with each of the four niches of the central pillar featuring statues of the Buddha and three bodhisattvas. The "gabled" roof is divided into panels by bands painted brown that mimic the structure of a wooden hut.

Like contemporary caves in South Asia, most of the Mogao caves' walls are covered by paintings describing the life of the Buddha and various manifestations of Buddhist doctrine. The predominant colors are blue, green, red, black, white, and gold. Stylistically, the art is an amalgam of Indic, Central Asian, and Chinese influences, although the overall style may be recognized as being far more South Asian than later Chinese Buddhist art and architecture.

In 400 CE, Buddhism was supported by the Northern Dynasties (386–581 CE). For the Southern Dynasties (420–588 CE), Confucianism was still dominant even though some learned monks studied Buddhist ideas in order to make them compatible with Daoist philosophy. The end of the Northern and Southern Dynasties saw the beginning of a large influx of foreign immigrants, most of whom were traders or Buddhist missionaries from Central Asia. Some settled in China and held official posts; they adopted the Chinese way of life but maintained their own social customs and practiced Buddhism. By the time China was united again under the Sui (581–618 CE), the country had already experienced decades of relative political stability and social mobility. This prepared the way for one of the most prosperous epochs in its history—that of the T'ang Dynasty (618–907 CE).

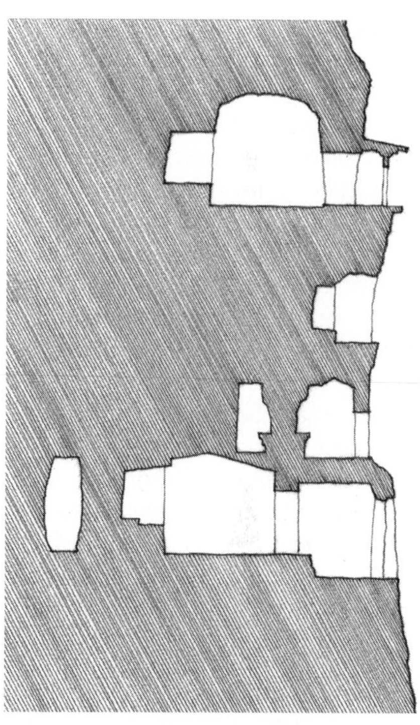

**8.21 Section through cliff at Mogao Caves**

8.22 Interior, Cave No. 10, Yungang Caves

8.23 Cave No. 10, Yungang, near Datong, China

### Yungang Caves

Some 1000 kilometers east of Mogao, in present-day Shanxi Province, the Yungang caves were constructed in the late 5th to early 6th centuries under the imperial sponsorship of the Northern Wei Dynasty (386–534 CE). Unlike the Mogao Caves, which were inhabited by monks on a trade route, the Yungang caves were a new type in that they were built adjacent to the Wei capital Datong. They had little resident monk population and were meant for worship primarily by the urban population of Datong. A Northern Wei minster ordered the construction of the first five of the caves. These contained colossal statues of the seated Buddha, in the manner of the Bamiyan. In an environment where imperial patronage of Buddha was fiercely contested, these caves may have been intended as representations of the five Northern Wei emperors as a way to compete with Confucian ideologies or even deified emperors of the Southern Dynasties.

While most of the caves at Yungang are focused on the image of the Buddha, it is worth noting that one of the caves (number 29) has a vertical column rising from the floor to the roof and articulated as a multistory tower with a series of projecting eaves. Small images of Buddha are located between the floors. This is an early manifestation of the Chinese pagoda (or *ta*) conceived, by Mahayana Buddhist thinking, as a magnification of the *chattras* of the South Asian stupa.

Under Mahayana Buddhism, the esoteric abstractions of the stupa were slowly replaced by a more graphic and literal iconography. First, the figure of the Buddha was considered to be equivalent to the stupa, an idea that was often expressed by superimposing a Buddha figure directly onto the stupa as at Ajanta. In China, as the *ta* emerged as the dominant form, the figure of the Buddha was inserted into the pagoda, either as a single colossal standing figure or several at each level (see discussion of the Mu-ta in 600 CE and the Guanyin-ge in 1000 CE).

8.24 Partial plan of Yungang Cave complex

8.25 Mosaic of Jesus the Christ

**EMERGENCE OF CHRISTIANITY**

When Christianity was officially recognized in 326 CE, it did not spell the end of paganism. Furthermore, many traditions were carried over, but the fact is that Christianity's monotheism brought a vibrancy and authenticity to religious practice that had long been lost by the old temple culture of the Greeks and Romans. Christianity had begun as one of several Hellenistic alternative-style religions that were based on a more intimate relationship with the divine. The rise of the cults of Isis and Dionysus, of Zoroastrianism and Mithraism, not to mention the Gymnosophists of Upper Egypt and the Theraputae in Alexandria, as well as the growing populism associated with mystical religious practices, meant that for a long time, few could have predicted the success that the Christians would achieve, even when Constantine converted on his deathbed. But when he did so, the Roman title Pontifex Maximus now meant that whoever was emperor was also the head of the Church and the vicar of Christ. As to the Church's competitors, they were bit by bit folded into the Christian world or condemned as heresies. The religious pluralism that flourished in the 5th century, and out of which Christianity itself had emerged, was quashed by the end of the 6th century. Judaism alone was given some leeway, but it too was under pressure. Christians were forbidden to marry Jews, and synagogue building for the most part was stopped.

This does not mean that there was a single unified doctrine. On the contrary, in the 1st century CE, as the Church was figuring out how elastic it was on various issues, debates raged about the nature of Christ, about Mary, as well as a host of other issues. The choice of architectural style must also have caused considerable discussion. For practical and ideological reasons, it was impossible for the new religious architecture to follow in the footsteps of temple architecture. The wide variety of solutions in the early days of Christian architecture are a testament to the search for a proper fit between architecture and liturgy. In an earlier age one could not possibly have mistaken a tomb for a basilica or a bathing establishment. Roman architecture created clearly defined architectural environments for the various urban functions. But already by the 3rd century CE, distinctions were rapidly disappearing and being reformulated, as with Maxentius' "basilica," which was modeled on an imperial bath building. In early Christian architecture, when house-churches were no longer needed, this trend was accelerated as various forms were studied and reevaluated for their compatibility with the developing liturgical needs.

The impact of Christianity on Roman buildings was, of course, a negative one. The Imperial Forum was abandoned; temples were chopped down for building materials; walls were added between columns to create churches. More often than not, stones from Roman buildings were fired in large kilns to make lime for mortar. As late as 1606, Paul V demolished the Temple of Minerva in the Forum of Nerva to obtain building material for the construction of the Aqua Paola fountain. Christian fanatics went to Baalbek to destroy idols, but they were, in fact, initially beaten back. Pagan rituals continued there until about 380 CE. But bit by bit, the Christian emperors tightened their grip. The sanctuary was eventually destroyed and the remnants redesigned as a relatively humble church. The liquidation of the sculptures was so complete that not a single example has been found. In fact, so devastating was the antipathy to the pagan world that it took a thousand years, until the 15th century, before interest in its existence was anything more than fleeting.

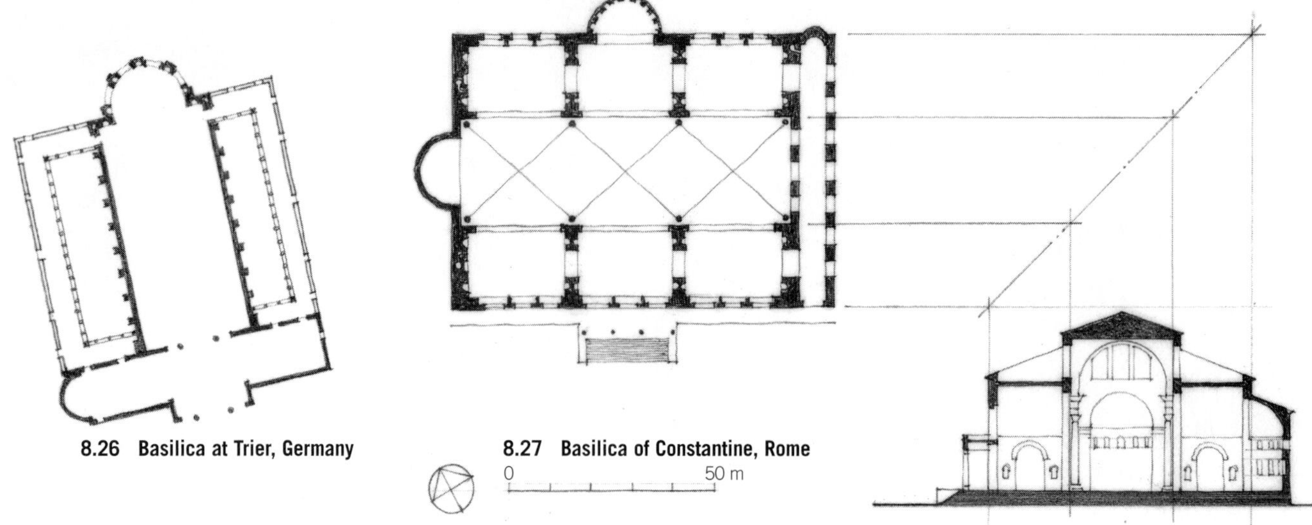


**8.26 Basilica at Trier, Germany**

**8.27 Basilica of Constantine, Rome**

To add to the complexity of the times, when Constantine left Rome in 326 CE and formally dedicated Constantinople as the "new Rome" in 330 CE, Rome became almost overnight a backwater. Constantine founded the new city not so much as a Christian one, for he converted only on his deathbed, but rather as a place where Christianity and paganism could coexist. This was not possible in Rome where the Christians were demanding complete allegiance from their sovereign. Seen from the perspective of Rome, however, the construction of Constantinople was a disaster, but seen from the perspective of the eastern provinces, it was a natural reascendancy. Unlike the European parts of the Empire, which were too spread out and with too many different tribes settling in various regions to have any unity, the east was naturally cohesive. The division of the Empire had other consequences, for suddenly there was not one capital or even four but actually six; along with Constantinople, there was Antioch, Nicomedia, Milan, Trier, and Cologne, all of which were now refurbished as imperial residences. Milan became an imperial residence from 353 CE onward. It was suddenly a major architectural center. Five new churches were built, three of them standing to this day at nearly their full height.

In 380 CE, however, Emperor Gratian made Trier his residence, bringing the flow of money to the north. Emperor Honorius, however, favored Ravenna and transferred the Imperial See there in the early 5th century CE; it became the residence of the Christianized Ostrogoths under Theodoric (490–526 CE) and his successors. Sumptuous new buildings were soon on the drawing boards. As for Constantine's considerable building activities in Constantinople, however, little remains. Most of what we know, when it comes to architecture in this early period of Christianity, derives from the remnants that have survived in Syria and Egypt and from buildings in Europe.

Without an imperial presence, Rome had to fend for itself. In 410 CE, she was sacked for three days by a band of Visigoths. The emperor of the West, Honorius, sat helplessly in Ravenna, and the emperor of the East was even further away in Constantinople. For protection, the Romans hired Odoacer, a German chieftain, but in 476 CE, he proclaimed himself king, defeated the Roman general Orestes at Piacenza, took Ravenna, and deposed Romulus Augustulus, who was the last official emperor of the West until the coronation in 800 CE of Charlemagne.

The Roman administration of Italy continued to function under Odoacer, who retained the chief officers of state. In 488 CE, Zeno sent Theodoric the Great, king of the Ostrogoths, into Italy to expel Odoacer. In 493 CE Odoacer consented to a treaty and was invited to a banquet where he and his officers were assassinated, leaving Theodoric master of Italy. Theodoric eagerly imported the most skilled masons and mosaic artists from the east while adopting the conservative Roman basilica-styled plan for his churches. But this did little to calm the anxieties in Constantinople, and in 534 CE, Justinian sent an army to bring Italy and North Africa into its sphere of control. In 536 CE, even Rome was taken, but in 568 CE, the Visigoths were back and were laying waste to northern Italy. As water poured into Rome from the aqueducts that had gone into disrepair, the unused land reverted to swamps, spreading malaria that made large parts of the area around Rome into the unsalutary plain that it remained until the 20th century. In 680 CE, the bubonic plague broke out. Rome's population dropped from about a million at the time of the Roman Empire to as low as 30,000 by the 6th century. The large parts of Rome that were now abandoned or used as farms came to be called the *disabitato* (the uninhabited areas).

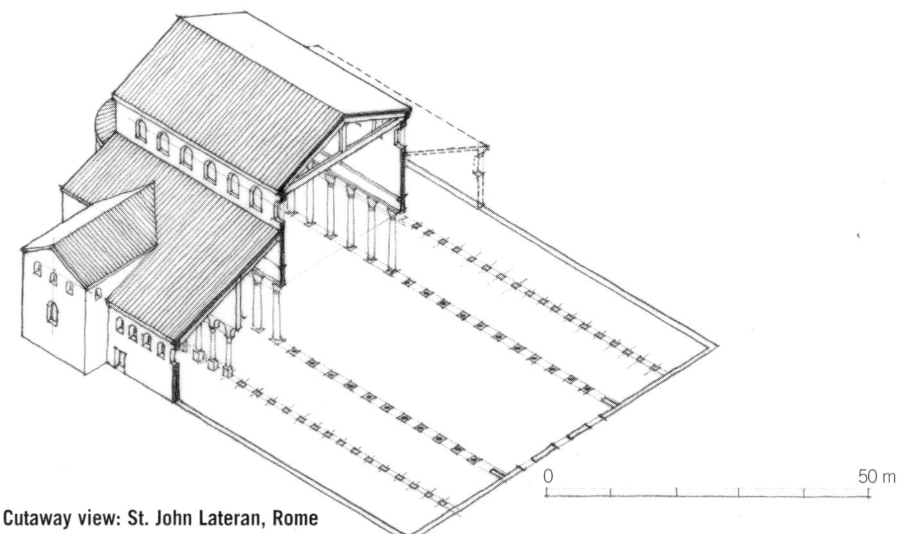


8.28 Cutaway view: St. John Lateran, Rome

**St. John Lateran**

It has long been held that early Christian architecture evolved out of the atrium or *tablinium* of the Roman houses where early Christians met. Admittedly, until the 4th century CE, Christian architecture as such did not exist, as services were in houses and in catacombs; but the argument that claims that the basilica evolved out of the Roman house, persistent in ecclesiastical circles, creates the illusion of a linear evolution of form that the physical evidence does not support. The basilica that became so important was an imperial form and imposed as a pattern on church building by Constantine, the first example being the Church of St. John Lateran, built from an imperial palace in Rome in 314 CE. For this church, the basilica was a logical choice. Though little of the original building is left, its form is well established. It consisted of five aisles, with the central one higher to let in light from a clerestory. Two rows of 15 huge columns created the colonnade 75 meters long. The whole was covered with a wooden roof. At the end there was a large apse, where the clergy would sit. They were separated from the populace by a columnar screen. The transept that one sees today is a medieval addition. There were no columnar embellishments, and the facade and indeed the entire outer surfaces were not of much architectural significance. In fact, it would be several centuries before the idea of a facade, which had been nurtured by the Romans, would return as an important design element in Western churches.

Though the exterior of the building might strike one as primitive, the interior was opulent. The roof beams shimmered in gold foil, and the walls were ornamented with mosaics high above the red, green, and yellow marble columns of the nave. Seven golden altars and offering tables stood in the sanctuary. Chandeliers of gold and silver lit the sanctuary. A hundred years later, Rome saw the construction of St. Sabina (425–432 CE), a mature and stately replica of St. John Lateran. Its larger windows show a greater confidence in masonry construction.

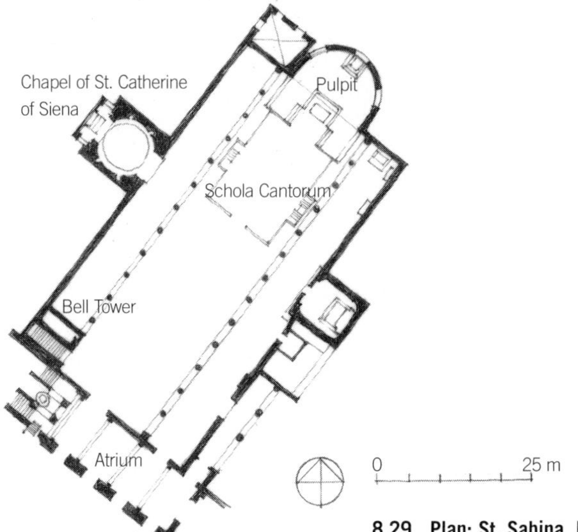


8.29 Plan: St. Sabina, Rome

8.30 Interior of St. Sabina, Rome

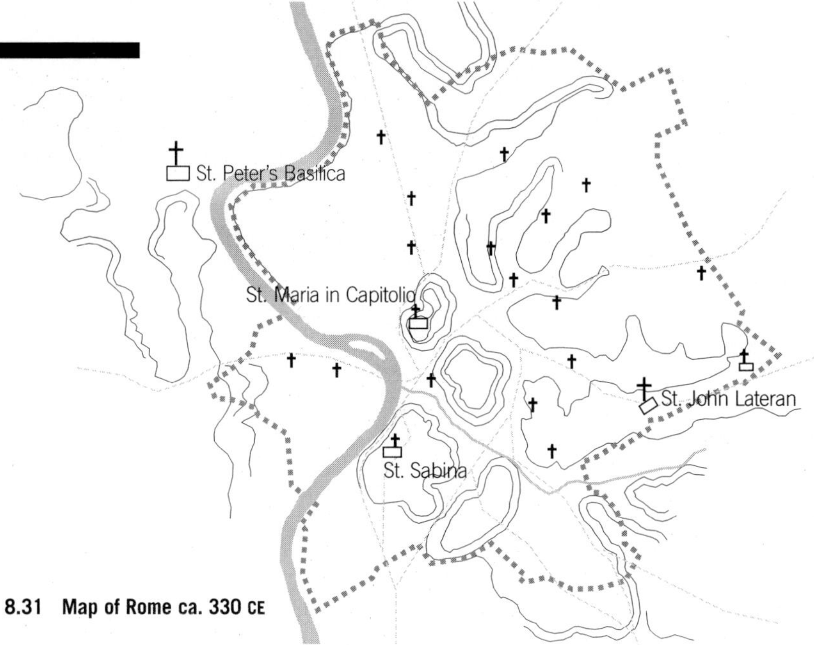


8.31 Map of Rome ca. 330 CE

### Martyria

Though the city of Rome was no longer a political and economic power, it became an important religious and pilgrimage center, much like Jerusalem, for it had the burial places of Peter, Paul, and numerous other martyrs. In making their tombs an important part of veneration, gone was a dark and uneventful Hades, or the idea of death as a privileged realm of pharaonic afterlife. Death was now seen as a source of personal renewal. The cult was to become so strong and such a part of Christian religious practice that the possession of even a piece of a martyr's body—an arm or even a finger—was enough to stand in for the whole.

The main precedent for this was Buddhism, which already, around the 1st century BCE, began reliquary practices, certainly an innovation in the history of religion. For the Christians, the martyrs were, however, not only important to devotional practices but also to the historical narrative of Christianity's success. And indeed, the new notion of history with simple people doing heroic things—far different from history-as-mythology or history-as-royal-lineage—would have profound impact on later developments.

Since many of the graves in Rome were at the outskirts of the city or in cemeteries outside of the walls, as was St. Peter's grave, the Christianization of Rome created an entirely new and unheard-of geographical profile in the history of Western urbanization. It was no longer a forum, agora, or palace that dominated the city and its image but the dozens of monasteries, baptisteries, and churches scattered in clusters in the farthest reaches of the city and its environs.

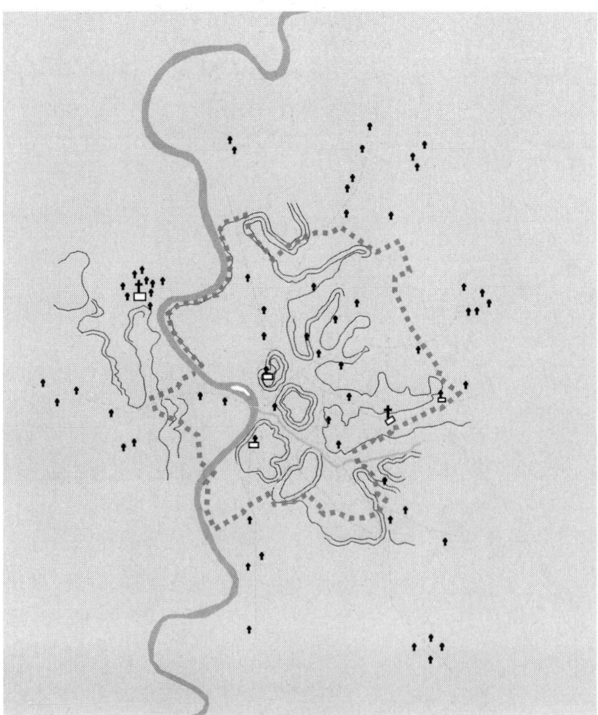

8.32 Christian sanctuaries outside the city walls of Rome

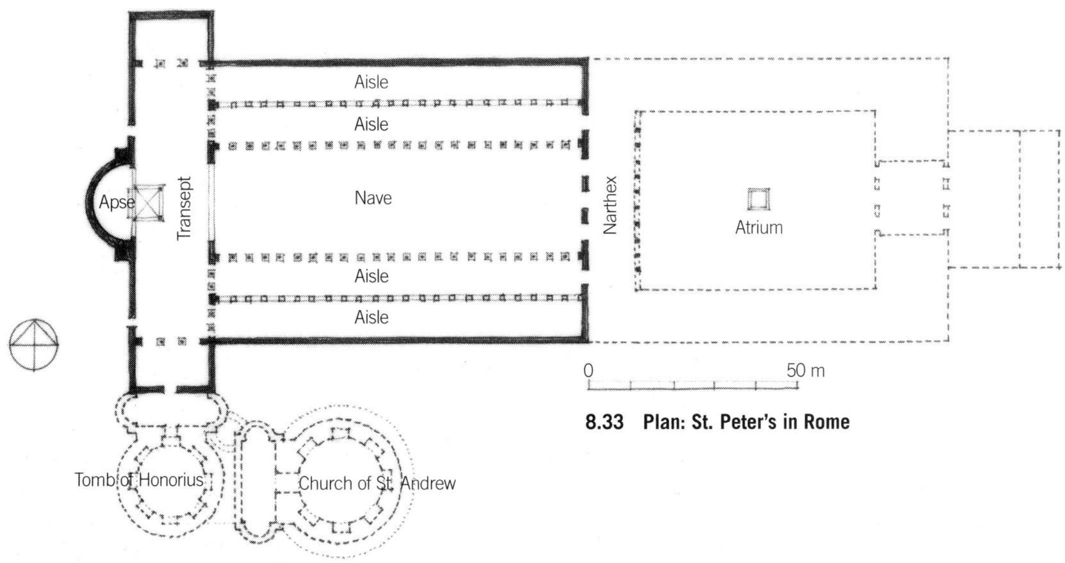


**8.33 Plan: St. Peter's in Rome**

**St. Peter's in Rome**

The Church of St. John Lateran, in Rome, had been established by imperial fiat as the political, religious, and administrative center of the Church. But it was the tomb of St. Peter that was attracting large crowds of worshippers and the principal event was a feast commemorating the martyrdom of the saint. Constantine founded the original church of St. Peter over the tomb around 333 CE. Though a basilica, St. Peter's had a slightly different shape than St. John Lateran, reflecting its status as a *martyrium*. A broad flight of stairs led to the atrium built on a vast platform over the sloping ground. The platform was built over a Roman necropolis with the tops of the various tomb structures cut off and the intermediate spaces filled in. The church itself, because of its use, was considerably longer than St. John Lateran, totaling 112 meters in length.

The nave can be described as a covered street with colonnades on both sides. The columns were not built for the church but were taken from pre-Christian Roman buildings. The nave became a place where those who could afford it could be buried. Floors were soon carpeted with graves. In that sense, it was part street, part graveyard, and part sanctuary; on feast days it became a site of boisterous family celebrations (a practice that was eventually banned).

The rather dark nave, illuminated only by high clerestory windows, led not to an apse, as at St. John Lateran, but to a large transept, which was a space practically unto itself. At its focus, over the tomb of St. Peter in the crypt below and just in front of the apse, was a baldachino (canopy) resting on four columns. Though today, the nave and transept combination might seem common, that was not the case in the 4th century. The transept only became ubiquitous after the Carolingians made it a central part of their churches in the 9th century. At St. Peter's, the transept differentiated the more popular *martyrium* church from an imperial basilica like St. John Lateran. To understand the significance of this building, one has to remember that the use of concrete had by this time been forgotten and that vaulting was thus impossible. The art of stone masonry itself was diminished; even for a building commissioned by the emperor, the columns had to be taken from Roman buildings. Despite the limitations, and perhaps even because of them, the building achieved a directness and majesty as one of the first buildings in the evolving Mediterranean world that was meant at its inception to highlight the mass appeal of the new religion. This was no dark and intimate "house of the gods" in the Hellenistic tradition. Nor was it a place of personal reflection in the Buddhistic sense, but rather a space in which large-scale communal ritual overlapped with the message of imperial glory.

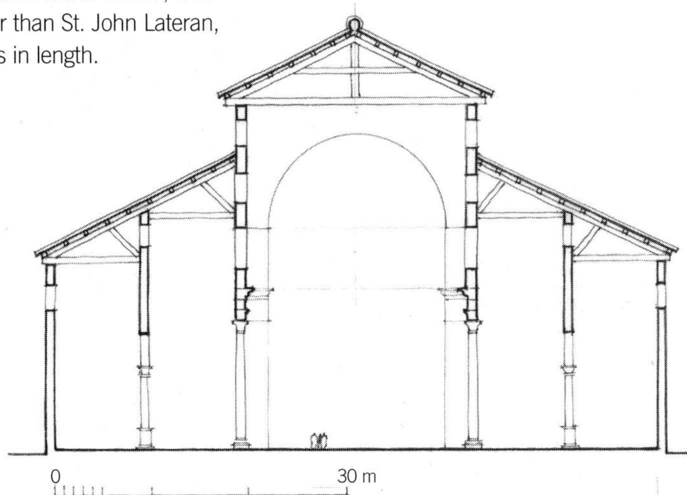


**8.34 Section: St. Peter's in Rome**

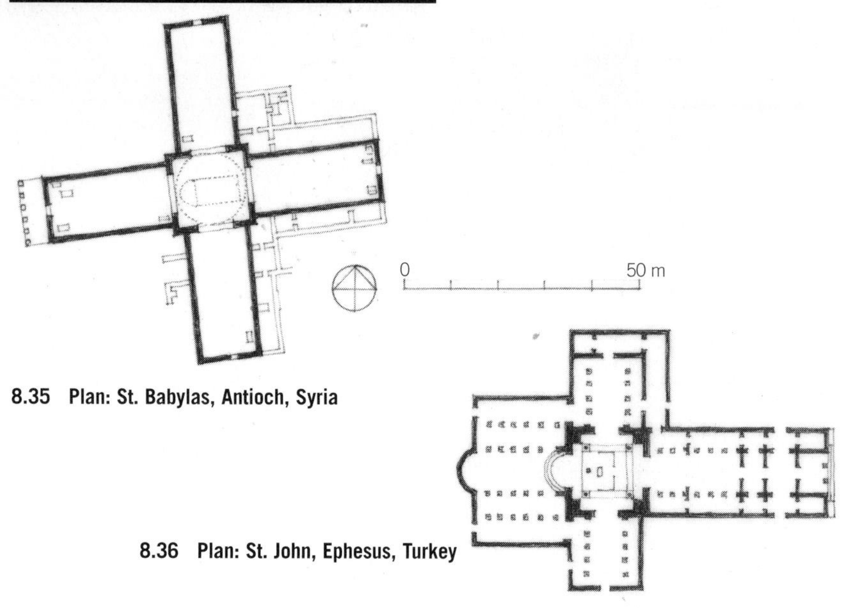


8.35 Plan: St. Babylas, Antioch, Syria

8.36 Plan: St. John, Ephesus, Turkey

8.37 Interior, Baptistery at Ravenna, Italy

**First Baptisteries**

The combination *martyrium*-basilica was soon to be found in various places. In Antioch, St. Babylas was built in 378 CE as part of the tomb of the local martyr. Four aisleless arms with timber roofs converge on the center square, which was surmounted by a pyramidal timber roof. A baptistery was later built against one of the side arms and a sacristy against the other. These were, of course, new types of spaces, and they challenged the architectural form of the basilica, which was in its Roman days a structure without rooms. Fitting these spaces into the basilica scheme was to become the main design problem in the coming millennium. Here they are simply stapled to the side of the building. At St. John in Ephesus (450 CE), they are bent around the northeast corner. At St. Mary in Ephesus (400 CE), the baptistery was appendaged to one side of the atrium.

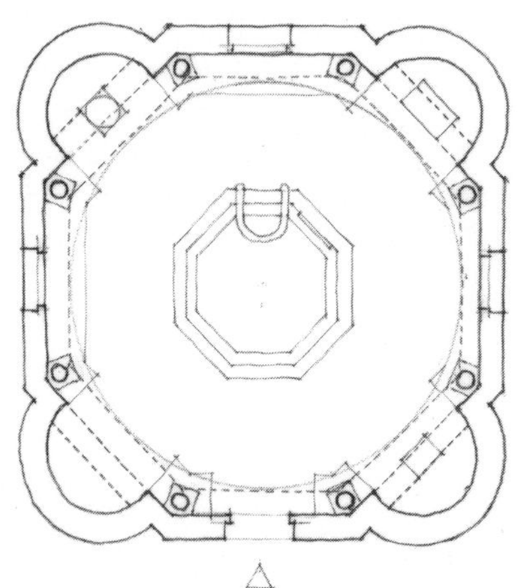

8.38 Plan: Baptistery at Ravenna

Though baptism was a sign of renewed life and potential salvation, symbolizing a person's entry into the community of the Church, the actual practice of baptizing a person was a flexible one. Running water was preferred, but if that was not possible, water in a basin was accepted. And if there was not enough water to fill a basin, then pouring water on the head three times was also acceptable. As a result, there was a great deal of flexibility about the location and nature of the space dedicated to this ceremony. Some baptisteries were square, others rectangular; some had apses, others none; some were vaulted, others not. Soon, however, baptisteries became recognizable architectural elements and among the earliest, the most spectacular was the Baptistery at Ravenna (400–450 CE), the octagonal shape of which soon came to be emulated throughout Italy and elsewhere. The Baptistery at Nocera (5th century CE), east of Naples, had a cupola that rose directly from a circular drum buttressed by the walls and arches of an ambulatory defined by column pairs. It is similar to St. Costanza in Rome (330 CE), which was, however, not a baptistery but rather a tomb that was converted to a church in the 13th century.

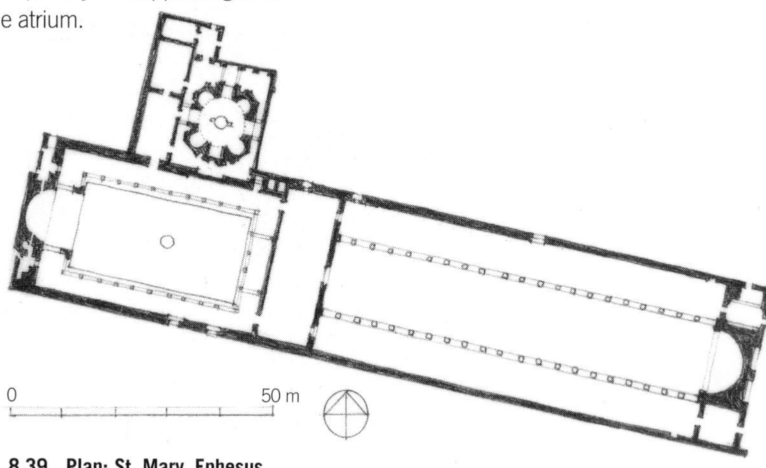


8.39 Plan: St. Mary, Ephesus

**POST-CONSTANTINIAN AGE**

The splitting of the Roman Empire into four parts under Diocletian in 293 CE was envisaged as a partnership so that each could better deal with the crises of the Empire. When the Christian Emperor Theodosius reformalized that division into East and West 100 years later, in 395 CE, the force of events was to lead the Empire into a schism. The rapidly shrinking importance of the Western Empire forced it into dependency on the East and not without a good deal of resentment. But Rome certainly needed all the support it could get. It was sacked in 410 CE by the Visigoths and again in 455 CE by the Vandals, who had set up their kingdom in North Africa. And when central and northern France was lost to the Franks after 460, northern Italy was open to invasion by various groups, including the Ostrogoths, who converted under Theodoric (495–526 CE), who set up his rule in Ravenna.

In the East, the Christian empire remained relatively unscathed from invasions. Nonetheless, the 5th century was very different from the Constantinian age that preceded it. The unity that Constantine had sought to impose on his dominions, in theology and in architecture broke down, leading to an era in which each region began to develop its own particularities. In the East, *martyria* became large freestanding structures. In the West, martyr's graves were enclosed within churches. The architects in some places preferred columns; in others, piers. Some architects used transepts; others did not. The location of rooms like the sacristy, the archives, and the library added further variations.

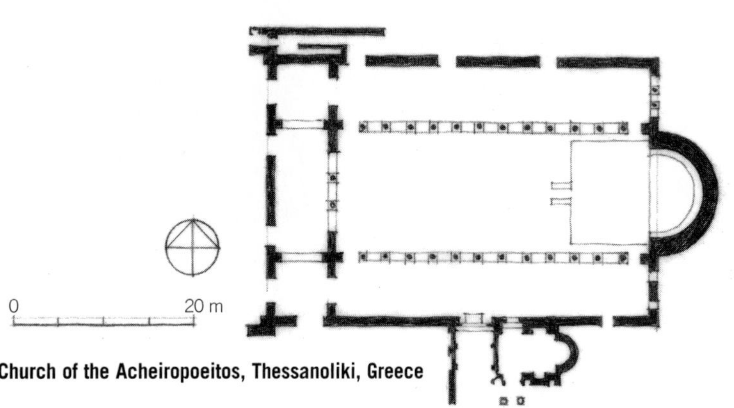


8.40 Plan and section: Church of the Acheiropoeitos, Thessanoliki, Greece

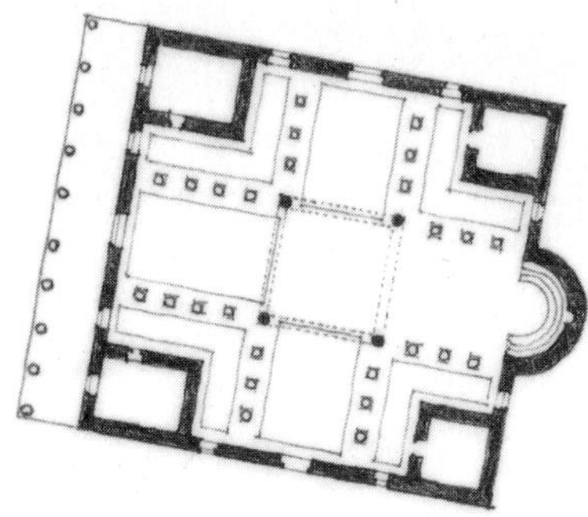

8.41 **Plan: White Monastery (Deir-el-Abiad), near Suhag, Egypt**

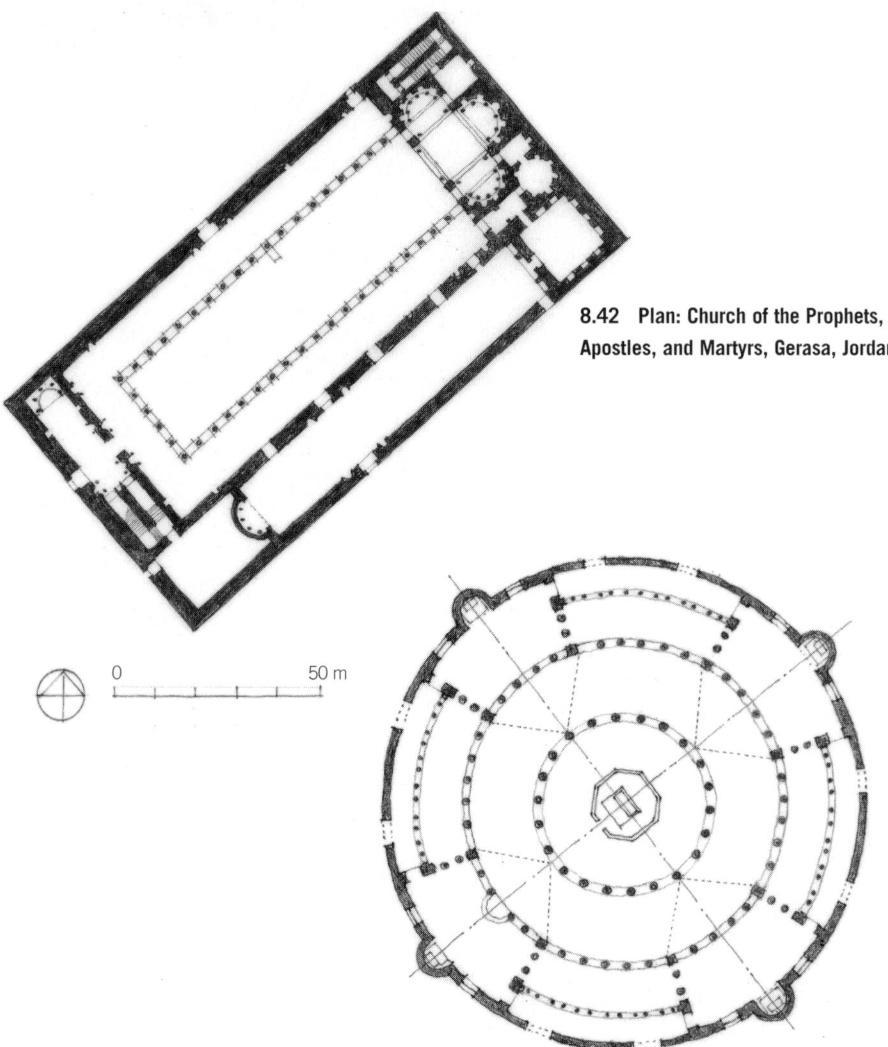


**8.42 Plan: Church of the Prophets, Apostles, and Martyrs, Gerasa, Jordan**

**8.43 Plan: St. Stefano Rotondo, Rome**

The Church of the Acheiropoeitos in Salonica (470 CE) is almost classical in its clean lines and broad command of space: The White Monastery (Deir-el-Abiad, ca. 440 CE), not far from the city of Suhag in Egypt (about 500 kilometers south of Cairo), takes on an Egyptian flavor in its compact boxlike shape with its various rooms, including an unusual *triconch* at the head. The narthex is placed not at the west, but along the south. The Church of the Prophets, Apostles, and Martyrs in Gerasa (465 CE) is a brilliant essay on the theme of a square within a square. In Rome, St. Stefano Rotondo (468–483 CE) embodies a complex intersection of cross and rotunda. The Roman churches, St. Stefano aside, tended to be the most conservative. St. Sabina (422–432 CE) and St. Maria Maggiore (ca. 432 CE) preserved the tradition of a colonnaded basilica.

**8.44 Nave, St. Maria Maggiore, Rome**

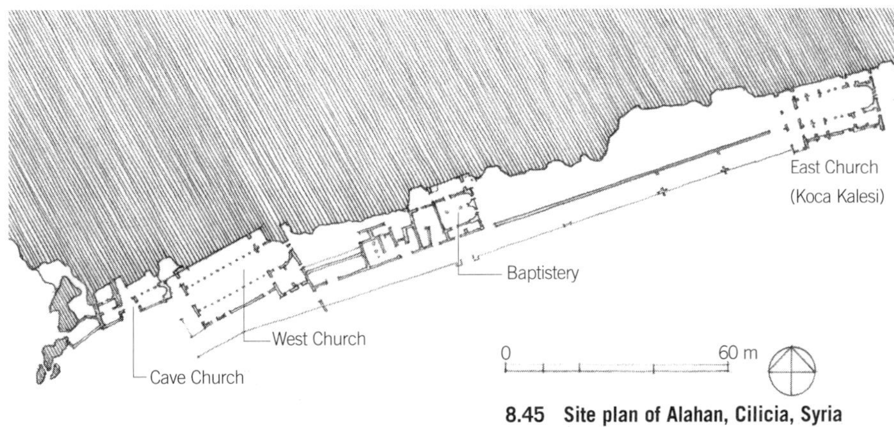


8.45 **Site plan of Alahan, Cilicia, Syria**

8.46 **Structure of Koca Kalesi, Alahan, Turkey**

**Alahan Monastery**

For a brief and fragile moment in history, the art of stone masonry that had been perfected by the Egyptians and Greeks hung in a precarious balance. In Constantinople, stone was replaced by brick. Even the Hagia Sophia made only sparing use of structural stone. Further to the west, because of the use of concrete, Roman architects had not built with stone for centuries. Stone was only used as a veneer. When the art of mixing concrete was forgotten, European architects resorted to rather primitive-looking rough stone walls. In 633 CE, Islamic armies conquered Syria and, not yet having established the architectural traditions for which they would become famous, drove the masons into exile. The use of dressed stones remained restricted to a small geographical location that stretched from Cilicia along the southeastern coast of Turkey, to northern Syria, and across to Armenia.

Because the region is now split into Syria, Turkey, Georgia, and Iraq, a comprehensive history of the architecture of this region is still lacking. But the fact remains that around 400 CE, it was in this small region that the most skilled masons in Eurasia were working, and their efforts would have important influences on Islamic and Christian practices alike.

The skills of Cilician and Syrian masons were known long before the region became Christian, and so it was no wonder that Cilicia soon developed a thriving Christian architecture, especially after the ascendancy of Emperor Zeo (r. 474–491 CE), who came from the Cilician city of Tarasis. Cilician builders had the advantage of a local volcanic mortar similar to the *pozzolana* that was used by the Romans in the making of concrete.

One of the most important Cilician sites created during the reign of Zeo was at Alahan, where several churches were built along a terrace against a rocky hillside. It includes a cave church at the western end of the terrace, near a basilica, with the eastern basilica 140 meters away. The lay community was separated from the monastic brothers by a wall with a colonnade that fed directly into the narthex. The monks who inhabited the area under the cliff took a stair carved out of the cliff up to the gallery.

On the eastern end was a domed basilica structure, Koca Kalesi, with a facade that is still relatively intact. It is built next to the cliff wall, and in fact part of the narthex is carved out of the rock. The western part of the church contains two transeptlike bays that probably supported a central tower with triple-arched windows punctuating the north and south faces. The inner corners are filled with squinch arches, supported by slender colonnettes. The whole is too light to support a stone dome, and thus it is thought that it supported either a light, brick dome or perhaps a wooden one.

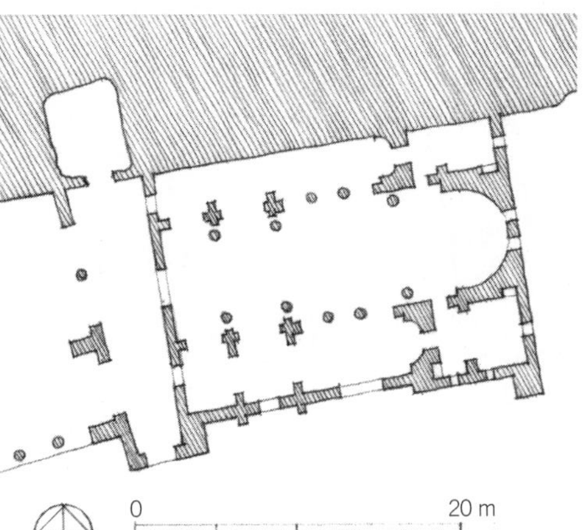


8.47 **Plan: East Church (Koca Kalesi), Alahan**

8.48 **Qalat-Siman, Syria**

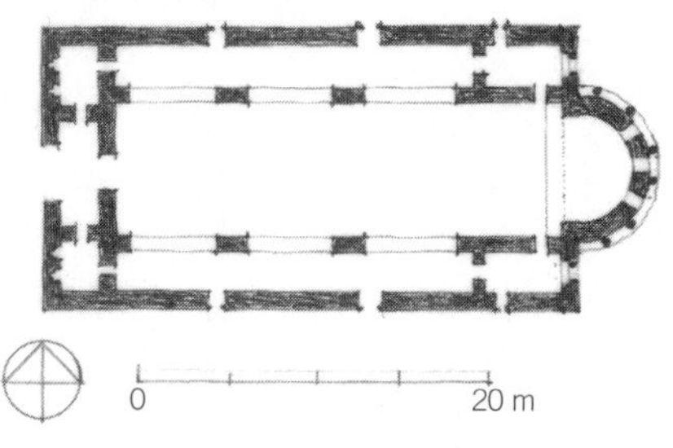


8.49 **Plan: Qualb Louzeh, Syria**

When Theodore of Cyrrus wrote his *Historia Religiosa* in the 5th century CE, he noted that St. Symeon the Stylite sat atop a pillar at Qalat-Siman for 40 long years and attracted "Ishmaelites, Persians, Armenians, Iberians, Himyarits, Spaniards, Britons, Gauls and Italians." When Symeon died in 459 CE, a large monastic and religious city emerged in Qalat-Siman, northwest of Aleppo. At the center of the complex was an octagonal structure protecting Symeon's column. Attached were four basilica-like wings. The eastern arm terminated in three apses, resulting in a peculiar hybrid of church types. Despite this, the entire complex is built of stone with a sensitivity unparalleled in the west. The facade consisted of a large central arch flanked by smaller ones. It was ornamented at ground level with pilasters and attached columns tied together with string courses.

The church in Qualb Louzeh, Syria (500 CE), halfway between Aleppo and Antioch and just south of Qalat-Siman, has a plan that is strikingly simple and compact. The piers are fluted and topped by Corinthian capitals. Round-headed windows are combined with rectangular ones. The church is much smaller than parish churches in Rome, but the thorough classical workmanship and the feeling for monumental stone forms kept alive traditions that were fading in the West.

The close connection between Syria and Cilicia is borne out in the construction of the Monastery of St. Symeon Stylite the Younger, near Antioch. The plan was allegedly traced by an angel and then a multitude of Cilician masons appeared, bringing their sick. They were probably migrant workers seeking employment on a seasonal basis. Season after season, they put in work in return for being healed. As to the plan, it is another remarkable Syrian-style fusion of cross, *martyrium*, and basilica, with the interstitial space of the precinct filled with smaller churches and ancillary rooms.

8.50 **Plan: Monastery of St. Symeon Stylite the Younger, near Antioch, Turkey**

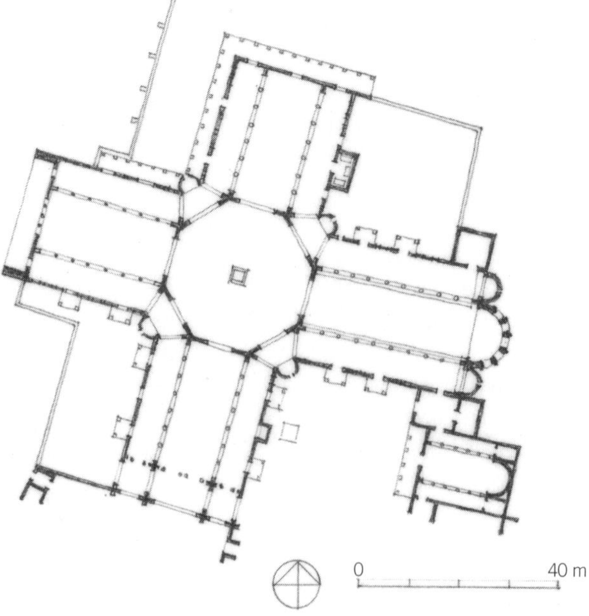


8.51 **Plan: Qalat-Siman**

8.52 North Church, now known as Bodrum Camii, Istanbul, Turkey

8.53 Tomb of King Theodoric, Ravenna, Italy

**Tomb of King Theodoric**

The Tomb of King Theodoric (ca. 520 CE) near Ravenna suggests the presence of Syrian stone masons by the calm manner in which the large ashlar stones and arches are articulated. It is located one kilometer from the center of Ravenna, beyond the ancient town walls, in an area used as a graveyard by the Goths. Though the foundation was of concrete, the construction itself is of dry masonry. No mortar or cement was used. In fact there is an uncanny resemblance between the arches of the tomb and the apse of the so-called North Church of Bodrum (ca. 480 CE), with its string course of Corinthian capitals. The lower story externally forms a decagon containing in each of its sides a recessed rectangular niche with an arched head. Internally it has the shape of a cross with equal arms. The upper floor is similar, except that it has a circular interior. It is thought that the upper floor had a porch all the way around, the columns resting on the top of the wall of the lower part like a continuous balcony.

Since there are no stairs leading to the upper floor and traces of an access stairway have never been found, it is presumed that the upper room was the funeral chamber to which the remains of the king were perhaps brought by a temporary stairway. The dome, 10 meters in diameter, consists of a huge single piece of Istrian limestone with 12 handles on the top, used no doubt to lift the stone into place.

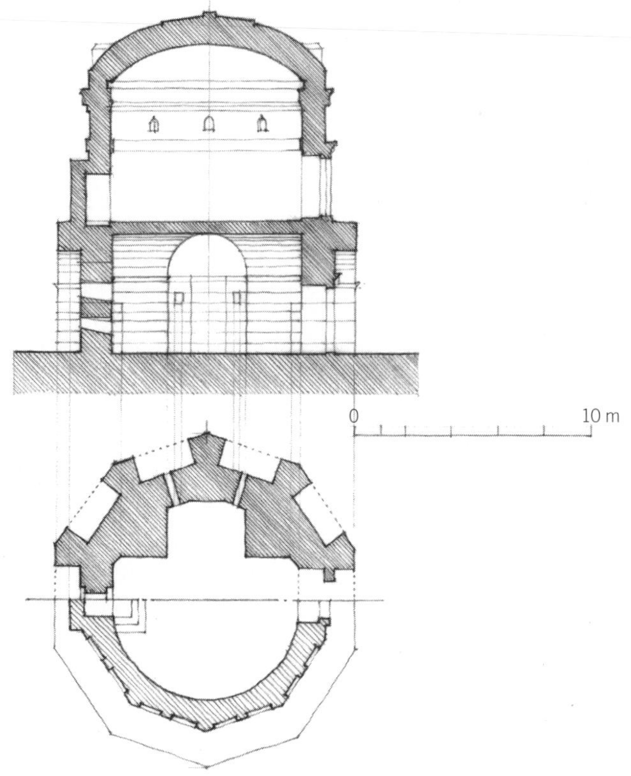


8.54 Plan and section: Tomb of Theodoric, Ravenna

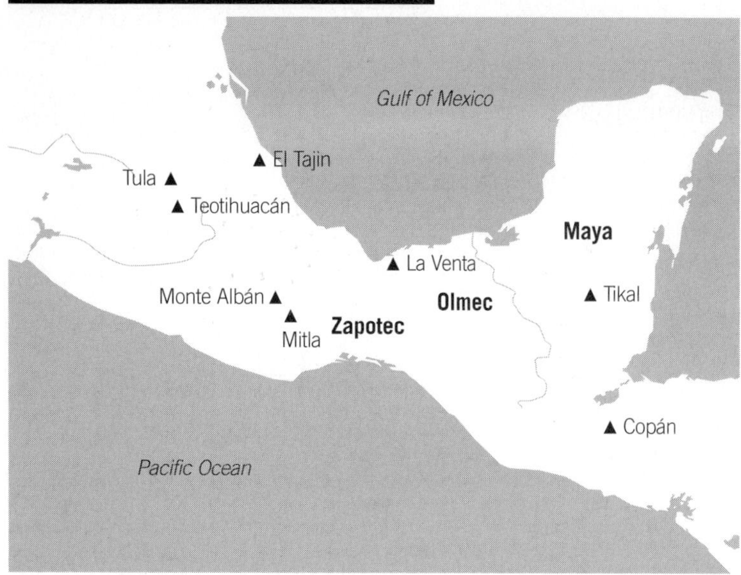


## ZAPOTECS OF OAXACA

480 kilometers south of Mexico City, in a valley formed by the coming together of three mountains, lies the dramatic and spectacular Zapotec capital, Monte Albán. The entire semiarid valley of Oaxaca had been inhabited since 1500 BCE, up until the Spanish invasion, by the Zapotec people. By 1000 BCE, a Zapotec elite had emerged, with connections to the Olmecs in the north. By 500 BCE, the valley had an estimated 25,000 residents, making it one of the most populous concentrations in America. It was supported by several types of irrigation projects, including artificially terraced hillsides irrigated by canals fed from permanent springs. The ubiquitous forest of today is far different from the tended landscape of the Zapotecs.

The Zapotecs believed that the universe was divided into four great quarters, each associated with a color—red, black, yellow, or white. The center was blue-green, which they considered to be a single color. The east-west axis of the sun was the principal axis of their world. Their religion was animistic. They believed that everything was alive and deserving of respect.

As in Hindu cosmology, the Zapotecs distinguished living things from inanimate matter by the possession of a vital force called *pee*, or "wind," "breath," or "spirit." *Pee* made things move to show that they were alive, like a bolt of lightning, clouds moving in the sky, the tremor of the earth, the wind in one's hair, and even the foam on a cup of chocolate. Inanimate things could be engaged with technology, but those with *pee* had to be approached with ritual and sacrifice, particularly something living like a beating heart.

Zapotecs recognized in a supreme being—without beginning or end—with whom no human came in contact; it was never represented. Humans did, however, come into contact with "natural" forces, the most powerful and sacred of which were *Cociyo*, or Lightning, the angry face of Sky (one of the four quadrants), and *Xoó* or Earthquake, the angry face of Earth. Even time was alive and considered cyclical. The Zapotecs had two calendars—a solar calendar with 18 months of 20 days, plus 5 days to bring it to 365, and a ritual calendar or *piye*, composed of 20 hieroglyphs or "day signs," which combined with 13 numbers to produce a cycle of 260 days.

Social structure was stratified into two layers: the commoners and the nobility. They had different origins. The commoners were born of commoners; they lived, worked, and died. Members of the nobility were descended from venerated ancestors, conducted wars, brought home captives, and were buried in tombs from where they ascended to the sky to become "Cloud People." Men had multiple wives, and under ideal circumstances, primogeniture was the law.

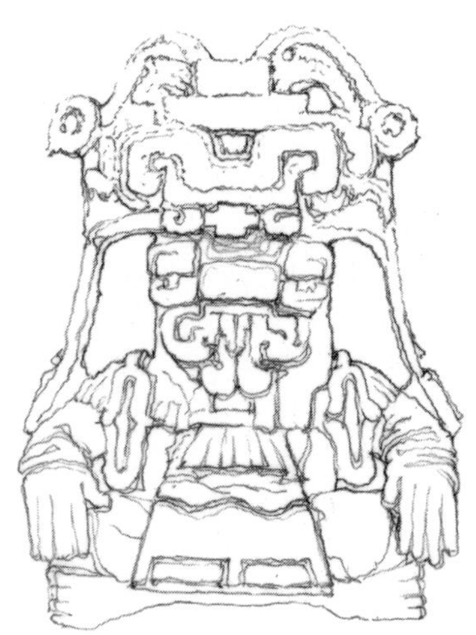

**8.55 Xoó: Lightning and Earthquake motifs in Zapotec culture**

8.56 Monte Albán, near Oaxaca, Mexico

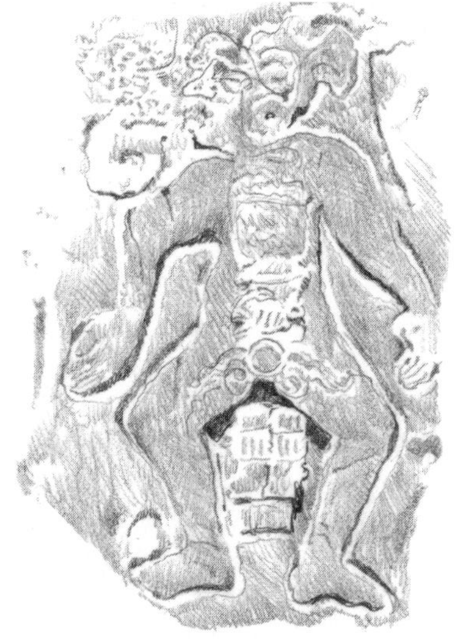

8.57 Example of a danzante figure

### Monte Albán

Around 500 BCE, at the height of their prosperity, the Zapotec elite decided to construct a brand-new administrative center. They picked a previously unoccupied escarpment dramatically located in the heart of the valley of Oaxaca. The valley is actually composed of three subvalleys that join together in the shape of a "Y." The 400-meter high escarpment on which Monte Albán is located sits more or less in the center of this "Y" and is visible from miles around.

Monte Albán was built in successive phases, and it is difficult to gauge what the earliest structures looked like. The oldest structure is the Temple of the Dancers (Monumento de los Danzantes, ca. 400 BCE), which consists of a triple set of platforms in the southeastern corner of the site. It is decorated by a series of "dancing" figures, so-called because they seem to be depicted in strange, rubbery postures as if they were acrobats of extraordinary ability. Over 300 of these figures have been identified at Monte Albán. Given their closed eyes and exposed mutilated genitals (a sign of ritual humiliation), these figures are believed to represent the earliest set of rulers subjugated by the Zapotec elite.

In the Monte Albán II period, from 100 BCE to 200 CE, a ring of about 155 settlements throughout the Oaxaca valley seems to have been brought under a single state centered on Monte Albán. The Grand Plaza at Monte Albán was constructed at this time by leveling an area of 300 by 200 meters. It was oriented to the cardinal directions and paved over with white stucco. The northern and southern ends of the plaza were bound by huge terraced platforms that form large palace enclosures of their own. The northern platform was built over a span of time and was repeatedly enlarged and modified. The platform has two sunken patios, each with steps and platform mounds on axis. The southern edge of the plaza was marked by a somewhat smaller platform, also built by incorporating older platforms.

8.58 Carvings of *danzante* figures at Monte Albán

8.59 **Observatory at Monte Albán**

The whole area of Monte Albán was densely occupied, and archaeological evidence suggests that by 300 CE, all the slopes surrounding the complex were occupied by residences for the elite, some of whom were buried in nearby tombs.

The period 200–700 CE finds the Zapotecs at the height of their prosperity, and this is the phase to which most of the structures at Monte Albán—as they have survived—can be dated. In the center of the plaza is a group of three conjoined buildings facing east–west; they were indisputably the focal temples. While the platform of the central temple has steps on both sides, it actually opens only to the east and consists of a double chamber, separated by a partial wall and columns. Later Zapotec temples usually had two chambers, an outer (less sacred) chamber to which worshippers could come and an inner (more sacred) chamber where the priests performed their rites. Those rites included the burning of incense and the sacrifice of animals and humans. Priests also performed autosacrifice, offering their own blood by piercing parts of their body. Some rituals involved the use of hallucinogenic mushrooms and drugs.

The main temple structure is flanked on either side by two smaller, lower temples, each facing north and south. A fourth building, detached from this group, is rare in Zapotec architecture. It is the only one set at an angle of 45 degrees to the site's main axis. Its ground plan resembles an arrowhead, with the steps forming the blunt end. It opens to the northeast and may have been oriented to the bright star Capella and used for astronomical purposes. A vaulted tunnel crosses the front part of the structure and leads upward.

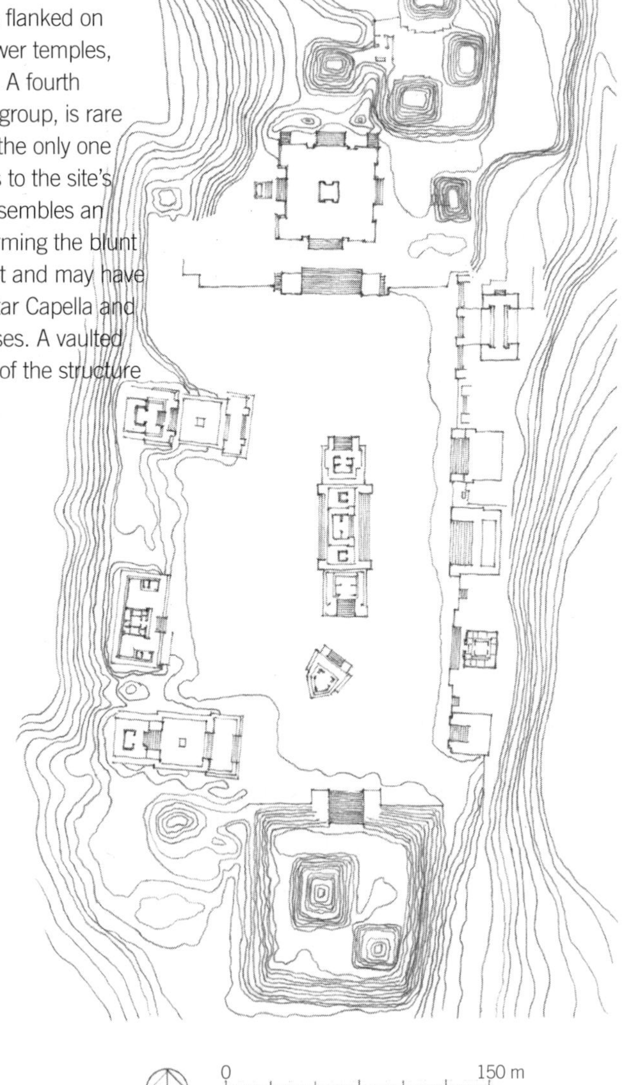


8.60 **Site plan: Grand Plaza of Monte Albán**

8.61 Ball court: Monte Albán

There are three large complexes on the western side of the plaza. Building complex M consists of two buildings separated by a patio with a small altar and the usual monumental stairway on axis. Building complex K, further north, is similar to M. In between the two, Platform Mound L consists of a platform with a triple-chambered temple and two smaller chambers flanking it.

On the eastern edge of the plaza, the Temple of the Dancers is flanked by two similar platform mounds with their own enclosed forecourts. On the western edge is a ball court and a series of platform mounds, all linked together creating a continuous edge. Building P contains an internal stairway leading to the top of the building; the stairway is reached by an underground tunnel that passes beneath the plaza to the central range of buildings, allowing the priests to reach them unseen. However, the most important building is the so-called Palace S. It is in the form of a low platform, reached by a wide staircase; from this platform, access to the interior was by means of a monolithic archway leading to a blank wall that skirted the entrance around it, before opening up to the interior court. The interior consists of an open courtyard surrounded by a series of small rooms.

Monte Albán recreates the Zapotec conceptual order on several different scales. Its location marks it as the place of privilege at the center of the cosmological landscape. Then the complex itself replicates on a diminished scale the very relationship of the escarpment on which Monte Albán was built, to the larger valley of Oaxaca, with the main ceremonial temple in the middle surrounded by a "mountainous" ring of platform mounds. And then the sunken patios in the north platform repeat the order of a valley surrounded by pyramids, again with a central platform. Unlike the artificial mountain volcanoes of the Olmecs, the Zapotecs created a miniaturized landscape that is both a sacred geography and its representation.

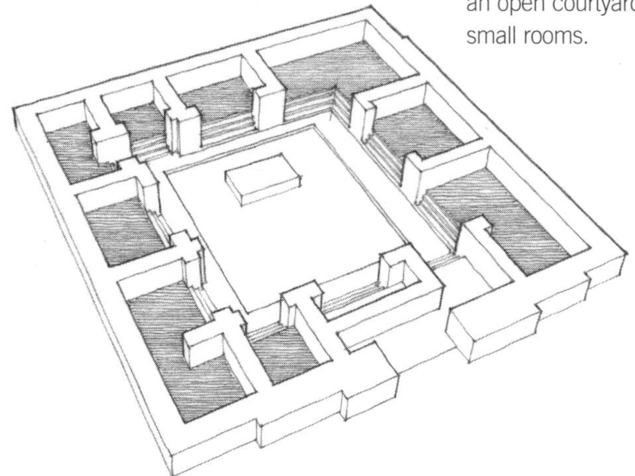

8.62 Palace S at Monte Albán

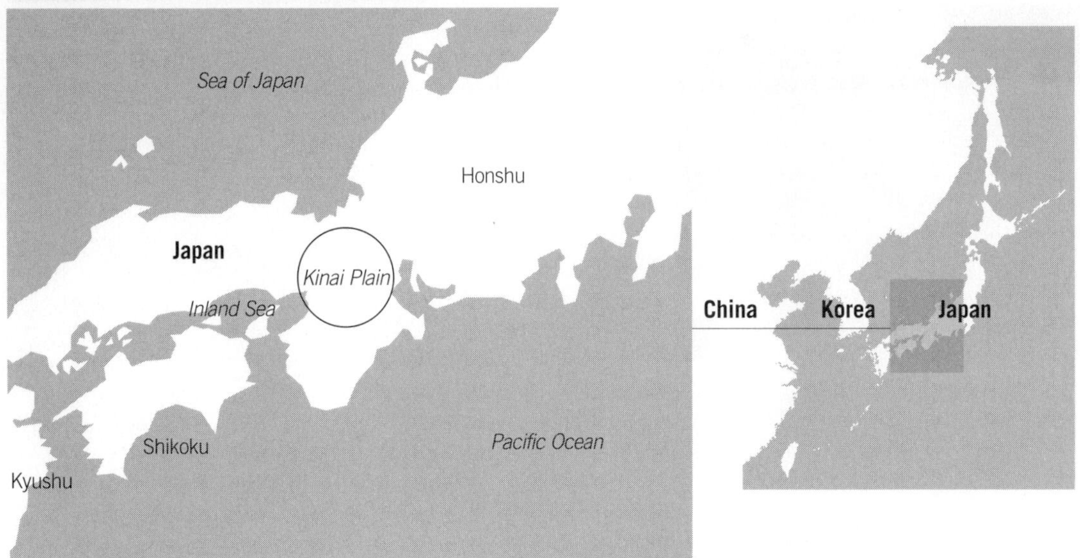


## KOFUN PERIOD: JAPAN

In the late fifth century, Japan's Yamato clan managed to wrest control over much of the Honshu and Kyushu islands, thereby establishing Japan's first royal family, a blood-line that has continued unbroken to this day. The Yamato centralized the government and most importantly organized the collection of grain. Each new king built a new palace and was buried in his own huge earthen tombs. By the 8th century Buddhism had come to Japan and the tomb building came to an end. This pre-Buddhist period from 300 to 700 CE is known as the Kofun period.

Made in the shape of a keyhole, the Kofun tombs were constructed by modifying a small hill and were generally surrounded by a moat. The round part held the tomb, and the rectangular portion was used for rituals and ceremonies. Generally they were 100 meters long, with the largest, the Hashihaka tomb in Nara, measuring almost 280 meters. The actual burials changed over time, becoming more elaborate. Early on the wooden coffin was buried directly in the tomb summit or in a pit lined with stone slabs and covered ceiling rocks. Later, stone coffins were used, and, finally, in the Late Kofun period, stone chambers with horizontal entrance passages were constructed. These allowed reentry into the chamber, leading to their development as family repositories, with multiple burials.

**8.63 Aerial view of the burial mound of Emperor Nintoku, Osaka, Japan**

Clay cylinders, called haniwa, were distributed all over the surface of the Kofun tombs. The haniwa may have originated as substitutes for burial sacrifices of attendants of the deceased as in China and Central America. Half-embedded in the earth for stability, they were generally just simple cylinders, 40–50 centimeters in diameter and about a meter tall. These hollow clay tubes served as stands for offering vessels in the ritual ceremonies. The tops of Haniwas were made in a variety of forms: houses, human figures, animals, and a multitude of military, ceremonial, and household objects.

**8.64 Burial mound of Emperor Sujin**

# 600 CE

In 600 CE, on the eve of Teotihuacán's collapse, the civilizations of Central and South America were at their zenith. With Monte Albán still a powerful state further north, a whole host of Mayan city-states, dominated by Tikal, Calakmul, Copán, Tonina, Palenque, and Yaxchilan arose in the Yucatan. Although bound by trade, family ties, and a common culture, these Yucatan states competed ferociously for dominance. The Maya developed the most advanced calendar in the world. In the Andes, around Lake Titicaca, Tiwanaku emerged at the center of an extensive empire.

In Eurasia, this period was—compared to the dramatic difference in global politics between 200 and 400 CE—a period of consolidation, in which the relationship between imperial power and the new religions of the world was being tested and enhanced. The Byzantines, for example, were in the process of purifying Christianity from its multiple divisions, creating and establishing the norms on which the fusion of religious and imperial power rested. New architectural forms were developed using brick domes, concrete by this time having been forgotten. Hagia Sophia was the most ambitious and splendid architectural accomplishment of the age. Though the Byzantines were the dominant force in the Mediterranean, they had to negotiate with powerful invaders from the north, some of whom, like Theodoric, set up a Christian-styled kingdom in Italy based in Ravenna. Rome and further north in Europe were at this time little more than a hinterland, with religious ideas there beginning to be developed based on the mysticism that would eventually distinguish Western Europe from the cultural and philosophical domination from the east.

The plains and deserts of Syria and Persia, though still nominally under the control of the Sassanians, was in a state of unrest with Muhammad founding the last of the great modern religions, Islam taking Mecca in 630 CE. With the Syrian heartland in turmoil, Armenia was experiencing a moment of growth as the new mediator between east and west. It would play an important role in the history of architecture. Whereas the Byzantines had shifted to using brick, and architecture in the European West was made of rough stones, the Armenians alone were preserving Greek and Hellenistic traditions of fine masonry craftsmanship. In the area that is now northern Syria, Eastern Turkey, Georgia, and Armenia itself, stone churches of great precision were being built, with important implications for Islamic and Christian architecture in the next centuries. The South Asian dynasties were advancing their transformation of Buddhism into Hinduism and engaging in a whole slew of experimental temple designs to respond to the developing Hindu liturgy. The Kalcuris, and then the Chalukyas in the Deccan, and the Pallavas in the south, developed their own range of rock-cut and structural stone temples. But if Buddhism was slowly disappearing in India, it was emerging as a powerful force in China, Korea, and Japan. After the competitive reigns of the Wei rulers, the Sui and then the T'ang emperors managed to control most of China. They invested heavily in large public work projects to enable trade to develop building roads and canals. Engineering as a consequence advanced in great measures. New monasteries were built and a new form, the *ta*, or the pagoda was developed out of the Indian stupa. Buddhism, which had entered Japan from Korea, was being fused with preexisting Shinto concepts to produce a form of esoteric Buddhism that, from the start, created a tradition of high architectural accomplishment, such as Horyu-ji Temple in Nara. The first building of Ise Jingu, Japan's holiest Shinto shrine, also dates to this time.

# 600 CE

◂ **Tiwanaku**
First settled 400 BCE

Southern Andes: Peak of Wari and Tiwanaku Cultures
6th–10th centuries

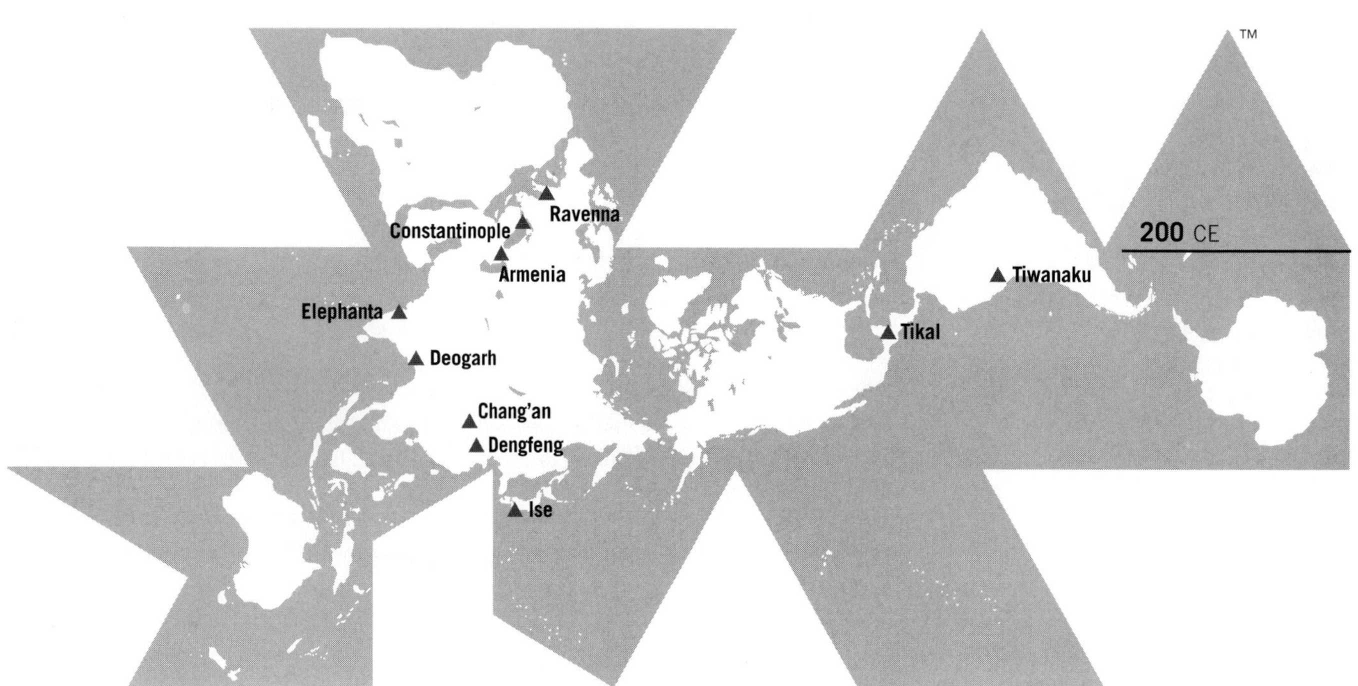


China: Eastern Han Dynasty
25–220 CE

Sixteen Kingdoms Period
304–439 CE

◂ **Ise Shrine**
Rebuilt every 20 years since ca. 500 BCE

Maya: Dynastic city-states
ca. 250–900 CE

▲ **Tikal Temple Complex**
700–900

Byzantine Empire
330–1453 CE

▲ **SS. Sergius and Bacchus**
525–530 CE

▲ **Hagia Sophia**
532–537 CE

▲ **St. Vitale in Ravenna**
538–545 CE

▲ **Church of the Vigilant Powers**
645–60 CE

▲ **St. Hripsime Church**
7th Century

**400** CE — **600** CE — **800** CE

India: Rise of Regional States
500–1300 CE

▲ **Vishnu Temple at Deogarh**
Early 6th century

▲ **Five Rathas**
7th century

▲ **Shore Temple at Mamallapuram**
700—728 CE

▲ **Shiva Temple at Elephanta**
540–555 CE

▲ **Durga Temple**
675–710 CE

Period of Northern and Southern Dynasties
386–589 CE

T'ang Dynasty
618–907 CE

▲ **Songyue Temple Ta**
523 CE

▲ **Daming Palace**
Begun 634 CE

Korea: Koguryo Kingdom
37 BCE–668 CE

▲ **Hwangnyongsa Temple**
Begun ca, 553 CE

Kofun Culture
ca. 3rd century–538 CE

Asuka Period in Japan
ca. 538–710 CE

Nara Period in Japan
710–794 CE

▲ **Horyu-ji Temple**
7th century

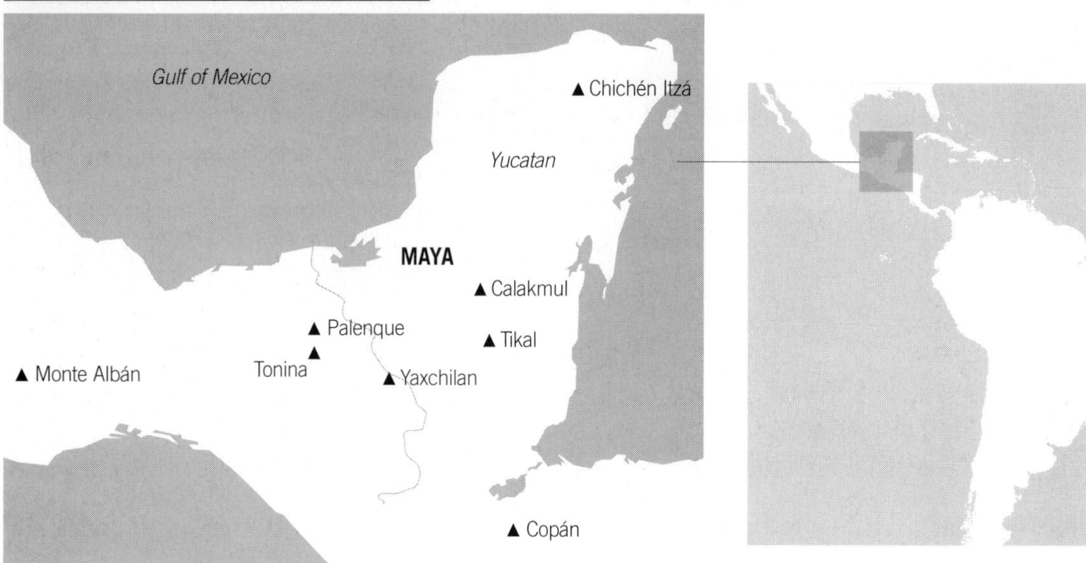


## MAYA OF THE YUCATAN

For their first 1000 years, the Mayan city-states of the Yucatan Peninsula were generally subservient to their more powerful neighbors to the north. But around 530 CE, Teotihuacán's influence as the superpower of Central America started to wane. Its gods were no longer worshipped and tributes went into decline. Immediately, the Mayan city-states asserted their independence and began to build their cities, and in particular, their ceremonial complexes, to their own tastes. Almost equally immediately, they began to battle each other for regional supremacy. After a century of unceasing warfare, Tikal, Calakmul, Copán, Tonina, Palenque, and Yaxchilan emerged as the dominant city-states of the Mayan lowlands (the lowlands are the regions around and including modern Guatemala). Tikal and Calakmul, in particular, fought each other incessantly during the 6th and 7th centuries. The archaeological record shows that their wars created a veritable buffer zone, 80 kilometers wide and 20 kilometers deep, between them, where there was no inhabitation of any kind. This is unusual in Mayan history, because all the Yucatan city-states were connected to each other by causeways. At the end of the 7th century, Tikal emerged the victor of this conflict.

Despite their conflicts, the Mayan city-states were interconnected by trade, kinship structures, sacrificial rituals, and architecture. Distinct from that of Teotihuacán and Monte Albán, their language and science were in many ways more advanced than that of their more powerful northern neighbors. They developed a comprehensive writing system, designed a highly accurate Long Count calendar, and could predict solar eclipses. They recognized that Venus was both the morning and the evening star. Their science was driven, of course, by the dictates of their cosmology and mythological understanding of the cycles of their universe. For instance, they believed that Venus was responsible for pulling the sun into the dark underworld in the evening and then resurrecting it in the morning. That is why they tracked it with precision. In addition, sacrificial bloodletting was an essential and central part of their religious and royal public spectacles.

Beginning around 830 CE—dated as the year 10.0.0.0.0 in the Mayan Long Count calendar—the Maya suddenly and unexpectedly abandoned their cities. Many of the Maya are believed to have died from some form of catastrophic economic and agricultural collapse. Some moved to the highlands of the Yucatan, others went into the higher valleys of Central America.

### Tikal

Tikal's recorded history begins in 292 CE, when Balam Ajaw (Decorated Jaguar) came to power. At its peak around 700 CE, Tikal was home to about 80,000 people. Surrounded by corn fields cultivated with intense labor, the houses of the residents were spread evenly over a 16-square-kilometer area. They were clustered into groups of about four to seven, all raised on high platforms and organized around a courtyard. A high level of civic organization and hydraulic engineering was critical to Tikal's survival. The swampy land had to be sectored by building raised causeways. This enabled the land to be cultivated, and the causeways used for travel. More permanent platforms had to be built for the dwellings; for these, stone quarried at some distance had to be hauled with help of the wheel. And finally, stone-lined cisterns had to be constructed to collect fresh water, which was securely funneled from the surrounding buildings to maximize catchment. The construction of water tanks was important since the dry season lasted from January to April, during which time water needed to be stored, conserved, and rationed. Tikal, like Uaxactún before it, was built on a set of broken hills, located directly on the watershed divide between the Gulf of Mexico and the Caribbean Sea. Perched at the high point of the region, therefore, Tikal's Temples enjoyed a commanding view of their surroundings.

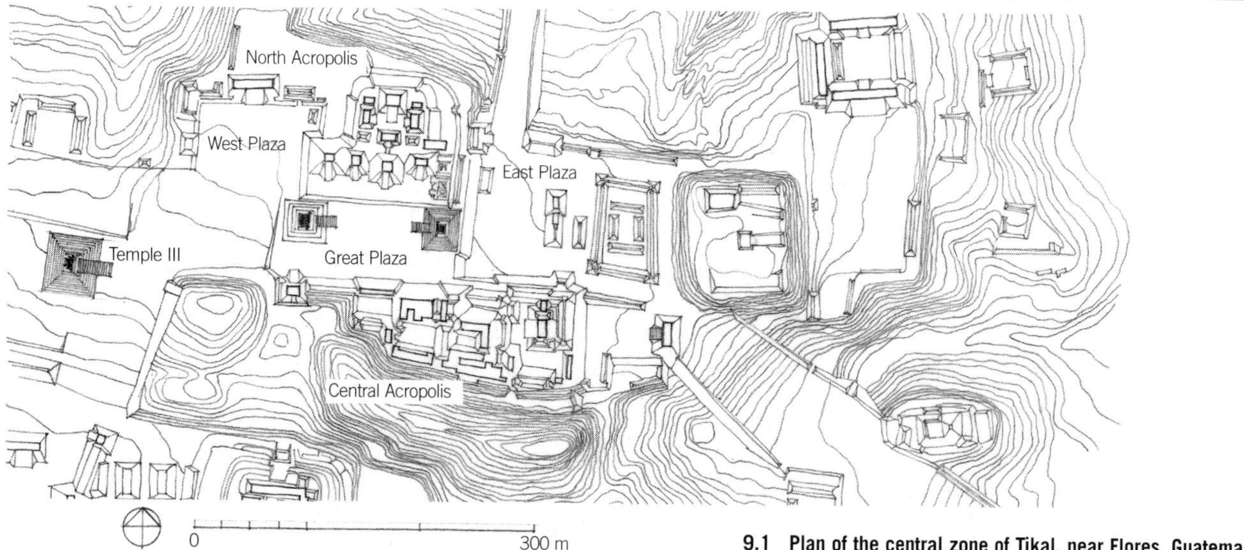


**9.1 Plan of the central zone of Tikal, near Flores, Guatemala**

Though the central buildings of the Maya were used for ceremonial and religious functions, and also sometimes as markets, the city itself was quite spread out in the form of an urban settlement. Whereas the priestly class and ruling elite probably lived in the palaces associated with the shrines, the rest of the Mayans visited the centers for specific purposes. Though temples were constructed with specific orientations and functions in mind, ceremonial centers, as a whole, were not expanded according to pre-planned rules or geometries, giving them a somewhat ad hoc appearance. There may, of course, be reasons for the slightly disjointed and angular arrangement of buildings and open plazas, but these have been lost to time.

The North Acropolis, the oldest complex of Tikal, was "reskinned" many times. When a ruler of some significance died, he was buried in the Acropolis and a new stone layer was added to it. The new mass was carefully set to ensure that the addition did not damage the older structure. Small vaults were built for the burials, each with its own shrine. Stairs provided access to these chambers for ancestral rites, which had to be performed by later rulers. A section through the Acropolis, therefore, is a veritable textbook of Tikal's thousand-year history.

The Plaza is a flat stone platform approached by climbing six wide steps. A set of stelae describing Tikal's rulers and dating their achievements are lined up along its northern edge. Temples I and II were constructed simultaneously in 734–736 CE by Yik'in Chan K'awiil. (K'awiil also built Temples IV and VI.) The Tikal ruler, Jasaw Chan K'awiil I, died in 734 CE and was buried in a spectacular ceremony beneath Temple I.

Unlike most Central American platform mounds, whose colossal size completely dwarfs the shrine that sits atop them, the shrines of Tikal rival and even dominate their substructures. A cursory study shows that the width atop the shrine of Temple I is just a little less than that of the structure's base. This makes for an extremely steep profile. But as a consequence, the visual focus of the entire composition is the entrance of the shrine, which is wider than the steps leading to it. Nowhere else in Central American architecture does one find this particular set of architectural proportions at work.

Unlike the clay and stone interiors of earlier Mayan pyramids, the interior of this one was built with large blocks of stones, carefully and accurately fitted in the supporting walls. To keep water from leeching into the interior, the surface was sealed with mortar. The brickwork that covered the entire pyramid served more as decoration than for protection.

Southeast of the Great Plaza is the so-called Central Acropolis, which held the royal courts and residences. It consisted of a series of courts connected at the corners, with simple adjoining buildings sitting on platforms. The palace courts, although adjoining the central ceremonial complex, were visually screened off from their surroundings. They were entered at the corners.

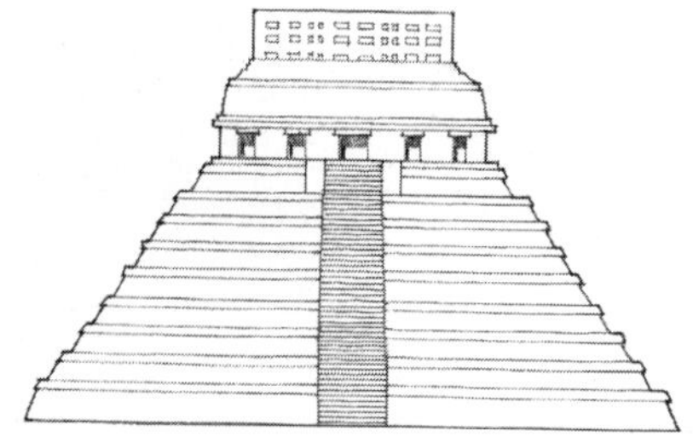

**9.2 Temple of the Inscriptions, Palenque**

9.3
**Temple I (Temple of the Great Jaguar), Tikal**

Tikal's urban core is a spectacular assembly of more than a hundred stone temples. Their engineers constructed Tikal's base by building up the higher zones into platforms with mud and stone. Three zones in the middle were connected over time by causeways to form a triangle. Additional causeways connected to adjoining platforms and the rest of the urban area. The largest of these zones is focused on a giant stone platform, the Great Plaza. To its north is the North Acropolis, which faces the Great Plaza. Its eastern and western ends are anchored by the so-called Temples I and II respectively. Further west and slightly to the south is Temple III; and even further west, connected by a causeway, is Tikal's largest temple, the 70-meter-tall Temple IV.

Astronomy determined the location of the main temples. They are connected by sightlines. Standing on top of Temple I, looking west, the peak of Temple III marks the setting of the sun at the equinoxes. From the same position, a sightline to Temple IV marks sunset on August 13, "the day the world began," according to the Mayan calendar. Further north, two adjacent platform mounds, called the Twin Pyramid Complex, are oriented exactly along the cardinal directions. Their collective steps add up to 365, corresponding exactly to one calendar year. They were constructed at the end of a 20-year period of the Mayan calendar, signifying the successful completion of that period.

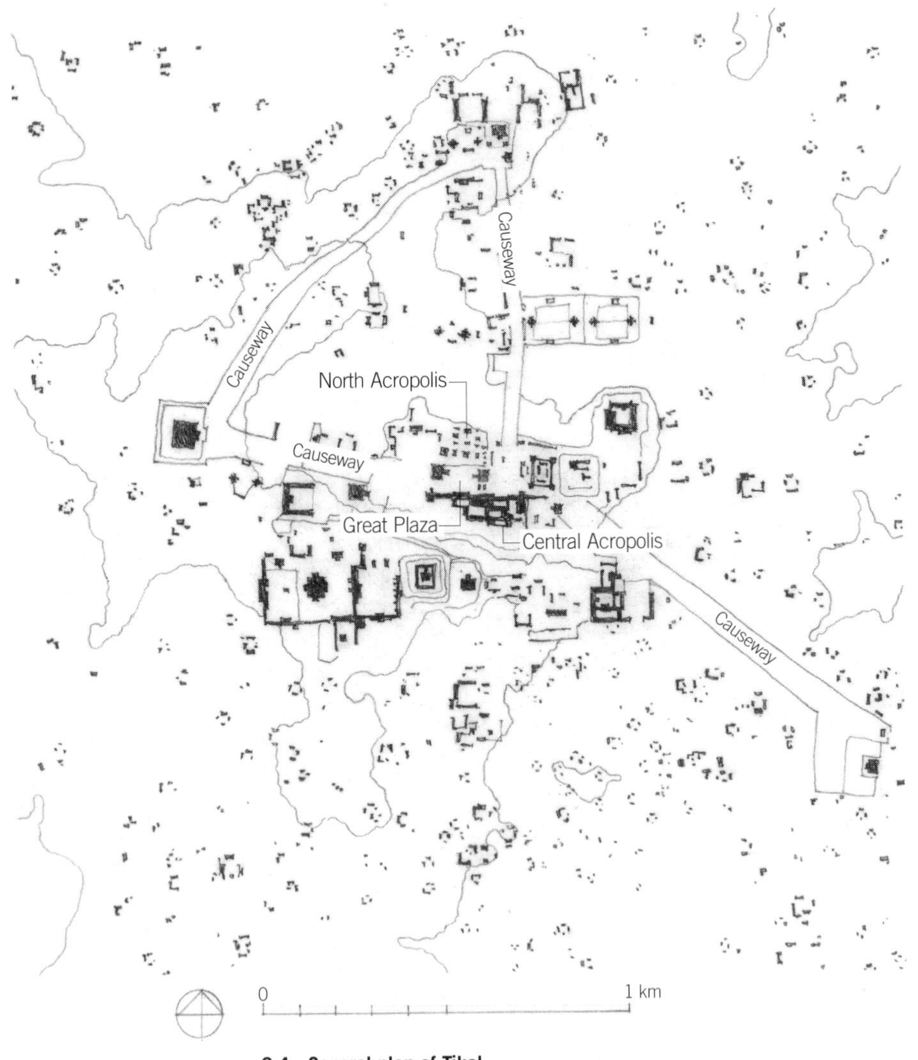


**9.4 General plan of Tikal**

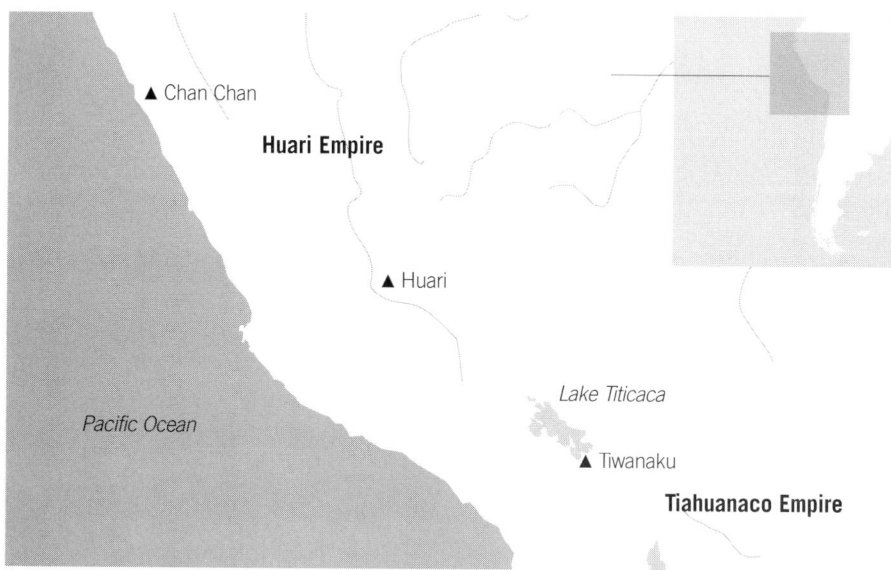


**TIWANAKU**

Tiwanaku lies in a highland valley in the southern Andes 3660 meters above sea level, near the south shore of Lake Titicaca. Inhabited from roughly 1000 BCE to 500 CE, it was not only the capital of a network of cities but also the regional ceremonial center, maintaining its preeminent position as such until about 1000 CE. It was not so much the city as the lake, which was seen as the place of origin from whence the primeval couple were sent out to call the Andean cultures from the springs and rivers, rocks and trees. Lake Titicaca was known as the *taypi*, or the zone of convergence between the principles of *urco* (the west, high, dry, pastoral, celestial, male) and *uma* (the east, low, agricultural, underworld, female). Tiwanaku was the central representation of the *taypi*, and elite who lived there were viewed as the guardians and representatives of this sacred order.

The ceremonial center was surrounded by an immense artificial moat, with water diverted from the Tiwanaku River, that evoked the image of the city core as an island. On crossing the moat and entering Akapana, the visitor moved from the space and time of ordinary life to that of the sacred.

The Akapana was a low-terraced platform mound, with a base 200 meters square and a height of 17 meters. The bulk of the earth used for the infill presumably came from the moat created at the edge of the sacred precinct. Vertical stones, approximately 3.5 meters on center, infilled with stone blocks perfectly cut and joined with characteristic Andean precision, mark the edges of the terraces and form the retaining walls.

The highest terrace was covered by thin layers of a bluish-green gravel, brought in from the Quimsachata range just south of Tiwanaku. From here, a complexly engineered drainage system connects the top of Akapana to the Tiwanaku River and ultimately to Lake Titicaca. On the summit of Akapana was a sunken court.

Associated with the Akapana are four temples—the semisubterranean, the Kalasasaya, the Putuni, and the Kheri Kala. The semisubterranean temple is open to the sky—a negative space lined with standing sandstones and masonry infill and axially linked to the Kalasasaya, a large terraced platform with a megalithic staircase on the south centered on the Portal of the Sun and a monumental stone sculpture, the so-called Ponce Monolith. The Kalasasaya was also furnished with its own central sunken court, like the Akapana. On the morning of the spring equinox, the sun rises and bisects the semisubterranean temple and appears in the center of the Kalasasaya's staircase.

**9.5 Megalithic entrance to the Kalasasaya mound, near La Paz, Bolivia**

9.6 **Interior, SS. Sergius and Bacchus**

## AGE OF JUSTINIAN

The time period between Constantine was one of consolidation for the Christians. Constantine's attempt to create an empire that was primarily imperial, and only then Christian, with a lot of paganism still mixed in, had become an empire that was primarily Christian. For Justinian (483–565) the Imperium Romanum was to be identified with the Christian *oikoumene*, and the triumph of Christianity was as sacred a mission as the restoration of Roman supremacy. To this effect, he reintroduced Roman Law, but with the dogmatic exclusiveness of the Christian religion. All other religions were denied legal protection. Pagan temples were torn down and strict laws passed to consolidate and unify the Christian domination of the empire. In 529 CE, he closed the Academy in Athens, many of its scholars seeking to take refuge in Persia, taking with them the fruits of Greek learning. This was largely to stem the multiplication of ideas and theories in theological debates and to enforce a return to a unified doctrine. This multiplicity had reflected itself in architecture as well. Justinian was also able to recover Italy and Africa. Bridges, fortifications, aqueducts, churches, markets, and whole cities sprang up in the wake of Justinian's conquests.

An excellent example of Justinian's architecture can be seen in Constantinople, in the church dedicated to St. Sergius and St. Bacchus, two soldiers in the Roman army who were martyred in the early 4th century CE and became the official patrons of the Byzantine armies. Several important factors, often ignored in conventional accounts, should be taken into consideration. The building, though we now see it as a freestanding structure, was originally part of a larger complex that included Justinian's private residence and palace. Furthermore, the slightly thicker walls to the south belonged to another church dedicated to St. Peter and St. Paul, begun in 518 CE and built by Justinian's uncle, Justin I. When Justinian became Caesar in 525 CE, he appendaged the new construction onto that one.The two churches were connected at ground level by means of three large arched openings (which later changed into windows when the Church of Peter and Paul was removed). Such church composites were not uncommon in the east, though rare in the west. The narthex on the west extended across both churches, which shared a common atrium in front. Furthermore, to the north, there was a monumental entrance, presumably from the former palace, so that there was a cross axis from north to south, connecting the two buildings. For reasons unknown, the Church of Peter and Paul fell into disrepair, was demolished, and by the 16th century was gone—as were most of the remnants of Justinian's palace.

The original context is important as it explains some of the curious and also sometimes-overlooked aspects of the design. To provide an entrance for the priests from the southwest into the apse at the back of the church, the eastern facade was tilted a bit, with the space left for a porch perhaps still visible in the setback of the facade at that corner. The resultant tilt impacted the orientation of the apse and thus of the central nave. To the west, the tilt was not implemented, because the narthex had to align with the Church of Peter and Paul. The plan is distinguished by its extraordinary openness. Unlike western churches, which channel the churchgoer into the nave from the west, we have a system that permits more fluid pathways into and through the church. Another feature of the plan that is often overlooked and that applies to the discussion of both SS. Sergius and Bacchus and the Hagia Sophia is that there are no separate rooms to the right and left of the altar where the sacred meal is prepared and where the bishop dons his garb, the *prothesis* and the *diaconicon* respectively. These are typical in all later Byzantine churches, but they are not present in early Justinian ones. The result in both buildings is that the central structure holding the dome is freed from the surrounding architecture in a way that is actually not characteristic of Byzantine design. The presence of multiple doorways and the absence of a *prothesis* and *diaconicon* requires some explanation, as does the liturgical use of these buildings.

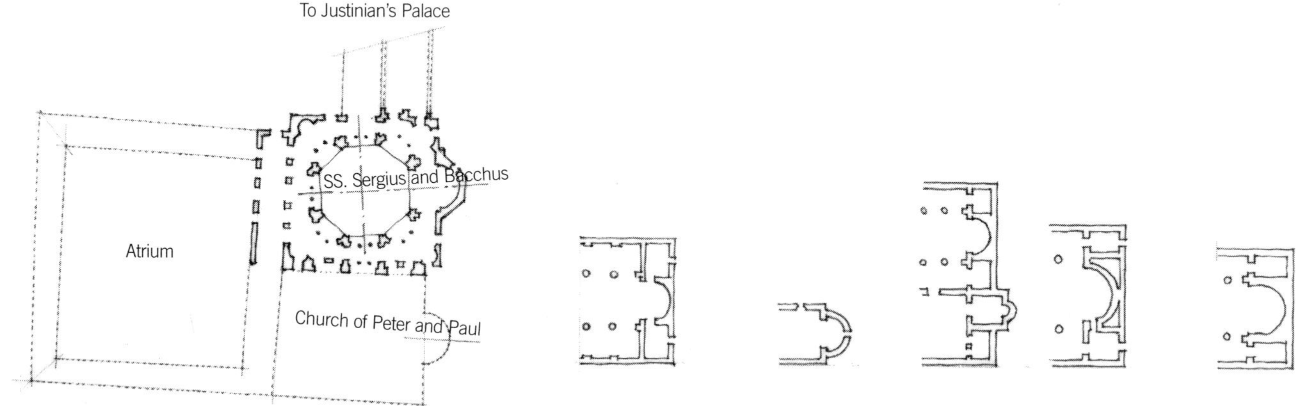


**9.7 Original context for SS. Sergius and Bacchus**

**9.8 Examples of North Syrian sanctuary plans**

**SS. Sergius and Bacchus**

One could compare SS. Sergius and Bacchus and Hagia Sophia with churches in Syria, where a single apse is flanked by rooms, and with the Roman plan, which is distinguished by its simplicity; both churches had galleries, with access gained by staircases located outside the body of the church. No other early Christian architecture makes such extensive use of galleries. And finally, the apse was not a podium with an altar, as in the west, but a semicircular tier of benches called a *synthronon*. One is still visible in the church of St. Irene, which stands just to the northeast of the Hagia Sophia and which was used before Hagia Sophia as the city's principal church. (The upper floor and vaults are 8th century constructions.)

Since it was never redesigned as a mosque, the apse has remained as it was. A final component of Justinian liturgical space was an elevated *ambo*, or reading desk or pulpit, approached by stairs from east and west, from which the Bible would be read. The word *ambo* is derived from the Greek verb, *amabainein*, which means, "to go up." It was usually set near the center of the nave but often slightly to the east of the axis. The *ambo* was surrounded by a low screen and a slightly elevated path to the altar, known as a *solea*, (from the Latin meaning "higher"). It was often marked out by a low screen as well.

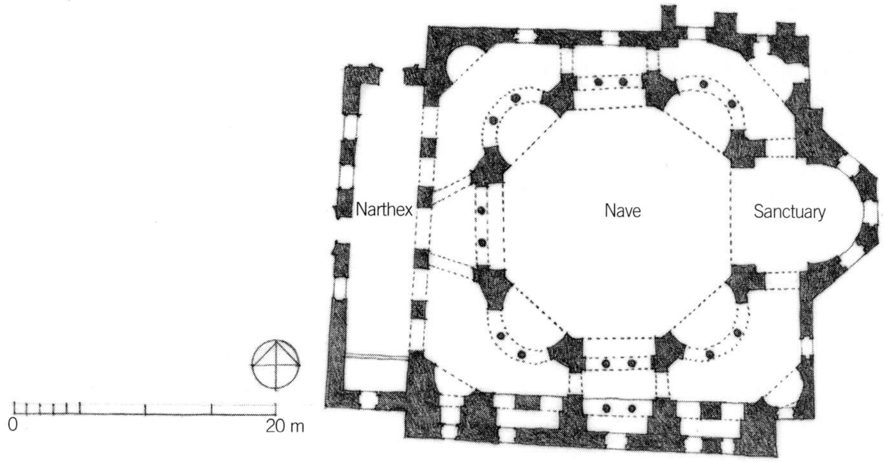


**9.9 Plan: SS. Sergius and Bacchus, Istanbul, Turkey**

As to how the spaces were used, one should not project current medieval liturgical uses one finds in Greek Orthodox churches onto these spaces, even though there are clearly numerous similarities. In Justinian's day, the populace gathered closely around the *ambo* in the nave. Furthermore, the preparatory rites of the *prothesis* for the First Entrance that are common today did not seem to exist in the Justinian age. The entrance ritual was more straightforward but also grander. The people gathered in the courtyard, and there they made their offerings of bread and wine to the church. Once the bishop had blessed the entrance and had himself entered, he was followed by the deacon who carried the bejeweled and bound volume of the Gospel—which stood for Christ himself—accompanied by candle-bearers and incense-bearers and a subdeacon carrying a cross. The rest followed. This entrance, the First Entrance, had numerous symbolic meanings, including the rejection of disbelief, and signifies the first appearance of God and the conversion to faith. In Rome, the order is reversed. There, the priests enter first and await the arrival of the bishop. In Constantinople, the bishop would go past the *ambo* and into the *solea* or sanctuary, defined by the short barrier of the iconostasis to the altar, where the Gospel would be placed, and then to the *synthronon* where he would give the initial blessing signifying the glorification of Christ.

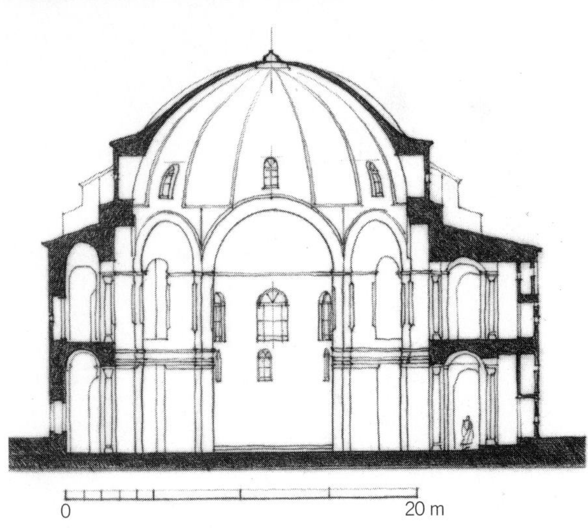

**9.10 Transverse section looking toward the sanctuary: SS. Sergius and Bacchus**

**9.11 Sixteen-sided dome of SS. Sergius and Bacchus rests on 8 double-storied piers.**

If the Emperor was present, he would have arrived earlier than the bishop and joined him at the narthex, at the head of the procession. His honor guard with soldiers and crossbearers would, however, have been allowed into the church to define the path. After leaving a gift of gold at the altar, he would have proceeded to the south aisle, where his throne was located. The interaction between emperor and priesthood was an essential and defining moment in the integrity of the Empire and Church, with their meeting and common participation in the ceremony a sign of the unity of earthly and divine realms. At SS. Sergius and Bacchus, the emperor's spot was in the northeast of the gallery, from where he could overlook the proceedings.

The bishop made his entrance already vested—thus the absence of the *diaconicon*, which came later as a space in which the bishop applied his vestments. The atrium served as the place where the people gathered. The narthex was a more formal space used to organize the procession once it had arrived. Once the procession had commenced, the congregation could also enter, which they did by streaming into the space from the various entrances in a manner of popular commotion.

Following the blessing, the readings took place from the altar and from the *ambo*, with the Gospel carried to the *ambo* with great solemnity and excitement. After the reading and the sermon came the Great Entrance, or as it was called at that time, "The Entrance of the Mysteries," which had as its object the transfer of the Eucharistic bread and wine from their place of preparation to the place of offering on the altar. Like the First Entrance, it is described through a language of various metaphors, but it is commonly related to the second coming of Christ and was the ceremonial climax of the liturgy. Today, a table or niche on the north side serves for the *prothesis*. In Byzantine times, there is no evidence of this custom. It seems that the act of bringing the bread and wine offered by the congregation started outside the church in a special room of a building called the *skeuophylakio*, which was used to hold the sacred vessels in which the food was transported. In other words, during the service, the wine and bread brought by the congregation was prepared out of sight and, in the process, "became" the flesh and blood of Christ and then was carried into the church.

At the Hagia Sophia, the *skeuophylakio* was located to the north of the building and was most likely the round building at the northeast corner. The bread and wine were brought in through a side door. At SS. Sergius and Bacchus, the atrium and the *skeuophylakio* are no longer present and the location of the latter is unknown without archaeological work.

It should also be noted that the space inside the church was segregated according to the sexes, but it is not clear how it worked at the time. It seems that the Empress and her court viewed the liturgy from a special place in the gallery, but whether all women were in the gallery or only in some part of it, or whether women had a place on the ground floor, has not been fully determined.

We turn now to the space itself. Over the center rises a sixteen-sided pumpkin dome brought down on eight double-storied piers, screened in the interstitial spaces by pairs of columns on both levels. These screens alternate in a rhythmic manner, being straight in the direction of the principal axis and curving outward on the four spaces at the corners.

**9.12 Interior, St. Vitale, Ravenna, Italy**

**9.13 Plan: St. Vitale, Ravenna**

**St. Vitale, Ravenna**

The plan type was a recent one that had been developed in Cilicia at the so-called Domed Ambulatory Church in Dag Pazari, which some scholars date to the 480s and which has an ambulatory. Another church even further south, dedicated to the Virgin Mary, is also of the same box-in-a-box type, and it dates perhaps to the 420s. Also similar is the cathedral in the city of Bosra (511–512 CE), located 140 kilometers south of Damascus and dedicated to the same saints. Those buildings, however, were of stone, whereas SS. Sergius and Bacchus was built of brick embedded in a thick mortar. It was much lighter and probably easier and quicker to build, but it was also susceptible to lateral forces and earthquakes. This also meant that the supporting walls could be opened up with windows and that the buttressing, in effect, could be concealed in a supporting cast of semidomes and quarter-domes. There is considerable debate as to whether this technique came from Mesopotamia or whether it was homegrown, but until hard evidence is presented, one can conclude that whatever the sources, the technique once established here would soon be developed yet further, as in the Hagia Sophia. Another possible earlier source comes from late Roman times. An octagonal "church" was found in Gadara, but excavations have shown that this building, like a similar one in Gerasa, was a *macellum*, or market, that had been converted into a church.

A building that is often given as a parallel structure to SS. Sergius and Bacchus is St. Vitale (538–545 CE) in Ravenna, built during the brief time in the 6th century when it was the seat of Theodoric's rule as titular head of the Western Empire. It was financed by a wealthy local banker whose monogram appears on the capitals of the ground floor and was clearly iconographically linked to Constantinople. The central area is an octagon supported by piers, between which double-height bays swell out and away from the center. The surfaces were richly decorated with marble panels and mosaics in the Byzantine style. Though the double-shell plan with its wedge-shaped piers is similar to SS. Sergius and Bacchus, one must note the addition at St. Vitale of the *prothesis* and *diaconicon* to the north and south of the apse. The sanctuary is also given greater prominence and is more remote from the central space. The ambulatory and gallery were not vaulted (the present vaults are medieval), placing greater emphasis on the piers, which are buttressed to their backs. To compensate for the mass of the piers, the architects replaced the rhythmic alternation of semicircular and straight screens with a continuous row of semicircular niches, which are deeper than the ones at SS. Sergius and Bacchus and thus give the space an airier feeling. It was perhaps a matter of preference. One is more elastic and intimate, the other more organized and formal.

**9.14 Section: St. Vitale, Ravenna**

9.15 Interior: Hagia Sophia

### Hagia Sophia

While opinions regarding the spatial compositions of SS. Sergius and Bacchus and St. Vitale may differ, about the Hagia Sophia, in Constantinople, opinions are united. It was from the date of its opening one of the greatest buildings in the Western world. Little is known for certain about the predecessors of Hagia Sophia. It was originally dedicated by Constantine in 360 CE and rebuilt after the fire of 404. But after the ruthless suppression of his political enemies in the Nike uprising, in which even that building was damaged, the emperor Justinian called in the mathematician Anthemius of Tralles and Isidore of Miletus to design the new structure. In five short years (532–37 CE) they produced a daring and lofty domed structure whose fabric is still largely intact today.

Sheathed in marble and gold, its splendor made it one of the most talked about buildings in the Christian world. One visitor, Procopius, writing in the 6th century when the building was newly finished, stated "the dome must surely seem not to rest upon solid masonry but to cover the space beneath with its golden dome suspended from heaven."

Some of the skeptics thought they were right when an earthquake destroyed the dome in 557 CE, barely 20 years after the dedication; but undaunted, Justinian had a new one built, though it was more steeply pitched.

The structural system is simple but ingenious. A 30-meter square forms the center. At the corners, piers rise up to support four arches, between which are pendentives that hold a dome scalloped with 40 ribs. Windows line the base of the dome, making it seem to float. The east and west arches are closed off with a screen of columns and windows. The undersides of the east and west arches, however, are as if blown away, allowing one to look into vast three-apsed buildings on both sides.

The only difference between the east and west is that, on the eastern side, the final 8 meters of the apse boldly project from the perimeter wall that otherwise, like a box, contains its precious spatial cargo. The deep galleries on the north and south, which form spatial corridors parallel to the nave, help create the sense of drama that pervades the building. From a structural point of view, they serve to divide the buttressing into segments.

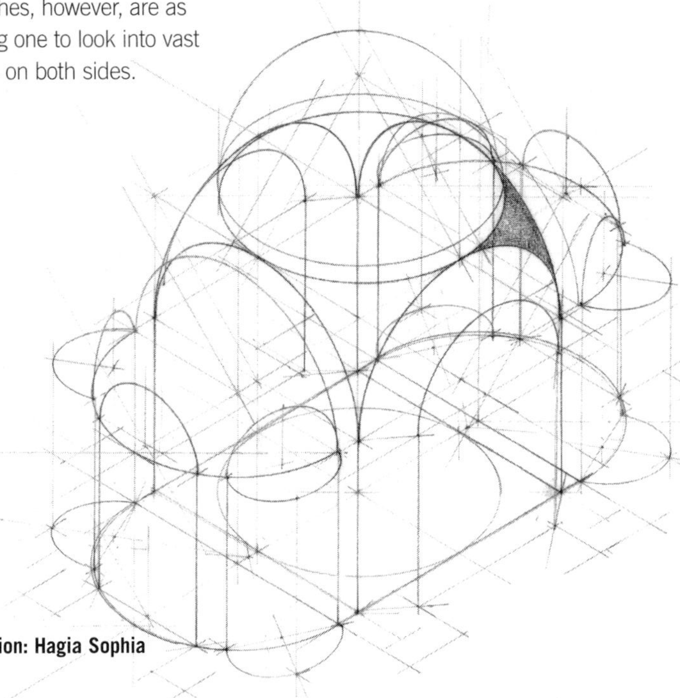

9.16 Spatial composition: Hagia Sophia

9.17 **Side aisle: Hagia Sophia**

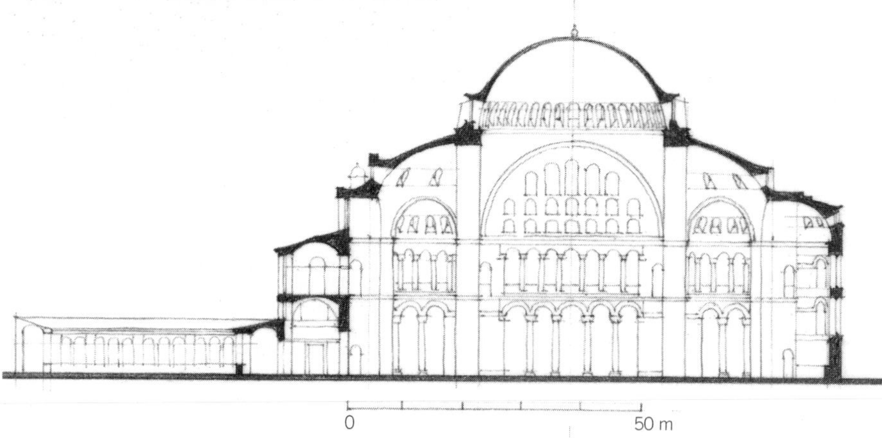


The vaults, made of brick, are thin and lightweight. Still today there is considerable uncertainty about the statics that govern the building's integrity, for the semidomes are too thin to be of much assistance. But the combination of supporting half-domes, quarter-domes, and massive piers were enough, and in the days before computers and earthquake-impact studies, the audacity of the system is remarkable. Later, from the 8th century on, various types of buttresses were added to the exterior to prevent problems.

The use of windows is similarly complex. The window at the east end of the apse, the lights along the base of the dome, as well as those on the north and south, allow light to stream directly into the nave. But the large windowless openings under the supporting arch at the west end are filled only with grill work. Under the north and south tympana, the colonnaded columns stand in the shadows, backlit from the windows in the outer wall.

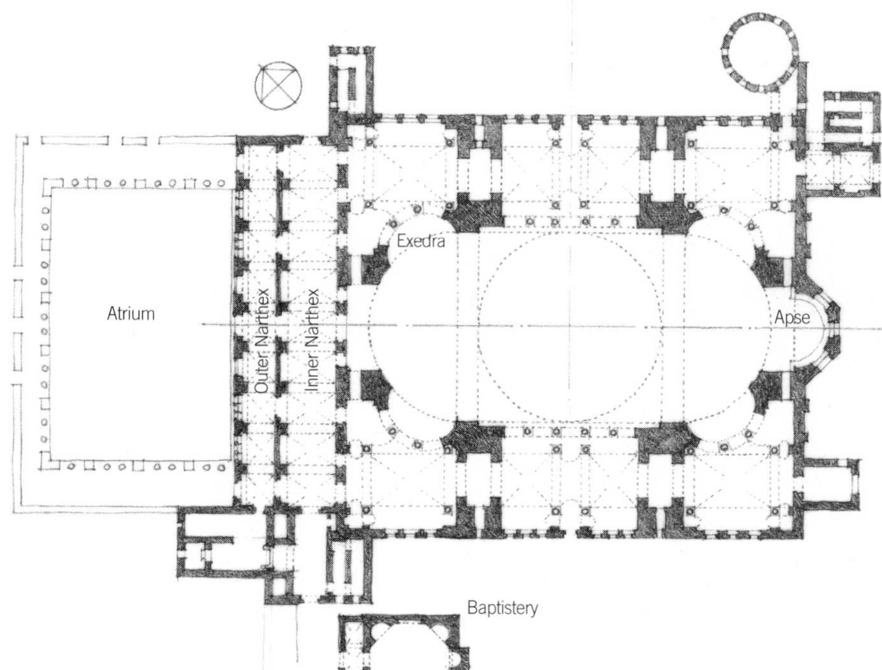


9.18 **Plan and section: Hagia Sophia, Istanbul, Turkey**

9.19 View of semidome, Hagia Sophia

9.20 Mosaic, Hagia Sophia

As impressive as the structural system of Hagia Sophia was, the architects made every effort to make it appear effortless. Today's experience of the building can in no way compare to the original. Destroyed mosaics and even 18th-century decorations may be reminders of how time spins its web through the fabric of buildings, but they also make it difficult to imagine the Justinian splendor. In the 7th century, the marble cladding and mosaics would have obliterated any sense of oppression or weight. From the dark-gray marble of the pavement to green marble with white veins, dark-blue marble with yellow veins, and reddish columns, to the silver and gold of the mosaics, the eye moves from surface to surface, as if structure simply did not exist. And, as to the dome, the first one was covered with a gold mosaic. The second one had a large figure of a cross embedded in its decoration. The windows were filled with glass tinted blue, red, green, brown, yellow, and purple. The light was thus a subdued one. Even the patterned marble floor, unlike the floor of the Pantheon, denies a sense of stability and has been described by ancient commentators as a wavy sea.

Though a good deal of the marble panels have survived, few of the mosaics have, since most were taken down or plastered over during its conversion to a mosque. (Hagia Sophia was secularized in 1935).

From the outside, with its staggered heaping of volumes, a visitor would not in any way expect a space of this dimension and scale. In fact, once one enters past the narthex, the space rises so forcefully that one feels one is at the bottom of a vast canyon with the floor of the church a type of stage on which the Procession of the Entrances was performed. As to nighttime illumination, it must also have been impressive. From the base of the dome, brass chains swept down to support a metal ring equipped with flat silver disks pierced to hold glass vessels holding oil lamps. Within this vast candelabrum was hung another but smaller crown of lights and higher up a great silver disk acted as a reflector.

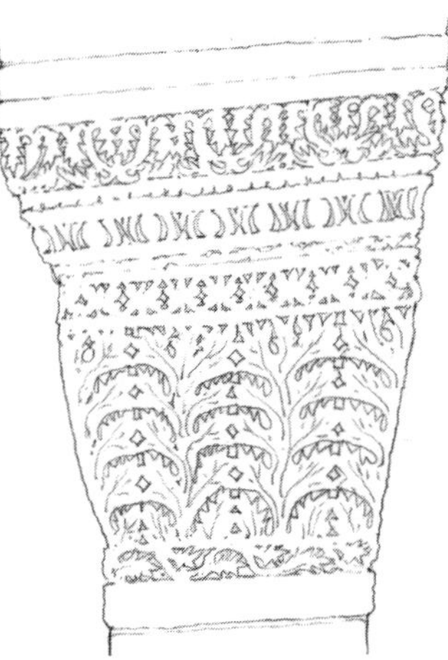

9.21 Composite capital: Hagia Sophia

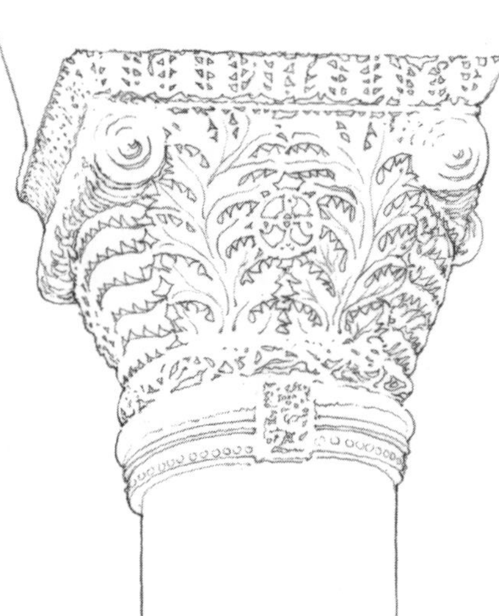

9.22 Composite capital: Hagia Sophia

9.23 **Detail of capital, Hagia Sophia**

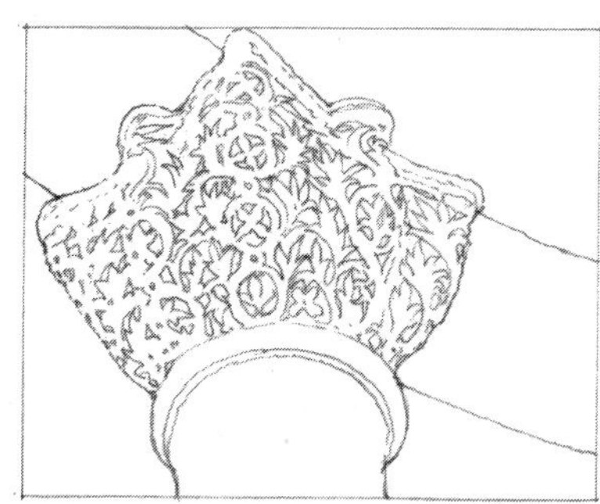

9.24 **Capital used at SS. Sergius and Bacchus**

**Byzantine Capitals**

There are two types of capitals used at Hagia Sophia, composite and Ionic. The composite capital that had emerged during the Late Byzantine Empire, mainly in Rome, combines the Corinthian with the Ionic. Composite capitals line the principal space of the nave. Ionic capitals are used behind them in the side spaces in a minor position with respect to the Corinthian or composite orders, as was to be their fate well into the 19th century, when buildings were designed for the first time with a monumental Ionic order. At Hagia Sophia, though, these are not the standard imperial statements. The capitals are filled with foliage in all sorts of variations. In some, the lush small leaves appear as if they were caught up in the spinning of the scrolls. Clearly a different and nonclassical sensibility had taken over the design.

At SS. Sergius and Bacchus and other churches of the time, we see the full emergence of this experimentation. Since post-Renaissance classicism in Europe so radically dismissed these efforts as outside the norm of the "classical" tradition, one has to note that the "classical" tradition was more open to experimentation than one might at first think.

Furthermore, after the fall of the Roman Empire in which standardized models were often used, local craftsmen were obviously invited to test their skills. That many of these craftsmen were using northern motives or were themselves Christianized Visigoths is more than obvious. The capitals at St. Vitale in Ravenna show wavy and delicate floral patterns of foliage that had been used to decorate belt buckles and dagger blades. Their inverted pyramidal form has the look of a basket. At the Basilica Eufrasiana in Parenzo along the Adriatic, we find a double-tier design with birds at the corners and delicately carved grape vines below. At Salonica, we have capitals that also consist of abstract curved patterns in conjunction with some that have leaves looking as if they are being tossed around by the wind. The capitals at SS. Sergius and Bacchus have a delicate stenciling in which the swirling tendrils of acanthus stand out against the blackness of a deeply cut background. Like the spaces around them, they swell in and out.

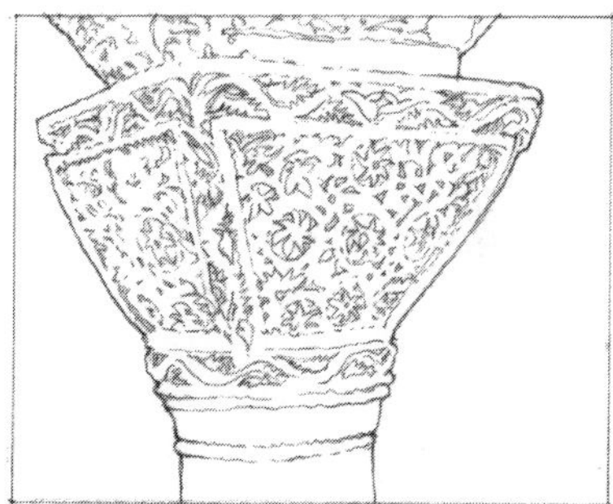

9.25 **Capital used at St. Vitale**

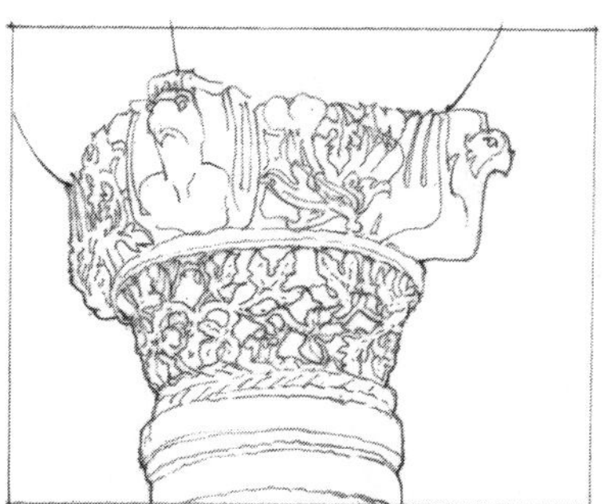

9.26 **Capital used at Basilica Eufrasiana**

9.27 **Capital used at Salonica**

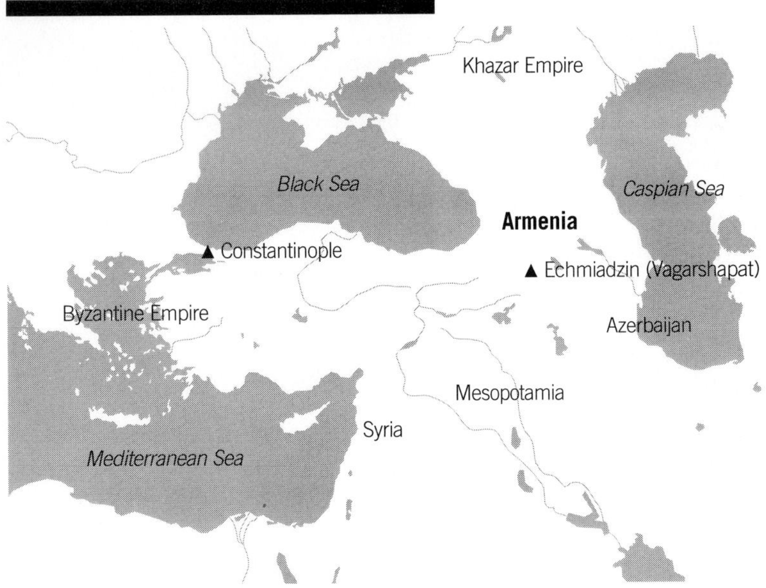


## ARMENIAN ARCHITECTURE

The area defined by the Caspian Sea to the east and the Black Sea to the west was an important geographical hub. Merchants could unload goods from China on the shores of the Caspian, where they would be taken through Armenia to the Black Sea, from where almost any destination in Europe was reachable. The trip from China to Rome would have gone through fewer contested territories in the year 600 than it does today. Such a location was both the cause for the rise and fall of the Armenian Kingdom. Descended from the Urartu, the Armenians were controlled by the Persians, then by Alexander, the Romans, and then by the Persians again. Despite all this, and given the Armenian desire for autonomy, the period between the 4th and 9th centuries was highly creative. In the 6th and 7th centuries, with Arab regions to the south and Vikings to the north still in disarray, Armenia was a safe link between east and west. But by the 10th century, with the expansion of Islam and Christianity into large, far-flung yet interconnected domains, options for trade multiplied significantly to the detriment of Armenia, which was able to survive only until 1375.

The significance of Armenia in the history of architecture lies, once again, in the quality of its stonework. One has to remember that the Byzantines had given up stone for brick (Hagia Sophia is basically a brick building). The use of concrete, furthermore, had been forgotten by this time. The Armenians alone maintained the classical Hellenistic tradition of clean surfaces and volumetric complexity. Furthermore, unlike Byzantine architecture, which emphasized the interior over the exterior, the Armenians maintained a strong focus on the objectlike quality of the building, and this would have an important impact on the later development of church architecture in Europe, when Armenian masons went to the west in search of work.

The history of Armenia's Christian architecture begins in 301 CE when Dertad III (the king of Armenia under Roman suzerainty) was converted to Christianity by St. Gregory the Illuminator, a native Armenian. He made Christianity the state religion. In general, the Armenian liturgy resembles that of the Eastern Church except that its language is classical Armenian and not Greek. The distinctive look of Armenian architecture developed quite rapidly. Buildings tended to have forms that were simple and solid-looking. From the earliest date, they were volumetrically and planimetrically small masterpieces in spatial organization and composition. Furthermore, the carving and placing of the stones was excellent and indeed, at the time, would have been far superior to other stone buildings in Europe and Asia.

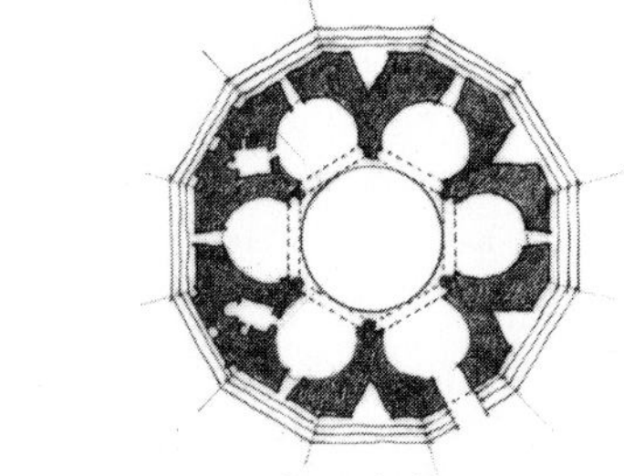

Central plan

Cruciform plan

Inscribed trefoil plan

**9.28 Typology of Armenian churches**

9.29 Church of the Vigilant Powers, near Echmiadzin, Armenia

### Church of the Vigilant Powers

Many of the early churches were built with the local dark, ash-colored tufa stone, with some blocks measuring more than a half-meter high and almost 2 meters across. Windows are small but always well integrated into the volumetric whole. The interiors were thus dark with light coming in mostly from above.

Particularly remarkable is the Church of the Vigilant Powers (Zvartnotz) near Echmiadzin, begun in 642 CE. Though only the lower portions remain, it can be reconstructed with reasonable accuracy. From the outside, it consisted of three telescoped cylinders, 37 meters across at ground level. The external walls were enlivened by blind arcades. Within, wedge-shaped piers held four large exedrae, three of them composed of six columns and the fourth closed to become an apse. The piers rose to form arches that supported a dome on squinches. Windows were smaller at the bottom than on top where they formed a continuous band, thus creating a luminous center and a darker periphery.

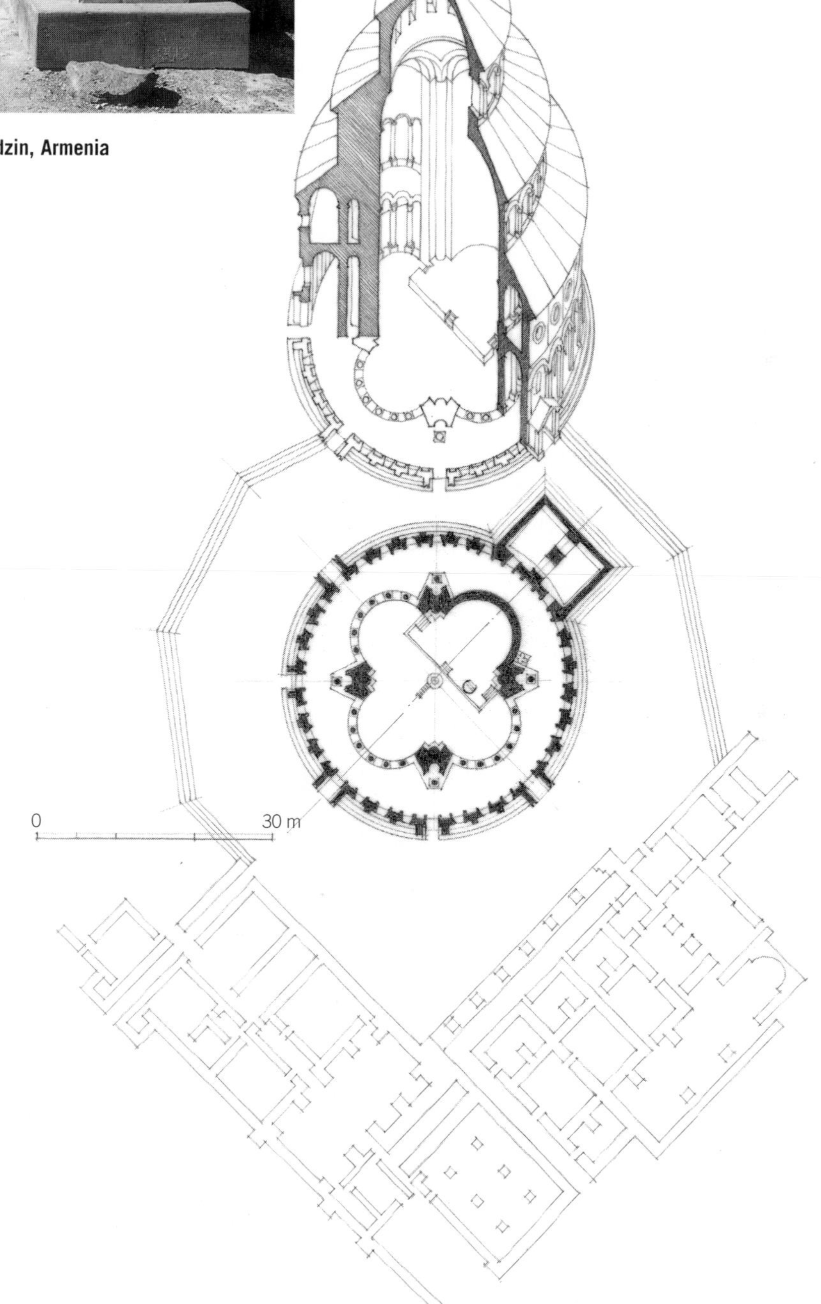


9.30 Plan, elevation, and section: Church of the Vigilant Powers

9.31 St. Hripsime, Echmiadzin, Armenia

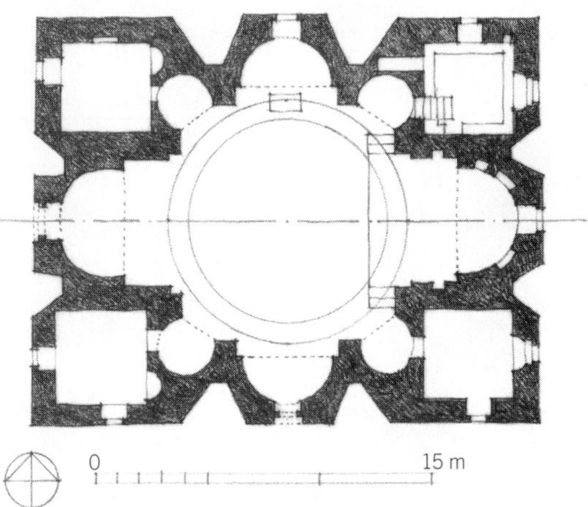


9.32 Plan: St. Hripsime

**St. Hripsime**

One of the most refined examples of Armenian architecture can also be found in Echmiadzin. St. Hripsime was the second church built by St. Gregory the Illuminator during the first quarter of the 4th century. It was replaced in 395 CE by a small chapel. The present church edifice was built in 618 CE. The building is constructed of dark ash-colored tufa stone bonded on the interior with concretelike mortar. The whole rests, like a Greek temple, on a stepped stylobate. The interior organization is that of a quatrefoil plan with niches in the cardinal directions. In addition to these, there are niches on the diagonal corners, creating a fluid and dynamic space on the inside. The diagonal niches, having the form of three-quarter cylinders, may also have been intended to strengthen the abutment of the dome. They are pierced and give access to four subsidiary chambers that flank the eastern and western niches. Barrel vaults intervene between the axial niches and the central square. These vaults, which are wider along the main axis, accentuate the east-west direction. The whole composition is bound together to form a well-proportioned rectangle with large triangular recesses that contribute to the rhythmic impression of the composition. The center of the composition rises to a dome resting on a windowed drum. The drum is 16-sided on the exterior and has 12 windows at its base. The beauty of the St. Hripsime edifice derives from the simplicity and harmony of its different parts.

9.33 St. Hripsime, Vagharshapat

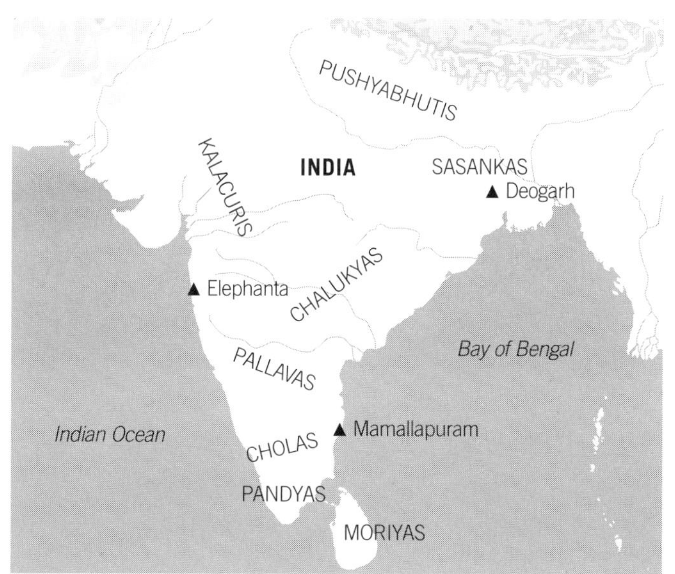

**9.34 Vishnu Temple, Deogarh, India**

**RISE OF THE TEMPLE KINGDOMS**

During the 6th and 7th centuries, at least 36 distinct kingdoms were in power in South Asia. The subcontinent was not "fragmented," but rather, as in Europe, composed of a series of disparate independent entities. With Buddhism pushed to the margins, however, Hindu architecture in South Asia now entered an experimental phase, with brick and rock-cut temples competing with new structural-stone temples for prominence throughout the subcontinent. In the north, Harshavardhana (606–647 CE) was the last major empire builder in pre-Islamic India, consolidating Hindu temple building in the north. In the kingdoms of the Chalukyas, the Pallavas, the Cholas, and the Pandyas, new experimental temple forms were being explored. Although an invasion by the Huns of North India dispersed the Buddhist monks from Kashmir, they continued to prosper in major universities like Nalanda and Ujjain and in Sirpur in Central India. Emblematic of the syncretism of the time, Sirpur has shrines dedicated to Hindu deities such as Shiva and Vishnu adjacent to compounds dedicated to the Buddha. The oldest statue of a female deity, Haritiki, has also been found here. One Buddhist *vihara* at Sirpur shows concepts overlapping with new emerging Hinduism: nine rooms are clustered around a 12-pillared court, influenced by the precise geometric logics of a mandala. A Buddha statue originally stood in the center.

The plinth of Hindu Vishnu Temple at Deogarh (early 6th c.) was divided according to a nine-square mandala, with the main area occupying the central square. The four directions are represented by stairs on all four sides, with the shrine facing west, as is appropriate for a Vishnu temple. At the corners were originally four subsidiary shrines, also square in plan, that were interlocked with the platform. This is an important early example of the attempt to design by means of interlocking geometries, the cerebral exploration of which was to become the defining characteristic of Hindu temple form in the centuries to come.

Vishnu Deogarh's entrance portal is one of the masterpieces of Gupta art. It consists of a series of progressively recessed highly sculptured jambs. The *ghana-dwaras* (blind-doorways) on the three other sides of the temple also contain superb Vaishnaite relief sculpture organized in a counterclockwise sequence and manifesting various aspects of Vishnu's divinity.

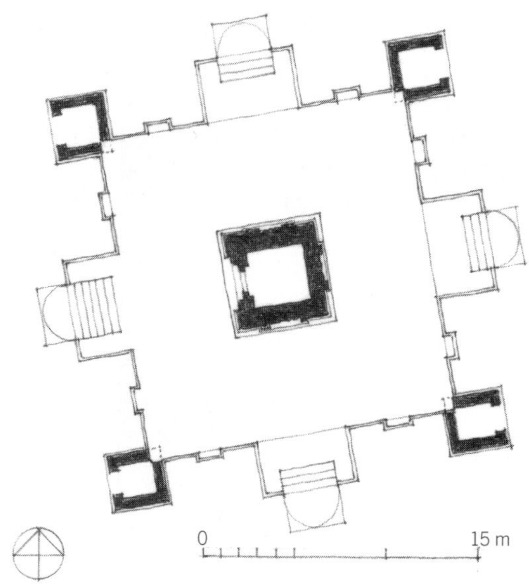


**9.35 Plan: Vishnu Temple, Deogarh**

9.36 Cave of Shiva, Elephanta, near Mumbai, India

**Shiva Temple at Elephanta**

The 6th-century Gupta period Shiva temple is one of seven caves built on the island of Elephanta, six miles East of the modern city of Bombay (Mumbai). They were built by Hindu monks, living away from the centers and even the corridors of civilization, in the manner of the Buddhist monks. Cut into the steeply receding slope of a stone outcropping, the Shiva temple shows an attempt to resolve the problem of multiple spatial and visual vectors into a coherent whole. It has a cruciform plan with a large central-colonnaded, roughly square hall projecting out one bay on each side to create entrances on the east, north, and west sides, and a large sculptural niche on the south, which is the also the mountain side. The two axes seem to be equal, with the east-west axis, the ceremonially superior one, marked by the main garbh-griha. The north-south axis, aligned with the main entrance, terminates in three gigantic Shiva sculptures in deep recessed niches. This triptych, much celebrated in the annals of art history, occupies the entire width and height of the end wall and, compared to the rough-hewn character of the rest of structure, was carved with greater care.

At the west end of the hall, the *garbh-griha* was conceived as a square chamber with portals on all four sides, which, of course, suggest four axes centered on its sculptural deity, a *shivalinga*. There are thus three competing centers at Elephanta—the center of the hall, the Shiva triptych, and the *cella*. But in the end, it is the *cella*, a minicruciform structure in itself, that dominates the entire composition, not by being the forced center of everything but by its subtle location that exploits its possibilities as a freestanding element.

In actual experience, the east-west axis is the most prominent; from the eastern entrance, one can see through the *cella* to the other side, highlighting in silhouette the distinctive hump of the *shivalinga* enshrined at the center of the *cella*. A dramatic silhouette provides focus. The Shiva triptych on the south is in deep shadow and, in the absence of artificial lighting, is visible only from nearby.

9.37 Plan: Cave of Shiva, Elephanta

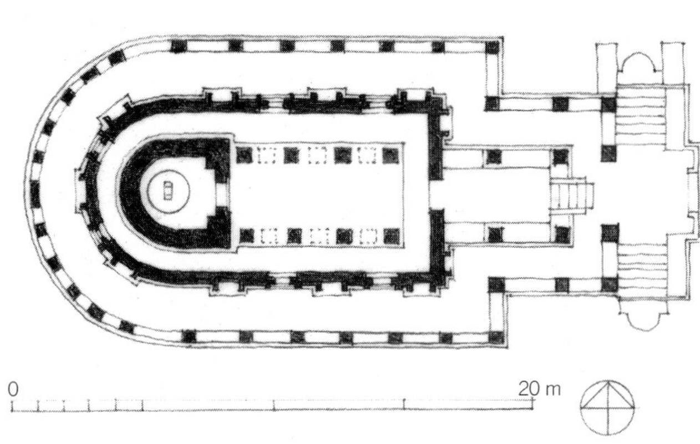


9.38 **Plan: Durga Temple at Aihole, India**

9.39 **Five Rathas, Mamallapuram**

**Durga Temple and the Five Rathas**

One of the most experimental of the Chalukyan temples in Western India is the so-called Durga Temple (675–710 CE) at Aihole. It is unusual in two respects. First, it has an apsidal end clearly derived from the Buddhist *caitya* halls, and it ably accommodates the *parikrama*, or circumambulation function, by providing an enclosed corridor around the general arc of movement. There are a few examples of similar apsidal temples in India, but they are rare. Second, the Durga Temple has a secondary envelope wrapping around the main shrine, which is unique in Hindu temple architecture. Usually the plinth, at most, will echo the outline of the main shrine, but at the Durga Temple, a second aisle was created and left largely unadorned, with large openings formed by simple piers. The veranda created by the intermediate space makes for an interesting study, with a simple, light-filled, airy "functionalist" outer perimeter, contrasting against and protecting the heavily ornamented and sculpted interior wall, which belongs to the main body of the temple.

Contemporary with the Chalukyas, with whom they had frequent commerce, the Pallava are one of the most distinguished dynasties of the South. The second Pallava ruler, Narsimhavarman II, is known for having built at Mamallapuram not only one of the largest port cities of the time in India but a series of stone monuments that form something of a petrified stone city on the coast.

The oldest and most famous of his constructions are the so-called Five Rathas (Mid- to late-7th century CE) and the Shore Temple at Mamallapuram.The Five Rathas are a group of five miniaturized stone temples accompanied by life-size sculptures of a bull, an elephant, and a lion. Four of the temples are carved out of a single, large piece of rock. It is unclear why they were made. They may have been an experimental study of typological possibilities or displays of sculptural prowess in stone intended to rival woodwork. One can note, however, that miniaturization is a constant theme in Hindu temple design. Every temple is a miniature, or a model, of the Hindu cosmic order. And then, the "decorative" module of a temple on a *shikhara* is also a miniature of the temple of which it is a part. In other words, on every scale—from the minitemple on a *shikhara* to the temple itself, and then in the full-scale reality of the Hindu cosmos—the same form repeats itself, as in fractal geometry. Beyond being a symbol of cosmic order, they also symbolized the worshipper's personal wholeness.

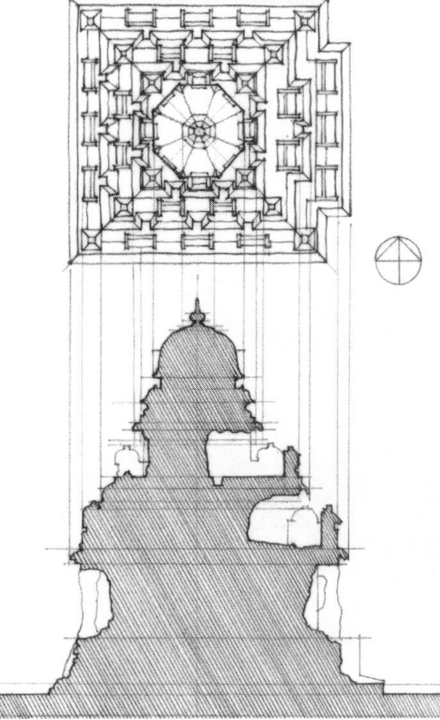
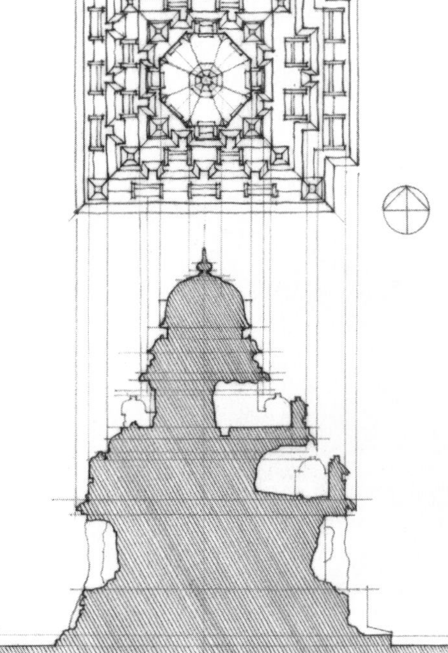


9.40 **Plan and section: Dharmaraja Ratha, Mamallapuram**

9.41 Shore Temple at Mamallapuram, India

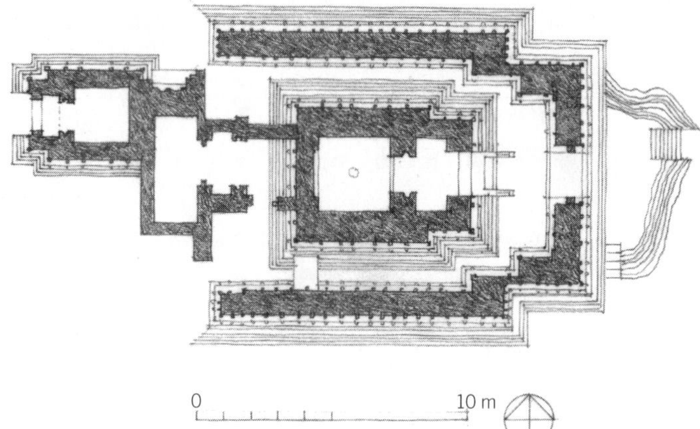


9.42 Plan: Shore temple at Mamallapuram

**Shore Temple at Mamallapuram**

The Shore Temple at Mamallapuram (700–728 CE), so-called because it overlooks the Bay of Bengal, is one of the oldest structural stone temples of South India, attributed to the Pallava king, Narsimhavarman II. Situated on the beach at the very edge of the Bay of Bengal, the temple is actually an amalgam of three different shrines. The main shrine is dedicated to Shiva and faces east. The second shrine, with a smaller *shikhara*, is also dedicated to Shiva but faces west. Between the two, attached to the back wall of the smaller Shiva shrine and entered from the east, is a small third shrine, dedicated to the reclining Vishnu, with no superstructural presence. The Vishnu shrine, probably the oldest on the site, is on axis with the larger Shiva shrine, although there is no direct communication between the two.

The entrance is through a gateway, or *gopuram,* covered by a transverse barrel vault. Although most of the exterior arrangements of the temple have eroded, there is ample suggestion that water may have been channeled into pools in the temple and may indeed have also entered into the Vishnu shrine, which would have been appropriate since the reclining Vishnu figure is mythologically described as lying in the primordial ocean.

The *shikharas* are similar to the nearby Five Rathas, with a strict pyramidal outline and pilastered wall. The individual tiers of the Shore Temple's *shikharas* have been kept distinct and separate, with the deep overhanging eaves casting dark shadows without blurring the levels. Both *shikharas* resolve themselves into octagonal capstones with long finials.

9.43 Shore temple at Mamallapuram

Most later Hindu temples, dedicated to more than one deity, will be lined up hierarchically or organized radially around a dominant center. The Shore Temple's bi-axial configuration of the two Shiva shrines, which are separated and yet linked by the small Vishnu shrine, represents an effort to balance the multiple competing liturgical requirements.

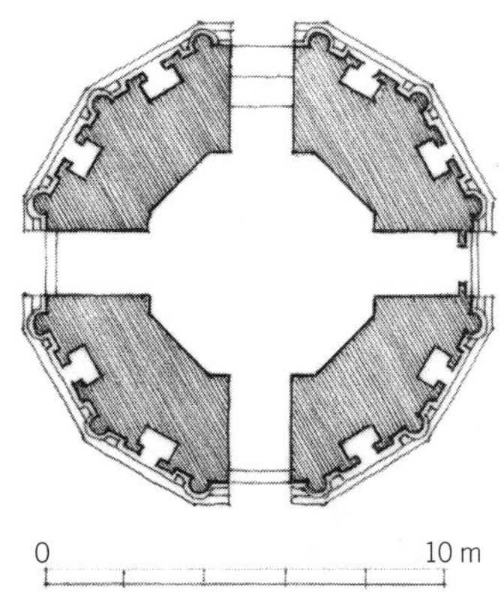


**9.44 Plan: Songyue Temple Pagoda, Dengfeng, China**

## SONGYUE TEMPLE TA (PAGODA)

Architecturally the Chinese translated the South Asian stupa into the *ta* (or pagoda, which is what the Portuguese called the Hindu temple *shikharas*, which is what they mistook the Chinese *ta* to be.) The Chinese term *ta* is itself a transformation of the Sanskrit stupa into *dagoba*. While the stupa is a round earthen mound, the *ta* is a tower. Both the *ta* and the stupa share the same purpose, to house at its core a buried relic. But the *ta* is a tall, multilayered structure, whereas the stupa is generally squat and solid. Where the stupas emphasize the fullness of the mound's body and focuses on the mystery within its earthen core, the *ta* magnifies the vertical axis and makes a display of the many levels of heavens inhabited by many Buddhas. It is important to realize that the *ta* was not just a mistranslation. It was how the Chinese chose to represent the stupa. Even Hsuan Tsang, for instance, who had seen and carefully recorded innumerable stupas in India, specifically chose the form of a *ta* when building his own monastery in Chang'an, the Wild Goose Pagoda (652–704 CE), a 7-story, 20-meter-high structure, originally made of mud and brick. Though the form may have been inspired by Han Chinese watchtowers, the *ta* never functioned as watchtowers. Rather they served like beacons visible from a distance.

Part of the explanation behind the *ta* may lie in the fact that whereas stupas began during a phase of Buddhism that deemphasized representation, the *ta* emerged after the establishment of Mahayana Buddhism, which permitted representation. The *ta*, in fact, symbolizes outright the multiheavened cosmology of Mahayana Buddhism. In the stupa this cosmology is referred to through the small *chattris* (or umbrellas) at the summits. The *ta*, essentially, is a *chattri* magnified to huge proportions.

**9.45 Songyue Temple Pagoda**

The Songyue Temple Ta (523 CE), in Dengfeng of Henan Province, is China's oldest and largest surviving *ta* or pagoda. Located in the middle of a river valley, it is a 12-sided polygon, 40 meters high, and consisting of 15 bodhisattva levels, surmounted by an obtuse finial. The whole is made of brick, including the corbeled overhanging eaves of the main body. The overall form is parabolic with a slight suggestion of entasis. The lower story of the base is unornamented, with an entry facing south. The second story is slightly cantilevered, with engaged columns at the corners and lotus-bud capitals that seem to be of Indian origin. The four sides face the cardinal directions and have openings leading to a central space; the other sides have arched niches, like the Mahabodhi Temple Complex in India. The arches are decorated with lion motifs. The Songyue Temple Pagoda was originally plastered, possibly white, and would have stood out against the hills. As it is, the pagoda, along with others with which it forms a family, sits in dramatic relation to its surroundings, as its undisputed focus. Unlike most later pagodas, the Songyue Temple Pagoda is not accessible. The individual stories—much too small to ever have been intended for human occupation in any way—are entirely representational, complete with a door and two windows carved into each of the 12 sides at each story.

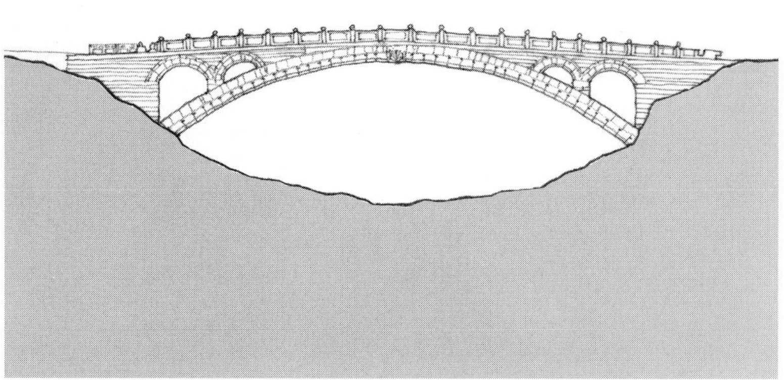

**9.46 Stone Arch Bridge on the Jiao River, near Zhaozhou, China**

## SUI AND T'ANG DYNASTIES

After a long period of competitive warfare, the Sui (581–618 CE) and the T'ang (618–907 CE) succeeded in establishing centralized dynasties that controlled much of the Chinese territories. In an effort to integrate the economies of their territories they made determined investments in public works, in particular the building of canals and roads. Their engineering achievements can be seen in the segmental stone-arch bridge they built over the Jiao River near Zhaozhou on the main north-south trade route. The Jiao River was more than 40 meters wide at this point. The steep approaches of their older semicircular bridges were impractical for wheeled vehicles, while their post-and-lintel technology was not sufficiently advanced. The problem of sinking multiple stone piers into the swift flowing river made a multiple arched structure impractical. Li Chun, the engineer of the bridge, constructed the Zhaozhou Bridge using a series of 28 adjacent arcs, each containing 43 wedge-shaped stone voussoirs, tied together with nine reinforcing iron rods, welded with a cap to pull the stones together. In addition, he countersunk dovetail-shaped iron keys into the outer voussoirs, along with a thin stone course at right angles to the sides of the arches. To enhance stability the bridge has a slight camber so that the thrust falls toward the center, and six of the exterior stones were cut to allow them to overhang, forming hooks to prevent the voussoirs from falling outward.

In the next four centuries the T'ang engineers constructed bridges using not only the segmental arch and open spandrel construction but also arched, suspension, and cantilever technology. Most of their inhabitable structures, however, were made of wood, which have largely perished. Some, however, survived in the literary record. The Yongning Monastery Pagoda (built 516 CE, burnt 534 CE) was well celebrated and carefully described. Part of a larger complex, this nine-story structure, 161 meters tall and 46 meters wide, was raised on a 2.2 meter base made of pounded earth. It had a solid central core made from timber posts with earthen infill. It had nine bays on each side and a high gilded finial. Like surviving Japanese Buddhist pagodas, it had a square plan and gently tapered toward the top, although most of its decorative elements, like ogee-arched windows, were probably based on Indian models.

### Daming Palace

Though the Sui and T'ang emperors were generous patrons of Buddhism, their own authority continued to derive from the Confucian ordering of the world as had been established during the Han dynasty. Spatially the authority of the emperor was of course represented by the palace, constructed axially at the head of the city. In the long reign of Gao Zong (650–683 CE), however, the power of the emperor was further magnified with the creation of another palace beyond the boundaries of the city. The Daminggong, the Palace of Great Light (*gong* means palace), is in its own special compound covering three square kilometers. It was organized axially in a series of interconnected courts, forming a four-part complex:

1. Entry square about 500 meters square
2. Hanyuan Hall (Hanyuandian) in front (south side) of the entry square
3. Xuanzheng Hall at the back (north side) of the square
4. Northern third containing the emperor's court, reception areas, residences, gardens, and temples.

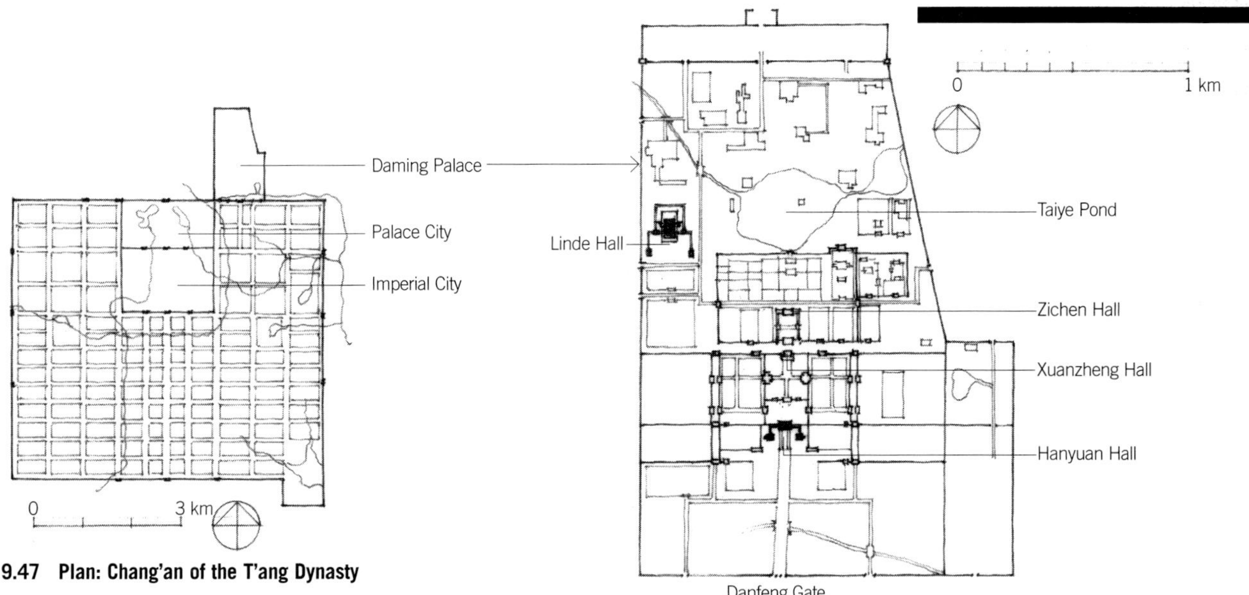


**9.47 Plan: Chang'an of the T'ang Dynasty**

First in Daminggong's axial sequence was the Hanyuandian, or the Enfolding Vitality Hall, the main gate where imperial rites were performed. This huge, imposing gate faced a gigantic square, where ceremonies with a large number of participants and spectators were held. Fifty-eight meters wide, the Hanyuandian, quite large in itself, was staged by a long cascading stair in its forecourt that exaggerated the lead-up to it. This stair, called the Dragon-Tail Way, was a classic example of the horizontal elongation of space, a hallmark of Chinese palace design. The Hanyuandian's 11 by 4-bay structure supported a double-hipped roof. It was flanked by high pavilions on either side that were raised, on their own bases, higher than the main hall.

Three-hundred meters beyond Hanyuandian was the Xuanzheng (political) Hall, from whose sides extended the wall defining the inner perimeter of the palace complex. Here, the emperor held court on the first and fifteenth day of each lunar month. Beyond its arcades lay all the main offices of the imperial bureaucracy. Two purple palace gates led to the internal compound of the palace complex, which consisted of a series of pavilions strung together by rectilinear arcades. Beyond the palace complex lay the Taiye Pond and a large open area with occasional pavilions and compounds, which can be thought of as the garden complex.

West of the main palace area was the Linde Hall (Unicorn Virtue Hall), which was used for "banquets and less formal receptions." The hall consisted of three interconnected structures that abut one another on their long sides to form a larger complex that is 58.2 meters wide and 86 meters deep, accompanied by a panoply of surrounding arcades and pavilions. Literary sources record that theatrical performances were held in the arcades, and polo matches took place in front of the first hall.

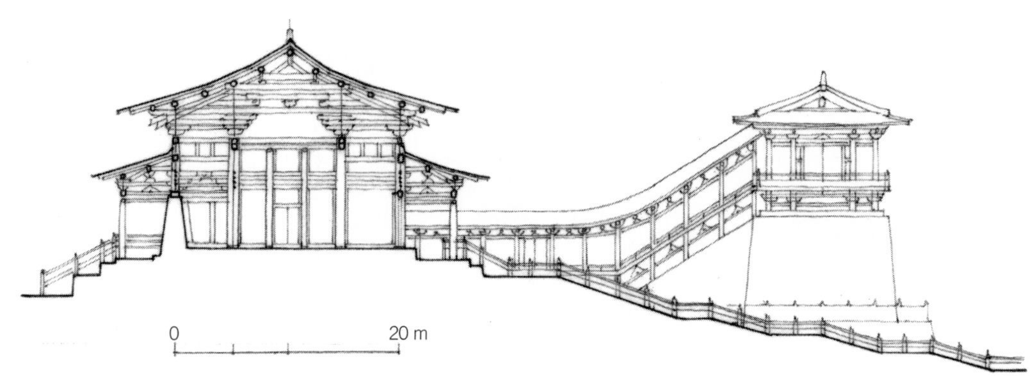


**9.48 North-south section: Hanyuan Hall, Chang'an (Xian), China**

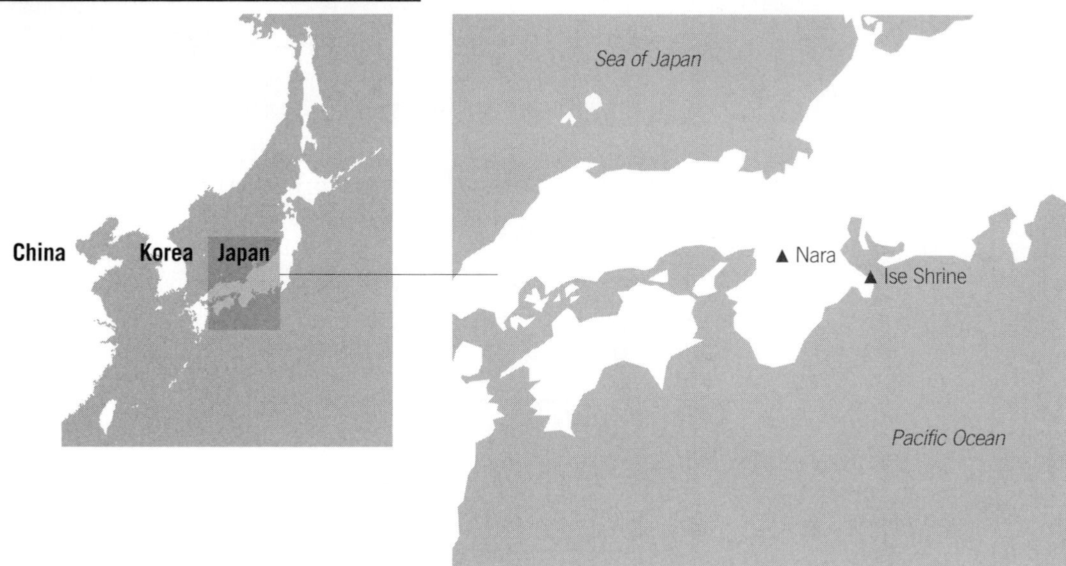


## NARA PERIOD: JAPAN

By the 8th century CE the various clans of Japan had cohered into a single political unit under an emperor, with the northern islands the last to be brought into this unity. Rice was the principle commodity. Japan's native religion at the time was Shintoism, a form of animism in which every aspect of nature was revered. There were no creeds or images of gods, but rather a host of *kami* (an honorific for noble, sacred spirits). *Kami* were both deities and the numinous quality perceived in objects of nature, such as trees, rocks, waters, and mountains. The *kami* that are still venerated at more than 100,000 Shinto shrines throughout Japan are considered to be creative and harmonizing forces in nature. Humans were seen not as owners of nature, or above and separate from it, but as integral participants in it and indeed derived from it. The Buddha was received as a great *kami*, but a *kami* could also be attributed to the spirits of deceased emperors, heroes, and famous persons. In the 6th century, the emperor came to be deified as a living *kami*, and his divinity surpassed that of other *kami*.

*Kami* receive tribute at shrines in the form of food offerings, music, dance, and the performance of traditional skills such as archery and sumo wrestling. Ceremonial purity is strongly encouraged and bodily cleanliness is an absolute necessity. In its most elemental architectural form, a shrine would be a simple unadorned structure in which the *kami* were thought to dwell. Before the shrine stands a detached portal, known as a *torii*. Only priests could approach the *kami* during special rites in which they acted as mediators between human beings and the *kami* world. The earliest Shinto sanctuaries were simple piles of boulders or stones that marked the sacred dwelling place of the deity and the place were the kami were thought to dwell.

### Ise Jingu

The unification of Shinto's animism with the spirit of the emperor set the stage for a remarkable building that still exists to this day, the Ise Jingu (Shrine), dedicated to the tutelary *kami* of the Japanese imperial family. It has no parallel in the entire history of global architecture. Every 20 years for the last 1500 years, the shrine has been rebuilt, identical to the one before, but with virgin old-growth timber. The Ise Shrine that stands in Japan today was built in 1993. In a sense, it is therefore only 18 odd years old. Yet, at the same time, it can be dated to the year 500 CE. The sacred necklace of *magatama* (jewels representing the soul spirit, which enter the body of the possessor) is the symbol of succession from the Sun Goddess and is the emblem of the emperors of Japan even today. This necklace is kept at Ise. As such, Ise Jingu is Japan's most deeply revered shrine.

**9.49 South gateway to the Ise Inner Shrine**

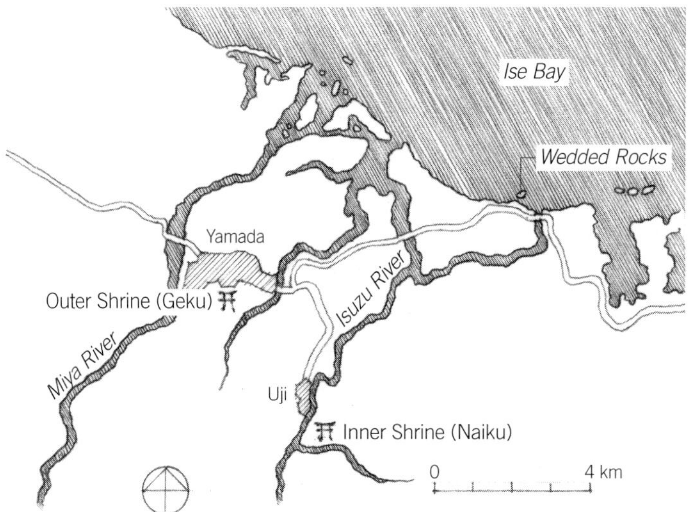


**9.50 Location Map: Ise Shrine, Japan**

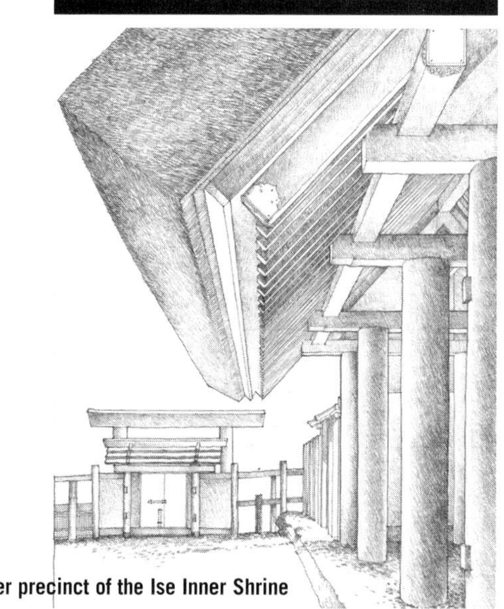

**9.51 Inner precinct of the Ise Inner Shrine**

Set deep in a forest, the Ise Shrine is a huge complex that actually consists of two shrines—the Inner Shrine (Naiku) and the Outer Shrine (Geku)—and a wide array of lesser sanctuaries distributed around a narrow, verdant coastal plain on the east coast of the Kii Peninsula in southern Honshu.The area, relatively warm even in the winter, is crossed by the fast-flowing Isuzu River. Naiku is dedicated to Amaterasu Omikami (Heaven-Illuminating Great Kami), the traditional ancestral deity of the imperial house, and Geku is dedicated to Touke Okami (Abundant Food Great Kami). Originally unconnected, the two were joined into an institutional unit in the 9th century. The Ise complex additionally houses about 120 separate shrines, including a number of tiny sanctuaries dedicated to the spirit of a single rock or the deity of some bubbling spring as per Shinto practices.

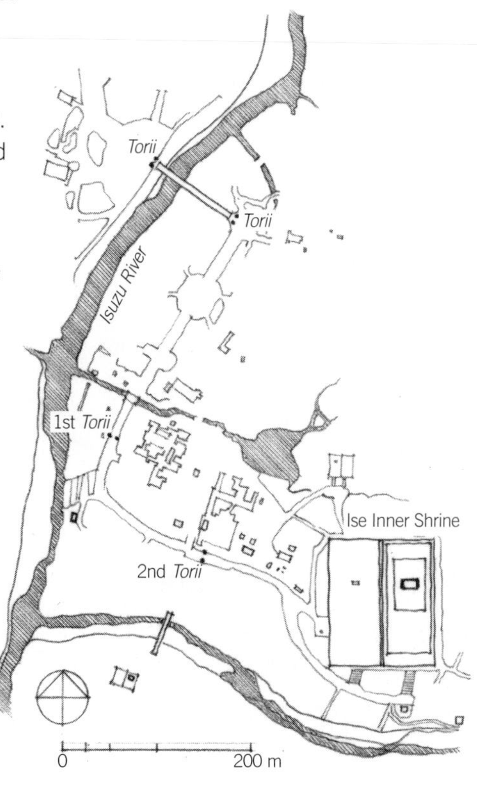


**9.52 Area Plan: Ise Inner Shrine**

The path to the Naiku is carefully scripted, marked today by a series of *torii* (derived from the Sanskrit *torana* for gate). One accesses the Naiku precinct by crossing the Uji Bridge, which is constructed from fragrant cypress wood, over the Isuzu River. At each end of the bridge is a freestanding *torii,* a symbol marking the presence of a sacred shrine. From the bridge, the pilgrim proceeds to the right along a broad street covered with gravel and flanked by carefully tended gardens. At its end is another *torii,* and after that there is a large stone basin with water for purification rituals. Then the path turns east and rises up the gentle slope through another *torii,* this time surrounded by tall cedars and zelkova elms, creating the sense of entering a dense forest. Moss covers the ancient rocks along the path. Finally, the path curves to approach the Naiku shrine from the south. The final approach is made by way of 21 stone steps that lead to the *torii* of the outermost fence. A fine silk curtain hanging across the entrance is all that marks the beginning of the prohibited zone. The innermost shrines are open only to the temple priests or the imperial family, and even then only in a highly regulated and hierarchical fashion. Only the reigning emperor has access to the innermost shrine, the Shoden, and the rest of the family's distance from the Shoden is a measure of their distance from the throne. Everyone else worships from the outside.

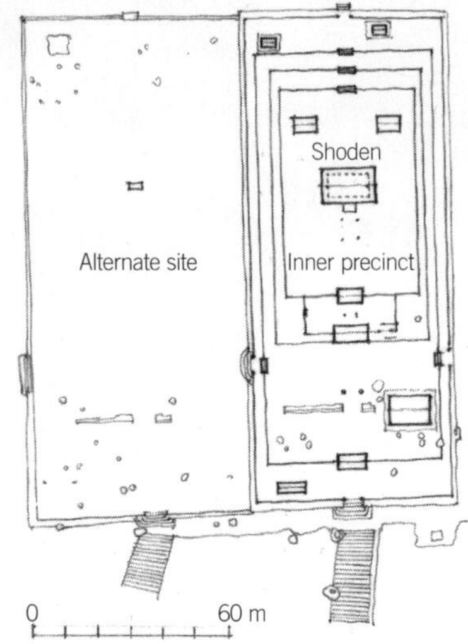


**9.53 Plan: Ise Inner Shrine**

0
10 m

**9.54 Elevations: Shoden, Ise Inner Shrine**

The Naiku contains three structures organized axially—the central shrine, the Shoden, and behind it on either side the two treasuries. The 15-meter-by-10-meter Shoden sets the tone for the entire shrine. Raised off the ground by columns set directly into the ground (without a foundation), the Shoden is a meticulously crafted and ornamented wooden structure, three bays wide and two bays deep, built entirely without nails. It has a deeply thatched reed roof and entrance on its long side that is accessible by an externally placed flight of stairs.

Straight, squared timbers are used for the rafters, which descend sharply from the ridgepole. The side gable ends have no opening. At the middle of each gable end stands a solitary pillar, free of the wall, that supports the ridgepole.

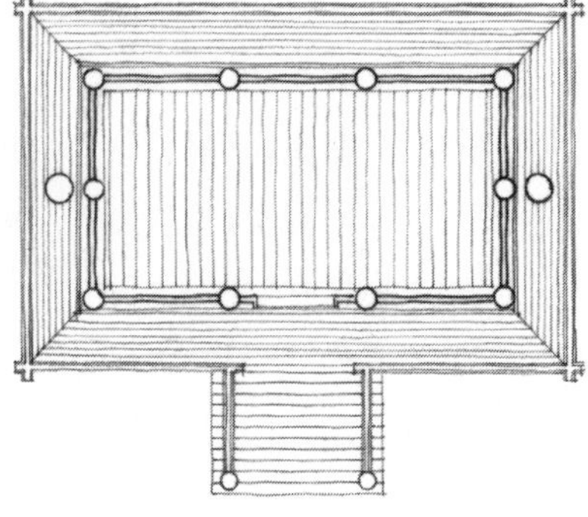

**9.55 Plan: Shoden, Ise Inner Shrine**

The ritual process of rebuilding the Ise every 20 years is known as *shikinen sengu* ("the transfer of the god-body to a new shrine in a special festival year"). The reconstruction alternates between two adjacent sites. While one site is in use, the other is thus always empty, covered by white gravel. When the floor of the previous Shoden is relocated, a small wooden pillar, known as the Shin no Mihashira, or "heart pillar," is left buried in the old shrine compound and a small shed, the *oi-ya*, is built over it to protect it from the elements.

There could be several possible explanations for the *shikinen sengu* ritual. The most prosaic is the need for periodic maintenance of buildings made with highly perishable materials. The idea of renewal might also be tied to Shinto beliefs, and may be described as the desire to show reverence to the great *kami* by revitalizing its earthly residence. In a metaphysical sense, a belief in the transience of material objects as opposed to the permanence of form, a metonym for the nature of the *kami*, is ritually enacted. But most fundamentally, perhaps, the rebuilding renews the social contract with the imperial family, the core of whose legitimacy lies in the long line of its unbroken ancestry.

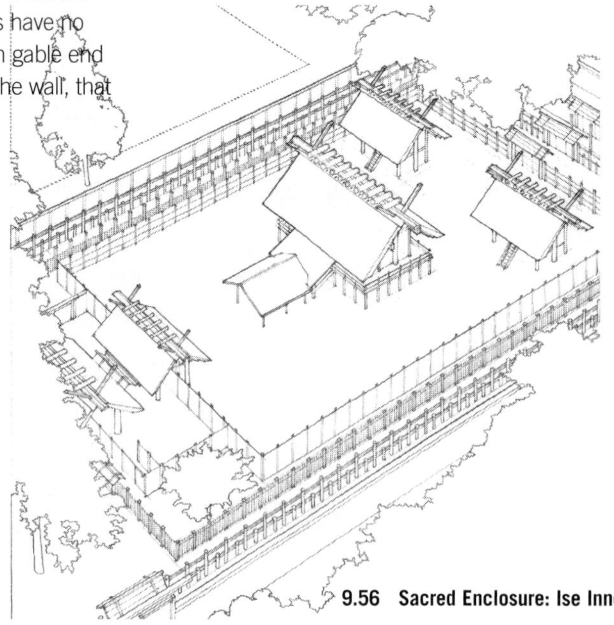

**9.56 Sacred Enclosure: Ise Inner Shrine**

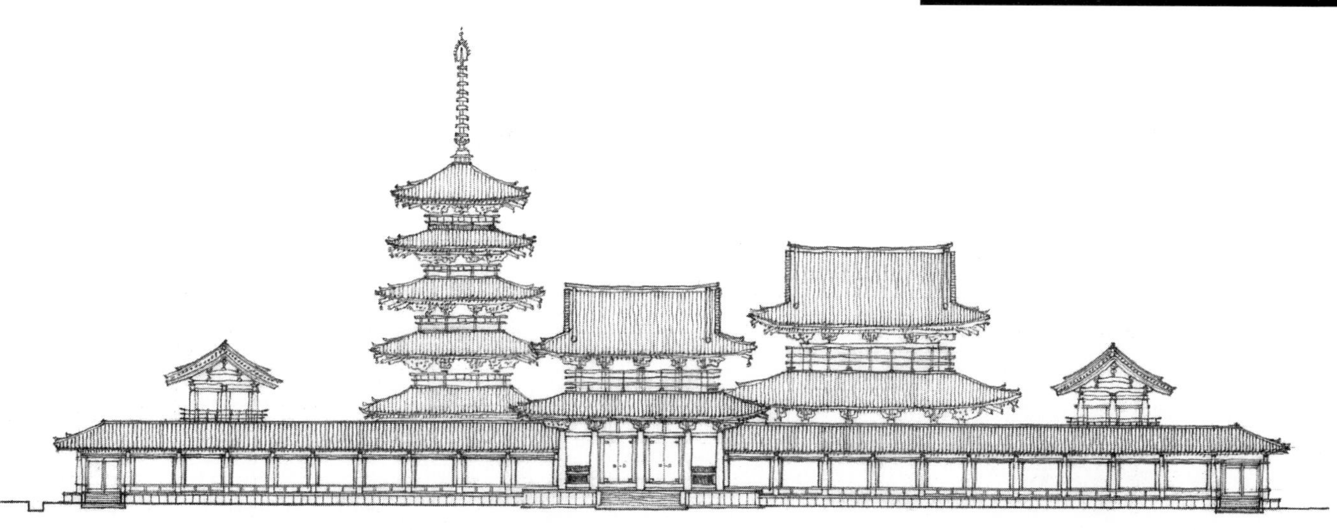

9.57 **Elevation: West Precinct of Horyu-ji Temple, Nara, Japan**

**Buddhism's Arrival in Japan**

From Korea, Buddhism first crossed into Japan round 552 CE, in the reign of the Emperor Kimmei (509–571 CE). Along with their teachings, the Koreans brought with them their architecture, which defined the early period of Japanese Buddhist architecture. These complexes, like those in China and India, functioned as places where monks lived, underwent religious training, and studied sutras. The earliest Buddhist temples of Japan, such as the Monastery at Shitennoji (593 CE), were derived from traditional Korean temple plans with the pagoda and the main hall aligned on axis with the entrance or middle gate. At the Hwangnyongsa Temple in Korea, it is rigorously symmetrical and organized with great precision. There are seven basic elements known as the Shichido Garan. These were: (1) the pagoda (*to*); (2) the main or golden hall (*kondo*); (3) the lecture hall (*kodo*); (4) the bell tower (*shoro* or *shuro*); (5) the sutra repository (*kyozo*); (6) the dormitory (*sobo*); and (7) the dining hall (*jikido*).

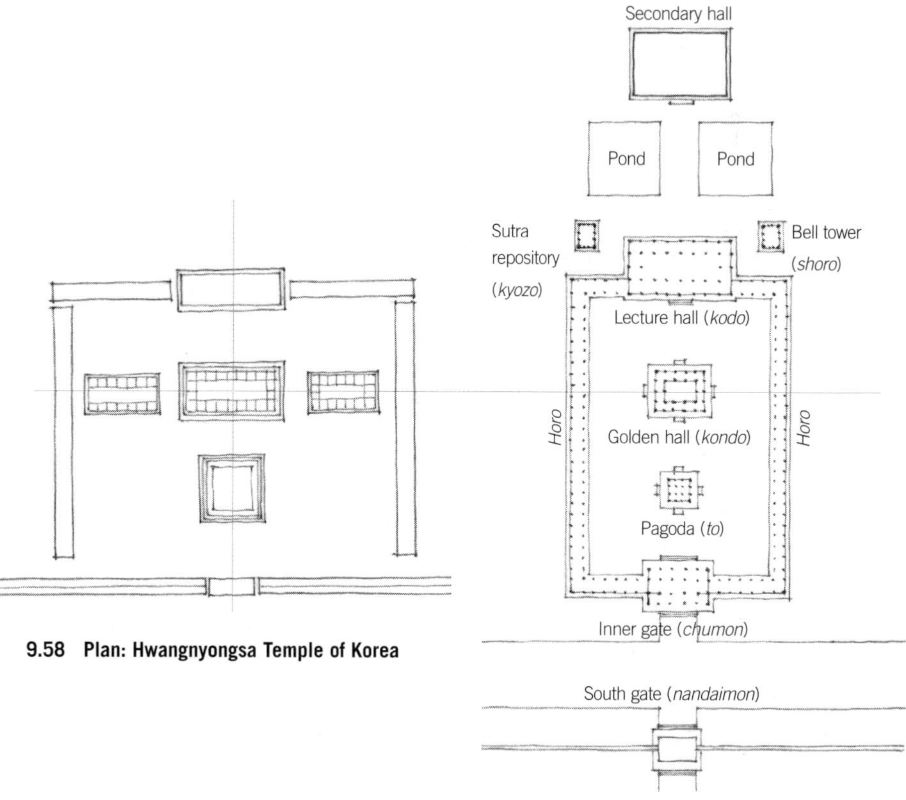


9.58 **Plan: Hwangnyongsa Temple of Korea**

9.59 **Plan: Early Buddhist monastery at Shitennoji, Osaka, Japan**

9.60 Courtyard of West Precinct: Horyu-ji Temple

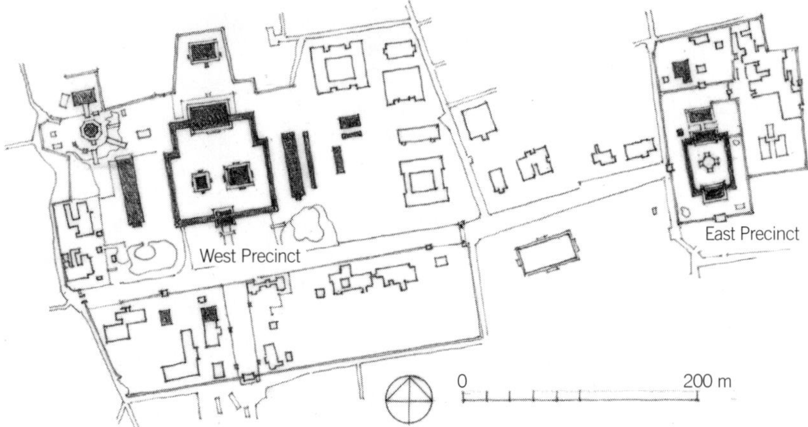


9.61 Plan of the Horyu-ji Temple Complex

**Horyu-ji**

Following the so-called Taika reform (645–9 CE), the Japanese royalty, came to prefer the Chinese rather than the Korean precedents and adopted a degree of flexibility. When Horyu-ji (*ji* means temple) at Nara was built late in the 7th century, the Golden Hall and the pagoda were aligned along the east-west axis and bisected by the axis of the Inner Gate. The tall pagoda was balanced by the width of the Golden Hall. The cloister was wide enough to give both sufficient breathing room. The eastern wing of the precinct has one extra bay to accommodate the width of the Golden Hall, which lies at the center of the composition. Instead of an insistent axiality, with the largest pagoda in front dominating the others, the new plan produced a spatially dynamic situation since both buildings, which are unequal in size and form, simultaneously come into view on entrance and have to be balanced for proper effect. This also created the situation of a dynamic balance between the verticality of the structures and general horizontality of the forms. Inside the Golden Hall is the triad of the Buddha Sakyamuni with two attending bodhisattvas made by the celebrated sculptor Kuratsukuri no Tori in 623 CE to commemorate the death of Prince Shotoku. The Four Heavenly Kings were made around 650 CE by the sculptor Yamaguchi no Atai Oguchi.

The five-by-four-bay proportions of the Hall make it appear almost square. It is a two-story structure with two deep, overhanging eaves, upturned at the ends, complemented by a later-built shallow porch eave on the lower level. It sits on a low base, with small stairs on all four axes and a hipped gable roof marking the crest. Like in Greek architecture and in most contemporary wooden temples, the columns at Horyu-ji display entasis and have their greatest dimension in the middle and the smallest at the top. The Middle Gate roughly repeats the organizational scheme of the Golden Hall, but on a simpler scale. It is four bays wide and three bays deep, and because it has a row of columns down the center, one enters the complex slightly off axis.

The five-story pagoda is based on the three-bayed square module. In the center is the ceremonial axis-mundi column, which is presumed to be spliced somewhere in the middle. Each succeeding story recedes as it rises and culminates in the tall finialtower with the traditional arrangement consisting of upside-down bowl and lotus flower, preceding the seven *chattris* of the upper worlds, and finishing with water-fire and illumination finials. The original precinct was expanded by extending the northern end of the enclosure to include a Lecture Hall (*kodo*) in the early 8th century.

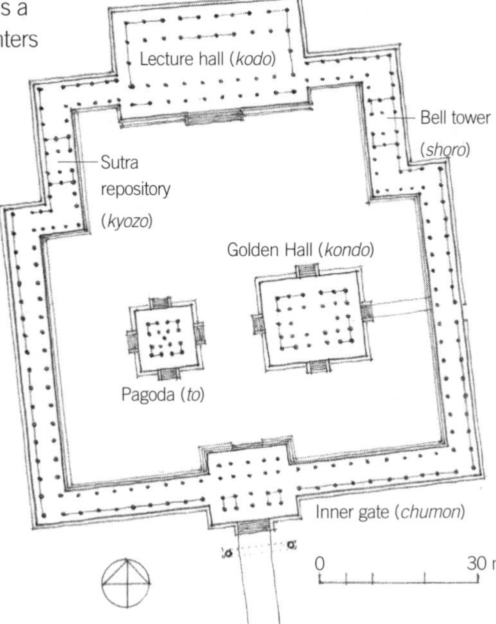


9.62 Plan: West Precinct of Horyu-ji Temple

# 800 CE

In 800 CE, China's T'ang Dynasty (618–906 CE) was unquestionably the principal superpower in the world. Only a couple of monastic halls with wood architecture survive, but just the map of Chang'an tells us of their building capacities. At the terminus of the Eurasian silk route, Chang'an was not only an economic hub but home to a wide array of religious and intellectual persuasions.

Meanwhile South Asia, distributed across several kingdoms, was a hotbed of intellectual and religious activity. The Hindu kingdoms built a diverse array of rock-cut, stone, and brick temples. Simultaneously they continued their patronage of Buddhist monasteries that matured into universities of international repute. Monks from China, Sri Lanka, Japan, Southeast Asia, and Indonesia came to study at Nalanda, Paharpur, and Amravati.

South Asian traders plying the sea routes along the Andaman coast took their Hindu and Buddhist concepts to Southeast Asia. There, one of the most advanced Asian civilizations of the time, at least architecturally, arose in Indonesia at the intersections of the Chinese and Indian trade routes. The Buddhist Shailendra kings of 9th-century Indonesia built Buddhist and subsequently Hindu stone temples of extraordinary achievement. In the short space of 100 years, they built not only one of the finest Buddhist stupa shrines ever, Borobodur, but also one of the largest and most complex Hindu temples of the time.

In Cambodia, Jayavarman III established a new Hindu kingdom in 802 CE and built a capital called Hariharalaya on the flood plain of the Tonle Sap lake. This became the foundation of 600 years of occupation of Cambodia by the Khmer kings, built upon advances in irrigation technology. The Khmer built a hybrid civilization, with their mythology coming from India, but their forms from Indonesia.

Islam was spreading on the backs of highly skilled armies, moving rapidly into West Asia, North Africa, and finally to Spain, where a kingdom of great splendor and learning was created. Its principal architectural form was the mosque, which in the early days of the religion was a simple hypostyle hall oriented toward Mecca. But buildings meant to compete with the Byzantine's were also constructed, such as the impressive Dome of the Rock in Jerusalem. The Umayyad caliphs, in Spain, made Córdoba its capital and erected a splendid mosque there. In 750 CE the Abbasid dynasty that replaced the Umayyad founded a new capital, Baghdad, making it one of the great urban foundings of the age.

In Europe, Charlemagne was crowned Holy Roman Emperor (800 CE). The architectural accomplishments in comparison to other places in the world were, however, slight, as technology and the philosophical arts were in serious decline. Nonetheless, Charlemagne, eager to assume the legacy of the Roman Empire, set out to copy Roman architecture, leading to a style known as Romanesque, which would become the foundation for architectural developments for centuries to come. Just as important was the creation throughout Europe of a loose network of monasteries associated with feudal rulers that became an important imprint of power from Germany to Italy. The only religion without geographical claims was Judaism, but it had learned to incorporate itself into the world of other cultures, with communities in Cairo, Damascus, and all along the Mediterranean playing important roles in facilitating trade and commerce.

All in all, in the 9th and 10th centuries, the Eurasian map started to foreshadow the modern world with distinct kingdoms stretching continuously from the Pacific to the Atlantic, linked by trade routes. This was also a period of urban innovation: Hariharalaya was the new capital of the Khmer, Baghdad the new capital of the Islamic Abbasids, Córdoba the new center in Spain, and Aachen the new center of the Holy Roman Empire. And of course Chang'an was the largest city in the world.

In America, a new generation of Mayan city-states had arisen in Guatemala, Honduras, and El Salvador starting around 250 CE. The impact of Central America's civilizations continued to be felt in its outermost reaches with the establishment of cities like Pueblo Bonito by the so-called Anasazi of North America.

Period of Northern and Southern Dynasties
386–589 CE

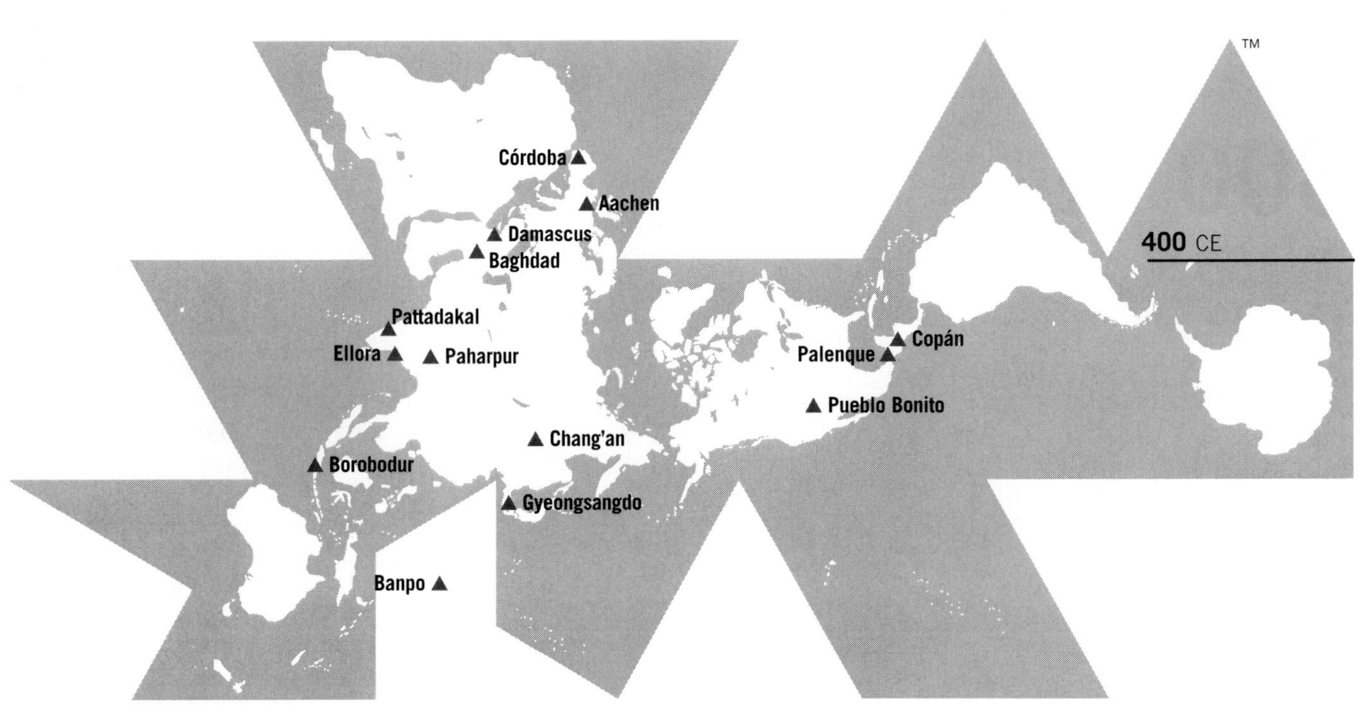


Pre-Pueblo Cultures
ca. 1000 BCE–700 CE

▲ **Quirigua**
2nd–10th centuries

T'ang Dynasty
618–907 CE

▲ **Chang'an: The T'ang Capital**
581–906 CE

▲ **Nanchan Temple**
782 CE

▲ **Foguang Temple**
857 CE

Silla Dynasty
668–935 CE

▲ **Buseoksa Temple**
676–1000 CE

South Asia: Pallava Dynasty
to 740 CE

Chola Dynasty
ca. 860–1279

▲ **Kailasnath at Ellora**
600–1000 CE

▲ **Virupaksha Temple**
733–44 CE

**Sumstek Gompa** ►
11th–13th century

▲ **Mahavihara of Nalanda**
6th–7th century

▲ **Rajasimhesvara Temple**
early 8th century CE

▲ **Somapura Vihara**
7th century CE

**600** CE — **800** CE — **1000** CE

Pre-Angkor Period in Cambodia
ca. 550–802 CE

Angkor Period in Cambodia
802–1431 CE

▲ **Candi Prambanam**
835–856 CE

▲ **Phnom Bakheng**
ca. 900–921 CE

▲ **Borobodur**
842 CE

Umayyad Rule
651–750 CE

Abbasid Caliphate
750–1258 CE

▲ **Dome of the Rock**
632–691 CE

▲ **City of Baghdad**
ca. 762 CE, capital of Abbasid Caliphate

▲ **Great Mosque of Samarra**
852 CE

▲ **Umayyad Mosque**
709–15 CE

▲ **Great Mosque of Córdoba**
787 CE

Merovingian Dynasty in Central Europe
482–751 CE

Carolingian Dynasty
751–911 CE

Holy Roman Empire
962–1806 CE

▲ **Abbey of Fulda**
790 CE

▲ **St. Gall**
816–836 CE

**Abbey Church of St. Riquier** ▲
Completed 799 CE

▲ **Palatine Chapel**
792–805 CE

Byzantine Empire
330–1453 CE

▲ **Theotokos Tou Libos**
10th century

▲ **Germingny-des-Prés**
806–811 CE

▲ **Koimesis in Nicaea**
9th century

Maya: Dynastic City-States
ca. 250–900 CE

▲ **Palenque**
ca. 600–800 CE

▲ **Copán**
ca. 600–900 CE

Pueblo Cultures
ca. 700–1600

▲ **Pueblo Bonito**
Begun 920

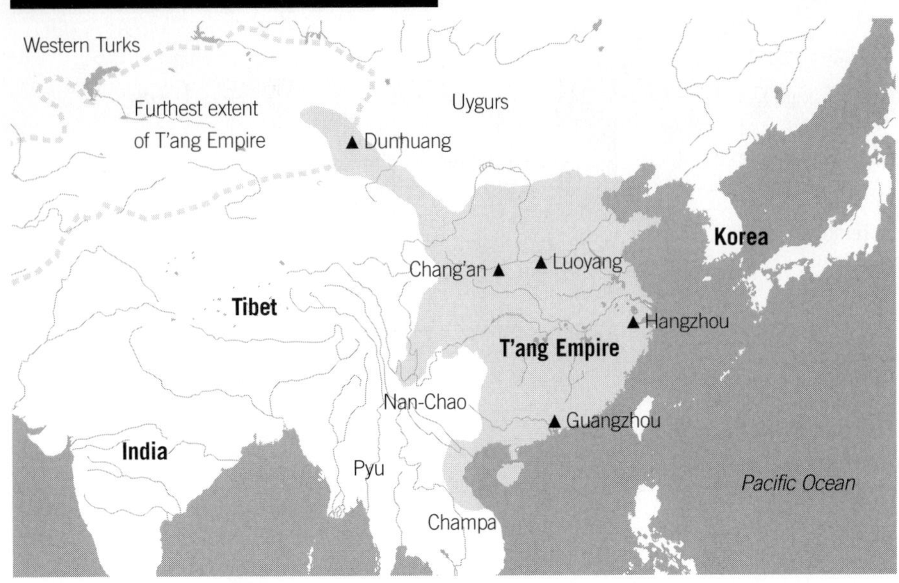


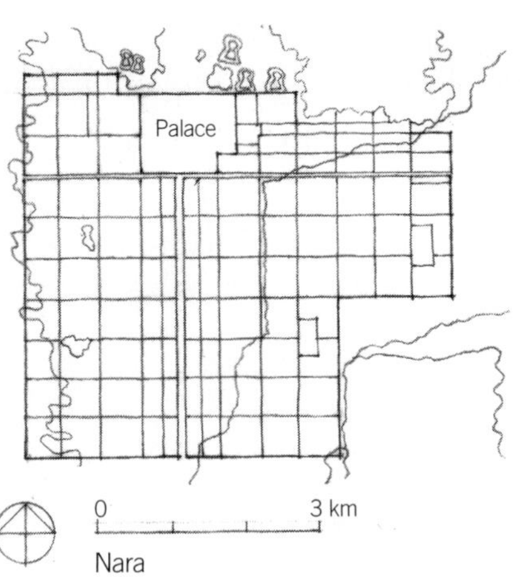


**10.1 Plan grid of Heijo-Kyo (Nara), Japan**

## CHANG'AN, THE T'ANG CAPITOL

Located at the terminus of the Silk Route, Chang'an (Forever Peace) was first established by the Han Dynasty in 200 BCE, when they moved their capital west from Luoyang. But in 24 CE, in the middle of the Han reign, Chang'an was looted and burned. It was reduced to a provincial city, and Luoyang was reestablished as the Han capital. In the 4th century, Chang'an experienced a revival not as a political capital but as a center of Buddhist learning. Late in the 6th century, the first emperor of the Sui dynasty, Emperor Wen, reestablished Chang'an as an imperial capital. The Sui rebuilt the city a few miles south of the old Han city and called it Daxing (Great Prosper). This was the city that, under the T'ang, was to become famous as China's *urb primus* of the first millennium, its commercial, intellectual, and political capital and the Eurasian destination of the Silk Route. Trade, not only external but internal, boomed under the T'ang. They connected all their major cities by road and canals. Chang'an, Luoyang, Yangzhou, Chengdu, Guangzhou, Youzhou, Bianzhou (now Kaifeng), and Mingzhou (now Ningbo) were all part of the network. Guangzhou and Mingzhou were foreign trade ports. An ancient form of bill of exchange, known as *fei qian* (flying money), was introduced by the T'ang. Merchants who sold their goods in Chang'an could get *fei qian* drafts with which they could draw money in other places.

In 750 CE, Chang'an, with a million residents, was a veritable cosmopolis. A stela inscribed in 781 CE documents the introduction of Nestorian Christianity by Syrian priests in 635 CE. The last of the Sassanian princes, Firuz, found refuge here around 670 CE. Manichaeism came with the Persians fleeing Islam around 694 CE. Predominantly, however, T'ang Chang'an remained a place of Confucian and Buddhist advancement. Thousands of Buddhist scholars and pilgrims, such as Faxian, came to live in Chang'an's hundreds of Buddhist monasteries. In 840 CE, the Japanese pilgrim Enin found monks from South and North India, Ceylon, Kucha (from the Tarim Basin), Korea, and Japan, as well as the Chinese monks, building pagodas, temples, and monasteries. Hsuan Tsang's Wild Goose Pagoda was constructed to hold all his manuscripts in the 7th century. Enin also noted that the city's prized relics were four teeth of the Buddha, three of them from India, Khotan, and Tibet, and the fourth, reputedly, from heaven. On major festivals to honor the dental relics, each monastery turned out with offerings such as medicines and foods, rare fruits and flowers, and all kinds of incenses. Individual donations were also commonplace. One man donated one hundred bushels of nonglutinous rice and twenty bushels of millet. Another man provided biscuits. Another donated enough cash for the meals.

Chang'an was the primary model in the history of city planning, not only for the development of later Chinese capitals, like Beijing during the Ming and Qing dynasties, but also for the major capital cities of Korea and Japan, such as Nara and Kyoto. Chang'an went into decline in the middle of the 9th century after a series of rebellions resulted in officially sanctioned persecution of its population, particularly the Buddhist. The city lost its primacy after the collapse of the T'ang dynasty in 906 CE.

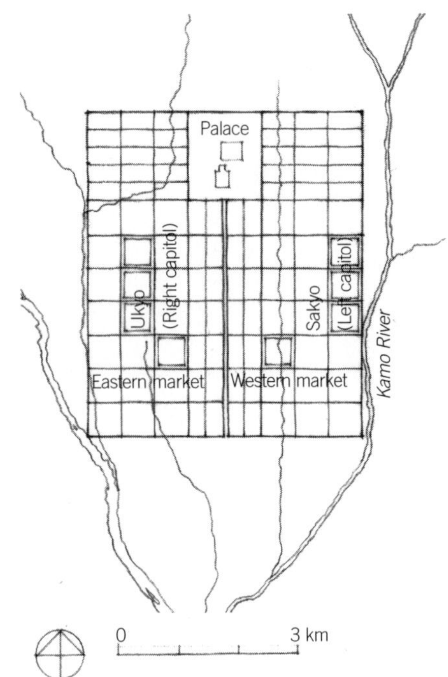


**10.2 Plan grid of Heian-Kyo (Kyoto), Japan**

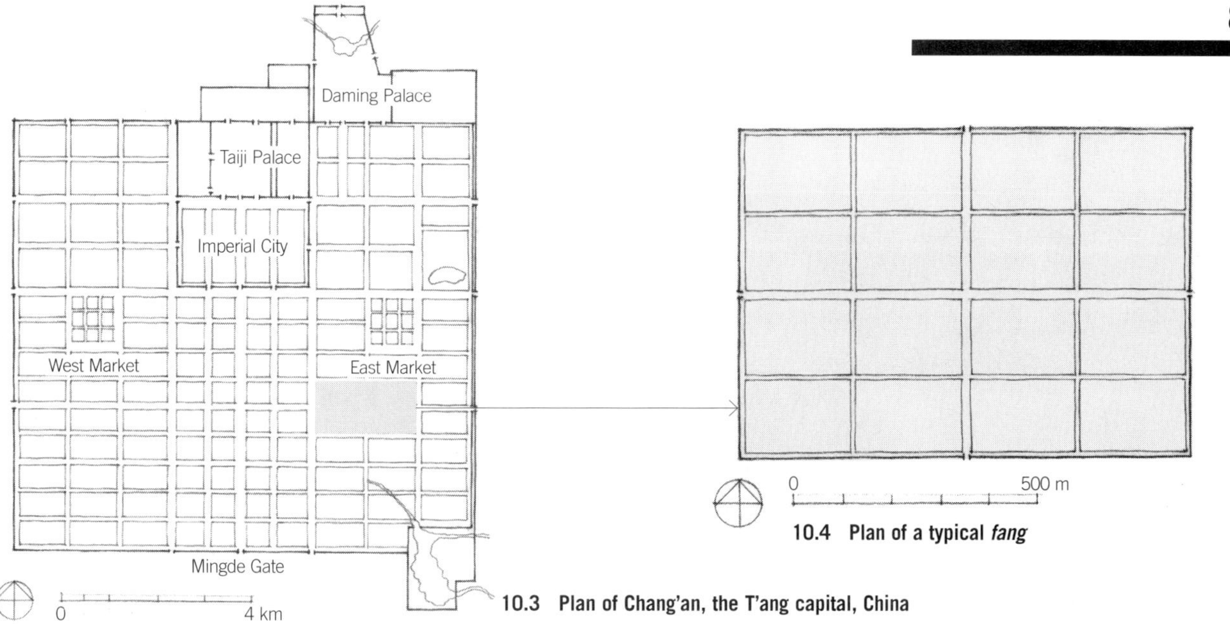


10.3 Plan of Chang'an, the T'ang capital, China

10.4 Plan of a typical *fang*

The construction of Chang'an was overseen by the Sui imperial engineer and planner Yuwen Kai (555–612 CE). Kai had also earlier engineered the Grand Canal in 605–606 CE on the orders of the Sui emperor Yang Di (r. 604–617 CE) to transport grain from the alluvian southern plains to the relatively impoverished (but militarily strong) north. Although overscaled to match its imperial ambitions, Chang'an's master plan was based on Zhou period descriptions of the Wangcheng ideal city (see section on 800 BCE). The Sui interest in Wangcheng was part of the interest in a modernized renaissance of older Chinese ideals, in particular Confucian ideal, intended in part as a foil against the rising tide of Buddhist practices. Some 8.65 kilometers by 9.72 kilometers in size, its outer walls were punctured by three gates on each of the western, southern and eastern walls. Mingde, the central southern gate, was its main entrance. The city gates opened onto monumental streets, the largest of which was 220 meters wide (from the Mingde gate) and the rest about 140 meters each. Four canals distributed water to the city.

The city's module was based on the dimensions of the imperial palace. The Taiji Palace (the palaces and halls for imperial meetings) was located at the north end of the central north-south axis, occupying no less than five percent of the entire city. Just south of it was the Imperial City (offices of the government and national ceremonial halls).

The rest of the city was divided by east-west and north-south avenues into 108 neighborhood blocks called *fangs*. In spite of its population, the colossal spread of the city ensured that the density of the *fangs* was not very high, especially as compared to Teotihuacán and Rome at their heights. The *fangs* contained all of the temples, commercial buildings, public parks, and housing. Each *fang* was its own minicity, with its own inner transportation network, walls, gates, and corner towers. There were two major commercial areas in the Outer City called the West Market and East Market, each occupying two *fangs*. These markets were the subject of many literary descriptions, many devoted to the global range of goods that were available in them. The areas around Qujian Lake and the Xingqing *fang* were famous scenic districts.

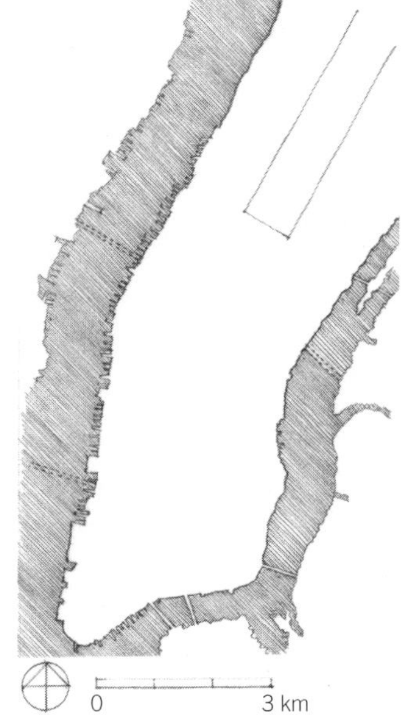


10.5 Outline plan of Manhattan, New York City, drawn at the same scale as 8th century Chang'an (shown above)

10.6 Main Hall, Nanchan Temple, Wutaishan, Shanxi Province, China

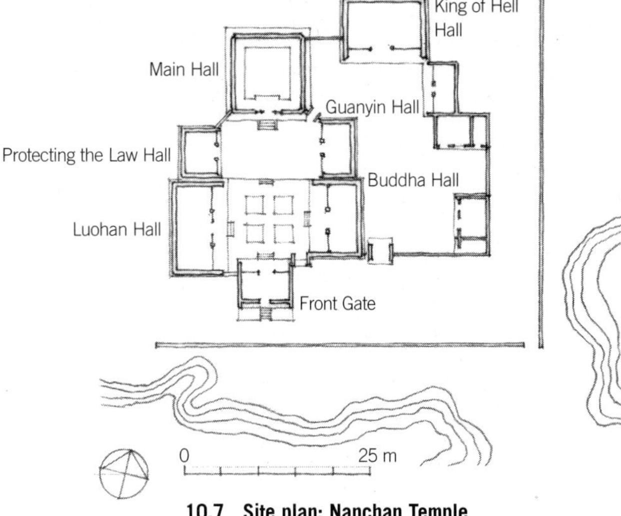


10.7 Site plan: Nanchan Temple

**Nanchan and Foguang Monasteries**

Of the thousands of wooden monasteries built during the Sui and T'ang period, the Nanchan and Foguang monasteries, located far north of the capital on Wutai Mountain in Shanxi Province, are two of the few to have survived into our time. They also show the sinification of Buddhist architecture. The older Nanchan Temple is a relatively modest structure from the T'ang period that was rebuilt in its present form in 782 CE. Its Main Hall is dedicated to the bodhisattva Manjusri. Manjusri, which means "Gentle Glory" or "Sweet Splendor," was a semimythical figure who was seen as the personification of Transcendent Wisdom. According to tradition, Manjusri was born without a father and mother and was thus free from the pollution of the common world. The word bodhisattva means "enlightenment being."

The Foguang Temple (857 CE) was a more ambitious construction. Unlike the three-bayed hall of Nanchang, with its simple hip-and-gable style (*xieshan*) roof, the Foguang Hall is seven-by-four bayed and has a roof format that was known as the first-class hip style. The columns divide the hall into an inner *cao* (space), and an outer *cao*.

As was with the transformation of the stupa to a *ta* (pagoda), the Chinese also transformed the monastery format; in this case it clearly derived from the palatial architecture of the time. The courtyards were named after their principal buildings, for example, the pagoda courtyard, the *chan* (meditation) courtyard, *vanaya* (discipline) courtyard, *purea* (land) courtyard, etc. The overall styles of Nanchan and Foguang temples, however, are very similar, with low-pitch roof slopes, deep eaves, and dominating brackets.

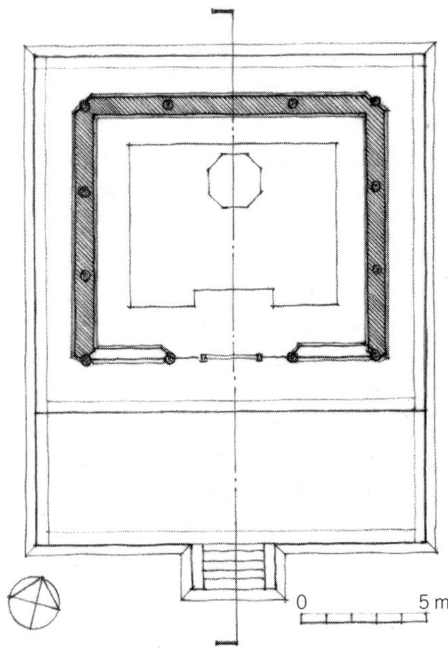


10.8 Plan of Main Hall: Nanchan Temple

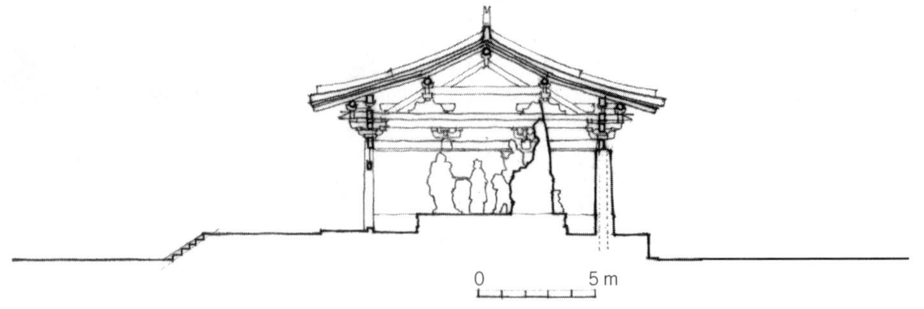


10.9 Transverse section of Main Hall: Nanchan Temple

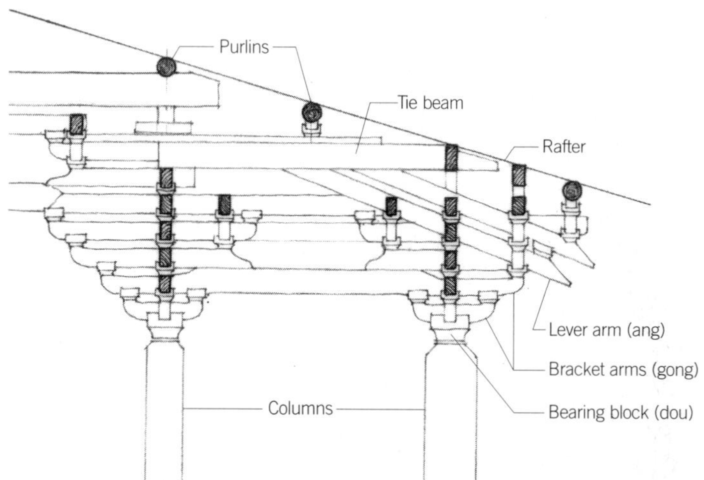

**10.10 Detail of bracket system: Main Hall, Foguang Temple**

**10.11 Main Hall, Foguang Temple, Wutaishan, Shanxi Province, China**

Chinese wood roofs are described on the basis of the number and types of bracket-sets and beams deployed. While bracket-sets are a complex addition to the number of horizontal and vertical (and diagonal) composite elements called *dou-gong*, the beams are designated by their position and the number of rafters they span. *Dou-gong* bracket sets differ in size and number, depending on their position, location, size of roof, and stature of the building. Bracket sets of this complexity never developed in India, Mesopotamia, or areas to the west where walls played a more important role in the structural stability and expression of a building. In the west, wood beams needed to be attached with skill, but architects did not need to have to worry about a building twisting, which is a common problem with structures set up on columns or posts. The brackets not only keep the top part of the building stiff from rotational forces but also supplied flexibility in case of earthquakes. The technology was developed early on by the Chinese, but it was by no means static. It went through several developmental stages. By the 15th century, engineers learned how to simplify the bracketing systems and began using them more for the purposes of tradition than out of structural necessity.

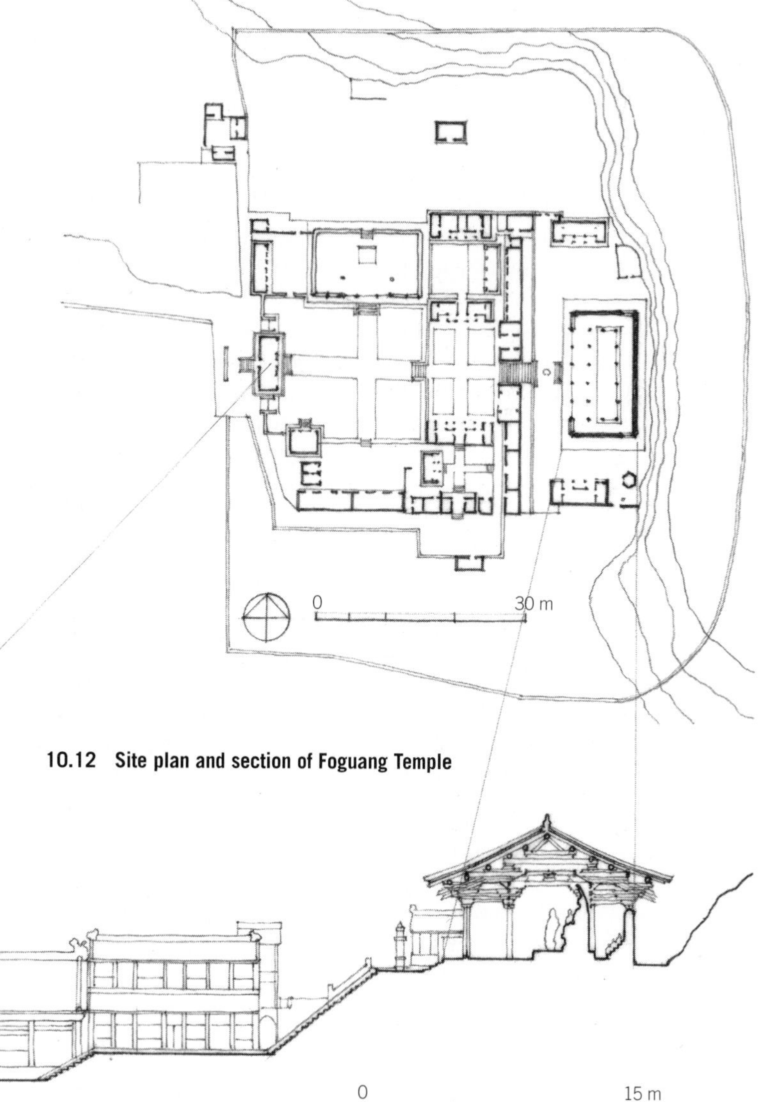


**10.12 Site plan and section of Foguang Temple**

10.13 Buseoksa Temple, Gyeongsangdo, Korea

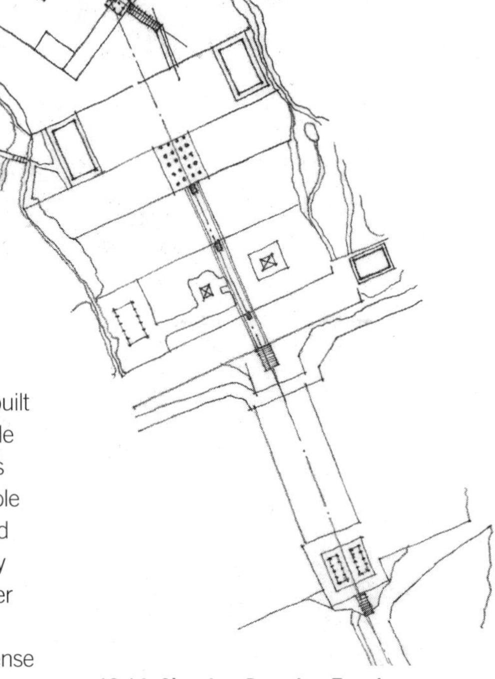

10.14 Site plan: Buseoksa Temple

## KOREAN BUDDHISM

By the end of the 7th century the Silla dynasty (668–935 CE) controlled most of the Korean peninsula. It defeated the Kaya Federation in 562 CE and, thanks to an alliance with the Chinese T'ang court, it also succeeded in conquering the kingdoms of Paekche in 660 CE and Koguryô in 668 CE, thereby unifying Korea for the first time under a single kingdom with its capital at Kyôngju. Even after the Chinese troops had withdrawn into Manchuria, the Silla maintained close ties with T'ang China through trade and diplomatic exchanges. The Silla officially adopted Buddhism as the state religion, enabling it to spread rapidly, even to Japan. Nonetheless, the introduction of Buddhism into Korea was met with some resistance, which was only successfully solved when native gods were in essence seen as apparitions into which Buddhist gods had temporarily projected themselves. Certain shamanistic gods, for example, were made into bodhisattvas incarnate. A similar tension persisted in Japan between Shinto traditions and the new modern Buddhist concepts. As Mahayana Buddhism evolved in India and China, several different sects evolved in Korea as well, particularly those influenced by Tibetan and Chinese esoteric or Tantric Buddhism, which were accessible only to the initiates.

Among the various temples that were built during this period was Buseoksa Temple (676–1000), begun in 751 CE, that was the center of Silla Buddhism. The temple was burnt by the Japanese in 1593 and restored in 1969–73. It was founded by the monk Uisang in 676 CE, the founder of the Consciousness-Only school, an idealistic system of thought in which sense perceptions have no objective reality. It is the mind or the consciousness of the perceived that holds and contains the universe. Buseoksa, or Temple of the Floating Stone, is so-named because of a large rock beside the western hall that appears to float above the stones underneath, perhaps symbolizing its defiance of gravity.

The monastery rests on a forested slope defined by a series of terraces accessed by paths, stairs, and gate houses. From the entrance of the Cheonwangmun Gate there are 108 steps between it and the Anyangmun gate, the number of steps representing redemption from agony and evil passions through 108 cycles.

The Anyangmun Gate is actually a pavilion floating out over the edge of a terrace, with the entrance to the terrace from underneath it. Anyangmun means "entrance to heaven," and it is the culmination of the spiritual path. With spectacular views into the valleys and landscape beyond, it sits opposite the Muryangsujeon Hall, with its Buddha, dating from about the year 1000.

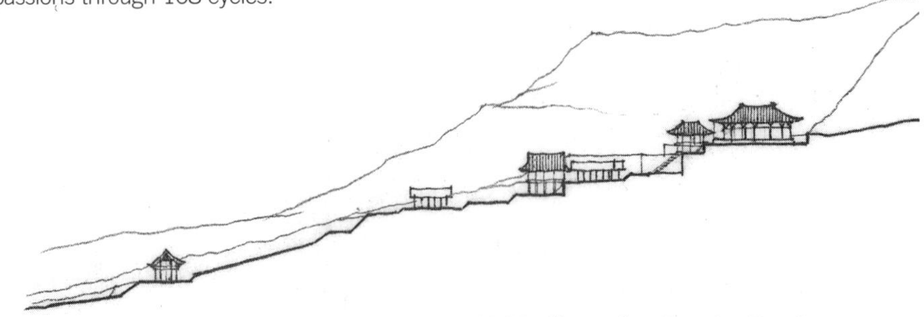

10.15 Site section: Buseoksa Temple

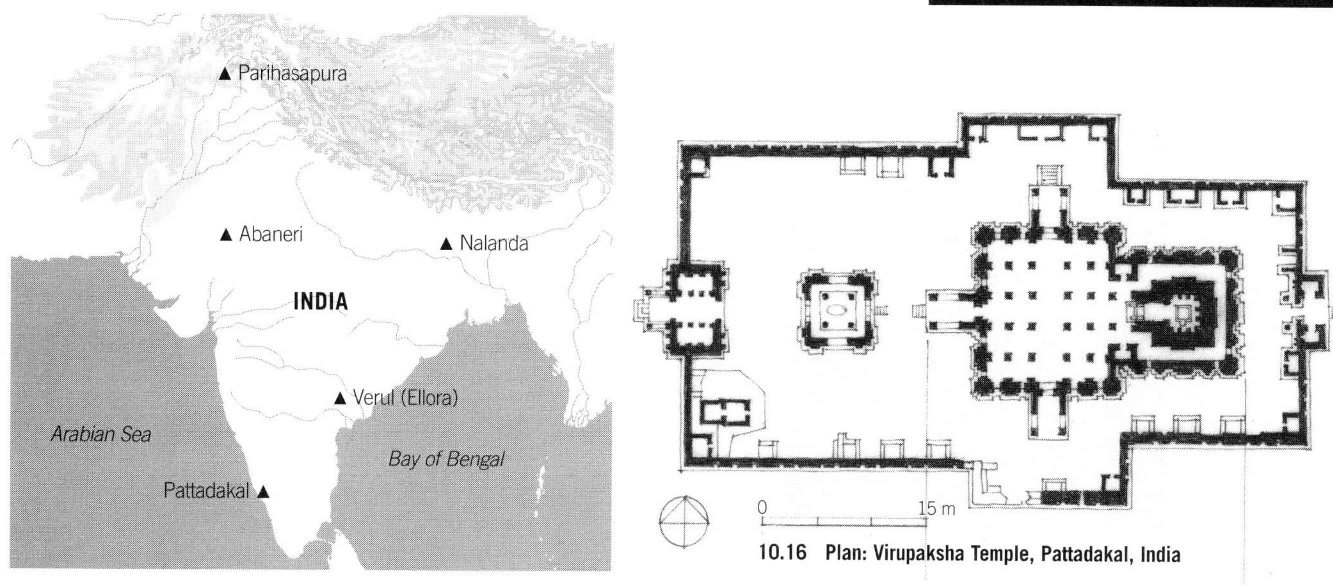


**10.16 Plan: Virupaksha Temple, Pattadakal, India**

**SOUTH ASIAN HINDU-BUDDHISM**

While South Asia's Buddhist *viharas* played host to what was by now a pan-Asian movement, South Asia itself was ruled by a series of diverse kingdoms with many religious affiliations. Since the Gupta period, there had been no single major "empire" in place in South Asia, and as a consequence a wide range of intellectual and philosophical positions received patronage from various rulers and merchants. There was something of an intellectual fervor in place with different religions and sects building competitive universities (*shilas*) and temples to express and explore their ideas. In general, while the Hindu kings dominated most of the country, Buddhist rulers were strong in the east and northwest. For more on this, Susan and John Huntington have compiled one of most extensive and carefully researched accounts of South Asian temple architecture in *The Art of Ancient India*.

In central India, the Chalukyas continued their stylized exploration of the structural rock temples. Their finest example was the Virupaksha Temple at Pattadakal (733–744 CE), built by Vikramaditya II's queen, Loka-Mahadevi. Unlike the experimental architecture that preceded it, the Virupaksha tried to balance ritual requirements with a formal order that is governed by the axial dictates of a geometrical plan.

The Virupaksha temple sits within a generous walled enclosure, with the main entrance on the east marked by a shallow *gopuram* vestibule, echoed on the west by a smaller but similar opening. The temple wall is designed to designate two spaces—an entrance court focused on the small, square Nandi shrine in the middle, and a secondary space that leads around the pillared *mandapa* and main shrine (or *vimana*), creating a passageway designating the *parikrama*. The Nandi shrine faces west with the supplicants, in the direction of the main shrine, and in that sense, the shrine stands in the court with all the other supplicants.

The *mandapa* consists of 12 freestanding columns that are extended into the edges either by pilasters or by columns of attached structures through careful composition. Three porches, two of them with steps to the ground, project out from the *mandapa*. The main *vimana* consists of the square thick-walled *garbh-griha*, surrounded by an enclosed circumambulatory path. The *garbh-griha* projects out, forming a neck in the direction of the *mandapa* and lining up with the innermost columns to form a vestibule framed by niches on either side.

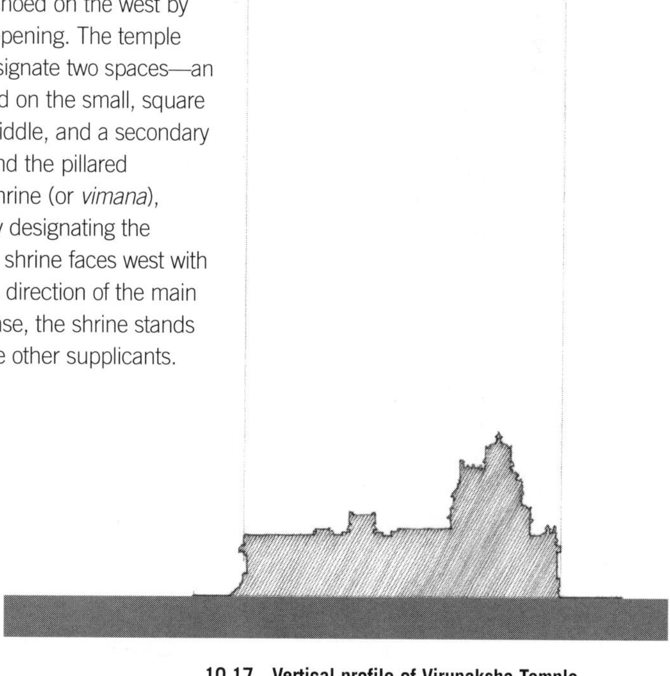

**10.17 Vertical profile of Virupaksha Temple**

10.18 Temple of Kailasnath at Ellora, near Aurangabad, India

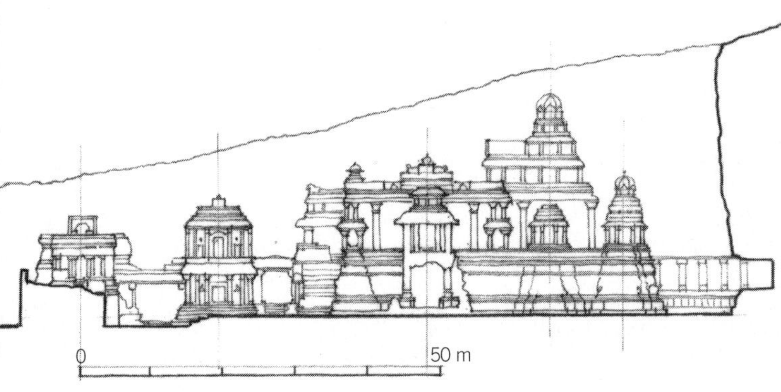


10.19 Longitudinal section: Kailasnath, Ellora

### Kailasnath at Ellora

Control of the Deccan was wrested away from the Calukyas around 750 CE by the Rashtrakutas, who ruled for about two centuries until 973 CE. The Rashtrakutas quickly established their military superiority and captured the all-important trade routes that connected the western region to the rest of the subcontinent, in particular, the *dakshinapatha*, or southern route. On the *dakshinapatha*, at Verul (contemporary Ellora), the Rashtrakuta ruler, Krishna I, ordered the construction of what was to be not only the largest rock-cut temple of its time but ever after. Fifty meters wide, more than 90 meters deep, and 20 meters high, Kailasnath is in the middle of the three-kilometer-long wall of basalt that has 34 caves carved out of it (12 are Buddhist, 17 Hindu, and 5 Jain, dating from 600–1000 CE). Kailasnath is conceived as a representation of the mythological mountain abode of Shiva, Kailash mountain. Unlike the Buddhist rock-cut structures that were always essentially elaborations of a cave, Kailasnath is an independent entity, a freestanding colossal sculpture revealed from the matrix. Since it is still surrounded by the rock from which it was hewn, there is a palpable sense of excavation to Kailasnath, as if it were still a work in progress.

Two "victory towers" have been left on either side of the mass of the Nandi chamber. They not only provide the vertical axis of the composition but their length also visibly measures the mass of the rock that has been excavated.

From outside, the temple is almost entirely obscured by its two-storied entrance *gopuram* (flanked by Shaivite and Vaishnavite figures on either side) on the west that leads, through a vestibule, into the main space. The ground floor is dominated by the immense presence of the excavated mass, since the body of the temple at this level is mostly solid and cannot be entered. Toward the back, the perimeter is ringed by a colonnade of square pillars whose only purpose seems to be to support the overhanging rock above. In the midst of an elaborate sculptural program, the lower rock mass of the main shrine has life-size elephants carved into it, as if they were supporting the temple above.

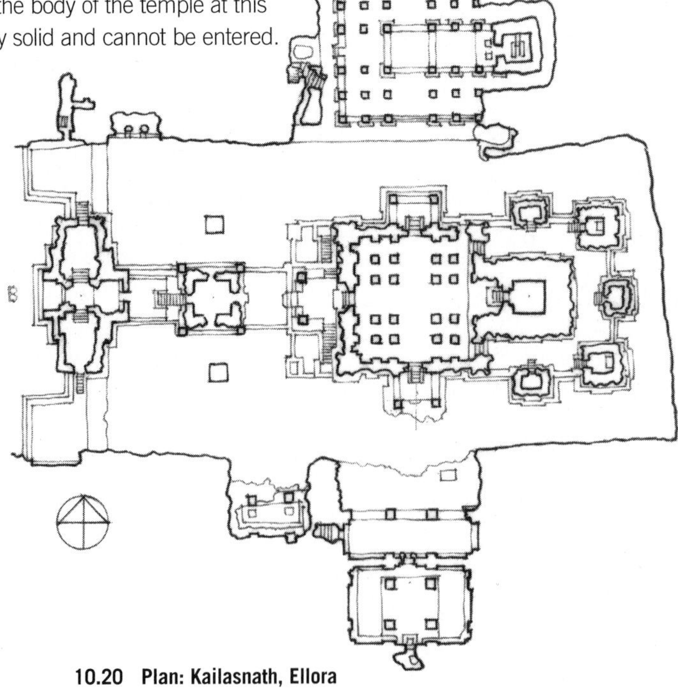

10.20 Plan: Kailasnath, Ellora

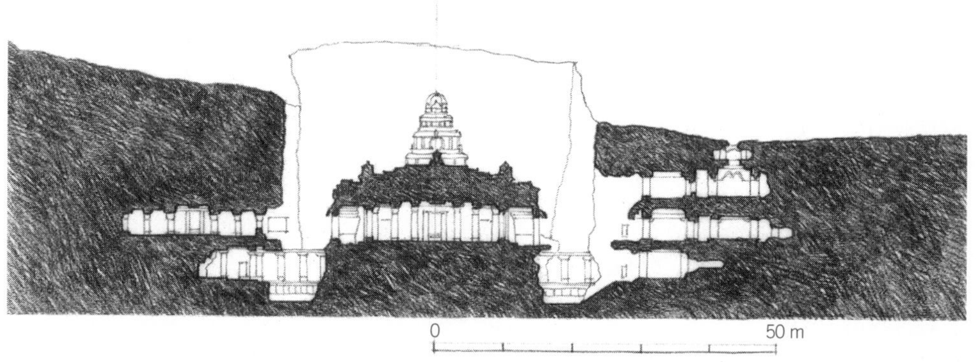


**10.21 Cross section: Kailasnath, Ellora**

Access to the main level of the temple is from a pair of symmetrical stairs on the west that emerge into the entrance vestibule of the shrine. The *mandapa* had 16 columns clumped into groups of four, creating a cruciform central space that opens into smaller porches on the north and south. The main *garbh-griha* is the traditional windowless square chamber with thick walls and a *shivalinga* for its image. A distinctive characteristic of Kailasnath is the ring of five subsidiary shrines that open onto the *parikrama* surrounding the main chamber. Bridges connect the main shrine with the Nandi chamber and the entrance *gopuram* as well. The *shikhara* of the main shrine is completely in the southern style, with its four-tiered pyramidal shapes resolving into an octagonal finial. The subsidiary shrines are also excavated and use the same vocabulary.

**10.22 Detail: Temple of Kailasnath, Ellora**

Kailasnath, however, does not end with the main shrine, gigantic as it is. Toward the north, on axis with the *mandapa*, is another rock-cut temple, Lankesvara, complete with a 16-pillared *mandapa* and *garbh-griha*, that almost rivals the main shrine. To the south, there are two additional shrines, also rock-cut, one of which extends almost 25 meters into the rock.

Most discussions on the construction process of Kailasnath assume that gigantic trenches must have been dug into the rock, clearing out the main mass of the temple, followed by a process of excavating and sculpting. A more counterintuitive possibility is suggested by the fact that subsidiary shrines, in particular the one to the north, are excavated so deep into the rock that one can imagine that they might have employed the same process for the main shrine. Since Kailasnath is derived from rock-cut cave temple precedents, conceptually, it makes sense as well to excavate the sacred cave and then, in an act of superseding the infinity of the mountain around the traditional caves, to "uncover" the exterior in the form of a complete temple. There is no room for error, since rock cannot be replaced. Simply making the temple had to have been an act of dedication.

The Rashtrakutas would, of course, also have been very familiar with the constructed temples of the Chalukyas, their predecessors, and the Pallavas and Pandyas, their contemporaries to the south. The reason for their decision to dedicate the full extent of their resources to the creation of a gigantic rock-cut structure is unknown, but it must have had something to do with reasserting the value of the traditional way of making a monumental ritual structure in the face of the imminent modernity of the structural stone temple.

**10.23 Detail: Temple of Kailasnath, Ellora**

10.24 Rajasimhesvara Temple, Kanchipuram, India

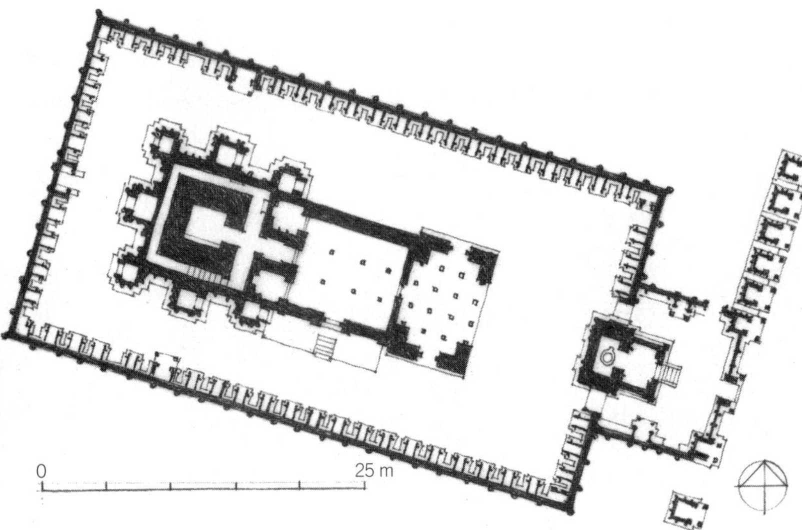


10.25 Plan: Rajasimhesvara Temple

### Step Well at Abaneri

Like the Ghats of Varanasi, the step wells of western India celebrate the act of descending to reach water. In the 9th century the Pratihara Dynasty of Rajasthan built a square step well at Abaneri, 35 meters on each side and about 25 meters deep. It descends down on three sides in a cascading rhythm of symmetrical switchback steps whose function becomes an exhilarating exploration of geometric possibilities.

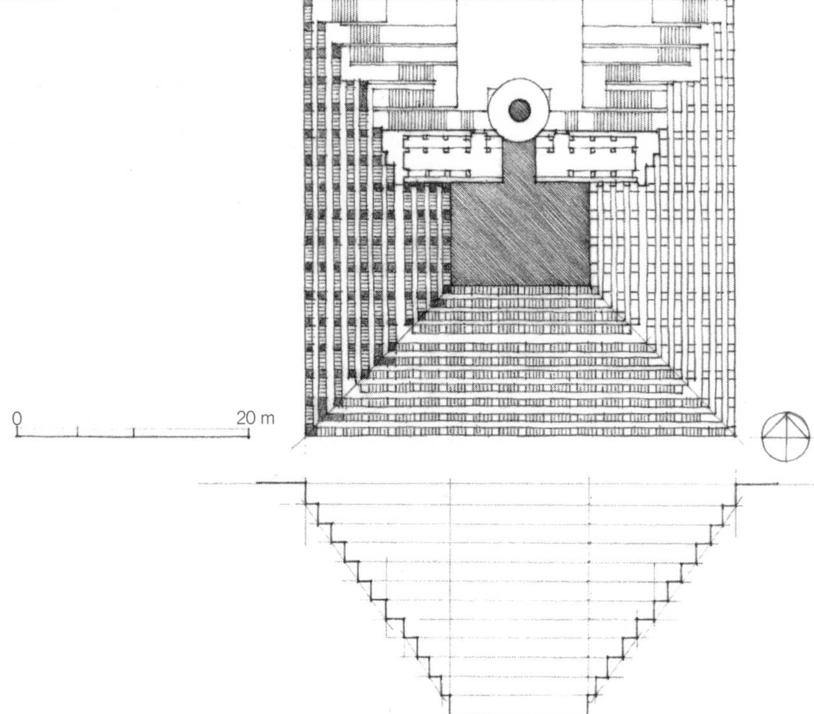


10.26 Plan and schematic section: Step well at Abaneri, near Agra, India

### Rajasimhesvara Temple

In South India, the Pallava king, Narsimhavarman (the builder of the Shore Temple), built the Rajasimhesvara Temple as his largest structure in his capital Kanchipuram (700–730 CE). Rajasimhesvara is bound by a stately perimeter wall, with more than 50 shrines lining its interior wall. On the east, the entrance is formed by a large antechamber within which, aligned with the main perimeter wall, is a smaller subsidiary shrine built by Narsimhavarman's son, Mahendravarman III. The entrance is surmounted by a barrel-vaulted *gopuram*, with seven shrines in a line to its north, suggesting that another compound wall of shrines may have been contemplated but never built. The main shrine is focused on a square *garbh-griha* dedicated to Shiva, contained in a thick wall that primarily supports the superstructure, with a narrow, unlit *parikrama* path. The shrine itself is surrounded by nine semidetached shrines, with the two on the east bifurcated to form an entrance into the main *garbh-griha* and one on axis to the south. Originally, this whole structure, with its gigantic four-story *shikhara*, stood as an independent structure, but was later added to with the creation of an intermediate hall toward the east, so that the two eastern subsidiary shrines can now only be accessed through the hall.

10.27 Rajasimhesvara Temple

10.28 Mahavihara at Nalanda

**Mahavihara at Nalanda**

Almost every Buddhist pilgrim to India made a stop at Nalanda, the Mahavihara (Great-Vihara) of the time. Mahaviharas like Nalanda were multidisciplinary universities devoted not only to the preparation of Buddhist practitioners but also to the study of the secular disciplines. Officially established by the Gupta king Kumara Gupta I (415–455 CE), Nalanda boomed in the reign of Harshavardhana. Nalanda had more than 2000 monks and about 10,000 disciples. Theravada, the school of Buddhism followed mainly in Sri Lanka, Myanmar, Thailand, and Cambodia, was developed here. Besides the various schools of Buddhism, including Hinayana, Mahayana, and Tantric, courses on the Indo-Aryan Vedas, Hetu Vidya (logic), Shabda Vidya (grammar), Chikitsa Vidya (medicine), etc., were also taught at Nalanda. Hsuan Tsang in fact spent most of his time at Nalanda studying law.

Ten quadrangles, covering 14 hectares, all lined up in a block and packed next to each other, give us a sense of the density of Nalanda. Made of brick, each *vihara*, 50 to 60 meters long, had a central courtyard (some with a shrine) ringed by two and three stories of cells for the monks, about 30 to a floor. The *viharas* faced a row of freestanding *caitya* temples, also made of brick, each with long central stairways leading to a platform on which stood the main shrine, with subsidiary shrines at the corners. Only a fraction of the *mahavihara* has been excavated.

Aryabhatta, the 5th-century astronomer and mathematician (born in 476 CE, Kerala, India) came to Nalanda as a boy to study astronomy. Aryabhatta was one of the earliest people to support the theory that earth is a sphere, preceding Copernicus by a millennium. His main work, known as the Aryabhattiya, was translated into Latin in the 13th century. It included methods of calculating the areas of triangles, volumes of spheres, and square and cube roots. Aryabhatta also wrote about eclipses and proposed the sun as the source of moonlight. Another 7th-century Indian astronomer, Brahmagupta, calculated the circumference of the earth as 5000 *yojanas*, or about 36,000 kilometers, only 4000 short of true distance. The number zero, called *sunya*, (meaning "void" or "empty") was invented at this time. *Sunya* passed into the Arabic as *sifr*, meaning "vacant." In about 1200 this was transliterated into Latin with the sound but not the meaning kept, resulting in *zephirum* or *zephyrum*.

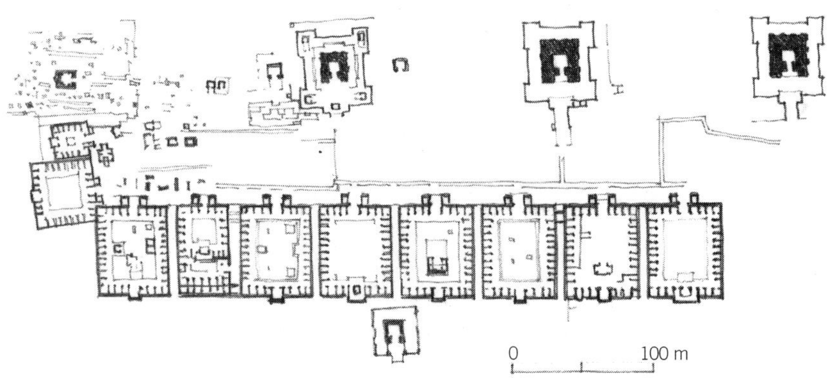


10.29 Plan: Mahavihara at Nalanda, India

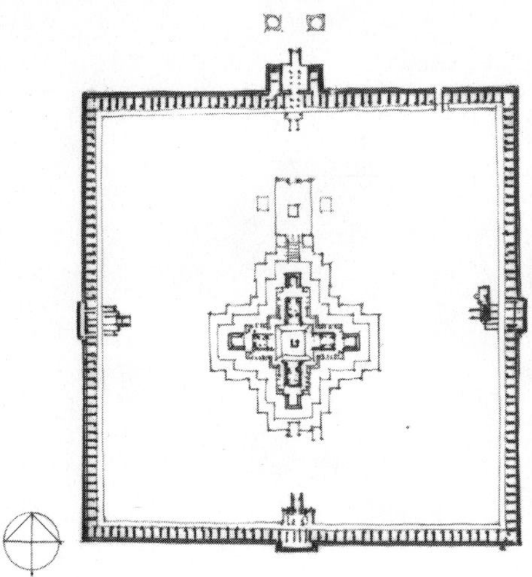

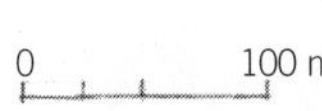


10.30 Plan: Somapura Vihara, Paharpur, Bangladesh

10.31 Sumstek Gompa

**Somapura Vihara**

After Harshavardhana, the Pala kings of Bengal maintained Nalanda for four centuries until the 11th century. The surviving ruins date from the Pala period when most of the stupas were literally built over. Indeed, the Pala and Sena kings built Buddhism into a powerhouse in eastern India with several monastic universities besides Nalanda, such as at Vikramsila and Somapura. So numerous were the *viharas* that the name of the modern state in this region, Bihar, is a contraction of the sanskrit describing the Land of the Viharas.

The two elements of Nalanda's design, the *vihara* quadrangles and the *caitya* temple, were integrated into a single complex at Somapura Vihara (ca. 800 CE) of Bengal. With a distinct cruciform shape, its *caitya* temple is more than 100 meters from north to south and sits in the middle of a vast quadrangular courtyard, 300 meters on a side, the edges of which contain 177 cells that may have served as shrines or monk cells. Facing north, the stupa sits on three terraces with jagged edges constituting a stage for the central shrine (which is missing).

The whole complex is made of burnt brick with decorative terra-cotta finishes that narrate Mahayana tales from the life of the Buddha and other bodhisattvas. The sculpture also reveals that sex-based Tantric Buddhism, which relied on the release of foundational energies through sexual and other types of intercourse between the male and female, was an important influence at this time. The order and configuration of the terraced stupa are based on Mahayana mandala diagrams of the kind that are still found in Nepal and Tibet.

**Sumstek Gompa**

One famous example from Kashmir to have survived largely intact to this day is the Sumstek Gompa in Alchi. Located on the high-altitude road from Srinagar to Ladakh, the Sumstek Gompa is a three-tiered structure depicting the native traditional architecture of Ladakh combined with the delicate wood carvings of the Kashmiri style. The interior, which is profusely adorned with murals depicting Buddhist motifs and bodhisattvas, glows from the warmth of the colors. Its adjoining Dukhang (assembly hall) contains a statue of Avalokiteshvara made of pure gold. In a style reminiscent of Ajanta, its walls are painted with scenes of turbaned men and multiple-braided women, drinking, riding, fighting, and wearing garments of Central Asian origin, although their features are decidedly South Asian. Most of what survives dates to the 11th century CE and was built by Padmasambhava.

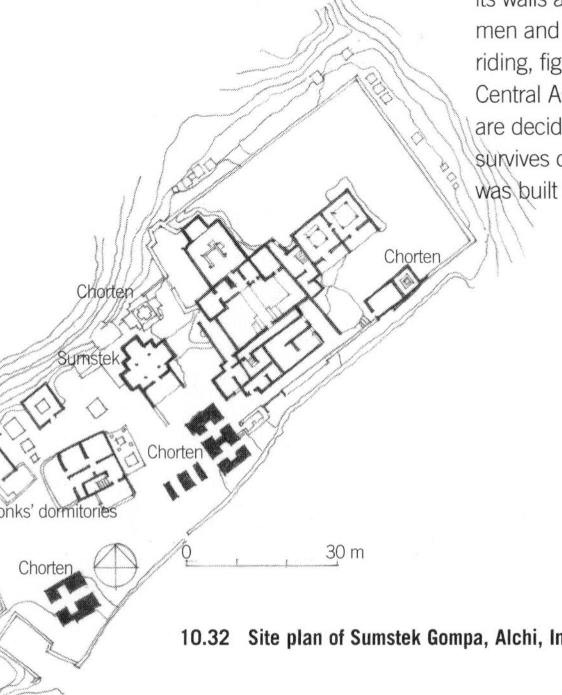


10.32 Site plan of Sumstek Gompa, Alchi, India

10.33 View of Borobodur, near Yogyakarta, Indonesia

10.34 One of the seated Buddhas in the upper terraces of Borobodur

## INDONESIA AT A CROSSROADS

Indian civilization travelled to Southeast Asia in the backpacks and cargoes of traders, beginning as far back as the 1st century CE. While the missions sent by Asoka in the 3rd century BCE reached as far as Sri Lanka, it was the traders plying close to the Andaman coast who gradually transformed the Mon people of Cambodia and then moved down the Malay peninsula and spread into the islands of modern Indonesia. As the Hindu-Buddhist kingdoms gained strength in South Asia, the volume of seaborne trade increased exponentially. At the same time, the Chinese traders of the Sui and T'ang dynasties came down the Vietnam coast to trade with Southeast Asia and South Asia. In the midst of this traffic, at the intersections of civilization, the Hindu-Buddhist Shailendra kings of 9th-century Indonesia used their new wealth to catapult their kingdom from one of the farthest outposts of seaborne trade between China and India into a conceptual center of the Hindu-Buddhist cosmological universe. Within the short space of 100 years, they built not only one of the finest Buddhist stupa shrines ever, Borobodur, but also a scant 20 miles away, one of the largest and most complex assemblages of Hindu temples of the time, the Prambanam complex. For more on this, Diagoro Chihara has compiled one of the most usable summaries of Southeast Asian architecture.

### Borobodur

The great "cosmic mountain" at Borobodur (790–850) was started in the reign of the Shailendra king Indra and completed in that of Samaratunga. Though based on earlier experiments, Borobodur is unique in its formal organization and articulation. It is approximately square in plan (122 meters north to south and 116 meters east to west), and it is roughly aligned to the cardinal directions. The plan follows a typical Buddhist mandala diagram with a biaxially symmetrical order composed of a series of jagged terraces giving way to round ones in the middle. Borobodur is at one level a quintessential stupa, having been built onto a solid mound, and at another level, it is a three-dimensional pedagogical process.

10.35 One of the sculpted panels on the lower square terraces of Borobodur

The building is neither a temple nor a monastery. Rather it is something of a university that one goes to, not to invoke divine beings but to participate in a didactic journey, to learn—by moving through its spaces—a progression of lessons by which means the successful student can attain a state of *bodhi* or perfected wisdom, just as the Sakyamuni Buddha did 2500 years prior. The essential experience consists of an orchestrated sequence of four galleries followed by three terraces, preceded by one large plinth or preterrace. The first four terraces are square and the latter three are round. The whole experience culminates in the central stupa, which is completely solid and cannot be entered.

As the Buddhist pilgrim approaches it, the complete profile of Borobodur is clearly visible with its levels of galleries and rounded stupa terraces orchestrated hierarchically around the central stupa, forming the outline of a gently swelling mountain. The destination, the central stupa, seems clear. As the pilgrim gets closer, however, the central stupa disappears and seems to retract into the monument, and it is replaced by a forest of smaller stupas and sculptures with a more human scale.

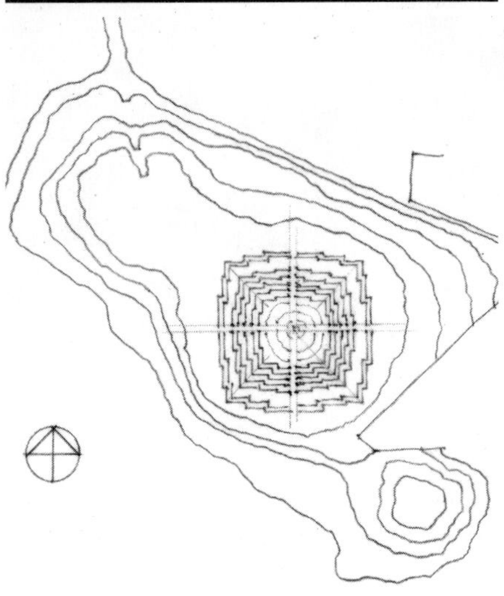

10.36 **Area Plan: Borobodur**

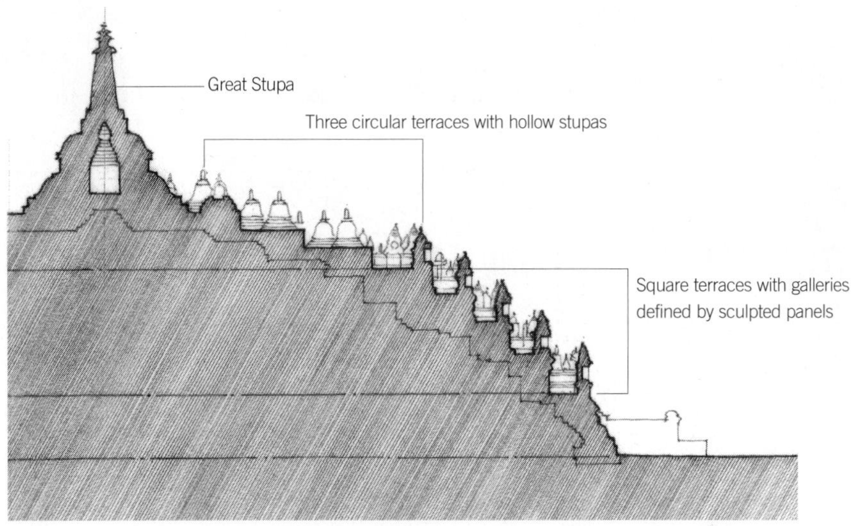


10.37 **Partial section showing the three levels of Borobodur**

Since nirvana is not a place or a thing, it has no description. Rather it is a state that must be achieved by the pilgrim through a personal journey. As governed by the mandala, this journey must be completed by a pilgrim in 60 conceptual steps. The journey begins by circumambulating the four lower galleries, which have two rows of sculpted panels on each side, organized sequentially to tell stories from the life of the Buddha. These narrow galleries are staggered so as to block all lines of sight and focus the pilgrims on the panels. Only after they have cleared these four levels can they ascend to the round upper levels, where there are no enclosing walls. Instead, they encounter the bell-shaped hollow stupas, each one of which contains a different sculpture of the seated Buddha displaying one of the mudras—the characteristic symbolic gestures of Buddhism. The openings on the lower stupas are diamond-shaped and large, while those on the ones above are square, smaller, and fewer in number. While each side of the *candi* (temple) in the lower level is one step, each bell-shaped stupa takes a whole step toward the end. At the final stage, pilgrims arrive at the stupa whose solidity symbolizes the *shunyata* or nonpresence that is aspired to by the Buddhist pilgrim who seeks nirvana.

It is important to note that the lowermost terrace of Borobodur was added at a later date, hiding a row of friezes behind it. It has been speculated that this lower terrace was probably added to stabilize the structure, since it is heavy (as it is made of yellowish-brown andesite, a dark volcanic rock that originates from Mount Merapi) and may have begun to slip. One of the controversies concerning the meaning of Borobodur is whether it was supposed to have a large stupa in the middle that would have dominated the whole edifice. While it is possible that it may have been planned and then abandoned when the foundation of the lowest terrace began to slip, it is just as possible that the designers conceived of it as it now stands.

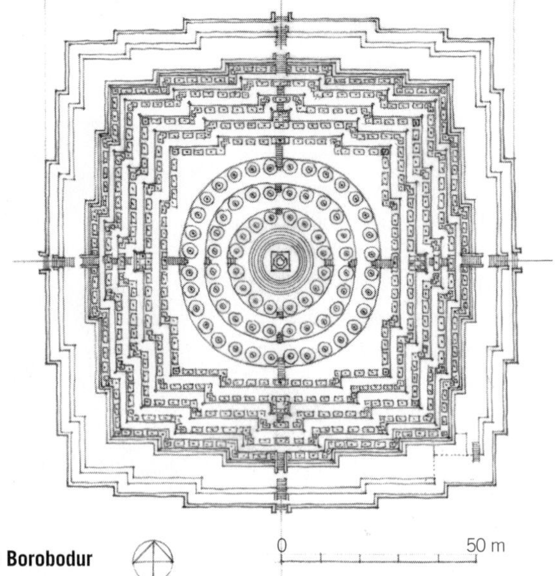


10.38 **Plan: Borobodur**

10.39 **Loro Jonggrang, Prambanan, Indonesia**

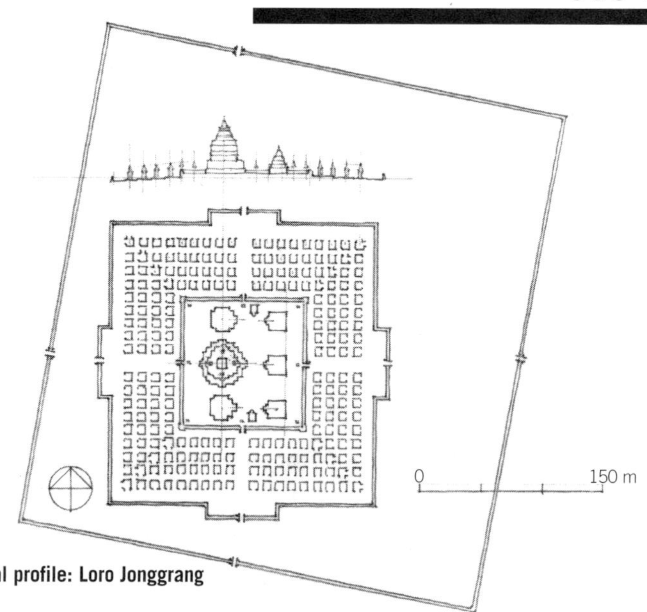


10.40 **Plan and vertical profile: Loro Jonggrang**

**Candi Prambanam**

In about 835 CE, after Samaratunga's death, his young son Balaputra's right to accession was usurped by his sister's father-in-law, Patapan of Sanjaya. Patapan replaced Buddhism with Hinduism in the Shailendra kingdom. As Borobodur was quickly forgotten, Patapan immediately initiated the construction of a series of Hindu temples that were continued by his son, Rakai Pikatan (or Jatiningrat). Their herculean efforts to quickly and spectacularly establish the new official faith are littered across the plains of Prambanam, not far from Borobodur.

One of the most impressive of these is Candi Prambanam, known popularly as Loro Jonggrang (Slender Virgin). Built around 850 CE, Loro Jonggrang's three central shrines, facing East, are dedicated to the Hindu trinity, Brahma, Vishnu, and Shiva, with Shiva at the center. (Ideas of divine kingship were also attached to the temple, especially with the burial of the remains of the king of Mataram Balitung (d. 910 CE), who claimed to be a reincarnation of Shiva. Three subsidiary shrines, for the corresponding animal "vehicles" or *vahanas* of the temple deities, face westward toward the main group.

The shrines sit on a platform, accessible from all four sides. Around the platform, 224 small shrines are arrayed in concentric rings, with extra widths for passages leading to the center. These small shrines are oriented in ranks of 18 to face outward, with the ones at the corners designed with two orientations. A wall encloses the complex with access gates on each side. Originally, this whole complex was surrounded by another perimeter wall, oriented not to the cardinal directions but northeast and southwest, measuring about 390 meters on a side. Except for its southern gate, not much of this enclosure has survived.

Prambanam's shrines are articulated as two-story structures divided by a band of molding. Their profiles are most like those of the Pallavas of Southern India, which emphasize slender verticality, with distinct and clear horizontal layers as in the Shore Temple. Prambanam's two-storied base, however, is significantly taller in proportion to its plan, as compared to its South Asian precedents. The bulbous profile of the individual *salas* or superstructures of Prambanam is also a nod in the direction of Borobodur, not far away. The plans and tripartite elevational orders of Hindu and Buddhist structures of Southeast Asia were very similar and could easily be adapted, one for the other. The two cosmologies were often articulated in parallel as well. As a consequence, it is not unusual to mistake a Hindu temple for a Buddhist one, and vice versa, in particular in latter-day Cambodia.

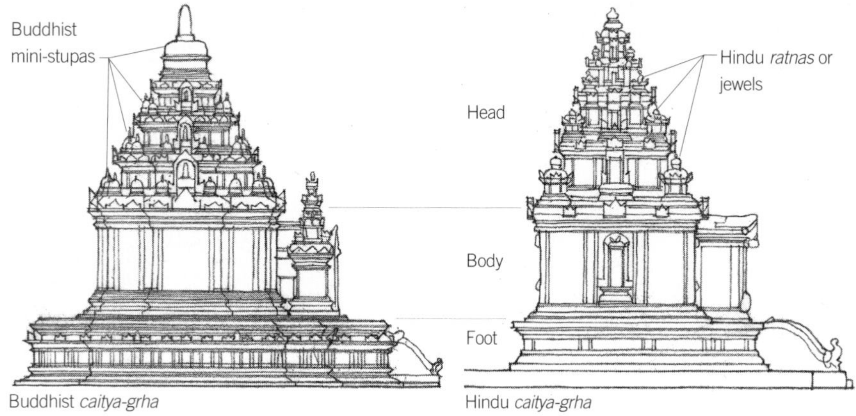


10.41 **Comparison of Buddhist and Hindu temples (after Diagoro Chihara)**

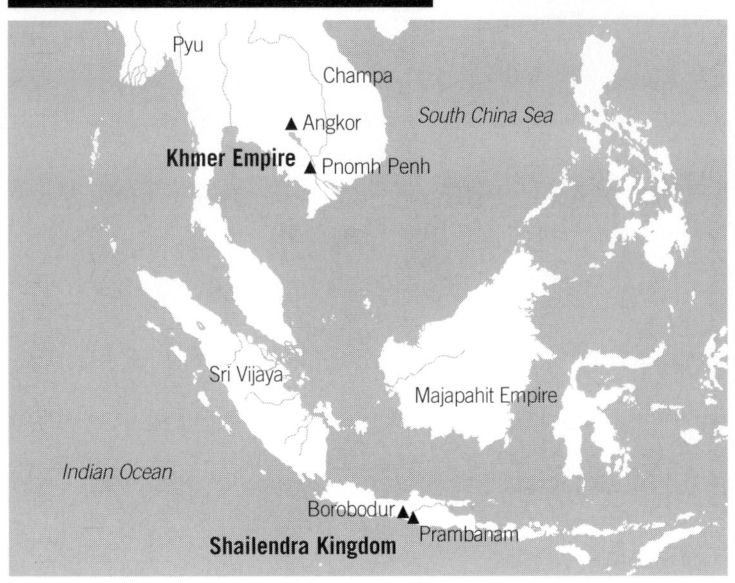

**10.42 View of Bakong Temple**

**HINDU KINGDOMS OF CAMBODIA**

The area of modern Cambodia, inhabited since prehistoric times, was held by various regional kingdoms who came to be Indianized in the 9th century, adopting Hindu cosmologies and ideas of governance. Their court language was derived from Sanskritic sources. In 802 CE Jayavarman II (r. 802–834 CE) established the first major Khmer kingdom, just south of the Dangrek mountain range, in a vast flood plain. Jayavarman III located his new capital, Hariharalaya just beyond the northern shores of the Tonle Sap, the great lake of Cambodia. The Tonle Sap was central to the areas economy. Several rivers flowed south from the Dangrek mountains, one of which was the Mekong. At the height of the Mekong's flood, its water backed up its tributary into the Tonle Sap, flooding the entire region. The Khmer learned how to harvest this water through canals and gigantic tanks called *barays*, which, after the floods had receded, provided a continuous, controllable supply of water for year-long rice cultivation. Causeways connected the city to the mountains and mountain passes to the north and west, about 60 kilometers away.

Hariharalaya was laid out in the shape of a square, the city centered around a series of temples. The largest temple, today called Bakong, was built by Jayavarman III in 881. While the Khmer cosmology and mathematical geometries came from Hindu India, their forms were transformations of Indonesian precedents. Dedicated to Shiva, Bakong's tower rises about 15 meters above its 18 meter high terraced base. Made of sandstone blocks, it displays a thin attenuated profile. The larger precinct contains a series of additional shrines, most made of brick, which were added around 1000 CE. The moat surrounding the enclosure was accessed by a causeway that had snake sculptures on both sides, serving as a balustrade. The snake represented Naga, the king cobra that was central to the foundational myths of Vishnu and Shiva.

Within the square temple pyramid, a structure likely derived from the *ratha* architecture at Mamallapuram, embodies the relationship of this earthly structure to the cosmos. The low pyramid steps upward, culminating in a central tower, a visible landmark that represented the king's centralized power. The combination of platforms and tower was unique to Khmer architecture. An extremely complex, sophisticated system of numerology—number of towers, steps, and ascending hierarchy of sculptural groups—reinforces the association with Shiva and the king's universal rule through an identification with the lunar year. The dynamic composition that results is but a foreshadowing of the famous Angkor Wat temple of the 12th century.

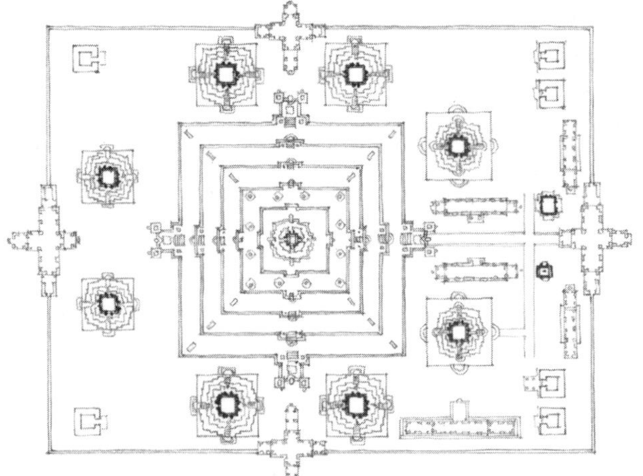

**10.43 Plan: Bakong Temple, near Siem Reap, Cambodia**

10.44 Section through "Temple Mountain" at Bakong Temple

**Phnom Bakheng**

In 889, King Yasovarman (r. 889–910 CE) moved his capital 15 kilometers to the northwest of Hariharalaya and called it Yasodharapura. Like Hariharalaya, Yasodharapura was laid out as a perfect square, four kilometers on each side, between two rivers. The Khmer kings built a gigantic *baray*, 2 by 8 kilometers in size, just to the east of the city walls. At Yasodharapura's precise center, there was a natural hill (which presumably was the motivation for picking this location). On the top of this hill, Yasovarman built his primary royal temple, Yasodharesvara, known today as Phnom Bakheng. Phnom Bakheng sits on a platform, created through cut and fill, at the summit of the hill. Its five terraces, a man-made mountain on top of the natural mountain, culminate in a plateau with four shrines around a central Shiva shrine. Another 103 shrines are distributed geometrically on the terraces, bringing the total to 108, an auspicious number by Hindu astrology. A sophisticated system of numerology—number of towers, steps, and ascending hierarchy of sculptural groups— reinforced the temple's association with Shiva. As at Bakong, Phnom Bakheng was surrounded by a moat, and the terracing creates a spherical profile. From the summit, the temple affords expansive views, in particular toward the mountains in the north. Some of them seem to have the outline of Naga to protect and define the vast flood plain.

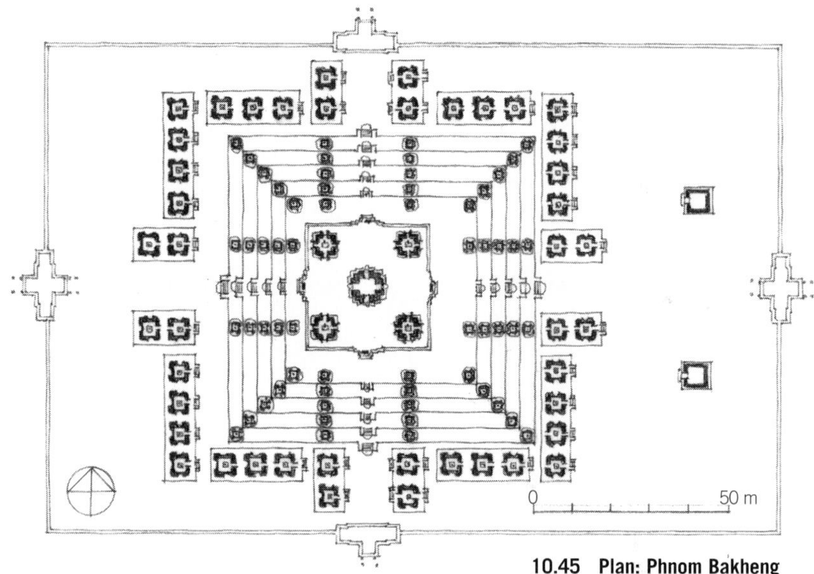


10.45 Plan: Phnom Bakheng

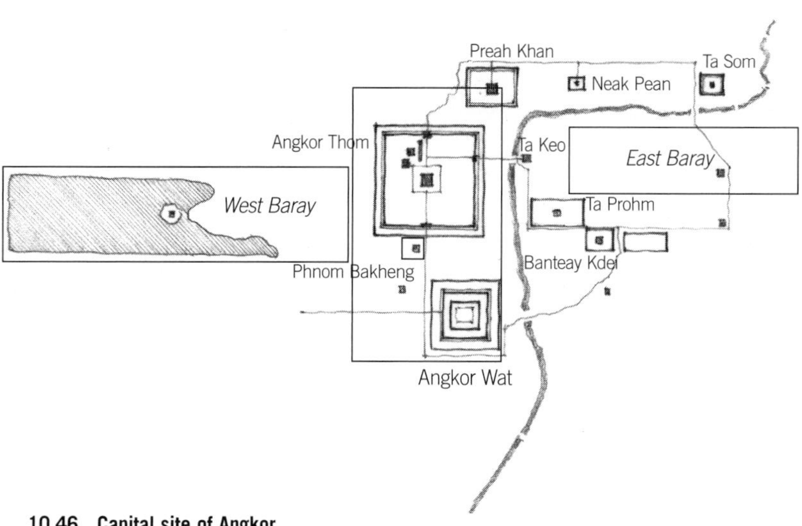


10.46 Capital site of Angkor

10.47 **Detail of stonework at Borobodur**

10.48 **View of stonework at Borobodur**

**Construction in Southeast Asia**

Monolithic stone architecture never made it to Southeast Asia from India. Instead the Javanese and Cambodian kings adopted the more advanced technique of building with brick and dressed stone from the very beginning. Whenever possible, as in Indonesia, fresh volcanic stone that had been carried downstream by rivers was cut and dressed close to the building sites, which were generally near rivers. At other places, sandstone from mountain quarries was transported to building sites on rafts during the monsoons, when the water levels were high and flooded vast areas of the land.

At Borobodur the individual stones were cut to a uniform height (22 centimeters) but were left with irregular widths and depths. This allowed them to be laid in courses, while ensuring that the maximum amount of available rock was consumed. No mortar was used, and the only real bonding technique used was the occasional shiplapping to hold the vertical stones in place, particularly on the external surfaces. Secondary stones were used as infill. These were generally irregular, and no special attention was paid to their bonding.

Where the depths of stones had to be uniform, such as in the two-stone-thick freestanding gateways of Borobodur, stone dowels were wedged between the stones to hold them together. On gallery floors, wedge stones were driven into the gaps of shiplapped joints so that all the stones were compressed together for a tighter fit.

10.49 **Wall section at Angkor Wat**

While sandstone was used on the mainland, andesite, basalt, tuff, and limestone was more common on the volcanic islands. Brick construction was common, used both for simpler and monumental buildings. Laterite was a common building material as well, particularly on mainland Southeast Asia, where they were cut and hardened into construction blocks. Not a rock as such, laterite is produced when a wide variety of rocks are severely weathered under strong oxidizing and leeching conditions. This occurs most commonly in tropical zones.

While bricks and laterites were often left exposed, they were also commonly finished with a stucco called *vajra-lepa* ("diamond plaster"). On the exterior, the *vajra-lepa* was generally molded into delicate patterns, and in the interior it was usually covered with dry frescoes. *Vajra-lepa* was often used on stonework as well. The corbeled arch was the roofing technique of choice. (True arches, occasionally found in India, such as at the Mahabodhi Temple, were mainly used in Burma in later centuries.)

**RISE OF ISLAM**

By the 7th century, Arabia, given its extreme climactic and geographic conditions, was at the periphery of the great cultural centers of its age. It was mainly inhabited by nomadic Bedouin Arabs who served as traders or exploited the land's meager resources. Jews had a strong presence in the area as well as Christians and Arabs, especially in Syria. The center of Arabian religion, which focused on nature and heavenly bodies, was in Mecca. Mohammed (ca. 570–632) began a bitter and prolonged struggle with Arab tribes and their polytheism, advocating instead a brand of monotheism based on a universalist and egalitarian sociopolitical basis in contrast to the tradition of tribal politics. His success in attracting followers was legion, and he eventually conquered Mecca and transformed it into a holiest of holies. All adult Muslims are required to visit it at least once in their lives. Mohammed was, however, more than the founding prophet of Islam; he was also a farsighted statesman, political arbitrator, and a gifted military commander, setting the stage for a fusion of religion and politics that was to define Islamic culture for centuries to come. By 711 CE, Muslim Arab armies were attacking north India to the east as well as North Africa to the west and by the end of the 9th century, Islam had grown into the largest civilizational entity west of China.

Since Mohammed had made no arrangements for a successor, dissension arose as to how to govern this vast territory, and the conflict between the Abbasids and Umayyads sealed a divide in Islam that lasts to this day. The Abbasids, descendants of Mohammed's uncle, al-Abbas, based their claim on the caliphate on the theological aspects of their rulership. The Shiites joined with the Abbasids in the 8th century, as they too believed that the caliphs ruled by divine designation and thus possessed spiritual authority. The Umayyads also saw themselves as heirs to the Islamic state, but interpreted the caliphate as a constitutional necessity working for the temporal welfare and protection of the community. The conflict between the theological and political interpretation of rulership remains contested to this day. It was initially the Umayyads who were dominant, ruling from their capital in Damascus. Able administrators, they ruled for a brief but certainly important period over the whole of the Islamic realm, the only time that it was so unified.

Worship did not require a building or even a consecrated space, rather it is based on five injunctions or "pillars," one of the most important being the five daily prayers facing Mecca. The month of Ramadan is also important, since during that time Muslims commune with themselves, give thanks to God through fasting, and make donations to the needy, fulfilling the third pillar.

The typical mosque has a courtyard through which one enters and that contains a well or fountain where one washes one's hands, head, and feet. The hall of worship was, in most instances in the first centuries of Islam, a space consisting of rows of columns so that the congregation could form rows facing the *qibla* wall—a wall that stands at right angles to a line drawn to Mecca. The imam, or prayer leader, stands in front of a mihrab, or niche, in the middle of the *qibla* wall. In some mosques, the bay just in front of the mihrab is elevated and roofed with a dome. To the right of the mihrab is a stepped pulpit, the *minbar*, made of wood or stone, from which the imam can deliver a sermon (*khutba*), usually on Friday. Almost all mosques have a minaret from which the faithful are called to prayer. There is no prescription as to where they are to be located or how many there need to be.

Tarik Khana (ca. 760 CE) in Damghan in northern Iran is one of the oldest still-extant mosques. Its rectangular shape encloses a courtyard and prayer hall. Massive round brick columns almost 2 meters in diameter support arcades of tunnel vaults. The Aksa Mosque in Jerusalem (702 CE), shows the development of an axis and transept emphasizing the *qibla* that becomes even more pronounced in the El-Hakim Mosque (991 CE) in Cairo.

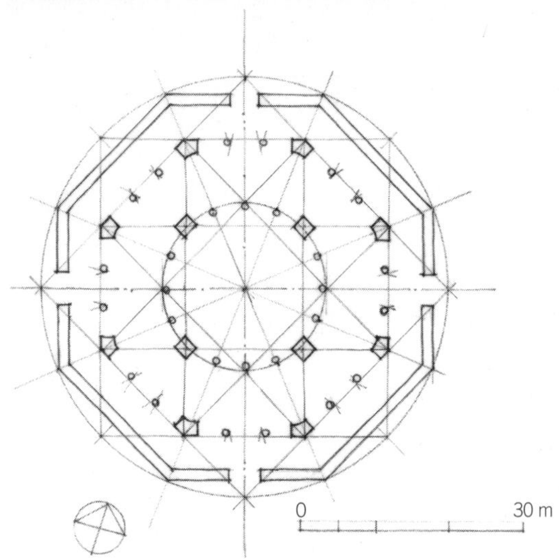


10.50 **Plan: Dome of the Rock, Jerusalem**

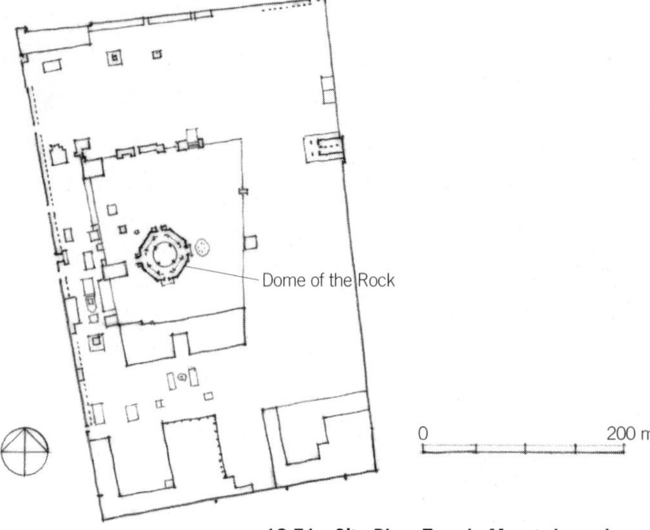


10.51 **Site Plan: Temple Mount, Jerusalem**

**Dome of the Rock**

With the Islamic conquest of Palestine and Jerusalem in the third decade of the 7th century, Caliph Abd al-Malik brought in the best masons and craftsmen available to design a building, the Dome of the Rock, which is today the oldest Islamic building to have survived intact in its original form. Completed in 692 CE, it encloses a huge rock at its center, the highest point of Mt. Moriah from which, according to tradition, the Prophet Mohammed ascended to heaven at the end of his Isra' (or Night Journey) to Jerusalem. In the Jewish tradition, this is the Foundation Stone, the symbolic foundation upon which the world was created, and the place of Abraham's Binding of Isaac. This same location is also where numerous important events in the life of Christ are believed to have occurred. The site is therefore holy to the Jewish, Christian, and Islamic religions.

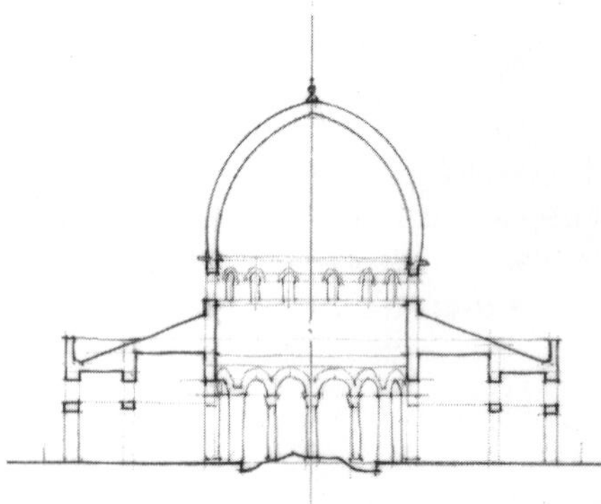

10.52 **Section: Dome of the Rock**

The building, which is Byzantine in conception and Sassanian in ornamentation, can be entered on all four points of the compass. The dome reaches 20 meters across the rock and is borne on a drum that rests on a double system of pillars and columns, the middle one circular, the outer one octagonal. The two rings, composed of piers and columns, are rotated with respect to each other so that the four piers of the inner ring face the arches of the outer octagonal ring, creating a dynamic interplay between square and circular geometries.

The dome and drum are not of brick or stone, but of wood. The dome is covered with golden copper-alloy plates and the drum with shimmering mosaic patterns of blue, red, green, and gray. The interior, in the Byzantine manner, was decorated with mosaics with a marble veneer in the lower section. Though technically a mosque, the building is much more. It is not only a geometrical and paradisiacal enclosure and a celebration of a spot of particular reverence but also a parallel to the Ka'aba in Mecca. Unlike that building, which can be circumambulated but not entered, this one can indeed be entered and yet, because of the presence of the rock, the center of the building remains in essence inaccessible. Furthermore, because one is gazing not at a rock but at the peak of the mount, one has the feeling of the architecture suspending one in space around that peak.

The history of the building site has been much debated. The site was first consecrated by the Israelites who built the First and Second Temple. After the Second Temple was razed to the ground by the Romans in 70 CE, Emperor Hadrian built a Temple to Jupiter there that was perhaps connected to an octagonal structure that, so it has been suggested by some, served as the foundation of the Dome of the Rock, but this has not yet been archaeologically proven. The crusaders consecrated the building as a Catholic church, but with their defeat, it reverted back to Islam.

10.53 **Dome of the Rock**

10.54 **Courtyard: Umayyad Mosque, Damascus, Syria**

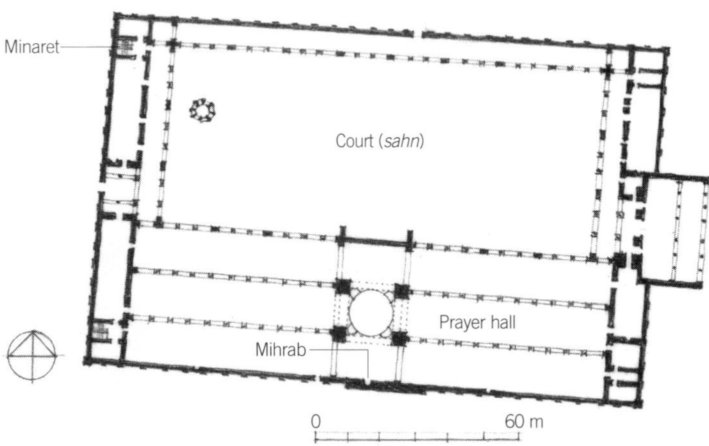


10.55 **Plan: Umayyad Mosque, Damascus**

**Umayyad Mosque**

Though the Arabs were initially illiterate, their conquests put them in touch with an array of civilizations such that they began to assimilate other cultures into their own, much as the Romans had with the Greeks, except that the transition was accomplished with astonishing rapidity and determination. From the Indians, who at that time were leading in the field of mathematics, they adopted numbering systems; from the Persians skills in construction; from the Byzantines, skills in vaulting; and from the Armenians, skills in stone masonry. The center of this learning was Damascus, built up by al-Mansur, who lavished the wealth and power of the new empire on the city. According to an Arab chronicler, Abu al-Wafa Ibn Aquil, Baghdad was filled with palaces, gardens, foundations, and mosques.

To house the books translated from Greek, Byzantine, and Indian, as well as to house the growing collection of works by Arabic scholars, Caliph al-Mamun ordered a library to be built. Known as the House of Wisdom (opened in 1004), it became the most outstanding single repository of knowledge since the great library of Alexander. Libraries were set up in other cities. Soon Arab intelligentsia were making breakthroughs in everything from medicine and chemistry to optics and philosophy. In 807 Sultan Harun ar-Rashid (766–809) sent Charlemagne a brass clock with moving ball and brass horsemen who stepped out of windows on the hour. There was nothing remotely similar in all of Europe.

The Umayyad Mosque in Damascus (709–15 CE), another monumental work of architecture in the Islamic history of that time, was built on a religious site dating back to an ancient Aramaic temple dedicated to the god Hadad. The Romans built a Temple of Jupiter on the site, a building that was transformed to a church in the 4th century (the Cathedral of St. John), situated on the western side of the temple. After the Islamic conquest of Damascus in 661, during the reign of the first Umayyad caliph, Mu'awiya Ibn Abi Sufiyan, the Muslims at first shared the church with the Christians. The caliph eventually negotiated with Christian leaders to take over the space, and in return he promised that all the other churches in the city would be safe and that a new church, dedicated to the Virgin Mary, could be built by the Christians. Damascus itself was completely rebuilt in the shape of a rectangle bisected by a Hellenistically inspired colonnaded road running north and south and crossing at the center, where the principal buildings were positioned.

The plan of the mosque is a 97 meter by 156 meter rectangle with three gates that connect the building to the city from the northern, eastern, and western sides. The mosque is defined by three halls, or *riwaqs*, that run parallel to the *qibla* wall. They are supported by two rows of stone Corinthian columns. These large and classically proportioned arches support a second smaller colonnade on which the massive wooden beams of the roof rest. The location of the mihrab is enhanced in the center by an octagonal 36-meter-high Nisr Dome (Dome of the Eagle). In the eastern part of the mosque a small, marble structure between the columns of the *riwaq* holds the tomb of St. John the Baptist, who in Islamic tradition is known as the prophet Yahya. The building was richly outfitted with marble paneling and mosaics. In the beginning of the 8th-century Caliph al-Walid bin Abd al-Malik addressed the citizens of Damascus thus: "Inhabitants of Damascus, four things give you marked superiority over the rest of the world: your climate, your water, your fruits and your baths. To these I wanted to add a fifth: this mosque."

Originally, the mosque was abutted by a palace on its southern flank, with a special entrance next to the mihrab.

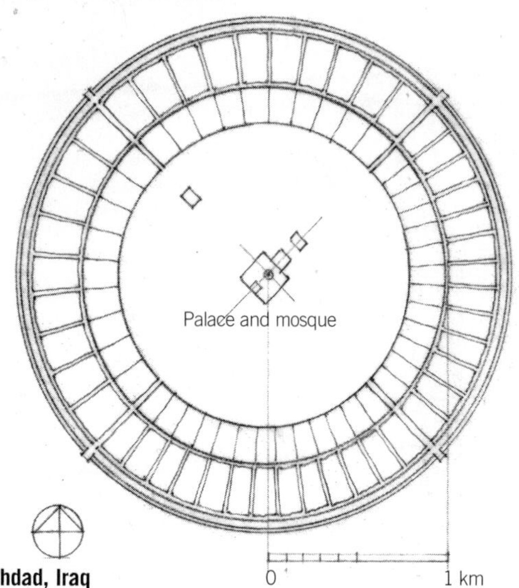


**10.56 Plan: City of Baghdad, Iraq**

### Baghdad

When the Umayyad Dynasty, which had its center in Damascus, fell in the mid-8th century, the new rulers, the Abbasids (r. 758–1258), who eventually became the champions of Sunni orthodoxy, a policy that helped them to unify an increasingly cosmopolitan Muslim empire, constructed a new capital city, Baghdad, to the west of Damascus and on the banks of the Tigris River. Engineers from the entire Islamic world were called to the site to help in its planning and construction from 762 to 766 CE.

The layout, one of the most remarkable examples of town-planning to have come down to us, was a simple circle about 3000 meters across. The walls were built of bricks and ornamented with colorful tiles. Two rings of residential zones lined the inside walls, leaving a vast area open in the middle for the palace and mosque. The walls were punctured by four gates. Though there are other smaller, regional examples of circular cities, this is by far the most elaborate. The city prospered, and with a population of about two million, it became a center of science, literature and art, like Damascus. Nothing of the city has come down to us. It perished as a consequence of numerous sieges and inundations. The Abbasid Dynasty ended when Baghdad fell to the Mongols in 1258.

With the wealth that came to the Abassid rulers, palaces of great size sprang up throughout the region, such as the fortified Palace of Ukhaidir in the desert about 200 kilometers south of Baghdad. It consists of a rectangular enclosure approximately 175 meters by 170 meters, with a gateway at the center of each, round towers at the corners, and semicircular towers spaced regularly between them. The main entrance led to an autonomous royal enclave (approximately 60 meters by 80 meters) positioned close to the north wall. It had a large courtyard and a barrel-vaulted *iwan* throne room, behind which was the royal apartment. Around that complex, there were packed four residential suites, each with its own courtyard.

The palace possessed its own mosque and bathhouse, located in the southeast of the complex. In the space between the palace and the outer walls, there would have been gardens. Though today we see the mud brick of the interior construction, these surfaces would have been lavishly decorated with carved stucco and paintings, often of flowers and vines arranged in panels.

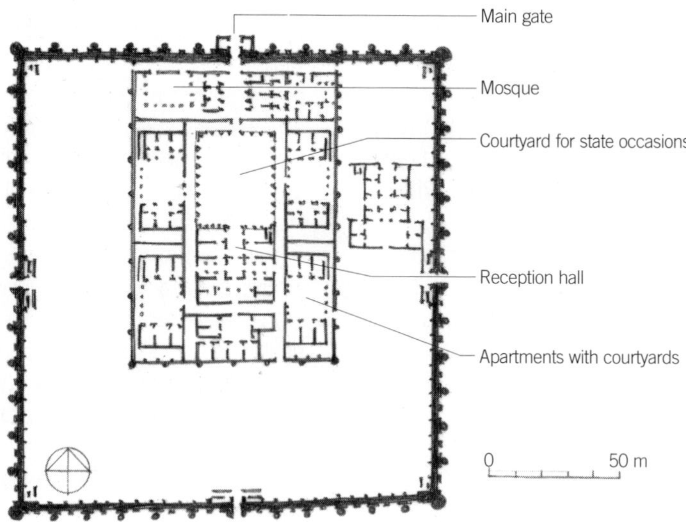


**10.57 Plan: Palace of Ukhaidir, Iraq**

10.58 Minaret, Great Mosque of Samarra, Iraq

### Great Mosque of Samarra

In 836, the Abassid capital was moved to Samarra, some 40 kilometers north of Baghdad. Samarra soon ranked among the greatest of the early Islamic cities. Though it remained the capital only until 892 CE, it prospered for centuries, reaching an area of 50 square kilometers. The caliph's residence itself took up 173 hectares on a cliff overlooking the Tigris River. Equally impressive were the two mosques, the Great Mosque of al-Mutawakkil (848–52 CE) and the Mosque of Abu Dulaf (860), both designed to look like desert fortresses. The bastioned walls of the Great Mosque of al-Mutawakkil measured 240 by 156 meters, and for centuries it was the largest mosque in the world. There were sixteen doorways that fed into the vast interior. On the inside, there were four hypostyle structures (one prayer hall and three porticoes) arranged around a large courtyard. Unlike in Damascus, where the three minarets were placed in the corners of the enclosing wall and one in the middle of the wall, here the minaret is a freestanding element placed on axis in front of the principal north entrance of the mosque. It had a helicoidal shape that reached 50 meters to the summit, with an external staircase.

Though contemporary texts are silent about the architectural articulation of these mosques, it has been suggested that they reflected the evolution from a more egalitarian society of early Islamic times into the more hierarchical society of the Abbasid period, where Persian ideas of kingship were increasingly adopted by Islamic rulers. Another reason may be that the mosque as an institution was less attached to the ruler than to the *ulama*, or religious leader, indicating a split between religious centers like these and the desert palaces, which were the centers of secular power.

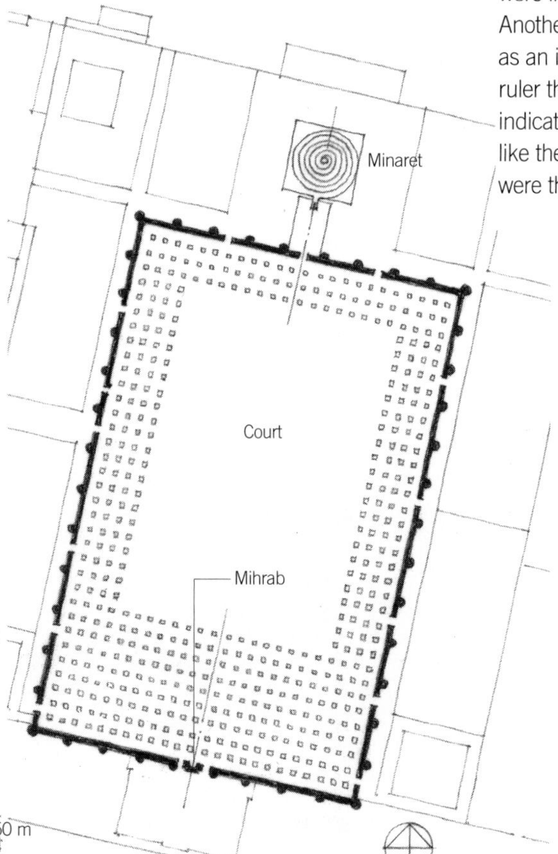


10.59 Plan: Great Mosque of Samarra

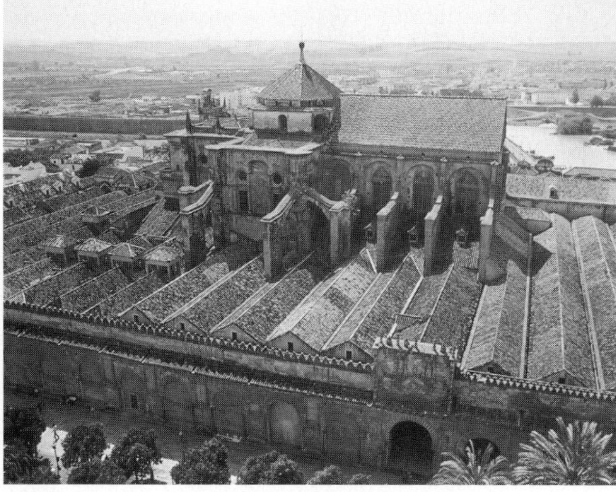

**10.60 Roofscape, Great Mosque of Córdoba, Spain**

### Great Mosque of Córdoba

Arab forces occupied Alexandria in 643 CE and crossed the Straits of Gibraltar in 711. From there, they made forays over the entire Mediterranean into Italy and France, driving out the monks from Monte Cassino, south of Rome, in 883. In the mid-7th century, however, the Muslim world had lost any real political unity when the Abbasid caliphate began to disintegrate and rival caliphates were established in Cairo and Córdoba in the mid-10th century. Originally, the Spanish territories were administered by a provincial government established in the name of the Umayyad caliphate based in Damascus. But when that dynasty was overthrown, its last surviving member fled to Spain as Emir Abd al-Rahman I. Under him, Córdoba became a quasi-autonomous capital of a vibrant Islamic culture. By the end of the 10th century, it had become the largest city in Europe with a population of about 100,000. It was also an important center of Arabic learning that was to make crucial contributions to European civilization.

The first building of significance designed under Abd al-Rahman I was the Great Mosque of Córdoba (784–6 CE). Only the southwest part, the original prayer hall, still survives more or less unaltered. The mosque, modeled loosely on the Umayyad Mosque in Damascus (705 CE), consisted of the walled-in courtyard opening up onto a hypostyle structure, in this case, of twelve bays with ten columns each. At the time of its initial construction, the Great Mosque, along with the Dome of the Rock in Jerusalem, would have been among the earliest examples of monumental Islamic architecture. There was nothing equivalent in scale and detailing in Europe.

**10.61 Dome structure: Great Mosque of Córdoba**

The wooden roof of the mosque, eventually replaced by arches, was supported on a two-tiered arch system. The principal shape of the arch was that of a high horseshoe. In it, however, were nested free-spanning, buttressing arches. The voussoirs alternate red and white stone, creating dramatic diagonal vistas. The overall result is a dramatic three-dimensional feeling.

Some of the capitals are spoils taken from destroyed churches and Roman civic buildings, and indeed, the unusual siting at the perimeter of the city may come from the fact that it was built over the ruins of a Roman warehouse. The building thus signals that the rulers had come to terms with certain aspects of the existing architectural tradition, which they incorporated with great ingenuity into their design. The horseshoe-shaped arches are thought to have been adapted from the remains of local Visigoth architecture.

10.62 **Entrance facade, Great Mosque of Córdoba**

10.63 **Hall of the Great Mosque of Córdoba**

Over time, the structure of the Great Mosque was lengthened and widened, but always with reverence for the initial design. The minaret topped with a domed pavilion was one of the first tower minarets in Islam. It was constructed to rival the Christian bell towers, which had been pulled down. A particularly important part of one of the later additions was the remarkable set of three domes added to the bay in front of the mihrab (962–966 CE), with the central one quite spectacular. Unlike Roman domes, which were primarily spatial elements, or Byzantine domes, which were props for spatially ambiguous mosaics, this dome emphasized a combination of geometric logic and decorative detail. The octagonal base closes itself toward the peak of the dome with the help of lobed arches that form two intersecting squares. These squares, in turn, create an octagonal frame that holds a petaled, umbrella-shaped dome. The result is not a dome in the sense of unified object but a series of spatial layers that act horizontally and vertically. Light filtering in through the screens of the lower register of arches contrasts with the dark niches at the corner. The mosaics, executed by Byzantine craftsmen, were of plants and vines in geometric patterns.

10.64 **Great Mosque of Abd al-Rahman I, 784–848 CE**

10.65 **Plan: Great Mosque of Córdoba**

10.66 Interior, St. Maria de Naranco

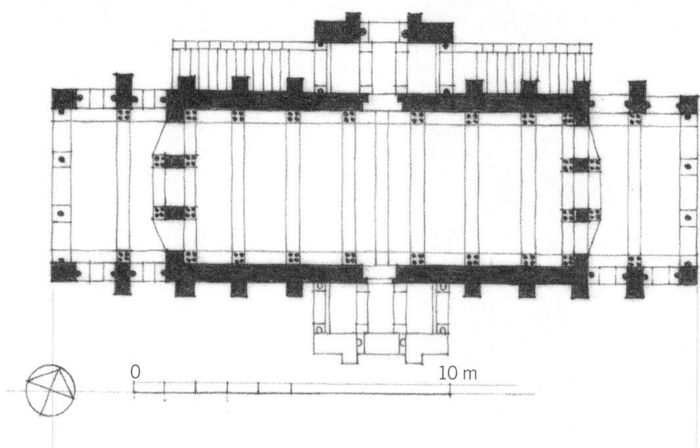


10.67 Plan: St. Maria de Naranco, Spain

**St. Maria de Naranco**

The Muslims had come to Spain in 711 CE as a small invasion force under Tarik Ibn Ziyad. With the ineffectual Visigoth kingdom crumbling before them, Islamic armies were able to extend themselves into France, with the area to the north and south of the Pyrenees, for a while, hotly contested. Eventually, however, the Muslims were able to control only the southern two-thirds of the Spanish peninsula. In the mountainous region of northwestern Spain, a Christian kingdom established itself for the entire duration of the Islamic presence in Spain. This Kingdom of Galicia, also known as the Asturian Realm, established itself juridically in 713 CE with Oviedo as its principal city, which remained its capital until 914.

One of the most interesting Asturian churches is St. Maria de Naranco, a few miles north of Oviedo. Dedicated in 848, it was not in the shape of a traditional church. Rather it was a long hall over a vaulted undercroft to be used by King Ramiro I and his royal magnates, with the people gathered outside the church and listening to the liturgy through the open-ended compartments. At each end, there is a loggia defined by meticulously worked arches. The sidewalls of the hall were decorated with arcades and ornamented by pairs of attached columns, which help thicken the wall to take the thrust of the vault above. Such vaults at the time were rare. While the building has both Muslim and Visigoth features, the hall shape itself was typical of German courtly structures as are the capitals. But the elegant proportions as well as its siting reflect Islamic influence.

10.68 Transverse and longitudinal sections: St. Maria de Naranco

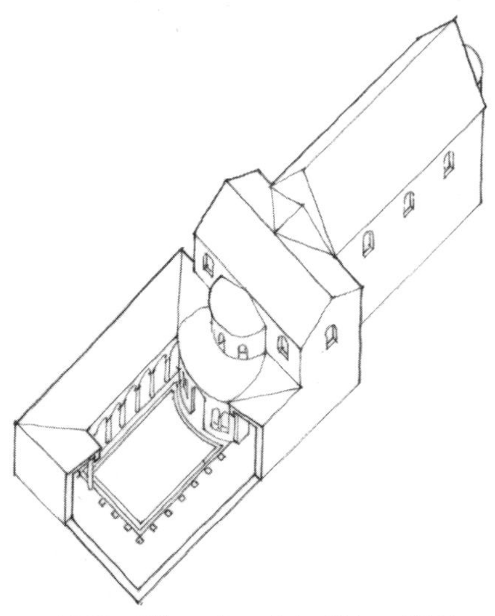
**10.69 Oblique view of the Abbey of Fulda**

## CAROLINGIAN EMPIRE

By the age of Charlemagne, the civilization of ancient Rome had become a distant memory, its culture, architecture, and art belonging to the past. Even the process of making concrete, the material so important to Roman vaulting, was forgotten. But the idea of the empire did not die; it was an illiterate Frankish king, Charlemagne (742–814) who first revived it. Long before his coronation in St. Peter's Church in 800 CE, the Carolingian Church had established a close relationship to Rome, but it was only with the coronation that Roman liturgy became the norm. For this, Charlemagne turned to the Benedictine Rule. When St. Benedict (489–543 CE) formulated his rules, it was an age in which temporal rule had broken down. As a counterbalance to the chaos, St. Benedict envisioned the monastery as a devout Christian family of men. The waking hours were devoted primarily to worship and work, primarily manual labor. The rules that governed this community acted as a type of ersatz constitutional system. The system was, however, inconsistently applied. But with Charlemagne the importance of the rules was reaffirmed as a way to regularize monastic life from a patchwork of devotional practices, some still residually connected to pagan religion. As a result, monasteries became successful financial, territorial, and educational institutions and, indeed, soon became the mainstay of stability and order in the fragile geopolitical structure of the Holy Roman Empire.

A religion that had formerly lived within the limited confines of what was left of the Roman Empire was now becoming more than a regional, Mediterranean phenomenon, and with the ascension to the throne of Charlemagne, the destiny of the Franks and, indeed, of all of Europe changed. A bold thinker and an excellent commander, he was able to dominate a large area of Europe. Originally, in the 5th century, the kingdom had centered around the city of Cologne, but a century later it moved its seat to Paris, which was the titular capital of the Franks. Charlemagne fought against the still un-Christianized Saxons to the east, against the Slavs to the south, and against the Muslim rulers in Spain. Charlemagne's Christian opponents resided in the Lombard regions of Northern Italy, the conquest of which opened the way for his control of Northern Italy and then Rome.

A new unified era was thus created, but it was a unity that came not from Rome or Constantinople but from the north. The seat of religious power was still, however, in Rome, and therein lay a peculiar ambiguity about the location of power that was to beset European politics for centuries. This split would not be resolved until the Enlightenment in the 18th century.

Though the type of government Charlemagne set up developed into a feudal system with its strict hierarchy linking serf, landlord, and count to the king, Charlemagne's kingdom lacked a firm centralized bureaucratic structure. The nature of Charlemagne's rule was one of constant mobility. He moved from place to place to assert and to expand his authority. The result was an important expansion of architectural works that put the imprint of his rule onto the landscape. In Italy, just north of Rome, he founded the monastery of Farfa as a southern outpost of the empire; to the east, he founded Lorsch and Fulda.

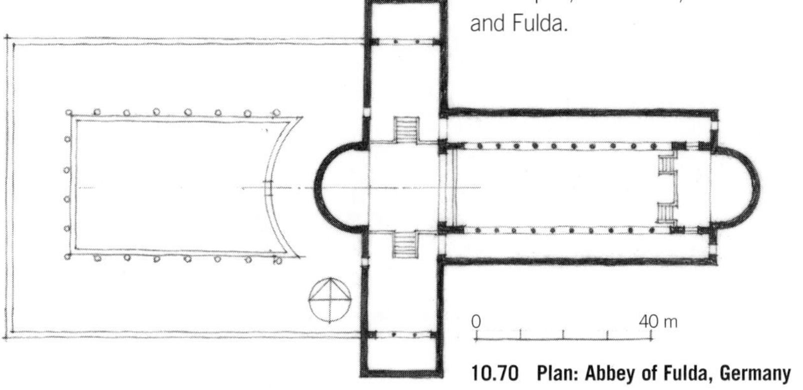

**10.70 Plan: Abbey of Fulda, Germany**

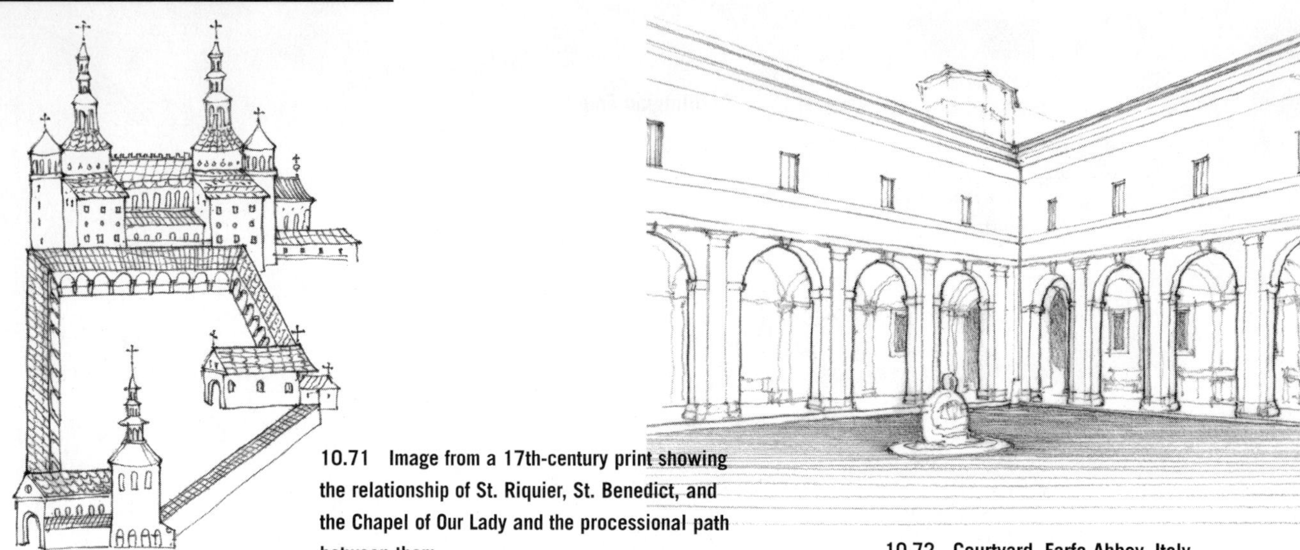

10.71 Image from a 17th-century print showing the relationship of St. Riquier, St. Benedict, and the Chapel of Our Lady and the processional path between them.

10.72 Courtyard, Farfa Abbey, Italy

In creating a new east-west connection from Fulda to St. Riquier as well as a north-south axis from Aachen to Rome, Charlemagne was able not only to promote his kingdom but also to conduct trade as had never been experienced since the demise of the Roman Empire. Architects could, of course, no longer rely on concrete, and so churches in this era show a particularly stark and simple volumetricity. Windows are small, roundheaded, sparsely ornamented, and positioned high in the wall. It was an architecture that did not tax the spatial imagination and yet it was one that yielded powerful forms and dark mysterious interiors. It was also an architecture that spoke a language of clarity. Walls were not only thick but solid-looking. The transept, a minor element in the 5th-century basilica churches of Rome, became integral to the design. This would set in play the need for innovations in vaultings and then for an increasingly intricate relationship between inside and outside that would become the fundamental architectural issue of subsequent medieval European architecture. But vaulting at the time was to a large extent a thing of the future. Most Carolingian buildings had wooden roofs.

The reconstruction of the Imperial Benedictine Abbey of Farfa (ca. 681 CE) shows an excellent example of this arrangement. Located north of Rome, it was designed as the place from which the Carolingians and the Romans could keep an eye on each other while at the same time coordinate their agendas. It was a powerful institution with its abbots ruling the surrounding area as princes. The building's apse was flanked by two round towers. The entrance courtyard was modeled purposefully on St. Peter's Church in Rome.

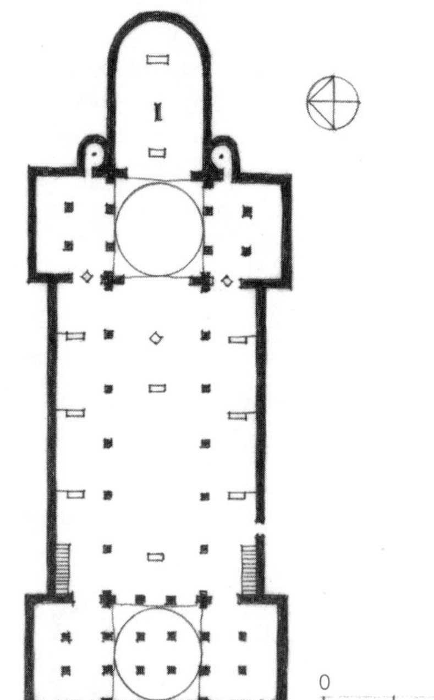


10.73 Plan: Abbey Church of St. Riquier, France

The Abbey Church of St. Riquier in northern France, not far from Amiens, though it too is no longer extant, can be reconstructed from descriptions and old views. Completed in 799 CE, it followed the basic plan, with towers soaring from cylindrical bases. It had a population of about 300 monks and 100 novices, not to mention the servants and serfs. The abbey was dedicated to the Holy Trinity and was connected to two smaller sanctuaries dedicated to St. Benedict and the Virgin Mary, all connected by walls and porticoes. Conforming to the new liturgy, there was a processional path through the church, which was designed to allow visitation of the various altars in sequence. (The church contained a collection of 25 relics.) This processional movement through the church was to become a mainstay of medieval religious practice. Also new was the addition behind the altar of an autonomous spatial zone that accommodated the monks. This church behind a church, or choir, was to become an important element in church design of the Middle Ages. Also significant was the design of the tower over the transept crossing.

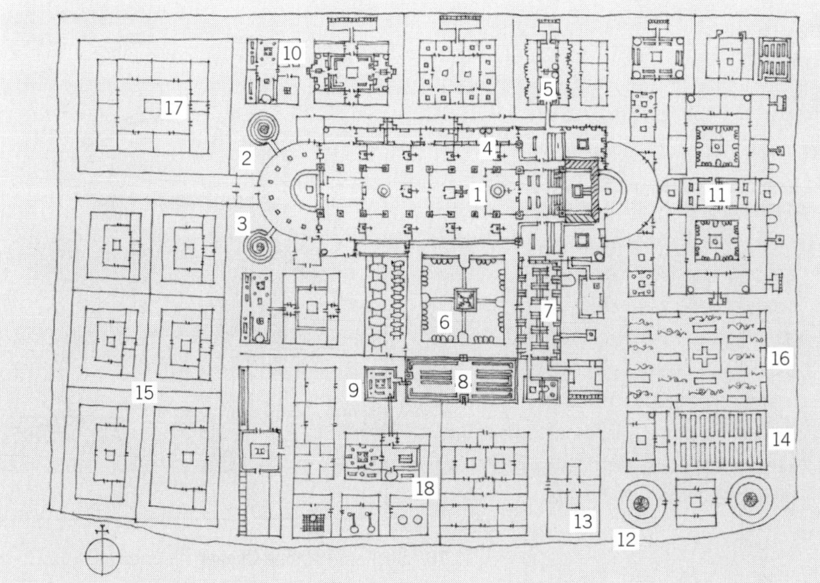


**10.74 Plan of St. Gall**

1. Church
2. Tower of St. Michael
3. Tower of St. Gabriel
4. Guest lodgings
5. Abbot's house
6. Cloister
7. Monks' dormitory
8. Monks' refectory
9. Kitchen
10. Brew house
11. Novitiate and infirmary
12. Henhouse
13. Granary
14. Monks' garden
15. Monks' orchard and cemetery
16. Sheep, goats, and cows
17. Knights and vassals
18. Workshops

**Plan of St. Gall**

In the 17th century, a medieval plan for a monastery was found that, so it was determined, was produced between 820 and 830 CE. It was a copy of an earlier plan and made under Abbot Gozbert for the building of the monastery at St. Gall in Switzerland. The monastery had originally been founded by an Irish monk, Gallus (ca. 612), but it had fallen into disrepair. Gozbert used this plan for his refurbishing campaign. The plan, drawn with red lead on smooth calfskin faces, provides a remarkably comprehensive snapshot of a monastic structure, in this case an institution of about 40 buildings inhabited by about 110 monks, with an equal number of lay people who served as support staff.

The site is organized into three zones: to the west, at the bottom of the plan, one finds the areas open to the lay population; the monastery proper is in the middle zone; and at the top, there is the garden, the infirmary, and the cemetery. To the left of the road that accesses the church entrance, there was a reception hall and dormitory for pilgrims. To the north of the church there were special buildings for the abbot and novices.

The church was a nave church with no transept. Its rounded entrance was flanked by freestanding towers. These were not bell towers, as that was a later development. At the top of one tower was an altar to St. Michael and on the other was an altar to St. Gabriel, the celestial guardians representing the forces of light against those of darkness and evil.

Though the draughtsman did not show the thickness of the walls, he did show doors, chimneys, and ovens and labeled each room. He even labeled the vegetables that were planted in the garden, such as onions, leeks, radishes, and fennel. The monk's cloister, the spatial core of the plan, was an open yard about 30 meters square with arcaded walks giving access to surrounding buildings, such as the dormitory, refectory, and the storehouse for the wine and beer kegs. The north walk, broader than the rest, was used as a chapter house for daily meetings, and it contained benches. It was connected to the east wall of the church with a special entrance that allowed the monks access to the alta, which was screened off from the public.

The plan was drawn using a module of 40 Carolingian feet, the *numeri sacri*, as that is the dimension of the crossing of the church's altar. The church length was five times that amount, or 200 feet, the depth of the side aisles, half that amount, or 20 feet. By means of further halving one comes to 2.5 feet, the smallest base measure applied in the plan.

10.75 Palatine Chapel, Aachen, Germany

As the burial place of Charlemagne, as well as the setting for imperial coronations, the Palatine Chapel became a dynastic shrine and an icon of imperial power. It is also likely that it was viewed as an incarnation of the heavenly Jerusalem. It cannot be a coincidence that the circumference of the inner octagon comes to 144 Carolingian feet, just as the walls of the heavenly Jerusalem described in the Book of Revelations came to 144 cubits.

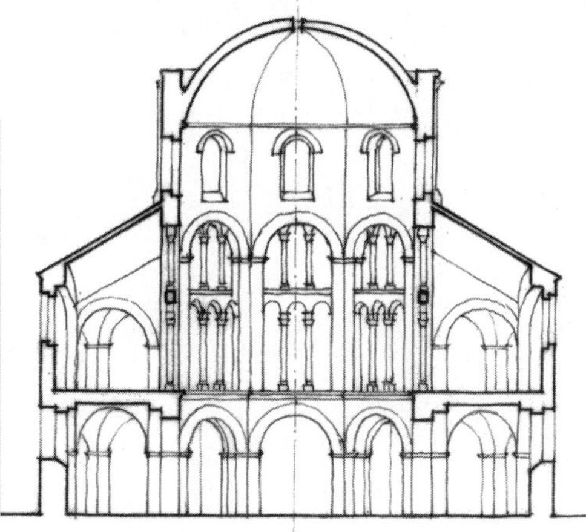

10.76 Section: Palatine Chapel 0 15 m

### Royal Palace at Aachen

The most important partially surviving example of Carolingian architecture is the Royal Palace at Aachen (Aix-la-Chapelle), begun in 792 CE, to the west of Cologne. Today only the Palatine Chapel exists, but at the time, it would have been the largest new building complex in the Christian world. The layout was bold and meant to be, in essence, a three-dimensional diagram. To the north was a cavernous audience hall. To the south and parallel to the audience hall was the chapel. Linking them was a 120-meter gallery punctuated in the middle by a monumental gatehouse. Here we see in direct visual form, the separate and yet united realms of church and state. The chapel was fronted by an entrance atrium. Linking the atrium to the chapel was a *westwork*, or what Carolingian writers called *castellum*, an important innovation of Carolingian architecture. As its name suggests, it was literally a piece of a castle appendaged to the church, which allowed the emperor to make official appearances at the upper-level tribune facing into the courtyard. The throne was also located there, directly over the main portal. From it, the emperor could look into the space of the chapel from his privileged vantage point.

Basilica

Gallery

Inner court

Outer court

Gallery

Westwork

Atrium

Palatine Chapel

0 50 m

10.77 Plan: Palace at Aachen

The Palatine Chapel consisted of a tall octagonal shaft of space, surrounded by annular galleries. At the ground floor, the octagon was defined by plain, undivided arches that held a cornice that separated the lower from the upper arches. On that cornice, the openings were defined by elegant arcade screens between tall arches leading up to a groin vault. To fight the lateral thrusts of the dome, the architects added lateral vaults at the gallery level that seem to have been inspired from observing Roman theater construction. The design, in its simple organization of piers and columns, has the appearance of a Carolingian attempt to revive Roman aesthetic sensibilities. The use of variegated marbles for the paneling and the voussoirs also reflected an awareness of St. Vitale in Ravenna, with which this building most certainly sought to compete, even though at St. Vitale, the shimmering and curved surfaces create a more ephemeral effect. Nonetheless, at the Palatine Chapel we see the beginning of an internal facade and of the search to bring unity to various architectural elements—the openings, cornice lines, revetments, and columns—while holding true to liturgical needs.

10.78 Theotokos, icon of the Virgin Mary

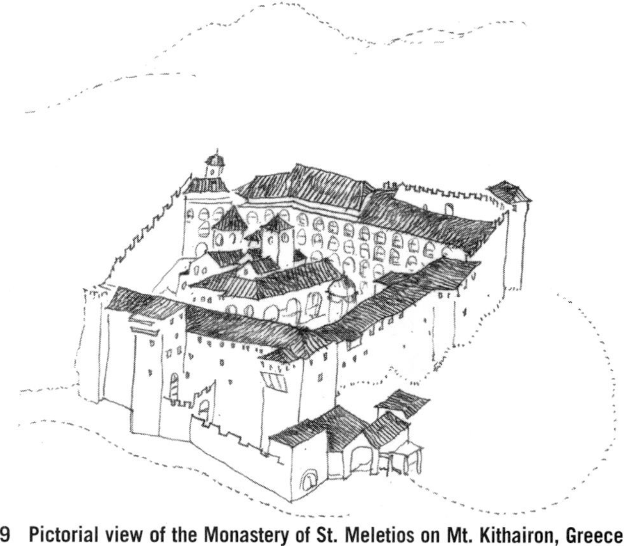

10.79 Pictorial view of the Monastery of St. Meletios on Mt. Kithairon, Greece

## BYZANTINE EMPIRE

The Byzantine Empire, despite some successes against the Arabs to the south and the Bulgars to the north, experienced a period of decline that began at the end of the 6th century. Mismanagement and the iconoclastic controversy on the question of whether images were to be used in religious services weakened the empire. With the creation of the alliance between the Roman Papacy and the Frankish Kingdom, the Byzantine Church was becoming increasingly isolated from Europe. Nonetheless, once the period of Byzantine iconoclasm came to an end, Nicephorus I (802–11 CE), was able to introduce a period of relative stability, especially once the Slavs had converted in the 10th century, choosing Byzantine orthodoxy over the Latin Church in Rome. The bishop of Constantinople thus became the spiritual father of the Rus, Bulgarians, Serbians, and the Slavs who were still in partial control of the Peloponnese. The later conversion of the Hungarians also helped. Resulting from all this, by the time of Basil I (867–886), was an upward trend in politics, literature, and art. A great deal of effort was made to expand the Imperial Palace in Constantinople. It was reported that in 830 CE, a Byzantine envoy went to Baghdad and was so impressed by the splendor of Arab architecture that he urged the emperor to build a similar palace. The palace soon became one of the great architectural complexes of the world.

The revival of Byzantine culture brought with it important changes in the political-architectural relationship. Unlike in the Justinian era, during which most of the major architectural monuments had been conceived as public buildings, the architecture of this period was to serve the imperial elite. As a result, major architectural projects were rare. The churches of this period, generally part of a larger monastic complexes, were thus considerably different from their Western counterparts in that they were not firmly linked to each other. Instead, they were relatively autonomous units, privately endowed, and performing important local services, such as running orphanages and hospitals. In exchange for the endowment, the founder obtained perpetual ad memoriam Masses and services and the right to participate in the monastery's internal affairs. Though schools were sometimes associated with these monasteries, they were located outside the walls together with the administrative offices. Today, most of the monastic enclaves have disappeared, leaving only the church as freestanding object. Mt. Athos Monastery and Mt. Kithairon Monastery of St. Meletios, however, give us an indication of the monastic enclosure.

The change to individual patronage created a shift toward a more internal view of religion. And for this reason, if we compare Byzantium with the great learning centers in India, Spain, and the Benedictine monasteries of the Carolingians, religion in Byzantium was still so attached to devotional practices that the powerful relationship between religion and learning that was developing in other parts of the world did not take place.

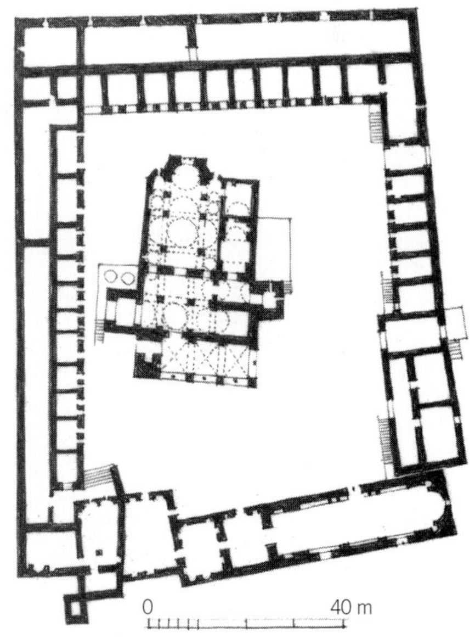


10.80 Plan: Monastery of St. Meletios on Mt. Kithairon

**10.81 Interior: Church of Christ Pantokrator, Istanbul**

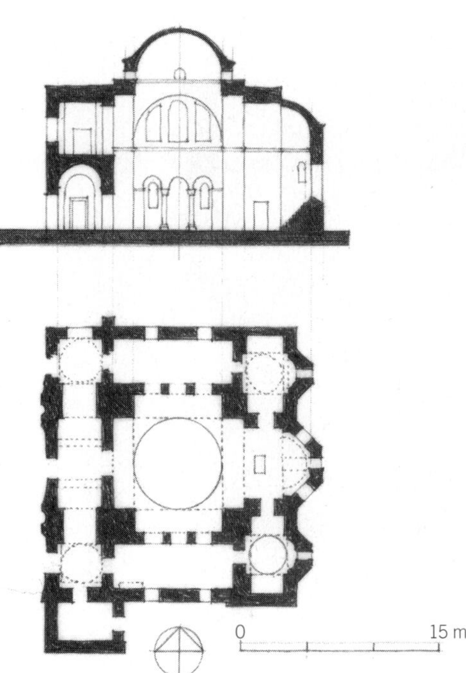


**10.82 Plan and section: Koimesis at Nicaea, Greece**

### Theotokos Tou Libos

By 800 CE, the Byzantine church had begun to take on its characteristic form of a dome resting on four columns placed in a square. The interiors were outfitted with more sumptuous mosaics. But because the interiors have been despoiled variously by the Venetians, Mongols, or Turks, there are few available today for study. An early example of the domical or Greek-cross church plan is Koimesis in Nicaea (Iznik), from the 8th century. Four strong piers mark the corners. They shelter small groin-vaulted bays of equal depth. A dome on pendentives rises from the peaks of the barrel vaults and is enclosed in a low drum, which is pierced at the cardinal points by small windows. The eastern arm opens up to the chancel, which is flanked by side chambers with *absidioles* that, on the outside, register as polygons. This cross-shaped, domed nucleus is enveloped north and south by barrel-vaulted aisles and galleries. To the west, there is an *esonarthex* surmounted by a gallery. The exterior, typical of post-Justinian architecture, reads as a graduated mass culminating in the dome, but the parts are tightly fused into each other. A more developed version of the cross-domed plan was used by Emperor John II Komenos in his Church of Christ Pantokrator (Zeyrek Camii), built 1118–43.

The dome was not only an important part of the composition but also was painted with an image of Christ looking down at the worshipper. For the Byzantines, art was inseparable from theology, with the presence of other icons either on the surface of the wall or as separate devotional objects. The scale of the churches thus emphasized spatial intimacy. Subtlety was valued over size. All in all, more so than in the west, the church was an image of the universe. The bishop's entrance into the church symbolizes Christ's coming into the flesh. Candles, incense, music, reliquaries, gold and silver utensils, and shining mosaic walls helped create a world based on mystery and awe.

Similar to Koimesis, and making the transition from Justinian to the Byzantine style that would become prevalent in subsequent centuries as a dome on four columns is the Church of the Theotokos Tou Libos (now called North Church and part of St. Mary Panachrantos), built in 907 by Constantine Lips, a high official in the reigns of Leo VI and Constantine VII Porphyrogenitus. It was associated with a convent and a hospice for travelers. The sacristy and vestry to the right and left of the apse are still pronounced but now more organically fused into the side aisles. The church had an upper level with two small chapels above the two corner bays at the west end of the *naos*. A south church was added some 80 years later.

**10.83 Interior: Theotokos Tou Libos**

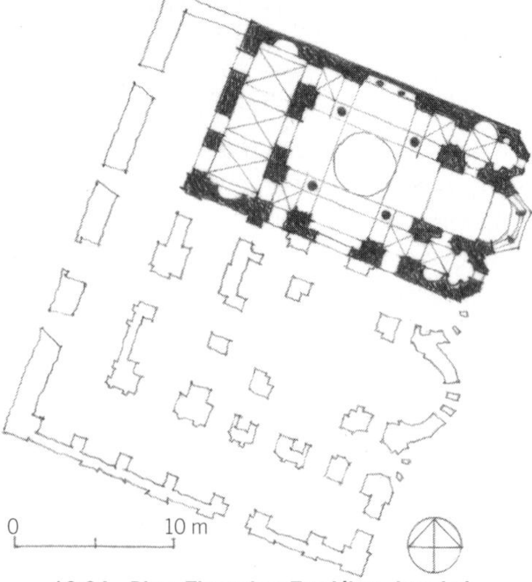


**10.84 Plan: Theotokos Tou Libos, Istanbul**

10.85 Germigny-des-Prés, France

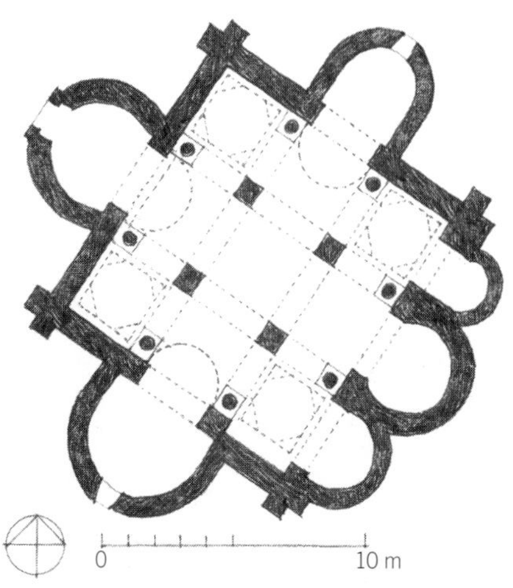


10.86 Plan: Germigny-des-Prés

**Germigny-des-Prés**

An important influence on European architecture in the west came from the direction of Armenia. Because of the continual attacks by White Huns, Khazars, Arabs, Byzantines, and later by Mongols, Armenian architects and workmen often sought to exercise their craft in other places. Armenian masons were brought to Cairo, for example, to design the walls and gates of that city. In 806–811, the Armenian architect, Oton Matsaetsi, built the church of Germigny-des-Prés in France. One of the most elegantly designed small churches of the time in Europe, it consisted of a box divided on its interior into a nine-square grid with four piers in the center and attached columns against the perimeter walls. The main and transverse axes, ending with apses, have tunnel vaults. Horseshoe-shaped arches exist both in plan and elevation. The entrance cuts through the western apse. One can easily sense the similarity between this church and St. Thaddeus near the town of Tadios in Azerbeijan, which still today attracts thousands of Armenian pilgrims from all parts of the world during the three-day-long Feast of Thaddeus. Though parts of the original building have been destroyed and rebuilt after earthquakes, both are excellent examples of a masterful integration of volume and space.

The Church of the Holy Cross (consecrated 921), originally unencumbered by ancillary buildings, makes its impression by its symmetry and equilibrium. Unlike Byzantine churches, which were composite in nature, Armenian churches aimed to maintain a tight bond between interior and exterior. This means that the Sacristy and the Vestry, instead of being separate spaces to the right and left of the altar, are embedded in the mass of the wall. The interior, however, was never just a reflection of outer form. It is as if the interior and exterior are squeezed against each other. The Church, as is also typical of Armenian architecture, presents the buildings in simple elemental forms, cubes, cylinders, cones, and pyramids. The dome is conical on the outside but within, hemispherical. Walls are made of an aggregate of pebbles and mortar, much like concrete, and dressed with blocks of closely fitting pink sandstone. The plan, with its four apses, is known as a *tetraconch*, even though the east and west exedrae are deeper than the north and south. The exterior is decorated with bas-relief sculpture depicting biblical scenes. The lighting on the interior is indirect and the windows are small. The main light source is around the drum, above which the dome seems to float, as if it were on a ring of light. The wide side apses swell the space outward at ground level, with small concavities at the corners, between the piers, adding further illumination. The entire interior was originally painted with religious scenes.

10.87 Church of the Holy Cross, on the island of Aght'amar in Lake Van, Turkey, near Gevash (Wostan)

**10.88 Pueblo Bonito, Chaco Canyon, USA**

## PUEBLO BONITO

Borders that have been drawn in more recent history cause the ruins of the southwestern United States to be often viewed as separate from those of Mesoamerica. In reality, the settlements in places such as Chaca Canyon and Mesa Verde made up the northern frontier of the Mesoamerican world and were not separated from its influence. However, because they were on the frontier, thousands of miles from Teotihuacán and Tula, they developed a very self-defined culture. Inhabiting a harsh desert environment, the Anasazi people did not have the advantage of a food surplus that could support the vast architectural undertakings that were going on further south. Instead they had to breed drought-resistant forms of corn, which along with beans and squash, would sustain them. The Anasazi also had to create an architecture that was appropriate to their climate.

Since the word *anasa'zi* is a Navajo word meaning "ancient enemy," the Pueblo people, who are direct descendants of the Anasazi, prefer to use the Hopi word *Hisatsinom*, meaning "the Old Ones." Around 600 CE, they began to change from a migratory farming culture to a sedentary one, learning to build permanent houses with an increasing level of sophistication in their architecture and time-consuming building techniques. The best known *Hisatsinom* settlement of the Chaco Canyon is Pueblo Bonito (Spanish for "beautiful town"), one of the largest towns in North America at the time and a prototype for other settlements. It was located beneath a massive cliff, part of which has since caved in. By 1100, there were 12 major Pueblo cities and hundreds of small clutches of houses—one of the most impressive urban structures north of Mexico and bespeaking a high level of social organization.

Pueblo Bonito had a D-shaped plan with masses of rooms and circular ceremonial structures called kivas surrounding two large plazas. The rows of rooms each rose one story before stepping back from the one below, giving the whole an impression of a terraced amphitheater. And, indeed, it has been suggested that one of the city's characteristics was to provide a place for viewing ritual dancing. Housing from 800 to 1200 people, the pueblo covered four acres and, at some points, reached five stories in height.

Kivas were an essential part of the *Hisatsinom* culture and architecture. They represent a local building type with a very long history and broad distribution. They had originated as circular storehouses, often nothing more than deep pit houses, plastered on the inside with smooth adobe. But they soon evolved to become semisubterranean temples, serving as communal spaces to perform and view ritual dances. Each kiva was the province of a social unit, with any one village possibly having several such units. They were only for men, with women allowed only on special occasions. In Pueblo Bonito, among the regular-sized kivas, there were two that were over 18 meters across and that probably served the entire city. Though Pueblo Bonito's kivas were built above the ground, the subterranean effect was maintained by constructing rooms all around and filling in any empty spaces with earth. They were equipped with a central firebox, a low masonry bench around the wall, and four wooden posts. Some had an underfloor ventilating system and a subfloor vault to the west of the fireplace. The flat roof had a smoke hole in the center and served as an entrance by means of a ladder. The sandstone masonry walls at Pueblo Bonito consisted of a loose rubble center faced on both sides with artfully placed sandstone bricks.

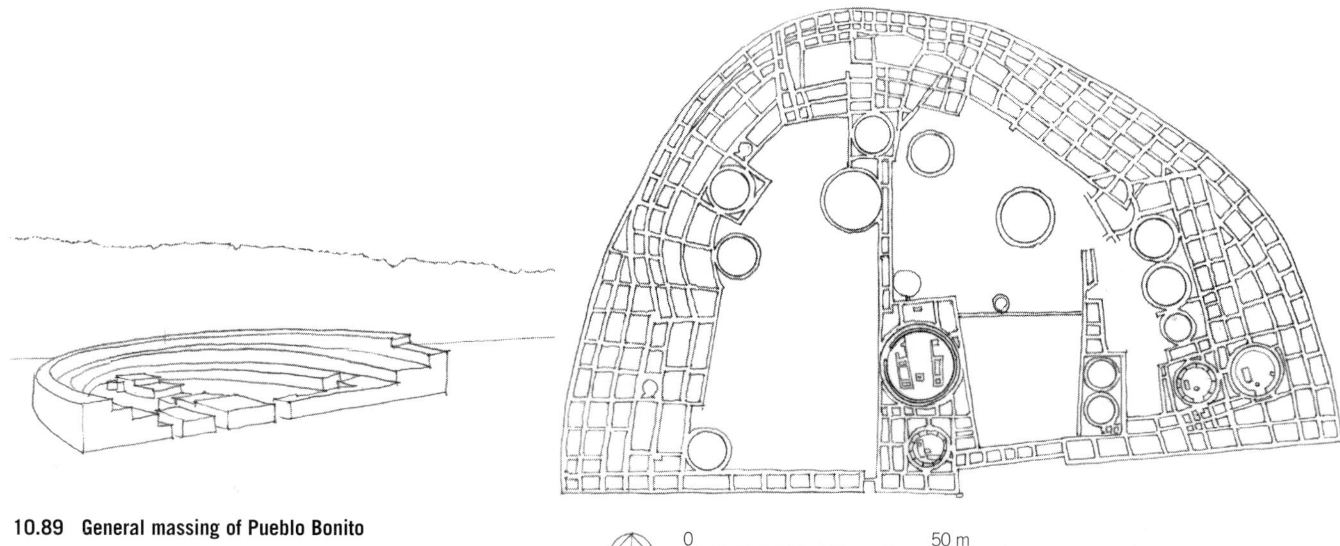


10.89 **General massing of Pueblo Bonito**

10.90 **Plan: Pueblo Bonito**

Construction of Pueblo Bonito began about 920 and was built up and modified over the course of three centuries. Early research attempted to relate the construction of Pueblo Bonito directly to more contemporary Pueblo architecture, where the structure reflects the social order of its inhabitants. The evidence, however, indicates that this was not the case at Pueblo Bonito. It is, however, clear that this city would have required a complex coordination of labor and materials. Tens of thousands of pine beams, used for wall supports and roof structures, came from a forest 96 kilometers away.

Pueblo Bonito also seems to have been aligned with the cardinal directions and with the solstice. Its overall orientation is north-south, which became typical of all structures erected by the *Hisatsinom*, but the architecture integrates the sun and the moon and the midpoint and extremes of both cycles into its layout. These facts, along with the rigidly patterned placement of doorways, the modularity in building proportions, and hundreds of other details, cause some researchers to believe that the master plan for Pueblo Bonito was likely conceived by one person or a small group of people and that there was a controlling hand and eye behind its construction. Though the highly disciplined architecture could suggest a strong hierarchical social order, the *Hisatsinom* were believed to have had a fairly egalitarian society.

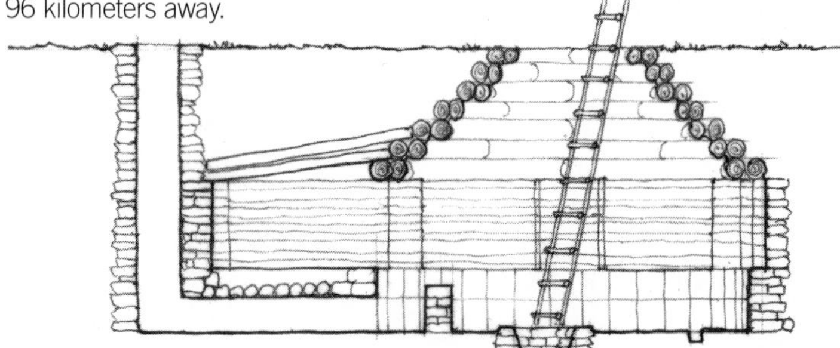

10.91 **Plan and section of traditional kiva**

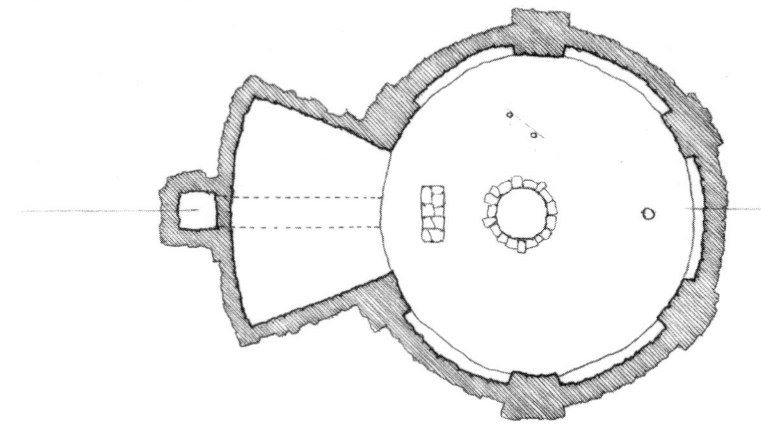

**10.92 Temple of the Foliated Cross, Palenque**

### MAYA CITY-STATES

In the 8th and 9th centuries, the Mayan city states of the Yucatan dominated the peninsula. In the period 600–750 CE, the city of Palenque, located in the foothills of the Chiapas altiplano, began to expand under the leadership of the great king Pacan and his two sons. The Otulum River passes through the city, and via a long corbel-vaulted tunnel, water was diverted to the palace. Unlike the solid masses of most Maya buildings, the Palenque architects set corbeled vaults parallel to one another, which not only created greater interior spaces, but also stabilized the whole structure. This is one reason why they have aged so well. The rooftop ornamental superstructure was also made as a roof-comb, which further reduced the overall weight of the structure.

Palenque is set into the hillside and laid out to take advantage of the contours and natural cleavage formed by the Otulum River. The central palace is the most remarkable of the Palenque buildings. It sits on a broad platform that is centrally located to visually command the site. On one side, the palace dominates the edge of the Otulum River; on the other, its platform and profile define the edges of the central plaza of Palenque.

The palace complex opens up toward the hills, although the monumental stairs are on the north and west sides. This would indicate that access to the palace, as one might expect, was carefully regulated. The interior is dominated by two courts that take up half the complex and are separated by a single double-vaulted, long building that was the original core of the palace. The south half of the palace is labyrinthine, with a dense network of interconnected chambers. Visually, the palace's most recognizable structure is the four-story tower that rises just outside the west courtyard. It is unique in Mayan architecture, and its purpose is still undetermined.

To the southwest of the palace complex is the so-called Temple of the Inscriptions (683 CE), which is famous because its foundation contains the tomb of K'inich Janaab Pakal. Unlike most tombs in the bases of pyramids, as at Tikal, which are totally interred within their superstructure, Pakal's tomb remained accessible from a stairway at the top of the temple. In the access stairway, we therefore find the explicit spatialization of one of the cardinal ideologies of Mayan religious practice, primarily, that rulers and generations to come ruled because of their connection to their ancestors and that honoring and maintaining an ongoing relationship with those ancestors was critical to their being and welfare. The stelae on Pakal's sarcophagus shows him passing through the underworld in the process of becoming an ancestor.

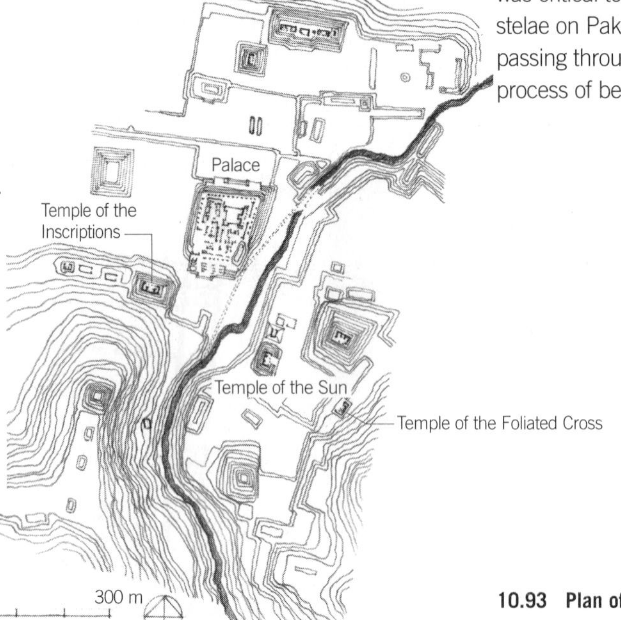


**10.93 Plan of Palenque, near Chiapas, Mexico**

10.94 **Ball court, Copán, Honduras**

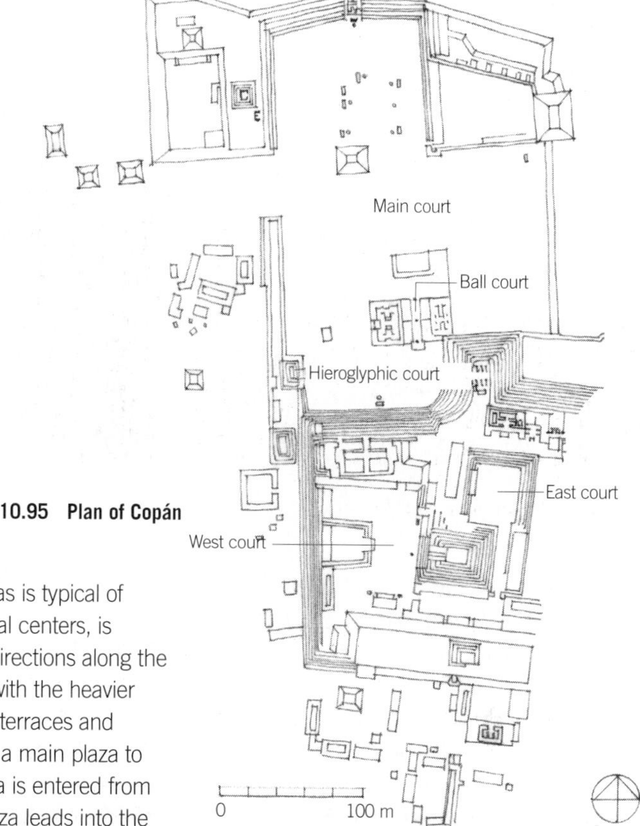


10.95 **Plan of Copán**

## Copán

Located in a mountain valley of the Copán River on the western edge of Honduras, Copán is the southernmost of the major Mayan cities. One of the largest Mayan centers, Copán was the capital of a state covering several hundred square kilometers between 400–820 CE. The site is about 600 meters above sea level, above the jungles and rain forests of the lowland Maya. Although occupied for about 2000 years, the main visible buildings were built in the period 600–800 CE.

The excavated ruins cover about 40 acres and consist of the main acropolis and five plazas. Like the ancestral complex of Tikal, the main structure at Copán is an agglomerative megacomplex, built over a period of 600 years, which has formed into a gigantic platform with an assorted collection of masonry temples, palaces, ball courts, plazas, tombs, carved stelae, and altars dating mostly from 695–800 CE.

Like the acropolis at Monte Albán, the surrounding mountains of the Copán River valley offered rich possibilities for dramatic landscape alignments. In particular, the Copán ball court, which sits between the main plaza and the acropolis, is aligned so that a view through it, which is also the main view from atop the acropolis, seems to exactly echo the angles of the steep hills beyond.

The Copán main group, as is typical of Mesoamerican ceremonial centers, is oriented to the cardinal directions along the longer north-south axis, with the heavier concentration of built-up terraces and palaces to the south and a main plaza to the north. The main plaza is entered from the east. A subsidiary plaza leads into the vast rectangular space of the main bounded plaza, with a low, three-level platform mound in the middle. A ball court and a subsidiary platform abut the south end of the main plaza, just before a monumental set of stairways leads up to the higher levels of the royal complex. A platform pyramid sits in the middle of the high terrace, which is edged by a series of palaces and tombs. The northern edge of the main plaza extends out into a T, forming another pyramid. The steep western stairway is a famous hieroglyphic stairway, whose 2,200 glyphs relate the story of the last Copán dynasty.

10.96 **Maya hieroglyphs at Copán**

10.97 Detail of stela at Quirigua, Guatemala

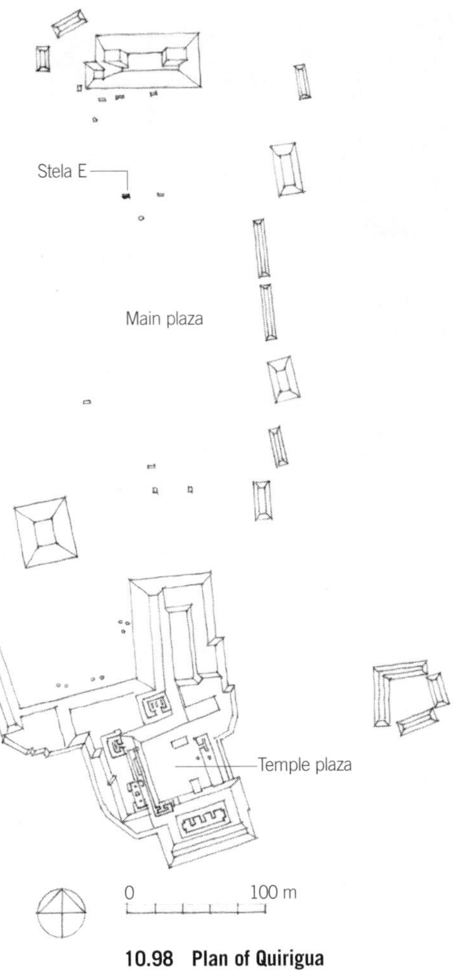


10.98 Plan of Quirigua

## Quirigua

Cauac Sky became king of Quirigua in 725 CE, while it was still a part of the state of Copán, but after he defeated and captured Eighteen Rabbit, king of Copán, in 738 CE, Quirigua became independent. Cauac Sky, who ruled for 60 years and is immortalized in a huge 10-meter high stela in the middle of the central plaza, is responsible for most of the building there.

10.99 Stela E in the central plaza of Quirigua

Situated in the Maya lowlands about 100 kilometers from the Caribbean Sea, Quirigua extends over 4 square kilometers on the floodplains of the Motagua River. Today, only the largest structures rise above the 1 to 2 meters of alluvium deposited over the 1000 years of abandonment. Its core is a gigantic, rectangular Great Plaza, oriented north-south and studded with some of the largest Maya stelae and monoliths ever. Its main platform mounds and palace group are clustered at its south end. Their interrelationships and urban composition is classic and skillful. A freestanding, solitary pyramid sits off-center at one end of the great plaza; its other side lines up with a much smaller, better defined plaza, with a ball court in its center. A monumental flight of stairs at the southern edge of this ball-court plaza leads to the main set of terraces and platform mounds that support the principal palaces. The Jade Sky Palace at the southernmost and highest point of the complex lines up on axis with the Great Plaza, forming its visual terminus, although access to it is carefully regulated. Both the palaces front their own private raised plaza, which they share with another, so-called Palace 1B5. The embankments and shape of the western edge of the acropolis indicate that the Motagua may have flowed along its edge at one time, so that the palaces would have directly overlooked the river.

# 1000 CE

Around the turn of the millennium, the most extensive and complex temple building programs occurred in South Asia. Across the length and breadth of the subcontinent, thousands of temples arose. No single kingdom but rather several orchestrated this, each vying for wealth, influence, and showmanship. These included older kingdoms, like the Pratiharas, and new kingdoms, like the Gangas in the east and the Chandellas in the central plains, and the Solankis in the far north. Eventually the Cholas, in the south, would control a territory that reached from the Ganges in the north to the island of Sri Lanka in the south.

China was now also divided. The three principal areas were controlled by the Song in the central plains, the Jin and the Western in Xia, the northwestern regions, and the Liao in the Manchurian north. Though the Song territories, crisscrossed with a network of newly established towns, developed a strong mercantile economy, the Liao, who had adopted Lamaist Buddhism, created new hybrid monasteries, thereby establishing the first firm Chinese connection to Tibet. In Japan, meanwhile, a shift in power from the emperor to the aristocracy, was accompanied by the growth of a new form of Buddhism, popular in contemporary Song China, known as Pure Land Buddhism.

In the Islamic world we begin to see the political and religious patterns that were to determine the power gambits of these regions for centuries to come. Islam had divided itself into four different political entities with the differences between Sunni and Shi'ite becoming irreversible. From west to east, we find the Berber Almoravids, who took control of Spain and linked it with their home base around Marrakech; the Shi'ite Fatimids, who controlled Algeria and Egypt; the Sunni Seljuk Turkomans, who had subdued Persia and whose leader became the new caliph in 1055, and finally there was the largely Sunni Ghaznavid Empire, stretching from Afghanistan to northern India. All were great mosque and palace builders. The architecture of the Seljuks remains the most impressive, however, given that they imposed a particularly coherent political, religious, and economic architecture on their territory. It enabled the Silk Route to flourish and to become Eurasia's economic engine until the advent of colonialism.

In Europe, the struggle for dominance was similarly multipronged, led by the Ottonian kings in Germany and the Normans in England. Both used a combination of religious and military institutions to stamp their authority on the land. The Ottonians fused the monasteries with market places, whereas the Normans reorganized the entire legal and religious landscape of England using a combination of cathedrals, castles, and monasteries. Given their connections to the Mediterranean, they blended continental and Islamic features, partially creating the base of what would later be known as Gothic architecture. Also developing was a monastic geography with the Cluniacs, controlling a complex network of monasteries across France, Italy, Germany, and Spain, creating rapid developments in architectural language. At the same time another type of religious geography emerged as a result of the developing pilgrimage routes that linked and spread architectural knowledge from place to place. Italy, on the fragmented margins of early medieval European culture, was slowly developing its own original architectural expressions, including the baptistery, which was located at the center of the town, and the duomo or cathedral, which was paid for through city funds rather than—as was common in France and England—through royal patronage and taxes. In the Yucatan Peninsula the Maya were at their height. In the valley of Oaxaca the Zapotecs continued to build new cities, and in the north the Toltecs built a powerful new dynasty destined to define the form and shape of the cultures that the Spanish conquistadors encountered 500 years later.

## 1000 CE

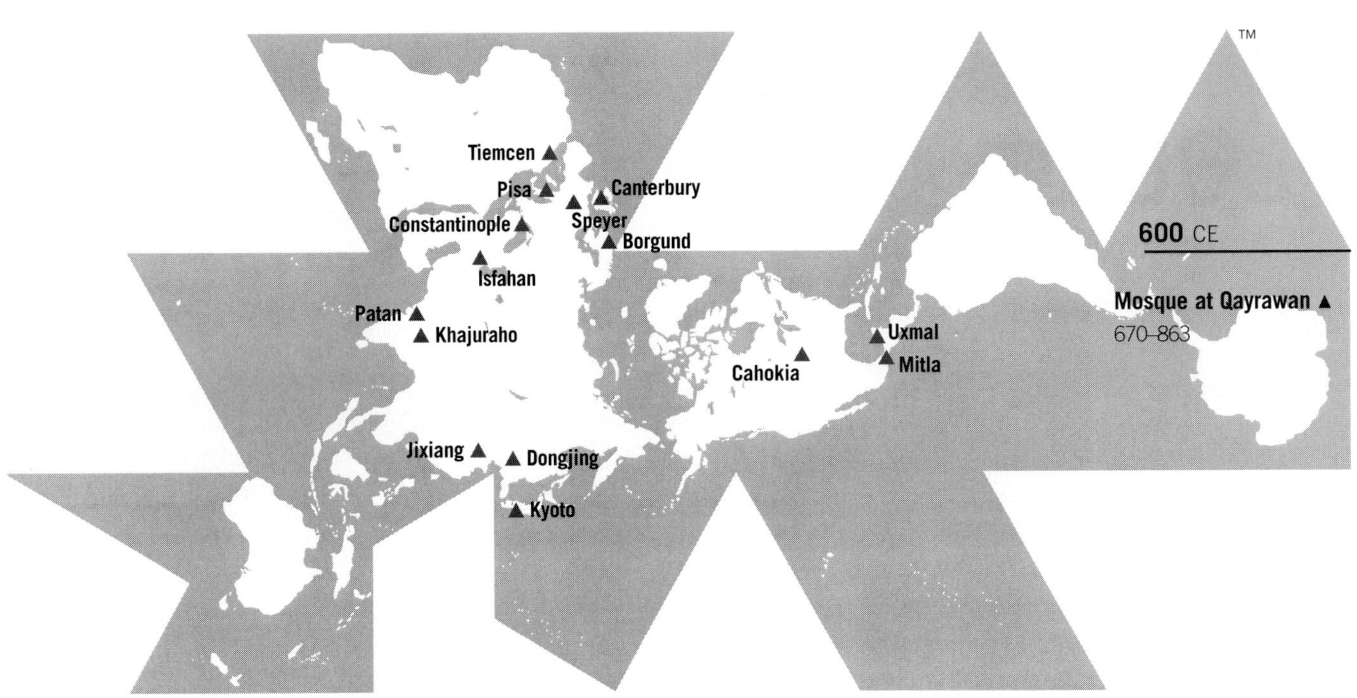


Dynastic city-states
ca. 250–900 CE

South Asia: Rise of regional states
ca. 500–1300

▲ Rajarajeshwara Temple
Late 10th century

▲ Khandariya Mahadeva Temple
1000–25

▲ Sun Temple at Modhera
1022–27

▲ Lingaraja Temple
ca. 1100

T'ang Dynasty
618–906

Northern Song Dynasty
960–1127

Southern Song Dynasty
1127–1279

▲ Dulesi Monastery
ca. 984

Japan: Late Heian Period
ca. 900–1185

▲ Yingxian Timber Pagoda
1056

▲ Byodo-in
1053

Abbasid Caliphate
750–1258

Fatimid Caliphate
969–1171

Umayyad Caliphate
929–1031

**800** CE — **1000** CE — **1200** CE

▲ Great Mosque of Isfahan
8th–16th century

▲ Al-Azhar Mosque
970–72

▲ Mosque of Tinmal
1153–54

Sultan Han ►
1229

Byzantine Empire
330–1453

▲ Sanahin
10th–13th century

▲ Church of Christ Pantokrator
1118–43

Ottonian Dynasty
936–1024

St. Michael in Hildesheim ▲
1001–33

▲ Cathedral of Ani
989–1001

▲ Speyer Cathedral
1040–1137

▲ Abbey Church of St. Foy
Begun 1050

Norman Rule in England
1066–1154

▲ Canterbury Cathedral
1042–1185

▲ Krac des Chevaliers
ca. 1100

▲ Durham Cathedral
1093–1133

Italian city-states
Late 11th–early 16th century

◄ Church of the Holy Sepulchre
ca. 335–12th century

▲ Cathedral of Pisa
1063–1118

Baptistery of Parma ▲
1196–1270

▲ Santiago de Compostela
1075–1128

Kievan Russia
ca. 860–1240

▲ Church of the Tithe
989–96

▲ Borgund Stave Church
12th century

Toltec-Chichén city-state
ca. 1000–1200

▲ Mitla
750–1521

▲ Uxmal
800–1000

▲ Cahokia
ca. 700–1100

Mississippian Cultures
ca. 800–1600

## 1000 CE

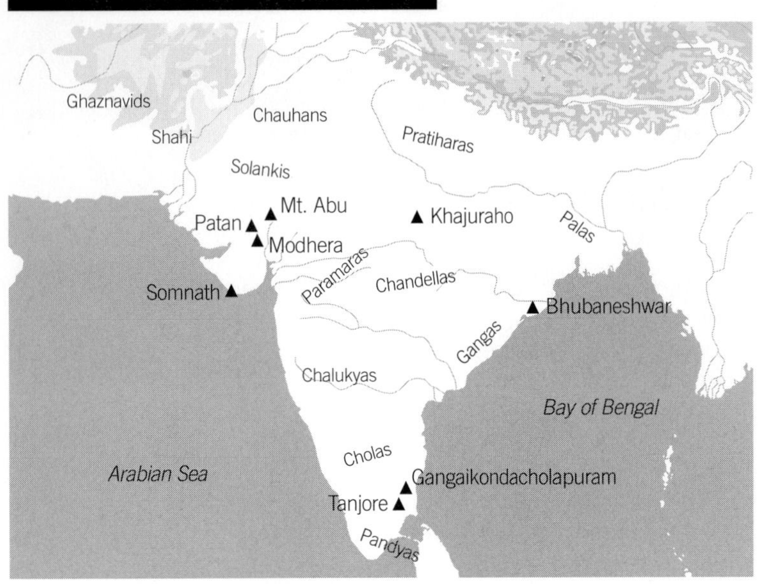


The largest Rajput kingdoms were those of the Pratiharas, the Chauhans, the Solankis, and the Paramaras. The Shahi in the northwest and the Chandellas in central India were some of the more important new regional kingdoms.

### RISE OF THE RAJPUT KINGDOMS

Harsha's descendents were unable to retain control over his empire, resulting in what is known as the tripartite struggle. Between 800 and 1000 CE, the Gurjara-Pratiharas from the west, the Rashtrakutas from the Deccan Plateau, and the Buddhist Pala kings from the east were locked in battle for control of the central Gangetic plains. Kanauj, Harsha's capital, with all of the major trade routes travelling south, east, and north passing through it, was the prized possession. The three contenders, by turn, had managed to capture Kanauj; but two centuries of warfare had weakened all three so much that they all collapsed more or less simultaneously.

The resultant power vacuum in northern India created the opportunity for a series of new kingdoms to step into the limelight. Some of these, like the later Chalukyas, were vassal states who had declared independence. More significantly, as Romila Thapar notes, this was a time when a large number of semitribal and tribal communities, who had lived subjugated lives at the edges of the established powers, began to emerge as their own kingdoms. Collectively the kingdoms of the 10th and 11th centuries are all known as the Rajput kingdoms because of the caste identity they all adopted (*raj-put*, "royal-son").

Hinduism was also undergoing a revolution at this time. The older Vedic religion, which was abstract in nature and centered on large fire sacrifices, began to be challenged by so-called Bhakti (devotee) cults that promoted the worship of Shiva and Vishnu. These cults argued against the elitism of Vedic Brahmanism, advocating instead a devotion to a single deity—conveniently available in the form of an image in a local temple—as the means of attaining religious merit. Everyone could be a bhakti. As these cults spread, a series of new subcastes were created in the 9th and 10th centuries to accommodate these new groups. Because of this, the Hindu caste system, which formerly was basically a distinction between those with caste (Brahmin) and those without, started to become the extremely complex map of occupational identity and social hierarchy that it is today. Caste at this time was also made flexible, and upward mobility was not only possible but encouraged. All it required was the appropriate moral conduct and the performance of rituals appropriate to the acquired caste, and perhaps an advantageous marriage. Most of the tribal communities were given the lowest or Sudra caste. But their kings, to be rulers, had to acquire the Kshatriya or warrior caste, as only Kshatriyas were allowed to rule. To belong to a Kshatriya caste the Rajputs had to first establish a mythical lineage and second, more importantly, build and support temples. Temple building made them the haloed keepers of their caste.

Many Brahmins, recently out of work following the tripartite collapse, eagerly supported this construction, launching one of the largest temple building campaigns of all time.

The largest Rajput kingdoms were those of the Pratiharas, the Chauhans, the Solankis and the Paramaras. The Shahi in the northwest and the Chandellas in central India were also regionally important new kingdoms. It is important to note that though they accepted caste identity, the Rajputs for the most part maintained their tribal languages and customs as well. The new culture they created with the Bhakti cults modernized Hinduism in a constructive way. New temple forms came into being, regional deities and gods were accepted into the expanding Hindu pantheon, and worship was conducted in regional languages. Modern India still has about 22 official languages (and over 500 dialects) with distinct lines of separation. As such it is better to think of India and Indian history as one does of Europe and European history. While the various regions share certain cultural aspects, their identities are as diverse as those of European countries. To think of a unified "Indian architecture" is as useful and as useless as thinking of "European architecture."

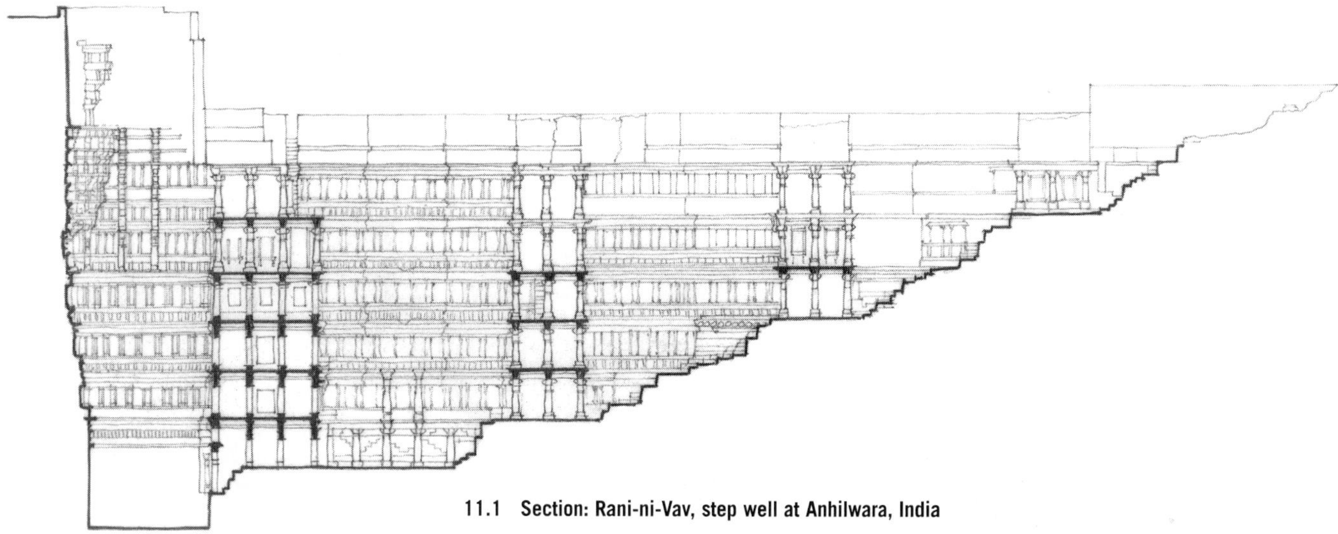

11.1 Section: Rani-ni-Vav, step well at Anhilwara, India

## SOLANKIS

Of the various Rajput Kshatriyas of western India, the Solankis, who ruled in Rajasthan and Gujrat, were among the most zealous of temple builders. They made their money trading not only with the other kingdoms of south Asia but also with central Asia through ports in Kutch. Trade was important because the Solankis' land, deprived of major river systems, was largely arid. The Thar Desert was part of their realm. Access to and distribution of fresh water, therefore, was critical to life. Wells, in fact, became the essential aspect of their architecture, but the Solankis wells were no simple affairs.

The step well called the Rani-ni-Vav, or Queen's step well, was built at Anhilwara (Patan) in the 11th century in memory of Bhimdev I (1022–63) by his widowed queen Udayamati. It functions as a long stairway leading down to the water table. The entire excavation is lined with a multitier, colonnaded facade supported by elaborately carved stone columns and beams. It was partially roofed, with light filtering even into the deepest parts, 28 meters below the surface. The reason for such splendor was that the Rani-ni-Vav (*rani*, "queen"; *vav*, "well") also served as a supplementary palace for the queen and her attendants.

The natural temperature of the earth, combined with the evaporative effects of the wind passing over the water, made the step well into a subterranean world of cool repose in the blistering summer months. In a more symbolic sense, the step well was also another version of the ghats of Varanasi, or the water tank of the Sun Temple at Modhera, except that the step well was fully inhabitable. Much of Solanki architecture was destroyed by invading Islamic armies. The Rani-ni-Vav survived intact because it was intentionally filled in with earth by the retreating Solankis.

11.2 Rani-ni-Vav, step well at Anhilwara

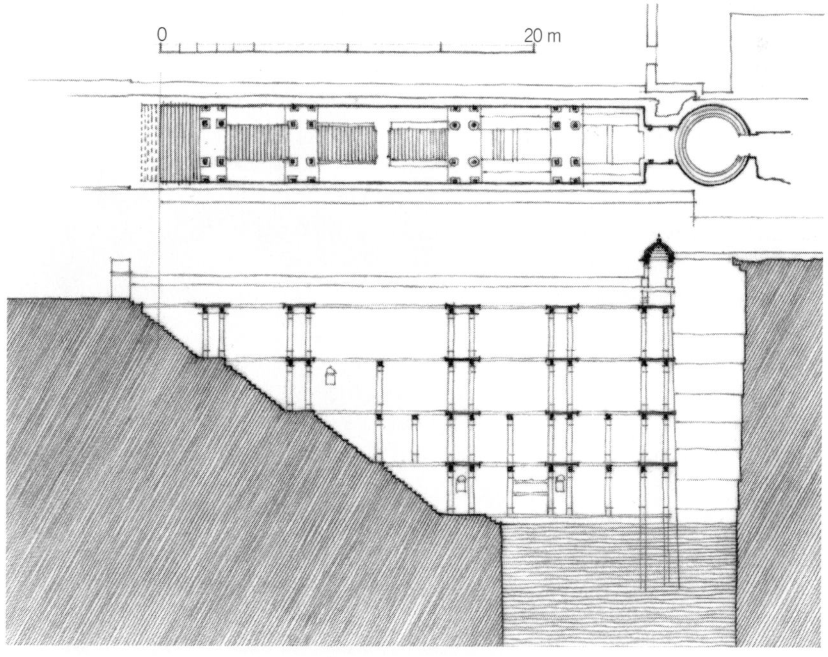


11.3 Plan and section: Step well at Vayad, Gujarat, India

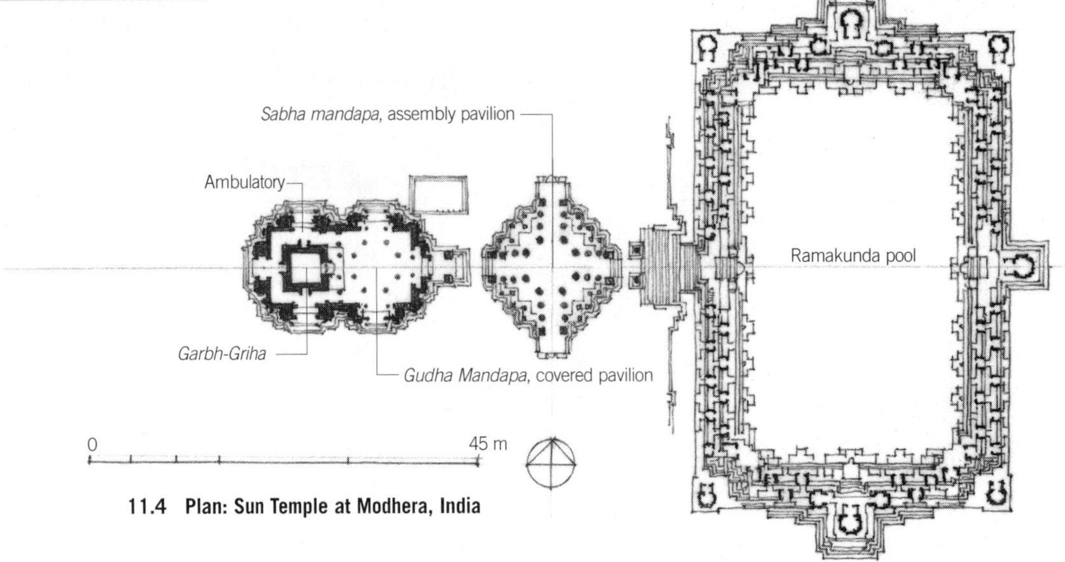


**11.4 Plan: Sun Temple at Modhera, India**

**Sun Temple at Modhera**

Though they were principally Shaivite, the Solankis claimed lineage from the Pandus, the solar family of Vedic India, described in the classic epic the Mahabharata. Solar cults, connected with fire worship, were important to their tribal ancestry and became particularly important at this time. The migration of new Magha or Shakdvipi Brahmins from the northwest and the presence of the Zoroastrians may have further promoted the cults.

The Solanki royal temple, dedicated to Surya, or the Sun, was made from golden sandstone and consists of a tripartite axial arrangement. The main shrine is in the west, a rectangular water tank in the east, and a *mandapa* in between, all integrated into a single composition. The *mandapa* is connected to the steps surrounding the water tank by a freestanding gateway or *torana*, which also marks the top of a flight of steps that lead down into the tank.

While the aesthetic expression of all the elements of the temple is in itself quite remarkable, in particular the delicate richness with which all the columns, brackets, cusped and wavy arches, and roofs are carved, its distinction lies in the manner in which it optically functions to connect the building elements. If one stands on the western edge of the tank and looks eastward toward the main temple, the view seems to be of one building composed of the steps leading upwards to the *mandapa*. But the conical top belongs to the shrine in the distance and the entrance of the *mandapa* is actually the gate in the foreground.

**11.5 One of the intricately carved pillars at the Sun Temple at Modhera**

The self-consciousness of this effect is evidenced by the fact that the access steps are themselves a separate element, excavated out of the ground, between the edge of the tank and the *torana*, designed primarily to effect the optical connection between the two. The steps, in other words, are free of the orders of the temple and tank, and they are actually an element practically unto themselves. One may also note that there is an echo between the implied triangular profile of the temple and the inverted V of the steps, and also between the conical dome above and the steps at the base of the inverted V that widen out into the tank, all creating an uncanny reflective effect, even when there is no water present.

11.6 Chausat Yogini Temple

**Tantrism**

Unlike the Solankis, who had learned kingship at the edges of the Pratihara kingdoms, the Chandella Rajputs were Gond tribals who were brought from obscurity into the caste through the Bhakti cults. They created a new kingdom in the central Gangetic Plains, just south of Kashi. Though the Chandellas readily adopted their acquired caste identity, they remained invested in aspects of their old animistic practices, particularly in the rites associated with female fertility. Because of that, their practices, which were derived from Tibetan Mahayana Buddhism, veered more in the direction of the tantric wings of the bhakti movement. Tantra means loom in Sanskrit, and refers to the tradition of handing down knowledge from teacher to student by word of mouth. For this reason, tantric Buddhism makes elaborate use of mantra or symbolic speech, made up of words or phrases that are repeated over and over.

The religion required secret initiations by a guru or leader. It was important that a woman be present at every ritual because the female was the initiator of the action; the male could only be activated through union with the female. Routinely condemned by the caste Hindus, the tantrics can be seen as an extremist version of the Bhakti movement. At the same time, given their radical opposition to the Brahmanical hierarchic ordering of society, they can also be seen as the radical critique of the newly emerging Hindu orthodoxy of their own day.

About a kilometer from Khajuraho was an early Chandella structure, the astonishing Chausat Yogini Temple (mid-9th century), the name meaning literally the "temple of 64 women saints." One of many such temples found in northern India, it consists of an empty quadrangular enclosure surrounded by 64 small shrines, each with their own individual pyramidical *shikharas*, with the main opening on one of the smaller sides to the north. The center of the Chausat Yogini is visibly empty or open, in contrast to a typical Hindu temple dedicated to a male deity, which has the dominant temple in the middle.

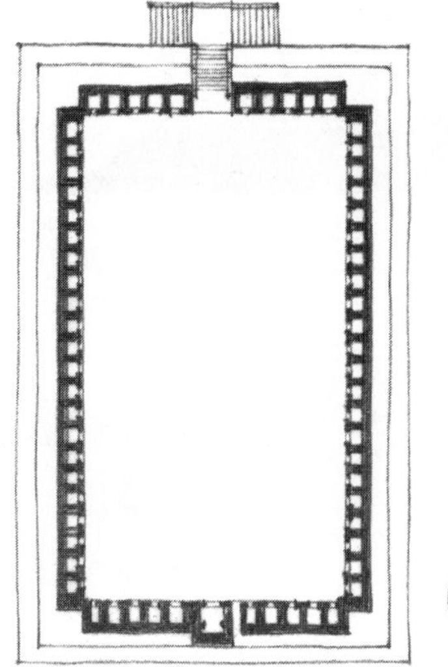

11.7 Plan: Chausat Yogini Temple at Khajuraho, India

11.8 **Lakshmana Temple *sikhara***

11.9 **Lakshmana Temple**

### Chandellas

In a brief period of about 175 years, the Chandellas, who called their kingdom Jejakabhukti, built more than 80 temples in and around their capital of Khajuraho (ancient Khajjuravahaka) to establish their caste identity. The crispness of their forms and the close continuity in their order and language indicates that there must have been a core group of architects or perhaps even a single architect-in-charge.

Two of the main royal temples of the Chandellas were the Lakshmana (950) and the Khandariya Mahadeva (1000–25) temples. Dedicated to Shiva, the Lakshmana rises on a high platform that ensures that, like all the other Khajuraho temples, it is visible from a long distance in the surrounding flat countryside. Independent subsidiary shrines are located at the four corners of the platform, suggesting a sense of enclosure and defining a sacred precinct without actually constructing a wall.

Access is highly dramatic. First the platform yields a tongue that becomes a stair that descends to the ground. The temple itself is preceded by its own cascade of stairs. The profile of the temple was itself something of a stair to heaven. The main temple consists of three *mandapas* preceding the main *shikhara*. The *mandapas* are articulated in horizontal layers, while the main *shikhara* emphasizes its verticality.

One distinguishing characteristic of the Khajuraho temples is the manner in which their architects orchestrated the front elevations, not mathematically or geometrical, but perspectivally when viewed at human height from the ground. The front elevations of the *mandapas* are designed such that from the perspective of the human eye they all nestle into each other perfectly. This is similar to the kind of orchestration designed by the architects of the Sun Temple at Modhera. The objective of this careful orchestration was not just aesthetic. The superstructure of every Hindu temple is conceived as a model of the universe. Its purpose is to disclose to the believer the inherent order and beauty of that universe.

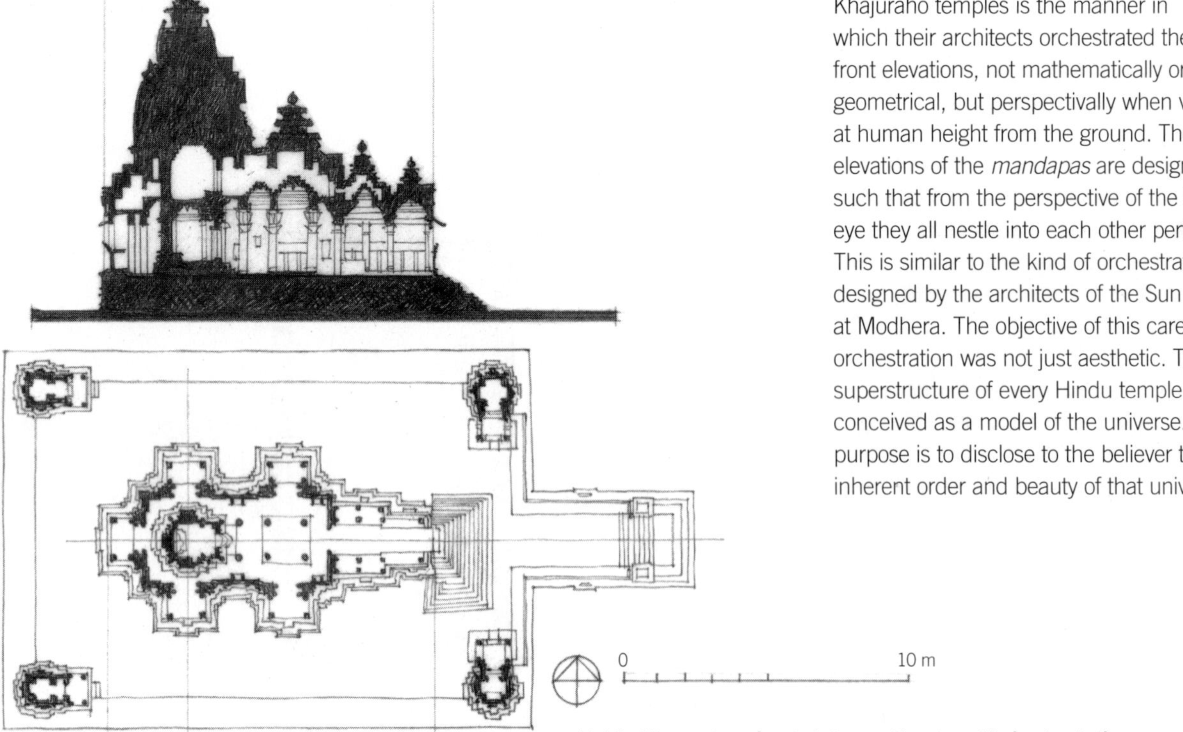


**11.10 Plan and section: Lakshmana Temple at Khajuraho, India**

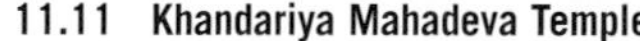

11.11 Khandariya Mahadeva Temple

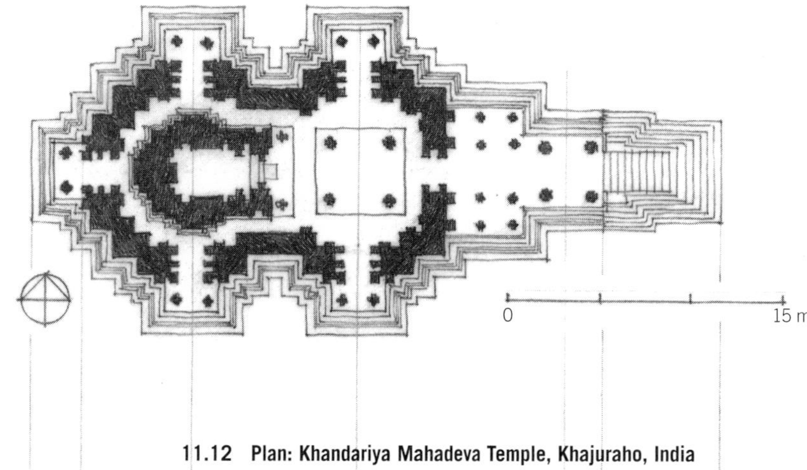


11.12 Plan: Khandariya Mahadeva Temple, Khajuraho, India

**Khandariya Mahadeva Temple**

The Khandariya Mahadeva Temple (1000–25), like the Lakshmana, sits on a high platform that it shares with another smaller temple, the Jagdambi, dedicated to the goddess Parvati. There are no corner shrines, so the profile of the Khandariya and its partner is silhouetted against the sky without interruption. Balancing the composition between the two temples is a single small shrine, at the center, raised up somewhat on its own small plinth. At 30 meters, including the platform, the Khandariya rises higher than all the other temples, but its strength lies not in its size but in the quality of its architecture. Its profile is designed to represent the rhythms of a jagged mountain range, both in its outlines and in the composition of its parts. Unlike the Lakshmana, the Khandariya's four *mandapas* are articulated with distinctive mini-*shikharas* that cluster around the *shikhara*. These mini-*shikharas* produce a sense of a rising wave as found in nature or as described by fractal geometries. The slight widening at the base, the strong horizontal protrusions of the porches, as well as the tightly bound faceting at the intersection of the *shikhara* and the *mandapa* make for an extraordinarily powerful composition.

The porches, because of their height, give the visitor a sense of elevation above the quotidian. The interior of the sanctuary, however, is appropriately deep and dark, like a cave. But unlike many Hindu temples, it is lit by large openings located well above eye level. The effect is particularly spectacular in the circumambulation route where the light coming from a high source casts dark shadows between the folds of the sculptures, bringing them into sharp relief. The openings are furnished with platforms and steps for attendants and musicians.

The Khajuraho temples are famous for their so-called "erotic sculpture." Sexual acts of almost every kind are carved with the same attention to detail and fullness as all the other sculptures, representative of the Chandellas' interest in Tantrism. It is important to note that this sexual sculpture, while present in abundance, is neither highlighted nor hidden; that is, it is just there, as an important part of the assemblage and a part of the wide variety of life that is depicted in the sculptural program.

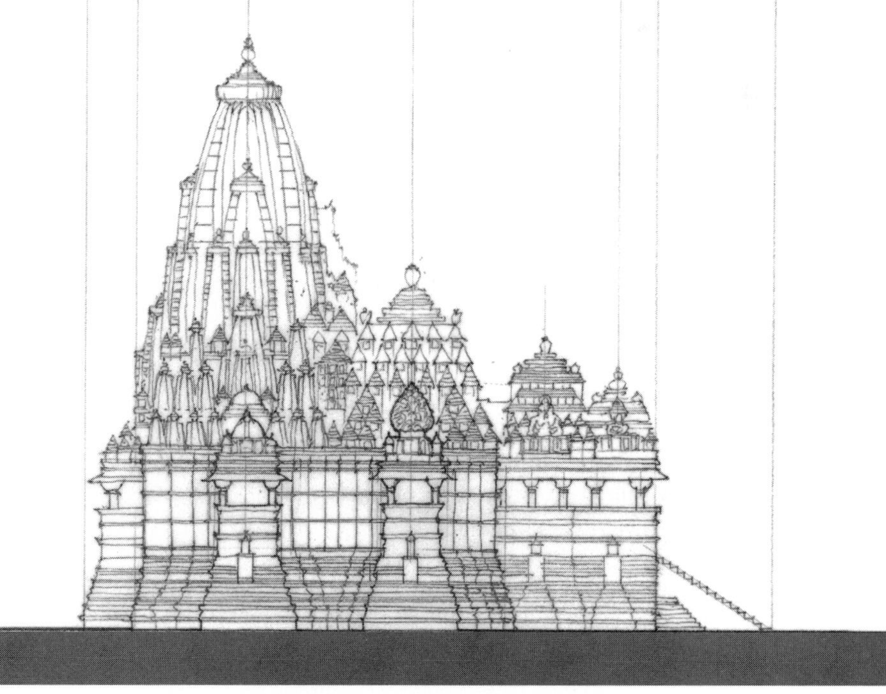

11.13 Elevation: Khandariya Mahadeva Temple

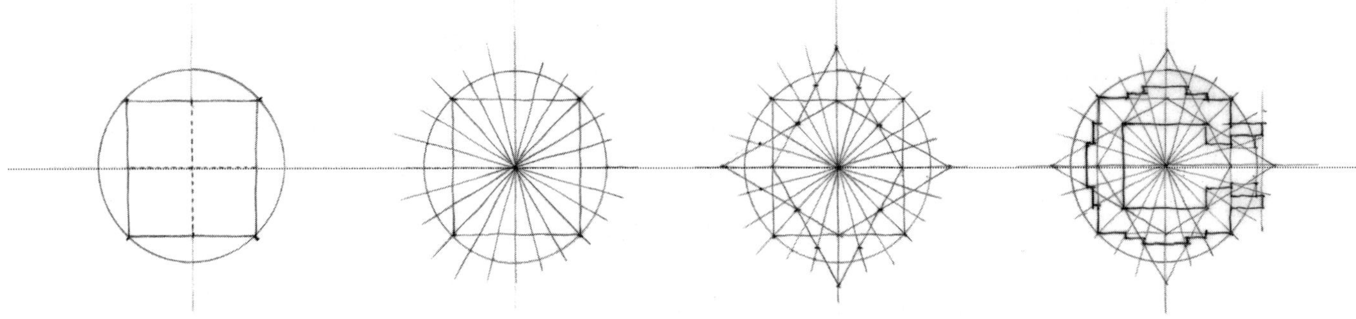

**11. 14 Geometric evolution of an Orissan temple plan (after Andreas Volwahsen)**

**Vastu-Shastras**

In the 10th century, the building boom required that temple design and construction be systematized. The Brahmins used to monopolize the astrological and mathematical knowledge that determined temple design, and the lower Sudra caste artisan guilds, called *shrenis*, guarded the construction techniques in their oral traditions. With the loosening of caste, the Brahmins and artisan *shrenis* for the first time collaborated to publish a series of technical manuals under such titles as *Vastu Shastra* (Construction Treatise) and *Shilpa Shastra* (Sculpture Treatise), which give us a first look at the highly codified language of temple design and construction.

A chief Brahmin, known as Sutradhar, designed the temple and supervised construction. His design was derived from an astrological diagram called a mandala. A mandala was a graph that mapped the positions of stars, planets, deities, and the sun with respect to a particular site. The Sutradhar chose from hundreds of mandalas, depending on the principal deity of the temple and the religious persuasion of the community. The head artisan in charge of construction was known as the Sthapati, or master builder.

From the chosen mandala, the actual form of the temple was derived through a series of geometrical maneuvers designed to express the potency of the various planets and deities occupying the grid of the mandala. Radiating lines, weight given to the primary directions, as well as special triangles, determined the location of the building's various parts. A complex system of faceting, known as *rathas*, determined the detailed articulation of the temple's surface. The purpose of the *rathas* was to enable multiple deities to share a single surface—in the vertical and horizontal plane—by suggesting superimposed layers. The final form was inevitably a heavily faceted pyramid. The sculpture and painting were done basic form

In the end the cosmic order expressed by a temple offered a vision of a pyramidal universe, cascading down in waves from a single point of origin, that in itself was without form or substance. The objective of the worshipper, in apprehending this vision, was to devote himself or herself to ascending to that formless center, a task assisted by devotion to the temple's resident deity.

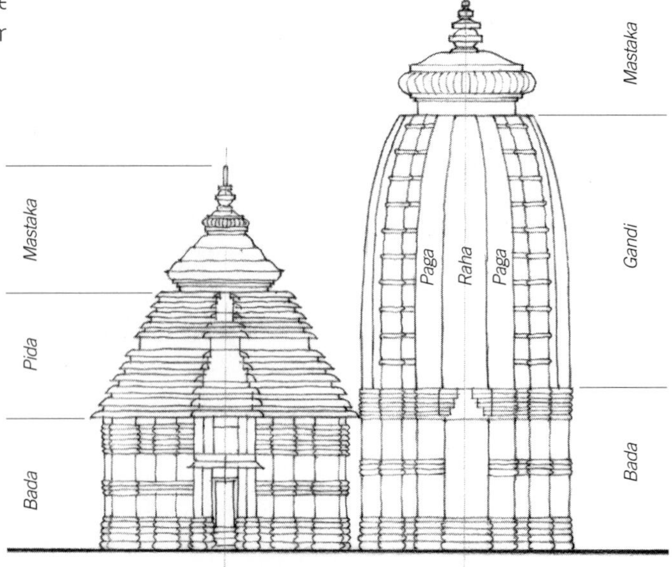


**11.15 Elevation: Orissan temple**

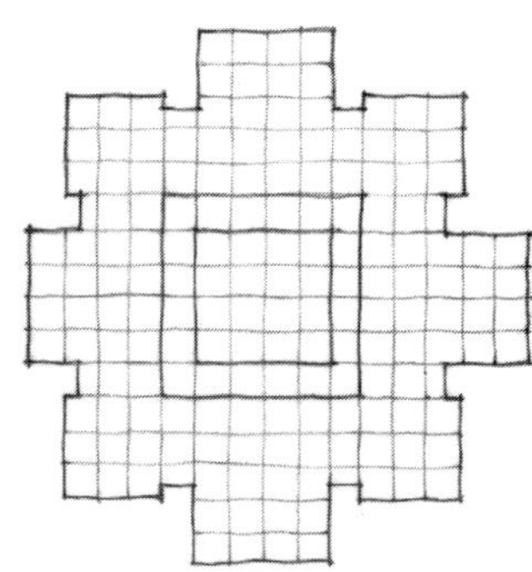
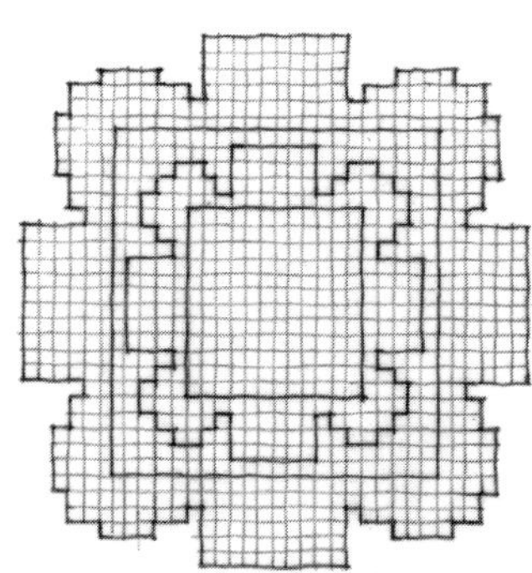

**11. 16 Vastu Purusha mandala: the basis for Orissan temple construction**

The city of Bhubaneshwar, Orissa, the capital of the Shailobhava (7th c.), the Bhaumakara (8th c.), the Somavamshi (9th c.), and most famously, the Eastern Ganga Dynasty (10th–13th c.), was once home to about 7000 Hindu temples. They were distributed around a sacred pool called the Bindusagar. Today a few hundred still stand, dating from the 7th to the 13th centuries. As Hinduism matured as a religion, the ruling dynasties grew in power, and their ritual practices became more and more elaborate, the temples of Bhubaneshwar also grew in size and complexity to accommodate to their patrons.

A study of select plans, in chronological order, shows the Orissan architects grappling with the problem of articulating and harmonizing two basic masses, the rekha deul, with its *garbh-griha* and tall pyramidal *shikhara*, and the *jagmohan* or *mandapa* (the preceding hall for rituals), which is larger in plan but always shorter in height (and may not even have a pyramidal roof).

The architects of the Eastern Ganga Dynasty went to great lengths to publish their *Vastu Shastra*. The detailed vocabulary they used to describe every element in the order of the temples gives us some indication of the underlying symbolism of the temple's vocabulary and the conceptual precision of their designs.

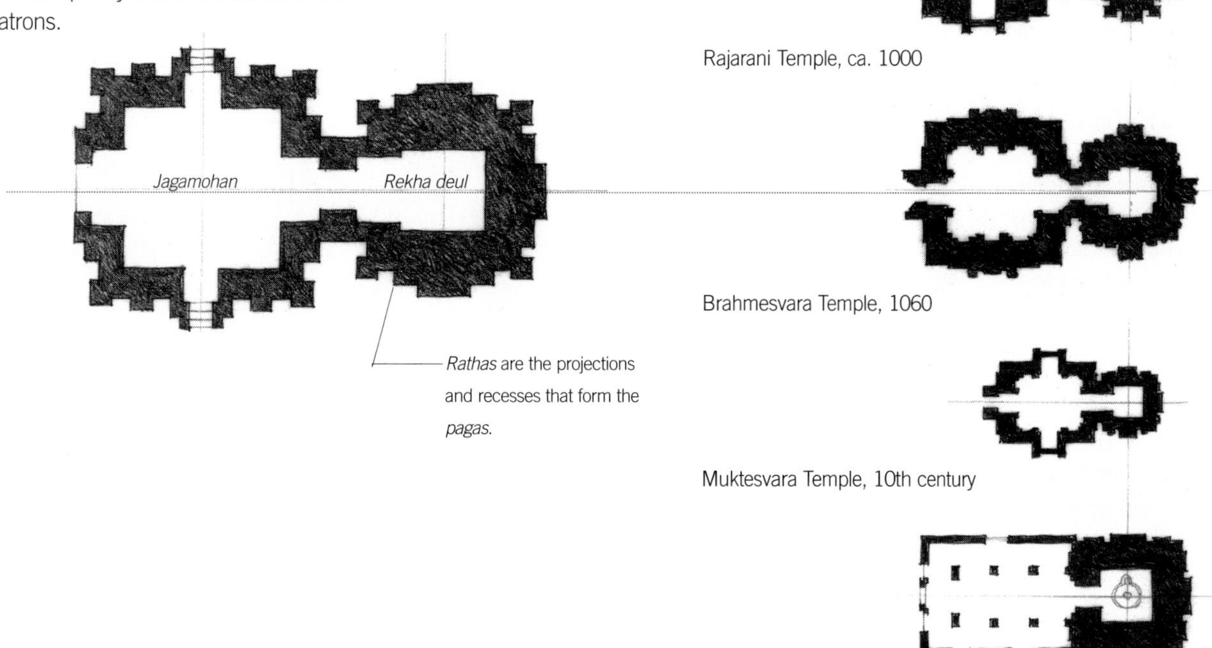


**11.17 Comparison of the *rekha deul* and *jagamohan* of four Orissan temples**

11.18 Lingaraja Temple, Bhubaneshwar, India

### Lingaraja Temple

As the "king" of the Bhubaneshwar temples, the Lingaraja (literally, "the phallus-king") (ca. 1100) was the largest designed for royal patronage. It was distinguished not only by its size but also by the presence of three *jagamohans* all lined up in row. The rituals that would normally have been conducted in a single hall were here separated out, not only to enable them to occur simultaneously but also to create the sense of a mini-pilgrimage in their performance. These *jagamohans*—a primary *jagamohan*, a *nat-mandir* (dance hall), and a *bhog-mandapa* (collective ritual performance hall)—were all about the same size, though each has a distinctive plan suited to its function. The *jagamohan* has a fully articulated exterior, making it a shrine in itself. The *nat-mandir* is airy and open, so that its activities could be visible and heard in the surroundings. The *bhog-mandapa* duplicates the *jagamohan*, and it was probably added later to facilitate rituals by larger groups who could not access the innermost shrine. The Lingaraja's 37.5-meter-high *rekha deul*, which dominates the silhouette for miles around, has a distinctive profile—first rising almost vertically and then only toward the top, curving inward before yielding to a recessed neck that supports a wide *amalaka* resting on the backs of lions, indicating royal patronage.

The Lingaraja now sits in the middle of a quadrangular compound that is dotted with innumerable small subsidiary shrines that were added over time to the main sequence to increase its potency. This proliferation is common in active Hindu temples and is described as the *parivar*, or literally the "family," of the main shrine, which is expected to change and grow in time as does a prosperous family around a reigning patriarch. Though the Lingaraja is now decommissioned, the nearby Jagannath Temple in Puri, also built by the Gangas in the 12th century, continues to be in use, and as a result, its *parivar* has grown. The compound is now completed saturated with subsidiary shrines, many built recently.

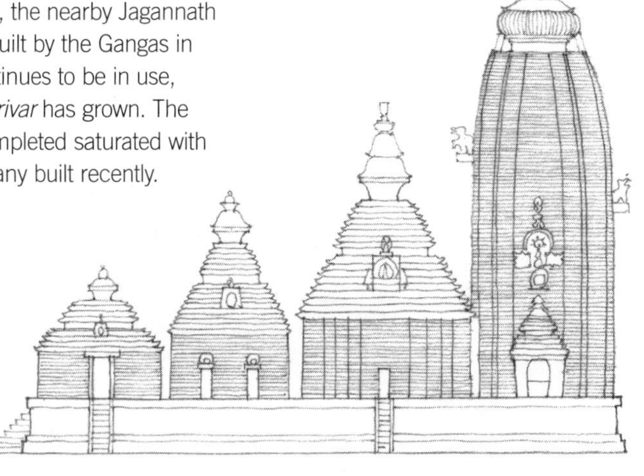

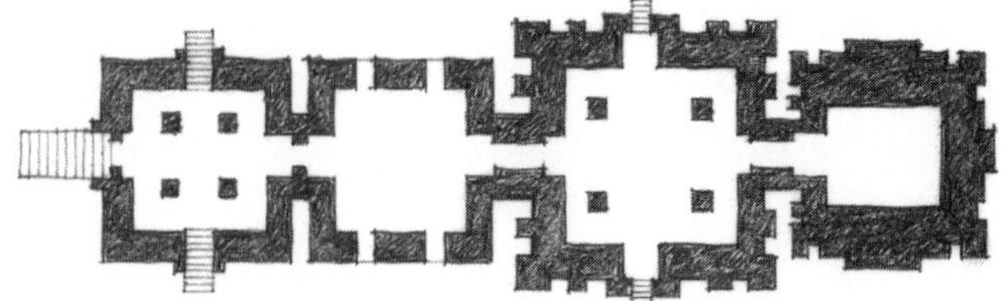


11.19 Plan and elevation: Lingaraja Temple

**11.20** ***A Teaching Session*** **(detail from a Shravanabelagola painting)**

**JAINS**

Many of the ministers employed in the Rajput courts were neither Hindus nor Buddhists, but Jains. This is because the Jains were often the best financial experts and bankers available, an unintended consequence of their religion. Jainism originates in the teaching of the Mahavira, a contemporary of the Buddha from the 6th century BCE. (Jain is a corruption of the Sanskrit *jina*, meaning conqueror, the title given to Mahavira in Jain texts.) Like the Buddha, Mahavira preached a doctrine of asceticism and meditation, but uniquely Mahavira stressed absolute nonviolence. He insisted that all forms of life or *jivas* were equivalent and that respect for all *jivas* was an essential for the purification of the human *jiva* or soul. Strict ascetic Jains, known as Digambars ("sky-clad," or naked) were expected not only to be pure vegetarians but were also expected to eat only a fruit or vegetable that had broken off its plant of its own accord. All root vegetables, like potatoes and beets, that entailed killing the whole plant were prohibited to all Jains. Furthermore, Jains could not be farmers by profession either because working the land inevitably harmed earth insects and worms. As a consequence, Jains turned to nonorganic professions such as jewelry making, trading, and banking. These professions made them literate, good managers and quite often financial experts, and they were therefore greatly sought by the courts. They also became great librarians and patrons of the arts.

Like the Buddhists, the Jains challenged Hindu caste hierarchy and refuted Vedic orthodoxy, particularly the Brahmin's claim to privileged access to higher knowledge. So Jain ideas and institutions alongside those of the Buddhists were severely attacked by the Hindus in the 9th and 10th centuries. Shaivite and Vaishnite Bhakti cults blamed them for negating life and being too abstract and impractical for the common man. They destroyed many of their temples. But unlike the Buddhists who wilted under the critiques and eventually disappeared from India, the Jains managed to survive the rising tide of Hinduism (and later iconoclastic Islam) in part because of their economic and political clout. Today there are almost 3 million Jains in India, mostly in western India and Karnataka. That Hindu India today is largely vegetarian is largely due to their influence.

As with the Buddhists, the Jain orders were codified in a series of councils, with the most important one held at Valabhi in 466 CE. At this council a less strictly ascetic sect of Jains was given official recognition, known as the Svetambaras (or "white cloth-clad"). The Digambaras and Svetambaras were subsequently divided into several subsects. Both sects believe in the leadership of 24 Tirthankars (literally "ford finders"), who are said to have appeared on earth to show Jains the way to the true religion. With Adinath as the first, the historical Mahavira was listed as the last of the Tirthankars.

Like the Mahayana Buddhists of Central and East Asia, the Jains built colossal monolithic statues of their Tirthankars and spiritual leaders. In 966 CE Chamundaray, a Jain minister of the Ganga Dynasty, built at Shravanabelgola, Karnataka, a 17.38-meter-high statue of a naked Gomteshwara Bahubali, the first man said to have attained enlightenment through Jain practice. It sits on top of a hill visible from a distance. Every 12 years the statue is covered with milk, yogurt, ghee (clarified butter), and saffron, along with gold coins.

**11.21 Bahubali statue**

11.22 Interior, Dilwara Temples at Mt. Abu, India

11.23 Interior, Dilwara Temples at Mt. Abu

**Jain Temples at Mt. Abu**

From the 10th to the 16 centuries, Jain ministers employed in Rajput courts paid on a scale matched only by royalty to build five Jain temples at Mt. Abu, Rajasthan. Vimal Shah, a minister of Bhimidev I, the Solanki Maharaja of Gujarat financed the first of them, Vimala Vasahi, in 1026. In 1256, the brothers, Vastupal and Tejpala, ministers in the Vaghela court, paid for the most elaborate of them, the Luna Vasahi. The temples were rebuilt several times, following each wave of Islamic iconoclasm.

The temples are clustered at the summit of a hill, oriented east-west. Each sits on its own terrace. A series of irregularly shaped smaller terraces provide access. Jain temple plans are modeled on Hindu precedents, with a main *garbh-griha* preceded by a *mandapa*, or worship hall. The central deity, however, is one of the Tirthankar; Vimala Vasahi to Adinath, Luna Vasahi to Neminatha. Later thinking insisted on adding all the Tirthankars to each temple. As a result the individual temples came to be surrounded by a quadrangle composed of rows of minishrines. (The original 24 Tirthankars were expanded to 52 and then 74 after the 12th century.) The *mandapas* of the minishrines are joined to form a cloister. Into the residual space between the quadrangle and the temple, the Jain architects inserted an open pavilion, held up by highly ornate columns, that became the recipient of the most lavish sculptural attention.

The temples are a local white *arasa* marble, carved the way one can work wood. The climax of the sculptural program are the columns and ceilings of the open pavilion. At the Vimala Vasahi 12 multifaceted piers, linked by flying arches that hold up a deeply domed ceiling. Sixteen female figures, personifying various aspects of learning, are attached in a ring around the perimeter. The exterior wall of the Vimala Vasahi is completely unornamented, masking the sculptural explosion inside.

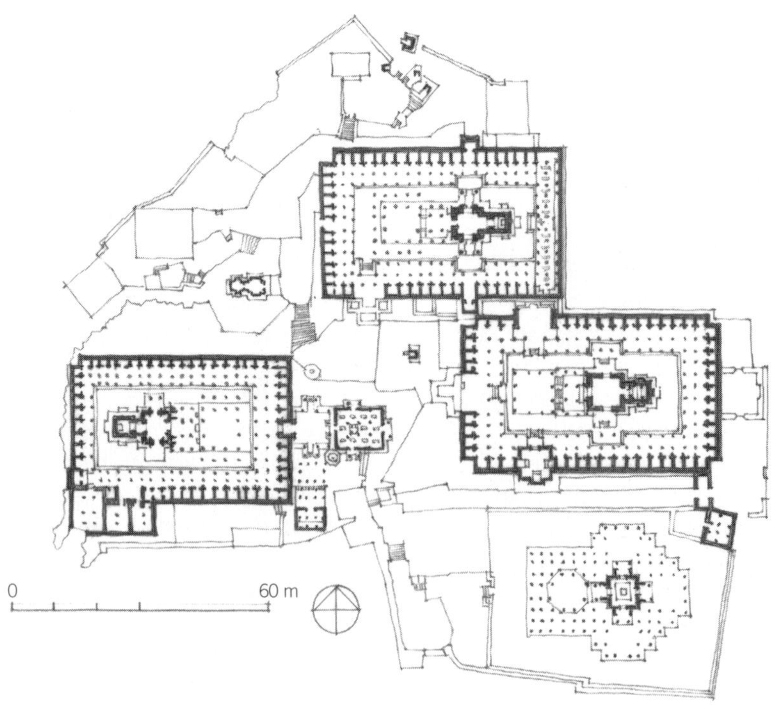


11.24 Plan: Jain Temples at Mt. Abu

**11.25 Portrait of Rajaraja Chola I, Sarabai Museum**

**Cholamandalam**

Unlike in the north, the social revolution brought about by the Shaivite and Vaishnite *bhakti* cults did not result in the proliferation of small competing kingdoms in the south. Rather, the south came to be dominated by a single power, the Cholas, who combined military strength with an effective strategy of wealth generation and governance to bring about a social and economic revolution of their own. The new Chola doctrine became the basis of modern Tamil identity.

The Cholas were aggressive military campaigners. First, in the mid-8th century, they teamed up with fellow feudatories, the Pandyas, to defeat the reigning Pallavas. Then, early in the 9th century, they annexed the Pandyan territories and built themselves a new capital at Thanjavur. In the second half of the 9th century, the Rashtrakutas and the Chalukyas by turn came down from the Deccan Plateau to challenge them, but Rajaraja I (985–1004) defeated them both in their homelands. Lightning attacks, conducted on horseback, was their successful strategy. With no large kingdom dominating the north, the Cholas, with complete control of peninsular India, were the largest power of the subcontinent. Immediately they embarked on an aggressive campaign of temple building across their territories, not only to spread Shaivism but also to consolidate their economic base.

Rajaraja I next turned his attention to trade. By the 9th century, Arab and Jewish traders had settled along the Arabian coast. Under the protection of local rulers, they brought in horses from Western Asia and traded them for Indian goods such as textiles, spices, medicinal plants, jewels, ivory, horn, ebony, camphor, aloe wood, perfumes, sandalwood, and condiments. Rajaraja I deposed the local rulers and began to buy directly from the merchants. He is said to have bought 2000 horses every year. He also, of course, started to collect taxes on the trade. But the largest profits were still collected by the Arab traders who plied the sea, and pirates were a constant problem. Rajaraja I launched a series of naval attacks on Arab staging grounds in the Maldives and Sri Lanka and brought the Arabian shipping lanes under his control. Sri Lanka became a vassal state. For the last ten years of his life, Rajaraja I devoted his time to building his royal temple in Thanjavur, which he called Dakshinameru, or Mt. Meru of the South.

Rajaraja I's son, Rajendra I (1014–44), who was coregent for his father's last ten years, modeled himself after his father. He first sent a military land expedition all the way north to the Ganges to establish tributary relations with the northern states and to secure the eastern ports. Then, he turned his attention to the most lucrative cash cow, the seatrade with China, conducted from the ports on the Bay of Bengal. The Mongol conquest of Central Asia had cut off the land routes between India and China, resulting in a boom in the sea-borne trade. The Chinese and Indian ships, however, had to make their way past Shrivijaya (Indonesia), whose kings tried to capitalize on the situation by replacing the Chinese and Indian intermediaries with their own. An incensed Rajendra I dispatched a heavily armed naval fleet across the Bay of Bengal and defeated Malaya and Shrivijaya. Although Indian traders plied these distances routinely, this was the furthest an army from India had ever travelled. With that the Cholas were unquestionably the superpower of the Southeast Asian region. Trade boomed and their influence spread.

Early in the 11th century, the Khmer kings sent a mission to, and even modeled themselves after, the Cholas. In 1077 the Chola king Kulottunga sent an embassy of 72 merchants to the Southern Song court. The Cholas called their extended sphere of influence the Cholamandalam, the "Chola vision-world." The Cholas built the largest naval force India was to ever have. When the Islamic rulers came to dominate the subcontinent, they funneled trade through northern land routes and, indeed, discouraged ship building and maritime trade. As a consequence, by the time the Portuguese arrived, early in the 16th century, there was no Indian navy to speak of.

11.26 Vijayalaya Cholisvaram Temple at Narttamalai, India

11.27 Shiva Nataraj

With the combination of conquered territories, vassal states, and trading outposts, the Cholas managed a sort of international corporate empire. Their focus was more on control of wealth than on occupation of land. At the center of this Cholamandalam, its instrument of governance, was the *kovil*, the Chola temple. In Tamil language *kovil* (*kov*, "god-king"; *il*, "home") means both temple and palace. By suggesting a continuity between the king and god, the Chola kings both boosted the image of the king as semidivine and at the same time used temples as surrogate courts, embodied with financial and judicial powers. For every economic unit (like a village or a district) the Cholas built a temple. The temple's construction engaged the entire community. While the temple's basic endowments of agricultural land or villages were made by the king, the actual land for the building was donated by the local elite. Donations for building materials were made by the merchants. Construction was done, both for cash and in kind, by the lower caste artisans. Provisions, such as images, lamps, oil, etc., were obtained through individual donations.

As representations of the king, temples (strictly the temple deity) had judicial, administrative, and religious power. Temples were also run like a corporation. They had the authority to make land-grants and to invest their assets as they considered fit. They were of course landlords, but they also became banks. They lent money at 12 to 14 percent interest, making mostly microagricultural loans, although the larger temples increasingly invested in trade. Major contributions and investments were inscribed on the walls of the temple for all to view. In this way the Chola temples became the financial centers of the community. Village assemblies also came to be held in them, and they were often responsible for the formal education of upper-caste boys.

Temples were administered through boards, consisting of elite stakeholders, as authorized by the king. The Brahmins, of course, were the only ones allowed to conduct rituals. But the lower castes could play the music, prepare the garlands, and lead the processions. Temples, in fact, maintained a huge permanent staff that included musicians, artists, artisans, and dancers (including *devadasis*, women dancers dedicated to the temple for life.) The community's cultural institutions, in other words, were also the preserve of the temples.

**Vijayalaya Cholisvaram Temple**

The Chola's chose the image of Shiva Nataraj, or the Dancing Shiva who orders the movement of the world with his dance, as their representative royal deity. As the enabler of order in the world, this was an effective surrogate image for the king. From this it followed that temple architecture was also a surrogate image of the royal ordering of the world. Although derived from Pandyan precedents, the Chola temples conveyed a vision of a well rationalized, logically articulated universe. A canonical system of arranging all the deities in the temples niches was initiated, and subsidiary shrines were orchestrated in a standardized order.

The small Vijayalaya Cholisvaram Temple at Narttamalai, built early in the 9th century, already had a crisp order. The *mandapa* had a simple flat roof and was clearly distinguished from the main *shikhara*, which had the largest mass, two circular upper stories rising above a crisply articulated square enclosure. Its surface relief is uncluttered; its niches were articulated as distinct bays with ample breathing room for each image; and pilasters follow, unfolding with a relentless rhythm all around the ground floor, and binding the two masses of the main building together. The temple sits at the edge of a stone escarpment at the high ground of the surrounding countryside. The temple overlooks and can be seen distinctly from the agricultural land and the villages that surround it and to which it belongs.

**11.28 Dakshinameru (Rajarajeshwara Temple), Thanjavur, India**

While regional temples served the more quotidian purposes of governance, Rajaraja I's royal temple at Thanjavur was designed to embody a vision of kingship at the scale of an empire. Rajaraja I projected himself as a Cakravartin, a king destined to bring order to the world, a demi-god in the grace of Shiva-Nataraj. He called his temple the Dakshinameru, the Mt. Meru of the South, distinguishing his world from that of the north. (Dakshinameru is now generally know as the Rajarajeshwara or the Brihadeshwara Temple). It was the location for major ceremonies of royal initiation and legitimation, linking the icon, the deity, and the king. The daily rituals of the deities mirrored those of the king, including the daily morning round of the sacred enclosure and the sunset retreat to the bedroom. Dakshinameru maintained a staff of 600 *devadasis*—treasurers, accountants, record-keepers, watchmen, musicians, readers of texts, and craftsmen of every sort, besides of course scores of Brahmin priests. This is still the largest temple in India.

The temple was located next to a river that was channeled to make a moat symbolic of the cosmic ocean. An outer enclosure was built somewhat like a fortress, entered on axis through a five-story *gopuram* or gateway. A second three-story freestanding *gopuram*, set on a long and low platform, gave access to the main quadrangle.

The towering mass of the main *shikhara* dominates the vast quadrangle. The *shikhara* rises 63 meters in 16 severe, crisply articulated stories. A rationalized rhythm of consistently applied pilasters, piers, and attached columns articulate the entire surface. The interior is hollow but not meant to be occupied. The circumambulation route that goes around the massive *linga-yoni* in the *garbh-griha* is repeated on the upper story and is occupiable. This is a rarity in Hindu temples, an allusion to the idea that Rajarajeshwara offered "access" even to the realm of the gods.

Even the ground story (that symbolically corresponds to the earthly realm) is articulated as two stories, indicating more than one celestial dimension of the royal temple, a reference to the semidivine claim of the Maharaja. The main temple is preceded by two cojoined, dimly lit hypostyle *mandapa* halls. The *antaral*, or vestibule where the priest would be, is compressed between the *mandapa* and the *garbh-griha*. Subsidiary shrines are arranged along the cloistered edge. Additional shrines were added later.

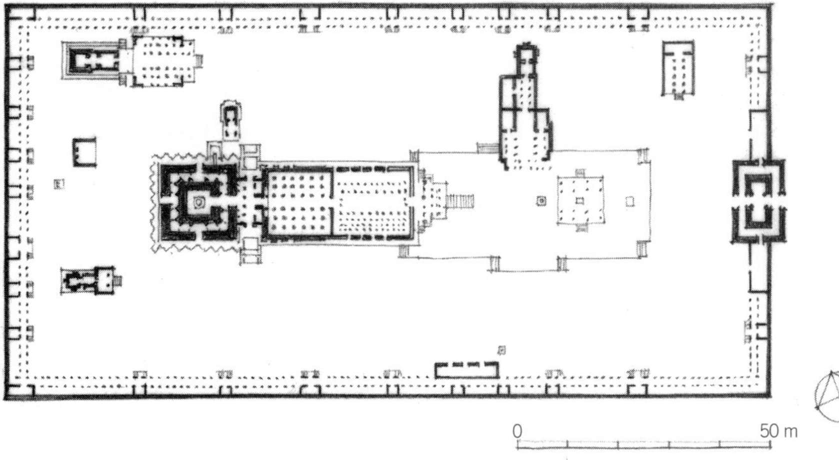


**11.29 Plan: Rajarajeshwara Temple**

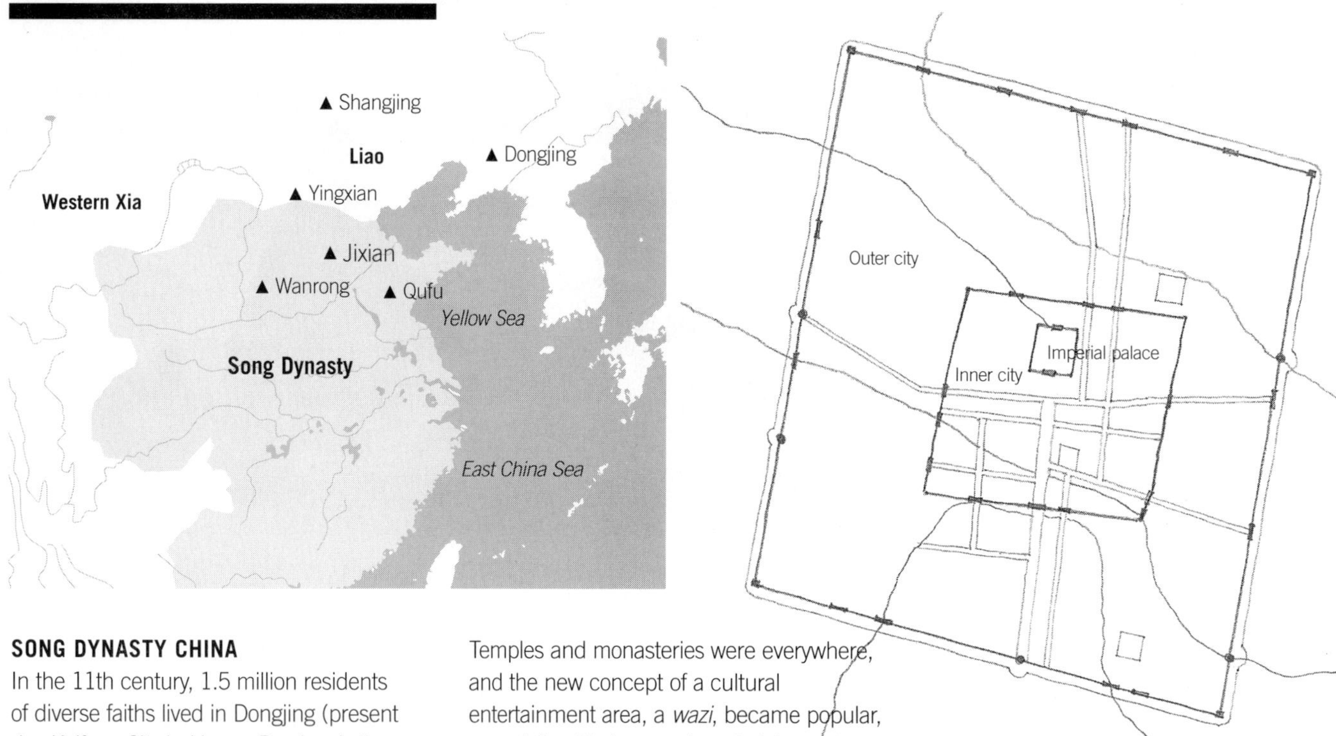


11.30 **Plan of Dongjing, China**

**SONG DYNASTY CHINA**

In the 11th century, 1.5 million residents of diverse faiths lived in Dongjing (present day Kaifeng City in Henna Province), the Northern Song capital, in a city spread out over 7.5 square kilometers. Unlike the cities of the T'ang, Song dynasty cities were more than just administrative centers; they also served as centers of trade, industry, and maritime commerce. Because Dongjing was not divided into activity-specific wards, merchants could set up shop anywhere they pleased. All the major streets and intersections, as we learn from paintings of the time, were bustling with activity. Besides the extremely wide imperial ways, there were four rivers with high bridges that enabled boats to pass freely so that goods could be transported in and out of the city in cases where transport by cart was too difficult. The Song created very successful networks between their large and small cities, facilitated by the use of paper money and wood-block printing that enabled a mercantile economy to boom. The cultivation of tea and cotton became widespread. Gun powder was used for the first time and canals were dug. The compass and movable type were invented. Under the Song Dynasty, Daoist and Buddhist traditions came to be closely aligned; but it was Confucianism, influenced by Buddhist practices, that reemerged as a major ideological force.

Temples and monasteries were everywhere, and the new concept of a cultural entertainment area, a *wazi*, became popular, especially with the creation of night markets. A Song scroll, *Upper River during Qing-Ming Festival*, contains a detailed description of the bustling city. Unlike in earlier Chinese capitals, the imperial palace complex was located in the middle of the city, and it was developed in a much looser fashion than others with multiple sequences of imperial buildings. Public courts, located in front toward the south, followed by private palaces in the back were not forced into a single hierarchical axis; instead they were dispersed throughout the area in an array of axial arrangements in response to the growing needs of the court.

11.31 **Portion of the Song Dynasty scroll entitled *Upper River during Qing-Ming Festival***

11.32 Yingxian Timber Pagoda, China

## Mu-Ta

More than one hundred early pagodas from the Song, Liao, and Jin dynasties have survived into modern times because most were made of brick. Of the timber pagodas, few have lasted the ages, with the exception of the Yingxian Timber Pagoda, built in 1056. It is often referred to simply as the Wooden Pagoda, or Mu-ta. The Mu-ta was built by Daozong to commemorate the death of his father, Xinzong (1031–55), the seventh Liao ruler. Access to the 67-meter-high *ta* was through a monastery with a monumental Mountain Gate (Shanmen) and a large 55-meter-long forecourt that is no longer extant. Terraces (*yuetai*) of different shapes and sizes lead up to the octagonal stone base. The lowermost story consists of three independent rings of wooden pillars. The smallest pillars in the outermost ring support the lowest eaves. The two interior rings form the inner and outer *cao* with a giant seated Buddha figure in the center. Other than the lowermost level, where the columns are encased to create an enclosure, all the upper stories are open, with the central altars alternating between square and octagonal plans. The imagery of each story (the figures and their arrangement with respect to each other and in space) is independent and self-contained, so that each level can be conceived as an individual mandala. The arrangement of the fifth story, for instance, represents the composition of the Womb World Mandala.

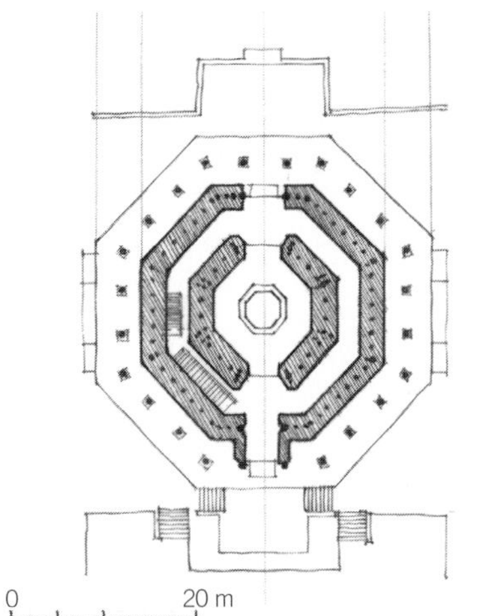


11.33 Section and plan: Yingxian Timber Pagoda

Virtually a skyscraper of its time, the Mu-ta was one of the most advanced structural achievements of its time. Like the Guanyin-ge, each story of the Mu-ta is a separate structural entity (none of the pillars go more than a story) tied together by 54 different types of bracket sets. On the exterior, each story of the Mu-ta is represented by eaves, held up by a neat arrangement of structural *dou-gong*. In the interior, however, the structure is held together by a complex mesh of post and beams, radial *dou-gong* brackets, and cross bracing that ultimately forms a thick nest in the form of a torus between the external skin and the central space. It is this mesh that has enabled the Mu-ta to withstand a millennium unharmed.

**11.34 Mural from a Liao Dynasty tomb**

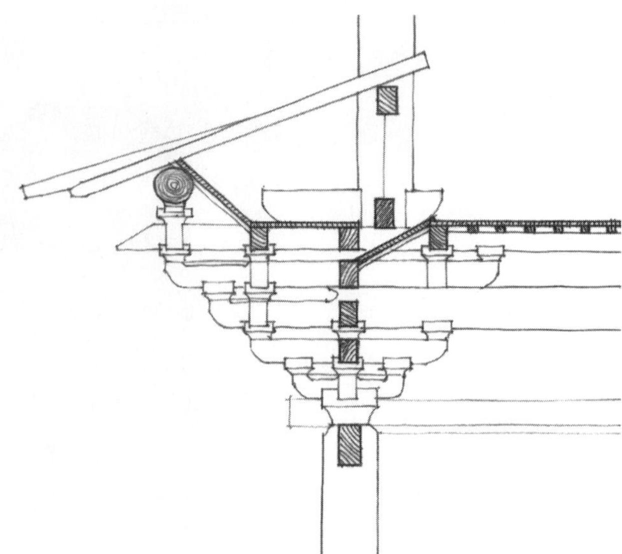

**11.35 *Puzuo* bracketing, Guanyin Pavilion**

**Liao Dynasty**

Nomadic herdsmen from Mongolia, the Khitan (Qidan), established the first of China's "foreign" dynasties (947–1125). They named their dynasty the Liao, which means "understanding" or "awakening." Ultimately, they controlled a territory that reached from the Mongolian border into Manchuria, below the Great Wall. Though they posed a threat to the Northern Song (960–1127), they acted as a buffer between the Song territories and the northern peoples during this period. They became a center for the mutual exchange of culture, using their wealth to build several capital cities, as for example, Shangjing. They maintained a two-tier social structure, however, adopting the T'ang system of governance for the Chinese but maintaining their own tribal governance for themselves. Within Shangjing, for example, the structures of the non-Mongolian peoples were made of permanent materials, while the ruling Liao continued to live in tents.

While as nomads they had left their dead on trees to rot, the Liao were quick to adopt the Chinese system of building masonry tombs for royalty. Located just outside their cities, these tombs consisted of multichambered underground burial vaults and several platforms above ground for descendants to perform sacrifices to appease the spirits of the dead. Each had a long Spirit Path, a paved road leading to the tombs, flanked by larger than life-size statues of mythical and real animals and other ceremonial objects meant to guard and guide spirits. Interiors were painted at times to reflect interiors of tents and wooden structures. One of the curiosities of the Liao tombs is that they all contain one panel with the painting of a woman in the act of stepping through the door. Its meaning remains unclear. Bodies were drained of fluids and filled with vegetable products, embalmed, and often covered with a suit made of fine metal.

**Dulesi Monastery**

The Liao had nomadic connections with Tibetan Buddhism, which they continued to support. In 984 ce, a nobleman from Jixian, Hebei, built a Buddhist monastery, Dulesi (Solitary Joy), dedicated to Guanyin, the bodhisattva of compassion and mercy. Dulesi Monastery was rebuilt several times, but its central structures, the main gate (the Shanmen) and the prayer hall (Guanyin-ge) are original to the Liao. (The suffix *-ge* refers to multistory buildings that are accessible only from the front and that, like this one, house colossal statues.)

The complexity of Dulesi's wood construction shows that the Liao were well versed in Chinese building systems. As in the Mu-ta, the Guanyin-ge's columns rise more than a single story, and each story is a distinct structure wedged into the one below. (Diagonal struts to increase stability were added later by the Qing.) Chinese wood roofs are described on the basis of the number and types of bracket-sets and beams deployed. Bracket sets (called *puzuo* or *dou-gong*) are classified by the number and complexity of their horizontal, vertical, and diagonal elements. Beams are designated by their position and the number of rafters they span. In the Shanmen, four four-rafter beams and four two-rafter beams hold up the roof. The structure uses 24 different types of bracket sets, with the most complex ones at the corners.

**11.36 Dulesi Monastery, Jixian, Hebei Province, China**

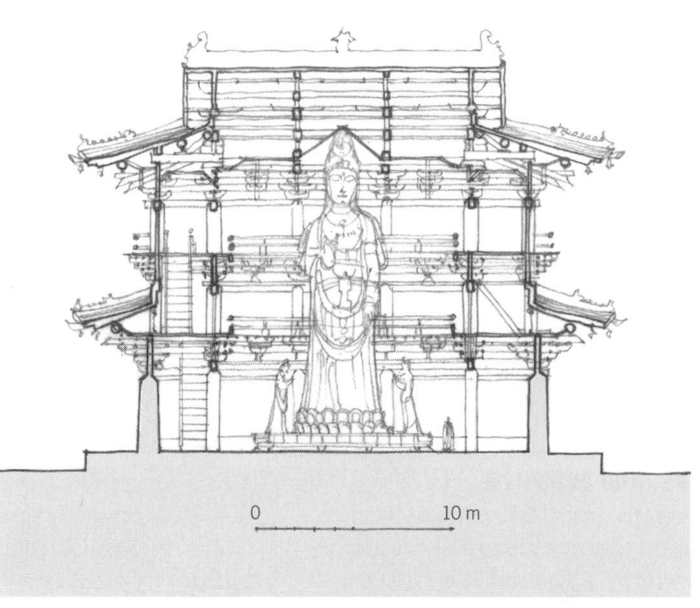


**11.37 Section through Guanyin Pavilion, Dulesi Monastery**

The three-by-two bay Shanmen (mountain gate) is aligned with the Guanyin-ge. Four-meter-high wood columns rise from granite bases. The columns taper from a 51 centimeter base to 47 centimeters at the top and bend slightly inward. Thirty meters separate the Shanmen from the Guanyin-ge. The line of sight is such that the top of the roof of the 22-meter-high Guanyin-ge is distinctly visible from the Shanmen, allowing the entire structure to assert its full impact upon entry.

The plan is divided by columns into an inner space and a circumambulatory vestibule, known as the outer and inner *wai* and *nei cao*, respectively. In the middle of the space, accessible by stairs, is the 16-meter-high Guanyin, the tallest wooden Buddhist sculpture in China (which probably predated the Liao).

The Guanyin's eyes are aligned with a pair of windows in the upper story and can be seen from outside when the windows are open. In addition, the Guanyin's eyes align with a masonry pagoda located 350 meters away on axis. Although this White Pagoda (reconstructed 1058) is completely symbolic, this optic connection was a reinterpretation of the Mahayana Buddhist practice of superimposing statues of Buddhas on stupas to emphasize the identity between the two.

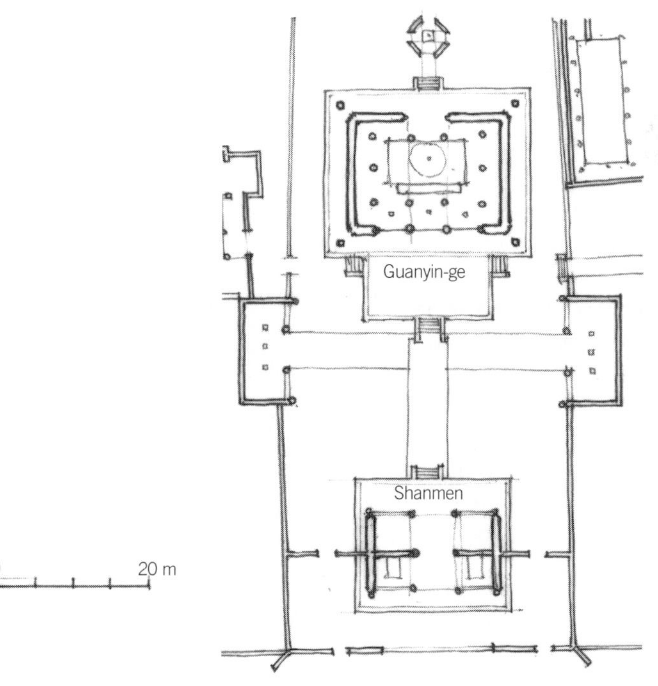


**11.38 Plan: Dulesi Monastery**

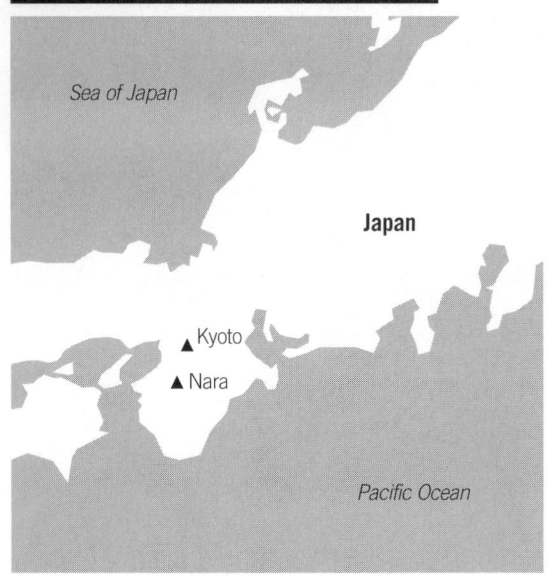

11.39 Phoenix Hall at Byodo-in, near Kyoto, Japan

## PURE LAND BUDDHISM

Around the year 1000, as power shifted from the upper classes to the aristocracy, a new form of Buddhism known as Pure Land Buddhism came to dominate Japan. Since Pure Land Buddhism was open to all, it offered a means by which the Japanese aristocracy could gain access to Buddhist teachings without becoming complete ascetics in monasteries. Originally developed in India in the 2nd century CE, Pure Land Buddhism was based on the concept that a devotee could attain rebirth in a Sukhavati ("equanimous or pure land") of his or her choice by following a prescribed set of personal meditations. These meditation were to focus on a particular set of "visualizations"—that is, a set of prescribed scenes, that took the worshipper to that place through a series of steps. Its core teachings were contained in the Visualization Sutra, a sermon believed to have been given by the Buddha to the virtuous Lady Videhi, who sought to be released from her world full of material attachments and demons. Because of its association with Lady Videhi, Pure Land Buddhism was promoted, in particular, by women. Pure Land visualizations were usually depicted in paintings, sculptures, and mandala diagrams. The act of transcribing sutras and redrawing visualizations was enough to earn a devotee merit. Now transcriptions were done as architecture, by remaking plans implied in mandalas into real buildings. This made the temple itself into an object of worship.

In 1053 a nobleman, Fujiwara no Yorimichi, (990–1074) converted a preexisting villa in Uji, near Kyoto, into a transcription of the Taima mandala. This visualization is known as the Byodo-in, or the Temple of Equanimity. In Buddhism, *byodo* (equal) refers to the condition of possibility that is open to all. The Phoenix Hall (Hoo-do) is all that remains of the original temple. Hoo are mythical phoenix-like birds, sculptures of which are atop the roof of the hall.

The Taima mandala depicts the Buddha seated on a C-shaped platform on a lake surrounded by bodhisattvas. Built on an artificial island in a lake, the Phoenix Hall replicates the Taima mandala in plan with winglike extensions on the right and left. Accessed only from the back by a bridge, the Phoenix Hall was meant to be primarily viewed from across the lake, as a visualization that a devotee focused on during meditation.

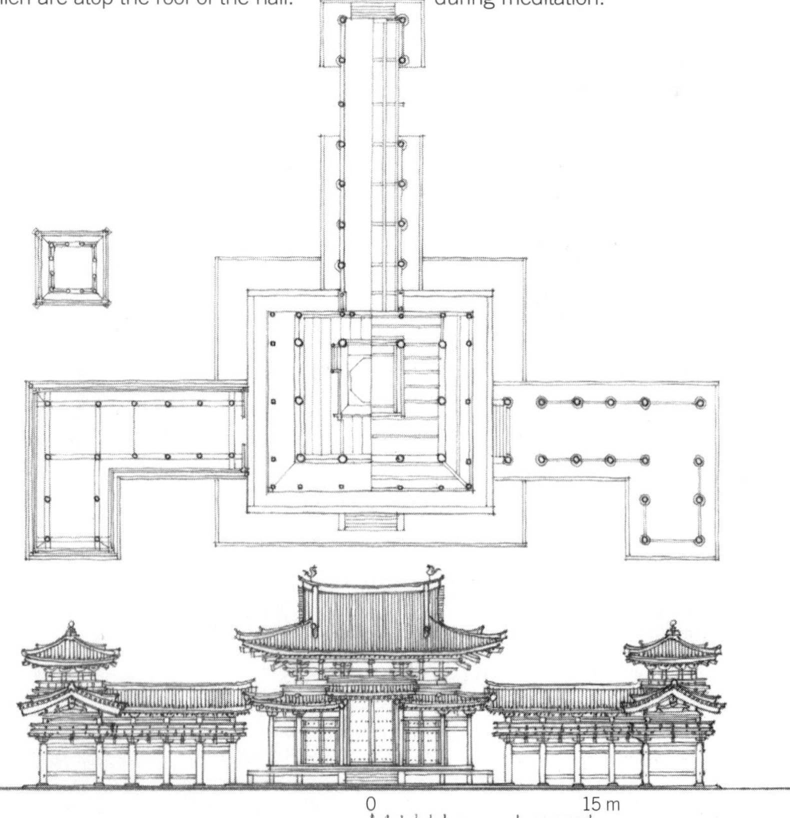


11.40 Plan and elevation: Phoenix Hall at Byodo-in

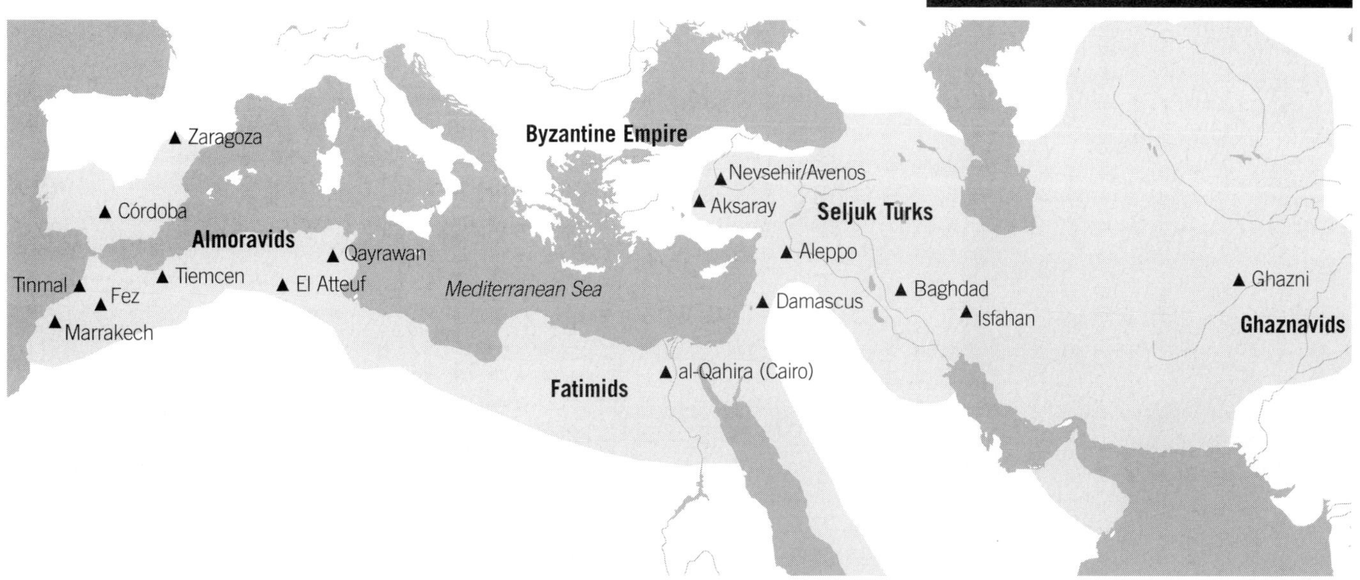


## SELJUK TURKS

Turks in the 10th century were a pastoral people living in Central Asia east of the Caspian Sea. Abandoning their homeland, they moved into Afghanistan and Iran. Accepting the faith of Islam along the way, they created a number of Turkish-Islamic states, one being the Ghaznavids, who settled in what is now western Afghanistan. Another tribe, the Seljuks (named after a tribal leader), drove further westward, penetrating into Iran, Syria, and eventually into the ethnically diversified Anatolia, held nominally by the Byzantines. The Seljuks consolidated their power over eastern Anatolia in 1071. The presence of the Seljuks was a major factor in bringing about the Crusades. And yet, despite the problems with the crusaders, the Seljuk period was one of relative calm, with Persia, in particular, seeing one of its most prosperous periods. The stability and success of the Seljuk regime was the achievement of the politically skilled Vizir Nizam al-Mulk, a cultured Persian, a brilliant administrator, and a significant political philosopher, whose work *The Book of Government* is a classic of Islamic literature.

The Seljuk Empire, at its peak, spanned a region from northern India to the Aegean, allowing the ancient trade routes of Anatolia to be connected with those to China, creating what is now called the Silk Route. The opening up of the Silk Route not only brought in enormous wealth but also promoted the development of industries, like the manufacture of paper. Paper originally had to be imported from China, but in the 8th century, it was being produced in Baghdad and Damascus and exported to Europe. Though Anatolia was not itself directly on the Silk Route, which ended in the ports of Syria, Anatolia profited from it, as it was one of the world's major suppliers of tin, an important element in the production of bronze as well as other metals. During Seljuk times, textile and leather exports were also important, as they were shipped to both Europe and the east. Once a year there was a vast commercial fair called Yabanlu Pazan (Bazaar of the Foreigners) held for forty days not far from Kayseri, in the center of Anatolia, at a place where several caravan routes converged.

The Seljuks distinguished themselves from earlier Islamic societies by their strict military hierarchy and attendant financial and landholding prerogatives that were closed to all but a few exceptional local recruits. The principal elements of their political program were: the mosque, the madrasa (Arabic for "school"), the *ribats* and *khanqahs*, the sufis' lodgings, and the mausoleum to commemorate their deeds.

Tiles were important decorative elements of Seljuk architecture. The technology for tilemaking emerged out of the century-old tradition in Iran and Iraq, which was brought to Anatolia by the Seljuks. The tiles consisted of an underlying paste with a high silicate content over which a thick mixture containing kaolin and feldspar was spread. Monochromatic tiles were used for fill and borders; others were designed as large custom-made plaques for a particular place in the composition.

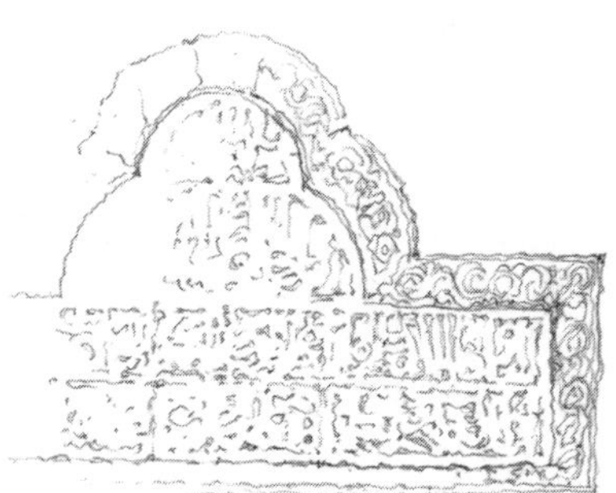

**11.41**
Representations of the human form are banned in Islam, but images of birds and animals as well as sphinxes and centaurs—often linked to ancient totemic worship still prevalent in Anatolian lands—were frequently embedded in the composition. Calligraphic inscriptions of Koranic verses were often used along the cornices or to frame portals.

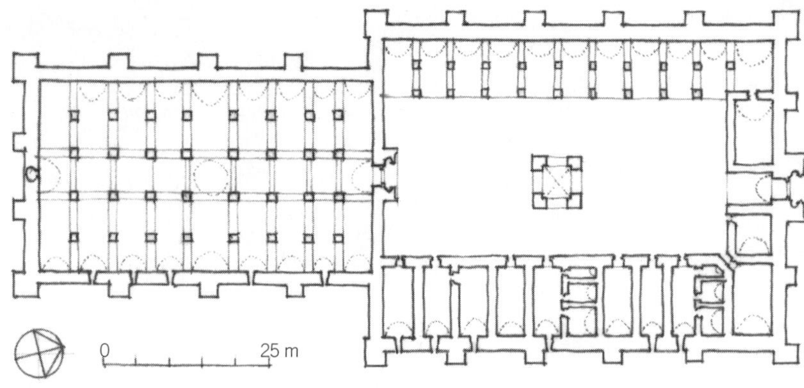


**11.42 Entry portal: Sultan Han, Kayseri, Turkey**

**11.43 Plan: Sultan Han, Kayseri**

### Sultan Han

Among the finest and most characteristic of Seljuk buildings are the caravansaries (derived from two Persian words meaning "a palace for caravans"), or *hans*, constructed during the 13th century to encourage trade throughout the empire; several dozen of them survive in good condition. These huge stone buildings, some 119 of which are known to have been erected, were made to shelter and protect not only the caravanners but also their camels, horses, and donkeys, along with their cargoes, and to provide needed services. Though caravan resting places had existed for centuries, this was the first large-scale systematization of mercantile transport across the desert. The services that the caravansaries offered were free of charge for the first three days. One of the basic rules was that travelers who came to the establishment were to be treated equally without regard to race, creed, or social status.

Though plans of caravansaries may vary, they were typically square or rectangular buildings with thick stone walls and a large courtyard in the center that was surrounded by one- or two-story arcades, accommodating bathing services, storage, treasury, and stables, as well as rooms for physicians, cooks, blacksmiths, and musicians. Though the exterior walls were plain and devoid of decoration, the portals were elaborately decorated with bands of geometrical designs and Koranic inscriptions. At the center of the caravansary was often a small mosque or prayer-room, usually raised above ground level on a stone platform. At the far end of the courtyard, opposite the main portal, was a large vaulted hall, usually with a nave and three side aisles. It was lit by narrow windows in the stone walls and had a stone cupola centered above the nave; it served as a shelter for goods and caravanners during bad winter weather.

The Sultan Han, grandest of all, covering 4,500 square meters, is west of Aksaray, a center in the Cappadocia region on the Konya highway. Designed by a certain Muhammet of Syria, the doorway is particularly spectacular. The outer frame is covered with a delicate floral pattern. The tympanum over the door, which has an abstract geometrical pattern, looks as if it were eaten away by the encrustations of an open conically shaped stalactite vault.

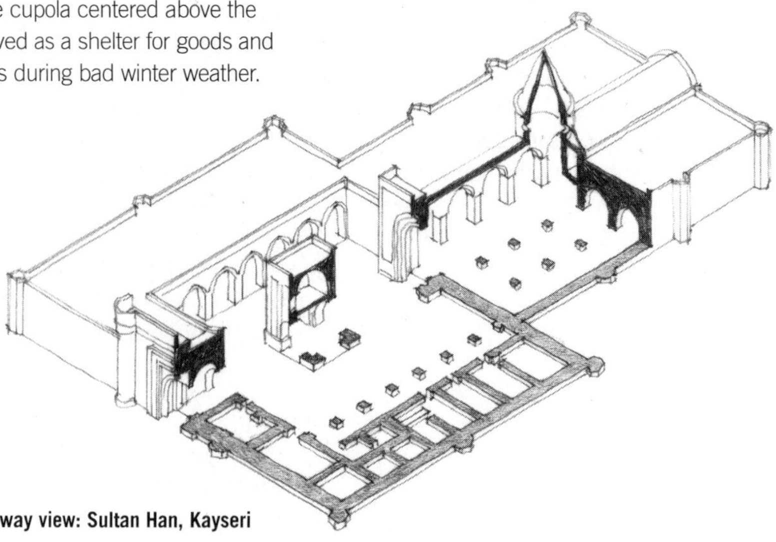

**11.44 Cutaway view: Sultan Han, Kayseri**

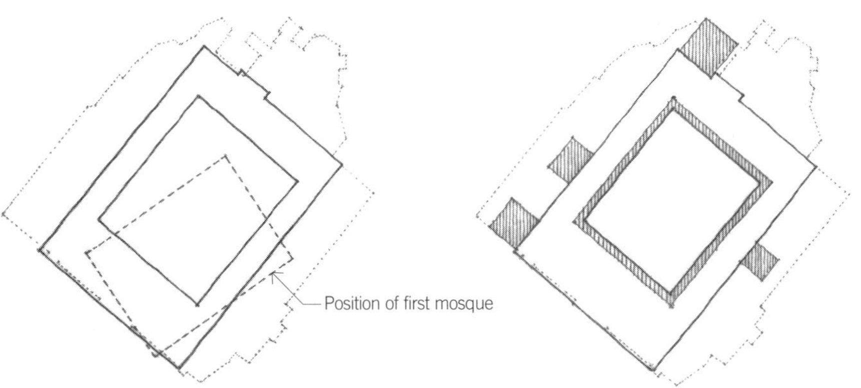

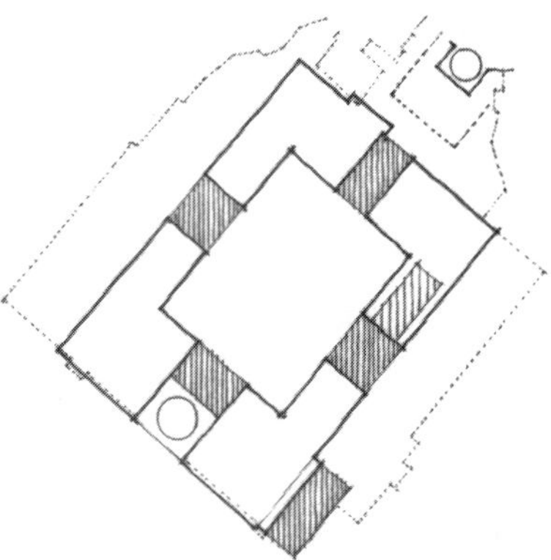

Abbasid Mosque, 8th–9th century

Mosque after enlargement and additions of the Buyid Period

Four-*iwan* mosque, ca. 1150

**11.45 Development of the Great Mosque of Isfahan, Iran**

**Great Mosque of Isfahan**

The Great Mosque of Isfahan (Masjid-i Jome or Friday Mosque), in the northern part of the city, was one of the most influential of all early Seljuk religious structures. Though the building is known as a "four-*iwan* type" because of the *iwans* that face each other across an open courtyard, the building was in actuality the result of numerous architectural transformations. The primary building substance dates to a mosque built in the 840s that stood over an even earlier mosque, built in 772, which in turn was built over the foundations of a Christian church. The mosque was a conventional hypostyle-courtyard mosque, typical of early mosques. But beginning around 870, it was thoroughly revised. The central space was reduced somewhat by the addition of a new facade running around all four sides. An elegant *qibla* dome was built and, to the north, an annex with a domed sacred area, literally an "inviolate zone," the original purpose of which is not precisely known.

In the time of Sultan Sanjar (1096–1157) four *iwans* were added to the courtyard, in essence imposed on top of the older system. The old columns were thickened or removed, as was required; the original columnar rhythms are still best visible in the areas to the right and left of the northern *iwan*. In the 1350s, buildings were added to the outer flanks of the structure, a madrasa was added to the western flank and a *musalla* (a temporary place in which worshippers congregate to perform their prayers) to the eastern one; these are only the most prominent changes made to the building over time.

In its original pre-Islamic form, the *iwan* was a type of stage for the enthroned king, but with the Seljuks it was used for several purposes; in a madrasa, for example, it was a lecture room. At the Isfahan Mosque they are grand portals, becoming the very symbol of the mosque on the other side.

**11.46 Courtyard: Great Mosque of Isfahan**

11.47 Iwans: Great Mosque of Isfahan

11.48 Closeup of muqarnas: Great Mosque of Isfahan

The Isfahan *iwans* are not identical. The main one, at the southwest, leads to the dome in front of the *qibla*. The side *iwans* have no particular relationship to the spaces behind them and lead nowhere except through doorways at the sides. To the north, which was formerly the old entrance into the mosque, the *iwan* with its barrel vault points in the direction of a *haram*, a special sanctuary where contending parties could meet to settle disputes, which originally was freestanding on three sides but was eventually roofed over and connected with the neighboring buildings. The particular reason why the mosque orientation would be interrupted by the use of the four *iwans* is not known, but the building is an ideal space composed of principal elements, with the *iwans* as a symbolic armature arranged in precise relationships to each other.

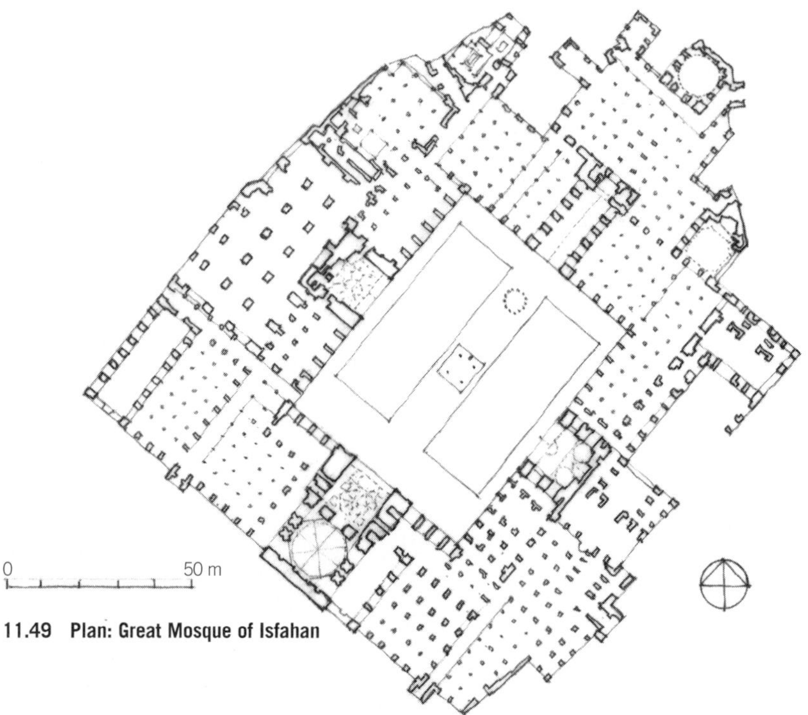


11.49 Plan: Great Mosque of Isfahan

11.50 Section: Great Mosque of Isfahan

**11.51 Gök Madrasa, Sivas, Turkey**

**11.52 Courtyard: Madrasa al-Firdus, Aleppo, Syria**

### First Madrasas

If the caravansaries were the central element of the Seljuk economic policy, the madrasa (Arabic for "school") was an important element of Seljuk political ideology, initially serving to promote the Islamicization of the Anatolian population, which until the 13th century was still predominantly Christian. The madrasa served subsequently to enforce and unify the Seljuk's Sunni beliefs. The madrasas were thus an important element in the campaign against the Shi'ite Fatimids of Egypt. Though many mosques had spaces and annexes that were used for classes as well as for residences for students and teachers, separate institutions for higher studies were still relatively rare prior to the Seljuks. Madrasas were built in almost all parts of Asia Minor. The origin of the madrasa is not clear. Some link it with the Buddhist *vihara*, and, given that the eastern areas of Islam had been saturated with Buddhism for centuries, there is some plausibility in that argument. Another possibility is its association with the courtyard house, a tradition that goes back to ancient times.

As with the caravansaries, the Seljuk madrasa followed a standard form. They were rectangular, compact, and relatively windowless, appearing as solid rectangular objects in the landscape. Portals, however, were often grandly and richly carved. Their central courtyard was lined with classrooms around a central *iwan*. Siting, financing, and local traditions determined the particulars. The great al-Nizamiyya Madrasa (1067) in Baghdad, which coincided with the entry of the Seljuks into Baghdad in 1055, is a four-*iwan* type. In Aleppo, the Madrasa al-Firdus (1235–41) shows the masonry skills typical of the north Syrian region.

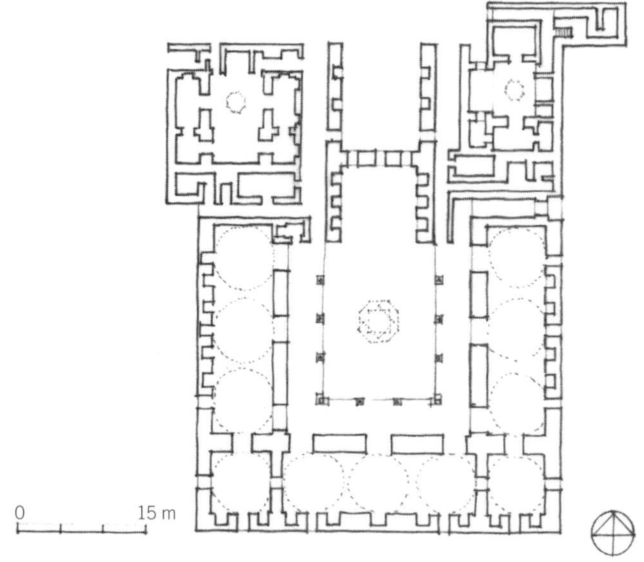


**11.53 Plan: Madrasa al-Firdus, Aleppo**

**11.54 Mosque at Qayrawan, Tunisia**

Marrakech gets the name Marra Kouch, which means "Land of the Kouch-men." Kouch was the name given to warriors with dark complexions from modern Mauritania.

### Mosque at Qayrawan

By the middle of the 9th century, Muslims were the uncontested rulers of North Africa and its Saharan and trans-Saharan trade routes. But given the heterogeneous population of Berbers, Romans, Christians, Africans, and Arab conquerors and their families, turbulence was an ever-present possibility. Initially North Africa was controlled by the Umayyads from Damascus, but eventually, as in Spain, local regimes came into power, such as the Fatimid, based in Egypt, and the Aghlabids, based in Tunisia. The Fatimids were eventually supplanted in western Africa by the Almoravids, Berbers from Western Sahara, who eventually came to control Spain, meaning that by 1000 there existed a single Moorish empire spanning the Straits of Gibraltar and circumscribing the area of Morocco, Algeria, and Tunisia, an area known as Maghreb (Arabic for "west"). They founded the city of Marrakech in 1062 as a portal to the southern trade routes. It was, however, the subsequent rulers, the Almohads, who began construction of the Kutubiyya Mosque.

North African mosques had a plan that developed from the Spanish prototype, with the Mosque at Qayrawan (constructed in stages from 670–863), however, serving as a particularly important model. The Kutubiyya Mosque in Marrakech, though built 400 hundred years later, differs little from the Qayrawan mosque.

It has a low hypostyle hall organized around a T shape composed of the raised aisle facing the *qibla* wall and a central axial aisle that connects the mihrab to the courtyard. Even the number of aisles—seventeen perpendicular to the *qibla* wall—matches that of Qayrawan. Clearly there is an intentional link to a more ancient brand of Islam. But the rough quarry stone minaret, square in plan, towers 70 meters in the air, nearly twice the height of the minaret at Qayrawan. The result is a minaret with a vertical architectural presence that balances the horizontality of the prayer hall. The tower is five times taller than it is wide, including the slim lantern that defines the top. Each of these five units, which correspond to five stacked interior rooms, is articulated on the facade with a framed register. Each register is different, though a motif of interlacing polylobed arches and blind openings is consistent throughout. The stone patterning, unlike the Almoravids, is nonfloral. The patterns result from the interlacing of simple repeated geometric shapes to create the appearance of a light web or net texture, known as *shabka*.

0 50 m

**11.55 Plan: Mosque at Qayrawan**

11.56 Plan of *qubba*: Al-Barubiyyin, Marrakech, Morocco

11.57 Al-Barubiyyin, Marrakech

### Muqarnas

*Muqarnas*, also called stalactite or honeycombed vaulting, are one of the most ubiquitous features of Islamic architecture between the 11th and 15th centuries, appearing around the Islamic world, including South Asia, in a variety of materials, including brick, stone, stucco, and wood. The term's origin and meaning, as well as the historical development of the form, are not known for certain and are much debated. It is likely that it developed out of squinches that eased the transition between the square and circle of the dome. It is also possible that the *muqarnas* developed out of a fascination among Islamic artists for complex geometrical patterns, which were being applied to the surfaces of doors and window moldings as well as to book illustrations and calligraphy. Though they do not have an explicit symbolic value, they seem to allude to the geometry of the heavens. It has also been suggested that the dome is a spatial analogy to the theological philosophy of the Ash'ari Sunnis that emphasized an atomistic cosmology in which God was responsible for preserving the created world from one instant to another. Geometric ornamentation and stereotomic composition possessed an allegorical dimension that linked the splendor of human efforts with the wonders of God's creations. An early example is the Shrine of Imam Dur in Dur, Iraq (1085). The building consists of an elongated cube on which rests a series of octagonal tiers that telescope and rotate toward the final dome.

Among the more developed examples are the madrasa al-Nuriyya (1168) with its more integrated effect and the Mausoleum of Zumurrud Khalun in Baghdad (1200), which is permeated by small openings, creating a scintillating and ephemeral weightlessness. The dome (*qubba*) of al-Barubiyyin in Marrakech (1117) is another early example of a complex dome structure. Its eight-pointed star seems to almost float free from the enclosing frame. The four corners have *muqarnas* of their own, producing a dynamic three-dimensional effect. One of the most spectacular of these domes is the one in the Alhambra over the Hall of the Two Sisters (1356–59), which projects both chaos and order at the same time. It is not surprising that the earliest stone *muqarnas* come from Syria. At the portal of the Ayyubid Palace in Aleppo (1210), it is integrated into a portal and in essence is split open to reveal its section, demonstrating complete mastery over stone in two and three dimensions.

11.58 Section: Shrine of Imam Dur, Samarra, Iraq

**11.59 Al-Azhar Mosque, Cairo, Egypt**

**11.60 Entry portal: Aqmar Mosque, Cairo, Egypt**

## FATIMIDS

The Fatimids, who had established themselves at Mahdiya in Tunisia, may have lost Algeria and points to the west, but in their expansion to the east, they were successful, sweeping through the Nile Valley, across Palestine, and into southern Syria, controlling a considerable part of the Middle East for more than 200 years. Most Egyptians at that time were Sunni Muslims, which the Fatimid, who were Shi'ite of the Ishma'ili sect, opposed. The Fatimid caliphs, who considered themselves to be divine rulers sent by God to ensure the prevalence of Islamic justice, refused to recognize the legitimacy of the Sunni Abbasid caliphates, ruling from Baghdad. It was the Fatimid vision and mission to convert the whole Muslim world to their faith and overthrow the Sunni caliphate.

One of their principal architectural expressions was the construction of the city of al-Qahira, the modern city of Cairo, the core of which was essentially a palace city for the caliph and his court and the office of the state bureaucracy and the military. A street ran along a north-south axis with the great East Palace standing at the center and the al-Azhar Mosque to its south. The al-Azhar mosque (970–72), though it has been much renovated and enlarged, still maintains its North African hypostyle hall with wooden roofs. A striking feature is the central axis, which breaks the rhythm and emphasizes the *qibla*. The minaret is placed on axis on the south side of the courtyard.

The mosque in its final form, with various functions appendaged to its rectangular hull, became almost a city unto itself. It still remains an important center for Islamic theological scholarship in the Muslim world. The building is named "the radiant" in honor of Mohammed's daughter, Fatima al-Zahra, from whom the Fatimid dynasty claims descent.

Though descriptions testify to the sumptuousness of the Fatimid palaces, little of their palace architecture survives; but one can get a sense of Fatimid-era architectural skills in studying the facade of the Aqmar Mosque in Cairo (1125). Based loosely on the triumphal arch motif from classical times, it has a central portal flanked by tall niches that are surmounted by *muqarnas* panels and by blind niches. An inscription runs across the top. Moldings and decorative friezes are used to tie the parts together.

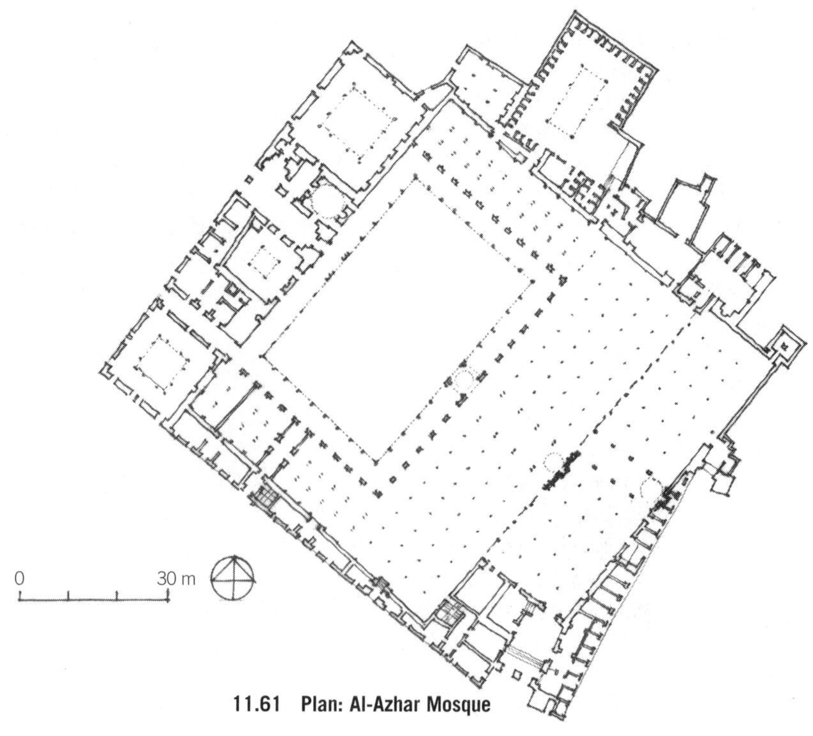


**11.61 Plan: Al-Azhar Mosque**

11.62 **Great Mosque in Tlemcen, Algeria**

11.63 **Mosque of Tinmal**

**ALMORAVID DYNASTY**

The Almoravids who ruled Spain and Morocco were replaced by another Berber tribe, the Almohads, whose base was even further south in the Atlas Mountains and who espoused a particularly puritanical form of Islam. The economic centers of both these regimes was no longer Spain but Fez with its cosmopolitan populations of Berbers, Arabs, Andalusians, and Africans. The Almohads were active builders of religious, military, and civilian structures as well as powerful promoters of crafts. Almohad textiles were shipped throughout the Islamic world and were sold in Christian Europe as well.

The architectural styles of the Almoravids and Almohads are related, but there were important differences. The Almoravids adopted the more refined Spanish style, as in the Great Mosque in the city Tiemcen (1082), on the Moroccan-Algerian border, an important nexus in north-south, east-west trade routes, was inspired by the Mosque of Córdoba. The *qibla* dome is supported by slender ribs with delicately carved filigree patterns in between, making it seem to float in the open sky above. The Almohads, who practiced a strict ascetic interpretation of Islam with no deviation, developed a mosque type that adhered to a strictly circumscribed architectural plan, such as the Mosque of Tinmal, (1153–54), located 100 kilometers southeast of Marrakech in the Atlas Mountains.

The wider central aisle and transept in front of the *qibla* wall, combined with the entrance courtyard, create a spatial figure within the plan. There were no minarets on the front but rather a square tower directly over the *qibla*. The fortlike exterior belies the delicacy of the interior articulation.

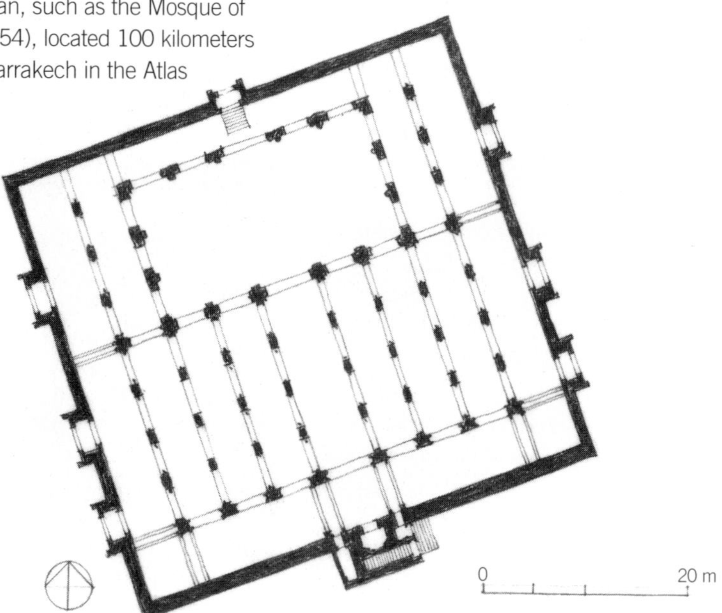


11.64 **Plan: Mosque of Tinmal, Morocco**

11.65 Church of Christ Pantokrator, Istanbul, Turkey

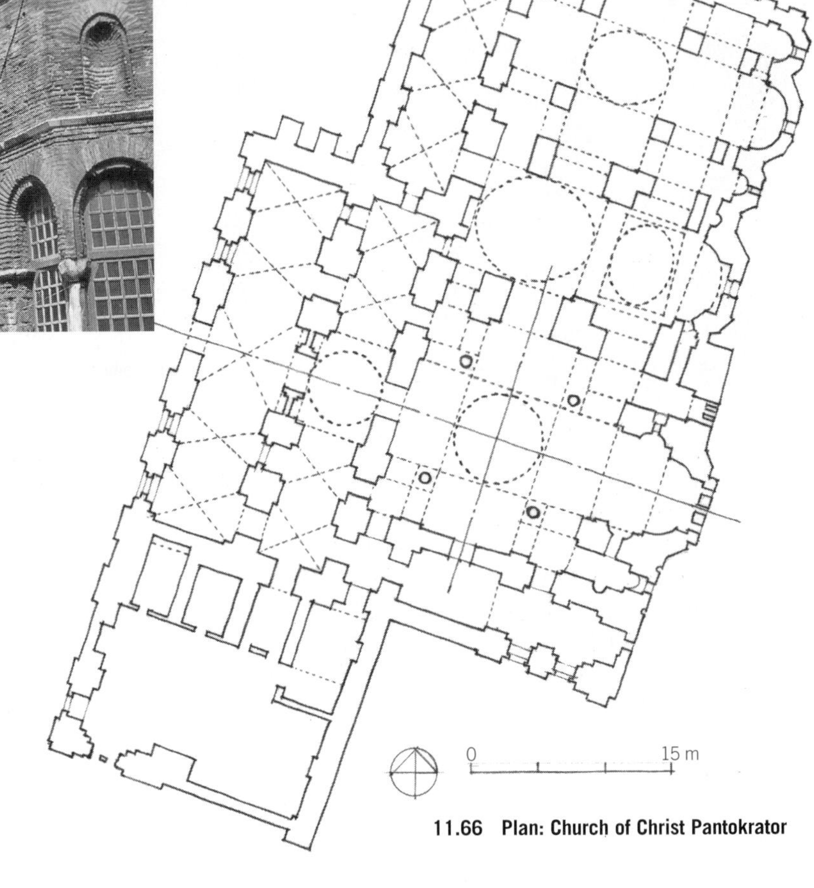


11.66 Plan: Church of Christ Pantokrator

## BYZANTINE REVIVAL

By the year 1000, the Byzantine Empire had rebounded under Basil II, due to successful military campaigns and a restructuring of the administration. Church building also began to rebound. Formally, little changed, with the central element a dome resting on four columns placed in a square. New, however, was the desire to create compound churches by adding new ones to older ones and opening up a passageway in between and uniting them with a new narthex. This can be seen at the Church of Christ Pantokrator (known in Turkish as Zeyrek Camii), which was built 1118–43 by Emperor John II Komenos and which has three churches. The South and North churches were built first by Empress Eirene. After her death, John decided to join the two churches, with a third dedicated to the Archangel Michael but also serving as a mortuary chapel for his family clan, the Commenus. Over the centuries, many Byzantine emperors were buried there. The building, on that account, was much renowned in Constantinople. It was, as was customary, associated with a monastery and a hospice, in this case one for old men. The South Church is a four-column type. The columns, now gone, were of red marble. The North Church is similar, with a dome carried on a high drum. The middle church also had a dome, creating a complex labyrinthine interior.

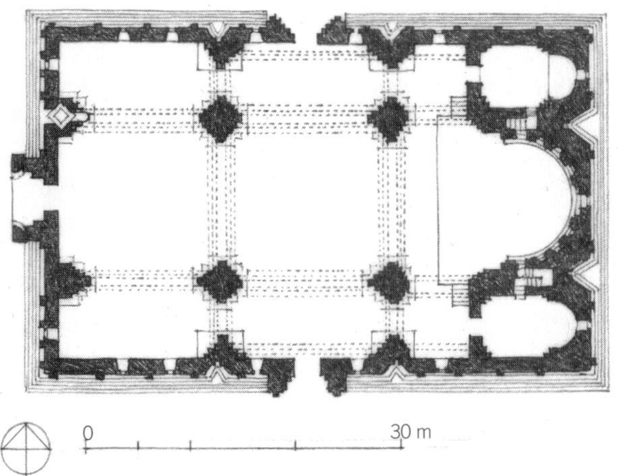


11.67 Plan: Cathedral of Ani

11.68 Cathedral of Ani, Armenia

11.69 Plan of Sanahin complex, Lori, Armenia

An important influence on Byzantine architecture came from the direction of Armenia. During the period of the Arab caliphate (654–861) all church-building in Armenia had stopped, but when independence was regained, Armenia saw a reawakening of its architectural culture until 1045, when it was invaded from the north by the Turks. But in 1080 Prince Ruben founded a new kingdom in Cilicia and Armenia (sometimes known as the Fourth Armenian Kingdom). The close relations this kingdom established with European countries played an important role during the Crusades. Intermarriage with European crusading families was common among its aristocracy. Many French terms entered the Armenian language.

A well-preserved monastic compound, Sanahin (also St. Amenaprkitch) gives us an indication of an Armenian monastic institution. Once again, unlike Byzantine aggregates, where buildings tend to fuse into each other, the complexes in Armenia maintained volumetric and functional clarity. The composition in this case is designed along two rectangular lines with facades facing westward.

The churches (begun in 934) have between them a barrel-vaulted corridor or academia, where pupils could sit on the stone benches while the teacher walked up and down the space, as was the custom in peripatetic schools. Appendaged to the front of both churches are *gavits*, dating from about 1210, which came to be used around that time. In these vaulted spaces, on the west side of the church, the novices could assist the Mass. However, their principal utilization was as meeting halls. Laws and ordinances were carved on the internal walls. They also served as special places to bury the nobility. The southern church has four columns, whereas the northern one has three naves. They were illuminated by an oculus in the vault.

The Cathedral of Ani (989–1001) deserves to be also listed among the principal monuments of the time because of its pointed arches and clustered columns and piers. It was spectacularly sited on a bluff overlooking the Arpa and Akhurian rivers. The architect responsible for the building was Trdat (987–1001), whose fame was such that he was summoned to Constantinople to repair the dome of Hagia Sophia, which was damaged by an earthquake in 989. Continuing their tradition of architectural innovation, Trdat rested the dome on a drum with four pendentives descending between the arches, which rest on four piers. Smaller arches span the side aisles.

The Armenian word *gmbet*, usually translated as "dome," means more precisely "the vault of heaven." The vision of Gregory the Illuminator (b. 239), the patron saint of Armenia, also played a part in the acceptance of the dome. He wrote that he saw a figure of light descending from heaven associated with a magnificent building that had the form of a dome on four columns. We also see the emergence of decorative detailing based on floral and geometric designs to form blind arcades and to articulate openings and cornices. This would become another design feature that was to spread to the west, to Italy in particular.

11.70 Section of Sanahin church

## 1000 CE

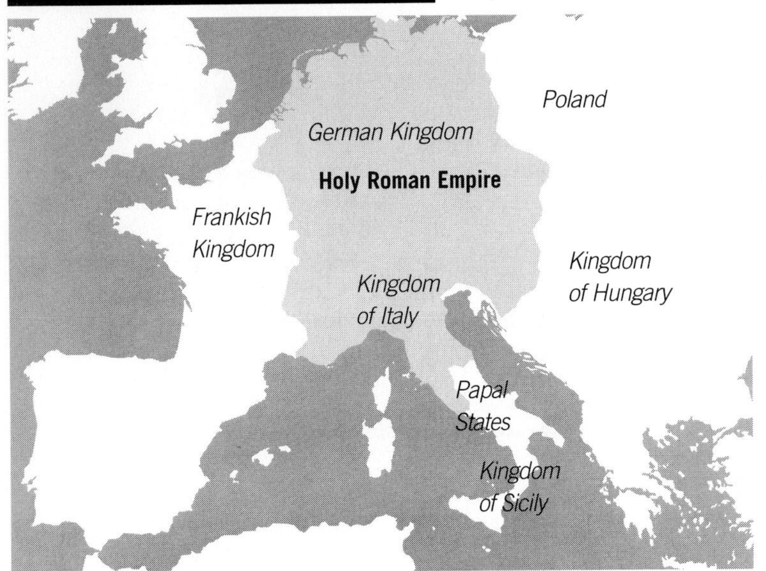


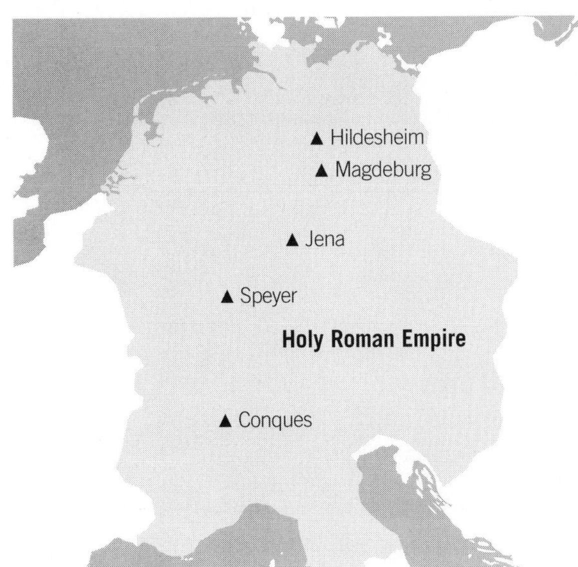


### OTTONIAN GERMANY

For several decades, under Charlemagne, virtually the entire Western world—such as it was defined at that time—had been brought together under a single political domination governed by a homogenous group of bishops and judges, scions of the dominant families. But with the division of Charlemagne's empire after his death, the Viking raiders in the north and Muslim incursions in the south, the quality of life in Europe deteriorated. Communities were scattered, libraries destroyed, and monasteries ruined. But by the year 1000, the situation had begun to improve, partially because by then the feudal system had been established throughout most of Europe. It divided society roughly into three groups, the serfs and agrarian laborers, members of religious orders, and the aristocracy, whose power was hereditary, who collected the taxes, and who took responsibility for military protection of the land.

By the year 1000, the balance of power had also shifted from France to the western part of the kingdom and the Christianized Germans under the Ottonian Dynasty (919–1024). The princely realm of Germany, like that of France, had no capital in the modern sense. Rulers moved from place to place, adjudicating legal cases as they went, trying to hold together the network of relationships on which the kingdom depended. The absence of a single capital city differentiated the European notion of governance from almost every other state in the world.

The German Empire aspired even more to be heir to the Roman mantle than the Carolingian Empire had. Though Charlemagne had received the title Imperator Augustus from the pope, the phrase Romanum Imperium only began to appear on documents after 1034. Despite the overt connections to Rome, Ottonian rulers also admired Constantinople. Mothers and wives of the aristocracy were often Greek princesses, and the emperor took over the Eastern notion of *basileus*, or "sovereign," complete with the concomitant conception of authority and its emblems of power—the golden cape and the sphere held in the right hand. The Greeks brought with them artisans as well as Byzantine and Armenian architects and stone masons, whose quality workmanship had a positive impact on Ottonian architecture.

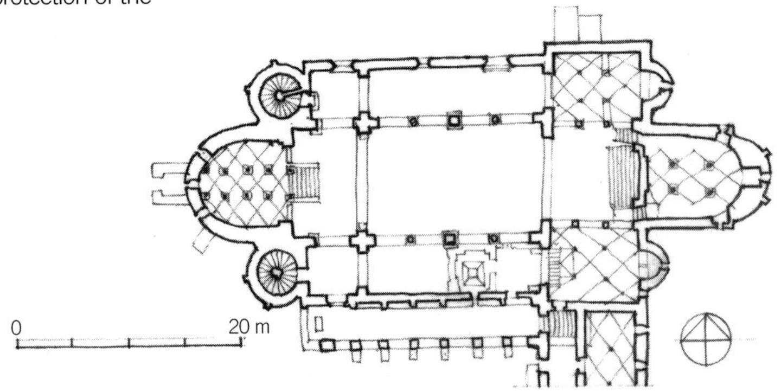


**11.71 Plan: St. Cyriakus, Gernrode, Germany**

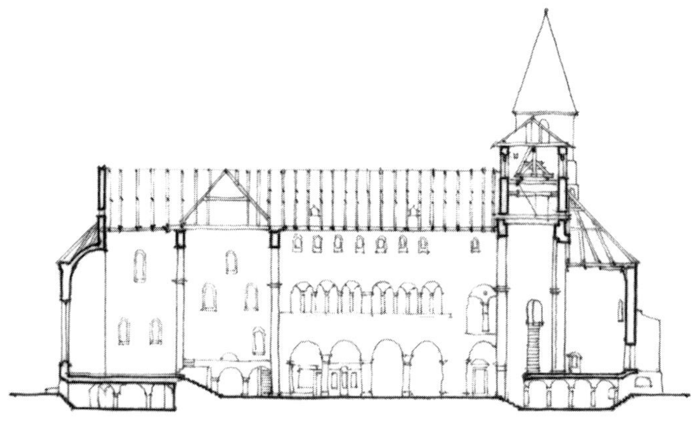

**11.72 Section: St. Cyriakus, Gernrode**

As a way to cement imperial control over their territory, the Ottonian kings combined the founding of monasteries with the founding of market centers. Like the Carolingian churches, Ottonian ones consisted of volumetric masses. But the uncluttered external surfaces and the integrated relationship between the crossings and transepts of St. Cyriakus in Gernrode (960) and St. Michael in Hildesheim (1001–33), for example, impart to the buildings a complex simplicity that the earlier Carolingian church, St. Riquier, lacked. St. Michael's has a nave that stretches between two almost identical transepts. The entrance to the church, leading up from the marketplace, was broadside on the southern flank. The plan of the nave has a ratio of 3:1, with the rhythm established by piers with two columns interspersed between them. The building, which has no westwork, reflects the gradual reduction of importance of the westwork.

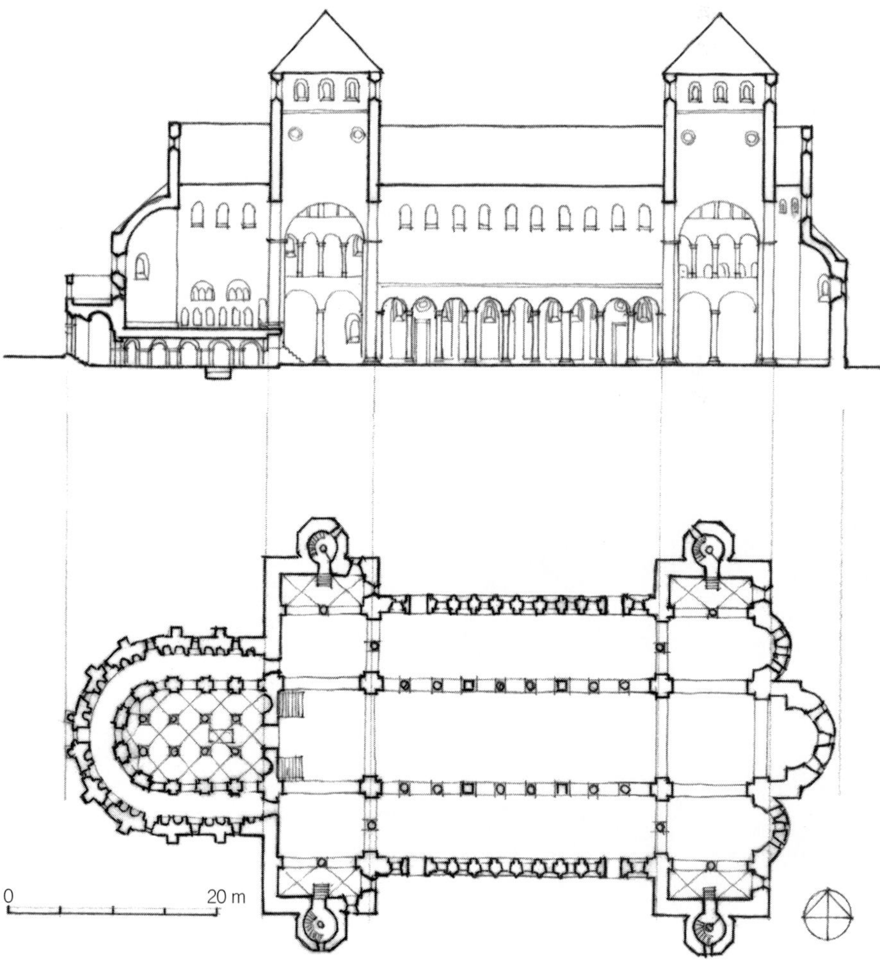


**11.73 Section and plan: St. Michael in Hildesheim, Germany**

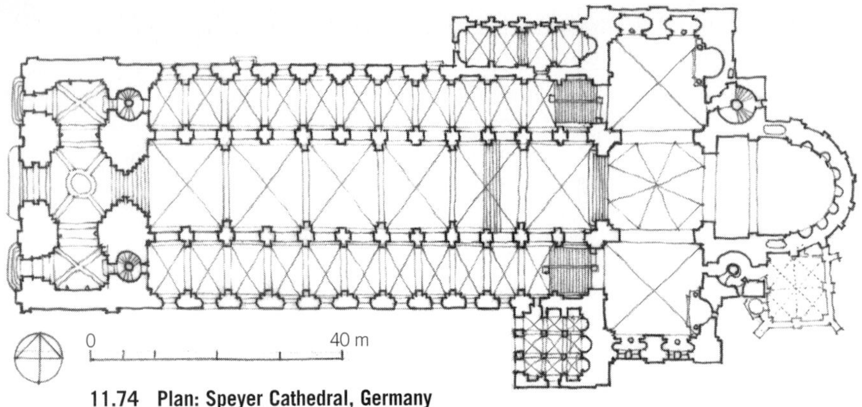


11.74 Plan: Speyer Cathedral, Germany

The word *cathedral* comes from the Greek word that designates a professor's chair from which a lecture was given. Early Christian bishops used a cathedra not only as a symbol of their power but also as a place from which to preach, even though that practice was eventually abandoned. The first use of the word in regard to architecture dates from around 800 CE. A *cathedral*, in that etymological sense, is thus an elaborate framing device for a bishop's chair. Some ancient chairs still exist, such as the so-called Chair of St. Peter, which is preserved in the Vatican Museum.

**Speyer Cathedral**

Despite the problems of the times, the increased trade and competition among the cities led to a rapid increase in architectural production, and that in turn led to a rapid development of the architectural language. Particularly important was the introduction of stone vaulting. The implications were profound, spatially, structurally, and symbolically. To support the vault, the builders could have decided to build thicker walls, but instead they interpreted the side aisles as structural buttresses for the vault, transforming the interior of the building into a tripartite space visually coordinated with the vaults over the aisles.

11.75 Abbey Church of St. Foy, France

One of the earliest churches built in the new manner is the Speyer Cathedral, begun around 1040, with the vaulting completed around 1137. Abandoning the squat compositions of Carolingian and Ottonian architecture, the nave elevation of Speyer was defined by a series of high arches mindful of a Roman aqueduct. Windows at the top bring light into the nave. Even more significant was the presence of a single attached column that rose from the floor to the base of the vault, some 32 meters from the floor, higher than any other vault at the time. The crossing is defined by an octagonal tower. The tall proportions allow the building to seem more compact and controlled, and to some eyes, more Roman, especially when compared to Hildesheim's static arrangement of volumes. There can be no doubt that the third Abbey Church of Cluny, begun about 1088, was erected in open rivalry to Speyer. The interior nave of Speyer has since been rebuilt, but St. Etienne in Nevers (1063–97) is more or less comparable.

Despite its innovations, Speyer can also be seen as the end stage of the Romanesque style, for at that very same time, a remarkable new development was taking place at the Abbey Church of St. Foy at Conques, begun around 1050. As at Speyer, the tall, soaring, barrel-vaulted nave imparts the impression of a single structure as opposed to a box with a roof on it. As at Speyer, the high side aisles served as buttresses for the vault. And, as at Speyer, the nave, at least in the lower part, combined its structure with arcaded openings. But the architects here added buttresses on the outside to further strengthen the walls. Though small, they are enough to effect the clear differentiation between wall and column that defines Carolingian and Romanesque architecture. The wall begins to look more and more like a series of piers.

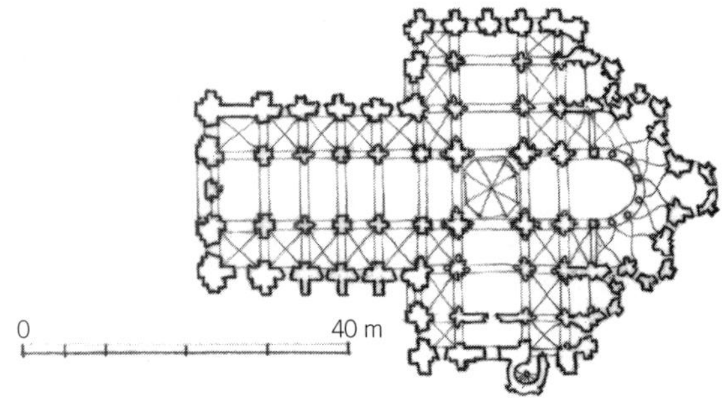


11.76 Plan: Abbey Church of St. Foy

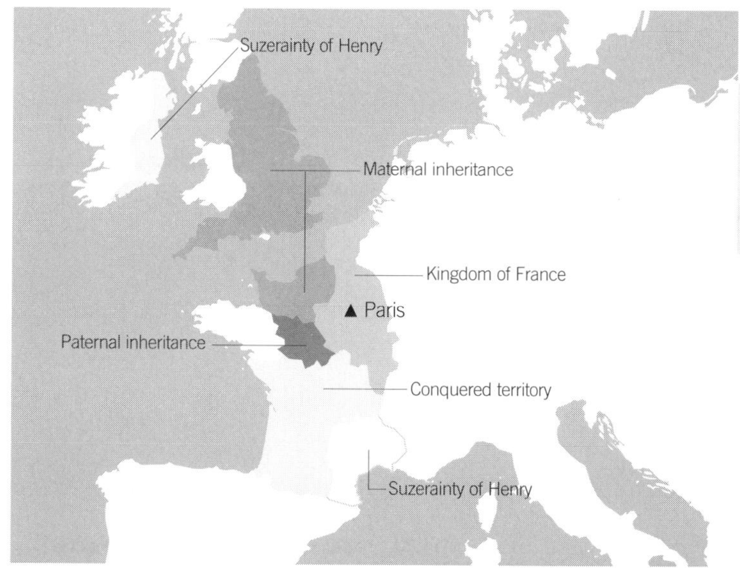


The Normans, a warrior people from the northern French coast, overran England and southern Italy and settled in Scotland, Wales, the Byzantine Empire, and (after the First Crusade) the Levant. Norman power was extended by strategic marriage alliances.

**NORMANS**

In 911, Charles the Simple validated the Norman possessions around Rouen, which the Normans had begun to occupy in the 9th century. The Normans, with amazing adaptive energy, renounced paganism and absorbed local customs and language. They furthered the development of the Romanesque style, of which the Cathedral of Caen is the prime example. In 1001, Richard II, Duke of Normandy, had invited the Italian abbot, William of Volpiano—accompanied by a colony of Benedictines, with their well-established traditions of design and masonry construction—to restore the Abbey of Fécamp. Soon a uniquely Norman style developed that not only incorporated Norse decorative motifs but also drew on the Islamic influences brought to England and France from the Norman holdings in Sicily.

In various waves, the Normans conquered parts of southern Italy, Sicily (1061), northern Africa, and then England, following the Battle of Hastings (1066). The new rulers transformed the entire religious, mercantile, and political geography of England, but given the dispersal of their holdings, from England and northern France to southern Italy and Sicily, the Normans became a clearinghouse of different stylistic and cultural trends that bridged many classic divides. The influence of Islamic masons, who were brought to England to work on the cathedrals, is not in dispute.

Most importantly they transformed the village- and agrarian-based geography of the Saxons into one based on towns with a castle at the center, in the middle of a larger farming district or borough, to serve as the basic instrument of their government. Unlike in Germany, where castles were generally on defensible ridges or mountains, in England, where mountains were not a prominent geographical feature, they were at the core of the urban layout. Town markets were created and an aristocracy took shape, promoting an international luxury trade in commodities such as fine cloth and wine. It has been estimated that about 400 to 500 new towns were laid out in this manner, creating a pattern of urban centers that was to survive virtually unchanged up to the Industrial Revolution and, in parts of the country, survives today.

The Normans introduced not only a strong mercantile society but also a change in the notion of kingship. Roger the Great, in the chronicles of the time, is represented as the royal deputy of Christ. The small Saxon churches that dotted the English landscape could no longer measure up to such grand claims. Most were torn down and in their stead, the Normans designed a religious landscape around powerful state-supported bishoprics, each of which needed a sumptuous cathedral. Architects and masons were brought in from the continent as were successive waves of continental monks—Benedictines, Augustinians, Cistercians, Cluniacs, and Carthusians—who were just as important from a religious point of view as from an economic one, their well-organized farms producing surpluses for the markets. The Cistercians, for example, were associated with irrigation and large-scale sheep farming. By the end of the 12th century, 600 new monastic institutions of varying practices had been set up.

**11.77 Norman knights**

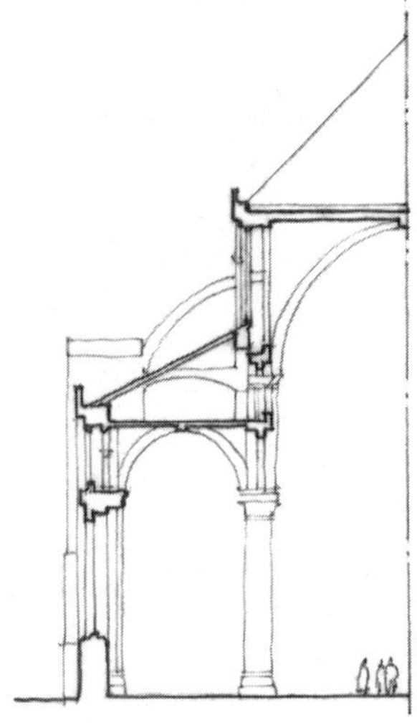

11.78 Section: Choir of Canterbury Cathedral

### Canterbury Cathedral

Among the new bishoprics Canterbury was the most important as its bishop served as vice-regent of the king. When Canterbury Cathedral was destroyed by an accidental fire in 1067, one year after William the Conqueror landed on the south coast of England, Lanfranc, the first Norman archbishop of Canterbury, initiated a rebuilding that was based on the new cathedral of St. Etienne in France. When a fire destroyed the choir in 1174, the architects, William of Sens and William the Englishman, erected a new choir and a presbytery that it doubled the length of the church. The newer part existed on a higher elevation, with the stairs serving to separate the more sacred areas to the east. The project shows how England adopted French construction techniques, specifically the concept of the flying buttress, the six-partite vault, and other Gothic features, with the nave itself, of course, remaining from the time of Lanfranc. The nave was, however, rebuilt in the late 14th century. The church houses, among other sacred objects, the relics of St. Thomas, originally placed at the center of the round chapel at the eastern end of the building.

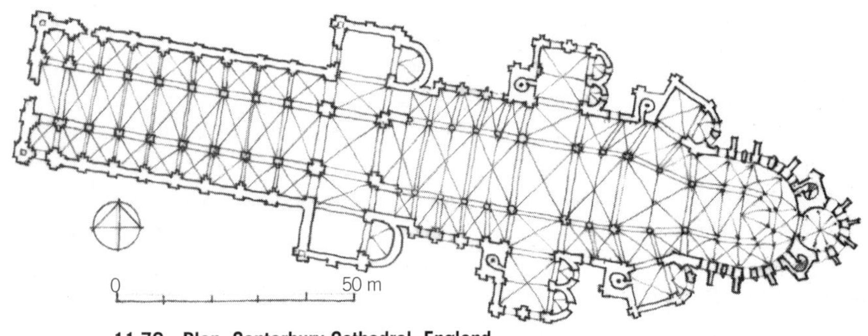


11.79 Plan: Canterbury Cathedral, England

11.80 Interior vaulting: Canterbury Cathedral

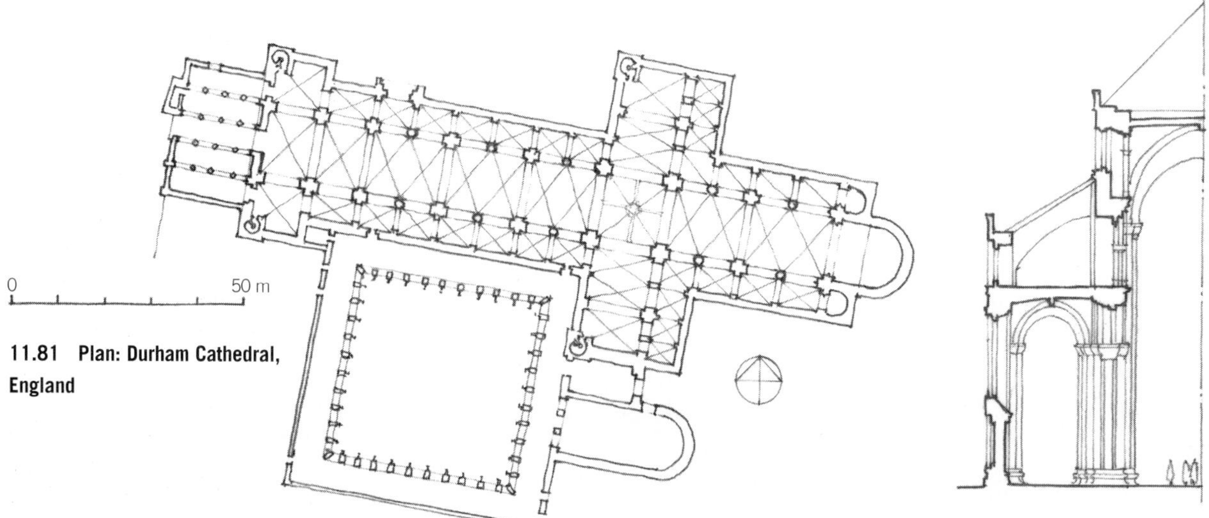


11.81 **Plan: Durham Cathedral, England**

11.82 **Section: Nave of Durham Cathedral**

### Durham Cathedral

Durham Cathedral (1093–1133) is important for its architectural features, specifically, its rib vaulting (the first of its kind in England), its pointed arches, and its high standard of masonry. Durham shows the specific Anglo-Norman style as a blend of the English decorative tradition with Norman architectural skills, and it marks the development from a more monumental and simple scheme, as we can see in Gloucester Cathedral (begun 1089). The choir and the nave of the three-aisled church were built between 1093 and 1133, but the west towers were not completed until 1220. In comparison with the nave of Gloucester, which also has heavy round columns carrying the arcades, Durham, in the manner of Speyer, introduces the idea of attached half-columns that guide the eye to the ceiling. Even though the loftiness of both churches had been a feature of Romanesque architecture, what is novel here is the structural openness of the wall. A basic principle of Norman building was the reduction of solid walls to a thick but open skeleton of arches. The arches were not just interruptions in the wall but were defined in a regularized way with surrounds framed by attached half-columns and horizontal string courses.

The north transept of Peterborough Cathedral (1117–40) is a typical example. The openings do not deny the weight and mass of the wall, as would become the tendency later, but rather, illuminated from behind, they seem to release their load gradually as the wall ascends.

The decoration of the columns with its zigzag and chevron motifs also made extensive use of color, specifically black and red, which was an influence from Islamic architecture that came into the country through the crusades and the Norman-Arab connections in Sicily and northern Africa. Geometric patterns, such as we see in Peterborough and other features of the inner decoration can later be found in several other cathedrals in northern England, suggesting that the same masons moved on to work in Scotland.

Durham Cathedral is considered a forerunner of what is now called the Gothic style largely because of the fusion of the ribbed vault and the pointed arch, which are considered essentially Gothic features. The so-called Galilee Chapel (1153–95) in front of the west facade is unique with its five parallel halls, longitudinal arcaded walls without any subdivision into bays. This layout resembles one encountered in Islamic mosques and once again shows the cross-fertilization of ideas introduced from the Mediterranean.

11.83 **Nave of Durham Cathedral**

11.84 Aerial view: Cefalu Cathedral, Sicily, Italy

11.85 Exterior detail: St. Maria Nuova at Monreale, Sicily, Italy

### Cefalu Cathedral

When Roger d'Hauteville conquered Sicily in 1060, he found a culture that had been under Arab influence since the late-9th century. The Normans not only availed themselves of the practical and technological innovations of the Muslims but also integrated them into their administration and even into the army. Soon Apulia, Capua, Sicily, and finally parts of northern Africa came under Norman domination. Specifically important was the control over the Straits of Messina, the trade route to the Bosporus.

The first major church was built at Cefalu; it followed a typical early Norman footprint, with a nave with side aisles, a wooden ceiling, and a massive transept in the east. It is a heavy and somber building that contrasts sharply with St. Maria Nuova at Monreale (mons regalis or "royal mountain"), south of Palermo on the slopes of Monte Caputo, and that was started only a hundred years after Cefalu. Islamic influences are apparent on the outside decoration of the apse, with its intertwined arches and the terra-cotta ornamentation. The Great Mosque in Córdoba (10th century) and the Bab Mardum Mosque in Toledo (around 1000) show similar interlocking arches. The cathedral also shows Byzantine influences, particularly the exquisite mosaics, which cover the interior walls of the cathedral and are second in quality only to those in Hagia Sofia in Istanbul.

The stylistic synthesizing is also evident in the areas of western Italy that the Normans controlled as well. Amalfi, in fact, became a seafaring republic, rivaling Genoa, Venice, and Pisa, from the 9th to the 11th centuries. At its height it had trade representatives in Mahdia, Kairuan (Cairo), Alexandria, Beirut, Jerusalem, Antioch, and Constantinople. At the Cathedral of Amalfi, the original Norman building underwent various expansions, including the "Cloister of Paradise," which was clearly influenced by Islamic motifs.

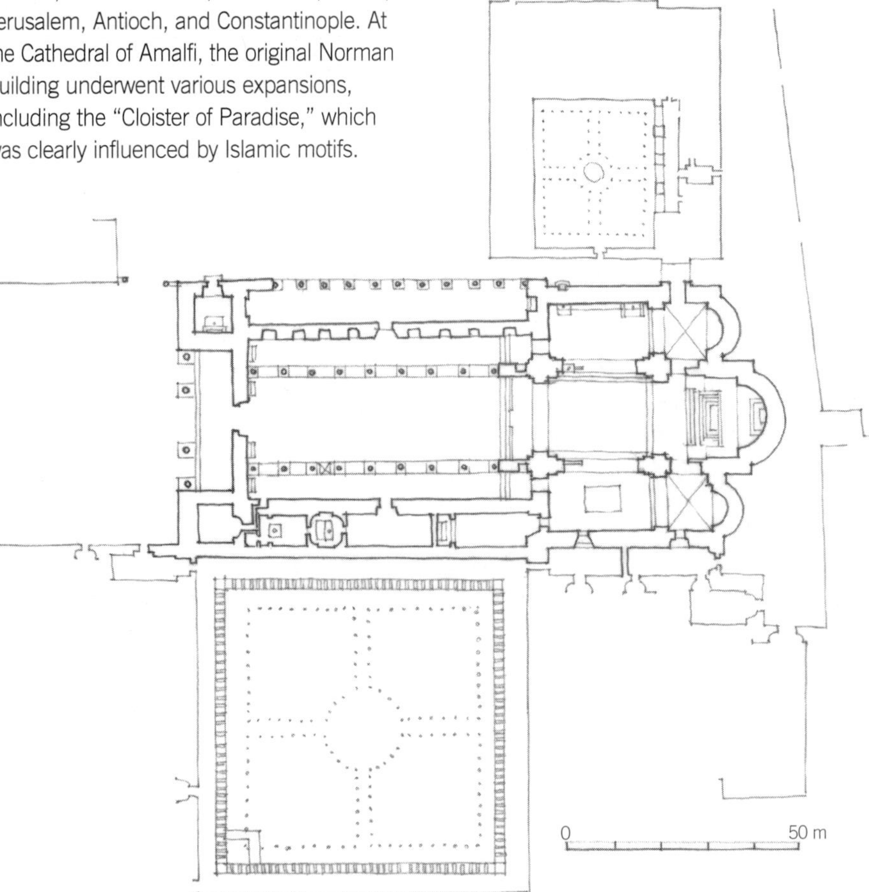


11.86 Site Plan: Cefalu Cathedral

11.87 **Krac des Chevaliers**

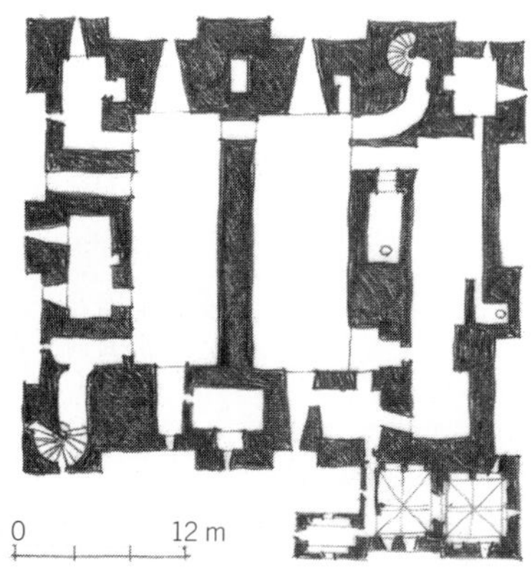


11.88 **Plan: Dover Castle, England**

### Dover Castle

In the British Isles, castles had become a necessity in the late 9th century as a response to Viking incursions, but under the Normans, castles, built on licenses extended to loyal vassals by the king, played an important part not only in warfare and in deterring local rebellion but also in protecting and strengthening the economic fabric of the kingdom. Each major landowner had a castle as his principal seat. Many fortifications were near a river, which provided water for the moat. Protecting roadways, river crossings, or ports, castles were designed with different degrees of complexity, depending on cost, need, and the constantly evolving state of the art, which in turn was a response to evolving weapon technology.

Dover Castle, begun around 1180, was almost cubical in form, measuring roughly 32 meters in all directions. There was a well in the basement to guarantee a water supply and chambers in the interior for storage of supplies. The idea was to minimize the size of the openings, or loops, as they were called. The loops were in this case not planned for positioning armaments; that would be a later development. The principal defensive position was the roof. Eventually, by the early 13th century, the square plan had to be abandoned because advances in siege technology made corners vulnerable to attack.

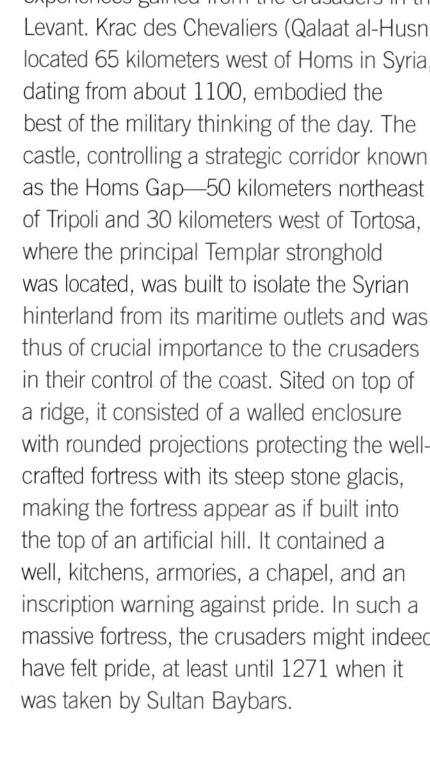

The Normans were not slow to profit from the experiences gained from the crusaders in the Levant. Krac des Chevaliers (Qalaat al-Husn), located 65 kilometers west of Homs in Syria, dating from about 1100, embodied the best of the military thinking of the day. The castle, controlling a strategic corridor known as the Homs Gap—50 kilometers northeast of Tripoli and 30 kilometers west of Tortosa, where the principal Templar stronghold was located, was built to isolate the Syrian hinterland from its maritime outlets and was thus of crucial importance to the crusaders in their control of the coast. Sited on top of a ridge, it consisted of a walled enclosure with rounded projections protecting the well-crafted fortress with its steep stone glacis, making the fortress appear as if built into the top of an artificial hill. It contained a well, kitchens, armories, a chapel, and an inscription warning against pride. In such a massive fortress, the crusaders might indeed have felt pride, at least until 1271 when it was taken by Sultan Baybars.

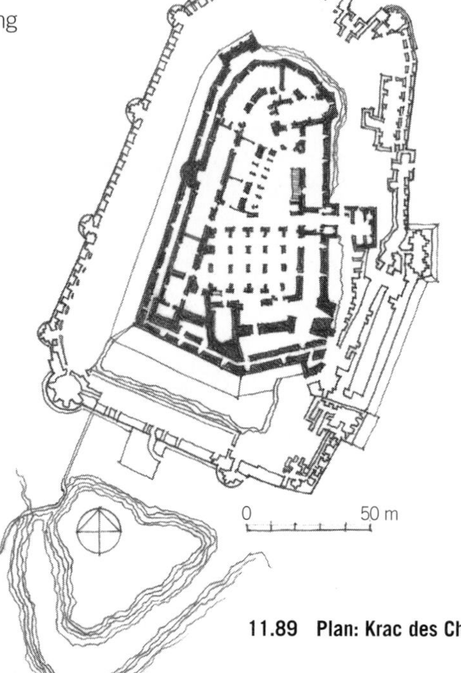


11.89 **Plan: Krac des Chevaliers, near Hamah, Syria**

# 1000 CE

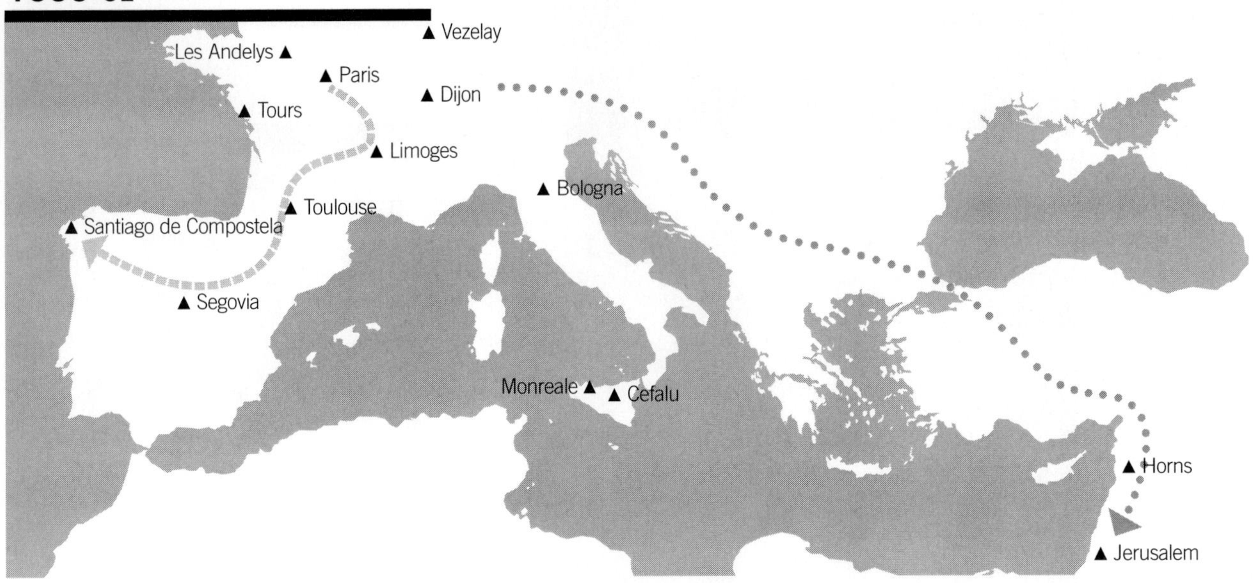


## PILGRIMAGE CHURCHES

The 11th and 12th centuries saw a growth in the popularity of religious pilgrimages, usually to sites where miracles had occurred. Pilgrims sought out these churches mainly for the relics they housed, which were thought to beam out a benevolent or curative aura. Possessing relics—a finger, foot, or even a head of a saint—became central to a particular church's identity, and churches vied with each to collect as many such relics as possible. Major ones were the tomb of St. Peter in Rome, the tomb of St. James at Santiago de Compostela, and the tomb of Christ in Jerusalem. Most pilgrims went on their own volition, but some pilgrimages were acts of penance imposed for exceptional misdeeds. The trips, exhausting and often dangerous, became the source of stories and ballads, such as Geoffrey Chaucer's *Canterbury Tales*. Other accounts give us some of the earliest descriptions of church architecture in the west.

The most venerated pilgrimage site was the Holy Sepulchre in Jerusalem. The original church, constructed by Constantine, was consecrated in 335 CE to protect a tomb held to have been that of Christ. Constantine's church was torn down by the Persians. The crusaders then began a church that, with changes and additions, is the basis for the church as it stands today. It retained the circular design, though on a larger scale. Appendaged to it is a two-bay nave that opens onto a courtyard. The conical roof has an oculus at the top. The shrine itself, a rectangular structure, was destroyed by fire in 1808; the current one dates from shortly thereafter.

It is a customary ritual to await daybreak on the morning of Easter eve in the Church of the Holy Sepulchre, at which moment are extinguished the earthly lights to welcome the coming of the light from heaven for the reception of which a special silver lamp is prepared. Once it appears, the bells are rung, and the fire is transferred to other lamps so that it can be transported to other churches.

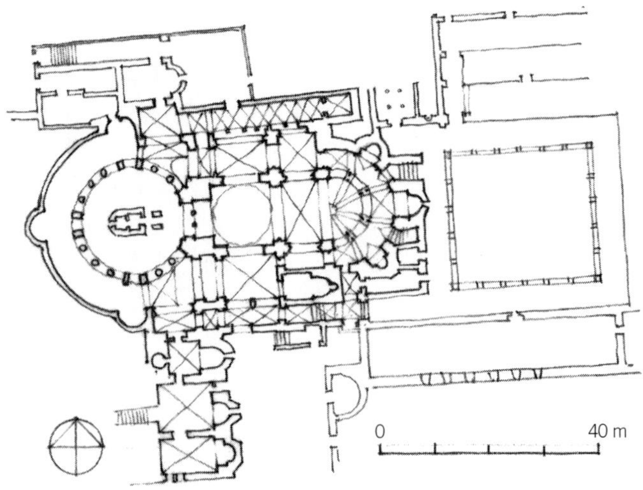


**11.90 Plan: Church of the Holy Sepulchre, Jerusalem**

11.91 Basilica of St. Sernin, Toulouse, France, view of apse

The descriptions of the Holy Sepulchre led to the construction of models in the west, such as St. Bénigne at Dijon (1001), Neuvry-Saint-Sépulchre (1045), and the Church of La Vera Cruz in Segovia. As none of these replicas are alike, it is clear that a precise imitation was not as important as other features. Among these copies is the frequently restored Church of St. Stefano at Bologna. Erected in the 5th century, it was rebuilt in 1180 in the shape of a dodecagon. The tomb chamber has an altar on top and is approached by two staircases.

11.92 Interior, Church of St. Stefano, Bologna, Italy

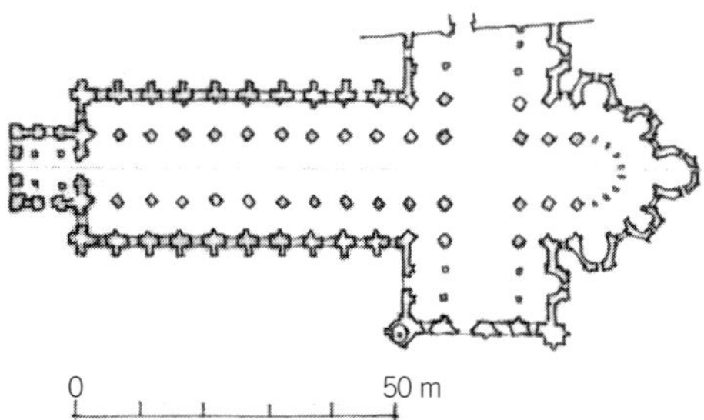


St. Martial, Limoges

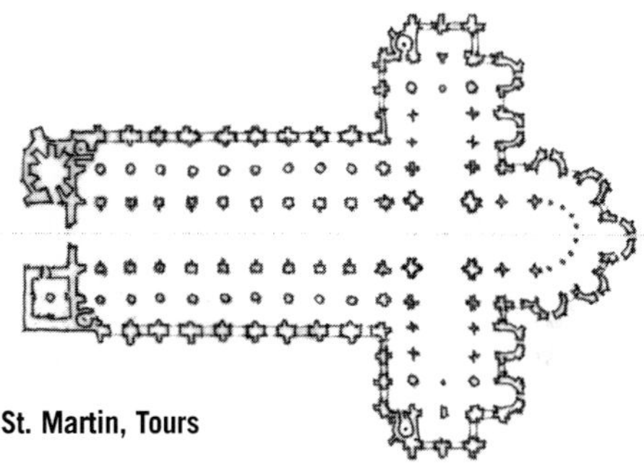

St. Martin, Tours

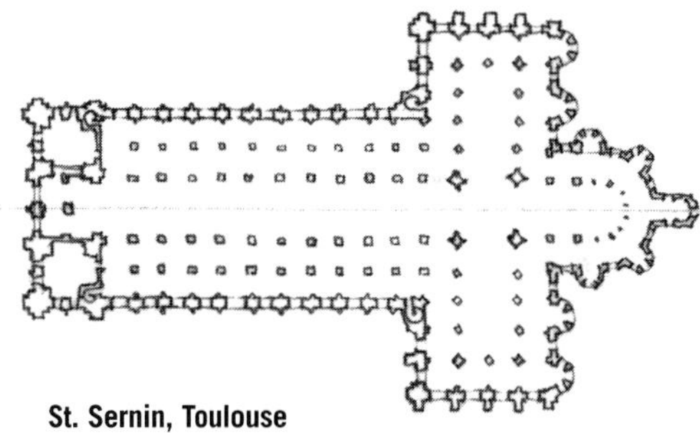

St. Sernin, Toulouse

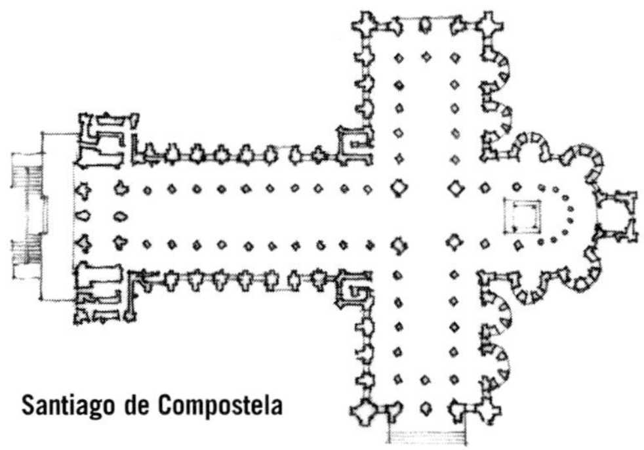

Santiago de Compostela

11.93 Comparative plans of four pilgrimage churches

## 1000 CE

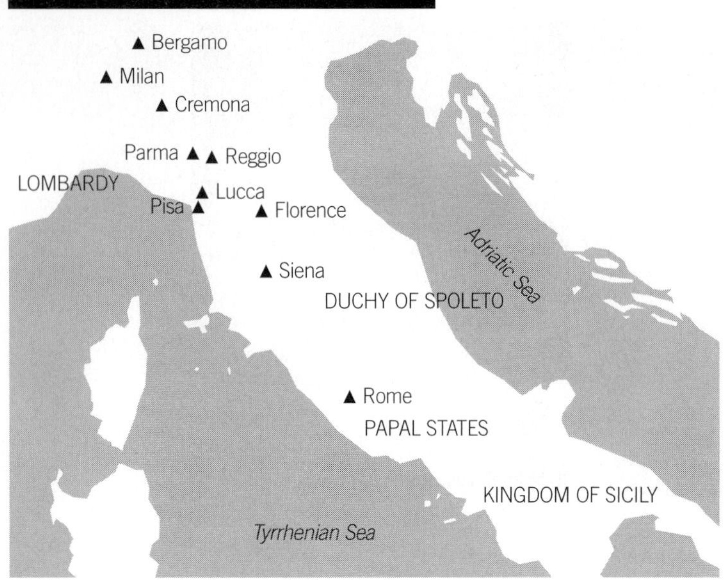

**11.94 Modena Cathedral, Italy**

### ITALIAN CITY-STATES

Charlemagne traveled to Italy only four times, each time for less than a year, setting a precedent of absentee monarchism that persisted for centuries. This allowed north Italian states, seen by the kings as the southern fringe of their empire, to survive as neither independent of nor fully integrated into the empire. Nevertheless, the cities were bustling places. Lucca was growing so fast that houses were being built along the approach roads; soon a good portion of the population lived outside the walls in so-called bourgs. And between the cities, villages—called variously *vici*, *loci*, *casalia*, or *villae*—came to be established. Because of this, monasteries, with some exceptions, were not able to develop such a hold on the local population as in northern Europe. To be sure, the cities did not look very impressive. Roman civic buildings and temples had been left to rot, or they were used as quarries. Churches built after 600 CE were small. Only a limited amount of farming occurred within city walls. The forums had lost their civic value and became marketplaces. In 1006, a series of disastrous famines and plagues carried off thousands of people. Due to the weak centralized power of the emperors, combined with the rising status of the cities, more and more power was ceded to the city bishops by the emperors to maintain support and control.

The bishops of Modena, Reggio, Bergamo, Cremona, and other places were given unprecedented powers. In 904, the bishop of Bergamo, for example, was granted the right to build city walls and to rebuild them with the help of the citizens. The results of this transfer of authority were complex and in the long run dangerous to the imperial state, as bishops were not able to maintain their hegemony over urban society. The new relationship between bishops, local aristocracy, and merchants resulted in a tense but vibrant urban economy that eventually set the stage for architectural productions unlike any seen since the days of the Roman empire. Cities now began to vie with each other in the construction of duomos and baptisteries that showed off the wealth of the city and the status of the church. The principal churches during this time were in Venice (begun 832), Pisa (begun 1063), Modena (begun 1099), Cremona (begun 1118), Siena (begun 1196), and Verona (begun 1139).

The architect of the Modena Cathedral was a man named Lanfranco, *mirabilis artifex, mirificus aedificator*, about whom, however, little is known except that he came from Como, where a school of builders had been established. Compared to other Romanesque buildings of the time, the structure is lighter and the lines stripped to their essentials. The building was clad in white Istrian stone and articulated by blind arcades. The central division is emphasized by a rose window and a baldachino-style central portal.

The work is ornamented with sculptures by the stone mason Wiligelmo, showing, among other things, Adam and Eve working the land to gain redemption. The portals also depict biblical and mythological events, including monsters and centaurs that warn not only of the diabolic threats awaiting man outside the city of God but also the threats that come from outside the Christian world, for Sicily had already fallen, first to Islamic troops, then to Arab colonizers. The archbishop's palace and administrative center was connected to the cathedral by means of a private passage. The building was commissioned by Queen Matilda di Canossa (1046–1115), one of the most powerful women of the entire Middle Ages, with a fortress in the heart of the Emilian Apennines, and a strong supporter of papal policy against the emperors. Matilda commissioned or had a hand in the commissioning of several other buildings in the Po River Valley, including the Rotunda of San Lorenzo in Mantua (1083), the Benedictine abbey of San Benedetto in Polirone Po (1077), as well as Cremona Cathedral (1107–17) and Piacenza Cathedral (1122).

11.95 **Detail: Cathedral of Pisa, Italy**

11.96 **Cathedral of Pisa**

**Cathedral of Pisa**

The Cathedral of Pisa was founded in 1063 after the victory of the Pisan fleet over the Saracens near Palermo. Pisa could now attempt to fulfill its ambition to become the Venice of the western Mediterranean and to develop a greater visual presence. The cathedral was consecrated in 1118, but it was completed only after considerable alterations in the 14th century. Stylistically it was a variation of the Mediterranean basilica plan with influences from Armenia, Syria, and Islamic architecture. The building also had imperial-Lombard overtones, especially in the facade with its four registers of freestanding gallery work. In the nave, the granite columns were taken from Roman temples on the Isle of Elba, the capitals range from imperial Roman to Byzantine temples; the walls have marble paneling inspired by Byzantine practice; and the dome in shape and manner of construction, rising on the inside from very high and narrow pointed arches, looks Islamic.

The building does not follow the trend of the great pilgrimage churches, in which structure and surface were becoming increasingly unified. In fact, it defied that trend in its celebration of surface. The elegant and costly marble sheathing that wraps around the exterior has little if any correlation to inner structure.

The massive volume of the building becomes light and airy, even though the openings are few and small in the typical Romanesque manner. The plan is also far different from French cathedral architecture, which aspired to a unity of form and structure. Here the double-aisled nave is intersected by a transept formed by two single-aisled minor basilicas, set front-to-front, with a domed crossing between. Each of the minor cross basilicas is provided with an apse of its own. The plan is thus a type of composite of basilicas to give the illusion on the exterior of a nave with transept.

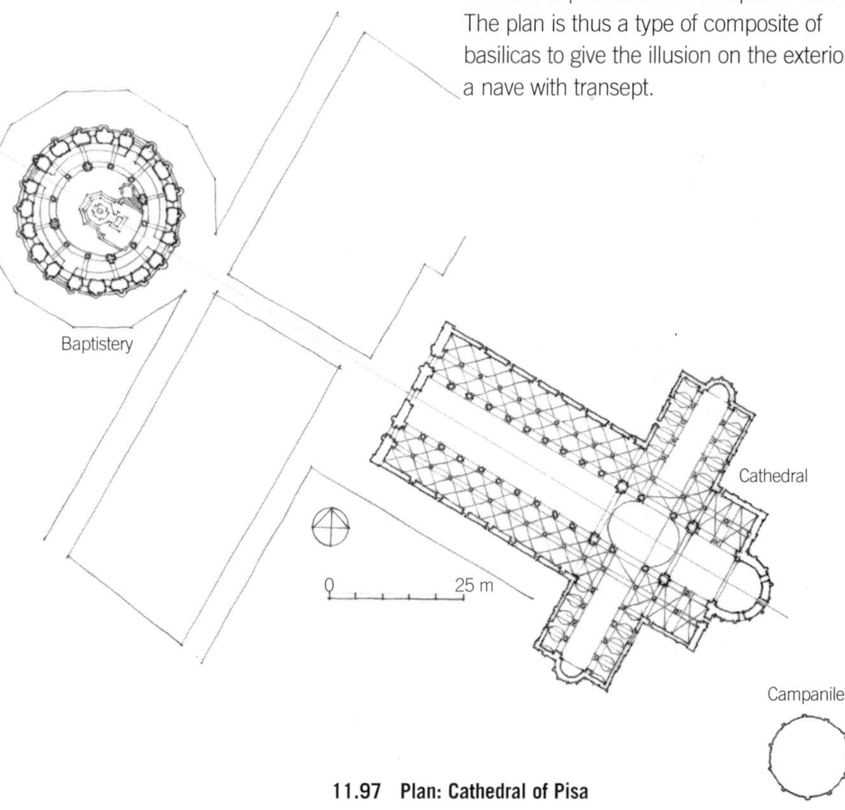


11.97 **Plan: Cathedral of Pisa**

11.98 **Baptistery at Florence, Italy**

11.99 **Baptistery at Pavia, Italy**

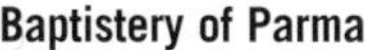

### Baptistery of Parma

Parallel to the emergence of Italian urban cathedrals was the growth of baptisteries, conceived as bold, freestanding structures in the piazza in front of or next to the church. Their usually octagonal shape had its roots in early Christian mysticism and imperial Roman symbolism. By the 10th century, with the revival of learning, numerology had risen into a science of its own, built on the numbers embedded in the concept of the Trinity, the twelve apostles, the Holy Spirit (3 + 4), the number of perfection (3 x 4 x 5), and so forth. The number eight and the octagonal form were especially important. In an inscription on the cathedral baptistery in Milan, the connection between number, geometry, and architecture is aptly expressed.

> He erected an eight-choired temple for use by the saints and an octagonal font is worthy of its number. This number proved fitting for the elevation of a housing of the holy baptism, which gave back to the people true deliverance, raising them again in the light of Christ, who loosened the bonds of death, and (who) from their graves raised the lifeless....

Architecturally the most significant baptisteries are at Florence (1060–1150), Pisa (1153–1265), and Parma (1196). The Baptistery of Parma, modeled on the Rotunda of the Anastasi in Jerusalem and begun in 1196, has corners that look like giant-order piers with loggias and a blind arcade on top spanning the interstices. The lower level consists of generous arched openings and blind arches. The eight great piers and the sixteen columns on each register are standard referents to the Holy Sepulchre in Jerusalem. Although the imposing mass of the buildings is Romanesque, its sculptural decoration reflects the Gothic advances made in France. This is most clearly seen in the prominence accorded to the Virgin Mary—the main portal is dedicated to her—and in the changed representation of Christ from a severe judge to a more humane figure, which was the sign of the new religious mentality.

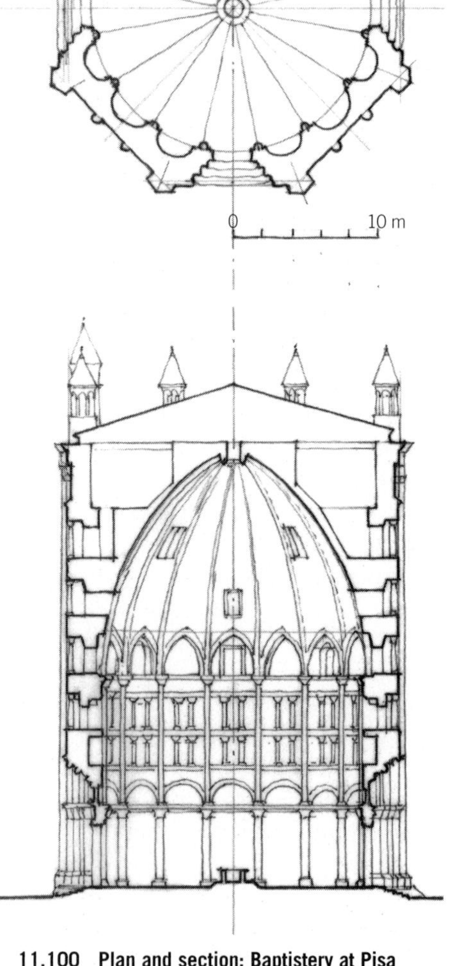


11.100 **Plan and section: Baptistery at Pisa**

**11.101 Kaupanger Stave Church, Norway**

## MEDIEVAL SCANDINAVIA

Most stave churches in Scandinavia were built during the 12th century, after the Viking campaigns had come to an end. The conversion of Norway to Christianity was not due to missionary activity, as in Ireland and elsewhere, but came about through the efforts of the Viking kings. Olav Trygvason, who was king toward the end of the 10th century, was the first to build churches in Norway, probably with the help of a master builder brought over from the British Isles. Gradually, however, local craftsmen were drawn in and wooden buildings appeared. Once totaling about 800, today there are only some thirty of these unusual buildings extant.

ke the Viking ships, the stave churches ɜrive from a building tradition developed defy the harsh elements. A low wall flat stones raised the buildings above ound level. Beyond that, columns, anks, and supports were dovetailed, ɜgged and wedged, never nailed. Thus e structure was a flexible one that could ;pand or contract depending upon damp dry weather. To tighten the structure, a ɔntinuous belt of cross braces was added the periphery of the building. The interiors ɜre modestly ornamented and very dark, th small strips of light occasionally forcing eir way from the window in the west gable from the small peepholes along the top the longitudinal walls. Religious services ɜre intimate and illuminated by candlelight. ɜalm books were not in use then.

**11.102 Borgund Stave Church, Norway**

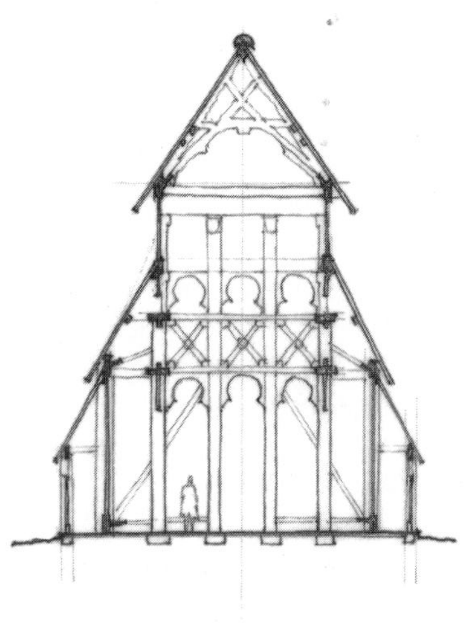

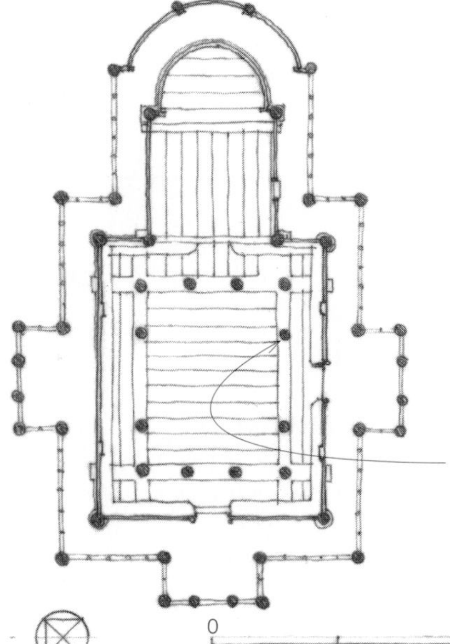


**11.103 Plan and section: Borgund Stave Church**

The word stave, from the Nors *stavr*, refers to the load-bearing posts that make up the structure.

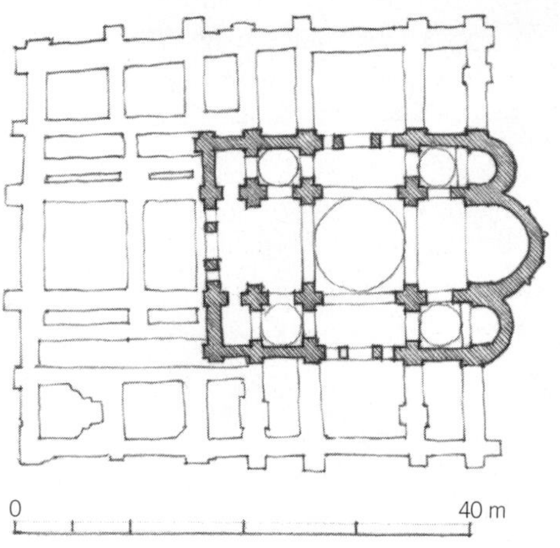


11.104 Plan: Church of the Tithe (Desyatinaya), Kiev

## KIEVAN RUSSIA

The rise of craftsmanship—metal shaping, metal casting, weapon production, wood and stone carving, cobblery, bread making, etc.—led to the emergence of the first fortified settlements among the Eastern Slavs, along the rivers of the Valdai plain, in the 8th and 9th centuries. Centralization of power under the Rurikovichi Dynasty, of presumably Norse origin, accelerated the decline of the patriarchal clan organization and gave rise to the development of a bourgeois society ruled by a prince and noblemen. Kiev soon became the center of a great waterway system of rivers, principally the Dnieper, linking Scandinavia and Byzantium. This allowed for a consolidated and planned development of trade routes —the Dnieper and the Volkhov rivers connecting the White Sea to the Black Sea, and the Volga River connecting the Caspian sea to the north—serving as the highways of the age. The trade in furs, hides, wax, honey, wheat, spices, metals, fabrics, and artisanal products contributed to the increase in the wealth of the cities and the development of civic infrastructures.

Though the Hungarians made an alliance with the Latin Church, the Slavs and Rus converted in the 10th century to the Eastern Church. The decision, according to medieval legend, was inspired by the beauty of St. Sophia in Constantinople and the elaborateness of Christian religious rituals, as reported back to Russia by emissaries sent to compare the different religions.

This is borne out by the fact that the first masonry structure in Russia, the Church of the Tithe (Desyatinaya, 989–96), was erected by Byzantine masons. It was built in alternating layers of stone and flat brick in a mortar of lime and crushed brick. Though little of it is preserved, 20th-century excavations revealed fragments of mosaics and fresco decorations and allowed for a reconstruction of the plan—an "inscribed cross" epitomized in the church of Nea Ecclesia in Constantinople (881) and a prototype for Russian medieval masonry churches. More original was the Hagia Sophia of Kiev. It had numerous domes and was a type of church within a church, with its inner surfaces ornamented with rich mosaics.

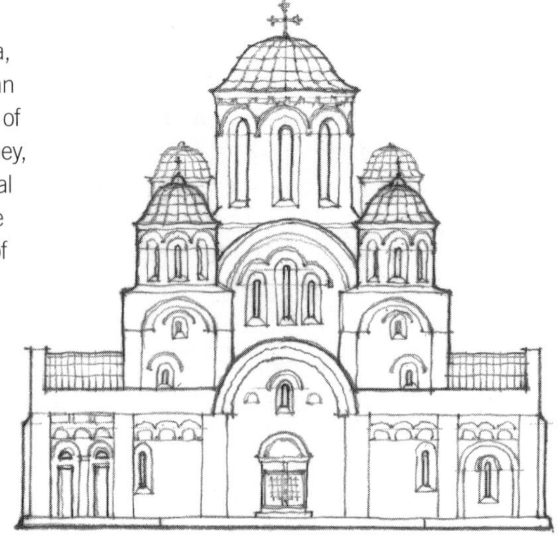

11.105 Elevation: Church of the Tithe (Desyatinaya)

11.106 Monastery, Selime, Cappadocia, Turkey

11.107 Monastery, Selime, Cappadocia

### Cappadocia

In Anatolia, the Cappadocian monasteries and churches, of which there are some six hundred, often are held to have appeared at a time when the Christian community was facing increasing threat from Arab invaders from the south, but in reality the rock-cut churches were begun centuries earlier, even though their dates are not known with certainty. From both archaeological and stylistic evidence, it seems that most were built between 800 and 1080. By that time, the Byzantine armies had rebounded from their initial losses against the Arabs. Nevertheless, once the Seljuk Turks had taken most of Cappadocia by 1090, church-building stopped.

Though some of the rock-cut churches served the local community, most were the sites of small hermit communities of maybe ten or so individuals; some might have been occupied by single monks. The volcanic rock made the carving relatively easy, with a small group of workmen able to carve a church in one or two seasons. It is thought that a tunnel was dug to the rear of the space and that the workmen then carved down and out to the prescribed dimensions. The soft rock made precise architectural details impossible, but the plans are clearly modeled on the conventions of built architecture, with columns, ribs, and ceiling beams carved out of the stone. The wall surfaces were painted with scenes of the Bible, the lives of the saints, or with geometrical forms. One such monastic compound is the Hallac Dere monastery. The core of the complex is a three-sided courtyard, entered from the open south side. The entrance vestibule leads to a pillared hall with a domed room at the back that might have served as a meeting room. The church was oriented toward the south. The capitals are simplified cushions with decorative scrolls at the edges. The surfaces were not painted but ornamented with line drawings and decorative patterns along borders and openings.

11.108 The Dark Church, Goreme, Cappadocia

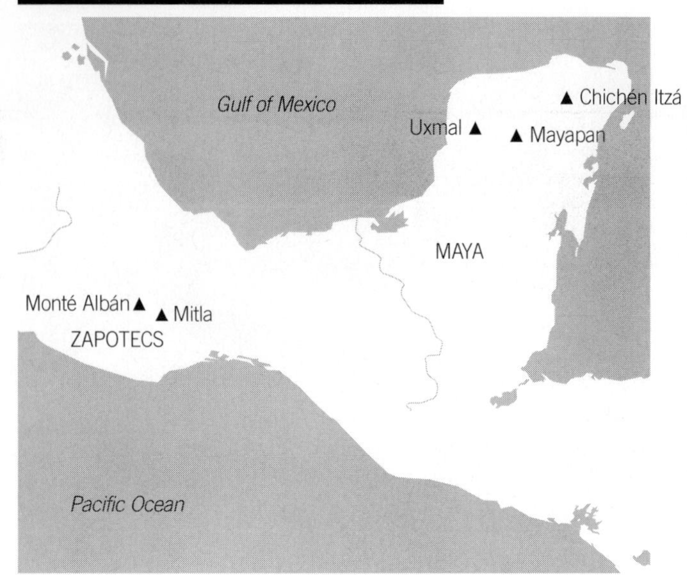

**11.109 Temple of the Magician, Uxmal, Mexico**

## MAYAN UXMAL

Immigrant groups from Tikal established Uxmal in 751 CE. In the 9th century, Uxmal was one of several Mayan city-states competing for territory, but by 900 CE it had become the regional capital and most likely the largest contemporary Mayan city. A network of stone roadways, called *sakbehoob*, connected Uxmal to other cities such as Nohpat and Kabah. Chichén Itzá was a major ally.

Uxmal's elite lived in a sprawling palace complex located at the area's highest ground, a broad and wide terrace. A stone wall, with regularly spaced openings, enclosed the area. At the southern end of the complex, built into a small mound, was the main platform mound, wedged between a gigantic platform with the so-called Governor's Palace to its east and a series of rectangular courts to its west. The platform mound faced north. Its broad stairs would have been visible from a distance. The northern edge of the palace complex was dominated by a huge quadrangular palace, the so-called Nunnery (890–915 CE). To its immediate east, the largest structure, a steep platform mound with a rare oval-shaped base, was the Temple of the Magician. Scores of other buildings, arranged in quadrangles of various size and shape, were distributed through the complex; most were residential units; and a few were platform mounds. Similar structures outside the wall were dispersed across a much larger urban residential area.

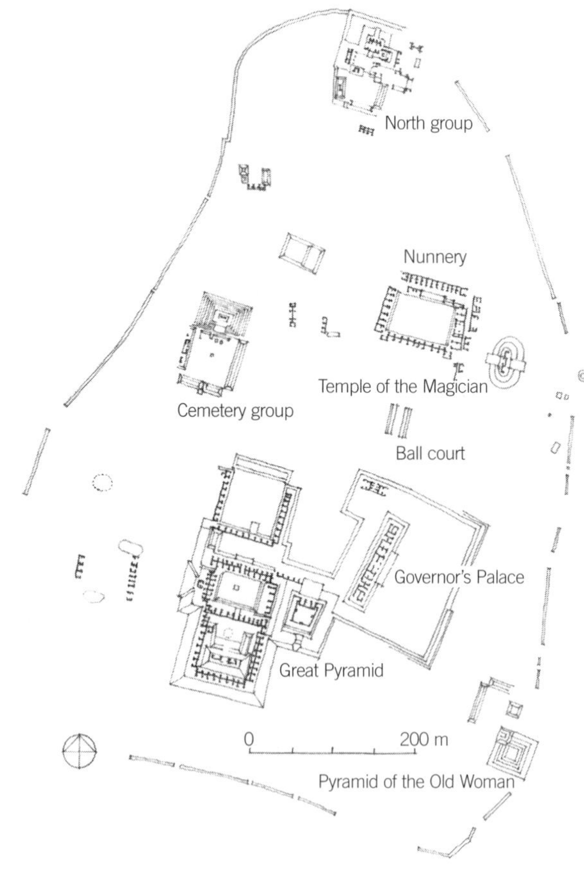


**11.110 Uxmal palace complex**

**11.111 Ball court at Uxmal**

Chan-Chaak-K'ak'nal-Ajaw, also referred to simply as Lord Chak, ruled Uxmal in the late 9th century. He commissioned the Governor's Palace, the Nunnery quadrangle, and very likely a rebuilding of the Temple of the Magician. The Temple of the Magician, originally built in the 6th century, was reconstructed at least four times. While the exact reasons for its unusual shape are still uncertain, its dramatic profile dominates the setting, contrasting the orthogonal geometries of the Governor's Palace and the Nunnery quadrangle.

Standing alone, an entity unto itself in the city, the Governor's Palace was both the royal residence and a sort of council house, or Popol Nah. Its huge terrace was linked to the main platform mound at the corner, signifying their continuity. Although the platform was accessible only from the west, from the middle of the complex, the main structure of the Governor's Palace, an astonishing 100-meter-long building, faced east away from the center, overlooking a distant vista from across a vast platform. The rising sun would have brightly illuminated its 24 rooms that were clustered into three segments. Narrow passages with steep triangular roofs separated them. Each room was a set of two, one opening onto the front, and the other behind it, against a back blank wall.

The broad frieze on the Governor's Palace is its chief glory. Made from over 20,000 individual stones depicting serpents, thatched huts, masks of the rain god Chak, human busts, and other geometrical motifs, the frieze is a kaleidoscope of Mayan mythology. A gigantic stone sculpture above the main entrance shows Lord Chak on a throne surrounded by serpents.

The friezes on the four buildings of the Nunnery quadrangle together depict the Mayan cosmography, or the order of the universe as conceived by the Uxmal. The southern building, also known as the *itzam nah* or the "conjuring house," bears the icons of the Lords of Xibalba, the underworld. The south building of the Nunnery quadrangle axially aligns with the ball court, the symbolic gate to Xibalba. The eastern frieze depicts the cyclic themes of world creation, while the western frieze depicts scenes of war, sacrifice, death, and rebirth. Together the eastern and western friezes symbolize the diurnal and annual journeys, or "lives," if you will, of the sun and its compact with the earth, inhabited by humans. The northern building, built on the highest platform of the quadrangle, has a frieze that depicts celestial figures symbolic of the world of "heaven." In the middle of the quadrangle there originally stood a stone column, representing the *wakaj-chan*, or "world tree," and an altar representing the first stone of the cosmic hearth.

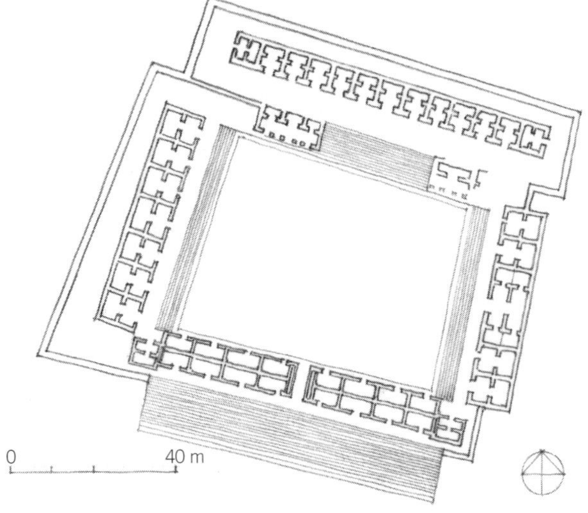


**11.112 Plan of the Nunnery quadrangle at Uxmal**

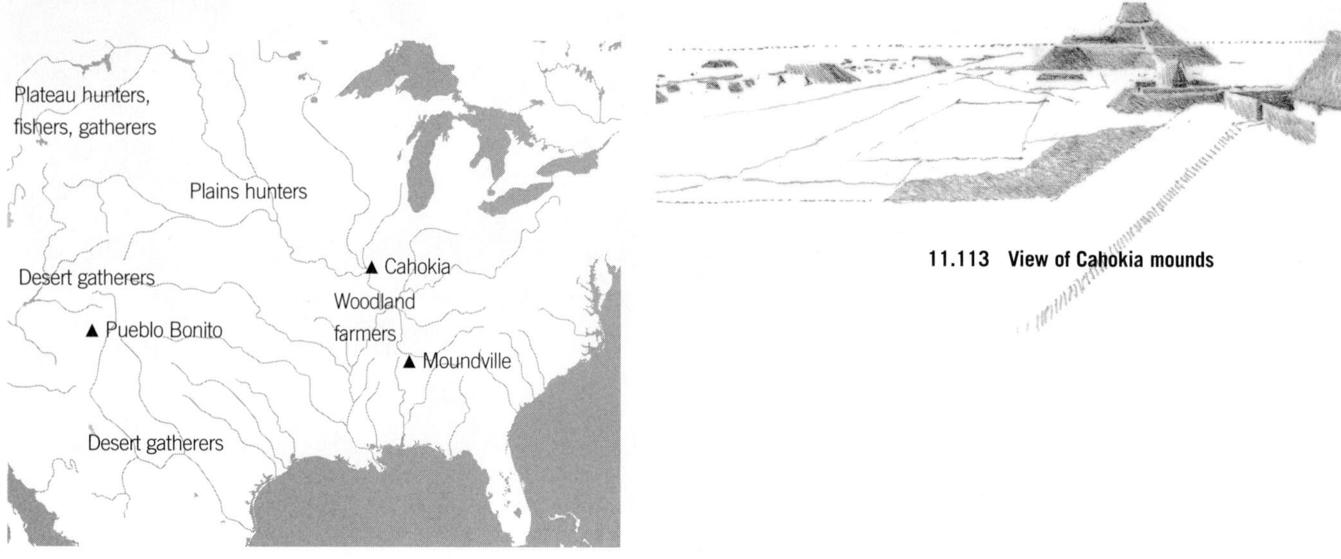


11.113 View of Cahokia mounds

## CAHOKIA

In the 10th and 11th centuries, native Americans constructed earth mounds throughout the Midwest. Several settlements were located along the Mississippi River system. The largest of these was at Cahokia, near St. Louis (700–1400 CE). From their central location, the Cahokians not only benefited from the Mississippi's alluvial deposits, but they also traveled vast distances by walking, running, or canoeing, bringing in copper from the Upper Great Lakes, mica from the southern Appalachians, and seashells from the Gulf of Mexico.

In settlements built around approximately 120 earthen mounds, 20,000 people lived in Cahokia at its peak in the 12th century. Its center was the so-called Monks Mound, the largest platform mound of North America. Monks Mound was surrounded by terraces and smaller mounds roughly on axis. The Cahokians seemed to have known of Central American advances in astronomy. They built several calendrical circles with posts of red cedar. A first circle of 24 posts was enlarged to one of 36, then to one of 48, and finally to one of 60 posts. Their last and largest circle was built only to an arc of 12 posts, but if completed would have had 72 posts. While this is still being researched, it seems that these circles were designed to mark the equinoxes. At the equinoxes, the post marking sunrise, due east, aligns perfectly with the front of Monks Mound.

Other native American mounds were in shapes of birds and animals. The Serpent Mound in southern Ohio was built by the so-called Fort Ancient people around 1075. (This date is still in dispute.) The 1.5-meter-high mound was built on a base of clay and stone in the form of a serpent devouring an oval-shaped "egg."

Current theories suggest that the shape was designed both as a calendar and a symbol. Lunar alignments correspond to six of the seven coils of the serpent and the head and oval point to the sun's northern setting point, during the summer solstice. A line linking the center of its coiled tail to the base of its head also aligns with true north. The serpent, usually identified as the moon and the underworld, could be interpreted as swallowing the sun represented by the oval.

11.114 Site Plan of Cahokia, near St. Louis, Missouri

# 1200 CE

The history of religions is never static, and this is especially true during this period. In Japan, Buddhism developed into a variant known as Pure Land Buddhism, which is based on the concept of visualizations as the path to liberation. Itsukushima Shrine in Japan brought out the delicate balance between Pure Land Buddhism's attempt to achieve a balance between outer landscape and inner meditation. In China, Mahayana Buddhism continued to take the form of large state-sponsored monasteries with the pagoda (*ta*), a veritable skyscraper, serving as a vertical representation of the many levels of enlightenment. In Pagan, in modern Burma, Buddhism came to be associated with didactic panels placed inside the temple superstructures as well as with a desire for dramatic internal illumination. In Cambodia, the Khmer rulers shifted from being Shiavite Buddhists to Vishnaites, because the latter better served their developing ideology of royal divinity. Scale was no issue. The Khmer-built Angkor Wat remains one of the largest religious buildings in the world. In South Asia, Hinduism continued its transformation into religion with a multifaceted pantheon. The Orissan kings emphasized the sun god in a temple that had at its symbolic center an enormous stone chariot. The Hoysalas developed temples with a star-shaped plan to accommodate multiple deities.

In the Christian world, the situation was equally diverse and fluid. One finds the almost simultaneous development of large urban cathedrals that fuse the powers of the Roman Church with those of the state (Gloucester Cathedral in Norman England), pilgrimage churches with their emphasis on the Virgin Mary (Notre-Dame of Reims in France), and churches belonging to a new type of religious order, mendicants who renounced the wealth and ostentation of the great cathedrals and who preferred instead simple and modest buildings (e.g., the Dominican Church of Toulouse). In Italy, the urban cathedrals and mendicant churches formed composite, though somewhat contradictory, liturgical spaces. The Ethiopians, who maintained the great tradition of rock cutting, created an entire liturgical landscape based on Jerusalem.

This was the time period of an amazing cast of architectural patrons: Emperor Huizong (1100–25) in China; Prime Minister Taira no Kiyomori (1118–81) in Japan; Suryavarman II (1113–45) in Cambodia; King Kyanzittha (1084–1113) of Burma; Qutb-ud-Din Aibak (1150–1210) in northern India; King Narasimhadeva (1238–64)) of the Orissa; King Lalibela (1185–1225) in Ethiopia; Mohammed I (1238–73) of Islamic Spain; and Frederick II (1194–1250) of the Holy Roman Empire.

If one follows the dots on the map, it becomes clear that there is a major gap in the area from Central Asia to the Near East, in largely Islamic lands, where architecture was in a virtual standstill from 1220 on to about 1330 because of the Mongolian disruptions. Mongolian armies invaded south into China and Burma and westward into Russia and Anatolia, altering the economic and political landscape everywhere they went. The Song in China, the Seljuks in Anatolia, the Delhi Sultanate in north India, and the Novgorod Empire in Russia all came to a rather sudden end. The only Islamic region to prosper, well out of the range of the Mongolians, was Spain and North Africa, where one finds in Fez and Granada new mosques and palaces. The most spectacular of the palaces was the Alhambra.

Once the destructive fury was over, the Mongolians were quick to adapt to local customs and ways, becoming Buddhist, Confucian, or Islamic, both Sunni and Shi'ite, depending on where they were. In China, where they founded the Yuan Dynasty, the consequences of this in the history of civilization would become apparent in the following century; but by the early 14th century it is apparent that by eliminating regional rivalries, the Mongolians lowered the risks of trade and enabled the orderly transfer of goods across the great distances of the Eurasian continents. This eventually enabled the quickening of the Eurasian economy that reached its zenith in the 15th and 16th centuries.

In Central America, the Toltecs, claiming descent from Teotihuacán, established a militaristic culture that was to define the region's civilizations right up to the Spanish conquest. In the Yucatan, Chichén Itzá emerged as the primary city-state, the final moment of Mayan development before their final collapse around 1250.

# 1200 CE

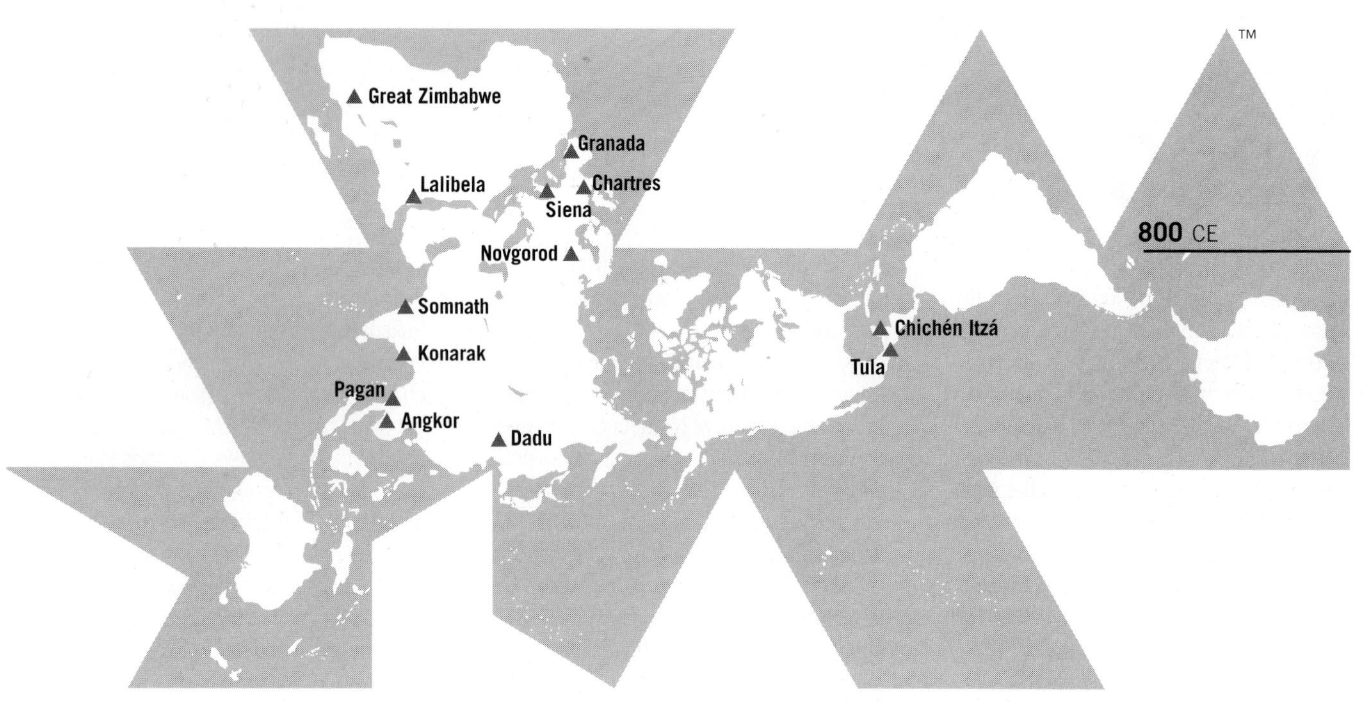
Great Zimbabwe
Granada
Lalibela
Chartres
Siena
Novgorod
Somnath
Konarak
Pagan
Angkor
Dadu
Chichén Itzá
Tula
800 CE
TM

Khmer Kingdom: Angkor Period
802–1431

▲ **Angkor Wat**
802–1220

▲ **Lokesvara Temple**
Completed 1191

Kingdom of Pagan
802–1431

▲ **Shwezigon**
Late 11th century

▲ **Ananda Temple**
1090–1105

Japan: Late Heian Period
ca. 900–1185

Kamakura Period
1185–1333

Nanbokucho Period
1336–1392

▲ **Itsukushima Shrine**
6th–13th century

Northern Song Dynasty
960–1127

Southern Sung Dynasty
1127–1279

Yuan Dynasty
1279–1368

◉ ***Yingzhao Fashi* published**
1103

**1000** CE — **1200** CE — **1400** CE

Delhi Sultanate
1210–1526

▲ **Quwwat-ul-Islam**
ca. 1200–1315

India: Hindu States
10th–12th century

▲ **Vadakkunnathan Temple**
11th–19th century

▲ **Kesava (Somnatha) Temple**
ca. 1268

▲ **Sun Temple at Konarak**
Late 13th century

Zagwe Dynasty
ca. 1137–1270

▲ **Churches of Lalibela**
13th century

▲ **Great Zimbabwe**
ca. 1250–1450

Holy Roman Empire
962–1806

▲ **St. Denis**
1144

▲ **Chartres Cathedral**
1194–1220

▲ **St. Croce, Florence**
Begun 1294

Crusades
1096–1270

▲ **Notre Dame, Paris**
1163–1250

▲ **Notre-Dame of Reims**
1211–90

Black Plague
1347–1352

▲ **Fontenay Abbey**
Founded 1119

▲ **Amiens Cathedral**
1220–35

▲ **Castel del Monte**
ca. 1240

▲ **Exeter Cathedral**
1280–1300

▲ **Palazzo Publico, Siena**
1297–1310

Republic of Novgorod
12th–15th century

▲ **Intercession of the Virgin**
1165

▲ **St. Paraskeva Piatnitsa**
1207

Nasrid Sultanate
1298–1492

▲ **Alhambra**
1338–90

Toltec-Chichén city-state
ca. 1000–1200

▲ **Tula**
ca. 950–1150

▲ **Chichén Itzá**
ca. 7th–13th century

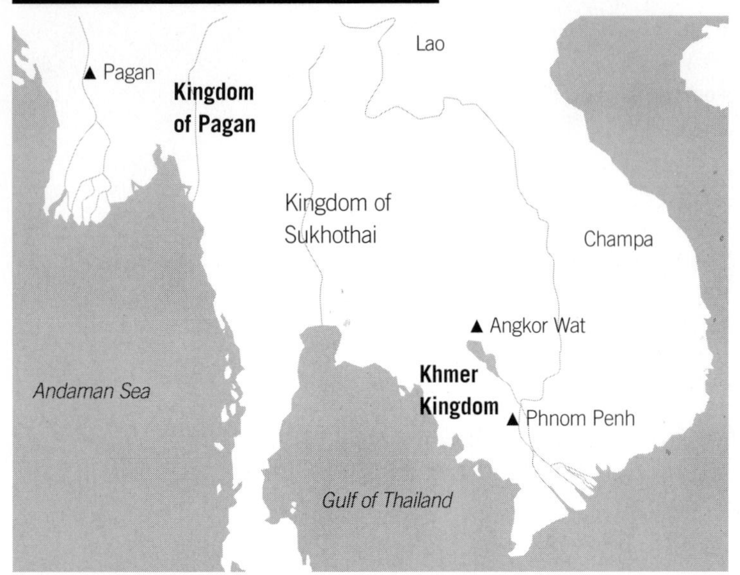

**12.1 Vrah Vishnulok (Angkor Wat), near Siem Reap, Cambodia**

## VRAH VISHNULOK (ANGKOR WAT)

By the 11th century, Yasodharapura, the Khmer capital located just north of the Tonle Sap lake had grown into a major city with about a million inhabitants. The *baray* system, with its controlled release of water that had been trapped in the monsoons, had made the flood plains to the west of the Mekong River into the preeminent rice-producing region of Southeast Asia. King Rajendravarman (r. 944–68) extended the city to the east with the construction of new temples. King Suryavarman I (r. 1001–50) added new palaces to the north and a vast new *baray* some 7 by 2 kilometers to the west. He also created a large new temple, Bapuon, just outside the gates of Yashopura. Bapoun became the center of a new square city, about as big as and overlapping Yasodharapura.

But all these temples, as vast as they were, paled in comparison to the one built by King Suryavarman II (1113–50), now known as Angkor Wat. For its construction a large part of Yasodharapura had to be cleared. Suryavarman II built many other temples in surrounding territories, but this is the only one he built in Yasodharapura itself. Its original name is Vrah Vishnulok, or "Vishnu's abode," but the French archaeologists who first worked on the site contracted the modern Cambodian *Nagara*, meaning "city" with *wat*, meaning a Buddhist shrine, to create the name. It is neither a city nor a Buddhist shrine.

The Khmers, by this time, had built hundreds of stone temples in and around Yasodharapura, but Vrah Vishnulok, measuring 1030 by 820 meters, was by far their largest. It was surrounded by a 200-meter wide and 2-meter deep moat that, like previous Khmer temples, signifies the primordial Cosmic Ocean: infinite, limitless, and original. Vrah Vishnulok, like the earlier temples, was conceived as a mandala based on an island-mountain rising in the middle of a vast primordial ocean, a representation, in this case, of the Hindu god Vishnu's abode. Suryavarman II was a great believer in Vishnu, having switched over from Shiavism to Vaishnavism. He particularly invested in the concept of the divine kingship, as a manifestation of Vishnu. Because Hindus believe that Vishnu manifests himself repeatedly as the lawgiver, he could be easily invoked to legitimize royal authority.

Vrah Vishnulok, dedicated to Vishnu, is therefore also dedicated to Suryavarman II. Its *garbh-griha* once held a statue of Vishnu as a facsimile of Suryavarman II. This also explains why this temple is entered from the west, unlike most of Khmer's Shiavite temples that face east. There is, however, much that is still unknown about the temple. Archaeological work on the Khmer civilization is still in its infancy. Its astrological notations (such as the columns on its balustrade being equal to the number of years in a Hindu age) as well as its esoteric astronomical measurements that are still being decoded by archaeologists. It is, however, generally assumed that the building is a map of cosmological space and time as understood by the Khmer.

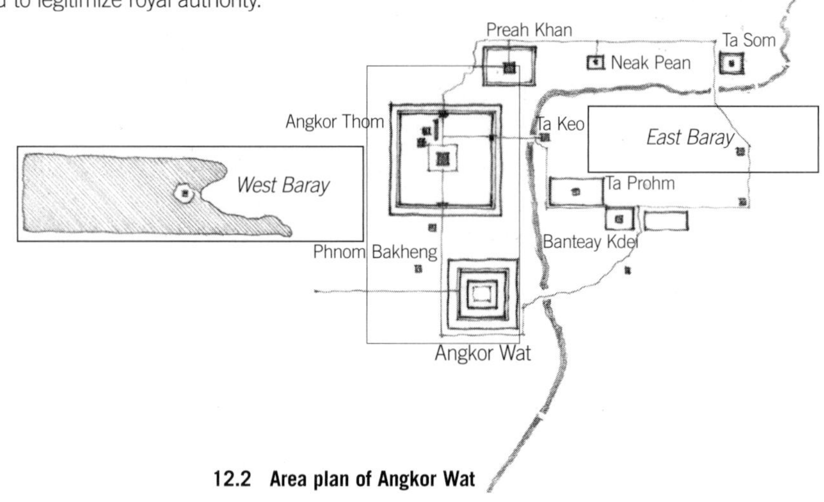


**12.2 Area plan of Angkor Wat**

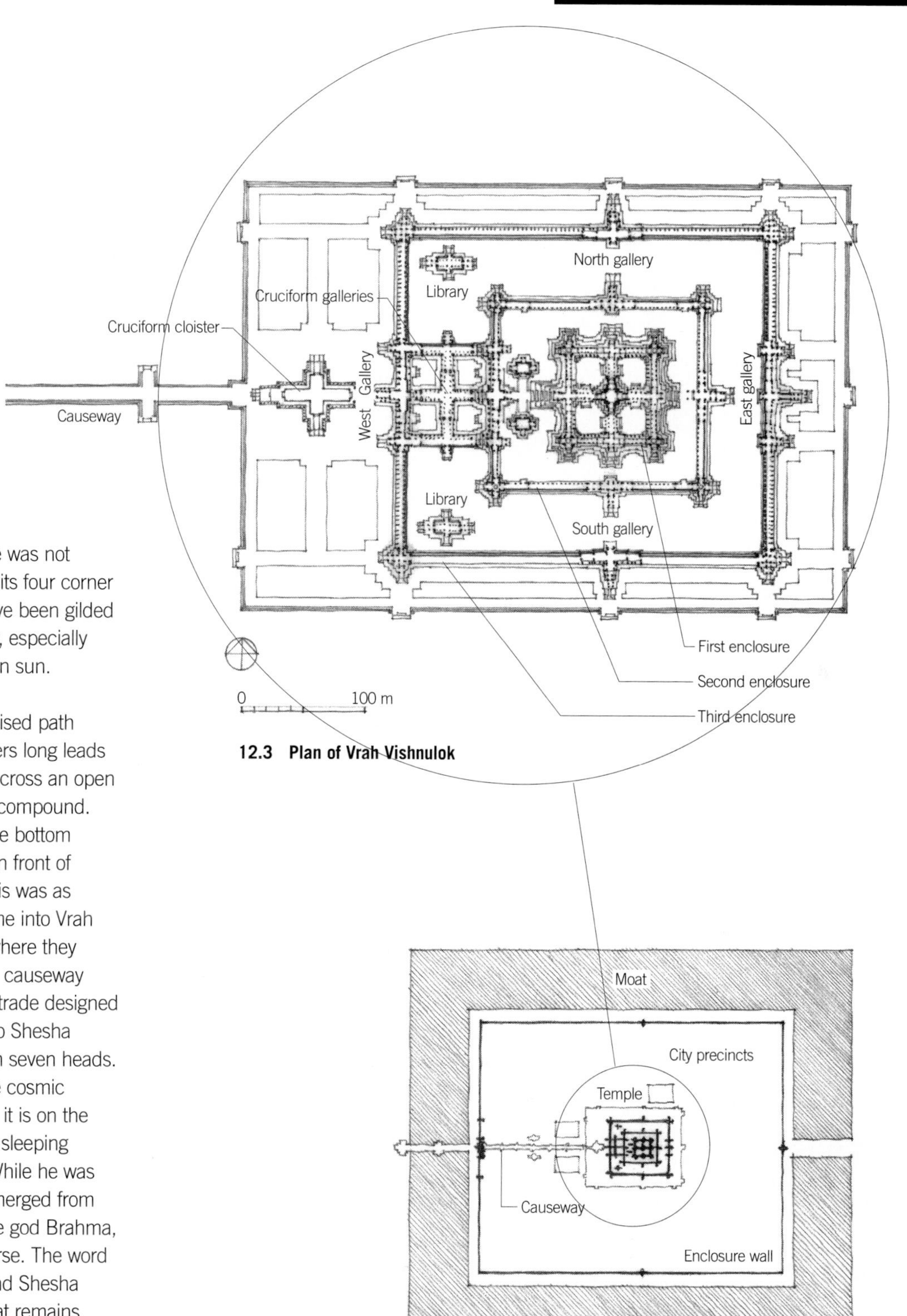


**12.3 Plan of Vrah Vishnulok**

**12.4 City of Vrah Vishnulok**

The outer surface of the shrine was not what we see today. Along with its four corner towers, it was presumed to have been gilded and would have shone brightly, especially when illuminated in the western sun.

A causeway in the form of a raised path 9.4 meters wide and 350 meters long leads across the "ocean" and then across an open field to the front of the temple compound. The causeway terminates at the bottom of an elevated cruciform altar in front of the entrance to the temple. This was as far as the common people came into Vrah Vishnulok, and this altar was where they made their sacrifices. Both the causeway and altar are edged by a balustrade designed as long serpents, a reference to Shesha Naga, the celestial serpent with seven heads. A critical role in the story of the cosmic ocean is played by Shesha, for it is on the coiled body of Shesha that the sleeping Vishnu dreams the universe. While he was dreaming, a lotus on a stalk emerged from Vishnu's navel on which sat the god Brahma, who actually created the universe. The word *shesha* means "remainder," and Shesha is supposed to be made of what remains after each cosmic cycle comes to an end. The destruction of everything produces a remainder, which is the critical scaffold from which the "dream" of life comes into being. The Shesha Naga was one of the most prominent symbols of the Khmer.

12.5 **Cruciform courtyard, Vrah Vishnulok**

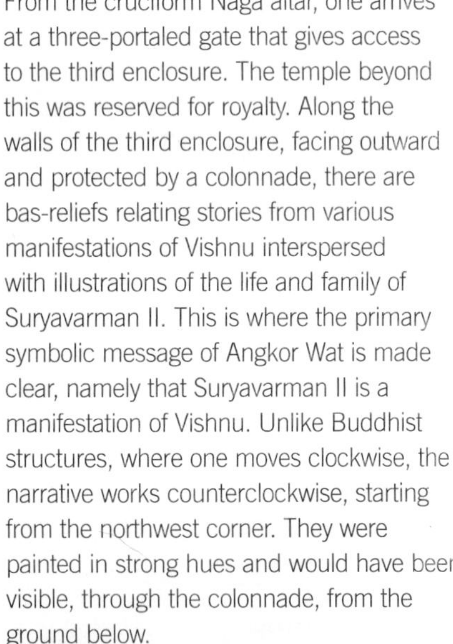

12.6 **Third enclosure gallery, Vrah Vishnulok**

From the cruciform Naga altar, one arrives at a three-portaled gate that gives access to the third enclosure. The temple beyond this was reserved for royalty. Along the walls of the third enclosure, facing outward and protected by a colonnade, there are bas-reliefs relating stories from various manifestations of Vishnu interspersed with illustrations of the life and family of Suryavarman II. This is where the primary symbolic message of Angkor Wat is made clear, namely that Suryavarman II is a manifestation of Vishnu. Unlike Buddhist structures, where one moves clockwise, the narrative works counterclockwise, starting from the northwest corner. They were painted in strong hues and would have been visible, through the colonnade, from the ground below.

12.7 **Quasi-Hellenic details in the interior of the so-called Library at Vrah Vishnulok**

One enters into the building proper through the so-called Cruciform Galleries, which are arranged symmetrically to the right and left of the axis. There are as well a pair of pavilion-islands, the exact function of which is unclear. From here one moves up through the different levels, each a smaller version of the cosmic order of ocean and island precinct, one "world" resting on another. Unlike Bakong (see 800 CE), the top of which was like being on a rounded-off mountain, the vertical scale of Vrah Vishnulok escalates and intensifies as one nears the central precinct, which in the final level looms above one like a peak, accessible only by long, steep flights of steps. The central shrine, the climax of the whole arrangement, is a tower that rises 43 meters above the floor of its gallery (that is itself 23 meters higher than the level of the moat). It is surrounded by four smaller corner towers. The main *garbh-griha*, which had the statue of Vishu/Suryavarman II, was originally accessible from all directions. There was also a well at its center, in which offerings could be thrown, that originally descended 23 meters below ground. Above, a linga-shaped opening almost rises the height of the entire tower. The well, also found in most Khmer temples, is not only a connection to the water-based authority of the Khmer rulers but also an inverted mirror of the cosmic mountain signified by the tower.

The influences from Prambanam and the architecture of the Shailendra kings are obvious in the overall massing and profile of Vrah Vishnulok. The influences from India are, of course, strong as well. The Khmer had sent an embassy to the Chola court in Thanjavur, from where they may have derived further inspiration (besides their own history) about divine kingship, and its manifestation in temples built at a grand scale. Divine kingship can also be traced to the Kushans and the Chinese. But the use of square piers and Greek and Persian decorative motifs in the galleries indicates that Vrah Vishnulok's details might also be viewed from within the sphere of Alexander's Hellenism. The cruciform "libraries" that flank the causeway seem particularly "western," even in the use of attached pilasters on the entrance porch. A good deal of scholarly work still needs to be done to properly understand this building's importance in the flow of architectural thought through South and Southeast Asia.

12.8 **Lokesvara Temple (Preah Khan), near Siem Reap, Cambodia**

**Lokesvara Temple (Preah Khan)**

In 1181 the new King Jayavarman VII converted to Buddhism and embarked on a rebuilding of Yasodharapura. He relocated its center from Bekong to a new temple called Indrapattha, known today as the Bayon, located just outside the old walls. Instead of the whole body, just part of the Buddha was graphed onto the many towers of the Bayon, a reinterpretation of Mahayana Buddhist practice. The gigantic face sculptures on the towers give to the Bayon a unique, enigmatic character. Jayavarman VII's new city, known today as Angkor Thom, was smaller than Yasodharapura, three kilometers square instead of four, and it probably served primarily as a palace compound since it incorporated the palaces that had been built there by previous kings. Among the astonishing buildings erected by Jayavarman VII is a Buddhist university to the north of the city, originally called Lokesvara, but known today as Preah Khan. At its height the Lokesvara temple complex had 1000 students and teachers. Surrounded by a moat, this huge complex comprises a vast axial network of corridors, chapels, libraries, and pavilions, brought into unity by the two axes that lead through numerous thresholds to the central sanctuary. The principal inner surfaces were stuccoed (some traces still remain) and presumably were painted in vibrant colors, showing didactic images. One of the fascinating structures is a two-story building with round columns, dating perhaps from the 13th century.

In the mid-15th century, the Khmer Kingdom was sacked by the Thais, and its vast wealth plundered. After that the Khmer abandoned Angkor Thom and moved south to Phnom Penh in 1431. The buildings, temples, and canals were eventually abandoned and soon overtaken by the jungle. The history of the architecture of Southeast Asia will not be better understood until more work is done here. What architectural skills were mastered here, what technologies were used, what type of mathematics underlies these buildings, what influences and associations with distant lands shaped its production and design are all still far from certain.

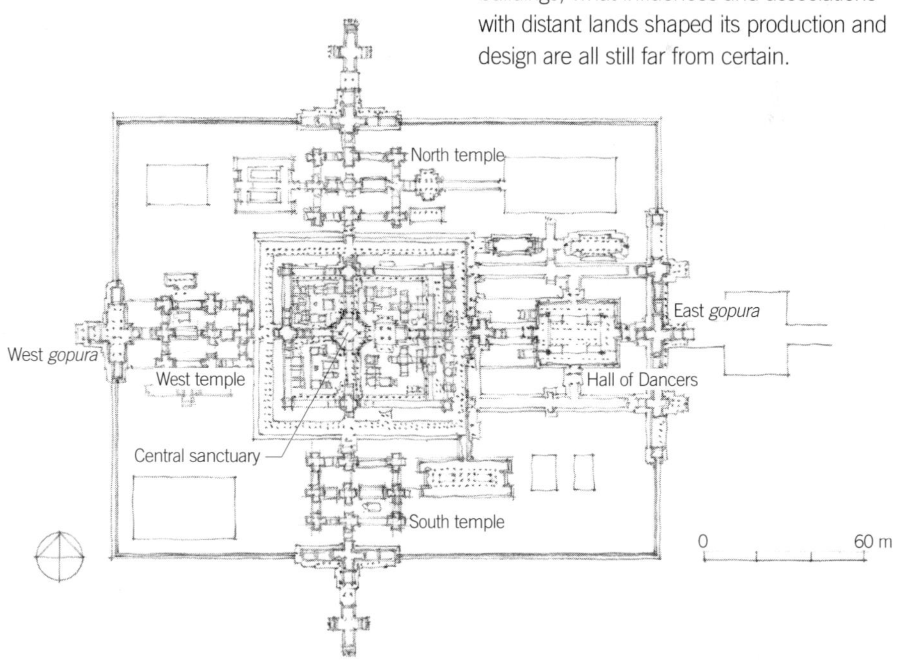


12.9 **Plan of Preah Khan**

12.10 View of Pagan, near Nyangu, Burma

12.11 Shwezigon, Pagan

### KINGDOM OF PAGAN

In the 12th and 13th centuries, there arose a Buddhist kingdom with a political and cultural identity that was a unique hybrid of its Asian neighbors. The kingdom of Pagan covered the area roughly equivalent to modern-day Myanmar (Burma), with its capital at Arimaddanapura, the City of the Crusher of Enemies, now known as the city of Pagan. For two centuries, Pagan waged war with the Cholas in peninsular India, while maintaining a close but carefully guarded relationship with India's eastern kingdoms. With a selectively chosen set of ideas and practices, the Pagan kings built more than 2000 structures, stupas, and temples (*gu* in Pagan) on the flood plain of the Irrawaddy River. Although all the Pagan stupas and temples are Theravada Buddhist, the Pagan kings, like their powerful contemporaries, the Khmers of Cambodia, adopted the modern-for-its-time Hindu idea that the Buddha was a manifestation of Vishnu and that a virtuous king could also be a manifestation of Vishnu. Unlike the Khmer, however, the temples of the Pagan kings were not dedicated to themselves as manifestations of Vishnu but to the Buddha.

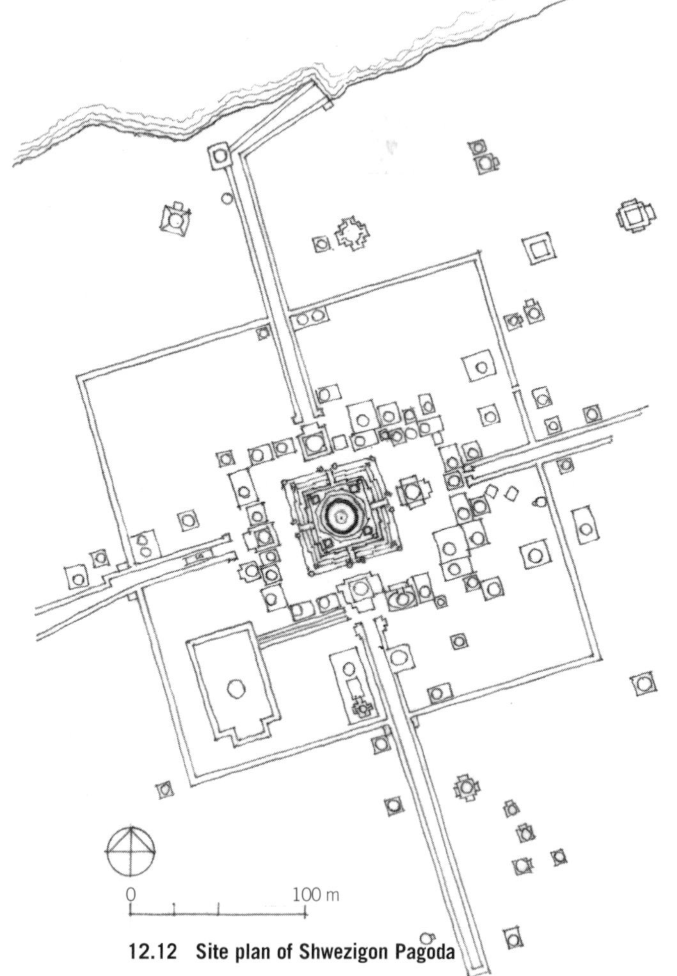


12.12 Site plan of Shwezigon Pagoda

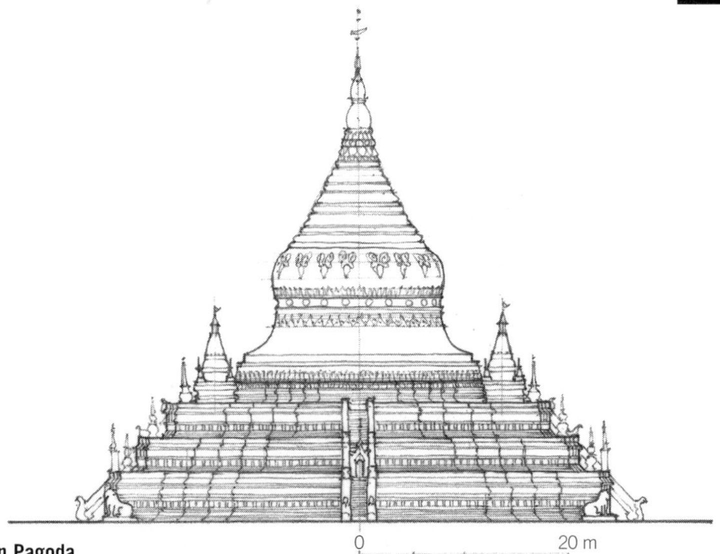


**12.13 Elevation: Shwezigon Pagoda**

Pagan, located on a bend of the Irrawaddy River, sits in the driest part of Southeast Asia. While the monsoons bring water to the rest of the surrounding area, the plain at Pagan is dry and dusty. This meant that water was readily available from the Irrawaddy but that forests did not have to be cleared. Furthermore, the alluvial soil was perfectly suited for an infinite supply of burnt bricks, of which all of Pagan's surviving religious structures were made. The earliest Pagan buildings, built in the reign of Anawratha, were terraced stupas, derived from Indonesian prototypes. The Shwezigon Paya (pagoda, stupa, or *zedi*), for instance, is a solid-core stupa that rises steeply, like a stepped pyramid, through five square terraces, culminating in a stupa form so completely merged with the umbrellas of its *chattri* above that the base below forms an almost conical shape. A steep flight of steps at the center of the four sides of the stepped base give pilgrims access to the terraces that, like those at Borobodur, contain didactic panels depicting tales from the life of the Buddha and other Buddhist texts.

Though the stupa is intended to be conceptually solid, there is within it a vast and complex network of narrow interconnected tunnels, many of which have terra-cotta inlaid panels. The tunnels were designed to enable post-construction donors to gain merit by paying to have dedicatory tablets embedded in its walls. The temple is presumed to have contained an important relic in its core, but it has not been found and is presumed stolen. Since the stupa was considered an extension of that relic, by embedding objects in its "force field," latter-day worshippers hoped to gain nirvana, or *nibbana,* as it was known in Pagan.

Around 1100, soon after his ascension to the throne, Kyanzittha (1084–1113) began construction of several large stupas. At the Ananda Temple (1090–1105), the Shwezigon prototype has been developed considerably. Though the temple has the customary square terraces, complete with glazed terra-cotta didactic tablets and corner stupas, it has no external staircases. From the square, ground-level substructure, the building rises in an escalating rhythm to the base of the superstructure and *shikhara.*

In this building, the didactic galleries have been incorporated into the body of the temple in the form of two concentric, tall ambulatories that are entered through broad spacious porches at the center of each side. In no other Pagan temple is there so extensive a program of Buddhist education. Light comes through the thick walls into the outer ambulatory from high windows in a regular rhythm. Passageways cut directly in front of the windows allow light to filter further in. Nonetheless, at the core, the illumination is still rather sparse and meant to contrast with the light that comes dramatically into the space from hidden clerestory windows. This light illuminates the Buddha statues located in niches in the central core, facing out in all four directions. (The statues at the north and west are original, and the others are from a later date.) The clerestory light into the innermost sanctum, never found in other Hindu temples, is a distinct Pagan invention designed to further core Buddhist symbolism—the solid core of the stupa is the same as the body of the Buddha, both of which are a source of enlightenment or nirvana.

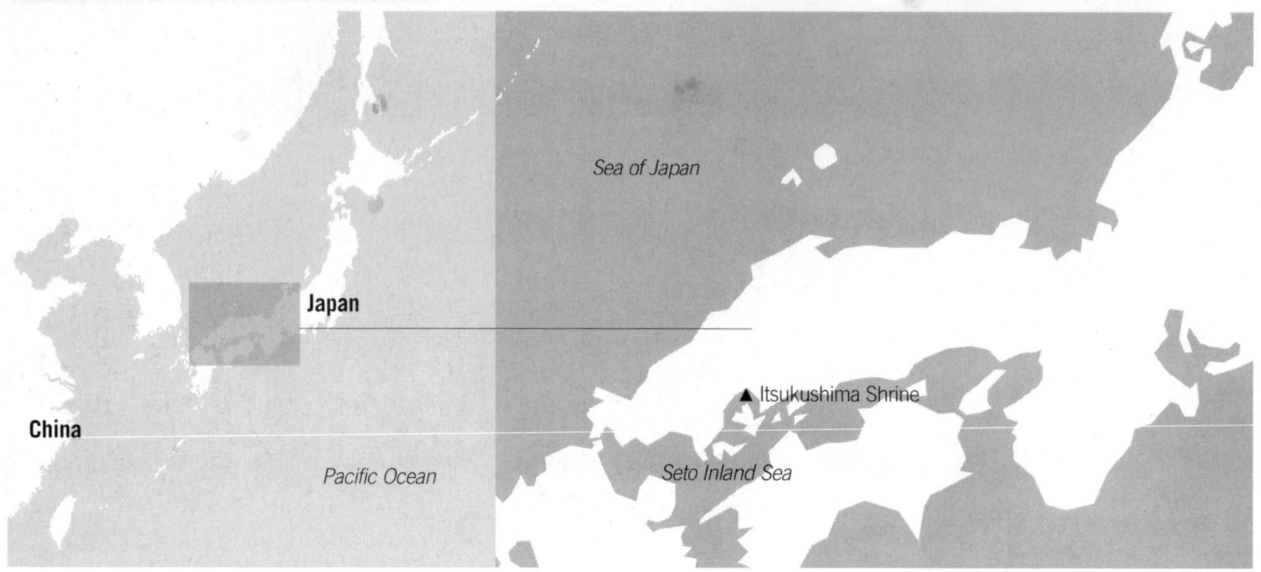


## KAMAKURA JAPAN

In the Kamakura period, Minamoto established a new capital near Edo (modern Tokyo); but their rivals, the Taira clan, continued to battle them from the south. In 1185 the armies of the Minamoto (or Genji) clan routed those of the Taira (or Heike) clan in the sea battle at Dannoura. With that the Minamoto established the first in a series of military governments whose reign is known as the Kamakura period (1186–1333). (In Japan, particular dynastic reigns have their own name as a period.) Frequent wars, natural disasters, and two attempted Mongol invasions in 1274 and 1281 gave this period a feeling of instability, which the Buddhists associated with the end of the predicted reign of Buddhism (*mappo*). The end of royal patronage of Buddhism opened the space for charismatic Buddhist monks to travel the countryside popularizing *nenbutsu*, or Pure Land concepts of Buddhism, which promised enlightenment for all who devoutly repeated the name of the Amidaba Buddha (similar to the rise of the bhakti cults in South Asia).

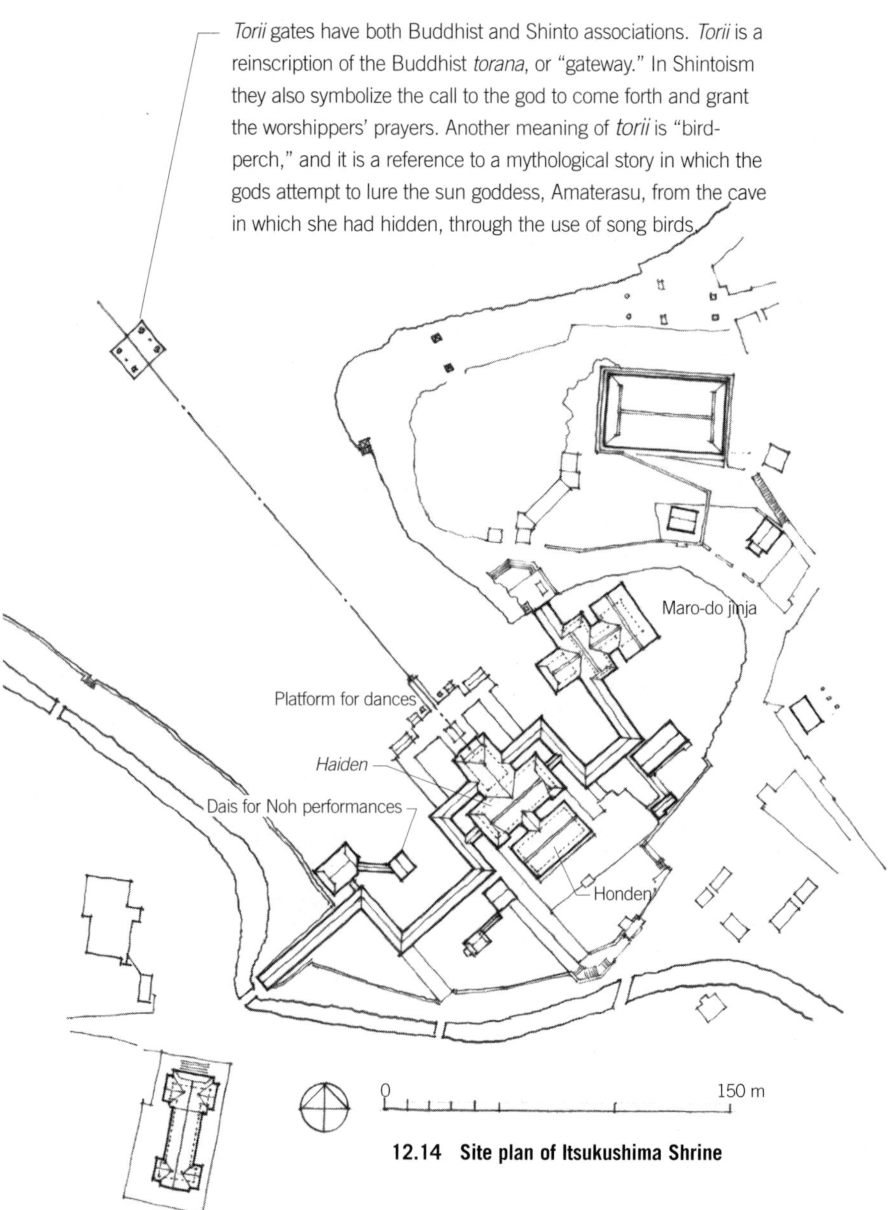


**12.14 Site plan of Itsukushima Shrine**

12.15 Itsukushima Shrine

12.16 Sanju-sangen-do, Kyoto, Japan

**Itsukushima Shrine**

Taira no Kiyomori (1118–81) of the Taira clan built a shrine on Itsukushima, one of the many islands in the Seto Inland Sea, a sacred Shinto site since the earliest times, and home to Ichikishima-Hime-no-Mikoto, the *kami* "who ensures safety at sea," and her two sisters. The original Shinto shrine dates to the 6th century, but it was rebuilt on a grand scale by Kiyomori beginning in 1168. Kiyomori also presented 33 illustrated scrolls of the Buddhist Lotus Sutra to the shrine, making Itsukushima a seamless blend of Shinto and Buddhist practices and architecture.

The shrine is positioned in a cove on the sheltered Seto Inland Sea, one of the most scenic areas of Japan. With its solitary vermilion *torii*, standing knee deep in the sea with the green mountain island as a backdrop, the shrine is regarded by many as an icon of Japanese culture and identity. The *torii*, located about 160 meters from the front of the shrine, stands 17 meters high and is spanned with a 24-meter beam. Two columns support the horizontal elements, and four short columns reinforce the structure against collapse. At high tide, the shrine appears to float, and it is in this that its Shinto character as a protective shrine merges with Pure Land Buddhism's ideas, which would describe it as floating on the infinite ocean on a lotus plant.

The associated beach shrine contains two sanctuaries, the *honsha* (the main shrine housing female deities) facing out toward the water and the *maro-do jinja* (the shrine for male guest deities) on the east, roughly perpendicular, facing west or inland. The two sanctuaries are wrapped by a long *kairo* (a roofed, semienclosed corridor) that winds intricately around the structures, connecting them to land. Each shrine has a *haiden* (worship or oratory hall), a *haraidono* (purification rites hall), and a *honden* (main hall), in sequential arrangement.

**Sanju-sangen-do**

In 1164 Taira no Kiyomori also built Sanju-sangen-do in Kyoto, an arresting example of committing to architecture one of the visualizations of Pure Land Buddhism. Sanju-sangen-do was designed as an extremely long (33 by 4 bays) structure to display, literally, a thousand life-size statues of the thousand-armed Kannon (a bodhisattva goddess of mercy), 500 on either side of a large central Kannon image. The statues are arranged in multiple rows and densely packed. Twenty-eight additional attendants, many of them directly derived from contemporary Hindu gods of India, are lined up in front. The forest of statues, arrayed as far as the eye can see, makes a strong impression, more fantastic than some earlier visualization structures, such as the Byodo-in.

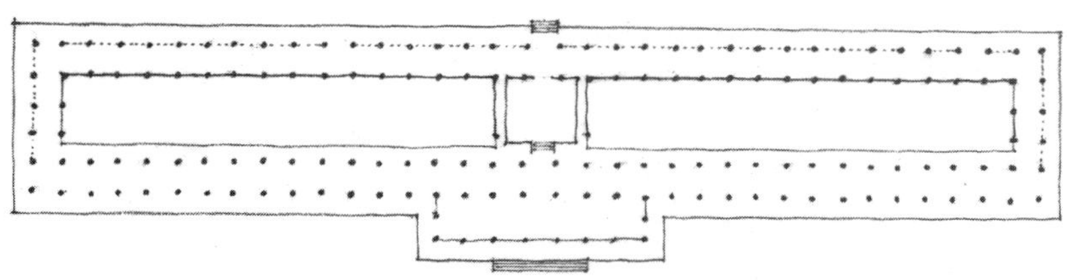

12.17 Plan of Sanju-sangen-do

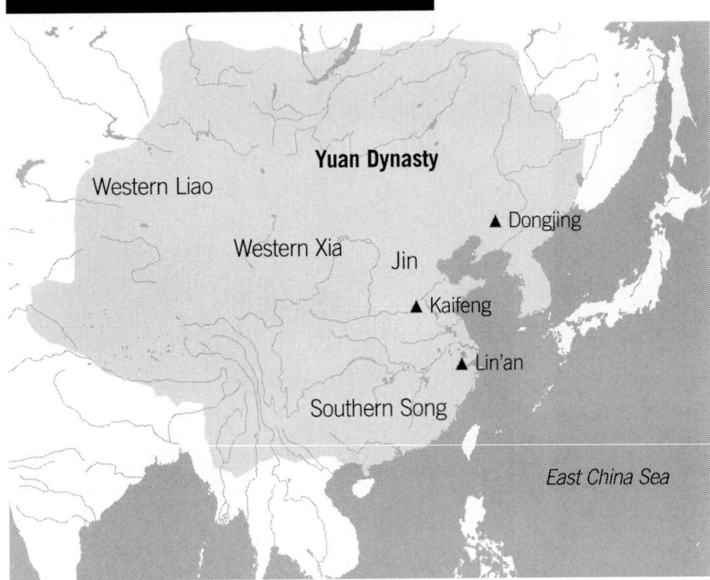


## SOUTHERN SONG DYNASTY

During the Song Dynasty, powerful mercantile families began to establish large estates distinguished by their elaborate private gardens. As the popularity of these gardens grew, wealthy merchants and noblemen tried to outdo each other with better designs. A garden at Dezhou, for instance, was renowned for its four distinct landscapes. Another garden had an artificial lake, with an island emerging from marshes, surrounded by artificial mountains and piles of rocks on which a palace was built. Little West Lake, a private garden in Lin'an, went so far as to "borrow" the views of an actual mountain outside its boundaries and in essence spliced it into its composition.

The same is true for Genyue (1117–22), a Northern Song garden in Bianliang (modern Kaifeng) that is focused on a high peak, Longevity Mountain, in its northeastern corner. A multitude of lower peaks, called Ten Thousand Pines, are also "borrowed." Interspersed in the garden are about 40 structures, including verandas, lodges, towers, platforms, and rustic huts, all linked by pathways that move up and down and wind around, framing the architectural structures within and against each other and the landscape.

Although the Song gardens can be described as inhabitable landscape paintings, it is important to note that their purpose was not to stand-in for the real thing. Rather, each garden was designed to enhance and intensify the essential qualities of the landscape and to achieve a perfected, "natural experience" that was, however, imbued with didactic messages.

The Song Dynasty period, known for its literary achievements, was one in which storytelling became a popular form of entertainment. The stories told by the professional entertainers were printed in storybooks, called *huaben*, which later inspired the longer novels of China, many about the battle between the virtuous and the unscrupulous to teach the consequences of behavior. This was related to the ideals of Confucianism and, during the Song Dynasty, Neo-Confucianism, which was an aggregate of Buddhist metaphysics and Confucian ethics. In this form, it was believed that through reason and study the whole world could be grasped.

**12.18 Mountain and river garden scenes from the Song Dynasty**

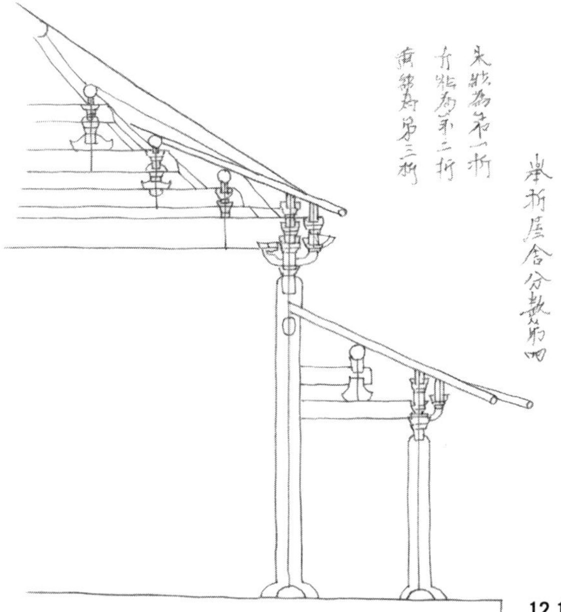

12.19 **Page redrawn from the *Yingzhao Fashi***

12.20 **Mountain and river garden scenes from the Song Dynasty**

**Yingzhao Fashi**

The Song emperor Huizong (1100–1125) was an emperor, aesthete, and an enthusiastic patron of the arts. A catalog of his paintings, the *Xuanhe Huapu*, published in 1123, lists over 6000 works in his collection. Art academies were established in his reign, and the collecting of antiques became popular alongside an interest in ancient history and culture.

In the Huizong reign the *New Yingzhao Fashi*, the detailed manual of architecture and construction, was commissioned and presented to the throne in 1103. It was called the "new" *Yingzhao Fashi* because the old one, dating to the T'ang, was no longer applicable to contemporary issues. The manual was not, however, intended as an aesthetic or philosophical document but rather to help the imperial administrators regulate, and reign in, the construction industry. Aesthetically, architecture under the Song and the Jin (and later under the Yuan) had become very ornamental and complicated. The size of the *dou-gong* decreased with respect to the overall height, but it increased in complexity and show. The placement of columns was even occasionally disrupted to accommodate more ambitious spatial arrangements. While all these transformations made for a much richer and more expressive architecture, it also resulted in a great deal of waste and corruption.

Because construction was controlled by powerful guilds that carefully guarded their knowledge, passing it on only in oral verse, buildings routinely ran over budget. The imperial court found that it could not reasonably predict the cost for and time to completion of building. Furthermore, the high demand for timber was causing rapid deforestation in the Song territories, and with the northern forests in the control of "barbarians," the imperial court felt that it would soon run out of timber. The *New Yingzhao Fashi* aimed to solve both these problems.

Li Jie was an intellectual, a painter, author of books on geography, history, and philology. In addition, as a superintendent for state buildings in the ministry of works (*gong bu*), he had carried out several building projects, which made him an ideal person for the job. For three years Li Jie systematically interviewed leaders of the construction guilds, documented their building principles and processes, and added his own rationalizations and explanations. He finally presented his findings in 1105 CE in the form of regulations that the government administrators could use to monitor construction expenditures.

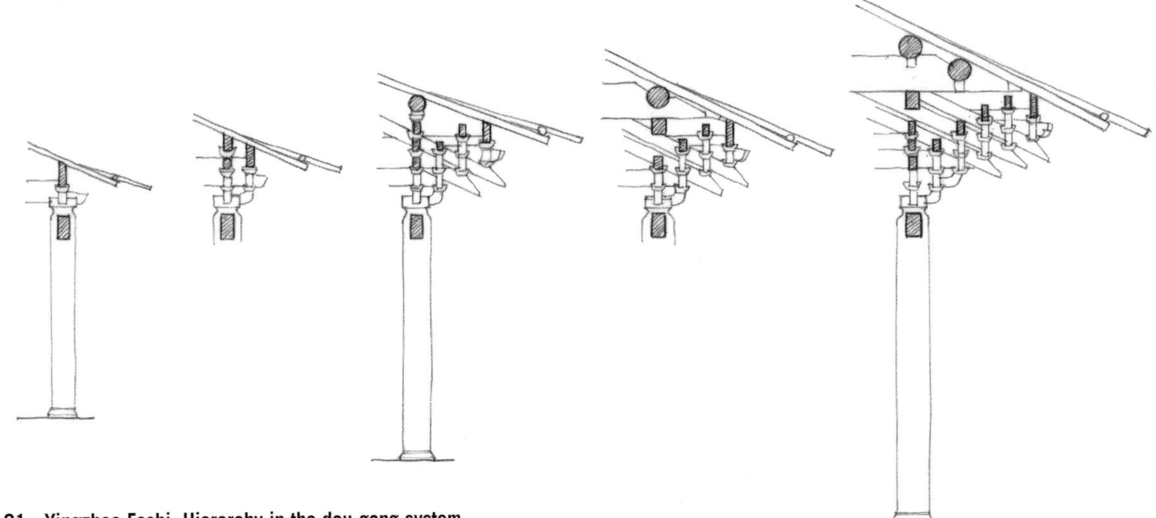

12.21 **Yingzhao Fashi: Hierarchy in the dou-gong system**

Li Jie's *Yingzhao Fashi* consists of 34 chapters, organized into five parts: basic data, regulations, labor work, materials, and drawings. Each part is subdivided into the following 13 sections: Moats and Fortification; Stonework; Structural Carpentry; Nonstructural Carpentry and Joinery (doors, windows, partitions, screens, ceilings, staircases, shrines, etc.); Stone Carving and Dressing; Turnery; Sawing; Bamboo Work; Tiling; Clay Work and Plastering; Decorative Painting and Coating; Brickwork; Brick and Tile Making and Kilns.

The *Yingzhao Fashi* described eight types of buildings but was concerned primarily with imperial and government buildings and not with buildings for the commoners, since only the former would be paid for by the administrator. Most of the drawings are plans (determining the basic size of a building), sections (determining quantities), and wood sections (instrumental in determining costs). All these were regulated by a proportioning system, known as the *cai-fen*. A *cai* was 10 *fen*, and a *zu-cai* was 21 *fen*. The standard proportions were in the ratio 2:3. Thus a standard wood section would be 10 by 15 *fen*.

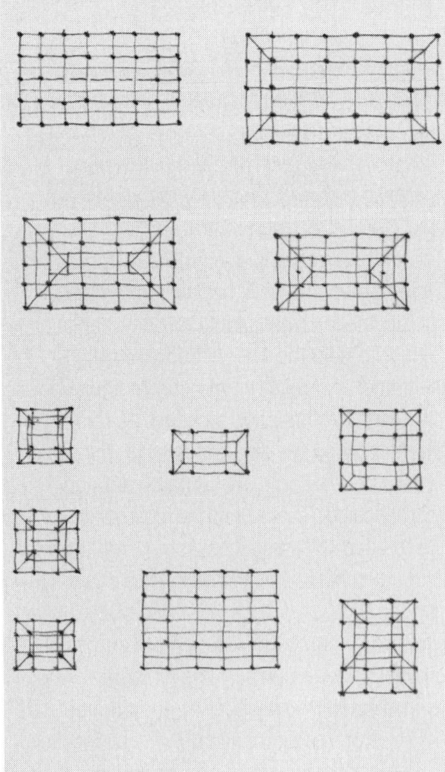

12.22 ***Yingzhao Fashi*: Hierarchy in plan layout**

**YUAN DYNASTY CHINA**

In 1215, after the Western Xia, Jin, and Song all fell to the military genius of the Mongols, Chengiz (Genghis) Khan was enthroned as head of a vast Mongolian empire; in 1264, Kublai Khan (1215–94), Chengiz's son, ascended the throne of China, choosing the Chinese name Yuan ("original" or "prime") for his dynasty. By 1279, with the surrender of the last of the Song territories, all of China was under the Yuan. The Mongols divided society into four classes, with the highest reserved for themselves and the lowest for the southern Chinese from the former Song regions. Outsiders enjoyed the middle status in China, between the Mongols and the native Chinese, to the great irritation of the Song. The Lamaist Buddhists, from Tibet and Nepal, and the Daoists found particular favor with the Mongols, as they had with the Mongolian-related Jin, 200 years before. The Muslims were welcomed and happily tolerated at the western border. Under the Yuan, one of the oldest mosques of China, the tomb of Tughluq Temur was built in 1363 in Huocheng, Xinjiang. While the Yuan introduced global civilization to China and modernized its military and economy, their architectural achievements were no match for those of the Song. They built new capital cities and strictly adhered to the planning principles described in the *Rituals of Zhou*. They also ordered the construction of numerous altars and temples throughout China, dedicated to ancestors and local deities.

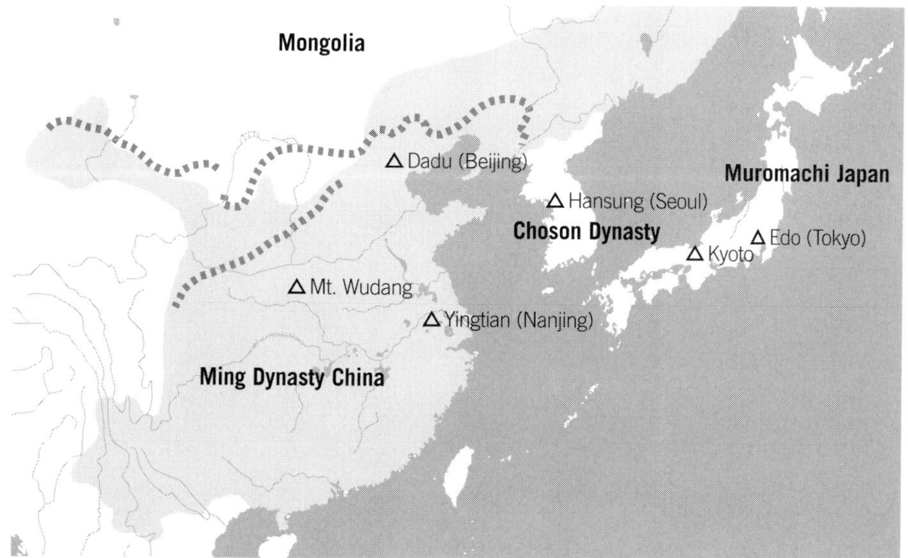


In 1267, Kublai Khan moved the capital to Dadu (Ta-tu, or Great Capital), the present-day location of Beijing—though, to the Mongolians, it was known as Khanbalig, the City of the Great Khan. Dadu was about 50 kilometers square, with an orthogonal arrangement of streets typical of earlier Chinese capitals. The urban center, consisting of the palace and the imperial quarters, was located south of the city center, with residential areas predominantly occupying the northern part. The palace, however, was nothing more than a mask. Within the palace, Kublai Khan, like the Liao kings before him, lived in resplendent tents of the kind the Mongolians were used to from their nomadic lifestyle. Marco Polo, visitor in his court, describes Kublai Khan's palace:

> You must know that it is the greatest palace that ever was. The roof is very lofty, and the walls of the palace are all covered with gold and silver. They are adorned with dragons, beasts and birds, knights and idols, and other such things. The hall of the palace is so large that 6000 people could easily dine there, and it is quite a marvel to see how many rooms there are besides. The building is altogether so vast, so rich and so beautiful, that no man on earth could design anything superior to it. The outside of the roof is all colored with vermilion and yellow and green and blue and other hues, which are fixed with a varnish so fine and exquisite that it shines like crystal, and lends a resplendent luster to the palace as seen for a great way around.

When Chengiz Khan died, he was buried in a secret, unmarked location in the deserts of Mongolia as per Mongolian tradition. (A team of archaeologists have recently located a site in Mongolia that is conjectured to be the mausoleum of Chengiz Khan.)

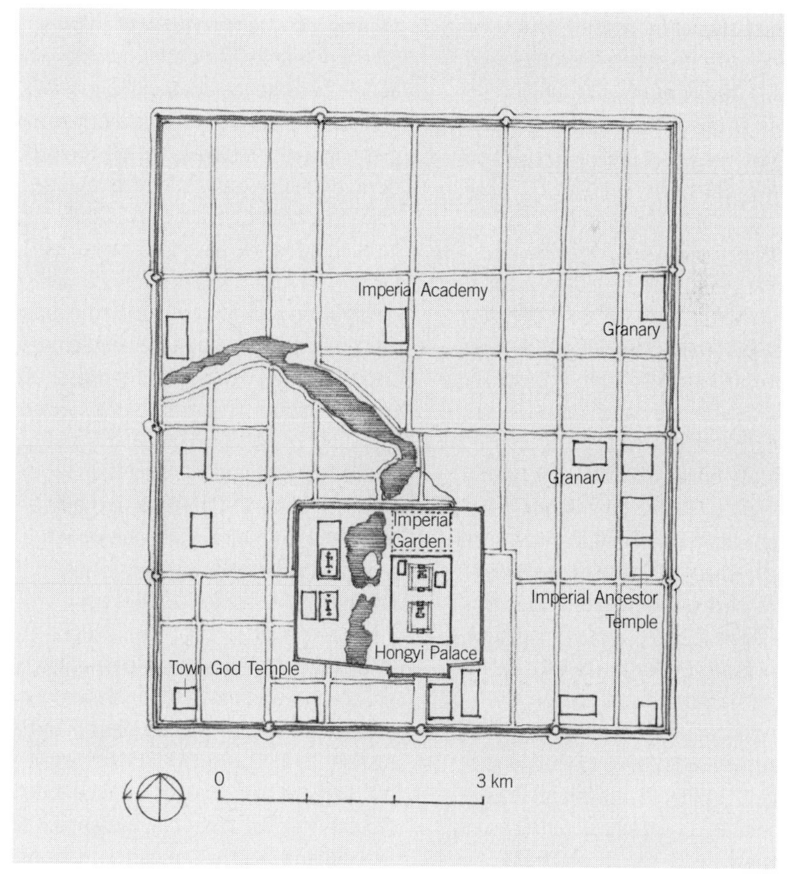


**12.23 Plan of Yuan Dadu**

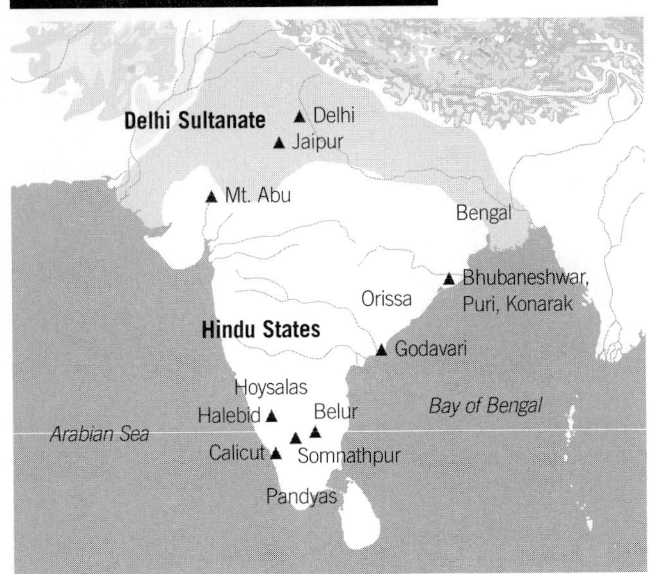

12.24 Temple columns, Quwwat-ul-Islam, Delhi, India

## DELHI SULTANATE

The 13th and 14th centuries were the last time Hindu civilization could be said to have been in full sway in South Asia, before it was largely overwhelmed by Islam. In western India, Jain devotees continued to build finely detailed temples. In the east, a new Orissan dynasty in Puri began construction of ambitious and imaginative temples, and in the south, the Hoysalas, the inheritors of the Cholas, pushed the temple plan to a new level of complexity. But another player had now entered the scene, Qutb-ud-Din Aibak, a Turkish general of Mohammed Ghori, who defeated the Rajput king Prithviraj Chauhan in 1192 and created an Islamic sultanate based in Delhi. Tension persists in the way historians describe and evaluate the Islamic rulers' relationship to their Hindu conquest. On the one hand, most Islamic rulers routinely massacred Hindus and systematically destroyed and desecrated Hindu temples. On the other hand, the Hindu population continued to thrive under Islamic rule, merging with it in many ways at the level of popular culture, underlining the more tolerant and even enlightened aspects of Islamic rule, particularly that of the Moghuls. One of the consequences of the tension, however, was the eventual partitioning of South Asia into India and Pakistan in 1947 by the British on the eve of their departure, an act whose ramifications are still in play.

### Quwwat-ul-Islam

South Asia's first major Islamic monument speaks unambiguously of its iconoclastic ambitions. In 1192, when Qutb-ud-Din Aibak occupied Delhi, he imperiously used the stones of the 27 Hindu and Jain temples he had razed to the ground to construct his new mosque, the Quwwat-ul-Islam (Might of Islam). The platform of the Hindu temple became the court of the mosque. The colonnade was constructed by reusing pillars from the temples, at times upside down or one on top of the other to raise them to a height greater than at their original location. Most still have their moldings intact. The main *qibla* wall, on the west, was constructed with five corbeled ogee arches, presumably by Hindu masons. Alternating bands of Islamic calligraphy and geometric moldings adorn every inch of the *qibla* wall.

In keeping with central Asian Islamic tradition, Qutb-ud-Din Aibak also built a tower, the Qutb Minar, just outside the mosque to commemorate his victory. Originally three stories tall, this now 72.5-meter-high circular tower, edged by alternating circular and acute-angled projections, was made of rubble masonry dressed in red and grey sandstone and white marble. Its inclined, conical volume give it a dramatic presence, as if rooted to the ground while its upper reaches appear tall and ephemeral. The five narrow balconies are supported by a multitude of small highly ornamental brackets.

Qutb's successor, Iltutmish (1211–1236), still using Hindu building materials, extended the *qibla* wall by three bays on either side and built a colonnade that enclosed the Qutb Minar. A hundred years later, King Al-ud-Din Khilji (1296–1316) decided to expand the complex by doubling the length of the *qibla* wall to the north and enclosing it in a courtyard large enough to hold a minaret designed to be twice the height of the Qutb Minar. Little of this was realized, and only the short stub of the tower remains.

In 1311, a new gate, called Alai Darwaza, was constructed by Al-ud-Din Khilji to the south. Despite being connected to the mosque at its northwestern edge, this elegant cubic gateway has the demeanor and proportions of a Roman triumphal arch, finished by Indian masons taking directions from their new Islamic rulers. A central arch is framed by equivalent bays, subdivided and screened arched openings, and blind windows, all of which are decorated with alternating bands of red sandstone and white marble with thin calligraphic and geometric inscriptions. A true dome sits atop squinches in a plain interior illuminated by small deep windows. The Alai Darwaza, which in its detailing exhibits influences from Seljuk artisans, was among the first monuments in South Asia to signal the arrival of a distinctly South Asian Islamic architectural way of building that was perfected eventually by the Moghuls.

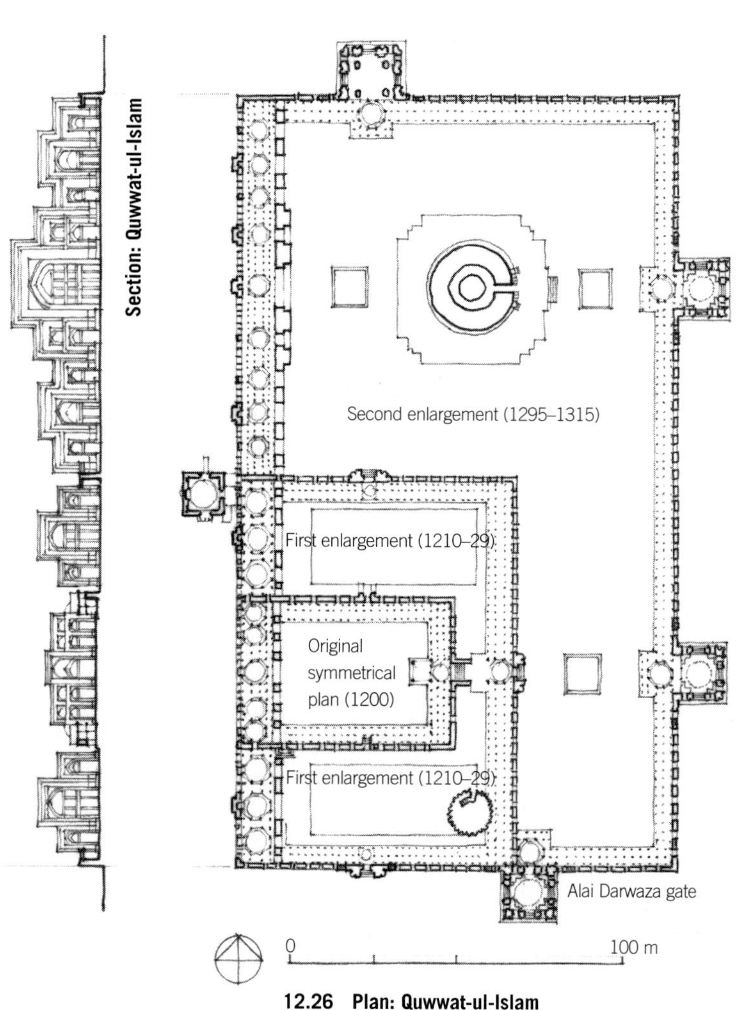


12.26 **Plan: Quwwat-ul-Islam**

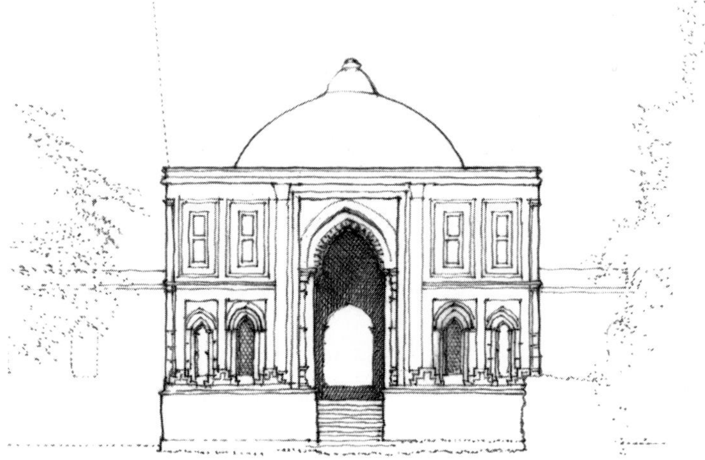

12.27 **Alai Darwaza gate, Quwwat-ul-Islam**

12.25 **Eastern gateway to Quwwat-ul-Islam**

**Tomb of Ghias-ud-Din Tughlaq**

In 1305, when Al-ud-Din Khilji added a ceremonial door to the Qutb complex, the points of reference for his architecture were Persia and Turkey. Twenty years later, when Ghias-ud-Din Tughlaq constructed his tomb in Tughlaqabad, he further simplified and abstracted the Alai Darwaza design, maintaining the largely unadorned battered walls and using minimal ornamentation. The central arch, however, has some sense of Hindu detail with its ogival-pointed arch form and crenelated outline, and similarly its tall marble-clad dome, imported straight from Persia, is topped with a form almost identical to the *amalaka* and *kalasha* found at the top of some Hindu temples. But fundamentally on the interior Ghias-ud-Din Tughlaq's tomb is a square box with a dome supported on pendentives—a construction system and symbolic language that was commonplace in the west but completely alien to the formal elaborations of, for example, the Sun Temple being constructed in Konarak at about this time.

12.28 **Chariot wheel, Sun Temple at Konarak, India**

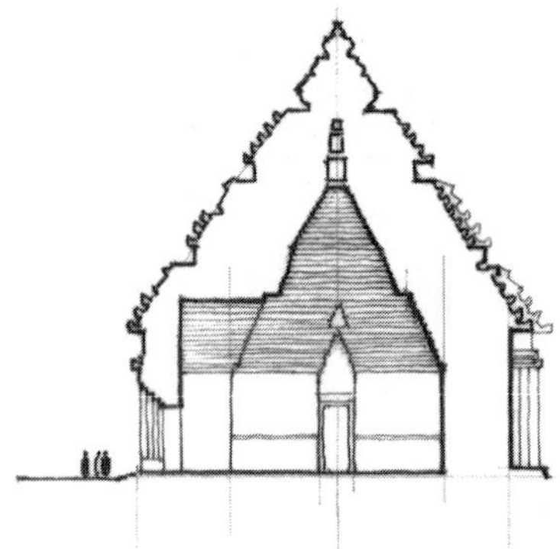

12.29 **Section: Sun Temple at Konarak**

### Sun Temple at Konarak

A new phase in Orissan history was ushered in by the later Gangas, who, unlike their Shiavite predecessors, were Vaishnavite in religious preference. Under them the Jagannath Temple in Puri (which is still in use and therefore inaccessible to scholars), the Ananta Vasudeva in Bhubaneshwar (1278), and the colossal Sun Temple at Konarak (1258) were built, all in the late 13th and early 14th centuries. The Ananda and the Jagannath temples are similar to the earlier Lingaraja Temple, with a sequence of three *mandapas* leading up to the main shrine or *deul*. The Sun Temple, however, takes the older single *mandapa* model, as at the Brihadeshwara Temple, and blows it up to stupefying proportions.

It was begun by King Narasimhadeva (1238–64) when he was only 18 years old. After a series of successful military battles on behalf of his father, Narasimhadeva I decided to dedicate the wealth he had appropriated from the conquests to a temple devoted solely to Surya, the Sun god, instead of preparing to honor the entire family of Shiva, as had been the case with the earlier temples of the Gangas. Not many Hindu temples are dedicated only to Surya. Along with the one at Modhera (and another at Martand, Kashmir) this temple represents one of the few instances when a more regional tribal god was given expression at a royal scale in Hindu architectural history. With that also came a full range of tantric sexual sculpture.

Like the Cholas, the Gangas took out their deities in procession in huge wooden chariots shaped like temples. Narasimhadeva's Sun Temple, however, reverses the conception and is conceived as a giant stone chariot to carry the sun in its daily and annual path across the sky. Twelve pairs of wheels, one for each month, were carved into the base and were accompanied by seven horses (three on the north, four on the south), one for each day of the week. Each wheel, more than three meters in diameter, had eight major and minor spokes with their own astrological significance. When seen from the side at some distance, the entire temple created the sense of an object on the verge of movement. The temple was consecrated on the birthday of the Sun god, a Sunday in the Hindu calendar year 1179 or 1258.

The *mandapa* has three sets of horizontal moldings in typical Orissan style, and the *deul* (which is now lost) was of the traditional vertical expression. It sits in the middle of a large compound measuring 180 by 220 meters. Three subsidiary shrines, or *nisas*, facing north, south, and west with cruciform prechambers, are attached to the base of the *deul*. There are also a multitude of smaller independent shrines, constituting its "family," as is typical of Orissan temples.

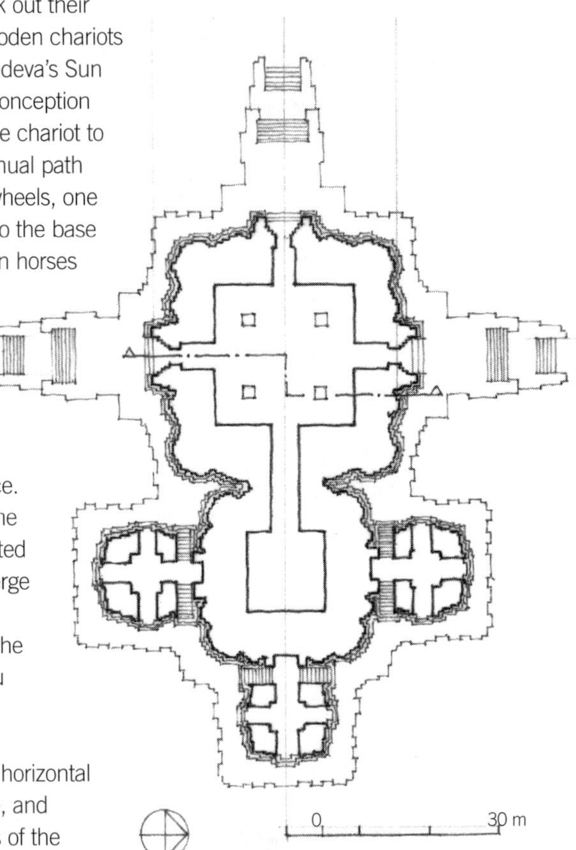


12.30 **Plan: Sun Temple at Konarak**

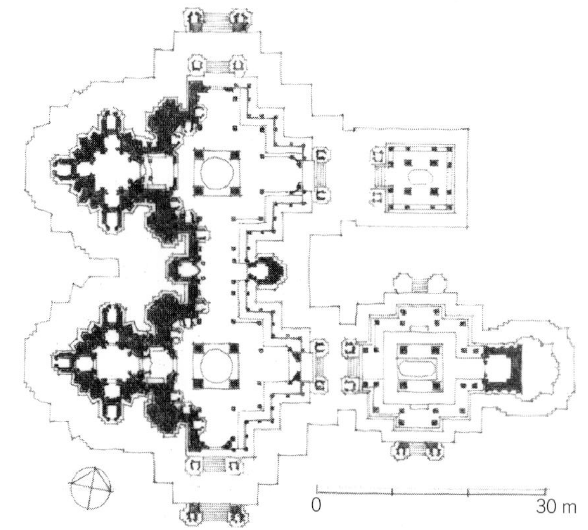

**12.31 Plan: Hoysalesvara Temple, Halebid, India**

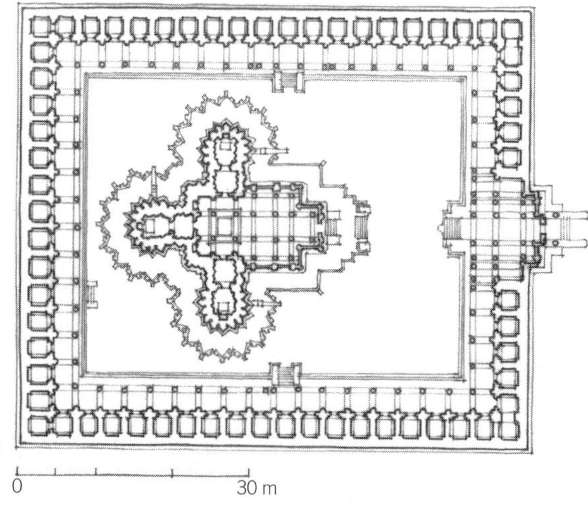


**12.32 Plan: Kesava (Somnatha) Temple, Somnathpur, India**

## HOYSALAS

To control the Arab trade the Cholas had conquered the Chalukyas in the 10th century. After the Cholas themselves went into decline late in the 12th century, the Hoysalas of Karnataka, erstwhile tributaries of the Chalukyas, used the opportunity to declare their independence. Hoysala culture reflected the influence of both. They took the systematic rational approach to iconography of the Cholas and adapted it to temples at the Chalukyan scale and form. For the Hoysalas this meant that they had to find a way of balancing several principal deities nonhierarchically into the main shrine of a temple (while the larger pantheon was still accommodated in the cloisters). The Hoysalas built about 80 to 90 temples from the late-12th to the mid-14th centuries. The important ones are from the reign of King Vishnuvardhana (1108–42) at the two Hoysala capitals, Belur and Halebid.

The Hoysalesvara Temple at Halebid (1121–60) is a composite of two star-shaped, identical shrines of equivalent importance and complexity. Both face east and abut each other. Their cruciform *garbh-griha* is expressed on the exterior with a multifaceted star-shaped perimeter and three subsidiary shrines opening to the south, west, and north. On the east their entrance forecourts lead to a cruciform *mandapa*, one side of which is linked by an extra bay where two small shrines were inserted.

The distance between the two shrines was calculated to ensure that each shrine could stand alone and be fully resolved (including in the full expression of its platform) and yet be linked at the first opportunity without any additional or superfluous bays. Even so, one could argue that the Hoysalesvara Temple is really two distinct temples linked together by a corridor rather than a single unit with multiple centers.

The Hoysala architects achieved their best resolution of multiple shrines at the Kesava (Somnatha) Temple at Somnathpur (1268) from the reign of Nrsimha III. Part of a larger Vaishnavite complex, the Kesava Temple is an ambitious structure, designed with three shrines that retain their individual identities and yet are merged into a single expressive unit with a shared *mandapa*. Enclosed by a low quadrangle with an entrance gate to the east, the Kesava Temple sits on a low-stepped platform that follows the outline of the temple.

**12.33 Kesava (Somnatha) Temple**

Three star-shaped shrines, each with its own prechamber, open onto a square court that is elongated to the east to form a colonnaded *mandapa*. Since each shrine is surmounted by a low superstructure and the *mandapa* is flat, the Kesava Temple does not have a dramatic skyline of the kind that, say, the Chandella temples at Khajuraho do. On closer examination, the plan and the detailing of the temple, however, are surpassed by none.

Uniquely, the Hoysala built with a hard, black schist that, though difficult to work with, could sustain deep cuts and take on a fine polish. With multiple tiers of deeply excoriated circular bands, columns seem to pulsate and swirl in space, as if they had just been removed from the wheel. Although most have been carved over, many of the columns have been left unadorned, which imparts to them an almost modern, mechanical quality, something rarely found in Hindu architecture.

**12.34 Vadakkunnathan Temple, Trichur, India**

### Vadakkunnathan Temple

Geographically the Western Ghats slice off the coastal region Kerala from the rest of South Asia in the same manner that the Andes separate Chile from South America. Politically, however, Kerala's Chera kings reigned largely under the shadow of the greater powers of peninsular India, such as the Pallavas and the Cholas. Control of Kerala was critical for trade. Kerala's hot and humid climate was ideal for growing spices, which were traded through their ports in Cochin and Calicut, through Arab intermediaries, with Byzantium and then later with China and Europe. In the 12th century, with the decline of the Cholas, Kerala broke up into a series of small kingdoms and principalities that came to be dominated by a minority group of high-caste Brahmins, known as the Nambudiri Brahmins. Without powerful royal patronage, the Nambudiri Brahmins maintained their cultural domination by marrying into the local lower-caste Nayar families, establishing a hybridized culture that made significant accommodations to the more populist practices of the Nayars, such as matrilineal traditions that favored women (including polyandry and primary right to inherited property). They accommodated local deities and cults, giving them a place of honor with Shiva and Vishnu in a series of temples they built that to this day define the characteristic of Kerala culture and architecture.

The Vadakkunnathan Temple at Trichur is one of the largest Nambudiri temples, started in the 11th century but modified and added to until the 19th. Perched on a beautiful hillock at the center of Trichur, the temple comprises nine acres surrounded by a reserved forest of hardwood teaks called the Tekkinkadu. The sacred area is enclosed by a rectangular enclosure called the *nalambalam*. A secondary colonnade creates a circumambulation route around the inner edge of the temple precinct. The main entrances are from the west; three of them are directly aligned with the temple's three main shrines, known as *srikovils*. The *srikovil* furthest to the north is dedicated to Shiva, the southern to Vishnu manifested as Rama, and in the middle, albeit the smallest at the place of privilege, the shrine unique to Kerala's local history, dedicated to Sankara-Narayana, the combined form of Shiva and Vishnu. Although the *garbh-griha* of all three *srikovils* is square, the outer forms of two are round. Each *srikovil* is accompanied by its own prayer *mandapa*.

While the walls of the three shrines are made of stone and are carved in the traditions of the Pallavas and the Cholas, the Nambudiri temples are unique for their graceful wooden roofs that dominate the structure and are visible from a distance. These roofs, covered with copper sheets, overhang well beyond the main structure, casting deep shadows, and with their smooth and gently curving forms sharply contrast with the richly crafted stone walls.

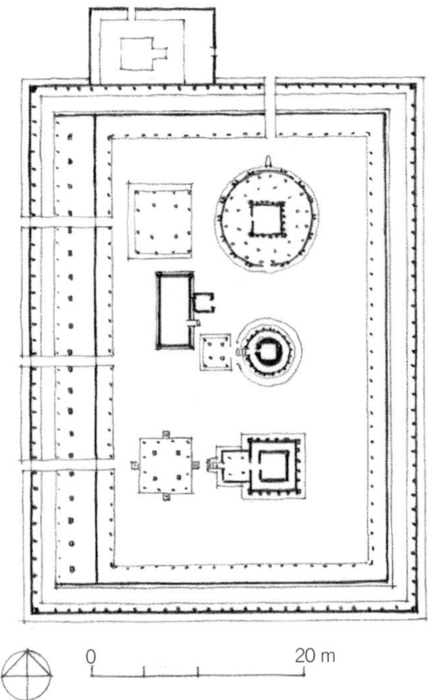


**12.35 Plan: Vadakkunnathan Temple**

**12.36 Site plan of Great Zimbabwe, Zimbabwe**

## AFRICAN KINGDOMS

The Great Zimbabwe (Great Palace) is one of a group of fortress complexes, dating from the 10th century, located on top of a granite bluff as well as in adjacent valleys in Zimbabwe not far from Maswingo. The complex housed a large population as well as the royal court, markets, warehouses, and religious shrines. The number of ruins is substantial and have yet to all be thoroughly studied. The kingdom drew its wealth from the abundant gold reserves in the region and the good agricultural land. The blocks of the walls were skillfully laid without mortar, with the walls ranging from 1 to 5 meters thick. At the heart of the complex is the palace itself. The Karanga ethnic group, whose ancestors it is now thought built the structure, called it Mumbahuru, meaning "house of the great woman." The building was not constructed as an isolated object in space but as an extension of the natural landscape. It contained an outdoor living space (*kgotla*) that served as a garden and as a place to keep livestock. The *kgotla* is also a place where descendents can establish communion with one another and with their ancestors. The visual focus of the building is a 6-meter-wide by 10-meter-high conical tower, the purpose of which remains unknown.

Though no premodern African palaces apart from the Great Zimbabwe have survived, the Husuni Kubwa, destroyed by the Portuguese, give us a glimpse into the scale of precolonial African architecture. Trade between Japan, China, and India had by this time blossomed, and the east African towns were the major distribution centers for the African continent. East Africans sold gold, ivory, and enslaved people to Swahili or Arab traders who lived in villages along the coast. Of these, Kilwa, off the south coast of Tanzania, was preeminent. It was established in the 11th century by believers of Shirazi Islam, an East African variant of Middle Eastern Islam. The rulers of Kilwa were not only eminent traders but controlled sources of gold in nearby Mozambique, evoking the interest of the Portuguese in the 16th century. Their arrival spelled the end of African control of trade routes. The palace is situated on a rocky promontory overlooking the Indian Ocean. Husuni Kubwa, which means large fortified house in Swahili, had several courtyards for different functions, with a distinct progression from private to public. The king's private courtyard had a sunken pool and next to it an audience court.

Palace court
Pool
Audience court
Domestic court
South court
0
30 m

**12.37 Plan: Palace of Husuni Kubwa at Kilwa, Tanzania**

12.38 Giorgis, one of the rock-cut churches of Lalibela, Ethiopia

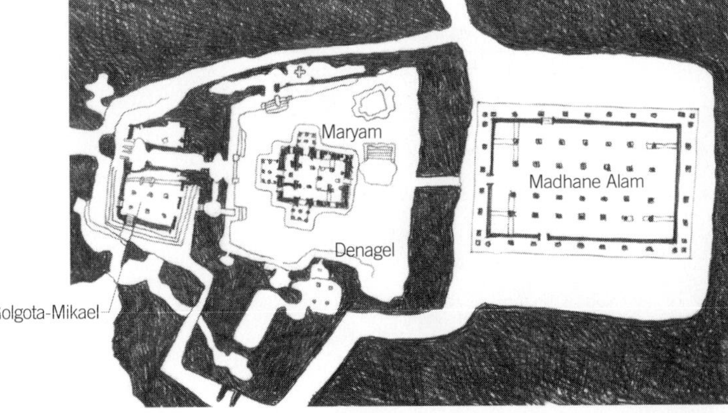


12.39 Plan: Biet Golgota, Mikael, and Selassie

**Rock-Cut Churches of Lalibela**

In Ethiopia, the Zagwe Dynasty (founded in 1137) was a period of prosperity that reached its peak under King Lalibela (ca. 1185–1225), who is credited with building a set of eleven churches cut out of solid red volcanic rock. They are located in his capital city, known originally as Roha (340 kilometers north of Addis Ababa) but renamed Lalibela after his death. The city is located on a ridge between two streams that flow into the Takkaze River. Though the Christian monarchy, under threat from the forces of Islam from the north, had retreated into these ridges from the old capital of Aksum to the north, they continued to control the Red Sea ports that linked central and southern African trade routes to the shipping lanes to India and elsewhere.

The churches, in their overall conception, represent Jerusalem and the Holy Land, which Lalibela had never seen but imagined from the Bible. They are divided into northern and eastern groups by a rock-cut channel called Yordannos (Jordan River). Bieta Madhane Alam is the largest and most impressive of these monolithic churches. Bieta Giorgis (St. George), carved into the shape of a cross, is situated apart from the other churches to the west. To get to the floor, one has to follow a deep, narrow trench leading in a wide circle through rock gates and chambers. The building is approximately 12 meters in height, length, and width and rests on a triple-stepped platform. It represents a wooden building, replete with delicately chiseled acanthus leaves and gargoyles. The interior has a cruciform floor plan with a dome above the sanctuary in the eastern arm of the church.

The eleven rock-hewn churches are: Madhane Alam, Maryam, Denagel, Selassie, Golgota, Mikael, Emanuel, Mercurios, Abba Libanos, Gabriel-Raphael, and Giorgis. Lalibela was buried in Golgota. The churches are still in use. In the heart of Golgota is the holy of holies with three niches and monolithic altars in front of them, reflecting the syncretism of beliefs. In the central niche a cross enclosed in a circle seems to represent the sun, which has vanished into the underworld. Two animal-headed figures are in the side niches, an ox and an ass, with the ox horns representing the moon and the ass said to signify the heaven, just as it was in the metaphor of Anu, the Mesopotamian god.

12.40 Section: Rock-cut churches of Lalibela

12.41 **Facade, St. Denis**

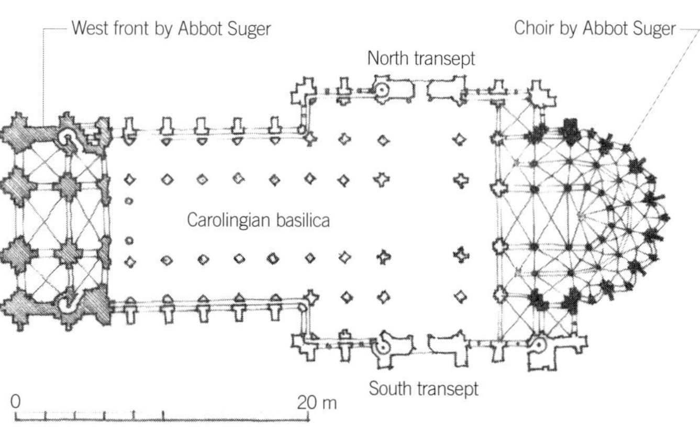


12.42 **Plan: St. Denis, near Paris, France**

**EUROPE: THE HIGH MIDDLE AGES**

In the span of only a hundred years prior to about 1270, the skylines of Europe changed profoundly. The spires and towers of some 600 major churches and cathedrals now marked their location in the landscape of cities from England to Italy, from Spain to Germany, and beyond. This energetic building activity was driven by a renewed religious fervor that terminated in the crusades but also left its mark in stone. Income from the selling of indulgences by the Roman church was one of the main sources of financing often augmented by other sources such as sending relics on tours. The bishops of Chartres, for example, sent its relics as far away as England to solicit contributions. The building of cathedrals was at the time by far the largest construction enterprise ever attempted in Europe. Chartres Cathedral, for example, was huge and able to hold more than 8000 people. Construction, technologically complex and often dangerous, frequently took many decades and not infrequently hundreds of years.

Unlike Carolingian churches with their imposing westworks and unlike Ottonian monastic churches, as at Hildesheim, that were associated with market towns and that may not have had a facade at all, St. Denis, consecrated in 1144, had a facade that served as a sacred threshold to its mystic interior.

The shift in focus dates to the Synod of Arras (1025), during which it was decided that sculptural programs could serve to help the illiterate contemplate what they could not understand through the written word. Statues once used only sparingly, and usually in relation to aristocratic worship practices, now stood row upon row along the facade. Compared with the Norman facade of St. Etienne (1067–87) in Caen, with its solid wall of stone facing the town, St. Denis seems to almost float above the ground in front of it. Depicted over the middle door was the Divine Son in the Vicinity of Judges. The church was begun on the west end rather than on the east, as was the custom because Abbot Suger wanted his towers to beam their message to the countryside.

Abbot Suger (1081–1155), one of the most powerful men in France and who was actively engaged in France's political life, played a large role in running the kingdom while King Louis VI was away on crusade. He wrote a book, *The Book of Suger Abbot of St. Denis on What Was Done During his Administration* (ca. 1144), that gives valuable insight into his design ideas. For Suger, the use of precious materials in the furnishings of the church, as well as the use of stained glass in the windows, was meant to draw a person's attention away from earthly concerns to higher, heavenly things.

The entrance was through triple portals with the central one larger than the others, recalling Roman triumphal arches and serving as a symbol of the Trinity. The Trinity had become important to theological speculation in the second quarter of the 12th century, and its restatement signified support for orthodox interpretation of the Bible and for papal authority. The tympanum over the door portrays Christ in judgment. The sculptures notwithstanding, Abbot Suger held that the religious experience was one of transcendence, symbolized by disembodied light. In the center of the facade there was a rose window, one of the first of its kind, a grand wheel of light. The relationship between the facade and the interior was foretold, so Suger argued, by the portal that tells you "what shines here within, through palpable visual beauty, the soul is elevated to that which is truly beautiful, and rising from the earth, where it was submerged, an inert thing, it is resuscitated in heaven by the radiance of its glory."

St. Denis was also groundbreaking in that it heralded an approach to building now known as the Gothic style. Although some of its features, such as the cross-rib vaulting and the flying buttresses, had been incorporated in prior churches, they were here all combined into an stylistic statement integrated with sharply pointed spires, rose window, clustered columns, pointed arches, cross-rib vaulting, and stress on luminosity.

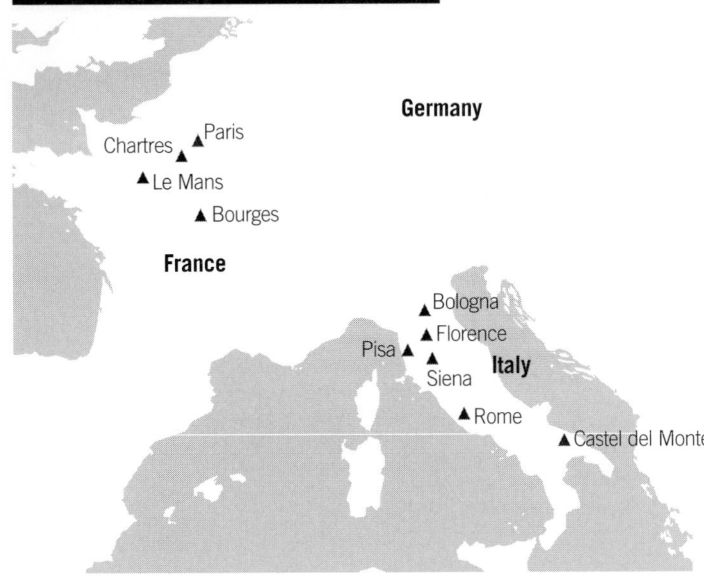

12.43 Chapter house, Lincoln Cathedral, England

**Chartres Cathedral**

Among the various aspects of architecture that changed during this period was the emergence of the interior elevation of the nave as an architectural unit in its own right, with architects seeking to balance the interplay of horizontal and vertical elements. At Notre Dame in Paris (1163–1250), there are four discrete horizontal levels—the ground-level arcade, over which run two galleries, called the tribune and the triforium, over which ran an upper, windowed story or clerestory. The windows of these cathedrals were, of course, not transparent but filled with stained glass, bringing into the interior a muted, shimmering light. At first the flying buttress was a pure structural necessity, as at Saint-Germain-des-Prés where they were added for reinforcement around 1180, but they were soon integrated into the design from the start. Some buttresses, as at Lincoln Cathedral Chapter House (1230–50), stand well back from the outer wall, but most were integrated into the outer sidewalls. The flying buttresses consist of a tower that supplies the necessary counterweight and an arch that transfers the lateral loads to the tower. Due to the flying buttresses, the interior of the church became uncluttered and emerged as a spatial unit. Nonetheless, the flying buttress sacrificed the legibility of the exterior for the interior, leading to the problem of how to integrate it at the planning stage of the building.

The epitome of the new style was Chartres Cathedral (1194–1220), where the nave on the outside is almost completely obscured behind an intimate tangle of buttresses. The interior, on the other hand, is almost canyonlike. The nave elevation has only three levels, permitting a strong vertical extension of the bays. To compensate for the added height two flying buttresses, one over the other, bring the load to the tower. The vaults, another important Gothic element, were composed of stone ribs with thin brick vaults between them that seem to be stretched like taut skin.

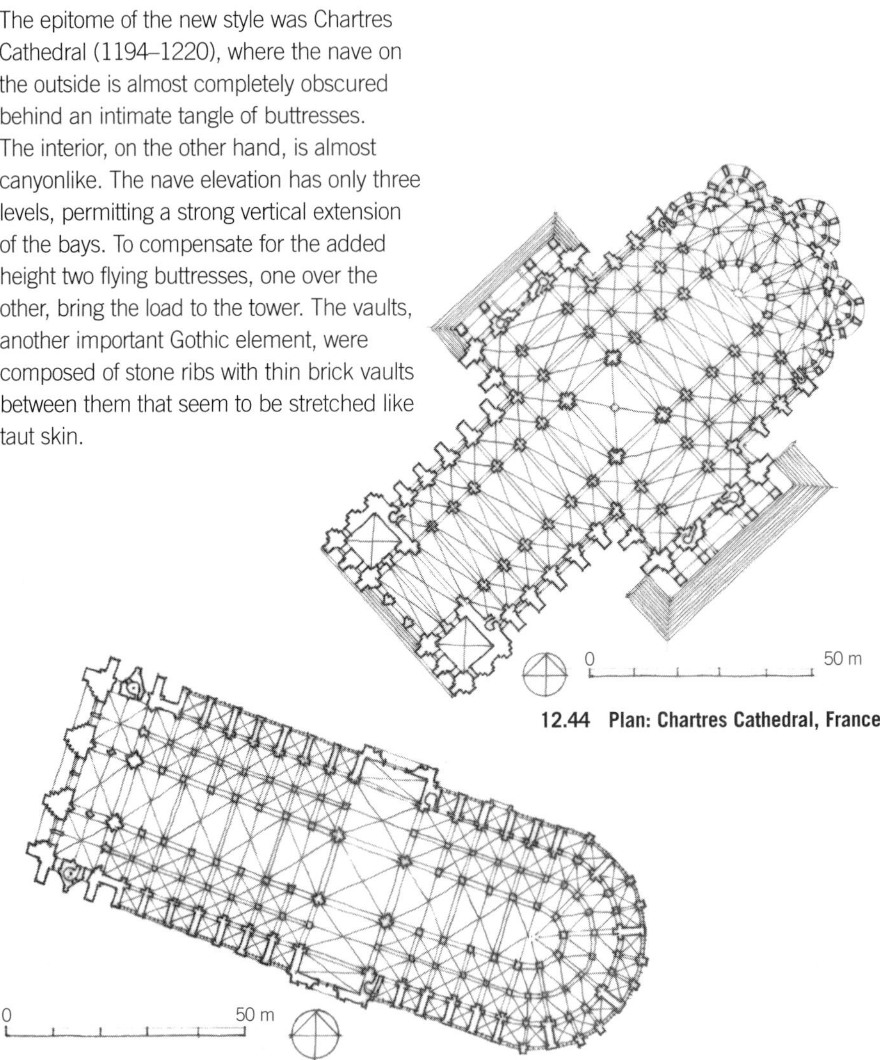


12.44 Plan: Chartres Cathedral, France

12.45 Plan: Notre Dame, Paris, France

12.46 **Amiens Cathedral, France**

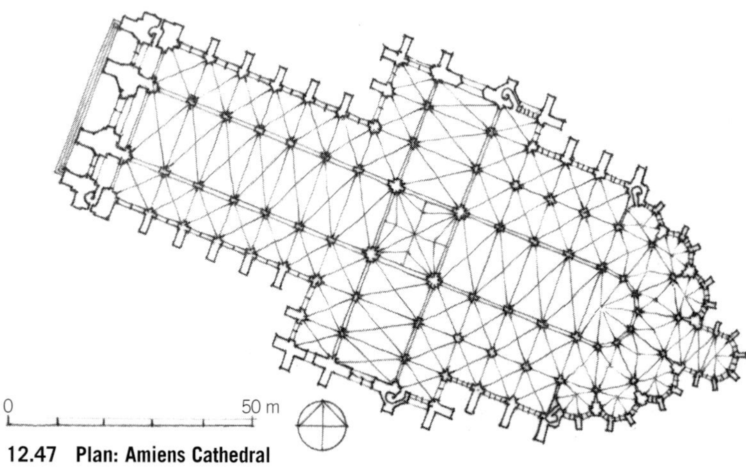


12.47 **Plan: Amiens Cathedral**

**Amiens Cathedral**

The Cathedral at Bourges (1195–1214), though begun only one year after Chartres, follows a slightly different model. Unlike Chartres with its clutter of buttresses, the slope of buttresses at Bourges was made to correspond to the steep slope of the roof, which along with the absence of a transept, allows the body of the nave to read as a unified form. The round *chevet* at the end rises in three stages with small high-peaked chapels seemingly suspended between the buttress piers. The interior is not as canyonlike as the nave at Chartres, because the tall arches create the illusion that the wall of the side aisle is the actual side of the nave.

The development of the Gothic style was far from linear. At Amiens Cathedral (1220–35) the architects were more conservative than at Bourges, following the Chartres model with its calmer interior and soaring verticality. This verticality is further enhanced by the integration of the crossing piers into the overall design of the inner facade. The introduction of four lights at Amiens in the upper clerestory, in preference to the usual two, further adds to the impression of verticality. Its tall nave arches and tall clerestory windows fuse the approaches of Chartres and Bourges, while preserving to some extent the unity of the nave. The calm interior is set off against the delicate luminosity of the *chevet*.

The new spatial idea was taken up by the architect of Le Mans Cathedral (the *chevet* was built 1217–1254), who extended the reach of the buttresses and extruded the chapels from between the bottoms of the buttresses. They appear as a collection of minichurches nestled next to the church itself. All of this was set off against the vigorous form of the transept. The aspiration for verticality occasionally led engineers to go beyond the limit of safety. When the vaults of the gigantic Beauvais Cathedral collapsed in 1284, the building had to remain incomplete.

Whereas Romanesque churches had round columns in the nave, Gothic churches, from Speyer onward, began to have columns that were composed of a columnar core with *colonettes* attached to it. The *colonettes* facing the nave continue upward to reach all the way to the vault, whereas the *colonettes* on the inside become part of the ribs of the vaults in the side aisles. As a result, Gothic supports were neither columns nor piers; rather they were columnar bundles working not only in the vertical dimension but also in plan as they would seem to be squares rotated 45 degrees, creating diagonal vistas through the building.

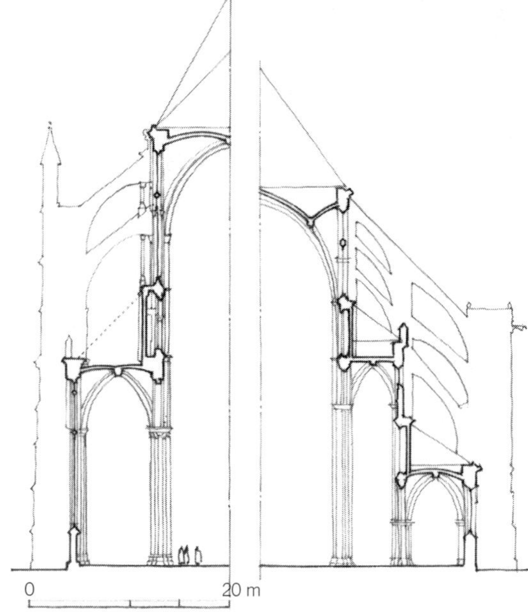


12.48 **Half-section: Naves of Amiens and Bourges cathedrals**

12.49 Cathedral of Notre-Dame of Reims, France

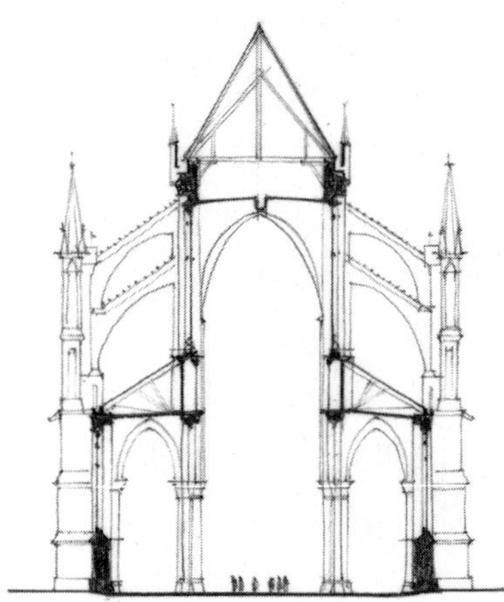

12.50 Section: Cathedral of Notre-Dame of Reims

**Notre-Dame of Reims**

By the second decade of the 13th century, the Roman church was able to tap into and direct a new populism that had first manifested itself in the popularity of the pilgrimage churches and the resulting transformation of church space from a place of liturgical requirements into a space of reliquary exhibition and theological display. On a philosophical level, the discussion changed from issues of belief and ritual to one of symbolism of light (God) and geometry (the ordered universe). Robert Grosseteste, who read Greek fluently and was familiar with Arabic scientific commentaries, argued that all of human knowledge stemmed from the spiritual radiance of uncreated light. Rose windows appeared in almost every church, sometimes opening so wide that they touched the framework of the buttresses, as at Auxerre Cathedral (completed around 1234). The apse of St. Thibault in Auxois (begun toward the end of the 13th century), where structure is no longer made of ribs and skeletal orders but of a veillike curtain of vertical elements, defies architectural logic altogether.

Statues of church saints placed in the facade were meant to narrate the ongoing vitality of Christian life. By rehabilitating the tangibly created world, Catholic theology slowly moved away from the old Platonic separation of body and soul that had worked so effectively in the days of the early church. St. Thomas Aquinas argued that the soul derived all its knowledge from the perceptual world.

Along with these new ideas was the emergence of the Marian cult. Mary, the mother of Christ, who had until then played a minor role in the Christian liturgy, was now taken into the heart of the popular imagination, her image standing alongside that of Christ's, a movement that paralleled the troubadour's chivalrous veneration of women. By 1220, at Notre-Dame in Paris, the theme had found its ultimate expression. Chartres had its own prized relic, the tunic that had ostensibly belonged to the Virgin Mary, a gift from Charles the Bald, who obtained it from Constantinople. At the Cathedral of Notre-Dame of Reims (1211–90), figures of Mary were visible in every part of the church, not only standing in for the saints but for the Christian church itself.

Cathedral construction was frequently thwarted by unfavorable relations between the church and the burghers who, since the 13th century, were not only prospering but demanding their own political and juridical rights. During times of unfavorable relations, the burghers preferred to make donations to parish churches, convents, and charitable institutions. The exception to this was the Cathedral at Amiens, where the citizens of the commune, enriched from international trade in blue dye, made significant contributions to the construction of the cathedral, which can be understood from the donor inscriptions in its upper windows.

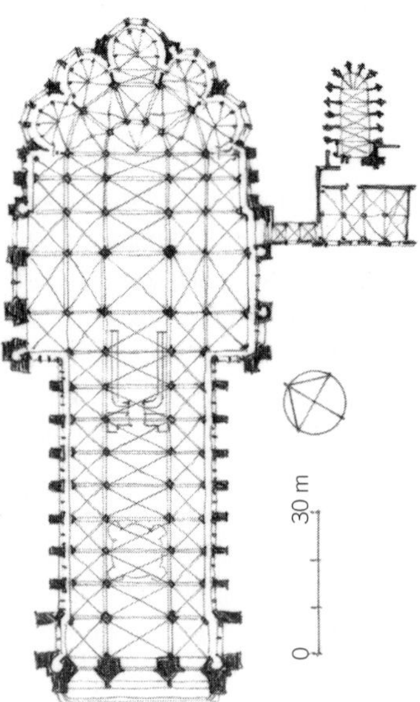


12.51 Plan: Cathedral of Notre-Dame of Reims

12.52 **Interior of Fontenay Abbey, near Montbard, France**

12.53 **Monastery, Fontenay Abbey**

## Cistercian Monasteries

Against the backdrop of 11th century religious populism and the increasing laxity of the Cluniac Order, a countermovement sprang up headed by St. Bernard of Clairvaux and others that urged a return to the austere rules of the early monastic days of St. Benedict, who conceived of the church as a workshop for prayer. Among the most prominent of the new reform orders was the Carthusian Order, founded in 1084, and the Cistercian Order, founded in 1115. The Cistercians had four so-called "daughter houses," namely Clairvaux, Morimond, Pontigny, and La Ferté. These in turn promoted the creation of numerous monastic offspring, so many that by the close of the 12th century there were 530 Cistercian abbeys in Europe.

Though Cistercians had a large number of recruits from the feudal nobility, one of the reasons for their success was that they opened their doors to artisans and peasants, their manual labor being conceived as an offering to the Creator. For this reason, Cistercian monasteries were as organized as any farm, with all the monks participating in the chores. Cistercians became known for their innovations in farming and herding. Their vineyards in Burgundy and the Rhineland became legendary.

Under St. Bernard's influence, all the details of existence were rigidly prescribed with frequent inspection visits. Cistercian monasteries were not sited along pilgrimage routes but in inauspicious, often swampy and inaccessible land. They had no crypts or towers and were built on rigorous geometrical principles. They had simple, vaulted naves. Lighting was dim and limited by rule to only five candles. Wall surfaces were clean and simple. Sculptural embellishments, such as those found in St. Denis, were forbidden. Bold or ambitious proportions and architectural bravura were not tolerated. Even ornamental pavements were frowned upon. The plans had square east ends in defiance of the ambulatory design of the great cathedrals.

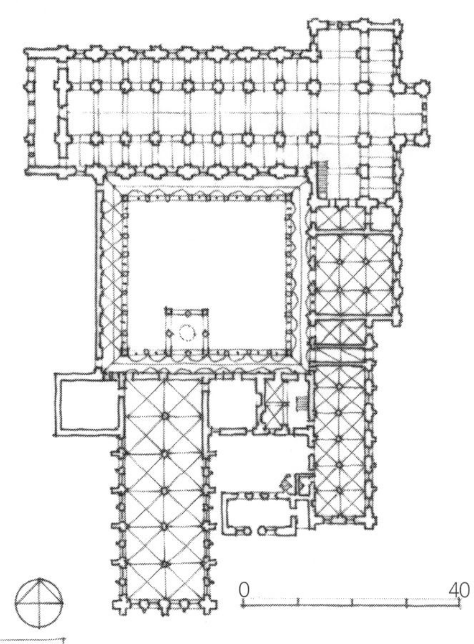


12.54 **Plan: Fontenay Abbey**

When the Cistercians adopted the ribbed vault around 1150, even though they were slow to explore its possibilities, they performed an act of major importance in architecture by disseminating this feature across Europe. The building that best represents the Cistercian aesthetic is the Abbey of Notre Dame, in Fontenay, Burgundy, founded in 1119, the oldest ensemble still in existence. Since there is no clerestory, the interior gains most of its light from facade windows and from the corresponding ones at the crossing and in the sanctuary. A tunnel vault with transverse arches defines the space of the nave. The building is meant to look and feel purposeful and dignified. On account of the tunnel vault, it possesses remarkable acoustical qualities. The refectory was placed in the customary Cistercian position opposite the fountain house on the south side of the cloister with the axis perpendicular to the church.

12.55 Castel del Monte, near Andria, Italy

**Castel del Monte**

The Holy Roman Empire, which had been taken over by the Ottonians, existed more in name than in substance, with the German princes fighting among themselves for regional advantage. The church was eager to see the German Empire weakened in this way so that its own authority would remain preeminent. That changed with Frederick II (r. 1212–50), who was granted the Norman crown as King of Sicily as his mother had been a Norman princess. At the age of twenty-six, he also became emperor. At the time, just as new religious ideas were altering Christian religious practices, so too, new notions of kingship were being developed, based to no small degree on the ideas of Aristotle, the bulk of whose writings were not known in the west until the end of the 12th century. These writings stimulated the development of a theory of state that required no appeal to theological premises. Though it would be centuries before that ideal could reach fruition, a generation of rulers now emerged who saw themselves as the head of their own institutional organization. In turn, for the first time, the Roman church was asked to pay taxes on its vast land holdings.

To secure his lands, Frederick II, who had grown up in Palermo, marched into southeast Italy and began an extensive building campaign, erecting some 200 buildings, principally fortresses and palaces. The most impressive of his works was the Castel del Monte in rural Apulia. This building, like Castello Maniace in Syracuse, the Castel Ursino in Catania, and the donjon at Termoli, is noted for its stark severity and pronounced geometric configurations. Displaying particular emphasis on the use of equilateral squares and octagons in planning, it is constructed from heavy rusticated stonework. The Islamic influences native to southern Italy and known to Frederick II from his childhood in Palermo remain a topic of debate. The strong Saracen population in southern Italy definitely influenced many Christian buildings known to be decorated with Islamic motifs, as in the case of Sicily's St. Maria Maggiore of Siponto. It should also be noted that, unlike Christian Europe, the Islamic Middle East maintains an abundance of octagonal and square buildings.

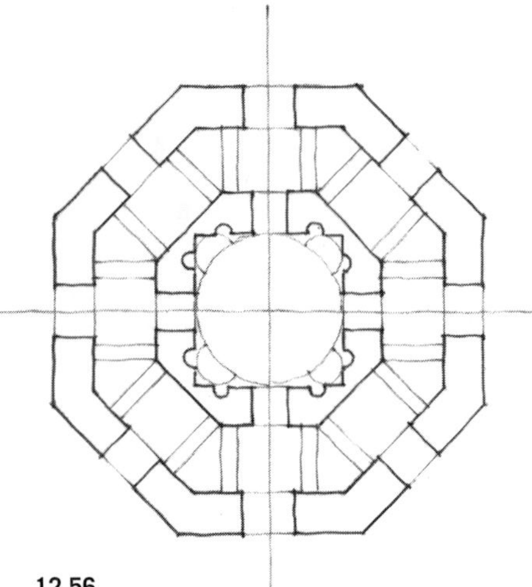

12.56
Mausoleum of Qubbat as-Sulaibiya at Samarra, Iraq

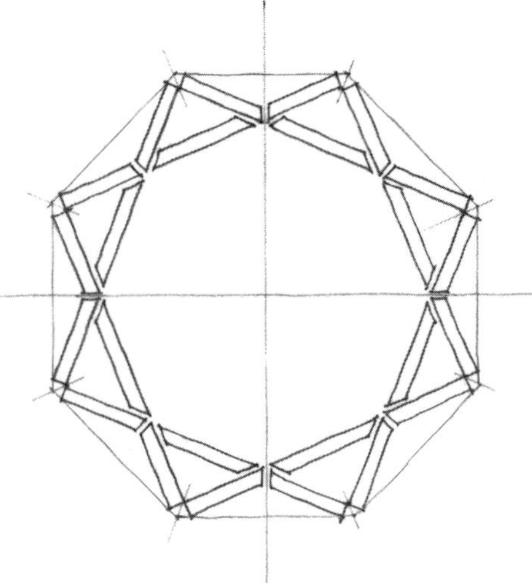

12.57
Ribs of the cupola of the Omayyad mosque in Córdoba, Spain

12.58 Interior court, Castel del Monte

The Castel del Monte is a remarkably complex object with no truly singular precedent in Europe insofar as the specificity of its shape is concerned. It has an equilateral octagonal exterior, containing an octagonal courtyard and eight octagonal towers. Mathematically the building is a *monohedron* with eight reflecting planes and eight rotations, forming a volume composed of eight symmetrical axes. The rooms surrounding the courtyard are necessarily trapezoidal, each containing a ribbed groin vault reminiscent of Cistercian architecture. Three of the eight towers contain staircases, while several others contain lavatory facilities; others serve no discernible purpose. Interestingly, two of the towers contain a six-ribbed vault, despite being octagonal spaces. It should also be noted that the wall containing the entrance portal is obviously smaller than the other sides of the octagon, a quirk that has not gone unnoticed. This has generally been defended as an intentional adaptation in planning.

In addition to the varied native influences of southern Italy and the Middle East, Frederick II was a strong supporter of the Cistercians and their austere Christian aesthetic. The building was perhaps designed by the Cistercian architect Philippe Chinard. The great Hohenstaufen halls of Frederick II's castles have been tied to Cistercian cloisters, and there are Cistercian buildings composed of clear geometric volumes and heavy masonry in a simple composition before the reign of Frederick II.

The influence of the Cistercians can also be seen in the interior decorations of many Hohenstaufen buildings, including the capitals and various other decorative and figurative elements necessarily European in character.

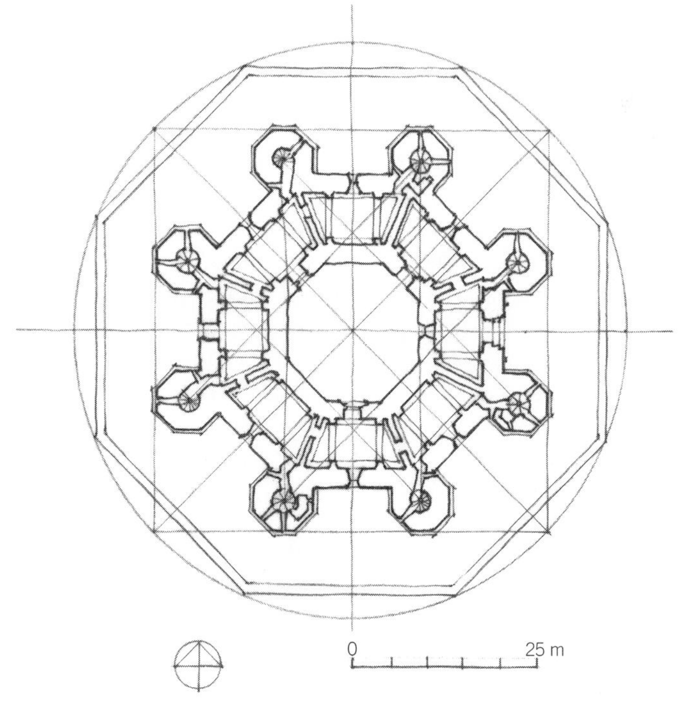


12.59 Plan: Castel del Monte

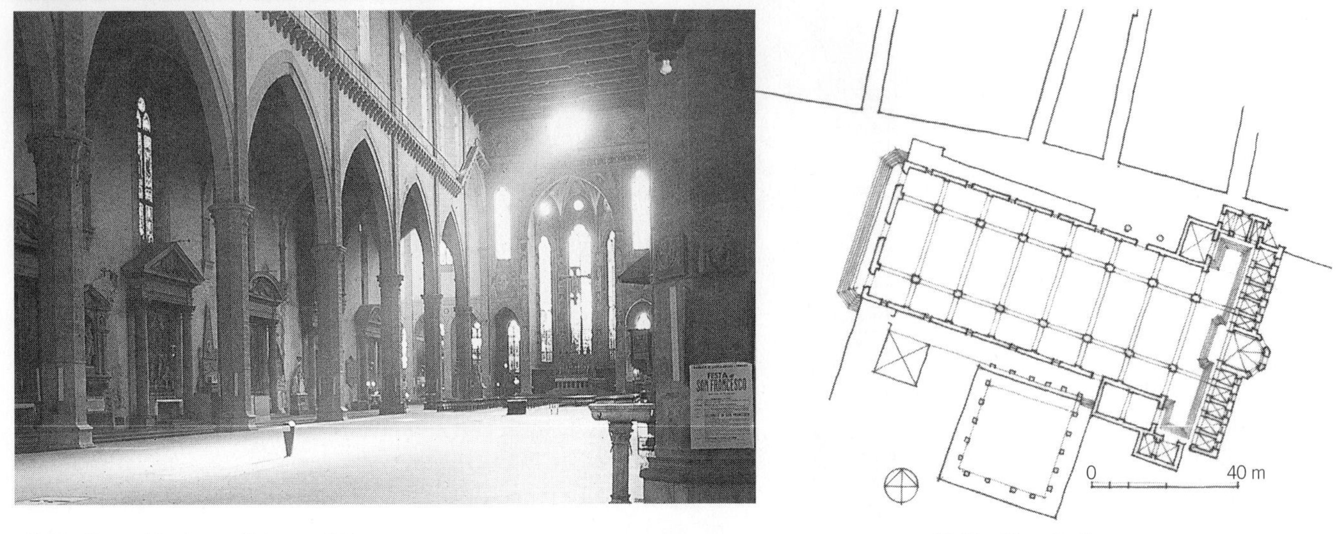


**12.60 Nave of St. Croce, Florence, Italy**

**12.61 Plan: St. Croce**

### Mendicant Orders

At the beginning of the 13th century, the Roman church saw its theological interpretation and hierarchical structure by a series of heresies, several of which revolved around the Gospel, which taught that access to the divine was not through a complicated hierarchy of church officials but through personal emulation of the deeds of Christ. For this reason, this particular reading of the Gospel had been repressed by the church fathers. St. Francis of Assisi was on the verge of being branded just such a heretic in 1206, when he abandoned worldly life, became an ascetic, and preached the Gospel. But Pope Innocent III, eager to bring the poverty sects under his control, allowed St. Francis to preach and informally approved his efforts in 1209 (officially in 1223), hoping to avoid a possible split in the church. Thus was born one of several mendicant orders that radically transformed church history.

In the early Middle Ages, monastics established their monasteries in the quiet isolation of the countryside as a counterpose to what they saw as the decadence of Roman cities. As a result, inhabitants of cities and villages often had to walk long distances to go to a church and were thus remote from the cosmic principles that supposedly united them as members of the Christian faith. The mendicants set up their monasteries in the hearts of cities, and in many places, for the first time, the rituals of religion were within reach of the commoner both physically and conceptually. Mendicant monasteries were not sites of calm reflection but served more as dormitories for the monks who would leave in the morning to perform various duties. The Franciscans became specialists in architecture and construction, helping to build fortification walls and infrastructure. The Dominicans, another mendicant order, were known as doctors, lawyers, and teachers, many becoming well-known philosophers. The Dominicans were also closely associated with the development of Scholasticism during the 13th century and were prominent at the great universities of Europe. In a sense, one can call the 13th century the second Christianization of Europe. If the first was fought in the name of conversion and was largely dynastic in structure, the second was fought in the name of reforming one's inner sensibility and sought popular appeal.

Because mendicants had no money, their churches were usually built for them by citizens. At first many were simple structures or converted barns. By 1233, there were Franciscan communities in every city of northern France. They were soon in every city in Germany and Italy as well. Mendicant churches were by definition simple and austere. The great ebullient forms of the cathedrals were spurned. The Dominican Church in Toulouse (1275–1292), for example, had no flying buttresses and was built entirely of brick. At the Franciscan church of St. Croce (begun in 1294), the architect Arnolfo di Cambio spurned vaulting and recreated the vast emptiness of Constantinian naves in a spare Gothic idiom.

**12.62 Dominican Church, Toulouse, France**

12.63 Entrance facade, Exeter Cathedral

12.64 Fan vaulting, Exeter Cathedral

**Exeter Cathedral**

The transition from the Romanesque to the Early Gothic lies to some degree in the systematization of the nave elevation and in the integration of the nave with rib vaulting. By 1300, architects, increasingly confident in their material, began to explore the decorative qualities inherent in structure, creating styles that historians variously call decorated, perpendicular, or flamboyant Gothic. Scholars have long wondered if the emergence of this new stylistic direction coincided with increased contacts with the East. It is known, for example, that England's Edward I (1272–1307) sent an emissary to Persia. At any rate Exeter Cathedral (1280–1300) shows a decorative unity, and one can say fullness, that earlier cathedrals did not have. The lower facade has become a veritable curtain holding the figures of the saints. With its abstracted crenellations it stands almost as an independent screen in front of the building. On the inside the crisp folded geometries of early 13th-century vaults have been replaced by the rippling shapes of the fan vaulting. The origin of fan vaults is not known.

It would be wrong to see the buildings in this style as belonging to a deterioration of the Gothic style, as is sometimes held. Instead, what we should recognize is the desire to integrate decoration and structure. A factor that contributed to the change was the fashion for more luminous interiors and more frequent use of white or clear glass, which enhanced the subtleties of a building's surface treatment. Furthermore, in England at least, cathedral builders did not aspire to the great heights that were typical of the French churches, preferring instead wider windows, lower buildings, and taller steeples. In other words, early 14th-century English cathedrals tended to have more coherent and yet more dynamic silhouettes. This can be seen at the presbytery of Gloucester Cathedral (ca. 1350). Unlike those parts of the building that were already finished, the new extension, actually a structure unto itself, has huge windows clearly visible on the outside. The buttresses are kept tight to the body of the church. On the interior facing the apse, the lightness and paperiness of the architecture has been so dematerialized that nothing is left except a thin filigree grid of supports.

The new direction received its grandest manifestation at the Cathedral of Milan (begun 1387), a wide building with a vast orchestration of vertical elements in white marble, reaching a crescendo in an octagonal tower that rises almost magically from the center of the building.

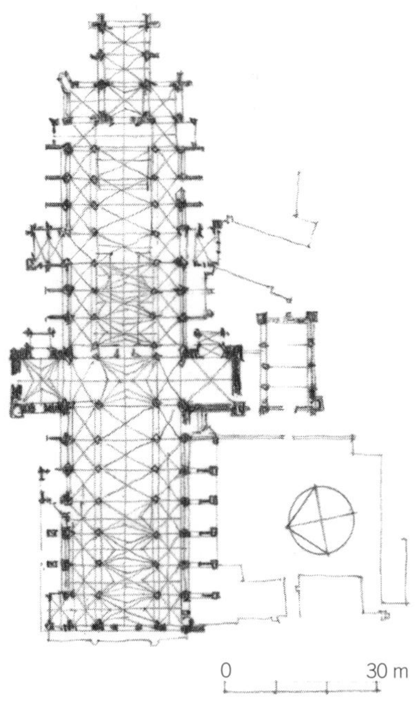


12.65 Plan: Exeter Cathedral, England

12.66 View of Gubbio, Italy

12.67 Town Hall, Gubbio

**Italian Town Halls**

In Italy, in the wake of faltering imperial control, a population explosion and an expansion of markets, the artisans, guild members, and merchants, known collectively as the *popolo*, banded together with men of rank and property, to dominate the political system. The rise of the *popolo* was rapid. In Milan, in 1190, the *popolo*, though the main source of communal revenues, was entitled to only one-fifth of government positions. By 1198, they were the dominant political force in the city. Often the first act of the *popolo* was to pass tax reform, systematize the law courts, and set up control of public monies. Beginning with Pisa in the 1080s, Bologna in 1123, and Florence in 1138, these fledgling city governments laid the groundwork for an urban consciousness that was to become the hallmark of Italian politics for the next two centuries. The formal acceptance of this new arrangement came in the form of the Peace of Constance (1183), a much overlooked treaty that paved the way for the modern notion of republic. With the German emperors no longer in a position to assert their power, they gave the northern Italian cities the right to elect their own consuls, to govern their own lands, and most important, to make their own laws. The cities also boldly chipped away at regalian rights, such as the imperial right of coinage, lucrative salt tax, and taxes from tolls that in earlier times had been collected by the church or by noblemen.

By 1300, 23 cities in northern and central Italy had populations of more than 20,000 and almost all of them claimed a degree of political autonomy. The form of governance varied and was rarely stable, with old aristocratic families still playing important roles. Siena was controlled by an oligarchy; Verona and Padua were ruled by tyrants; Florence was controlled by its leading mercantile families, the Medici in particular. Modena was controlled by the d'Este family. Rivalry between cities led to almost continual strife. Milan, Brescia, and Piacenza were almost continually at war. Pisa was defeated by the Genoese in 1284, but Lucca was subjected by Pisa in 1343. These wars made larger political units impossible, except in the south below Rome, an area dominated by Naples. Central to the new notion of governance was a town hall and a public piazza (*campo*) on which people could assemble. There was often also a special building for the head of the militia and police. For the first time in centuries, perhaps since the days of the Romans, buildings were built and conceived as an ensemble with a public space. The new town halls were coordinated urbanistically with the cathedrals that were being built in most cities. Cathedrals were begun at Pisa in 1063, Modena in 1099, Verona in 1139, and Siena in 1196.

The new governments required that the family towers that were present in the 12th century—and from which families often waged a type of urban warfare against each other—be cut down, thus radically curtailing violence. As a result of these changes, a new urban-institutional profile emerged unlike anything one would have found in France, for example, at the time. It was composed of the cathedral, town hall and piazza, and mendicant churches. The earliest town halls date to the end of the 12th century and are at Brescia, Verona, Modena, Pavia, and Bergamo. These were followed in the 13th century by town halls at Volterra, Todi, Como, Orvieto, Ferrara, Spoleto, Ancona Crema, Bologna, Piacenza, San Gimignano, Pistoia, Siena, Fano, Narni, Assisi, Gubbio, Rimini, and Montepulciano. Most of these town halls followed a simple prototype, a large meeting hall on the upper floor, with large windows facing the piazza and a balcony for the reading of proclamations. The ground floor was often open or had a loggia where silver, gold, or other elite merchants could work under the direct protection and supervision of the city. In the urban complex of Gubbio, the town hall and palace face each other across a piazza that is raised on a high undercroft to dominate the valley below.

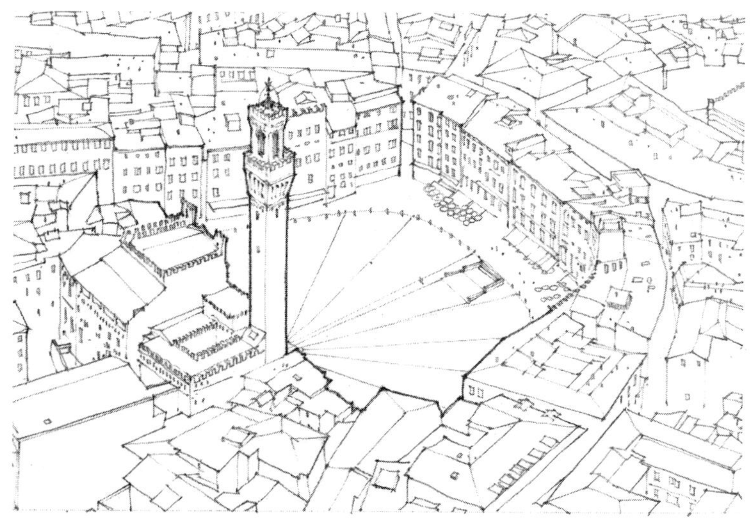

12.68 **Aerial view: Piazza del Campo, Siena, Italy**

12.69 **Palazzo Pubblico, Siena**

### Siena

In the 13th century, one of the most important cities in Italy was Siena, as it controlled the southern Tuscan wool industry and dominated the trade routes between France and Rome. It also maintained Italy's richest pre-Medici banks. Siena's power reached an apotheosis with the defeat of a much superior Florentine army at the battle of Montaperti in 1260. The city then embarked on an unrivaled urban redevelopment. From 1287 to 1355, the city underwrote the completion of a cathedral, a *campo*, and the town hall. The prosperity came to an abrupt halt with the Black Plague, which reached Siena in 1348; by the end of the year, two-thirds of the 100,000 population had died. The city never recovered and froze in its current constellation, constituting a snapshot of a late medieval Italian city. In its earlier days, the city had been divided into at least three factions, each one located on one of three spurs that reached over the hilltop. To unify the city, the *campo* was constructed more or less at the center of the city on unclaimed land that sloped steeply into a ravine. A large terrace was built over the ravine to form the *campo*. At the far end, a town hall was constructed—the Palazzo Publico (1297–1310), with four stories facing the *campo* and with elegantly proportioned reception and councilor rooms, many decorated with frescoes recounting important events in the history of the city.

The curve of the piazza was defined by a continuous row of palace fronts, most dating from the 14th century. At the base of the tower, one finds the Cappella di Piazza (1352–76), built to commemorate the deliverance of the city from the plague. Opposite the town hall is a Loggia della Mercanzia (1417), where merchants could meet. The Duomo (1196–1215) a few blocks away dominates the silhouette. As was common in Italy, areas of towns were organized around mendicant churches. In this case the principal ones are St. Domenico (1226), Sant'Agostino (1258), and St. Francesco (1326–1475).

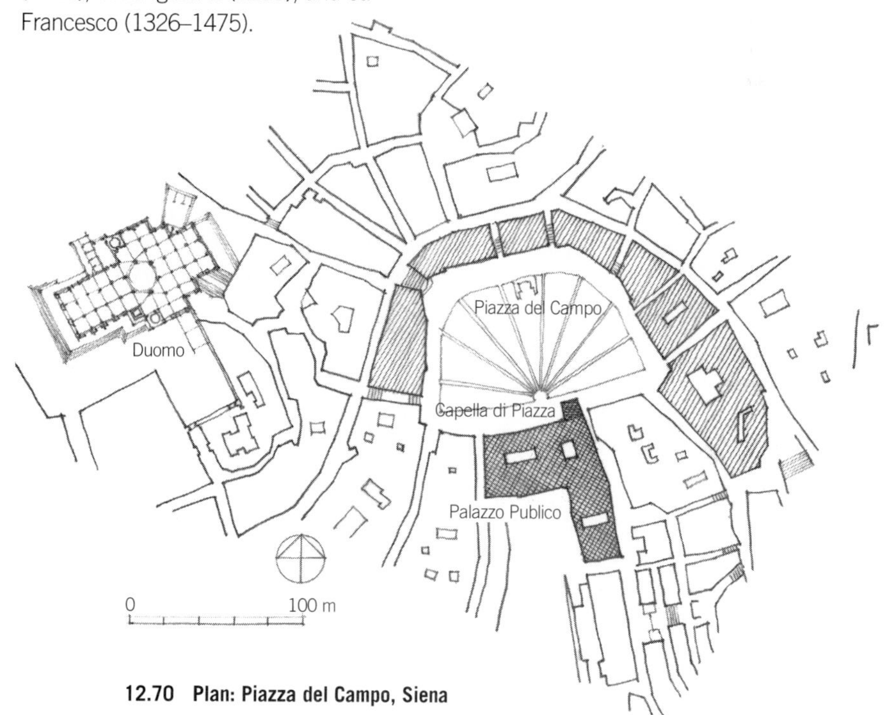


12.70 **Plan: Piazza del Campo, Siena**

12.71 Church of St. Paraskeva Piatnitsa, Novgorod, Russia

## REPUBLIC OF NOVGOROD

A gradual decentralization of power in the mid-11th century in Russia gave way to the development of autonomous cities and monastic complexes. The shift produced a church architecture suited to the tastes of each region. The greatest examples are to be found on the territory of Novgorod and in the area of Vladimir-Suzdal where the monastic clergy, together with leading merchant families, took the main role in the building of churches. The Church of St. Paraskeva Piatnitsa on the Marketplace, built in 1207 on the commercial side of the city and dedicated to the patron of the marketplace, was built on the site of two earlier wooden churches, as noted by William Brumfield in his book *A History of Russian Architecture*. The building shows a departure from the cubic scheme of the earlier churches. The plan is still an inscribed cross, but its arms are emphasized in the north, south, and west by three large covered porches. The porches are reached through a stairway and passageway within the north and west walls. This way, the builders avoided the building of galleries within the main volume of the building and established the model for a new type of structure.

Another important regional center was Suzdalia, located in the northeast of Russia in the upper reaches of the Volga River, in an area that had been colonized by the Slavic tribes in the 10th century. Among these early Suzdalian churches was the Church of the Intercession of the Virgin (1165)—about 1.6 kilometers away from the city of Bogolyubovo—and commissioned by Andrey Bogolyubsky who led a military campaign on both Kiev and Novgorod and who subsequently established his power as the grand prince of all Russia. The Church of the Intercession was built on an artificial hill overlooking the Nerl River. Paved with stones, the hill protects the church from flooding on its marshland site and also accentuates the verticality of the church arrangement. The massing consists of a square base on which the church seems to rest, with a tall drum and dome rising from the center. The elegance of the design is further achieved by retaining a sense of proportion through the use of pilasters on the facade and the high apses that extend to the vaults of the *zakomary* (arched gables).

In 1237 the Mongolians, called Tartars in Russia, invaded the region and destroyed all the chief cities with the exception of Novgorod and Pskow. The Tartars, also known as the Golden Horde, set up a state that lasted until 1480 in south and east Russia. Needless to say, building activity during this period came to a halt, and most of Russia experienced cultural decay and isolation from Europe.

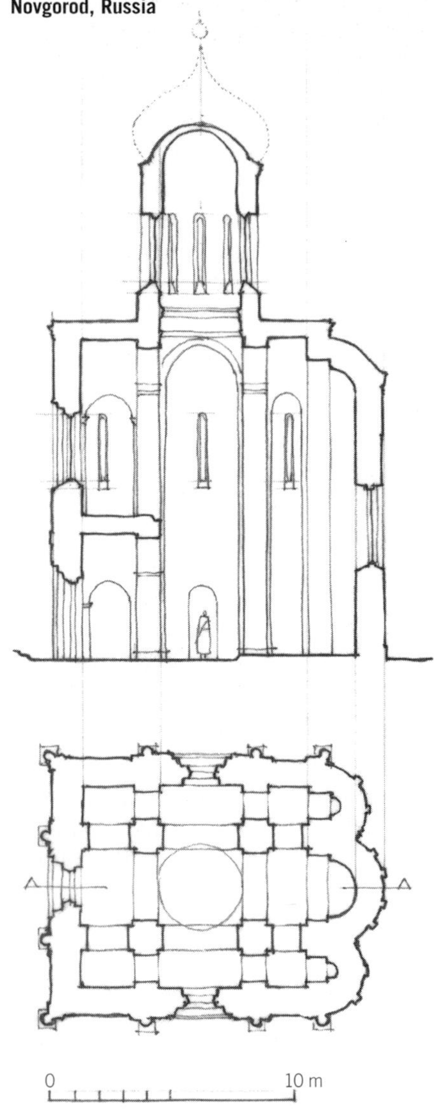


12.72 Plan and section: Church of the Intercession of the Virgin, Suzdalia, Russia

## NASRID SULTANATE

In 1260, the Mongols destroyed Aleppo and Damascus, massacring 50,000 inhabitants. With the Arabian heartland in turmoil, there were only two places in the Islamic world where architecture could develop, in northern India (which would eventually come under the sway of the Mongolian Timurid) and in the Spanish-Moroccan area far removed from Central Asia. It was extraordinarily prosperous, despite the fact that by the 11th century the unity of Spain and Morocco, as established by the Almohads, had dissolved. The Merinids ruled in Africa and the Nasrid Sultanate in Spain. Fez, the capital of the Merinid Empire, became a city of 200,000 people and had some 785 mosques, including the Great Mosque of Fez (1275), modeled on Granada and the Attarin Madrasa (1323–25) with its finely carved capitals and delicate wall treatments. It was in Spain, however, where the spectacular palace of Alhambra (Red City) was laid out (1238) by Mohammed I (1238–73).

Alhambra is first and foremost a fortification, defined by a defensive wall circuit mediated by towers and gates atop a natural acropolis surrounded by rocky terrain and the River Darro guarding the northern side. Alcazaba, the citadel on the westernmost tip of the Alhambra complex, enclosed within an additional triangular wall circuit, certainly exemplifies the military aspects of the complex. It served as an armory and was heavily fortified with a watchtower.

**12.73 Court of the Lions, Alhambra, Granada, Spain**

The palace was entered at the Bab al-Ghadur, renamed by Christians the Gate of the Seven Floors, which was located at the eastern end of the Alhambra's southern wall circuit. A second entrance, Bab al-Shari'a, renamed the Gate of Justice, stands to the western end of the same wall and is noteworthy for the carving of an outstretched hand in the keystone and an inscription above the portal of a key. Various interpretations have been made of these symbols, which are likely intended to legitimize the rulers' claims of authority. The palaces were decorated throughout with colored tile work on the floors and the walls at lower levels and elaborately carved stucco on the walls at higher levels. These designs combine geometric patterns with naturalist floral motifs into a highly developed style of calligraphy wherein Koranic verse and poetry become a visual art. The elaborate forms seen on the palace walls are often stylized script mirrored and transformed into an angular or curvaceous composition.

12.74 **Court of the Myrtles, Alhambra**

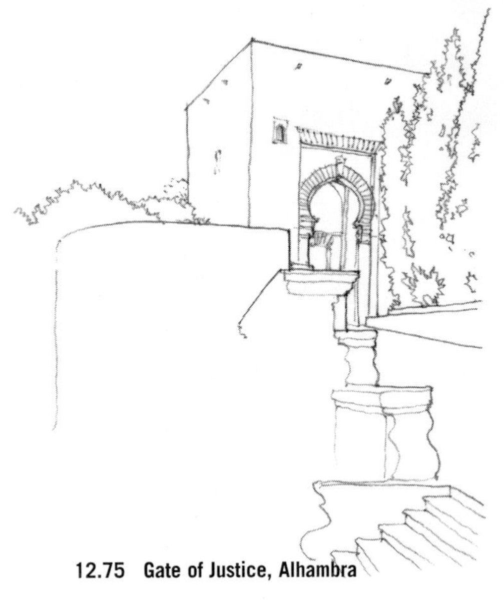

12.75 **Gate of Justice, Alhambra**

Though the original purpose of most rooms in the palace has been lost, the inscriptions on the walls are often the means by which their purpose is extrapolated. The floral motifs, called *ataurique*, either carved or painted, are found throughout the Alhambra, particularly in the *sebka* pattern characteristic of Islamic art. Honeycomb projections from the ceilings that resemble stalactites, known as *muqarnas*, are to be found throughout the complex.

The palaces are arranged to form a dense network of rooms, mediated by airy gardens with pools of water. Water was symbolically important as a signifier of luxury, but it was also connected to both physical and spiritual benefits. The Court of the Lions is much more formal in its layout than the adjacent Palace of Comares. In it, four channels of water, representing the four rivers of Paradise declared in the Koran, extend near-cardinally within the columnar portico surrounding the courtyard and into the palace itself on two sides. The lions, which gives the palace its name, likely come from an earlier palace built on this site and have been inferred by some to demonstrate an intentional recreation of the Temple of Solomon.

The use of materials in the palace is varied. Some of the walls are made of a type of concrete, others of brick. Ashlar stones were used at the gates and to reinforce the corners of the walls. The outside walls were stuccoed and sometimes painted to simulate stone or brick. Columns of marble were sometimes structural and sometimes not. Most of the marble came from the province of Almería and has a white brilliance that gives the columns an elegant and ethereal quality. As in Greek times, the shaft was left plain, but the capital was painted in bright colors. Though relatively similar to classical columns in proportion, the Alhambra columns, like those in the Court of the Lions, have numerous annulets in the necking below the capital.

As is common in Islamic art and architecture, geometries stemming principally from equilateral squares and the rectangular formations produced by the rotation of a radius from the base of the bisecting hypotenuse are commonplace, forming the basis of most of the Alhambra's construction in both plan and elevation. The two-dimensional ornament, particularly evident in the tile work, exemplifies this same fascination with geometries stemming principally from equilateral squares forming eight-pointed stars. The complexity of Islamic geometry in ornamentation is particularly evident in the ceiling of the Throne Room in the Comares Palace, in which all 17 mathematically possible tessellation groups for the mirroring of its patterned ornament are evident. It is worth noting that the full consideration of all 17 possible groups was not expressed mathematically until the 20th century.

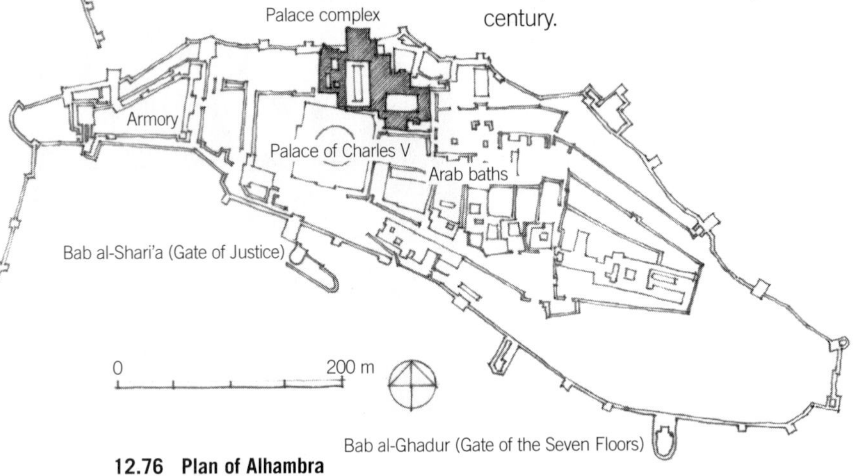


12.76 **Plan of Alhambra**

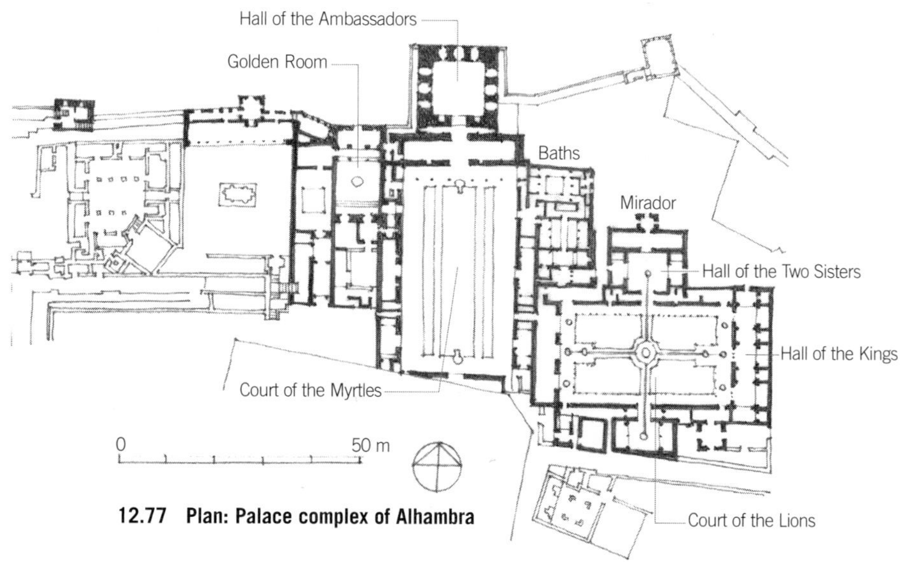


12.77 **Plan: Palace complex of Alhambra**

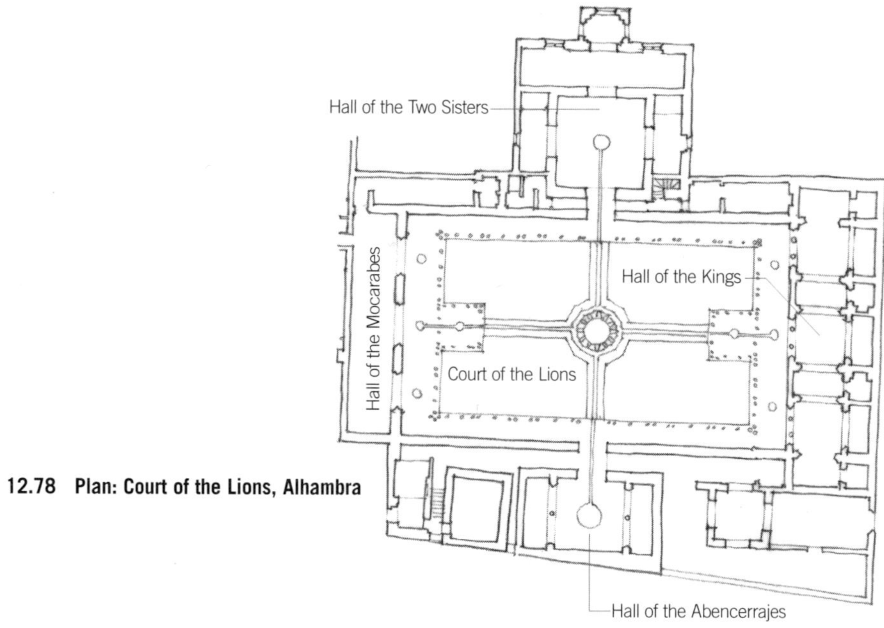


12.78 **Plan: Court of the Lions, Alhambra**

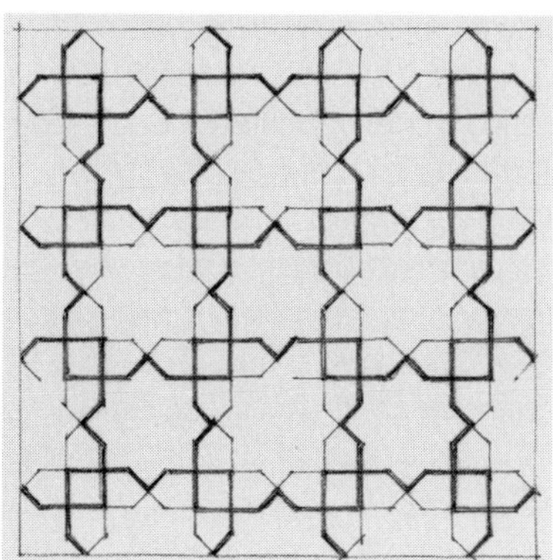

12.79 **Geometric motif, Alhambra**

While the Christians fought relentlessly to expel Islam from the Iberian Peninsula, they also seemed to have had respect for Islamic culture, as they preserved many Islamic buildings with little modification. Signs that the Alhambra remained the residence of the Spanish governors until 1717 are certainly evident, distorting many impressions of the Arabic Alhambra. The Palace of Charles V (designed by architect Pedro Machuca in 1527 and begun in 1533) intentionally sought to set itself off from the surrounding Islamic buildings as a gesture of deference. The mosque of the Alhambra, adjacent to the aforementioned Palace of Charles V, was refashioned as the Church of Santa Maria la Blanca in a Baroque style at approximately the same time. While there are other signs of the Spanish occupation, a handful of Islamic buildings and many other structures added to the complex by the Spanish kings have been razed.

12.80 **Giant Toltec figures at Tula, near Tula de Allende, Mexico**

**TOLTEC EMPIRE**

From the 9th to the late-12th century, the Toltecs, with their capital at Tula, located further north than any previous pre-Columbian capital of Central America, were the defining force of the region. They adopted an aggressively militaristic stance and extensively practiced human sacrifice. No subsequent dynasty failed to claim Toltec ancestry. Their myth of Quetzalcoatl (the Plumed Serpent) was the likely cause of the Aztec abdication to the Spaniard Hernán Cortes in the 16th century, when the latter's arrival was mistaken as the prophesied return of Quetzalcoatl. A Teotihuacán god, Quetzalcoatl was said to have sacrificed himself to enable the birth of the sun. He was also associated with Venus, the morning star, the predictable presence of the late evening or early morning that was linked to the sun's daily sacrifice, that is, its death and rebirth in the form of its passage through the underworld. Quetzalcoatl's story was merged with history. Ce Acatl Topiltzin, one of the earliest Toltec rulers, was driven out of Tula around 1000 by the warrior god Tezatlipoca, who demanded a constant supply of human hearts in sacrifice. Quetzalcoatl vowed to return to Tula from the east in one of his sacred years and take his vengeance, but meanwhile sacrifices to Topiltzin were required.

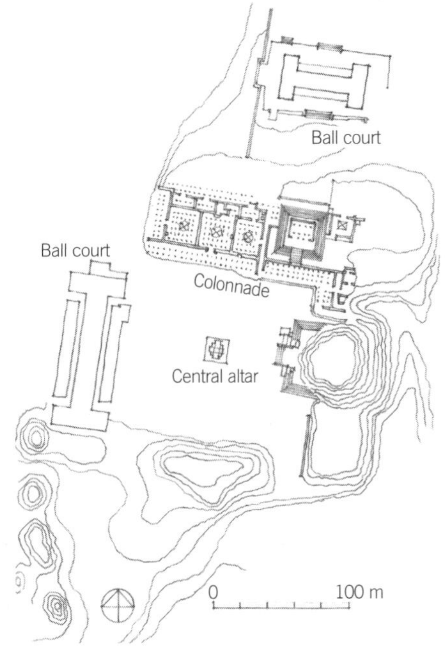


12.81 **Site Plan of Tula**

**Tula**

Tula had a population of about 40,000 by 1100. The Toltec architects designed with established methods, such as placing buildings around large plazas, using many-tiered platforms as bases, building newer structures atop older ones and painting colorful motifs on surfaces of buildings. The main sacred complex sat on a high artificial terrace, with the central plaza occupying an area 100 meters by 100 meters, partly enclosed by pyramids, palaces, and ball courts.

The substructure to Tula's pyramid was covered with thick white stucco, which may have symbolized the underworld. Although the temple at the top of the pyramid was destroyed, the stone columns that supported the roof still remain and were carved with images of Toltec warriors. Unique to Tula was the Coatepantli, or Snake Wall, a freestanding structure that encloses a passageway north of the base of the pyramid. Both sides of this passage consist of identical friezes—top and bottom bands of geometrically stylized snakes framing the central panels and depicting partly skeletonized men apparently being devoured by serpents. Only two other *coatepantlis* are known to exist, those at Tenochtitlán and at Tenayuca, suggesting that they were a feature of Mesoamerica only from 900 to 1500.

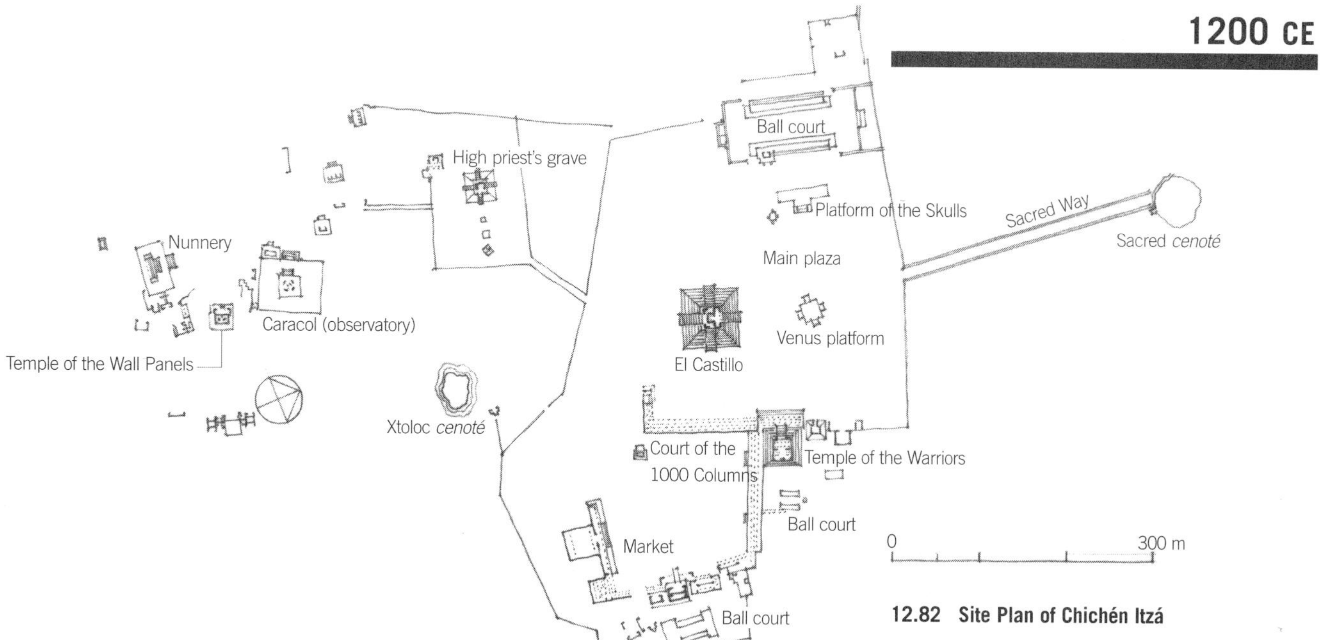


12.82 **Site Plan of Chichén Itzá**

**Chichén Itzá**

The architectural ideas of Tula were reproduced and refined in Chichén Itzá. Occupied at least since the 7th century, Chichén Itzá became the premier city-state of the Yucatan Peninsula in the 12th century. The first phase of its architecture was distinctly Puuc or pre-Toltec. In the 10th century, Chichén Itzá was reoccupied by the Itzá after a brief period of abandonment (probably due to drought), when its architecture became distinctly Toltec in style and conception. Since Chichén Itzá is very far from Tula the mechanics of the influence between the two are still a subject of discussion. The sudden efflorescence of Toltec architecture in Chichén Itzá has led some to speculate that the exiled Toltec ruler, Topiltzin Quetzalcoatl, may have in fact landed in Chichén Itzá, arriving there by sea in the 9th century.

Although sacrifice and a militaristic stance were central to the Itzá, their ceremonial complex is much more about the cosmic calendar and its measurement and meaning. The complex is organized around two *cenotés*.

*Cenoté* is the Mayan word for the deep water-filled sinkholes that the Itzá associated with the underworld. Since the soil and rock in the region is porous and does not hold water well, the eerie underground pools had both practical as well as religious meaning. Of the two in the city, the southern one was used for drinking water, and the northern one, connected to the surface by a ceremonial path, was used for sacrifices. The structures around the southern *cenoté* are the older ones. Here, the main structure is the Caracol, or observatory. A circular structure on a trapezoidal base (that is itself raised on a large rectangular platform), the concentric walls of the Caracol have tiny openings that align to track the movement of various stars and, in particular, Venus.

The northern complex revolves around its central structure, an impressive biaxially symmetrical platform mound, known as the Castillo. The Castillo, as we see it, hides within it an older platform mound, whose temple was accessed by a single stair. The temple, complete with its sacrificial sculpture, the *chacmool*, was carefully interred in the reconstruction or the symbolic "re-skinning" of the platform mound.

12.83 **The Castillo, Chichén Itzá**

12.84 **Ball Court at Chichén Itzá**

12.85 **Temple of the Warriors, Chichén Itzá**

The temple atop the outer layer of the *castillo* has its own *chacmool*. Hearts of sacrificed victims were placed on the belly of the *chacmool*, a Tula invention. The *chacmool* is a sculptural figure lying down facing up, legs drawn in, elbows on ground, with its upper back raised, head turned to a near right angle. He holds a vessel, disk, or plate on his stomach, where offerings may have been placed or sacrifices carried out. Although the complete origins of the chacmool are still undetermined, they proliferated from Tula times. Twelve have been found at Tula, fourteen at Chichén Itzá, and two in the Aztec capital, Tenochtitlán.

Besides being a sacrificial temple, the Castillo also functioned as a solar calendar. It has 91 steps on three sides and 92 steps on the northern side, adding up to 365 steps and depicting the number of days in the solar year. It is almost exactly aligned to the cardinal directions to enable a carefully conceived set of solar events on solstices and equinoxes. The Castillo's best known solar calendric effect occurs on the equinoxes when the balustrade of its northern stairway casts seven isosceles triangles as shadows that link together to form the body and tail of a serpent, with its head sculpted at the base of the stair. This is presumably a depiction of the ceremonial descent of Kukulkan, the Itzá's name for Quetzalcoatl, from the sky.

Kukulkan's descent is also presented in the Temple of the Warriors, marking the western edge of the plaza, a structure remarkably similar to the one in Tula. A forest of pillars, carved with warriors and originally roofed over with perishable materials, forms a long prechamber presumably to restrict access to the main pyramid where the rulers would have held audience. A single flight of stairs leads to a temple whose threshold is marked yet again with a *chacmool* and two columns depicting Kukulkan's descent. In the back is a bench where the king may have sat as captives were sacrificed against the *chacmool*.

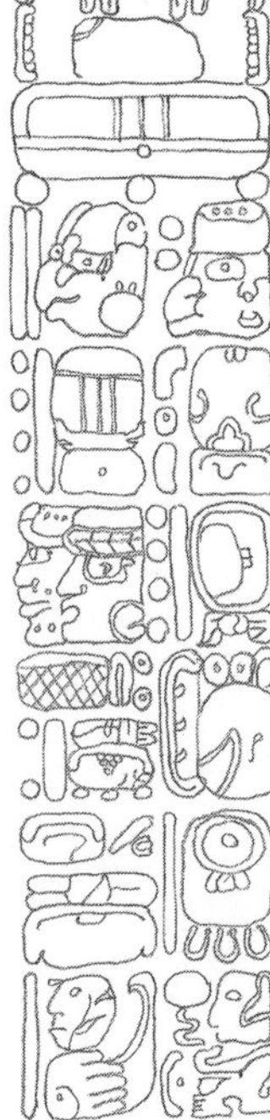

12.86 **Kukulkan's calendric drawings**

On the western edge of the plaza is Chichén Itzá's principal ball court, the largest known in pre-Columbian America. It is 146 meters long and 36 meters wide, with its hoops 8 meters high in the air, making it almost the size of an American football field, or so large that it is hard to imagine that it could have actually been used for sport and may in fact have been intended to depict a more ceremonial ball court of the gods. There are several other smaller ball courts in Chichén Itzá.

In the middle of the plaza, just east of the ball court, was the Tzompantli, with its relief of skulls that was used to display the impaled heads of defeated warriors, as at Tula. At the middle of the northern edge of the plaza lies the entrance to the path that leads to the sacred *cenoté*.

As was the rest of the Yucatan, Chichén Itzá was suddenly abandoned in the middle of the 13th century for reasons that are still not fully understood. However, the Castillo and its path to the sacred *cenoté* continued to be used by local inhabitants until the Spanish Conquest.

# 1400 CE

In 1250, a century after the fall of the Toltecs, Chichén Itzá was abandoned. Nahua-speaking migrant groups from the north, known as the Mexica (pronounced "me-shee-ka"), settled into the central valleys of Mexico, establishing new cities such as Acolhuacan, Tenayuca, Azcapotzalco, and Texcoco. After two centuries of conflict, the Tenochca concluded a military alliance with the Acolhua of Texcoco and the Tepanecs of Tlacopan, forming a powerful bloc linking most of central Mexico. Their capital, witnessed by Cortés, was Tenochtitlán, the site of contemporary Mexico City. To the south the Chimu kingdom controlled the territories of coastal South America in the 13th and 14th centuries. Here they exploited their arid climate to build one of the world's largest cities ever made from adobe. In the middle of the 15th century the Chimu were displaced by upstart rulers from the highlands of Peru, the Incas, with their capital in Cuzco. In their short life before they fell to the Spanish, the Incas dominated the trade routes of coastal South America, constructed long bridges with rope, and built roads and cities with some of the most intricate and precise random rubble masonry ever seen in history.

The year 1400 marks more or less the end of the great conquests from the Russian steppes. The great arrows on the maps showing the Gauls, the Huns, the Turks, the Mongolians, and numerous other tribes from the steppes are no longer there; the Eurasian world for the first time in 1000 years was not beset by migratory invaders. The migrational period from 400 to 1400 was so profound that its impact can be found in every corner of Eurasia, from North Africa and England to India and China. The only spots that were outside its sphere of direct influence were southern India and Indonesia. The impact of those invasions were not all negative, for whether it was Liao tribes in China, who adopted Chinese ways, or the Huns in eastern Europe, who converted to Christianity, these tribes contributed much to the civilizational and aesthetical imperatives that were already under way. One of the principal characteristics of this period is the emergence of a new wave of global urbanism. In fact, many of the cities that today are the center of much of our preservation efforts date from this period. In Korea, Seoul was being transformed into a great and impressive capital. In China, Beijing's Forbidden City was being built. Islam, of course, was also rebounding and expressing its wealth in mosques and schools and mausoleums from Egypt to northern India. Samarkand, the capital of Timurid, was expanded and was perhaps the leading economic city of the world. Close by was the bustling metropolis of Bukhara, the Shaybanid capital. Further to the east, the Mamluks were making considerable improvements to the city of Cairo.

It is a great irony that with the increased trade in the 14th century, there came the Black Plague, killing hundreds of thousands worldwide and placing a damper on European economic progress. Nonetheless, by the middle of the 15th century enough of a recovery had been made that the true face of the new post-steppe-invasion era could be seen.

The Italian Renaissance is unthinkable without understanding the new position of the Italians in the global economy. With the restoration of trade links to China, Italy, with its energetic mercantile city-states, was excellently positioned to link the great trade routes ending in the Levant. The Italians may not have had power in an overt way, for the Holy Roman Empire was still in the north, but by investing their newly found wealth in art and learning, they became the dominant cultural force in Europe. Venice, the principal port of international trade, minted its own coins and secured its position as the world's leading gold market. Florence also began to assert itself with the Medicis becoming the leading bankers in Europe. While much building activity was going on in Florence and Venice, London, Aachen, and Paris were falling into disrepair.

## 1400 CE

▲ **Chan Chan**
ca. 1000–1400

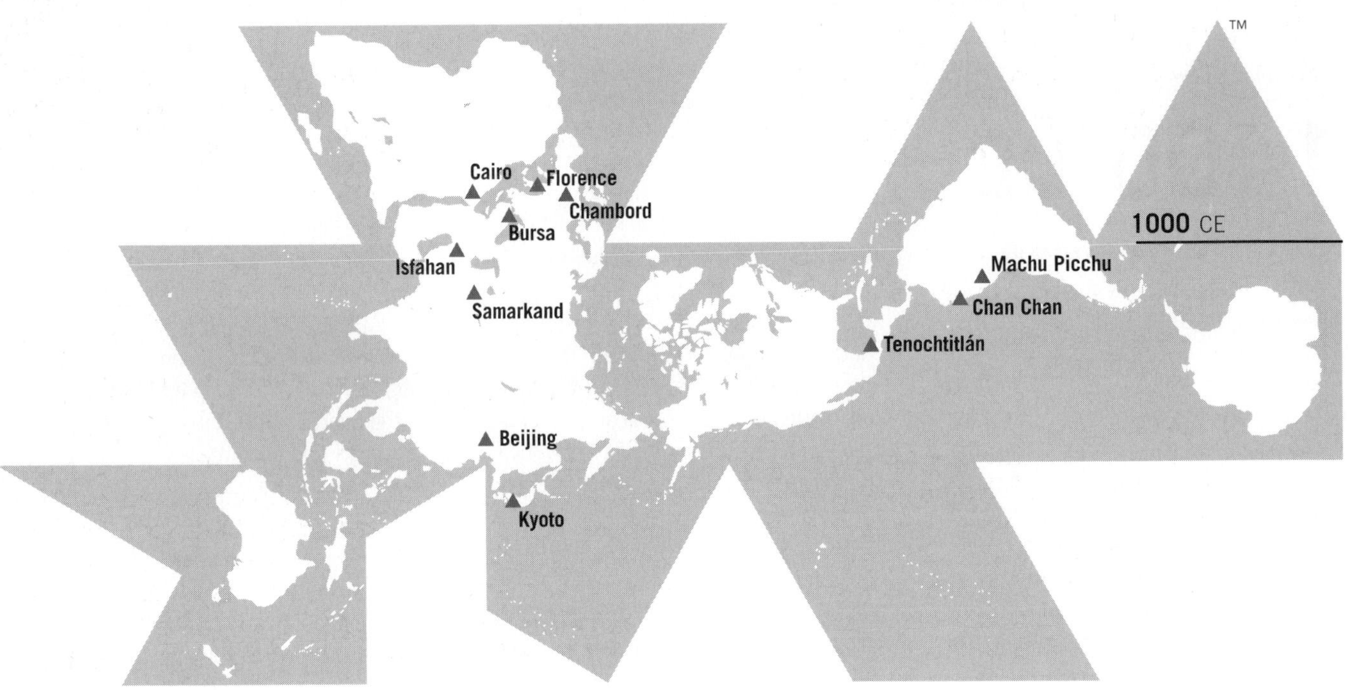

Aztec State
ca. 1350–1521

▲ **Tenochtitlán**
ca. 1325–1521

⦿ 1492
Columbus arrives in America

Inca Empire
ca. 1200–1532

Conquest Period
1500–1542

▲ **Cuzco**
15th century

▲ **Machu Picchu**
15th–16th century

China: Yuan Dynasty
1279–1368

Ming Dynasty
1368–1644

▲ **Forbidden City**
1420–1908

Japan: Kamakura Period
1185–1333

Nanbokucho Period
1336–1392

Muromachi Period
1392–1573

▲ **Kinkakuji**
1397

▲ **Ginkakuji**
1483–90

**1200** CE — **1400** CE — **1600** CE

Black Plague in China
1330s

Black Plague in Western Asia and Europe
1346–1351

▲ **Bibi Khanum Friday Mosque**
1339–1404

Timurid Dynasty
ca. 1370–1507

Delhi Sultanate
1210–1526

▲ **Jami Masjid at Gulbarga**
1367

▲ **Jami Masjid of Ahmedabad**
1423

Ottoman Empire
1281–1923

▲ **Topkapi Palace**
Begun ca. 1459

▲ **Beyazit Complex**
completed 1488

Egypt: Mamluk Sultanate
1260–1517

▲ **Complex of Sultan Hasan**
1356–63

▲ **Mausoleum Complex of Sultan Qaitbay**
1472–4

Italy: Papal and Autonomous City-states
12th century–1870

▲ **Cathedral of Florence**
Begun 1294

▲ **Medici Palace**
1444–64

▲ **St. Peter's Basilica**
Begun 1506

▲ **Rucellai Palace**
1446–50

▲ **St. Andrea at Mantua**
1472–94

France: Valois Rule
1328–1589

▲ **Château Chambord**
Begun 1519

# 1400 CE

To keep Tlaloc satisfied, human sacrifices were performed in front of the temple of Huitzilopochtili and the bodies thrown down the stairs, in a reenactment and continuation of the original sacrifice. The still-beating hearts were offered to Tlaloc on the reclining figure of *Chacmool*, resealing the alliance that enabled the cosmic order to be maintained.

**13.1 Tlaloc, Mexica god of rain and fertility**

## TENOCHTITLÁN

The Mexica capital Tenochtitlán was described in detail by Hernán Cortés before he destroyed it; his drawing of the city was presented to the Spanish king and widely circulated in Europe, thanks to the printing press. Cortés told of a city of 200,000 inhabitants on an island in the middle of a lake, connected by causeways to the shore. Gigantic stone towers dominated the city's center, at the intersection of the causeways.

The Mexica modeled themselves after the Toltecs and claimed descent from Teotihuacán. Although they often left conquered states free to govern themselves, they demanded heavy tributes and military support like a protocolonial ruler to maintain their own civilizational supremacy. Their Toltec-inspired rituals required extensive human sacrifice, resulting in constant warfare. In 1487, following an enlargement of the main temples, more than 20,000 prisoners of war were reportedly sacrificed in Tenochtitlán.

Tenochtitlán was founded in 1325 in a swampy area near the western edge of Lake Texcoco. According to Mexica mythology, they picked the site when an eagle with a snake in its claws settled there—an image that is still a part of Mexico's national emblem. In fact, the Mexica were likely forced to live on this undesirable land by the Tepanecs, another Nahua group, to whom the Mexica were first subservient but whom they eventually conquered. The Mexica drained the swampy 10-square-kilometer lake and built it into a gridded island city that was linked to additional settlements on the mainland by three raised causeways. A network of streets and canals, like those of contemporary Lin'an in China and Venice in Italy, teemed with boats transporting goods and people. Ceremonial art and luxury goods of the finest quality were traded and sold in Tlateloco, its central market. Two aqueducts brought fresh water into the city.

At Tenochtitlán's ceremonial center were the main temple—consisting of two stepped pyramids rising side by side on a huge platform and painted in bright red and blue—and palaces painted a dazzling white. Not far was the pyramid of Echecatl, the god of war. Ceremonial and governmental buildings were also in the vicinity, as well as a school for the sons of the nobility and priests, a warrior's council, a ball court, an intimidating *tzompantli* (or skull rack) for displaying the severed heads of the sacrificed, and several other pyramids and temples. A protective enclosure sealed the area.

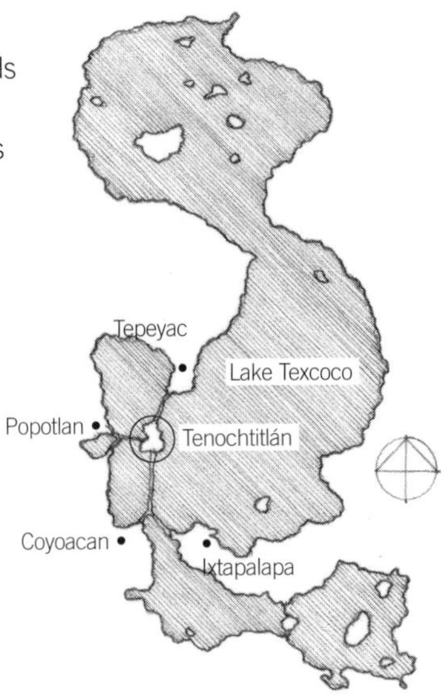


**13.2 Location of Tenochtitlán on Lake Texcoco, Mexico**

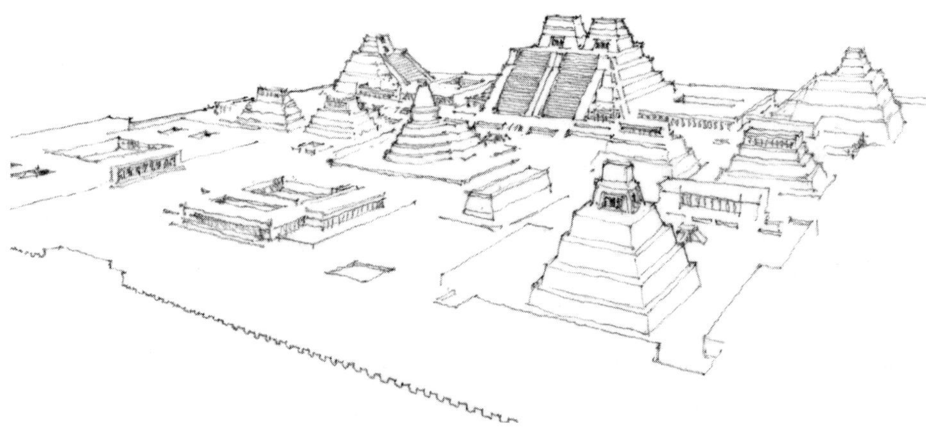

13.3 Pictorial view of the Great Temple of Tenochtitlán, Mexico City

Although a church was built on its foundations, we have detailed descriptions of the main temple, known today as Templo Mayor. Four roads converged at the temple, which sat on a vast base, representing the terrestrial earth. Large incense braziers, with serpent heads and cauldrons on all four sides, were set up to receive offerings. From its base, the temple rose in four platforms, representative of the celestial levels of the cosmos, until it reached the top level, where there were two temples dedicated to Tlaloc and Huitzilopochtili. Two parallel stairs led separately up to the temples, to the summit. Huitzilopochtili, whose temple was to the south, was the Mayan warrior god who fought his brother Centzon Huitznahua and his sister Coyolyauhqui immediately after birth. He defeated them and threw their dismembered bodies down the mountain, a sacrifice marked by a round tablet at the foot of the stairs.

Between 1325 and 1521, Templo Mayor was reconstructed seven times, with the older temple encased intact within each new larger building. Of all these, the second building has survived intact, including its two temples, complete with the stone to which the prisoners were tied before being sacrificed.

Like their predecessors, the Mexica were dedicated observers of the sun, the stars, the cycles of nature, the passing of the seasons, and the death of plant and animal life. And like their predecessors, their architecture and their rituals were intended to maintain the integrity of the cosmic order. The science of observation was certainly very sophisticated, though it is still incompletely understood. Templo mayor was constructed, however, so that it points about seven degrees south of east and that on the equinoxes, the sun rises exactly between the temples of Tlaloc and Huitzilopochtili. A monolithic Calendar Stone, which is 1.2 meters thick, 3.6 meters in diameter, and weighing over 24 tons, was found in 1790 under the main square. On its face is a representation of the sun god.

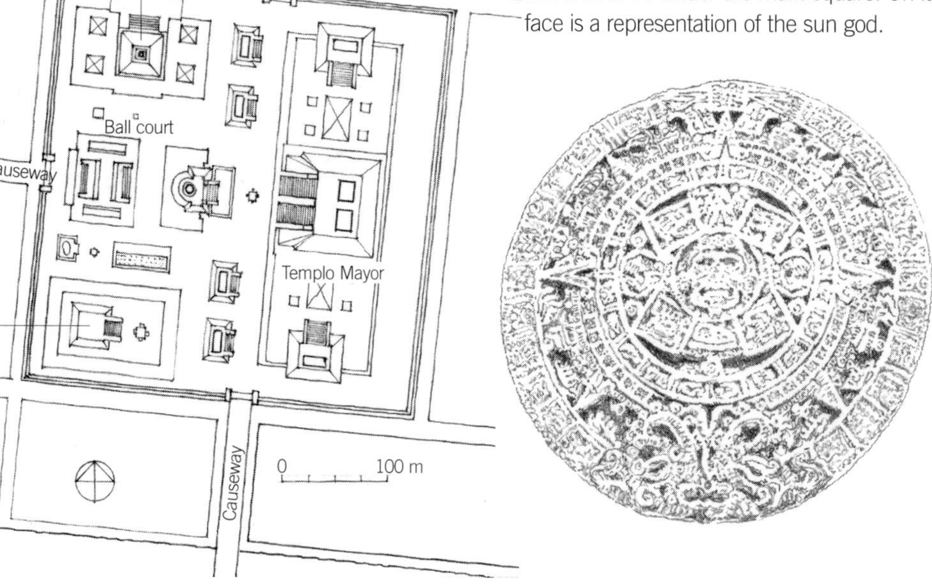


13.4 Plan: Great Temple of Tenochtitlán

13.5 Calendar Stone from Tenochtitlán

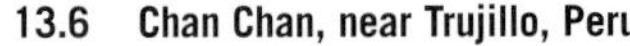

13.6 **Chan Chan, near Trujillo, Peru**

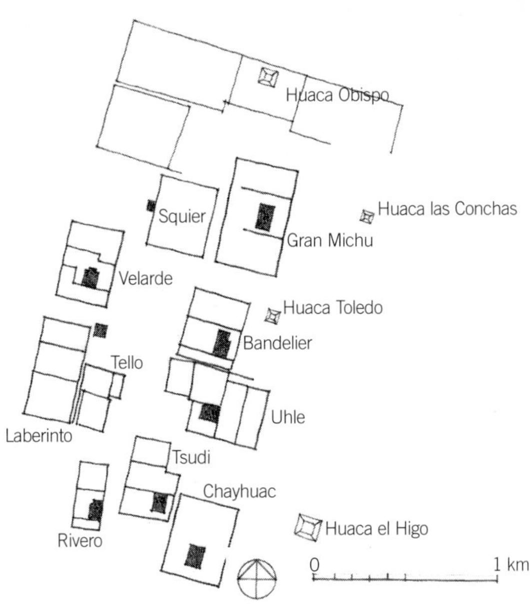


13.7 **Schematic plan showing the citadels of Chan Chan**

### Chimu: Chan Chan

In the coastal valleys of northern Peru, the collapse of the Wari kingdom around 1000 led to the emergence of the Chimu (850–1470). The Wari or Huari (750–1000) had built large rectangular enclosures laid out in a strict grid patterns in their cities, such as Pikillaqta and Jincamocco. The Chimu (also called the Chimor) eventually came to control the entire northern coast of Peru from the modern border of Ecuador to Lima. Like the Moche before them, they took advantage of the extreme aridity of the land to build elaborate structures out of adobe and sun-dried mud bricks. They were also extremely skilled metal workers. At the junction of the Moche and Chicama valleys, where Chan Chan was located, high quality mud and no rain made adobe a perfect building material. Unlike their contemporaries in North America, the Chimu did not confine their adobe technique to pyramids and mounds. The Chimu capital, Chan Chan, spread out across a large plain of the coastal desert, which was made arable by extensive irrigation. It covered 20 square kilometers and at its height is estimated to have had about 25,000 inhabitants.

A rectilinear plaza, 70 meters square and originally bound by low walls, defined Chan Chan's ceremonial center. Around it were about ten rectangular palace compounds. Each successive Chimu king, by custom, started a new family line and built a new self-contained complex, thereby enabling the older generations to continue in their place, while establishing his own identity. The palaces were all enclosed by a high adobe wall and had similar layouts. In the middle was a burial ground. Around it, large and small courts organized the spaces into minineighborhoods, complete with streets, residential quarters, temples, and irrigated gardens. Its main streets were 4 to 6 meters wide. The more important rooms were ornamented with low-relief mud friezes, depicting fish, birds, human and animal figures, and geometric motifs.

To the west and south of Chan Chan lived the poorer people; their houses were smaller and made from cruder adobe. To the north and east lay 14 pyramidal burial mounds, most of which have been extensively quarried for treasure. The largest of these was 180 meters square at its base and 45 meters high. Many of the pyramids were decorated with mud friezes.

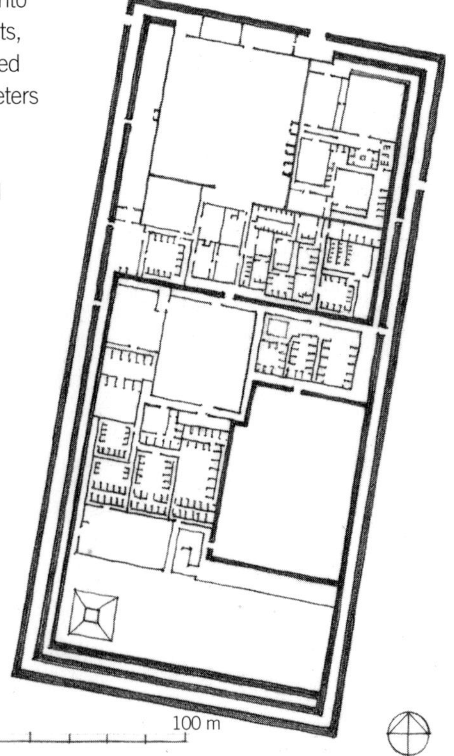

13.8 **Plan of the Rivero citadel at Chan Chan**

0 100 m

13.9 **Aerial view of Cuzco, Peru**

## INCAS

About 1460, the Chimu were defeated and Chan Chan pillaged by the Incan armies. Not much is known of the prehistory of the Incas, except that Pachakuti, who ascended the Incan throne in 1438, built an empire that brought the area of present-day Peru, Bolivia, northern Argentina, Chile, and Ecuador under Inca control. The Inca traded up and down the South American west coast, building stone roads and ingenious rope bridges to facilitate travel. Although they did not use numbers, the Inca developed sophisticated techniques of counting and calculating, using knots on strings. The versatile llama was their solitary beast of burden.

Cuzco, the Inca capital, was located in the Peruvian highlands. Four major roads of the empire terminated in the center, at the plaza of Cusipata. Under Pachakuti, Cuzco was transformed from a village of clay and straw into a city of stone. Wedged between the Tullumayo and the Huatanay Rivers, Cuzco's plan forms the body of a puma or jaguar. The head was represented by the fortress, the heart by the central plaza, and the tail by the confluence of the two canalized rivers. Further south another river, the Chunchulmayo, was called the "gut river," or the belly of the puma.

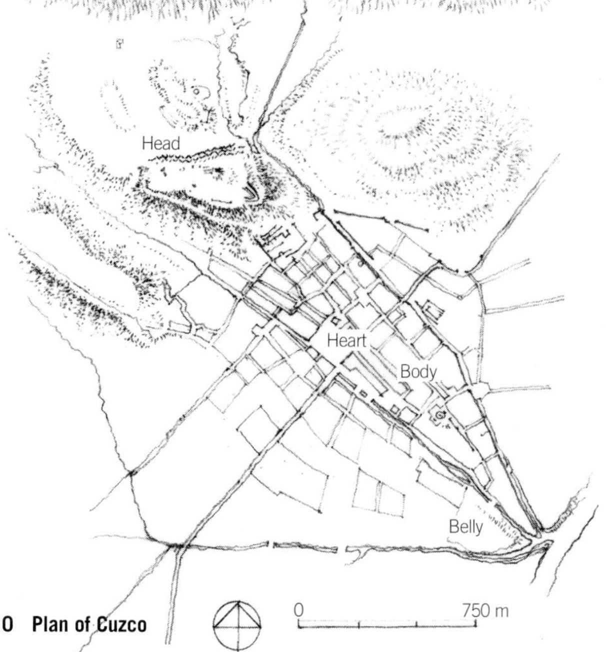


13.10 **Plan of Cuzco**

The plaza of Cusipata was surrounded by the main civic structure of Cuzco, the palaces, three temples, called *kallankas*, dedicated to the Sun (Qorinkancha), the Creator (Kiswarkancha), and the Thunder (Pucamarka). The Spanish city was built directly on the ruins of the Incan footprint so that the large blocks of stones that were cut to fit each other perfectly to make the palaces can still be viewed at the street level in Cuzco.

Cuzco itself seems to have had no defensive wall, but a few miles away on a hill there is an impressive structure, Sacsayuaman, that is presumed to be a fortress. It could also have been a temple to the sun, a water reservoir, or all of the above. It has three platforms, one on top of the other, followed by a triple row of toothed walls made from gigantic blocks of granite. Built into the natural contours, Sacsayuaman's walls were titanic and precise works of engineering. Some of their granite blocks weighed up to 200 tons and had to be hauled reasonable distances. Each polygonal block was individually shaped on site to fit absolutely exactly into neighbors. One cannot slip a razor blade into the joints. Additionally, water was drained with great care, with individual stones being shaped and aligned to create a ceremonial series of water spouts and channels.

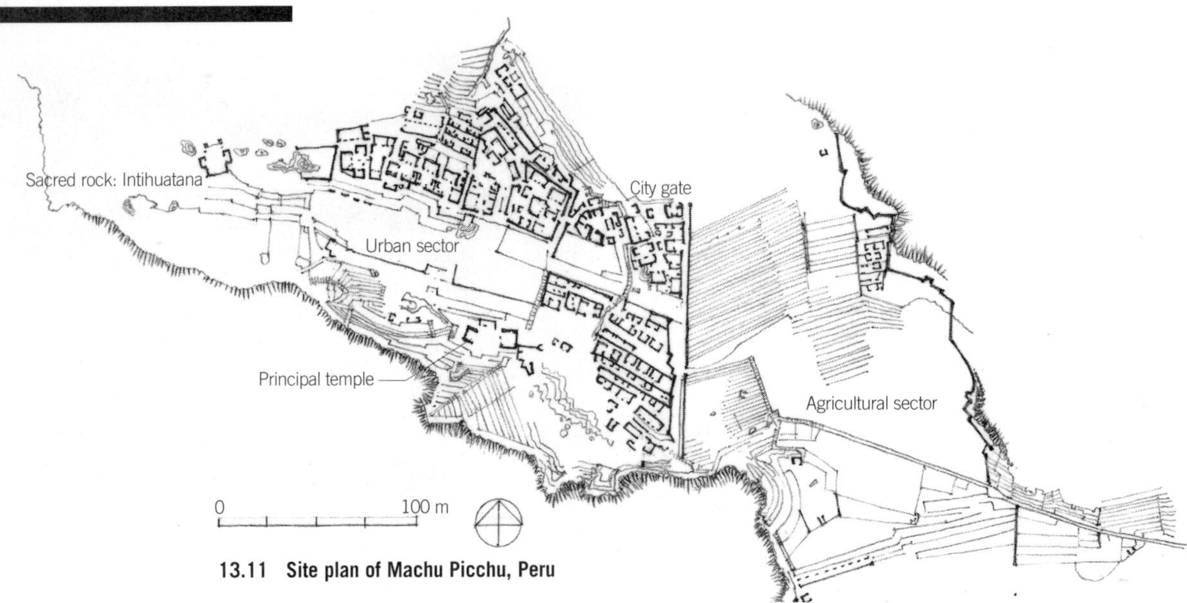


**13.11 Site plan of Machu Picchu, Peru**

### Machu Picchu

Machu Picchu is located between two steep peaks, 2750 meters above a gorge carved by the river Urubamba. It is the only Incan settlement to have survived intact, having been completely missed by the Spaniards. Seventy kilometers northwest of Cuzco, and discovered by Hiram Bingham in 1911, it was probably inhabited late into the 16th century, when it was gradually abandoned and forgotten. Some 200 buildings arranged on a series of parallel terraces on both sides of a central plaza constitute the core of the settlement. It is small; only about 1000 people could have lived there. Access to the site was difficult; it was a long trek up the steep gorges and entry was possible only from one carefully guarded check point. Because it was a magnificent site for solar and stellar observation, some have argued that the city was a royal retreat or perhaps even a special temple reserved for the elite.

The genius of Machu Picchu lies in the terracing and partitioning of the site, which fills a roughly east-west lying saddle between the two peaks. The saddle rises sharply in the south, and after a crest and a short flat plain, it slopes gently down toward the north and the east. It resembles a wave, with a stable spot at its precarious top. To shore up the land and to create spaces to build on, the Incan planners constructed terraces carefully, following the contours. At the eastern end, there is a sector of terraces with a complex network of irrigation channels that is assumed to have been used for cultivation.

**13.12 Incan stonework, Machu Picchu**

A long central plaza, gently terracing down toward the east, sets the stage. On either side of this plaza, distributed by a complex network of streets and stairs, lie the main buildings. Most of these are single-room dwellings clustered around courts, when possible, but usually arranged along narrow pathways defined by the terrace widths. They are all made from the characteristic Incan finely-fitted stone masonry, with wedge-shaped windows, monolithic lintels, and preconceived water drainage and harvesting systems. The granite used in the construction was quarried locally. Gable ends testify to perishable roofs long gone. There is, however, no evidence of any adobe construction, suggesting the highly elite and ceremonial function of the city. Nestled within this network are some surprising anomalies: a semicircular turretlike structure unexpectedly abuts the residential fabric and a series of baths line the central north-south pathway.

13.13 Machu Picchu, as it stands today

The high southwestern edge of the saddle is reserved for a temple, accessed by a long stair from the east. At the foot of the stair lies what is assumed to be a temple with three C-shaped rooms looking into a central court. At the top of the stair lies the main temple, the sacred center, dedicated to the sun. Three steps into an antechamber brings one to the final terrace, at the center of which lies a huge granite monolith known simply as the Intihuatana, or the "hitching post of the sun." The Intihuatana stone is something of a miniature Machu Picchu, with a series of small "terraces" culminating in a dramatic outcrop, resembling the peak just beyond. Intihuatana stones are believed to have once been dispersed throughout the Incan world, but they were destroyed by the Spanish who considered them idolatrous. Their exact meaning is uncertain, but they were likely miniaturized replicas of a sacred peak from which the sun could be imagined to be hitched by a rope, enabling its circular journey through the upper and lower worlds. Perhaps Machu Picchu's peaks were as close as the Incans thought they could get to that sacred peak.

13.14 Close-up of the urban sector of Machu Picchu

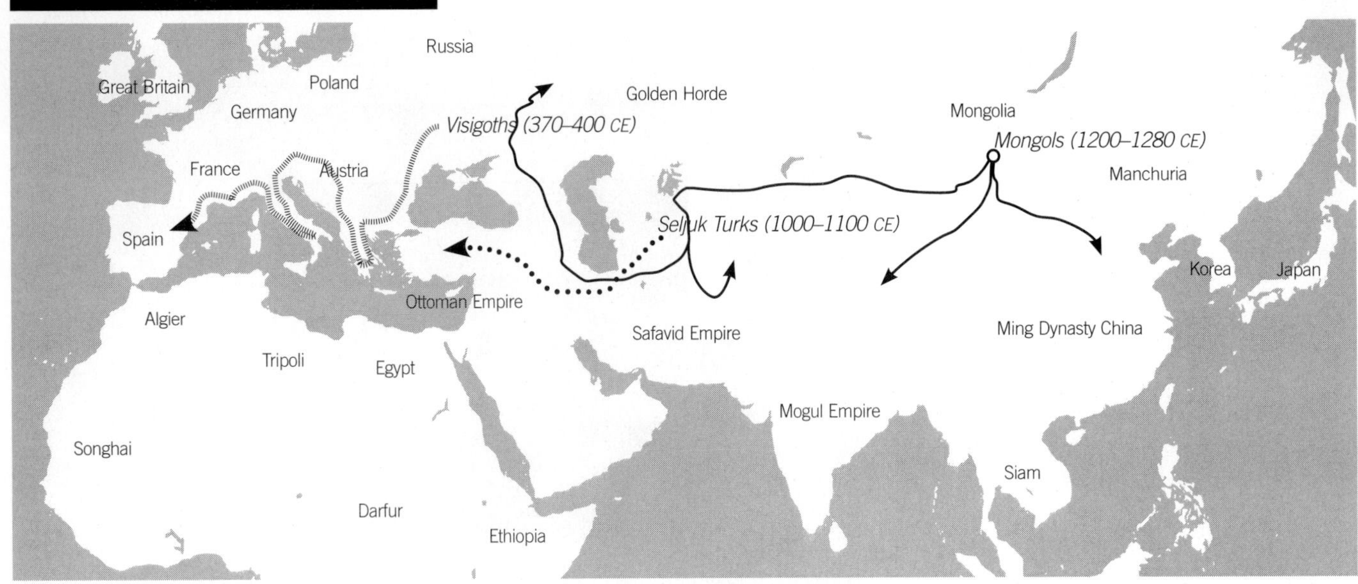


## NOMADIC INVADERS

From the 2nd to the 14th centuries Eurasian history was marked by continual flows of humanity—first from Germany eastward, then from the Russian steppe, and finally from Mongolia. They were fierce fighters all; the famous Greek sculpture the *Dying Gaul* is just as much a testament to the difficulties the Greeks were facing against invaders from the north as to the fierceness of those invaders. At first, the great world powers, the Romans and the Chinese, erected barriers. The Limes in Germany (from which the English word "limit" derives) is contemporaneous with the beginnings of the more famous Great Wall of China. All these walls, of course, did not hold. The reason for the expansions out of the Russian and Central Asian steppe are not clear. Climactic changes, overpopulation, or internal stresses and desire for better land, all figured in. Not all of the tribes left for the same purpose, and not all were simply out to plunder. The Visigoths were particularly cruel in their zigzag route through Europe to Spain, but the Lombards who settled in northern Italy eventually created a vibrant culture, and the Franks who settled in France founded a dynasty out of which rose the likes of Charlemagne on whose shoulders rested the future of Europe. If some of the first waves were particularly destructive, successive invaders settled and adopted local ways.

The Normans negotiated with the Franks to settle in northern France and eventually took over England. The Hungars, who had been a thorn in the side of the Romans, eventually made their peace with the Byzantine rulers and converted to Christianity. It was not only to the west that peoples moved. The Hephthalites or the White Huns (the color refers to how the Mongolians divided geographical regions) invaded Iran in the 5th century, proceeding into India where they remained a distinct group. They were the first of several waves culminating with the Seljuk Turks who swept southward to dominate a belt of territory from Anatolia to western Iran. The greatest explosion out of the northeast was from the Mongolians, who at their height around 1260 constituted an empire so vast that it defies the imagination even today. They intermarried and ruled, adopting Christianity to the west, Islam to the south, and Buddhism in China. Their world was eventually transformed by the Timurid, descendants of the Mongols, who ruled from Samarkand, and created an empire that ranged from northern Syria to western China.

Though the migratory waves dissipated by the 15th century, their impact was far from negligible. The rulers of the Shaybanid empire in Central Asia, the Safavid empire in Iran, and the Indian Moghul empire were all descendants from the Timurid rulers, and they produced a regional order that was amazingly stable for over 200 years, leading to a flowering of Islamic civilization in all three empires. Eventually, in China itself, the Mongol example was repeated by the Manchus (from Manchuria) in the 17th century, who established China's longest-lasting dynasty. The Manchu Qing self-consciously modeled themselves on the Mongols, conceiving a multiethnic and pluralistic empire that withstood the great colonial invasions of Europe until the early 20th century.

It could be argued that as powerful as were the early civilizations in Mesopotamia, India, China, and the Mediterranean, the story of that world, from about 200 CE onward, became increasingly associated with a different type of civilizational drive, one that at first seemed to be everything but civilizational. The Chinese, Romans, and Persians alike looked with horror at the migratory people from the north and embedded negative attributes of rootlessness and barbarism in their image of them, even though not a few of the tribes possessed well-developed agricultural skills and legal systems.

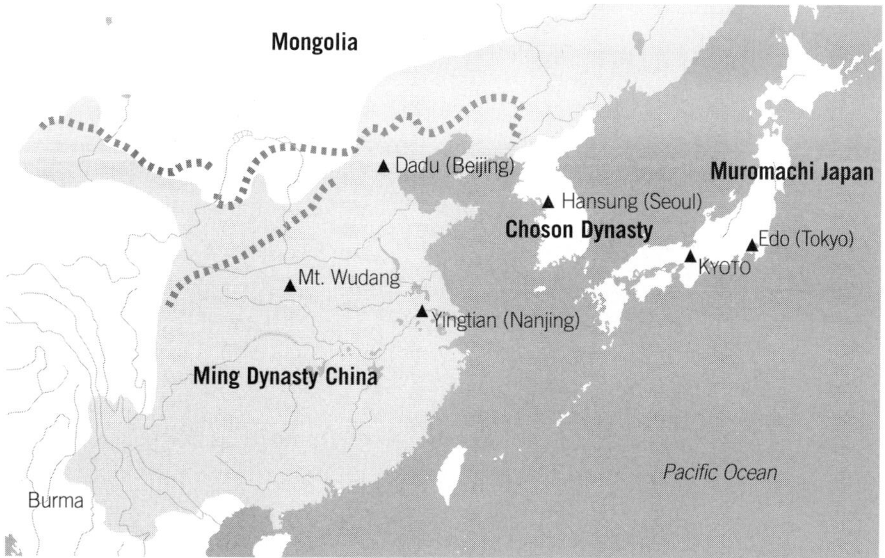


**MING DYNASTY CHINA**

In 1368, Zhu Yuanzhang defeated the last Yuan emperor and established the Ming ("bright" in Chinese) Dynasty. The third Ming emperor Zhu di (the Yongle emperor; r. 1403–24), moved the capital to Dadu, but renamed it Beijing, meaning Northern Peace. The Ming (1368–1644) were Han Chinese and considered the Mongolian Yuan foreign barbarians and so were eager to erase as many traces of Mongolian rule as possible. They exerted tight controls on its citizens and reintroduced Confucian practices.

But the Ming also continued the modernizing programs of the Yuan, expanded urban centers, and maintained the architectural traditions and construction styles. The bracketing system, however, had become by this time a largely ornamental device, as structural innovations enabled large roof spans to be supported without the old brackets. Techniques in glazing evolved significantly, enabling buildings such as pagodas, gateways, arches, and screen wall facades to be decorated with a more colorful effect. The elaborate carvings on doors, windows, and wall facings that the Ming are renowned for originated during Yuan rule, as seen, for example, in carvings on structures such as the archway at Juyongguan.

**Mount Wudang**

The Yongle emperor believed that his ascent to the throne had been aided by Zhenwu, a Daoist mythical warrior, so in 1412 he dispatched 300,000 workers to Mt. Wudang, Hubei, where the Daoists believe that Zhenwu attained immortality. Mt. Wudang is in an area of precipitous cliffs, with dramatic views, that is covered in mist year-round. Its thick forest cover is filled with caves, springs and grottoes. Zhu di's workers built a 60-kilometer long pilgrimage path in stone that winds its way up to the tallest peak, aided by 39 delicately constructed bridges. Along the way are 9 temple complexes, 2 monasteries, and 36 hermitages, all built into the natural contours of the land, often perched over and along cliffs. The Purple Empyrean Hall was the main hall of Mt. Wudang's largest monastery. Two terraces (only one short of the Forbidden City's Hall of Supreme Harmony) elevate the elegant double-eaved, hip-and-gable, five-bay hall. One of the main martial arts schools of China, Wudang kung fu, is associated with this area.

The route culminates at Tianzhufeng (Heavenly Pillar Peak), the tallest peak of Mt. Wudang. Here sits a small Golden Hall (1416) made by casting the roof and prominent parts of the three-bay structure in bronze. Within is the statue of the barefoot long-haired Zhenwu, surrounded by his Daoist retinue—the Dark Warrior, the tortoise with a two-headed serpent entwined around him, a golden youth, a jade maiden, and guardian spirits of water and fire. They were all cast in bronze. Above them a bracket set more complicated than any found in the *Yingzhao Fashi* was built to signify their stature and royal favor.

**13.15 Purple Empyrean Hall, Mt. Wudang, China**

13.16 Meridian Gate, Forbidden City, Beijing, China

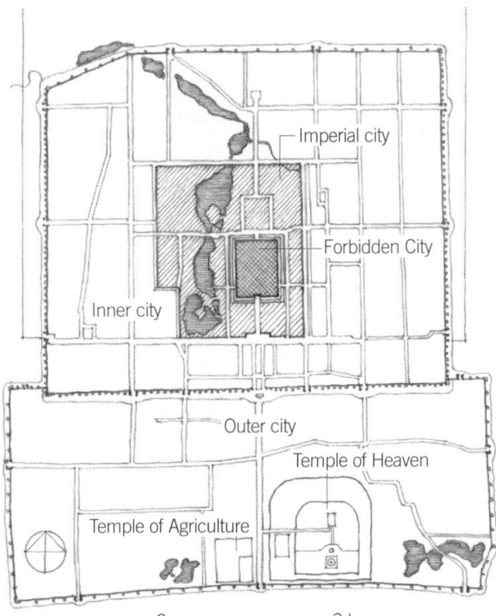


13.17 Plan of 15th century Beijing

**Forbidden City**

The Forbidden City, the enormous palace complex built by Emperor Zhengtong (r. 1436–49) in Beijing, is one of the most celebrated icons of imperial China. For five centuries, from about 1420 to 1908, the city was the hallowed seat of 24 emperors. The Forbidden City is particularly important since all pre-Ming palaces were destroyed. A central compound, the Palace of Heavenly Purity—built for the exclusive use of the emperor as the residence of the Son of Heaven—defined the core of the city and served as the conceptual center of the empire. Every gate in this innermost zone was guarded by trusted eunuchs. Since the emperor embodied both the authority of government and its justice system, access to him had to be both carefully circumscribed and, at the same time, projected well beyond his actual corporeality. This, in essence, was the dual purpose of the Forbidden City.

The Palace of Heavenly Purity consists of three pavilions on axis, on an I-shaped, single-step marble platform, preceded by a terrace facing south. It is surrounded by a wall, the innermost enclosure. Sixteen pavilions, housing the royal concubines, extended this innermost sanctum immediately to the east and west. Imperial gardens and additional palaces for members of the royal family make up much of the remaining structures.

Just south of the Palace of Heavenly Purity, a set of three halls perched on a three-step, I-shaped marble platform repeated the order of the innermost palace. This second triptych, much larger in scale, is the terminus and focus of the public sequence of the Forbidden City and as such is the public center of the empire. It is the largest group of buildings in the Forbidden City.

The emperor met daily with his officials in the Hall of Supreme Harmony. Only the highest officers had access to this hall, which was also the throne room of the emperor. Behind it, the Hall of Central Harmony and the Hall of Preserving Harmony only served supporting functions. Although the height, spans, and ornamentation of the Hall of Supreme Harmony are magnificent, the impact of the hall comes from the manner in which the deep overhang of the roof projects its presence into the vast space of the courtyard that precedes it, which any supplicant would have to traverse before reaching the throne. In front of the Emperor all supplicants had to kowtow—that is, they had to prostrate themselves, facing north. Only the Emperor looked down facing south—a relationship magnified in the orchestration of the roof and the courtyard.

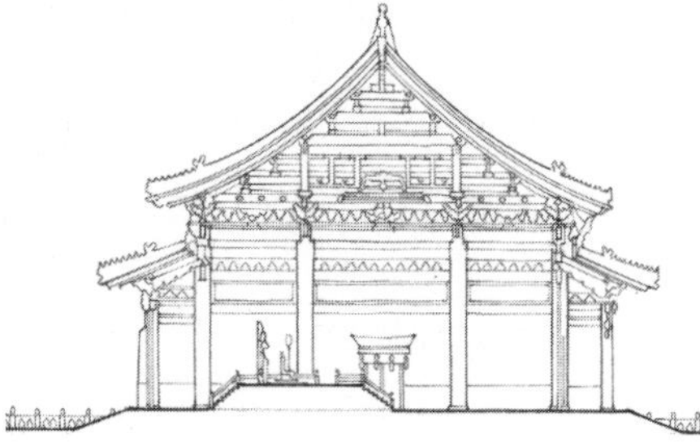

13.18 Section: Hall of Supreme Harmony, Forbidden City

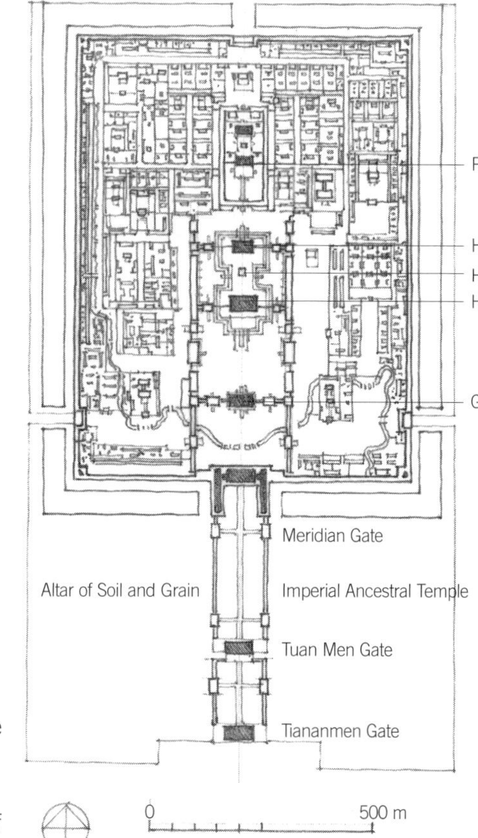


**13.19 Plan: Forbidden City**

The Forbidden City housed the imperial bureaucracy and its millions of records. The daily communiqués that arrived from the most distant parts of the empire were catalogued, interpreted, and presented to the emperor and his councillors for action when necessary. The offices of the bureaucracy were located in the corridors on either side of the Hall of Supreme Harmony.

Five marble bridges symmetrically straddle the Jinshahe or Golden Water River that winds its way around the Forbidden City. Just beyond them, further south lies the imposing Meridian Gate, the designated entrance into the Forbidden City, which aligns with the city's enclosing wall and moat (with turrets in the corners). This was where high-ranking civil and military officials gathered to wait for the emperor and where large triumphant ceremonies were conducted.

**13.20 Hall of Supreme Harmony, Forbidden City**

The U-shaped form (with five entrances and a tall platform with high pavilions) of the Meridian Gate connected the Forbidden City to the palatial entrances of the Song, T'ang, and even Han palaces. From here, the path became a long passageway, with three more gates along the way. Duanmen, or the Gate of Uprightness, was followed by Chengtian, from where the emperor issued imperial edicts, and then finally the Great Ming Gate or Da Mingmen, the main entry into the imperial city. The central gates, paths, and bridges could be used by no others, and when the emperor was carried along that path, all were required to avert their eyes.

As one travels down the main axis of the Forbidden City, the spatial experience transforms with the elevation of the ground plane. The first three gates rise high above the ground on imposing blank walls, giving one the sense of moving through an intimidating and cavernous space. On the other side of the Gate of Supreme Harmony, however, the view opens up, with the Hall of Supreme Harmony raised handsomely as an object in space on its three stately terraces. The terraces raise the viewer higher than anywhere else in the Forbidden City. From on top of the third terrace, the view south, which was the emperor's privileged view, is high enough to enable the emperor to see over the walls. From here all the gates and the length of the city can be apprehended in a single glance.

13.21 Imperial Vault of Heaven

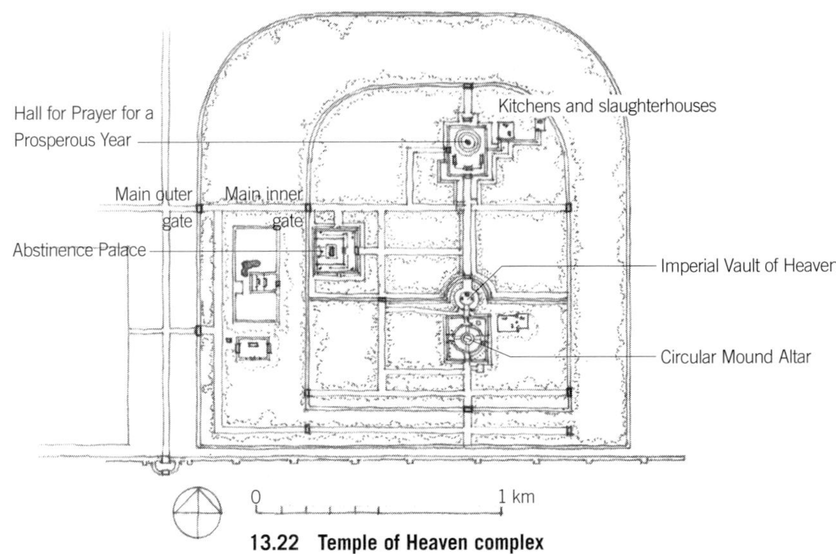


13.22 Temple of Heaven complex

**Temple of Heaven**

If the axis, courts, gates, great halls, and throne represented imperial authority, the emperor's connection with the altars and temples that he visited and that were all located outside the Forbidden City was the tactile embodiment of his status as a Son of Heaven. The oldest of the structures visited by the emperor were the Imperial Ancestral Temple and the Altar of Soil and Grain, located just beyond the Meridian Gate, to the east and west of the major axis. There were also the Altars of the Sun and Moon, located to the east and west of Beijing, and the Altar of Earth, to the north.

The south was reserved for the most important altars of them all, the Altar of Agriculture, intended to ensure the timely cycle of production, and the Circular Mound Altar, the enabler of the Emperors' mandate, in the Temple of Heaven complex. The Circular Mound Altar's focus is a three-tiered circular (conceived as the shape of heaven) platform located in a square (the shape of earth) enclosure. Just north of the Circular Mound Altar is the Imperial Vault of Heaven, and further north is the Hall for Prayer for a Prosperous Year. Elevated on three circular terraces of white marble, this temple has a triple set of conical roofs over a round space that is quite unique in Chinese architecture. Connecting the Circular Mound Altar and the Hall for Prayer for a Prosperous Year is a 360-meter-long raised walkway.

The sacrifice at the Temple of Heaven complex occurred every winter equinox. The emperor prepared for the event by fasting for three days prior, living in the Abstinence Palace located at the western edge of the complex. The Abstinence Palace is one of the few remarkable Ming buildings made with perfect stone vaults. Only the buildings for the dead (the Ming tombs) and this one were considered "unworthy" of a wooden roof, but yet they were built in a manner worthy of their imperial stature. At 3 AM on the day of the equinox, the emperor traveled to the Circular Mound Altar, approaching it from the south, that is, facing north in the position of a supplicant.

The entire altar, basically a type of ritual platform, was illuminated by hundreds of lanterns, incense burned everywhere, and in the middle, representing heaven, was a tablet, facing south, moved there especially for this ceremony from its resting place in the Imperial Vault of Heaven just beyond to the north. The emperor prostrated himself and kowtowed to the heavens more than 50 times in a carefully scripted ritual that only he could perform as witnessed by all present. Heaven's displeasure with the emperor, manifested by bad omens and natural or political catastrophes, was always considered a sign of the withdrawal of his mandate to rule.

13.23 Circular Mound Altar

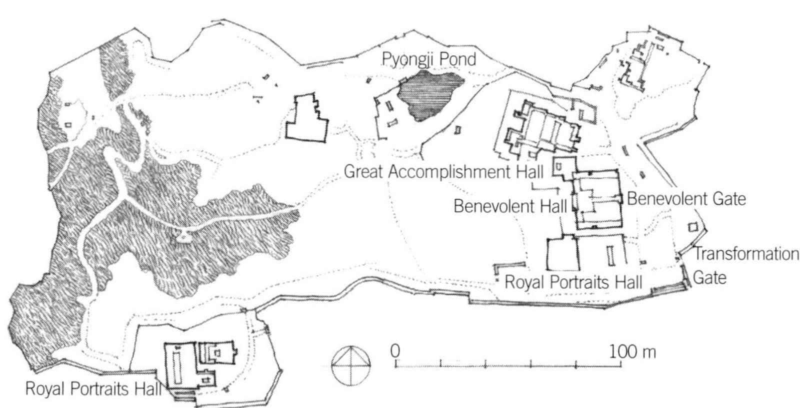


**13.24 Site Plan: Kyongbokgung Palace, Seoul, Korea**

**13.25 Kyongbokgung Palace**

## JOSEON DYNASTY

In 1392, Yi Songgye with the aid of the Ming Dynasty seized the throne and established the Joseon Dynasty (also known as the Chosun Dynasty) that was to last until 1910. Korea was known under the Joseon as Daejoseonguk (Great Joseon Nation). Though the Mongolians were defeated, aspects of Mongolian culture, here as elsewhere, remained embedded in Korean society. Confucianism, like in China, was reestablished as the state religion and a new capital was built, named Seoul, situated not far from the largest river of the peninsula and the focal point of overland transportation routes. Several palaces were built in Seoul, the most important being Kongbokgung (or Changdokkung) Palace (Palace of Shining Happiness, 1394). For the siting of the palace, the surrounding topography was carefully studied from the standpoint of both Confucian ideology and feng shui. Feng shui was very much respected in the making of the principal roads connecting the main gates of the city by way of the four cardinal directions. Straight lines were not always the rule, as can be seen in the east-west and north-south thoroughfares, which are slightly curved.

According to feng shui, a building should face southward and should have mountains on the left and right, symbolizing an azure dragon and a white tiger respectively. The palace was thus situated in the north sector of the city, in the foothills of Paekak Mountain, facing south to the northern mountain peak called Nam Mountain. The deity on Paekak Mountain was female, whereas the deity on Nam Mountain was male. Paekak, which symbolized royal authority and was the most highly valued in terms of feng shui, was closed to the common people and protected from any private use. The Nam, however, was open to the common people. Because there was no natural mountain to the east of the palace, an artificial hill was made to compensate for the shortcoming in topography. In its original form, the palace had about 500 buildings. They were burned during the Japanese invasions of 1592. (About ten 19th-century reconstructions remain.)

The palace had a public portion (toward the south) and the more private part (toward the north) consisting of several stroll gardens, strung together by a series of carefully composed follies for repose. One of these is particularly famous. Organized around a shallow, quadrangular water tank, with a high ridge on one side and several small pavilions distributed along the tank's edges on the other three sides, the folly is skillfully understated, as if it were nothing more than a reinforcement of natural elements already present in the landscape.

The throne hall (*injongjon*), facing east and surrounded by its own wall, was a large two-story building, built in 1405. It sits on the top of a series of low stone platforms that seem particularly well proportioned in respect to the slope of the eaves. Stone tables in the courtyard indicate where each rank of official should stand for formal ceremonies. The bays are 5 meters square except for those on the central axis, which are 6.7 meters square. The throne sat on a high platform at the back of the middle bay. It was connected in the north to the government building, where the king worked and in the south to a portrait hall, or Sonwonjon Shrine, where the former kings' portraits were enshrined. On each king's birthday, a memorial rite was held there, emphasizing the principle of continuity.

13.26 **Kinkakuji, the Golden Pavilion, Kyoto, Japan**

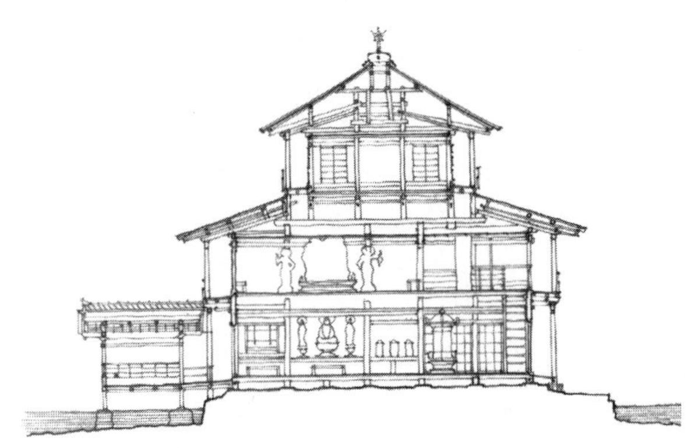

13.27 **Section: Kinkakuji, the Golden Pavilion**

## MUROMACHI JAPAN

After two centuries of domination by aristocratic regents and military rulers, the young ambitious Japanese emperor, Godaigo (r. 1318–39), enlisted the help of Ashikaga Takauji (1305–58) to reclaim the court in 1333. But when Godaigo refused to name Takauji as shogun after their victory, the latter forced the emperor into exile (1335) and placed his own representative on the throne.

As shogun, Takauji made two important decisions that changed the course of Japanese history: he reinstated Kyoto as the capital and reestablished links with the Chinese Song Dynasty, links that had been broken since Kublai Khan's failed attempt to invade Japan in the 13th century. Profits from the China trade were important to the shogun's power. Song culture infused itself into Japanese society and with that came a blending of cultural elements that laid the foundation for a form of Buddhism known as Zen, the word a corruption of *chan* or "meditation." Zen emphasized sustained meditation, rather than, say, visualizations as the course to nirvana. The Zen monasteries were built in the Karayo (traditional Chinese) style, more complex in detail and more delicate in effect.

### Kinkakuji

In 1394 the Muromachi shogun, Ashikaga Yoshimitsu (1358–1408), Takauji's grandson, gave up his government position to become a monk and to retire to his private estate, the central focus of which was a three-story viewing pavilion known as Kinkakuji, or the Golden Pavilion. It sits at the edge of a carefully designed pond in whose reflection the pavilion both doubles in size and seems to float like a lotus flower. The outlines of the pavilion are visibly Song, if compared to paintings of the time. The first story contained a public reception room and an access point for pleasure boats. It is sturdy, clearly defined, and rectilinear, and it is followed by a deeply recessed second story, intended for private discussions and protected by the gentle sweep of an upward turning eave. The stunning views from its balcony were carefully designed, as was the rest of the estate, with small islands in the foreground, framing and enlarging the background. As with Song estates, the surrounding distant landscape was also incorporated into the visual composition of the garden. Finally, the third story, Yoshimitsu's private refuge, resolves the pavilion in an upwardly turning roof with a more pronounced swell that culminates in a bronze phoenix finial.

After Yoshimitsu's death, Kinkakuji was turned over to the Rinzai sect of Zen Buddhism to be used as a monastery and temple, at which time it was enlarged considerably. Yoshimitsu originally wanted to gild the pavilion (thus its title), but for most of its life it remained in wood. In 1950, the pavilion was destroyed by a mad arsonist. When it was reconstructed in 1955, its upper two stories were gilded to honor Yoshimitsu's original intentions.

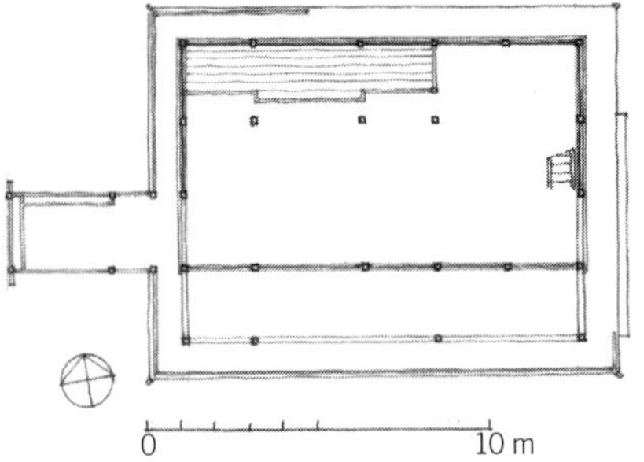


13.28 **Plan: Kinkakuji, the Golden Pavilion**

13.29 **Teahouse, Kinkakuji, Kyoto**

13.30 **Ginkakuji, the Silver Pavilion, Kyoto, Japan**

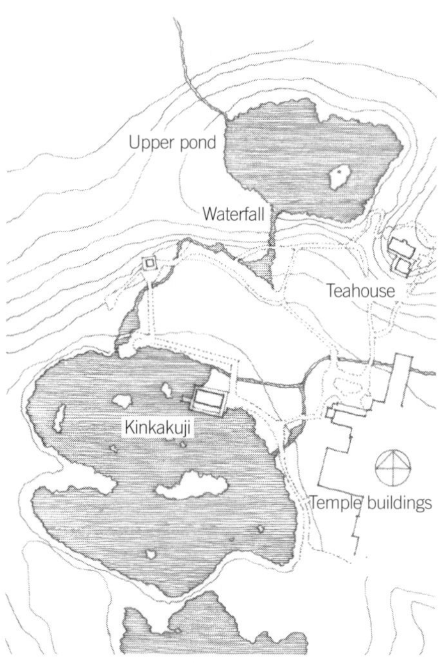


13.31 **Site Plan: Kinkakuji**

### Ginkakuji

Ginkakuji (Silver Pavilion) was built as a retirement villa by Yoshimitsu's grandson, the shogun Yoshimasa, in 1482. In a tribute to Kinkakuji, Yoshimasa intended to cover two stories of his pavilion with silver. While neither Yoshimitsu nor Yoshimasa realized their goal of gold and silver buildings, the names have endured. In time, Ginkakuji became a center of what is known as Higashiyama culture that blends the contemplative conundrums of Zen Buddhism with the aristocratic tastes of the samurai nobility, a mix of Chinese Song and Japanese Heian court traditions. In Yoshimasa's original design, the two-story pavilion stood, carefully composed, at the edge of a pond. Small bridges, tiny islands, and exactingly planted and pruned shrubs and trees—these were all conceived in the usual Song-inspired syntax of the time. The whole composition was designed to generate carefully framed views from a promenade that makes its winding way around the pond and from the various subpaths and meditation walks that lead from the pond to the side of the hill. The views were supposed to evoke fabled descriptions from Japanese literature.

Ginkakuji's fame lies in the additions made by Zen Buddhist monks during the Edo period in the 17th century, the palace having been turned over to Zen Buddhists after its patron's death.

Since sand had to be stored on site to maintain the gardens, the Zen monks decided to use it to build two sculpted mounds next to the pond and in stark contrast to it. One is low and carefully raked to form a plateau, and it is called the Sea of Silver Sand, so named for its appearance in moonlight. The other mound rises as a perfectly shaped, truncated cone, arresting at first glance if only for its sheer size. The cone evokes the profile of Mt. Fuji, but may also refer to the sacred mountain in the middle of a Buddhist mandala. From different points on different walks around Ginkakuji, the cone, uniform in color and outline from all directions, functions as an object of constancy in the changing assembly of views. As one moves around, the two mounds set in play a visual drama, the exact meaning remains open to interpretation; along with the garden and pond, it is designed to sustain the meditational inquiries of a Zen Buddhist mind.

One can argue that ultimately it was Ginkakuji, more than Kinkakuji, that evolved into a meditation garden of the kind that the Zen designers became famous for. The assembly of its views is more restrained and subtle, and since they are bound by a much smaller space, their experience is far more intimate and immediate.

**13.32 Plan: Bibi Khanum Friday Mosque, Samarkand, Uzbekistan**

### TIMURID DYNASTY

Chengiz Khan and his successors' campaign of conquest had altered the whole situation in Eurasia and above all in the Islamic cultural region of Central Asia. The occupation of Persia and the fall of Baghdad in 1258 unleashed a period of disarray and confusion. This led to infighting and anarchy and ultimately to a yearning for order and discipline that saw for example the rise of the dervishes as a Sufi branch of the Sunni in which Islamic practices mixed with displays of loyalty and passion. The Sufis were to become a major force in the 16th century under the Moghuls in South Asia as well.

One of the earliest post-Mongolian states was created by the Turkish-speaking Timur (1336–1405), who succeeded in conquering a vast territory. He was a brave soldier but also a ruthless and notably cruel commander. He unified Persia, Iraq, and Transoxiana by expelling local potentates and clearing the countryside of robbers, bringing forth a new wealth and economy to the region that much favored the flow of trade. While not themselves heterodox or Shi'ite, the Timurid rulers accorded respect to the Shi'ite figure of Ali, the prophet's son-in-law whom they considered the founder of their civilization's mystic brotherhoods. Furthermore, with a generosity unthinkable in later generations, empress Gohar Shad built her Shi'ite subjects a splendid shrine in the city of Mashhad, still a major pilgrimage center in modern Iran.

Consistent with Timur's passion for grand structures, imposing appearances became the main priority of his architectural program, with the facade developing into a virtual freestanding architectural form. High drums and external domes stabilized by brick ribs were often placed over the structural inner domes. The combination of portal and dome produced buildings of great spatial drama.

Timur set up Samarkand, already a major metropolis along the Silk Route, as his capital. It soon possessed large suburbs with fountains and canals. In the factories, the citizens wove silk and cotton; Persian craftsmen worked saddles and decorated copper; Chinese craftsmen produced the first paper outside of China itself. The 13th-century population exceeded half a million. Between 1339 and 1404, Timur built in Samarkand one of the biggest mosques in the world. Known as Bibi Khanum Friday Mosque (measuring 109 by 167 meters), it was entered through a high portal with round corner towers, its arches spanning nearly 19 meters. The principal elements of the plan—the entrance portal, the mosque, and the lecture halls—are all enlarged into monumental forms and then framed by the repetitive elements of the mosque. The colossal entrance portal even protrudes from the exterior wall, with two minarets projecting out even further.

The cylindrical shafts of the minarets, rising from the ground rather than emerging from the top of the *iwan* and sitting on decagonal socles, provide the earliest surviving example of minarets flanking a portal. Behind this lay a spacious courtyard at the back of which stood the dome-covered main building of the mosque, towering 44 meters into the air. The basic plan is the four-*iwan* type that had been developed in an ad hoc way in Isfahan some 400 years earlier. This building, of course, was a unit from the very start and the hypostyle hall here forms the connective tissue holding together the monumental elements.

Of a similarly grand scale was the Ulugh Beg Madrasa in Samarkand (1417–20), which opens up to the main square on axis to the Bibi Khanum Friday Mosque. It is one of the largest madrasas in Central Asia, with an enormous entrance portal flanked left and right by dome-covered lecture halls with four axial niches. Slender round minarets mark the corners. The square courtyard has four *iwans* and a large mosque at the rear with additional lecture halls to the right and left. The building became the prototype of many later madrasas.

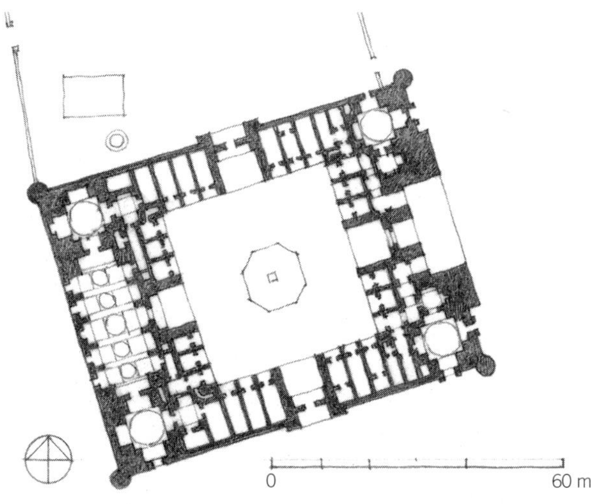

**13.33 Plan: Ulugh Beg Madrasa, Samarkand, Uzbekistan**

**13.34 Ulugh Beg Madrasa**

Among the numerous impressive buildings in Samarkand is the Shrine of Ishrat Khaneh (1464), built a kilometer or so to the east of the city near a cemetery. The grand, recessed portal rising over the rest of the building leads directly into a domed hall, the height of which is enhanced by an ornamental tower-and-dome. To the right and left of the principal axis are a string of chambers of various sizes. A crypt is located just below the main dome. A staircase from the rectangular room in the right-hand group leads to the crypt below the domes.

The Timurids developed a new type of dome support. Instead of the square hall and octagonal squinch, which had been developed in Islamic architecture over the previous centuries, the dome was set on two pairs of overlapping arches, as can be seen at the Shrine of Ishrat Khaneh. The dome was thus smaller than in the older system, but the whole now had a dynamic plasticity, both outside and inside. This technique had originated in Armenia, where it was known since the 12th century. From there it spread to Russia, and it is quite possible that captured Russian or Armenian building masters might have been responsible for this aspect of Timurid architecture.

Though decorative tiles were used in Islamic architecture from early times on and had been developed by the Seljuks, the complete sheathing of buildings in colored tiles, characteristic of Persian architecture today, dates only from this period. Prior to the 13th century, most monumental decorations were made of stucco that was painted or gilded. But only under the House of Timur in the late 14th century did the various ornamental motifs appear, fired in ceramic tiles, that utterly blanketed the structures. Though the color blue predominates, the range of possible colors was quite wide, including turquoise, white, yellow, green, brown, aubergine, and black.

The designs, based on intricate geometric patterns and interlaced with stylized script from Koranic verses, were wrought with astonishing delicacy, with the craftsmen conceiving space as a complex three-dimensional color field. A particularly beautiful building is the Blue Mosque of Tabriz in northwest Iran, completed in 1465 and named for the luminous cobalt ground of its ceramic facing. The tradition reached its apogee in the 17th century in the Winter Prayer Hall of the Royal Mosque of Isfahan (1612–38).

**13.35 Bibi Khanum Friday Mosque**

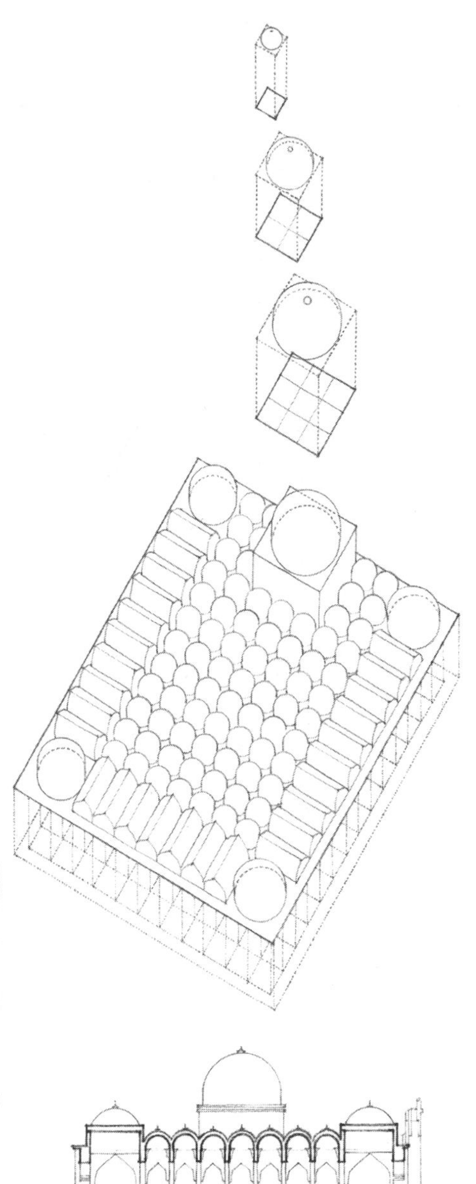

## DECCAN SULTANATES

In 1400 central India was controlled by a familiar patchwork of diverse regional kingdoms, but this is the first time that most of these were ruled by Islamic kings, known as the Deccan Sultanates. With a first opportunity to establish and build their new Islamic institutions, they conceived an array of innovative architectural projects. Most of the Deccan sultans were affiliated with the sultans in Turkey, for political reasons. Qutb-ud-Din Aibak's dynasty (1206–90) had controlled the entire Indo-Gangetic plain of North India from their capital in Delhi. Their successors, the Khiljis (1290–1320), did spectacularly better and brought central India, that is, the entire Deccan Plateau from Gujarat in the west to Pandua in the east and Gulbarga in the south, under their control. The Khilji's successors, the Tughlaqs (1320–1413), however, were unable to manage this vast empire and bungled a series of ill-conceived administrative projects. Timur, sultan of Samarkand, took the opportunity in 1398 to launch a raid from across the Himalayas and found Delhi bereft of its defenders. In the subsequent chaos, the governors and regents of the Deccan Plateau, many of them Khilji appointees, declared independence, establishing the Deccan Sultanates. The sultans took pains to distinguish themselves from the weak court in Delhi and instead turned to West Asia, not only for trade but for the occasional help in shaping their material culture and architecture.

### Friday Mosque of Gulbarga

In Gulbarga, the capital of the Bahmanid Sultanate (1347–1542), Sultan Muhammad I tried to import his architecture as puritanically as possible. He used Rafi bin Shams bin Mansur, an architect from Iran, to build his Friday Mosque (1367). Without any courtyard or *iwan*, the mosque with its central hall (66 by 54 meters) is covered with 63 small cupolas; the *qibla* wall to the west features a high dome surrounded by twelve smaller and lower domes. An unusua aspect of the interior is the extremely wide span of the arcades, with very low imposts that were to become more common in south Indian Islamic architecture later on but were unheard of at this time. There is a Persian mood and even a basilicalike feel to this mosque.

**13.36 Interior arcade, Friday Mosque of Gulbarga, India**

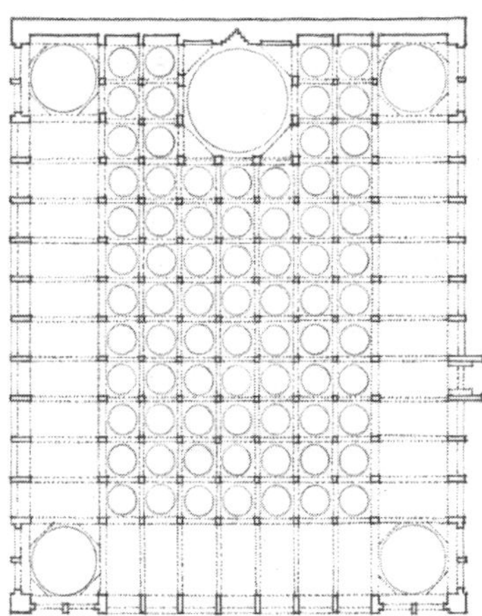

**13.37 Plan, section, and pictorial view: Friday Mosque of Gulbarga**

13.38 **Jahaz Mahal, Mandu, India**

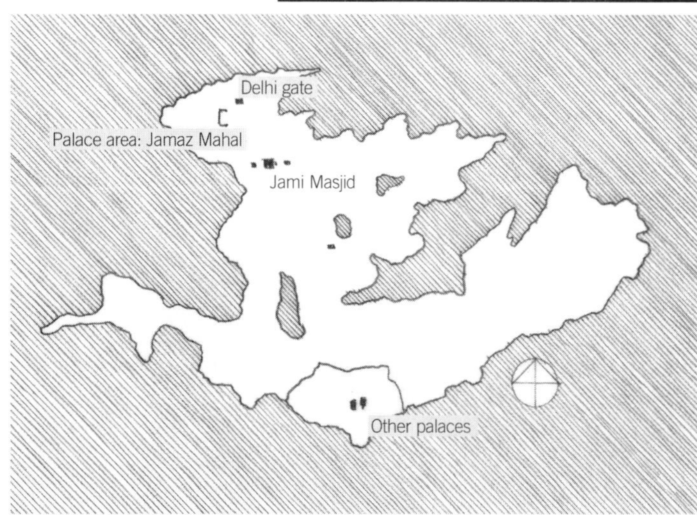


13.39 **Plan of Mandu**

## Mandu

Gushang, the Sultan of Malwa, was more experimental. He built a new fortress and capital in the Vidhyan Mountains at Mandu (1406), and for his important buildings, he decided on simple, handsome, cleanly articulated cubic volumes with hemispherical domes. The innovation found their best expression in the palaces, of which Jahaz Mahal is best known. Sitting at the edge of a man-made lake, the building is actually a dam built for the lake with a palace integrated into it. Designed to take maximum advantage of the water, through channels and cisterns, the palace has some of the characteristics of maritime architecture. The name of the palace, Jahaz Mahal, means "Ship Palace." The palace's primary focus is an elaborately foliated water tank, surrounded by a triple arcade at the northern end, which was used by the kings and their queens for its cooling breezes.

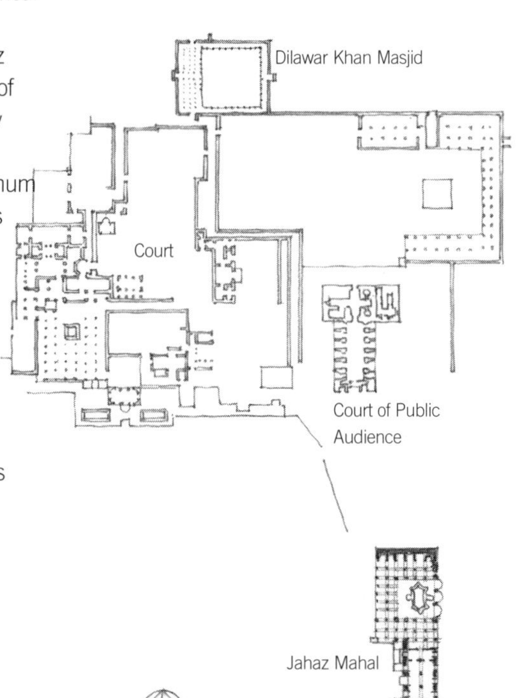


13.40 **Plan: Royal Palace complex, Mandu**

## Pandua

In Bengal, the Gaur and Pandua Sultans started out building fairly conventional stone-clad mosques and mausoleums. But stone is scarce in Bengal, and it rains incessantly. Brick was always the material of choice here, as we know from the Buddhist monasteries of the Pala kings. Even stone-clad mosques such as the Adina Mosque in Pandua (1364) were made of brick before being clad. In 1425, when the Sultan Jalal al-Din Muhammad Shah (r. 1414–32) began construction on his mausoleum, he decided to make it out of brick. This square building with corner turrets and an octagonal room surmounted by a hemispherical dome has an unusual twist to it. Inspired by the curved roof of local vernacular bamboo-and-hay structures, Muhammad Shah's architects incorporated a curved cornice into the profile that not only helps shed water but gives the mausoleum a unique shape. The move was propitious, for from here onward Bengal buildings began incorporating the curved cornice in every structure, creating a uniquely Bengali architecture that was imitated around South Asia in later centuries.

13.41 **Inner court, Jami Masjid of Ahmedabad, India**

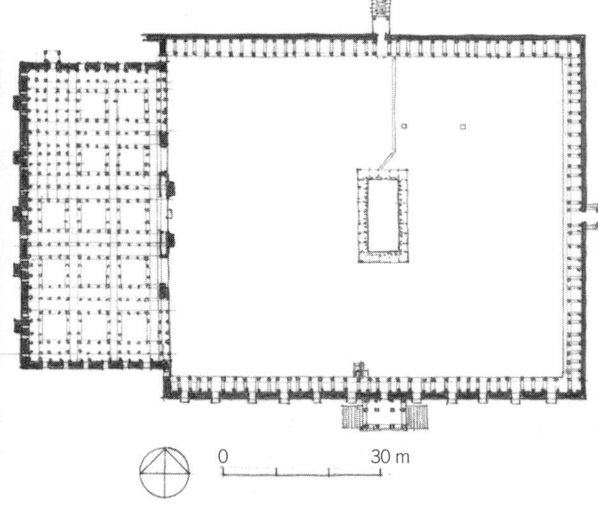


13.42 **Plan: Jami Masjid of Ahmedabad**

**Jami Masjid of Ahmedabad**

In 1398, Ahmed Shah (r. 1411–42), a former governor of the Tughlaqs in Gujrat, declared himself independent and in 1410 founded Ahmedabad as his new capital on the Sabarmati River. Ahmedabad went on to become very prosperous, particularly under Fath Kahn Mahmud (1459–1511), who expanded the kingdom in all directions. Under the Delhi sultanate and the Tughlaqs, it had been, of course, standard practice to demean the demolished Hindu temples by reusing the columns, upside down or in pieces, to hold up the new mosque. The curious characteristic of Ahmed Shah's architecture is the manner in which this mark of repression became the expressive language of the new architecture. For his new Jami Masjid (Friday Mosque) built in 1423 in Ahmedabad, Ahmed Shah embraced the new aesthetic created by the demeaned Hindu columns and authorized the construction of new columns not unlike the ones that were pillaged, thereby legitimizing this new architectural syntax.

The heavily ornamented columns not only peek through pointed arches of the court walls but are also magnified and attached to the sides of the central arch of the *qibla* wall in the form of minarets. The result is one of the finest mosques of western India, with the arched screen and pillar portico of the western *qibla* wall combined to create the effect of a finely composed and restrained but carefully detailed building, an effective combination of arch and trabeation. This hybridized way of building continued to characterize Ahmedabad's Islamic architecture, until it fell to the Moghuls late in the 16th century.

13.43 **Court arcade, Jami Masjid of Ahmedabad**

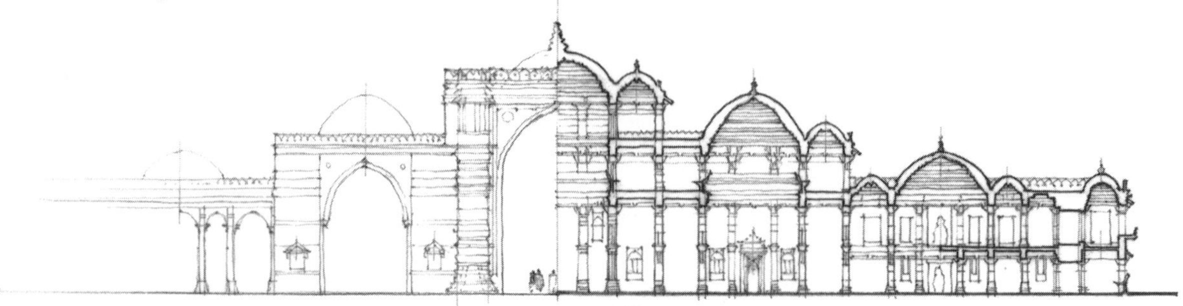

13.44 **Section through main prayer hall: Jami Masjid of Ahmedabad**

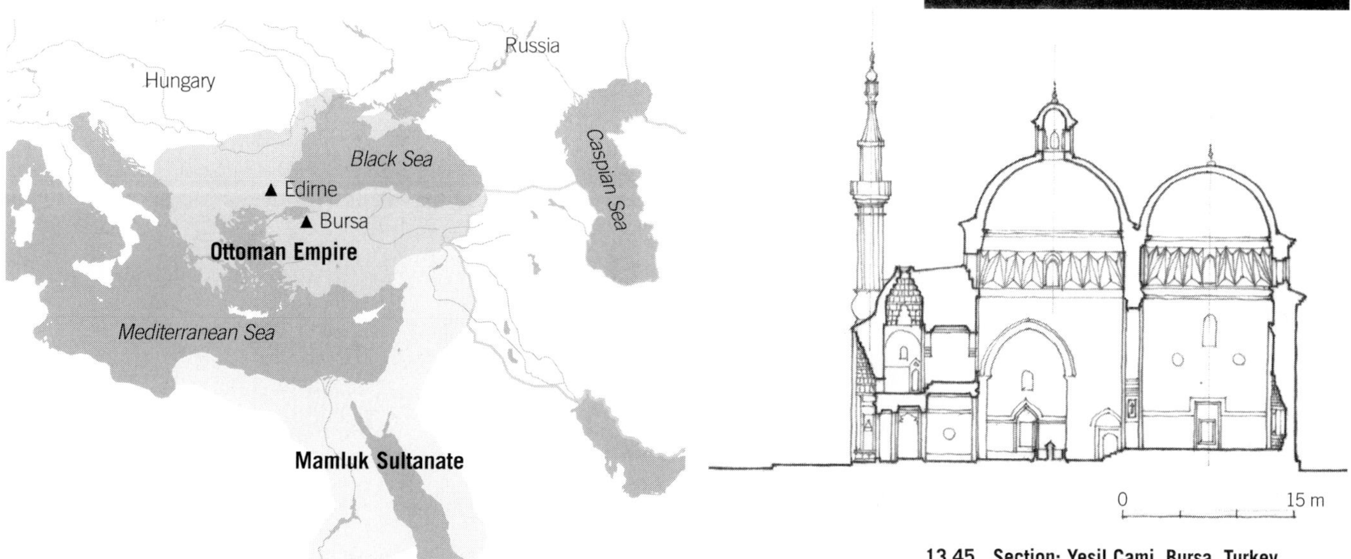


**13.45 Section: Yesil Cami, Bursa, Turkey**

**OTTOMAN EMPIRE**

By the early years of the 14th century, the Seljuk empire, following the attacks of the Mongolians and the disruptions of Timur, had dissolved into a series of small regional dynasties, interspersed by newly arriving tribes of nomads. Among these were the Osmanlis, or Ottomans, as they came to be known, who lived in the area of Bursa. Their leader, Osman Bey (1258–1324), whose followers captured Bursa from the Byzantines in 1326 and used it as their capital, took over the existing Byzantine administrative structures. From there, the Ottomans began to expand rapidly. In 1371, they reached Serbia, and in 1453 they conquered the main prize, Constantinople, bringing the Byzantine Empire to an end. The Ottomans were so strong that no single European country could challenge their position, despite repeated and coordinated attacks through the following centuries.

Ottoman mosques were not designed as introverted, walled rectangular enclosures, as they had been under the Seljuks. Instead, the early Ottoman mosques emphasized the singular hemispherical dome, resting on a square plan, that was entered through a three-bay loggia with a minaret to one side. This prototype was expanded with side rooms, vestibules, and loggias. Sometimes the dome was given an enclosed forecourt, becoming more complex but never more complicated.

One of the best examples of this type of royal mosque is Yesil Cami, in Bursa (1412–19). From an ornate marble portal one passes a low, square vestibule that leads by way of a short barrel-vaulted corridor to the central hall. The main prayer hall, or *iwan*, behind the hall is raised from the central hall by four steps, the side *iwans* by one step each. Both domes sit on belts of "Turkish triangles" that negotiate the change from square to circles. At the center of the main hall, which has an oculus, there is a pool. The royal family would have ascended the stairs near the entrance to gain access to the royal box. It is composed of two sections, a domed antechamber that opens onto a barrel-vaulted rear chamber that, in turn, looks onto the interior of the mosque.

Whereas Seljuk buildings tended to be conceived as isolated rectangular objects that were brought into relationship to each other only by way of addition. Ottoman structures, from early on and in step with the advanced architectural thinking of the 15th century in India and Italy, were designed as institutional complexes that brought the building and public space into dialogue. At the Yesil Cami Mosque, the various parts of the institution—the madrasa, the imaret (or hostel for pilgrims), *hamam* (bath), and *türbe* (tomb)—are spread out in the immediate area of the city.

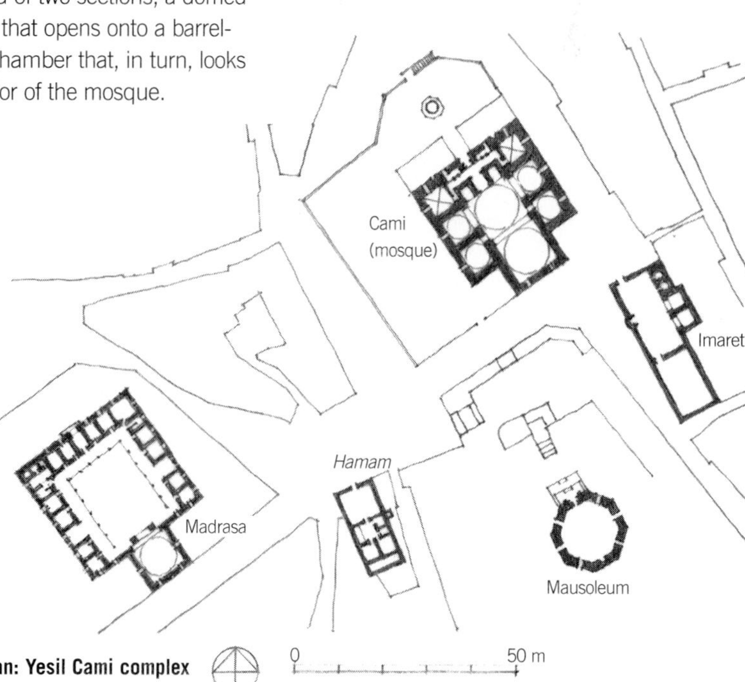


**13.46 Site Plan: Yesil Cami complex**

13.47 **Beyazit Medical Complex, Edirne, Turkey**

13.48 **Courtyard, Beyazit Medical Complex**

**Beyazit Medical Complex**

In the spring of 1484, the 37-year-old Ottoman ruler, Beyazit II, on his way with his army to the Balkans, arrived in Edirne and ordered the construction of a number of buildings, among them a mosque and a medical center known as the Beyazit Medical Complex (completed in 1488). The five principal elements of the composition are carefully walled off because of the number of horses, mules, and camels that would be grazing nearby. The buildings form an irregular U-shape, with the mosque and its court at the center, facing in the direction of the street.

The mosque is uncompromisingly square, half the width of the 50-meter broad courtyard. The dome, lofty and growing dramatically over the entrance, was illuminated by a large central wheel carrying three tiers of oil lamps, all suspended by a single chain from the center of the dome. Flanking the mosque are two square *tabhanes* with nine domes, each *tabhane* having four corner rooms opening onto *iwans* off a central court.

This plan is closely related to that of the Cinili Kiosk and is, therefore, distantly related to the concepts of Central Asia. The minarets are set in the angle corners of the *tabhanes* protruding from the walls of the courtyard. How the *tabhanes* were originally used is not certain, but it is generally thought that they served as temporary lodgings for members of the dervish orders. Beyazit had mystical leanings and was described as a man who loves simplicity peace and retreat. The dervish orders were also increasing in number in the 15th century.

To the east of the mosque were two buildings that served as refectories and kitchens. The hospital on the western side of the complex is a hexagonal structure, with its own small courtyard and forecourt. The hexagon was domed, and in the center it had a fountain to soothe the nerves of the ill. It is quite likely that musicians played here or possibly they made use of the sofa in the principal *iwan*, which forms a stage at the far apse end of the hexagon. The whole complex employed 167 people and was staffed by three doctors, two eye specialists, and two surgeons, as well as a dentist.

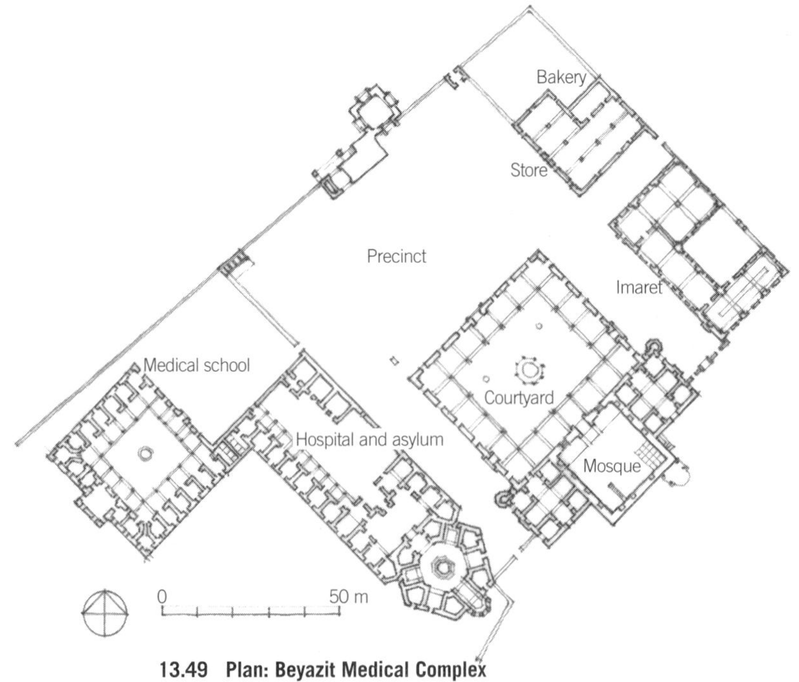


13.49 **Plan: Beyazit Medical Complex**

**13.50 Topkapi Palace, Istanbul, Turkey**

### Topkapi Palace

The Topkapi Palace in Istanbul served as the main royal residence and seat of the imperial Ottoman administration from the second half of the 15th to the mid-19th century. The building has a protracted history beginning around 1459 with its commissioning by Mehmed II (1432–1481). The palace, surrounded by water on two sides and by high walls on the third, was not conceived according to a rational or mathematical system, as a mosque would be, and it is often seen as a haphazard aggregate of buildings. Nonetheless, it was planned according to a logic related to the definition of a sultan. The Ottoman sultan was defined as beyond any relation of reciprocity, and ceremonies stressed the unbridgeable gap between master and subject, thus the insistence in this palace on the privacy of the sultan. The Moghuls, elaborating on Timurid and Mongolian models, had more accessible private zones, as in Europe, where the ruler could entertain his or her guests. The Topkapi Palace, however, with its clearly delineated boundaries, was designed, as explained by the architectural historian Gûlru Necipoglu, to instill a sense of sanctity and respect as much as fear and awe.

The building was begun under Mehmed II and added onto and expanded by subsequent sultans. It is located at the very tip of Istanbul, overlooking the sea, defended by an irregular walled-off enclosure roughly 700 by 1500 meters. The main entrance was just behind the Hagia Sophia, to one side, the church having been converted to a mosque. The Imperial Gate was the first of three main ceremonial double gates that one had to pass. The first court was a vast open area, and the most accessible, that contained workshops, storage areas, dormitories, kitchens, a bakery, and baths. It also contained a mint and various offices of the government. This court also served as a waiting area for dignitaries as well as staging area for processions.

The courtyard was also the site of a special ceremony to impress foreign dignitaries, held four days a week, in which the courtiers lined up in orderly rank, dressed in their finery. Visiting ambassadors had to walk through thousands of richly clad soldiers and courtiers standing in mandatory silence, an intimidating backdrop for diplomatic negotiations. The tree-lined path that transverses the court was meant to be used by all except the sultan. The huge kitchens on the other side reminded visitors of the largesse of the sultan who, in distributing free food to his courtiers and ambassadors, was following an ancient Ottoman custom. The courtyard was also used for executions, which the sultan could observe from a window in the Tower of Justice.

At the second gate, the visitor would have had to dismount to gain access to the next court, called "the arena of justice," and the beginning of the palace proper. It was a completely enclosed space, uncluttered by freestanding buildings and unified by a continuous marble colonnade. It housed the Tower of Justice, Council Hall, and treasury clustered at the far left corner of the court. A loggia, raised on a platform, in front of the Council Hall overlooked the space. On the inside of the hall, from the back, the sultan could watch the proceedings from behind a curtained window. The hall was low and unassuming, because it was modeled on a tent known as the "consultation tent," which was used by the imperial council during military campaigns.

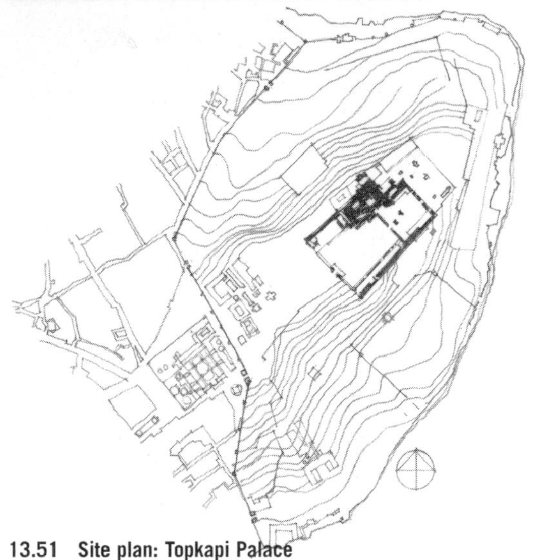

13.51 Site plan: Topkapi Palace

13.52 Topkapi Palace, Istanbul

The Third Gate, or the Gate of Felicity, is the site of the sultan's public appearance and was thus especially sacred. On particularly important occasions, the sultan would greet visitors under its airy canopy. Behind the gate was the Chamber of Petitions, a square, one-story structure surrounded by loggias, which served as an audience hall, a building that is technically within the private precinct but still conceptually a part of the second courtyard. The third court was raised on high retaining walls, as the land slopes down below it toward the north. The throne room was located at the far leftmost corner. The buildings in this court were designed to take in the vistas of the surrounding landscape. One description points out that the sultan, from his belvedere, could watch each part of his flourishing capital and the sea, teeming with ships.

The residential quarter was located to the east of the second and third courts in a compact mass huddled close to the walls of the court. There were special areas that housed pages and slaves—males, females, and eunuchs—who were all part of the sultan's retinue. It also housed the harem. And in the northernmost corner were the royal apartments.

The palace is not organized by axis, nor are the buildings grand in the traditional sense. Rather the buildings are organized through diagonal vistas and angled approaches, with the open areas of the courtyards meant to contrast with the ad hoc intimacy of the residential quarters.

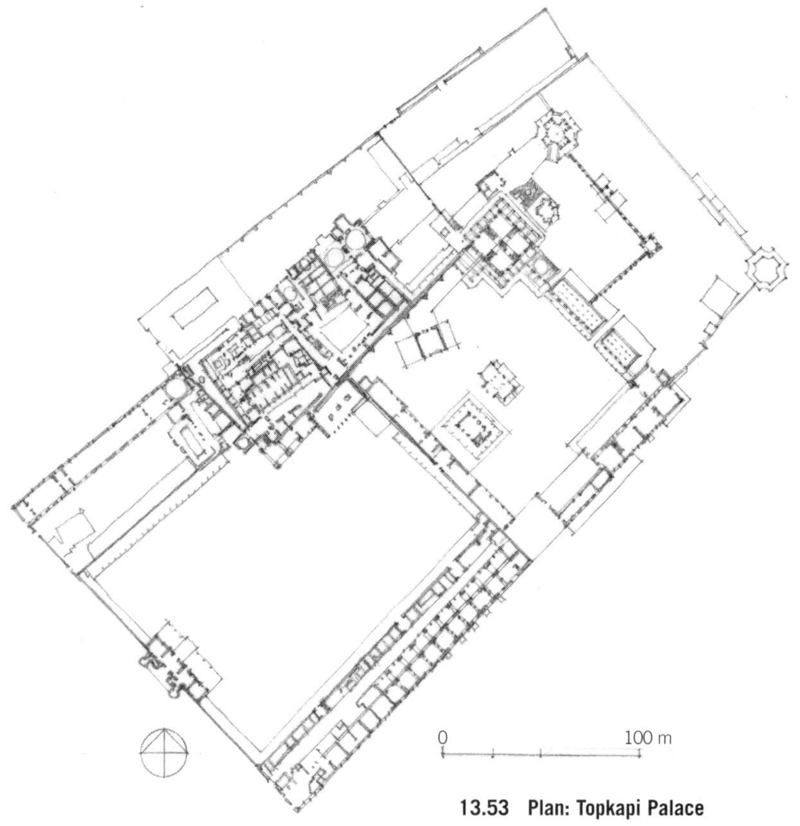


13.53 Plan: Topkapi Palace

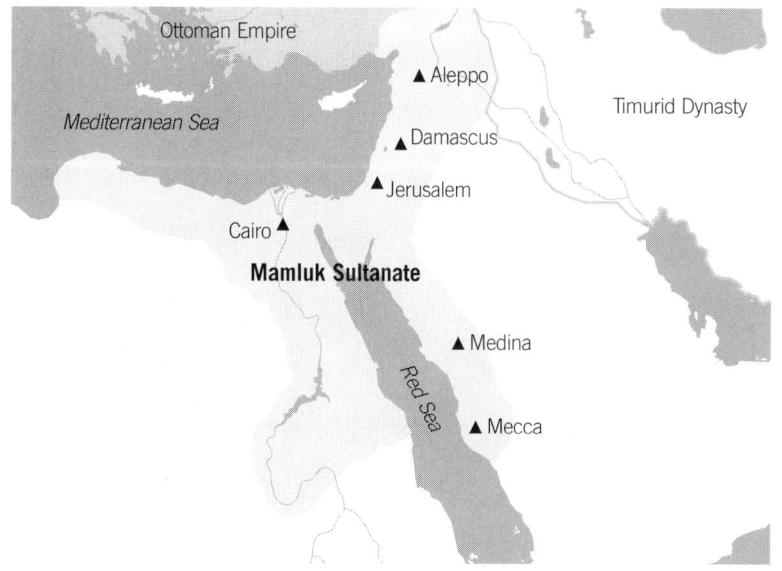

13.54 Portal, Complex of Sultan Hasan

## MAMLUK SULTANATE

The Mamluks, who came to rule Egypt from 1260 to 1517, were not Arabs but originally Turkish, Kurdish, and Mongolian slaves who had been raised as fighters in the army of the Ayyubid, themselves Kurdish Turks from Syria. The word Mamluk comes, in fact, from an Arabic word meaning "the owned." But with the collapse of the Ayyubid rule in Egypt, and following a period of warfare and transition, the Mamluk general, Baybars al-Bunduqdari (1260–77), established the dominance of the Mamluks in Egypt, pushed back the Mongolians as well as the Christian crusaders in the Levant and Syria, and regained control over the holy cities of Mecca and Medina. Under the previous Ayyubids, the center of power had been in Damascus; but under the Mamluks, Cairo's importance was restored. Though a military elite, they turned out to be savvy traders, establishing ties with Venice and Genoa, as well as with Constantinople. Mamluk bureaucracy was made up mostly of Coptic Christians and Jews, who had filled such administrative roles for centuries.

The almost 50-year reign of Baybars' successor, al-Nasir ("the victorious," in Arabic) Muhammad, resulted in several major architectural commissions, including a madrasa-mausoleum (1296–1304) that, though intended as his burial site, is actually the burial site of his mother Bint Sukbay.

The Mamluks, with a ready supply of well-trained masons, extended and enhanced the tradition of Fatimid palace architecture, establishing a series of important new religious institutions along the main road leading to the citadel. The greatest example of Mamluk architecture is the Complex of Sultan Hasan, a colossal project, begun in 1356. It contains a cruciform congregational mosque with four madrasa and a mausoleum of an imperial scale, as well as an orphanage, hospital, bazaar, water tower, baths, and kitchens. The service block is set at an oblique angle to the mosque and the religious spaces.

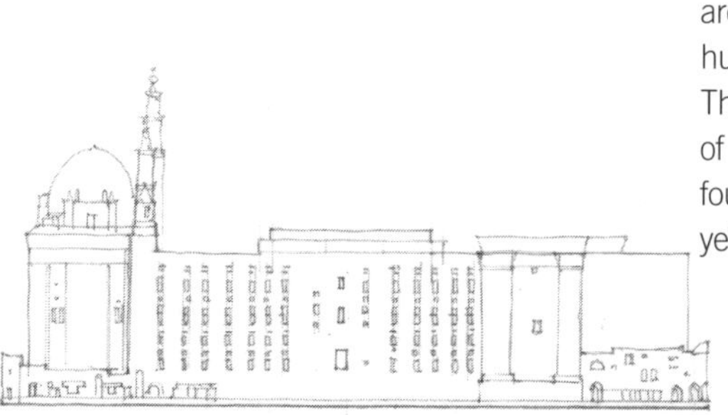

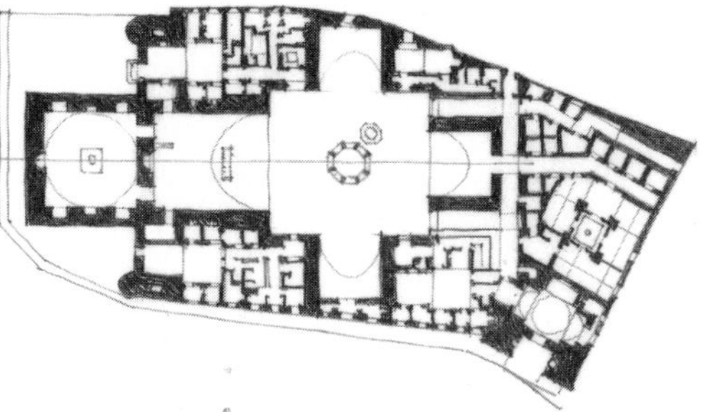

13.55 Plan and elevation: Complex of Sultan Hasan, Cairo, Egypt

The portal of the complex, rising 37 meters high, is crowned by a *muqarnas* cornice. The decorations include such Chinese motifs as chrysanthemums and lotus flowers. The central court was paved and had a fountain at the center. The four madrasas are located in the corners between the arms of the *iwans* and each has its own small courtyard. The southeast *iwans*, the largest of the four, was spanned by an enormous vault, considered at the time one of the wonders of the world. The mihrab and surrounding *qibla* wall are paneled in marble slabs of contrasting colors. Doors flanking the mihrab lead to the tomb beyond. In it, the walls are paneled with marble and the *muqarnas* of the dome are gilded and the whole illuminated by hundreds of specially designed glass lamps. The building not only makes maximum use of the site but redefines the Central Asian four-*iwan* type, making it more intimate and yet also more monumental.

13.56 Dome, Mausoleum Complex of Sultan Qaitbay, Cairo

13.57 Mausoleum of Emir Hairbak, Cairo, Egypt

**Mausoleum Complex of Sultan Qaitbay**

The buildings tended to be made of ashlar, inlaid with marble on the facade and in the interior and decorated with ornamental string courses and reveals. The capacity of the designers to impose order onto complex urban sites, however, was unique. The program included a madrasa, which was usually an open court faced by one or more *iwans*, cells for the students, a mausoleum for the patron, as well as service rooms of various types. No two buildings are alike, testifying to the fluid imagination of the architects. The asymmetry of these buildings, however, was not always a matter of necessity but, one can easily state, an aesthetic decision. An excellent example is the Mausoleum Complex of Sultan Qaitbay (1472–74).

Sultan al Ashraf Qaitbay (r. 1468–96) was known for the efficient manner in which he ran the country and the stability he created. He was particularly interested in architecture during his reign and promoted more than 60 projects of all kinds of buildings, not only in Cairo, but also in Mecca, Medina, Damascus, and Jerusalem. The Mausoleum Complex, with no other buildings surrounding it, houses the madrasa and the burial *qubba* of the sultan and balances the minaret tower on the right with an open loggia on the left. The dome is made up of three separate elements: the square-planned building at the bottom; an intermediate volume with vigorously shaped scrolls at its corners that make the transition to an octagonal platform; and the dome, resting on a drum on that platform.

Compared to the simple windows on the body of the building, some designed to look like they were carved out of the wall, the dome was given a particularly refined and elaborate decoration in which two patterns, an interlaced geometric star pattern and a floral arabesque, are combined. On the interior, we find *pietra serena* paneling, a surface treatment similar to what one can find in northern Italian churches. The love for asymmetry was developed further at the Mausoleum of Emir Hairbak (1502), which integrates the street facade with the axis of the mausoleum.

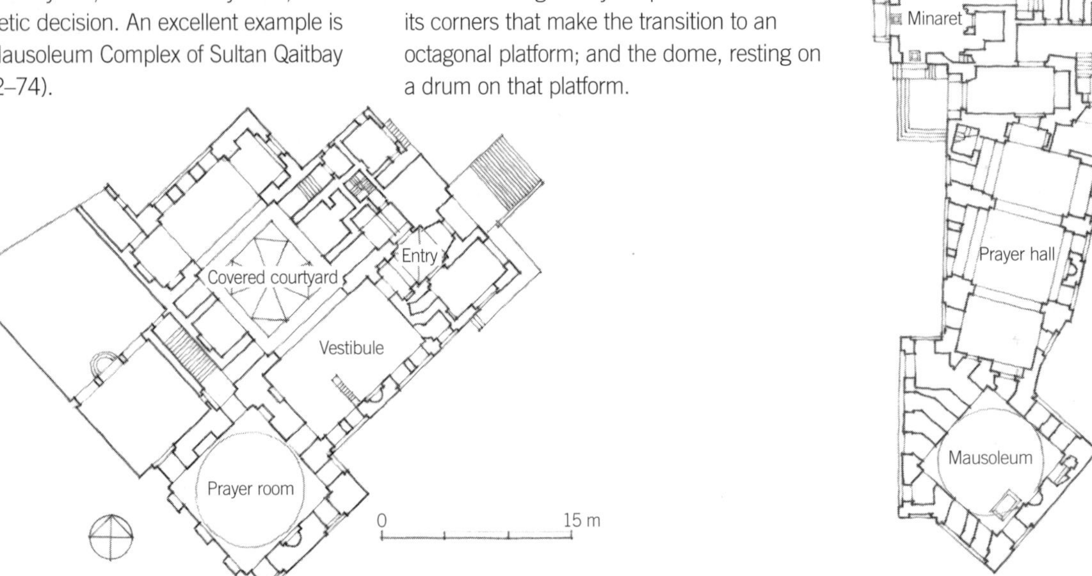


13.58 Plan: Mausoleum Complex of Sultan Qaitbay

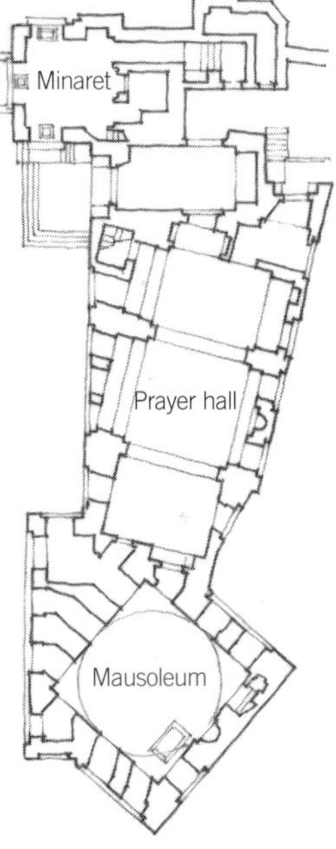


13.59 Plan: Mausoleum of Emir Hairbak

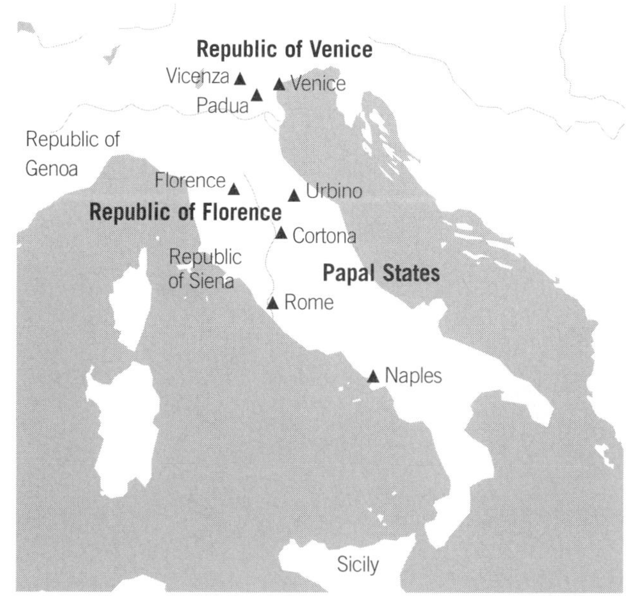


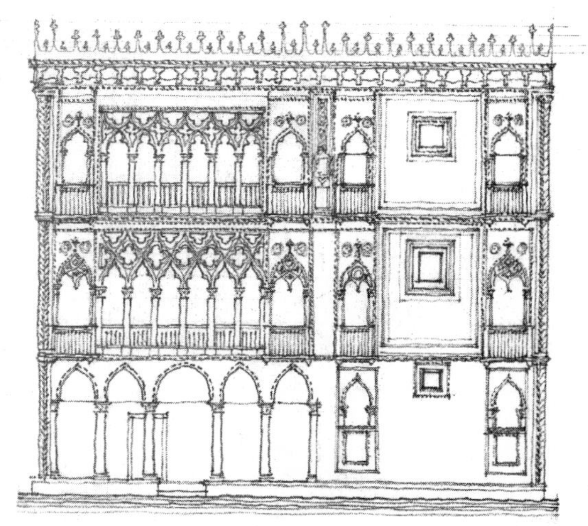
**13.60 Ca' d'Oro, Venice, Italy**

## REPUBLIC OF VENICE

The Black Plague (1350–1425) carried off 35 to 65 percent of the rural and urban population of Italy. Milan, for example, had a population of 150,000 before the plague in 1300. In 1463 the population was 90,000, and it was still under 100,000 in 1510. The political result was that only a handful of cities were able to right themselves and become dominant in the political landscape; these were Venice, Florence, Milan, and Naples. They rebounded to no small degree because they were able to tap into the new post-Mongolian era, pan-Eurasian spirit of enterprise. If one followed the Silk Route westward across Asia, through the lands of Timur, the Fatimids, and the Ottomans, one would come to Islam's principal European trading partner, Venice, whose empire was essentially a commercial enterprise, the vital organs of which were its warehouses, ships, barges, and packhorses. The Venetian world comprised a field of investment and interest that stretched from Bruges and London to Aleppo and beyond. All goods traveling to Germany, Sicily, and England had to pass through the port of Venice. By 1423, the Venetian gold ducat was being minted at a million a year. The state budget of Venice at the time was equivalent to that of France and England, and if one considers that Venice and its environs had a population of 500,000 whereas France had fifteen million inhabitants, there is no doubt that Venice was indeed Europe's strongest economy from the late-14th century onward or for about a hundred years. The material goods that came through the Venetian ports were distributed throughout Europe with the aid of the Florentine banking families, in particular the Medicis. Even though Florence is regarded as the traditional home of the Renaissance, it is in fact more accurate to see both Venice and Florence as common hubs of an economic and cultural renaissance.

Among the various new palaces that came to line Venice's canals, the most exquisite is the Ca' d'Oro ("house of gold)," a reference to the gold leaf that was applied to its exterior detailing. Stone for the facade was brought at great cost from Istria and had to be set on thousands of oak piles sunk deep into the sand and mud of the lagoon.

The facade of the palace consists of three superimposed galleries. Whereas the tracery of the loggias on the *piano nobile* and second floor had quatrefoil openings over the columns, the lower colonnade is noticeably more classical with its simple rounded and pointed arches. Though the exact origin of the quatrefoil shape is not known, the form was used on the Doge's Palace next to Basilica di San Marco in Venice and was clearly meant to show its owner's status as a member of the political elite. Throughout the facade, at corners and edges, and defining various architectural elements, there are decorative bands that make the façade appear as if it were almost woven into place. The palace was built for Marin Contarini, a Venetian aristocrat and one of Venice's leading cloth and spice merchants.

13.61 Cathedral of Florence, Italy

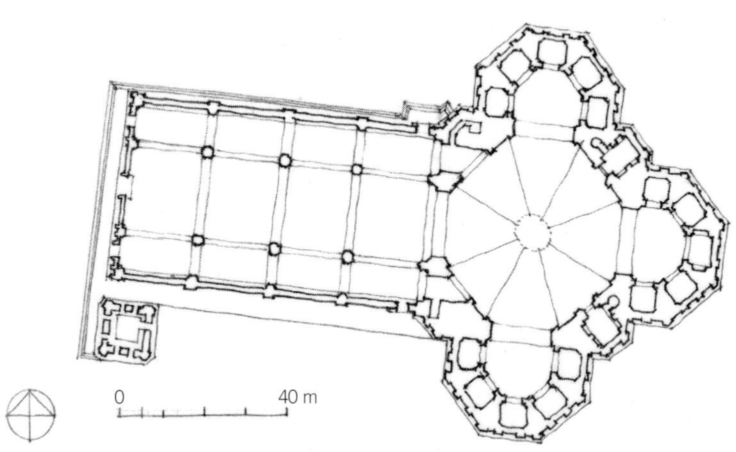


13.62 Plan: Cathedral of Florence

### Cathedral of Florence

The Cathedral of Florence, begun in 1294, was among the last of the great Italian city cathedrals. The plan, designed by Arnolfo di Cambio (1232–1300), was an unusual one, calling for a broad nave leading to an octagonal, domed apse. The fusion is eastern in flavor and perhaps meant as a homage to the city's founding saint, St. Reparata, who was martyred in 250 CE at Caesarea. The new building, however, was dedicated to the Virgin Mary. The design specification for the Duomo explicitly banned buttresses from the exterior. In the latter part of the 14th century, the architect then heading the construction, Giovanni d'Ambrogio, attempted to introduce Gothic-styled buttressing, but it was taken down and d'Ambrogio lost his job. In the 1350s, the Florentines, wanting to outdo the churches of Pisa and Siena, decided to expand the length of the nave. The new plan, which required that some already-completed elements of the building be torn down, maintained the same design idea, but on a larger scale. The new dome was as wide as the Pantheon in Rome but elevated some 60 meters in the air. Furthermore, whereas the Romans used a combination of brick and concrete, the Florentines had only bricks, the use of concrete, of course, having been forgotten.

No one knew how to complete such a dome. The stone vaults of the aisles required massive piers, but their impact was lessened by the height of the arches. There is no triforium. Instead a crenellated entablature creates a hard line between the arches below and the billowing vaults above.

On the outside, the three parts of the octagonal east end were designed to appear closely packed to the body of the church, with the skin modeled on the 13th-century Baptistery to the front of the building. By the time Filippo Brunelleschi was first consulted on the cathedral, the body of the church had more or less been finished, leaving a gaping hole where there should have been a dome. To make matters more difficult, a drum had been built with large round windows in the sides, meaning that lateral thrusts could not be brought to the ground through side vaults, as at the Hagia Sophia. Construction was at a standstill.

It would have been impossible to build a wooden framework strong enough to support such a dome during construction, which was why each successive architect concentrated his efforts on every part of the building except the dome. In 1418, a competition was announced to solve the problem. It was among the earliest public competitions in the history of architecture. Brunelleschi won by proposing an ingenious system by which the dome could be constructed with only limited use of wooden scaffolding. The problem he faced was not only how to build the dome but also how to minimize the lateral thrusts of a dome without using external buttressing.

13.63 Section: Cathedral of Florence

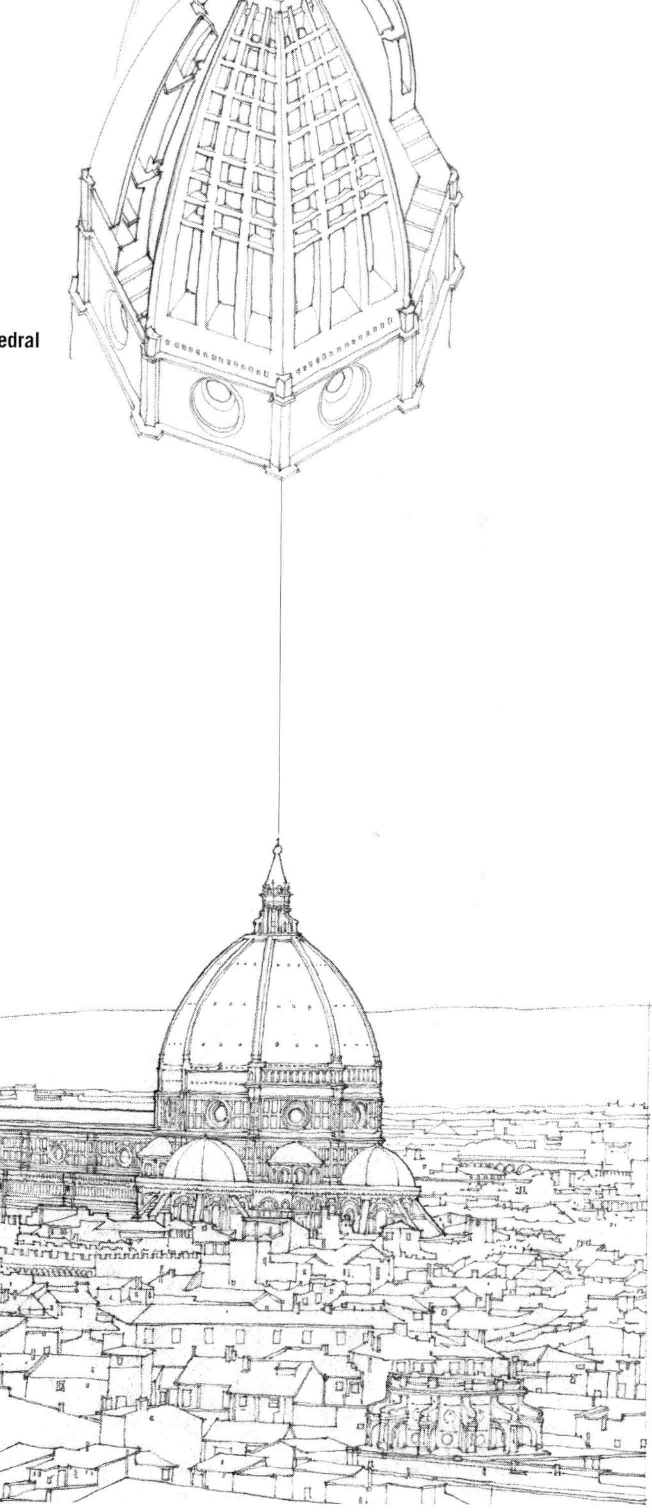

13.64 **Latticework for the dome of Florence Cathedral**

Brunelleschi created a curving rib-lattice structure, with a large metal chain at the bottom of the dome, resolving any residual horizontal thrust. The lattice was built of brick laid in herringbone fashion to insure cohesion. The elegance of this method was that the first phase of construction did not require a support structure since each layer, as it spiraled closer to the center, would cohere to the one below. A centering platform suspended from the dome itself was constructed only in the last phase. The dome did not come to a complete close but terminated with an oculus about 7 meters in diameter. To make sure that the ribs were in compression, a heavier-than-normal lantern had to be constructed over the oculus. Begun in 1446, it was also designed by Brunelleschi.

13.65 **View of Florence showing the dominance of Il Duomo over the urban landscape**

13.66 **Loggia dei Lanzi, Florence, Italy**

13.67 **Foundling Hospital, Florence, Italy**

### Florentine Loggias

The narrow streets of Italian cities consisted of hard materials, stone and brick, and because many of these cities were confined by city walls, open spaces such as parks and gardens were at a premium. Loggias were thus highly valued and served both functional and symbolic purposes. A loggia is a roofed-over outdoor space. Unlike an arcade, which covers pedestrian traffic, a loggia is a place to assemble rather than to traverse.

From the 14th century onward, Italians began to use increasingly complex rituals, celebrations, and public events to mark visitations by dignitaries, the departure of ambassadors, and even the coronations and marriages of distant kings. The Loggia dei Priori (now called Loggia dei Lanzi; 1376–82) played an important part in those events. It was constructed perpendicular to the entrance of the Palazzo della Signoria, or the town hall, and consisted of three lofty arches rising from a stepped platform. The columns, sitting on a short, ornamented plinth, are composed of pilasters bound together into one massive shaft 10 meters in height, terminating in a rich and beautiful capital of the Corinthian order.

Another type of loggia was for public services, like the one next to the Baptistery, which was used by the clergy to give out alms. Another one, associated with the Church of San Marco, served as a hospital. The most spectacular was the Foundling Hospital (Ospedale degli Innocenti; 1419–24; finished 1445), built by the Silk Guild, one of the most important guilds in Florence.

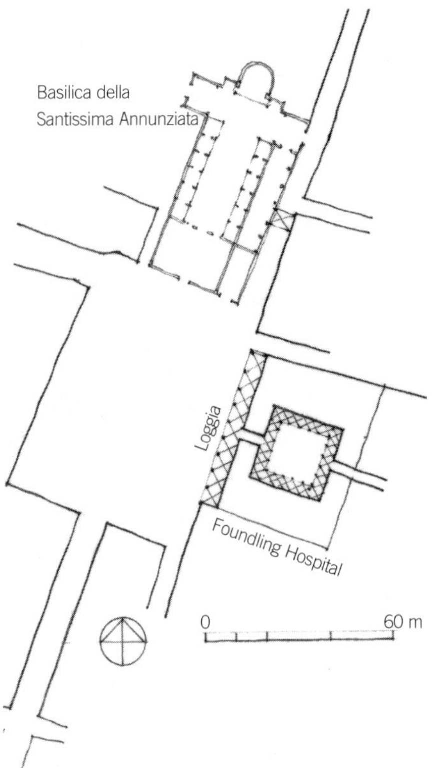


13.68 **Plan of Piazza Santissima Annunziata**

Ever since 1294 the guild had committed itself to the care of infants (*innocenti*). Though it had set up wards and hospitals, this building was specifically for abandoned children. A special door was built in the facade with a rotating panel so that a child could be deposited anonymously. By the year 1640, more than 1600 infants and children lived there, along with 40 priests, nurses, and administrators.

The loggia that constitutes the building's facade was designed by Brunelleschi, and even though its prototypes were medieval, its style was markedly new. The columns brought into view a new architectural sensitivity, modeled more carefully on classical precedent. The columns are the earliest examples of archaeologically correct Corinthian capitals in the 15th century. However, had Brunelleschi wanted to be more truly Roman, he would not have set the columns on thin plinths only 5 centimeters high. The facade consists of a long unbroken entablature. The arches are semicircular rather than pointed. Rondels, with babies in swaddling clothes depicted in them, decorate the space between the arches.The vaults, also spherical, were originally covered with a sloping wooden roof, but eventually an attic level was added but not under Brunelleschi's supervision.

13.69 Medici Palace, Florence, Italy

13.70 Section: Medici Palace

**Medici Palace**

The first Medici family member to come to prominence was Giovanni di Bicci (1360–1429), whose fortune was passed on to his son, Cosimo I de' Medici (1389–1464), who ruled over a vast banking and mercantile organization. In 1422, a political crisis led to the expulsion of Cosimo and his family. But after a year in Venice and the ensuing flight of capital from the city, he was invited back, and for the next thirty years he was the de facto ruler of the city, even though he never had the official title. With the rule of his son, Lorenzo de' Medici (1469–92), the pretense of political liberty could no longer be maintained, but his tenure was one of great artistic achievement.

The Medici Palace, commissioned in 1444 by Cosimo and completed about 20 years later, was designed by Michelozzo Michelozzi (1396–1472) though influenced by Brunelleschi's principles.The building is not what one might call "classical" or Roman, for it continued the prototype established in the 14th century by palaces built by the Davanzati. Though it is much wider than earlier palaces, the Medici Palace has only three stories and is topped by an enormous classical cornice that was meant to optically tie the volume together, though it makes the top floor appear to be almost crushed.

The ground floor is heavily rusticated in a manner that imitates the rustication of fortresses built by Emperor Frederick II in the middle of the 13th century in southern Italy. The windows have roundheaded openings, with strongly marked voussoirs placed symmetrically in the design; a string course separates the ground floor from the *piano nobile*. The story above that is entirely smooth, creating a strange effect in combination with the heavy cornice. If the outside appears purposefully medieval, the plan shows a new type of architectural thinking. The courtyard is actually a four-sided arcade. At the back of the courtyard, opposite the entrance, the arcade blends into a large open-air space that served as a reception loggia, leading to the garden behind the palace. Because of its scale, elegance, and built-in loggia, the courtyard has the appearance of a private piazza.

A quasi-public staircase to the upper level leads from one side of the courtyard to the principal rooms on the *piano nobile*. The idea of a grand ceremonial staircase as a principal architectural feature was a later development initiated by the construction of the Strozzi Palace. Construction of that palace began in 1489 under the supervision of Simone del Pollaiolo, using a model made by Benedetto da Maiano. Unlike the Medici Palace, which sits at a corner, the Strozzi bought an entire city block so that the building sits like a freestanding fortress in the city. Entrances on three sides lead to a courtyard.

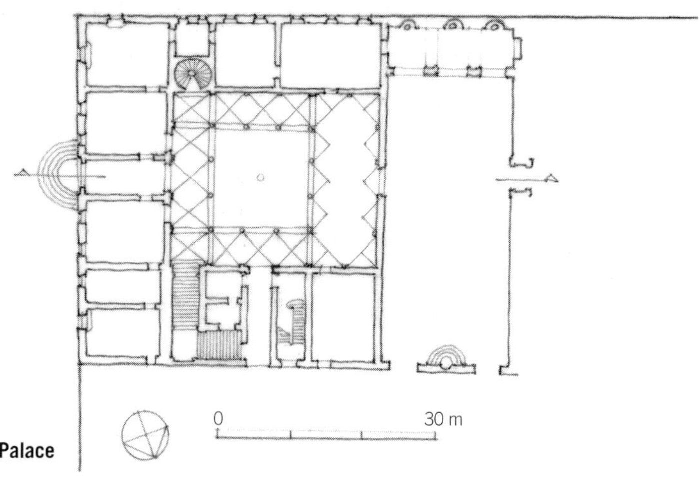


13.71 Plan: Medici Palace

13.72 Pazzi Chapel, added to the cloister of St. Croce, Florence, Italy

13.73 Interior of the Pazzi Chapel

## ITALIAN RENAISSANCE

The word Renaissance (from the Italian rinàscita, "rebirth") was coined in the 19th century to describe the cultural and intellectual changes that took place in Italy during the 15th century. The term refers in particular to the growing infatuation by the Italian intelligentsia with Roman antiquity, whether through the writings of Cicero and others or through the study of Roman ruins. It also refers, in the field of painting, to the discovery of perspective, which had been approximated by painters like Giotto di Bondone (1267–1337), but which was first described mathematically by Leon Battista Alberti (1404–72) in 1435. Whereas the discovery of painting provides a relatively clear mark between the Middle Ages and the Renaissance, the difference in architecture is less obvious. Medieval practices continued to intermingle with classically inspired ideas for a century. Nonetheless, Brunelleschi's Pazzi Chapel (begun 1429) set the tone for a type of architecture that emphasized the use of columns, pilasters, and entablatures, all unified by a proportional system that governed the heights, widths, and intercolumniations of the pilasters.

Though the detailing of the columns and bases was inspired by Roman buildings, Brunelleschi was still not using the orders in their distinctive categories of Doric, Ionic, and Corinthian. That emerged only somewhat later and was first insisted upon by Alberti in his treatise *De re aedificatoria* (1452), now known as the *Ten Books on Architecture*. Renaissance architecture is thus just as much about changes in practice as in the emerging theorizing of the discipline. Key was the discovery (ca. 1415) of a copy of a manuscript of Vitruvius's *Ten Books on Architecture* in the library of St. Gallen in Switzerland. Alberti studied the manuscript and used it as an inspiration for his own work. Covering a wide range of subjects, from choice of materials to the history of architecture and from different types of buildings to the philosophy of beauty, Alberti's treatise was written not only for architects but also for patrons eager to understand the logic of representation through buildings.

There are other phenomena that are part of what one understands by the words "Renaissance architecture." The difference between the architect and the craftsman was now accepted, and architectural drawings were now more common. Sebastiano Serlio (1475–1554) wrote a treatise, of which five books were finished, that was more visual than Alberti's treatise, which had no illustrations. Serlio's book had dozens of drawings, showing a variety of built and unbuilt projects. It was enormously popular among the many patrons and architects eager to emulate the splendors of antiquity.

Questions about the nature of ancient Roman architecture and about the proportional systems that the Romans used were not easy to resolve and led to a wide range of interpretations. Some architects, like Brunelleschi, were less Roman than others, and, in fact, it was only with Neoclassicism in the 18th and 19th centuries that rigorous adherence to antique models was seen as a virtue. Nonetheless, the Renaissance did require a rigorous attention to proportion and as a result, facades become flatter and volumes more regularized. The vertical dimension began to be articulated by horizontal layers of columns, entablatures, and cornices. Niches and aediculae now entered the architect's vocabulary as secondary elements to be placed between pilasters. Windows were framed and often pedimented.

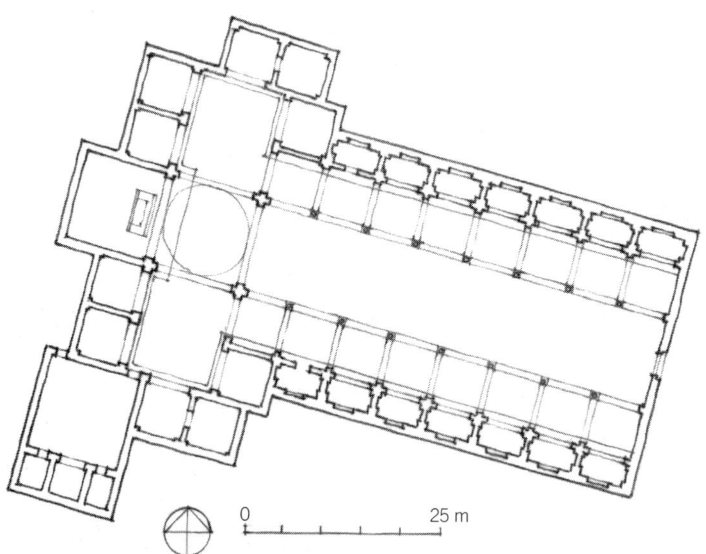


**13.74 Plan: St. Lorenzo, Florence, Italy**

**13.75 Nave of St. Lorenzo, Florence**

**St. Lorenzo**

The drama of this building, begun in 1421, lies in the stark contrast between the *pietra serena* (dark stone) and the whitewashed walls, creating the impression of a structural system in which the pilasters —though not loadbearing—are meant to be read as structural. Unlike French and English Gothic architecture, where the load-bearing function of architectural elements disappeared in column clusters, here the difference is clearly spelled out between what carries the load—or at least seems to carry it—and what does not. Even so, this is not a pure Roman-inspired building, for the prototype for the colonnaded nave is found in the early Christian basilica. The restraint and orderliness of the nave was also akin to Franciscan churches of the late 13th century, and the Latin cross plan, with square chapels on the side, harkens back to the Cistercians. In that sense, one can see this as a complex fusion of early Christian, Cistercian, and Franciscan motifs, but built according to a classicizing motif. Working within the constraints of that classical system forced Brunelleschi to confront the problem of "turning the corner," one of the persistent issues in classical architecture. On inside corners, only a few leaves of a pilaster are visible to indicate the presence of a structural support hidden in the wall.

Furthermore, the giant-order pilasters, in turning the corner between the transept and the nave, are partially obscured by the lower order ones. Yet another problem is that the pilasters along the wall stand higher than the columns, because the floor of the chapel is three steps up from the floor of the nave. This means that they should have been thinner, but that would have looked odd. To solve the problem, and not wanting to raise the nave columns on bases, Brunelleschi had the pilasters reach directly to the entablature; but on the columns in the nave, he added a *dosseret* above the capital to equalize the distance. They are decorated with patterns that reduce their structural appearance.

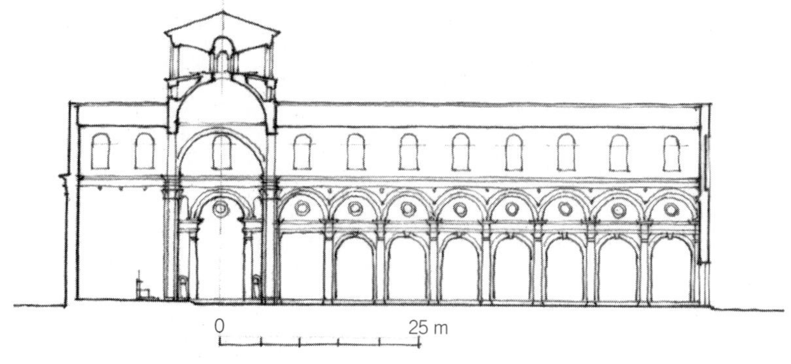


**13.76 Section: St. Lorenzo, Florence**

13.77 Santo Spirito, Florence, Italy

### Santo Spirito

Brunelleschi attempted to solve the problems he encountered in designing St. Lorenzo at the Church of Santo Spirito (1436). First, the nave columns and wall pilasters rest on the floor at the same level. Brunelleschi also tried to resolve the corner problem by creating an arcade around the entire perimeter of the Latin cross and thus allowing the large crossing piers to be the only complicating factor. The traditional apse had to be forsaken, however. The chapels that line the walls are reduced in size to be little more than niches. The only problem he encounters is at the reentrant corners, where the niches have to be squeezed together. As to the corners, he fused the arcade of the nave with the giant-order pilasters of the crossing so as to keep the two scales from competing with each other. But to tie everything together, he floated the entablature above the tops of the arches, a nonclassical solution if ever there was one.

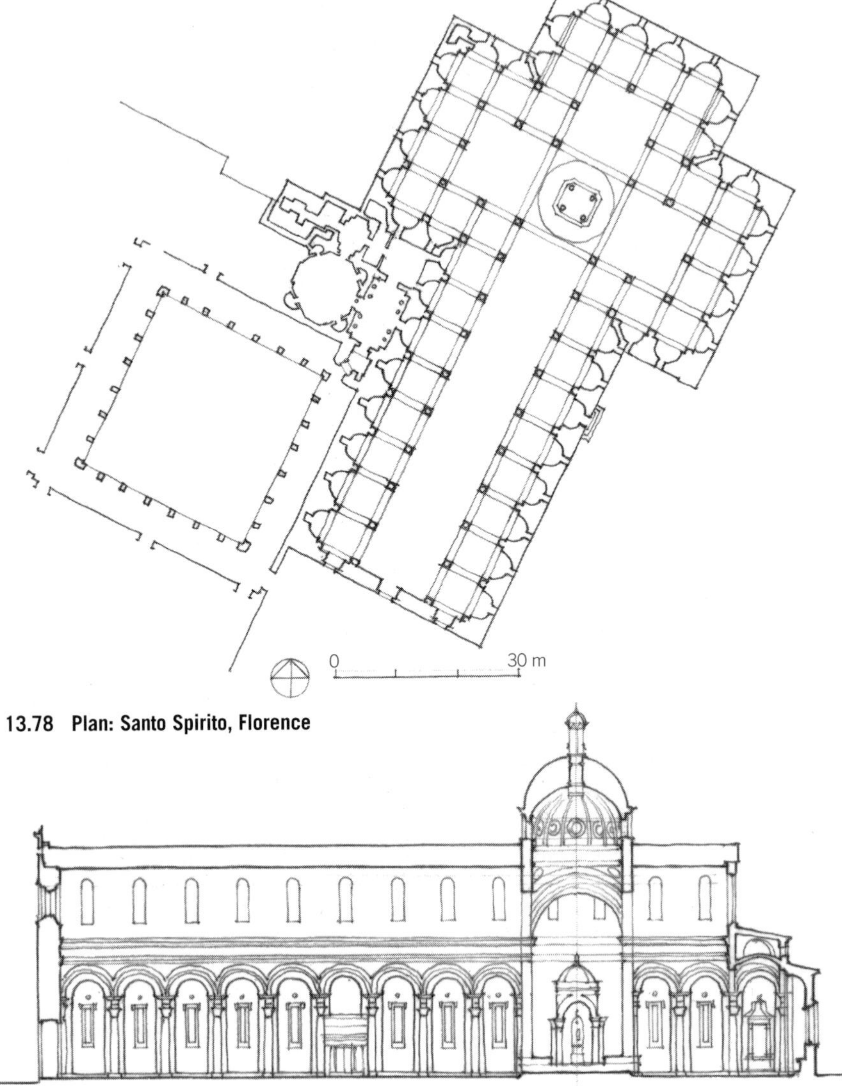


13.78 Plan: Santo Spirito, Florence

13.79 Section: Santo Spirito, Florence

13.80 **Elevation: Rucellai Palace, Florence, Italy**

13.81 **Rucellai Palace**

One can compare here the difference between humanistic and Gothic architecture. Whereas the humanistic mind demanded harmony of the elements, the scholastic mind demanded a maximum of explicitness. Whereas the humanistic mind emphasized proportion, the Gothic mind demanded visual coherency. In other words, Brunelleschi, in order to achieve proportional unity, had to sacrifice visual coherence by implying the presence of columns through the means of pilasters or even a few leaves of a capital stuck into a corner. In a Gothic building, such a differentiation between visible and invisible did not exist—nothing in that sense was "suggested." But that does not mean that form was reduced to its mere basics. Gothic architecture was just as much a search for clarification of form as it was a search for form's unfolding. In that sense, it had a hard time serving representational demands for buildings other than churches, where the parts were complexly intertwined into each other. In Renaissance architecture, a few pilasters added to a façade might be all that was needed to differentiate a building belonging to an elite patron from a structure inhabited by lower-tier citizens. Renaissance architecture struggled to strike a balance between the real and the illusionary.

**Rucellai Palace**

Unlike most architects, who rose up through the trades and guilds, Leon Battista Alberti had a law degree from the University of Bologna and was a noted humanist and scholar. He worked in the curia of the popes, but that was, in essence, his day job. His real passion was studying the classics, producing treatises, such as those on painting, architecture, as well as writing dozens of small plays. His architectural treatise remained a standard text used by architects and patrons for centuries. Though drawing on Vitruvius, it was an up-to-date compilation of important information on almost all aspects of architecture and design. Adherence to classical ideas was important, but Alberti also wanted the architect to understand the needs of the client. Alberti also differentiated the architect who can hold all the ideas and details about the building in his head from the craftsman who operates under the instruction of the architect. Though this split existed to some extent already in the Middle Ages, architecture for the first time becomes a field of study differentiated from the crafts.

The Rucellai Palace (1446–50), designed by Alberti, gave to the Florentines their first taste of a truly "humanist" facade. It is, however, more show than reality, because the facade is little more than a veneer placed over Rucellai's medieval palace. Nevertheless, it was a portent of things to come. All three zones of the facade are articulated by pilasters that, together with the unbroken entablatures that mark the different stories, form a grid over the entire surface. Window openings are placed within each intercolumniation. At street level the socle has a bench along the entire stretch of the facade.

The initial design called for five bays; in a later expansion, further bays were added. The pattern of the voussoirs, stones, and pilasters do not conform to actual stones, but they are grooved out of the variously shaped stones of the veneer. Unlike at St. Lorenzo, where the pilasters appear to be a structural system, here, because the pilasters and the wall are of the same material, the pilasters read less forcefully and perhaps as less "real." On the other hand, they show a desire to unify the facade in its two dimensions. Introducing such coherency to a facade had been reserved for churches and had until then rarely been applied to palace design.

13.82 **Piazza at Pienza, Italy**

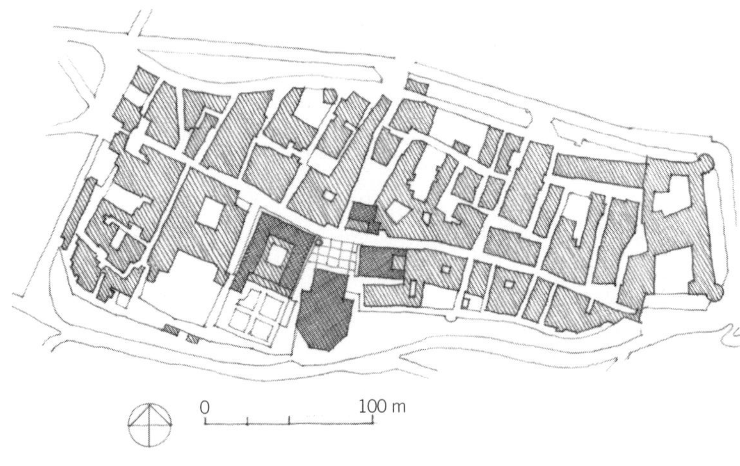


13.83 **Site plan of Pienza**

## Pienza

In Europe's early Middle Ages, the pope controlled mainly Rome, but as the centuries progressed, the various popes cobbled together alliances with feudal lords that soon allowed them to control a territory reaching all the way to the Adriatic Sea. During the 14th century, when the papacy, in a period known as the Schism, was split between two or more popes and pretenders, there was little the popes could do to profit from their territorial claims. But when the Schism was resolved in 1420, the popes began to feel the desire for grander architectural expression. The fabric of Rome had been seriously neglected over the centuries, and the papal palace was itself relatively shabby.

The first pope to undertake serious architectural improvements was Nicholas V (1447–55), who renovated the Capitoline, rebuilt churches, and planned improvements for the Vatican. It was, however, the next pope, Andreas Silvius Piccolomini (Pius II), who integrated papal architectural ambitions with the emerging notions of humanist classicism. He built an elegant retreat for himself (1459–64) in his hometown Pienza, a rustic hilltop village south of Siena. The town's original name, Corsigniano, was changed to Pienza in honor of its new patron.

The task of grafting a papal retreat onto a medieval village was made difficult by the fact that the center of the village, at the top of the hill where the best views were, was extremely narrow. The architects needed to build undercrofts to support parts of the new church and palace. In the whole, the ensemble reconstructs an idealized version of a late medieval town, with the duomo at the top, a piazza in front, the papal palace to the right, and the bishop's palace to the left. A loggia and a "town hall" are at the front. The village, of course, had never needed a town hall, and this one was built for the sake of illusion.

The pope's Piccolomini Palace, is similar to the Rucellai Palace, which, however, it predates. It is for this reason and others having to do with the personal relationship between client and architect that the building, and perhaps the entire project, seems designed by Alberti. There is no attempt to unify the design of the various buildings by means of a single surface treatment. Instead, each building is clearly recognizable as belonging to a certain type or function. The trapezoidal shape of the piazza is partially explained by the topography. The road that cuts through the site is at the top of the curving spur of the hill, which falls off steeply to the south, so much so that the garden of the papal palace and the apse of the church had to be built up on massive foundations. It is also possible that the layout was meant to create a dynamic interplay between views along the street and the facades of the various buildings.

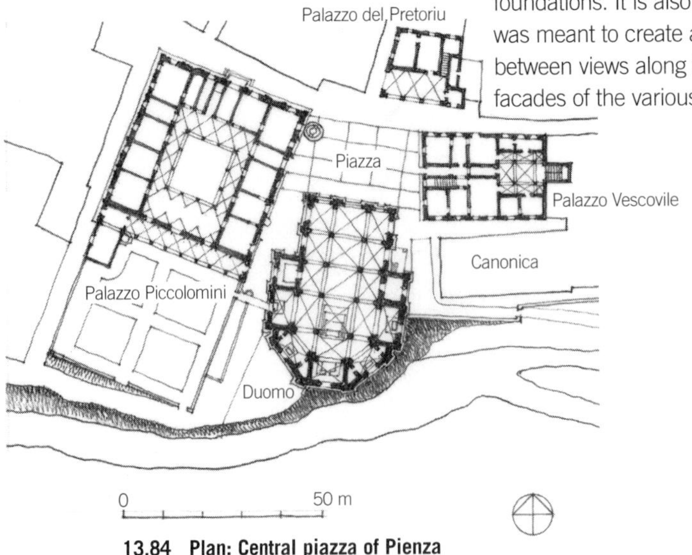


13.84 **Plan: Central piazza of Pienza**

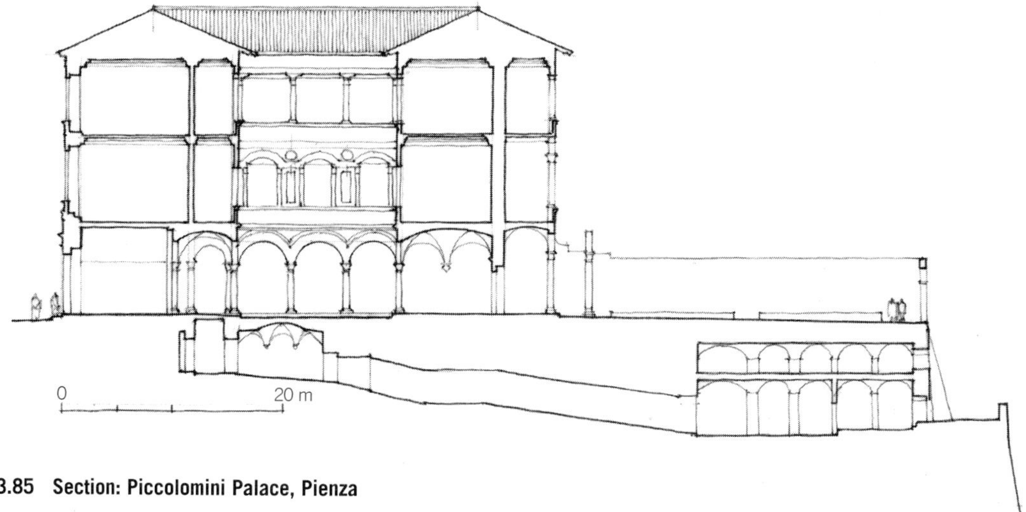


**13.85 Section: Piccolomini Palace, Pienza**

The palace rests at the very top of the hill so that a garden, supported by an undercroft, used for stables, storage, and service, seems to float high over the valley below. The surface of the palace is articulated by three stories of pilasters placed on continuous and unbroken entablatures. The lower order is Doric, while the upper two are a very simplified Corinthian. The lower level, including the pilasters, are covered with rustication, creating an ambiguity between structure and skin. The upper-level pilasters are more conventional. Each story is slightly lower than the one underneath, giving the whole a groundedness that it might not otherwise have. The palace is dominated by a square courtyard with a three-story loggia at the far end that, in turn, opens to the garden loggia. The building is, therefore, a U-shape closed off by the loggia screen in order to become a square. This is emphasized at each corner where the facade meets the loggia. The facade appears literally to be read as the thickness of a pier. The use of a loggia screen reflects the personal taste of Pius II, who reveled in nature and landscape. There is also a clear separation between the public and private faces of the building.

**13.86 Piccolomini Palace, Pienza**

The facade of the church consists of four piers between which are nested arches supported by columns tied together by horizontal cornices at their top and midpoints. To accommodate the proportions of the attached columns, the architect set them up on high dadoes, which make the building seem unresolved. The problem of integrating horizontal and vertical and unifying larger and smaller scales would become one of the most important issues in Renaissance and Baroque facade design. Since the elements of the facade fit rather uncomfortably with each other, it has been thought unlikely that it was designed by Alberti but rather by Bernardo Rossellino (1409–64), known more as a sculptor than an architect. Despite its problems, the facade was one of the earliest fully Renaissance facades. It builds on medieval prototypes, but in its attempt to integrate columns, piers, entablatures, niches, arches, and aediculae into a single composition, it set forth a compositional topic that was to remain primary until the advent of the modern era.

13.87 St. Andrea, Mantua, Italy

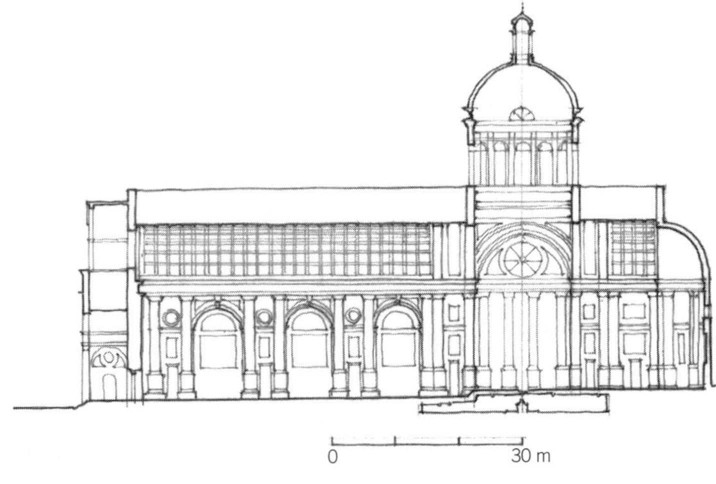


13.88 Section: St. Andrea, Mantua

**St. Andrea at Mantua**

For St. Andrea at Mantua (designed ca. 1470, built 1472–94), Alberti abandoned the long tradition of side-aisled churches for a single barrel-vaulted nave with side chapels. Such a broad open space could be easily justified for a church that was to hold large crowds of pilgrims on the annual showing of the blood of Christ. The blood, actually a dried substance held in a vial, is located below the church at the crossing and is retrieved during the ceremony by a hole in the floor at that spot. If the vial turns to liquid, it is seen as a good omen. The crypt, fittingly, is designed as a Greek cross. The facade, one of the first true church facades of the Renaissance, faces onto a small piazza and is based on a Roman triumphal arch. The theme of triumph is carried on into the interior elevations of the nave. Alberti's use of the giant order was novel for the Renaissance. The problem was how to coordinate the facade with the height of the barrel vault of the nave behind it. Alberti made no attempt to compromise the front, so he created an arched opening that shields the upper-level window. The barrel vault on the interior was another novelty. There are no side aisles. Instead, the arches set between the giant order of the nave elevation open onto side chapels, which are also barrel vaulted. Between these spaces, Alberti placed smaller domed altars.The giant order, though not itself structural, marks the presence of the buttress piers that support the vault. The oculi in the faces of the piers help define the location of piers to their right and left. Integrating the buttressing into the building in this way shows Alberti's talent in exploiting structural elements for spatial organization.

The same is true for the minor order in the side chapels that, together with the ribs, mark out the geometry of the space. This is far different from Brunelleschi's "structural system," which is basically applied to the wall's surface. Strangely the unity of the two scales at St. Andrea is avoided to some degree on the facade where the lesser order is pulled away from the giant order by a few centimeters, perhaps to accommodate the necessary width of the opening, thus once again showing some of the difficulties of working with the classical system.

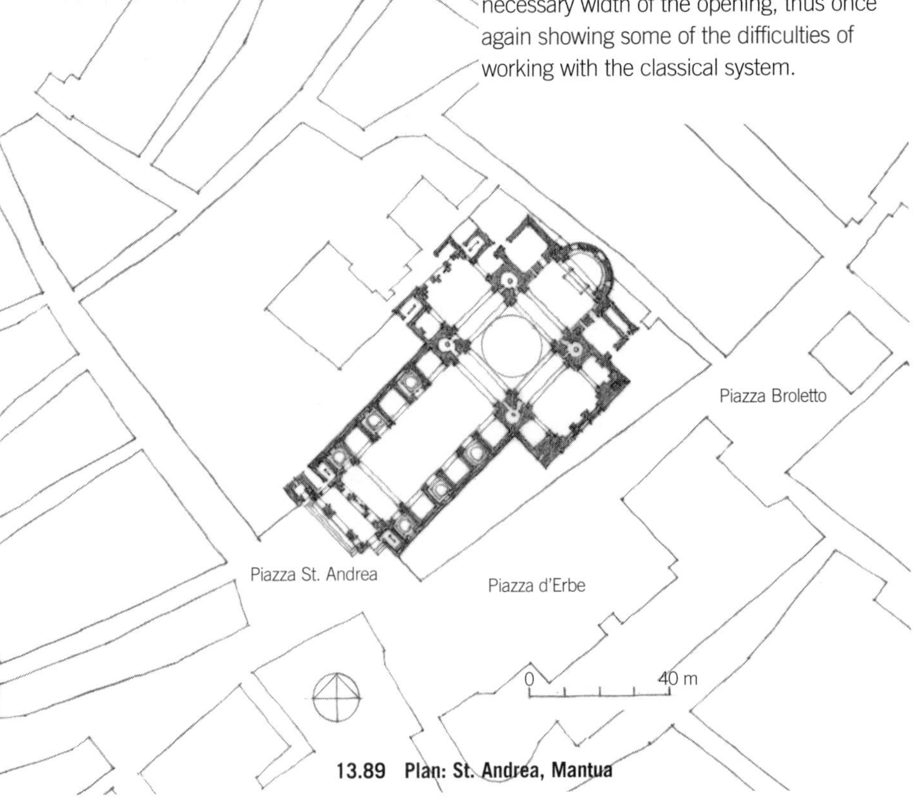


13.89 Plan: St. Andrea, Mantua

13.90 Villa Medici, Poggio a Caiano, Italy

**Villa Medici**

Though urban palaces were the norm for the elite, the Medici were among the first to create a villa that was not just a fortified stronghold. One of the several that were used by the Medici family, the Villa Medici, known as Poggio a Caiano, was among the most important, standing on the top of a small hill a few kilometers to the west of Florence. It had a wide view over the plain between Florence and Pistoia. Originally a fortress, it was rebuilt, beginning around 1485, into a villa by Giuliano da Sangallo. It also seems to be the earliest attempt to recreate a classical *villa suburbana* as described in texts by Pliny and Vitruvius. On a large vaulted platform, containing the service rooms and spaces needed for the farm, rests the villa proper, an H-shaped, simply ornamented, two-story building with views of the surrounding fields and of Florence. The whole was framed by an enclosing wall with its gardens in between. The curved double staircase replaced the initial design, which had a straight stairway leading to the top of the platform.

Functionally, the main rooms are aligned along the central axis with a large barrel-vaulted room at the center, straddling the main axis and decorated with frescoes. An apartment suite with an antechamber and bedrooms was at each corner. The loggia, with its temple-front design at the entrance, was built for Giovanni de' Medici (son of Lorenzo, 1475–1521), who became Pope Leo X. The building was often used as a summer residence of the Medici family and increasingly for official receptions and the welcoming of important personalities, such as Charles V, who stayed there in 1536. In the 1570s, frescoes, alluding to the history of the Medici family, were added to the walls of the great hall.

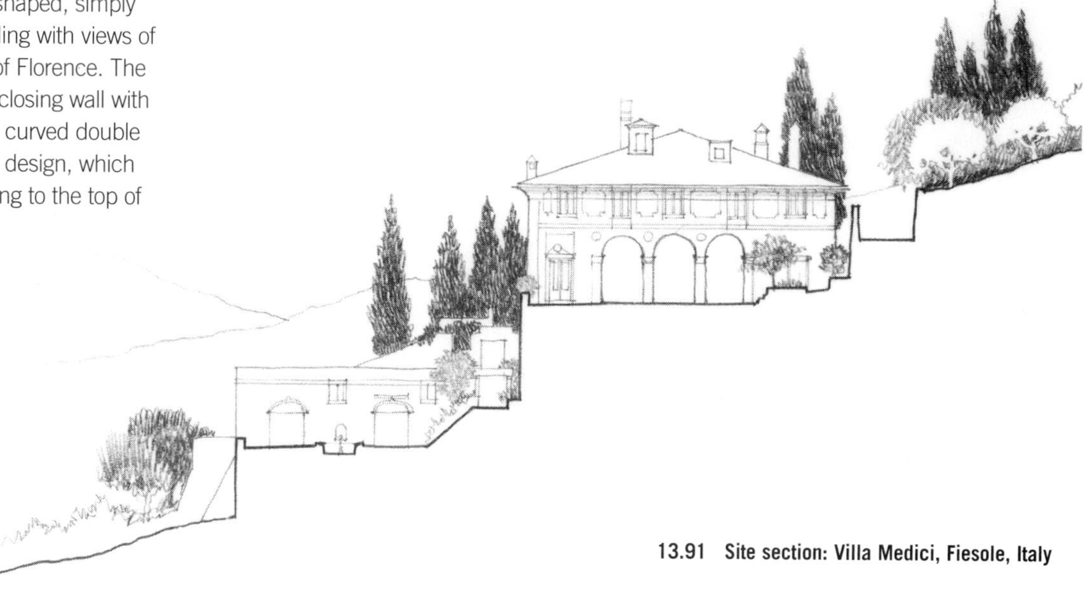

13.91 Site section: Villa Medici, Fiesole, Italy

13.92 St. Maria dei Miracoli, Venice, Italy

13.93 St. Maria del Calcinaio, Cortona, Italy

**Miracle Churches**

One of the consequences of the Black Death, from a religious point of view, was the surge of devotional practices associated with the Virgin Mary. Though these had been strong in France, in Italy, one saw the development of a particular form of devotion, to paintings of the Virgin. These paintings were not icons in that they were not made at the outset to possess miraculous powers. Instead, most were quite humble in origin and made for private use, becoming miraculous owing to particular circumstances.

In 1409, for example, a certain Francesco Madi had a small altarpiece painted by one Maestro Nicolò. It was a modest painting of the Virgin Mary holding the Christ child. He was proud of the painting and hung it on the street corner where he lived in Venice; it hung there for 70 years unnoticed. On the evening of May 23, 1481, a young lady was savagely attacked as she rounded the corner. But when it was over, the crowd that had been drawn to help her noticed that despite the knife thrusts, she was unharmed. The next morning the news had spread over the entire city and soon large crowds convened under the painting hoping that its protective powers would rub off on them. The number of people was such that the city had to move the painting and provide it with a church specially designed so that it could be seen by all comers.

The plan of the building, St. Maria dei Miracoli (1481) is a very simple, rectangular barrel-vaulted box, but the building is clearly a special one. It is paneled outside and inside with rare, multicolored marbles, and has the appearance of an enormous jewel box. The "box" is combined at the eastern end with a small quasi-centralized building that houses the painting, which is elevated on a high platform so as to be clearly visible from all parts of the interior. Unlike most Venetian churches that are at the center of their neighborhoods and are thus not along the canal, this one was placed alongside a canal to indicate its special status as belonging to the entire city.

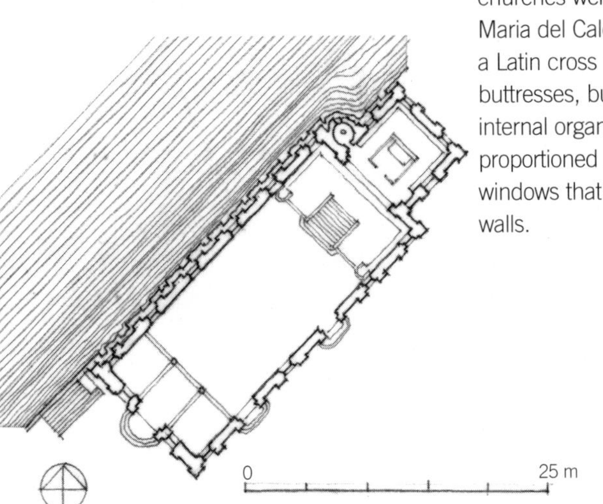


13.94 Plan: St. Maria dei Miracoli, Venice

From the late 14th century into the 16th century, numerous churches in Italy were designed around similar paintings that were thought to perform miracles. How and why this practice came about and reached into the popular imagination at that time is not known, but since most of the paintings were of the Virgin Mary, it could be presumed that this was an extension of the Marian cult that had begun in the 13th century. The dedication to the miraculous Virgin of Guadalupe in colonial Mexico is a later development of this same phenomenon. Most of the buildings that house these images have plain and spacious interiors uncluttered by columns and aisles. In all, the painting of the Virgin Mary presides at the altar. Many of these churches were centralized, but not all. St. Maria del Calcinaio, Cortona (1485) has a Latin cross plan. There are no external buttresses, but only thin pilasters to indicate internal organization. The nave is generously proportioned and well illuminated from the windows that are carved out of the thick walls.

13.95 San Pietro in Montorio, Rome

13.96 St. Maria della Consolazione, Todi, Italy

**St. Maria della Consolazione**

The Greek cross format exerted a strong fascination for Renaissance architects, and largely because it was seen not so much as an icon as it might have been for the Eastern Church, where the Greek cross plan had been first established, but as a materialization of the mathematical ideas that bind the intangible with the tangible. Architecture, with its equipoise of harmonic relationships and strict geometry, revealed the perfection and omnipotence of God's truth and goodness. Renaissance architects were also rediscovering the circular temples of the Romans. The relatively small Tempietto of San Pietro in Montorio (1499–1502) by Donato Bramante (1444–1514) was one of the first buildings in Rome designed in the Renaissance manner. A ring of Doric columns topped by a balustrade surrounds a cylindrical volume that rises over the one-story high colonnade topped by a dome. The crypt gives access to the site where Peter was said to have been crucified. The existing courtyard of the monastery in which the building is located, was meant to have been redesigned into a circular form. The Tempietto was, however, more a marker than a church, as only a few people can gather in it at one time.

One of the important champions of the centralized church was Leonardo da Vinci, who experimented with a wide range of possibilities, most consisting of a square, almost cubical box with apses on all four sides. In some, the apses take on complex shapes that allow for different formal arrangements between primary and ancillary spaces. All are surmounted by a dome, usually a replica of the duomo of Florence.

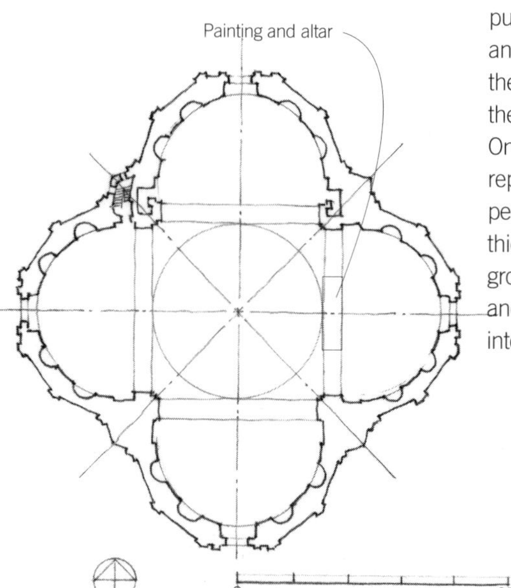

13.97 Plan: St. Maria della Consolazione

The Greek Cross received its strongest development in the context of miracle-working-painting churches, as these churches did not need baptisteries, monastic appendages, or administrative buildings. One example is St. Maria della Consolazione, a few miles outside of the town of Todi, built by a relatively unknown architect Cola di Caprarola but almost certainly influenced by drawings of Leonardo. The plan consists of a square under the dome with semicircular apses on all four sides. The miracle-working painting sits on a special altar in the eastern apse indicating that, though the building is biaxially symmetrical, there is a clear east-west emphasis. The airy interior seems to push out against the bones of the pilasters and ribs. The interior is quite luminous since there are windows all around and even in the base of the hemispherical apse vaults. On the exterior, the internal "structure" is replicated, except that the corner piers, perhaps for structural reasons, were thickened. There are no windows at the ground level, which creates a sense of mass and density that contrasts with the light-filled interior.

**13.98 Model for St. Peter's Basilica made by Antonio da Sangallo the Younger**

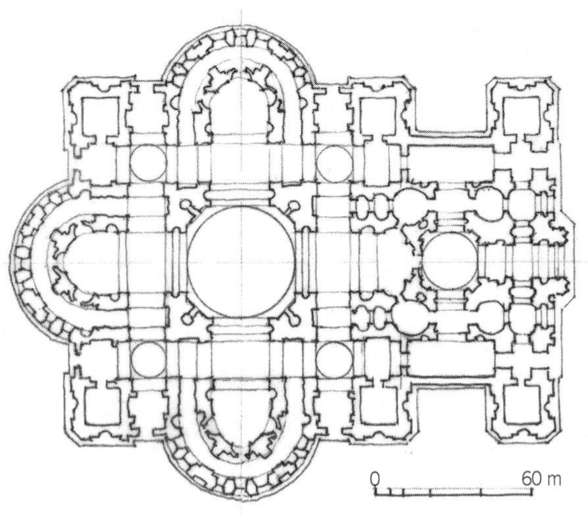


**13.99 Plan of St. Peter's by Sangallo**

### St. Peter's Basilica

The history of the building of St. Peter's Basilica in Rome is certainly one of the most complex in the history of western architecture. The decision by Julius II to tear down one of the most venerated sanctuaries in Christendom and erect a new building was a bold one, with the pope appointing Bramante, who had just finished designing the Tempietto of San Pietro in Montorio. Like the Tempietto, the new St. Peter's was a *martyrium*, but unlike that building it had to be large enough to accommodate the huge crowds. And, given that the Hagia Sophia, its counterpart in the East, had fallen into the hands of the Islamic Turks, the building had to serve as a symbol for all of Christendom.

Bramante (who worked on the project from 1505 to 1514) made a series of plans, some of the drawings of which still survive, allowing a close look at his design progress. The buildings he proposed were suitably ambitious; they even ignored the problem of the Vatican Palace, which was sited directly next to the old basilica, implying that the Vatican Palace would have to be removed and a new one built. Bramante's first plan (ca. 1505) shows a four-sided building sitting in a large courtyard open on all four sides. Each arm of the Greek cross ended with an apse projecting outward from the surface of the building. Four large towers were to rise from the corners. The building had remarkably little wall surface, with the architectural structure being a residue between the spaces.

**13.100 Medal showing Bramante's intentions for St. Peter's Basilica**

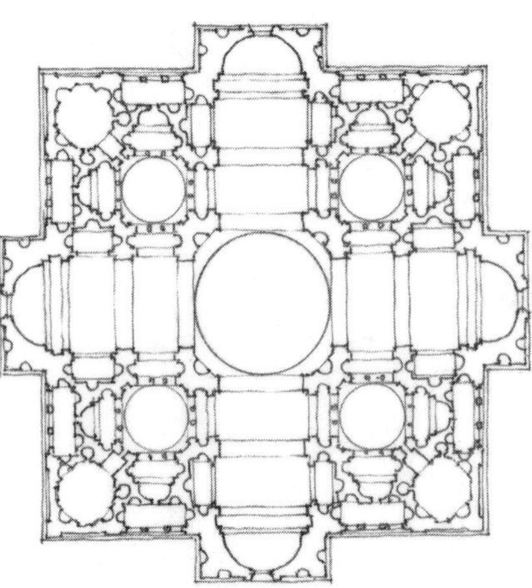

**13.101 Plan of St. Peter's by Bramante**

A contemporaneous design was made by Antonio da Sangallo the Younger (1484–1546), who produced a large wooden model of the basilica. He thickened the piers to provide more support for the dome and added to the front a T-shaped structure—consisting of a facade and domed ceremonial space—transforming St. Peter's into a longitudinal structure. Little was done, however, until the project fell into the hands of Michelangelo Buonarroti (1475–1564). By then the decision to transform the building into a combination centralized-longitudinal church had been set. A subsequent plan by Bramante (ca. 1512), with a thickening of the walls to support the domes, shows a compromise in the direction of mass and stability, but it still betrays his skill in unifying space and mass. The four piers under the dome cohered into unified elements. The corner towers were balanced by luminous, domed ancillary spaces that have been cleared of columns so as to read as a fluid progression of niches and pilasters. The composition is dominated at the center by a pantheonesque dome sitting on a forestlike ring of columns that served as a drum. The plan was approved in 1505, and in April 1506 the foundation stone was laid. For ideological and structural reasons, Bramante lengthened one arm of the building to form a nave with a centralized crossing. At his death in 1514, he had, however, completed only the four main piers that were to support the dome. Even though the design would undergo subsequent revision by Michelangelo, these piers determined the basic spatial layout of the church.

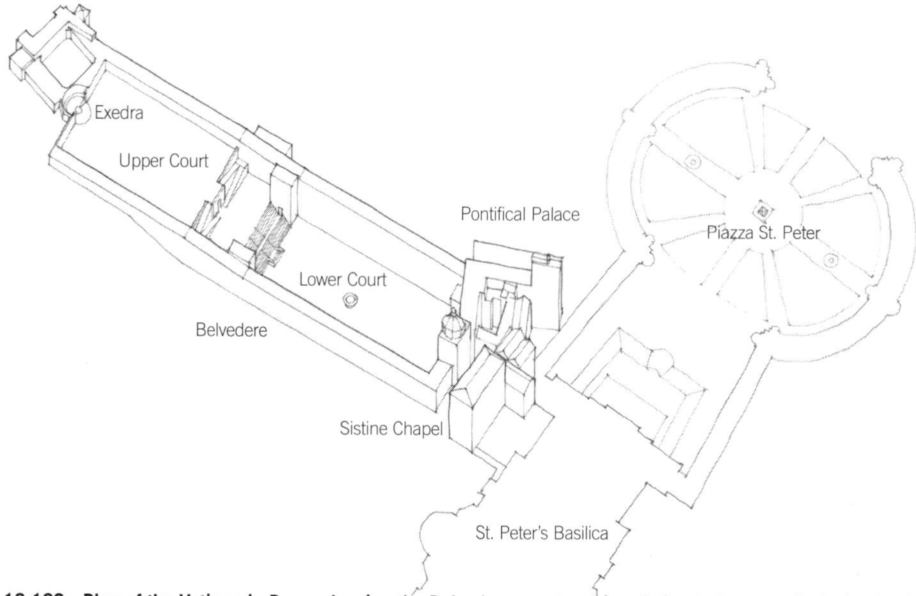


**13.102 Plan of the Vatican in Rome showing the Belvedere courtyard in relation to Bramante's design for St. Peter's Basilica**

**Vatican Belvedere**

Bramante's initial plan called for a new papal palace as well as a new St. Peter's, but at some moment the decision was made to maintain the old palace, despite its awkward position in relation to the new church. In 1505, Bramante received the commission to design a vast rectangular courtyard that would connect the palace with a villa, the Belvedere, built some decades earlier and located some 300 meters to the north. The building is essentially a covered street, but the structure also served for leisure, relaxation, and entertainment. It was the largest construction in Rome since the days of antiquity, a fact that was not lost on its patron.

There are three parts to the building. The section closer to the Vatican is three stories high. The part closest to the villa, which is at a higher elevation, is just one story high (a second floor was added later) and framed a formal garden. The two structures were connected at the center by a series of terraces. The lower space was a gigantic stage set, for the midlevel terraces and the lower level were connected by a large stretch of steps that served as outdoor seating facing the Vatican. The privileged viewing position, however, was from one of the upper level papal apartments in the Vatican.

In the previous century, an architect would probably have designed the whole as a single colonnaded unit, but Bramante chose an approach based on a visual design methodology. The upper terrace has a triumphal arch motif that allows it to be seen from the distance of the papal window. The ground plane of the upper terrace is tilted slightly upward to the end wall so that the building does not seem to disappear into the perspective. Furthermore, the axis is designed as a series of interweaving forms and visual plays. The circular fountain in the lower court is answered by the apse in the *nymphaeum* in the retaining wall, which, in turn, is echoed by the large curved indentation in the facade of the back wall. Spectacular events were held in this space, from tournaments to mock naval battles, with thousands of people lining the galleries and sitting on the steps.

**13.103 Belvedere courtyard, Vatican City, Italy**

13.104 Facade detail: Library of Venice, Italy

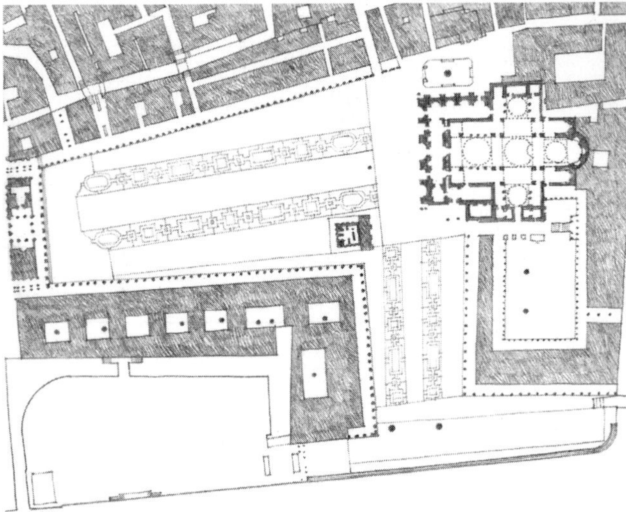

13.105 Plan: Piazza San Marco, Venice

**Piazza San Marco**

In the early 15th century, the buildings between Piazza San Marco and its L-shaped extension, the smaller Piazzetta that ran to the water's edge, were a dilapidated set of inns, government buildings, stalls, market booths, money-changing offices, and even public latrines. A mint, located facing the water, had been established much earlier for the production of gold and silver coins, the minting of coins being an important manifestation of the autonomy and prosperity of the Venetian state. In the 1530s, the boom in the Venetian economy necessitated a renovation of the area. The resulting buildings were at the time a showcase of the civic ambitions of the new humanist architecture. The north side was rebuilt first, with a long arcade at the ground floor, and filled with shops to be rented out.

In 1536, Jacopo Sansovino was given the commission to redesign the mint. Money for the its construction was raised by taxes on salt, the shipping of which was an important element of the Venetian economy, as well as by selling 23,000 people as slaves that had been captured in various wars. Both the courtyard and the facade have three orders—a rusticated base surmounted by a Doric *piano nobile*, surmounted by an Ionic order. Whereas the facade is entirely rusticated, the courtyard is more urban, with only the lower floor rusticated. The facade was among the first to break down the volumetric integrity of the column by rusticating the columns as well as the walls, a device that has a classical precedent in the Porta Maggiore in Rome (52). The windows are tightly packed against the columns, with the cornices encroaching into the space of the columns.

Next to the mint and turning the corner toward the Piazza San Marco, across from the Doge's Palace, Sansovino designed a library that was begun in 1537. Apart from palaces, this was one of the first major civic buildings designed in the new humanist vein. The choice of a library on this site was remarkable as most libraries were located in monasteries, but Venice possessed one of the richest collection of Greek manuscripts then in existence and the decision was made to celebrate it on the public piazza. Sansovino, as explained by Deborah Howard in her book on the Italian architect, chose a purposefully different style from the Mint, taking the theme of the medieval colonnades of the Piazza, yet deploying it in the latest manner.

The building is 21 bays long, with a Doric order at the ground level surmounted by an Ionic *piano noble*. A crowning balustrade carries a row of skyline statues. At the upper floor, the space between the columns is taken up not by windows but by arched openings resting on columns. Those columns, like the larger ones, spring from the same height, namely, at the top of a balustrade zone that echoes the cornice above. The result is a building that appears to have no walls. The strong horizontal stress exerted by the cornice and the balustrade of the *piano nobile* was offset by the verticality of the columns and the statues.

**13.106 Piazza San Marco: The Doge's Palace is on the left and Scamozzi's Library is on the right. The entrance to the piazza is framed by the Lion's Column and the Column of St. Theodore.**

13.107 Château of Chambord, near Blois, France

**FRENCH CHATEAUS**

The 15th century, as well as the first half of the 16th century, in France was a period of relative weakness compared to Italy. The economy was still feudal, and scientific and industrial innovations were lagging. The Black Plague had killed thousands, and due to the Hundred Years' War large tracts of farmland were left fallow. Furthermore, the struggle between the aristocratic classes had left the royal finances in disarray. High taxes imposed both in Paris and in the countryside fed a spirit of revolt. A turning point in France's international fortunes came only with the ascension of Francis I (r. 1515–47). Though Francis I was not a particularly astute military planner, he did gain tracts of land in northern Italy and in the process became a great admirer of Italian art and learning. In 1516 he invited Leonardo da Vinci to spend the rest of his life in his court, offering him his own little palazzo, Clos Luce, near the royal residence at Amboise. Sebastiano Serlio was also brought to France.

An urban culture such as was familiar to Italians did not exist in France. The kings did not even live in Paris, which was not to become the capital until the 17th century. Instead, in a tradition dating back to Charlemagne, they moved from place to place, living in an assortment of châteaus usually close to hunting grounds. One such place was Chenonceau (1513–21), with its extensive woods and gardens. Between 1527 and 1547, Francis I built, however, no less than seven chateaus near Paris. Some were hunting lodges, others places of residence, but even these were located near huge game-filled forests. Of these Chambord was the largest and most elaborate, and it is believed that Leonardo had a hand in its design. But since Leonardo died in 1519, in the year the chateau was begun, it could only have been in its planning. Construction went on even though the royal treasury was empty.

The building consists of a square castle or *dogon*, with round towers at the corners, the whole structure framed by a large rectangular building, still partially unfinished. The *dogon* is not in the center but clamped against the northeastern facade of the larger structure. The chateau represents the unity of royal authority and cosmic symbolism. The double spiral staircase that rises through the center of the building, and which is attributed to Leonardo, brings one to the roof of the building, a world unto its own. With its complex coves and turrets and views of the hunting grounds, it was used as an place for outdoor entertainment.

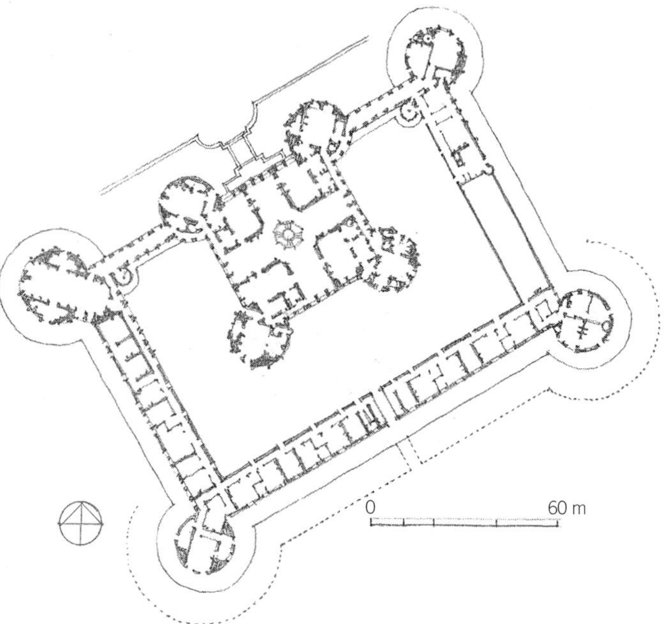


13.108 Plan: Château of Chambord

13.109 **Vaulting of the Church of Our Lady at Ingolstadt, Germany**

**Liebfrauenmünster at Ingolstadt**

The Renaissance introduced a type of architecture that, once it had been accepted by the elite, spread northward to France, Germany, and England. But it would be wrong to think that Gothic traditions simply died away or that the story of 15th- and 16th-century European architecture is one only of humanism's supremacy. One need only remind oneself of the Cathedral of Milan or Brussels City Hall (1402–54), as well as many other buildings in various parts of Europe that were built in the Gothic manner despite the possibilities of an Italianate alternative. One of the most complex Gothic structures during this era is the Liebfrauenmünster at Ingolstadt, built largely during the 15th century. Beneath a complex set of ribs in the vaults, the architects, Erhard and Ulrich Heydenreich, suspended a second level of ribs of a type never seen before. Though they appear to be ribs floating through space, they are carved to appear like closely cropped vines, complete with protruding nubs and twigs, growing out of the vaulting ribs and in some cases emerging directly out of the walls.

As to the ribs, they are sinuous and rubbery and occasionally cropped. Both layers are governed by geometry, but a geometry that is so inventive and arresting that it clearly defies structural necessity. Basketry also comes to mind, the architectural term being, however, *astwerk*, or "branch work." This type of architecture was not limited to vaulting. At Augsburg Cathedral, standard framing devices suddenly seem to sprout twisting and intertwining branches that grow upward over the frames.

Even though the interplay between nature and architecture might be unproblematic and possibly even humorous for a modern viewer, one must remember that in medieval theology nature was associated with forbidden realities and lower urges. Forests, in stories, were places where dark forces lurked. But Renaissance ideas were softening these attitudes. The garden, a rarity in medieval architecture, was suddenly a central element in the program of palaces, even papal palaces like the Piccolomini Palace in Pienza; but whereas the Italians accepted the garden as something framed, if you will, by proportion, the Germans in the 15th century began to explore nature as an architectural form. In that sense, these vaults are more an extension of Gothic ideas than an experimentation with Renaissance ones.

13.110 **Vaulting of the Church of Our Lady at Ingolstadt**

# 1600 CE

By the year 1660, the lands that had been overrun by the Mongolians and Timurids had rebounded, and, at the traditional Eurasian center, three new empires developed—the Shaibani Uzbek empire in central Asia, the Safavid empire in Iran, and the Indian Moghul empire, with their great capitals at Bukhara, Isfahan, and Delhi respectively. It was the strength and power embedded in this land-based Eurasian geography that had driven Spain and Portugal, at the outer fringes of that map, to seek alternate routes to the markets of the east. Their poverty was the mother of invention.

Though the European conquests are often discussed as part of an "age of discovery," one has to note that at this moment the old economy and soon-to-be-new one were still largely contemporaneous. The Moghul empire emerged as the single most important power in South Asia. To their west, the Persians had united the areas between Kandahar and the Zargos Mountains, and the Ottomans controlled the flow of goods between the east and Europe, until the Portuguese and the Spanish circumvented the problem by searching for a maritime alternative. The power behind that alternative strengthened with the creation of silver mines in the second half of the 17th century when the Spanish discovered rich deposits of silver in Bolivia and Mexico. Within 100 years, it has been estimated, the world silver supply doubled.

The impact of Spanish money in the realm of architecture manifested itself first in the Roman Church. Though the Spanish had little to show for their money except the austere palace of Philip II, El Escorial (begun 1563), it was the Roman Church that benefited most, at least in the short run. The entire city of Rome, in fact, was practically a building site, with large bishops' palaces, churches, and gardens being built. Rome's most famous artist, Michelangelo, was designing not only St. Peter's Basilica but the Campidoglio as well. The Counter-Reformation, and the Jesuits with their new church headquarters in Rome (1574–84), aimed at reasserting the Church against the Protestants, with Spain serving as both a military wing of the Church and its direct or indirect economic beneficiary. In the early decades of the 17th century the building boom propelled Giovanni Lorenzo Bernini and Francesco Borromini into the light of architectural history. To the north, in France, Holland, and England, the new architectural sensitivities were only just beginning to make their imprint. The Dutch, who had become the captains of the world and who had created a new notion of governance based almost solely on their mercantile prowess, had few grand architectural ambitions and the French and English were still just learning the Italian styles.

Apart from Rome, the story of Eurasian architecture is largely non-Western. In Japan, the Tokugawa shoguns consolidated their power by building defensive castles and palaces from which they subjected the regional rulers to their new power and customs. The Ming emperors turned their attention away from the sea and expanded the Great Wall to its largest extent yet to ward off the persistent Mongol threat. In India, there was no more ambitious patron of architecture than Jalal-ud-Din Akbar, who not only built the Moghul empire but endowed it with new mosques, palaces, and even a new city, Fatehpur Sikri, in north India. The Moghuls, though dominant, were not the only power in South Asia. To their south, the Deccan sultanates continued to jockey for power. Furthermost south was Vijayanagar, the last major Hindu kingdom, founded in 1336 by the Sangama brothers, Harihara and Bukka. Though Vijayanagar succumbed to the armies of the Deccan sultanates in 1565, the latter did not have time to savor their victories; they, in turn, were overwhelmed by the Moghuls under Aurangzeb early in the 17th century. In west Asia the ambitious Persian rulers matched Jalal-ud-Din Akbar's efforts by building the enormous extension of Isfahan. The Ottomans, led by Suleyman the Magnificent, were also at work, redesigning Istanbul to match their new ideas, adding mosques and palaces of unprecedented scale.

## 1600 CE

China: Ming Dynasty
1368–1644

Voyages of Zheng He
1405–33

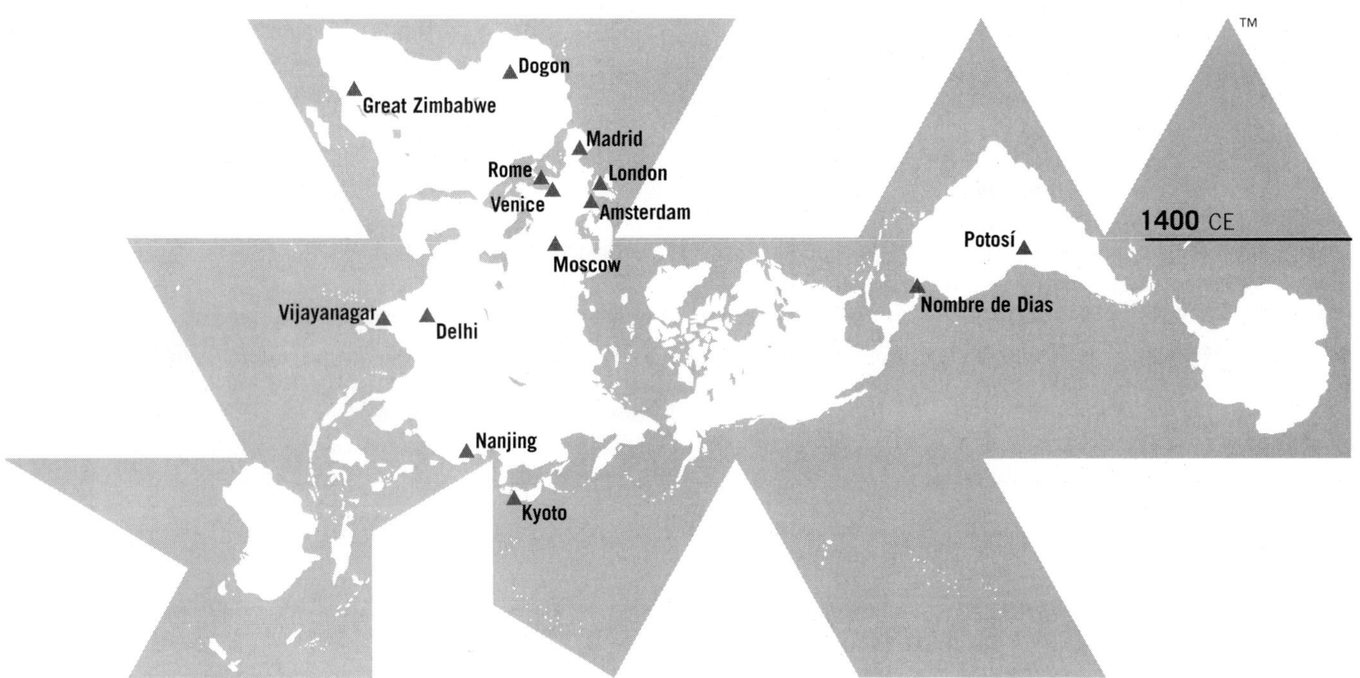

Muromachi Period
1392–1573

Momoyama Period
1573–1615

Edo Period
1615–1868

▲ **Himeji Castle**
1346–1610

▲ **Nijo Castle**
1601–3

⦿ 1633
Closure of Ports

Moghul Dynasty
1526–1858

▲ **Humanyun's Tomb**
1565

▲ **Fatehpur Sikri**
1569–74

Kingdom of Spain
1516–1700

▲ **El Escorial**
Begun 1557

**1500** CE — **1600** CE — **1700** CE

Italy: Papal and Autonomous City-states
12th century–1870

▲ **Villa Farnese**
1547–9

▲ **Il Gesù**
1568–84

▲ **Villa Rotonda**
Begun 1552

▲ **St. Carlo alle Quattro Fontane**
1638–67

▲ **St. Ivo alla Sapienza**
1642–50

▲ **St. Andrea al Quirinale**
1658–70

Netherlands: United Provinces
1581–1795

▲ **Zuiderkerk**
1603–11

▲ **Amsterdam Town Hall**
Begun 1648

France: Bourbon Rule
1589–1792

▲ **Place Royale**
Begun 1605

England: Elizabethan Age
1558–1603

▲ **Hardwick Hall**
1590–7

▲ **Banqueting House**
1619–22

▲ **Archangel Michael Cathedral**
1505–9

Russian Empire
1547–1917

Migration and establishment of the Dogon peoples
15th–16th centuries

▲ **Great Zimbabwe**
16th century–ca. 1650

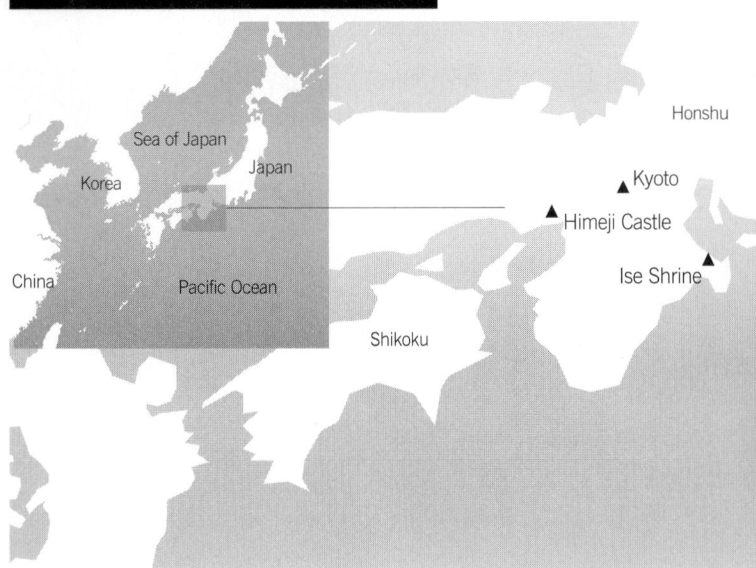

**14.1 Himeji Castle, Himeji, Japan**

**TOKUGAWA SHOGUNATE**

Around 1600, Japan was ruled by three Tokugawa shoguns—Oda Nobunaga, Toyotomi Hideyoshi, and Tokugawa Ieyasu—who unified and pacified the country after a century of upheaval and civil war. The shoguns continued to patronize Zen Buddhism and, under Ieyasu, reconstructed the major shrines and temples of Kyoto, such as Nishihonganji, Choin-in, and Kiyomizudera. The shoguns governed by means of a culture of authority centered on elaborately staged rituals of power and submission. The opposing trajectories of the minimalist thrust of Zen practice and the studied displays of power give to this period its signature characteristic, which has come to define the core of Japanese architecture—the creation of a culture, and an architecture, that appears to be simple and almost casual but is in fact carefully conceived and constructed with incredible precision.

In 1577, the shogun Oda Nobunaga (1534–82) sent his trusted lieutenant and subsequent shogun, Hideyoshi, to construct a castle in Himeji, some 150 kilometers west of Kyoto, to control the routes connecting the newly acquired western territories. Two gently sloping hills overlooking the north end of Japan's Inland Sea serve as the locus of the castle compound, which consists of a *honmaru* (inner citadel) and its defensive terrace.

Resting on the top of a sloping stone base, some 14 meters high, the main tower (known as the Great Tenshu) rises seven floors, a wooden skyscraper of its time. The entire structure is held together, from basement to the uppermost seventh story, by two massive pillars, which pass through and lock together each level of the building. The east pillar is made from a single trunk of silver fir (28.4 meters tall), while the second is a composite. This technology was taken from pagoda designs. Mastlike pillars at the center, known as the *shinbashira* or "heart-pillar," hold the structure together. The Himeji, in fact, is a type of bulked-up, inhabited pagoda—a symbolic allusion that certainly would not have escaped a visiting warlord.

Its exterior elevations consist of a carefully orchestrated rhythm of triangular and flaring gables, creating a visual signature for the Tenshu, which eventually came to be imitated in all subsequent castles built in Japan. The walls are white, whereas the roofs are covered with gray tiles embellished with white plaster to secure them against the winds.

In Japanese, the suffix *-jo* means "castle." Himeji Castle in Japanese is thus Himeji-jo. The suffix *-ji* means temple.

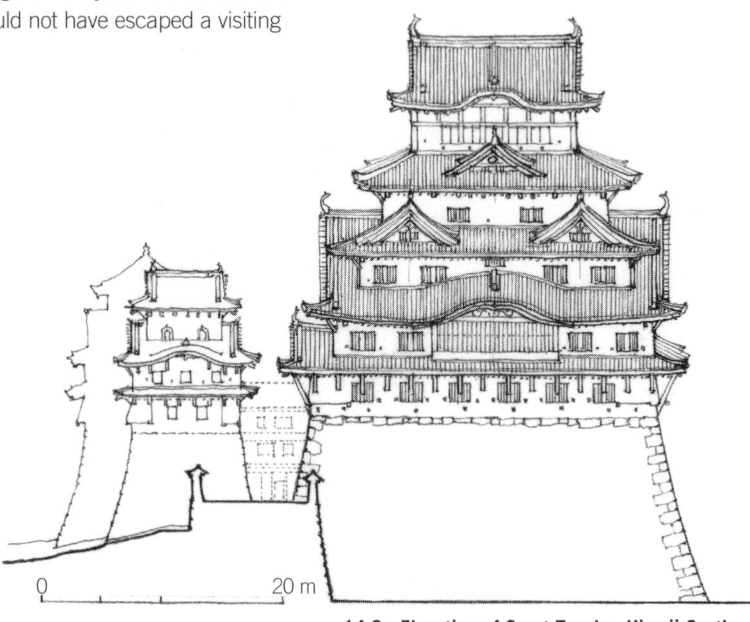


**14.2 Elevation of Great Tonshu, Himeji Castle**

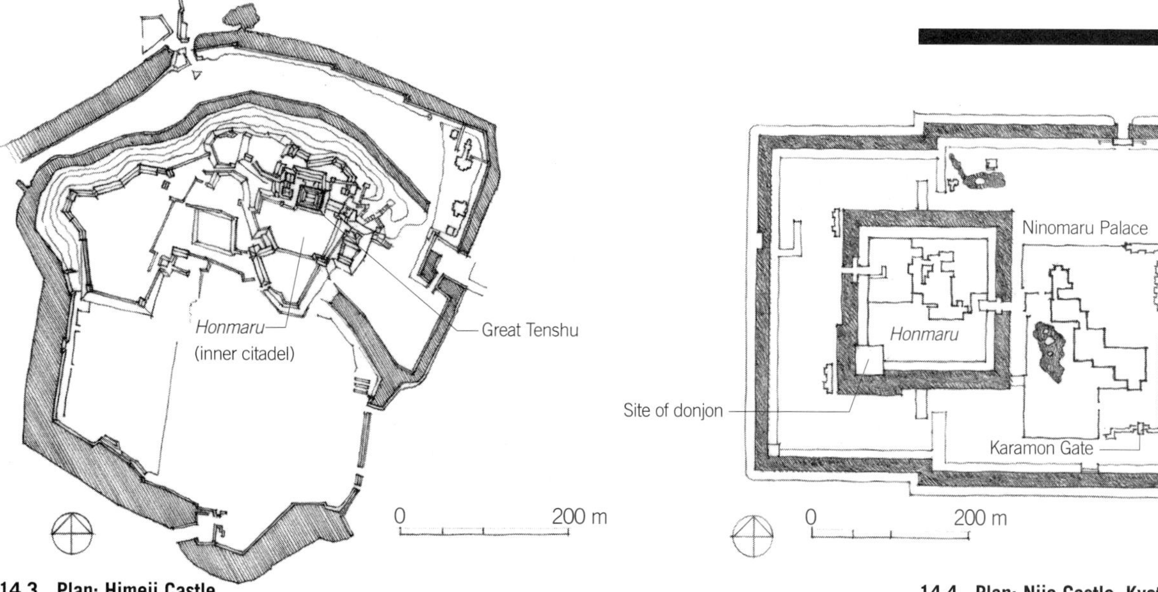


**14.3 Plan: Himeji Castle**

**14.4 Plan: Nijo Castle, Kyoto, Japan**

### Nijo-jo

If Himeji Castle expressed authority vertically, Ninomaru Palace in Nijo Castle, located in the heart of Kyoto and built after the shogunate was secure, was designed to stage authority through a carefully orchestrated syncopation of waiting rooms and meeting halls. The shogun Tokugawa Ieyasu began building Ninomaru in 1569, immediately after he was made shogun by the emperor. Its purpose was to force all the daimyo of the region to gather and pay obeisance to him. In 1624–6, the palace was redesigned in preparation for a visit by the emperor, Go Mizuno, in 1626, the first visit by an emperor to a shogun's palace. The new design was coordinated by Nakai Masatomo, the master carpenter by title responsible for government projects in Kyoto.

A high stone wall with a moat surrounds the 500 by 400-meter site and contains two compounds, each within its own perimeter walls, one for a castle (now destroyed) and the other for the palace. Of post-and-beam construction, the Shoin-style buildings of the Ninomaru Palace are capped by a series of massive clay-tiled roofs joined at various angles. Only the main gate and entrance hall are roofed in cypress-bark shingles. Most of the woodwork has been left unpainted. Entry is through a gate, the Karamon, in the southern compound wall that leads into a courtyard with two gateways, one to the stroll garden on the left, and the other to the palace, directly ahead, but just off axis. The wall behind the Karamon steps back, suggesting the presence of hidden depths to the court, whereas the wall to the garden is angled, creating the illusion of a perspectivally larger space.

The Tozamurai (waiting rooms and government offices), the Shikidai (secondary audience space), and the Ohiroma (main audience space) are the three main buildings of the palace. Added to this are the Kuroshoin, meant for informal audiences with the shogun, and the Shiroshoin, the royal residence. There was also a service building in the back (at the north), with kitchen and baths connected to the main structure by means of a network of corridors. In plan the palace functions as a series of layers organized by a diagonal spine—a corridor that defines the edge between the garden and the internal spaces. All the main spaces of the four buildings are connected to this corridor. Movable screens can be used to close or open any part of the palace or its corridors. Every plank of this garden corridor was fitted with tiny iron springs that distinctly creaked, even at the lightest of steps, so that when the screens were closed the occupants of the internal spaces would always know if anyone was outside, or if the shogun approached.

**14.5 Entrance to Nijo Castle, Kyoto**

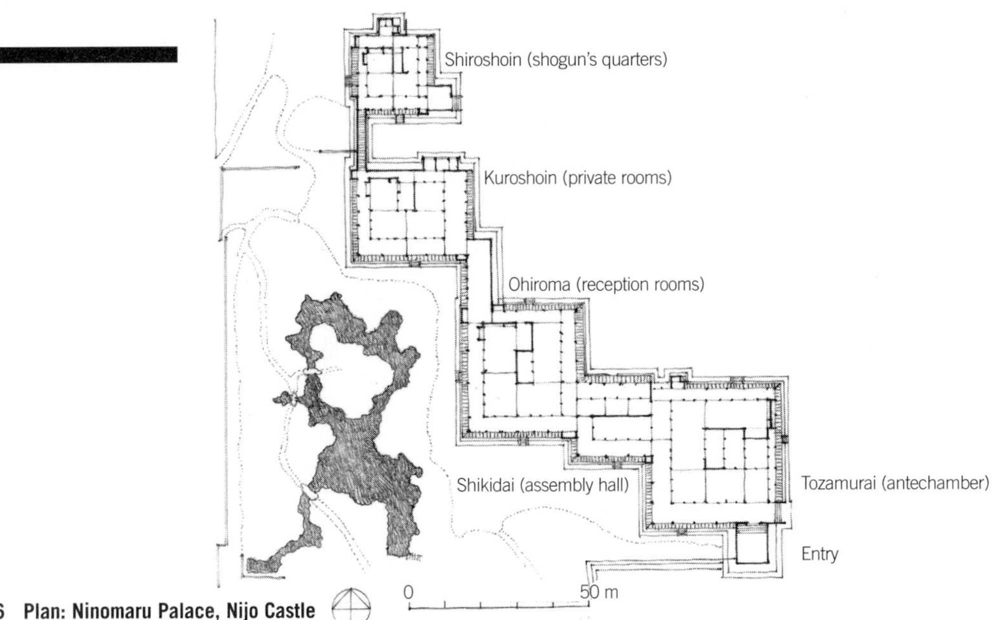


**14.6 Plan: Ninomaru Palace, Nijo Castle**

A visitor entering through the Kuramayose would be shown to one of the three waiting rooms of the Tozamurai. With no real view of the garden, the screens of these would usually be closed. Inside, the visitor would be confronted with a large painting of crouching tigers and panthers, life size, lurking in bamboo groves. Here the hustle and bustle outside could be heard but not seen, as the visitor would wait to be called for his audience. This was the theater of intimidation.

Most visitors would have their audience in the Shikidai with one of the shogun's councillors. Here, the main room was made intentionally long and narrow and offered only a partial view of the garden; the room's design was intended to focus on the councillor, who would sit at one end. Behind him the knotted branches of two large pine trees, evergreen and symbolic of the perennial authority of the shogun, are painted with bold strokes jumping freely across the structural elements in defiance of any containing frame. This was the theater of substitution, the culmination of most journeys, with only the hinted presence of the shogun.

The three spaces of the main audience hall, the Ohiroma, were organized in an L-shape to build in visual hierarchy even in the main audience hall. The visiting daimyo or councillors sat in the *gendan no ma* (lower chamber), separated from the *jodan no ma* (upper chamber) by a single step. Lower-ranking visitors sat out of sight in the *san no ma* or third chamber. The shogun entered from the north and sat in the middle of the northern half of the *jodan no ma*, facing south. There was thus considerable distance behind him and the visitors.

**14.7 Garden of Nijo Castle**

Behind and to his east was the *chigidana* (staggered shelves), gilded in gold with a painting by the famous painter Kano Tan'yu, marking the place of authority. Directly behind him was the *tokonoma* alcove, or display space, with a twisted bonsai pine, its highest branch rising vertically on center. When all the screens were shut, this would be the only place with direct light, which would backlight the shogun. Directly to the shogun's left, on axis, was a special, elaborately decorated door; above him, the coffered roof was raised; and to his right, if the screens were open, he would be able to see the island in the middle of the lake, the only spot in the entire palace where this was possible. Thus, although the shogun sat on the floor on a mat at a spot that was not distinguished in any way, it was staged from every direction so that the moment the shogun occupied it in person, its centrality would be immediately clear.

The Kuroshoin was organized much more informally, although it had the same three L-shaped chambers for the shogun and the audience, only much smaller. The shogun's sleeping quarters in the Shiroshoin were small and simple.

14.8 **Yomeimon, Toshogu Shrine, Nikko, Japan**

In Japanese the relationship between power and architecture is often codified in the language. *Mon* or gateway is part of the word *kenmon*, which describes a person of authority. It literally means "power gate." The word *mikado* (honorable gate) is used in reference to the emperor. A *kinmon*, or "prohibited gateway," could only be used in the imperial palace where access was restricted. Already in the 9th century the building of gates was forbidden to people of low rank.

### Nikko Toshogu

It is testimony to the power and ambitions of the Tokugawa shoguns that Ieyasu, soon after his death, was deified as a tutelary *kami*, or a living spirit, of Japan in 1617. As such, Ieyasu was considered divine and on par with the emperor. As is appropriate to a *kami*, Ieyasu was buried high on the sacred mountain Nikko. The mausoleum and shrine was known as the Nikko Toshogu, and it was built by his grandson, Iemitsu (1604–51), the third and most powerful of the Tokugawa shoguns.

The Toshogu occupies the side of a hill and was built in the *gongen-zukuri* form, with extended verandas carried on bracket sets and paired triangular and cusped gables at the front. Toshogu's access gate opens onto an irregularly shaped compound with a series of subsidiary buildings. From here the path tends to the left before turning north again to face the main shrine, still somewhat up the side of the hill. A *torii* marks the path that leads to the first terrace. Another stair through another gateway leads to the second terrace. From here, finally, twelve steep steps lead up to the Yomeimon, the gate of the inner shrine. This was as far as the daimyo were allowed to go to pay obeisance to Ieyasu. Only priests and members of the Tokugawa family were allowed to enter the shrine itself, just as the imperial family had sole access to Ise's inner shrine.

In the Yomeimon the visitor encounters a spectacular explosion of color and structure. Two layers of highly ornamented bracket sets support a balcony and a Heian-style, hip-and-gable tiled roof. The pristine surfaces of the frame, painted with white lime and accented with gilded metalwork, stand in stark contrast. Phoenixes, peonies, dragons in clouds, and imaginary birds of paradise compete for space with 22 separate figural compositions depicting Chinese themes. Shinto guardian angels sit on each side of the entrance, and a sculpture of Zhou Gong Dan, the Duke of Zhou, cited by Confucius as the paragon of the virtuous ruler, is placed directly above the front entrance.

The Nikko shrine itself is a three-part construction, with the worship hall (*haiden*) connected to the main hall (*honden*) by the *ishi no ma*, or "stone-floored corridor." The shrine's decoration is more restrained and dominated by a single-woodshop tradition. Forked finials (*chigi*) and billets (*katsuogi*) ride on the ridge of the Honden, as was typical of all Shinto shrines.

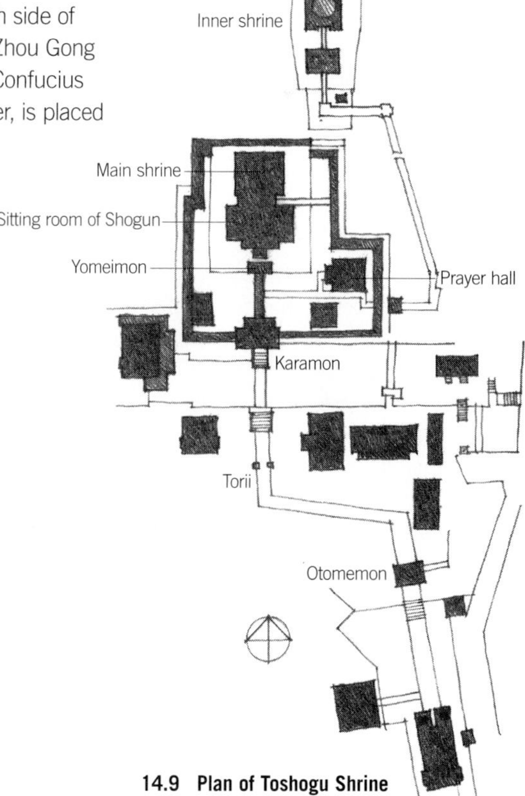


14.9 **Plan of Toshogu Shrine**

14.10 Dry Garden at Ryoanji Temple, Kyoto, Japan

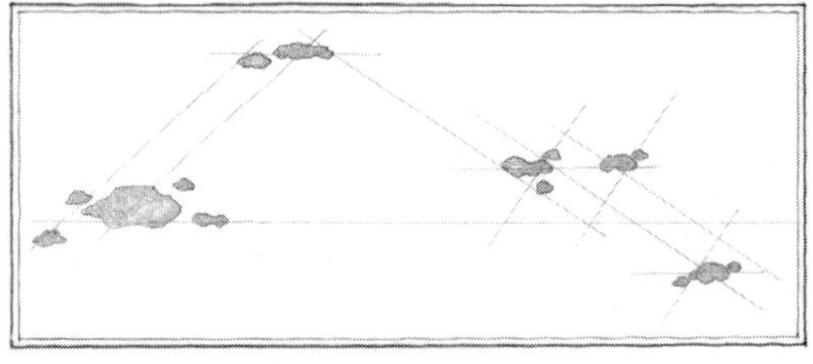

14.11 Plan of the Dry Garden at Ryoanji Temple

**Ryoanji Temple**

The Zen monks invented the dry meditation garden as a practical necessity. Earlier Japanese garden design had been based on Song Chinese examples, which were built on large estates with long stroll paths that had views created from the natural landscape and constructed ponds, islands, mountains, and even rivers, complete with waterfalls. While the miniaturization of natural elements was a part of the design strategy, these gardens relied on size for their effect. In the 15th century, however, when the shoguns began to reduce plot sizes to accommodate larger populations in their cities, such full-fledged gardens were impossible. The newer generation of gardens, made by Zen masters, were designed around the careful staging of views that give the impression of space and depth where, in actuality, there was neither. In the process, they created the dry garden, so called because they employed abstract means of representation, using, for example, white pebbles and moss to signify large bodies of water. The Zen monks particularly enjoyed creating visual koans, or quizzical conundrums, that could be meditated upon.

Ryoanji, the Temple of the Peaceful Dragon, contains the most famous of Japan's dry gardens, created around 1480 by an unknown designer in the estate of one Hosokawa Masamoto, located in the northwestern foothills of Kyoto. The southern half of the estate contains a pond with an island and a circumambulatory stroll path. A paved stone path, with a prominent jog halfway through it, leads to the *hojo*, or the main pavilion. The *hojo* is subdivided into three southern and three northern chambers, with a walking platform around it. A moss garden, perhaps simulating rivers, occupies the narrow stretch to the north of the *hojo*. To the south of the *hojo* is the 337-square-meter, rectangular abstract dry garden with the visual koan.

The dry garden has a bed of white gravel, carefully raked to form bands running in the east-west direction. Against this backdrop, there were placed 15 natural stones, clustered in five groups. The gravel around them is raked to respond to their presence in various ways. The precise meaning of this koan is left open to interpretation; perhaps the white field is an ocean and the rocks islands. The rocks could also stand for a tigress, leading her cubs across a river, another common interpretation. In the end, of course, the garden is not meant to convey a singular interpretation but to serve as an aid to meditation, with the empty space between the stones just as important as the stones themselves, or perhaps even more so.

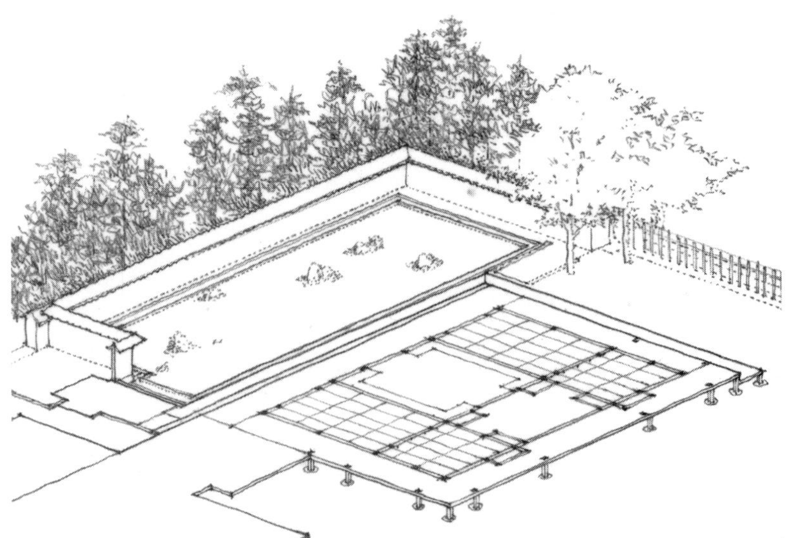

14.12 Pictorial view showing the relationship between the Ryoanji Temple and the Zen dry garden

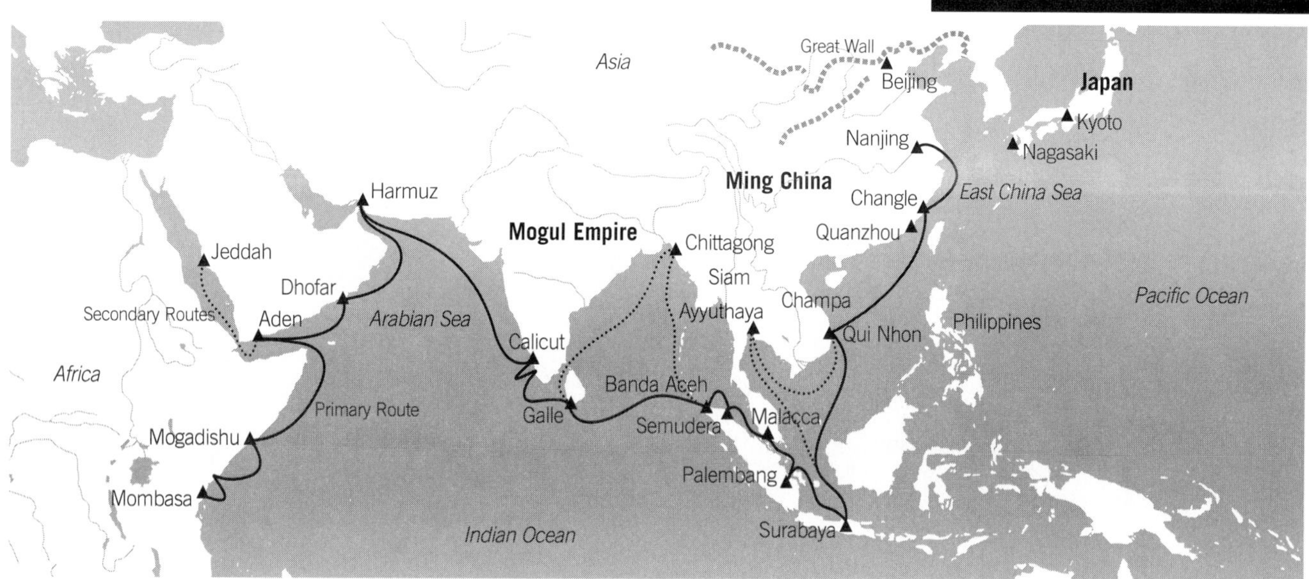


**Voyages of Zheng He**

The first Ming emperor, Taizu, also called the Hongwu emperor, sponsored a series of famous naval voyages between 1405–1433 with at least seven of those traversing the "western ocean," which could be the Indian or the Pacific ocean. The voyages were commanded by Zheng He (1371–1435), a Muslim from China's Yunnan province, whose father and grandfather had traveled to Mecca for hajj and who, therefore, knew of the Islamic cartographic advances. Zheng He's mission was not economic but diplomatic, seeking to establish ties with other nations. Some of the voyages had as many as 300 ships and 27,000 sailors in all, and they reached as far as Mombasa in Africa.

The Chinese economy was integrally tied to trade and these voyages were meant to expand China's trading horizon. The Chinese also traded with the Dutch, who controlled Java, as well as with the Spanish and Portuguese. It is estimated that as much as one-third of all the silver extracted from South America was brought to China to pay for porcelain, silk, and other luxury goods. To feed this export economy, huge kilns were built at Jingdezhen in Jiangxi Province, which produced annually an estimated 100,000 small ceramic pieces and 50,000 larger pieces. Still preserved as ceiling decorations in the Santos Palace in Lisbon are 260 Chinese plates and bowls.

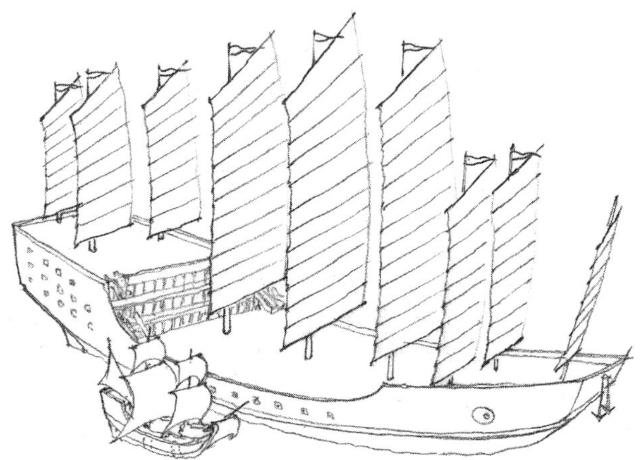

**14.13 Ming Dynasty treasure ship in comparison to Vasco da Gama's São Gabriel**

In 1449, the Mongolians ambushed an expedition led by Emperor Zhengtong, wiped out the Chinese army, and captured the emperor. Stability returned only in 1457 when Zhengtong recovered the throne. The Mongol threat, yet once again, shook the Ming court to the bone. They resolved to disband the expensive explorative sea voyages and instead to concentrate on fortifying against the Mongolians. In 1474 the Ming general Wang Yueh insisted on and received approval to extensively rebuild the Great Wall. Almost 40,000 troops were set to work to build not only vast segments of the wall but also its accompanying fortifications, signal towers, and stockades. The Ming Great Wall occupies the rest of the last range of hills before the mountains level off in the northern deserts of Mongolia. In retrospect, the long-term possibilities of Zheng He's naval expeditions, one might say, were traded in for the immediate and urgent securing of the Great Wall system.

In Ayutthaya, the old capital of Thailand, just north of Bangkok, there is still a living temple dedicated to Zheng He. Certain Chinese ethic groups living in Thailand trace their ancestry to a Chinese princess and her entourage, left here by Zheng He on one of his voyages.

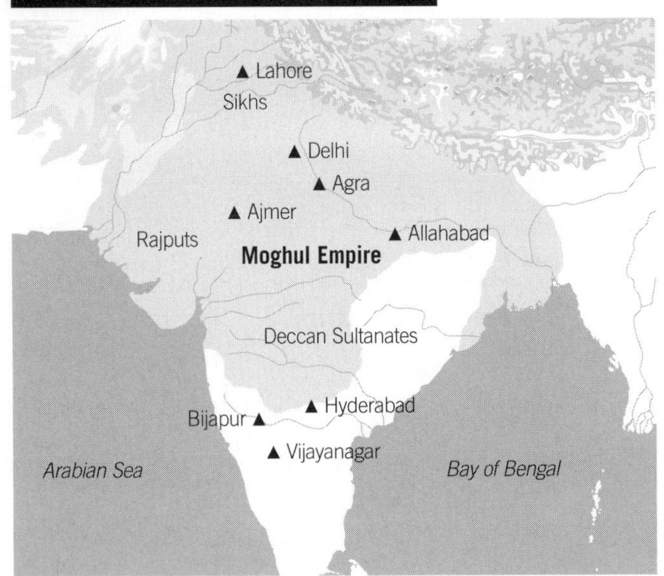

14.14 **Humanyun's Tomb, Delhi, India**

## MOGHULS

Timur's successful raid on Delhi in 1398 paved the way for Babur (the Tiger), to make a similar journey to Delhi from Samarkand in 1505. Unlike Timur, however, Babur came to stay. He deposed Sikander Lodi, the last of the sultans to rule from Delhi, and established the Moghul Dynasty. Babur's son, Humanyun, lost the throne in 1540 to Sher Shah Sur, an Afghan and former ally of the Moghuls, who ruled from eastern India. Although he ruled for a scant 15 years, Sher Shah Sur established a centralized administration whose foundation the Moghuls were able to later expand upon. Humanyun reclaimed the Delhi throne in 1540, but when he died a year later, he was succeeded by the 18-year-old Jalal-ud-Din Akbar (1556–1605), whose long reign firmly established the legitimacy of the Moghul empire. At its height in the late 17th century, the Moghul Empire extended from the Himalayas to the Kaveri. The Moghuls were Sunni Muslims who claimed direct descent from the Timurid empire in central Asia with strong connections to the Persians. They were also influenced by contemporary reform movements, such as Sufism, particularly under Akbar, and constantly struggled to reconcile their heritage with Hindu India. By contrast, the Deccan sultans had been Shi'ite with strong affiliations to Turkey.

### Humanyun's Tomb

Humanyun's principal wife, Begai Begum, brought in a Persian architect living in Bukhara, Mirak Mirza Ghiyas, to design the tomb (1570). Faced with red sandstone, it sits in the middle of a square garden divided into quadrants by causeways, which are further divided into nine smaller sections in the manner of the *chahar bagh*, or four-garden, plan of Persian gardens. Set into the axis of each causeway is a water channel, with small, square lily ponds at the intersections. The eastern wall was built directly on the Yamuna River. (Over time the river moved off to the east.) Its main gate was on the south, although entrances were built in the center of all four walls. The tomb has two platforms, a low first platform with chamfered ends, followed by the second main platform, which contains secondary arcaded and vaulted chambers.

Stairs from the central arch lead to the upper platform. The tomb itself is an octagon with eight surrounding chambers on two levels. A bulbous dome, covered in marble, sits on a high drum. Passageways connect all the chambers, an unusual feature that may be associated with the Sufi practice of circumambulating the burial chamber. A false tombstone, marking the actual tombstone below, sits under the main dome and is raised on gigantic piers. The entire interior is plastered and painted in white and a delicate orange-red that closely matches the red sandstone used on the exterior.

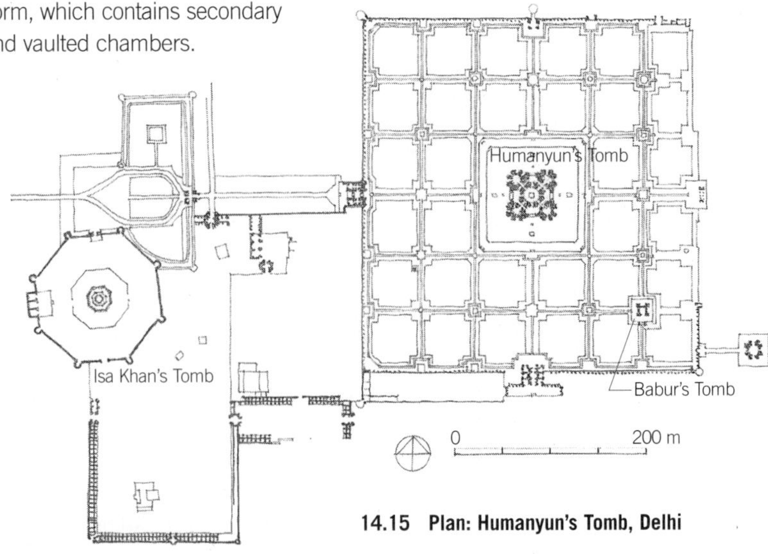


14.15 **Plan: Humanyun's Tomb, Delhi**

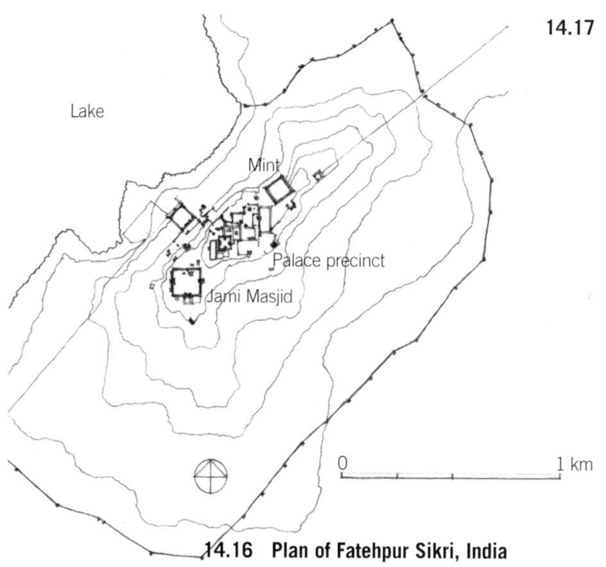


14.16 Plan of Fatehpur Sikri, India

14.17 Gateway at Fatehpur Sikri, near Agra

**Fatehpur Sikri**

If Jalal-ud-Din Akbar was responsible for consolidating the Moghul empire, establishing its system of governance and promulgating its new social and religious ethos, then his grandson Khurram Shah Jahan (1628–57) was its beneficiary. One was an uneducated and idiosyncratic idealist, the other an indolent and cultured aesthete; both were responsible for using their vast wealth for two of the finest architectural creations of south Asia, the city of Fatehpur Sikri and the mausoleum of the Moghul empress, Mumtaz Mahal, known as the Taj Mahal.

Fatehpur Sikri's origins lie in Akbar's close connections with Sufi thought. Salim Chisti, a renowned Sufi mystic, lived on a stony escarpment, 48 kilometers west of Agra, where Babur had once built a mosque to give thanks for his victories in India. Akbar is said to have traveled to Salim Chisti on foot to beg for the gift of a son, who was promptly born a year later to his Hindu Rajput wife, Begum Jodha Bai. To give thanks and to live in close proximity to his mentor, Akbar decided to build a new mosque and palace complex on the long and narrow stony escarpment, known then simply as Sikri (from *shukri*, or thanksgiving, in Persian).

Begun in 1561 and abandoned a mere 14 years later for reasons that are still unclear, Fatehpur Sikri is assumed to have been designed, or at least closely directed, by Akbar himself. Akbar was an exceptional and, in many senses, a very modern thinker. Although he was illiterate, he was very curious about the empire he had just created. He surrounded himself with books, philosophers, and aestheticians and searched for a philosophical and religious practice that could, to his mind, resolve the multiplicity of and contradictions among beliefs in his world.

Akbar explored his interests through personal practice. He had all the major Hindu epics translated into Persian, complete with illustrations; he prostrated himself to the sun, kept a perpetual flame, and rose when lamps were lit, in accordance with Zoroastrian sun and fire worship; he observed Christian, Hindu, and Muslim holy days as well; he restricted animal slaughter on Jain holy days, accepted prostration before himself, and sought to perform miracles of healing. Meanwhile, his fundamental Sunni faith remained constant, but he was very influenced by Sufi mystic thought and is reported to have had several mystical experiences.

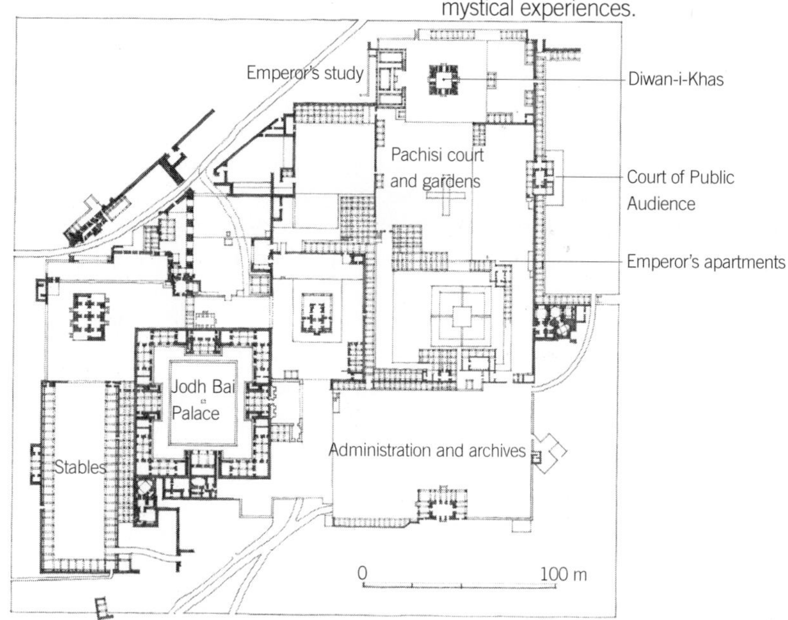


14.18 Plan: Palace precinct, Fatehpur Sikri

14.19 Jami Masjid, Fatehpur Sikri

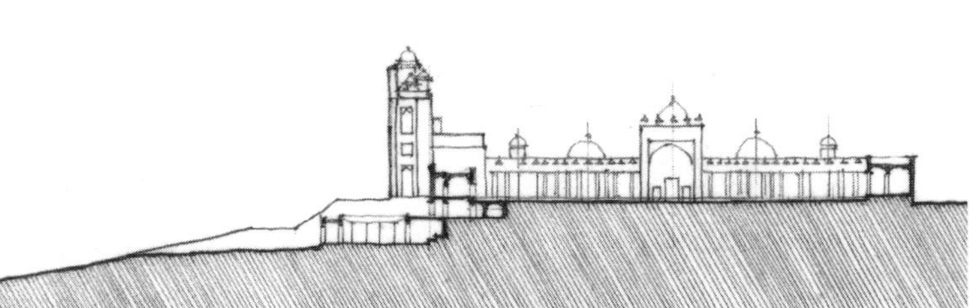

14.20 Section: Jami Masjid, Fatehpur Sikri

The first and largest structure to be built at Fatehpur Sikri was the Jami Masjid or Friday Mosque, built for the use of Sheikh Salim Chisti, the basic raison d'être for the city's construction. Until the late-19th century, the largest mosque in south Asia, the 165-by-133 meter Jami Masjid has a huge courtyard, with gates on three sides and to the west the *qibla* wall, centered on an *iwan* with a central dome, flanked by two smaller side domes. The mihrab, *minbar*, and the entire end of the western wall are elaborately decorated with inlay work of stone mosaic and glazed tiles with azure blue and gold inscriptions. Other than the *qibla* wall, the rest of the mosque is made of red sandstone with occasional marble inlay. The sandstone, faceted like wood, is used in the columns structurally and not as cladding, an innovation that gives to the colonnade a delicacy denied to clad stone piers. Indeed, structural red sandstone columns are used throughout Fatehpur Sikri, and where thicker walls were necessary, they were all clad with the same red sandstone (with the occasional marble and semiprecious stone inlay) giving the entire complex a unity of expression.

In 1573, Akbar rebuilt the southern gate of the mosque after his much sought-after victory over Gujarat. Renamed Buland Darwaza, or Victory Gate, the 54-meter-tall gate is so tall that it ran the risk of overwhelming the *qibla* wall of the mosque to which it is just an entrance. The skill of Sikri's designers is found in their handling of the Darwaza section, which they carefully designed to ensure that it is a triumphal and majestic proclamation of victory on the outside without overshadowing the interior. First, they exaggerated the external height of the Darwaza by building a lofty flight of stairs in front of it to take advantage of the mosque's location at the very edge of the escarpment. When one thinks one has begun a long journey up the lofty Darwaza, one is actually still climbing the side of the escarpment. Its impact on the mosque is mitigated by the stepping down of the section; while the exterior elevation rises to the full height, the interior elevation finishes below the height of the *qibla iwan*. The result is that, from the inside, the external height of the Darwaza appears only as a distant silhouette and not a part of the mosque itself.

Since the mosque had to be oriented due west, it is at an angle to the escarpment's orientation. While the mosque is thus at odds with its context, the multiple courts that make up the royal palace are aligned with the Jami Masjid's orientation rather than with that of the escarpment. In a sense, the entire palace complex can be seen as an expressive continuation of the liturgical identity of the mosque.

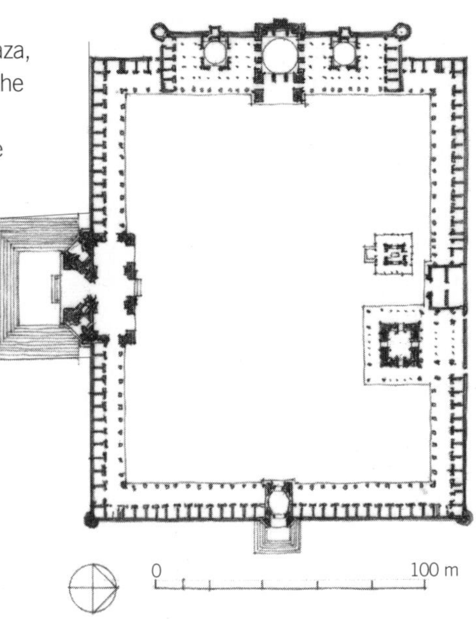


14.21 Plan: Jami Masjid, Fatehpur Sikri

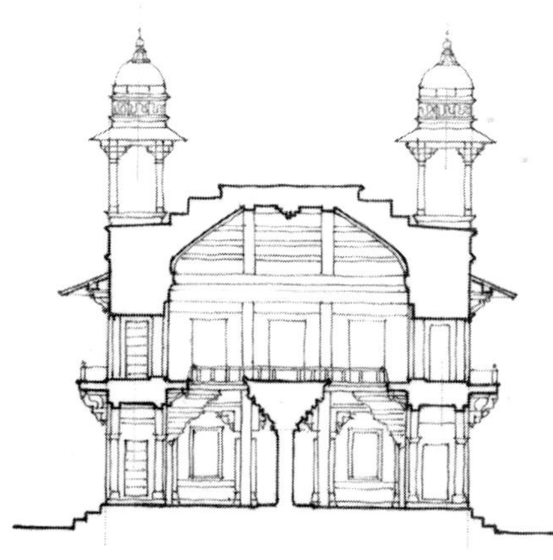

14.22 **Diwan-i-Khas: Section**

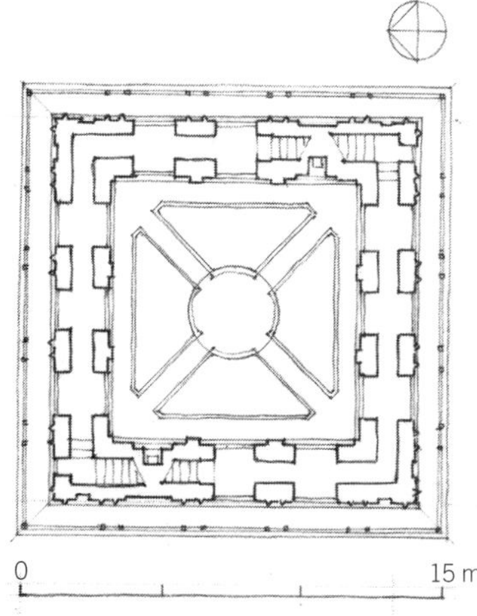


**Upper-story plan**

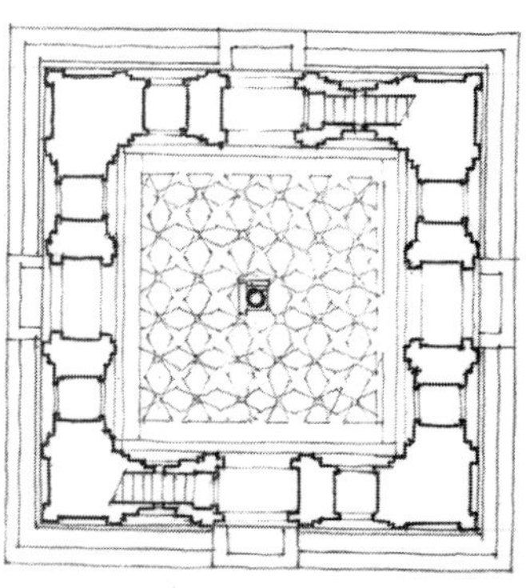

**Ground-floor plan**

### Diwan-i-Khas

Fatehpur Sikri's most important building is the emperor's quarters, with its audience hall, the Diwan-i-Khas. Divided into numerous subsections by level changes and the placement of subsidiary buildings, it is anchored on the south by the emperor's apartment. This simple three-story, trabeated structure, with a throne room in the center against the wall, was brightly painted and connected to other parts of the palace by several discreetly screened corridors.

In front of it, a little off-center, is the Anup Talao, or the "incomparable pond," a shallow, square water tank. It is focused on a small central terrace, accessed on axis by four narrow terraces, the first of three cruciform patterns in the Diwan-i-Khas. In the middle of the northern half of the main court is inscribed the cruciform arrangement used to play the dice game of pachisi, named for the highest number, 25, that can be achieved by a single throw of the dice. This oversized game board may have more symbolic associations connected with numerology than be for actual use.

Beyond this, framed on center, is the solitary object-in-space building, clearly the most important structure in Fatehpur Sikri, and also, as it turns out, the most mysterious. This two-story square box, with four *chattris* at the corners, made entirely out of red sandstone, is known as the Diwan-i-Khas. A deep overhanging *chajja* casts a prominent shadow over the upper-story elevation. At 13.18 meters, the width of the building is the same as its height taken to the top of the *chattris*, making it symbolically a perfect cube. But the drama at the Diwan-i-Khas is in the interior. In the double-height space of the interior, located in the center of the overall volume and supported by a single pillar with a mushroom of sandstone brackets, is a round platform, hovering, as it were, in midair. It is connected at the corners with narrow bridges forming a cruciform pattern. A narrow balcony runs around the interior at the second-story level.

The Diwan-i-Khas has no known precedent and was never copied again. A common assumption is that it functioned as an idiosyncratic audience hall, with the emperor listening to supplicants from above and consulting with ministers at the ends of the bridges. Another interpretation holds that it was meant as a spatial representation of Islam's core concept, the Five Pillars that define the faith, namely the unity of God, daily prayers, giving to the poor, fasting, and the hajj. Of these, faith is described in Islamic literature as the central pillar, supported by the other four. If one conceives the corners of the Diwan-i-Khas, with the *chattris* and the quarter-round corner brackets that support the bridges as pillars, then the entire edifice could indeed be seen as an embodiment of Islam's Five Pillars.

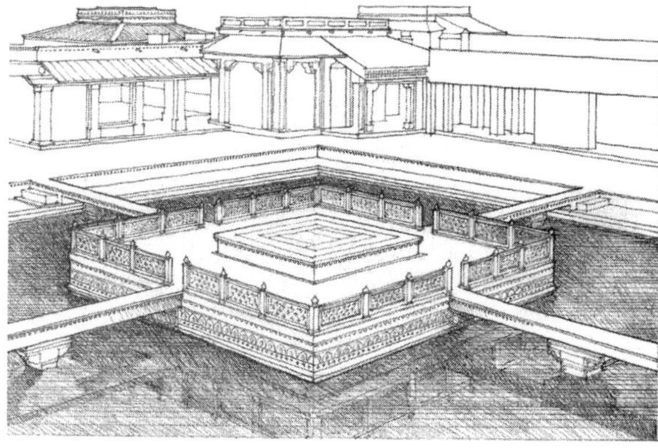

14.23 **The emperor's apartments at Fatehpur Sikri**

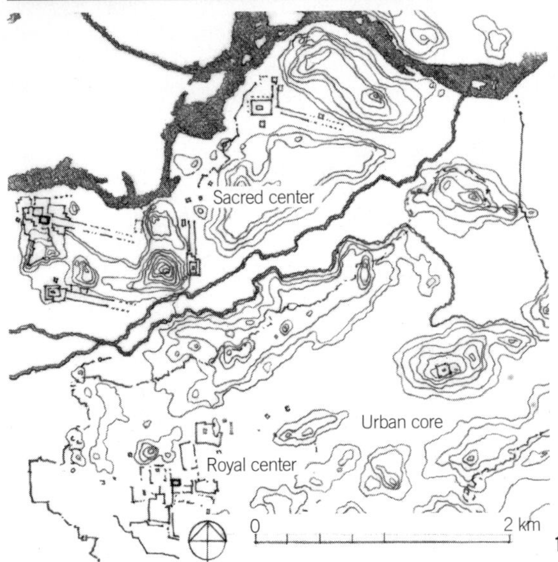


14.24 Site plan of Vijayanagar, India

14.25 Rampant horse column: Vitthala complex, Vijayanagar

### Vijayanagar

The brothers Harihara and Bukka Sangama established their capital Vijayanagar in 1340 on a rocky plateau on the southern bank of the Tungabhadra River. Former generals of the Moghuls, the brothers had converted to Islam but reconverted to Hinduism when they established Vijayanagar (City of Victory). Though defenders of Hinduism, they copied much from the architecture of pomp and circumstance of their Islamic neighbors. Their temples were based on Tamil prototypes. The 15th-century Ramachandra Temple, in the royal compound of Vijayanagar, consists of a small square *garbh-griha* with an attached antechamber, leading to a larger square *mandapa*, with three pillared porticos. The main level of the temple is divided into panels with framing pilasters. The layered pyramid of the *shikhara* is distinctly separated from the main level by a horizontal course, culminating in an octagonal finial. It is enclosed by a perimeter wall with three entrances. The Vijayanagar interest in procession is indicated by the staging of the main east entrance. Here a short *gopuram*, aligned with the temple, leads into a forecourt whose cross axis is framed by pillared halls. A small, axially placed water tank shares the center of the court with another Vijayanagar signature form, a field of columns (eight in two rows in this case) aligned with the temple entrance.

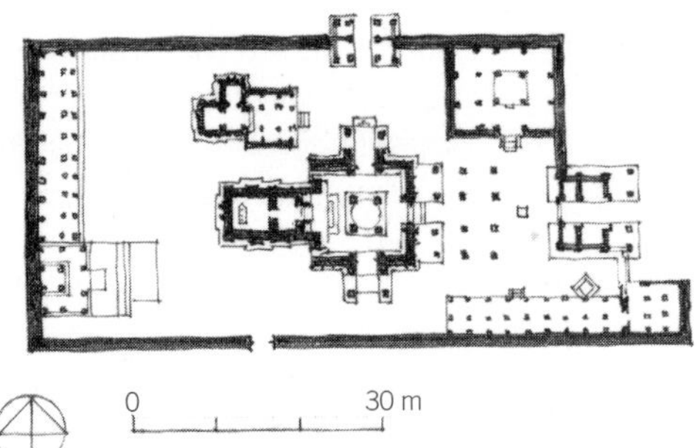


14.26 Plan: Ramachandra Temple, Royal Center, Vijayanagar

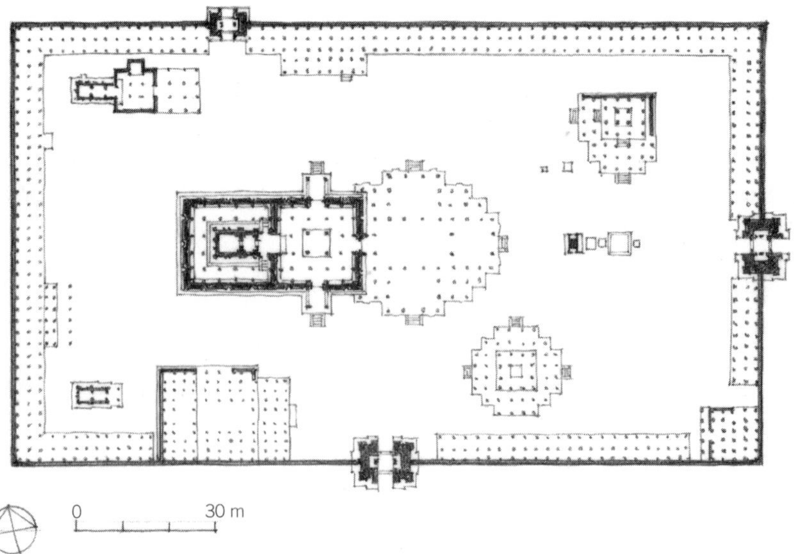


14.27 Plan: Vitthala complex, Sacred Center, Vijayanagar

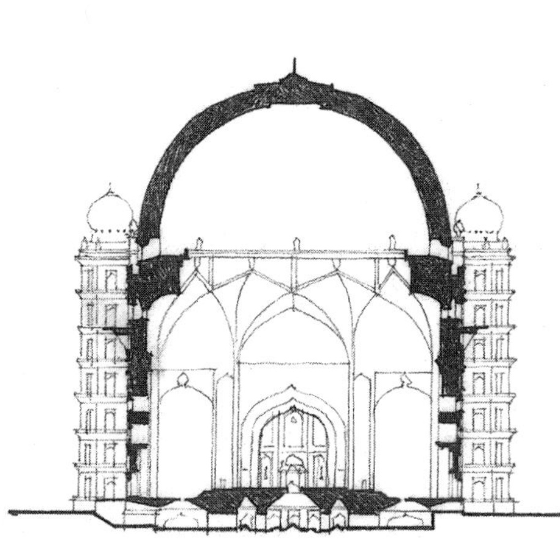

14.28 Section: Gol Gumbaz, Bijapur, India

14.29 Gol Gumbaz

The Vitthala complex, whose main shrine was built around 1554 during the era of Sadshiva, enjoyed extensive royal patronage. While the main *garbh-griha*, its circumambulation route, and its first 16 pillared *mandapa* are not out of the norm, its distinction lies in its second open *mandapa*, accessed from three sides and adorned with highly ornate monolithic columns and groups of *colonettes* with slender fluted profiles clustered around shafts. A stone replica of a wooden chariot, complete with wheels, stands in front of the temple. Off to one side is a stepped, open colonnaded hall, with a raised platform in the center for fire sacrifices. On either side of the entrance steps the temple has columns that are modeled in the form of *yalis*, or rampant mythical horses in fiercesome poses. The Vijayanagar kings maintained a precious supply of horses through trade with the Arabs (which made control of the western ports, such as Goa, very important). Besides the usual panoply of mythical beasts in Hindu temples, such *yalis* became standard in the Vijayanagar and later Nayak temples, testimony in part to the significant role played by horses in the Vijayanagar's history.

**Bijapur**

After the combined forces of the Deccan sultans defeated the Vijayanagar in 1565, they went on a building spree. Most benefiting from the fall of Vijayanagar was the Bijapur dynasty, founded by Yusuf Adil Shah (1489–1510), who built Bijapur into a citadel with 10 kilometers of walls and six gates. Whereas his buildings were rather austere, that was not the case with Ibrahim Adil Shah II (1580–1627), whose buildings are sumptuous and celebratory. Ibrahim II modeled his architecture on the example of his contemporary, the Moghul emperor Akbar.

The most exceptional of Bijapur's buildings is the Gol Gumbaz, the largest single-chambered building ever constructed. It was a tomb built by Ibrahim II's successor, Muhammad adil Shah (1627–57), for himself. Eight intersecting pointed arches, springing from two rotated squares, support both a round platform and the gigantic hemispherical dome. Built with horizontal brick courses, cemented with thick layers of lime mortar, the dome is 3.5 meters thick at the base, has six small openings, and a flat section at the crown. Its supporting walls are largely plain and unornamented. An unoccupied niche is in the eastern wall, the main entrance to the west, and in the middle, directly below the intersections of the arches, is a simple platform with the tombs of Muhammad and his family at the center. Outside there are four corner turrets, more like stubs, with simple domes.

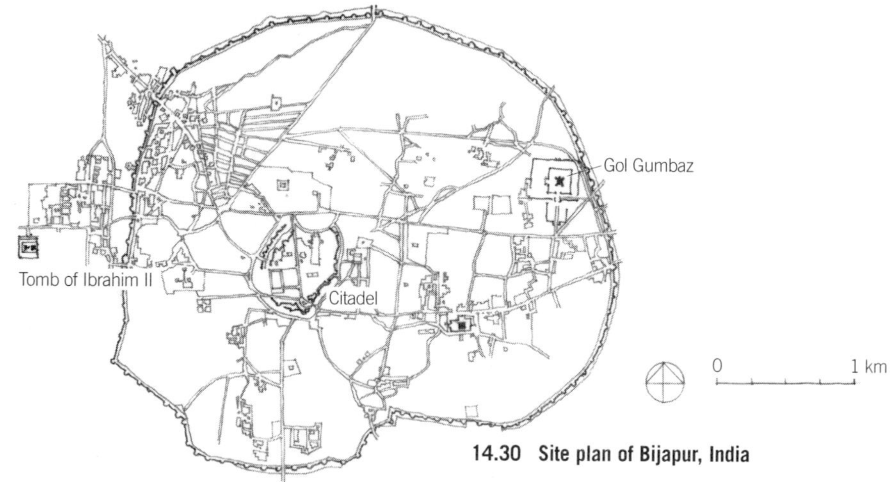


14.30 Site plan of Bijapur, India

14.31 Tomb of Ibrahim II, Bijapur, India

### Ibrahim Rauza

Ibrahim II's tomb and mosque complex (Ibrahim Rauza; *rauza* means "garden") was built originally for his wife but eventually held his own grave as well as those of his family. Enclosed by a quadrangle about 125 meters square, the tomb and mosque sit off center on a single platform. On the western side, the freestanding mosque has five arches three bays deep, with a bulbous dome over the central bays. A deep parapet supported by closely spaced brackets rounds out at the corners in a profusion of brackets that spiral into tall, thin minarets that culminate in small bulbous domes supported like balls on a bed of flower petals. The central dome also appears to be a sphere supported by tall lotus petals. The four corner minarets define a spatial field, twice the height of the primary building, at the center of which is the central dome with its own minarets at the corners. Ibrahim II's tomb on the eastern side butts against the edge of the compound and, although it has seven arches on each side that vary rhythmically in width, the overall vocabulary of the building is in harmony with the mosque. Together, the tomb and the mosque define a court, almost perfectly square, that is animated by a shallow water tank shifted off center toward the mausoleum.

14.32 Section: Tomb of Ibrahim II, Bijapur

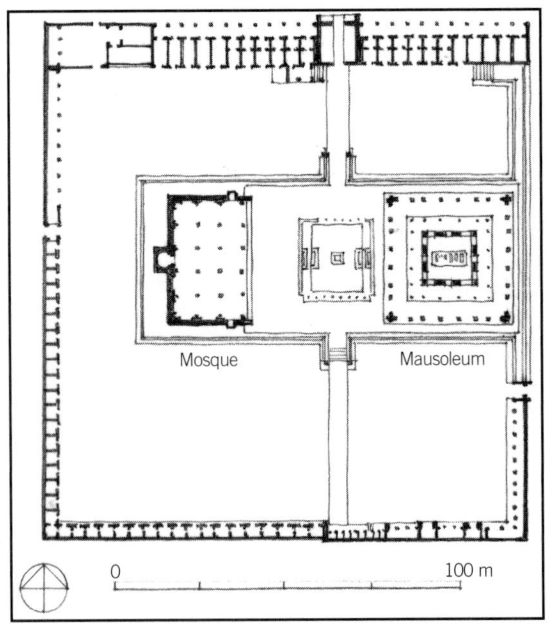


14.33 Plan: Tomb of Ibrahim II, Bijapur

14.34 Sheikh Safi Tomb-Mosque, Ardebil, Iran

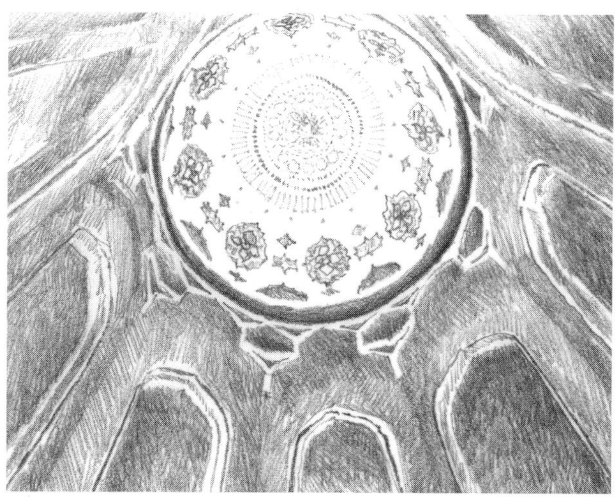

14.35 Interior dome: Sheikh Safi Tomb-Mosque

**Sheikh Safi Tomb-Mosque**

Of a militant Islamic Sufi order, the Safavids first appeared among Turkish-speaking people in Iran; they had their home base at Ardebil, west of the Caspian Sea. In 1501 the Safavids seized Tabriz and made it their capital. They also conquered Armenia, Azerbaijan, and Khurasan. Particularly important to them was the tomb-mosque form such as that of Sheikh Safi, completed in the middle of the 17th century in Ardebil. The city was the birthplace of the eminent religious leader Sheik Safi (1251–1334), from whom the Safavid dynasty descended. Sheikh Safi was the founder of a Sufi order known as the Dervish Brotherhood. The main objectives of the Brotherhood were the elimination of the then-rampant anarchy and the reorganization of a new state. The Safavids drew on both the mystical emotional force of the Sufi and Sufism's appeal to the masses. Ismail, a descendent of Sheikh Safi and who was later crowned as the shah of Persia in Tabriz (1501), was a member of this order. He created an immense empire and succeeded in subjecting the many principalities that had formed after the fall of Timurid state. In 1510, he conquered Baghdad.

The tomb-mosque structure, begun in the 14th century and added to in subsequent centuries, is entered via a long garden to which the buildings are joined at an angle. These are centered around an inner courtyard, measuring 31 by 16 meters. At one of the narrow ends is the mosque Jannat Sara (meaning the House of Paradise), an octagonal structure of 16 wooden pillars with window recesses and without a mihrab. The facade is bold and simple, with elegant green-and-blue tile work ornamenting the surface and with inscriptions in the Kufic and Riqa script serving as a frieze. The space is entered to the left, the right door leading to service rooms. Screening of the large central opening separates the inside and the outside.

At a right angle to the mosque lies the tomb proper, consisting of a mausoleum and a prayer hall with rectangular niches. The palacelike facade is of brick with vertical zones in blue tile and an entrance to the left. The mausoleum is composed of a tall circular tower with a dome. It has a circumference of 22 meters and is about 17 meters high.

The centralized building alongside the mausoleum, with a dome on a low drum, is the 17th-century Porcelain House (Chini Khane; *Chini* means "China" and *khane* means "niche") in which the Chinese ceremonial wares of the sanctuary are preserved. The walls had wood paneling with openings of various forms and sizes, reaching all to the way to the vaults, in which the porcelain pieces were individually displayed. Filling out the plan were kitchens and living rooms for priests, pilgrims, and the poor. There is also a Khanaqah (House of Dervishes), Cheragh Khaneh (House of Lamps), Shahid Khaneh (House of Martyrs) and Chelleh Khaneh (the place where devotees isolate themselves during the forty days of Lent).

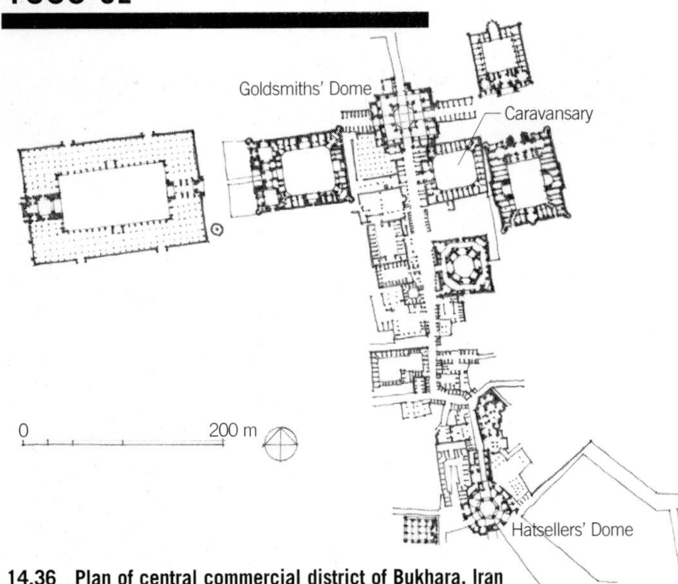


14.36 Plan of central commercial district of Bukhara, Iran

14.37 Goldsmiths' Dome (Taq-i Zargaron), Bukhara

### Shabanids of Bukhara

In 1507, the Timurid kingdom fell into disarray, with the realm splitting between the heterodox rulers of Safavid in Iran and the staunchly Sunni Uzbek Turks, who remained masters of Samarkand and who formed a confederation centered in present day Kazakhistan. Though most of the tribal masses clung to nomadic or seminomadic lifestyles, the cities, as the seats of the political elites, began to thrive once again.

Principal among these cities was the ancient city of Bukhara, which began to equal Samarkand as a mercantile center of central Asia. It was located at the heart of a region called Transoxiana ("beyond the Oxus River"). Watered by that river, which was just to its east, its soil was highly fertile and had been prized since remote antiquity. The Chinese already knew of its existence in the 7th century. The city was to remain important well into the 18th century when, after long periods of prolonged feudal infighting and rivalry between various rulers, the city went into decline and was eventually conquered by the Russians in 1868. An English trading agent who was there in 1558 commented on the large size of the city, and indeed in the previous decades the rulers constructed many commercial structures, such as bazaars, caravansaries, bridges, and underground water reservoirs, as well as mosques and schools.

Shibanid architecture was markedly more plain than the expensively clad and often enormous structures of the Timurids. This had as much to do with economic reality as with the large scale of their building operations. Bricks were often covered with stucco, and tiles were used only on the facade or in the principal rooms. In spatial terms, however, Shibanid architecture was not lacking, and the luminous interiors do justice to the simplicity of the form.

Several building ensembles were built in the center of Bukhara as part of the larger commercial and religious rebuilding of the city. The Kalayan Mosque, also known as Pa-yi Kalan (Foot of the Kalan), dating from about 1514, comprised a minaret, mosque, and madrasa. The mosque was at the time one of the largest in central Asia, measuring 130 by 80 meters and accommodating 120,000 worshipers.

The development of the north-south artery through the center of Bukhara took place between 1562 and 1587. The most characteristic element was the *chürsü*, a type of retail market structure that had a central domed space surrounded by vaulted lanes and workshops. These domed market halls (*taqs*), which brought together traders of similar types of goods, were arranged in rows along the streets and had a distinctive presence in the city. The northernmost one is the Goldsmiths' Dome, which, despite its name, was the retail emporium for textiles. There was as well a special dome for moneychangers. The domes were encircled by gallery markets and linked to commercial facilities, baths, and other public institutions. There was also a caravansary and a warehouse. *Khanqas*, the meeting houses of the Sufi dervish brotherhood, are also to be found in Bukhara. This is where the dervishes lived, prayed, and received pilgrims. One such place is associated with the tomb of Baha al-Din, the founder of an important order. It consists of a large central building with four axial portals and a domed central hall.

**SPANISH CONQUEST OF AMERICA**

Spain in the early 15th century was on the very margins of the global economy that stretched from China to Venice. It had little domestic production. Its economy was on the verge of collapse. The plagues of 1362, 1363, 1367, and 1374 were followed by the collapse of Spanish banks and unrest among the peasants and urban citizens, which led to a rapid decline by the middle of the 14th century. A century and half of great cathedral building came to an end. The expensive campaigns of Ferdinand V and Isabella I of Castile against the Moors decimated the treasury. Unable to afford the highly taxed prices of the land routes to the East, the Spanish and Portuguese were willing to sail literally over the edge of the earth in search of spices, a core commodity for the luxury market at the time. At first the expeditions, despite the excitement of Christopher Columbus's discovery of the Americas, brought little to the Spanish coffers; nor can one even talk yet of a Spanish Empire, which came into being with Charles V (1500–58), who, due to family ties, came to control the Netherlands, Spain, and Austria. With Spain still of little value, Charles's prime interest was northern Italy, which, after taking Rome and Florence, he came to dominate by 1530. Pope Paul III (Alessandro Farnese, r. 1534–48) was particularly pro-Spanish. It was this alliance between Charles V and Rome that more properly set the stage for the Spanish Empire.

Charles's holdings constituted an empire in a very different sense than any before. There was no central capital and no periphery but rather a network of territories held together by a complex set of royal ties, marriages, and economic interests. The holdings in the Americas were just one part of this rather unwieldy picture. With dominions spread out over Europe, Charles V set up a postal communication system (operated by the Tassis family) that was the most expeditious in the world.

The conquest of the Inca by Francisco Pizarro was more promising in regard to gold than the conquest of Mexico by Hernán Cortés. The Spanish were at first content with robbing the Inca and panning for gold, using tens of thousands of slaves. But then rich deposits of silver were found in the city of Potosí in Bolivia in 1545 and at Zacatecas (Mexico) in 1548. By 1650, Potosí was the largest city in the Americas with a population of 160,000. Soon Spain became the world's leading silver producer (the Spanish crown received one-fifth of the silver) and in the end produced 50,000 tons of silver, a quantity that doubled the existing stock of silver in Europe. The result was that with so much money flowing so fast, the entire economic structure of Europe and indeed the world had to bend to this new reality. And it was not only silver that Philip II of Spain controlled. The salt flats in Portugal and the Caribbean, which produced most of the maritime salt consumed in the west, belonged to the Spanish; and through Brazil, Philip II controlled most of the sugar available to Europe.

As goods filtered their way through the European markets, the wealth that it left in its wake created the beginnings of Europe's commercialization and industrialization. The colonization of the Americas under the Spanish should, therefore, not be seen simply as one of conquest and subjugation in the traditional sense of imperial expansion. The military expenses of the Spanish were relatively modest compared to other expenses at the time, especially expenses in fighting the Ottomans. Instead, the empire was brought into existence by a collaboration of powerful elites, international bankers, and enterprising traders who operated across national divisions.

This was not the first global economy, but it was certainly a very new type. The traditional notion of centers linked by trade routes had given way to a network energized not so much by the flow of money but by the flow of investment and debt. Credit based on anticipated revenue became the oil in the wheel of the new economy. At the harbors and ports, it was not money that changed hands but commodities and pieces of paper. The new economy created an inflation the likes of which had never been experienced before. As a consequence, an increasingly economically disenfranchised lower class arose, which, from the point of view of the aristocrats, needed to be controlled by the authority of religion and state.

**14.38**
Portion of a map of Tenochtitlán drawn by Alonso de Santa Cruz, ca. 1555

**14.39**
With a force of around 400 infantry, 16 horsemen, and a few small cannons, Hernán Cortés invaded and conquered an Aztec empire populated by six million people.

A Christian population yoked to an export economy governed by an absolutist ruler was the Spanish formula for its new colonial society. It had at its center a system of *encomienda*, a form of feudalism, in which Spanish settlers (*encomiendos*) were given large tracts of land along with a population of several hundred native Americans. The *encomiendos* introduced European beasts of burden, farming techniques, and manufacturing processes, along with extensive mining, that worked on the basis of an unlimited supply of forced labor. New towns were created to support the *encomienda* economy and to connect it to the ports. The towns were laid out on a regular grid with a plaza in the center. Church and administrative buildings usually faced onto the plaza.

The Franciscan, Dominican, and Augustinian friars who came to America hard on the heels of the conquistadors were focused on a mission far different from that of the initial colonizers, namely to claim the natives for Christ. They built the first churches, intermixing the conventions of church liturgy with local pre-Columbian practices. They were also the first to actually defend the rights of the natives as children of God. A central figure in that respect was Bartolomé de Las Casas, a former *encomienda* turned Dominican friar who vehemently protested the cruel and harsh treatment of the natives by the *encomiendos* to the King of Spain. "Were they not human, children of God, deserving of our protection?" demanded de Las Casas. In response the Spanish king enacted a series of laws that, among other things, prohibited enslaving the native Americans and gave them certain rights. These laws were, however, never enforced, with the local settlers successfully arguing that the economy would grind to a halt without slavery. The viceroy of Peru was in fact assassinated when he tried to enforce the laws, so Charles V had to withdraw them.

### *Atrio*

The Spanish-American churches built by the friars emphasized simplicity and directness, focusing more on techniques of communicating the Word to the native population than on celebrating the church itself. Simple boxes with thick walls, often buttressed on the exterior, provided a sturdy frame for the Franciscan House of God. Windows were few and usually very high. The walls were unsegmented and left bare or at best painted with simple illustrations in a style not unlike that of the pre-Columbian temples. A simple stone table served as the altar, raised by a few steps from the floor of the nave. Behind this was placed a reredos, an ornamented screen that visually illustrated Christ's trials.

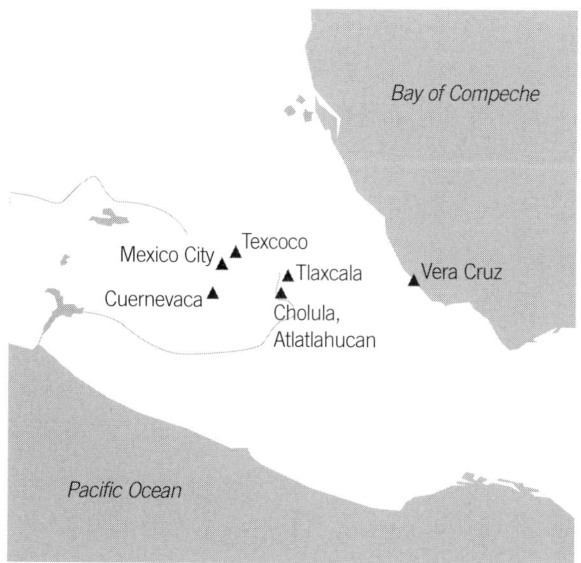

**14.40 Example of an *atrio***

The real innovations were on the exterior. To accommodate the large populations, which were not allowed inside the churches by law, the friars developed the concept of the *atrio*, a large open court walled along the edges, that used the facade of the church with a built-in outdoor chapel to conduct Mass at its west end. Corner chapels with the sensibility of a turret, an elevated gate, and a large cross in the middle gave to the *atrio* the sense of a festive plaza, not unlike the plazas that fronted the pre-Columbian pyramids. Within, the friars devised elaborate processions, complete with stopping places that began at the church and rotated counterclockwise around the *atrio*.

**14.41 Plan: Franciscan Church complex at Cholula, Mexico**

Hundreds of *atrios* were built by the best Franciscans in the 1560s and 1570s, with some of the classic examples at Cuernavaca, Cholula, and Atlatlahucan. The Catholic church, however, became very uncomfortable with the unorthodox practices of the friars. The outdoor *atrios* not only contravened the basic principle of the House of God as a place with a roof but also favored processional activities that often evolved into songs and dances that resembled pre-Columbian rituals much too closely. While the friars were interested in transforming older religious icons into Christian icons (such as the amalgamation of a number of female goddesses into the Virgin of Guadalupe), the Spanish church opposed these hybridizations. In 1574, the friars were subjected to the office of the viceroy and the administrative strictures of the dioceses. Their sacerdotal privileges were revoked, the building of monasteries was stopped, and the *atrios* were deemed unfit for service. Their spirit, nevertheless, survived within the Latin American church, evolving into one of the most progressive churches in the world.

For the Spanish, the results of their success were double edged. Though the impetus was to bring back spices at a cheaper rate, the Spanish found no spices in the Americas, only metal and sugar, and as a result, the Americas never developed as an effective economic benefit to Spain, which was poor in natural resources. Cocoa and tobacco, which were sent back to Europe, did not become popular until the 17th century, by which time it was no longer the Spanish who controlled these commodities.

Within 50 years of the Spanish conquest, roughly 95 percent of the indigenous population had perished due to warfare, slavery, and disease. The rapid depopulation of the Americas because of disease made it difficult to find able-bodied men to work in the mines. This, combined with the expulsions of 120,000 Jews from Spain in 1492, many more tens of thousands from such Spanish territories as Sicily, the expulsion of the Moors from Granada in 1570, the failure of Spanish industry to maintain its momentum, the destruction of the Spanish fleet in 1588, and a policy of ruthless taxation, left Spain in a perilous financial situation. With the Spanish faltering, it was the French, who, at first, gained the most from this new world economy, since they had the foresight to study and to thoroughly revise and rationalize their productive capacities.

14.42 **El Escorial, near Madrid, Spain**

### El Escorial

Though the history of 16th-century Europe centers on the Spanish, Spain had no capital. Valladolid in the north of the country served for the most part as the residence of the court. In 1526, Charles V built a palace inside the Alhambra, designed by Pedro Machuca, who had been a painter practicing in Italy. Though elegant, it was too far to the south. So in 1562 Madrid was made the seat of Spain's royal court, with Philip II building for himself a vast palace, known as El Escorial (begun 1563); it is located 50 kilometers northwest of the city on the slopes of the rugged Guadarrama Mountains that separate Madrid from the plains of Castilla y León. The word *escorial* (slag heaps) refers to the heaps of slag (*scoria*) that were left by ancient iron miners on the site. Philip II, a deeply religious king and a fierce advocate of Catholicism, designed his palace in the form of a monastery to symbolize the strength of his faith.

The palace covers a large area (205 by 160 meters), with the buildings laid out on a grid with inner courts. Dominating the composition is the axially placed church and its forecourt. The church, built in somber, gray granite, has a Doric order at ground level. All other pilasters are embedded in the articulation of the wall, giving the building a solid and massive appearance.

Apart from the arcade below, the facade is reminiscent of St. Sebastiano by Leon Battista Alberti in Mantua. Perhaps the reference to a saint who, despite being tortured, remained alive, was appropriate for a king who was known to have been brooding and obsessive. The royal suite of apartments is located around a private courtyard, with Philip's bedroom, modeled on a monk's cell, looking out into the chapel. Through the centuries the building has served as the mortuary for the Spanish kings with stacks of sumptuous marble and bronze sarcophagi in the royal tomb chamber.

The building is an anomaly when compared to contemporary palace construction elsewhere in Europe. Grandeur, splendor, ostentation, and ornamentation were eschewed. Instead the building was a self-conscious statement of an ideological "return" to a simpler life. It was, of course, not a true life of simplicity, for Philip II was certainly for a while among the most powerful and wealthiest of monarchs in Europe. And yet the building was meant to serve as a penitential offering by a king whose inner desire was to be a hermit. It was a combination of royal retreat, heavenly city, and neomedieval utopia.

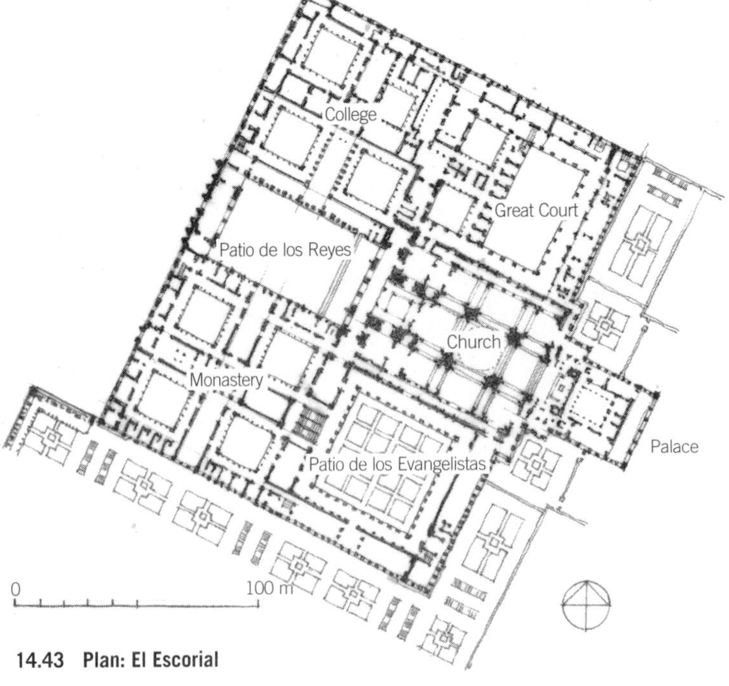


14.43 **Plan: El Escorial**

14.44 **Facade, Capitoline Museum, Rome, Italy**

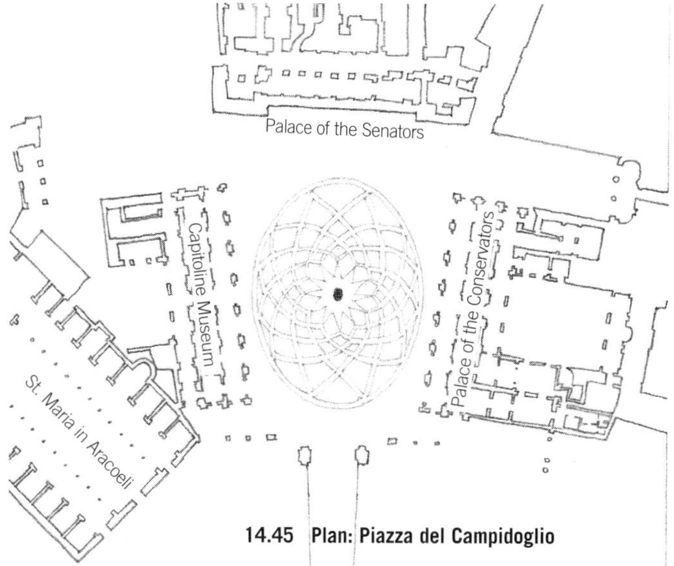


14.45 **Plan: Piazza del Campidoglio**

## ITALIAN HIGH RENAISSANCE

The situation in Rome in the beginning of the 16th century was bleak. In 1537, the city had been sacked by the German and Spanish troops of Charles V. But more fundamental was the success of the Protestant Reformation. Begun in 1517 by the German professor-priest Martin Luther, it rapidly picked up steam to threaten the hegemony of the Catholic church. The newly rising European urban middle class was particularly supportive of the Reformation as it had grown tired of the politics and corruption, not to mention the hypocrisy of the popes. The religious rebellion soon became a political rebellion sinking Europe into a quagmire of wars that would intermittently occupy the Europeans for over a century. To answer the Protestant charges, the Church convened the Council of Trent (1546–63) and promulgated several reforms, including imposing greater discipline on the religious (priests, monks, nuns) to align practices with Christian dogma and morality. The Church also allied itself with Charles V, whom it had originally viewed with suspicion, in the hope that he could restore the Church to its previous position through military might.

In an effort to reaffirm the splendor and dignity of the much-tarnished Roman Curia, Pope Paul III (Alessandro Farnese; r. 1534–49) initiated a series of bold building campaigns. Chief among them was the construction of a piazza on Capitoline Hill, the nominal site of the Roman Senate. The papal route from St. John Lateran Church on the outskirts of Rome to the Vatican went through the forum, up the hill, and over the Capitoline Hill.

Though the area was of no particularly great importance to the political ideology of the papacy, its dilapidated but venerable structures were an embarrassment to Paul III on the occasion of the ceremonial visit of the Emperor Charles V to Rome in 1536. The two main buildings on the site were the Senate and, flanking it to the south, a building used as a type of town hall where Rome's guilds had their offices and where their representatives, called *conservatori*, met. It is today known as the Palace of the Conservators (Palazzo dei Conservatori).

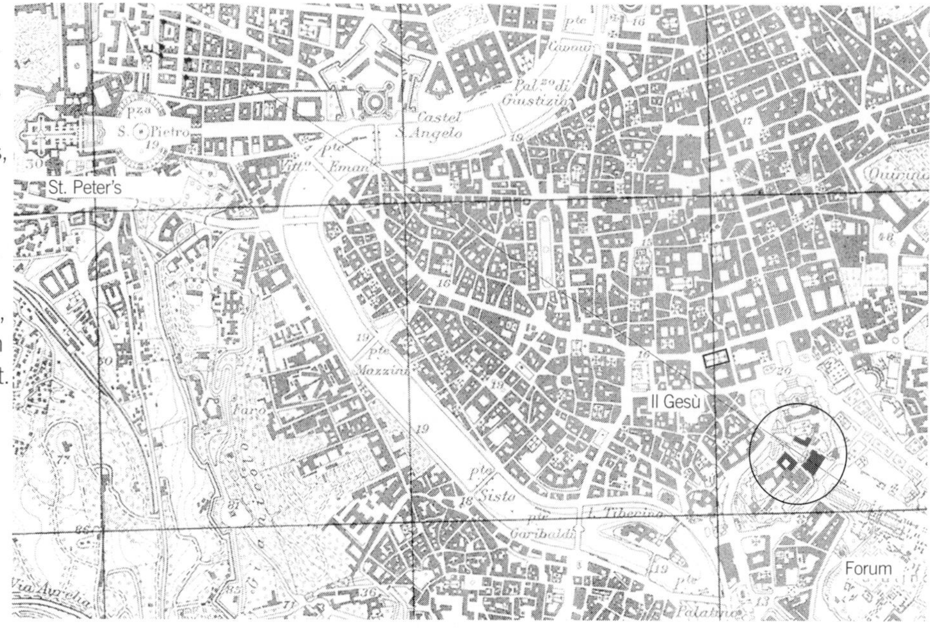


14.46 **Location map: Piazza del Campidoglio**

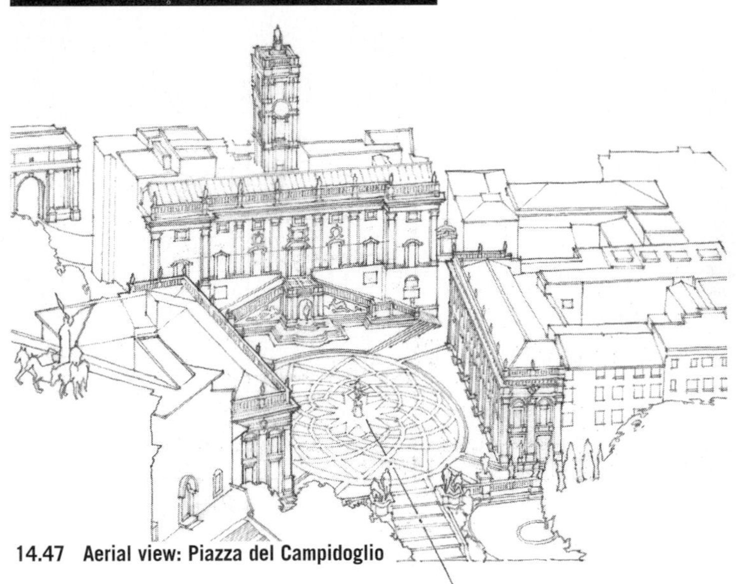

14.47 Aerial view: Piazza del Campidoglio

14.48 Arcade, Capitoline Museum

**Campidoglio**

Michelangelo Buonarroti (1475–1564), who drew up the plans for Piazza del Campidoglio (begun 1538), transformed the disorderly complex into a symmetrical composition with a piazza and three palace fronts. The piazza was designed as a trapezoid with the entrance up from the forum, along the northerly side of the Senate. The Via Sacra passed through the piazza, then descended a broad gentle stairway. In the name of symmetry, Michelangelo added a building, known as Palazzo Nuovo, with no programmatic requirements, except to hold a few offices, to face the Palace of the Conservators. This astonishing fake building, serving only as a framing device for the space, was erected in 1646–50 by Carlo Rainaldi but according to Michelangelo's designs. The double flight of steps attached to the facade of the Senate was one of the first times one saw such a combination of facade and stairway, the dynamic effect of its form helping to unify the three facades. It had a *baldacchino* at the summit to be used for ceremonial occasions.

The two palaces that define the cross axis of the piazza have porticoes at their ground levels that extend the space of the piazza under the buildings. There are no arches, as would have been more standard and more structurally sound. But Michelangelo shunned the vault as an architectural form, preferring instead the pier and lintel. Also rather novel was the use of the giant order for the pilasters supporting an unbroken entablature, with a balustrade above the cornice to define the principle rhythm of the facade.

14.49 Partial facade: Piazza del Campidoglio

The pilasters of white travertine are offset against the orange-tinged bricks of the wall. The windows are minicompositions in their own right, emphasizing the placement of the great hall of the *piano nobile*, overlooking the new piazza.

At the center of the piazza there is an shallow oval indentation, out of which rises a gentle hill; its surface ornamented with a rotating twelve-pointed blossom pattern hints at a zodiacal symbolism, as suggested by James Ackerman. The ideological content of the piazza was brought to the fore by the sculptural program. A figure of the mother wolf who had nursed Romulus and Remus was placed over the entrance of the Palace of the Conservators. The most important sculpture was a statue of Marcus Aurelius (and one of the best preserved bronzes from Roman times) brought to the site from the Lateran Palace, serving here to emphasize the new civic face of papal power. In the Middle Ages, enemies of the city had their heads decapitated and placed in his open hand. Sited at the top of the mound, and thus at the center of the universe, he represents the strength and power of law.

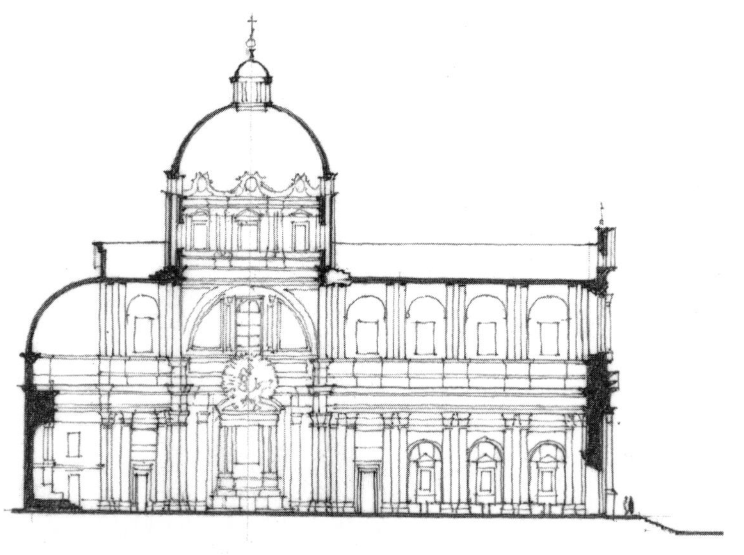

14.50 Longitudinal section: Il Gesù, Rome, Italy

14.51 Entrance facade: Il Gesù

**Il Gesù**

Despite its identification with Spain, the Society of Jesus, otherwise known as the Jesuits, owes its formation to France and to the University of Paris. It was formed in 1534 by Ignatius Loyola and six of his followers, all students at the university. Loyola, a major force behind the Counter-Reformation, founded the Society of Jesus "to enter upon hospital and missionary work in Jerusalem and to go without questioning wherever the pope might direct." Though Pope Paul III established the Jesuit order in 1540, it was still relatively inconsequential until after Loyola's death, after which time it began to develop rapidly. The principal difference between the Jesuits and other orders that had traditionally emphasized communal religious devotion was Loyola's relaxation of a prescribed monastic life and an emphasis on a more active apostolic mission. The Jesuits were not lay brothers, but priests organized around a centralized authority. Prayer and meditation had to be balanced with service and teaching. The Jesuits hoped to unify religious teaching with academic learning, and by 1575 they had established 14 educational institutions in France, with about 1000 members and with some of the colleges having a student population of more than 800. At the time, the universities of Europe, though controlled to a greater or lesser extent by churchmen, were relatively secular institutions.

The Jesuits also exploited the trade links to set up colleges in various parts of India, Africa, and the Americas. The first missionaries arrived in Peru in 1568. In 1610, Philip III (r. 1598–1621), proclaiming that only the "sword of the word" should be used to subdue the Paraguayan Indians, made extensive use of the Jesuits in South America. In 1592, when Cardinal Odoardo Farnese visited the Jesuit college in the Piazza Altieri, 27 languages were being spoken in the refectory. From early on, the Jesuit order attracted important noble patronage, including Marguerite of Austria—wife of Octavio Farnese, the nephew of Alessandro Farnese (Pope Paul III), who supplied funds generously and gave to the church the use of his architect, Gianomo Barozzi da Vignola (1507–73), to design il Gesù, the Jesuit mother church, in Rome.

The site for the Jesuit church was a prominent one just below the Campidoglio and at an important intersection of the papal route through the city. Vignola's design was eventually modified, however, by Giacomo della Porta, whose facade was finished in 1577. In its plan and structure, il Gesù was more influential than any other Roman church of the late-16th century. Its broad, barrel-vaulted nave was suitable for preaching to large congregations. The choir was clearly cut off from the nave to emphasize the distinction between priests and laity. Side chapels, sold to individual families, ensured proper endowments.

The interior walls were initially conceived as bare. This simplicity was mandated in the order's leadership and was common in early Jesuit churches. The facade was also significant as it pointed to new formal solutions that were to be taken up by Baroque architects. The lower order, based on the theme of pilaster pairs, is elevated on high dadoes with a similar dado zone separating the upper and lower orders. The central axis is emphasized by framed niches, as well as by the attached columns to the right and left of the door.

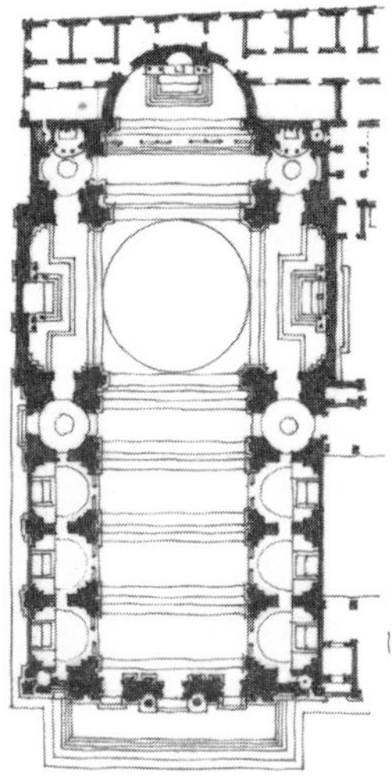

14.52 Plan: Il Gesù

14.53 Villa Farnese, Caprarola, Italy

14.54 Interior court, Villa Farnese, Caprarola

## Villa Farnese

The year 1559 saw the accession of Pius IV (r. 1559–65) and the beginning of a new era of guarded optimism in the Roman situation. The English Queen Mary was married to Philip II in 1554, and there was hope in Rome that England—which had split from Rome under Henry VIII—would be reunited with the Church and that the nascent Protestant sympathies there could be crushed. More importantly for Rome, it was a city awash in Spanish gold and silver. There was more unearned wealth than anywhere else in Europe. Rome thus also attracted the poor and most probably had the largest collection of vagabonds of any major European city; some suggest that one in four of Rome's population was a beggar.

By the end of the century, the city had become a gigantic workyard. Architects, painters, and sculptors hastened to find employment. Art, technically, was used not as an end in itself but as a means to glorify the Church in its struggle against the Protestants. In truth, by the end of the 16th century, power and money were held in the hands of a small church oligarchy that was encouraged by the papal government to build fine houses and villas. These included the Villa and Palazzo Borghese (Cardinal Camillo Borghese, Pope Paul V, begun 1605); Palazzo Barberini (begun 1628); Villa Barberini (Cardinal Bonifacio Ferreri, enlarged 1641); and the Villa Pamphili, (Giambattista Pamphili, Innocent X, 1644).

Setting the tone for this building campaign was Alessandro Farnese (1520–89), grandson of Paul III, who commissioned a villa in Caprarola, to the north of Rome while still a cardinal. The designer was Baldassare Peruzzi. It was by no means a standard villa, for it was designed as a *rocca*, a large fortified country residence, even though its castlelike attributes were more a question of style than necessity. The pentagonal shape with angular bastions may have come from designs made by Antonio da Sangallo the Younger, for whom Peruzzi had worked in the designing of St. Peter's in Rome. In 1556, Cardinal Farnese commissioned Vignola to complete the building and solve some of the still-open questions with respect to circulation and planning, transforming Peruzzi's simpler building into one suited for papal life. Vignola was also responsible for the street that was cut through the town. Work was begun in 1559.

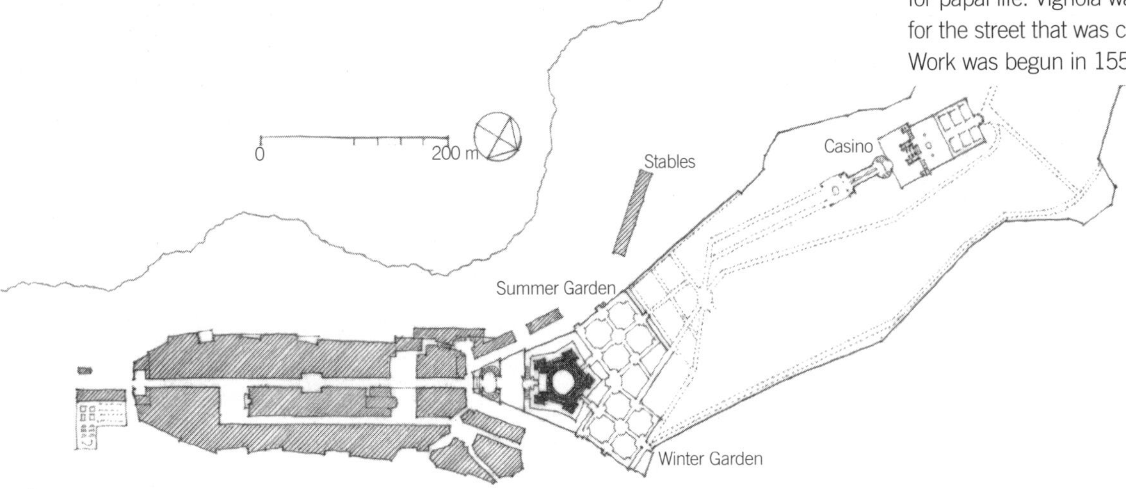


14.55 Plan of Caprarola and the Villa Farnese

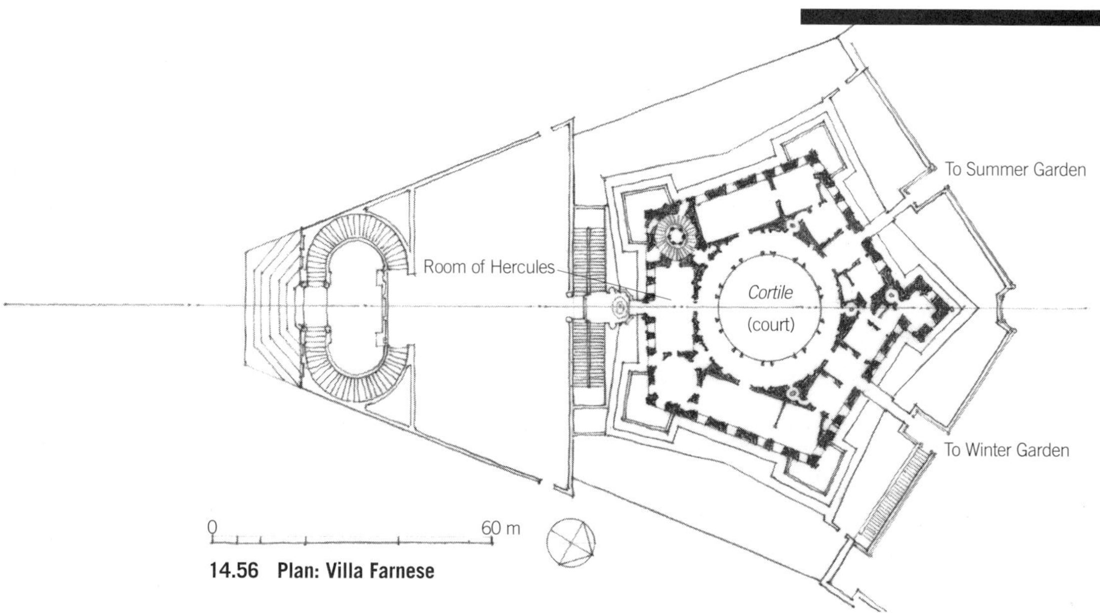


**14.56 Plan: Villa Farnese**

The building was positioned at the top of a hill, facing southeast over a wide terrace down a long axially placed street that was carved through the center of the small town of Caprarola. In essence, the design made the village an extension of the architectural layout. Farnese organized splendid hunts, and it is possible that the villa was built for this purpose. But the palace was also a place where dignitaries were to visit, and this may be the first building that was planned specifically for a carriage approach. From the piazza in front of the building a large portal led to a circular carriageway in the basement that allowed the carriages to drop off people indoors at the foot of a grand spiral staircase and then drive around the corridor and out. Much of the basement was cut out of the tufa rock, including the great cistern that lay at the very center of the composition. The basement also houses the major service rooms, the kitchen, pantries, and ovens.

On the exterior, a symmetrical pair of curving stairs, flanking and framing the carriage portal, mount to a polygonally shaped terrace at the back of which symmetrically designed scissor-back stairs lead to a small oval staircase that in turn leads to the main door.

Overlooking the piazza from the level of the *piano nobile*—and the culmination of the arrival sequence—was a grand loggia with five open bays (now enclosed by windows) that offered a splendid vista over the city and surrounding landscape. It was called the Room of Hercules, the classical association of Hercules having been associated in the late-16th century with the sites of Latium around Rome and a favorite theme exploited in the gardens of the popes. Lavishly decorated with wall paintings on the theme of Hercules and the grandeur of the Farnese, it served as the summer dining room. At the opposite end from the spiral staircase is a round chapel.

There were two principal apartment suites on the *piano nobile*, to the right and left of the great salon and entered from the circular courtyard, forming a linear chain of five rooms, with the more public rooms to the front. The three smaller rooms beyond served as the Cardinal's bedroom, wardrobe, and study.

From the dressing room a wooden bridge over the moat provided access to two square-shaped gardens set into the hillside. The northern suite to the right of the entrance served as Farnese's summer apartment, the other as his winter apartment. The idea that a villa should correspond to the changing of the seasons had been laid out by Vitruvius and was developed in the Renaissance in various villas. At Caprarola, this practice determines the layout of the entire complex.

Ingeniously inserted in the tower of the rear-angled bastion were the various private living conveniences required in a luxurious palace—the bathing rooms, a library, and at the top a dovecote. The circular court is two stories high with a ground-floor arcade below and an arcade with coupled Ionic half-columns attached to the piers pierced by rectangular openings above.

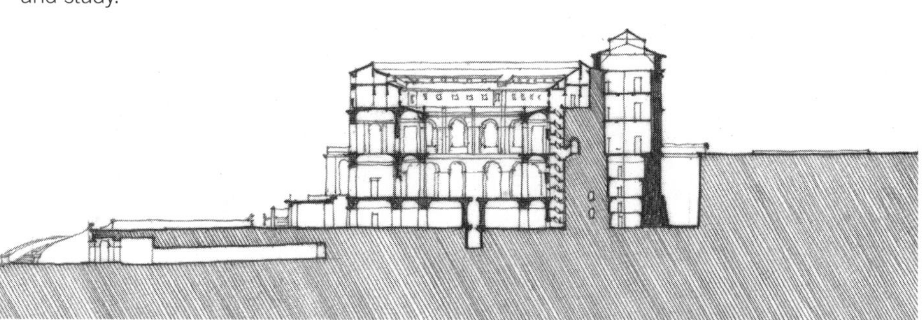

**14.57 Section: Villa Farnese**

**14.58 Interior, Il Redentore, Venice, Italy**

**14.59 Elevation: Il Redentore**

### Il Redentore

The 16th century saw a dramatic decline in Venice's dominance of the Eastern spice trade. Genoese ships, preferred by the Spanish, replaced the Venetian galleys; Antwerp had become Europe's most important port, and Portugal, using its new shipping lanes around the Cape of Good Hope, had brought the cost of pepper down considerably. In 1505, pepper that was imported from Venice over the old route cost 20 Flemish *groates* a pound while Portuguese pepper cost only about 16 *groates*. Furthermore, the immensely costly Turkish War (1570–73) was followed by a plague (1575–7) that took about one-third of the city's population. Nonetheless, Venice managed to hold on to its economic position largely because of the farms in the Veneto, the lands in the Po Valley that were under its control. By 1630, it has been reckoned that 35 percent of patrician income came from Venice's mainland estates. In the early 17th century, the long-maturing crisis approached a climax. The Thirty Years' War (1618–48) in Germany disrupted overland routes to northern markets. And another plague (1630–31) and the Turkish War of 1646–69 left Venice a shell of its former self. The 1560s was thus the high before the low, and it was during this time that Andrea Palladio (1508–80) rose to prominence. He designed churches, villas, palaces, and the town hall of Vicenza. Even if he had not become a leading theorist, his work alone would have outnumbered that of any other Renaissance architect.

Palladio was originally named Andrea di Pietro della Gondola and trained as a mason, but under the influence of the humanist poet Giangiorgio Trissino, who became his first patron, the talented young mason was given a new name in honor of Pallas Athene. In 1541, he visited Rome with Trissino and made extensive studies of the ancient buildings, publishing his findings in 1554 in a treatise, *Le antichità di Roma*. In 1545, he was given his first major commission, the rebuilding of the Basilica in Vicenza. A flood of commissions soon followed for palaces, villas, and churches, leaving an indelible mark on Venice and the Veneto. In Venice he designed the conspicuously located St. Giorgio Maggiore (1565–80) and the Redentore.

The Redentore was built in fulfillment of a vow on the deliverance of the city from a devastating plague of 1575–6. There are several similarities with the Gesù—the elevation of the church on a podium, the separation of the choir from the altar, the almost complete absence of nonarchitectural ornament and the chaste whiteness of the whole interior. The integration of the giant order and the minor order, used in the side chapels, creates a clear hierarchy and interdependence of all architectural elements with each other. Though the columns and pilasters have no structural function, they appear more substantial than those in Brunelleschi's churches. The facade, though seemingly simple at first glance, is a complex composition with semiattached columns and square piers forming the main temple front. A minitemple front, though large in real terms, is nestled between the central columns, with yet another layer encompassing the outer bays.

**14.60 Plan: Il Redentore**

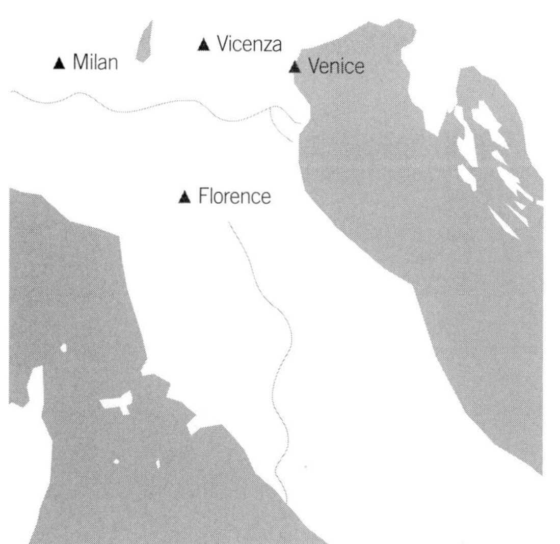


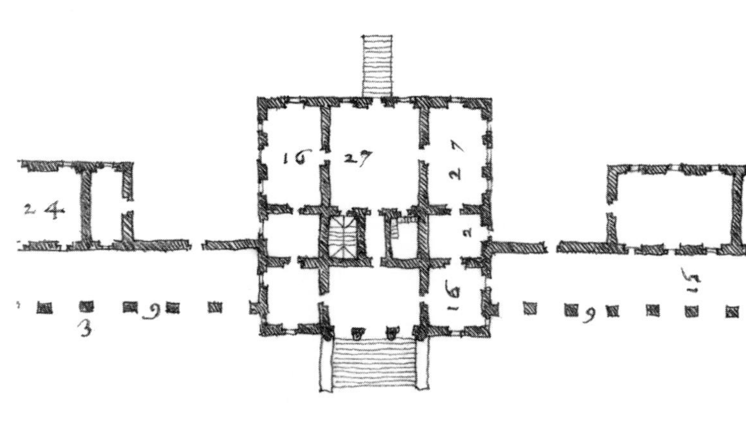

14.61 Plan: Villa Emo, Treviso, Italy

**Palladian Villas**

Though Palladio was highly learned in antique architecture, he was not a slave to imitation. In fact, it was his combination of Roman architectural vocabulary with a clarity in his syntax that made his buildings appear so novel. Architects prior to Palladio had certainly aimed for symmetry and proportion, but none achieved the directness of Palladio, who carefully included even the length-height-width ratio of the rooms into his thinking. The villas Palladio designed for the great Venetian families were far different from those of the popes in Rome or of the Medici in Florence, which were designed for peace and tranquility. These were in part working farms that did more than just provide the villa with oil and grain; they were an important part of the new Venetian economy. To facilitate smooth traffic through the building, there are two staircases leading to the grain-storage rooms in the attic, one for those going up and the other for those going down.

From among Palladio's numerous villas, the most distinguished are Villa Barbaro (1549), Villa Foscari (La Malcontenta, 1560), and Villa Emo (1599). All, except Villa Barbaro, have splendid, elevated temple-front facades, giving access to a great hall.

The layout is always symmetrical and simple, and the rooms too are governed by simple proportions (1 by 1, 2 by 3, 3 by 4, etc.). Windows and internal doorways are often aligned, adding even more cohesion to the interior. Palladio, however, added nuances that have intrigued architects for centuries. At Villa Cornaro, the temple front is recessed on one side but projected forward on the other. Villa Foscari, reached by boat from the Venetian lagoon, became a model for palaces, villas, and houses throughout Europe and the Americas.

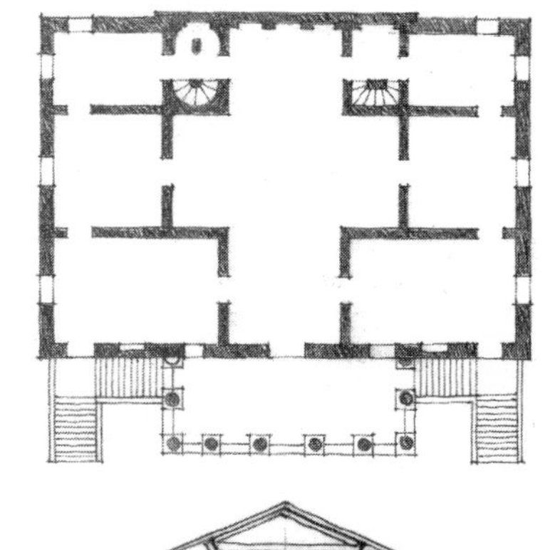

14.62 Plan and elevation: Villa Foscari, Malcontenta, Italy

Without doubt, Palladio was the most systematic and system-conscious of the great Renaissance architects, as evidenced by his *The Four Books on Architecture* (1570). Leon Battista Alberti and Sebastiano Serlio had begun that tendency with their treatises, but Palladio's approach was different. Alberti, in his *Ten Books on Architecture* (1452), attempted a comprehensive study of the field of architecture and dealt with everything from where best to get materials to the different types of building. Serlio, in his *Five Books on Architecture* (first volume appearing in 1537), showed how the classical system could be put to use to generate an almost infinite variety of plans. Palladio emphasized the systematization of the plan itself. Whereas Serlio's treatise allowed the patron a good deal of options, Palladio's did not, or at least not outside a narrow set of rules. And yet what makes Palladio's architecture so likable was that it was never rigorous and never produced uniform or boring buildings. Method and system did not impede creativity.

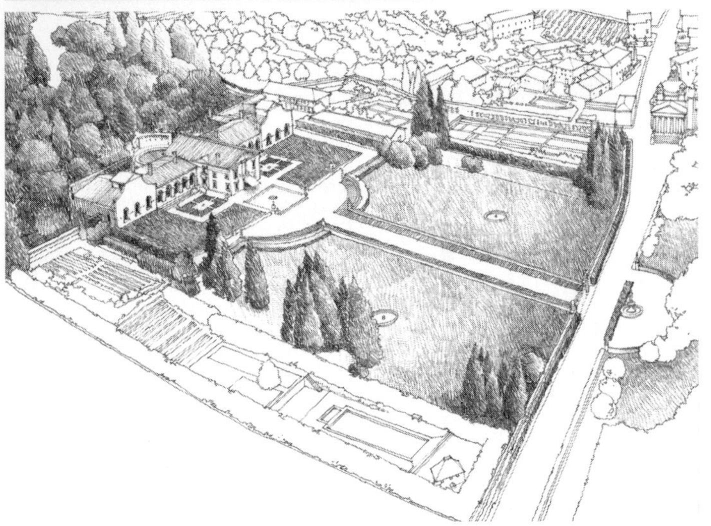

14.63 Villa Barbaro, Maser, Italy

14.64 Villa Rotonda, near Vicenza, Italy

### Villa Rotonda

Villa Rotonda (1566), though having many of the attributes of a working farm, was designed for the papal prelate Paolo Almerico as a type of retirement estate. The building's design is unusual for Palladio in that it is doubly symmetrical, standing on the top of a low hill artificially enhanced with retaining walls. At the center of the building was a rotunda—originally planned with an open oculus—with identical suites of rooms at each of the four corners. Each facade had a temple front. The principal material was brick, stuccoed over and painted white. Stone was used sparingly, given their cost in times of economic stress—and mainly for the capitals or for the ornamentation around windows. The villa, elevated on a basement that is disguised by its stairs, is itself built out on an artificial terrace. The entrance facing the northwest loggia is recessed into the hill so that from the villa looking back over the entrance, one sees the chapel on the opposite side of the small road. To the north there are orchards going down toward the river. Cut out of the woods to the south is a *giardino segreto*, which can only be reached from the basement. Only on the east side is the view of the landscape from the villa unobstructed.

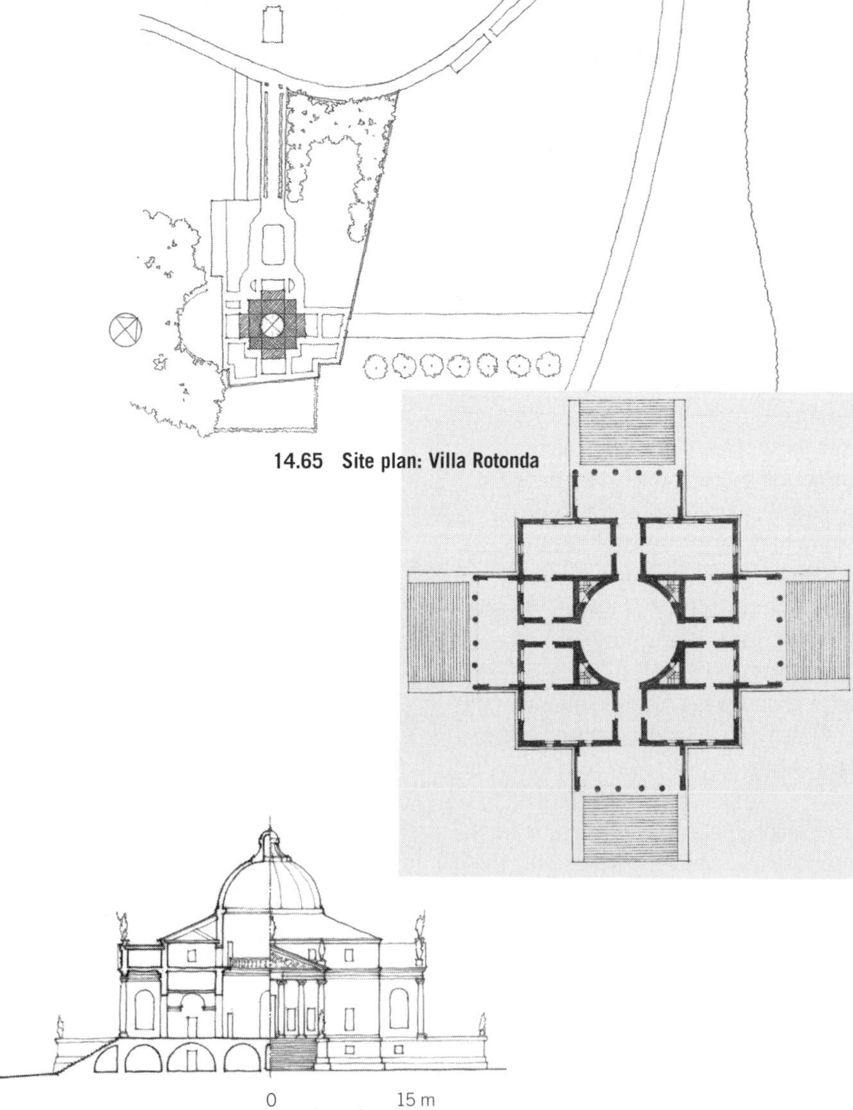


14.65 Site plan: Villa Rotonda

14.66 Plan and section-elevation: Villa Rotonda

14.67 Uffizi, Florence, Italy

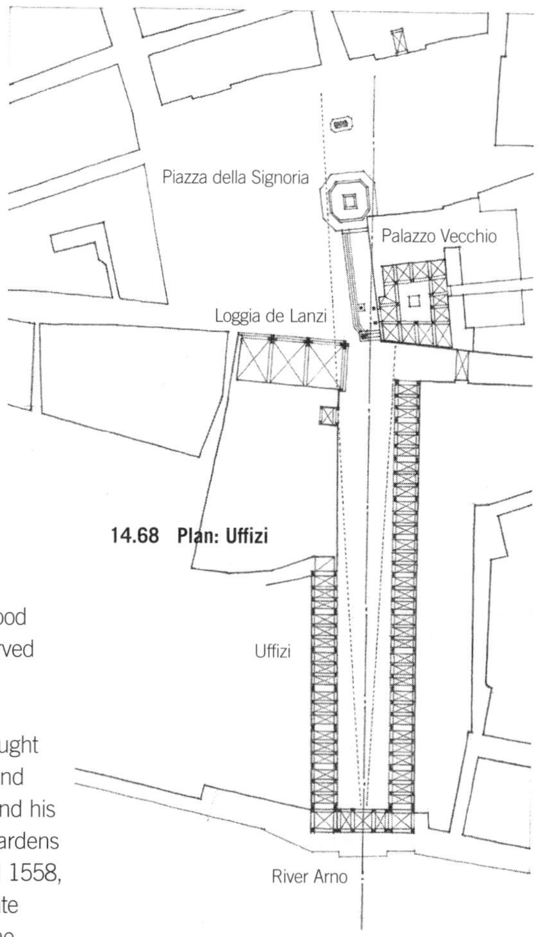


14.68 Plan: Uffizi

### Uffizi

At the end of the 16th century, the vitality of life in Italian cities had been exhausted by the course of numerous wars as well as by the slow but unstoppable drift of money and power to the North European powers. Yet for the French, who were the principle European beneficiaries of Spanish money, Florence was still an invaluable point of connection to the old Eurasian economy. Securing a link to Florence also allowed the French to monitor and control Italian politics. In 1533 Catherine de' Medici became the wife of Henry of Orléans, future king of France, and in 1600 Marie de' Medici married Henry IV of France. By the 17th century, it was French, not Italian, that was spoken at the court of Florence. Cosimo I de' Medici (1519–74), seeking to balance the French with the Spanish, married Eleonora of Toledo, daughter of the Spanish ambassador to the kingdom of Naples. Cosimo set the style for his new absolutist rule by grafting onto the old city a new, quasi-royal profile.

Indicative of the new notion of statehood was the Uffizi (or "offices"), which served as administrative headquarters of the region. Cosimo moved his residence across the river to the Pitti Palace, bought in 1549 and subsequently enlarged and remodeled several times by Cosimo and his descendants. He added the Boboli Gardens behind the palace between 1550 and 1558, but just as importantly he built a private corridor from the Pitti Palace, along the Ponte Vecchio that crossed the Arno River, to the Uffizi and then to the Palazzo della Signoria, from whence he ruled, creating a uniquely-styled unity in these buildings, allowing him to define his presence in the city without ever having to be seen.

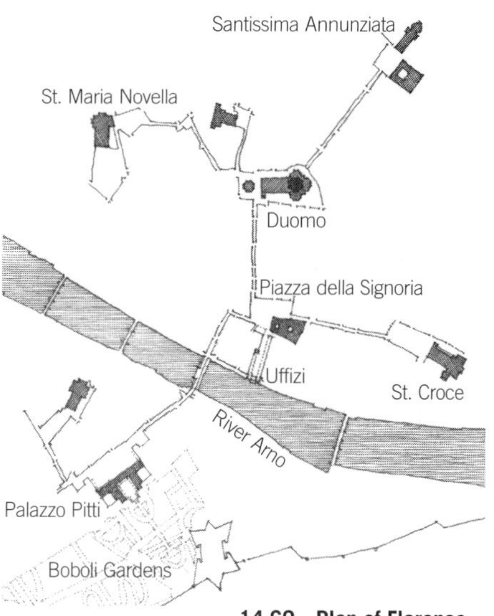


14.69 Plan of Florence

The Uffizi (1560–65) was an unusual structure, built three stories high along both sides of a long streetlike piazza that connects the Palazzo della Signoria with the River Arno. At its terminus, there is an airy loggia overlooking the Arno, which was designed by Giorgio Vasari (1511–74), who is better known as an author or painter but who also undertook several architectural projects in the style of Michelangelo. There are no vaults in the ground floor arcade but, rather, columns and entablatures, as at the Campidoglio. The building is grafted into the medieval fabric and thus has no visible "outside" of its own, except for the central hollow which is part piazza and part elongated courtyard.

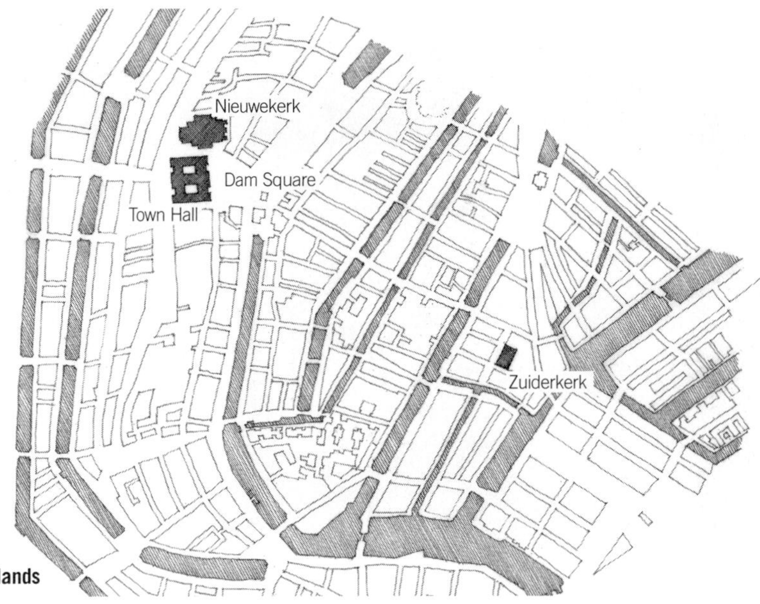


14.70 Plan of Amsterdam, Netherlands

## AMSTERDAM

Though Holland had the fastest-growing economy in Europe at the time, having become the mercantile hub of the Spanish Empire, this was not reflected in its architecture. Because they were for the most part Calvinists and their beliefs dictated simple church structures, they did not build churches until they had reached independence from Spain. Following the destruction of Antwerp by the Spanish, Amsterdam, a relatively unimportant city until 1579, quickly became one of the leading international ports of Europe, developing a cityscape that included the town hall in Dam Square (now the Royal Palace), the Westerkerk, the Zuiderkerk, as well as a large number of canal houses commissioned by leading mercantile families.

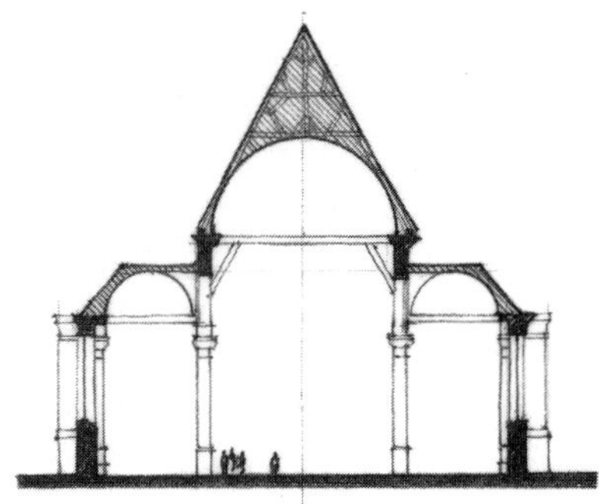

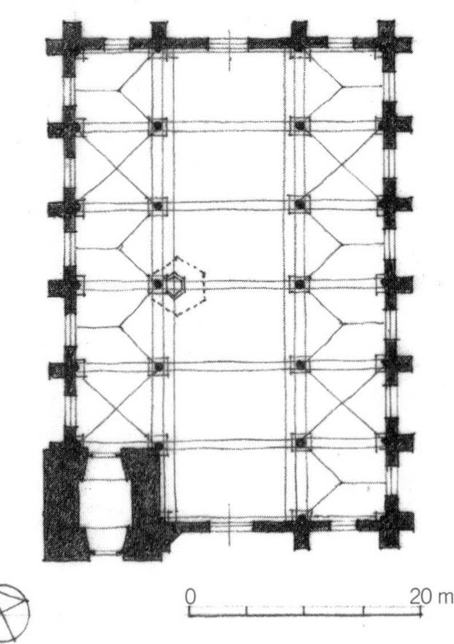


14.71 Plan and section: Zuiderkerk, Amsterdam

The first church in Amsterdam specifically built for the protestant community was the Zuiderkerk (1603–11). It is a simple six-bay rectangle that is pseudo-basilican in plan, meaning that, though it has a nave and side aisles, it has no apse, thus reflecting the more community-oriented nature of its religious services. The buttresses on the outside are reduced to a minimum in a way that was meant to be reminiscent of the Gothic hall churches. It also had a wooden vault. The tower is squeezed into one of the corners.

Though longitudinal in plan, the use of the space was transversal, as the pulpit for the Bible readings was placed in front of the middle column of the western arcade. The columns are dark and contrast with the whitewashed walls in a manner that was clearly meant to imitate 15th-century north Italian Renaissance churches. In this way they harkened back to an ideal of a simpler late Medieval-early Renaissance life, presumed to have been untainted by the grandeur and corruption of the church of Rome. Zuiderkerk was followed by the Westerkerk (1620–31), which created a more unified whole with a clear division between the main axis—with the tower serving as entrance—and the cross axis with the pulpit.

14.72 Amsterdam Town Hall

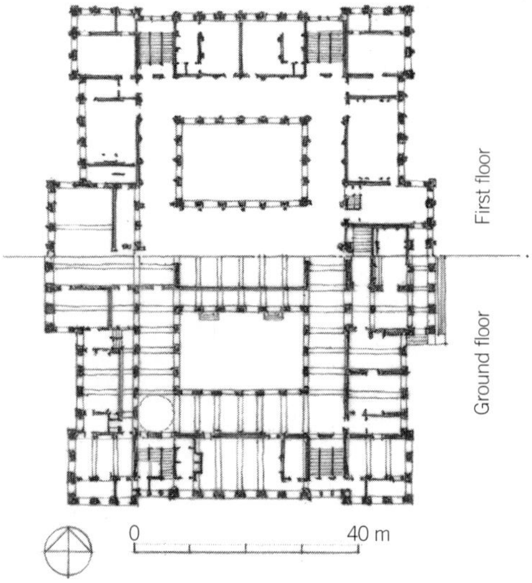

14.73 Plan: Amsterdam Town Hall

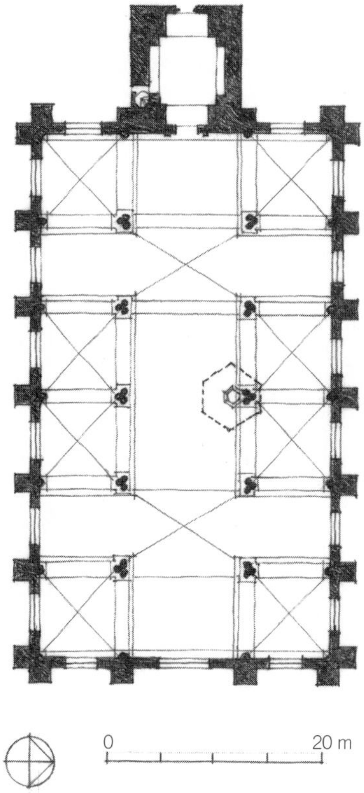

14.74 Plan: Westerkerk, Amsterdam

### Amsterdam Town Hall

For the Dutch, it was not gold that was to be extracted from the colonies but cocoa, tobacco, and sugar, which turned out to bring more profit than all the bullion of the Americas combined. In Amsterdam, the new center of the Dutch world, and a city entirely dedicated to making money, palaces, monasteries, and castles were not part of the cultural fabric. Instead one found rows and rows of townhouses facing onto a relatively straight arrangement of parallel streets and canals. By the end of the 17th century, the city had grown from 20,000 to 200,000 in the span of just over 100 years. The city's exchange bank, Wiselbank, founded in 1609, was for a long time the greatest public bank in northern Europe. By the end of the 17th century, over 16 million Dutch florins were lying on deposit in its vaults, including the florins of other European governments.

The bank was in the first floor of the new town hall, designed by Jacob van Campen (begun in 1648). On the facade of the building, a statue of Atlas lifts the globe on his shoulders above a pediment in which the nations of the world offered up their goods to an allegorical Amsterdam. Inside, the marble floor of the huge barrel-vaulted Burgerzaal, lit from the sides by two courtyards, was inscribed with maps of both the heavenly and the terrestrial worlds. Though it is almost 100 meters long, its facade looked like two palaces stacked on top of one another. This should not lead us to understate its significance, not only in the city itself, as an expression of Amsterdam's ascension in world politics, but also as an opening up of the role civic architecture was to have in the future urban profiles of Europe. The town hall was one of the first applications of Italian Renaissance style to a monumental civic structure, and it was in many respects to remain the model for town halls well into the modern era. The building faced onto one of the few public squares of the city called the Dam, which had as its focus a tall square building known as the Wage (or the public weigh-house). Here and in the nearby markets, as a description put it in 1664, almost the whole world seemed to be assembled to buy and sell—Poles, Hungarians, the French, the Spanish, Muscovites, Persians, and Turks.

14.75 Place Royale, Paris, France

14.76 Plan of 17th-century Paris

## PLACE ROYALE

When Henry IV came into power in France in 1589, Paris was hardly the city that it is today. Despite the nominal authority of the crown, France essentially functioned as a highly decentralized confederacy of autonomous provinces. Paris had suffered several wars; the absence of kings, who preferred to live in the countryside chateaus; and the general downturn of the economy in the 16th century. In Paris, there was not even a royal palace. In deciding to make Paris a capital city and the seat of newly forming, centralized nation-state, Henry IV initiated a series of urban projects that were also intended to boost the city's economic standing. One such project was the triangular-shaped Place Dauphine in Paris (1609–14), designed to provide accommodations for bankers and merchants. It was located at the westernmost tip of the Île de la Cité as a highly visible indicator of its importance, its narrow entrance forming, however, a tranquil and enclosed precinct within.

Another experiment in urban design and mercantile enhancement was the Place Royale (today the Place des Vosges), begun around 1605 on open land at the edge of the city. It was originally planned with three sides for shops and apartments and the fourth for a range of workshops for the manufacture of silk. Though some silk was still imported from China, much of it also came from Vigevano, Italy, where silk production was mastered in the late-15th century. Henry IV was eager to reduce France's dependence on foreign production, but French silk production never succeeded because of the climate, and eventually the whole square became a residential address attracting the cream of Parisian society.

Presiding over the square at both ends were special pavilions for the king and queen, as the place was intended as a setting for royal pageants. Indeed the space was inaugurated in 1611 by a masque and tournament held in celebration of the marriage of Louis XIII to Ann of Austria. It was a setting that was also suited to the nobility and rich bourgeois, who had taken up the fashion of strolling and riding in carriages. Originally, therefore, the place was not paved but covered with a lawn and fenced in, an idea unknown to the Italian Renaissance.

14.77 Aerial view of Place Royale

14.78 Wollaton Hall, near Nottingham, England

**ELIZABETHAN ENGLAND**

Though England, too, benefited from the shift away from the Mediterranean to the Altantic, its growth in the first half of the 16th century had been hampered by complex internal conditions, poor management, and restrictive policies. Its maritime operation existed mainly in fishing, smuggling, and plundering. The period of Queen Elizabeth I's reign (1558–1603) was, therefore, not vainly referred to as England's Golden Age. She adopted modern notions of management, transforming feudal magnates into office holders. Overseas foreign investments resulted in a growing propertied class, with wool and textiles becoming an increasingly large part of the economy along with the production of lead, salt, and soap. The population increased from three to four million between 1530 and 1600, providing a large reservoir of potential indentured labor. The English destruction of the Spanish armada in 1588 established them as a sea-power to be reckoned with. The result was a thirst for a culture equal to France and Italy. All in all, 16th-century Englishmen were the first of their nation to become generally aware of the vast world around them.

As to architecture, however, the English had a long way to go. Houses were relatively plain and rugged and showed no fine paintings, apart from portraits. Nonetheless, the change in English culture was rapid and profound. Old houses were set out with chimneys, walls were paneled, windows glazed, and old timber-framed buildings were faced with stone. A particularly important innovation at the time and one that affected the development of Elizabethan-era architecture was the use of coal in glass firing. And here, once again, immigrants played an important role.

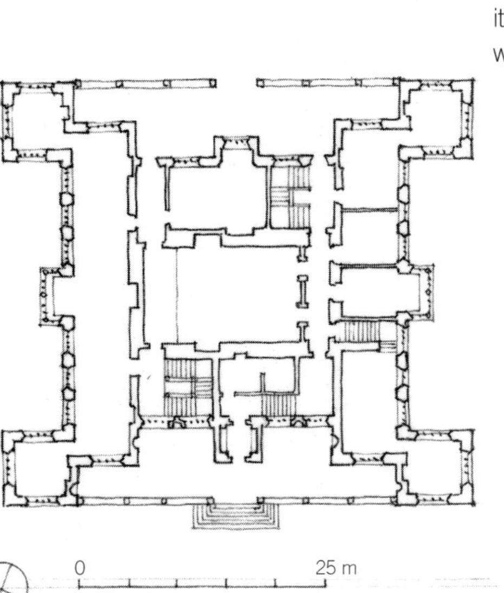

14.79 Plan: Wollaton Hall

Jean Carré, who was from the highly contested area of the Lorrain and whose patent for plate glass was granted in 1567, was attracted to England along with other Lorraine glassmakers; soon furnaces were being built in scattered parts of the country with prices beginning to fall almost at once. The market responded with enthusiasm. Wollaton Hall (near Nottingham, 1580–88), the home of an important coal magnate, was already a splendid showcase for the new industry. It sported at the top, a special room called the Prospect Room, with no particular purpose other than to show off its towering fenestration. One could contrast this type of fenestration with Titchfield Priory (Hampshire, 1537–40), which, even though it is only the gatehouse that survives, still has windows in the Gothic medieval manner.

14.80 **Hardwick Hall, Bolsover, Derbyshire, England**

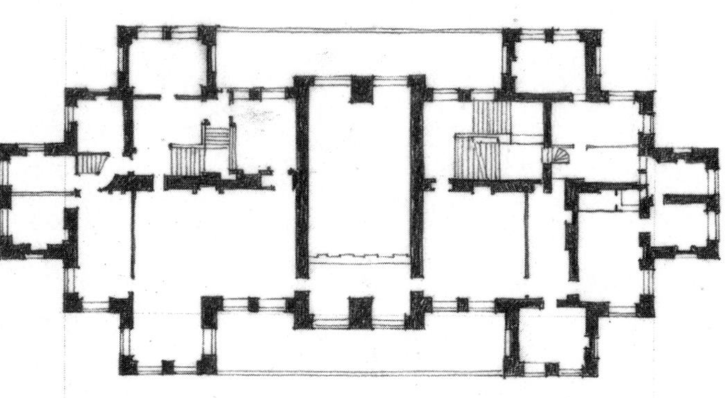

14.81 **Second-floor plan: Hardwick Hall**

**Hardwick Hall**

Hardwick Hall (1592–97) in the English heartland at Bolsover in Derbyshire is less ostentatious and more unified than Wollaton Hall. Its tall windows are simply and tightly framed against the unadorned wall. Volumetrically, the building is an ingenious fusion of a three-story building with six four-story towers. Compared to Barlborough Hall (Derbyshire, 1583) and Montacute House (Somerset, ca. 1599), the building in its simplicity and directness reflects a penchant for volumetric clarity that was to become ever more the norm in English residential architecture. However, as was characteristic for English manor houses, the symmetry on the outside was not enforced on the inside, where the designers preferred to operate with greater flexibility. Apart from the front and back porticoes and the connecting hall, the building, designed by Robert Smythson, was laid out to suit the needs of the client, Bess of Hardwick, Dowager Countess of Shrewsbury, a woman of considerable standing in Elizabeth's court. Upon the death of her husband, George Talbot, the 6th Earl of Shrewsbury, the biggest tycoon in England, Bess became one of the richest ladies in England, well able to dictate her preferences in architecture.

The ground floor contained the kitchen and service rooms as well as a chapel. To the right of the Great Hall, a staircase led to Bess' principal quarters, with anterooms leading to her bedroom at the corner. On the other side, there was a great chamber, which served as the dining room. Another suite for relatives and guests was on the third floor.

The second and third floors both have long galleries along the back facade. The long gallery on the third floor is fully integrated into the plan with the "withdrawing chamber" located on the central axis. The prototype for such a gallery was the Queen's Gallery in Hampton Court (1536–7), which was built as a place where the ladies of the court could watch the hunting in the park. At Hampton Court, the Great Gallery was an independent wing attached to the queen's lodgings. At Hardwick it is integrated into the design. The interior of Hardwick was mostly finished with whitewash. The color in the house was provided by the rich tapestries, numerous table carpets, and the gilded and colored furniture. The floors were covered in reed mats, as was common at the time.

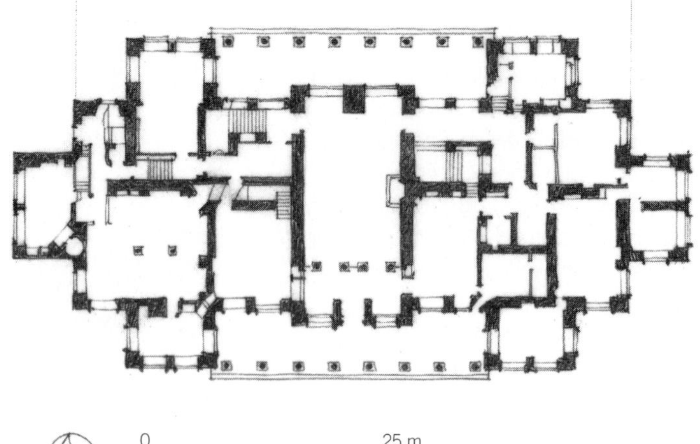


14.82 **Ground-floor plan: Hardwick Hall**

14.83 Interior, Banqueting House, London, England

### Banqueting House

Inigo Jones' second visit to Italy in 1613–14, during which he studied the buildings of Andrea Palladio in particular, prepared the young architect for his most ambitious project, the Banqueting House. The first Banqueting House, appendaged to the Royal Palace in London, was built in 1581 and served for dining and theatrical entertainment. A second one was built in 1606 but was destroyed by fire in 1619. The Banqueting House designed by Jones in 1619 was less a place for banquets than a royal audience hall, reflecting a greater emphasis on royal authority. This was the first public structure in the mature Palladian style in England. At the ground floor, the windows between the pilasters were an alternating sequence of triangulated and segmental pediments; while at the upper floor, the windows are all unpedimented, yielding an intricate yet calm design. The central three bays are emphasized by the use of attached columns, and the corners by pilaster pairs. The whole is raised on a low rusticated basement that matches in height the balustraded frieze on top. To understand the building's importance, we have to keep in mind the symbolic significance of the Italian motifs as an attempt to extend the architectural language born during Europe's mercantile revolution in the 15th century. But whereas Italian architecture developed in a culture of regional princes and rich merchants, it was now being associated with the centralization of the state.

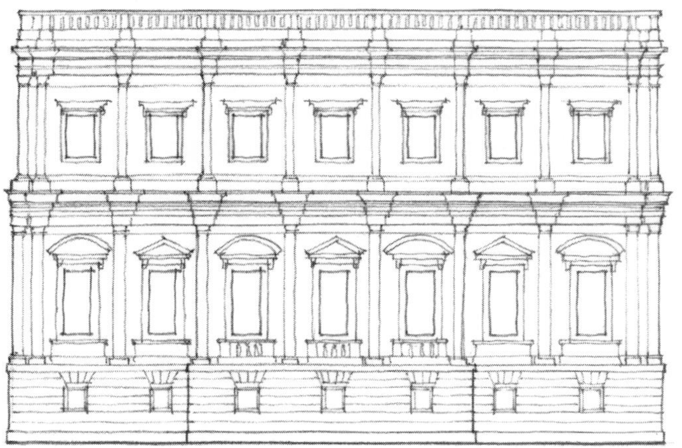

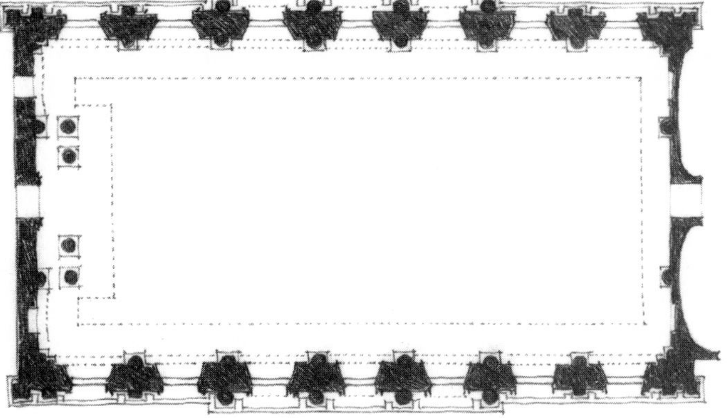

14.84 Plan and elevation: Banqueting House

**14.85 Plan of the Kremlin, Moscow, Russia**

**14.86 Cathedral of the Assumption, Moscow**

**KREMLIN'S NEW CHURCHES**

The Byzantine Church, in a desperate move to relieve Turkish pressure on Constantinople, agreed to reunite with the Roman Catholic Church (the Union of Florence, 1439). The Russian Church, a delegate of which was present at the signing in Florence, chose, however, to repudiate the treaty and to maintain the Russian Church as defenders of the Orthodox faith. This sense of renewal, along with the consolidation of central Russian lands against the disintegrating Golden Horde, spurred on an unprecedented building campaign, especially under Ivan III (1462–1505).

Despite the Russian insistence on the decoupled relationship with the West on matters of church doctrine, Ivan III sent an envoy to Italy in 1475 to seek out Italian architects who could assist in the planning and execution of his various construction projects, none more important than the redesigning of the Kremlin, the hilltop fortification compound at the center of Moscow, the city the rulers had used as their place of residence since the 12th century. One set of Italian engineers began repairing and updating the Kremlin walls as well as parts of the palace within.

The most important Italian architect to arrive was Aristotile Fioravanti (1420–85), who had worked in the service of Francesco Sforza in Milan. He designed the Cathedral of the Assumption or Repose of the Virgin (Uspenskii Sobor), a church that came to be used for the crowning of Russian rulers and the investiture of the patriarchs of the Russian Orthodox Church. Though the design was closely monitored by the Russian clergy, ever on guard against any possible heresy or the slightest sign of "Latinity," the church brilliantly fuses Italian and Russian motifs.

The cathedral was designed as an open nine-square grid, added to the front of the iconostasis, which was incorporated into the gridded system. Pilasters thicken the walls to give the volume a typical Italian flavor. The strict lines of the cornices dampen the profile of the semicircular *zakomary* gables. On the inside, there are groin vaults over all the crossings except for five, which have tall drums and gilded domes. The pentacupolar silhouette is not typically Italian but Russian, and in this way the Italian and Russian elements are brought together. Fioravanti's technical expertise allowed him to create a better finish to the limestone walls and better bricks and mortar for the building's structure, yielding a thinner but more durable structure.

One of the final churches begun by Ivan III was the Cathedral of the Archangel Michael (begun 1505) on a site a hundred meters to the south of the Cathedral of the Assumption. It was to be used as the burial site for Russian rulers. The architect, Aleviz Novyi, had arrived in Moscow in 1504 after completing a palace for the Crimean khan, Mengli-Girei, at Bakhchisarai. He was possibly Alvise Lamberti da Montagnana, a student of Mauro Codusi, the noted Venetian architect.

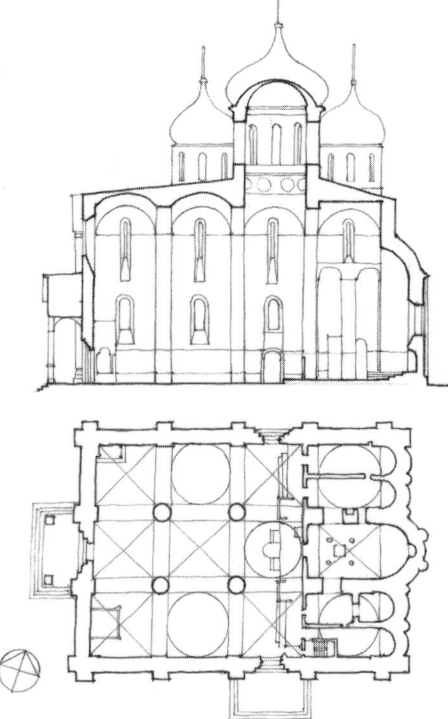

**14.87 Plan and section: Cathedral of the Assumption**

14.88 Church of the Archangel Michael

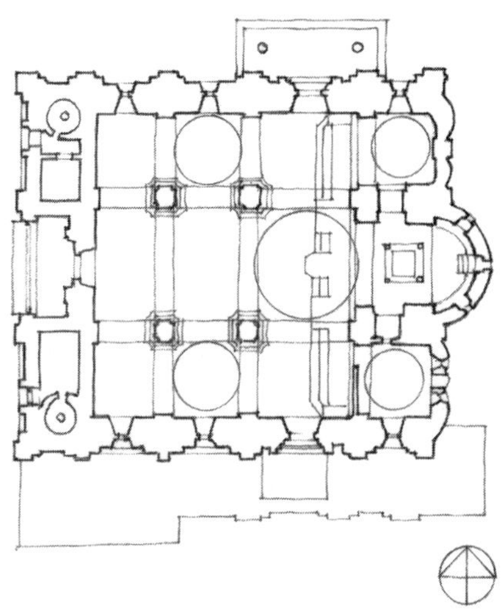

14.89 Plan: Church of the Archangel Michael

The architecture clearly reflects a Venetian style as opposed to the more Lombardian style of Fioravanti. The facade is of a standard tripartite division; whereas the side facade has an *ababa* rhythm. Instead of unadorned piers, as at the Cathedral of the Dormition (in the city of Vladimir, 1158–60), there are two registers of pilasters, some of the earliest examples of the neoclassical style in Russian architecture. Much like the Cathedral of the Dormition, we see a fusion of eastern and classical motifs, especially in the series of shell arches that form the crown of the building.

Indeed, it was the intent of Ivan's architects to remain firmly rooted in the Russian tradition. In that sense, one can see very clearly how classicism came to be sublimated into regional idioms so as to maintain, for political purposes, a continuity with the past. Though the impact of Italian classicism was muted in subsequent decades by the return to the onion dome and the reintroduction of color, the impact is undeniable.

14.90 South elevation: Cathedral of the Dormition

14.91 Cathedral of the Dormition, Vladimir, Russia

### Church of the Ascension

Following Ivan IV's conquest in 1554–6 of the Khante of Astrakhan at the mouth of the Volga on the Caspian Sea, one of the most important Eurasian trading arteries came into Muscovy. Just as importantly, the conquest gave a boost to the Russian Orthodox Church, which had been facing challenges to its wealth, institutions, and even to its doctrines from various religious groups. The new churches being built at the time are known as tower churches and have become some of the more distinctive examples of Russian architecture. One of the most noted examples is the Church of the Purification (latter half of the 17th century), which was built in Aleksandrova Sloboda, in the compound from which Ivan himself ruled.

Built over an earlier structure, it consists of a two-story polygonal arcade supporting tiers of *kokoshniki*, an open octagon, and on top, a tent roof with cupola, soaring to a height of 56 meters. The building thus moves away from the religious traditions embedded in the pentacupolar tradition toward a dynastic message, reaching its apotheosis at the Church of the Ascension at Kolomenskoe (some 10 kilometers southeast of the Kremlin in Moscow [1529–32]), which consisted of a two-tier arcaded church reached by external staircases, on top of which rose an astonishing structure consisting of the body of the church, three tiers of flattened *kokoshniki*, and an octagonal drum supported by a tent tower on top.

Though it is now common to use the label "baroque" to describe the architecture of the 16th and 17th centuries, one has to remember that this designation is relatively recent, having been formulated in the later 19th century. Nonetheless, the word does have value in pinpointing certain important changes in attitude about architecture and indeed about life in general during this period. We will restrict use of the term to describe a style that developed as a medium for propaganda during the Counter-Reformation, spanning the decades between 1620 and 1670.

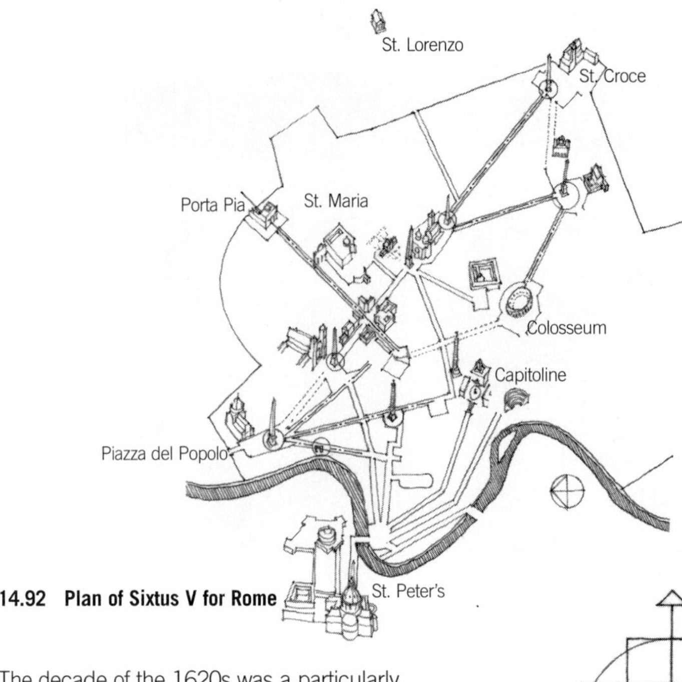


**14.92 Plan of Sixtus V for Rome**

## BAROQUE ITALY

The origins of the baroque were predominantly in Rome and the architects who most contributed to its creation were Giovanni Lorenzo Bernini (1598–1680) and Francesco Castelli Borromini (1599–1667). It is important to differentiate Roman baroque from European baroque. Baroque Rome waned after 1648 under Pope Alexander VII. From that time forward the papacy ceased to be a major power in European politics. It was the French and Austrians who now possessed a good deal of Europe's wealth, with the baroque style coming into its own at the Place Vendôme in Paris and the Château de Vaux-le-Vicomte by André Le Nôtre (1656–61). In Austria, it is exemplified by the castle of Schönbrunn Palace (1695). Eventually the Baroque became an architecture of the late-17th-century European capitals—Rome, Paris, London, and Vienna—giving to these cities a profile that is today still very much part of their modern identities.

The decade of the 1620s was a particularly promising moment in Church politics. Catholic forces destroyed an alliance of Protestant princes at the Battle of White Mountain (1620), near Prague in the present-day Czech Republic, while missionary work was carrying the word to the Far East and the Americas. The relationship of the Church with Spain, the military enforcer of Church politics, was secure, or so it seemed at the time. There was a mood of celebration and a sense that the Protestant revolution could be put to rest. The heroes of the Counter-Reformation (many of them Spanish) were canonized—Charles Borromeo in 1610, Ignatius de Loyola, Francis Xavier, Filippo Neri, and Teresa of Avila, all in 1622, and Gaetano da Thiene in 1629, and this, in itself, was a signal for new churches and chapels dedicated to the new saints.

In church architecture, the Greek cross, which was sometimes favored in the Renaissance because of its symmetry, was rejected for the conventions of the Latin cross, which was liturgically more satisfying in Counter-Reformation eyes since it allowed for a clear separation between clergy and laity, this was one of the primary distinctions between Catholic and Protestant churches of the time. Furthermore, the sacramental altar could be given a more central and monumental position.

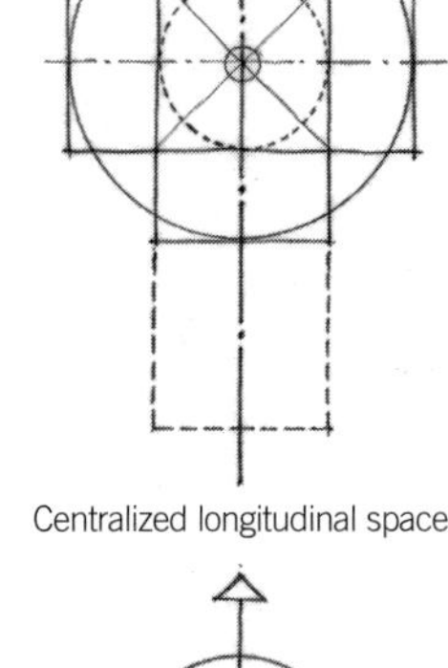

Centralized longitudinal space

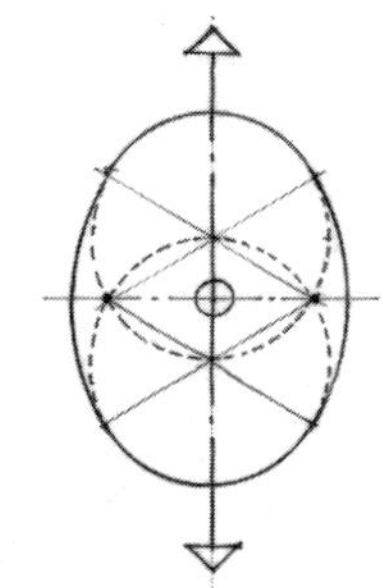

Elongated central space

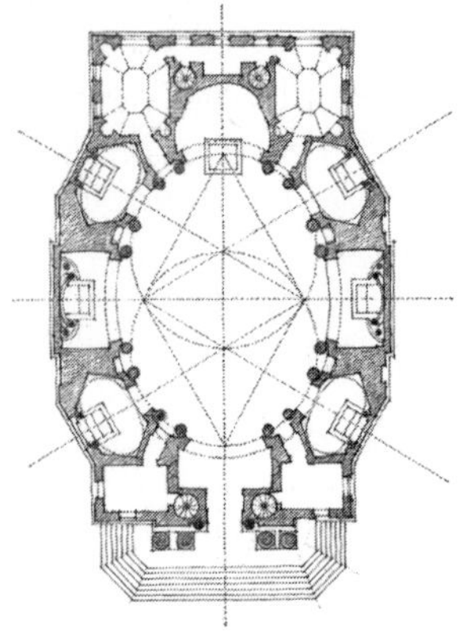

**14.93 Plan of an elliptical church by Borromini**

In 1585 Pope Sixtus V introduced a plan for the urban transformation of Rome that was based on a series of grand avenues connecting the prominent religious landmarks of the city and that was to become the progenitor of similar schemes in other cities. There was no longer a single main focus, as in the Renaissance, but a multitude of foci. One could argue that the superimposition of this type of clarity and organization onto the city corresponded to the new expanded world as understood by the European powers at the time. An important element in Sixtus's plan for Rome was the Piazza del Popolo, a long triangular space inside the walls of one of the city's main gates. Two churches similar in design, St. Maria di Montesanto (1678) to the east and St. Maria dei Miracoli (1681) to the west, were added to the piazza to define its southern end and serve as a secondary gateway into the city.

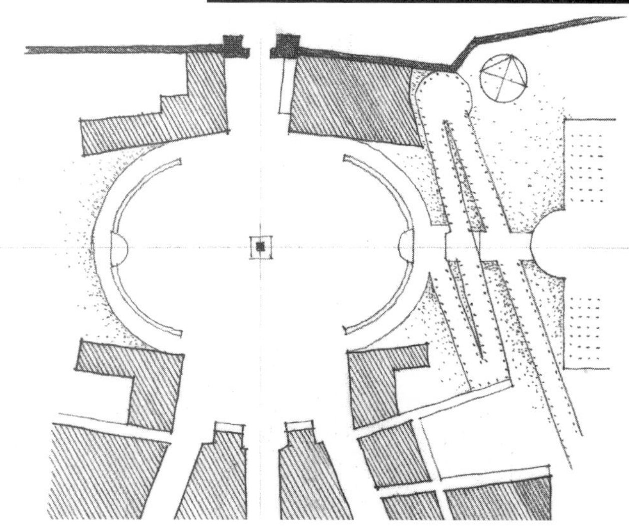

**14.94 Plan: Piazza del Popolo, Rome, Italy**

The preference, as was established at Il Gesù, was for a longitudinal nave unencumbered as much as possible by side aisles. Transepts were minimized or nonexistent, allowing the use of rectangles and ovals, which also helped to create the sense of community that was to be inculcated in these churches.

From the point of view of form, baroque architects preferred curves to straight lines, using niches, walls, pilasters, and attached columns in a seamless way that made architecture seem pliant and rubbery, not framing the liturgical celebrations but a part of it. It seemed that the very substance of the building was being shaped by the powerful and mysterious forces of the divine. We find not only the use of curves and ovals but also an appreciation of rhythmic movement through space as well as an intensification of its visual dynamics with the use not only of painting but also of sculptural putti who inhabit the higher reaches of the space. Unlike the medieval cathedrals where stained glass filtered and modulated the light coming into the nave, baroque windows were of plain glass and devoid of any tracery. Light had to blend in with the architecture and illuminate certain areas. It was not blinding light but rather a mysterious and diffuse light, with windows concealed by screen walls or pilasters. One often enters a baroque church and finds it quite luminous without first noticing any windows at all.

Many of the elements of baroque architecture were, however, not new. Michelangelo and Palladio had both used the giant order. Baldassare Peruzzi and Gulio Romano had created trompe l'oeil effects in their frescoes. But the Baroque architects did not hesitate to go from one medium to the other when called for to fulfill the Counter-Reformation need to expound the mysteries of the faith and extol the virtues of the martyrs. Though treatment of walls and pilasters varied a good deal, careful thought was given to the effects of color and lighting. Italians preferred colored marbles of rose and pinks, highlighted by whites and blacks. They made use of gilded and coffered domes, illuminated from a cupola. South Germans preferred a white- or cream-colored background, against which the furnishings were meant to stand out.

Painters created elaborate ceiling frescoes portraying visions of the Church Triumphant. There was also a tendency to intensify color in the upward direction. The Baroque architect was an impressario of appearances with sculpture and painting just as important as the architecture itself. It was, however, not all show and no substance. Bernini and Borromini were widely learned, and Guarino Guarini was theological and philosophical and a professional mathematician. All were well-acquainted with classical architecture, and so it cannot be said that it was lack of knowledge that prompted an aesthetic that broke with the classical norm. Rather it was a new way of thinking about architecture, one that brought the articulation of space up to date with recent developments in mathematics and geometry, working not platonically but very much through the senses.

**14.95 Piazza del Popolo, Rome**

14.96 St. Andrea al Quirinale, Rome, Italy

14.97 Section: St. Andrea al Quirinale

**St. Andrea al Quirinale**

Up until the late Middle Ages in Europe, little if anything was known of architects or leading masons in respect to life and training. By the early 15th century, however, the leading artists and architects come much more into view. Already with Brunelleschi, biographies were written indicating his level of fame. Michelangelo and Leonardo da Vinci were already famous by the end of their lifetimes. Giorgio Vasari (1511–74) compiled the first history of Renaissance artists in his *Lives of Seventy of the Most Eminent Painters, Sculptors, and Architects.* But none had achieved the level of popular fame as Bernini; when he went to Paris, people lined the streets to see his carriage pass by.

The core architectural works of Bernini are San Tommaso da Villanova at Castel Gandolfo (1658–61), St. Andrea al Quirinale in Rome (1658–70) and St. Maria dell'Assunzione at Ariccia (1662–64). All of these are central-type designs have plans that are simple geometrical forms based to no small degree on the architect's unqualified reverence for the Pantheon. In other words, though a building like St. Andrea is a transverse oval, its referent is still a classical one. The building had to be pushed back to allow for a small piazza in front of the church where carriages, which had become increasingly large over time, could pull up to the front. (The courtyard has since been removed.)

The church sits directly opposite Palazzo del Quirinale, which was an official apostolic residence but now is the home of the president of modern Italy. Intended as part of a monastic complex set up by the Jesuit order to train novices, the building was dedicated to recently appointed saints of the Jesuits—Andrew Avellion, Francis Xavier, Stanislaus Kostka, and Ignatius Loyola. It was thus in Bernini's eyes a type of Pantheon of the Jesuits. The massive Corinthian pilasters form the entrance, out of which projects a curved entrance canopy. The convex curve of the projecting porch is cradled in the middle of a concave-shaped piazza that mirrors the shape of the central oval in the interior. On the interior, a series of niches fill the body of the wall, with the central apse dedicated to St. Andrew and marked by flanking pairs of marble columns. The other four saints were positioned in the squarish niches on both sides of the principle cross axis.

The color scheme and the use of light are striking. The Corinthian pilasters that mark out the principal spatial configuration are in white, whereas the spandrels, lesser pilasters and the freestanding columns on the side of the central apse are covered in delicate, white-speckled, rose-tinted marble. Light from a concealed window streams down into the apse, illuminating a spectacular picture frame supported by cherubs and solar rays, all in gold. The dome over the oval glistens with golden decorations evoking the heavenly space to which St. Andrew ascends. It is patterned between the ribs by finely worked hexagonal coffers. Perched over the windows at the base of the dome are figures of putti and the fishermen who were St. Andrew's companions.

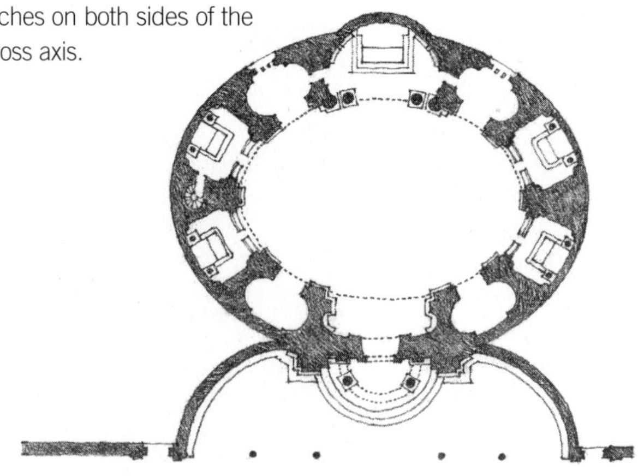

14.98 Plan: St. Andrea al Quirinale

14.99 **Transverse section: St. Carlo alle Quattro Fontane, Rome, Italy**

14.100 **View of ceiling: St. Carlo alle Quattro Fontane**

**St. Carlo alle Quattro Fontane**

St. Carlo was dedicated to another newly created saint of the Counter-Reformation, St. Charles Borromeo, (1538–84), who had been Archbishop of Milan and Papal Secretary of State under Pius IV. He was canonized in 1601. This church thus belongs to the new type of Counter-Reformation urban monastic order, in this case the Discalced Spanish Trinitarians, whose function it was to collect money to buy the freedom of Christians captured by the Moors.

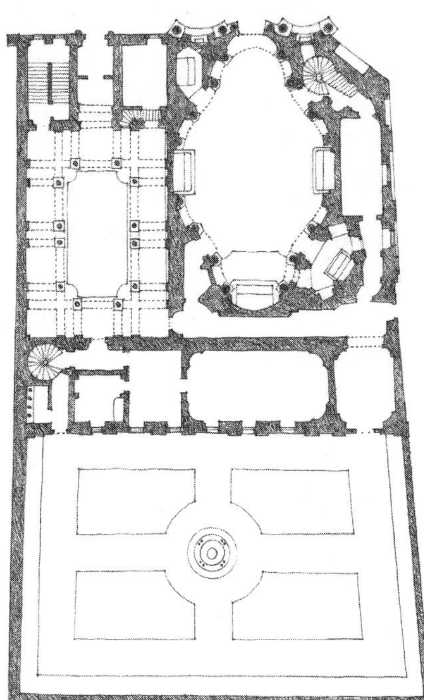

14.101 **Plan: St. Carlo alle Quattro Fontane**

Borromini was given the commission in 1634, but the building was not finished until 1682. The church is located at an intersection known for its four fountains, thus the name. The body of the church is nestled in an "L" formed by the entrance to the compound on the left of the church and a back wing of rooms. Of the church, only the front facade is visible and that is merely a skin added to the outside of the building, given that the church engages the street at its narrowest.

The design of the interior is an ingenious compromise of form and pragmatism. It is based on the prototype of a dome and four apses, but the apses have been flattened so that the spaces of the apses and that of the dome become almost one, brought into unity by means of a ring of Corinthian columns that appear embedded in the soft mass of the walls. The inner surface of the oval dome is coffered with interlacing octagons, crosses, and lozenges. Though, once again, there is much that links the two great artists, Bernini and Borromini, the latter, one can clearly see, worked unremittingly with the language of geometry. Bernini was certainly most interested in geometry, but in many respects, he was more the classicist. Borromini brings the classical orders and requirements into alignment, however, with an almost neomedieval fascination with geometric complexity. If Bernini was attracted to the historical symbolism of Rome, Borromini was attracted to the symbolic potential of space itself.

Despite the spectacular nature of the facade, one has to recall that Borromini designed it to fit within a set of other facades that, though purposefully less remarkable, are all part of a single unit. In fact, one of the questions one can pose is: where does one facade begin and the other end? The church facade hinges to the corner facade with its fountain below and bell tower above, which in turn leads to the side facade of the monastic building, where the pilasters projecting only a few centimeters serve to create a background rhythm for the whole. To the right of the church facade, Borromini designed the monastic facade and courtyard so that it reads as separate and distinct from the church and ties in with the neighboring structure on its right. In other words, what is remarkable is that the church is not a freestanding element proclaiming itself as separate and distinct from the urban fabric but rather consciously fitted into its environment. The two-story entrance courtyard to the monastery is also a play of geometrical inversions; but, in keeping with the ideology of austerity, it is designed with all elements in plain white, giving the whole a remarkably modern feel.

14.102 St. Ivo alla Sapienza, Rome, Italy

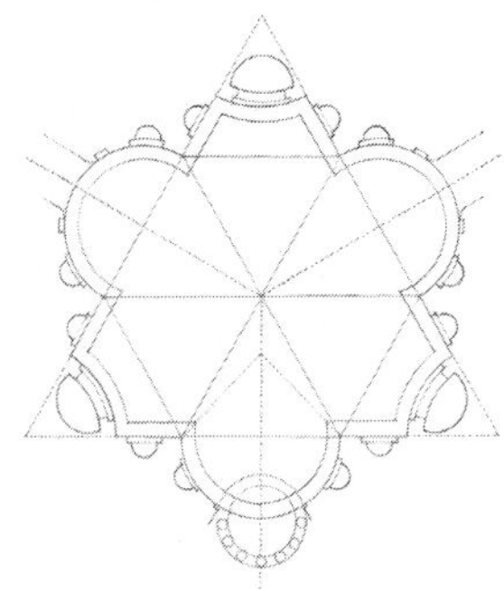

14.103 Plan geometry of St. Ivo alla Sapienza

## St. Ivo alla Sapienza

St. Ivo alla Sapienza (1643–8) is somewhat different from St. Carlo, from an urbanist point of view, because the institution, a law school, filled the whole city block. La Sapienza was originally founded in 1303 by Pope Boniface VIII. The block was torn down and the new building constructed with a church dedicated to St. Yves (1253–1303), the patron saint of lawyers. Nonetheless, here, too, Borromini designed the building as if it were fitted into an older structure by using the institutional spaces as part of the "frame" for the church, which sits at the back of a long courtyard piazza, seemingly embedded within the fabric of the building. The church was designed in plan as two intersecting triangles, with circles added at the perimeter to add or subtract space. The result is a space that is centralized and yet axial. Its simplicity is ingenious. As at St. Carlo, the facade and the space of the church just barely intersect. In fact the church has no facade in the traditional Renaissance sense, since it is here nothing more than an elaboration of the courtyard facade. The church has a high drum on which the dome is placed. The dome is surmounted by an ornate cupola with a spiraling top.

14.104 View of ceiling: St. Ivo alla Sapienza

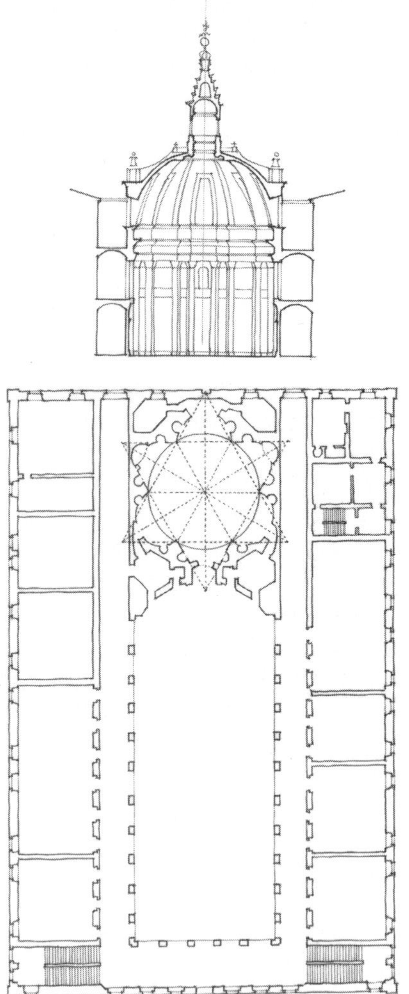

14.105 Plan and section: St. Ivo alla Sapienza

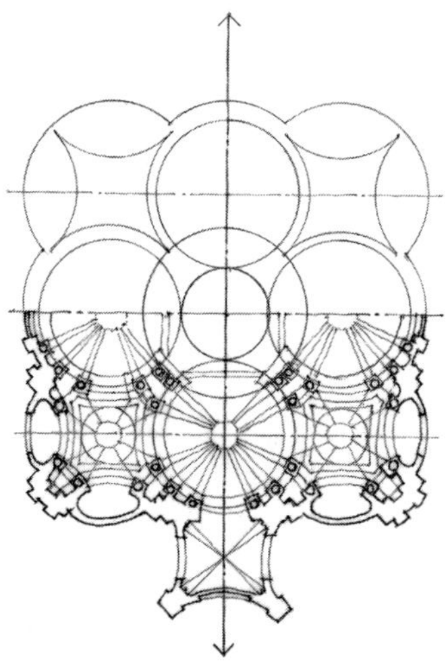

**14.106 Plan: San Filippo Neri, Turin, Italy**

**14.107 Section: San Filippo Neri**

### San Filippo Neri

Born in Modena, Guarino Guarini taught mathematics after having joined the Theatine order, a Counter-Reformationist teaching movement founded in the southern Abruzzi. When the Theatines were invited to Paris, they introduced to the astonished French a new attitude to religion involving elaborate representations and theatrical devices. The Theatines, unlike other orders, took their architectural designs from members of their own order, and it is in this context that the young Guarini encountered the architectural profession. He also had the good fortune of doing his studies in Rome in the 1640s, during the years in which Bernini and Borromini were at their most active. His work, however, deviates from the trajectory set out by them in so far as it was influenced not only by medieval precedents that he assiduously studied but also by Islamic architecture. The telescopic disposition of vertical space is characteristic of Mudéjar architecture, as exemplified in La Seo (the Cathedral of Saragossa) begun in the 12th century.

Guarini also studied Gothic architecture, which, as explained by Harold Alan Meek, though much undervalued in Italy, had made a rebound among intellectuals as part of a protest against the preponderance of Roman taste. Not Gothic, however, was Guarini's insistence that the upper ribs float in space, as at St. Lorenzo in Turin (1668–87), where their support to the ground is visually incomprehensible They are held up by four massive piers tied together at the level of the squinches by diagonal cross arches, with the whole system disguised so well—and so purposefully—that the corner chapels' round openings seem to point to nothing behind them but air.

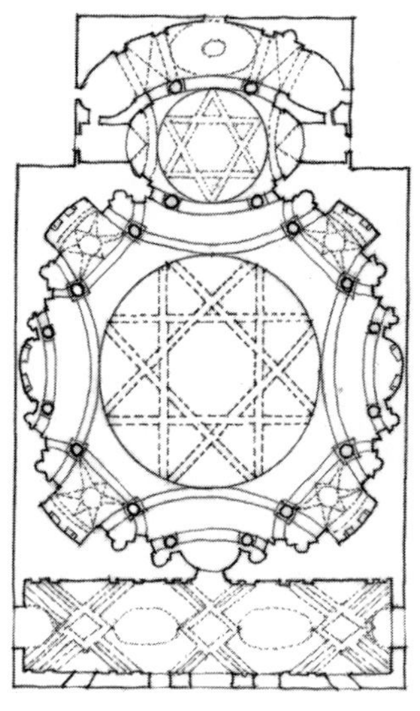


**14.108 Plan: St. Lorenzo in Turin, Italy**

The centralizing urge on the part of Guarini in subsequent works was resisted by the clergy, since it was seen as liturgically awkward. The resolution created by Guarini and used subsequently by others was to create a type of elongated centralized system, either with an ellipse or by multiplying spaces along the axis. The Church of the Immacolata Concezione in Turin is a case of the latter, whereas San Filippo Neri in Turin is an example of the former. There triangular projections break up the nave into three lozenge-shaped spaces. Though one can see some similarities to a study-plan that Borromini made for one of his churches, as has been noted in the scholarship on this church, Guarini's plan is unmistakably different, not only in the separation and reintegration of the elements, but also in the relationship between primary and secondary spatial elements. In Borromini, the secondary elements are still part of the inner spatial surface, whereas in Guarini the secondary spatial elements are almost autonomous and yet appear as continuous when one is in the nave, seemingly suggesting a further continuation of space where there is none.

**14.109 Church of the Visitation, Paris, France**

### Church of the Visitation

Jules Hardouin Mansart (1646–1708) was a grandnephew of François Mansart, under whom he studied architecture and whose family name he later adopted. He was favored by Louis XIV who made him his court architect and ennobled him in 1699. He was to become one of the most dominant architects of the age. Influencing his work was the architecture of Salomon de Brosse (1571–1626), whose facade of St. Gervais (1616–21), added on to an older Gothic church, showed the development of a bold and new monumental style. The tall nave of the Gothic church required an unusual three-story solution. Unlike what might have been common in the Renaissance, where attached columns below are often flattened into pilasters above, Salomon de Brosse used attached columns in all three horizontal zones. This enhanced the sculptural drama of the facade. In fact the absence of pilasters freed the wall to come into its own plasticity, even in the stacking of the three equally sized large openings on the central axis of the facade. The unusualness of the facade, the robustness of the columns, and the simplicity of the Doric temple front with columns set forth a vigorous reinterpretation of the classical norms that Mansart with his flair for innovation extended into his own work.

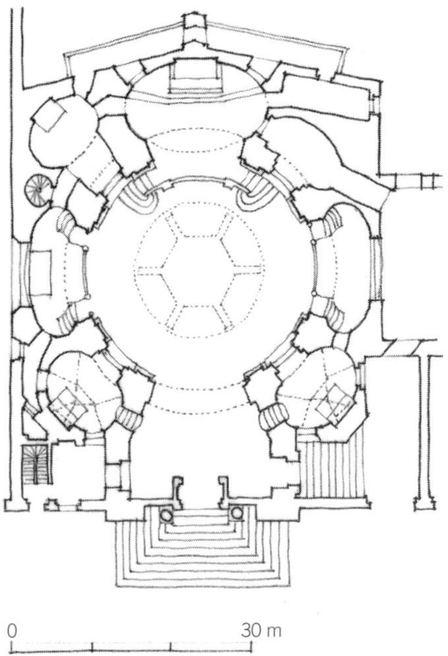


**14.110 Plan: Church of the Visitation**

Among Mansart's first designs was the relatively small Church of the Visitation (designed 1633). It was built for the "Daughters of the Visitation of St. Mary" (also known as the Visitation order), founded in 1610 by François de Sales, a Jesuit priest, known for his devout life and inspiring sermons. The church building is circular but, as at St. Andrea in Rome, not technically "centralized." It is rather, in conformity with Counter-Reformation expectations, a stretched circle. The altar is placed in an ancillary space behind the circle almost on par with the side chapels. But that is not the only unusual aspect of the building. The entrance is marked by what seems to be an autonomous pavilion squeezed against the mass of the church. Small walled courtyards to the right and left of the facade allowed the facade to register as a sacred portal. Perhaps the most fundamental aspect of the design is the prominence given to the plain wall surface. The orders were used sparingly, in a way that let the whole seem a composition of pure forms.

**14.111 Dogon house structure, Mali**

## DOGON OF MALI

The African continent below the Islamic north consisted of a complex web of social and political organizations. Some societies, like the Asante, Yoruba, and Tutsis, maintained large states, whereas the Mbuti and Efe of central Africa and of the Kalahari Desert continued a life of hunting and gathering. Despite the tendency to see African society as self-contained and self-supporting tribes, the reality is that various groups had long and extensive contacts with one another through trade. Neighboring societies may have borrowed elements of each other's rituals over the centuries in a manner that makes it impossible to trace the precise origin of particular rituals. During the 1700s, aggressive Islamization from the north deeply impacted and changed west African nations, such as the Bambara, but full Islamization, still a matter of political friction to this day, was never achieved, often creating a hybrid religious culture.

The Dogon, at the southern edge of Islamized Africa, live above, along, and below the Bandiagara Cliffs, a 150-kilometer-long sandstone escarpment in south-central Mali. The name *Dogon* was given to these people by the French in the early 20th century, even though they are not a homogeneous group but a mosaic of different cultures, as is clear from their language, which consists of numerous dialects. From their own mythical stories, it is thought that they originally moved into the area in the 11th century, with other groups moving into the area up until the 15th century. The Dogon at some moment encountered an older preexisting culture, the Tellem, whom they incorporated into their society and who moved with them. The Tellem are the smithies for the Dogon, and they are responsible for making the important ancestor statues that are commissioned by Dogon elders for their ceremonies. The Tellem are held in awe because of their magical powers, but they are seen as lesser in the highly stratified society of the Dogon. Despite differences, the various groups have lived in remarkable peace over the centuries.

In Dogon society an individual's status is determined by position within family groups and by hierarchies based on age and rules of descent. Religion involves the worship of ancestors as well as spirits. The Dogon believe, however, in one god, Amma, who is all knowing and all powerful and who upholds the balance between the living and the dead. Each clan will have its own altar (*taba*) to Amma. The Léwé cult, dedicated to agricultural renewal, is the principal cult that reenacts the departure from their ancestral homeland. Its main symbol is the snake that comes out of the earth of the ancestors and that accompanies the tribes on their journey. These and other ceremonies are overseen by the priests. All the rites and ceremonies involved masking, and they were performed by males personifying supernatural beings and speaking their special language.

**14.112 Dogon toguna**

14.113 Dogon city

Dogon society is spread out over a vast area of cities, villages, and clan compounds. Some of the larger cities have more than 5000 inhabitants and are composed of densely packed compounds. These compounds (called *ginna*) have different typologies, but they mostly consist of walled enclosures and squarish towers topped with conically shaped straw roofs. Another type is composed of two rectangular volumes separated to make a courtyard with entrance at one end and a round cylindrical kitchen at the other. In the cliffs, the compounds have a more compressed beehive arrangement. All compounds have granaries, divided up for different purposes, which are usually tall cylindrical structures with a door at the top and small portals below. The word ginna also applies to the house of the oldest in the clan who descends from his clan's ancestral founder. The house will be larger and more complex than the others in the compound and will be based on the number symbolism of one and seven, which includes the female number of four and the male number of three. At the social apex is the priest (*hogon*) and his house is appropriately large and visible. Its facade is painted with totem images. Civic buildings are known as *toguna*. They are basically artificial forests composed of high piles of sticks and straw held up on wooden but sometimes stone posts. They are low to the ground so it is not possible to stand up under them. They are places for sitting and talking.

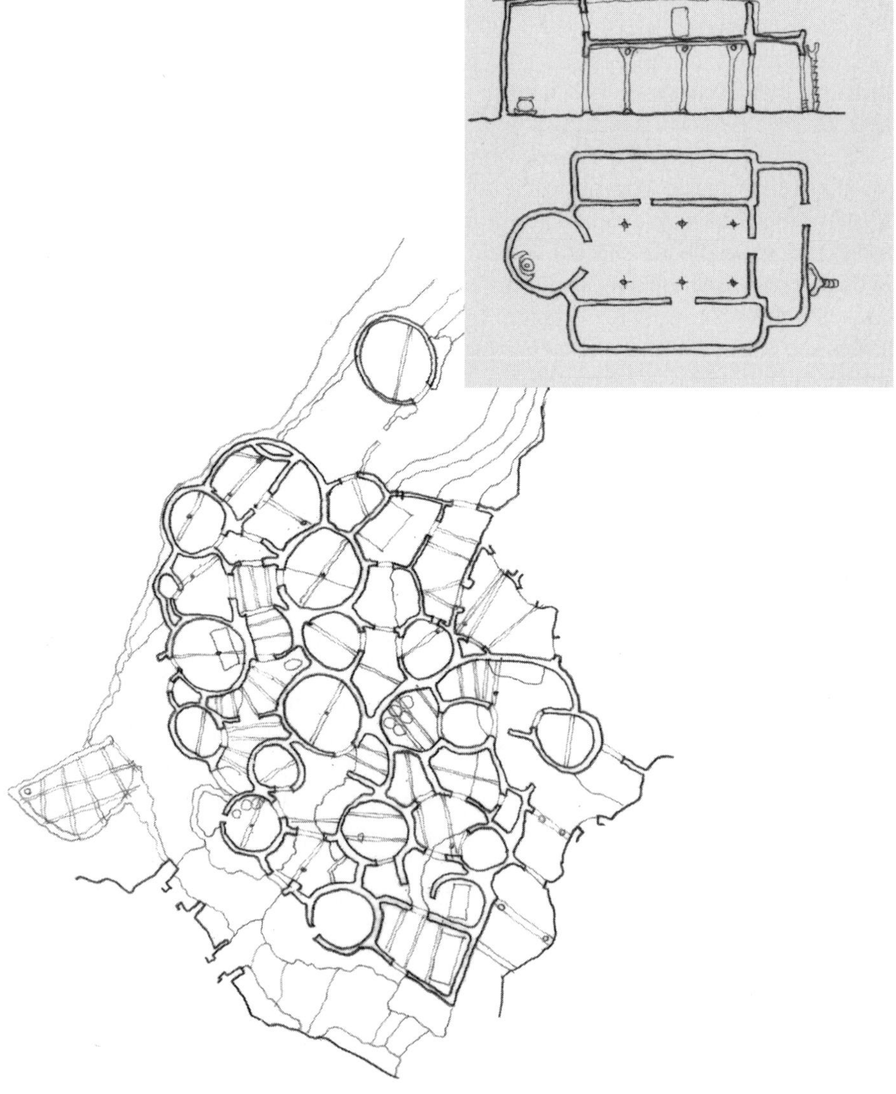

14.114 Plans and sections of typical Dogon housing clusters

# Architecture of the Eurasian Power Bloc

In the 17th century, the Eurasian world from Japan to Western Europe was an economic power bloc, built on land-based and coastal trade. From one continent to another, wealth, ideas, and people travelled with traders, migrants, and armies. This was the Old World undone by the new European command over ocean trade.

Imagine a traveler in 1652 starting a trip through Europe and Asia to study the latest developments in the field of architecture. Starting in Japan he tells the story of how he is led through the Ninomaru Palace in Nijo Castle, located in the heart of Kyoto. He then visits the austere Katsura Imperial Villa and is introduced by his hosts to the newly developed intricacies of the Zen tea ceremony. Crossing into Korea, he visits the Kyongbokgung Palace in Seoul (begun in 1394), led there by a Mongolian serving in the Manchu empire, which had reduced Korea to a vassal state. Traveling with a Mongolian commander into the heart of Manchuria through Mukden, its capital, he visits the still relatively recently designed Forbidden City, which is being refurbished by the new Manchu rulers who had just taken Beijing. The times are just stable enough to travel to the nearby Ming tombs. On the way he discusses with his guides the pros and cons of their international seafaring voyages and whether or not they should be continued.

He then works his way southward into the rugged highlands of Tibet to visit Potala Palace, built by the supporters of the fifth Dalai Lama, who carved out an important political territory for themselves in the Himalayas. Descending down in the fertile plains of the Ganges, he travels through area controlled by one of the Islamized descendants of the Mongols, Akbar the Great. He makes his way past Man Madir, one of the grand 16th-century palaces of the Tomara Dynasty in central India, to Delhi and its expansive palaces. He inspects the great planned city, Fatehpur Sikri, laid out by Akbar in 1573, and then he goes up the Yamuna River to see the just-completed Taj Mahal. He then heads to Kandahar and crosses into Persian territory, following the trade routes to Isfahan, where he sees the vast urban extension of Isfahan with its enormous city square, sumptuous mosques, and broad royal gardens. There he meets traders from as far away as England. From Isfahan, he crosses the Argos Mountains into areas newly controlled by the Ottomans and following the old Seljuk caravan routes and makes his way to Antioch on the Mediterranean, where he takes a ship to Istanbul.

The city, taken by the Ottomans in 1453, was in the process of being rebuilt by its new lords. He admires the great Hagia Sophia, but his guide explains to him the superiority of the recently built mosques by Sinan and in particular of the Suleymaniye Mosque. From Istanbul, he takes a merchant ship to the somewhat faded port of Venice and is told there of economic hardships and of Dutch competition while being led to see the churches of St. Giorgio Maggiore by Andrea Palladio. He then follows a group of pilgrims to see Rome, a city awash in Spanish money. The dome of the Vatican in Rome, one of the most demanding and exciting building projects in all of Europe, was just being finished. In front of the church, he sees a vast area that had just been cleared to make way for Bernini's colonnaded Piazza of St. Peter's.

He takes the time to visit the recently finished building by Francesco Borromini, St. Ivo della Sapienza and to discuss with its priests the efforts to strengthen the Counter-Reformation. From the Roman port of Ostia, by boat to Marseilles, and then northward, he works his way through France. He admires the new wealth of the aristocracy and sees some of the great chateaus on the Loire, the Place Royale in Paris, and the facades of some churches, but otherwise French architecture has yet to develop into anything rivaling what he had seen elsewhere.

To see the wealth of the Europeans in action, he goes to Amsterdam, a city with neither grand palaces nor dominating churches but a bustling port and world metropolis. He visits the city hall and is shown the great bank as well as the world maps inlaid in marble on the floor. He takes time to visit his first Protestant churches and is told of terrible religious wars. In crossing the English Channel, he visits the newly built Banqueting House (1619–22), one of the first buildings in England to be designed in the modern Italian manner, a structure representing an ambitious but—from the point of view of the Chinese, Moghuls, Ottomans, and Dutch—still relatively marginal power, namely England. The major export commodity of England still was wool, and its foreign policy was driven more by pirating than by politics.

# 1600 CE

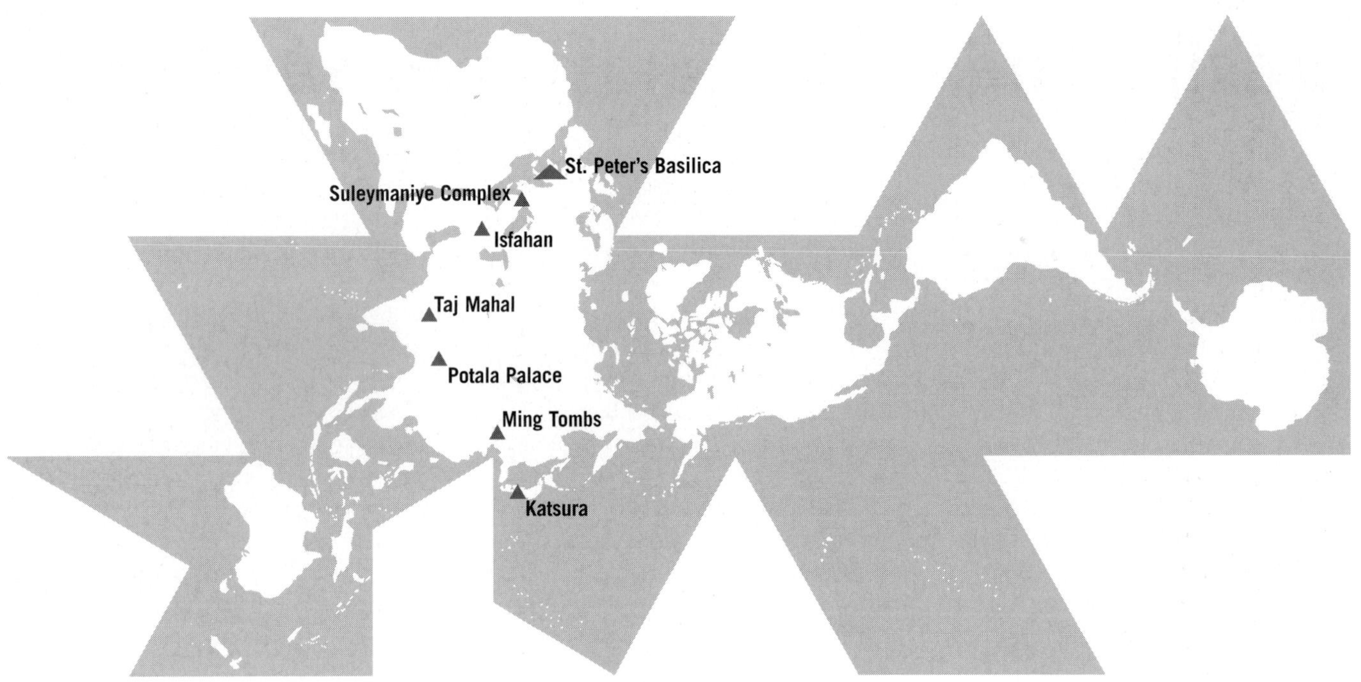
St. Peter's Basilica
Suleymaniye Complex
Isfahan
Taj Mahal
Potala Palace
Ming Tombs
Katsura

14.115 **Suminoe pine, Katsura Imperial Villa, near Kyoto, Japan**

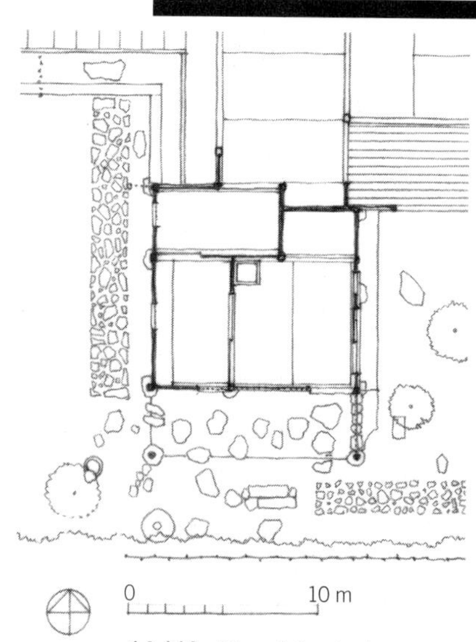


14.116 **Plan: Taian teahouse**

**Katsura Rikyu (Katsura Imperial Villa)**

In contrast to the Shogun military commanders who, in developing their aristocratic ambitions, created sumptuous displays of power, the older aristocratic families, now largely disempowered, began to adopt an introspective and pseudorustic aesthetic influenced by the ideals of Zen Buddhism. The most celebrated example of this new aesthetic—now considered by many modern architects as "the essence" of Japanese architecture—is the Katsura Imperial Villa. It was built by the nobleman Hichijonomiya Toshihito (1579–1629) and his son Toshitada (1619–62). Underlying the design is the ceremonial teahouse. In the 17th century, serving and drinking tea had become the center of lavish rituals at courtly ceremonies, with the focus on the display of the quality tea ware and the presentation ceremony upstaging the tea itself. In the latter part of the 16th century, Sen no Rikyu (1522–91), a patron of the Zen monks in Ginkakuji, transformed the ceremony into a simple, precisely choreographed, and highly personalized exercise known as *wabi-cha*. His famous dictum was "one moment, one meeting." The ceremony, which was to contrast with the extravagance of the shogun, was to be free from all distractions, past and future, and lead to a state of immediacy.

Rikyu designed one of the first known rustic, or *soan*, teahouses named Taian, in Yamazaki, south of Kyoto. The approach path followed a carefully designed zigzag route. All along the path, and in particular at a point of turning, there were studied views of the garden. The final approach to the teahouse was from an angle, with its three-quarter view blocked and framed by a carefully pruned trees that obscured part of the teahouse and broke the view in two. This was all meant to help the participant clear his mind and focus on the present.

The interior space was defined by a simple bench providing a place for the participant to sit and wait until the ceremony was ready. Entrance was through a door (*nijiriguchi* or "crawl-in door") so small that one had to bend to enter it, assuming a posture of submission. The main space (*chashitsu*) had two tatami mats with another one for the preparation of the tea (*katte*), and a fourth serving as an ancillary space. The roof is flat and low except over the main space where it rises several inches. In the corner of the main space there is a hearth for boiling water. The entire structure is made from simple unworked materials.

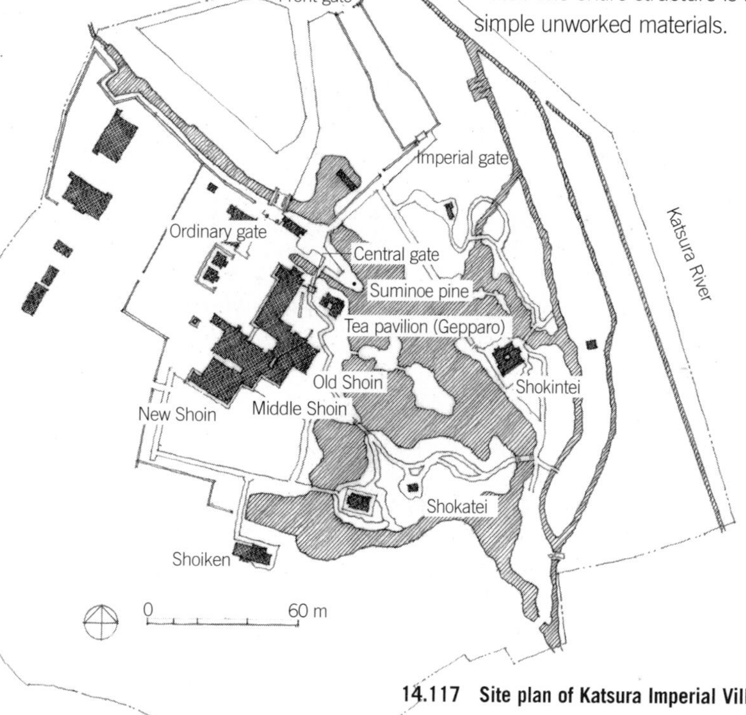


14.117 **Site plan of Katsura Imperial Villa**

14.118 **Central gate: Katsura Imperial Villa**

14.119 **Garden gate, Katsura Imperial Villa**

The Katsura Imperial Villa is a 7-hectare estate on the western bank of the Katsura River, located in a suburb of Kyoto. The main building comprises three interlinked *shoins* (or sections) referred to as the Old, Middle, and New Shoins, staggered at the western edge of an irregularly shaped pond with several islands. The Old Shoin, furthest to the north, was built by Prince Toshihito and the other two by his son, Prince Toshitada. The New Shoin, along with a special gate and access path, was built on the occasion of the Emperor Go Mizuno's visit to Katsura in 1663. Seven teahouses are roughly distributed around the garden in a semicircular arc and linked by a stroll path. In its outlines, therefore, Katsura is nothing more than a nobleman's country villa with a stroll garden. Katsura's genius lies in its detailing, its use of materials, and the way in which the walking path, like the access path of Rikyu's teahouse, has been delineated to unfold the experience of Katsura.

The palace has two main entry gates. The commoner's entrance into Katsura is through a simple bamboo gate located at the far end of an austere but immaculately constructed bamboo fence. Nothing of the interior is visible from the outside. Even as one walks in, one's view is carefully screened by a hedge. Katsura's front gate was built for imperial visits. It was patently unassuming and opened onto a straight, unedged gravel path lined with trees, leading to another gate framed in the center of the picture plane. In both gates, the entrance into Katsura is a study in quietude.

14.120 **Plan: Imperial Villa, Katsura**

Past the second gate the gravel path turns sharply right for 50 meters or so, the longest stretch of straight path at Katsura. Although the entire garden is to the left and the villa dead ahead, the view down this Imperial approach is carefully screened by bushes and trees. As one moves, small openings reveal views of the garden, a glimpse of the main teahouse, a look at the boathouse, a bridge over a water view, until it reaches the northern edge of the villa where it makes a sharp turn to the left. This is where the visit to the villa really begins.

A narrow promontory, edged by a thick hedge, juts out into the pond, with a miniaturized Suminoe pine tree in its middle. The framed view of the tree draws attention to and blocks the view of the garden beyond. The miniaturization of the tree also makes the promontory seem longer than it is and introduces the notion of self-consciously constructed symbolism in the landscape. The Katsura garden is not just picturesque, it is a stage set prepared for a filmic experience of space and time.

14.121 Stepping stones: Katsura Imperial Villa

To the right of the Suminoe promontory, over an arched wood and earth bridge, is the Central Gate, a visitor's first encounter with architecture. A simple freestanding wall with a rectangular opening extends out to the west from a subsidiary building (which contains the commoner's entrance). The gravel path terminates with a single large, uncut stone at the threshold, followed by four dressed stones arranged in a square. From there, a loose arrangement of uncut stepping-stones crisscrosses the straight path made from cut stones and signals the signature theme of Katsura's walkways yet to be experienced, that is, the studied orchestration of stepping-stones to generate a haptic and tactile experience.

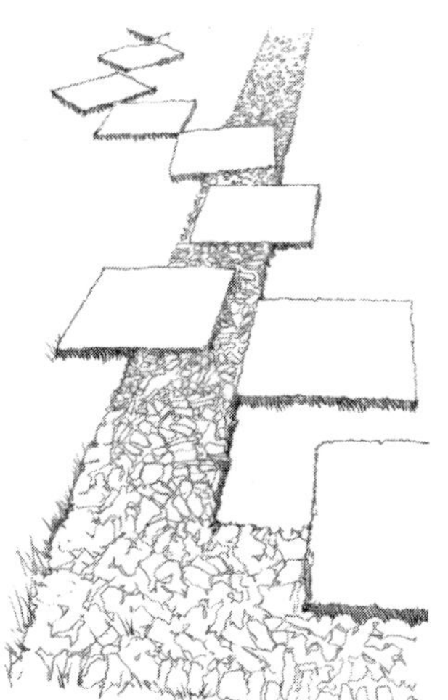

14.122 Garden path: Katsura Imperial Villa, Kyoto

From the Central Gate, stepping-stones lead to the entrance of the Old Shoin, called the Imperial Carriage Stop. Here, another freestanding wall with an opening, projecting out from the Old Shoin to the north, offers an alternative route, a second carefully staged path leading east to the Gepparo, the teahouse closest to the Shoins. The stepping-stones winding through the opening have the quality of mysterious footprints; they invite you to follow them.

The final step up into the Old Shoin is another uncut stone dramatically set against the straight lines of the wooden steps of the entrance porch. Another of Katsura's signature themes is the elaboration of the villa as a simple hut, like Rikyu's Teahouse, built directly within the natural landscape (not unlike the palatial residential architecture of the time). Every entrance into the villa is from large uncut stones, and every exterior post, at least on the garden side, sits directly on a stone as its foundation. As at Rikyu's Teahouse, all the wooden posts and beams were left unpolished and unadorned, some with their bark intact.

The geometry that governs the plan of the three Shoins is derived from the dimensions of the tatami and the sliding shoji screens covered with translucent rice paper. The planning of the spaces is orchestrated as a series of interconnected rooms, with all the important rooms facing east onto the garden. The supporting rooms are to the west and are connected to secondary structures. The Middle and the New Shoins are connected by a special intermediate section called the Music Room. An external veranda runs along the eastern edge of the villa, edged by sliding screen doors that can be opened and shut to modulate the light and to connect the exterior and the interior.

14.123 Detail: Katsura Imperial Villa, Kyoto

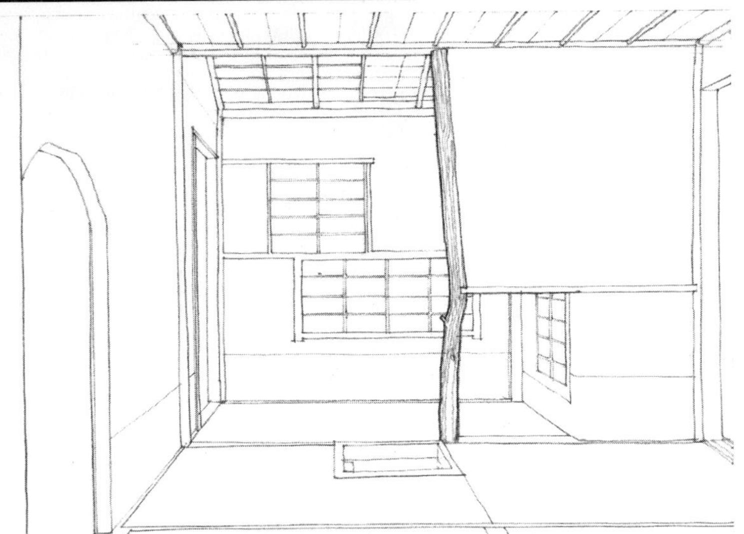
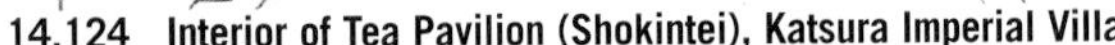

14.124 **Interior of Tea Pavilion (Shokintei), Katsura Imperial Villa**

14.125 **Ceiling structure of the Gepparo, Katsura Imperial Villa**

The spatial and visual focus of the Old Shoin is an east-west cross axis formed by the pantry, Spear Room, and its main space (the Second Room) with its external bamboo deck called the Moon-Viewing Platform. (The Katsura River was known as a scenic place for moon viewing in August.) The framed view from within the Shoin and the open view from the platform are both carefully designed. A miniature stone pagoda in a clearing on the southern edge of the Island of Immortals is the view's stable point amidst a dense arboreal landscape. Its focus is the still water of the pond, which at night would reflect the rising moon on the east and by day, the trees along its irregular edges. In autumn, the trees are ablaze with color and in winter with snow.

Katsura's "main event" is the walk around its stroll garden. The garden is traditionally credited to Kobori Enshu (1579–1647), a tea master and garden designer, although this has been disputed. Many walks are possible, but the common walk circumambulating the pond in a clockwise direction begins to the north of the Old Shoin, moves down the Imperial Approach, winds through the northern garden with the Outside Resting Place, around the Shore, to the main teahouse (the Shokintei), on to the large island with the Shoiken and Orindo tea-houses, then across the Riding Ground and Moss Garden, and back to the Middle Shoin. It is, of course, the journey rather than the destination that is important. Most of the path is on individual stepping stones made from uncut rocks, each one placed with great care. Although each stone is completely horizontal and always no more than a comfortable stride apart, the fact that they are not a continuous walkway and can suddenly make unexpected twists and turns forces one to be very aware of not only where one is walking but the very act of walking. The stepping-stones simulate and provoke the haptic and meditational experience of intentional walking, as required by Zen-inspired practices.

Intersections are an art in themselves. When the dressed stones of the straight paths, surrounding the *shoins*, meet the stepping-stones, the latter dance around and through the former with a studied irreverence. But when they encounter the cascade of pebbles that make the "sand" of the shore, they march through them like a determined walker on the beach. Sometimes they seem to have inherent purposes; the stepping-stones march straight across the wet moss garden, next to the Middle Shoin, while the straight path is forced to skirt around the edge. At other times, they are simply functional. Along the way, stone lanterns mark terminals and places of rest. One of the most famous uses of the lantern is at the terminus of the spit that projects out into the pond from the shore. Here at the end, a single lantern, known as the Night-Rain Lantern, marks the terminus of the path not to be taken.

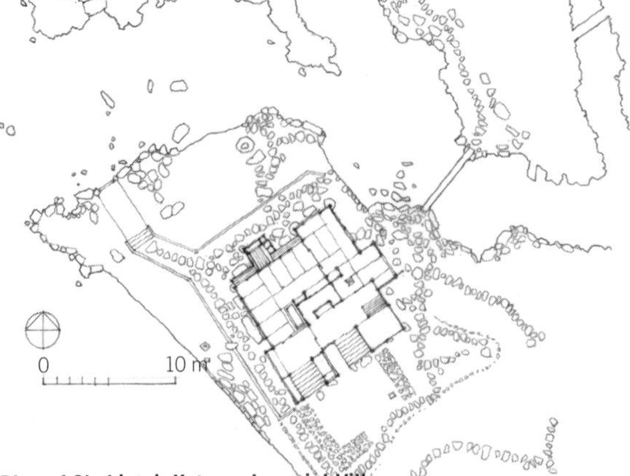


14.126 **Plan of Shokintei, Katsura Imperial Villa**

14.127 **Ming Tombs, near Beijing, China**

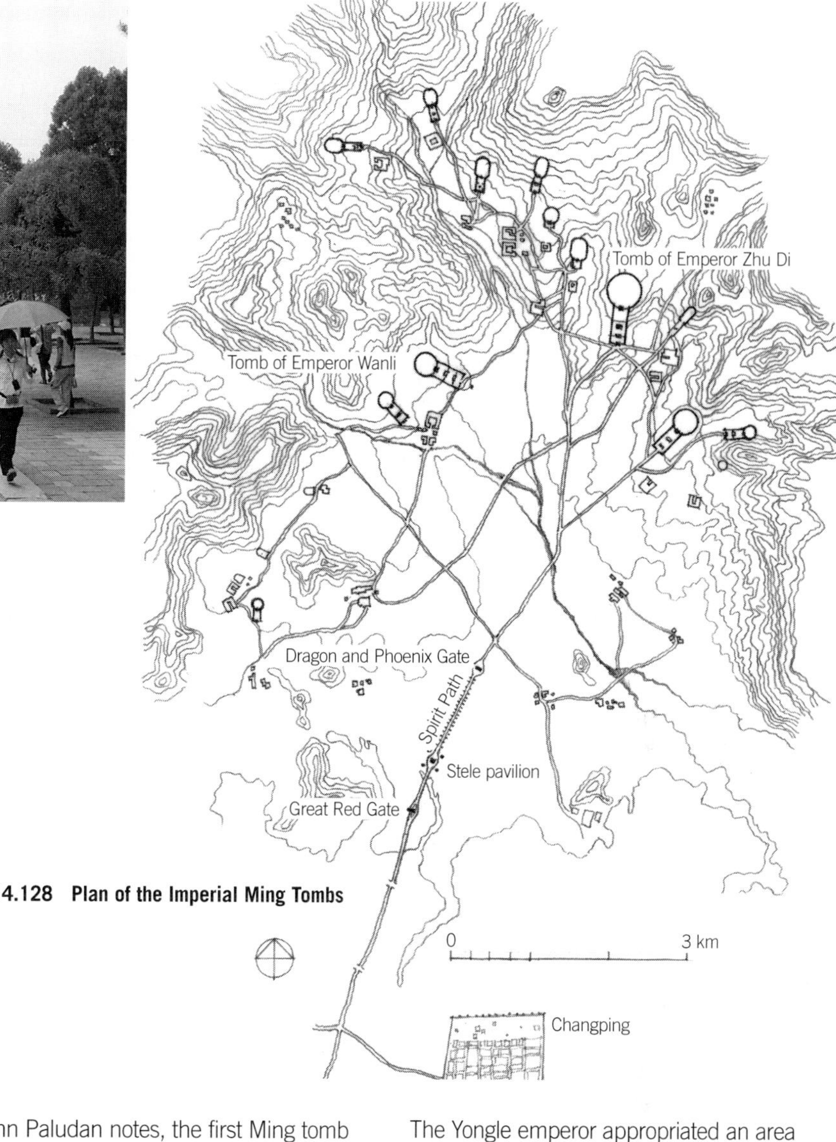


14.128 **Plan of the Imperial Ming Tombs**

## Ming Tombs

So efficient was the Ming bureaucracy that the fact that the seventh Ming emperor, Wanli (1573–1620), was reported to have been indolent and pleasure-seeking seems not to have affected the prosperity of his empire. Official ceremonies and presentations were simply made to an empty throne in his stead. A large proportion of Wanli's time, along with an estimated 8 million *taels* of silver, was spent in the design and construction of his tomb, which began in 1585 when he was only 22 years old. Much more than personalized egocentric attempts at guarantees for an afterlife, tombs, and in particular royal tombs, were an integral part of the Chinese cosmology. Spirits of dead ancestors of even the common people had to be fed and cared for or else they were liable to visit misfortune upon future generations. The emperor's death, however, was particularly special in that he became part of heaven itself, and the tomb's architecture had to represent that transition. Many of China's royal tombs, going back to that of the First Emperor, Shi Huangdi, have still not been excavated. The thirteen Ming tombs, of which only Wanli's has been excavated, are among the most famous and best preserved, and they are clustered in the valley of the Tianshou Mountains in the Changping county of Hebei province, about 80 kilometers northwest of Beijing.

As Ann Paludan notes, the first Ming tomb built here was that of the third Ming emperor, Zhu Di, known as the Yongle Emperor, in 1409. Zhu Di moved the Ming capital to Beijing and built the Forbidden City. The Ming, continuing T'ang and Zhou funerary practices, designed their tombs to consist of three parts—a long Spirit Path leading up to the tomb, a shrine for ceremonies and sacrifices to the dead, and the burial mound itself. However, unlike their predecessor, the Song, the Ming did not build a separate Spirit Path for each tomb and instead clustered all their tombs in a single valley off one Spirit Path with a single approach. The Ming also did away with the practice of sacrificing for the emperor "accompanying" concubines and servants and so did not need a separate chamber for them.

The Yongle emperor appropriated an area of about 330 square kilometers, which was defined by a perimeter wall that encompassed a large area, including a valley, the base hills of a mountain range, and rivulets feeding into a river running to the south. This area was protected by a prohibition against the cultivation or cutting of trees, and a village was established near the entrance to house the people employed to maintain the land.

14.129 Ming Tombs, near Beijing

14.130 Underground chamber, Tomb of Emperor Wanli, Ming Tombs

Conceptually, the Ming tombs are a part of the same spatial-symbolic order of the Forbidden City and the Altar of Heaven. This order is in part feng shui but mostly a spatialization of a social and spiritual order focused on the emperor; the symbolic order of Beijing was designed to enable the institution of the emperor, as a governmental and spiritual center, to be functional and visible. In the tombs, however, there were no quotidian needs, no citizenry to be governed. Here, it was only the reigning emperor and his relationship with the ancestors, represented in the city by the empty space of the Altar of Heaven, which had to be spatialized, making for the purest representation of the intersection of the terrestrial world and the heavenly one. Each succeeding emperor was expected to visit the tombs of his predecessors on each of the anniversaries of their deaths.

Site selection was critical. The Yongle emperor picked the site for his tomb so that it was nestled at the base of the intersection of two low-mountain ranges. This fit the dictates of feng shui, which required that two mountain ranges (the tiger and the dragon) provide a protective back to the site to block evil northern spirits. (In the Forbidden City the mountain is represented by the small artificial hill just beyond the north wall.)

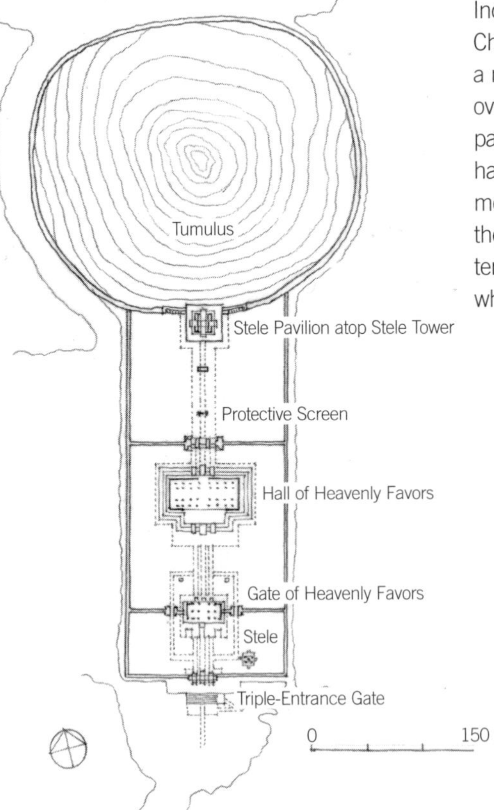


14.131 Plan of the Tomb of the Yongle emperor (Changling)

The north-south axis was defined by the creation of the Spirit Path. As he did at the Altar of Heaven, a visiting emperor would have approached the site from the south, the direction of supplication. The entrance was marked by a five-portal, stone ceremonial gate, called Pai Lou, composed of six monolithic columns, adorned with animals derived from native Chinese, Buddhist, and Indic sources. Unlike the convention in China, where every building or structure has a name that was always written on a tablet over the central entrance, the tablet on this particular gate was left empty, for it would have been inappropriate, so it was held, for mere mortals to announce the presence of the Sons of Heaven. *Pai lou* is the generic term for gateways commemorating people who have led virtuous lives.

14.132 Stele guarding the entrance to the tomb of Emperor Wanli

14.133 Spirit Path, Ming Tombs, near Beijing

About a kilometer beyond the Pai Lou was the Great Red Gate, the official entrance to the tomb grounds. The building, square in plan, has a solid base cut through, with tall tunnel vaults in its axes that, at their center, frame a huge 10-meter-tall monolithic stele held up on the back of a tortoise. Poems, written by later emperors in praise of their ancestors, were carved on the stele. At this gate, the emperor dismounted and proceeded on foot. Just to the side of the gate, there was a pavilion, no longer extant, where the emperor and his retinue of about 1000 attendants rested and changed into the appropriate robes. From there, the emperor began his long walk down the Spirit Path.

As in earlier tombs, the main event of the Spirit Path is its array of statues of mythical and real beasts and eminent nobles and generals aligned on both sides. Twelve pairs of animals and six pairs of men symbolize an eternal guard, arrayed in the same manner in which the honor guard was prepared in the Forbidden City for ceremonial occasions. The animals are in pairs, one resting and one standing. At the end of this segment of the Spirit Path there is a small three-portal gate, with the center blocked to prevent the passage of evil spirits.

Once one passes through the sides of the gate, the Spirit Path continues with a gentle curve to the left, leading to a triple bridge across the river, straight to the Yongle emperor's tomb. Subsidiary paths to the other tombs fan out from the main path, like the branches of a tree.

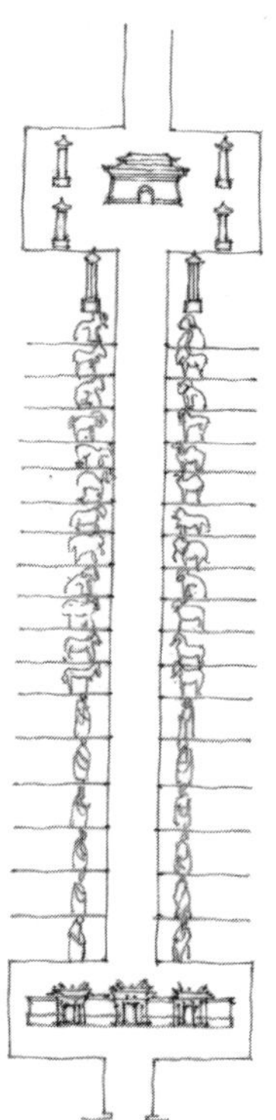

14.134 Spirit Path, Ming Tombs

The tombs are a long distance from the main entrance, a walk of almost 6 kilometers from the Pai Lou. This walk, through a flat plain filled with carefully chosen fragrant trees, was often the subject of painting and poetry. As in the Forbidden City, and Chinese imperial architecture in general, the Path, as a monumental extension of space in the horizontal axis, was made at a scale appropriate only to the emperors. The horizontal extension of space was considered to be the measure of a building's significance. In an obvious sense the Spirit Path repeats the axis of the Forbidden City. But in another sense, it is the Forbidden City, with its fake mountain at the northern end, that in a sense copies the sacred axis embodied in the Spirit Path.

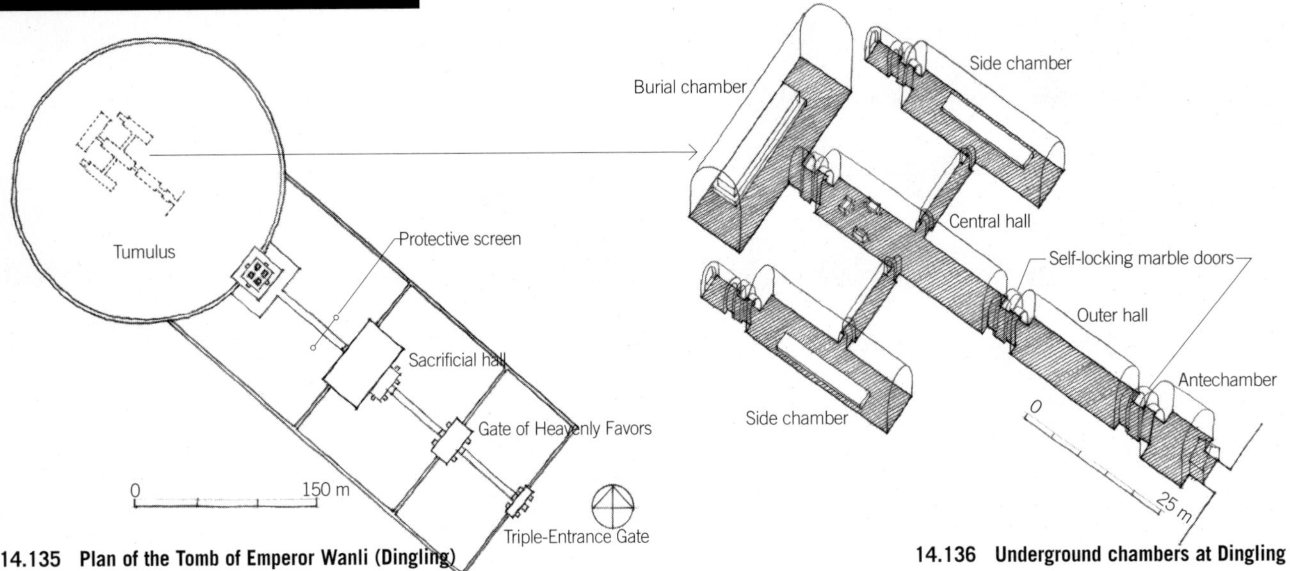


**14.135 Plan of the Tomb of Emperor Wanli (Dingling)**

**14.136 Underground chambers at Dingling**

The thirteen tombs consist of a sequence of rectangular enclosures for rituals and sacrifices, terminating in a round or oval burial mound. The enclosures signify the terrestrial and the circular mound, the heavenly. Where the wall of the last enclosure and the wall of the circular enclosure meet, one finds a Stele Tower with a pavilion on top of the base that gives access to the mound. Most of the tombs have only one or two enclosures, and only the largest three—Changling, Yongling, and Dingling—have three. Changling, the oldest and largest, begins with a triple-entrance gate that leads into an enclosure, which originally held a structure for the emperor and his retinue to finally adjust their clothes. This led through a gate into the main court for sacrifices, which contained the Hall of Heavenly Favors, almost identical to the Hall of Supreme Harmony in the Forbidden City, enabling the emperor to be honored in death as he was in life. Three marble terraces support the great hall (67 by 30 meters) with three stairs leading to it. Inside, 60 columns made from single trunks of old-growth timber called *machilus nanmu*, nearly 13 meters high, support a double-eaved roof without any diagonal struts. The *dou-gong* on the exterior is ornamental, not structural. The coffered ceiling is painted in blue, green, red, and gold. Both the Hall of Heavenly Favors and the Hall of Supreme Harmony are the largest halls in China.

The tomb mounds are defined by fortified earthen mounds with 3-meter-wide walls, buttressed on the outside to hold in the earth with no visible entry markers. They are planted with thujas and oak trees (since the roots are believed to be able to nourish the dead). At the apex of the hill, one finds a small tumulus in the shape of a cone or long ridge.

The tumulus is only representational, because the actual tomb is far below the surface. Seen from the approach axis, the stele gate, the mound, and the mountain profiles are all part of the one symbolic entity. The tumulus of Emperor Wanli's tomb, for example, lines up directly with the peak beyond. The approach to the offering table, which stands just in front of the base of the stele tower is not flat but actually a series of transitions marked by gates and thresholds.

The actual tomb of Emperor Wanli, located 27 meters below the surface, consists of three sacrificial enclosures and four interconnected barrel-vaulted chambers. Three run parallel to each other and one at right angles at the head, and that is the main chamber. Whereas the side chambers were empty, and were probably intended for concubines and family members, the central one contained three thrones replete with ritual objects. The burial casket of the emperor, the empress, and the highest concubine (elevated to empress when her son became the next emperor) were found intact in the head burial vault. The vaults were all made of pure white marble, polished smooth. Once again, this tradition, which goes back to the tombs of the Han emperors, shows that though the Chinese had certainly mastered masonry skills, they chose to use it only for their tomb structures. One of the few places where a stone vault was used in a building above the terrain was in the Fasting Palace of the Altar of Heaven, where the emperor prepared himself for the all-important calendric rituals. That room was, in essence, a type of tomb, for the emperor was expected to use it to purify himself through abstinence and fasting.

14.137 **Potala Palace, Lhasa, Tibet (China)**

**Potala Palace**

Buddhism was introduced into Tibet by Mahayana monks travelling from India and Nepal in the 8th century. By the 10th century, Nepal had begun to thrive as a regional power, capturing significant territories in Mongolia and China. The growth of the Tibetans was, however, checked by the Chinese well into the 15th century. Although China's non-Han dynasties, the Liao and in particular the Mongol Yuan, supported Tibetan Buddhism, they made sure they were politically subservient. The Ming paid only lip service to Tibetan Buddhism since their focus was on the revival of a Confucian and Daoist state. As a consequence, the Tibetans split into a number of competing sects, variously identified by the color of their habit as the red, white, and yellow sects. But when the Ming dynasty began to lose power, the Uigher Mongols, under Altan Khan, the descendants of the erstwhile Yuan dynasty, converted to the Tibetan yellow sect; after that, Tibetan Buddhism or Lamaism spread quickly among the Mongols of central Asia.

In 1641, Altan Khan's grandson, Gushri Khan, defeated all the other Tibetan sects and proclaimed Ngawang Losang Gyatso (1617–82), the fifth Dalai Lama, not only the spiritual head but also, for the first time in Tibetan history, the political head of Tibet. Just then the Mongolian Manchus had taken over from the Ming, and one of their first diplomatic acts was to invite the fifth Dalai Lama to the Chinese court, where he was received with full honors.

One of first acts of the fifth Dalai Lama was to establish a new capital and build a new palace that was identifiable as the seat of both the spiritual and political power of the Buddhist world. This was the Potala Palace, the vast and majestic, palace cum mausoleum, located on a hill in the middle of the valley of Lhasa, Tibet's "forbidden city."

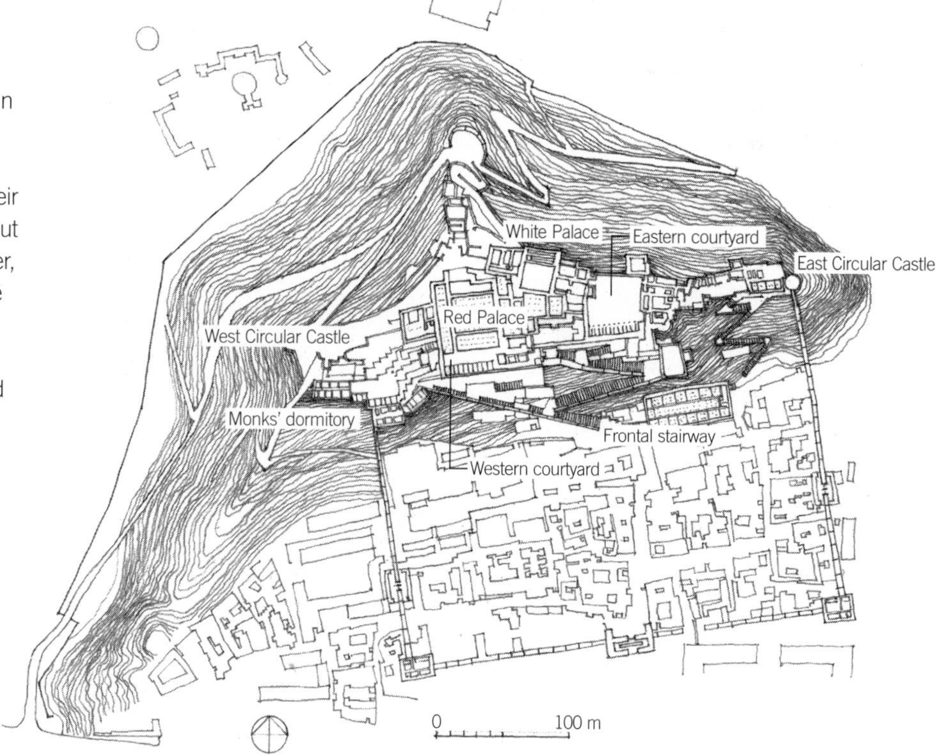


14.138 **Plan: Potala Palace**

As the residence of the dalai lamas, considered to be living manifestations of the Buddha, the Potala Palace is the sacred center of Tibetan worship. The name Potala derives from the name of a sacred mountain, the Kailasnath, home of Shiva in the Hindu cosmology. As such, the palace is just as much a pilgrimage site as a royal residence.

**14.139 South elevation: Potala Palace**

The Lhasa River is a tributary of the Tsangpo, which becomes the Brahmaputra when it swings south around the Himalayas and into India. At an elevation 130 meters above the valley, Marpo Ri hill stands above a widened river bed at the bottom of a ravine, in the middle of which stand two steep, rocky outcrops. On the higher and larger of these, known as Red Hill, sits the Potala Palace, 360 meters long and 110 meters wide and reaching to a maximum height of 170 meters. It is oriented east-west, with the front facing south toward the inner city. The setting is dramatic. A jagged towering mountain range forms a towering bowl. In the middle, the rocky outcrop and the swiftly flowing Lhasa are at the center of what literally seems like the roof of the world.

Since it was meant to be defensible, the palace's primary massing is that of a fort. Thick, battered brick walls, painted white, rise steeply directly from the rock surface in a series of terraces that take over the entire summit of the Red Hill. The walls step back and forth to accommodate the changing contours and to generate openings for the access paths.

Solid and impenetrable at the bottom, the walls are opened up in its higher reaches by dark windows, which are few and simple at first but at higher elevations become larger and more richly embellished. The walls are topped by a prominent red coping. The visual terminus is a series of small golden Chinese-styled roofs that are not so large as to be the solitary focus but prominent enough to ensure that the eye comes to rest on them, providing a speck of metallic brilliance in a landscape dominated by gray rock. Long ramps, visible from the distance, wind their way up the side of the hill. Their slow ascents mark them as self-conscious processional paths, leading to a place of pilgrimage

The current palace was built in two major phases. First the main ramparts and the western part of the main palace, known as the White Palace, were built. This was partially rebuilt and a Red Palace constructed that became the primary residence of the dalai lamas.

The White Palace houses large ceremonial halls for prayers, rooms for visiting dignitaries, and offices, while the Red Palace houses the audience hall as well as burial stupas for the dalai lamas. The roof of the palace opens onto a flat terrace where one finds the Chinese-style pavilions, gilded in copper, one for each dalai lama, burning inside. At the foot of the Potala Palace, a square walled enclosure contains a network of governmental buildings.

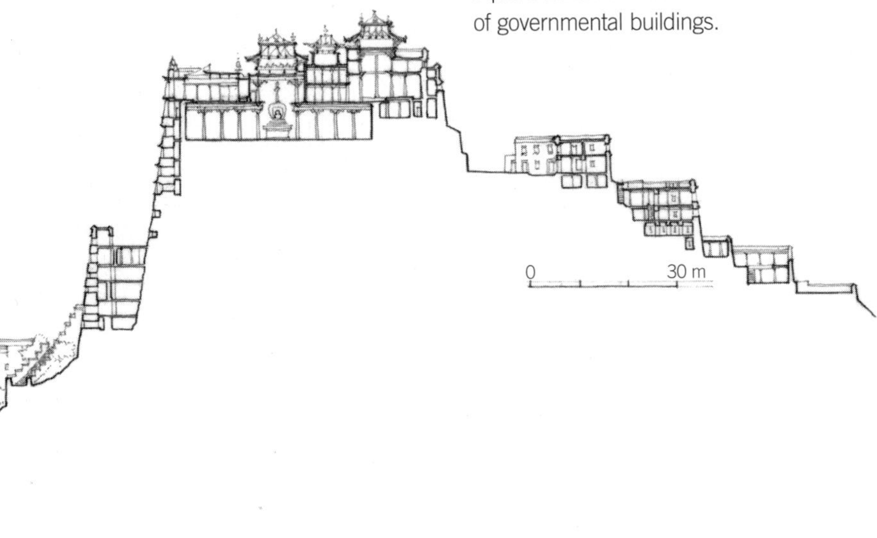


**14.140 Section through Potala Palace**

**14.141 Potala Palace, Lhasa, Tibet**

Access to the Potala begins at the end of the lower quadrangle, at a column erected to mark the completion of the Red Palace. The first ramp leads to subsidiary structures in the west, but then it switches back and heads up toward the White Palace. After another switchback, it comes to a point where the entrances into the Potala, which have been hidden until now, suddenly reveal themselves, nestled between the staggers of the walls. A stair to the east leads to the entrance of the White Palace and another, directly opposite, to the Red Palace. The high walls of the Potala itself are at hand, and for the pilgrim this is the first arrival threshold. Several more are to follow.

The usual entrance is through the White Palace. A tall rectilinear opening, with three open stories above, leads into a dark space with four columns. From here the path turns left, proceeds down a narrow corridor, turns right, and arrives at a small curved court, where the second threshold to the palace is located. A flight of stairs and a two-column vestibule leads to another corridor, from which a left turn drops one into the eastern courtyard, the ceremonial arrival space of the Potala. This is the pilgrims' third and final threshold.

This courtyard is surrounded by a two-story enclosure and dominated by the canted mass of the White Palace at the northwestern corner. A central stairway leads into the six levels of the White Palace, highlighted by characteristic Tibetan windows made from brightly painted wooden frames and elaborately carved sun screens. The elaboration and size of the windows increase with each story, terminating in the cornice. Internally, the main structural frame is made from wood, with rooms organized around a courtyard on the upper levels. This mode of construction and elevational representation is typical of Tibetan architecture, a consequence of its long intercourse with Nepalese architecture and culture.

The Red Palace contains pillared prayer halls and the salt-dried and embalmed remains of eight dalai lamas, marked by eight white stupas called chortens. The largest and most elaborate of these is, of course, the stupa for the fifth Dalai Lama.

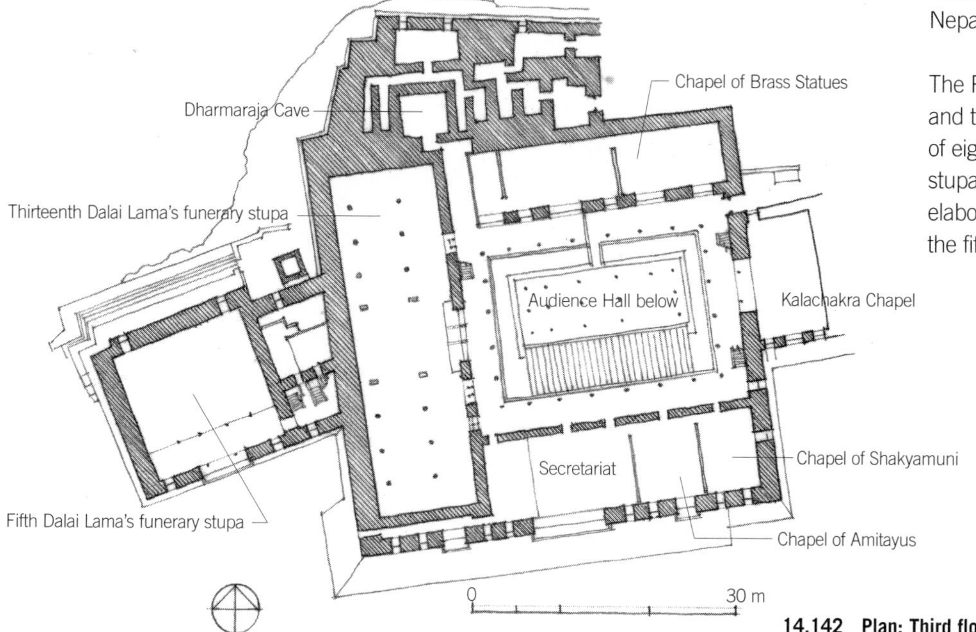


**14.142 Plan: Third floor of the Red Palace, Potala Palace**

14.143 Taj Mahal, Agra, India

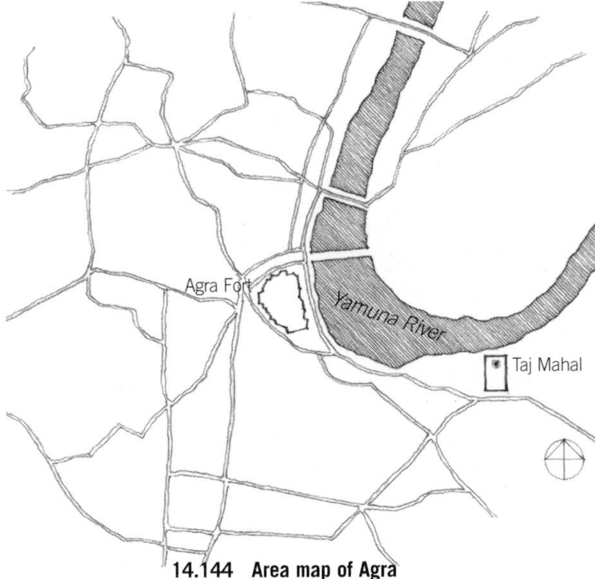


14.144 Area map of Agra

**Rauza-I-Munavvara (Taj Mahal)**

Having inherited a vast and prosperous empire, Shah Jahan (1628–58) enjoyed the dividends of peace. He was dedicated to poetry, art, literature, and most of all to architecture, expending vast resources to build palaces, mosques, and tombs all across his empire, especially in Delhi, where he built a brand-new city called Shahjahanabad. In the latter half of his reign, however, the bulk of Shah Jahan's energies were devoted to the creation of the funerary tomb for Mumtaz Mahal, his favorite queen and granddaughter of the fabled Nur Jehan. The tomb was known to the Moghuls as the Rauza-I-Munavvara (or the Illumined Tomb, as documented by W. E. Begley and Z. A. Desai), because of the luster and transparency of its marble. Later it was also referred to as Rauza-I-Mumtaj-Mahal, which the English contracted to Taj Mahal in the 19th century.

Mumtaz Mahal died unexpectedly in 1631 while giving birth to her 14th child. Twenty-thousand workmen labored for 15 years on the tomb. On every death anniversary of Mumtaz, Shah Jahan staged the Urs celebration at the Taj Mahal. (Urs celebrations involve prayers and song in praise of the deceased, usually a saint.) The first Urs occurred on June 22, 1632, even before the tomb was completed. Shah Jahan was also buried on Mumtaz's right, feet facing south, and closer to the Ka'aba, as required by Islam. The Taj Mahal thus is truly the tomb of both Mumtaz Mahal and Shah Jahan.

Controversy surrounds the question of who was the architect of the Taj Mahal. The historical records list several people responsible for the tomb, or parts of it. Ismail Khan from Turkey may have designed the dome. Qazim Khan from Lahore cast its gold finial. Chiranjilal, a local lapidary from Delhi, was the chief sculptor and mosaicist. Amanat Khan from Shiraz was the chief calligrapher. Other specialists included sculptors from Bukhara, calligraphers from Syria and Persia, inlayers from south India, stonecutters from Baluchistan, and so on. Thirty-seven men can be counted in the creative nucleus. The Taj Mahal in this sense was a global project. Yet, given that Shah Jahan personally supervised the design and approved every aspect of the project, he must be recognized as the chief architect of the Taj.

Although the bulk of the building material is from south Asia, the Taj Mahal's ornamental materials came from around the Eurasian world. Its marble and red sandstone came from the hills of Makrana, near Jaipur, Rajasthan. From central Asia came Nephrite jade and crystal; from Tibet, turquoise; from upper Burma, yellow amber; from Badakhshan in northeastern Afghanistan, lapis lazuli; from Egypt, chrysolite; and from the Indian Ocean, rare shells, coral, and mother-of-pearl. In addition, topazes, onyxes, garnets, sapphires, and bloodstones were among the 43 types of precious and semiprecious stones from around India that were used.

The main tomb is sited on the southern bank of the Yamuna River on a vast platform, 103 meters square and 7 meters high, erected on arches. To its west stands a diminutive mosque, made of sandstone, with three modest marble domes. To its east is an identical structure, placed there to provide symmetry. Reflected in the wide waters of the Yamuna, which flows slowly in Agra, the Taj Mahal appears like a surreal and ghostly apparition, an unreal concatenation of domes and minarets, rising well above the flat plain. Although considered to be the Taj Mahal's back side, the Moghul emperors usually accessed it from the water, via a barge built especially for this purpose. It docked at the northeastern edge of the platform, from where a stair leads up to the tomb.

The land-based access to the Taj is from the southern garden side. The simple and discreet red sandstone walls of its perimeter betray little of the drama that awaits inside. A small gate in the middle of the wall leads into a quadrangular enclosure with spaces for maintenance workers and shops. Stepping out beyond the wall is the main gate of red sandstone and marble, a rectangular *iwan* surmounted by a string of closely spaced *chattris*. In the center, a single large pointed arch opens onto the entrance bay that telescopes down into the actual entrance arch itself. From here, through the entrance opening, the main body of the Taj Mahal is perfectly framed.

14.145 View of main gateway to the Taj Mahal, Agra

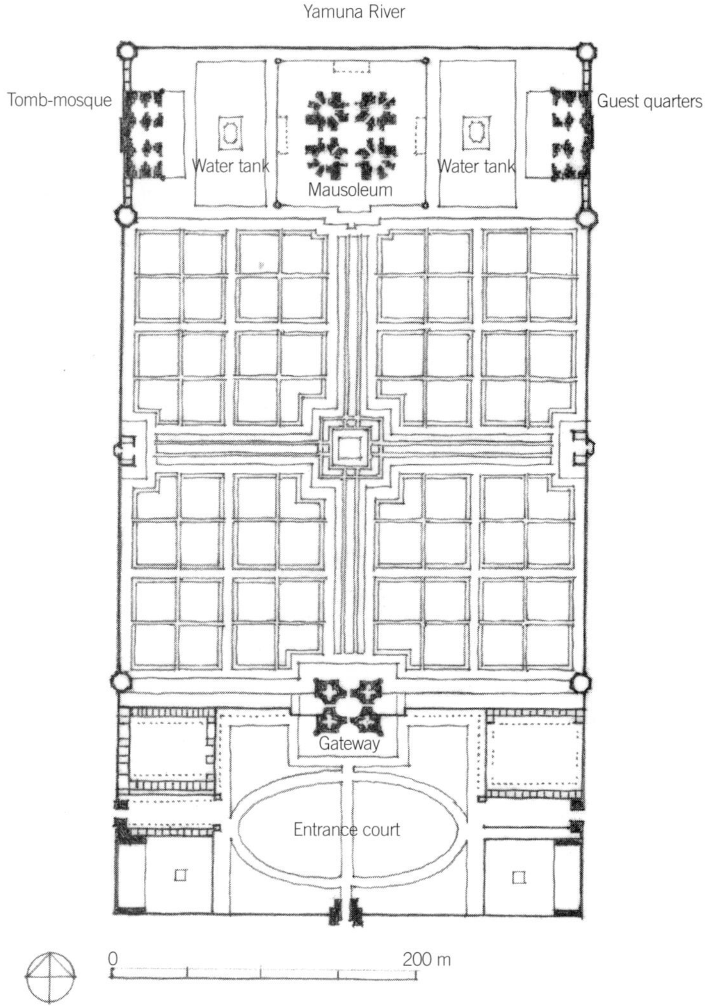


14.146 Site plan: Taj Mahal, tomb of Muntaz Mahal

Once through the gate, the full frame of the Taj Mahal jumps into focus. The tomb of Mumtaz Mahal and Shah Jahan is placed at the end of its garden with a 92-meter-square garden to serve as foreground. Even at that distance the Taj Mahal fills the frame. The backdrop, given the hidden presence of the Yamuna, is empty or, rather, always filled by the color of the sky. Water channels, with fountains down their middle, are wide and generous. They reflect the tomb and further magnify it. Deciduous and evergreen trees fill the garden.The slender, three-story minarets create an implied cube that contains the Taj Mahal. They make the tomb three dimensional. The double dome of the tomb, however, rises above the minarets so that conceptually it is only the dome and the outer dome (conceptually the dome of heaven) that rise above the imaginary plain supported by the minarets.

The translucent white marble that covers the entire surface of the tomb, absorbs and reflects the light. In the mornings and evenings, it has a reddish hue; during the day, a subdued white with a slight bluish tinge; and on moonlit nights, it is bright white. On bright days, the light blurs the edges of the tomb, making it shimmer. Since every surface is covered in the same white marble, even the shadows are softened. At dusk and dawn, the Taj Mahal appears to float weightlessly, like an ethereal, uncanny apparition.

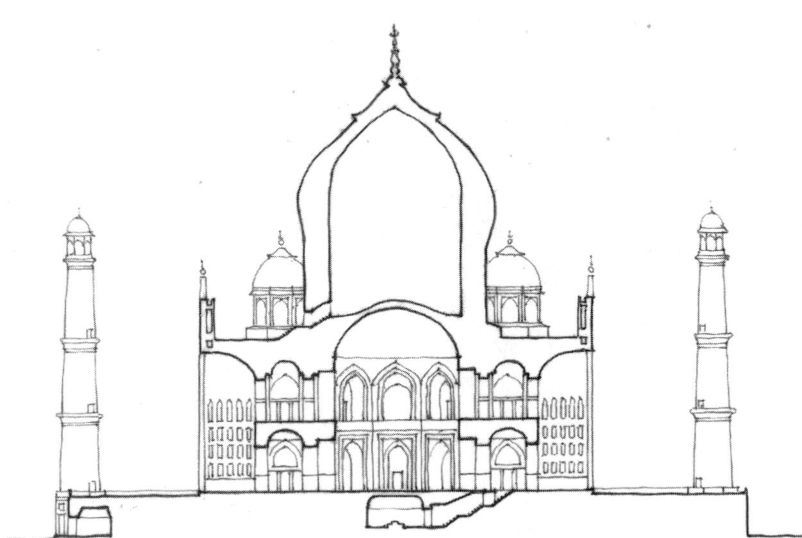

14.147 **Faux tombs of Mumtaz and Shah Jahan, Taj Mahal**

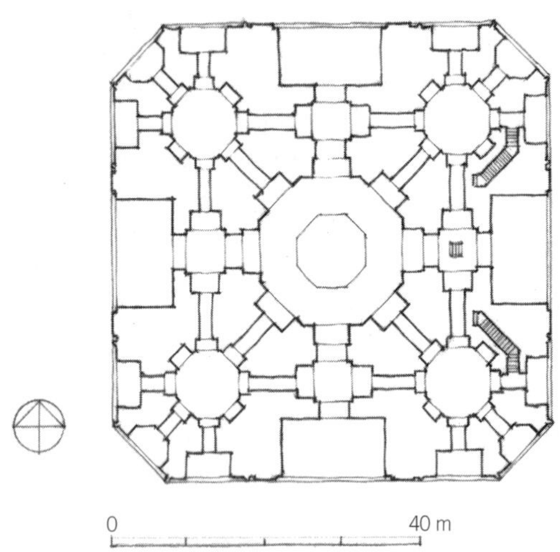


14.148 **Plan and section: Taj Mahal**

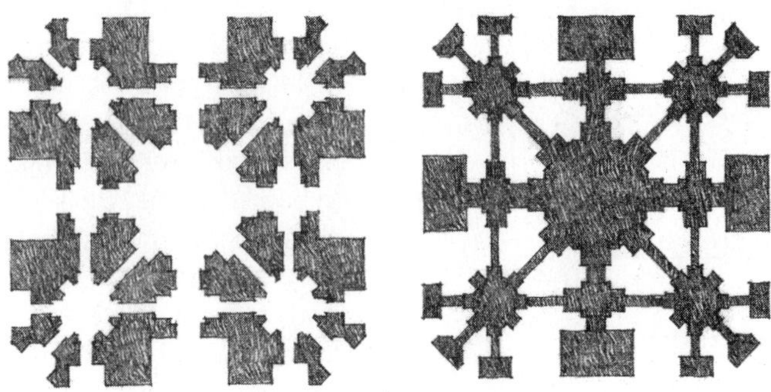

14.149 **Mass and space rendered as figures: Taj Mahal**

In plan, the Taj Mahal's central chamber is surrounded by four corner spaces connected by corridors to permit circumambulation. At the ground-entrance level are the faux tombs of Mumtaz and Shah Jahan, with the actual burials in a crypt directly below (accessible by a stair). The section reveals that the outer bulbous dome is raised exceptionally high on a drum, well above the inner dome, so that actually the volume contained in the upper dome is equivalent to the volume below. Because of the high drum, the outer dome rises well above the central *iwan* of the elevation, making it the undisputed center of the composition (unlike, for instance, Humanyun's Tomb, where the side chambers compete with the central dome, making the overall structure more squat than tall). The side *iwans* are considerably lower; they are faceted only on the outer side and not on the inner side (as at Humanyun's Tomb); and the articulation of all their horizontal elements have been decidedly subdued in favor of the vertical. Indeed, a distinguishing characteristic of the Taj Mahal's massing is that in elevation all the elements are clustered and hierarchically arranged to ensure that they do not compete with each other and instead build up the centrality of the main dome. Even the *chattris* have been clustered right next to the central dome, almost as if they were supporting domes themselves. If one draws an imaginary line along the edges of the central dome and the *chattris*, one makes a triangle or a pyramid, framed by the four minarets.

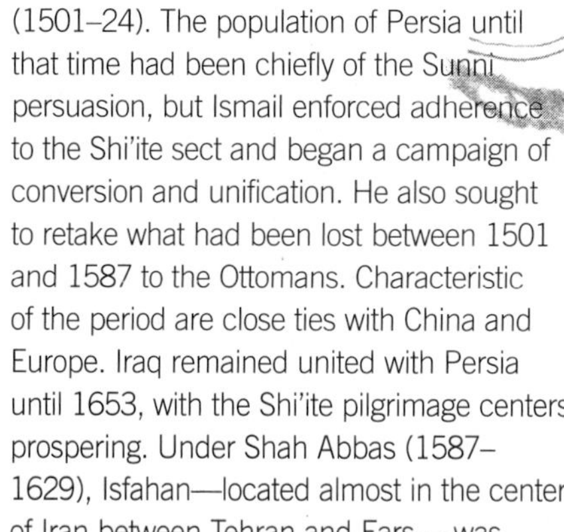

**14.150 Plan of Safavid Isfahan, Iran**

### Isfahan

The Safavid control over their territories had waned under internal and external challenges to their authority, until the accession to the throne of Shah Ismail I (1501–24). The population of Persia until that time had been chiefly of the Sunni persuasion, but Ismail enforced adherence to the Shi'ite sect and began a campaign of conversion and unification. He also sought to retake what had been lost between 1501 and 1587 to the Ottomans. Characteristic of the period are close ties with China and Europe. Iraq remained united with Persia until 1653, with the Shi'ite pilgrimage centers prospering. Under Shah Abbas (1587–1629), Isfahan—located almost in the center of Iran between Tehran and Fars— was made the capital (1598) and rebuilt into one of the largest cities of the world and the focus for all the artistic energy in the country. Transferring the capital away from the insecure borderland to the center of the country was part of Abbas's policy of state consolidation.

Isfahan, with a population of about half a million, soon became a grand cosmopolitan center with English and Dutch merchants, European artists, and diplomats (hoping to secure alliances with the Safavid court against their common enemy, the Ottomans). A famous half-rhyme *Isfahan nesf-eh jahan* (Isfahan is half the world) was coined in the 16th century to express the city's grandeur. The new layout was the most extensive urban planning in the world west of China.

**14.151 Main square of Isfahan**

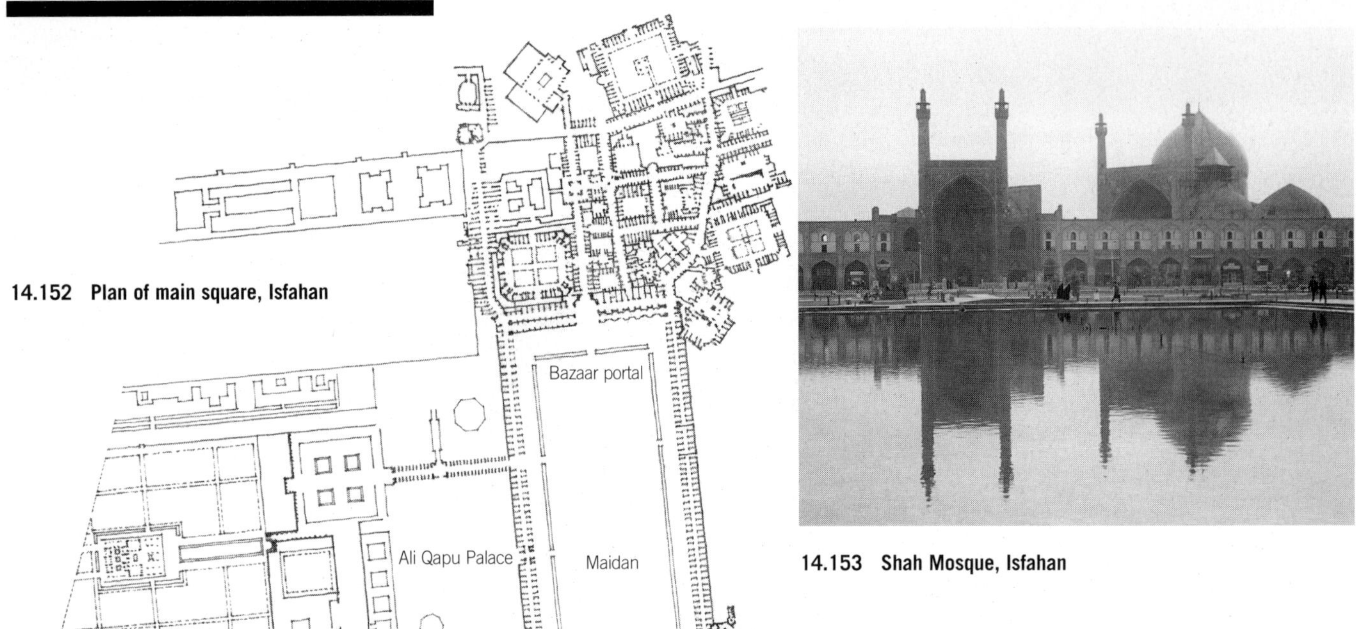


14.152 **Plan of main square, Isfahan**

14.153 **Shah Mosque, Isfahan**

Previously, the central square of the city lay next to the old Friday Mosque, believed to have been built on the site of a Zoroastrian fire temple. Though many of the old buildings were restored by Abbas, he instructed his planners to create a new urban center to the south of the old city center and named it Naqsh-I Jahan (Design of the World). It consisted of a vast, rectangular open space that served as the city's new civic and commercial center. To its west, there was a monumental boulevard, Chahar Bagh Avenue, some four kilometers long with canals, fountains, and trees, and flanked by palaces of the nobles. The boulevard stretched across the Zayanda River with a 300-meter-long multitiered bridge, which connected the city to several garden estates (*chahar bagh* means "garden retreat") to the south. These estates were large walled enclosures with pools, promenades, and pavilions. The central element in the composition and linking the commercial district with the avenue was the Imperial Palace in its own walled precinct, the Naqsh-I Jahan garden.

The new square—still today one of the largest in the world (512 by 159 meters)—was the symbolic center of the Safavid Dynasty and its empire. It was used for festivals, markets, and games of polo. At night 50,000 earthenware lamps hung from poles in front of the buildings to illuminate the square. It was designed with two stories of shops around the perimeter. The long modular facades decorated with polychrome glazed tiles were broken only by the monumental entrances to four buildings: the Masjid-i-Shah Mosque in the south, the Sheikh Lotfollah Mosque in the east, the Ali Qapu Palace in the west, and the Great Bazaar to the north. A royal mint and a royal caravansary were also included in the ensemble as well as baths and a hospital.

The Masjid-i-Shah Mosque, begun in 1611, is set at a 45-degree angle so as to face in the direction of Mecca. Its entrance portal mirrors the entrance to the bazaar to the north. The mosque uses the four-*iwan* scheme, with a central courtyard 70 meters square and surrounded by two-story arcades noted for a calm balance between volumetric organization, decorative detail, and unifying symmetry. The architect was Muhammad Riza. The plan is distinguished from many other such buildings by its unusual concern for symmetry. The domed sanctuary is flanked by rectangular chambers covered by eight domes that serve as winter prayer halls. These halls lead to rectangular courts surrounded by arcades that also serve as madrasas. The entrance portal is a tour de force of tile decoration, executed in a full palette of six colors (dark blue, light blue, white, black, yellow, and green). Glittering tiers of *muqarnas* fill the half dome, some panels of which are decorated with stars and vines scrolling from vases.

14.154 **Suleymaniye Complex, Istanbul, Turkey**

14.155 **Suleymaniye Complex, Istanbul**

**Suleymaniye Complex**

Mimar Sinan (1491–1588), who constructed nearly 200 buildings in Constantinople, changed the face of the city, creating Istanbul's unique silhouettes of mighty domes and slender minarets. Raised as a mason, he worked his way through the ranks to become chief architect of the court. Though Sinan was fired by the vision of a domed building modeled in the style of the Hagia Sophia, his brilliance was in fusing Seljuk features, such as the emphasis on portals, and the stone mastery of the Anatolians with the structural logic of the Byzantine domes into a seamless and novel unity. This is nowhere better expressed than in the Suleymaniye Complex, begun in 1559, commissioned by Suleyman the Magnificent (1520–66) in the wake of military successes in Iraq and the Balkans. The walled complex (216 by 144 meters) was terraced up a hill to take advantage of the view overlooking the Golden Horn to the north, and it contains, among other things, four madrasas, a medical madrasa and a hospice, a caravansary, a bath, as well as a bazaar.

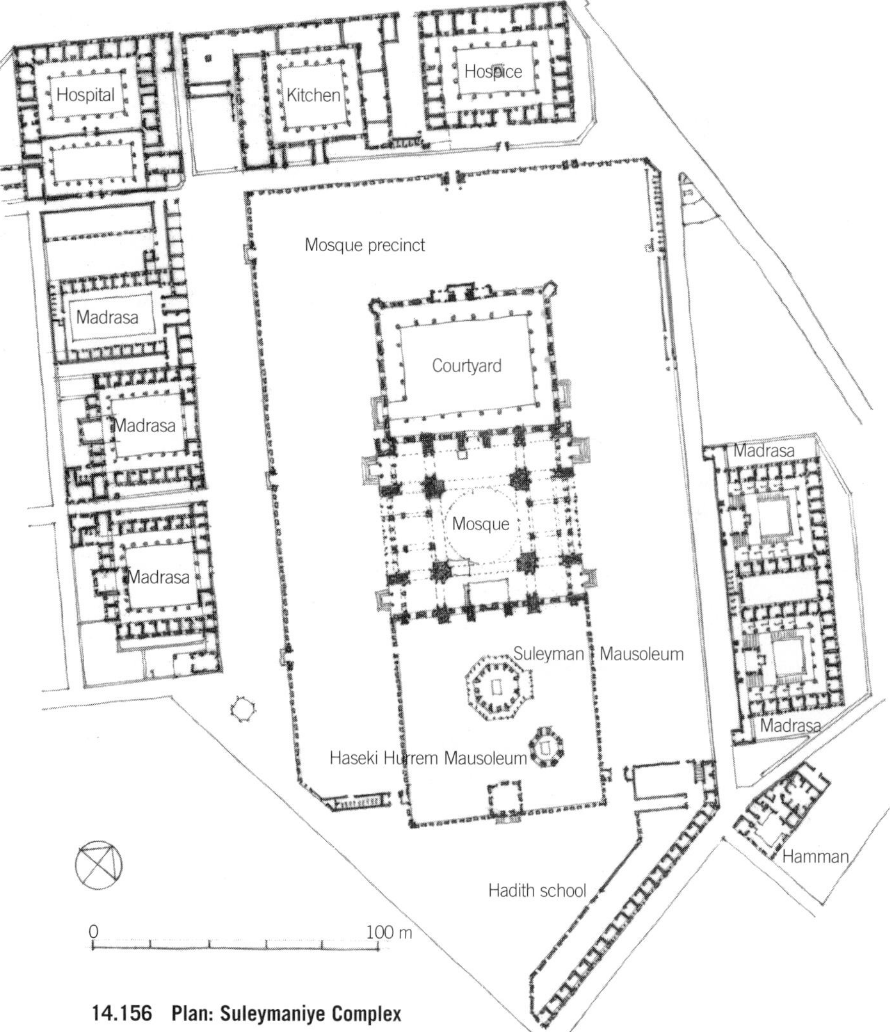


14.156 **Plan: Suleymaniye Complex**

**14.157 Elevation and section: Suleymaniye Mosque**

The composition of the mosque is obviously modeled on the Hagia Sophia, and in this it was similar to a trend epitomized already by the designer of the Beyazit Mosque (1501–6), except that with Sinan as the architect, the composition is considerably tighter. The building is also, in many respects, very different from its Justinian model. It is dominated by a dome 48 meters high with two flanking half domes on the principal east-west axis and arches on the cross-axis. The weight descends to the ground by means of four massive columns of granite.

On the exterior the forecourt has a colossal portal with a tympanum framed by half columns and minarets at the corners. Construction was organized by a court management office that, in consultation with the sultan, planned and oversaw the building project. Workers were Muslim as well as Christian and were organized according to skills. The decorative tiles were made in Iznik, the carpets in Anatolia and Egypt, and the colored and noncolored glass (the latter, a technological innovation of the time) in Venice; the limestone and granite came from the quarries on the Sea of Marmara, and the lead for the window grills and doors came from the Balkans.

While the Hagia Sophia was dark on the inside and had a mysterious effect, Sinan's building, lit from floor to dome in more equal measure, is pervaded by a sense of order and discipline. The windows are numerous and wide, and since the galleries are pushed back, sunlight piercing through the windows of the sidewalls reaches directly into the central space. Also, unlike in Hagia Sophia, where the surface of mosaic and gilding seems to blanket the structural forms, at Suleymaniye Mosque, the architectural volumes are clearly legible and enhanced by a corbeled gallery at the level of the springing of the arches (somewhat similar in effect to the arch style at St. Maria del Fiore in Florence) that unifies the central unit underneath the domes.

Sinan's mosques were followed by commissions such as that by Sultan Ahmed for a mosque built by Mehmet Agha, which is also known as the Blue Mosque (1606–17).

**14.158 Interior view of vaulting in the Suleymaniye Mosque**

**14.159 St. Peter's Basilica, Rome, Italy**

**St. Peter's Basilica**

Donato Bramante's piers for St. Peter's Basilica were completed by 1512. His design was, however, too big even for the Vatican and his successors spent half a century reducing its scale. Very little was done, however, until 1535, when the work on a new model was begun with the planning done by a team of architects that included Baldassare Peruzzi and Antonio da Sangallo the Younger. But few of these plans were brought to fruition until 1546, when Michelangelo was put in charge of the design by Paul III. By the time of Michelangelo's death in 1564, the exterior and the interior of the south transept was complete. As it stands today, St. Peter's is the product of many architects working at different times on the basis of Michelangelo's design. Michelangelo reduced and contracted the preceding plans. Compared to Bramante's plan, Michelangelo's is strikingly simpler. No longer was there a proportional declination of space from large to small. Instead, there was a single square with four apsidal ends to the Greek cross. A longitudinal orientation was given to the plan by the addition of a colonnaded portico on the front. The correlation between inside and outside was obscured, however, by the fattening of the mass to the right and left of each of the external apses, creating the appearance of a continuous succession of pilasters.

In comparison to Bramante's design, which was intended to be read from the top down, its unifying form, dissolving into filigree patterns of niches, columns and vaults, Michelangelo's building was meant to be read from the bottom upward, with the strained relationship between the outside shape and the dome hinting at the mystery of the divine presence within the building. The walls were not the outer form of volumetric elements added together but a dynamic balance between form, structure, and space, with an alternating rhythm of dilation and contraction. Furthermore, unlike Bramante's building, with its large dome looming over a static mass, Michelangelo's building at the rear, though difficult to access for the common person, appears as an undulating cliff surface that moves both toward and away from the center.

Originally, the dome was to have been lower, since Michelangelo planned it as hemispherical on the model of the Pantheon; but in the course of construction under Giacomo della Porta, who inherited the project after Michelangelo's death in 1564, the dome was heightened to make it an ogival form akin to the Duomo of Florence. The dome sat on a tall drum with windows set between strongly buttressed fins disguised by attached column pairs, with the image being one of ascension rather than load bearing.

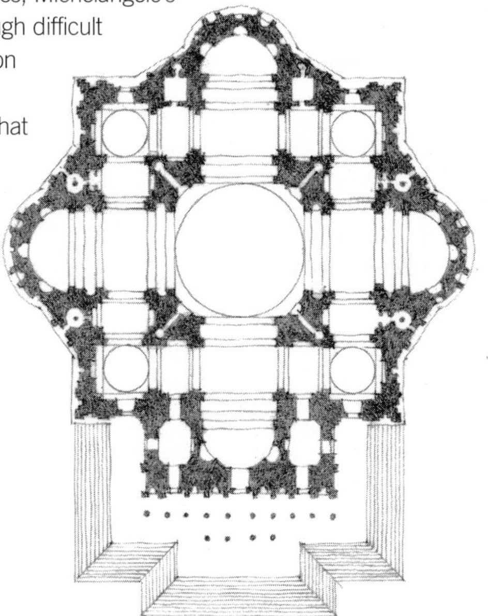

**14.160 Michelangelo's plan for St. Peter's Basilica, begun in 1546**

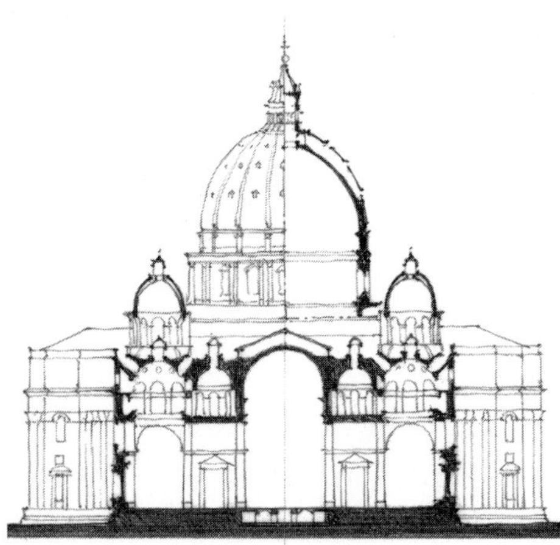

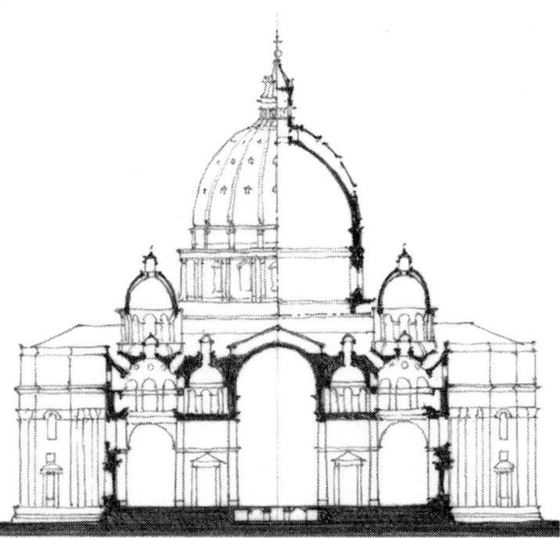

14.161 **View of nave from dome, St. Peter's Basilica**

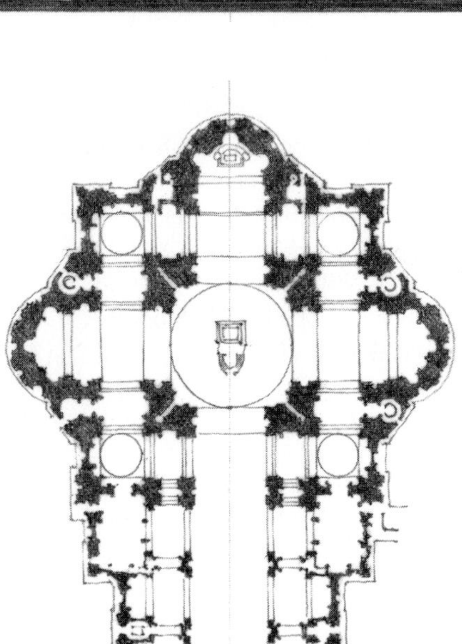


**14.162 Section and plan: St. Peter's Basilica as completed by Michelangelo Buonarroti and Carlo Maderno**

The idea of creating a building standing free in a large vast courtyard was an impossibility, given the vastness of the building and the encroachments of the papal palace and gardens. We must, therefore, remember that the building is primarily seen from the front and yet, when Michelangelo died, there did not exist a definitive plan for the facade, which seems to have been modeled relatively straightforwardly by Michelangelo on the Pantheon with six columns (instead of the Pantheon's eight) supporting a pediment. A series of architects were put in charge of the work; but until 1605 the front of the old basilica was still in place and was serving as the entrance. But that too was eventually demolished, and before long the last vestiges of the medieval basilica had disappeared.

In 1603, Pope Paul V appointed Carlo Maderno chief architect of St. Peter's; in 1607, he extended Michelangelo's building by three bays. His facade elaborated on the basic theme of Michelangelo, but the design is not considered a success. The windows and openings of various sizes and proportions seem to crowd out the interstitial spaces between the columns. But in all fairness to Maderno, the two end bays were not part of his design. It was decided that the facade needed two end towers, and even though the facade was extended to accommodate these towers, the towers themselves were never added, as structural difficulties prevented their completion.

In 1626 Pope Urban VIII called upon Giovanni Lorenzo Bernini to begin work on the great *baldacchino* over the papal altar. So impressed was he that in 1629 he appointed him Architect of St. Peter's. Thereafter, for at least forty years, the greatest of the baroque architects was engaged upon the basilica's embellishment. The partnership between Urban VIII and Bernini matched that between Julius II and Michelangelo as one of the greatest patron-artist relationships in the history of architecture. But the scheme to redesign the piazza in front of the basilica came from the mind of Alexander VII. The first stone was laid in 1657, and the piazza was finished in 1666.

There were a number of factors that had to be taken into consideration. The old entrance to the Vatican was 120 meters northeast of the portico and had to be retained. Also, a covered processional way for state visits to the pope had to be constructed and the loggia for the time-honored papal blessing over the central entrance had to be kept within view of the greatest possible number of people, especially at the Easter celebration. And finally there was a great Egyptian obelisk that had been brought to Rome in 37 CE, and it was moved to its present site in 1586.

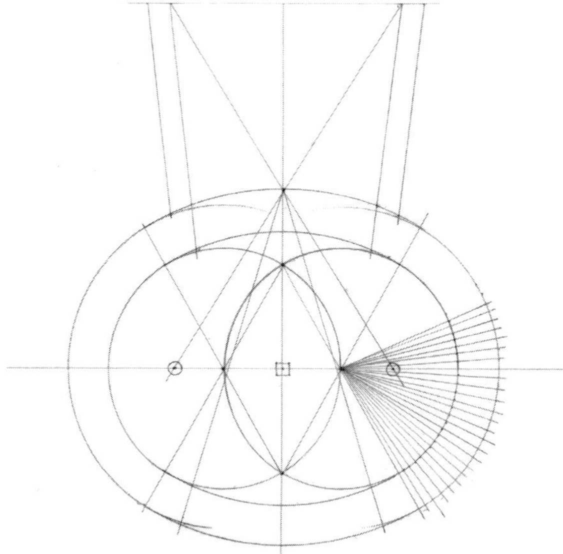

14.163 Bernini's geometric solution for laying out St. Peter's Square

14.164 View of St. Peter's Square from the dome

Bernini's solution was to create and interlink two piazzas, a trapezoidal one in front of the church and a great oval set one parallel to the facade. The trapezoidal space was defined by corridor wings connected to the facade of St. Peter's. In this way the basilica seems to be brought forward and the height of the facade accentuated. The oval was constructed in a relatively conventional manner out of a series of circular arcs. The colonnade consisted of two rows of columns pairs that were designed to flair out from the center.

As obvious as the plan may seem today, it was in reality the end result of a design process that began with the side arcs being further out from the center in a way that emphasized their circularity. Bernini also experimented with a single large circle. Only over time did he come to the decision to make an oval; even so, the space is so vast that it is perceived as circular, and that may indeed have been Bernini's intent with the preexisting obelisk serving as its center.

Though it is true that an ellipse was known as a conical section, it was at the time generally thought to be a question of mathematics. It was certainly not used here, given that Bernini was more interested in the symbolic power of the Pantheon than in contemporary mathematics. From the two centers of the ellipse, the viewer of the great curve would see a single row of columns with statues of saints lining the balustrades, creating a new and powerful "pantheon," instantiating the power and history of the Church.

There had been nothing like Bernini's freestanding oval colonnade in any previous architecture, and the fact that he placed an Ionic entablature on Doric columns seemed more than forgivable. The solid strength of the columns, in fact, contrasts with the verticality of the slender Corinthian columns of the facade.

14.165 Aerial view of St. Peter's Square

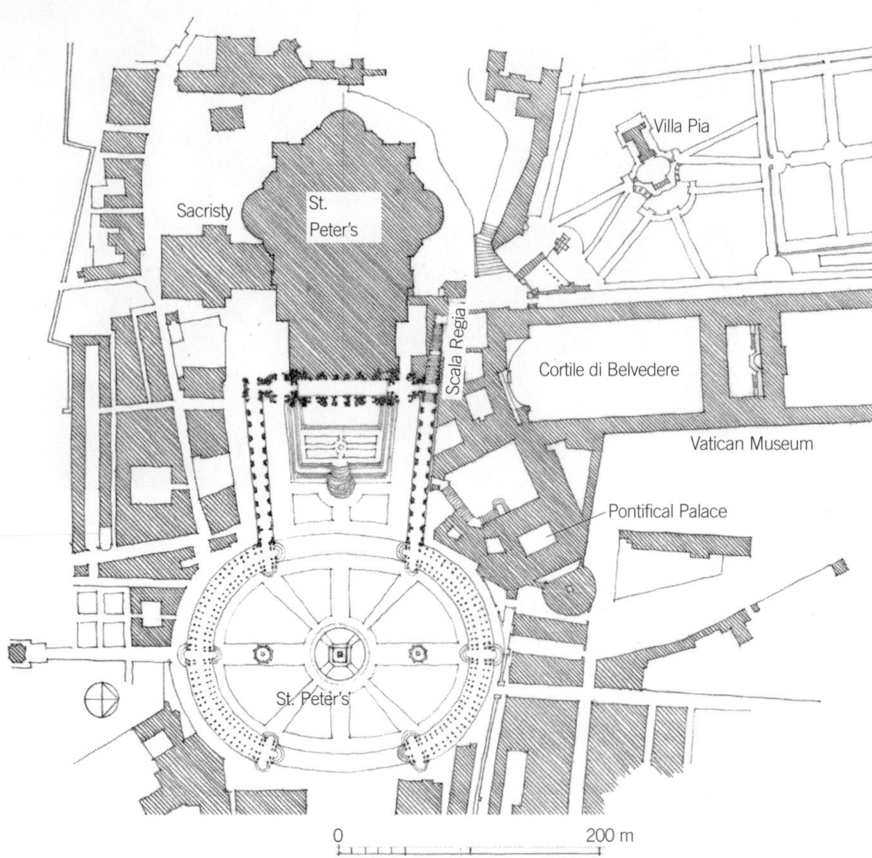


**14.166 Site plan of St. Peter's Square**

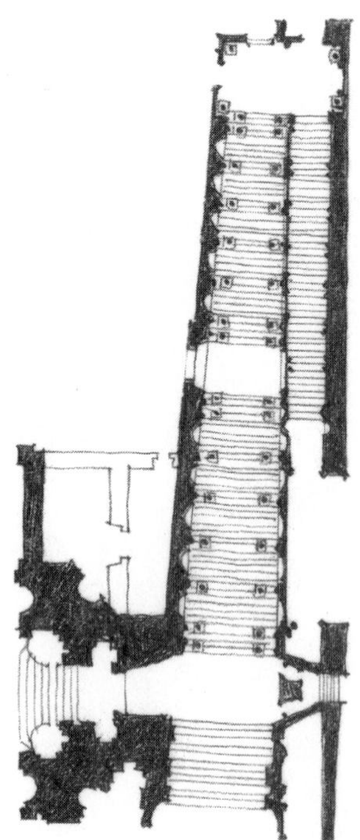

**14.167 Plan of the Scala Regia**

The program for the site required an important asymmetry in the plan to accommodate a suitable entrance into the Vatican Palace. Bernini solved this by incorporating the entrance into the northern colonnade, its southern equivalent being a blank facade. The entrance opens to the Scala Regia, designed by Bernini in 1663–66 to bring dignitaries up to the papal palace. The aisled and vaulted stairway is an architectural triumph over the awkward siting. Though the space provided was neither straight nor wide nor adequately lit, Bernini overcame each obstacle by using tricks of perspective that create an impressive approach to the papal apartments.

When Bernini died in 1680 the connection of the great oval to the street leading up from the Tiber River had not been determined. Bernini had planned a building that would partially close off the piazza, creating a greater sense of enclosure, but it was never built. In 1935, under Benito Mussolini, the area was cleared out and given its current monumental design.

# 1700 CE

By the early 18th century, cities like Samarkand, Bukhara, and Aleppo, which had once been at the heart of the Eurasian trade, had become increasingly marginal to the new world economy of the maritime ports that were set up by the European powers. One need only think of such major metropolises as Macau, Hong Kong, Singapore, Bombay, Calcutta, Madras, Cape Town, Senegal (originally St. Louis), Rio de Janeiro, Buenos Aires, Boston, New York, and Quebec City to remind ourselves of the global scope of this phenomenon. At the foundation of the system was the fort and the plantation. Local populations were transformed into work forces, and when these were in short supply, enslaved and indentured laborers from Africa and Asia were brought in on ships.

In Europe, it was the French who first translated colonial power and wealth into large-scale architectural projects, none grander than Versailles (1668). Aristocratic privilege and high-bourgeois mercantilism resulted in large residences reflecting the social pretensions of their owners and the new economic conditions. New building types, such as bourgeois apartments (or hotels), coffee houses, parks, and theaters, sprang up to nourish the new culture. It was also a time of unease. Religious persecutions were at their height and tensions between the European powers over control of the global economy resulted in a series of costly wars. The Dutch War (1672–78) concluded in favor of the French; but later the War of Spanish Succession (1701–14) created an important power shift in the direction of Austria and England, paving the way for places like Schönbrunn Palace (begun 1695) and Blenheim Palace (1705–22). Russia, too, was a rising power, redefining itself in the European model, both culturally and architecturally, with its impressively scaled new capital of St. Petersburg, founded in 1703.

Throughout Europe, the baroque style, as it came to be known, became dominant with thousands of churches built or refurbished. Huge palaces were built first in France and then in Austria, Italy, and Germany, with long allées and gardens stretching far into the landscape. The increasing centralization of governments also led to the creation of new state institutions, like hospitals and asylums.

China and Japan were, however, still economically and politically balanced against the colonizing West. The Qing annexed parts of central Asia and Tibet to make the largest Chinese empire in history. To accommodate China's diverse populations, the Qianlong emperor developed a pan-Asian conception of empire, building dozens of new palaces and gardens and reestablishing the Yuan-era link with Tibetan Buddhism. Since Chinese currency was based on the silver standard, European traders, anxious for Chinese goods, were pouring silver into the empire. In Japan, the Tokugawa shogunates were in the midst of redefining the culture, creating a world that followed a strict code of behavior that was, in many respects, astonishingly modern, as the rising middle class sought ways to articulate institutions suitable to its needs despite the restrictions placed on it by the shoguns.

In India, in the brief period of time as the Moghul empire weakened and before the full colonization of India, the various regions experienced a moment of liberation as local governors took the opportunity to proclaim independence. Shuja-ud-Daula in northern India, the Nawab of Oudh in Bengal, the Sikhs in Punjab, the Rajputs in Rajasthan, and the Marathas in the Deccan were wrestling for power at the same time the colonizers began to build on their coastal footholds and started to acquire hinterlands. As a result, though this was a turbulent time in India, it was also a time of tremendous exploration from a cultural and architectural point of view. The Sikhs, a reformist movement, took root in northwestern India and established a formidable kingdom. Darbar Sahib (Golden Temple) in Amritsar was their most important shrine. The Mallas of Nepal, meanwhile, enjoyed relative immunity from these global events next door; but their royal square in Patan embodied its own global history.

In contrast to the energy in Europe, India, and east Asia, building activity in west and central Asia slowed down. This was so pronounced that most books dealing with Islamic architecture end around 1750. The result was that East and West, both strong and viable, split around an increasingly economically marginalized center.

# 1700 CE

▲ **Elmina Castle**
Begun 1482; taken over by Dutch in 1637

▲ **Haciendas**
Begun ca. 1529

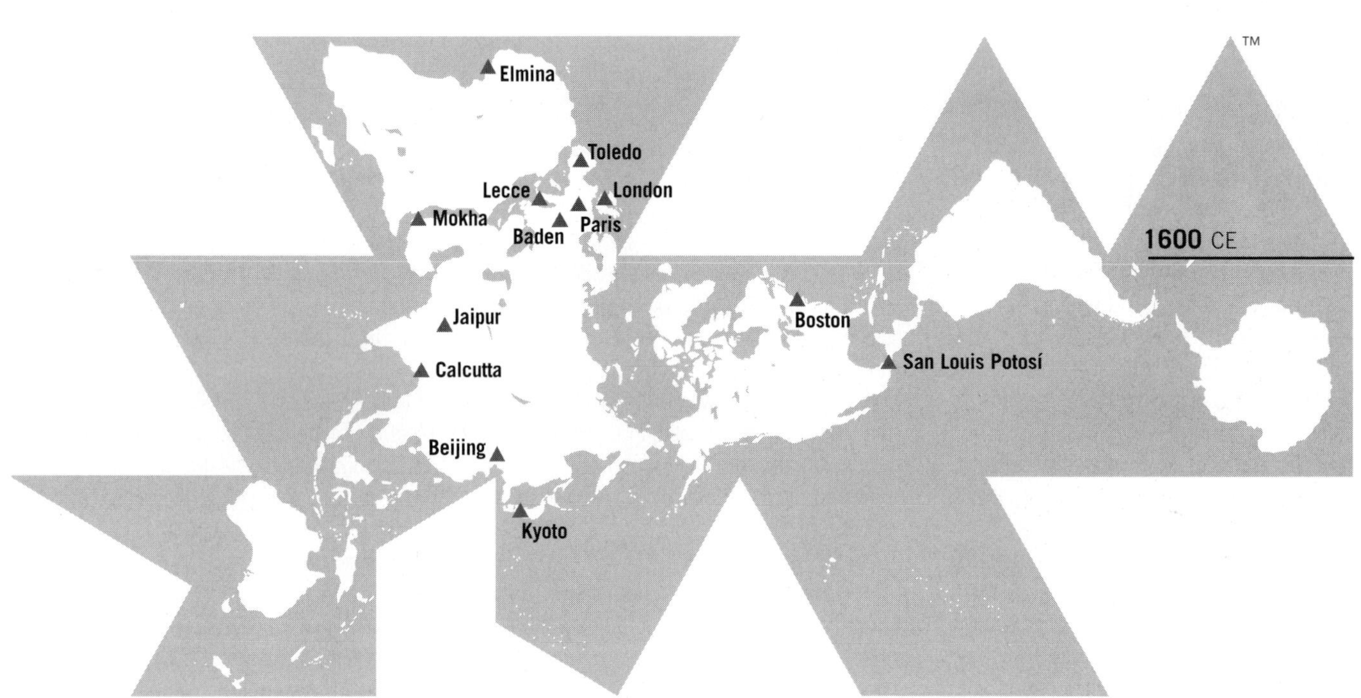


China: Ming Dynasty
1368–1644

▲ **Fort Manoel**
ca. 1682

Central America: Viceroyalty of New Spain
1535–1821

France: Bourbon Rule
1589–1792

▲ **Hôtel de Sully**
1624–9

▲ **Hôtel des Invalides**
1670–91

▲ **Versailles**
1661–1756

▲ **Place Vendôme**
Begun 1698

England: Stuart Rule
1603–1714

Hanoverian Rule
1714–1901

**1650** CE — **1700** CE — **1750** CE

⦿ Thomas Savery invents the steam engine
1696

Sir Isaac Newton's *Principia* published ⦿
1687

⦿ Abraham Darby produces high-quality iron
1711

⦿ Benjamin Huntsman develops crucible method for making steel
1740

▲ **St. Stephen Walbrook**
1672–9

▲ **Blenheim Palace**
1704–20

▲ **St. Paul's Cathedral**
1675–1710

▲ **Stowe Gardens**
Begun ca. 1680

▲ **Palace of Schönbrunn**
Begun 1695

▲ **Karlsruhe**
Laid out 1715–19

Qing Dynasty
1644–1911

▲ **White Stupa, Beihai**
1651

▲ **Yuanmingyuan Gardens**
1720s

Japan: Edo Period
1615–1868

▲ **Sumiya**
1670s

South Asia: Moghul Dynasty
1526–1858

▲ **Meenakshi Sunderesvara Temple**
16th–17th century

▲ **Durbar Square**
Rebuilt 17th century

**Hawa Mahall** ►
1799

**Darbar Sahib** ►
Rebuilt 1764

## 1700 CE

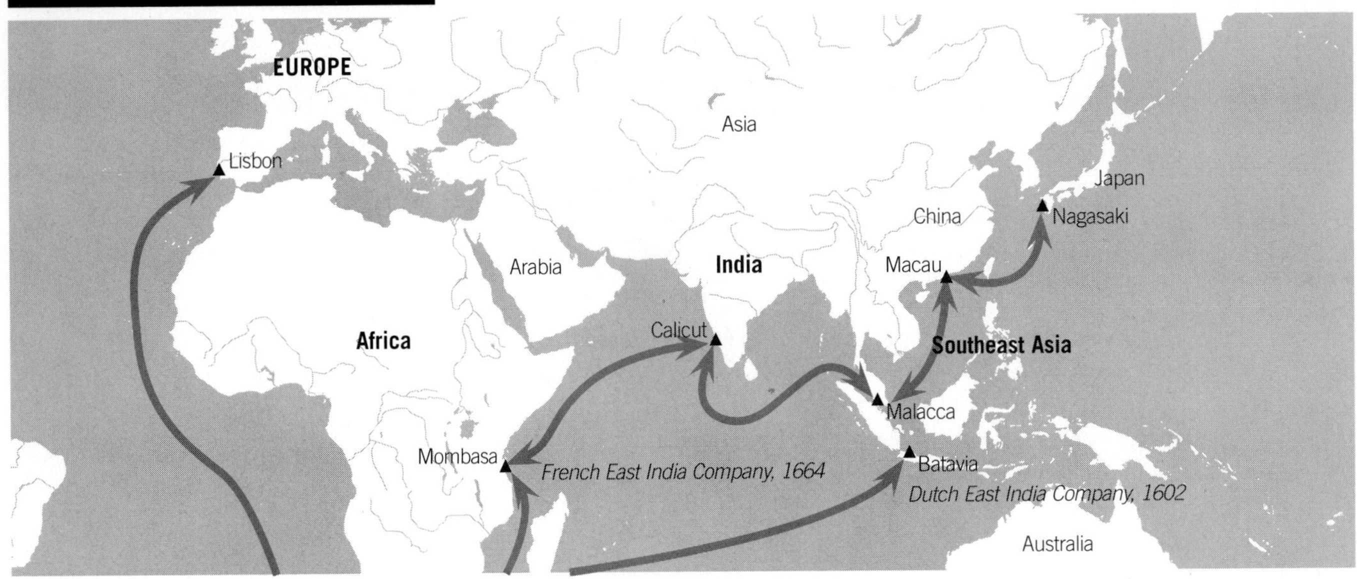


### COLONIALISM

By the end of the 17th century, the European powers had established a network of lucrative trade links around the globe. Struggles between the principal competitors, first between Spain, Holland, and Portugal, and then between Britain and France, were almost constant. There were basically five different colonial models more or less unique to the particular givens: Africa; Central and South America and Indonesia; North America; India; and east Asia. Africa's colonization was based almost purely on the extraction of gold, ivory, and human beings. African traders brought the "goods" to the ports where the exchange took place. The slave trade had been a part of African economy for centuries, but the Europeans magnified it to such a degree that the history of Europe, Africa, and the Americas was irrevocably altered. It is estimated that more than 20 million people, and possibly as many as 40 million, were exported as slaves from Africa, with Portugal, Spain, France, Holland, England, and the New World all participating. The Spanish brought the first slaves to the Caribbean in the 1520s. The Dutch brought the first slaves to North America in 1619, one year before the landing of the fabled Mayflower.

For the continental powers, Portugal, Spain, and France, the enslaved were to serve as workers on the plantations and haciendas to replace the decimated native American population. These farms, the development of which constituted a second type of colonial geography, were efficient to build and control, and they involved a minimal outlay of capital. They had to be managed, of course, with a firm grip. The Dutch, who came to Indonesia in 1511 and who defeated Sultan Hasanuddin of Goa in 1667 and Prince Trunojoyo of Madura in 1680, also promoted the plantation system. To control production and raise prices, the Dutch burned down the clove gardens of the locals. The Spanish, in southern Italy, built fortified agricultural centers or farms, known as *masseria*, specializing in olive and grape production.

The legacy of the plantation system was unambiguously negative. In Mexico, even by 1910, seventy percent of all arable land was held by just one percent of the population. Almost every country or region that was colonized by the plantation system had later to struggle to create secular, scientific, and cultural institutions on par with other places and then often only with modernization programs initiated in the 20th century. New Orleans, founded by the French in 1701, did not have a major university until well after the States became independent.

For the English, the dominant spheres of their interests—New England and India—presented diametrically different situations. Unlike the inhabitants of India, who were in possession of a vibrant and militarily strong culture, the native Americans in the New England area were in a period of decline. One did not find, as one did in Louisiana and Georgia, the large chiefdoms, which were not easily bullied by the Europeans. This perceived vacuum within the global colonial geography provided the opportunity for Europeans to settle with impunity, reveling in the notion that they were living in virgin territory. The influx was diverse. By 1700, from Maine to Virginia, one would have found villages and towns with a mixture of Dutch and English Puritans, French Calvinists, Catholics, Swedes, Spanish Jews, and, of course, English Anglicans. New England was thus an international mercantile-agrarian civilizational project, unique in the colonial world. By the early 1700s, one found courthouses, schools, churches, roads, and two universities—Harvard, founded in 1636, and Yale in 1701.

India, because it was remote, densely populated, and urbanized, did not receive influxes of European settlers. Furthermore, officers of the British East India Company, during the early time period, had to approach Indian rulers with the appropriate respect to negotiate trade and protection treaties.

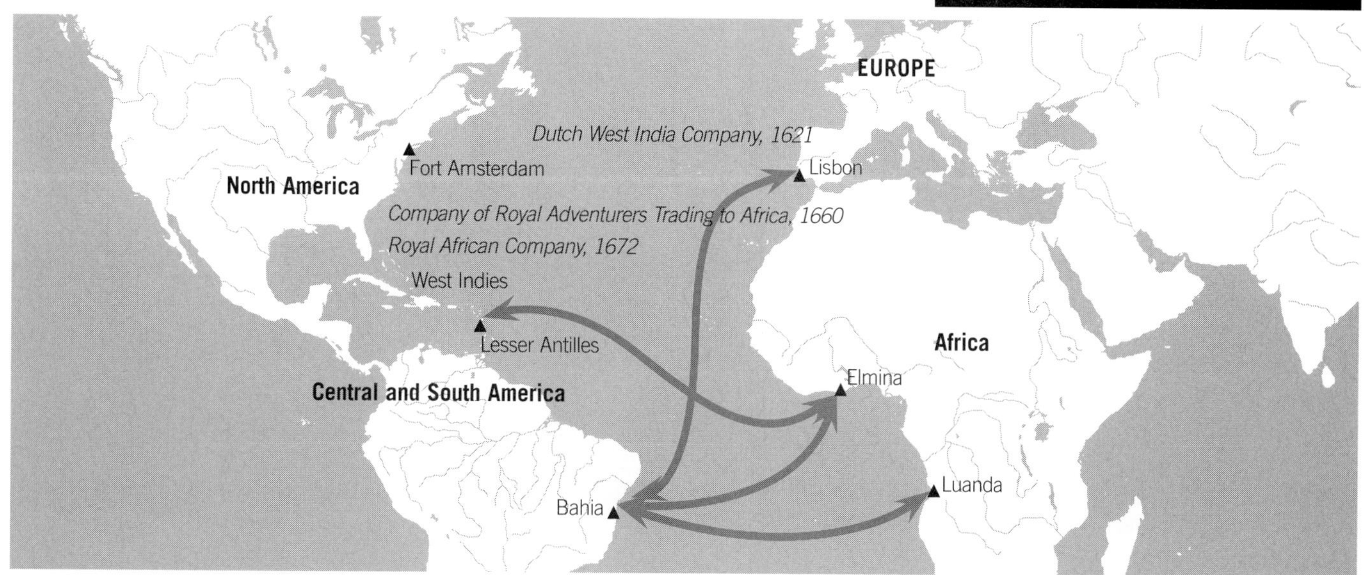


When, in 1690, the Moghuls finally allowed the English to found an outpost, it was on the swampy mouth of the Hooghly River. Nor was the security of Calcutta a foregone conclusion. Just as the Dutch were having difficulties in Indonesia, in 1756 Calcutta was sacked by Siraj ud Daula, the regional ruler of Bengal. To operate to their best interest, the English had to pit one regional faction against another, and through this practice they soon became the masters, ultimately partitioning the subcontinent some 200 years later into India and Pakistan along largely religious lines in a way that was to guarantee regional strife in perpetuity.

China presents a different story. The Chinese under the Qing Dynasty did not want or need European goods, as they were economically and militarily quite strong.The English, however, wanted tea, which in the 19th century had become an essential part of English cultured life. They also wanted to pay for the tea with the opium they grew in India. The Chinese naturally resisted and attempted to close their ports. Trade, nonetheless, was forced onto China until by the mid-19th century, following complaints of "hardship" by the English merchants and opium suppliers, the English invaded, launching the Opium War of 1839–42, which forced the Chinese to open its ports and pay England an indemnity of 21 million dollars. In this way China was brought to its knees, certainly another sad chapter in the history of colonial arrogance.

Japan, well aware of what was happening in India, also closed off its ports, beginning around 1639, with the exception of Nagasaki and then under highly controlled circumstances. Since both the Chinese and Japanese economies were thriving, trade with Europeans carried more obvious risks than benefits.

One should not forget that west and central Asia, largely Arabic and Islamic countries, were of limited interest to colonial powers from the 18th century onward. The Ottoman empire was seen primarily as a convenient bulwark against Czarist Russia. Persia was of even less consequence to the Europeans, and slowly shrank under the pressure of Russia. The strain of economic decline, governmental disinterest, and the absence of a viable mercantile class made the jump to modernism politically difficult and ambiguous for Islamic and west Asian countries. Egypt in the 1880s and Turkey in the 1920s were the first two countries in the region to attempt to create a bourgeois class of any density. It was only with the discovery of oil in the early 1900s and its industrialization in the 1930s and 1940s that foreign powers began to attempt to reassert influence—and their right of interference—in the Arab world, and this is, of course, an ongoing historical development.

In the 18th century, just as the colonial project was unfolding and flooding Europe with great wealth, one saw the emergence of a philosophical movement, largely centered in France, England, and Germany, that challenged the arbitrariness of power as well as the prevalent colonial attitude of dogmatism, intolerance, and state censorship. The Enlightenment philosophers attempted to rethink their attitudes toward "primitive cultures" as well as European civilization and its history, formulating in the process a newfound faith in reason as a way to come to terms with a world that had grown extraordinarily complex. Progress, they hoped, could be understood and produced rationally as long as the history on which it was based was removed from religious interference and political agendas. The Enlightenment thus had its roots in the colonial encounter and tried to design alternative civil and institutional models in tune with its philosophical speculations. Its successes and failures in that respect are still being debated.

15.1 Elmina Castle, Cape Coast, Ghana

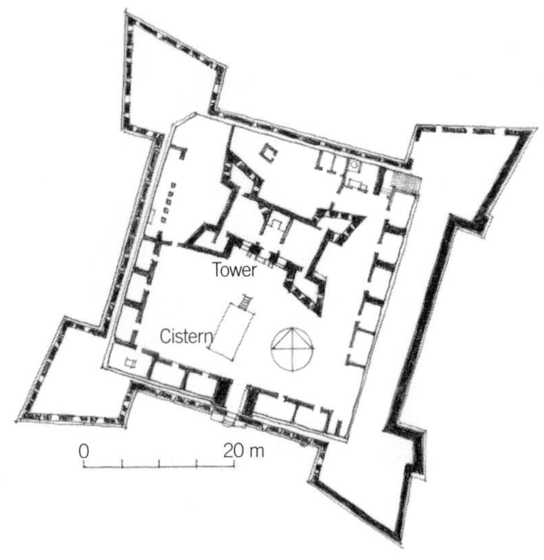


15.2 Plan: Fort Commenda, Ghana

**Colonial Forts**

To enforce the policy of extraction as well as to protect ports and trade routes, the colonial powers embarked on a worldwide fort-building campaign. Many hundreds if not thousands were built, 60 alone along the west African coast. Africa had been a supply source of enslaved laborers for centuries. Islamic rulers, for example, owned slaves captured in holy wars. In fact, some of the first slaves brought to India were brought there by Arabs. For the most part, enslaved men were used in the government and by the military; the women in domestic households or in the fields. But in reaching around the west coast of Africa, Europeans opened a whole new chapter in the history of slavery and their operation functioned at an unprecedented scale. Some forts served the sole purpose of holding captured slaves. The Portuguese Elmina Castle, in Ghana, on a promontory overlooking the mouth of a river, set the pattern for subsequent buildings. The rectangular castle was located in the protected core of a set of perimeter walls. A church and an administrative center faced each other across the inner courtyard. Corner bastions projected past the surfaces of the building so gunners could protect the entrances and flanks. In 1637, it was taken by the Dutch, who rebuilt and expanded it as a slave collection point.

By 1700 new technologies and military strategies required a different type of fort. Success now lay not in the height of the walls, as of old, but in the ability to shoot sweeping fire from within the fort while deflecting mortar and cannon shot coming from the outside. Fort cannoneers did not want to lob the ball high, as it would merely plunge into the earth. Instead, the cannon ball was shot low to the ground, so that it would bounce and ricochet through enemy lines. The glacis served as an artificial sloped terrace where this danger would present itself to any attacker.

When combined with ditches and bastions that provide raking angles, the geometry of an 18th century fortification becomes quite complex, as can be seen in Fort Manoel, (ca. 1682). It was located on Manoel Island in Marsamxett Harbor to the northwest of the principal city of Valletta, which it protected in Malta. Fort Manoel was used as a model for forts built throughout the world, particularly by the English and French, the main superpowers of the age. The English Fort Commenda, in Ghana, begun in 1686, for example, is a similarly advanced, but somewhat simpler version. These forts would remain the norm for the next 200 years, until the advent of aerial bombardment.

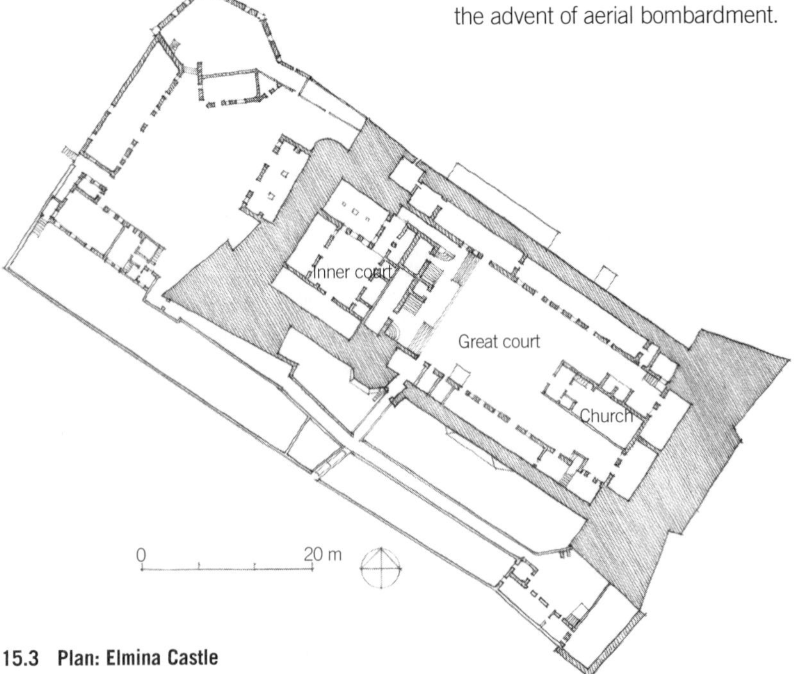


15.3 Plan: Elmina Castle

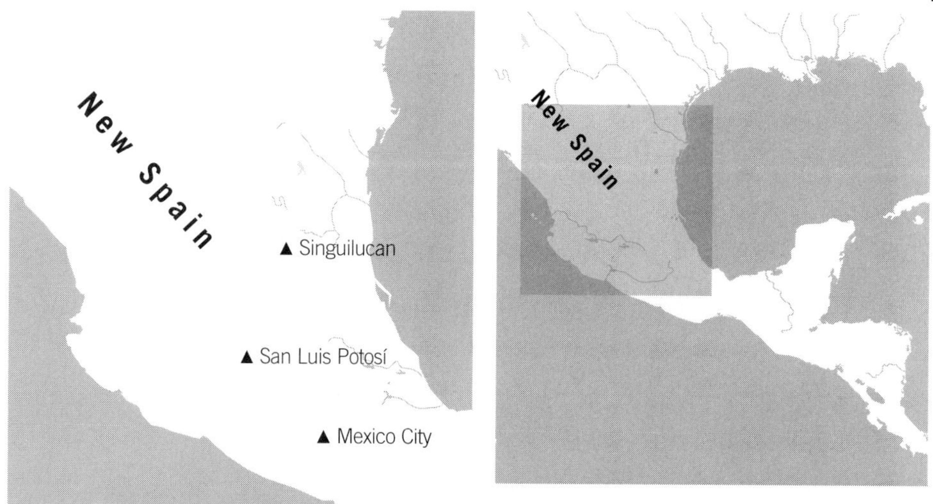


**Haciendas**

The hacienda system is thought to date to 1529, when the Spanish crown granted to Hernán Cortés the title of Marquis of the Valley of Oaxaca, the present state of Morelos, Mexico. The grant included all the Indians then living on the land and the power of life and death over them. The native Americans, like the slaves who soon arrived from Africa, were bound to a particular hacienda for life, as were the lives of their descendants. Not all haciendas focused on producing export commodities, but by the 18th century, the system, stretching from Mexico to Argentina was the primary means of export production and, in some cases, the core of subsequent urban developments. One should also include in this geography Louisiana, which was settled by the French.

Haciendas came in various sizes, but in some cases they reached the size of a small country like Holland. Peotillos, 55 kilometers from San Luis Potosí in Mexico, controlled an area of 193,000 hectares. Most specialized in one or two products, Peotillos, for example, specialized in grain. In the Andes, maize, wheat, barley, beans, and a variety of vegetables were produced; in areas where water was abundant, sugarcane was grown, as well as rum and other liquors. Other haciendas focused on livestock, cacao, coffee, tobacco, cotton, rubber, and a variety of woods.

Since the hacienda was often remote from metropolitan centers it had to accommodate a wide range of functions. In some cases it had its own marketplace, cemetery, and jail. Its architectonic form follows a common scheme involving courtyards for different purposes. The main residential building was designed around its own private courtyard or patio.

The link between the *patio de campo* and the more restricted areas was through a corridor known as a *zaguán*. Some patios were organized around quarters for the workers and their families; others contained workshops, warehouses, granaries, stables, cowsheds, or spaces related to the production of pulque, a highly marketable liquor.

The word hacienda comes from an Old Spanish term (*facienda*) derived from the Latin *focere*, which means "to make something."

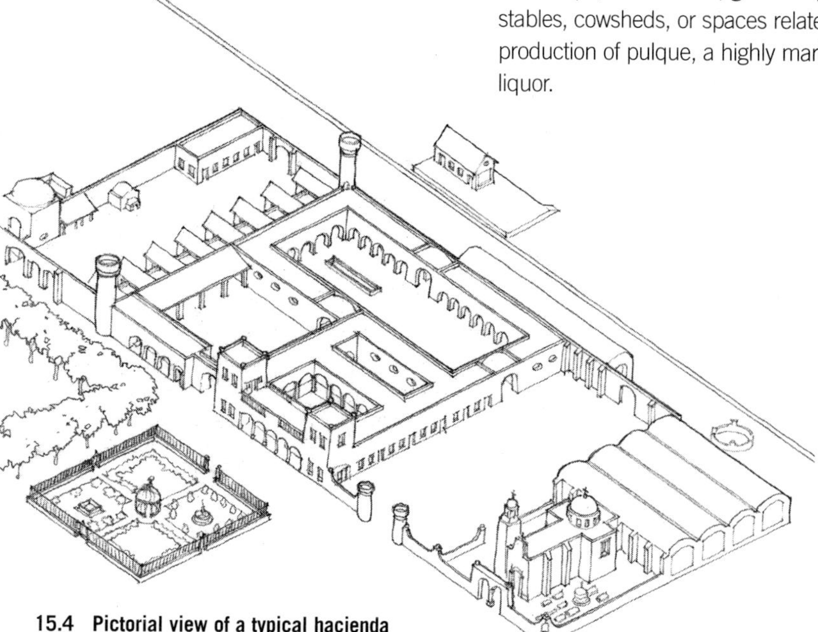

**15.4 Pictorial view of a typical hacienda**

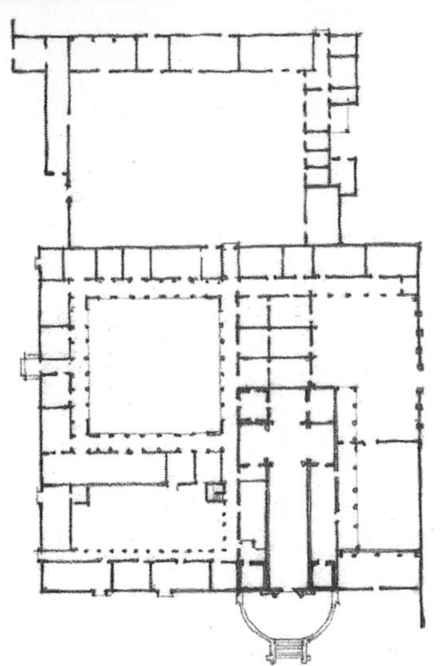

15.5 Plan: Brazilian hacienda, Santa Catalina

15.6 Example of a Brazilian hacienda

**Brazilian Haciendas**

In Brazil, the development of sugar and coffee plantations generated, as early as the 17th century, a proliferation of *fazendas* (the Portuguese equivalent of hacienda), in the northeast of the country. As in other places, the high death rate of the native population necessitated a new labor force, a need that was met by the importation of Africans as slaves who were continuously replaced in a steady stream, totaling over 3 million. Thus, a new type of construction was added to the architecture of the *fazendas*—the *senzala* or slave quarter, a large dormitory warehouse, divided into small spaces to house the slaves and their families. The symbolic and economic center of the *fazenda* was, of course, a large square area or patio where the coffee was dried. The big house was located on one side of the square, usually positioned on higher ground, overlooking the entire area.

***Masseri***

Colonization was largely a European imposition on non-European lands. An exception was in Southern Italy, which was under Spanish domination until the arrival of French troops under Napoleon. Lecce, an important center in Apulia, was an independent city-state until 1463, when it and the surrounding territory came under the control of the Kingdom of Naples, which in turn was an extension of the Spanish Empire. Anti-Spanish uprisings were brutally suppressed. The area, a leading producer of olives and wines, was organized by a system of plantation estates known as *masseri* (or *masseria*, for a single farm). The buildings, like haciendas, had courtyards for agricultural purposes, but the main house was far different than the hacienda with patio, largely because of worries about raids by the Ottomans. The buildings were a cross between a palace and a fort. They were often solidly built of stone, with a long external staircase leading to the *piano nobile*. The top of these stairs was sometimes constructed in wood so that in case of invasion, the staircase could be separated from the house in a last-ditch effort at defense. The farms, which dotted the landscape, brought wealth to their owners, who lived in cities such as Lecce and Bari, which were outfitted with Spanish-style baroque churches and palaces.

15.7 Example of a *masseria* near Lecce, Italy

15.8 **Kaffeehaus Jüngling, Vienna, ca. 1838**

**Coffee Houses**

The expanding middle class, with its ravenous taste for novelty food stuffs and luxuries supplied by the colonies, rapidly reshaped European culture. The diet changed considerably, with tomatoes, potatoes, and corn, as well as tobacco from the Virginias, chocolate from the Spanish Americas, and sugar from the Caribbean, becoming indispensable consumer goods in a very short time.

Coffee came to Europe from Africa by way of Arab traders. It is thought to have been first produced in Yemen. The drink caused a great deal of controversy in the Islamic world, because some authorities thought coffee was intoxicating and, therefore, should be forbidden. As a result, its consumption was initially associated with subversive political activity. From the beginning, however, the social significance of this beverage rested in the fact that it was consumed in public by an exclusively male clientele in a new establishment, the coffee house, usually located on major commercial arteries. The coffee house of Ipshir Pasha in Aleppo (1653) is a rare early coffee house to have survived to our day. It consists of a courtyard and a covered hall, with windows overlooking the street to the south. Domes of varying shapes cover the hall. The end of the Turkish trade monopoly came in 1616, when the Dutch East India Company stole live seedlings and planted them in Java and elsewhere. The French subsequently founded plantations in the Caribbean, leading to a rapid expansion of the drink's popularity. The opening of the first Parisian café was in 1672. The Kaffeehaus Jüngling in Vienna, from about 1750, had a completely glazed two-story wooden facade overlooking a piazza set out with tables and illuminated by a large lamp.

Tobacco smoking was brought to Europe via the Spanish army, and, as explained in Woodruff Smith's book on the topic of consumption and respectability during this period, it was eventually taken up by members of the upper classes who thought that it enhanced their reasoning capacities. Thus, along with coffee houses, we see the emergence of gentlemen's smoking rooms in the houses of the elite. The habit that still persists in Europe of drinking coffee and smoking stems from this time and from the rapid development of a colonially produced cuisine that came to distinguish European culture. As to sugar, it too was incorporated into newly emerging rituals of consumption. Europeans began to put sugar into tea and coffee (first in France, so it is thought), thus combining—if one throws in a piece of chocolate—a culinary experience that embodies Europe's global-economic imperative. One also saw the emergence of sugar bakers, usually imported from Germany and Switzerland, who often created a whole "sugar course," in which an entire meal was replicated in sugar for the guests to view and, of course, to nibble on before it was taken away and the real meal served.

The times of meals began to change to accommodate the transformation of taste. Until then dinner, the principal meal, was served at midday, but the custom of drinking tea and eating chocolate in the afternoon caused it to be shifted to later in the evening. It soon became the custom to start the day with coffee and chocolate, and this became what is now called breakfast. Whereas coffee houses were associated with boisterous male conversation, tea became domesticated into a ceremony presided over largely by women, often on silver tea sets, silver being yet another colonial commodity. Compared to 1717, when 700,000 pounds of tea were imported, three million pounds were imported by 1742. Furniture was designed to accommodate the new rituals, such as a "conversation chair" that allowed one to lean back in a more relaxed position, and high-backed padded chairs also made their appearance. There were those who complained about the modernization of taste, but there was no turning back.

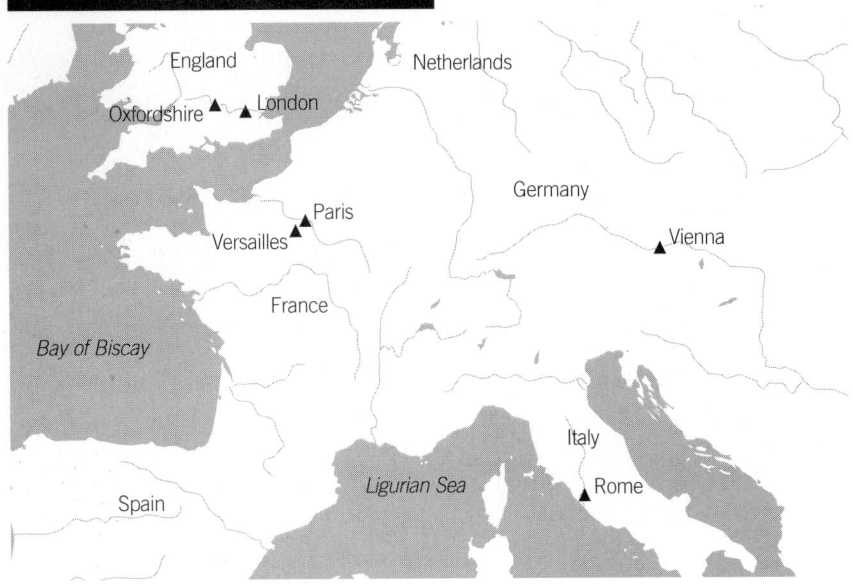


## FRENCH CULTURE OF EMPIRE

With the decline of Spanish sea power, the French acquired the Isle of Bourbon (1642) for use as a commercial base in the Indian Ocean. In west Africa, they took over the mouth of the Senegal River, where they became involved in the slave trade. In the Caribbean, they set up sugar plantations. The French also settled Canada, founding Quebec City (1608) for the fur trade, and later at the mouth of the Mississippi River, New Orleans (1718), forming a T-shaped area running through the heart of the vast North American continent. The money flowing into France created an inflation the likes of which had never been experienced in the global economy before, making, in essence, the poor even poorer. For the elite, however, it brought unimaginable wealth, which was spent in lavish constructions beginning around 1660. Playing a part in this was the optimistic temper of the 1680s, when France basked in a short-lived peace following the successful conclusion of the Dutch War in 1678, which made France and England the primary colonial powers of the world. What the French brought to the colonial project, unlike the Spanish, was planning. Their success, especially under Louis XIV, who took over rule in 1661, was in combining absolutism with an effective government bureaucracy, based on the division of government into committees, subcommittees, and bureaus run by various ministers and secretaries of state, all supported by an elaborate tax collection system.

The rationalization of the national economy was the undertaking of Jean-Baptiste Colbert (1619–83), Louis XIV's chief adviser on political, economic, naval, and religious matters. He was responsible for many of the innovations that, though cumbersome, created the base for France's economic prosperity. An edict was issued, for example, that all lace sold in France must be made in France. The freight tax was eliminated to facilitate the cheaper transportation of goods. Understanding the interrelationship between the global and the national economy was Colbert's innovation. It made the French elite the richest people in Europe.

Colbert also understood that the affairs of politics were directly tied to matters of economics, and economics in turn was dependent on knowledge. He had extensive studies made, for example, of ship building, navigation, and armaments to make the French fleet the strongest in the world. But he also founded the Royal Academy of Science in 1666 and the Academy of Architecture in 1671, among other institutions, all aimed at serving and advising government administrators and ministers. Because there was, however, no accountability in the system and because the king could still spend almost at will, it is no accident that when Colbert died, the system began to collapse under the weight of corruption and mismanagement.

As a consequence of these changes, a new social order emerged in which aristocrats, impoverished by civil and foreign wars, were being supplanted as arbiters of taste by the flourishing bourgeoisie and in particular by the nouveaux riches, as the French called them, who adopted aristocratic airs but who needed to be educated in the proper dress and etiquette codes. Changes in fashion, hairstyles, cuisine, and artistic nuance required constant attention. The emulation of the nobility also entailed a good level of conspicuous consumption, especially by financiers who bought ennobling titles and large country estates. Writers like Jean-Baptiste Molière parodied this phenomenon. His play, *Le bourgeois gentilhomme*, of 1670, blends lowbrow hilarity with stinging satire aimed at a "respectable" society all too eager to learn the finer points of language and dress. The central figure, Monsieur Jourdain, a financier, hired instructors in the arts, fencing, and philosophy but always reveals himself as bourgeois to the core.

The origins of French polite society lay in the Italian courts of the 15th century. When the French king, Francis I (1494–1547), invaded northern Italy, he was struck by the level of decorum he encountered in Italy, such as the use of elaborate introductions, the formalities of courtly interaction, and the public displays of power and wealth.

**15.9 René Descartes's illustration, *Mind and Body***

Though the French quickly learned Italian manners, it was not until the explosion of wealth in the mid-17th century that one saw the attempted transfer of courtly protocols into the upper levels of society, where it was refashioned according to a different set of needs and expectations. Instead of hunting, the principal pleasure of the aristocracy, it was now attending a theater, conversing in a parlor, strolling through a private garden, or waltzing in a glittering ballroom that defined the enrichments of upper-class life. As a result of the newly expanded horizon for artistic patronage, one saw a tremendous outpouring of artistic production. This was the age of Jean-Baptiste Molière (1622–73), Henry Purcell (1658–95), George Frederick Handel (1685–1759), and Johann Sebastian Bach (1685–1750). Antonio Canaletto amazed viewers with his highly realistic paintings of urban squares and Giambattista Tiepolo, too, with his dramatic ceiling paintings of mythological events taking place among softly billowing clouds. Courts vied for the best painters, sculptors, and designers. It is no accident that Immanuel Kant (1724–1804), the noted German philosopher, worked on the question of "taste." He did not challenge the privileges of the rich in that respect but hoped that the forces of tastemaking, once properly understood, could in fact become integrated into the history of civilization.

It might appear ironic that a century that saw the proliferation of flamboyant artistic excess and the emergence of harsh class distinctions, not to mention abject forms of colonial arrogance, was known as the Age of Reason. But this contradiction is resolved when we consider that the rise of European modernity derived from many sources and had many facets. In this pregnant moment in history, not all factors followed each other in logical sequence but occurred in a sort of eruption of concurrent events and interlocked phenomena, such as the rise of philosophical rationalism and state-sponsored industrialization, theories about cause and effect, and philosophies of cognition.

Francis Bacon (1561–1626) and René Descartes (1596–1650) brought to the fore a world of experimentation and deductive reasoning that tried to come to grips with the emerging awareness of the complexity of the world, whether in the realm of science or practical knowledge. Though Cartesianism (Descartes's philosophy) was predictably condemned by the Church fathers, its followers were legion, and Descartes's physics and "method" were broadly accepted, even by some churchmen, in the guise of Aristotelianism.

Nor can we forget that the scientists of the age still had their religious attachments in some form or other. Even Benedict de Spinoza (1632–77) framed his "agnosticism" in a religious format. Other philosophers used rationalism to demonstrate the existence of a supreme being. We should, therefore, not confuse 17th-century rationalism with late-19th-century professionalism. While science and rationalism intruded into the social, intellectual, and aesthetical climate of the age, it often did so under the guise of traditionalism.

Nonetheless, the 17th century was a time in which almost every subject was theorized and analyzed. One saw the publication of René Descartes's *Discours de la méthode* (1637), Thomas Hobbes's *Leviathan* (1651), as well as the *Théorie de la construction des vaisseaux* (1667) by the Jesuit priest, Pierre Hotte, a professor of mathematics who sought to improve the art of shipbuilding. The slide rule, the barometer, the thermometer, and the compound microscope all came into being in the first half of the 17th century. Generally speaking, 17th-century science stressed mechanics as a governing principle in the same way that governments began to stress and extend their bureaucratic reach, both ultimately promising efficiencies of production. The world was suddenly filled not only with agency but also with the means to control and define agency and to give it spatial extension and measure.

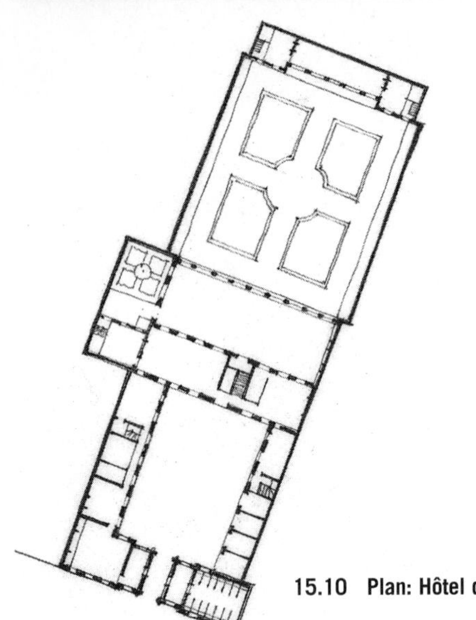

15.10 Plan: Hôtel de Sully, Paris, France

15.11 Hôtel de Sully, Paris

### Hôtel de Sully

The word hotel refers to an apartment for the urban elite as it came to be developed into a building type around 1630. The reason for its sudden emergence was that Henri IV (1553–1610), unlike previous French kings who preferred to live in rural chateaus, moved the court to Paris to establish a capital there. The court remained in Paris through the reign of Louis XIII (1610–43), who operated under the regency of his mother Marie de'Medici, and through the early years of the reign of Louis XIV. When he moved the court to Versailles in 1682, hotel construction shifted from central Paris to the western districts that were closer to Versailles.

Hotels, because of the social rituals associated with them, were designed around a specific set of spaces. A porte cochere allowed the carriages to enter the *cour d'honneur,* where the ritual of arriving, dismounting, and entering was played out. The main part of the building, facing the court was the *corps de logis* (principal living quarters), with the ground floor used for servants' quarters and service areas. The stables were located to one side of the courtyard, along with special rooms for the carriages. To the rear of the *corps de logis,* one found a garden, perhaps with a gallery, a long windowed room for taking in the views and discoursing.

Visiting rooms, ballrooms, and dining rooms, part of the *appartements de parade,* were on the main floor. The family living quarters, which were usually above, consisted of an antechamber, in which to meet visitors; the bedroom (*chambre*); and possibly a more private room for conversation or study, known as the cabinet. Servants lived under the roof. In the arrangement of the elements, symmetry was preferred, at least for the entranceway and courtyard, with much creativity going into establishing the necessary imprint in the often irregular urban sites of Paris with which the architects had to work. It is the Hôtel de Sully by Jean du Cerceau (1624–9) where we see a full-fledged urban palace. It was lived in by Maximilien de Béthune, Duc de Sully (1560–1641), superintendent of finances under King Henry III and later Henry IV's prime minister.

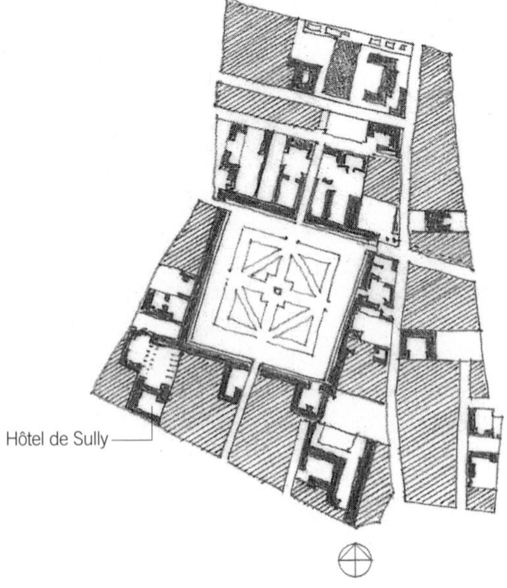


15.12 Plan: Place Royale, Paris, France

15.13 Place Vendôme, Paris

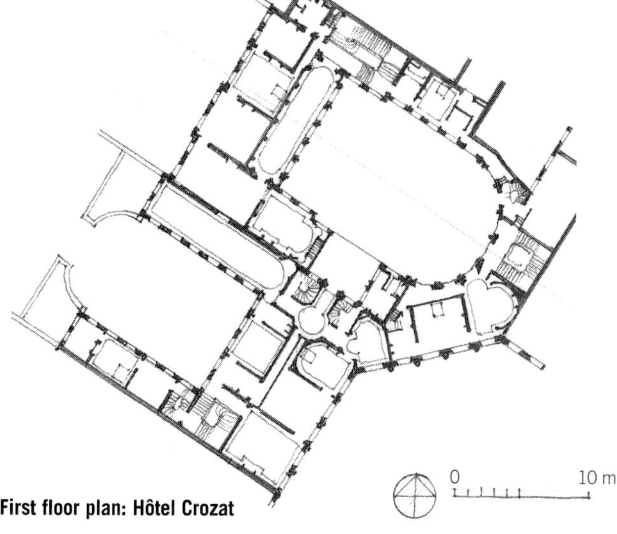


15.14 First floor plan: Hôtel Crozat

## Place Vendôme

Most of the early 17th-century hotels, though located near the Royal Palace, were relatively isolated from each other within the urban fabric of Paris. This began to change as the century progressed and architects sought to integrate the hotel with urban armatures known as "royal squares." Though these squares were called "royal," they were usually built on the initiatives of private individuals or municipalities, even though the climate for their creation was fostered by the King. In other words, they had to be consonant with the principle of royal dignity. Between 1684 and 1688 there were many more proposals for such squares than were actually realized. The first in Paris was the circular Place des Victoires (1684–87) with an equestrian statue of the king in the middle. This was followed by the Place Vendôme (commissioned in 1677) where the facades were all designed by Jules Hardouin-Mansart (1646–1708) and his disciple Pierre Bullet, and it was only later that the actual houses behind the facades were executed by various architects.

The Place Vendôme was different from the Place Royale as it was not a place where the king displayed his power and presence to the upper classes; it was rather on the order of a vast private courtyard. The double hotel for the wealthy financier Antoine Crozat (1702) and his son-in-law the Comte d'Evreux (1707) was located in one corner of the Place Vendôme. Crozat was a leading figure in royal finances. Both hotels have rooms in a remarkable variety of sizes and configurations; but typical of French design was the absence of corridors (except in the servants' quarters) to link the rooms along the main facade. The building was designed by Pierre Bullet.

When Louis XIV moved the court to Versailles, fewer and fewer hotels were built, but under Louis XV (1710–74), who was only five when he became king and who as a young man lived mainly in the Tuileries Palace in the center of the city, Paris once again—for a short while—saw the revival of royal squares and the flourishing of urban apartments. Place Louis XV, now Place de la Concorde in Paris (1763–72), linked the Tuileries Gardens and the Champs Élysées on one axis with the river, and the Church of the Madeleine, planned as a royal chapel (completed 1806–42), on the other axis. Its central area was actually designed as an island of sorts, surrounded as it was by a moat (now filled in). Squares were also built in cities other than Paris, such as the Place Royale (now Place de la Bourse) in Bordeaux (1729) and the Place du Palais, Rennes (1721–30).

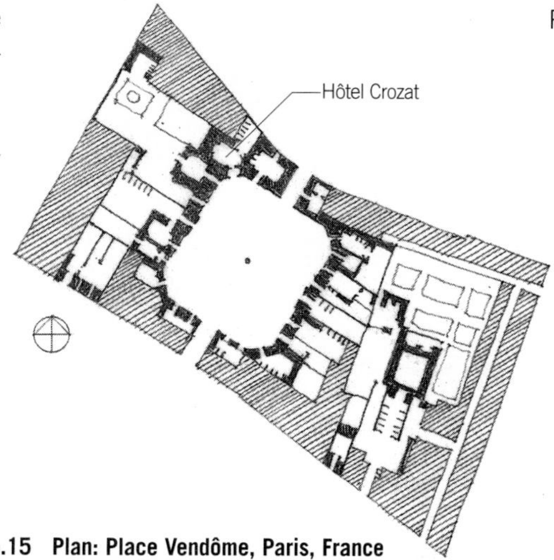


15.15 Plan: Place Vendôme, Paris, France

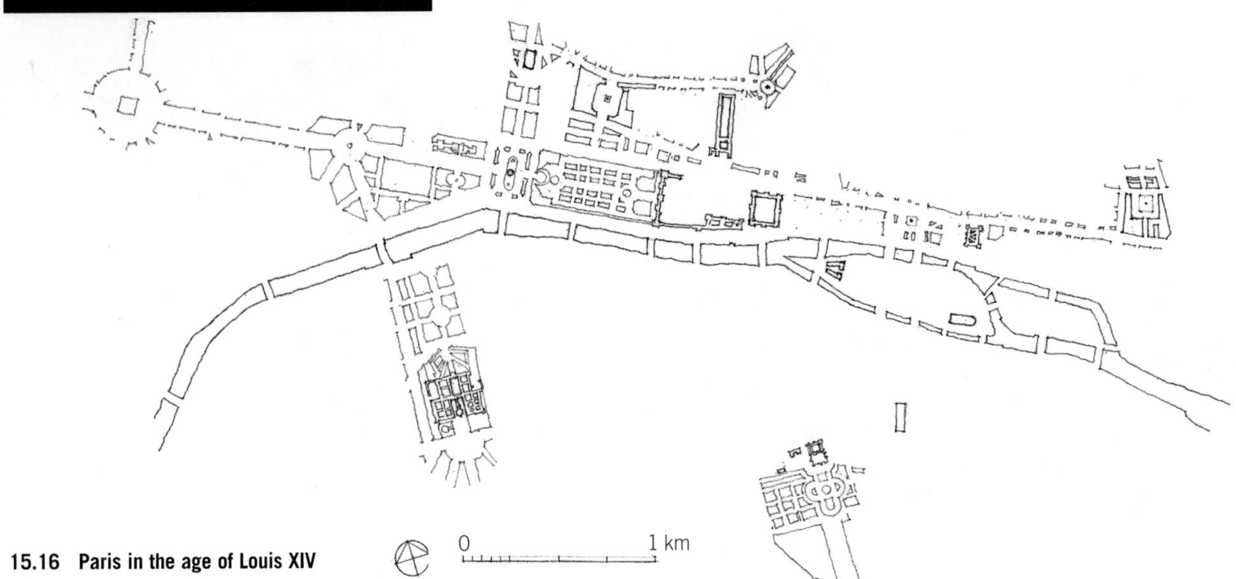


**15.16 Paris in the age of Louis XIV**

**East Facade of the Louvre**

The Louvre was originally a small fort built in the late 12th century under Philip II Augustus as a defense against the Normans. Charles V enlarged and improved it, but all of it was torn down in 1546 by Francis I, who commissioned a new hunting lodge to be erected under Pierre Lescot. Construction was started and then stopped. Jean-Baptiste Colbert hoped that Louis XIV, after his marriage to the Infanta of Spain, Maria Teresa, in 1660 would make the Louvre the seat of the royal household and the court. As a result, Louis Le Vau (1631–70), France's leading garden and chateau designer, took over the job of updating the Louvre into an urban palace in 1655 in collaboration with Claude Perrault. In 1664, a competition was held for the east facade of the Louvre and submissions were made by Claude Perrault and even by Giovanni Lorenzo Bernini, who was especially invited to Paris to study the site. Bernini proposed a Roman-style facade that would hide all the previous construction. His design was rejected, however, for one that was, so it seems, a synthesis of the ideas of Perrault, Le Vau, and perhaps others. Given the complex history of the project and the number of architects involved in the final design, it is an astonishingly successful building. The high ground floor, with its narrow, minimally detailed windows, serves as a podium for the main floor with ranges of coupled, freestanding columns, which form a screen for the building behind, creating a linear loggia.

Just as successful was the overall composition, a central pedimented projection integrated with the columnar screens to its flanks and unpedimented end pavilions with pilasters instead of columns marking the far ends. Such an arrangement was quite novel. One could compare it with Palazzo Porto-Breganze designed by Andrea Palladio (built by Vincenzo Scamozzi, 1575), which is more unified in appearance, or Villa Barbaro (1549–58), where the pieces are more differentiated. The Louvre struck a balance of unity and differentiation that was much admired in its own day, and much imitated.

The building is also significant from the point of view of the history of technology. The columns carry straight entablatures that are actually a series of disguised arches held together partially by tie rods.

The structure was completed by 1670, but when Versailles was proclaimed the new royal capital in 1682, the funds for the remaining Louvre projects that had been foreseen began to dry up.

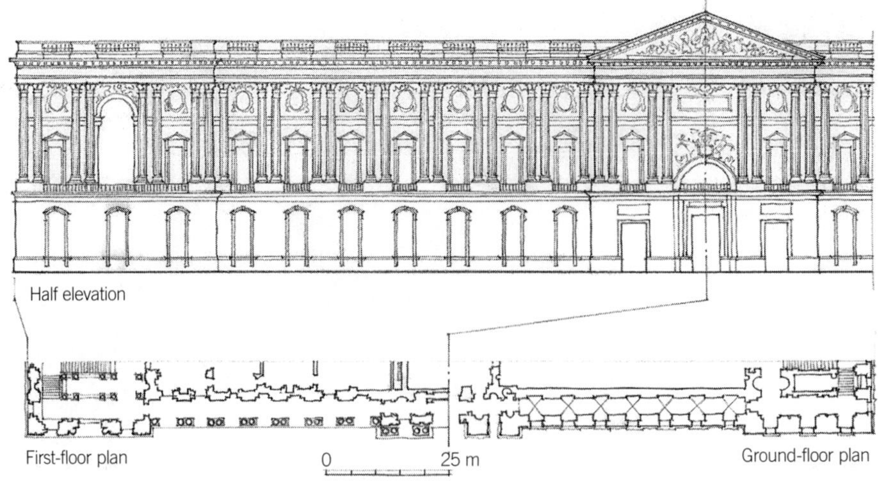


**15.17 East front of the Louvre, Paris, France**

15.18 **Chateau de Versailles, France**

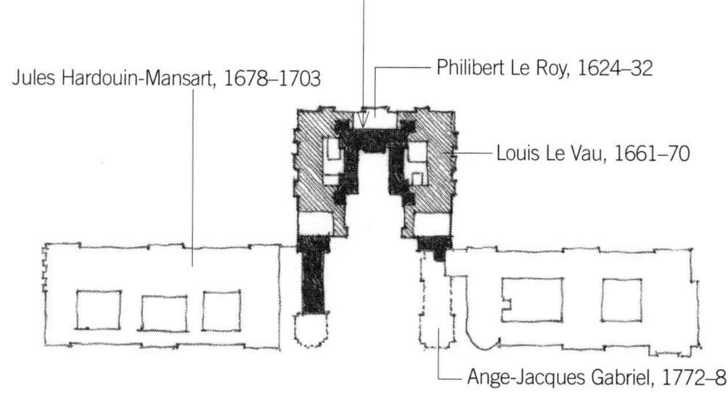


15.19 **Development of the Palace at Versailles during Louis XIV's reign**

## Chateau de Versailles

The site for Chateau de Versailles was an old hunting lodge about 20 kilometers southwest of Paris. The design by Louis Le Vau and Jules Hardouin-Mansart went through several phases, beginning in 1661 after André Le Nôtre had begun work on the gardens and fountains. In 1668, the king decided to expand the purpose of the chateau so that it could serve as a suitable residence for himself and his family. The problem was what to do with the old building, which was much out of date. The architects solved the problem by wrapping a new building around the old. The original palace still stands, but it is in essence embedded within the fabric of a new structure that consists of a series of forecourts, creating a telescoping U around a central court at the top of a gently sloping hill. In 1682 work had progressed far enough that the king could proclaim the palace the royal capital.

Three avenues led through the countryside to the front gate, but only the central and northern avenues lead to Paris; the southern avenue, a kilometer long, was added for the sake of symmetry. The terminus of the avenues brought one to the first gate, through which the carriages of the visitors passed. The carriages were stopped at the second gate, and everyone, except for the most distinguished, had to proceed on horse or foot to the last gate that led into the inner courtyard. On the ground floor of the palace there were apartments mainly for the royal guards and for administrative purposes. One room, to the right, was specially prepared for the reception of important visitors. It contained the grand double Stairway of the Ambassadors, resplendent with colored marbles and wall paintings. The stairway led to the principal reception rooms where the king lived. The apartments were arranged enfilade, that is, the rooms were arranged in an axial manner so as to provide a vista along the length of the suite. There were no corridors, except in the servants' quarters.

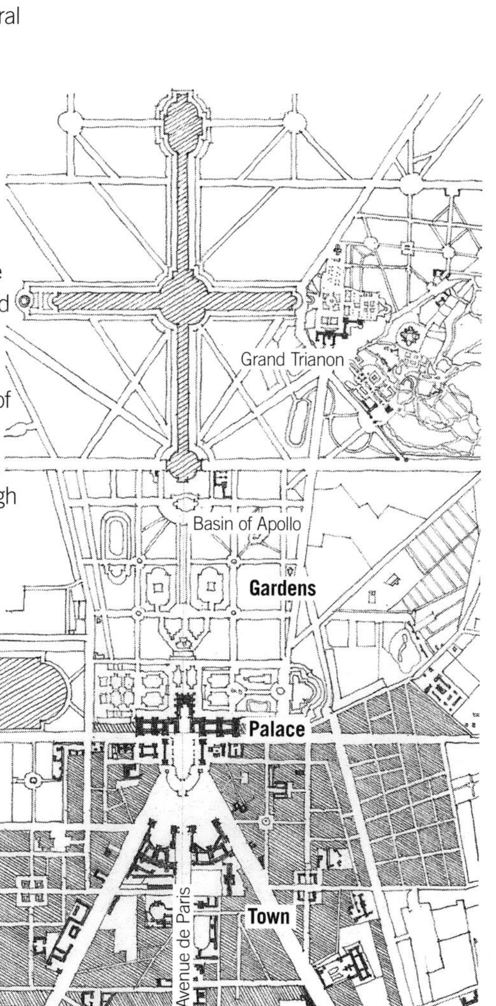

15.20 **Site plan of Versailles**

15.21 Hall of Mirrors, Palace at Versailles

15.22 Hardouin-Mansart's chapel at Versailles

The Conseil des Bâtiments, or King's Buildings Office, which was set up by Jean-Baptiste Colbert, was so well organized that after the untimely death of the palace's chief architect, Louis Le Vau, construction work never stopped. The king took a great interest in the building and spent a good deal of time discussing almost every aspect of it with the architects.

Le Vau had based his designs to some extent on his landscaping of the chateau of Vaux-le-Vicomte (begun 1657) outside Paris, built for Nicholas Fouquet, the finance minister of Louis XIV. Using a hill, he created a series of terraces and slopes with views back to the building. The land around Versailles, however, was much less auspicious. It lacked vistas, woods, and even water. Much of it was a bog. Water for the fountains and canals needed to be pumped uphill. The gardens were laid out on a grid and aligned with the palace at the far eastern end and aligned along a broad allée to a fountain at the far western end. Though no hill was available on the flat site, Le Vau was able to create subtle elevation changes by gently sloping the ground downward away from the palace toward the Grand Canal in the distance, creating a feeling of height and extension into space simultaneously.

At first the gardens were designed for traditional uses, like walks and pleasurable conversation, but Louis XIV introduced the idea of the fête, which included horsemanship events, banquets, plays by Molière, music, and fireworks. These events were not just for the elite but were recorded in publications that were part of the king's publicity and propaganda apparatus to enhance the fame of Versailles. As tastes developed for ever grander displays, the gardens went through several redesigns, in particular, at the western end with the Basin of Apollo, which shows Apollo rising from the sea (designed by Jean-Baptist Tuby). The theme of Apollo, elaborated on in a nearby grotto, was meant to emphasize the divine aspirations of the king.

Le Vau's replacement was Jules Hardouin-Mansart, who was not only the architect but also the administrator-coordinator of the system that had been devised by Colbert. Though the Buildings Office set an astonishingly high standard of performance, ironically, it often required the king's personal authority to resolve sometimes even the most trivial of questions.

In the early 1680s, Louis XIV became increasingly religious due to the influence of his pious mistress, Madame de Maintenon, whom he secretly wed in 1684 after the death of his first wife, Maria Teresa. In 1685, the king revoked the Edict of Nantes, which allowed for the toleration of the Protestant Huguenots that Henry IV had set in place. Though there are several chapels in the palace of Versailles, Hardouin-Mansart was commissioned to design an even grander one. The chapel consisted of a rectangular nave with apse but without a dome. It was Gothic in its proportions, purposefully so, and intended to demonstrate its connection with the Palatine Chapel. Much like Charlemagne's cathedral in Aachen, it had arched openings on the ground floor. The exterior is an elegant fusion of Gothic sensibilities with classical orders, the high pitched roof, the large windows extending to the pilasters, and the buttresslike thickening of the walls of the apse. The main floor was articulated by freestanding columns holding a straight entablature, influenced by the Louvre colonnade. The two buildings, the Grand Trianon and the chapel, show the global and historical imagination that was at work in the French royal ideology, all made possible by the elastic nature of baroque architecture.

15.23 L'Observatoire-de-Paris, France

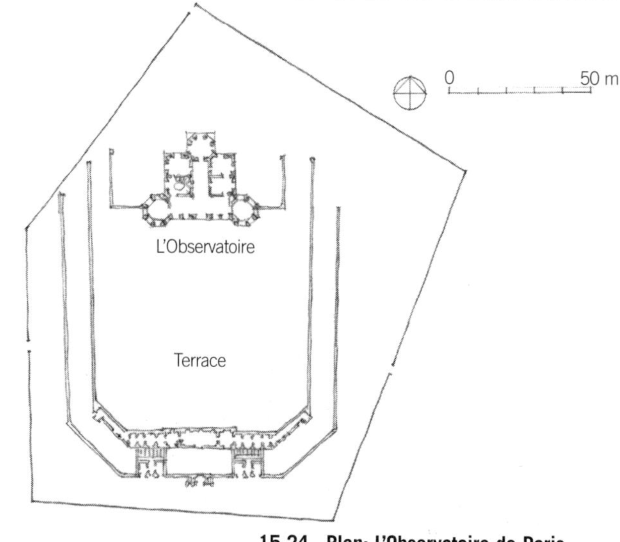


15.24 Plan: L'Observatoire-de-Paris

**L'Observatoire-de-Paris**

The foundations for theoretical discourse in architecture had been laid in the Renaissance by Leon Battista Alberti, Sebastiano Serlio, and Andrea Palladio, among others. One of the beneficiaries of the work of these Italian theoreticians and one of the most representative of the new generation of French theoreticians in the 17th century was Claude Perrault (1613–88). Perrault was a fervent believer in the exalted position of the age in which he lived. For him, the age of Louis XIV had reached the equivalent of the Age of Augustus. Perrault began as a member of the medical faculty at the University of Paris but shifted his interests to the realm of architecture. He was familiar with Greek and knew Latin, making a translation of Vitruvius that was brought out in 1673 in a spectacular folio edition dedicated to the king. Perrault also presented a copy to members of the architectural academy. It was the first authoritative and well-annotated French translation of Vitruvius, and it became the standard work on architecture in Europe. Though Perrault's own taste influenced the illustrations, he attempted to adhere as far as possible to the information in Vitruvius' text, setting an example for accuracy and attention to detail that was to become an essential aspect of the neoclassical mentality. His images emphasized the undecorated aspects of antiquity, resisting the temptation, prevalent at his time, to dwell on ornamentation and decoration.

A particularly heated debate revolved around the question of whether the perception of beauty was a result of custom or a spontaneous response, with Perrault arguing that beauty was not a fixed property to be revealed by the artist but a variable depending on custom, pointing out, for example, that one can find neither two buildings nor two authors who agree on any subject or follow the same rules.

Though Perrault had a hand in the design of the east facade of the Louvre, his principal architectural accomplishment was the design of the Observatoire (1667–72) for the Royal Academy of Science (founded in 1671). The selection of Perrault as architect was facilitated by his membership in the building council (Conseil des Bâtiments) and by the influence of his brother Charles who since 1664 had been serving as Colbert's assistant in that council.

The Observatoire, built in the southern outskirts of Paris, was by the standards of the day an austere building. There were no orders, no columns, and no pilasters. Simple string courses demarcating the stories and openings are either slightly recessed from the smooth wall surface or surrounded by barely projecting moldings. Each side of the octagonal corner towers was aligned with the sun's position at solstices and equinoxes and the eastern one was unroofed for the use of a telescope within. The building was put together with the greatest skill, and the staircase with its complex three-dimensional curving surfaces, all in stone, still astonishes today. The building was sited against a terrace that negotiated the change of terrain. The roof was meant to be used as a platform from which astronomical measurements could be made. A hole in the center of the floors of the main chambers allowed measurements of the sun's zenith to be made.

15.25 Elevation: L'Observatoire-de-Paris

15.26 **Courtyard, Hôtel des Invalides, Paris, France**

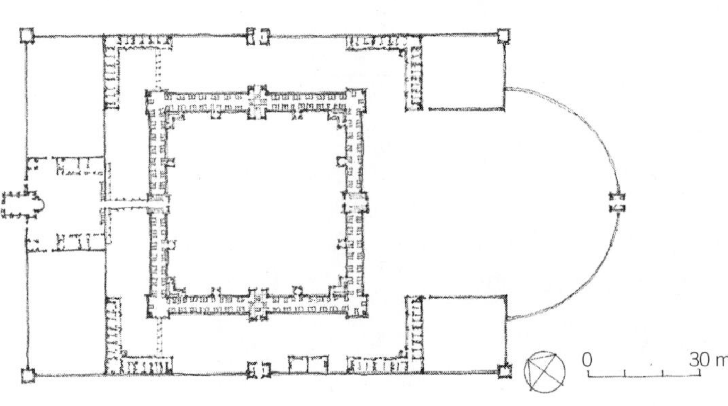


15.27 **Plan: Hôpital Saint-Louis, Paris**

### Hôtel des Invalides

In Europe hospitals had first appeared as a type of by-product of the pilgrimage drives and the crusades. There were several important ones in Italy. The Knights of St. John were well known for their hospitals on Rhodes and elsewhere. By the 18th century, however, hospitals were flooded not only with the thousands of soldiers who fought in the almost endless cycle of battles but also by the poor and the indigent who formed an increasingly large lower class. Plagues and epidemics added to the problem. In Paris a cholera epidemic in 1519 and the plagues of 1580, 1596, 1606, and 1630 struck down thousands. But because hospitals remained associated with religious orders and charitable institutions, there was practically no distinction between a hospital, a pesthouse, and a poorhouse. Furthermore, the sick were often unwilling to leave their houses for a hospital, concerned that while they were sequestered, their property would be pillaged or their income threatened.

To combat these conditions, Henri IV decreed the construction of the Hôpital Saint-Louis (begun 1607). It was outside the city walls and easily accessible from major roads. The wards consisted of wide, open corridors with patients' beds placed against the walls. Four of these corridor buildings were linked to form a large courtyard.

After the end of the Thirty Years' War in 1648 much of Europe was flooded with former soldiers, many of whom had lived their entire lives as soldiers and had difficulty returning to civilian occupations, posing a threat to civil and moral authority. To address the problem, construction was begun around 1660 on the Hôpital Général, which became a model for similar institutions around France. It was not so much a hospital as a pauper's house, where the poor could be segregated and controlled.

The most spectacular of these creations was the Hôtel des Invalides, begun in 1671 and finished in 1676. Behind its moat and expansive entrance front lies a large Royal Court, while ranges of buildings to the right and left are grouped around smaller courts. The north facade is articulated in typical French fashion by central and end pavilions that project forward. Apart from the entrance porches, there are no columns or pilasters on the main facade. The court has two stories of arches on piers relieved only by the pedimented pavilions at the center along the axis. There were special areas for sick and wounded soldiers, one for pauper soldiers and a barracks for older veterans.

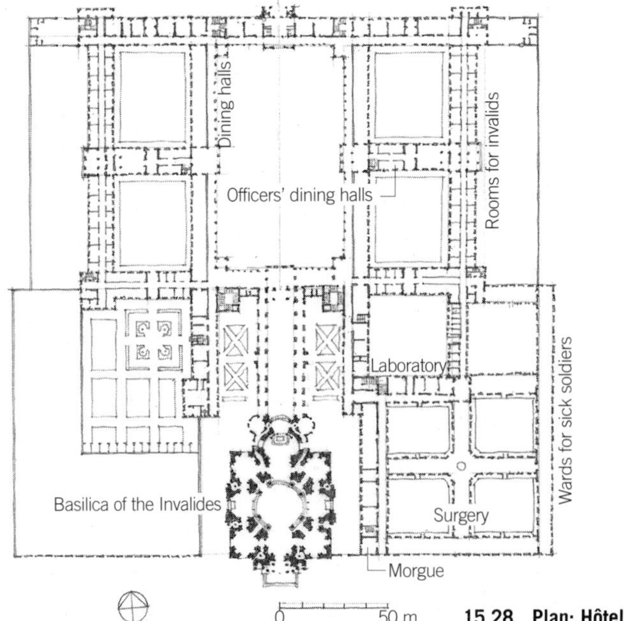


15.28 **Plan: Hôtel des Invalides**

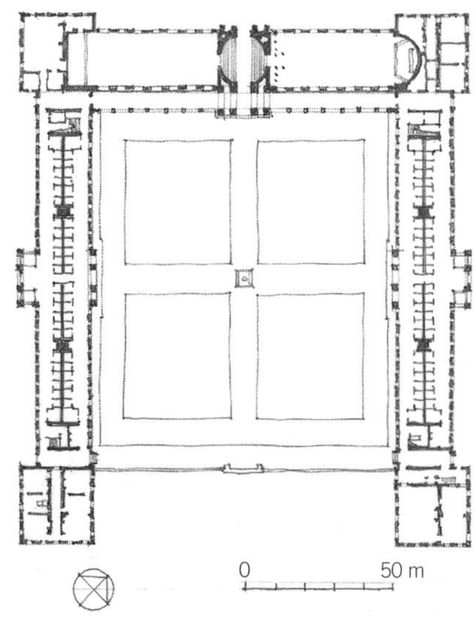


15.29 **Plan: Chelsea Hospital, England**

15.30 **Dome, Basilica of the Invalides, Paris**

By way of comparison, hospitals in England, built from public funds, tended to be simpler, given the political ambiguity of spending money in a way that many thought would seem to reward poverty. Chelsea Hospital (begun 1682) shows, however, the first awareness of French innovation regarding the problem of soldiers. Designed by Sir Christopher Wren, the cells were placed in ranges, back to back. At the end of the range a larger room was set out for the sergeants. Instead of an enclosed quadrangle, the wards faced each other across a large courtyard open to the Thames River, with a great hall and chapel linking the wards at the far end. The hospital's governor and lieutenant governor lived in river pavilions at the corners.

### Basilica of the Invalides

The sanctuary of the Invalides (1676–79) is actually a double church, a basilica, or Soldier's Church, attached to a central-plan domed edifice, with the dome rising majestically behind it. Both were designed by Hardouin-Mansart. On the facade, Hardouin-Mansart did not articulate his windows with Italian-styled balconied *aediculae*. The windows, instead, are left as mere openings carved out of the thickness of the wall. The dome sits on a high double drum and constitutes the culmination of the building's massing.

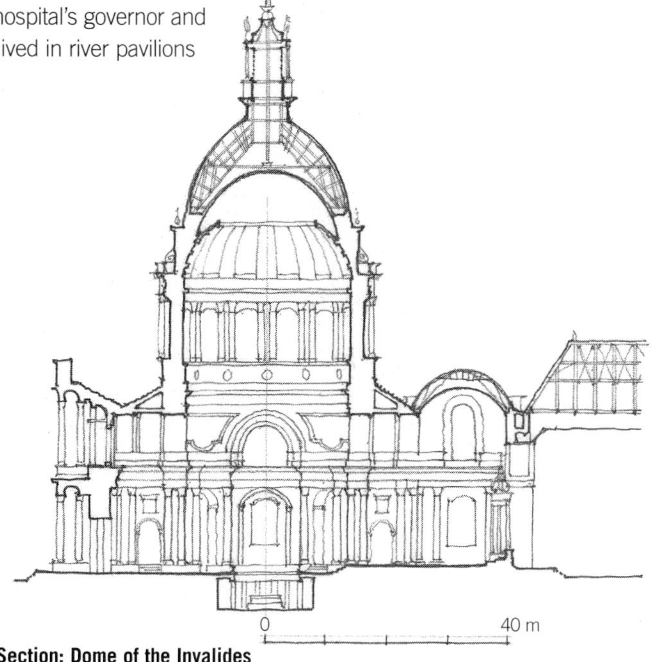


15.31 **Section: Dome of the Invalides**

The lowest dome is cut open to create a large oculus, revealing the underside of the second dome, which is painted with the sky and clouds and allegorical religious figures of the Charles de Lafosse painting, *St. Louis Giving Up his Sword to Jesus Christ*. The uppermost dome is supported by a lightweight wooden structure. This splitting of the dome into several shells makes the dome far different from Michelangelo's at St. Peter's, which is a double dome mainly for structural reasons. Here the dome is split not only to create an illusion on the inside—a type of vertical framing device into the glories of Heaven—but also to enhance its visibility from the outside.

Instead of being just a temple of martial glory, the church was a religious shrine dedicated to the sainted Louis IX, the 13th-century French king with whom Louis XIV was increasingly associated. The fortunes of the French government were decreasing toward the end of Louis XIV's reign and his reputation needed glorification, if not deification. The saint's statue, carrying over from the theme on the ceiling of the dome, appears in the left-hand niche of the main facade, along with Charlemagne's in the right-hand niche.

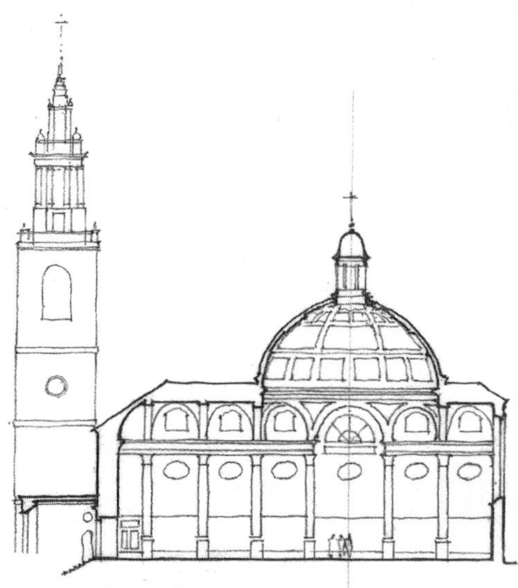

15.32 **Section: St. Stephen Walbrook, London**

**ENGLAND: HOUSE OF STUART**

In 1536, the English king, Henry VIII, dissolved the Catholic monasteries and abbeys and created the English Church. The English Church has many liturgical similarities to the Catholic Church, except that the King of England is its head instead of the pope. It was thus in every aspect a state religion. Puritanism, however, gained many adherents, and these formed a substantial element in the Parliament. The Parliament became so strong that during the English Civil War (1642–51) it executed Charles I (1649) and set up Oliver Cromwell (1599–1658) as ruler of the Protestant Republic, as some term this interim period. In 1660, the monarchy was, however, able to reinstate itself under Charles II. Despite the troubles, the external policies during this period were marked by rapid growth of trade and colonization. The Navigation Acts (1650 and 1696) aimed at protecting English shipping and ending the dominance of the Dutch in world trade. When Catherine of Braganza married Charles II in 1662 she brought to England, as part of her dowry, territories in Bombay and Tangier. In the second Dutch War (1665–7), New Amsterdam, founded in 1625 by the Dutch West India Company, fell to the English and was renamed New York after the Earl of York. In 1670, the British East India Company was given the right to autonomous territorial acquisitions.

In the meantime, at home, the antiquated housing stock in cities such as London gave rise to untold problems. London was subject to no less than 16 outbreaks of the plague, culminating in the Great Plague of 1665 that killed 17,000 people; in the following year London experienced the first great city fire of modern times. The fire lasted for five days and destroyed almost all of central London. Some 13,200 houses were destroyed and more than 80 churches, including St. Paul's Cathedral. Apparently, the fire also put an end to the plagues by killing off the rat population. Though the disaster presented an opportunity to rethink the layout of the city, it was decided to rebuild the city more or less along the lines of the old streets. The buildings were grouped into four types, depending on street location. The rebuilding of the churches was seized as an opportunity to place a strong Anglican imprint on the city. The Anglican Church was dominated by the landed gentry and so one must see the church as an extension of the interests of the ruling class.

Sir Christopher Wren was asked to design almost all of these church, some 51 buildings (beginning in 1670). Having no recent English prototypes to fall back on, he relied on Italian notions but modified them to fit the more restrained tastes of the English. The variety of Wren churches is immense, partially because many were built over the foundations of their predecessors, often with irregular lots and in cramped quarters. To help pay for the new churches, the government imposed a tax on coal entering the port of London.

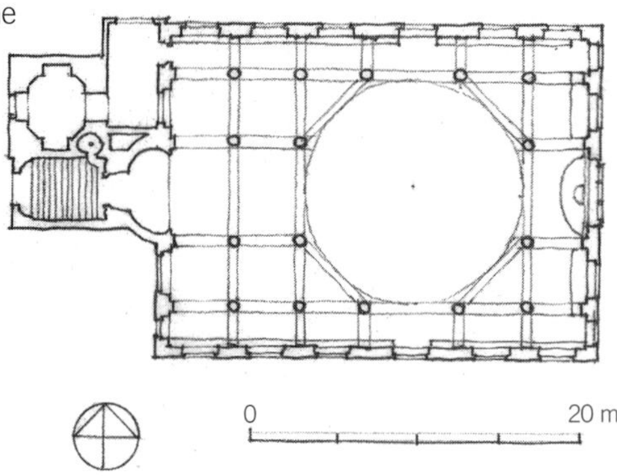


15.33 **Plan: St. Stephen Walbrook**

15.34 **Approach to Charnock's Tomb, Calcutta, India**

In reaction against Puritanism, Anglicanism placed considerable emphasis on the dignity of the service as prescribed in the Book of Common Prayer. But unlike Italian Counter-Reformation churches, which emphasized the spectacle of devotion, Wren's Anglican churches possess some of the simplicity and openness of Protestant churches. Wren experimented with a range of forms—centralized, longitudinal and square. Some churches had galleries. The individually designed steeples, however, became the most famous aspect of his designs. Steeples had been in disfavor since the introduction of the Italian Palladian style by Inigo Jones, who preferred towers and domes. Wren brought the steeple—a Scandinavian wooden architectural form—into the Palladian fold by creating a box for the bell chamber with openings and pilasters, on which the steeple rested. St. Stephen Walbrook is a typical case (1672–80). It is a cross-in-square church with a central dome, a forerunner of St. Paul's. The outside, mainly hidden behind the mansion house, appears plain, while inside we find a bright, classical interior. Eight Corinthian arches on high bases support the dome.

### Charnock's Tomb

In 1612, the British East India Company succeeded in replacing the Portuguese as naval auxiliaries to the Moghuls. This enabled them to open their first port at Surat on the western coast. At first India was seen as of limited mercantile importance, as the English wanted it mainly as a staging post for their trade ventures with China. But soon India became invaluable as a source of cotton textiles, muslins, taffetas, calico, and chintzes, as well as barreled indigo, molasses, saltpeter, and later, opium.

The first generations of English company officers were careful to maintain cordial relations with the Indians on whom they depended for trade. Many wore Indian clothes, and intermarriage was common. Company soldiers married the Christian women of the Armenian community in particular. Back in England, many of these early colonists were accused of having "gone native," a phenomenon that is well supported by the oldest English structures to have survived, two tombs, George Oxinden's in Surat and Job Charnock's in Calcutta. Oxinden was the governor of Bombay when it was transferred to the English, and his family tomb in Surat (ca. 1669) has no trace of English architecture. Charnock was the founder of Calcutta. His tomb (ca. 1700) is based on Moghul prototypes, as it is an octagonal structure with round openings on every side with a higher story and crenellations.

Charnock is supposed to have married a Hindu widow, whom he rescued from being burned at the funeral pyre of her husband, at the young age of 16. Charnock, who was 51, and his young bride must have made a strange couple, but they seemed to have lived a full life. They had three daughters who were among the first generation of Anglo-Indians, a community that was formidable yet culturally ostracized by both the English and the Indians.

A Frenchman who had also "turned native" and amassed a big fortune in trading, Claude Martin used his wealth to create a sprawling palace for Anglo-Indian children who had been abandoned by their English fathers. Constantia in Lucknow (1790) was Claude Martin's attempt to reimagine a Moghul tomb in the form of a multistory inhabitable space, out of a European architectural vocabulary, with decorations taken from both traditions. Uncomfortably poised on a platform (with round arches and pilasters instead of pointed arches), Constantia was a symmetrical structure with the hint of a dome created by freestanding intersecting arches. The skyline is composed of *chattris* made in the European style and an array of statues, like in Italianate Baroque buildings. It was a rare hybrid, an attempt to modernize Moghul architecture by making it fit new functions while re-presenting it in English garb, as it were, to clearly identify it with empire.

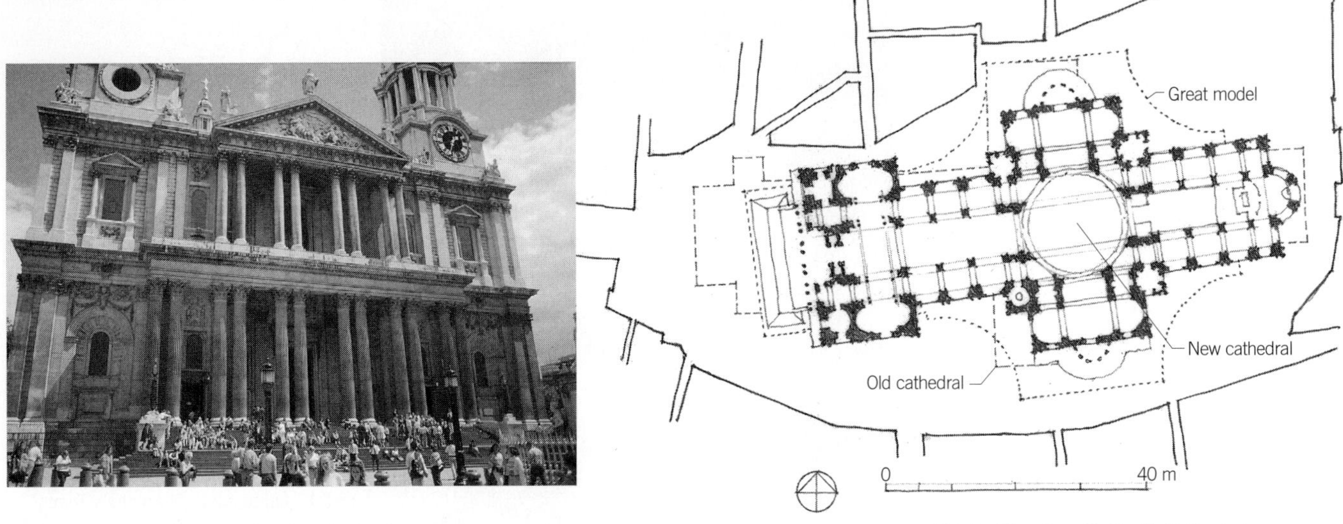


**15.35 St. Paul's Cathedral, London, England**

**15.36 Site plan: St. Paul's Cathedral**

## St. Paul's Cathedral

After the destruction of St. Paul's Cathedral in the Great Fire of London, many wanted to rebuild it in the old Gothic style. Wren, however, envisioned a building that transcended national taste and competed on a European scale. Several plans and revisions were made, including one known as the "great model," with highly original large concave exteriors. This was rejected for a more conventional plan. The church fathers also wanted a medieval-styled section, with low side aisles and a tall nave. As it is, the building (1675–1709) is in the shape of a cross, with the dome, one of the largest in the world, over the crossing. It is surrounded by three galleries on different levels. To disguise the low side aisles, Wren created a blind second story that also concealed the buttresses holding up the vaults. Without the false second story, the dome would have looked astonishingly out of scale. Even so, it looms large, resting on a ring of columns with eight cleverly disguised buttresses. On the interior one finds a giant pilaster order for the nave and a lower order for the secondary spaces, modeled loosely on St. Peter's. But unlike Michelangelo's lower drum, which fits compactly onto the body of the building, St. Paul's drum is both lofty and airy, rising almost incomprehensibly out of the center of the building. While Michelangelo's lantern appears as a bundle of forces collected into a relatively tightly wound package, Wren's lantern sits serenely on top of the dome as a small centralized *tempietto*.

The semispherical dome (flattened on top) consists actually of a wooden frame with a lead surface supported by a catenoid masonry stricture. Below that there is an almost spherical catenary vault. To create the impression of height so that, from the point of view of the perceiver, the inner and outer dome match, the columns supporting the dome lean toward the center.

On the facades, which seem to resemble a palace more than a church, the paired pilasters and *aediculae* rely heavily on Donato Bramante, as does the ring of columns at the base of the dome, which—unlike the ones on the inside—are not structural except that they add buttressing support to the base of the dome. The pairing of the Corinthian columns on the facade are taken from the Louvre. Wren had made a trip to Paris and had met with Hardouin-Mansart, Bernini, and others. He had also been to Italy to see the developments in Rome. The building can be seen as a purposeful synthesis, if not a celebration, of different design ideas. Whether it transcends these can be debated. It is useful to compare its dome with Hardouin-Mansart's dome for the Hôtel des Invalides. The interior of St. Paul's dome is painted so that it looks like a colonnade supports a dome higher up. The upper part of the conical vault is painted to extend the illusion through the oculus.

A catenary arch is the mirrored upward projection of a suspended chain. It is the most ideal form of vault, as it supports itself without the need for buttressing. This form of curve was distinguished from parabolas by Jacobus Bernoulli in 1691.

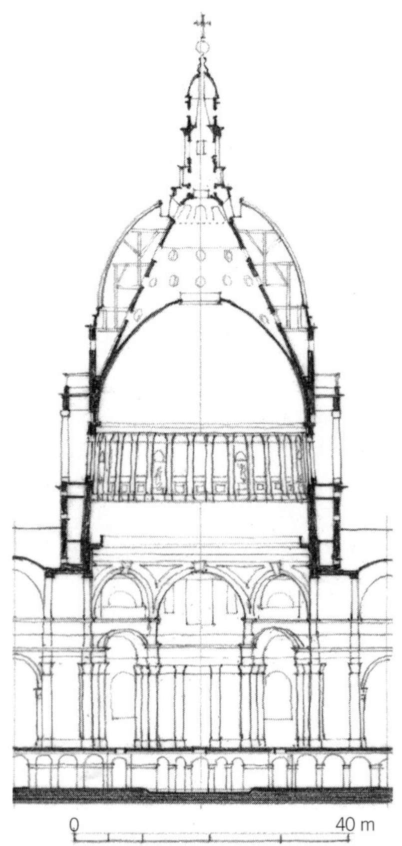


**15.37 Section through dome of St. Paul's Cathedral**

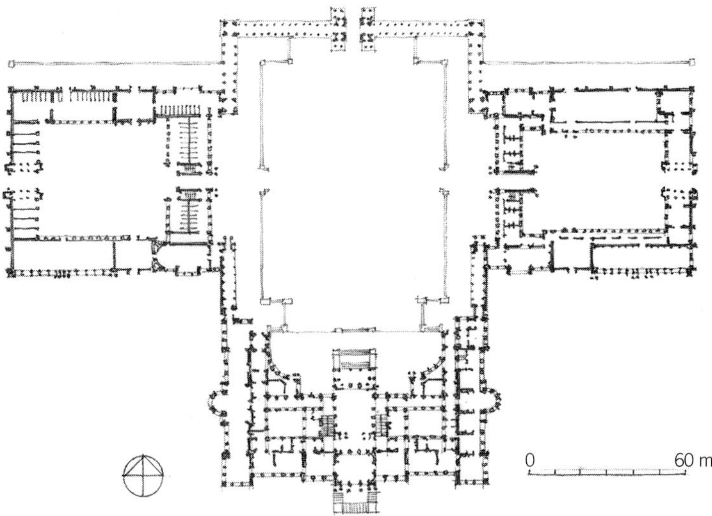


**15.38 Plan: Blenheim Palace, near Oxford, England**

### Blenheim Palace

The conclusion of the Wars of the Grand Alliance (1688–97), in which England, Austria, and others were successful against the French, resulted in a shift of power in the European world. The matter was not settled, however, until the War of Austrian Succession, which culminated in 1704 in a huge battle near the small German town of Blenheim. When it was over the English under the 1st Duke of Marlborough had routed the French. The success had clear implications in the global economy. Among other things, it enabled England to take over the lucrative French slave-trading network, throughout the Caribbean.

As a token of her appreciation, Queen Anne, with Parliament's hearty approval, rewarded the winner of the Blenheim battle, the 1st Duke of Marlborough, with a 15,000-acre piece of land and the funds to build himself a castle. The building was designed from the start as a public monument to the English victory. In its great hall there is a painting of the Duke in shining cuirass and blue mantle, kneeling before Britannia, who, seated on a globe, offers him a victory wreath. At Britannia's feet sits the goddess Plenty, with fruits pouring out of her cornucopia. Mars and Hercules look on with wonderment. Off to one side the muse of History holds a huge pen and is writing the words "*Anno Memorabilia* 1704" in a big volume. On the exterior, over the central portico, stands Minerva, the goddess of war, with a chained captive to either side.

The corners of the towers are capped with 12-meter-high pinnacles that portray the Duke's coronet crushing the French fleur-de-lis. Trophy piles carved out of stone, pikes, armor, cannonballs, and drums bristle atop the ends of the east and west pavilions while ferocious lions sink their teeth into the ruffled feathers of French cocks. The building was designed by John Vanbrugh (1664–1726), a personal acquaintance of the Duke of Marlborough. Vanbrugh had no formal training as an architect, but he worked closely with Nicholas Hawksmoor, an architect who had apprenticed in the office of Wren.

**15.39 Blenheim Palace**

The plan is simple and monumental. The Roman imperial portico on the north entrance facade might seem obvious enough, but it only barely disguises the enormous hall behind it. The principal living suites in the rear were not connected enfilade, as would have been the case in France, but were served by a circulation system that takes up quite a bit of space itself. On the west, there is a long gallery with views to a garden and a forest beyond. Though the building filled the fantasy of domination, many already in that time thought it extravagant. One must remember, however, that when Blenheim Castle came into being in 1705, absolute monarchy had reached its zenith in England and in France. Society believed in hierarchical order; reason, governance, and divinity had fused into one and this moment in time was reflected in Blenheim Palace.

15.40 **St. Mary Woolnoth, London, England**

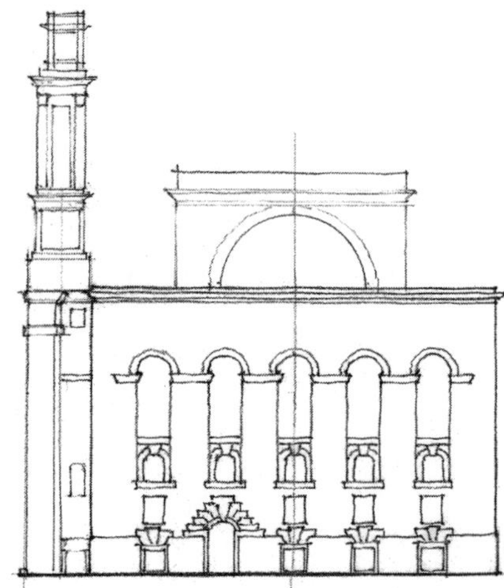

15.41 **Elevation: St. Mary Woolnoth**

**St. Mary Woolnoth**

The most imaginative of the English architects of that age was undoubtedly Nicholas Hawksmoor (1661–1736). Wren shared with his apprentice an interest in the architecture of Asia Minor and of the still barely known architecture of Greece and Egypt. But if Wren had an eye for compositional unity, Hawksmoor aimed to bring the elements of architectural composition into dynamic interrelationship. He pried features out of their expected contexts. Though we are inclined to see Hawksmoor's buildings as examples of the baroque or, in this case, the English baroque, as it is sometimes called, there are certain caveats since baroque religiosity was not a factor in his work. Nonetheless, it fit with the ambitions of Reverend Thomas Tenison (1636–1715), archbishop of Canterbury, who played a key role in the post-London-fire rebuilding. He saw the fire as an opportunity to restore the luster of the Anglican Church that had been weakened in an increasingly secular age, by emphasizing its basic theological tenets in combination with a grand architectural vision. The ascendency of the Tory Party in 1710, with its strong attachment to the king and the Anglican Church, was a further factor in setting the stage for Hawksmoor's church commissions.

The strangeness of Hawksmoor's buildings is a result of a design process that emphasized esoteric historical and philosophical meanings that might be known only to experts. In that sense, Hawksmoor spoke to a generation of designers that attempted to distance itself from amateur architects.Unlike Wren, who wanted to place England on par with the great baroque capitals of Europe, Hawksmoor was seeking a more personal idiom.

Hawksmoor's St. Mary Woolnoth (1716–24) is an astonishing building when compared with the stiff linearity of the English Palladian style that was starting to make its presence felt. The enfronting double-tower-facade appears as if two buildings were stacked on top of each other and the entirety surmounted by two symmetrically placed small bell housings. In the lower zone, the voussoirs around the openings are connected to horizontally banded rustication grooves that continue even around the corner columns. Over this structure, he placed a "base" on which rests an entablatured blind portico. It would be wrong to see Hawksmoor's architecture simply as playful or as baroque, when it is clear that he attempted to force the architectural elements, such as keystones, arches, pilasters, and columns, out of their traditional compositional frame, emphasizing them, and allowing them spatial and compositional independence.

French baroque, if one thinks of the east facade of the Louvre, aspired to a unity of mass and surface decoration. Here the surface decoration and the massing battle for supremacy. Not adhering to the limited Palladian interpretation of the antique, Hawksmoor studied buildings such as the Roman tomb of the Julii at Saint-Rémy. The two columns flanking the entrance are esoteric references to the Temple of Solomon, the reconstruction of which preoccupied many architects of the time, including Wren. Anglican theologians, at the time, were also interested in the Second Temple of Solomon as a way to reconnect to both biblical authenticity and the ethos of early Christianity. The upper portico was a reference to the Mausoleum of Halicarnassus, one of the ancient seven wonders of the world, which had been destroyed but for which Hawksmoor made a sketch based on descriptions by Pliny and Vitruvius.

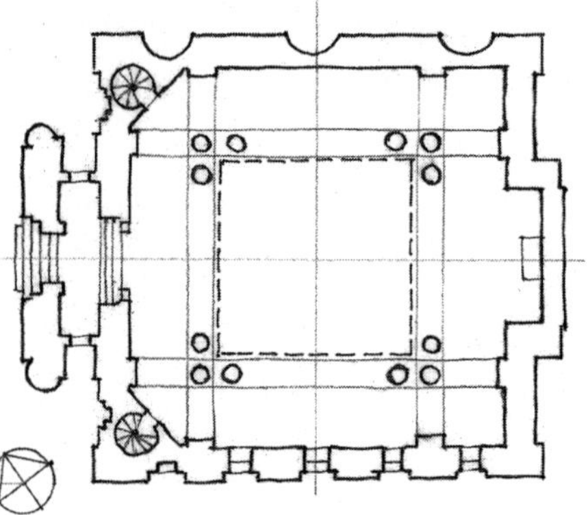

15.42 **Plan: St. Mary Woolnoth**

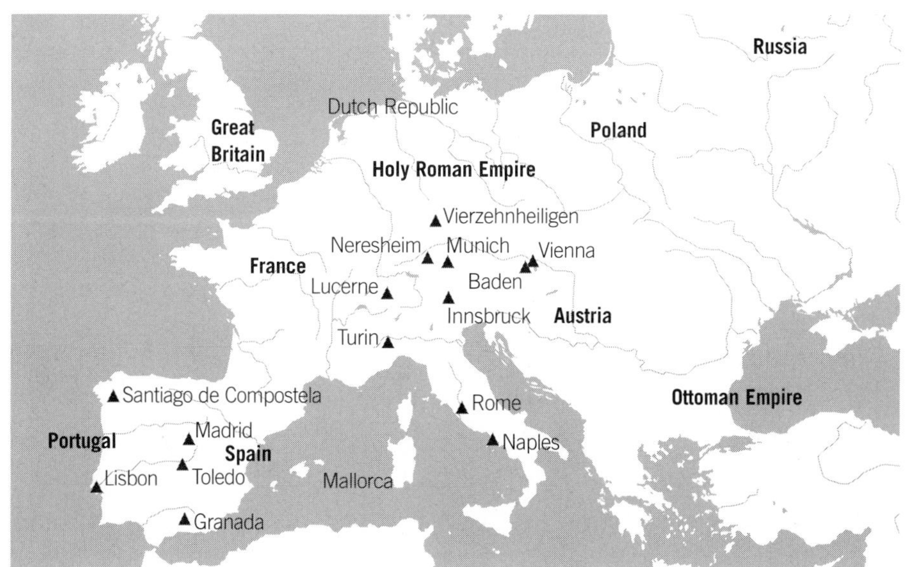

15.43 **Palace of Schönbrunn, Vienna, Austria**

## SPREAD OF THE BAROQUE

Under Louis XIV Paris enjoyed enormous authority in matters of the arts. But when Hardouin-Mansart died in 1708, French architecture, though still impressive, lacked an innovator of Hardouin-Mansart's level. By that time, however, baroque ideas had spread from one European court to another to become a European-wide phenomenon, with Sweden, Russia, Italy, Germany, and central Europe all sites of numerous large-scale building projects. Leading the way were the Austrians, who, surviving their struggles with the Ottomans and emerging as victors along with the English in the Austrian War of Succession, entered into European politics with significant leverage. Its rulers were Leopold I (1656–1705), followed by his son Charles VI (1685–1740), and then Charles' daughter, Maria Theresa (r. 1740–80). Among the several important architects operating in Austria, Fischer von Erlach (1656–1723) was perhaps the most outstanding. He had studied art in Rome and later in Naples, in close contact with Giovanni Lorenzo Bernini. His design for the Palace of Schönbrunn (1695) set the tone for a wave of palace buildings in Austria and Germany, all taking their impetus from Versailles. Most of the palaces featured a long approach axis that integrated the palace with the constructed landscape. The buildings had forecourts or a series of forecourts and were usually located near the perimeters of existing cities.

An example of the attempt to unify a palace with its surroundings beyond what Versailles even offered was the ambition of Margrave Karl-Wilhelm von Baden-Durlach, an important Protestant regional ruler, in laying out Karlsruhe in Baden (1715–19). The palace with its tower, the Bleiturm, in which the word *blei* refers to lead ammunition, sits at the center of a vast circular road that allows forests, gardens, palace, and the urban fabric to be integrated into a single geometric unit.

Thirty-two radiating alleys lead from the tower. Inside of the nine southward-oriented allées the palace was placed with its two symmetrical wings jutting out at oblique angles. Approaching from the front, the Bleiturm, centrally located behind the palace, has the appearance of a church tower. The building, which is partly of wood, was built by the engineer Jakob Friedrich von Batzendorf, a lieutenant in Karl-WIlhelm's unit guard, according to instructions given by Karl-WIlhelm himself.

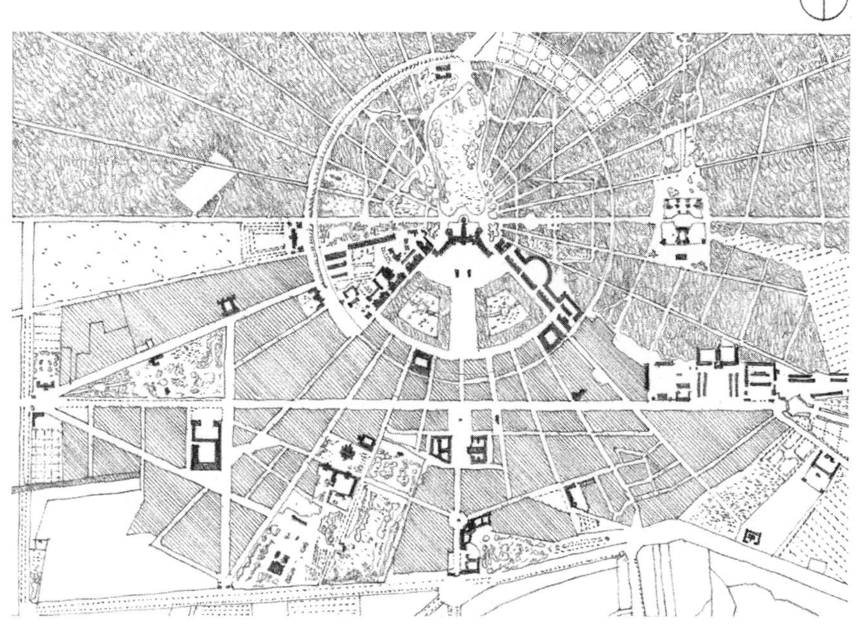

15.44 **Plan of Karlsruhe, Baden, Germany**

15.45 Valletta, Malta

15.46 Auberge de Castille, Valletta

### Valletta

Valletta on the island of Malta remains one of the greatest intact examples of baroque architecture and fortifications in the world. Since many European cities demolished their fortifications in the late 19th century to make way for urban expansion, there are few places that give such a complete picture of an 18th-century city still rooted in a late-Renaissance urban grid.

Malta was ruled independently by the Knights of Malta and served primarily as a bulwark against Ottoman incursions into the western Mediterranean. The Knights of Malta had originally been the Knights of St. John before they were expelled by Saracen armies, first from Jerusalem to Rhodes and then by the Ottomans to Malta. The Ottomans followed the knights there and laid siege to the island in 1565, but they were driven back. With the success against the Ottomans, new knights from the best noble families flocked to be enrolled, bringing in power and wealth. As the threat of invasion receded, the knight orders prospered. The relatively austere Counter-Reformation architecture that marks Valletta's early days was then abandoned for more elaborate baroque facades. The fortifications were also continually being updated and expanded. No major attacks were ever mounted against it, a testament of sorts to its reputation.

15.47 Site plan: Valletta

The Cathedral of St. John's (1573–7) reflects the ethos of the Counter-Reformation combined with clean military surfaces without windows. The plan is a very simple nave church, with side aisles used in this case as chapels by the various nations. Austere Counter-Reformation architecture did not last long as the baroque was enhanced and modified into a celebration of courtly power rather than religious restraint. Reflecting this is the Auberge of Castile (1744), with its broad front and elaborate entrance decoration. Generally, the Maltese baroque style mixes the decorative elements of the baroque with a lingering zest for sculptural and quasi-militaristic monumentality, as can be seen on the facade of the Auberge of Italy, which has at its corners powerfully articulated quoins.

**15.48 Zwinger, Dresden, Germany**

### Rococo and the Zwinger

Though architectural innovation was diffused throughout the European cultural landscape, the French were still at the center of the discussion about fashion and taste, creating around 1700 a style known as rococo. Flourishing for about three decades, until the advent of Neoclassicism, in the later decades of the century, its primary sphere was in the realm of the decorative arts, furniture, and ornamentation. It has its origins in the baroque and its insistence on the legitimacy of effect over structure. But the baroque, especially in architecture, tended toward the ponderous and oppressive. The rococo style, with its emphasis on gaiety, reveled in plant and vine forms, spirals, curves, and the playful integration of art and space.

The style is often associated with Louis XV (1710–74) who became king of France in 1715. The personality of the young king, who was informal and accessible, differed from that of his father, but we would seek in vain for any direct correlation between Louis XV and the new art form except to note that there was certainly a spirit of both gaiety and experimentation that made the rococo possible. The style came to be much disparaged, especially in the 19th century, and indeed the word rococo, though widely used today, was actually a derogatory term. In its own day, it was referred to merely as "modern."

In the realm of architecture, the rococo achieved its best expression not in France, but Bavaria and southern Germany. Examples include the Solitude Palace in Stuttgart, the church of Wies in Bavaria, and the Zwinger (1710–32), which was designed by Matthäus Daniel Pöppelmann in collaboration with sculptor Balthasar Permoser, in Dresden. The Zwinger consists of two symmetrical and mirror-reflected structures opening a space in between for a garden and fountains. They were connected on the side by a long gallery.

The structure was designed for August I, or August the Strong (1673–1733), who united Saxony and Poland, elevating Saxony into an important regional power. Like most royal personalities of the time, spectacle played a large part in the definition of power and the building certainly lived up to the demands placed on the architects. The central courtyard was used for court festivals, tournaments, and celebrations. The decorative motifs revolved around Hercules, a figure of which graces the highest point of one of the pavilions, holding the globe on his shoulders, and who was meant to be a reference to August I.

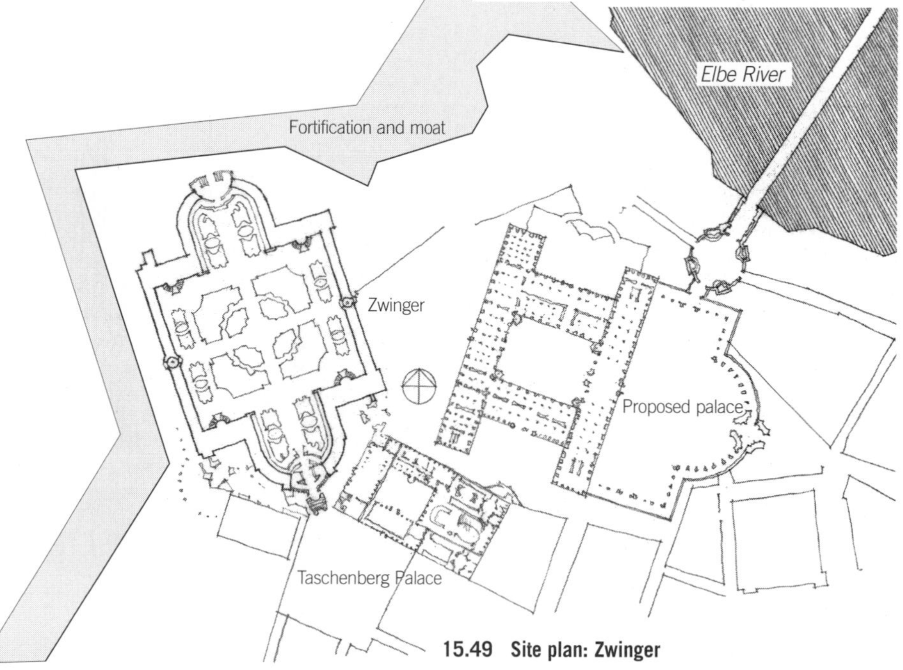


**15.49 Site plan: Zwinger**

15.50 Cathedral of Saragossa, Spain

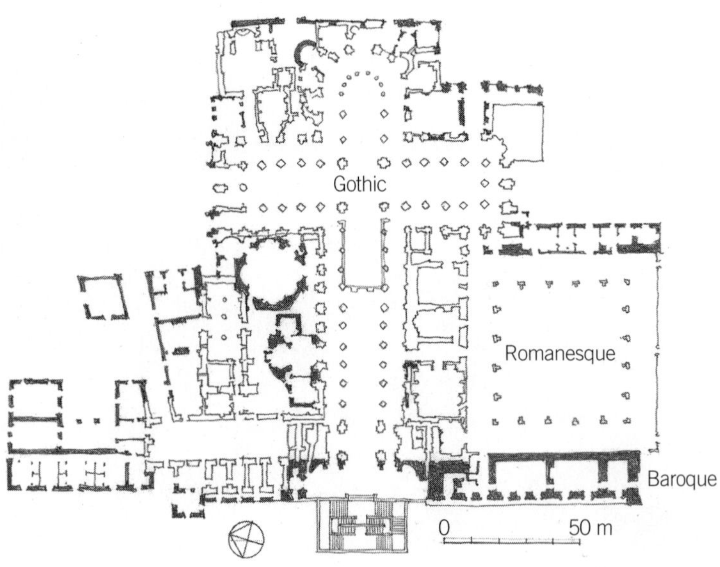


15.51 Plan: Santiago de Compostela, Spain

**Facade of Santiago de Compostela**

In 1665, upon the death of Philip IV in Madrid, the entire clergy of the capital marched through the streets. There were 1325 secular priests, 340 Franciscans, 180 Augustinians, 160 Dominicans, 130 Jesuits, 120 Mercedarians, 80 Carmelites, and 70 members of various hospital orders. But the future was not promising. Spain by then was economically defunct. Despite the problems, baroque architecture found its most flamboyant expression in Spain, Portugal, and southern Italy. The Spanish architects, similar to the south Germans, reveled in decorative illusion and created a realm in which gravity and structure seemed to play no part. Given the paucity of resources, architectural construction during this time was often limited to the facade, examples of which can be found in almost every land controlled by the Spanish, from southern Italy to Mexico. Throughout the Renaissance the facade was seen as an extension of the architectural intent of the interior. It was a type of essay on a theme that would play itself out upon entering. In the baroque style, the facade became an autonomous element related, however, to the pomp of the high altar. Though some architects like Johann Balthasar Neumann sought to downplay the altar, this was not the case in southern countries where the facade almost became the church itself, and especially in instances where baroque facades were added to existing old structures.

The supreme example is the facade of the Cathedral of Santiago de Compostela (1738), which was added to the old Romanesque church. It was fronted by a small elevated piazza with a grand staircase leading up from the Plaza del Obradoiro. At the lower level of the facade are still some residual Renaissance memories, but these are quickly surpassed the higher one goes, with the top of the facade formed by a crowd of volutes, balls, pinnacles, putti, and statues giving way to the tower bases stretching upwards on attenuated pilasters and ending at their tops in a veritable symphony of turrets and volutes.

15.52 Transparente, Toledo Cathedral, Spain

Narcisco Tomé's so-called Transparente (completed 1723) in a chapel in the Cathedral of Toledo is another example of Spanish baroque. For its construction, a space in the medieval vault was removed and the new design filled in. The Transparente caused an enormous sensation at the time of its opening, an occasion celebrated with a bullfight and public rejoicing. Its liturgical purpose was to celebrate the gift of the Holy Communion. Technically, it is neither an altar nor a chapel but a spatial-sculptural environment on the theme of the sacrament. Its purpose is to frame the Eucharist, opening at the back of the high altar of the cathedral. It can be reached by a concealed stairway behind some marble paneling. Two smaller columns hold up an entablature but the ends of the cornice curve outward like a pair of horns with angels flying and diving about above, framed by taller columns draped with vegetation. The entrance of the central cavity is crowded with figures, golden rays, and putti of unheard-of pomp. Higher up is a bas-relief of the Last Supper carved in alabaster and a representation of the Virgin's apotheosis. Higher still and beyond are more angels. Christ is seated on clouds, surrounded by prophets. The whole scene is lit by a large concealed dormer window from behind the onlooker.

15.53 Elevation: Vierzehnheiligen, near Bamberg, Germany

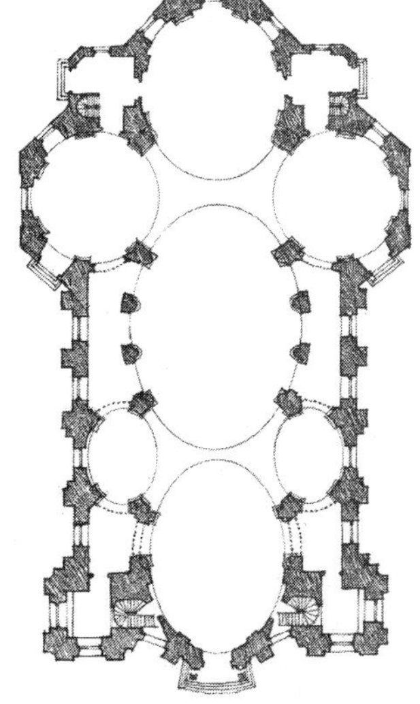

15.54 Plan: Vierzehnheiligen

15.55 Nave of Vierzehnheiligen

**Bavarian Baroque**

A compact geographical unit between the Danube to the north, the Alps to the south, the river Lech to the west and the Inn River to the east, Bavaria had been a dukedom since the late 12th century, and indeed it had been under the rule of the Wittelsbachs for almost all of that period. With a largely peasant population, and possessing only three towns with a population over 100,000, Catholicism was able to survive unimpaired through the wars of religion. But just as the Bavarians were resistant to Protestant ideals, they were also resistant to the aristocratic, urban Catholicism of Austria. The Bavarian country folk transformed the baroque into an exuberant and colorful architectural idiom filled with the perhaps sentimentalizing but emotionally-felt detail and imagery of their faith. The interior of the churches in villages and monasteries are usually painted white and are light-filled and airy with gilded overlays contributing to a dematerialized, buoyant effect. The dome, such an important element in Italian architectural composition, plays no major role in Bavaria.

Particularly significant were the ceiling frescoes, in which it appears that the barrier between earth and heaven has dissolved. The Church Militant looks upward at the splendor of the Church Triumphant. When viewed in the right light conditions, these frescoes can be overwhelming in the richness and variety of color, the marshaling of the figures—the apostles, the saints, the fathers of the church—positioned at decisive points in the composition, the angels and the putti flying, playing, sitting, leaning, adoring, against blue skies, among clouds floating in and out, and forming a playful, artistic expression all their own. Rarely is the treatment heavy and burdensome, yielding an astonishing thematic and symbolic unity.

Vaults were usually of brick, one layer thick, reinforced from the top with ribs. The bottom third of the vault was usually strengthened by an extra layer of brick mortar poured over the whole to produce a crude reinforced concrete shell. By avoiding stone, these vaults were quickly built and inexpensive to construct. Precise calculations were not required, nor were the elaborate lift machines that would have been necessary for heavy stones. They were also free from the problems of statics and often required support at only a few points.

15.56 Painted vault of Vierzehnheiligen

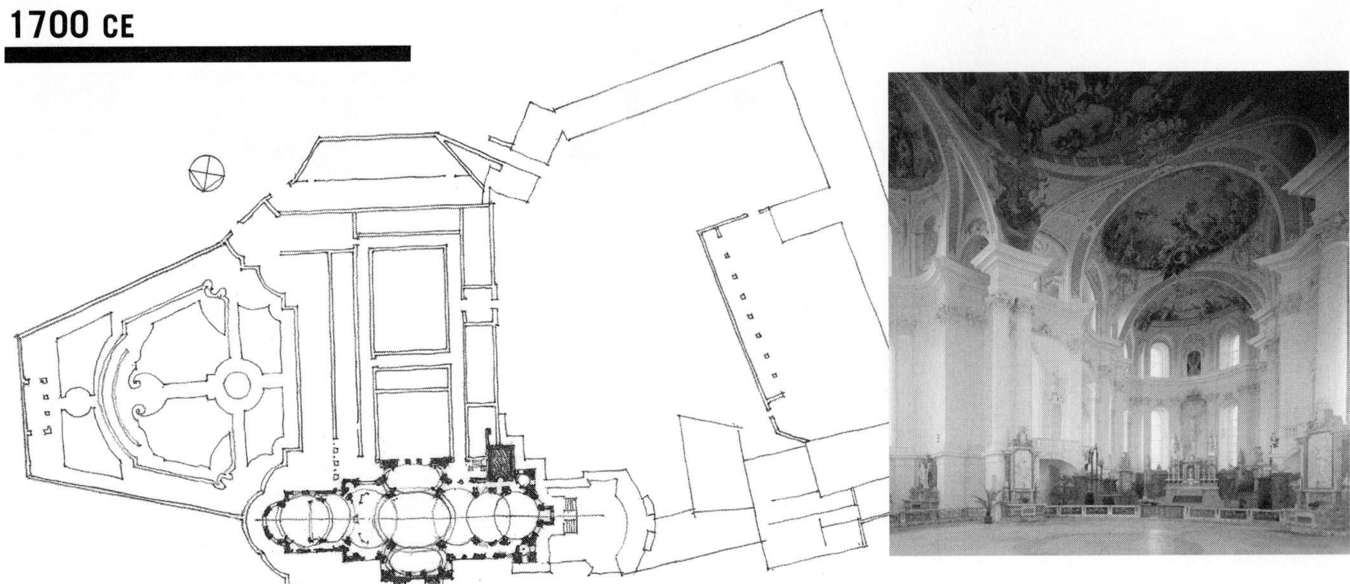

15.57 **Site plan of Abbey of Saints Ulrich and Afra, Neresheim, Germany**

15.58 **Interior: Church of Neresheim**

### Neresheim

The south German baroque is mainly the story of a few eminent architects, assisted by painters, stucco workers, and sculptors of no less distinction. Among these are Johann Michael Fischer (1692–1766) and Johann Balthasar Neumann (1687–1753). Neumann's most extraordinary work is perhaps the Pilgrimage Church of Vierzehnheiligen (1743–72) at a Franciscan monastery near the town of Bamberg that had become a pilgrimage site in the mid-15th century following a miraculous apparition.

Neumann's last and most comprehensively conceived major project, however, was the church of Neresheim (1747–92). It was not freestanding but integrated into the fabric of a Benedictine monastery and even included at its choir end an old tower from an earlier Romanesque church. On the interior, oval and circular vaults are supported on an undulating frame of columns, pilasters, arches, and piers. Light floods the interior.

Though the tendency when experiencing and studying a space like this is to think of it as decorative and plastic, one must remember that Neumann was an officer in the engineering corps and that his buildings were just as much a testament to his engineering as to his design skill. He used wall piers or short sections of wall turned at right angles to the nave as primary load-bearing elements, eliminating the necessity for a solid continuous outer surface. Vaults were carried by three-dimensional arches. The exterior shell of the church was relatively plain.

The oval at the crossing is placed lengthwise to the longitudinal interior, stretching between that part of the building used by the community and the choir at the rear, and is reserved for the monks. The oval is counterbalanced by smaller ovals that evoke the tradition of the transept without interfering in the spatial liturgical rituals, which did not require such spaces. The ovals are connected by curving vaults that leave one in doubt as to how they work structurally, with light from the large windows visually dissolving the borders of the different spatial elements. The interior has been described as serene, with the dominant tonality of white punctuated by a minimum amount of decoration.

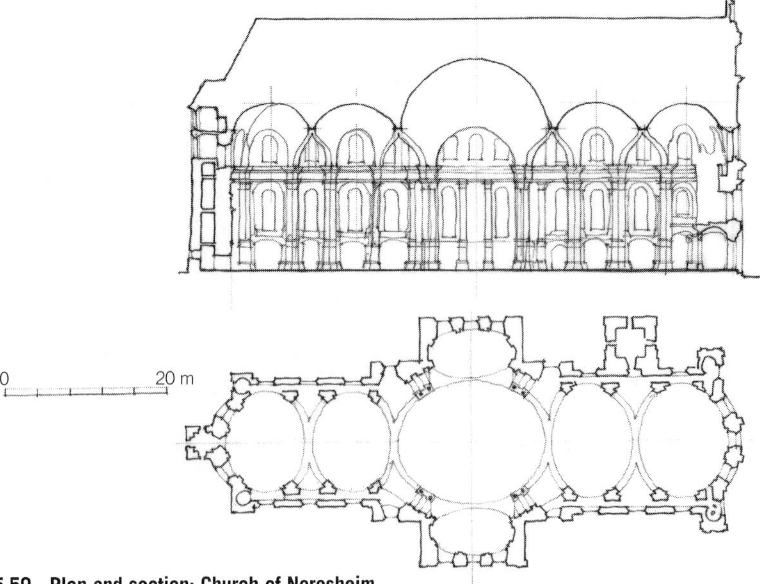


15.59 **Plan and section: Church of Neresheim**

15.60 **Chinese Teahouse, Sans Souci, Potsdam, Germany**

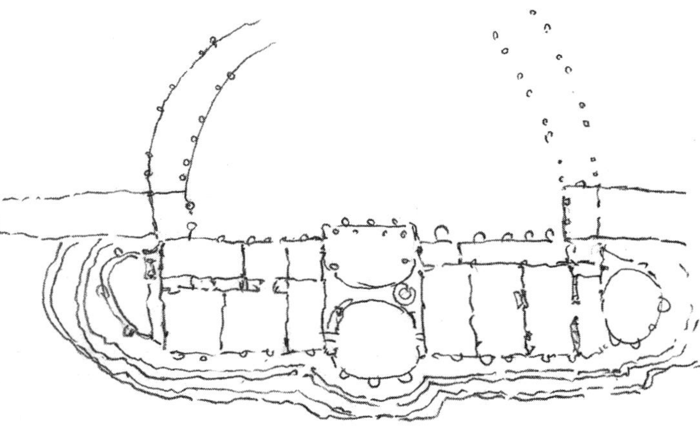

15.61 **Sketch of Sans Souci by Frederick the Great in 1744**

**Sans Souci**

The first detailed accounts of Chinese life arrived in Lisbon in the 1520s with others soon following, written by missionaries that were sent to China, India, Indonesia, and Japan. In 1585 Pope Gregory XIII instructed the Spanish priest Juan Gonzalez de Mendoza to set down all that was known about China. In *The historie of the great and mightie kingdome of China, and the situation thereof*, the first more broadly-read treatise on the subject, de Mendoza mentions palaces and gardens and describes houses so grand that they reminded him of Rome. But these bits of information were (and remained) saturated with myths and legends. The first book with more substantial content was *The History of That Great and Renowned Monarchy of China* (1655), written by Alvarez Semedo, who had spent 22 years in China. This was followed by the Dutch Jan Nieuhof's *Embassy*, which appeared in Latin, French, and English editions (1669) and was the first book with more than passing interest in Chinese architecture. Because of the use of wood in domestic architecture, Nieuhof found Chinese architecture lacking in beauty, as would any European trained that stone was the only material of strength and permanence.

The imperial palaces, however, did interest him, and he included several engravings of pagodas and palaces. These descriptions fascinated the upper class, and around 1675 Louis XIV built the Trianon de Porcelain, which, though in shape and form Western, had a roof with blue-and-white patterned tiles, creating what was thought to be a reasonable approximation of the porcelain pattern used at the famous pagoda at Nanjing. The building did not last long, partially because of leaks in the roof, but it set in play a series of royal Chinese pavilions or what the Germans called *Porzellankammern*, the most famous being the Chinese teahouse at Sans Souci palace in Potsdam (1757), built by the Prussian emperor, Frederick the Great (Frederick II).

The palace, which served as his summer retreat, had a vast park that contained several pavilions, one of which was the Chinese teahouse. The gilt columns, which support the roof, are in the form of palm trunks opening out in luxuriant sprays of shoots as they meet the entablature. Life-sized gilt Chinese figures sit at the base of the columns, playing musical instruments and engaging in animated conversation. Soon, Chinese pavilions, together with Turkish tents, were common in pleasure gardens of the time. Chinese porcelain was also making its way through the markets of Holland, adding more fuel to the fire with members of the gentry creating collections of their favorite pieces.

15.62 **Chinese Teahouse, Sans Souci, Potsdam**

15.63 **Stratford Hall Plantation, near Montross, Virginia, USA**

15.64 **Interior, Stratford Hall Plantation**

## GEORGIAN ARCHITECTURE

With the ascent of King George I to the throne in 1711 significant changes began to take shape in England, leading to the rise of the Whigs who, beginning in 1714, would dominate English politics for 70 years, with important consequences in the field of architecture. George I was actually a German from Hanover who ruled to a large extent through a prime minister, Robert Walpole, a Whig statesman who held his post through the reigns of George I and George II. The Whigs, who followed a pro-mercantile policy, welcomed the lack of interference from the king. And yet, despite the freeflowing mercantile spirit of the age, architecture during this time took on a notably uniform style that came to be known as Georgian. Though grand and stately, it was overtly simple and purposefully understated. Walls were unadorned brick, and windows and doorways were made of white wood. The facade was symmetrically arranged around the entrance, close to the ground or accessed by a short flight of steps. Grander homes might have a portico or pilasters. Some had quoins on the corners.

The significance of the Georgian style rested not in its search for architectural innovations, but its circumstance as the first style that one can truly label as national. The baroque, by way of contrast, was so widely disseminated that it cannot, despite regional variations, be seen as anything other than a European phenomenon. The Georgian style was unique to England and its colonies.

The practice of contrasting the brick with the white wood trim originated in Holland and thus reflected the strength of an aesthetic associated with England's Protestant majority. The Georgian style was also particularly attractive to the emerging mercantile aristocracy. Unlike in France, where the aristocracy played little role in the industrialization of the land, in England this was much more common. The landed gentry were heavily involved in coal and agricultural ventures, both in England and abroad.

The Duke of Chandos, for example, was involved in speculations that varied from an oyster fishery and a soap factory to land in what would later form part of New York State in the United States. This was also a time when Robert Clive's victories in India placed Madras and Bengal under British control. James Wolfe's capture of French-held Quebec in 1759 opened up trade in fish and fur.

Georgian-style buildings in England and Ireland range from Uppark (1690), built for the noted Whig politician Forde Grey (later Earl of Tankerville), to Bellamont Forest in Ireland (ca. 1725) by the gentleman architect Sir Edward Lovett Pearce. Georgian-style architecture also was used throughout the English-controlled American colonies. The Stratford Hall Plantation (1738) in Virginia, at the head of a large estate that grew tobacco for export to England, was designed for Thomas Lee, an important businessman in the Virginia colonies and for a time acting governor of the state.

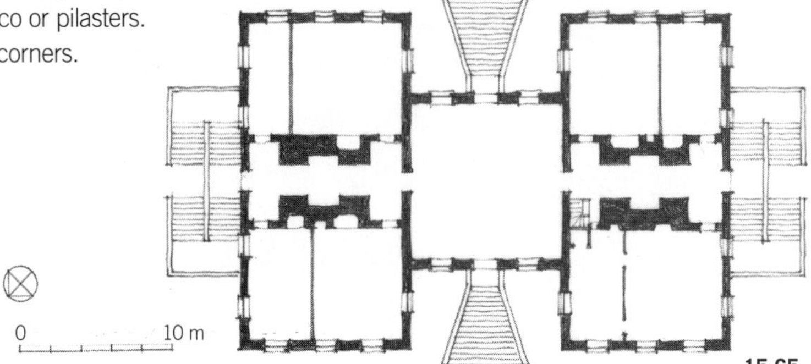


15.65 **Plan: Stratford Hall Plantation**

15.66 **Chiswick House, near London, England**

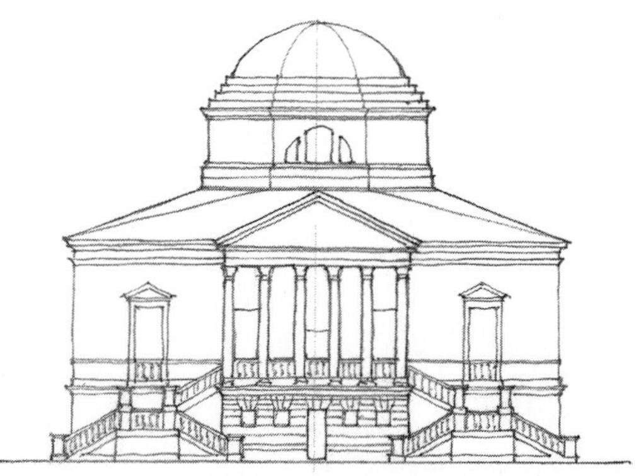

15.67 **Elevation: Chiswick House**

### Chiswick House

Underlying Georgian architecture was the Palladian Revival, which blossomed after the 1715 publication of *Vitruvius Britannicus*, written by the Scottish lawyer and architect Colen Campbell, who proclaimed the superiority of antiquity over what he argued were the affected and licentious forms of the baroque. The work of Inigo Jones was held in just as high esteem as that of Palladio. This book, together with the publication of the three volumes of *The Architecture of A. Palladio* (1715, 1717, 1725) by the Venetian Giacomo Leoni, sparked a Palladian movement that saw itself also as a proto-national style given that it could also be seen as an updated Inigo Jones style.

Palladianism invested a great deal of energy in substantiating the idea of the primacy of the natural law of proportion, still a rather novel idea in English design practice. Facade, plan, and volume had to be unified into a formal whole. And yet, despite this penchant for abstraction, the external detailing had to adhere closely to Palladio's works, thus the frequent use of rusticated bases, pilastered upper elevations, and pedimented entrances.

Palladio's legacy bore an aura of authority and exclusion and thus played into the class consciousness of the gentry. His treatises offered relatively cheap but prestigious models to imitate The role that print played cannot be underestimated, for the distribution of plans, plates, and treatises was an essential part of the Palladian style's success. It could be easily taught, mastered and copied.

The Palladian movement reached its height in the hands of Richard Boyle, otherwise known as Lord Burlington (1694–1753), an influential Whig politician. Upon inheriting a great fortune from his grandfather and after trips to Italy in 1714 and 1719, he began his career as a gentleman architect, hoping to promote neo-Palladianism as a nationally accepted style by influencing the Office of the Works to pick candidates of his choice for commissions. The most important of his buildings was his own (1723–29), Chiswick House, which was not actually a house but rather a pavilion for his library and for entertaining friends. The basic idea of the Chiswick House is that of Villa Rotonda, though the facade is modeled on Palladio's Villa Foscari. Certain aspects were also taken from Vincenzo Scamozzi, such as the obelisk chimneys, the octagonal rather than circular main hall, and the string course at the balustrade level that wraps around the entire building.

Palladian motifs became common in the palaces on the Strand, a long street that ran along the north side of the Thames River and that linked the old walled City of London, the country's economic capital, with Buckingham Palace (though it was still relatively modest at that time) and Westminster, the symbolic and political capital of the country. The presence of so many grand houses in this area gave London a very different character from Paris, where the hotels had to be carved out of the urban fabric.

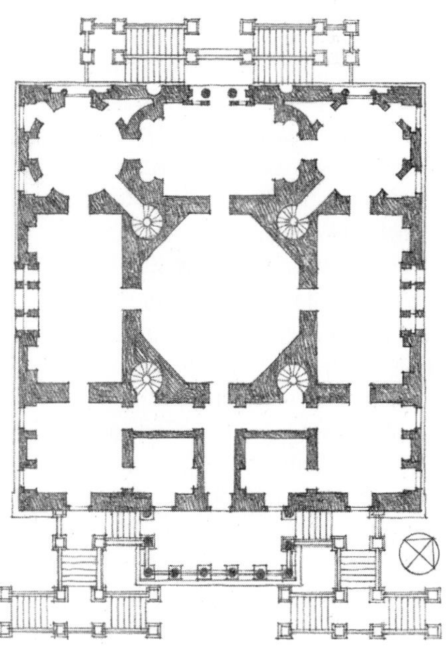

15.68 **Plan: Chiswick House**

15.70 King's Chapel, Boston

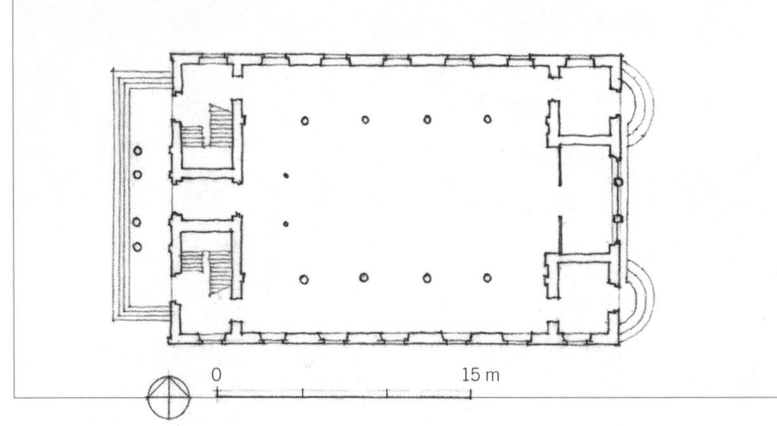


15.69 Plan: King's Chapel, Boston, Massachusetts, USA

### King's Chapel

There is nothing more revealing than a list of items carried in British ships to the Americas: drinking glasses, cups, teapots, pans, knives, candles, desks, paper, soap, medicines, and books. Such a massive export of cultural commodities not only for bare subsistence but also for the enhancement of daily life was to become a hallmark of the English method of colonial politics. Boston, one of the largest seaports of colonial Britain, boasted an impressive set of houses, warehouses, shops, and meetinghouses. The number of Britons on the north Atlantic coast increased nearly twentyfold between 1660 and 1670. The city became successful so fast that in 1684, the Royal crown, now considerably more powerful than it was just a few decades earlier, took control of the colony, paving the way for the establishment of the first Anglican parishes on the model of Sir Christopher Wren's London. The most important of these was centered on King's Chapel (1749–54). It was designed by Peter Harrison, who had just recently arrived from England. He was not a gentleman-architect like Lord Burlington, and certainly not a brilliant designer like Nicholas Hawksmoor. He was, however, thoroughly for the Georgian spirit that had made Palladianism its central credo. In the case of Harrison, he had learned Georgian Palladianism from books and publications and eventually became its prime representative in North America.

In Newport, Harrison also built the Redwood Library (1748–50) and the Touro Synagogue (1759–63), the latter commissioned by descendants of Sephardic Jews who had been expelled from Spain, Portugal, and France in the 15th and 16th centuries, and who had settled in various places throughout Europe. The members of the small congregation were attracted to Newport, because under governor Roger Williams they were assured freedom of religion. Harrison drew on the Bevis-Marks Synagogue of London (1701), which was a simple box with surrounding galleries on three sides; it, too, was designed for a Sephardic community.

The 12 columns supporting the women's galleries on the interior represent the 12 tribes of Israel. They are made of single tree trunks, the lower ones being Ionic, the upper ones Corinthian. There were no pews. Instead, the floor at the center was reserved for a table for the reading of the law. The men sat along the perimeter on the ground floor and the women above in the balconies. The building has a sense of intimacy and openness that Harrison had not been able to achieve in the King's Chapel.

15.71 Elevation: King's Chapel

15.72 **Stowe Gardens, Buckinghamshire, England**

**Stowe Gardens**

As discussed, there were two architectural trends in England in the early decades of the 18th century, neo-Palladianism and the baroque. This is clear if one compares the Chiswick House and St. Mary Woolnoth, which were more or less contemporary constructions. By the 1730s, both styles came under attack by a movement known as the "picturesque." Though Protestantism, with its call for moral moderation, played a part in this, it was also enmeshed in the rise of English nationalism and, beyond that, in the political debates raging between Whigs and Tories. The Whigs favored free enterprise as exemplified by the philosophies of James Watt and Adam Smith, who were champions of policies that catered to the needs of aristocratic landowners who wished to be as free as possible from royal whim. The Tories saw the role of the king in more beneficial terms as the symbol of all that was noble and lasting. Palladianism, generally speaking, had its supporters among the Whig elite, who saw in the style a parallel to their mercantile policies and social ambitions. It was a language of mathematics, proportion, and geometry, unencumbered by the arbitrary and the whimsical.

By midcentury, even though the Whigs remained in power, they came to be criticized by those eager for a more principled accounting in respect to England's colonial and mercantile policies. Corruption among the Whig elite made them an easy target, with critics hoping for a return to the conservative notion of royal privilege. The "picturesque" garden, as it came to be known, was to no small degree a direct consequence of this critique of the rationalism and modernity of Whig politics.

The term picturesque should, therefore, not lead us to think that these gardens were lacking in ideological content. Rather, the type of painting to which the term picturesque refers tended to commemorate some significant and unified human action, historical or mythical, that many of the conservative elite who favored a relationship between church and state thought had been lost in the corruptible world of the pro-mercantile Whigs.

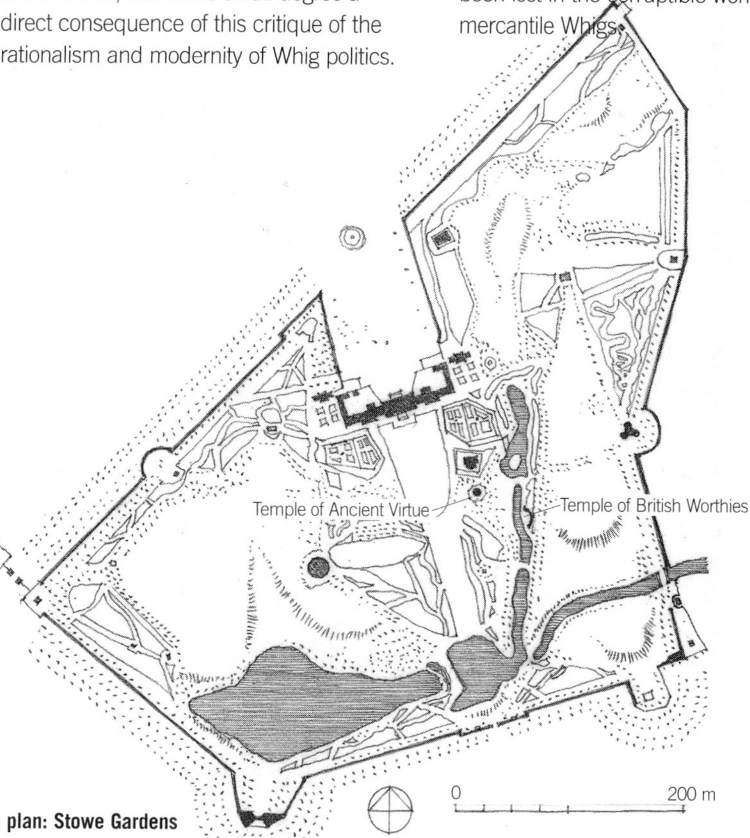


15.73 **Site plan: Stowe Gardens**

15.74 Temple of British Worthies, Stowe Gardens

15.75 Temple of Ancient Virtue, Stowe Gardens

**Temple of British Worthies**

Key to the success of the new gardens, therefore, was that they be experienced not only by their owners and friends but also by a wide range of personages drawn from the upper and middle class. At the time, garden tourism was on the increase and already an important part of upper-class social life. The "English gardens" tapped into and furthered that phenomenon.

The theoretical origins of the English garden lie in the writings and designs of Alexander Pope (1688–1744), eminent essayist, satirist, and critic of Whig policies. Among his achievements was the translation of the *Iliad* and *Odyssey* into English, the epics appealing to the English thirst for noble heroism. It is now commonly accepted that Pope, together with other literary friends of Lord Richard Temple Cobham (1675–1749), helped articulate the governing iconography of the Elysian Fields, based on the myth of Elysium, paradise for heroes of the gods. Imagery of the Elysian Fields was at the center of the design of the gardens of Stowe (begun in 1731), which were built for Lord Cobham, field marshal and politician. Cobham, forced to resign his military commission in 1733, joined the ranks of Whig opponents. It was then that he decided to create the garden.

Placed in the landscape was a Temple of Ancient Virtue, a round Ionic *tempietto* honoring the great law givers and writers of the ancient world, among them Socrates and Homer; near it as ironic counterthrust was the Temple of Modern Virtue, a ruined structure featuring a headless figure that was generally taken to represent Robert Walpole, head of the Whig party. The meaning of these two buildings is made clear to the visitor by the presence of a Temple of British Worthies, a shrine to great Britons arranged in two groups of eight along a curving wall, honoring William Shakespeare, John Milton, Queen Elizabeth I, Inigo Jones, and Alexander Pope, among others; not too far away is the Grenville Column, a memorial to the brother of Earl Temple, Captain Thomas Grenville, who died aboard Lord Cobham's ship fighting the French in 1747. At the top of the column, the figure of Heroic Poetry fingers a scroll with the words *Non nisi grandia canto*, her face turned toward the temple of British Worthies.

15.76 Temple of Modern Virtue

Other elements were added to the garden later, the Cook Monument, added in 1778, commemorating Captain James Cook's discoveries in the South Pacific, and the Seasons Fountain, honoring the visit by the Prince of Wales to Stowe in 1805.

To some extent the idea of a landscape, however artificial, conceptualized around a dignified, civilizational armature parallels the English colonial experience in the Americas. Unlike the French, who encountered strong resistance from the Indians and who, because they never had enough people in the colonies to suppress the Indians, began to study and to analyze their habits so as to cooperate with them in trade and then to lead them into conversion, the New Englanders, except in the Carolinas, found little organized resistance among the Indians who, at that particular place and time, were less socially unified than those in the French settlements in Canada or along the Mississippi River. While contact with the Indians led the French to study and ask questions about the origins of civilization, the English, at least those back home in their gardens, began to muse on the mythological underpinnings of European history. One could hypothesize that it was in the English gardens, with their often pedagogical and ideological notes, that we begin to see the first traces of what later was termed "Eurocentrism."

**QING DYNASTY**

The Manchus, a nomadic people closely related to the Mongolians, were long poised to take power in China. By the early 1600s, under their charismatic leader Nargaci, they had already built up a sizable kingdom in Manchuria, at China's northwestern periphery, incorporating areas of northern Korea and eastern China. In 1616 they built their capital at Shenyang based on the axial spatial models of Chinese capitals and palaces. Early in the 17th century, under the influence of the Mongols, the Manchus converted to Tibetan Buddhism. After the fall of the Yuan Dynasty in 1368, Buddhism had waned amongst the Mongols, but in the 17th century, with the rise of the fifth Dalai Lama, Tibetan Buddhism experienced a resurgence. With their Chinese-style capital and manners and their Buddhist religious practices, the Manchus were already a hybrid of the major forces of east Asia when they walked into Beijing's Forbidden City in 1644 to establish China's longest lasting dynasty (1644–1911). Shun Chih (or Shunzhi, r. 1644–62), the first Manchu ruler of China, named their dynasty the Qing, or the "pure" dynasty. The Qing were China's third foreign dynasty. But the Qing projected themselves not as foreign usurpers but as the legitimate inheritors, the rightful claimants, of the Yuan throne.

One of the Shunzhi emperor's first decrees was to rebuild the parts of the Forbidden City that had been burnt by the retreating Ming. His only specification was that ducts be built into the Hall of Supreme Harmony so that heat could be pumped into it. To stamp their identity onto the city, however, they renamed all the major gates and pavilions and changed the ceremonies associated with the Temple of Heaven to reflect the new Manchu cosmic order. As an ethnic minority in the capital, they were very careful to ensure that military and political power remained with the Manchu elite. Non-Manchu Han Chinese men were required to shave their foreheads and wear their hair in a long ponytail called the *que*. Differences between the Qing and the Han were also played out in the urban fabric. In 1649 the northern city, the traditional heart of Beijing, was reserved only for Manchus. As a consequence, all the Han Chinese had to move into the southern city, which had always been underdeveloped, but which, as consequence of the new influx, developed into the commercial heart of the city. New temples and monasteries were built. Theaters, teahouses, shops of all kinds, guild halls, academies of classical learning, and public buildings were constructed. As wood became scarce, many of the residential and other "lesser" secular structures were made from stone and brick.

While maintaining their political dominance, the Qing insisted that all religions and ethnic groups be recognized. Confucianism, Daoism, Buddhism, Lamaism, Islam, and even Christianity were all allowed to be practiced. In the 15th and 16th centuries, several royal emissaries from European nations, such as Portugal, England, and Holland, were sent to the Chinese court. But, as with the Ming, the Qing emperors received these emissaries with feigned courtesy. The idea that there were civilizations as powerful as theirs elsewhere in the world was beyond their purview. Tibetan Buddhism, however, received particular favor from the new rulers. In 1651 the Shunzhi emperor invited the fifth Dalai Lama to visit Beijing. In connection with that visit, Shunzhi ordered the construction of three Tibetan-styled white stupas, two of them in the Imperial City. One of these was the bell-shaped White Stupa, the gigantic landmark of the Western Park or Beihai. Beihai, east of the Forbidden City but within the city walls, had first been developed by the Yuan and the Jin, and under the Ming the waters were dammed to create three artificial lakes, with an island in the middle lake. Shunzhi placed the White Stupa on the highest point of the artificial hill on the island, so that it was clearly visible from a distance. It was bigger than the one previously erected at the Miaoyin Monastery (1271) by the Yuan.

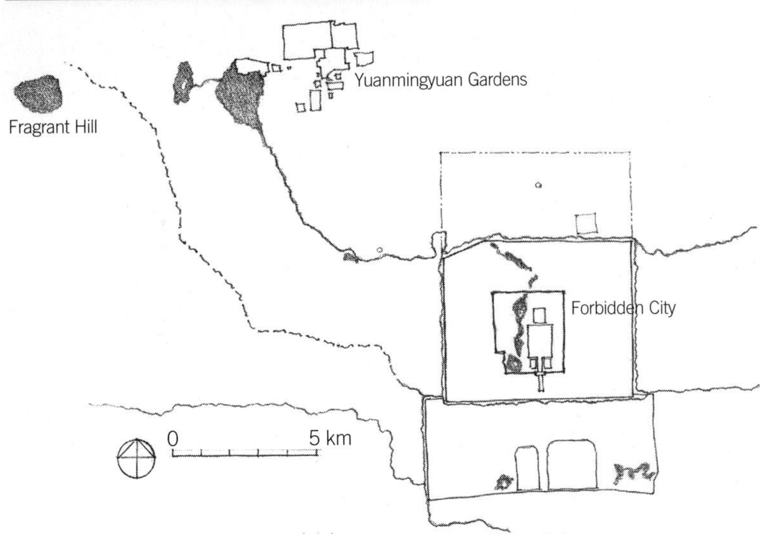

15.77 **Location of gardens northwest of Qing-dynasty Beijing, China**

15.78 **Remains: Yuanmingyuan Gardens, Beijing**

### Yuanmingyuan Gardens

By the middle of the 18th century the Qing had constructed more than 40 new palaces in the Forbidden City and in the privileged areas to its northwest, both within and outside the imperial city. They had also started building imperial tombs for themselves, following earlier imperial practices. But unlike the Ming emperors, who confined most of their court activities to the Forbidden City, the Qing were avid travelers and built several palaces and temples in distant parts of their empire. More than the Song and the Ming, the Qing were obsessed with large palatial gardens. The area to the northwest of Beijing was a largely flat plain with a gentle gradient toward the southeast, where the Yuan, Jin, and Ming had built summer retreats. The Qing converted these into huge garden palace complexes, exploiting numerous springs and rivulets that traverse the area. The Qing built waterways and reservoirs to ensure a perennial flow and distribution of water.

The largest of these gardens was the Yuanmingyuan (*yuan* means garden), built in the 1720s. Although its palaces and pavilions were similar to the axial courtyard structures of other palaces, such as those in the Forbidden City, their distribution and layout, at least in plan, is extremely fluid in contrast to the very formal axialities of the Forbidden City.

Entered from the south, the Yuanmingyuan was dominated by a palace with a small front lake and a larger back lake to frame it. The back lake had nine islands, each designed with its own pavilions, palaces, and scenic spots. North of this complex was a dense fabric of secondary buildings, laid out in a closely packed system of interconnected islands.

The eastern half of Yuanmingyuan was dominated by the large Fuhai Lake, in the middle of which were three small interconnected islands, representative of the three mythical islands of the Immortals supposedly located in China's eastern sea. Fuhai Lake was also surrounded by a string of nine connected islands with pavilions and hills designed for scenic views and strolls. Yuanmingyuan had 350 buildings organized into 123 building complexes.

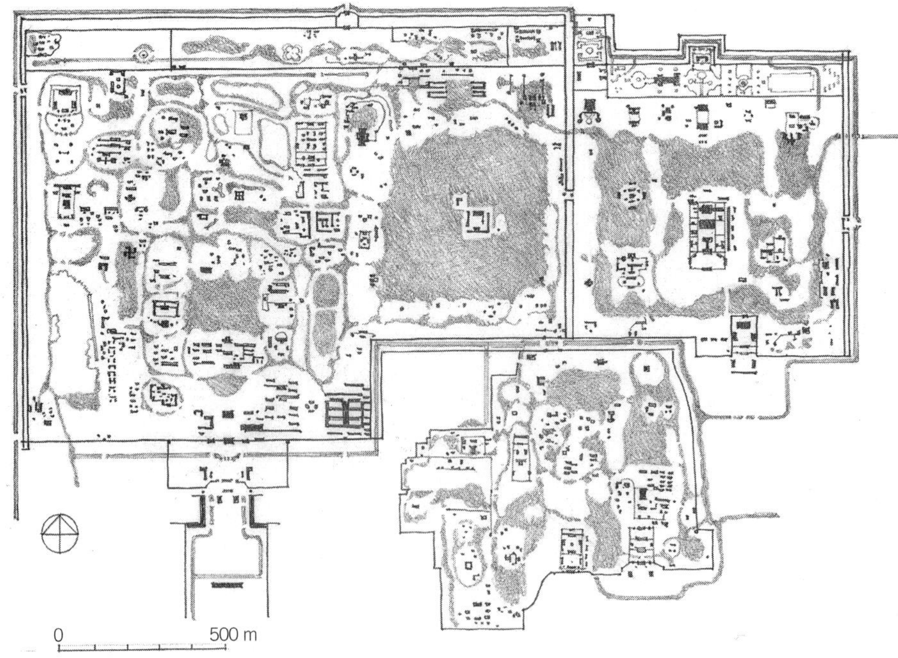


15.79 **Plan of three Yuanmingyuan Gardens**

15.80 View from Qingyi's stroll path

15.81 Qingyi garden pavilion, Beijing

**Qingyi Garden**

Later, Qianlong added a new garden, originally called Qingyi Garden (1750–64) and now known as the Summer Palace. Here he built another series of palaces and pavilions around a large oval lake that was separated from two smaller lakes by long narrow islands. A stroll path went around the lake and across all the small islands. In the middle of the main lake was a small artificial island, connected to the edge on the east by a long, arched, graceful bridge. The north edge of the lake was dominated by a huge palace and a Buddhist shrine complex, raised high on a solid stone platform, on axis with the central island. In the west the horizon was filled with a series of long mountains with distinct peaks. A pagoda and several pavilions are built on the crests of the peaks.

Chinese gardens were intended to evoke the spirit of the order of nature, distilled to its essence. The design skill lay in ensuring that every element functioned in a way that was thought to be harmonious with the whole from the perspective of viewing sites experienced in the process of strolling along the paths.

A garden's accomplishments were described as a function of its scenic spots. They were thought of as embodied poems and three-dimensional paintings. Symmetry was abhorred. At the same time, all the expectations and conveniences of a royal palace and seat of government were to be fulfilled. There are three palpable visual foci at the Summer Palace: the island in the middle of the lake, the Buddhist shrine at the northern edge, and the tall pagoda on the hills in the west. Although the Buddhist shrine is the largest element, the island is in the middle and constantly attracts the eye. And yet, as one walks around, one realizes that the pagoda in the distance always seems to be in the middle of all views, becoming, in fact, the best-remembered part of the garden.

The compositional ideas were derived from principles described in texts such as the Ji Cheng's *Yuan Zhi*, or "Gardening," written in the early 17th century. Ji Cheng invoked design concepts such as "suitability" "taking advantage," "refinement," "simplicity," and "changeability or unexpectedness," which were to be used to create places that have qualities such as "the real and the false," "assembling and spreading," "unevenness and neatness," "connecting and separating," "open and closed," and "level and solid." How these concepts were actually materialized required training in Chinese aesthetics. In addition, how the garden changed through the 24 hours of the day and in different seasons was to be anticipated and expressed.

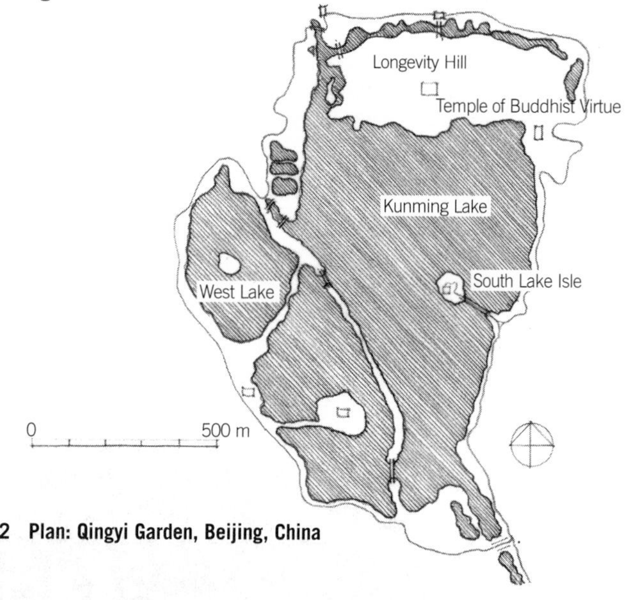


15.82 Plan: Qingyi Garden, Beijing, China

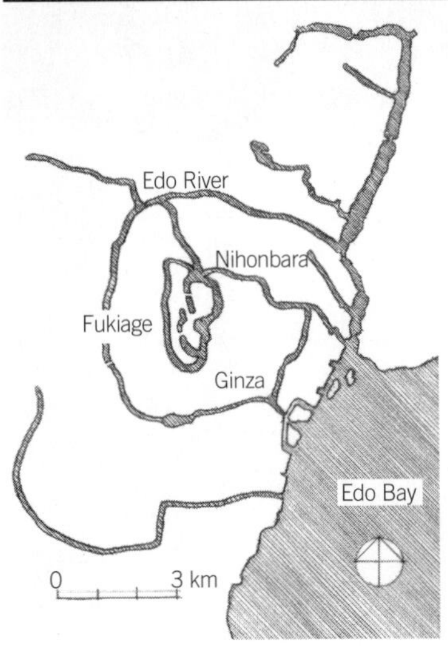


15.83 **Original spiral plan of Edo, Japan**

15.84 **Street in Edo (Tokyo) with shops, architectural drawing, 1876**

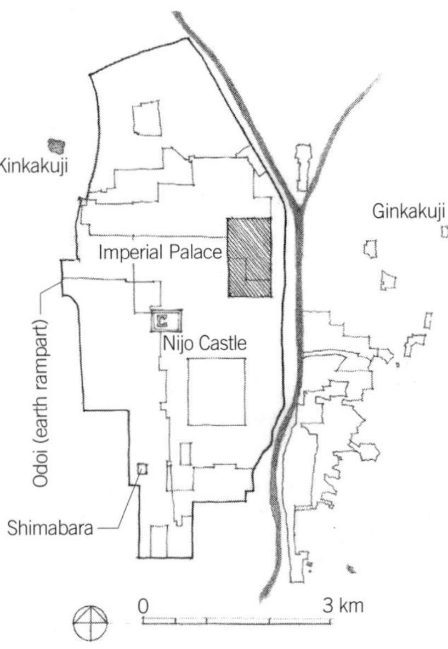


15.85 **Plan of Kyoto, Japan**

### Edo, Kyoto's Odoi, and Shimabara

The Tokugawa shoguns' political strength created a long period of relative peace that enabled trade and commerce to thrive, in particular with the Qing of China and with the Dutch and Portuguese who had just established new trading ports in Japan. The shoguns' vision of Japanese society, however, was not drawn from a mercantile world but from a militaristic image of a lost, well-ordered past. For the Tokugawa a highly ceremonialized and hierarchical code of conduct known as the Bakufu code, in which everyone had a designated place in the social fabric, was their preferred vision of society. One of the shoguns' problems, however, was to define their difference from the imperial family, to whom they were subservient by ceremony, but not in power. Their solution was to distance themselves. In 1603, the first Tokugawa shogun Ieyasu decided to rule from a new city, away from Kyoto, the imperial city. Under the Tokugawa, Edo (now Tokyo) became the de facto capital of Japan even though the emperor resided in Kyoto. They laid out Edo according to all the requisite Confucian-derived principles of imperial master planning. It was conceived as a spiral, though accommodations had to be made for geography. It was also developed in accordance with the need for security as well as symbolism, with its 32 major gateways guarding the various lines of approach to the center. Their distribution points were correlated with the 12 zodiac signs, integral to the Chinese astrological and calendrical system. In Edo, the populace was not allowed to mix. Each class was placed in different sections of the city. The *fudai* daimyo, the hereditary vassals who served as the Tokugawa retainers, were located to the northeast of the castle. Lower ranking samurai were spread in the subsequent sections of the spiral with the *chonin*, the merchants and artisans who serviced the feudal order, collected in the outmost part southwest of the city. Silver brokers lived in one neighborhood, gold brokers in another, and so forth.

Unlike Edo, where builders could start from scratch, in Kyoto, as Nicholas Fiévé has argued, the Tokugawa had to reform the city to meet the strictures of the Bakufu code. In the preshogunate Muromachi period (1336–1573), Kyoto's primary urban spatial division lay between the imperial spaces, which were distinctive and separate, and all the rest, which were hierarchical in size and prestige but integrated into the same urban fabric. Thus the temples, the homes of nobles and the commoners, the commercial establishments and the spaces of entertainment, all shared the same neighborhoods. Hierarchies were mixed. Civic authority was disaggregated, with individual areas under the "control" of their neighborhood, aristocratic family, or temple. One of the first acts of the new shogun appointed governor of Kyoto, Maeda Gen'l (1539–1602) was to build a new central thoroughfare, running north-south, that cut open some of the old blocks. This opened up new street frontage, which was quickly occupied by commercial establishments and houses. Then, in 1591, Hideyoshi defined the border of the city by building an earthen rampart (the Odoi). Trapezoidal in section, the Odoi was 9 meters at the base and between 3 and 6 meters high. It was topped by a wood and bamboo fence. A canal or minimoat 6 to 18 meters wide was excavated outside. The world within the Odoi was called the *rakuchu,* or the urbanized, world and the rest *rakugai,* or the outside world. All forms of internal enclosures and fortifications were then demolished, erasing all signs of the localized authorities. Some of the major Buddhist temples were moved outside the walls, in particular on the eastern hills. The members of the warrior class (the *buke*) were made to settle right next to the Nijo Castle and the Kyoto Governor's Palace, located just north of the castle. The members of the aristocracy were relocated to the peripheries of the imperial palace. The rest of the city was given over to the common man. Special quarters were also designated at the margins of the city for the lowest classes—the *eta* (the stained) and the *hinin* (the non-humans). In this way, the city came to be ordered according to the Bakufu code.

15.86 Facsimile of Tobei Kamei's block print: Shimabara geisha district

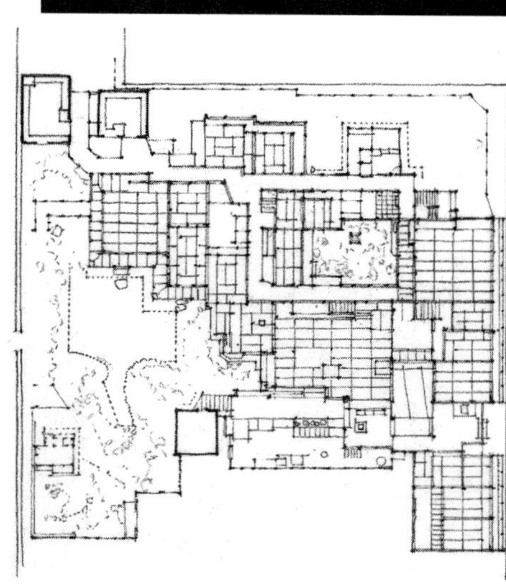

15.87 Plan of Sumiya, Kyoto, Japan

Kyoto's prostitutes, however, were a constant threat to the Bakufu code, because they conducted their business in the mixed public space of the street. In 1640 the prostitutes were ordered confined to a single area that came to be called the Shimabara. It was located in the southwest corner of the city, within the Odoi but far from its core and in the middle of one of the undeveloped stretches of land. The Shimabara was enclosed with its own cob wall, complete with a moat, whose purpose of course was not to prevent anybody from coming in but to keep the prostitutes from going out. A single gate on the east side controlled all movement in and out. Some 207 meters long and 246 meters wide, and with the nearest building in the city 400 meters away, this new prostitution quarter was in essence a miniwalled city, a zone of exclusion within the exclusive zone of the city. Here prostitutes of several classes catered to a clientele of every class. In general, the cheaper prostitutes were clustered closer to the main gate and the more exclusive ones toward the western end. With the merchants, warriors, and aristocrats sharing the same space and the same prostitutes, the Shimabara quickly became a place of sanctioned transgression. Architectural codes were also, therefore, open to violation here.

The more exclusive establishments of the Shimabara, the *ageya* (pleasure houses), catered to clients with high tastes, and their prostitutes were accomplished artists trained in the finest arts. Accordingly their houses adopted architectural forms and decorations that were prohibited by their lower-class status but appropriate to the high status of the clientele. This double standard was managed by making the exterior simple but creating individual spaces in the interior that were based on the residences of the upper classes, and even those of the shoguns. Indeed, the interiors were often extremely eclectic to respond to the varied status and tastes of the clients, with individual entertainment rooms, right next to each other built in completely different styles.

The only surviving example of a complete 17th-century *ageya* is the Sumiya (Place of Peace and Long Life), controlled by the Nakagawa family, who administered it for 13 generations from its very beginning in 1641. From the street its facade was simple but cleverly designed. The outer walls of both its ground and upper story were recessed by half a bay and fronted by wooden screens that ensured no one could look in but the guests could look out. They were also removable, so that when the street entertainers came calling or during festivals when the streets of the Shimabara became one big theater, the guests of the Sumiya could look straight out without hindrance.

In the interior one found a range of styles taken from those of the military mansions, town homes, and the teahouses. They were, however, willfully decorative and colored with great variety and exaggeration. The main reception rooms for the guests were located behind the exterior facade on the eastern edge of the building. This position corresponded to the typology of the houses of rich merchants. As in Shinden-style palaces, such as Ninomaru at Nijo Castle and the Katsura Imperial Villa, the entertainment rooms located near the garden were stepped back to ensure that each room had a special relationship to the garden, with individually framed openings designed for each space. The second floor had smaller rooms, for the more intimate relationships between the geisha and her clients.

15.88 **Pyoungsan Academy, near Hahoe Village, Korea**

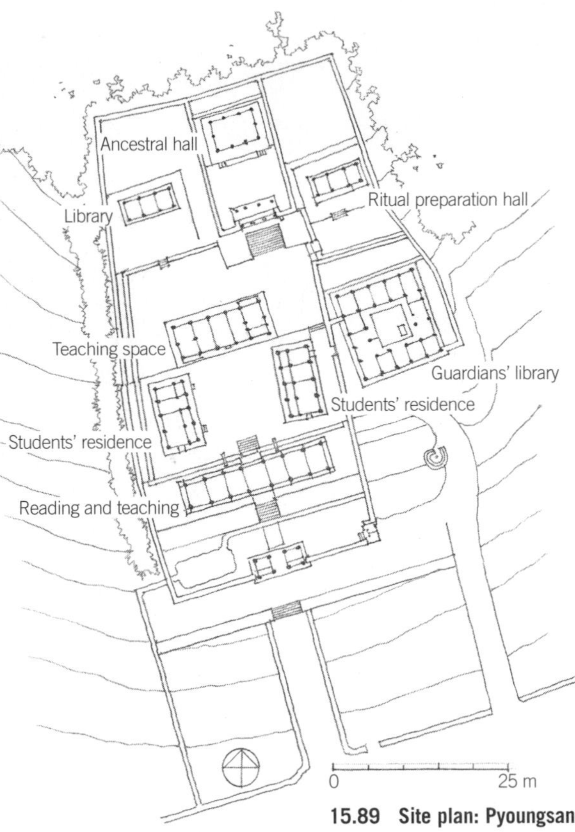


**15.89 Site plan: Pyoungsan Academy**

## KOREA: CHOSON DYNASTY

In Korea, the elite of the Choson Dynasty (1392–1910) attempted to suppress Buddhism in favor of Confucianism, but internal strife as well as Japanese attacks in 1592 and 1597 and Manchu assaults in 1627 and 1636 ravaged the country's economy. Nonetheless, Korea rebounded in the 18th century due to the strict enforcement of the class system, not unlike the Bakufu code, dominated by the *yangban*, who were government officials and administrators. Under them was a class of technicians, beneath them were the commoners (composed of farmers and merchants), and finally, at the bottom, "the despised people." In the strictest sense of the term, *yangban* referred to government officials or officeholders who had passed the civil service examinations that tested knowledge of the Confucian classics and their neo-Confucian interpretations. They were the Korean counterparts of the scholar-officials, or mandarins, of imperial China. The term *yangban*, means literally "two groups"—

that is, civil and military officials. Though its members had to pass the civil service examination, family members could be part of the *yangban* clan and thus share the aura of the elite as long as they retained Confucian culture and rituals. Though neo-Confucianism became the official state religion, the lower classes clung to more traditional Buddhism.

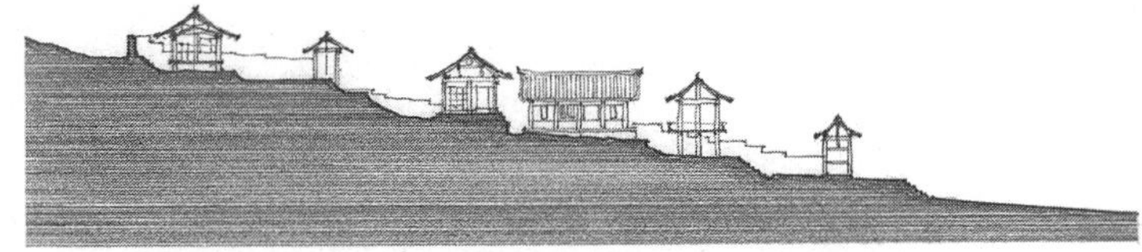

**15.90 Section: Pyoungsan Academy**

Pyoungsan Academy, located picturesquely along a bend in the Nakdong River in south-central Korea, was a private Confucian high school for the sons of that region's *yangban* elite. It was erected in honor of Ryu Song-ryong, who served as the prime minister during the destructive invasions led by the Japanese feudal lord, Hideyoshi. The building, modeled on pavilions that the members of the *yangban* class had began to erect called *chôngjas*—often along a stream or river at a particularly attractive scenic spot—which is an enclosed precinct rising up on a gentle slope.

One passes through a gate that allows a vista up the slope under the *chôngjas* and into the main court above, where the path leads. The view centers on the spot where the teacher would sit, with windows providing views further out. Flanking the court are student quarters. Access to the *chôngjas*, which seems to almost float above the earth, is along a simple, narrow wooden plank. Behind the school is the shrine in a separate enclosure and, to one side, a library. The caretakers' house is in a separate enclosure attached to the walls of the school. The teacher did not live at the school but in the nearby village.

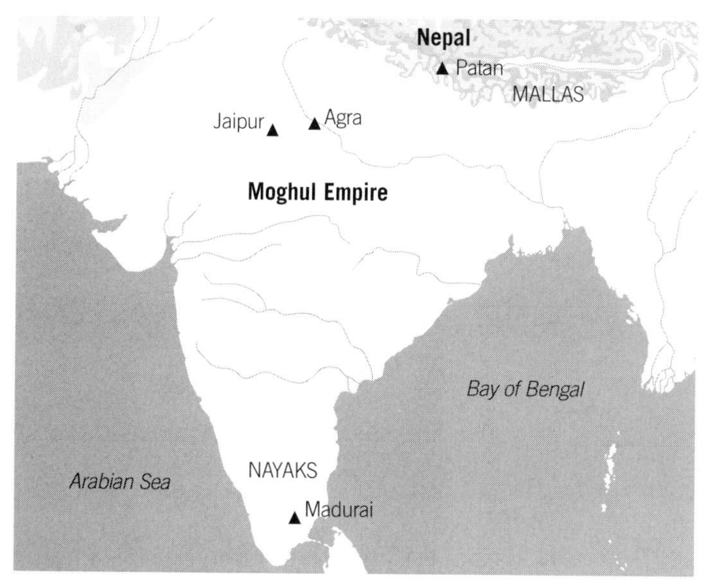

15.91 Meenakshi Sunderesvara Temple at Madurai, India

### NAYAKS OF MADURAI

In 1658 Aurangzeb deposed his father, Shah Jahan, and took over the Moghul throne. Under Aurangzeb's long reign (1658–1707), the Moghul empire in northern India expanded to its greatest extent, incorporating the areas of the sultanates of Bijapur and Golconda in the 1680s. Unlike his father, Aurangzeb was a competent administrator. He also insisted on stricter adherence to Sunni morality, both personally and in official policy. Discrimination against Hindus increased, and all experimental hybridized religious practices like those explored by Akbar were forbidden. Artisans and craftsmen fled. One of the beneficiaries of the artisanal diaspora were the Nayaks, erstwhile governors of Vijayanagar territories, who, after Vijayanagar's sack, established a sort of confederation of autonomous kingdoms with capitals in Madurai, Tanjore, Gingee, and Ikkeri. The Nayaks continued the Chola and Vijayanagar practice of treating temples as surrogate courts. Temple support, in fact, had been instrumental in the Nayaks' rise to power. The Vijayanagar kings had granted the Nayaks overlordship over several temples to help maintain the armies. After Vijayanagar's fall, the same temples helped the Nayaks come to power. Under the Nayaks the temple of Madurai and Tanjore became veritable cities unto themselves. Their gates were rarely closed, and urban life moved in and out at will.

The Meenakshi Sunderesvara Temple (1623–59) has two main shrines, the larger one dedicated to Shiva in the manifestation of Sunderesvara ("the beautiful one") and the smaller to his wife Meenakshi ("the fish-eyed one"). The temple's main deity, however, is Meenakshi, a local regional goddess who is important to the Tamils. Though she was married to Shiva after the rise of the bhakti cults, she continued to hold her dominance over the populace.

Spatially this duality is represented in procession. Although Sunderesvara's shrine has a well-defined axis leading to it, it is Meenakshi's more informally defined access path that has the important historical locations along it, most importantly the Lotus Tank, the mythical origin of the temple, and a corridor with painted panels depicting stories from the life of Meenakshi.

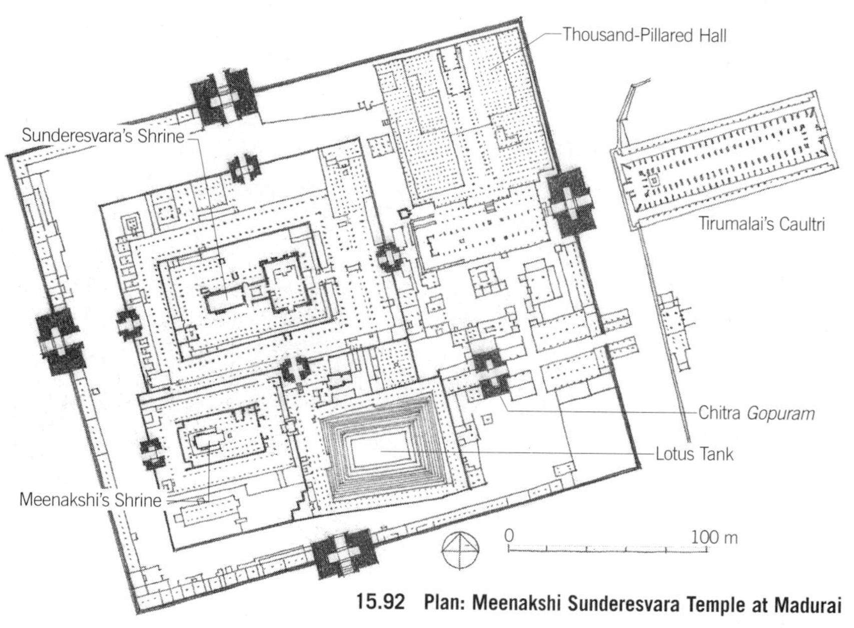


15.92 Plan: Meenakshi Sunderesvara Temple at Madurai

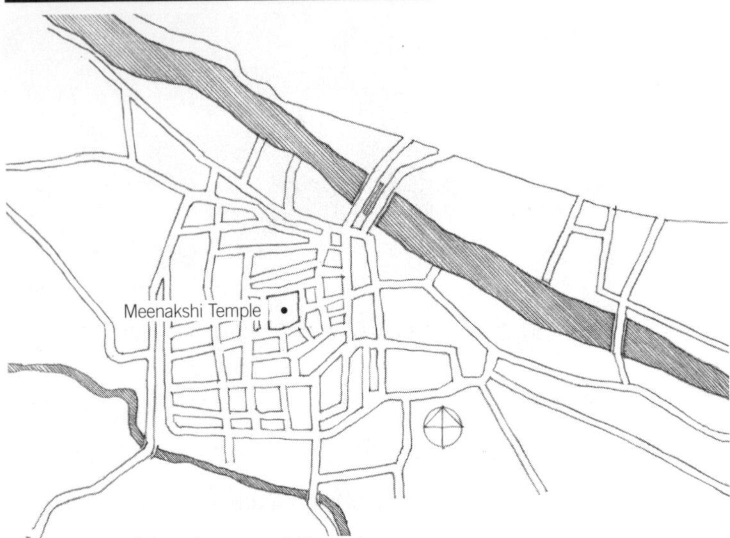


15.93 **Plan of the urban core of Madurai**

15.94 **Gopuram of Meenakshi Temple**

As it grew under the Nayaks, the Meenakshi Temple became a maze of concentric enclosures that nestle a diverse array of functional and ceremonial spaces, such as pillared halls, open courts, inhabitable corridors, and shrines, designed to accommodate the temples diverse civic and religious functions. Besides shrines, it has markets, private shrines, places for resting, dwellings for priests, ceremonial sites, and recently a museum.

As regents of the courts, Meenakshi and Sunderesvara priests had to perform several rituals, chief among them an elaborate annual procession that was meant to be visible to all, particularly the lowest castes who were not allowed into the temple. This procession celebrated Meenakshi's divine wedding to Sunderesvara (Shiva). Over a 19-day festival in April and May, Meenakshi is taken out in procession in a mobile structure into the crowded city streets, where she ceremonially defeats all the gods and earthly kings in one battle after another, until she finally meets Sunderesvara, whom she almost defeats and then suddenly realizes that she is prophesied to marry him. The streets where Meenakshi is carried are concentrically arrayed in three rings around the temple, continuing in that sense the already urban concentric order of the temple plan itself. (The Nayak temple at Tanjore is a more exact representation of this idea.)

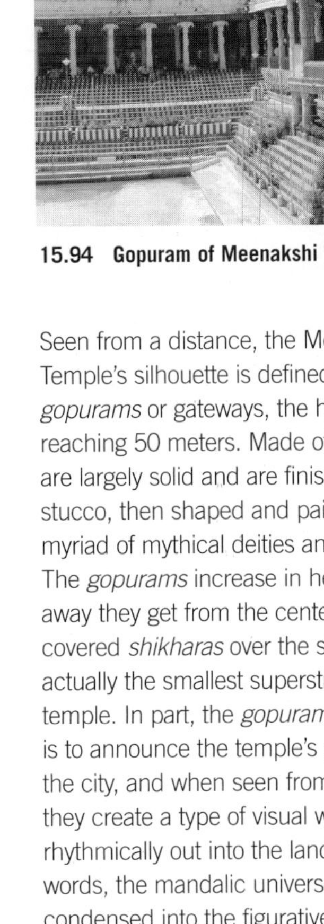

Seen from a distance, the Meenakshi Temple's silhouette is defined by its *gopurams* or gateways, the highest ones reaching 50 meters. Made of brick, they are largely solid and are finished in molded stucco, then shaped and painted into a myriad of mythical deities and creatures. The *gopurams* increase in height the further away they get from the center. The gold covered *shikharas* over the shrines are actually the smallest superstructures of the temple. In part, the *gopurams'* function is to announce the temple's presence to the city, and when seen from a distance, they create a type of visual wave radiating rhythmically out into the landscape. In other words, the mandalic universe that is usually condensed into the figurative representation of a Hindu temple's *shikhara*, was, under the Nayaks, expanded so far outward that it encompasses the geography of the entire city itself. And because Madurai sits in a river valley surrounded by a ring of low-lying hills, one can imagine the hills as the next layer of *gopurams*, implying mythical unseen mountains beyond.

15.95 **Section of the summit of a gopuram**

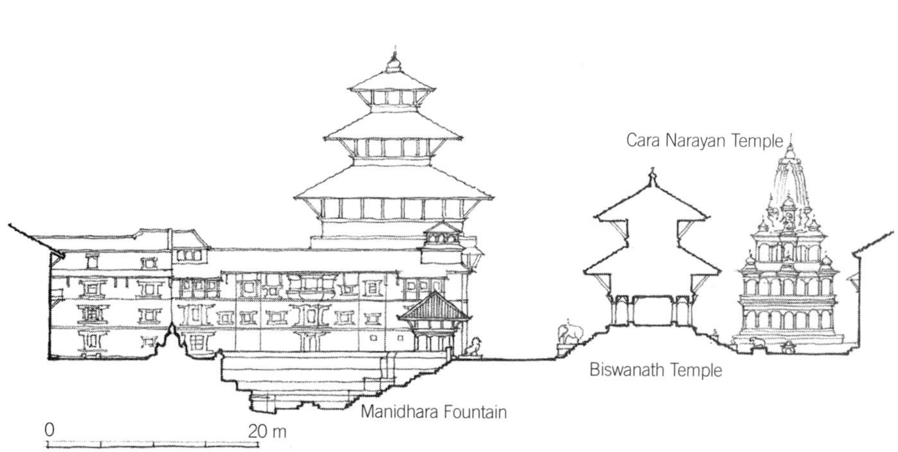

**15.96 Durbar Square: east-west section looking south**

**15.97 Durbar Square, Patan, Nepal**

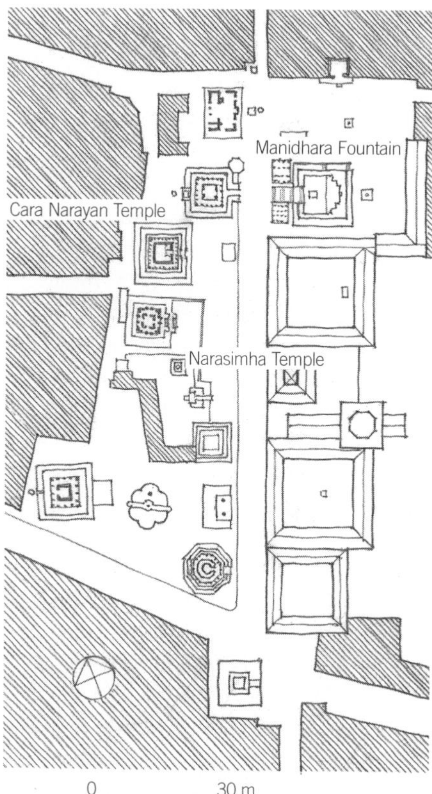


**15.98 Plan: Durbar Square**

## MALLAS OF NEPAL

At the other end of the subcontinent, the Himalayan kingdom of Nepal ruled by the Mallas went through a building boom in the 17th century as well. Nepal was originally populated as the midpoint between the north-south highway linking Tibet to India. Buddhist monks travelling through here spread Indian- and Tibetan-style Buddhism in Nepal, making it a unique blend of the two. After Islamic invaders occupied northern India in the 10th century, fleeing Hindu priests, royalty, and merchants added a new Hindu layer to Nepalese culture and civic polity. In the 13th century, these Hindu Malla kings established the longest lasting dynasty of Nepal. They ruled Nepal as a unified kingdom until 1482, after which it was divided into three independent kingdoms run by related Malla dynasties, with capitals in Patan, Kathmandu, and Bhaktapur. In the 17th century, the Mallas of Patan renovated and reconstructed their main Royal Court, known as the Durbar Square. Patan's Durbar Square marks the location where the ancient north-south route intersects with Nepal's main east-west artery. Its oldest structure, the Manidhara Fountain, was built in the 6th century as the core of a rest area for pilgrims. The square grew in importance when royal palaces and temples were added to it. Under the Malla, the royal coronations began to be performed in Durbar Square.

The eastern edge of the square was lined with a string of palaces abutting one another. On the western side an irregularly shaped open space is home to several freestanding temples that form the rough outline of an arc. Dispersed throughout are many freestanding pillars and small shrines. At its northern end, just beyond the palaces, the Manidhara Fountain forms its own urban place, wrapped around the negative space of its concavity. It is the delicate balance between the hard edge, the freestanding structures, and the negative space of the fountain that imparts to Durbar Square its unique urban character.

Most of Durbar Square as it exists today was rebuilt in the 17th century under successive Malla kings who, however, were careful to preserve some of the older structures, including the Manidhara Fountain and the Cara Narayan (1566) and Narasimha (1589) temples. These older temples were of the north Indian *shikhara* type that give Durbar Square, in spite of its regionalized reconstruction, a distinctive identity. Its eclecticism testifies to the variety of cultural influences that left their mark on it.

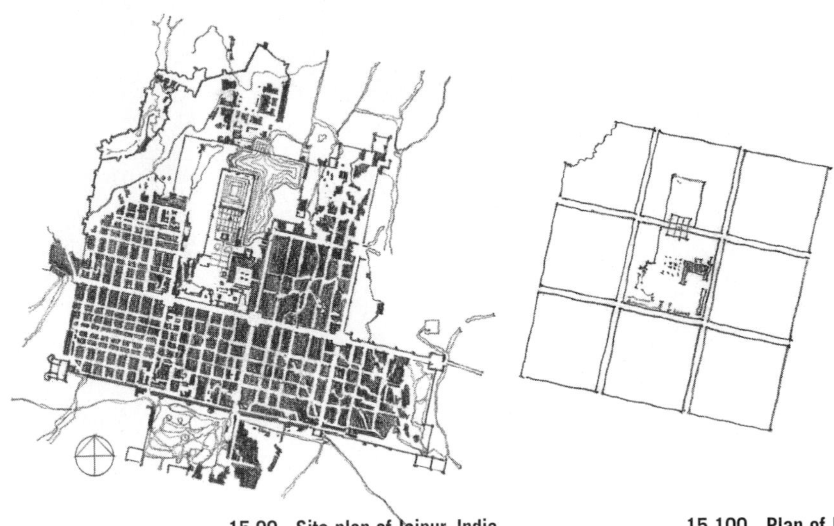

15.99 Site plan of Jaipur, India

15.100 Plan of Jaipur as a mandala

## END OF THE MOGHULS

Aurangzeb's death in 1707 provided an opportunity for regional kingdoms and disgruntled governors to declare independence. Although there was incessant competition and conflict, particularly with the Marathas conquering wide swaths of central India and repeatedly threatening their neighbors on all sides, the net wealth and prosperity of south Asia actually increased with the growth in mercantile trade and exchange, including with the newly established European trading posts on the sea. The lack of a "unified" empire in India at this time was therefore not a symptom of political and economic weakness but an indication of a time of prosperity and forwardness. All the art and architecture produced by these new kingdoms, those that continued to be Islamic and those that were not, was indelibly influenced by the Moghul example. For the newly independent, the Moghuls were the shining symbol to which they could aspire, even as they expressed their own distinct individuality. If modernity is the forward thrust of transformation, the production and exploration of the possibilities of the new in negotiation with the values of the status quo, then this was a time of great modernity in India. Jaipur serves as an example.

### Jaipur

Jaipur's Hindu maharaja, Sawai Jai Singh II (1699–1743), was a former general in the Moghul army; following the pattern well recognized in Indian history, he declared independence when the Moghuls became weak. His palace, located within Amer, a fort continuously occupied since the 10th century, was located on a hill overlooking the trading path from western India to Delhi. Amer was repeatedly rebuilt, among others by Sawai Jai Singh, who built a palace designed as a series of pavilions arranged around a quartered garden, complete with canals and fountains taken directly from Moghul examples.

By 1727, Sawai Jai Singh felt sufficiently secure to establish a new capital on the unprotected plain, on the site of one of his garden palaces. Designed with the help of the architect Vidyadhar, Jaipur was laid out as a square divided into nine smaller squares, seven of which were residential and two given over to palaces. It was conceived as a mercantile city, its walls meant only for the regulation of traffic and tax collecting. To entice settlers, Sawai Jai Singh ordered that shops be constructed along the entire length of main streets so that, to a visitor, it appeared to be well inhabited. At the intersections he constructed wide squares or *chowks*.

There is a theory that Jaipur was based on a nine-square mandala. Although not verifiable, the story is given credence because Sawai Jai Singh was an avid follower of Hindu astrology. To obtain the most precise observations of the planetary bodies he could obtain, he built state-of-the-art observatories in Jaipur, Delhi (built for the Moghul emperor), Varanasi, Ujjain, and Mathura. Sawai Jai Singh's observatories were based on similar ones built by Ulugh Beg in the 15th century in Samarkand, only these were larger, and since they were spread apart, their observations could be cross referenced for greater accuracy. Named Janter Manters, they make for a stunning, astonishingly modern sculpture park. (Janter Manter is a corruption of *yantra*, which means "instrument.")

15.101 **Hawa Mahall, Jaipur, India**

15.102 **Interior, Hawa Mahall, Jaipur**

### Hawa Mahall

In 1799 Sawai Jai Singh's grandson, Sawai Pratap Singh, built the Hawa Mahall, considered to be one of the signature monuments of Jaipur. The Hawa Mahall (literally, Wind Palace) gets its name because, as a palace, it was considered to be insubstantial, or made of wind, as it were. It earned this title because the structure was essentially a five-story-high screen wall, constructed at the edge of the palace complex, facing the street. It was built to enable the women of the royal household to observe the festival processions of the street, while remaining unobserved themselves.

Designed by Lal Chand Ustad, this structure derives from elements of Moghul palaces and mosques that often contained screened sections for women. At the Hawa Mahall, however, Ustad transformed the concept into a grand urban structure. Hawa Mahall was, if you will, a modern invention signifying new possibilities in urban experience, coming out of the Hindu reinscription of the Moghul experience.

15.103 **Janter Manter, Jaipur**

15.104 **Janter Manter, Jaipur**

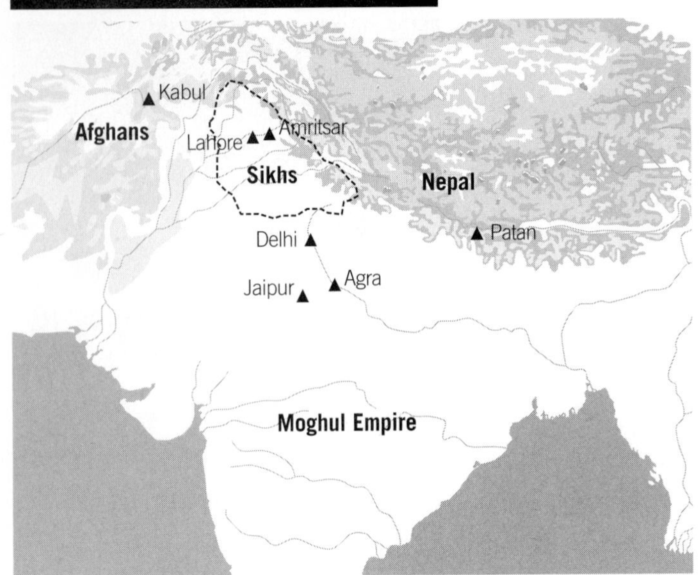


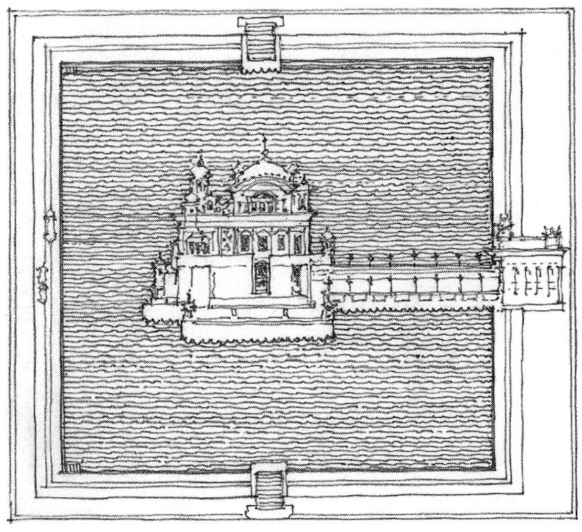
15.105 Darbar Sahib, Amritsar, India

## Darbar Sahib

In the 18th century the Sikhs, under Maharaja Ranjit Singh (1780–1839), expanded into a large empire encompassing the region of the five tributaries of the Indus and the Punjab. Founded by Guru Nanak in the 15th century, Sikhism was derived from Islamic sufi traditions and conceived of as a reformation of Hindu practices, eliminating idol worship and caste distinction and emphasizing the unity of God and the necessity of the intimate experience with the divine. The Sikhs offered themselves as an alternative to both Islam and the Hindus and accepted converts from both. The Sikhs were always involved in the political affairs of the Moghuls, falling in and out of favor with the Moghul court at various times. In 1699, Guru Gobind Singh (1675–1708), the last of their gurus, formalized the Sikh religion, enjoined the faithful to defend it by arms if necessary, laying the foundation for the idea of an independent Sikh state.

Darbar Sahib, or Golden Temple, built in Amritsar in 1764 during the reign of Maharaja Ranjit Singh, had long been an important place of Sikh pilgrimage and learning. In 1604 Guru Arjan Das installed the Granth Sahib, the Sikh holy book, here after its compilation. The Darbar Sahib has doorless entrances on all four sides as an indication of the building's accessibility to all. No formal rituals are conducted here, but hymns are sung day and night.

The lower story of the main structure is made of marble, whereas the upper story and domes are covered with plates of gilded copper (done in the 19th century). It sits on an island in the center of a sacred pool, 150 meters square, that is surrounded by a marble walkway (for ritual circumambulation) that in turn is separated from the outside world by buildings that house the various functions of the institution, such as its administrative offices, galleries, and dining halls.

A causeway leads from the Darbar Sahib to the edge, where one finds a three-story structure with a single dome, the Akal Takh, where the highest priests of Sikhism hold office. Every morning the Granth Sahib is ceremoniously carried from the Akal Takh to the Darbar Sahib to be installed; it is returned in the evening. Among the structures that lie outside the compound is the Guru-ka-langar, a three-storied building where 35,000 people are fed free daily.

15.106 Darbar Sahib, Amritsar, Punjab

# 1800 CE

The principal world power in the year 1800 was China. It may not have manifested itself as such, since it had no colonies. It extended its borders the old-fashioned way, conquering Tibet, Turkestan, and Mongolia. In size, population, production, and raw wealth, it had no equal. Its bold-thinking emperor, Qianlong, aimed to create a pan-Asian empire, unified around the ancient Indian ideal of *cakravartin.* Because Chinese architecture never underwent radical changes in its visual and formal vocabulary, there has been a tendency to see it as tradition bound, but that would be an all-too-simple reduction. Qianlong's purposeful use of imitation in constructing his new capital city, Chengde, was driven by the ideological innovation of constructing a vision of China as the center of a pan-Asian world. The Chinese world, however, went into rapid decline once the British forced the Chinese to accept ever more opium, against the Chinese imperial desires, in "exchange" for tea.

Europe was also undergoing a foundational revision as a consequence of the philosophical movement known as the Enlightenment, which revised ideas about nature, law, and government. Napoleon and his armies forced change not only in France but also in Italy, Austria, and Germany. The stranglehold of the aristocracy had been broken and its arbitrary aspects revealed. New building types relating to government and bureaucracy emerged. In that respect, one can compare the Somerset House in London (1776–1801), the U.S. Capitol (1755), the Four Courts in Dublin (1786–1802), the Virginia State Capitol (1785), the Government House in Calcutta, and the new Houses of Parliament in London (1840–60). The architecture of administration brought with it other forms of architecture, for example, of control, such as the panoptic prison. In the United States, the Enlightenment was, however, expressed with particularly utopian fervor, spurred on by the American Revolution and the sense that America was the land of untold opportunities.

The liberation of Greece from Ottoman occupation in 1829 added substance to these ideals, spawning a vigorous neo-Greek movement not only in the United States, but also in Germany and Scotland. In Europe Enlightenment utopianism was generally tempered if not co-opted outright by the lingering traditions of aristocratic privilege, producing an architecture generally known as neoclassical, the history of which took many turns and in some cases retreated toward a more conservative romanticism, especially in England. Nonetheless, traces of a more vigorous and austere neoclassicism, such as that pursued by the French architects Claude Nicholas Ledoux and Étienne-Louis Boullée, are to be found throughout Europe from 1800 onward. The reaction against neoclassicism and the spread of romanticism, developing into national romanticism after the Napoleonic Wars, became increasingly important as the century progressed.

Apart from China, Europe, and the European-controlled colonies, there were two areas that continued to develop architecturally but in very different ways—Japan and Thailand. Japan, like China, had closed itself off from European influence, but it maintained a strong architectural tradition, developing a "modern" architecture of the middle class, as in Kabuki theater. Thailand, which was never colonized, was, by way of contrast, more than willing to open itself up to Western influence, unifying borrowed elements into regionally developed forms of practice. In that sense the story of 19th-century urbanism has to include not only such new cities as St. Petersburg and Washington, D.C., and the redesigning of such older cities as Berlin, London, Paris, Dublin, and Athens but also Bangkok, the newly founded capital of Thailand. Thailand gives us a glimpse of what modern "eastern" architecture looks like that was neither colonized by the Europeans nor closed off in the name of tradition.

## 1800 CE

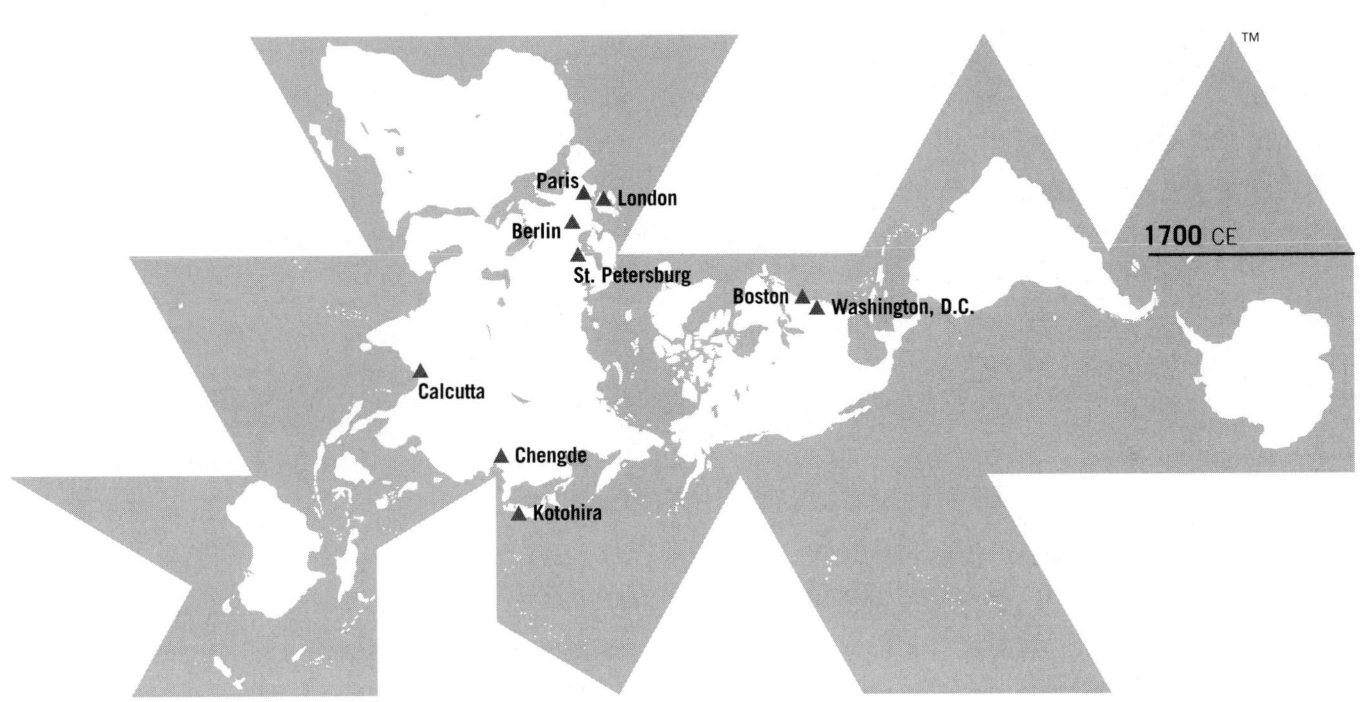


▲ **Bevis-Marks Synagogue**
1700

China: Qing Dynasty
1644–1911

▲ **Imperial Palace at Chengde**
1703–80

Opium War
1839–1842

Japan: Edo Period
1615–1868

▲ **Kanamaru-za**
1835

Neoclassicism
mid-18th to mid-19th century

▲ **Government House**
Begun 1803

▲ **Writers' Building**
1870

▲ **Shelburne House**
Begun 1763

▲ **St. Geneviève**
1757

▲ **Petit Trianon**
1761–8

▲ **Bibliothèque Nationale**
1788

▲ **Valhalla**
1830–42

**1750** CE — **1800** CE — **1850** CE

▲ **Salt Works of Chaux**
1775–9

▲ **Père Lachaise**
1804

**Schauspielhaus** ▲
1818–21

▲ **Altes Museum**
1823–30

▲ **Virginia Penitentiary**
1798

▲ **Pentonville Prison**
1844

▲ **Suffolk House of Correction**
1803

▲ **St. Madelaine Church**
1845–51

**Royal Scottish Academy** ▲
1835

▲ **Tennessee State Capitol**
1845–59

▲ **Beth Elohim Synagogue**
1840

▲ **Bibliothèque St. Geneviève**
1845–51

**Industrial Revolution**
17th–18th centuries

England: Hanoverian Rule
1714–1901

French Revolution
1789–1792

Napoleonic Wars
1795–1815

Victorian Era
1830–1901

American War of Independence
1763–1783

War of 1812

Joseph Bramah invents the water closet ⦿
1778

# 1800 CE

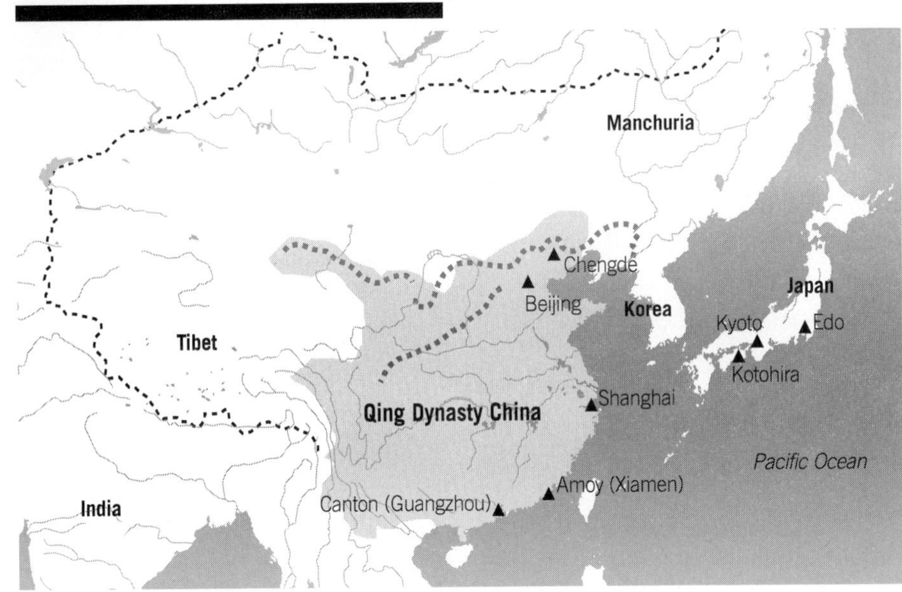

**16.1 Qianlong Emperor**

## QIANLONG EMPEROR

Though the Chinese exports of tea increased more than 50 percent in the first third of the 19th century and silk exports quadrupled, Chinese traders showed little interest in European merchandise. Instead, they demanded payment in silver. By 1800, China's asymmetrical trade with Europe meant that almost half of the Spanish silver mined in America wound up in Chinese coffers. The English, by way of contrast, were close to bankruptcy. Their solution was to force the Chinese to accept opium in exchange for tea, a policy they pursued so relentlessly that by the end of the 19th century, the Chinese economy went into a tailspin. This is arguably one of the great civilizational tragedies created by European colonialism.

But in the late 18th century, as wealth and food production grew, China possessed the largest and richest empire in the world. It was also ruled by a man who had a lasting impact on the shape of east Asian politics, Qianlong (r. 1736–96). Not dissimilar to his contemporary, Napoleon Bonaparte, who pursued a pan-European ideal, Qianlong saw himself as a pan-Asian emperor and not just of the Han Chinese. And like Napoleon, he was a military commander of great skill. In ten campaigns between 1755 and 1790, Qianlong expanded his empire to its greatest extent ever, bringing Mongolia, Chinese Turkestan, and Tibet under his control. Emperor to China's largest empire, with a diverse population, and a ruler of foreign origin himself, Qianlong aspired to establish a model of governance that would be pluralistic and moral. Qianlong's grandfather, the Kangxi emperor, had chosen to practice Tibetan Buddhism in private, even though he governed using Confucian Chinese principles. Unsatisfied by this arrangement, Qianlong decided to model himself after the Tibetan Lamaist conceptions of governance. His primary intellectual mentor was Rolpay Dorje, a Tibetan monk, who became the Grand Lama of Beijing in 1736. Under Dorje's guidance, as Patricia Berger has argued, Qianlong adopted the model of the *cakravartin,* expounded by the 1st-century Indian philosopher Nagarjuna, founder of the Madhyamika school of thought. *Cakravartin* derives from the Sanskrit *cakra,* "wheel," and *vartin,* "one who turns," and designates a ruler who enables the wheel of *dhamma,* or Buddhist law, to turn. Emperor Asoka, from the 3rd century BCE, was considered to be the *cakravartin.* Nagarjuna argued that as a *cakravartin,* Asoka was as meritorious of gaining nirvana as the most devoted Buddhist monk. This argument opened the gate for more secular, nonascetic ways of gaining merit in the Buddhist world. As a *cakravartin,* Qianlong was thus required to reach Buddhist Enlightenment not through world-renouncing asceticism, as had the Buddha, but through its very converse, through the just and rightful ordering of the human world, which in Qianlong's case, was his empire. Ultimately, Qianlong aspired to facilitate several paths to nirvana for his people, as Asoka did. Qianlong himself spoke several languages, and the court was officially polyglot. Edicts were issued in at least three languages. Qianlong saw himself as the mediator of all his different worlds, creating a new architecture that took all he considered to be significant from the different traditions and modernizing them into a synthetic whole. His reference was not to a single mythical past but to a vision that offered a complex, multinucleated concept of his empire.

As such, Qianlong embodied an ideal of empire and modernity that contrasted with the colonial model of empire based on the ideas of the "civilizing mission" that the English developed in the 19th century and that projected China as a static, ancient, and tradition-bound civilization and Europe as the bearer of modernity. While the English model eventually overwhelmed Qianlong's model, the policies of contemporary China are still to some degree attached to this pan-Asian vision.

**16.2 Imperial Palace at Chengde, China**

**16.3 Pulesi, Chengde**

### Chengde

As part of his pan-Asian vision, Qianlong embarked on an extensive building program, particularly in Chengde, to remake, as translations, sacred temples from various parts of his realm, assembled at one site as a well-ordered map of his empire. Chengde was conceived as essentially a symbolic capital, which by its very location—north of Beijing, beyond the Great Wall—its position reaffirmed the new pan-Asian world. Government, however, was still run from the Forbidden City.

Chengde was located at a remote Inner Mongolian oasis with lakes, green hills, and a multitude of small rivers at the foot of the Yanshan Mountains. Qianlong's grandfather, the Kangxi emperor (1662–1723), had already constructed a summer palace there. Besides enlarging the main palace and garden, Qianlong created about ten new temples in the surrounding areas, including Puningsi (1755), the Puyousi (1760), the Anyuanmiao (1764), the Pulesi (1767), the Putuo Zongcheng (1771), the Shuxiangsi (1776), and the Xumifushoumiao (1780).

These temples, dedicated to a range of Confucian and Buddhist deities drawn from various parts of the empire, formed a conceptual and religious-political arc around the palace. All these temples can be seen from the main hill north of the palace, so that they form a single scenographic whole. A self-conscious visual ensemble, Chengde was a spectacle. With the Han Chinese palace complex with its lake, gardens, and hills at its center and the Buddhist temples in an arc around it, Chengde was a veritable microcosm of the Qing empire, a map of the land.

But Chengde was more than a map of the empire. It was also an ordering of that map according to a Buddhist mandala. A critical feature of Chengde's landscape is a 60-meter-high rock formation called the Qingchui peak. Wider at the top than at the bottom, Qingchui looks like a huge pillar perched, unbelievably, at the summit of one of the eastern hills. Using the Qingchui "pillar" as the center, all the Tibetan Buddhist temples and the palace complex can be interpreted as "facing" Qingchui, not literally but by the geomantic logic of Chinese and Tibetan landscape architecture. In this reading Chengde as a whole was a mandala, with Quinchui standing in for Sumeru the sacred mountain, the Buddha's abode, at the center.

Shuxiangsi
Putuo Zongcheng
Xumifushoumiao
Puningsi
Puyousi
Anyuanmiao
Qingchui Peak
Pulesi
Punesi
Main Palace

**16.4 Plan: Summer Resort at Chengde**

16.5 Putuo Zhongcheng, Chengde, China

16.6 Potala Palace, Tibet (China)

### Pulesi

Chengde's temples, created as a microcosm of the Chinese world, were designed ostensibly as replicas of other temples of the empire but were, in fact, significantly transformed or modernized to reflect Qianlong's interpretation of their precursors. The Pulesi (Temple of Universal Happiness, 1767), for instance, is a hybrid building that merges the Tibetan conceptual order with Chinese formal expression. In appearance the Pulesi is like the shrine at the Temple of Heaven complex in Beijing; it is a round temple with a double eave and conical roof. In plan, however, it replicates a Buddhist mandala with a series of stepped terraces. The temple houses at its center an altar that is a building in its own right, a biaxial symmetrical structure that consists of an open box set on a tall base with elaborate portals facing the cardinal directions. The temple was built in honor of the representatives of the Kazak and other related ethnic peoples who came to Chengde for audiences with the emperor.

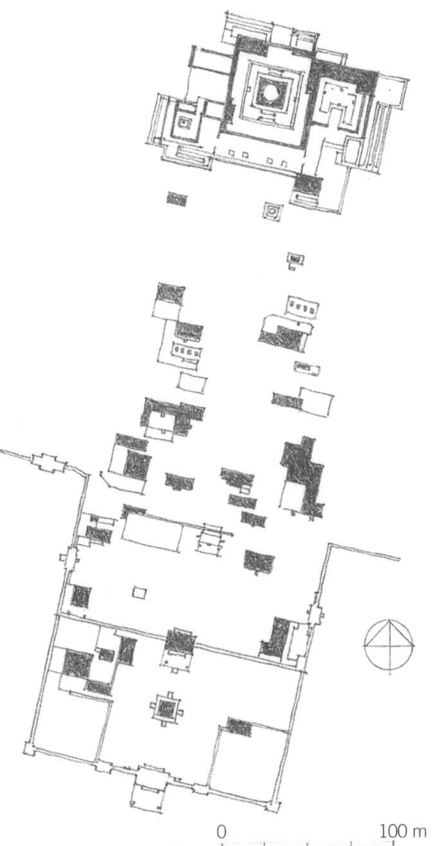


16.7 Site plan: Putuo Zongcheng

### Putuo Zongcheng

In 1771 Qianlong built Chengde's most visible structure, the Putuo Zongcheng. At the inauguration of the Putuo, the last of the Mongols, who had fled to Russia fearing the rise of the Qing, returned to Qing China, vindicating for Qianlong the rightfulness and justness of his rule as a *cakravartin*. Qianlong's founding edict states that the Putuo is based on Lhasa's Potala Palace, and inside there is a superficial similarity. Like the Potala, the Putuo consists of a series of lower white buildings rising up the side of a hill, culminating in the central red structure, the Dahongtai (Great Red Terrace), with the golden temple's roofs projecting over the summit. Yet like the Pulesi, the Putuo is not a copy of the Potala, but rather a modernization of it, reflecting Qianlong's claim to be a new *cakravartin*. The older Potala's massive white walls were support structures—in essence, buttresses holding up the terraces that house the red palace. The walls of the Putuo, by contrast, are enclosing walls, and the central Great Red Terrace is essentially a large open courtyard that houses within it, not visible from the outside, its main structure—a Chinese style temple pavilion, where Qianlong received the returning Mongols.

**16.8 Entrance facade: Shelburne House, London, England**

## NEOCLASSICISM

In mid-18th-century Europe, the heady mercantile era of the preceding century had given way to a desire for something more substantial. This was true in both England and France, but with different valences. In England, the critiques by the defenders of the picturesque had begun to sink in. But given that the royal court in England, unlike in France, played only a marginal role in determining aesthetic norms, matters of taste were largely left in the hands of the elite and well-to-do who, in turn, depended on artists and architects. And the Adam brothers, four in all, of which Robert (1728–92) became the best known, were in that respect the most influential. Their work had elements in keeping with the ideology of the picturesque insofar as it emphasized significant actions of great men, ancient and English. The brothers were members of the gentry, having learned about architecture from their father and from a family friend, Sir William Bruce, a man of considerable political standing. The Adam brothers were already successful architects when Robert made his first European trip. France left him disappointed, but Rome suited him better and there he met and befriended Giambattista Piranesi. When Piranesi published a self-portrait of himself and Adam on the dedicatory plate of what was to become his Campo Marzo, Robert Adam's fame was guaranteed.

Upon Adam's return from Rome, he realized that the Palladian manner he had developed in his early career would no longer do. Ornament had to be based on antique precedent not on Renaissance transmissions.

Composition of the rooms would have to be tighter. Above all, the Adam brothers sought to create a totally integrated architectural and spatial environment. The standard practice at the time was for the architect to design the building, whereas the interior finishes, such as wainscoting, decorating, and plastering, were assigned to specialists in these crafts. Furniture was bought by the client or ordered from an existing stock of designs. The Adam brothers sought to control the entire production, and to this end they even developed their own color schemes. They even had a few copies of their collected drawings tinted so that other architects could copy their method of coloring. Ceilings were important in their designs and were rarely given much thought in Georgian domestic architecture except perhaps for moldings at the perimeter and articulation of the corners. Adam's ceiling was covered with panels consisting of framed small ceiling paintings in a Roman cum Renaissance manner.

Shelburne House (begun 1763) was originally designed for John Stuart, 3rd Earl of Bute (1713–92), secretary of state of George III, but when Lord Bute was toppled from power, the house was sold to the young and rich 2nd Earl of Shelburne (1737–1805). Shelburne served in the government in various capacities, even as Prime Minister. He thought of himself as a man of principle who supported Adam Smith's free-trade ideas, but he also had great respect for the monarchy and was thus held in suspicion by the Whigs.

The exterior of the building is stately and overtly Palladian, but the interior is softer and more ornamental. Distinguished by delicate decorative pilasters and ceilings painted by Italian artists, it had an eating room with a series of niches in the walls for statues. After dinner the company would move to the music room, which was designed as an oblong connected at each end with a rotunda 11 meters in diameter. Some of the most important people in London gathered at the Shelburne house. Among those who were entertained there were Benjamin Franklin and David Hume.

16.9 Syon House, London, England

16.10 Interior of Syon House

### Syon House

The Syon House (1762–3), in Brentford, London, was named after Mt. Zion, which had been at one time a medieval abbey that had been closed down and its buildings sold. In time it fell by dint of marriage to the 1st Duke of Northumberland, formerly Sir Hugh Smithson, who, even though his political role was marginal, wanted it to be known that he was a man of great taste and culture. The task given the architect, Robert Adam, was to transform the shell of the old nunnery into a grand house, and this he did in a brilliant manner by designing, in 1761, a series of rooms leading from the entrance to the gallery at the back. The first was an apsed double-square room kept in a grisaille color scheme, decorated in the Doric order, placed lengthwise to the visitor. After turning right and going up the curved steps, one enters a green-and-gold square room decorated in the Ionic order. From here, one turned left to enter a long white-and-gold apsed room, Corinthian in style. Finally, by way of a red-and-gold plain *astylar* double-square room, one would arrive at the great gallery. At the center of the plan, a large circular, domed salon was envisioned; but it was never built. It would have been one of the most ambitious spaces for a private house ever attempted.

The restrained but richly surfaced neoclassicism of the four Scottish Adam brothers, all of them architect-designers, had by that time become an important part of the language of good taste. In 1732, the Society of Dilettanti was formed, an association of gentlemen with archaeological interests. The brothers were influenced by the discovery of Pompeii (excavated 1746–63). But the work of the Adam brothers is deeper than a surface application of archaeological fads. Nor should one perceive of it as a mere dilettante's passion.

Their practice was an integrated endeavor, defining the environment of the upper class from top to bottom and aiming specifically to give expression to the area between life and space, learning and politics, and architecture and decoration. In that respect, their work should still be seen in the context of the picturesque, which emphasized the unique aspects of significant human action. Their architecture served to inscribe self-confidence and self-discipline into the psychology of the elite to lay a basis for the exercise of authority.

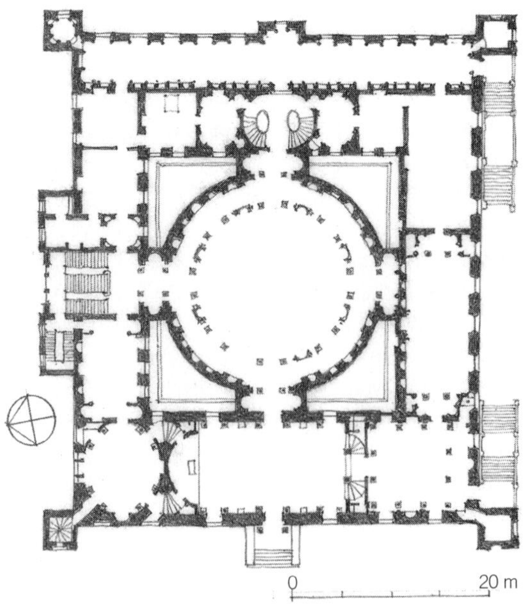


16.11 Main floor plan: Syon House

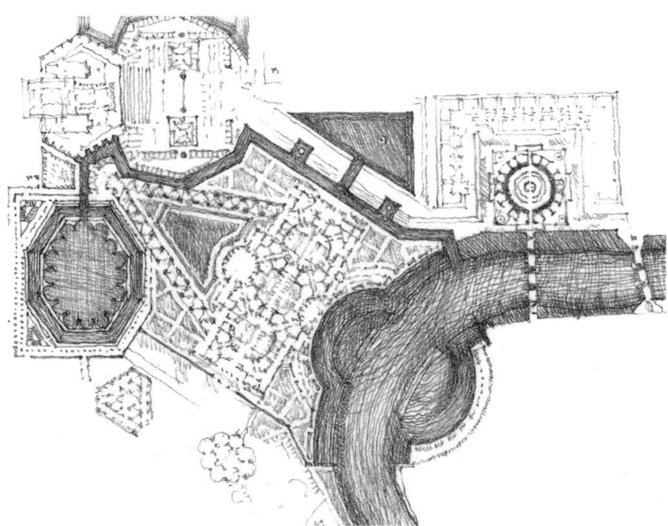

16.12 **Drawing of a fragment of Giambattista Piranesi's plan for Rome**

16.13 **Print from the Carceri series by Giambattista Piranesi**

### Piranesi and Romanticism

The 18th century was an expansionary age oriented toward accumulating wealth from far-flung global territories. It was also an age that had to adjust to the colonial project philosophically, economically, and politically. Naive historicism, like that of the neo-Palladians, gave way to a search for depth and ideals, whether that be in scholarly standards, academic affiliations, or archaeological truth, all of which, so it was thought, could bring authority and discipline into the field of architecture. The Enlightenment trajectory took different paths, depending on which aspect was emphasized, and the differences were spelled out in the contrast between Robert Adam and Giambattista Piranesi (1720–78)— the former working for a secure elite, living the life of an outward-looking member of an opportunistic colonial world, and the latter, with the faded glories of Rome in mind, taking a more sceptical view of history.

There were many who specialized in making copperplate engravings, but Piranesi elevated it into an idiom all its own. Scouring the often malaria-infested Roman *campagna* for pictorial possibilities, Piranesi created etchings of haunting intensity. Backlighting and unexpected and revealing angles brought into view broken stones, crumbling bricks, collapsed vaults, and overgrown facades.

This was a Rome far different from the one imagined in England, where it was embedded in a rhetoric of order and manliness. Piranesi's was a cataclysmic Rome approaching the end of time, with nothing left to show for its erstwhile grandeur except the overwhelming scale and melancholy of its ruins. Piranesi's work, one could argue, takes on the theme of the fluidity of time in contrast to the notion of a retrievable past as championed by the Palladians. The Colosseum is an empty crater, the Foundation Wall of Hadrian's Tomb, a vast battered cliff, and the people in his drawings are cripples, hunchbacks, vagabonds, and even grave robbers. The past, or rather the sad ruin left of it, is a mirror held up to shortsighted conceit.

In a sense, Adam and Piranesi, were two sides of the same coin: Adam in his zest for the exotic, Piranesi in his moody melancholia. Both admired the heroic, but from different political perspectives. Adam saw the Roman past as the legitimization of English civilizational supremacy and as a living model for heroic action. Piranesi saw the past as fragmented and beyond repair and as the backdrop to a meditative reflection on the end of civilization. These distinctions define the difference between neoclassicism and romanticism, the one reflecting a historical optimism, the other reflecting on the principle of historical loss.

16.14 **Drawing made from a Piranesi print of Roman ruins**

**16.15 Strawberry Hill, Twickenham, England**

### Strawberry Hill

Even though the picturesque in essence rediscovered ancient Rome while molding it to fit the needs of the English elite, the ideals of the picturesque resonated even more strongly among those who opposed resorting to the presumed rationalism of the ancients and the classical orders. They saw the Middle Ages as the more authentic and vibrant time period, emphasizing thus not the whites and blues and golds used by the Adam Brothers but reds, greens, and browns with purposefully dark and gloomy interiors and asymmetrical ground plans. Horace Walpole (1717–97), builder of Strawberry Hill (1749–77), used the word "Gothic picturesque" to define this style. Walpole was in many respects a counterculture person. He was well educated, and his wealth was created by his father, the prime minister Sir Robert Walpole, who also secured his election to Parliament, a post which he held until 1768. His father also found for him lucrative sinecures in the Exchequer and Custom House, which ensured a very comfortable income for life. But public life did not appeal to Walpole, whose principal passion was writing such Gothic novels as *The Castle of Otranto*. Walpole was also interested in the arts and wrote a four-volume history of art entitled *Anecdotes of Painting* (1761–71).

Upon the death of his father in 1745 Walpole settled at Strawberry Hill, an estate of some 40 acres at Twickenham, southwest of London, set among fashionable villas overlooking the Thames River and near the residence of his friend, the poet and garden enthusiast Alexander Pope. Expanding the existing house, he built a library, an armory, a gallery, a "star chamber," a "tribune," a sort of shrine, a china closet, bedrooms in several colors, and an oratory. There were towers, battlements, and stained glass rescued from demolished buildings. Walpole decorated the interiors in an uninhibited fashion, filling the house with art, paintings, sculpture, china, and heraldic symbols, both real and invented. Attention to structure was minimal, the fan vaulting in the gallery, a copy from Westminster Abbey, was made of papier mâché.

It would be wrong to argue that this was little more than a gentleman's fantasy, for the architecture of the Adam Brothers was just as much a gentleman's fantasy, even down to the custom-designed chairs that both Adam and Walpole made for their respective houses. Furthermore, Gothic architecture was beginning to be studied seriously. Yet the contrast between Adam and Walpole could not have been greater. Robert Adam was the consummate tastemaker for the metropolitan, insisting on a thorough conformity of design and life and an adherence to a prototype adjusted here and there in accordance with the needs of the client. Walpole built for himself alone. He sought out the strange and the unusual. And yet the building was designed as a demonstration piece on how to live presumably more intimately within an aesthetic environment of one's own making. Indeed, the house was much visited by the aristocracy and gentry, and after 1763 Walpole even began selling entrance tickets. Adam and Walpole represent the paradoxes associated with emerging modernism. Professionalism, or at least the beginnings of what we might call a professional practice, in the one and the deliberate and self-conscious search for personal expression and the desire for approbation in the other.

16.16
**Reproduction of the frontispiece to Marc-Antoine Laugier's *Essai sur l'architecture*, from *Allegory of Architecture Returning to its Natural Model*, by Charles Eisen**

**16.17 Maison Carrée, Paris, France**

**Marc-Antoine Laugier**

In France, the shift toward neoclassicism took on a more strident tone than in England, perhaps because the royal court was the principal tastemaker, with the Catholic Church playing an equally significant role as defenders of the baroque. Furthermore, the rococo, which had originated in France, was seen by many as bizarre and frivolous. French neoclassicism thus had a subtext of antimonarchism that was driven in part by a fascination with pagan naturalism. In that sense French neoclassicism was linked to the rethinking of the role of civic institutions. The philosophical movement of the Enlightenment gave substance to these critiques. In England, neoclassicism was less "revolutionary" and generally seen as the natural and proper environment for the elite.

In architectural circles, the argument came into the open with the publication in 1753 of Marc-Antoine Laugier's *Essai sur l'architecture*. Translated into English in 1775, it was a flashpoint of discussion about the nature of architectural production. Unlike Alberti's *Ten Books on Architecture*, Palladio's *Four Books on Architecture*, and Perrault's French translation of Vitruvius. Laugier's work pointed not to a classical past but rather to an earlier "rustic" past. Laugier spoke neither as an architect nor as a gentleman connoisseur. He was a Jesuit priest who had become famous as an impassioned orator.

In 1749, Laugier was invited to preach a sermon in the presence of the king, proof of his increasingly important role in the royal court. He preached yet again to the king in 1754, one year after the publication of his book and, one should add, in a climate of approaching revolt. Laugier, thinking perhaps of King Philip II of Spain and his humility, which was so forcefully expressed at the Escorial, thundered against the king's doubtful amusements and entreated him to give religion its due. His blunt address landed him in trouble with his Jesuit superiors who were eager to maintain a smooth relationship with the French royalty. Unlike previous writers, Laugier interpreted the classical principle of the balanced interplay between the whole and its parts as formed by architectural elements that ensured the actual solidity of the building. As a result, he frowned on the use of pilasters, which had been a staple of architectural design ever since the Renaissance. Even though his image of the ideal building was not based on Roman models, Laugier admired the Maison Carrée at Nîmes as the most perfect building of antiquity: "Thirty columns support an entablature and a roof which is closed at both ends by a pediment —that is all; the combination is of a simplicity and a nobility which strikes everybody."

It was not the classical temple as such that needed to be imitated but that which lay behind its design, the original "rustic hut" or *cabane rustique* as he called it, a word often mistranslated as "primitive hut." This "hut," according to Laugier, consisted only of columns, entablatures, and pediments. Vaults, arches, pedestals, and pilasters were not part of that system and should therefore, so he argued, not be used. Even arcades, another important element in classical architecture, were listed by Laugier as "abuses."

Laugier's book was highly controversial. He argued that architecture was not to be seen as performing the magical transition from the worldly to the heavenly, as had been attempted in the baroque style, but rather as serving as a self-critical and self-purging book that retold nothing less than the story of the "origins" of mankind. These "origins," which had to remain embedded in architectural design processes, were similar to the notion of "grace"—a sign of divine presence in all of mankind, even in nonbelievers, and at the same time the source for the development of a Christian life. In this sense his argument echoed the 15th century debate between Bartolomé de las Casas and Juan Ginés de Sepúlveda in Madrid, on the question of the status of native Americans.

16.18 St. Geneviève, Paris, France

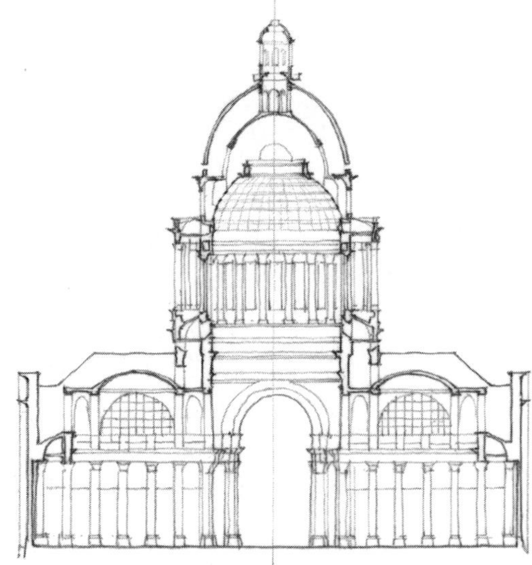

16.19 Section: St. Geneviève, Paris

### St. Geneviève

The Jesuits, who were sent from the Church to the French colonies in the Americas, had studied and written about the life and work of the native Americans. Laugier's "hut" was in many respects an indication of what the Jesuits had learned from people, who in their eyes were not "primitive," as had originally been argued, but actually noble; it was this, they argued, that prepared them for Christ. Also influencing Laugier's writings was the just-published *Discourse sur les arts et les sciences* (1750) by Jean-Jacques Rousseau (1712–78). In this astonishing book, Rousseau critiqued what he saw as the naïveté of the Enlightenment's careless atheism. Not only had reason in the hands of the more powerful crushed individual liberty, but it had also replaced simple virtues with a labyrinth of false truths. Reason did not lead to knowledge but to hypocrisy, and civilization led to class division, slavery, serfdom, robbery, war, and injustice. The only real progress was moral progress. It was a powerful and controversial critique of everything that the French intelligentsia had built up over the previous century.

Rousseau, a native of the Calvinist city of Geneva, marveled at the quite civilizational and devotional virtues of Swiss farmers and native Americans. It was Rousseau who coined the famous term "the Noble Savage" to describe the innate nobility of people like the Iroquois. The more conservative defenders of architectural convention rejected the notion of a noble savage and argued that it was still the Romans and Greeks who best translated nature into architectural form. But others saw a sanctioned opportunity for experimentation, and one of those was Jacques-Germain Soufflot (1709–80).

The dome of his St. Geneviève (Paris, 1757, which was later redesigned as a Pantheon for French luminaries) was still rather baroque, somewhat similar to Sir Christopher Wren's St. Paul's Cathedral in London. But novel was the clean-cut, neoclassical temple front with Corinthian capitals modeled on the Pantheon in Rome and self-consciously grafted onto the body of the building. Most baroque church fronts had little in common with Roman architecture. Soufflot also adhered to Laugier's call for an architecture in which every element has a structural rationale. There are pilasters on the interior but they are clearly linked to the structural grid established by the columns. The vaults, however, have a billowing lightness illuminated from the side through large windows, concealed on the exterior, however, behind a parapet. The contrast between the building's severe, clifflike exterior and the luminous, airy interior was meant to be a literal evocation of the Enlightenment's transformative power. The building was originally attached at its rear to a monastery, but made freestanding in the 19th century.

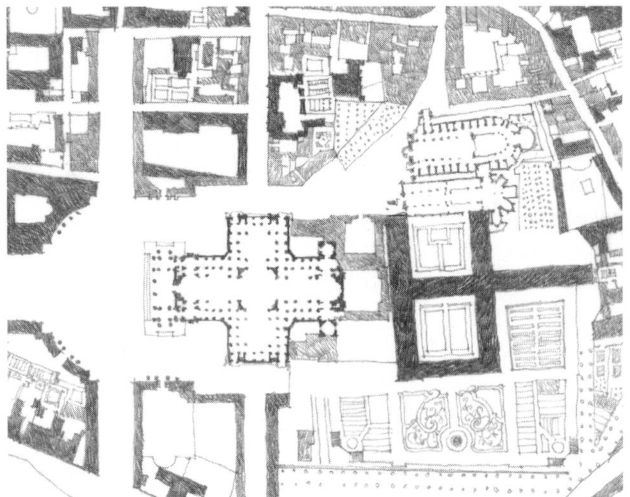

16.20 Site plan: St. Geneviève, Paris

16.21 Petit Trianon, Versailles, France

**Le Petit Trianon**

French intellectuals were impressed by the English picturesque garden and its mixture of elegance, informality, and exalted pedagogical mission. Voltaire was an advocate of English culture and often insisted on speaking English at the dinner table. He was certainly no populist. For him an enlightened monarchy was far superior to the chaos of democracy. This does not mean that neoclassicism shied away from the fashion-conscious world of polite society. On the contrary, it profited from the strength of bourgeois networks. By 1763 ladies had their hair done *à la grècque*, and one writer complained that young French gentlemen were often affecting an English accent.

It would be a mistake, however, to see the work of the French Enlightenment philosophers as completely antithetical to royal language, given the support it had from certain members of the French aristocracy. The critique of superficiality was expressed both outside and inside the court of Louis XV, as we have already seen with Laugier, with many writers and artists calling for a return to the standards if not of the ancients then at least of the time of Louis XIV.

At Ange-Jacques Gabriel's facade for the Petit Trianon in Versailles (1761–8) for Louis XIV, one can see just how quickly aspects of the new sensibility were absorbed. The volumetric simplicity, the absence of an axial imperative, as one might have expected from Hardouin-Mansart, and equally the absence of pilasters and quoins, except for the central four pilasters, was accomplished without any seeming loss of elegance.

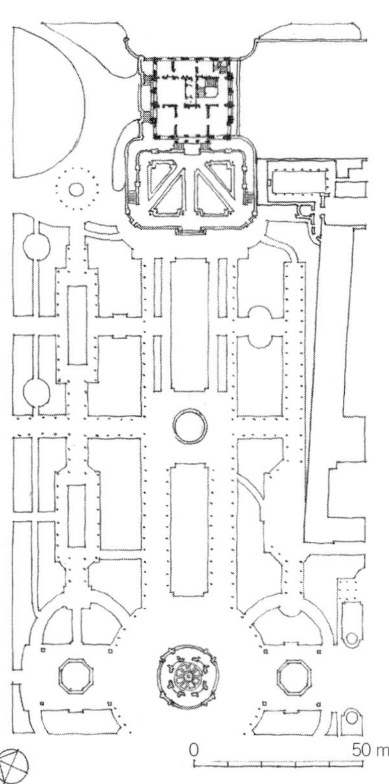


16.22 Plan: Petit Trianon, Versailles

In the European environment where global realities had increasingly become part of upper-class life, neoclassicism provided, as we have seen in the work of Adam, a language of stability and order that also reinforced the search for European self-understanding in the wake of the colonial experience. The term "neoclassicism," in wide use today, was invented in the mid-19th century. Until then, critics, theorists, and artists called it simply the "true style," one that was meant to challenge the fluctuations of taste. At its best, neoclassicism shared the Enlightenment's spirit of reform, whether it was scientific advancement in the age of reason or the new political philosophy that stressed the principles of human action. But neoclassicism, as a language of self-mastery, was also a language of the master over the production of others. Neoclassicism thus provided all too easily, the legitimization of empire as a structure imposed over colonialism, harboring an underlying and suppressed contradiction between a civilizational ideal and the political expediencies that were necessary to realize that ideal.

16.23 **Barrière de la Villette, Paris, France**

16.24 **Salt Works of Chaux, France**

**Salt Works of Chaux**

The most creative of the French neoclassicists of the time was Claude Nicholas Ledoux (1736–1806), who designed for the French crown a series of gates and toll houses—forty-five buildings in all—to mark the boundary of Paris and to impress approaching visitors. They also served as the place for payment of a much hated tax on the importation of salt (which had become very expensive) into the city. Like Wren's churches, each of the gatehouses is different from the next and yet each in its own way is varied and forceful. A few are left, including the Barrière de la Villette (1785–9), giving a good sense of Ledoux's austerely simplified architectural vocabulary. The central drum is supported by column pairs, serving as a screen, holding the arcaded bottom of a cylinder. Windows are without moldings and ornamentation is held to a minimum. The wide and low pediment—compared with the more historically accurate pediment of St. Geneviève—and the domeless drum are far outside the norms of classicism, but Ledoux, probably more than any other architect of his generation, was seeking to redefine architectural typology from top to bottom. His project for an agricultural lodge, for example, is a sphere placed in the center of a sunken courtyard and accessed on four sides by flying staircases.

Ledoux also designed various buildings for the Salt Works of Chaux (1775–9), located in the south of France between two villages near the forest of Chaux, not far from Besancon. The nearby forest supplied the wood needed to fire the kilns in which the salt was extracted from the brine. Ledoux's plan called for a semicircular arrangement of buildings with the house of the director at the center and the salt-extracting buildings to both sides. The circumference is occupied by curved storage buildings with the main entrance to the facility in the circle directly opposite the director's house.

The salt trade was among the grimmest aspects of life in 18th-century France; the forcible imposition of a tax gave rise to widespread smuggling and robbery, as salt was very much cheaper outside of France. The security of the salt works was thus essential. The entrance contained guardrooms and a small prison and is marked by a dense peristyle of six baseless Tuscan columns, with a squat attic above. Along the walls are openings out of which "flows" the thick saline water.

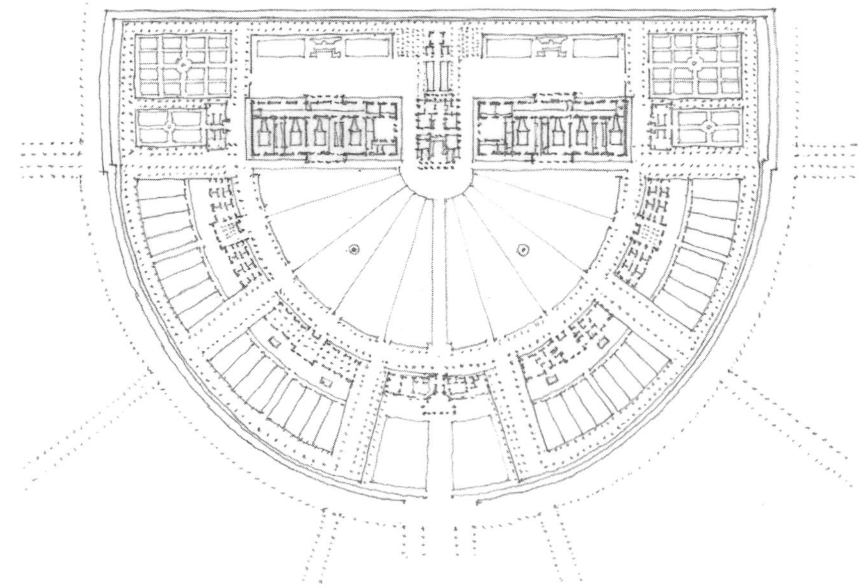

16.25 **Plan: Salt Works of Chaux, Arc-et-Senans, France**

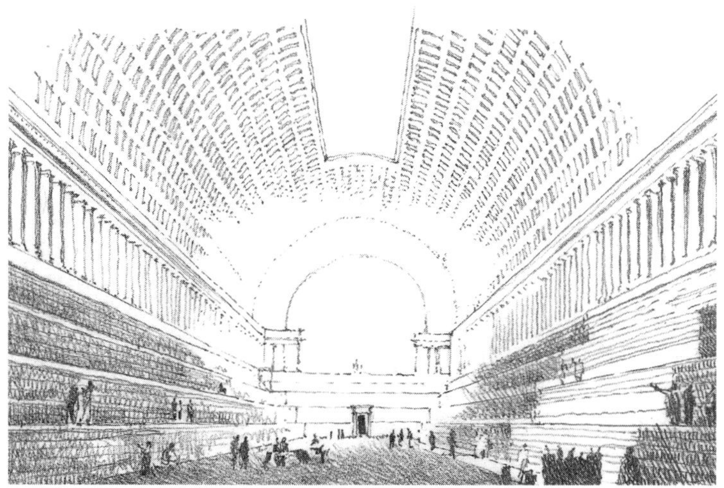

16.26 Boullée's idea for a Bibliothèque Nationale

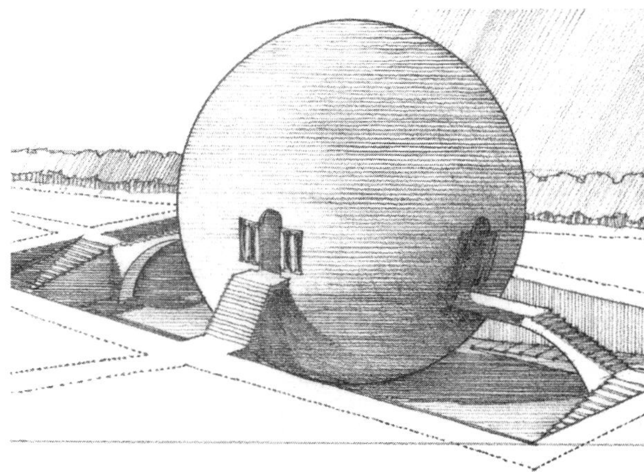

16.27 Claude Nicholas Ledoux's project for an agricultural lodge

**Bibliothèque Nationale**

The events leading to the French Revolution (1789–99) were manifold. The successors of Louis XIV had become increasingly self-involved and rigid, leading a frivolous and wasteful life in Versailles. Wars further weakened France, and its commerce with its colonies had dropped from 30 million livres in 1755 to four million in 1760. To understand the scale of this one should note that in 1751 the king spent 68 million livres, a quarter of the government's revenue, on the royal household alone. The descent was rapid. In 1760 the French commander in Canada surrendered to the English; in 1763, the French lost the French and Indian War and had to abandon their forts. In 1770 the Compagnie des Indes went bankrupt. The unmanageable national debt led internally to high taxes, while thousands of acres of farm land reverted to wilderness. Unemployment in Paris was close to 50 percent, and prices soared. Under these stresses and the concomitant food shortages, rural disturbances were common; but the actual opening salvo of violence, the first confrontation with the regime, was the bloody storming of the prison fortress known as the Bastille on July 14, 1789. More than any other architect, Étienne-Louis Boullée (1728–99) managed to straddle these complex political times. He won widespread acclaim during his lifetime for his series of inspired drawings that seemed to envision a postrevolutionary world.

Boullée's buildings have simple geometrical shapes, are monumental in scale, and often serve as backdrops for uncluttered neopagan devotions. His project for a Bibliothèque Nationale (1788), though often classified as an example of the neoclassical sensibility, has actually no standard classical features on the surfaces except for the entablature and the frieze of garlands. The main entrance, guarded by two large Atlas figures, gives admittance to a vast barrel-vaulted space boldly slit open at the top. The books are arranged on shelves against the walls of continuous terraces on the two sides of the interior of the building. Even more spectacular is Boullée's cenotaph for Sir Isaac Newton (1784). A sphere that represents the earth on the outside is on the inside a planetarium, with small holes forming the constellations. The entrance leads to a passageway that opens onto a shrine at the base of the inner void.

Both Ledoux and Boullée are often called "revolutionary" architects, but this is based on their architecture rather than their politics. Both straddled the fence in the French Revolution, even though they set in motion much of the aesthetic that for a short while governed the sensibilities of the age. Boullée probably made the transition better than Ledoux. Yet he too built little after the Revolution, but his place was more secure, and it was his vision that younger architects in the Academy of Architecture, where Boullée taught, aspired to emulate.

After the French Revolution, the history of neoclassicism took many turns, fusing with the Greek revival in Germany and Scotland and blending in with the eclectic stylistic preferences of the Victorians. Despite all of this, traces of a vigorous and austere neoclassicism, as was pursued by Ledoux and Boullée, are to be found throughout Europe from 1800 onward.

16.28 Section: Cenotaph for Sir Isaac Newton

16.29 **Virginia State Capitol, Richmond, based on Matthew Brady's Civil War photograph**

**NEOCLASSICISM IN THE UNITED STATES**

When the sons, daughters, and grandchildren of the European settlers revolted against English rule, what had at first started as a search for economic freedom became one of the Enlightenment's greatest moments. From an aesthetic point of view, the leading intellectuals were very much of the world of the Adam brothers and their ideal of a purified Roman majesty. Noteworthy, however, is that Americans, like the French at that time, were primarily infatuated with the Roman republic rather than with the Roman empire. It was a subtle but important difference, based more on fantasy than historical accuracy. The style of French postrevolutionary neoclassicism was known in particular to Thomas Jefferson (1743–1826), the drafter of the Constitution and the second president of the United States, who made a lasting imprint on American architecture of the period. Having lived in Paris for five years (1784–9) as minister to France, he came to admire philosophical developments in Europe and inculcated the idea that architecture was directly related to social reform. He was also the consummate gentleman architect, amassing a library of 130 books on the fine arts, certainly the largest in the United States. As an amateur architect, Jefferson, together with Charles-Louis Clérisseau, fused, if one will, Laugier and Adam, in the design of the Virginia State Capitol (1785). It was modeled on the Maison Carrée of Nîmes, one of the few Roman buildings that was accepted by Laugier as true to the standards of the "rustic hut." Clérisseau was a French architect prominent in the neoclassical movement and author of a work that included the first measured drawings of the Roman temple in Nîmes, which at the time was thought to have been a product of the earlier Roman republic, erected, so it was argued at the time, by self-governing free men. The Virginia State Capitol is thus based on a purposefully literal interpretation of a classical temple as an embodiment of republican ideals.

One could compare the Virginia State Capitol with the Government House in Calcutta. Both are examples of an "applied" Enlightenment, except that in the United States, the Enlightenment could be mapped onto a largely open landscape, given that the native populations that had survived the ravages of disease had been basically ignored or killed in battle. This was not the case in India, where native populations were an integral part of the success of the colonial economy. In India, once it became clear that buildings could not be just simple instruments of mercantile imperialism, classical clothing was necessary to link the colonial project to the language of eternal principles. This then transformed the direction of romanticism with its more paternalistic attitude toward the native population. In the United States, there was no such extensive encounter, meaning that neoclassicism could remain more abstract. Romanticism, as it developed in the United States, emphasized the natural beauty of the landscape, empty of history. One thinks in this respect of the paintings of Thomas Cole, such as *Landscape Scene from the Last of the Mohicans* (1827), which shows native Americans more as props than as people.

**16.30 Virginia State Capitol**

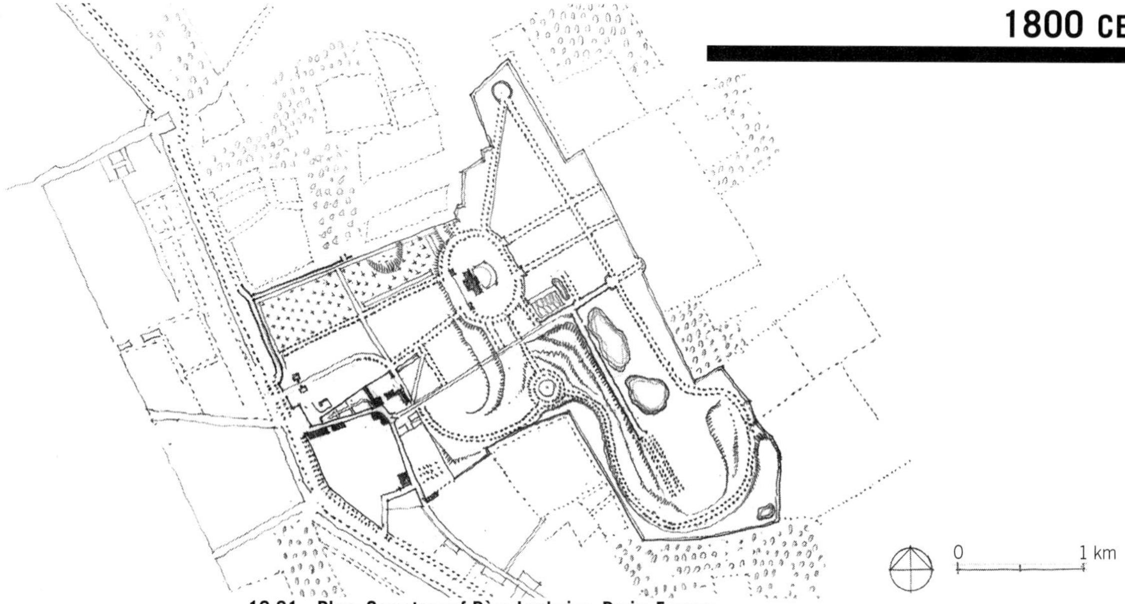

16.31 Plan: Cemetery of Père Lachaise, Paris, France

### Napoleonic Cemeteries

Whereas the English experimented with Enlightenment and then the romantic ideas in the governance of their colonies, the French, whose colonial empire had drastically shrunk by the mid-18th century, played the Enlightenment ideals out on the battlefields of Europe. Napoleon brought into European parlance concepts like liberty and justice, abstractions that were presumed universal and strong enough to replace defunct personalized regimes of the aristocracy. Though Napoleon marched through Europe, gaining adherents as he went along, he eventually succumbed to his own overreaching and to an alliance of Austrians, Russians, and English eager to keep Napoleonic ideas as far as possible from their domains. The impact of the Napoleonic era, however, was profound. It proved for a brief moment that nations could function without the paternalism of kings and princes. Napoleon was also responsible for emancipating the Jews in many of the lands that he came to control.

One of the most important contributions of Napoleonism to architecture was not in buildings but in cemeteries. Normally the soldier was an easily dispensable figure, fighting often as a conscript or as a mercenary. In Napoleon's army, death in battle was associated with the principle of national dignity, a theme that would become essential in the romantic period to come and, indeed, to the modern notion of nation as a whole. As a result, military death achieved a populism that it never had since antiquity. One has to remember that it was the custom that only the well-to-do were buried in or near a parish church. The poor were buried in pauper's graves.

But in 1803, after Napoleon made a decree that forbade burials in the city, a cemetery known as Père Lachaise was laid out on the outskirts of the city that was among the first examples of a garden cemetery. It was open to all. Graves, however, were to last for only 5 years unless permanent land was bought by the relatives who were also required to endow certain architectural features of the cemetery. The cemetery was laid out with trees bushes and winding paths; it had a central esplanade ending in a funerary monument. Père Lachaise became the model for cemeteries all over the world: the Glasgow Necropolis (1820), the South Metropolitan Cemetery at Norwood in London (1830s), and the Mt. Auburn Cemetery in Cambridge, Massachusetts (1831), are just a few examples.

16.32 View of the Cemetery of Père Lachaise

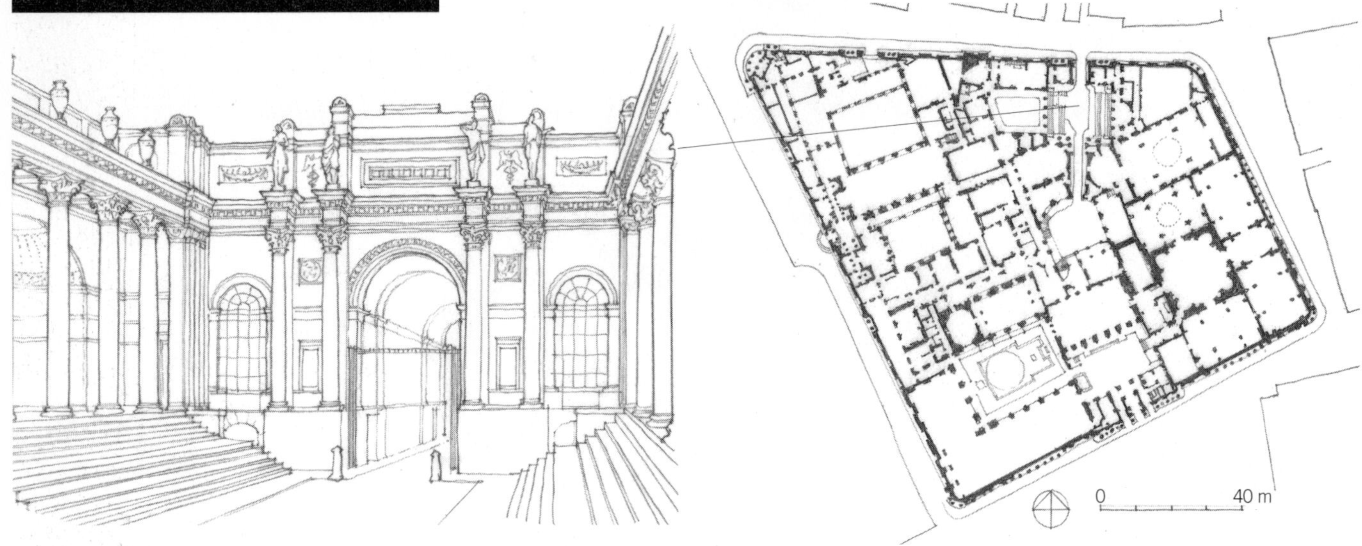


16.33 Lothbury court, Bank of England, London, England

16.34 Plan: Bank of England, London

**Bank of England**

By the early 19th century, the English economy was in a state of crisis and near bankruptcy, requiring it to borrow heavily from foreign banks. The French Revolution had spurred a major exodus of capital from London, and in the Napoleonic Wars, which began in 1799 and ended in 1815, Napoleon had hoped to cripple English hegemony by closing off its European ports. Rebuilding the Bank of England was important both literally and physically. The commission went to John Soane (1753–1837), the son of a bricklayer, who as a young apprentice in an architectural firm earned enough to travel to Italy where he was influenced by the work of Giambattista Piranesi.

Soane eventually began to receive small commissions, until he was appointed to the Office of the Works in 1791. Even though the Office of the Works favored a neoclassical style, a freer interpretation of classicism could survive in England, where neoclassicism had not risen to the level of state-sponsored aesthetic as it had in France during the time of Napoleon.

In designing the Bank Stock Office (1791–3), the first part of the bank to be built, Soane invented an architectural language based on flat vaults and pendentives to create a dynamic zoning of spaces. Unlike the penchant of other post-Enlightenment architects for the appearance of mass and weight, Soane's interiors seem papery and light. The building is a labyrinth of public spaces cleverly interconnected and yet it conforms to the requirements of an oddly shaped lot. Soane's designs, with its small passages contrasting with larger spaces, could be described as picturesque classicism. The building was criticized by both the conservatives and the anticlassicists, though its inventiveness has been championed in recent years as proto-Postmodern in its quirky and arbitrary dealing with classical forms. Soane's work should not be seen, however, as more ornamental than that of someone like John Nash (1752–1835), for Soane was quite taken by the arguments of Laugier and, following him, condemned the use of columns and pilasters in the same facade. He also avoided the decorative use of Greek and Roman ornaments, holding them out of place in a modern society. Novel was his use of segmental and semicircular arches, shapes that do not go comfortably together but that draw attention to the dramatic effect of light and shade.

Soane, predictably, was also an admirer of Sir John Vanbrugh (1664–1726), who in his estimation was the "Shakespeare of architects." In that sense he believed in the tragic nobility of architecture but simultaneously—and this would be the Romantic element in his work—in the break with the literal past. For that reason, Soane represented his bank as both a finished building and, remarkably, in a special drawing as a ruin, anticipating, if you will, the view backward from some future age.

**Calcutta and the Writers' Building**

Colonialism changed not only the lifestyles of the Europeans, but it also forced them to rethink their attitude toward governance and the divine, as well as their role in history, often to substantiate the colonial mentality, though sometimes to challenge it. This give-and-take spells itself out particularly clearly in the architecture of Calcutta where, by the late 18th century, some 200 years after the opening of its ports, what had initially started as a mercantile adventure had developed into a full-blown landholding enterprise. And yet, in spite of the East India Company's political successes and ample displays of wealth, the company, according to the banking statements in London, was still in debt in the early 1770s. (This is what prompted Frederick North, 2nd Earl of Guilford, to raise duties on tea to the Americas, triggering the Boston Tea Party.) The East India Company's officers were accused of corruption and profiteering, and in 1773, the company was reorganized to ensure greater accountability. This was in line with the new tendency to view power as a uniquely European privilege, based on the depth and nobility of its heritage. The company appointed a Governor General to preside over all the colonies, with an examiner, representing Parliament, keeping tabs on developments.

Thus was born, one could say, the ideological project of Indian colonization. But with new control came new opportunities for exploitation. Warren Hastings, the first governor-general of British India, from 1773 to 1786, expanded opium production for export to China. One of the significant buildings of this time is the gigantic secretariat and training school Hastings built for the clerks of the company (though they all had military-style ranks). Known as the Writers' Building ("writers" were clerks) this long, three-story structure was sited just in front of the fort, along the approach street that lead to its gates.

Given that the clerks enabled the company's work to be rationalized, it is only fitting that their domain was a remarkable essay in rationalization and functionalism (with only the slightest hint of classicism in the articulation of its central and side bays) with a single cornice running the entire length of the perimeter, interrupted only slightly by the central facade.

The present Writers' Building was designed in 1780 by a civil architect named Fortnam, as well as Thomas Lyon, an amateur architect and a carpenter. Trained architects rarely sought employment with the company at this time, and construction was mostly left to the engineers and gentlemen officers. The newly found power of a rationalized bureaucracy was also expressed architecturally in such structures as Sir William Chamber's Somerset House (1775–96), the first government office block in London.

**16.35 Writers' Building, Calcutta, India**

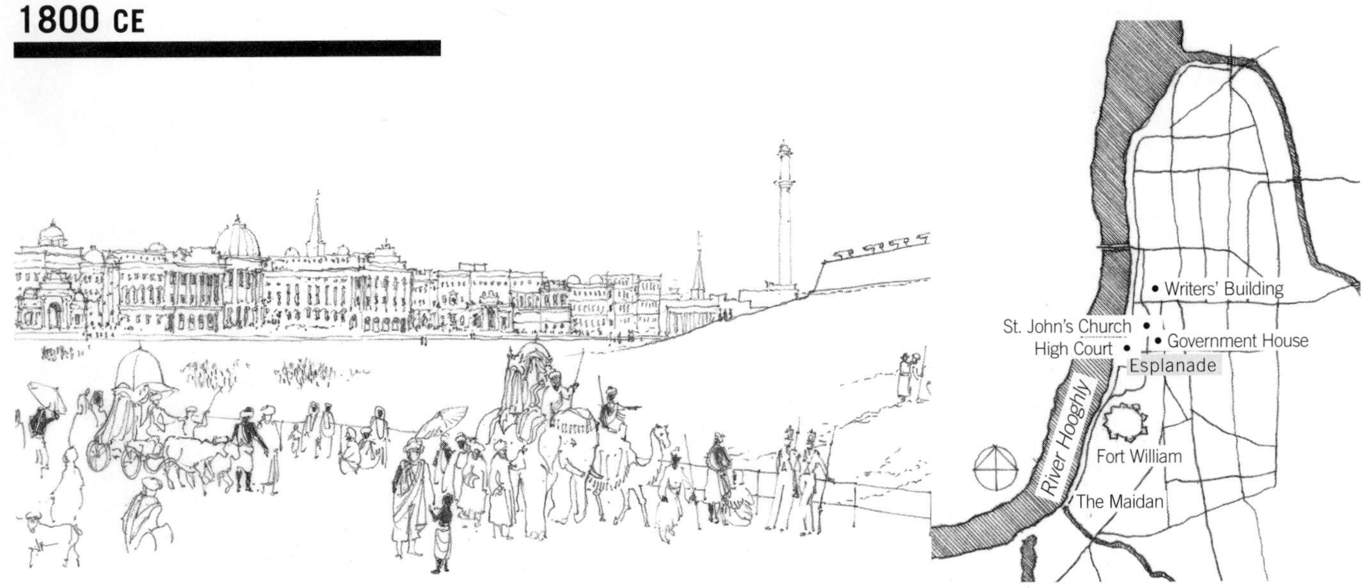


**16.36 View of Calcutta from the Esplanade, ca. 1850**

**16.37 Plan of early Calcutta**

**St. John's Church**

With the turn of the 19th century, English colonial policy underwent yet another change, as critics, influenced to some extent by an Enlightenment-inspired critique of the arbitrariness of power, forced the impeachment of Warren Hastings. For members of the new generation, such as Edmund Burke (1729–97), parliamentary oversight was not enough. There had to be a social contract, but one—in good English manner—that was attached to the principle of divine sanction, meaning that the purpose of the colonial administration had to be consonant with the "eternal laws" of governance. In England, the principles of good governance were equated, in particular by the Tories, with the power of the king and the aristocracy. National pride was also at stake. The newly formed United Kingdom (culminating in the conquest of Catholic Ireland in the 17th century) was legitimized on the basis of the Anglo-Saxon claim to be the sole inheritors of the "eternal and universal" laws and institutions of the Romans, considered at that time to be the only true instance of the civilizing genius. The perfect person to take over from the discredited Hastings as governor-general was Lord Charles Cornwallis (governor-general from 1786–93), the very embodiment of the fusion of Enlightenment legalism with aristocratic privilege, and this despite the fact that it was under his command as major general of British forces in the Americas that the colonies had become independent.

In an attempt to replicate the European aristocracy in India, Cornwallis created a class of Zamindars (landowners, from the Persian *zamin* or land, and *dar*, denoting to have or possess). In the earlier Moghul administration, land was collectively owned at the village level, and Zamindars were only tax collectors. Now that they actually owned the land, the Zamindars could parcel off pieces in response to market opportunities without consulting the disempowered peasantry. The results were disastrous. Enterprising company officers immediately exploited these opportunities for their personal ends, making quick fortunes.

**16.38 St. John's Church, Calcutta, India**

St John's Church, begun in 1787, demonstrates the shift away from the mercantile world of the early colonial period toward an Anglican-authenticated colonial regime. Based on the late-Georgian high steeple of St. Martin-in-the-Fields in London, it consisted of a simple box (a three-bay nave and galleries) with a Tuscan portico and a stone steeple and spire. Compared to its model, St John's steeple is stubbier, since one story was omitted; but the spire, as was its purpose, was unquestionably the most visible form on the skyline. Its symbolic importance equalled that of King's Chapel in Boston as a visible reminder of the authority of Church and King. The building was located on the official burial grounds of the East India Company to the south of the fort and close to the octagonal Islamic tomb of Charnock. Made from real stone, and not just brick, St. John's was meant to display, as it were, the solidity and permanence of the colonial administration, as well as its right to rule, and not just its power to do so. Doric porticoes were also added to Writers' Building around this time, to update the building according to the new ideas.

**16.39 Government House, Calcutta, India**

**Government House**

By 1800, a new generation of company officers took issue with the high-handed attitude of the governor-general and his Zamindar associates. They preferred to see the rural peasant as a person who did not necessarily need the corrupting sophistications of European rule. The natives—as they were called—were not to be thought of as a servant class but as limited junior partners in the Enlightenment project. Charles Metcalfe, one of the leading proponents of romantic ideals in India, admired in particular the Indian village (its ancient urban culture notwithstanding), thus enhancing the impression in Europe that the distinction between Europe and the colonies was a difference between cities and villages. Thomas Munro took this a step further in contemplating a future for India that could be developed out of its own true culture and institutions, under the watchful eyes of men like himself who would protect the natives while enforcing the process of collecting taxes. One of the consequences of this was that there was little attempt to "Christianize" the population as the Spanish had done in the Americas.

The attitude regarding India was summarized best by Charles Trevelyan, a young liberal, in the 1830s, who argued that India, "trained by us to happiness and independence, and endowed with our learning and political institutions ... will remain the proudest monument of British benevolence." For the liberals, passing on English civilization to the Indians, whose civilization was seen as defunct, had a singular objective. They claimed to hold custody of the Indian civilization until such time when the Indians were sufficiently "civilized" and self-disciplined. This task was commonly characterized as the "white man's burden."

Again, the definition of the governor-general changed. He was now seen first and foremost as a chief executive. In 1798, when Lord Richard Wellesley replaced Cornwallis as governor-general of British India, he set out to change Calcutta into the region's administrative center. He began construction of a new Government House (1803) to serve as his residence and office. The old governor's house was not particularly distinguished or well sited. To connect the new building with the older administrative center and the Writers' Building to the north, a new axially placed road was constructed. The building also faced in the opposite direction, to the expanding villa quarter to the south around the open space of a newly expanded fort.

The design was prepared by Charles Wyatt, an engineer in the company, who is presumed to have adapted it from the design of Robert Adam's Kendleston Hall, as published in Adam's book, *Works of Architecture, Vitruvius Britannicus*. With one central block connected to four smaller corner blocks by curving corridors and an oversized sweeping staircase toward the north, the governor's palace was designed from the start with spectacle in mind. With a tall Pantheonesque central dome (added somewhat later), each side of the facade is symmetrical and complete and stands as an idealized object in space. Its 26-acre territory was walled in, and entrances were marked with gateways that resemble triumphal arches. The strict neoclassical portico set up on a broad and imposing staircase sealed its identification with the eternal principles of Vitruvius, even though the entire structure was made in brick and Madras *chunam*, and not Italian marble.

16.40 Royal Pavilion, Brighton, England

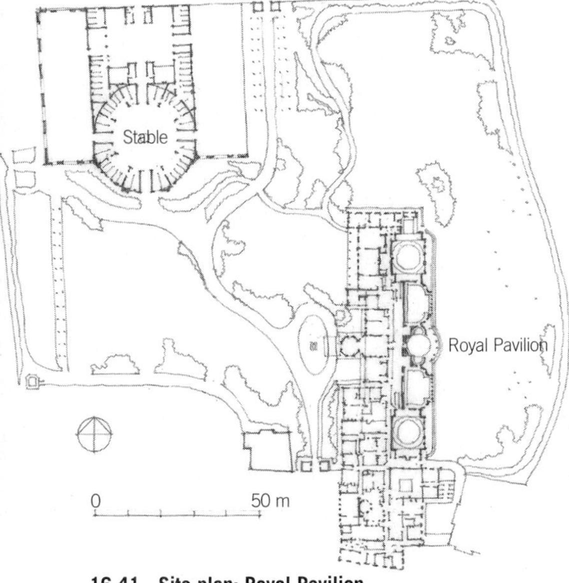

16.41 Site plan: Royal Pavilion

### Royal Pavilion

Gardens were often embellished with follies and other architectural curiosities, many of which played out the themes of colonial privilege, whether real or imagined. This was just as true for Sans Souci, as for the royal retreat at Brighton, then a small fashionable resort used by the Prince of Wales (1762–1830), the future King George IV. The retreat, however, should not be confused with English picturesqueness, as it had limited cultural pedagogical content. The prince, who as regent sided with the liberal Whigs, built stables in the "Indian manner," modeled loosely on Shah Jahan's 17th-century Friday Mosque at Delhi. On the inside, it had a large timber-framed dome divided into sixteen lotus-leaf panels of glass. It was a remarkable structure and one of the first glass domes in the history of architecture. Designed by William Porden, the plan and general form were modeled to some degree on the Halle au Blé in Paris, a corn market that had a shallow wooden dome (built in 1782, destroyed by fire in 1803), but this was not a market hall and the Halle lacked the grace and charm of the Brighton stables. What had begun as a curiosity, as a playful extension within the colonial imagination, became something that was neither eastern nor western, but nevertheless it was to presage a whole new level of spatial experimentation.

This also applies to the nearby Royal Pavilion (1818–22), which was built by none other than John Nash, who, though specializing in white neoclassical palaces and houses for the elite, had also become something of an expert on the Chinese style. As whimsical as the building may seem, it introduced a feature that was to presage the modern era. The dome was supported by a cast-iron structure, and indeed a good portion of the building was steel. Not having to design a neoclassical building, which would have had to adhere to well-established norms about structure and *firmitas*, Nash was able to create an architecture that was hung on a steel frame.

The Prince of Wales was an eccentric and self-indulgent man who was allowed to have his eccentricities, even with regard to his mild support of the Whigs as long as his father was alive. But once the prince became King George IV in 1820, he became a staunch defender of the Tory party. He hired Nash again, but this time to redesign Buckingham House in Buckingham Palace (1825). The eastern facade was added in 1847 in a manner befitting the king of a world power. He had been living in the Carlton House, which, though lavish, was seen as inadequate for the representational requirements of empire. By then, times had changed too, and even though the king's excessive ways continued, England, under the influence of reformers and evangelicals, had begun to seek more conservative and sober architectural expressions.

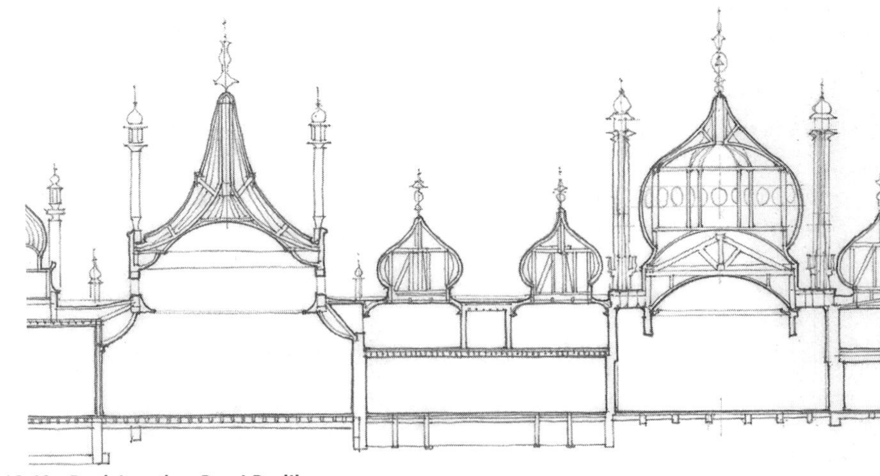
16.42 Partial section: Royal Pavilion

16.43 Eastern State Penitentiary, Philadelphia, USA

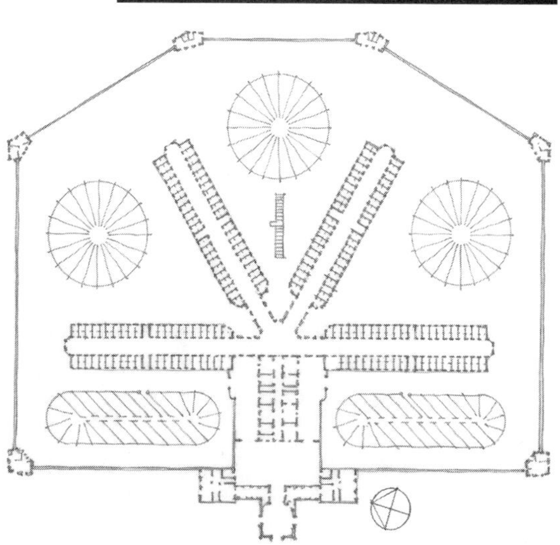

16.44 Plan: Pentonville Prison, London, England

**Panoptic Prisons**

The definition of criminality changed considerably between the 18th and 19th centuries. In the 18th century, criminals, the mentally insane, the poor, and the indigent were quite interchangeable. These unwanteds were thrown together in large halls and corridors. The Lunatics Tower in Vienna (1784) was nothing more than a cylindrical fortress. Overcrowding, filth, and brutal conditions made them into terrifying places. Law's purpose was to protect the elite, meaning that there was little incentive to deal out any kind of nuanced justice.

In England, around 1819, there were 220 capital offenses, ranging from murder to stealing bread. With the Enlightenment came the attempt to refine the force of law, but it was not so much the terror of the prisons that was so appalling to the minds of the early 19th-century moralists, as the fact that humanity could, in essence, be placed outside the reach of the moral life.

A connection had to be made between the reform of the body and mind of the prisoner and the legitimacy of the state, bringing forth the first modern jails, such as the Virginia Penitentiary (1798) by Benjamin Latrobe and the Suffolk House of Correction (Bury St. Edmunds, England, 1803). The latter had the prison's governor's house at the center as a way to demonstrate the new force of law that now ostensibly protected the prisoner from abuse while enforcing its own code of behavior. These new prisons were designed with isolated cells for the inmates grouped along open corridors of buildings that were like the spokes of a wheel, giving rise to the name, panoptic prison. A particularly clear example of the panoptic system can be found at the Eastern State Penitentiary in Philadelphia (begun 1821), organized according to a philosophy set out by the Pennsylvania Quakers that presumed that isolation would induce monastic self-reflection. Prisoners lived in a cell and could go outside into a small private courtyard. They were allowed out only for infrequent baths or medical emergencies. Visits were permitted only from officials. Masks and the use of numbers rather than names ensured anonymity if inmates had to be removed from their cells. Even the sewer pipes were arranged to prevent communication from cell to cell. All the while the prisoner's very movements were observed, either through the corridor or from the towers during exercises. Prisoners who were able were allowed to choose to perfect a few prechosen skills like shoemaking, basket-weaving, and broom-making, the idea being that these humble activities would reconnect them with the principle that being serviceable to society was the primary task of existence.

This system was much admired despite the fact that it soon became obvious that not a few inmates went crazy. Its English equivalent, the Pentonville Prison (London, 1844), designed according to Jeremy Bentham's design by which five radiating arms extend from a central hall from where the prisoners can be observed. Pentonville became the most copied prison in the world.

16.45 Suffolk House of Correction, Bury St. Edmunds, England

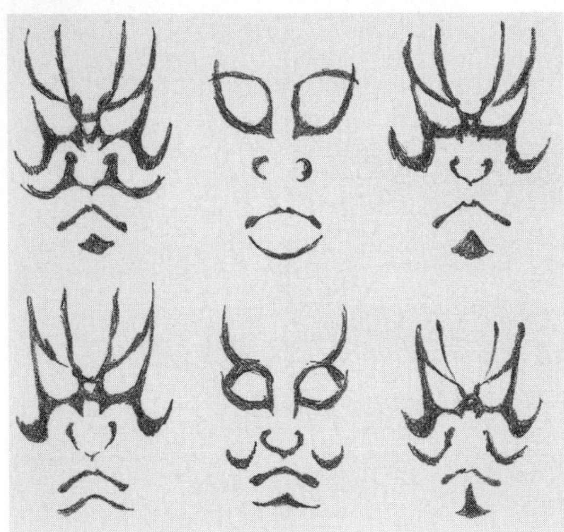

16.46 Examples of Kabuki make-up

16.47 Facsimile of Nishimura Shigenaga's *Interior of a Kabuki Theater*

### JAPAN: EDO PERIOD

The Tokugawa shoguns wanted to structure and ritualize upper-class life and society down to the last detail. They also closed Japanese society off from the outside, even though Chinese and some European ships were allowed into the port of Nagasaki. This was partially due to the legitimate perception that Japan would become another India if it allowed Europeans free access. It was also partially driven by a political goal to control the population.

The word "Kabuki" connotes "out-of-the-ordinary" and "shocking." The Kabuki theater evolved as a mix of the acrobatic, the comedic, and the sensual. In the Shimabara the street performers had been well integrated into the entertainment offerings. Alongside, the prostitutes had evolved their own routines to include comic sketches and elaborate dancing with sensual movements and erotic scenery. Early in the 17th century both these art forms were combined with the invention of the first Kabuki theater. Although banned by the shoguns in 1652, the scandal associated with the Kabuki only assured its notoriety as a liminal place between the openly erotic and the restricted. Here high officials interacted intimately with theater people who, though beautiful, accomplished, and expensively dressed, were social outcasts.

The earliest theaters were temporary structures similar to those used for special public Noh performances, except that they were much more plebeian than the high-class stages of the Noh. The Kabuki stages were in the open air, fenced-off areas, focused on a temporary stage with a gabled roof. Their placement was improvised to take advantage of existing situations, such as using the removable screens of the Sumiya that enabled the street to suddenly become a stage for the audience seated in the front rooms of the Sumiya.

Gradually the stages became more permanent, when a wooden wall was added behind the stage. As kabuki became popular with the more elite audiences, a separate space, literally raised above the commoners, in the form of raised boxes (*sajiki*) were added along the sides. These early theaters were equipped with enough spaces for dressing rooms, boxes, teahouses, and corollary entertainments. This could range from genteel conversation and private performances of music, dance, storytelling, impersonations, and skits to risqué banter and, of course, sex.

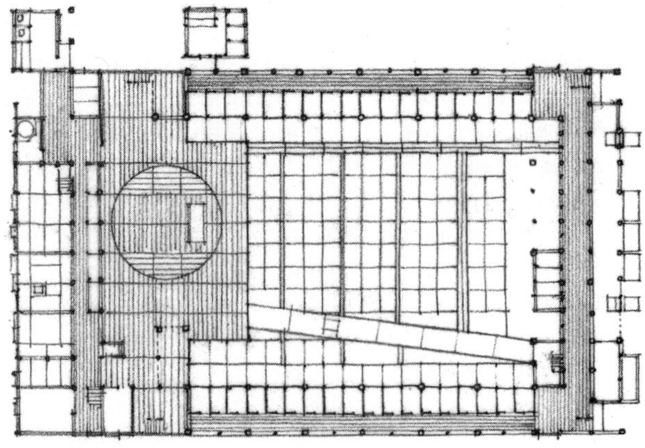

16.48 Plan of a Kabuki theater similar to Karamaru-za

16.49 **Interior of Kanamaru-za, Kotohira, Japan**

16.50 **Kanamaru-za, Kotohira**

**Kanamaru-za**

The mature form of the theater emerged in the late 17th century. With a single solid wall running around the perimeter, it had only a single entrance, cut low and small, to regulate flow. Only one person at a time could enter or exit, and then only by bending, as one entered a teahouse. The front facade additionally had shoji screens and wooden slats to curtail sight lines. A small tower with a drum, vertical banners, and platforms extending into the streets furnished the infrastructure for advertising. There was no lobby. The audience entered directly into the main audience space, known as the *doma*, which was basically an open lawn. In front was the main stage, roughly 12 meters square. To the sides, lifted on stilts, were the cubicles, with passages behind for the higher-class clients. The stage and the cubicles all had individual gable roofs. The stage roof was held up by corner pillars, with the gable end facing the audience, as in Noh stages. The main stage was supported by an extensive back stage area, including two side wings of different sizes, and an extensive preparation area almost twice as large as the stage itself. The backstage was also independently roofed.

By the 1740s ever-larger Kabuki stages were built throughout Japan. The entrance facade had more signage and acquired a small lobby area. There were now three entrances, two large ones for the elite and a smaller one for commoners. The whole was roofed over. An angled, raised corridor led to the stage front (the *hanamichi*). The backstage spaces became also differentiated, with specialized rehearsal rooms and two to three stories of dressing rooms for the performers, many of whom had acquired a star following.

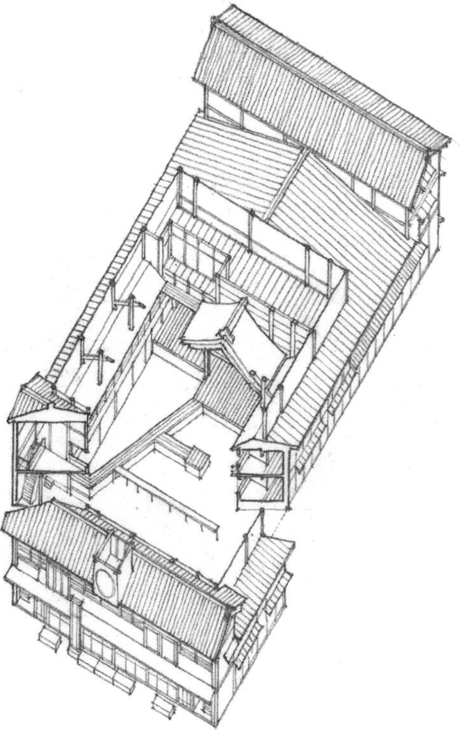

16.51 **Pictorial view of a Kabuki theater**

The seating was divided into individual spaces, called *masu*, by means of low wooden separators arranged in a grid. The *sazki* were based on tatami modules, and there were separate spaces built into the lobby to receive the shoes of the audience. The stage had two *hanamichi*, both at right angles to the stage and over to the side so as not to take up too much of the audience space. The stage itself had a round revolving segment that could be used to execute quick scenery changes.There are only a few extant Kabuki theaters from the 17th and 18th centuries. The Kanamaru-za (1835) is a good example of the fully developed Kabuki theater of the 19th century (although it is somewhat smaller than the largest theaters in the big cities).

## ROMANTIC NATIONALISM

Nationalism is such a ubiquitous term that one forgets that it is actually a modern term, springing from the end of the Napoleonic Wars. As important as Napoleon Bonaparte was in spreading the ideas of liberty and justice throughout Europe, the consequences of decades of war left Europeans in desperate need of stability. In 1813, Europe's diplomats met in Vienna to discuss the political future of Europe; they hoped that the borders could be stabilized. The Vienna Congress also stipulated that countries were to create constitutions, if they had not already done so—a promise some rulers broke to create stronger bonds between the aristocracy and the bourgeoisie. Prior to the Vienna Congress that bond was achieved mainly through the custom of marriage, which only tended to splinter and fragment the political landscape. It was hoped that countries with fixed national boundaries and with a working legal infrastructure would avoid war or have the means and recourse to avoid it. Though the ideals proved to be elusive, there is no doubt that the Vienna Congress helped create the modern notion of a nation-state, and it was certainly successful to the degree that it determined the future boundaries of Europe, boundaries that impact European politics to this day. Though various regional wars broke out during the 19th century, the Vienna Congress created so little dispute that Europe did not go to war for a century.

The new spirit of nationalism found an easy alliance with romanticism, especially in countries that felt that they had been victimized by the hegemony of other European powers. Romantic nationalism was thus particularly strong in Germany and Russia, which had been invaded by France under Napoleon. For the nationalists, history was more than just a gentleman's pastime. State boundaries had to make sense historically, linguistically, geographically, and now ethnically, and this led to an interest in local history and the development of regional antiquarianism. In Russia this led to a revival of the Russian language, for one has to remember that, until the defeat of Napoleon, the Russian aristocracy spoke mainly French. In Germany, one saw a fascination with the medieval, with the imagery of the forest, but also with ancient Greeks, with whom many romantics felt an affinity.

Later in the 20th century, romantic nationalism emerged in Scandinavia as a protest against Russian occupation and took the form of a revival of Nordic mythology.

In recent decades, with the post-Cold-War multiplication of new countries, romantic nationalism resurfaced to become a "global" phenomenon. Though it heralds the farmer and the workers, it is often an aesthetic that shies away from the political and thus appeals to upper-class tastes. As a result, romanticism generally is a conservative response in the lower classes and a liberal response in the upper classes. The traits are clearly identifiable: passion for one's country, combined with a feeling, real or not, of a past injustice at the hands of others. The past that romantics point to is often bucolic, quiet, and premodern—a cleaned-up fiction more than a reality.

**16.52 Congress of Vienna, 1814–15**

16.53 **Altes Museum, Berlin, Germany**

16.54 **Schauspielhaus, Berlin, Germany**

**Altes Museum**

In the course of the 17th century, the electors of Brandenburg expanded their territory so that by the end of the century Prussia had become more than a regional principality, it had become a major state. Yet, despite the War of the Austrian Succession (1740–8), which saw Prussia victorious against the Austrians, the Prussian army was crushed by Napoleon in the twin battles of Jena and Auerstedt. And in 1807 Prussia had to accept the harsh Treaty of Tilsit, by which it lost a sizable portion of its territory and, for a time, became a puppet of the French. The losses were regained when Prussia and its allies defeated Napoleon at Leipzig in 1813. It was in the wake of this post-Napoleonic enthusiasm that one can see the rise of the German romantic movement, especially in poetry and philosophy, which envisioned nature as a manifestation of the divine. The greatest German romantic painter, Caspar David Friedrich (1774–1840), created meditative landscapes that hover between mysticism and a sense of melancholy and solitude.

The defeat at the hands of Napoleon also led to a generation of thinkers who initially had been quite pro-French and who had hoped to retool the Enlightenment to fit the German context. Energetic reformers like Karl von Stein, the minister of commerce; Karl August von Hardenberg, Prussia's foreign minister; and Wilhelm von Humboldt, head of Prussia's department of education and arts helped transform Prussia into a progressive state by abolishing serfdom and the privileges of the nobility, introducing agrarian and other social and economic reforms and creating an exemplary system of universal education. Among the leading literary figures in Germany at the time were Johann Wolfgang von Goethe (1749–1832) and Friedrich von Schiller (1759–1805), who wanted to link German nationalism to the ideals of ancient Greece. This gave the German movement a different tenor than the nationalism one saw in France, which emphasized the idealization of political institutions and social arrangements. In Germany, the Enlightenment, in its more romanticized form, emphasized culture and personal self-cultivation and was thus drawn to ancient Greece. To that effect, Goethe reformed the court theater of Karl August, duke of Weimar, emphasizing the ennobling effect of the Greek playwrights.

The person who gave architectural shape to the romantic neo-Greek ideals was Karl Friedrich Schinkel (1781–1841). In 1803 he went to Rome to continue his training as an architect. There he met Wilhelm von Humboldt and they became friends. It was Humbolt who helped secure Schinkel's position in the Prussian bureaucracy; one of his first public projects was the design of the Neue Wache, or New Guardhouse (1816–18), a monument to the new citizen's army of Prussia. Until then, the only significant neoclassical building in Berlin was the Brandenburg Gate, inspired by the Athenian Propylaea. The Neue Wache, in an austere French manner, has a Doric porch flanked by two tower bases (rather than towers) that make the building appear to be a temple-gate combination. The tympanum shows the Goddess of Victory controlling and deciding a battle. The interior is a simple square room without a dome but a round skylight at the center.

Schinkel's other works included a theater, the Schauspielhaus (1818–21), the Altes Museum at Berlin (1823–30), Schlob Glienicke (completed 1827), and the Bauakademie (1831–6), to name but a few of the more prominent edifices. No other architect in Europe, with perhaps the exception of John Nash, wielded so much influence.

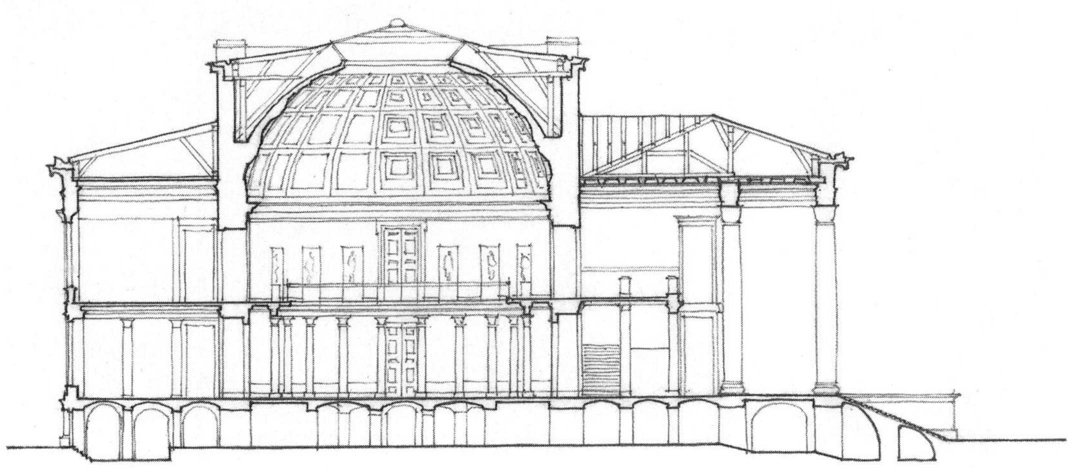

16.55 **Section: Altes Museum, Berlin**

Schinkel's most visible commission was for a public art museum sited very prominently opposite the Schloss (Royal Palace) in the very heart of Berlin. Altes Museum (1822–30), originally called the Neues Museum, embodied Schinkel's commitment to monumental civic architecture as a vehicle of the Enlightenment's cultural imperative. Though museums were beginning to be designed, most of them at that time were refurbished palaces; the building type, as an institutional element in the urban landscape, did not yet exist, mainly because before the bourgeois period that we are now entering, art collecting was still largely an autocratic privilege. Schinkel designed the building as a great block with two interior courtyards and a central space; the surmounting Pantheonesque dome was, however, not visible from the front. Instead, the front was a row of columns, like a great Greek stoa, elevated on a platform above the surroundings. At the top of the stairs, before one entered the rotunda, there was a loggia with large open-air staircases to the right and left of the principal axis. Art works were exhibited in long rectilinear units with column pairs forming a type of street down the middle. This was not a temple or sanctuary but rather a type of civic warehouse, with the central space fitted out with statues as if one were in an agora. It was a space designed for talking and holding conversations about the art, as much as for looking at it.

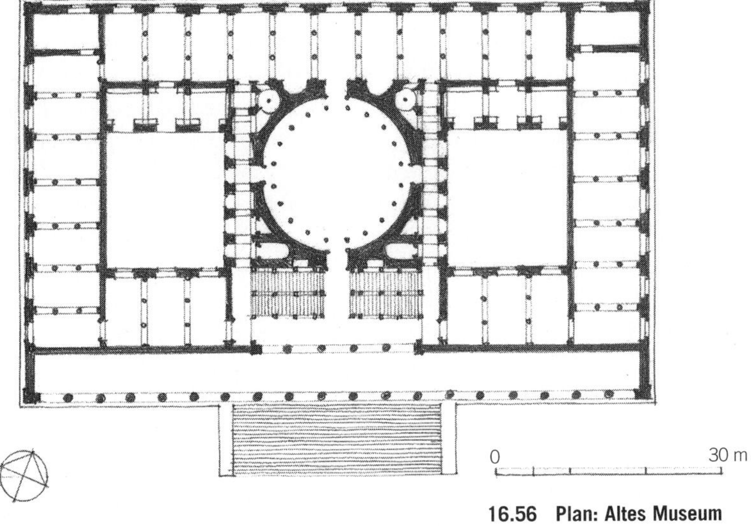


16.56 **Plan: Altes Museum**

16.57 **Entrance facade: Altes Museum**

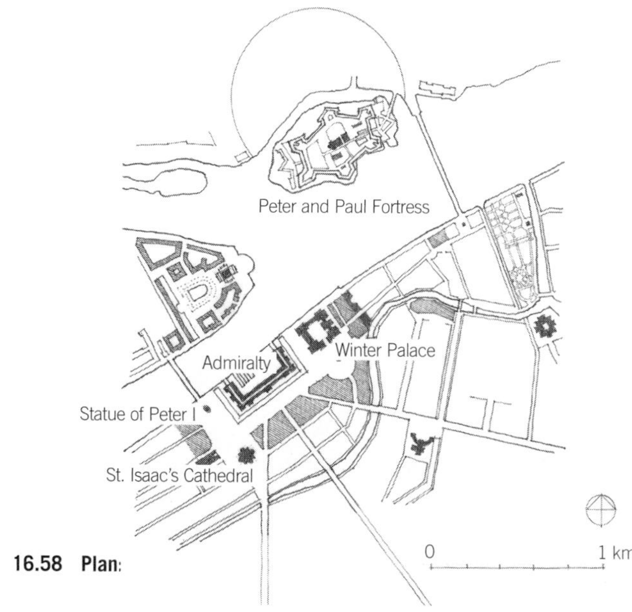


**16.58 Plan:**

**16.59 Aerial view of St. Petersburg, Russia**

### St. Petersburg

The two most important building sites of the time were in St. Petersburg and Washington, D.C. Both were designed as new capitals, and both were examples of the fusion of late baroque and neoclassical urban planning ideas carrying the imprint, however, of different political goals. In the 17th century, Russia was ruled by a coalition of forces that included the royal family, members of the nobility, church hierarchies, and military commanders who exercised control over the serfs. It was a time of numerous disturbances. There were urban riots in 1648, a revolt in 1662, a rebellion in 1669, and an uprising in 1668. But the difficulties were soon put to rest by Tzar Peter Alexevich Romanov I (1672–1725), who pulled Russia out of its isolation, turning the Orthodox Muscovite state into a secular, westernized empire against considerable opposition from many levels of society. This was realized through massive forced-labor enterprises as well as a series of wars, consuming as much as 90 percent of the state budget. The result, however, was an empire with acquisitions from the Baltic to the Caspian Sea and a modern army and navy, which roundly defeated Sweden. For the first time since the 13th century, Russia could sail down the Neva River to the Gulf of Finland and into the Baltic Sea.

To control access to the Baltic Sea, Peter needed a fortress, a project that eventually grew into one of the biggest building sites in Europe. St. Petersburg dates its beginning to May 16, 1703, when the cornerstone for the Peter and Paul Fortress was laid. 40,000 peasants were conscripted for the construction work along with Swedish prisoners of war. Work had progressed far enough by 1712 for relics from the Vladimir-Suzdal monastery to be sent to the St. Alexander Nevsky monastery, named after the 13th-century national hero St. Alexander Nevsky, who had received this name because he had beaten the Swedes on the Neva River. St. Petersburg now had its founding myth and was an instant religious as well as secular center. To speed things along, Peter, in 1714, even forbade masonry construction throughout the rest of Russia to ensure a supply of qualified workers and materials for St. Petersburg.

### Washington, D.C.

Washington, D.C., designed by Charles Pierre L'Enfant (1754–1825) in 1792, was different from St. Petersburg in that the important buildings were placed as an ensemble around conjoining squares in the Italian manner, with radiating streets emanating from the center, resulting in a complex overlay of different geometries. Over the base pattern of the urban grid, L'Enfant imposed a baroque styled web of avenues that is surprisingly idiosyncratic and that adjusts to the landscape and to the turns of the Potomac River. Over this, he imposed a third order, with the Capitol building and the White House not facing each other across an open mall but placed at the ends of an L, with the Capitol at the end of the longer arm of the east-west facing L. The intersection of the two arms lies along the Potomac so that the two buildings, backing their way into the urban fabric from the river's edge, achieve a sense of parallel prominence.

**16.60 Winter Palace, St. Petersburg, Russia**

16.61 U.S. Capitol, Washington, D.C., USA

16.62 U.S. Capitol, Washington, D.C.

L'Enfant's design calls to mind the gardens of Versailles because the grand avenues are like the allées. However, that the Capitol and the White House are also connected by one of the diagonal avenues, Pennsylvania Avenue, is a baroque device first articulated for Rome under Sixtus V in his attempt to link the great pilgrimage sites of that city. In that sense the city blends aspects of Versailles and Rome, bringing the Counter-Reformation ideal of the freestanding monumental building into line with the notion of a city as a landscape traversed by grand ceremonial approaches. The siting of both the Capitol and the White House away from the river's edge and fronted by lawns, derives from English country house prototypes and might also point to the Invalides (begun in 1671) in Paris, which, unlike the Louvre, was set at 90 degrees to the river at the end of a park, connecting building and river. This third element is unusual, for at St. Petersburg, the Winter Palace, which is modeled on the Louvre, sits alongside the Neva River.

The United States Capitol Building, begun in 1793, went through several stages involving William Thornton, Henry Latrobe, and Charles Bulfinch, in that order. The House and Senate chambers were placed right and left of a great rotunda that was envisioned as a museum, with niches sheltering statues of revolutionary heroes. The building seamlessly integrated allusions to a mythical Roman Republic past, universal geometries, and great historical events.

Beginning in 1855, the west front was rebuilt and a new dome (held up by a steel frame) was designed to rest on a high drum. It was far out of proportion to the building below, if one thinks of the conventions set in play by Michelangelo's dome for St. Peter's in Vatican City. But perhaps it was this strangeness that kept it from looking like a cathedral. The Capitol also went beyond the English country house to become something altogether new.

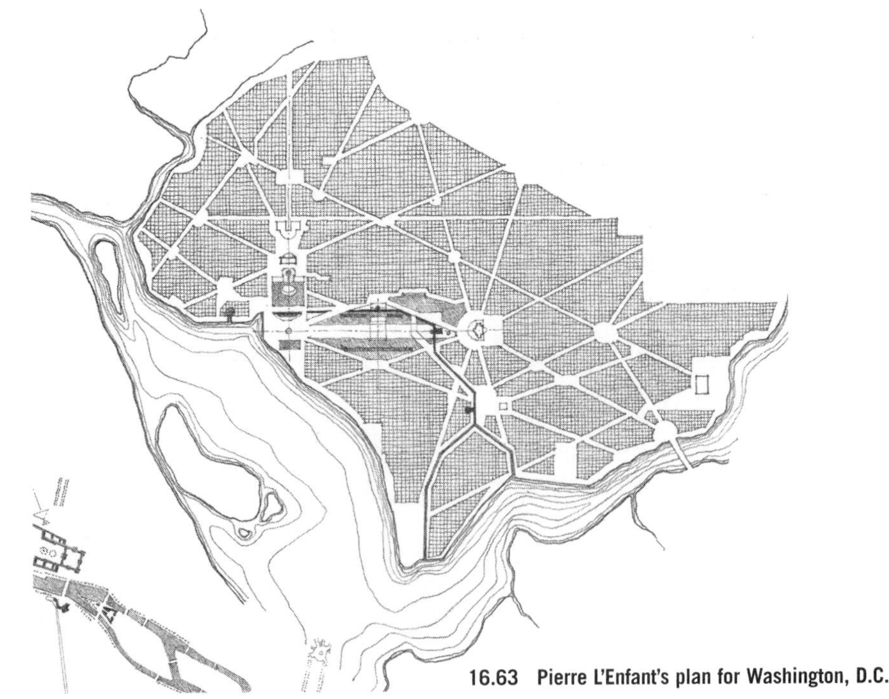

16.63 Pierre L'Enfant's plan for Washington, D.C.

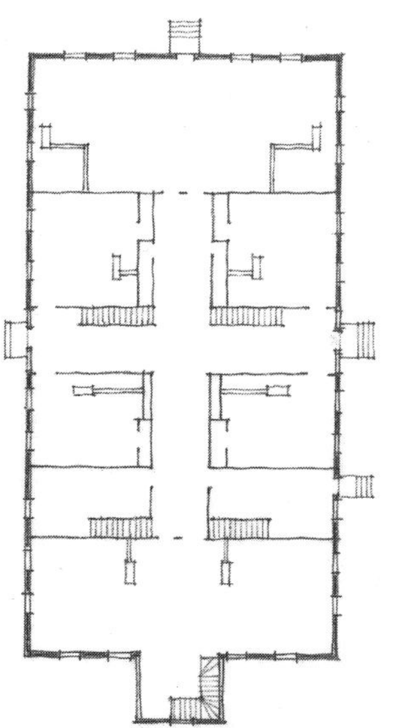

16.64 First floor plan of a Shaker communal house

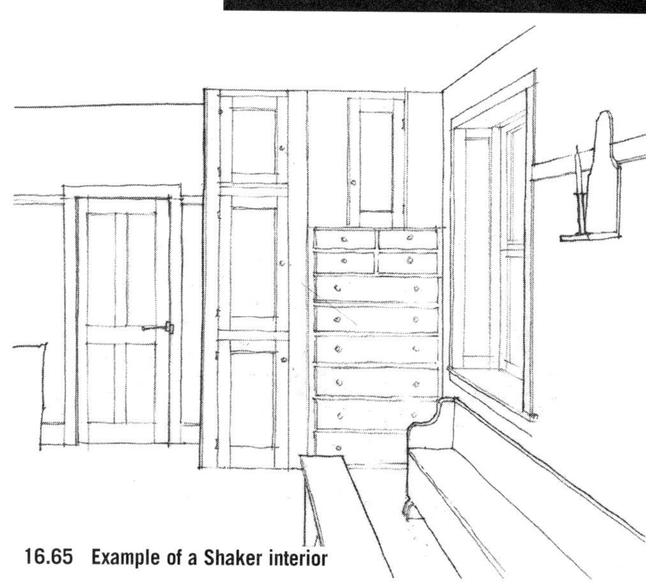

16.65 Example of a Shaker interior

**Shakers**

The 19th century saw radical changes in the social structure combined with a growing dissatisfaction with how the grand Enlightenment aspirations were playing themselves out, spawning a generation of utopian thinkers. Chief among them was Claude Henri de Rouvroy, Comte de Saint-Simon, an aristocrat, an officer in the American Revolutionary War, a real estate speculator, and journalist. His writings, including *Memoire sur la science de l'homme* (1813), *De la réorganisation de la société Européene*, with Augustin Thierry (1817), and *Le nouveau Christianisme* (1825), were highly influential. He advocated a semimystical "Christian-scientific" socialism envisaged around an elite of philosophers, engineers, and scientists who tame the forces of industrialization by means of a rational Christian humanism.Though Saint-Simon had adherents in Europe, and even influenced the thinking of Karl Marx and others, his movement to create new communities was rarely brought to fruition. In the United States, on the other hand, utopian ideals found a ready audience, with the creation of utopian communities reaching its height around 1840. Many were U.S. citizens but a substantial minority were emigrants from England, France, Germany, and Scandinavia. For most the ideal was a small tidy village with a range of craft industries.

The Shakers aimed at nothing less than transforming the earth into heaven. They were celibate, and their daily work and religious rituals were designed to foster a belief in both the earthly sphere, envisioned as a rural settlement, and a heavenly sphere, envisioned as a New Jerusalem. Between 1780 and 1826 the Shakers founded 25 settlements from Maine to the Ohio frontier. Communities were organized into communal households called families, which consisted of 30 to 100 persons in a similar condition of spiritual "travel." These families made the introduction of new members an orderly process. Cities adopted heavenly names, City of Peace, City of Love, Holy Land, and Pleasant Grove. Discipline was not imposed but a condition of divine respect. For example, anyone who slouched or nodded was required to make a public apology. Law required that one also sleep straight. Furniture reinforced the requirement for posture, and chairs were light and sturdy but had tall backs.

Shaker life was highly regulated. The women were responsible for brooming the house, whereas the men cleaned the workshops. Drawers were often installed recessed into walls so as not to collect dust or create clutter. In the houses, an invisible boundary separated the men's rooms on the west from women's rooms on the east. Double sets of stairs and doors articulated the division between male and female brethren. The furniture, clothing, and even the buildings themselves were made by members of the community. Members were physically surrounded by the handiwork of other believers. Despite the constraints, Shaker rituals involved dance and pantomime; imaginary garments were donned; and "visitors" appeared with particular messages to tell. Members who never raised their voices were suddenly singing and shouting and whirling in dizzy spirals from whence their name. The well-built and prosperous villages of the Shakers greatly enhanced the credibility of the communitarian strategy for social change, yet their unwillingness to engage in heavy industry eroded their prosperity after the Civil War, and their numbers declined sharply not least because of their belief in celibacy and the resulting lack of descendants.

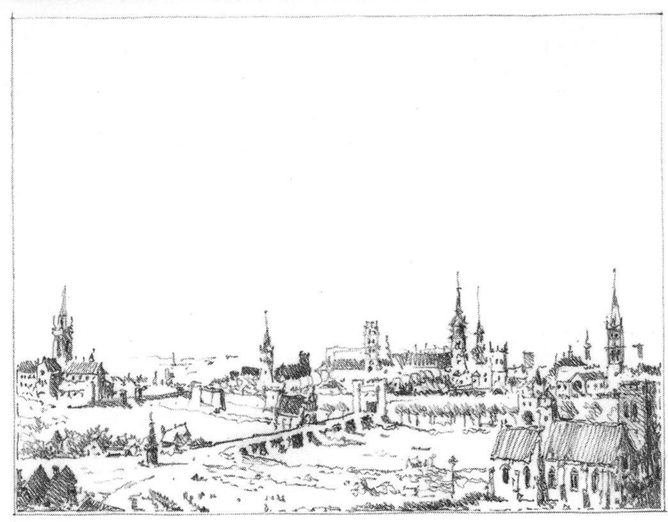

16.66 A plate redrawn from Pugin's *Contrasts*, showing a town in 1440

Pugin's book, *Contrasts*, has a plate showing a town as he imagined it was in 1440 and another one showing it in 1840. The former portrays a coherent city with intact walls and a church in the foreground; the latter shows a cluttered river, a jumble of church spires and smokestacks, and in the foreground a prison; the church is still there but now overgrown and neglected. It was an accusation against rationalism that would remain embedded in the image of modernity to this day, easily retrieved by those who see modern life as a downward slide into ethical and moral decline.

### August Welby Pugin

It is perhaps not coincidental that the two most important architectural theoretical works of the time came not from secularists but from secularism's critics, Marc-Antoine Laugier and August Welby Pugin (1812–52). Pugin's father, August Charles, Comte de Pugin, fled France during the Revolution and, as an authority on the Gothic style, took up work in the office of John Nash, who had to accommodate the growing demand for Gothic-style architecture even though he personally found it troublesome. The younger Pugin was already saturated in Gothic architecture, and had even converted to Catholicism, as the only true religion. With little hope for a commission, he set about writing *Contrasts*, which he published in 1836 at his own expense, no publisher having been found to publish such an explosive work. The book made his reputation, and soon commissions for chapels, churches, and even private houses came his way. "The history of architecture is the history of the world," he wrote, and, turning to the work of his own day, he asked whether "the architecture of our times, even supposing it solid enough to last, hand down to posterity any certain clue or guide to the system under which it was erected? Surely not ... It is a confused jumble of styles and symbols borrowed from all nations and periods."

The architect, he argued, should not just adopt any style the client wanted. Instead, architecture had to be based on principles (and in this he was the child of the Enlightenment), which included even the use of local materials in accordance with local traditions. This was what made "true" Gothic different from what he saw as the shallow Gothic of Horace Walpole or worse, the cold rationalism of the neoclassicists. Only Gothic, he argued, could provide the moral compass that one should expect from a Christian society.

Despite Pugin's conservatism, we should not see him naively as an antimodern. His convictions as to the need to consider regional traditions and local climate, as well as his belief in "honest" construction were all taken up by modernists once the Gothic imperative had played itself out. (One of his arguments against Italianate architecture was that it did not suit England.) A building, he maintained, had to show its various purposes, and this led to an appreciation for asymmetry and to an emphasis on articulating the differing parts of a building, an argument that modernists later would take up as well.

16.67 A plate redrawn from Pugin's *Contrasts*, showing the same town (illustrated above) in 1840

**16.68 Houses of Parliament, Westminster, London, England**

### Westminster

It was because of the growing confidence in the legitimacy of the neo-Gothic as genuinely English, that, after the old palace at Westminster burned in 1834, the decision was made by a parliamentary committee to rebuild in the Gothic style. Two hundred years earlier, a similar body had decided to rebuild old St. Paul's in the neoclassical style. A competition was proclaimed with the commission for the new Parliament building, which was eventually given to Charles Barry. Few can deny the brilliance of Barry's plan, with its lucid hierarchies that differentiate between public and private areas and the grandeur of the approaches to the great octagonal hall that separates the House of Lords from the House of Commons. An internal spine, which allows for a special sovereign's entrance at one corner of the building, was buffered by various open-air courts that allowed light into surrounding offices, libraries, and meeting rooms. The exterior—done almost uniformly in a soft, yellowish limestone—was designed in a Perpendicular Gothic style that replicated the taste of the 15th century. Despite the monotone treatment of the building's external mass, Barry was able to introduce picturesque elements to the skyline by the asymmetrical positioning of the vertical elements—the Victoria Tower, the lantern over the octagonal room, and Big Ben, Parliament's now-famous clock tower.

What is remarkable about this building may not be the building itself, but the debates that swirled around it concerning the role and purpose of architecture. The history of modern architecture is intertwined with the history of polemics, beginning with Charles Perrault's attack on beauty, carried forth by Marc-Antoine Laugier's attack on the classical orders, and extended into the 19th century by Pugin, the greatest defender of the Gothic at the time, who played a large role in the design and outfitting of the building. He envisioned it as a showcase of the Gothic style as a moral and aesthetic exemplar. Neoclassicism, with its cosmopolitan allusions that had met the expectations of the old elite, had here given way to a style that was assoiated not only with the new moralists but also with the monarchy of Queen Elizabeth I (1533–1603), whose rule was increasingly considered to be a golden age in which England saw the first flush of its global power. In other words, neoclassicism, though once the favorite language of colonial authority, was increaseingly seen as too generic and undifferentiated—one might say too European—to identify England, which was now the single most powerful colonial empire in the world, from its competitors.

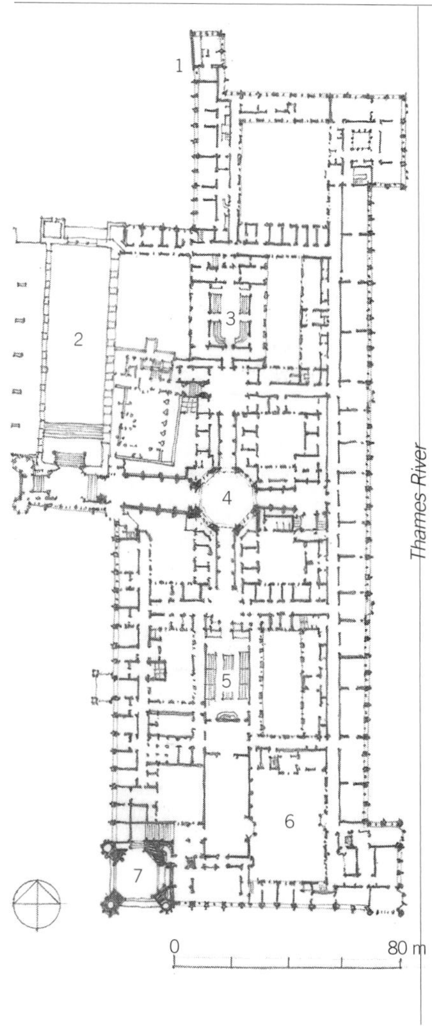


1. Clocktower
2. Westminster Hall
3. Chamber of the House of Commons
4. Central hall
5. Chamber of the House of Lords
6. Royal gallery
7. Sovereign's entrance

**16.69 Plan: Houses of Parliament, Westminster**

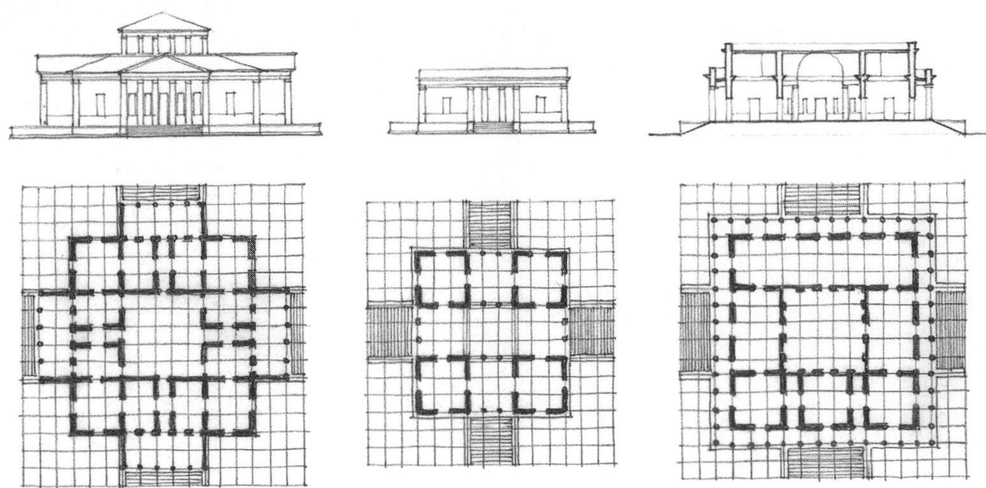

**16.70 Horizontal combinations from Durand's *Précis***

### Jean Nicolas Louis Durand

In France, the romantic movement had many representatives among the painters. Théodore Géricault (1791–1824), for example, used dramatic compositional techniques to bring out the themes of heroism, suffering, and endurance. But romanticism in France was slower to develop in the field of architecture. This was largely because architecture in France, unlike in England and Germany, remained tightly allied to state sponsorship and thus had to shun emotionalism and personalism. For that reason, post-Napoleonic French architecture, if anything, maintained the course of Enlightenment rationalism; the most important proponent of this tendency was Jean Nicolas Louis Durand (1760–1834), a pupil of Étienne-Louis Boullée and a professor at the École Polytechnique, which was founded in 1794. His work set the tone for French architecture for more than a generation. The purpose of the École was to provide engineers capable of meeting the needs of the revolutionary armies as well as provide plans for civilian public works in the remote corners of the new republic. No such school existed in England where the evolution of taste, remaining in the hands of the elite, was decentralized and often eclectic.

Durand's book *Précis*, first published in 1802, became a reference book used throughout Europe for half a century. In it, Durand rejected the emphasis on historical relationship, as with Robert Adam, between contemporary architecture and classical antiquity and instead argued that classical antiquity was regularized according to eternal principles of geometry, which could be copied; without that, one had to literally imitate Roman architecture. The plan had to be laid out on a grid and the function clearly expressed. "To please," he wrote, "has never been the purpose of architecture."

Instead the purpose has been "public and private utility, the well-being and the maintenance of individuals and of society." Durand's designs for walls, following Laugier, were freed from pilasters, moldings, quoins, and rustications. This should not be seen as "stripped down" classicism but as informed by a theory that links architecture with nature and reason. The square, which has no dominant axis, becomes the ideological and figural building block by means of which one begins to design a plan. It serves to link the columns in a grid and on a larger scale serves as a stabilizing geometry that defines the architectural formation. Like an ideal military unit, the building has to reflect order, clarity, and hierarchy.

Rationalism and civic dispassion had to be in evidence to demonstrate architecture's independence from aristocratic whim. In this respect, Durand represents a break from an insistence on tradition. Unlike picturesque and romantic notions of history, as the ground on which the future projects itself, Durand's architecture is strikingly "modern" as it insists on the primacy of program, even if in the service of the state.

If architecture was to be based on its own principles, it required a person who was trained as a professional architect. Benjamin Latrobe (1760–1820), a contemporary of Durand, who trained in England and then went to the United States to practice, took up Durand's argument, even going so far as to predict that the age of the gentleman architect was soon to end. Latrobe wrote a letter to one of his former pupils, Robert Mills—the first professionally trained architect born in the United States, admonishing him to insist on his professional rights. The architect, like a lawyer or doctor, Latrobe wrote, works by means of a contract and has to make his objectives as clear as possible. The architect should do nothing gratuitously when designing for the government; he should also make sure that the drawings are clearly understood by the client. Latrobe also admonished Mills to make sure that he himself authorized all payments to the builders so that the client cannot enter the scene and demand changes arbitrarily.

16.71 St. Madelaine Church, Paris, France

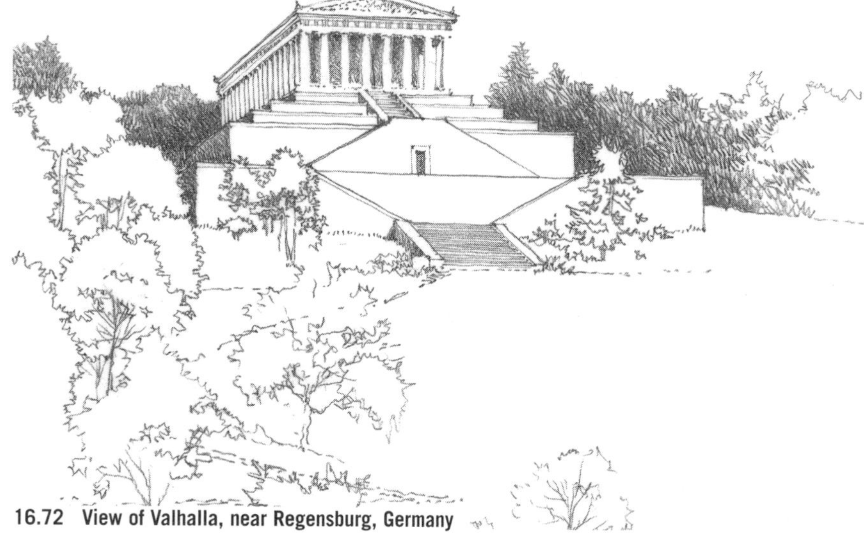

16.72 View of Valhalla, near Regensburg, Germany

**GREEK REVIVAL**

In the early 19th century, certain architects began to synthesize stripped-down classicism with Greek design, as in the St. Madelaine Church in Paris (1807–45), a building dedicated to the heroes of Napoleon Bonaparte's army, and, as we have seen, in Karl Friedrich Schinkel's Schauspielhaus (1818–21). The fascination with Greece received a boost in the 1830s, following the liberation of Greece from Turkish occupation. In 1830 England, Germany, and Russia signed the London Protocol recognizing the independence of Greece, with the Germans and the Bavarians placing themselves in charge of the military operation that would eventually free Greece from the Ottoman Empire in 1833, putting Otto of Wittelsbach on the throne, his reign guaranteed by the European powers.

The impact of the liberation of Greece on the European consciousness was indeed profound as it breathed new life into the neoclassical movement. Although today the Parthenon is one of the most revered ancient buildings in Europe, its artistic prominence came only slowly into focus in the course of the 19th century. In 1805, when Thomas Bruce, 7th Earl of Elgin, who had purchased the Parthenon frieze from the Ottomans, first approached the British Museum about buying the pieces, he encountered hesitation on the part of the authorities. A few years later, when Charles Robert Cockerell took the sculptures from the temple of Aegina, the English showed no interest in their purchase, and he sold them to Ludwig I of Bavaria, where they formed the kernel of the Glyptothek Museum in Munich. But with the liberation of Greece and the new enthusiasm for all things Greek, neo-Greek architecture took on a more strident form, as can be seen at Valhalla (1830–42), near Regensburg, which was designed by Leon von Klenze (1784–1864) as a hall of fame for German luminaries. Klenze, who had studied in Paris under Durand, also designed the Glyptothek (1816–30), with an archaeologically correct Greek front and a Roman-styled interior, following the methodology of Durand. Klenze was sent by Ludwig I to help design the new capital city, Athens, located to the largely uninhabited west and south sides of the ancient acropolis. It became the first capital city built to reflect Enlightenment and romantic ideals.

The Neo-Greek movement was relatively short-lived on the continent where it had to compete with other styles. But in Scotland, where the economy had rapidly developed in the middle of the 19th century due to an expanding hold on cotton trade and shipbuilding—Glasgow ships accounted for 85 percent of Britain's total tonnage—the country was eager to express itself as autonomous, even though it was part of England. The Greek style was thus an important expression of its national romantic fervor, as can be seen in the Royal Scottish Academy building (William Henry Playfair, 1835) in Edinburgh, Scotland, and St. Vincent Street United Presbyterian Church (Alexander Thomson, 1857–9) in Glasgow, Scotland.

16.73 Royal Scottish Academy, Edinburgh, Scotland

16.74 Old Shawneetown Bank, Illinois, USA

16.75 Market Hall, Charleston, South Carolina, USA

### Tennessee State Capitol

The most impressive examples of the Greek Revival were in the United States, where there was a particularly strong connection made between Greece and its own newfound nationhood. Once again one has to resist the temptation to see this simplistically as history imported into the open landscape of the Americas. The Americans saw their nation as the land of opportunity, where they could return to classical values without encumbrance of custom. *The Modern Builder's Guide*, which appeared in 1833 and ran through five editions until 1855, presented detailed engravings of the classical orders and their sources in ancient temples. The Greek Revival also expanded on the Hellenistic leanings of the architecture of the so-called Federal era (1780–1830), which was heavily influenced by the restrained classicism of the Adam Brothers. Unlike the Federal style, which was best expressed in the great houses of the well-to-do, examples of the Greek Revival include: the Old Shawneetown Bank (1836) in Old Shawneetown, Illinois; the James Dakin Bank of Louisville (1834–6) in Louisville, Kentucky; the Market Hall (1840) in Charleston, South Carolina; and William Strickland's Tennessee State Capitol (1845–59) in Nashville, Tennessee. The latter combined a temple with a huge version of the Greek Choragic Monument of Lysicrates in Athens. Also in Nashville a full-scale replica of the Parthenon was built in 1897.

These were not just isolated examples but part of a wave of neo-Hellenism that lasted for decades and that stretched up into Canada; it can be felt in even humble buildings as far away as Oregon. When the western half of New York State was conquered from the native Americans, place names were literally taken out of the *Iliad*. One can still go from Ithaca to Troy, to Syracuse, to Athens, to Rome, to Carthage, and even to Homer. In Nashville, Tennessee, a full-scale replica of the Parthenon was built in 1897. It was not painted in the vibrant colors of the ancient Greeks; it was left white as the neo-Grecs preferred.

The columnar Grecian mode was also easily adopted, especially in Mississippi and Louisiana, for plantation houses, where circumferential porches had been customary since the 18th century. Oak Alley (1836), near Vacherie, Louisiana, and the home of planter Alexander Roman, is a well-known example of the mode. The massive encircling columns support a continuous veranda on the second-floor level and the 28 columns are matched by an equal number of live oaks that line the formal approach to the house from the Mississippi River to literally play out the relationship between nature and form and, of course, to reinforce the ideology of elitism.

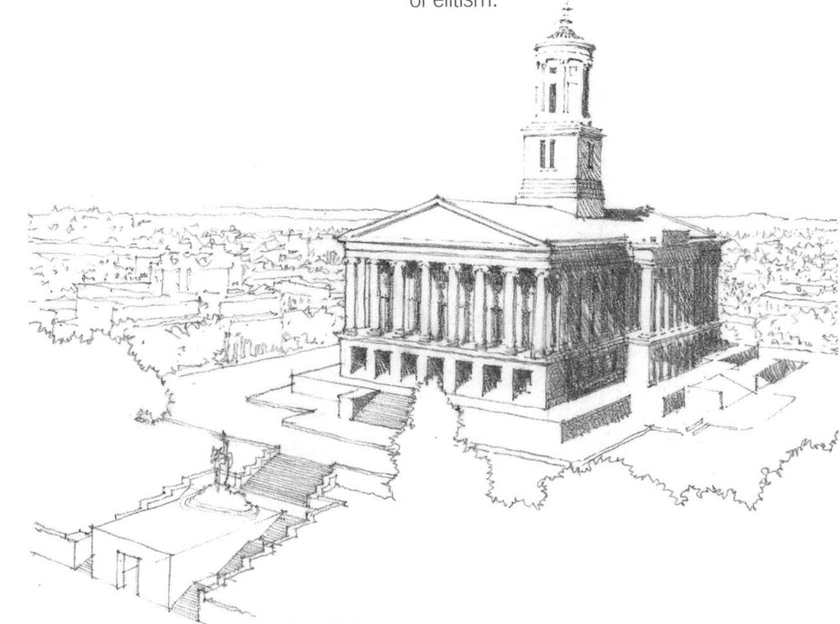

16.76 Tennessee State Capitol, Nashville, USA

16.77 Touro Synagogue, Newport, Rhode Island, USA

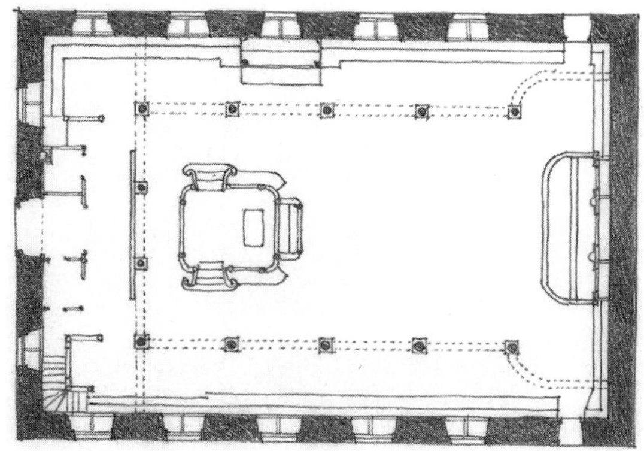

16.78 Plan: Bevis-Marks Synagogue, London, England

## SYNAGOGUES

Until the end of the 15th century, most Jews lived within the footprint of the old Roman empire, whether it be in Trastevere in Rome, Spain, or Thessalonica in Greece. This was the result of the great diaspora imposed on the Jews by the Roman emperor Titus, after his victory over the Jews and the destruction of the temple in 70 CE. Beginning with the Christian era, restrictions were imposed on Jews wherever they lived. They were not allowed to own land and excluded from affairs of the military, thus denying them access to aristocratic privileges.

Since banking was one of the few trades permitted, Jews were able to create a network that transcended local rivalries and in that capacity were often protected by kings and princes, who used them as private bankers. In Venice, Jews were allowed to come to the city principally because of their banking associations, but they were only allowed to live in a restricted area known as the ghetto, a term designating where Jews were required to live. An exception was in Lithuania where, from 1316 onward, Jews had a surprising amount of freedom.

With their expulsion by the Spanish in 1492 and by the Portuguese in 1496, the Sephardic Jews were forced to seek sanctuary in Poland, Amsterdam, Venice, Greece, Istanbul, and even Rome. In Amsterdam, a Sephardic synagogue was built in 1675 that has remained largely unchanged, and it is today one of the few tangible remnants of Amsterdam's once-thriving Jewish community. It is a large, rectangular brick building, with large round-headed windows on all sides that emphasize its vast interior space. It became the model for several later synagogues, including the Bevis-Marks Synagogue in London (1700) and the smaller Touro Synagogue in Newport, Rhode Island, the oldest synagogue in the United States. Jewish life in Germany improved slightly in the 18th century when courts invited Jews to come and serve as financial agents. In 1714, King Frederick William I of Prussia permitted the construction of a synagogue in Berlin.

The fate of Jews significantly improved, however, with Napoleon, who passed a number of measures supporting the position of Jews in the French Empire, and just as importantly in conquered countries; he abolished laws restricting Jews to ghettos or to certain professions. In 1797 when he invaded Italy, he threw open the gates to the ghettos. In 1807, like his contemporary Qing emperors of China, he sanctioned several religions as "official"—a first for a European ruler—and these included Judaism, Roman Catholicism, Lutheranism, and Calvinism. As a result of Napoleon's initiatives, Jews in other lands sought and eventually received emancipation in Germany in 1848, Great Britain in 1890, Russia in 1917, and finally in Spain in 1930.

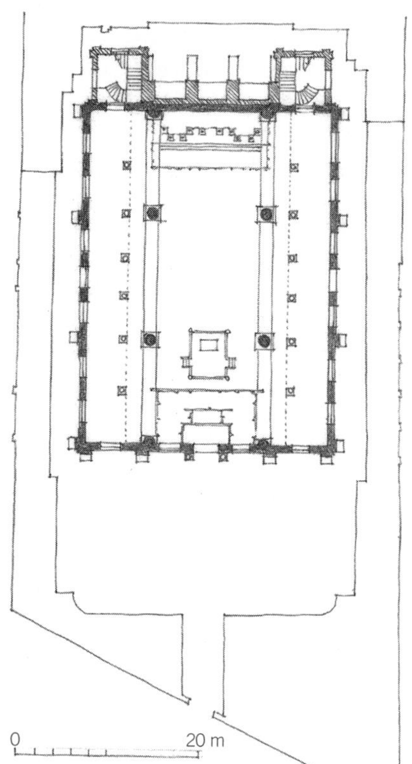


16.79 Plan: Sephardic Synagogue, Amsterdam, Netherlands

16.80 Tempio Israelitico, Rome, Italy

16.81 Interior of Beth Elohim Synagogue, Charleston, South Carolina, USA

The response by Jews to German emancipation was a building boom of unprecedented proportion. During the 19th century more than 200 large synagogues were built. It would be shortsighted to see synagogue architecture as part of the general European trend toward eclecticism. Synagogue eclecticism was a direct response to the new freedom from restrictions on what could be built. Furthermore, most of the architects were non-Jews who brought their own often romanticized expectations of what a Jewish space should look like to the table. Gottfried Semper (1803–79) designed a synagogue in Dresden (1840) that was on its exterior Carolingian-Romanesque, presumably to emphasize the aspirations of Germanness, but there was on the inside an order of columns with deep impost blocks copied from the Alhambra at Granada.

The emergence of the Judaic Reform Movement, intended to appeal to urban Jews, had a major influence on synagogue design. Reform Jews stressed the universal teachings of Judaism but also sought to modernize rituals that were difficult to maintain in a modern world. The Reform Jews also held that Jewish people were not in a state of permanent exile but contributing members of their community and nation. They considered every house of worship a temple, as holy as the original temple in Jerusalem. Pews were permitted, and prayer was in German. The organ was introduced.

16.82 Beth Elohim Synagogue, Charleston, South Carolina

The first reform synagogue was opened in Seesen in central Germany in 1810, and it was called a "temple" in keeping with Enlightenment ideals. Even though some of the synagogues took up the classical theme and were almost literally temples, as in the Seitenstettengasse Synagogue in Vienna (1826) and the Beth Elohim Synagogue in Charleston, South Carolina (1840), other examples in keeping with the general 19th-century preoccupation with origins were developed along Egyptian and Byzantine lines, as for example, the Tempio Israelitico (1882) in Florence. The prayer hall is almost square with galleries on three sides supported by columns with Moorish cusped arches. Every square inch of surface is covered with patterns and colored designs of abstract Islamic configurations, creating a soft reddish-golden atmosphere. Much as in mosques, synagogues did not display human figures.

16.83 Oriel Chambers, Liverpool, England

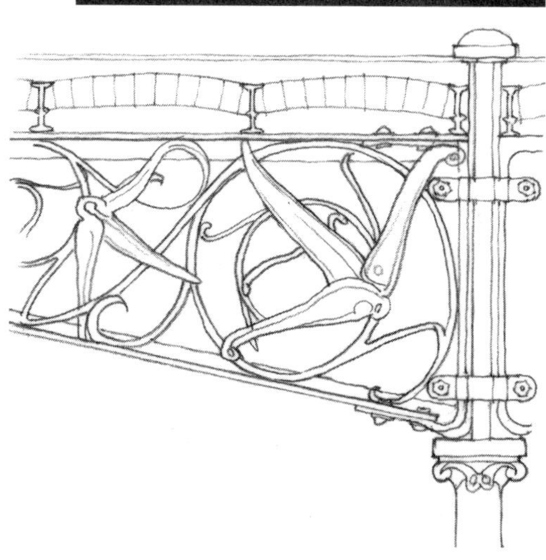

16.84 Viollet-le-Duc's decorative cast-iron detail has a rational foundation in the design of trusses.

**Eugène Emmanuel Viollet-le-Duc**

The mid-19th century saw the rapid expansion of the middle class, the fitful demise of the influence of the landed gentry, and the rise of a professional class. The Geological Society upgraded its membership from the "interested" gentry to one based on merit and scholarly accomplishment. Arguments that fossils were planted in the ground by god, still a viable theory in the 1830s, were no longer accepted in 1850. In architecture a similar revolution was taking place, led by a generation of theorists that included Eugène Emmanuel Viollet-le-Duc (1814–79) in France, Gottfried Semper in Germany, and John Ruskin (1819–1900) in England. Though different in many respects, all tried to rethink the principles of rationalism and technology, and all were writing at the same time. Ruskin's *The Stones of Venice* appeared first in 1851, the same date as Semper's *Die vier Elemente der Baukunst.* Viollet-le-Duc's *Dictionnaire raisonné de l'architecture française du XI au XVe siècle*, which was published in several editions, first appeared in 1854. Without doubt, the period represented a turning point in architectural discourse. Of the three, Viollet-le-Duc was also a strong advocate of the modern material of iron. Unlike other architects of his time, who were using cast iron by giving it a Gothic flavor to appease the demands of the followers of August Welby Pugin; Viollet-le-Duc made no such demand.

Neither was he advocating the technological rationalism of Sir Joseph Paxton in the Crystal Palace in London. Cast iron, and then iron, had emerged relatively quickly on the architectural scene, but the proper appreciation of its aesthetic was not yet obvious to mid-century architects. In the 17th and 18th centuries, baroque architects, because of the large domes and complex lighting effects, operated in a realm between architecture and technology. Neoclassicism, with its emphasis on image, made much fewer demands, technically speaking, on the architect. With the introduction of cast iron, that changed rapidly. The catalogues of architectural components published by the design office of British foundries began to grow thicker, and it was a short step from adding cast-iron balconies (of which the French Quarter in New Orleans, Louisiana, is an excellent example) to designing entire houses and structures out of cast iron.

By 1850 some were arguing for a congruence between material and form, as can be seen in the remarkable building, the Oriel Chambers in Liverpool, by the architect Peter Elkin, dating from 1864. The thin cast-iron frame holds glazed bay windows with no concession to ornamentation. Needless to say, at that time it was not well received; architects preferred to use cast iron mainly for floor supports. In that sense, the general approach of Quatremère de Quincy, who taught at the École des Beaux Arts, still prevailed. He critiqued the use of exposed iron in anything other than industrial buildings, setting a tone with long-lasting consequences. Iron received strong support, however, from the romantics who saw it as an opportunity to escape the strictures of the classical orders and to introduce a more local or regional flavor to architecture. Viollet-le-Duc tried to hold a middle ground, arguing against both the academy with its neoclassical allegiances and the autonomy of rational engineering. For him rationalism was not a question of numbers and efficiency but of style (in the singular), a style that emerged from a thorough familiarity with the history of architecture and with the visual and functional needs of the program. Restoring Gothic structures was not done simply in the name of historical survival but as a way to integrate style with design.

Viollet-le-Duc's approach is best exemplified in his design for an iron armature for a concert hall (1886), which even today strikes one as astonishing. Using the idea of a buttress but inverting it and placing it on the inside instead of the outside, he holds up a steel frame that in turn supports a thin masonry roof. Whether this was Gothic or not did not interest him.

Semper made an equally bold argument. The origins of architecture lie not in the Greek post and lintel and not even in the need to add a roof to the post and lintel, as Laugier had argued, to create the basic "vocabulary" of architectural design. Architecture began, so he argued, through crafts. From weaving a basket, primitive humans learned how to weave branches into walls and then close off the gaps with mud. From pottery, they learned how to make tiles and bricks.

For Semper, nature was not an abstraction producing regular geometries that needed to be emulated; nor was it for him a biological force in the sense that Gothic architects understood it, for instance, in modeling their vaults on tree branches. Instead, nature was wrapped up with our basic instinct for making things, which Semper understood as having both an economical and a moral component. At the Great Exhibition of 1851, he lavished praise not on Paxton's amazing technologically driven design of the Crystal Palace but on the display of houses from Trinidad, whose production yielded glimpses of an early stage of cultural development before industrialization derailed the processes by which craft develops form.

Because of this, Semper could be considered less interested in the technological than Viollet-le-Duc, and indeed, one has to remember that this particular moment in architectural theory was rather one of resistance to modernity, and yet one that was speaking in the name of the modern. At stake for him was not the moral abnegation of civilizational clutter, as it was for Marc-Antoine Laugier, but a cultural abnegation of civilizational clutter. To rectify this, he proposed museums as schools of public taste, a project given its most concrete realization in the formation of Vienna's Museum of Applied Arts.

**16.85 Caribbean hut, by Gottfried Semper**

**16.86 Concert hall, Viollet-le-Duc**

16.87 **Bibliothèque St. Geneviève, Paris, France**

16.88 **Transverse section: Bibliothèque St. Geneviève**

### Bibliothèque St. Geneviève

Among those who argued in favor of the use of iron was Henri Labrouste (1801–75). His Bibliothèque St. Geneviève (designed in 1843 and built in 1845–51), with its slender columns and billowing domes, coexists with stone walls, themselves without any trace of classical columns and pilasters. The distinction between the two floors is made on the outside by a thin entablature, with a continuous row of garlands suspended beneath it. Below, the wall is punctuated by relatively small, Romanesque-styled, round-headed windows. Above, from end to end, there runs an arcade, with pilasters forming a regular rhythm across the facade; it is distinctly Roman in flavor. The lower two thirds of the arcade are filled in to allow for a window in each bay. The whole is topped by a stripped-down cornice, lightly decorated in a neo-Grec manner. The building thus makes numerous historical references, but is no way historicist. Labrouste attempted to create an idiom that, through its reductivist aesthetic, could demonstrate a fluid connection between the old and the modern. To indicate the iron used on the interior, for those with a keen eye, Labrouste articulated the end bolts of the tie rods with round panels nestled between the archivolts. The building also has a picturesque component, for inscribed onto the panels in the arcades are the names of the authors of the books held in the shelves within.

In Labrouste's hands iron was a significant enrichment of the architect's tool box. In the vestibule, for example, the tall and solid piers contrast with the spindly cast-iron arches. But these arches were meant to evoke the branches of a sacred grove, an image reinforced by wall frescoes that show tree tops over the busts of famous literary figures. In that sense, the vestibule is a reference to the fabled Elysian Fields. Because Labrouste's position was not in line with the more conservative tastes of the academy, his career did not advance as fast as did those of his contemporaries. His use of iron as a form of vaulting became more common in the next decades and was used, for example, in the Paris church of Notre-Dame de la Croix (1870).

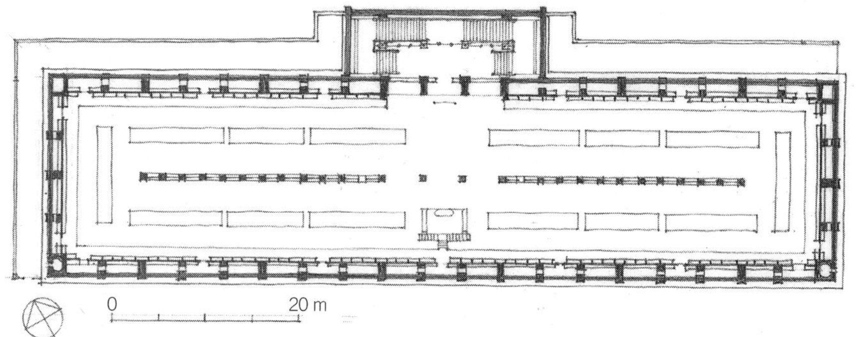


16.89 **Plan: Bibliothèque St. Geneviève**

16.90 Museum of Natural History, Oxford University, England

16.91 Facsimile of a drawing by John Ruskin of the Doge's Palace and Venice

**John Ruskin**

No Victorian era theorist was as widely discussed and read as John Ruskin, whose voluminous writings cover a host of topics. Ruskin preferred the simpler Italian medieval style to the more complicated northern Gothic, because he thought form should be determined by the material of which it consists and the way in which it is constructed. The early medieval period, he felt, embodied this ethos. Ruskin was, however, not opposed to the use of iron, unlike Pugin, but he much preferred conventional materials. He thus brought a new awareness to the aesthetic intensity of the architectural surface that was often lacking in neo-Gothic architecture. In his discussion of construction, he shied away from a builder's-manual approach and described in enormous detail the simplest aspects of masonry walls, arcading, and their basic elements. The fact that a wall is a series of layers, he argued, should be shown as distinctly as possible on the surface. Ruskin was not opposed to thin walls, but he wanted the thinness to be expressed in the paneling or in the use of a checkered pattern. In this way Ruskin begins to ask his readers to rethink their attitude to the past, looking not at the question of proportion in the abstract sense, nor at the question of Roman versus non-Roman origin, but rather at the physical and material rationale that underlies architectural reasoning.

His concern for the visual led him to prefer monolithic columns. He rejected the use of piers and buttresses, as they interfered with the visual impact of a form. Mass was not to be constricted by cold geometry, but was something to be molded freely with simple and grand outlines; Ruskin very rarely dealt with interiors, and thus rarely asked questions about program and function. In that way he succeeded in bypassing what till then had been called "theory," namely a discourse about proportion and program, thereby undermining it. For Ruskin, the shape of a building—as would have been significant for Durand—is less important than the architect's attitude toward designing it. Also, one could say that a building's tactile surface was just as important as the plan.

Ruskin was, of course, not an architect like Pugin, yet like Laugier he had a tremendous impact on architecture. Among other things, he taught his readers to use their eyes in understanding a building. The Ruskinian movement was felt in the United States in buildings like the Memorial Hall (designed by William Ware and Henry van Brunt, 1871–78) at Harvard University in Cambridge, Massachusetts.

After Ruskin, a generation of architects began to design in a way that conformed to his vision of the constructed world. This entailed a slow shift away from the enforced medievalism of Pugin to a more inventive style for which there is no particular name. Among those who worked in this direction was the firm of Deane and Woodward, which designed the interior of the Museum of Natural History at Oxford University (1853), using exposed Gothic-styled iron, demonstrating its expressive qualities down to the rivets holding the elements together.

16.92 Facsimile of a drawing by John Ruskin, Porta della Carta and Ducal Palace

16.93 Wat Pra Kaew, Bangkok, Thailand

16.94 Emerald Buddha, Wat Pra Kaew

## WAT PRA KAEW

By the late 18th century, the history of architecture becomes largely the history of European architecture, of European colonial architecture, and of Chinese architecture. Islamic architecture was on the wane, as was noncolonial architecture in India and elsewhere. There was one important and remarkable exception: Thailand. Thailand, or Siam, emerged as an important regional force in the 14th century under King Sukhothai who controlled the area roughly covered by modern Thailand. His capital was the island city of Ayutthaya, about 100 kilometers north of Bangkok. Though the Thai culture was largely Indic in origin (Ayutthaya is Thai for Ayodhya, the sacred capital of Lord Rama), the Thai learned their Sanskrit and scripture from the Khmer of Cambodia, building several Angkor-inspired temples and stupas in Ayutthaya. The Chinese admiral, Zheng He, came to Ayuttha, and left behind a Chinese princess and her attendant, who still survive in Thailand as a distinct community, and worship the princess and the admiral in a temple at Ayutthaya. In the mid-15th century, the Thai sacked Angkor and then, under King Rama I (1782–1809) of the Chakri Dynasty, established the city of Bangkok, or Ratanakosin, as his capital, on the Chao Phraya River, in 1782. The new Royal Palace was created as its new symbolic core in a compound a few hundred meters from the river's edge.

In the eastern section of the compound, a special structure was created to house the Emerald Buddha, a jade Buddha dated to 1434. Much venerated, it was brought to Bangkok in 1778 from northern Thailand. The compound is defined by a rectangular perimeter colonnade, with projections in the east and west, that contains a continuous wall fresco, painted on dry plaster, narrating the story of the Ramayana, the Hindu sacred text.

At the center of the compound, on a raised platform running east-west, are three huge closely spaced buildings, a golden stupa, a square Sutra repository, and a temple structure known as the Royal Pantheon. Also on the platform is a large stone model of Angkor Wat. Rama I had wanted the entire abandoned structure from Cambodia to be transferred to Bangkok, but when his emissaries returned with descriptions of its immensity, he decided to settle for a model. One has to remember that Angkor Wat is itself, like any Hindu temple, a model of the cosmos and as such the model is almost equivalent, in its philosophical significance, to the original.

The close proximity of these buildings is not because of lack of space. Each building in well-established Mahayana Buddhist symbolism is a representation of the other, and the proximity of each is intended to keep one from seeing any of the buildings as an autonomous structure; instead they were to be seen as substitutes, or even as metaphors, of each other. Whereas the stupa is covered with a single sheen of gold, the other two buildings are lavishly decorated on the outside with patterns made of mosaics, tiles, and fragments of glass and mirror. Colors used are reds, blues, and greens. The Wat Pra Kaew (Temple of the Emerald Buddha) stands to the south of the platform. It has a single interior space that is undivided by partitions, with the Buddha placed at the far end in a resplendent setting, high above human height, enshrined in a small golden temple. The walls are covered with frescoes. The roof trusses are made of wood.

16.95 Sutra repository and golden stupa, Wat Pra Kaew

The building and indeed the entire architectural ensemble is one of the most important in the Southeast Asia of this time, reflecting the cosmopolitan taste of its patron. The tiles on the outside of the building are done in a Persian style, while the mosaics were made by Byzantine craftsmen, and the Buddha hall is a type of Sistine Chapel, its walls painted with religious murals. The placement of the Buddha on top of a golden structure appears almost baroque. One should not interpret this as a sign of "oriental" eclecticism in comparison with the rigorous historicism of the European Enlightenment but rather as a modern fusion of different elements into something quite unique. Thailand was never a colonial country—a rarity in that part of the world—and thus its rulers had the freedom to explore and develop contemporary architectural ideas that were denied those countries that were placed under colonial imprint. So, whereas the architectural traditions began to dry out or became fossilized with the introduction of European-style buildings in India, for example, these traditions developed with a sense of freedom in Thailand, unfettered by the offended eyes of colonial overlords.

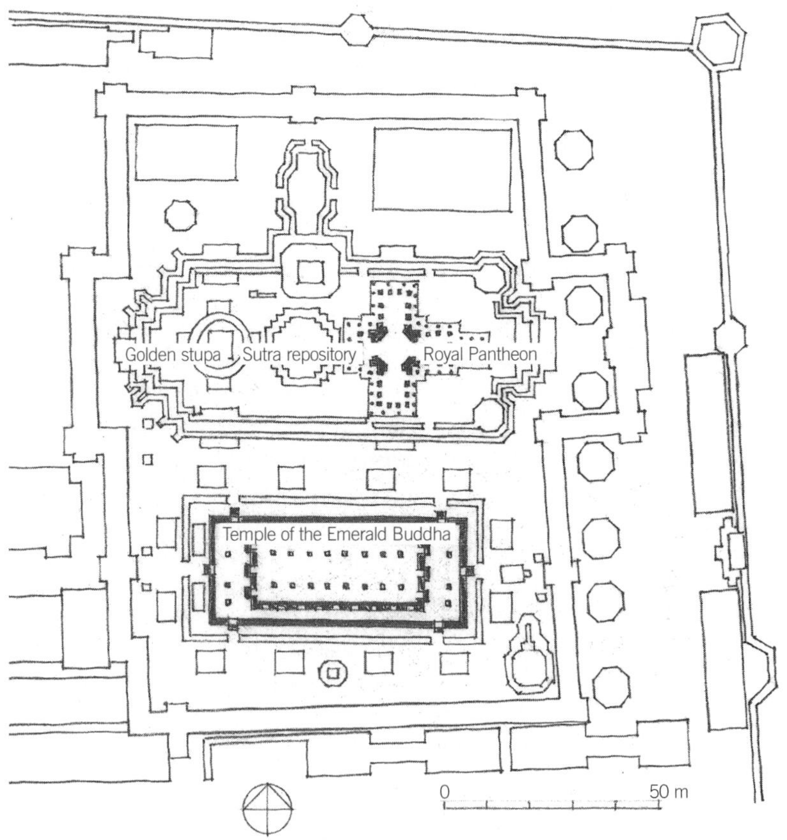


16.96 Site plan: Wat Pra Kaew

# 1900 CE

Between 1840 and 1900 the land area controlled by the European colonial powers rose from 60 to 91 percent, driven by a policy of landgrab and export-oriented cash-crop cultivation to be used for trade and to feed the industrializing economy back home. For the French, however, by the end of the 19th century, their colonies' yield rose only slightly compared to the escalating cost of running the empire. For England, however, colonization ushered in an era of unbridled prosperity making it the undisputed world power, especially after China was brought down in the middle of the 19th century through a policy of military action, political intimidation, and forced opiumization. By the late 19th century, England could act with impunity around the world. It invaded Egypt in 1882 to control the Suez Canal and South Africa in 1899 to take over the gold mines. By the turn of the century, England's wealth set it up for a showdown with Germany, which did not have a colonial empire but had industrialized heavily beginning late in the 19th century. The second half of the 19th century, because of the long rule of Queen Victoria (r. 1837–1901), has fittingly been called the Victorian era.

Political philosophers, Karl Marx (1818–83) in particular, shed light on the emergence of the increasingly tight relationship between government, power, and capital. Whereas Marx exposed the inner workings of capitalism, Charles Darwin (1809–82) brought out the inner workings of natural selection. In the arts, the young generation of the 1880s, led among others by William Morris (1834–96), began to rebel against the dehumanization of industrial production and the strictures of English society and demanded a simpler and, for them, more authentic way of producing art and craft. Frederick Law Olmstead (1822–1903) in the United States led a movement to bring nature back into architectural and urban design considerations.

Though England played the dominant role economically and in matters of domestic architecture, the French began to assert themselves in matters of urban culture. The center of Paris was thoroughly rebuilt under Napoleon III and became the model for urban redesigns in Europe and around the world. Argentina's exports, for example, may have largely gone to England, but when it came to streets and public buildings, the elite turned to Parisian models. The French Beaux-Arts, as a voice that combined bourgeois elegance and professional expertise (also known as the Second Empire style), was an international movement in its own right.

A perceptible shift occurred around the turn of the century, revolving around the split between public and private. Public architecture tended to be elaborate, formal, and yielding to the ornamental, whereas domestic architecture came to be dominated by the calmer ethos of the arts-and-crafts movement. Both, however, should be seen as part of the developing modernity of the times. Radical experiments were undertaken to invent new architectural styles and possibilities. With the development of art nouveau and expressionism in Europe and the inventions of Frank Lloyd Wright in the United States, the foundations of the world of modern architecture were set in place. In fact, between 1890 and 1910, architecture was significantly more experimental than it was in the 1930s. New materials like concrete were used to build new types of enclosures. The steel frame, developed in Chicago and New York, was challenging the norms of urban living and work. Particularly important to the transition to modernism was the expressionist movement, which in the span of the years before and after World War I articulated the first coherent alternative—though sometimes fanciful—to traditional architectural practices. By the mid 1920s, however, the modern movement, as it is generally understood, began to take shape in the buildings and theorizing of Walter Gropius, Ludwig Mies van der Rohe, and Le Corbusier, among many others, with the Bauhaus in Germany, the de Stijl architects in Holland, and the constructivists in the newly formed Union of Soviet Socialist Republics (USSR, or Soviet Union), the flash points for the developing aesthetic.

# 1900 CE

National Gallery, London ▲
1834–8

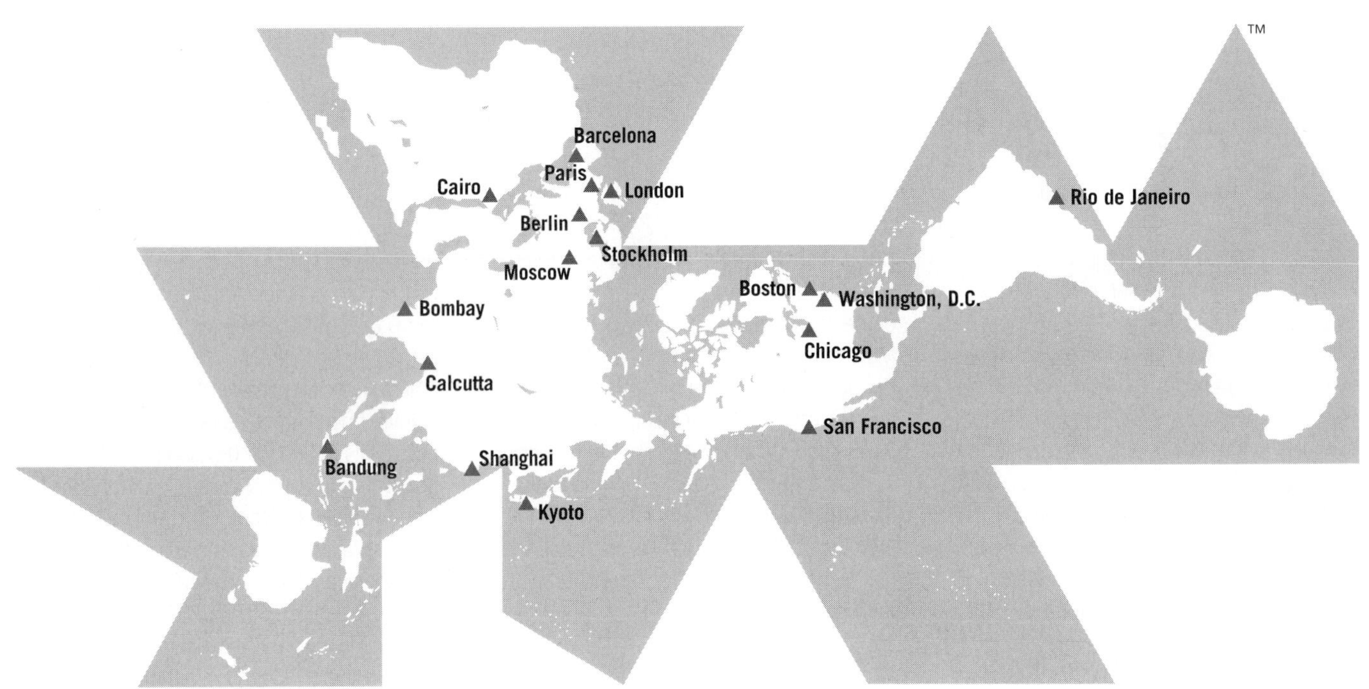

▲ **Crystal Palace**
1850–1

▲ **St. Pancras Station**
1863–7

▲ **Amsterdam Stock Exchange**
1898–1903

▲ **Bandung Institute of Technology**
1920

▲ **Galleria Vittorio Emanuele II**
1865–77

▲ **Victoria Terminus**
1878–88

▲ **Shanghai Bank**
1923–5

▲ **Central Park**
1853–83

▲ **Reliance Building**
1890–4

▲ **Wrigley Building**
1920–4

▲ **Trinity Church**
1872–7

▲ **Boston Public Library**
1887–93

▲ **Pennsylvania Station**
1906–10

▲ **Paris Opera House**
1861–74

▲ **Al-Rifa'i Mosque**
1869–80 and 1906–11

▲ **Mubarak Mahal**
1899

**1850** CE — **1900** CE — **1950** CE

American Civil War
1861–1865

World War I
1914–1918

Great Depression
1929–1933

World War II
1939–1945

▲ **Cornell University**
Founded 1865

▲ **Winslow House**
1893

▲ **Robie House**
1908–9

▲ **Gamble House**
1908–9

▲ **Taliesin**
Begun 1911

▲ **Hollyhock House**
1921

▲ **Isaac Bell House**
1882–3

▲ **Maison Tassel**
1892–3

▲ **Glass House**
1914

▲ **Villa Muller**
1930

▲ **Casa Batlló**
1904–6

▲ **25b, rue Franklin**
1903

▲ **Einstein Tower**
1917–21

▲ **Keith Arcade**
1927

▲ **Stockholm Public Library**
1920–28

▲ **Woodland Cemetery Chapel**
1918–20

▲ **Friedrichstrasse Office Building**
1921

▲ **Tatlin's Tower**
1919

▲ **Bauhaus**
1924–6

▲ **Villa Savoye**
1928–31

17.1 British Museum, London, England

17.2 Victoria and Albert Museum, London, England

**Metropolitan Board of Works**

The Victorian era was a time in which the bourgeois consciousness began to assert itself, both in its liberal politics and in its insistence on professional reasoning. The Victorians prided themselves on their growing morality. Slavery had finally come to a halt, as had child labor, but conditions in the factories and among the lower classes remained abysmal. But the age that produced Charles Dickens (1812–70), whose novels *Hard Times* and *David Copperfield* served as penetrating insights into the social conditions of the Victorians, also produced Charles Darwin (1809–92), whose *Origin of Species* (1859) and *Descent of Man* (1871) forever changed the science of biology. Even though the authority of the Anglican Church during this time was uncontestable, theological debates, the search for alternative religious experiences, and the rise of a professional class undermined established ways of thinking and created a period of continual debate and, for many, confusion. As a result of the rise of the middle class, new ideals were established that were to become the foundation of things to come, such as the desire to articulate the separation of work and home as well as the differentiation between the duties and tasks of men and women. Books on how to be a professional were just as common as those on how to raise children. Paralleling this was the emerging divide between public and private commissions and the styles associated with them. In the Georgian era, Palladian neoclassicism had generally served for both public and private buildings, but after the 1850s and the emergence of a more complex understanding of style, public and private architecture began to take on very different looks and, in fact, became increasingly polarized as the century wore on.

Turning first to the public commissions, one has to remember that grand public buildings were rare in London given that it had been to a large extent rebuilt after the fire of 1666. From the 17th century one might find an occasional guildhall or a few markethouses and from the 18th century some town halls. It was only in the 1820s that London's buildings came to betoken a monumental civic presence, with the new Privy Council and Board of Trade Building (1822–7), the General Post Office by Robert Smirke (1823–8), and the British Museum, also by Smirke (1823–46). It was a rather paltry civic presence. The problem was that metropolitan improvements were still largely haphazard and impromptu affairs, financed by a variety of sources.

In 1855, in an attempt to rectify the situation, the government created a Metropolitan Board of Works to augment the process by which decisions regarding the commissioning and building of public buildings could be made. The result was immediate. In fact, most public buildings in Great Britain, whether municipal offices, post offices, fire stations, schools or libraries, all date from after this time.

Among the most important Victorian era governmental buildings that put a new bureaucratic face on the empire were: the Admiralty (proposed 1852, built 1887), South Kensington Museum (1857), Colonial Office (1870–4), Home Office (1870–5), New Law Courts (1871–82), War Office (1898–1906), and the New Public Office (completed 1908). The massing of these buildings tended to be heavy, usually in a Renaissance-Italianate manner, with well articulated quoins and voussoirs, such as at the India Office (1863–8) and the New Government Offices (1868–78).

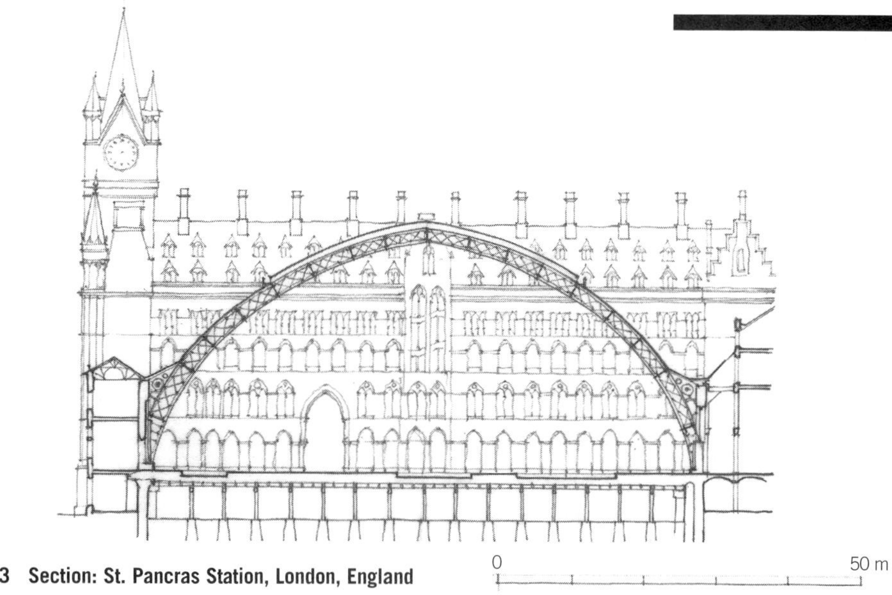


17.3 Section: St. Pancras Station, London, England

**Railroad Stations**

Claude Henri de Rouvroy, Comte de Saint-Simon (1760–1825), who was the first to identify the process of industrialization, did much to familiarize Europeans with the possibilities of new technology and steel. For most people in England and Europe, however, iron was best seen in the spectacular railroad stations of the time, which were not only marvels of engineering but also the sites that represented the new culture of mobility and exchange. Civil engineers now competed with architects as arbiters of taste. St. Pancras Station in London (1863–76), for example, contained a volume of space within its 80-meter span that defied anything architecture previously could have striven for. The large steel members were brought to the construction site by the railroad itself. In front of the shed, facing the city, there was a building that contained baggage facilities, waiting rooms, and offices of various sorts. By the 1880s, these terminals, not only in England but also in Germany, France, the United States, and even in the colonies, such as Bombay's Victoria Terminus (1888), had become the symbol of the age, leading even one commentator to write that train stations were to the European 19th century what monasteries and cathedrals had been to the 13th century.

Their rise can partially be explained by the fact that railroads were private companies in competition with each other. The need for impressive stations was because they were not only a symbol of corporate achievement but also, and more often than not, a means of outdoing a competing line. As a result, very few towns of any importance were served by only one railway company. London soon had several, but none connected to each other. There were differences in appropriate style for the front building, with its portico and waiting rooms, but the main prototype of shed-and-front building remained unchanged until well into the 20th century. The Anhalter Bahnhof (1872–80) in Berlin is a classic example.

In the colonies, where the English were monopoly owners of the railways, the stations were projected as symbols of civilizational advancement enabled by colonial rule. The Public Works Department of colonial India, staffed by officers of the trained English corps of engineers, took great pride in designing not only the large terminuses but also the thousands of smaller stations that were needed throughout India for material extraction and transportation of goods and people. While the larger terminuses were regaled with wide spans and rich decoration, the smaller ones were built using standardized and rationalized design schemes not only to optimize functionality but also to project a sense of militaristic order.

17.4 Anhalter Bahnhof, Berlin, Germany

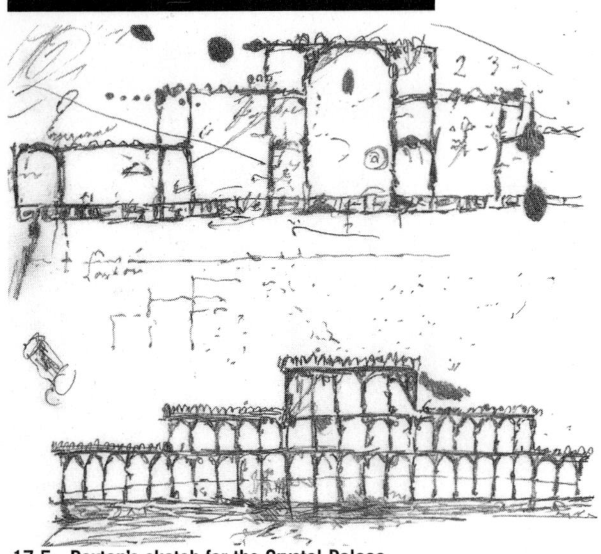

17.5 Paxton's sketch for the Crystal Palace

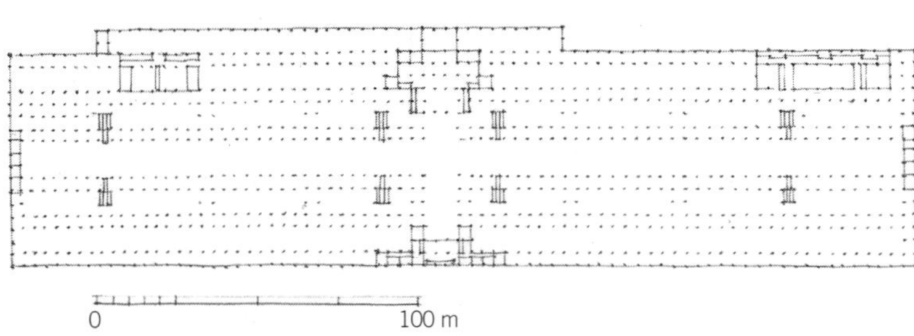


17.6 Plan: Crystal Palace, London, England

**WORLD FAIRS**

The first industrial exhibition was held in France in 1801 to search for buyers of material during an economic depression that followed the French Revolution. The English also had such fairs but at a smaller scale; their success led Henry Cole (1808–82), a leading advocate of industrial design and well known through his *Journal of Design and Manufactures* (1849–52), to argue that what was needed was not a national exhibition but a large international one that would showcase England's unique position in the global economy. The fair he organized was held in 1851, and it took place in a building that came to be called the Crystal Palace.

The design and engineering of the Crystal Palace was done by Sir Joseph Paxton, an innovative designer of steel and glass greenhouses. Unlike Henri Labrouste's Bibliothèque St. Geneviève, with its custom detailed iron elements, or St. Pancras with its massive beams, the Crystal Palace was composed of thin, relatively lightweight elements that were mass produced and assembled on site. Tension wires kept the structure from falling over. The effect was of a building that seemed almost to be woven, with compression and tension forces brought into the open as no other building had ever done before.

Paxton also understood that the structure had to be tall and inspiring and so designed its central element in the form of a long nave filled with exhibits, trees, and gardens. Under the Crystal Palace's roofs there was the first public display of English mass-produced machines and products. The colonies and distant lands were also represented, but their displays emphasized handcrafted products and raw materials. The contradiction between the two reflected the intellectual mindset of the time. The industrial bosses marvelled at the engineering and mass production; the arts and crafts enthusiasts pointed to the colonial products as evidence of what was lost to England. The masses came to gawk. No one had ever seen such a spectacle. The fair was a spectacular success. By the time the exhibition closed, after being open for just six months, more than six million people had seen it.

17.7 Interior: Crystal Palace

The unprecedented success of the fair set the stage for an endless series of repeats: the 1853 Exhibition of Dublin, the U.S. Crystal Palace in New York (1853), the Palais de l'Industrie (1855), the 1862 International Exhibition of London, the Dublin Exhibition (1865), and the Colonial and Indian Exhibition (1886). With these, one has to interlace the international exhibitions in Paris in 1855, 1867, 1878, 1889, and 1900, the Philadelphia Exhibition (1876), the World's Columbian Exposition in Chicago (1893), and the World's Exposition at Melbourne, Australia (1880). And then there were countless exhibitions held in the colonies, as for example, in Calcutta (1883), Jaipur (1883), South Africa (1887, 1893), Belgium (1894), Jamaica (1891), and Guatemala (1897). A cultural history of these exhibitions would map out the core topics of 19th-century modernity, including the mass-production of space and goods, the spectacle of display, the rituals of consumption, and the relationship between capital, nationalism, imperialism, and entertainment.

17.8 Galleria Vittorio Emanuele II, Milan, Italy

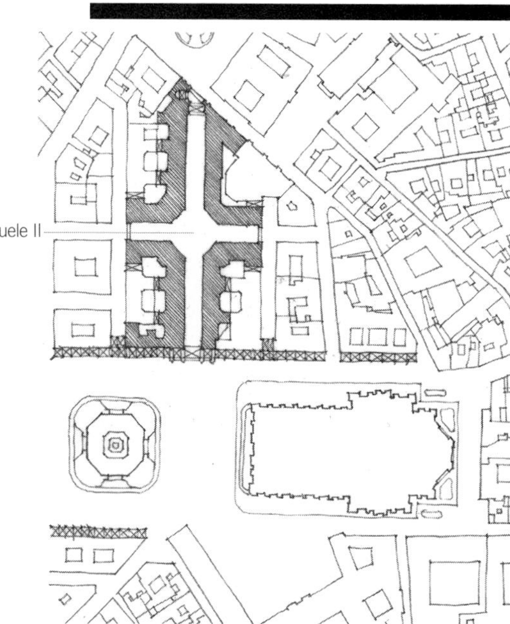

17.9 Milan: Piazza del Duomo

## THE PASSAGE

Besides train stations and industrial fairs, the building type that perhaps best epitomized the industrial revolution and its new culture of mass consumption was the shopping gallery. These buildings were places where one could see firsthand not only the wealth of the global marketplace but also the new materials of metal and glass. At the beginning of the 19th century most shops differed very little from those of medieval times—a window or counter faced the street, and there was a small enclosure where business could be transacted. The fall in the price of glass made large shop windows possible, and they soon appeared almost simultaneously at the end of the 1820s in London, Paris, and New York. In Paris, shopping streets—called a gallerie or passage—were soon designed with rows of shops under a single glazed roof. By the end of the 19th century these passages had grown in number and could be found in most European cities. At first, they were on a single floor, but soon they were on two or more levels. These galleries provided security for shop owners as well as convenience for shoppers. One has to remember that most 19th century cities were noisy and chaotic, and the galleries offered protected enclaves for bourgeois patrons.

Marking the zenith of this building type was the Galleria Vittorio Emanuele II in Milan, a building that became a symbol of the young nation. Its entrance was located facing the piazza in front of the Duomo, the facade of which had only been finished in 1806. The planning of the piazza had stalled for decades, but it was revived with the unification of Italy in 1859. Almost immediately the designing of the Galleria was put into motion, and when it was opened in 1867, it was seen as an engineering and urban marvel.

The four-part building, meeting at a great, glassed dome, is completely regular on the interior, but it dovetails with the older existing structures around it. The building has seven floors, not including the cellar, with a network of concealed intersecting supports, allowing for a flexible use of space. Staircases are located at the rear and are accessible through courtyards so as not to disturb the visual unity of the facades. The main staircases are located at the reentrant angles of the crossings. The third floor is reserved for club rooms, offices, and studios, while the uppermost floors are residential. More than just a shopping arcade, this building is an urban entity unto itself.

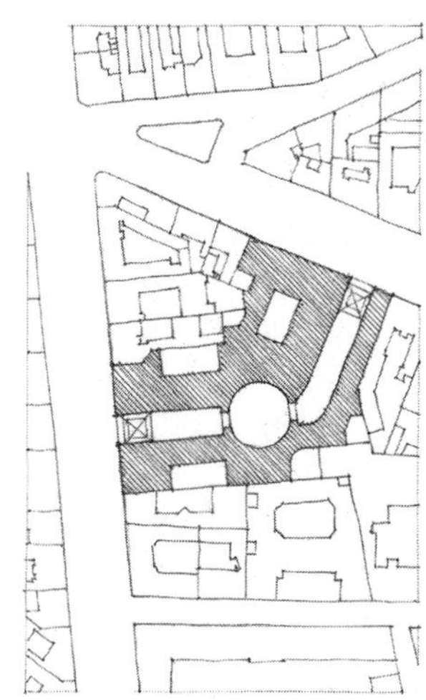
17.10 Berlin: Friedrichstrassenpassage

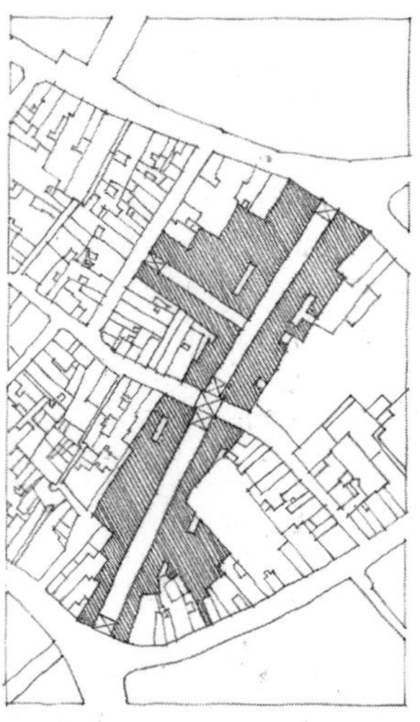
17.11 Brussels: Galeries St. Hubert

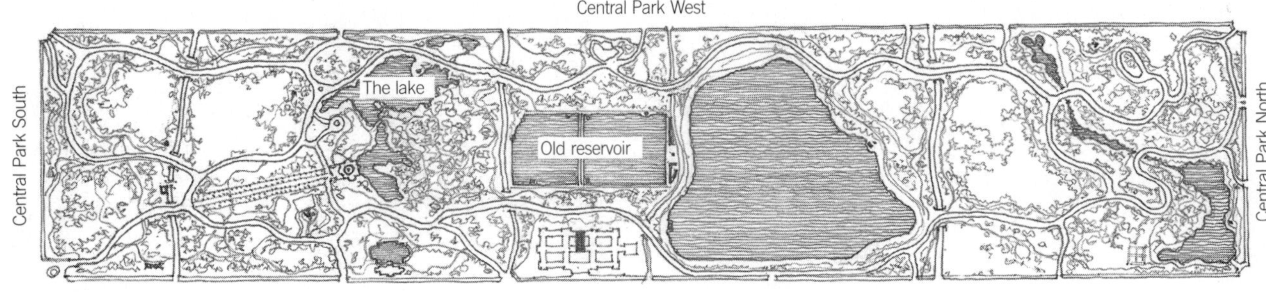


**17.12 Plan of Central Park, New York City**

### Central Park

By the early 19th century urban parks had become well recognized as an important aspect of a city's qualities. The gardens of Versailles were opened to the public in the 1830s. But no park could measure up to the ambitions of New York's Central Park (1853–83). A treeless garbage dump and shanty town was converted into a park some 2170 square kilometers in size. A vast amount of earth was removed, and the bed-rock blasted away if it did not conform. Four million cubic yards of soil and rock were then added and on top of that four to five million trees were planted. But it was not just the trees and plants that made it successful. The park contained meadows, forests, hilltop lookouts, castles, sheep farms, skating rinks, and eateries, supported by curving paths with elegant bridges, underneath of which is an elaborate drainage system. In its first year of operation, in 1872, the park attracted 10 million visitors.

Central Park was designed by Frederick Law Olmstead (1822–1903) and Calvert Vaux. Vaux, an English architect, came to the United States to work with Andrew Jackson Downing, an advocate of landscape design and a famous critic of industrialization and urbanization.

Downing (1815–52), influenced by picturesque ideas as well as the growing moralism of the early Victorian era, saw in the landscape more than just beauty. He also saw the garden as something other than a stage for monuments to heroes as it was at Stowe Gardens, Buckinghamshire, England. For Downing, landscape had a social purpose in that it enhanced moral value and even aided in the integrity of the family. The intimate house garden, he argued, should become the purview of the woman of the house, who should use it as a civilizing and protective veil around the house. He also wanted houses to blend as naturally as possible into the land.

One should also remember that at this time, the area around most large cities in the United States had been radically deforested to make way for farms. In 1845, when Henry David Thoreau lived next to Walden Pond, Massachusetts, in his attempt to get back to nature, the pond at that time was one of the few areas for many miles around that still had trees. Downing believed that one could bring nature to the city in the form of parks, but only if they were big enough so that the therapeutic experience of nature would not be diluted. Even though Central Park was an artificial landscape, it was built at such a scale that it could be experienced as "raw nature" but one that had been tamed and brought into balance with human needs.

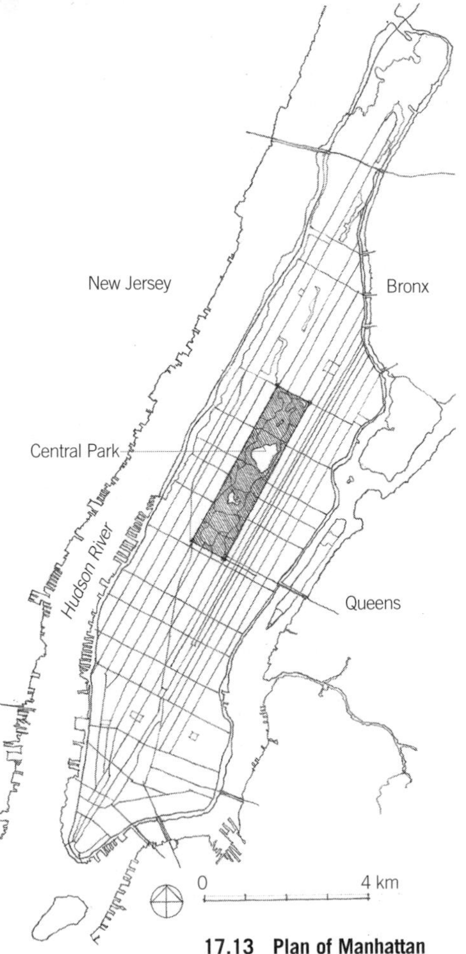


**17.13 Plan of Manhattan**

17.14 National Gallery, London, England

17.15 French-Egyptian Museum, Cairo, Egypt

## NATIONAL MUSEUMS

From the Renaissance on, history was more often than not explained as a sequence of great kings, queens, and military events. With the Enlightenment, history began to be perceived in terms of a civilizational dynamic and verifiable data. The original fixation on Rome and Greece expanded into a fascination with the history of Egypt, Mesopotamia, and India, with nations such as England, France, and Germany seeing themselves as the protectors and heirs of antique values. The national museums that now came into being exemplified the Victorian era's desire—and capacity—to master the logic of the expanding scale of history. The Louvre was among the first of these new museums, and it was transformed in 1793 from a private, royal collection into a public art museum open to all citizens free of charge. Subsequently Napoleon transformed the Louvre into an instrument of the state to strengthen the link between national identity and the history of civilization. The idea of the national museum was taken up by the Prussian king, Friedrich Wilhelm II, who built the Altes Museum in Berlin in 1829. By the end of the 19th century, the European conception of nation and empire were inextricably intertwined with displays of museums and exhibitions.

The discovery of dazzling, forgotten ruins, such as those of Angkor Wat by the French in the 1860s, became a competitive sport among nations. The principle of these discoveries was finders-keepers, with the finders becoming more famous than their discoveries; the Elgin Marbles, from the frieze of the Parthenon, was named not after the temple, but after the man who sold them to the British Museum, Thomas Bruce, the 7th Earl of Elgin.

One need only think of the span of time from the National Gallery in London (1861) to the Kyoto National Museum (1898), to the Estonian National Museum (1909), and to the National Gallery in Washington, D.C. (1931) to bring to mind museums that were designed to embody national ideologies. At the same time, museums were built in the colonies to expand the legitimacy of the civilizational mission and to enable native peoples to recognize themselves as differentiated subjects under the overarching and unifying umbrella of empire. The Government Museum of Chennai (1851) and Prince of Wales Museum in Mumbai (1914), as well as the French-Egyptian Museum in Cairo (1858) are but a few examples of the complex aspects of the history of colonialism.

In most cases, museums were conceived as neoclassical structures, because the claim to classicism was central to the concept of nationalism in the 19th century. The imprint of neoclassicism was so strong that even in the 20th century, modernism at first could do little to challenge it, at least in Europe and the Americas. In Europe there are few examples of museums not built in a neoclassical style until the advent of postmodernism.

17.16 Prince of Wales Museum, Mumbai, India

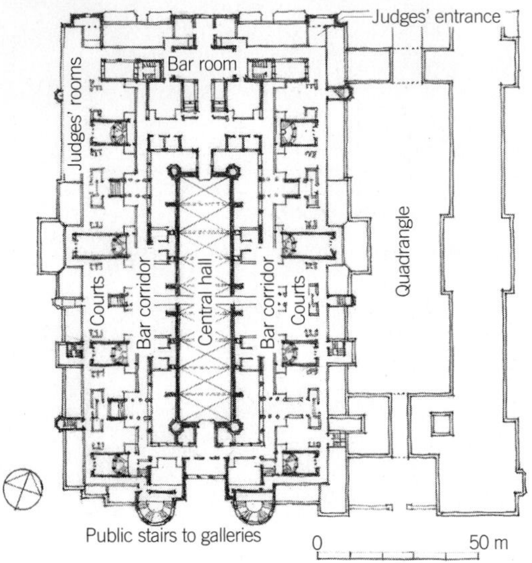


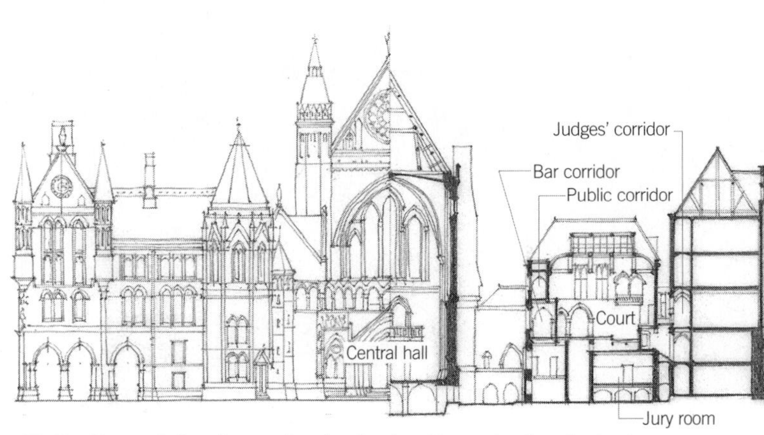


**17.17 Plan and elevation-section: London Law Courts, London, England**

**London Law Courts**

The Victorian era on the whole was still tied to the picturesque ideal that architecture had to be linked creatively to the past as an indication of the dignity of the present. But the Victorians were not attached to Rome or for that matter to Greece as the generation of Robert Adam and John Nash. They experimented with historical styles that resonated with the increased archaeological erudition of the time and with the diverse philosophical persuasions of their clientele. George Edmund Street, who designed the London Law Courts (1870–81), for example, used an early medieval style, not August Welby Pugin's high Gothic. Street chose this in appreciation of its more stern and primitive associations, despite the fact that the precedent was more French than English. Street, and many of the young architects of the time, were enthralled with the ideals of Gallic toughness.

The London Law Courts building was designed on the heels of significant reforms to the English legal code. With the crowning of William IV in 1830 and the return to power of the Whigs, the way was opened for an era of accelerated social progress. The Reform Bill of 1832 eliminated many inequities in representation. This was followed by child-labor laws that began to place controls on the hours of labor and working conditions for children and women in manufacturing plants. New police forces, which until then had existed in only haphazard form, were now in place, and they aimed to differentiate the different types of criminal activity in opposition to the more wholesale approach of the earlier generations.

The 1846 County Courts Act followed by the Judicature Acts of 1873 tried to make the court system more streamlined and more easily understood while at the same time expanding its reach. Church courts were closed down and replaced by divorce and probate courts. The high court also administered the voluminous new legislation dealing with property, bankruptcy, succession, copyrights, patents, and taxation.

With four different systems of circulation, the Law Courts building was quite complex and mirrored the new and expanded horizon of law. It had 18 courtrooms, with two of those larger than the others for the more prominent trials. A private corridor for the bar circled the building between the courts and the central hall. Judges were provided with their own corridor circuit, one-half level higher than that of the bar; it ran behind the courtrooms and gave direct access to the raised daises on which the judges sat in the courts. A circumferential corridor, running just under that of the judges, accommodated attorneys, with its own doorways into the courtrooms. The public, considered to be troublesome and boisterous, was segregated in its own corridor, which connected to the upper galleries of the courtroom. The large portal opening onto the Strand was used only infrequently for ceremonial purposes. One entered the building at specialized and monitored entrances that led to staircases and thus to the proper corridors. The great hall was not the central element of the circulation system but used only by those already inside the building. Given the tight packing of rooms and corridors, ventilation was a major concern, and so spaces and gaps were left in the composition to allow for outdoor ventilation and ventilation shafts. Whether the building lived up to its ideology of transparency or obfuscated it in a labyrinthine system is something that can be discussed.

17.18 **Victoria Terminus, Bombay, India**

17.19 **Government Secretariat, Bombay, India**

## COLONIAL BOMBAY

British colonial architecture in the first half of the 19th century focused on establishing the superiority of British civilization and, therefore, its right to rule, by building in classical styles. By this logic, there was no perceived value in Indian architectural history. It is even said that Lord William Bentinck, governor-general from 1828 to 1835, proposed to dismantle the Taj Mahal for its marble. That changed, however, in the 1860s, the events of 1857 playing a major role in the transformation. In May of that year, a widespread revolt broke out in almost all parts of British-occupied India. After a year-long struggle, the revolutionaries were overcome with great loss of life (as was also the case for the British), but England still held India firmly in its grip. Weak states were annexed, the Moghul emperor, nominally the ruler until then, was deposed and old cities like Lucknow that had supported the revolutionaries were drastically rebuilt to ensure that the British cantonments and forts could be defended with clear sightlines. The psychological impact of 1857 was long lasting, with the Indians settling into a period of quiescence with the English-speaking urban elites, known as babus, working hard to learn English and to internalize the culture and manners of the colonizers. It would require one of these babus, Mahatma Gandhi, to desire a paradigm-shifting concept of resistance—nonviolence—to trigger the process toward independence.

For the English, who envisioned an empire that would last in perpetuity, 1857 brought home the central contradiction of imperialism. Its "civilizing mission" had to be justified yet once more, but this time, lingering ideals of a romantic and contented native population made little sense. Instead, India became an extension of Victorian England, with its stress on institutions and civil bureaucracies. And so we see the construction of a Secretariat (1867–74), a Public Works Offices (1869–72), post and telegraph offices (1871–74), and, of course, a Law Courts (1871–78). Most were in the Victorian-Gothic style. The institutions that were created eventually became the building blocks of modern India.

During this time, the economy of India, with its vast labor force (3.5 million labor families in 1875) was also reorganized to make it better suited to the global industrial concerns of the English. Cotton and tea plantations became large-scale operations, with the port of Bombay emerging as particularly important in the second half of the century, especially after the opening of the Suez Canal in 1869. During the U.S. Civil War (1861–65), when the naval blockade by the northerners of southern ports meant that cotton could not be exported from the United States, Bombay became the prime exporter of cotton.

The most spectacular of India's Victorian-era buildings was F. W. Stevens' Victoria Terminus (1878–87) in Bombay. The design derives from Gilbert Scott's St. Pancras Station in London, although one could argue that with its fanciful Gothic detailing, polychromatic stone, decorative tile, marble, and stained glass, it exudes a certain un-English exuberance and excess, symptomatic perhaps of growing English interest in Indian ornamental details. Victoria Terminus, the largest British building in India at that time, was a success with the English public and—quite appropriately, given the city's success as a center of import and export—immediately became the iconic image of Bombay.

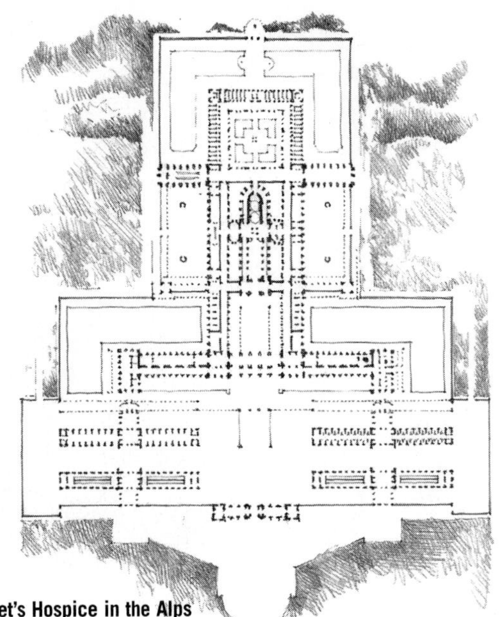

17.20 Premier Grand Prix, 1864: Julien-Azais Gaudet's Hospice in the Alps

### ÉCOLE DES BEAUX-ARTS

Throughout the 19th century, Europe's prime school for the study of architecture was the École des Beaux-Arts in Paris. Though it was intended for French, English, and U.S. citizens, by the end of the 19th century students from around the world began to study there, creating a cadre of devotees who spread the school's pedagogical system and architectural style to places around the globe. Its influence could still be felt in American architectural schools well into the 1940s. The Beaux-Arts was originally founded as the Académie Royale d'Architecture in Paris in 1671 by Jean-Baptiste Colbert, minister of Louis XIV, who envisioned it as a place that would refine the talent necessary for the complex building campaigns of the king. The French Revolution ended the royal academies, but in 1803, architectural education resumed. The main purpose of the education was to prepare students for state-sponsored architectural competitions.

Of particular importance to the Beaux-Arts conception of design was the ground plan. It had to be functionally clear and formally coherent, and it was usually composed of intersecting rectangles organized symmetrically along a central axis. There was a strong desire to balance buildings with courtyards and solids with voids. The arrangement of spaces, the differentiation between primary and secondary, was known as the *parti*.

The year 1840 marked an important landmark in the professionalization of architecture, when the Société Centrale des Architects was founded, an organization that made architecture into a profession similar to law and medicine. The Société spelled the end of the aristocratic system of patronage. It also spelled the end of the gentleman architect, though that tradition was stronger in England than in France. This is important to note, because even though the academic style of the French was much criticized by the moderns of the 20th century, the success of the École elevated architecture into an autonomous discipline. With that autonomy came new and complex theoretical questions about the nature of architectural production. Should one use new materials like steel and glass, and if so, how? What is the relationship between the identity of a nation, its history, and its architecture? By mid-century these issues became quite divisive. On one side stood defenders of idealized classicism, such as Quatremére de Quincy, and on the other were the romantics, such as Henri Labrouste, with their more flexible understanding of history. The conflict broke into the open with the appointment of Eugène-Emmanuel Viollet-le-Duc in 1863 as the professor of the history of art and aesthetics. His appointment was short-lived, however, and by the 1880s the school became known as a champion of an eclectic style that was picturesque in its massing but one that remained committed to the tradition of clean and rectilinearly organized plans.

Students who were enrolled in the school received much of their education outside of its walls. In fact, their principal learning took place in the atelier. The senior members of the field all employed students for cheap labor but in full awareness that they had to educate them in the principles of design. Naturally, quality varied as did style, and students therefore had to choose those with whom they felt most compatible. Lectures were given at the École, yet attendance was voluntary and no course examinations were given. Advancement depended on winning points in the monthly competition in composition, construction, perspective, and mathematics.

For a student, the pinnacle of success was winning the annual Prix de Rome, which sent the student to Rome to live at the Villa Medici for one year. The competition took place in three stages and lasted for several months. Students had to develop a twelve-hour sketch (*esquisse*) solving a design problem that had been set out by the professor of theory, leading to a more substantial presentation (*charrette*), named for the carts that the students would use to carry their material to the school. The authors of the best eight were then given about three months, usually until the end of July, to develop a *projet rendu*. It was from these that a winner was chosen. Drawings made for the final stage of the competition could be very large; some measured five meters in length.

17.21 Grand Staircase: Paris Opera House

17.22 Paris Opera House, France

**Paris Opera House**

Following a period of political unrest, a plebiscite was held in 1852 in France that gave supreme power, with the title of emperor, to Napoleon III (1808–73). He promptly canceled the independence of parliament and rolled back advancements that had been made in the name of universal suffrage, free press, and education. Public institutions were strictly supervised, the teaching of philosophy in the high schools was suppressed, and the power of the government was increased. The nation that had been created with great ideals of liberty, equality, and fraternity for all was now, for all practical purposes, a dictatorship.

Initially, the fortunes of France seemed restored. The country emerged victorious in the Crimean War (1854–6) and then went on to build the Suez Canal (1854–69). Napoleon III was eager to translate these successes into architectural form and even more than that to transform Paris into the leading capital of the world. For this he turned to Georges-Eugène Haussmann (1809–91), whose vision for Paris, like Napoleon III's, was unmistakably big. Unlike earlier urban designs that made straight boulevards through the city so as to enhance the placement of a royal palace, Haussman's new streets were designed for largely pragmatic considerations. They had to be built, however, by destroying large parts of old Paris and displacing thousands of inhabitants, mainly from the lower classes.

One of the centerpieces of the new Paris was the Opera House (1861–75), set at the intersection of several radiating streets. It was designed by Charles Garnier (1825–98), who was only 36 years old when he won the competition to design it. Earlier he had won the Prix de Rome, which guaranteed that even a son of a working man could have a potentially bright future in the professional class.

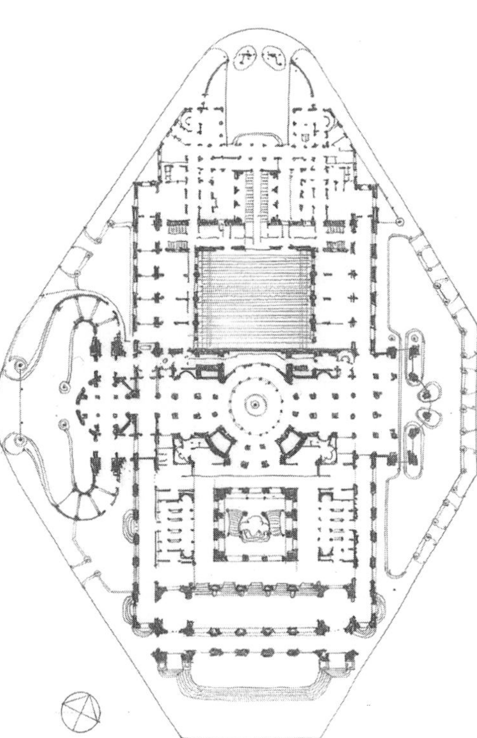

17.23 Ground floor plan: Paris Opera House

Garnier's design blends the double columnar colonnade from the Louvre with elements taken from Michelangelo's facade for the Campidoglio. It thus blends the royal symbolism that would have appealed to Napoleon III with the republican symbolism of Michelangelo's work. The front, when taken as a whole, could also be seen as a very wide triumphal arch. In that sense, it successfully negotiated the complex political situation in which it was situated without referring to Rome or Greece in any direct way. Like the London Law Courts, this building had multiple functions and circulation systems. The front facade entrances were for the public arriving on foot. The upper classes, arriving by coach, entered on the right-hand side. Performers and members of the opera administration entered at the rear. There was a special side entrance for the emperor, where he could roll up in his coach indoors. Structurally the building is of steel, but the steel is rendered invisible by stone and brick. The staircase that lies between the entrance narthex and the theater is itself a three-dimensional theater intended to allow operagoers to see and be seen, the encounters themselves becoming an elaborate social ritual of the time.

17.24 **Interior of a Victorian-era house**

17.25 **Victorian-era chair**

## DOMESTIC VICTORIAN ARCHITECTURE

While In France, state-supported architecture created an environment in which civic professionalism could flourish as practically nowhere else in Europe. Residential architecture rarely achieved much prominence and indeed there was little innovation in residential architecture in France, except in the creation of urban apartments, until very late in the 19th century. In England, where civic architecture was not regulated by the state, the architects turned to residential buildings as the primary way to enter the profession. The result was a rapid development of residential architectural thinking. The same was true in the United States, which is why much of the history of modern residential design focuses on these two places.

In the early decades of the Victorian era, the strict rule and order of the neo-Palladians gave way to compositions that were considerably more relaxed. They were tied less to the narrower focus on Palladio and more to a general interest in the Renaissance, which, by the 1860s, was becoming identified as a period unto its own, associated with the ideals of humanism, grace, and aesthetic contemplation. A later generation would see the Renaissance Italianate buildings as cluttered and spindly.

But for the Victorian architect, the value of these building lay not in their external appearance but in their plans that offered more flexible ways of organizing complex social and familial activities, while giving coherence, ideologically and philosophically, to the ideals of the bourgeois family. In the 1880s, the English middle class had grown in wealth and sophistication and was at the height of its prosperity and power.

The positive economic situation and stable internal politics meant that children of the Victorian era were noticeably less dogmatic than their fathers. They preferred the small scale to the large, delicacy and refinement to toughness and vigor. Chunky heavyweight furniture went out of fashion and practical, lightweight furniture came in vogue.

17.26 **Victorian-era chair**

The new generation may have broken with the past, but in terms of technology they were noticeably critical and looked to the emerging rationalism of their age with a certain suspicion. This generation was not one of ideological purists, even though they were the first English generation to be fully engaged in matters of social and political reform. A great emphasis was placed on education and a tremendous number of schools were built in the latter part of the century. Though morality was strongly emphasized, religion itself was downplayed or replaced by a preference for spiritualism or rendered absent all together. Life was not seen as defined by an abstract set of duties and obligations, but it had to be lived so as to protect oneself from the ugliness and crudity of the environment. More important than the product was the sensibility with which one approached it. And it is for this reason that the movement produced comparatively little theoretical literature. That would come a bit later with art nouveau.

17.27 Elevation: Studio House for Luke Fildes

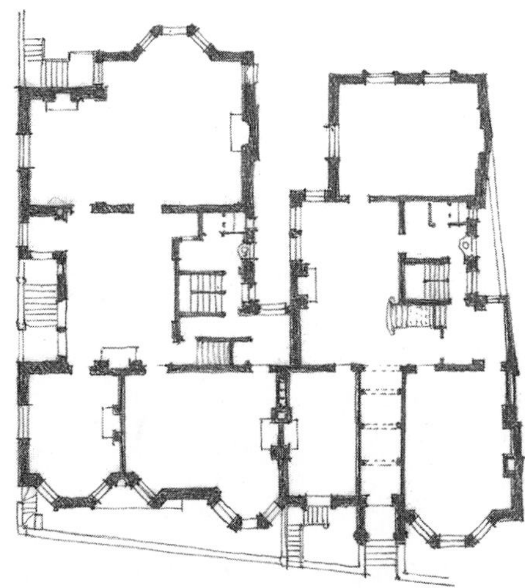

17.28 Ground floor plan: Lowther Gardens, Kensington

## QUEEN ANNE STYLE

One of the Victorian-era styles that developed during this time came to be known as the Queen Anne style. The style's connection with the 18th-century Queen Anne herself is obscure, but by the 1870s the basic bungalow forms had developed into more monumental structures with their own unique features, such as pedimented gables, sash and bay windows, picturesque massing, and sometimes wittily conjoined elements. The brick flue of a chimney, for example, might appear to run through a bay window of an upper floor.

One of the leading Queen Anne–style architects was Norman Shaw (1831–1913). Born in Edinburgh, Scotland, Shaw expressed the ideal of this search for a more relaxed interior design. His houses were to be lived in and not meant primarily for social ostentation. Windows were small or big depending on function and location. A studio house (1875–7) that he designed in Kensington, the fashionable western residential district just outside of London, shows this well. The entrance, protected by a balcony above, leads to a hall that, up a few steps, leads to the main floor, which consists of the dining and living rooms. The bedrooms and studio are upstairs with the staircase serving as a type of hinge linking the various aspects of the program. The building is in brick with white trim for the windows. In typical Queen Anne style two small windows illuminate the entrance hall and directly above them, hanging on to the facade, is the chimney that heats the bedroom suit above. Two very narrow windows emphasize its bulk. These contrasts between heavy and light were typical of Shaw's work. One can hardly doubt that there must be a connection between the work of Shaw and later of Adolf Loos, who was very familiar with English architecture.

As an example of a larger Queen Anne work, one can turn to Lowther Gardens (1877–8), Kensington, by John James Stevenson (1883–1934). Though he designed speculation houses, his designs show how the same plan type can be articulated to create a variegated whole by the way the gables are turned this way or that, by the articulation of the chimneys, and by the use of balconies and bay windows to tie together various elements.

By 1890, the Queen Anne style had run its course and architects who had favored it were moving either back to the more classical or toward an even freer form of expression. It is to the latter, and to men like Charles Francis Annesley Voysey and Charles Rennie Mackintosh, that the future belonged.

0 10 m

17.29 Plan: Studio House for Luke Fildes, Kensington, a borough of London, England

17.30 Trinity Church, Boston, Massachusetts, USA

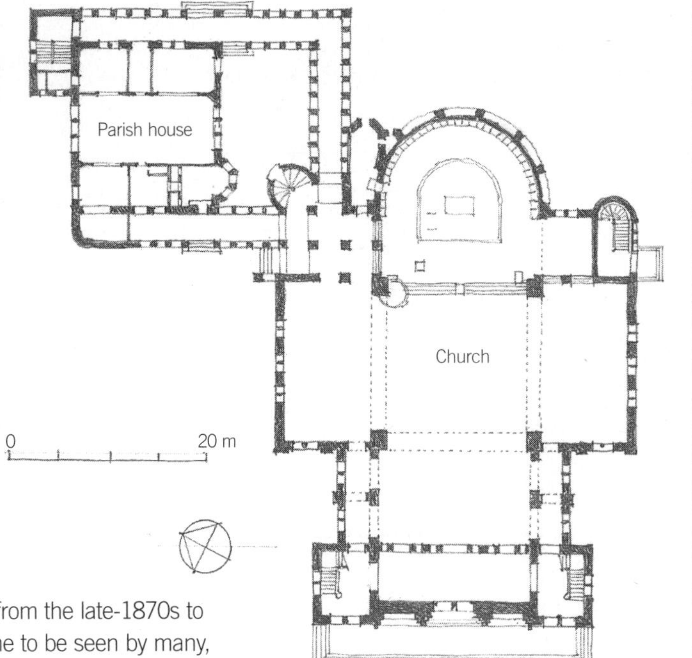


17.31 Plan: Trinity Church, Boston

### Henry Hobson Richardson

By the late 1830s, the Greek Revival had become without question the adopted national style of the United States, and it remained as such up to the Civil War. The simplicity, ideological coherency, and the ease by which one could copy its forms in brick and wood contributed greatly to its success. It had little competition from the Gothic style, which in the United States, unlike in Europe, had few major representatives. The result was a fluid movement from the Greek Revival to a French style known as "Second Empire," with its compositional emphasis on vertical pavilions and classically derived ornamentation. It remained an important subcurrent well until the advent of modernism. In the 1880s and 1890s, a group of architects, however, began to chart their own way, bringing out latent ideas of the picturesque while trying to match this aesthetic with the needs of the mercantile elite. These architects were Frank Furness, who operated out of Philadelphia; Louis Sullivan, who operated out of Chicago; and Henry Hobson Richardson, out of Boston. All developed very distinctive styles. Furness brought many of Eugène Emmanuel Viollet-le-Duc's ideas about integrating iron into the design to the United States. Sullivan brought bold simplicity, combined with rich ornamentation, to his buildings.

Richardson's work from the late-1870s to the mid-1890s came to be seen by many, however, as a style unto its own. When Richardson was young he had intended to become a civil engineer, but he switched to architecture while studying at Harvard in Cambridge, Massachusetts. In 1859, he went to Paris to study at the École des Beaux-Arts and remained there for five years. Because of his Parisian training, Richardson was well suited to serve the needs of the rising class of new businessmen who saw their ambitions mirrored in the world of cosmopolitan Paris. But by the 1870s, he began to be drawn increasingly to the English medieval style and to the picturesque, while attempting to find a means of combining the disparate and even contradictory aspects of his architectural interests. Richardson's plans, for example, maintain a clarity of form that was typical of Beaux-Arts while his attention to the tactility and color of the building's stone surface evoked sensibilities that were more in line with Queen Anne style and Ruskinian Gothic. In 1872 Richardson achieved national prominence through his selection as architect for Trinity Church in Boston.

17.32 Porch: Trinity Church, Boston

**17.33 Winn Memorial Public Library, Woburn, Massachusetts, USA**

The building's porch, facade, and crossing-tower step back in clear volumetric hierarchy. The porch, added after the building was built but to Richardson's specifications, was modeled loosely on the church of St. Trophime in Arles, France, whereas the tower, very wide and defining the entire width of the nave, was modeled on French and Spanish medieval buildings, including the 12th-century tower of the Cathedral of Salamanca. Reddish brown sandstone was used to define the architectural elements, such as voussoirs and string courses, against a backdrop of light gray granite. Though the building's style, in its massing and detailing, is neo-Romanesque, its plan is a Latin cross with an apse at the eastern end. The focus of the church is the tall and airy crossing. Stained-glass windows bring in a soft muted light that washes against the wall's golden surfaces, punctuated by reds, blues, and browns in an excellent example of the blend between the neo-Romanesque and the aesthetics of the arts-and-crafts movement. The stained glass, mostly in hues of blue and green, make the interior relatively dark. Illumination comes from a huge candelabra (now removed) hanging from the center of the crossing.

Richardson was fortunate that his mature career coincided with the rise of the American public library movement. The flowering of public education and the spread of interest in cultural developments in England and the United States led to the creation of many town lending libraries. Richardson's libraries have a looser exterior picturesqueness that was meant to contrast with the clarity of the plan, as, for example, at the Winn Memorial Public Library (Woburn, Massachusetts, 1876–9).

The plan is organized around a barrel-vaulted longitudinal library space with alcoves lining the sides for the bookshelves. It is appendaged onto a transeptlike reading room at the head of which is a picture gallery and an octagonal museum. The building is entered from the side along a tall tower with Gothic-style tracery in the upper ranges. Richardson was meticulous in his choice of materials. The walls are of red sandstone from a quarry in Massachusetts. The column bases and horizontal bands are of a cream-colored sandstone from Ohio, all set on a granite base. For the ornamental carvings of the capitals and corbels, Richardson brought in a Welsh sculptor.

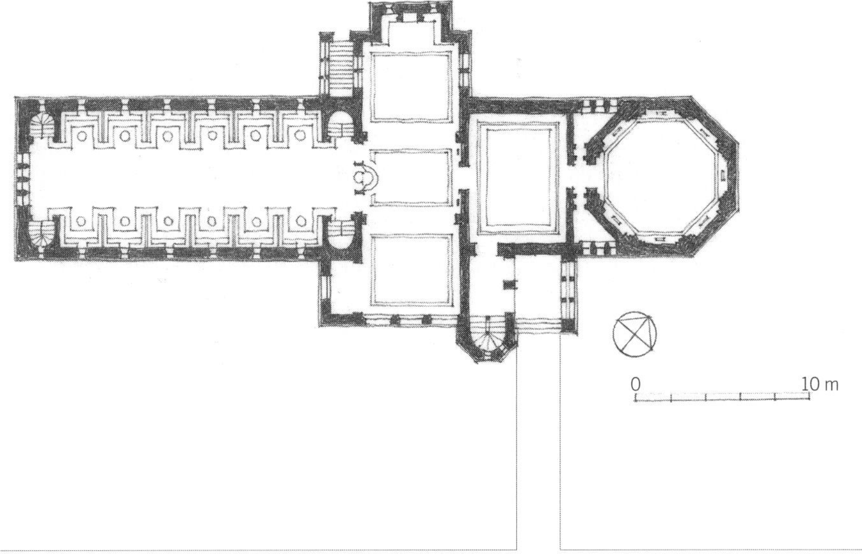


**17.34 Plan: Winn Memorial Public Library**

17.35 William Morris

17.36 William Morris textile design

## ARTS-AND-CRAFTS MOVEMENT

In England, the hopefulness of the 1870s began to evaporate by the end of the century. The emergence of Germany and the United States as political and economical rivals, the fiascoes of the Boer Wars, the stepped-up campaign for women's suffrage, and the continual drumbeat of workers' strikes and unrest had begun to sap the self-confidence and amiability of English society. The gulf between those clamoring for socialist reform and those arguing for a stronger imperial policy was creating bitter tensions. It was in this context that a movement sprang up that defined a middle ground between socialist capitalism. Known as the arts-and-crafts movement, it appealed to individuality, novelty, and good taste; but it refined these tendencies into a social and philosophical position that revolved around the critique of what many saw as the ethical vacuum at the center of England's mercantile culture. The concern of the arts and crafts was not on the end product of design, and certainly not on efficiency, but on the processes shaping the design. There had to be an intimate connection between design and production. This position was to have significant influence on later modernists, such as Henry Van de Velde, Hermann Muthesius, Adolf Loos, and Walter Gropius.

The arts-and-crafts artists were, for the most part, resistant to making connections to industry, as they were frustrated by what they perceived as the drift toward mechanization. Perfection of finish, symmetry, and precision were suspect since they represented the denial of the human element. But just because the movement critiqued capitalism and industrialism did not mean it was a friend of the socialists, who for their part paid little regard to the arts-and-crafts movement; their weapons were the trade unions not guilds of bookbinders and furniture makers. In reality, the arts and crafts appealed more to the disenfranchised bourgeoisie, romantic intellectuals, social utopianists, and to upper-class aesthetes than to members of the working class. In this it was, in essence, an extension of Victorian ideals. Different was the level of enthusiasm and the commitment to educating the middle class on the question of taste. Ruskin tried to launch a small community of like-minded people in Sheffield, but even though it failed, he did create a museum that contained carefully assembled objects intended for the edification of local laborers and schoolchildren, consisting of paintings, sculpture, prints, casts, and specimens in Sheffield.

The arts-and-crafts movement became quite widespread, reaching Belgium, France, Germany, the United States, and even some of the English colonies, particularly India. Some of the arts and crafts enthusiasts, like John Lockwood Kipling (father of the author Rudyard Kipling) in fact moved to India to dedicate themselves to the cause of preserving and promoting Indian crafts. Kipling promoted a new journal on Indian crafts and even started a school to train young craftsmen. The arts and crafts enthusiasts, however, had little influence on actual building in India, as compared to the work done by the Imperial Public Works Department.

17.37 William Morris' design for Kelmscott Press label

**17.38 Presentation drawings of Broad Leys by Charles Voysey**

**Morris and Lethaby**

When William Morris (1834–96) gave his first public lecture in "The Decorative Arts to the Trades Guild of Learning" in 1877 he was already known as a poet and decorator. In that year he had already opened show-rooms in London that displayed work from his business, known as The Firm. From it sprang the Arts and Crafts Exhibition Society (the source of the movement's name), launched in 1893 with a vigorous campaign of publication and exhibitions devoted to the applied arts. Louis Comfort Tiffany, famous for his lamps, was an admirer of Morris, as was Gustav Stickley, famous for his furniture. For these artists, the simple and the luxurious were not antithetical. Both sprang from the idea of the craftsman as artist and from the belief in individualism and individual commitment. Floating through this was not the abstract deism of the Enlightenment, but an ethos of religiosity, with strong leanings toward Christian simplicity and medieval quietude. Morris, who initially had planned to become a priest, was just as much a medievalist as a socialist.

Among the architects most closely associated with the arts and crafts were William R. Lethaby (1857–1931), Charles Francis Annesley Voysey (1857–1941), and in the United States, the firm of Greene & Greene. Lethaby, who began his career working for Morris & Co., designed several houses; but it is his Brockhampton Church (1901–2) in Herefordshire that is regarded as an important example of arts-and-crafts style. It was built of unassuming walls of red sandstone punctuated by a number of small, variously scaled windows. It was roofed with a steeply pitched concrete roof covered on the exterior with thatch, an unusual combination meant to protect the building against fire but without compromising the overall effect.

Voysey, who began his career designing decorative works and wallpaper, founded an architectural firm that designed numerous country houses for the well-to-do. They were picturesque in nature with an emphasis on pointed gables, tall chimneys, and sweeping roof lines. He used little surface ornamentation, and windows were designed to correspond to functional requirements, with larger windows for the living and dining rooms and smaller and more intimate windows above. In the United States, the arts-and-crafts artisans were mainly centered in New England and in California.

**17.39 Brockhampton Church, Herefordshire, England**

17.40 Mubarak Mahal, Jaipur, India

17.41 National Art Gallery, Government Museum of Chennai, formerly the Victoria Technical Institute Building by Robert F. Chisolm

## INDO-SARACENIC STYLE

Late in the 19th century, Gothic Revival architecture, with its overt message of English nationalism, seemed increasingly out of place in India. It was now clear to the English that India had an architectural history that was as deep as it was complicated. With scholars now studying Indian art and architecture, a new generation of architects began to experiment with a style that came to be known as Indo-Saracenic, which adapted the architectural vocabulary of Islamic or "Saracenic" architecture to create buildings such as town halls, libraries, and schools. The Indo-Saracenic paralleled the attempt in Egypt to create a Mamluk style.

Part of the Indo-Saracenic ideal was lodged in the colonial stereotype of the putative "decline" of Indian civilization. The English claimed that they had succeeded in conquering India because Indian civilization in general had gone into decay. One of the chief proponents of this idea was James Fergusson, the first historian of Indian architecture. Without any understanding of the functional or conceptual basis of Indian architecture, Fergusson classified and evaluated Indian buildings based on their formal properties and proposed that Indian architecture periodically went into "decline" and that it had thus to be revived by contact with foreign races.

For the arts-and-crafts high priest John Ruskin, the crucial index of decline could be mapped by differentiating between Indian craft and Indian art. While craftsmen, working in their native innocence, were seen as a positive example for the English, the Indian arts had, in his opinion, gone into decline accompanied by a decline in morality. This decline, according to Ruskin, accounted for the "worse than bestial" acts that Indian revolutionaries had supposedly been responsible for in the violence of 1857. At the same time, he feared that the decline in Indian crafts might be due to the corrupting influence of Europeans. His prescription was to reeducate native craftsmen in European aesthetics while preserving and reviving their craft traditions. European art with Indian craft in the service of modern colonial buildings was, therefore, the 19th-century recipe for a "modern Indian" architecture.

One of the most celebrated attempted translations of arts-and-crafts ideals into the practice of architecture in India was undertaken by Colonel Swinton Jacobs. An engineer by training, Jacobs worked in the "princely state" of Jaipur, in Rajasthan, for more than 40 years (1867–1912). (Princely states were nominally independent but governed by local rulers who were subject to the British Empire.) Jacobs believed that by training draftsmen to accurately copy full-size details from examples of Indian architectural history, they would come to appreciate the intrinsic quality of their own culture. His *Jeypore Portfolio of Architectural Details* (1890) was a collection of individual folio sheets that a craftsman could look at and study. All the examples were, however, drawn from Islamic architecture.

A building often attributed to Jacobs but probably designed by one of his personally trained disciples, Lala Chiman Lal, was the Mubarak Mahal, located within the palace compound of Jaipur in 1899. A ceremonial reception hall, the Mubarak Mahal was also a museum comprising a two-story cubic volume with projecting porches. It was a case study in Indo-Saracenic ornamentation: on the upper story a fanciful filigree of carefully executed ornamentation outlined the cantilevered balcony that ran around the entire perimeter of the structure, and on the lower story individual bays, conceived as display cases, self-consciously staged distinct ornamental details. The entire program, layout, and proportions and divisions of the structure, in short, its aesthetic, derived from the European tradition. Only in its details was it Indian.

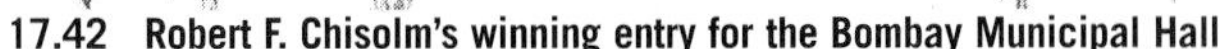

17.42 **Robert F. Chisolm's winning entry for the Bombay Municipal Hall**

17.43 **Jaipur Town Hall, India**

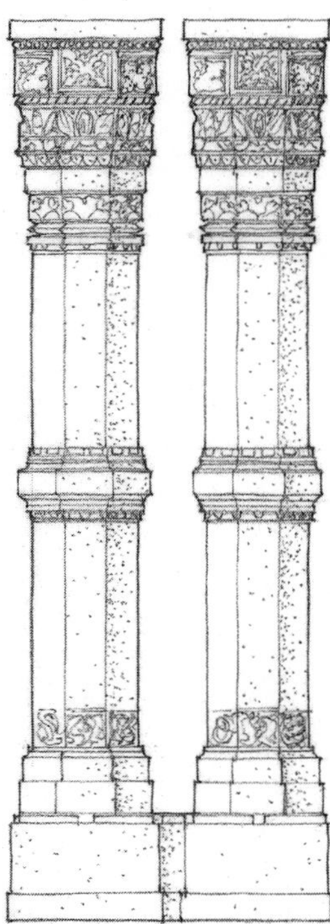
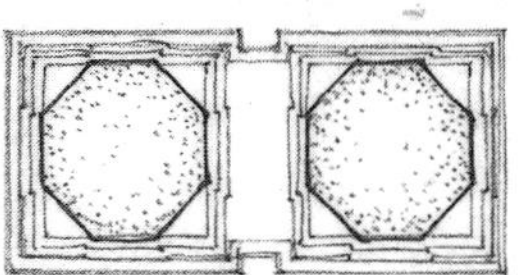

17.44 **Sample drawing from the *Jeypore Portfolio of Architectural Details***

Robert F. Chisolm belonged to the generation of professional architects who believed more in exploring their professional freedom than in following designs from ideological strictures. It was this search that led him inevitably to eclecticism. His unbuilt design for the Bombay Municipal Hall competition, for example, called for a three-story volume with a large central dome that was based on the Taj Mahal. Chisolm did not hesitate to open up the dome at the base with tall arched openings (which necessitated an internal structural system made of steel). Smaller domes on octagonal bases terminated the corners of the main cubic volume. The corners were further emphasized by the suggestion of turrets created by faceting the edges, with a string of moldings close to the ground that flare out slightly at the base, as, for instance, in the Hindu Victory Tower at Chittorgarh. The overall conception of the massing is reminiscent of Henry Hobson Richardson's Trinity Church in Boston. The centerpiece of the elevation changes at every level: a porch supported by paired columns on the ground floor, surmounted by a narrow balcony on the second floor, and finished with a wide, double-height arch surmounted by a Bengal-style drooping roof integrated into the cornice line. No part of the design was left untouched by the careful attention to detail.

Arts and crafts enthusiasts and the Indo-Saracenics did not make much of an impression on the local Indian maharajas in their personal commissions. Sawai Ram Singh (r. 1835–80) brazenly continued to have his workmen build imitation, hybridized, European-style buildings, such as his Town Hall in Jaipur. Singh was a wily character. He had used the typical colonial misrecognition of his relationship with his feudatories to his advantage, making his feudatories, who usually served as checks on his authority, submissive to him on the basis of the representation that he had among his English backers. For maharajas who, like the babus, had no paternalistic project in mind, the identifiable style of power was European.

17.45 Bandung Institute of Technology, Bandung, Indonesia

**DUTCH KAMPUNG**

While the English controlled India and most of the China trade, the Dutch continued their hold on Indonesia, in spite of several English and French attempts to dislodge them. However, late-19th century wars with France, the Acehnese, and the Javanese put the Dutch colonial government deeply into debt. In response, the Dutch set production quotas, fixed prices, restricted travel, and raised taxes under a policy called the Cultivation System (1830–70). It was a disaster and led to massive starvation in the midst of bumper crops of export commodities. A disgruntled young Dutch colonial officer, Eduard Douwes Dekker, captured the hardships of these years for the Dutch public in the 1859 novel *Max Havalaar*. The ensuing outrage back in the Netherlands forced the hand of the colonial authorities and in a series of legislative changes starting in 1870 the so-called Liberal Policy dismantled the forced cultivation of export commodities and opened the colonial economy to Dutch private enterprise. The Liberal Policy sparked a large migration of Dutch to the East Indies, leading to a forceful spatial assertion of European identity against native and immigrant Asian societies.

Using the garden-city model, the Dutch carved their colonial space out of the chaos, congestion, and filth of the native neighborhoods in the colonial towns across Java and Sumatra. Tall, single-story Dutch versions of the British Raj bungalow, with their wide verandas, were set in spacious gardens with outbuildings for kitchens and servants' quarters. The depth of eaves, ceiling heights, and oversized rooms represented creative adaptations to the harsh climate of the Indies.

The Dutch, learning from the English, were increasingly willing to create hybrid styles. In fact, the Indies-born but ethnically Dutch architect, Henri Maclaine Pont, was one of the progenitors of the Indische style of architecture dedicated to the fusion of Dutch and indigenous approaches.

Hendrik Petrus Berlage, the noted Dutch architect, characterized the challenge as one of pulling together the universal qualities of Western modernism with "the local spiritual aesthetic elements of the east." The quintessential exemplar of this was Pont's design for the 1920 Bandoeng Technische Hoogeschool (Bandung Institute of Technology). The technically sophisticated structural wood trusses are left exposed on the interiors of Pont's halls in keeping with the strictures of the arts and crafts movement, while the roof form is a free interpretation of the Sumatran Minangkabau slack-ridge system found in many regions of Southeast Asia. Within the context of the Ethical Policy instituted by the Dutch in 1900, Pont's aesthetic project constituted a new willingness to incorporate symbols more meaningful to all segments of colonial society.

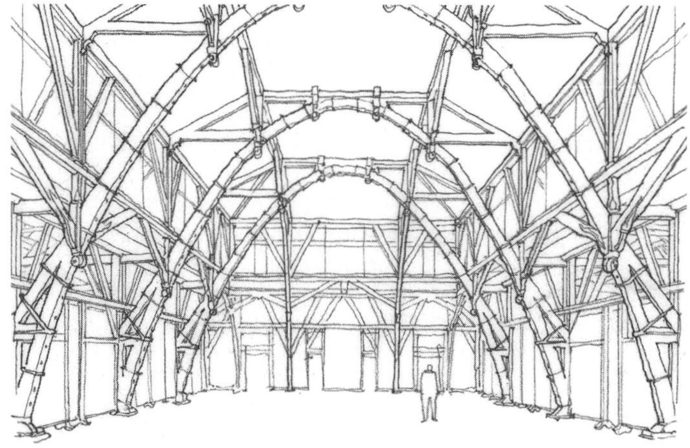

17.46 Interior: Bandung Institute of Technology

17.47 **Sultan Hassan, Al-Rafa'i, and Mahmoud Pasha Mosques, Cairo, Egypt**

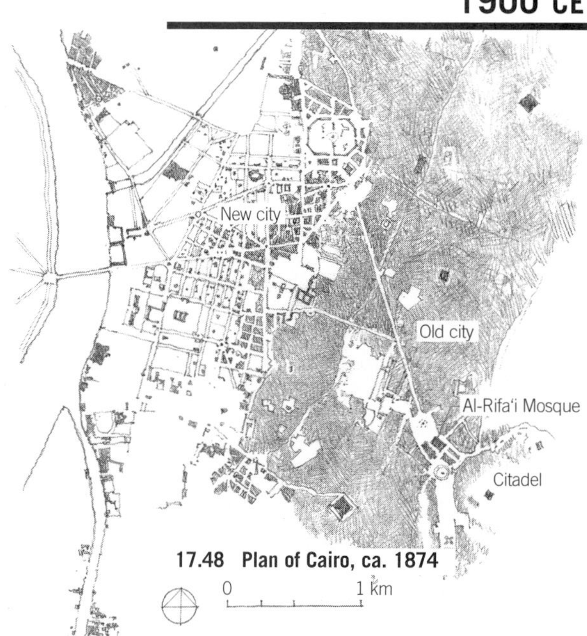


17.48 **Plan of Cairo, ca. 1874**

## Al-Rifa'i Mosque

Though the history of non-European modernism is generally thought to begin early in the 20th century with the spread of art deco (for instance along Bombay's Marine Drive), it actually begins in the second half of the 19th century and often still under the shadow of colonialism. This was true for Egypt, one of the first Arab countries to attempt to reinvent itself by means of modern ideas. Later in the century, Japan saw in Egypt an antecedent to their own modernization program.

Before British colonization of Egypt, which began in 1882, the neo-Mamluk style had proved itself convenient when Egypt proclaimed itself independent from the hegemony of the Ottoman sultanate and wanted an image that was both modern and Egyptian. Sa'id Pasha (r. 1854–63), Muhammad 'Ali's son and third successor, and especially Isma'il Pasha (r. 1863–79), his grandson, were the architects of Egypt's freedom from the Ottomans. Isma'il was fascinated by French culture to the point that he adopted French manners in his personal life and encouraged his entourage to follow suit. He also was an impatient modernizer who wanted to turn Egypt into a piece of Europe despite all adverse circumstances. The country's foreign debt, however, spun out of control. Bankruptcy was declared in 1879, leading to its occupation by the British in 1882.

Isma'il's passion for Europeanization was exemplified by his grand urban projects in Cairo, inspired by his visit to the Exposition Universelle in Paris in 1867. Back in Cairo, he wanted to turn his capital into another Paris, complete with wide, straight avenues planted with trees, palaces, planned gardens, pavilions, and all the amenities of modern city life, such as theaters, cafés, and even an opera house. He commissioned his minister of public works, 'Ali Pasha Mubarak, a member of the academic mission of 1844–49 to France and one of the most influential figures in modern Egyptian history, to draw the city's new master plan.

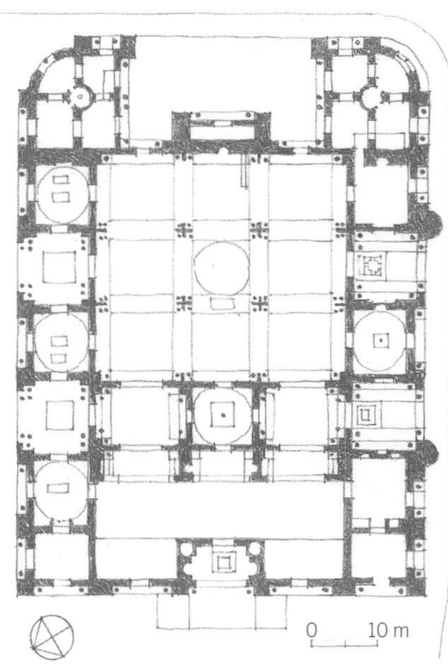


17.49 **Plan: Al-Rifa'i Mosque**

With the exception of two boulevards—Shari Muhammad 'Ali and al-Sikka al-Jadida (New Avenue or Shari' al-Muski)—that cut across the old city's dense fabric and required the razing of many medieval structures, the new city extended westward toward the Nile, along a north-south axis with streets radiating from central squares to form star patterns à la Haussmann. This Parisian-style Cairo was built in haste to impress the European monarchs who had been invited to Egypt for the inauguration of the Suez Canal in 1869, among them Empress Eugénie, wife of Napoleon III.

After the English set up a puppet state in 1882, the neo-Mamluk style, also known as neo-Islamic, remained the dominant motif, relating contemporary Egyptian architecture to a glorious phase of its history. One of the monumental examples, as studied by Nasser Rabbat, the noted scholar of Islamic history, is al-Rifa'i Mosque, constructed in two stages between 1869–80 and 1906–11. The first stage was designed and supervised by the Egyptian architect Hussein Fahmi, the second by the Austro-Hungarian Max Herz, with others hired as consultants and interior designers.

17.50 Gamble House, Pasadena, California, USA

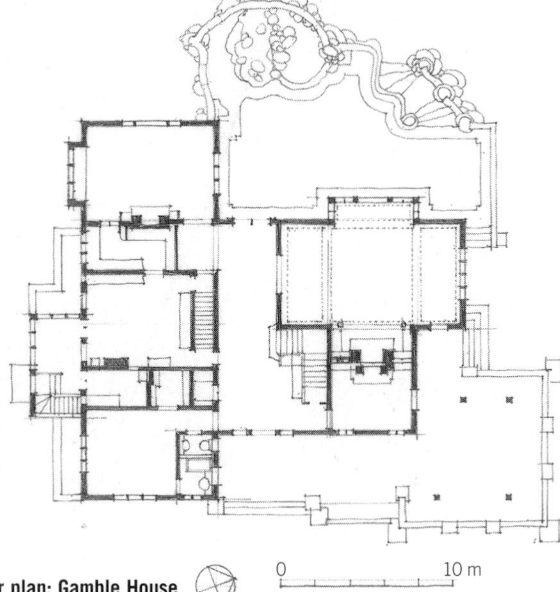


17.51 First floor plan: Gamble House

## ART AND CRAFTS IN CALIFORNIA

In California art and crafts underwent its most vigorous transformation and its longest period of vibrancy. It fused with Spanish-Mexican motifs, as well as elements from the Italian Mediterranean and the Far East. Linked to its development was a public school system strongly committed to manual-arts education and in particular to the belief that the union of head and heart through handicraft yielded therapeutic value. Local libraries organized sketch clubs and hosted exhibitions of local craft production.

Elements from the local landscape and flora were also quite strong in the California arts and crafts. Whether depicting the golden poppy, the Torrey pines, the redwood, or the sublime majesty of the Yosemite, California's arts and crafts artists extolled the state's natural beauty and were much more intimately associated with the outdoors than their counterparts in England and the northeastern United States. Many of their houses exploited the fine views and outdoor living afforded by the natural settings.

These arts and crafts houses featured deliberate blurring of interior and exterior space through the use of decks, pergolas, porches, and terraces. The English-styled medievalism in these houses gave way to an aesthetic of primitivism, as embodied, for example, in the writings of Jack London (author of *The Call of the Wild*, 1903), whose own house in Sonoma's Valley of the Moon was a prime example of arts and crafts domestic architecture: redwood, timber with bark left on, huge halls, and giant fireplaces. The Gamble House by Charles Sumner Greene and Henry Mather Greene (Pasadena, California, 1911) is an excellent example of the use of Japanese motifs. The stepping-stone path across the yard, the battered retaining wall, and an airy elevated porch are all Japanese inspired.

The house rests on a broad terrace that surrounds the house and extends the space of the living rooms outward toward the gardens and lawns. The house was designed in relationship to the existing majestic eucalyptus trees. As had been common in arts and crafts, but rarely achieved at this scale, furniture, built-in cabinetry, paneling, wood carvings, rugs, lighting, and leaded stained glass were all custom-designed by the architects.

The plan was defined by a large hall staircase that bisected the entire building, with the living room and den on one side and the dining room, kitchen, and guest bedroom on the other side. The principal upstairs bedrooms had sleeping porches overlooking the garden. Unlike a shingle style with its steeper pitched roofs, the roofs here are very flat, emphasizing the horizontal layering of space and creating shadows from the overhangs. On the interior the heavy wooden beams were left exposed, but they were smoothed and polished to bring out the material's yellowish warmth. The ceilings are plain white in the Japanese style and stand out against the wood framing. Art nouveau touches on the lamps and stained glass and rugs add a layer of urban sophistication. The house was designed as a retirement residence for David and Mary Gamble of Cincinnati, Ohio. David, a second generation member of the Procter & Gamble Company, had retired in 1895.

17.52 Watts Sherman House, Newport, Rhode Island, USA

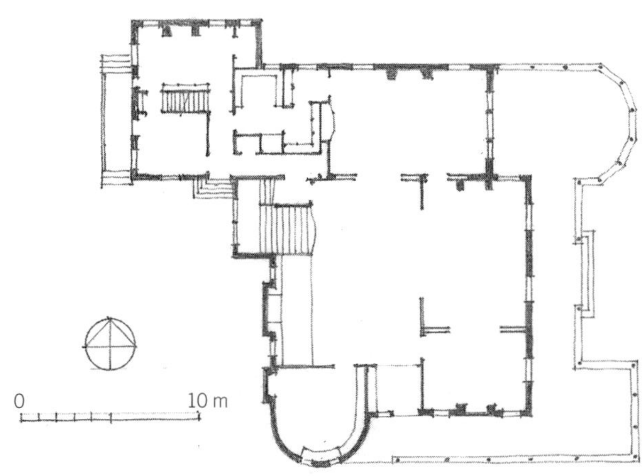


17.53 First-floor plan: Isaac Bell House, Newport

### SHINGLE STYLE

Unique in the United States, and parallel to the art and crafts movement but more closely allied with the Queen Anne style, was the development of what is now called the shingle style. Houses designed in this manner show an inventiveness in plan, with elements not merely touching each other but seeming to pass through or overlap with each other. The firm that developed this style more than any other was McKim, Mead, and White (founded in 1879), which was eventually to become one of the leading design firms in the United States.

William Rutherford Mead (1846–1928), who had an affinity for the Renaissance, and Stanford White (1853–1906) had little formal training, but they worked their way up as apprentices. Charles Follen McKim (1867–70), by contrast, had studied at the École des Beaux-Arts. Between the three of them, they produced a style of architecture that brought out the best of each. Their first commissions were for summer houses for the New England elite in areas remote from the bustle of the big city.

One of their innovations was to take the rooms of the servants' quarters out from under the attic and place them in a compact block or wing, against which the more openly designed living rooms of the first floor were contrasted. One can see this in the Robert Goelet House (Newport, Rhode Island, 1882–3) and in the Isaac Bell House (Newport, Rhode Island, 1882–3). In both houses the staircase was situated in a large room that served as a circulation center and as a spatial extension of the neighboring rooms, like the study and drawing rooms. Even though it was common to raise the first floor above the level of the ground, the use of porches made the house appear as if were resting on an elevated terrace, protected from the sun and rain by generously proportioned overhangs and roofs. The vertical surfaces of the houses were completely clad in shingles, using a variety of possible patterns to differentiate certain elements like the gable front. The interior surfaces were usually covered with dark wooden paneling. The Watts Sherman House (1874) by Henry Hobson Richardson, by way of contrast, is closer to the Queen Anne and the arts and crafts styles. The rooms are arranged in a more formal way and less open to the hall, and the servants lived in the attic.

The shingle style began to fade in the late 1890s, by which time U.S. architects trained in Paris at the École des Beaux-Arts were returning home with a notion of architectural space that did not conform to the relaxed openness of the shingle style. The new preoccupation in the United States with monumentality met the expectations of the more class-conscious elite and ultimately put an end to arts and crafts and its related aesthetic phenomena. McKim, Mead, and White played a dominant role in this shift, becoming the leading representative in the United States of the Beaux-Arts, neoclassical style.

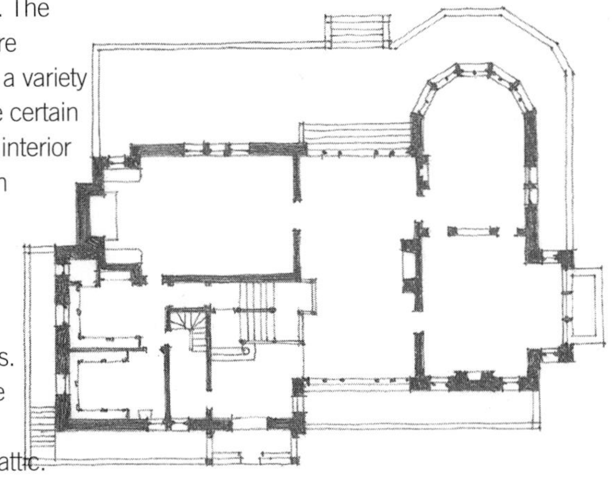

17.54 First-floor plan: Watts Sherman House

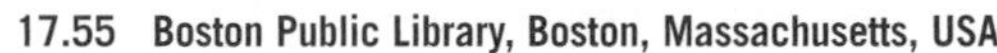

17.55 **Boston Public Library, Boston, Massachusetts, USA**

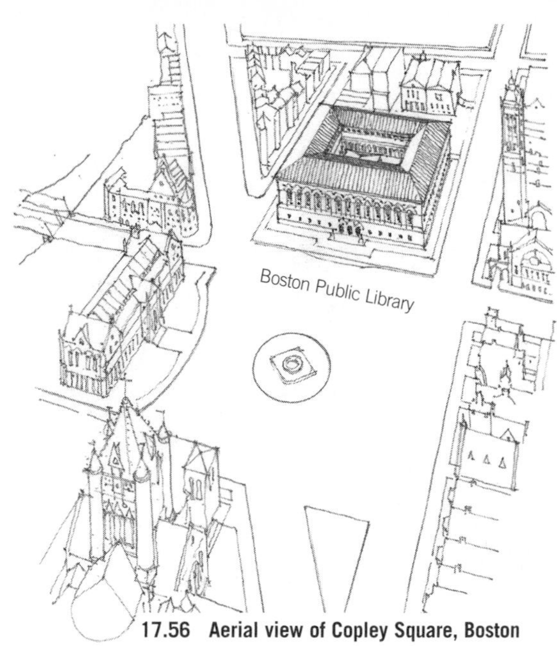


17.56 **Aerial view of Copley Square, Boston**

### CITY BEAUTIFUL MOVEMENT

The economic depression of the mid-1890s forced U.S. corporations to look abroad for markets, and this helped set the stage for a rapid expansion of the U.S. economy. The architectural mood changed accordingly from darker, heavier, and Romanesque-inspired motifs, such as that used by Richardson, to the lighter and more ambitious motifs of the French Beaux-Arts. The turn to classicism was energized by the World's Columbian Exposition of 1893 in Chicago, which was staged to celebrate the 400th anniversary of Christopher Columbus's arrival into the Caribbean. It championed a brand of neoclassicism that was monumental and civic in scale. Most of the exposition buildings were of stucco and painted white, thus its nickname—the White City. It came to be seen as a model of what cities should aspire to, especially since its integrated urban environment of buildings, parks, and walks stood as a challenge to the haphazard urbanism of the age.

Washington, D.C., was practically the only U.S. city with a street and boulevard system that had been properly planned for future growth. Inspired by the exhibition, city fathers began to draw up planning measures following some of its principles. The movement came to be known as the "city beautiful." These cities included Cleveland, San Francisco, Chicago, Detroit, Baltimore, and St. Louis, among others. Though few plans were actually implemented and the ones that were only partially completed, they consisted of a main skeleton of streets and nodes in combination with public buildings and parks. Most successful were the individual buildings that fell under this rubric. At the turn of the century almost every major metropolis, in fact, came to have its share of "city beautiful" architecture, whether it be train stations, banks, markets, or town halls.

Pennsylvania Station, New York City (1904–10), featured a block-long columnar screen, a drive-in unloading street, a central waiting room modeled on Diocletian's basilica in Rome, and a steel-and-glass hall and circulation platform, leading down to the various levels. The building was designed by the firm of McKim, Mead, and White, one of the leading champions of the French Beaux-Arts in the United States. Another example of their work is the Boston Public Library (1897), which faces across Copley Square to Richardson's Trinity Church on the other end. Drawing on Henri Labrouste's Bibliothèque St. Geneviève, with an arcade set up on a high base, the architects created in their use of fine marbles, mosaics, painting, and color one of the finest public buildings at that time in the United States. It had a monumental entrance that led up to the main reading room, which spanned the entire length of the facade.

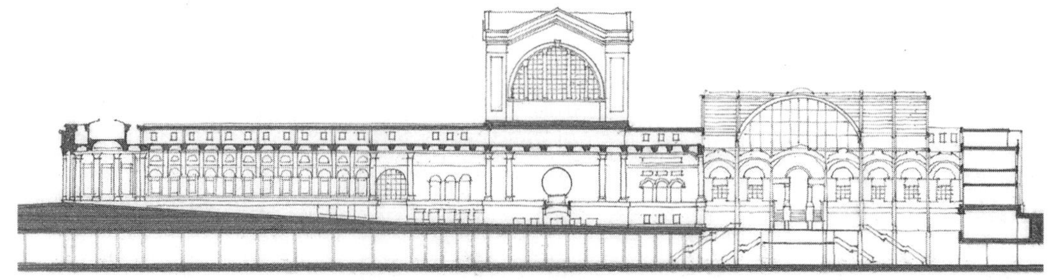

17.57 **Section through Pennsylvania Station, New York City**

**17.58 Palace of Fine Arts, World's Columbian Exposition of 1893, Chicago**

## RISE OF PROFESSIONALISM

Although the eclecticism of the late 19th-century Beaux-Arts was often perceived in the 20th century as a symptom of cultural decline, it is more instructive to associate it with the rise of the professional architect, one no longer tied to the aristocratic mandate to copy a single style. Firms were free to integrate an iron roof with a Romanesque facade if they so desired. The French played an important role in this deregulation of style. In the previous generation neoclassicism, though it can be found in many parts of the world, was either made by Europeans or brought by Europeans to places where they colonized or settled. But the late 19th-century Beaux-Arts, though still a European commodity, was imported into Argentina, Egypt, Mexico, Japan, and elsewhere, as it was associated with not only the sophisticated taste of the French but also with the principles of professionalism, nationalism, and modernization.

In England, professionalism was slower to develop than in France. The Royal Institute of British Architects (RIBA) was founded in 1834, but between 1841 and 1881, the number of architects quadrupled, and with that the professional architect came to dominate the scene, forging theories to conform to their tastes and interests. Even William Butterfield (1814–1900), though often associated with the aesthetic philosophy of Ruskin, belonged to this new generation. One sign of this was the rise in the number of architectural drawings necessary for the construction of a building. For the first church that Butterfield built, he required only nine drawings; but for the chancel of St. Mark's Dundela, completed in 1891, the contract was accompanied by about 40 drawings, including working details and fittings down to the bootscrapers. The proliferation of drawings spoke to the rising importance of the contractual relationship between architect, craftsman, and client, as well as to the increasing complexity of architectural production. By the middle of the 20th century, a building of any magnitude would require potentially 1000 drawings, accompanied by a detailed book of specifications.

In the United States, though the American Institute of Architects (AIA) had been formed in 1836, growth of the architectural profession did not really take off until after the Chicago World's Fair (World's Columbian Exposition) of 1893. The exposition buildings, designed on a monumental scale and integrated into a master plan, served to demonstrate what professional architects could accomplish. The architects of the exposition included Daniel Burnham, Richard M. Hunt, Henry van Brunt, and Charles F. McKim, all AIA leaders. The Tarsney Act passed by Congress in that year established the requirement for limited competitions for federal commissions, with institute members advising the treasury secretary, the federal official responsible for governmental building appropriations. Though the Tarsney Act was never fully implemented, the status of the professional (as opposed to an architect working as an employee of the government) was increasingly secure. By 1895, the AIA had more than 700 members. Daniel Burnham's architectural firm in the first decade of the 20th century was the world's largest and had become, as discussed by the historian Mary Woods, the model for countless later firms that utilized global business techniques. This new professional class had little patience with the mid-century battle between classical and medieval revival styles. That does not mean that Hunt, for example, who was schooled at the École des Beaux-Arts in Paris and who was an important advocate of architecture as a professional endeavor, was indifferent to style; rather, he had left the sectarian debates for a more fluid and individualist appropriation of the architectural vocabulary of the time.

17.59 Wainwright Building, St. Louis, Missouri

17.60 Monadnock Building, Chicago

17.61 Reliance Building, Chicago

**SKYSCRAPERS**

If there is one building type that represents the confluence of new materials, new strategies of construction, and new attitudes to capital and representation, it is the skyscraper. It did not appear particularly suddenly, for it took considerable time for its function, production, and even purpose to be synthesized. Questions about how to design the steel frame were the least problematic part of the building. Elevators needed to be improved and their operation guaranteed. The same was true of the plumbing, electrical, and heating systems. In other words, the key to the success of the tall building lay not in one or the other technology but in the capacity to integrate different technologies. At the 1900 Paris Exposition, the designers of the U.S. exhibition chose to promote just this, using as an example the recently erected 18-story-high Broadway Chambers Building in New York City. The exhibition presented a four-meter-high model of the building with an exterior skin in plaster that would be removed to show the underlying steel frame, complete with mechanical systems, boilers, pipes, and furnaces. It was an eye-opening object lesson of an emerging architectural ideal.

From a financial point of view the idea was relatively straightforward. An investor would arrange for the financing of the building and get the use of the prime floors, usually the lower ones, and rent out the upper stories to other businesses. That many early tall buildings were built by banks, insurance companies, or newspaper businesses is telling, since they used the building as both an investment and a home office, as well as a means of advertising. Though the technology of steel framing was well established by 1890 (many buildings of that time would look as modern as buildings of today during construction), the primary challenge for the architect was the facade. Many early designers assumed that a classical or Gothic front was still the appropriate response, but in Chicago, which in the 1890s had more tall buildings than any other city in the world, a group of designers were beginning to challenge that notion. Among the most innovative was the firm of Daniel Burnham and Company, which designed the 15-story steel-and-glass Reliance Building in 1894, with the principal design credit going to John Root and Charles B. Atwood.

Instead of a heavy cornice that was still seen in buildings like Dankmar Adler and Louis Sullivan's Wainwright Building in St. Louis, Missouri (1890), the Reliance Building is topped with a thin square lid, and the top floor, which houses machinery, converts into a type of frieze. Bay windows reach out into space, giving the building an inner dynamic, as if it had been pushed out against the stiff modularity of the columns. The insistent verticality of the Wainwright Building has been replaced by a layered look; but instead of appearing heavy, one floor almost seemed to float over the next, assisted in this not only by the delicate ornamentation of the floor spandrels but also by the fact that the building's spandrels were all lined with white terra-cotta tiles, giving it an ethereal presence.

17.62 Wrigley Building, Chicago

17.63 Monument of Lysicrates

## Wrigley Building

The Reliance Building was more the exception than the rule. A look of modernity in tall buildings was not insisted upon and, in fact, went counter to the idea that these buildings were meant to advertise wealth and culture. For that very reason, most tall buildings after the World's Columbian Exposition were clad in historical styles. A typical example is the headquarters building in New York (1912) of one of the largest and most innovative corporations in the United States, the telephone giant, AT&T. It had a Doric ground floor and Ionic upper floors, and it was designed by the Beaux-Arts-trained architect, William Welles Bosworth, who had studied at the Massachusetts Institute of Technology (MIT), an institution that was one of the first in the United States to model itself on the Beaux-Arts in Paris. Corporate representation at the turn of the century was a form of modernity in its own right. In that sense, the skyscraper was similar to the train stations of the 1860s, which competed against each other in size and lavishness.

The Woolworth Building (1911–13) in New York City, designed by Cass Gilbert in a Gothic style, was at the time of its construction the world's tallest building. It was built for Frank W. Woolworth, owner of the famous five-and-dime chain. The whole was sheathed in elaborate terra-cotta tiles with equally elaborate Gothic-inspired detailing. The interior lobby had mosaic-covered vaults. Corporations thus saw in the Beaux-Arts style the capacity to turn out designers who could work in an increasingly complex synthetic world.

17.64 Clock tower, Wrigley Building, Chicago

One of the reasons Beaux-Arts modernism survived so long in the United States was not because of the hold that the system had on academe, as is often argued, or at least that is not the only reason. Beaux-Arts modernism was the language par excellence of corporations eager to promote themselves. Historical awareness and reference to great architectural accomplishments of the past were an integral part of this ambition. That was the reason Bosworth chose to model his columns in the lobby of the AT&T building on those of the Parthenon and also why, at the top of the Wrigley Building (1920) in Chicago, which was designed for the famous producer of chewing gum, the architects placed a reconstruction of the Monument of Lysicrates in Athens (334 BCE). It was not only the monument as a token of Athenian sophistication that was at stake here but the fact that the French government in 1887 had just completed its restoration. The Clock Tower presented an image that capitalism wanted to project of itself as making history whole again and of integrating wealth with a European cultural ideology.

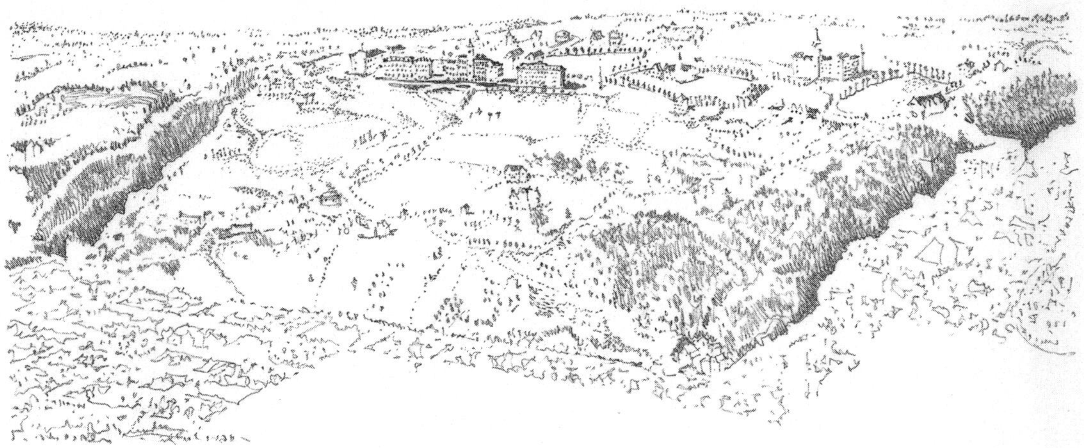

**17.65 1882 view of Ithaca, New York, showing the early campus of Cornell University**

## CAMPUSES IN THE UNITED STATES

The Land Grant Act of 1861, signed into law by President Abraham Lincoln, had a major impact on the history of U.S. education. It stipulated that each state was to have its own university paid for by the sale of government land. No such educational policy had ever been attempted before and no one could have foreseen its consequences in shaping advanced education in the United States. Despite differences from state to state, the early schools (known as land-grant schools) shared certain basic goals, including the promotion of practical education, the right of education for all social classes, and the freedom of students to choose their course of study. By the 1870s almost every state had one such university. Among the earliest were Cornell University, Ithaca, New York, and the University of California, Berkeley. By the turn of the century, dozens of private universities had also been built, and because of the rapid professionalization of the sciences in the 1880s, a new generation of technical institutions emerged. MIT, founded in 1863, was among the first, but soon there was also the Illinois Institute of Technology (1890), the Carnegie Technical Institute (1900, later Carnegie Mellon University), and the California Polytechnic State University (1901). The net result of this combination of public, private, and technical universities was a university system unique in the world.

In terms of architecture, many universities at first looked to Germany, where state-sponsored institutions had large but often rather simple buildings. Students were expected to live in apartments, with relatives, or in clubs, and for this reason, German universities were located in major cities. In the United States, toward the end of the 19th century, the social elite began to see the academic experience in much broader terms. Competition for students and professors as well as the desire to see education in more rounded terms led to the design of campuses, with sports facilities, dormitories, and a parklike atmosphere.

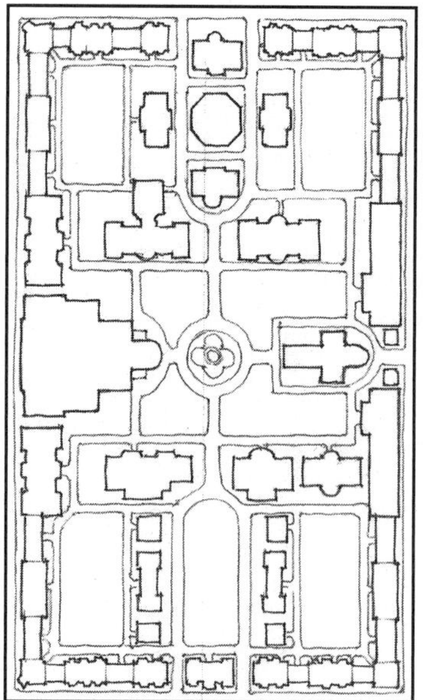

**17.66 Early plan for the University of Chicago campus**

Universities were soon being designed by the top firms in the country, and their designs are still today some of the most impressive accomplishments of that era. Designs came in three basic categories: Georgian, Gothic, and neoclassical. The Georgian style, leaning on the tradition of Harvard University, had individual buildings, usually in brick, for the various departments arranged around a quad or "green," as at Cornell University. More modern was the Gothic style that aimed for an integrated relationship between study, life, and sports. Examples can be found at Princeton University, Princeton, New Jersey, and the University of Chicago, where there was not a central "green" but a loose arrangement of buildings in the landscape. The neoclassical was also used, as at Columbia University in New York City, (the centerpiece of the urban campus, Low Memorial Library, designed by McKim, Mead, and White and built in 1903), at the University of Michigan (its central campus designed between 1904 and 1936 by Albert Khan), and at MIT (1913–16), which was designed by William Bosworth, where buildings were arranged around a central axis with a domed library, modeled on the Pantheon, at the symbolic head of the composition.

17.67 Art nouveau doorway in Paris, France

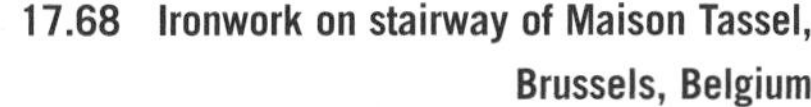

17.68 Ironwork on stairway of Maison Tassel, Brussels, Belgium

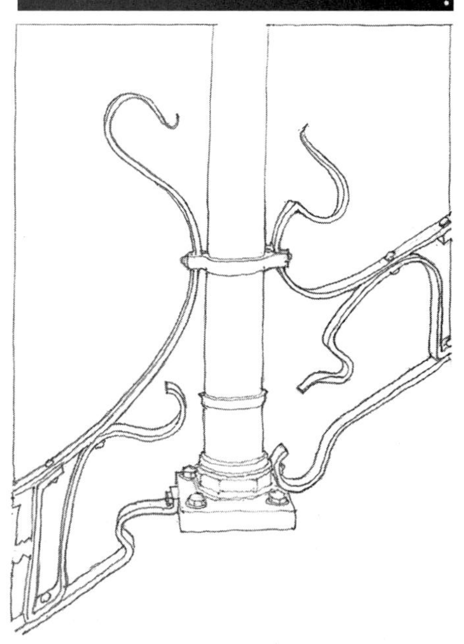

## ART NOUVEAU

By the 1890s in Europe, the supremacy of French Beaux-Arts and English Victorian styles were being challenged in places that were somewhat remote from the English and French fields of influence, namely in Spain (Antonio Gaudí), Scotland (Charles Rennie Mackintosh), Belgium (Hendrick Petrus Berlage), Austria (Otto Wagner and Joseph Hoffman), and Germany (Peter Behrens). In these places we can begin to see some of the sources of movement that later came to be known as modern architecture. One has to remember that in France state-sponsored architecture limited the experimentation that could be undertaken. In the United States, though private commissions were more important than state-sponsored ones, the Beaux-Arts system, which had spread throughout the U.S. academy by the first decade of the century, had all but stopped independent developments (with the exception of Frank Lloyd Wright). It is, therefore, no accident that it was in Belgium that a new style emerged known as art nouveau (or *Jugendstil* in Germany), which was built on a high-bourgeois aesthetic that had been developing since the mid 19th-century. It had parallels with the arts and crafts movement in England, but there were important differences.

Whereas the arts and crafts movement aimed to heal the rift between humans and product, art nouveau was more interested in issues of creativity. There were many overlaps, with not a few artists working in both camps. Art nouveau artists, however, tended to avoid the heavy, neomedieval look of the arts and crafts, preferring sinuous organic shapes and plantlike motifs. By the end of the century, art nouveau had drifted toward virtuosic displays of form, complicated intermingling of materials, and an interlacing of structure and ornament. It was unabashedly expensive.

A great number of art nouveau artists were endowed with dual talents. Antonio Gaudí was an enthusiastic Wagnerian, and Peter Behrens started out as a painter. William Blake, Dante Gabriel Rossetti, William Morris, and Aubrey Beardsley have left us poems, as great a value as their creations in the field of art. Algernon Charles Swinburne composed poems on paintings by James Whistler, which were written on gold paper and then displayed in specially designed frames. Oscar Wilde's *Salomé* became the libretto for an opera composed by Richard Strauss. Edvard Munch painted sound waves, and his paintings were once described in the leading art nouveau journal *Pan* as "emotional hallucinations of music and poetry."

Art nouveau artists were also profoundly theoretical, seeking to answer questions about the nature of aesthetic production and its direct relevance for the individual and society. Unlike previous theorists, like Gottfried Semper, John Ruskin, and Eugène Emmanuel Viollet-le-Duc, who emphasized the relationship between aesthetic and cultural production, art nouveau theorists were intensely interested in the question of artistic creation. Walter Crane, August Endell, Hector Guimard, Henry Van de Velde, and Adolf Loos all offered theoretical works aside from their artistic creations.

17.69 Armchair designed by Peter Behrens

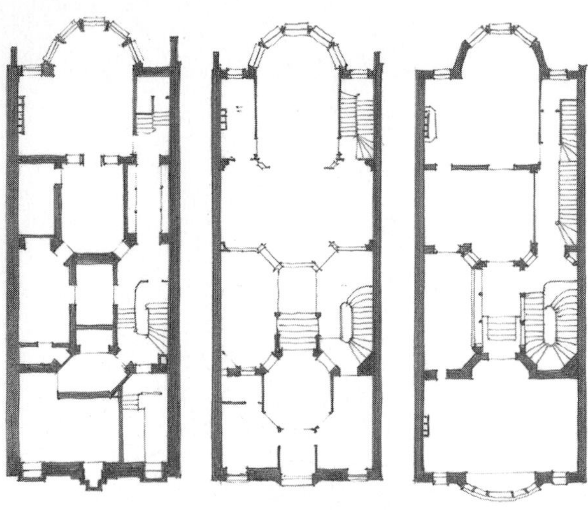

17.70 **Floor plans: Maison Tassel, Brussels**

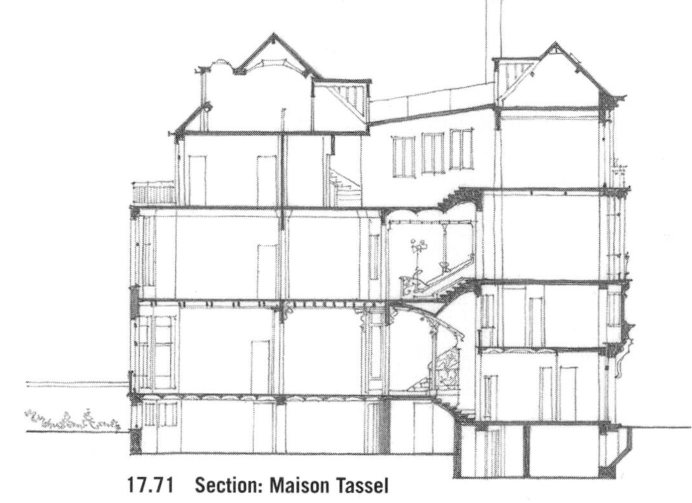

17.71 **Section: Maison Tassel**

### Maison Tassel

Though westerners had purchased Chinese and Japanese tea sets, plates, and bowls for well over a 100 years and had tried to imitate certain Chinese building types, like the garden pavilion, art nouveau saw in the East a common fascination with ornamental patterns. So inherent was the connection that S. Bing, whose shop in Paris, d'Art Nouveau, gave its name to the whole style, had begun as an importer of Japanese arts and crafts, and was himself the owner of one of the important private collections of japonaiserie. In London, the painter James Whistler is remembered as the first and most brilliant promoter of the Japanese style. He and others admired, in particular, the work of Utamaro, whose woodcuts were known for their asymmetrical distribution of masses, curving lines, and absence of compactness. Furthermore, the idea already put forward by William Morris of coordinating a painting, its frame, the artistic effect in the room, and indeed the shape and proportion of the whole room was reinforced by the perception of Japanese architecture as one of coordinated unity. For the art nouveau, archaeological correctness was not important. Japanese themes could be fused with Greek, Celtic, and later, after Knossos had been excavated in 1900, with Minoan motifs.

It could be said that though art nouveau expressed itself in the surface, it was far from superficial. In its rejection of perspective and fascination with flatness, it foreshadowed a desire to rethink the relationship between representation and abstraction. Nature was no longer a remote system of regulating realities as it was for the Enlightenment but a sensuous play of living forms. It eagerly took up biological forms. Ornamentation was no longer a sin but the medium by which one could reach behind the static world of appearances. The door handle by Victor Horta loops in and around itself, like a hardened piece of liquorice candy, one strand of which springs out into space to almost accidentally form a handle.

17.72 **Maison Tassel, Brussels**

Victor Horta (1861–1947), active in Belgium, was probably the greatest of the art nouveau architects. In Maison Tassel (1893), Horta brought out the expressive quality of iron, which he used both inside and outside of the house, in the form of weightless ribbons, spiraling and twisting into space. Since the floors were supported for the most part by iron columns, rooms could open into one another and be distributed in a novel manner. Horta rejected the standard Brussels building type, with the staircase to one side of the building. Instead, the staircase, combined with a lightwell, is placed at the center. This allowed him to vary the elevations of the floors in the front and back, with four floors in the front along the street and three in the back, with the main rooms oriented to the center. Interpenetrating space, as well as the use of mirrors to enhance the feeling of space, make the interior seem a world unto itself, a sanctuary from the outside life.

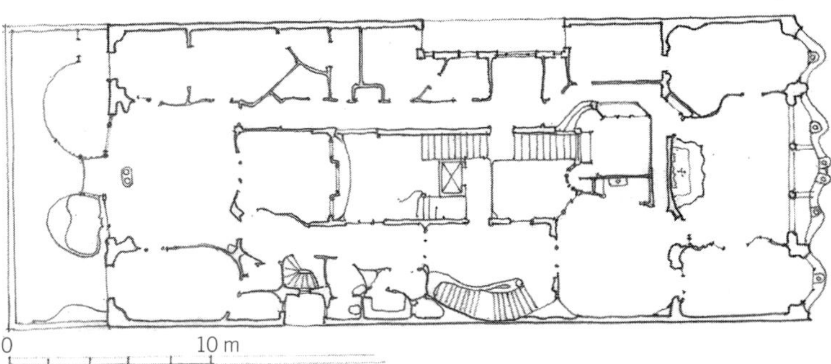


17.73 **Plan of principal apartment: Casa Batlló, Barcelona, Spain**

17.74 **Casa Batlló, Barcelona**

### Casa Batlló

Antonio Gaudí (1852–1926), despite his obvious talent, was not a particularly good student at the school of architecture at Barcelona. The academic styles and rationalization of construction did not appeal to him. He preferred the story of history and economy. After a period in which he apprenticed with various local architects he set out on his own. One of the characteristics of his work, apart from his unusual genius for space and light, was the delight he took in color. His architecture, more than any produced in the 20th century, has to be seen to be appreciated. Le Corbusier and Frank Lloyd Wright were consummate colorists, but for Wright, color was a question of patina, whereas for Le Corbusier, color was a question of spatial articulation. For Gaudí, color was thoroughly tactile in nature and could be linked, as Cèsar Martinell in his research has pointed out, to folk sensibilities, Mediterranean mosaic art, and Spain's Islamic past. Gaudí used colored stone and glass, polychrome glazes, broken tiles and plates, and exploited the shadings of stone and brick.

Gaudí was very much a perfectionist, working out every project in great detail. The facade of Palau Güell (1886–90) was completely redrawn 28 times, and some of its details changed completely. This explains why it took him four years to perfect the columns of the nave of Sagrada Familia (1882 to 1926).

Due to the richness of Gaudí's forms, it might seem that he was preeminently sculptural, but this too would be a mistake. According to him, the priorities of the architect are situation, measure, material, and only then form. Already in his first works, he was creating hyperbolic and trumpet-shaped helical forms, but always in combination with his refined sense of construction.

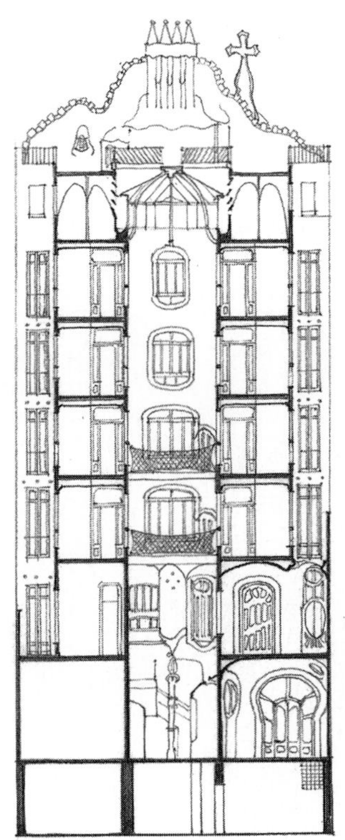

17.75 **Section: Casa Batlló, Barcelona**

Already as a young architect, he could imagine structural possibilities that seemed to defy conventional wisdom. One worker once waited hours after a particularly precarious-appearing corbel had been constructed to see if it would fall. It still stands today.

Casa Batlló (1904–6), commissioned by the manufacturer Batlló as a renovation of an existing building, became one of the most unusual modernist architectural masterpieces in Europe. Gaudí modified the inner court, introducing a staircase with a tautly undulating outline. And, on the facade, he created wavy forms surfaced with ceramics in shades of blue. The enigmatic, masklike balconies and the stained-glass windows evoke floral, animal, and geological motifs. The roof of glazed brick appears like the scales of a dragon, pierced by the tower, that has at its top a head of garlic that morphs into a three-dimensional cross, perhaps an allusion to St. George and the killing of the dragon, a story with much local resonance. At the level of the *piano nobile*, the great soft forms that seem to be made more of mud than of stone are held up by thin, bony colonnettes deformed in their middle and ornamented by vines.

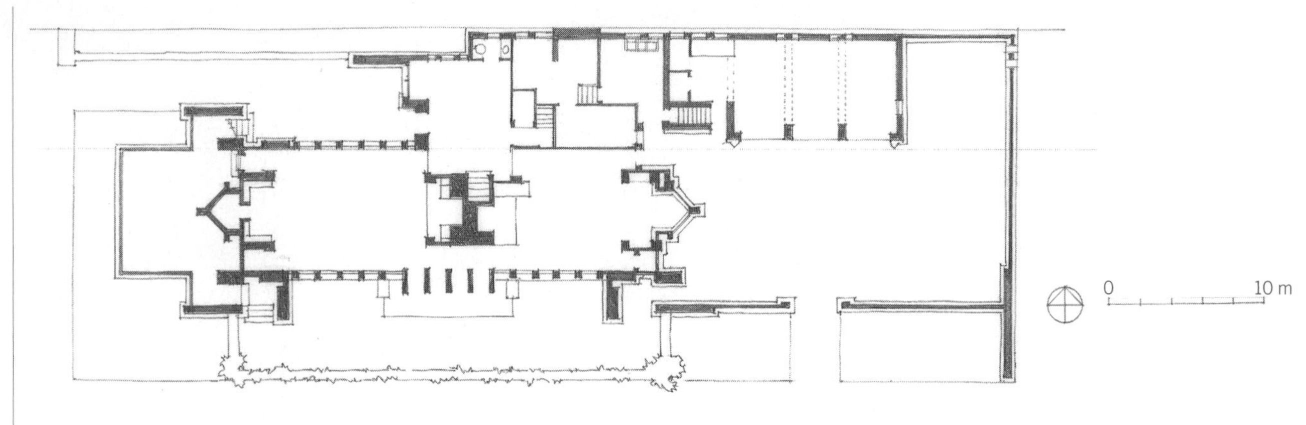


**17.76 First floor plan: Robie House, Chicago, Illinois, USA**

**Frank Lloyd Wright**

The long and complex career of Frank Lloyd Wright (1867–1959) can be divided into several phases: from the time he opened his office in 1893 to the Robie House (1908–10); the Taliesin phase (1911–14); the phase from the design of the Imperial Hotel to Falling Water (1934) and Taliesin West (1938); and from the Johnson Wax Administration Building (1936) to the Marin County Civic Center (1957) and the end of his life in 1959. His production was vast with about 400 houses and a dozen or so other major buildings.

By the time Wright designed the Robie House (Chicago, 1909), his style had become quite distinct when compared to the Victorian mansions that were very popular. Furthermore, unlike other architects who changed style slowly or at the behest of a client, the transformation Wright made was one driven by a search for abstraction. At the Robie House we still see its shingle style origins in that the service rooms are packed into a massive block against which the building rests. The hip roofs have been flattened so that they practically disappear. But the fireplace has now become the spatial and visual hub of the building, freed from encroaching walls and linked only to a staircase.

From the street, no entrance is visible. Instead the house screens itself from the street and seems almost defensive, while at the same time the design emphasizes the linearity of the street. The bands of white stone parapets form a series of plateaus, rising to meet the dark-edged roof lines, with the bands of windows shielded in the shadows. The interior of the main floor opens onto a balcony that runs along the entire southern exposure. And in good arts-and-crafts fashion, every aspect of the house was designed, from the carpets to the light fixtures.

It would be interesting to compare the Robie House with the Steiner House by Adolf Loos, for there are more similarities than meet the eye. Both give the client an interior environment that is intimate and richly detailed and that is coordinated down to the last detail. Both are also abstract and mute to the outside world. The principal difference, and one that was to remain a difference between European- and American-styled modernism, was its relationship to the garden. The American tradition, building on the shingle and bungalow style, as well as on the philosophy of Andrew Jackson Downing, was not adverse to incorporating porches and platforms into the building, all of which were relatively rare in European domestic design until after World War II.

**17.77 Robie House, Chicago**

17.78 Taliesin East, Spring Green, Wisconsin, USA

**Taliesin**

After a trip to Italy in 1909, Wright began to build at first a retreat and then a home in Spring Green, in southern Wisconsin, that came to be called Taliesin (1911–14). The name refers to the *Book of Taliesin*, a collection of poems and prophecies attributed to a 6th-century Welsh court poet. The building marked a significant departure from Wright's earlier homes, which were constrained by their suburban lots and tended to be designed to move from formal to informal spaces. Taliesin, on the top of a broad hill and with ample space to expand, was designed without this polarity. It was a highly personal expression, but it was also infused with what Wright thought was a uniquely American sensibility to the landscape. It was not "on" the hill, he claimed, but "of" the hill, for it was not easy "to tell where pavement and walls left off and ground began," surrounded as it was by low walled-garden courts, reached by stone steps.

The house reflects Wright's experiences in Italy where he saw for the first time the great garden villas of the Renaissance and in the baroque style. It was, therefore, not just a house but a country estate, house, farm, studio, workshop, and family seat, all in one.

The house was low and horizontal, with ungabled hip roofs placed in rhythmic response to the surrounding hills. The walls were of roughly dressed stone laid in textured horizontal courses, as if partially natural and partially manufactured. The house allowed the occupants a sense of being embedded in the surrounding landscape, given the slope of the land. It was, Wright explained, a "natural house," by which he meant not that it was like a cave or log cabin but that it was "native in spirit" to the place.

Taliesin's plan organization can be described as a geometric ordering of the landscape, with each part joined to the next in a meandering pattern of solids and voids that winds its way down the hill. The principal living block is a rectangle that has been eaten into by voids or expanded outward by terraces and rooflines. Subtle shifts of alignments create a dynamic within the house that is enhanced by placing the access points to the rooms at the corners.

Later, in the 1930s, Wright built another home and office for himself in the Arizona desert called Taliesin West.

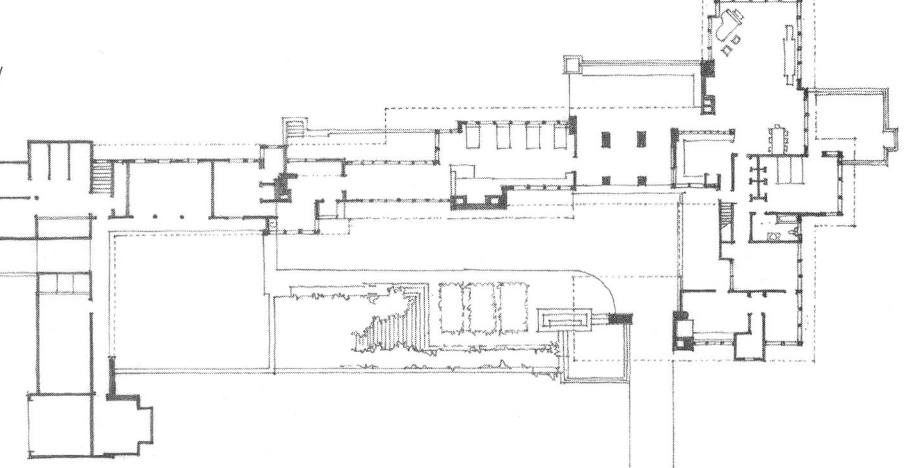


17.79 Plan of Taliesin East

17.80 Lucknow University Library, India

**Walter Burley Griffin**

Newly united in 1901, Australians, under the prime ministership of Edmund Barton, were looking for a national expression. Some attempts at transforming an arts and crafts and art nouveau–derived interpretation of Australian flora and a Richardsonian-derived idea of civic buildings (such as Edward Raht's Equitable Life Assurance Society Building in Sydney, 1895) were finally rescinded in favor of a more progressive modernism, as can be seen in the design of Canberra, Australia's new national capital. The winning entry of the 1912 competition was by a young, little-known architect from Chicago, Walter Burley Griffin. Strongly influenced by Frank Lloyd Wright's houses and Daniel Burnham's master plans, Griffin called himself a landscape architect to emphasize what he claimed was the organic derivation of his design. His proposal also drew on the city beautiful movement, however, in that it featured a picturesque ordering of the landscape with intersecting axial geometries. He proposed to use the irregular basin of the site to create a series of interconnected water tanks and a lake, showcasing the main government center and capital. The rest of the city was spread out axially, with star-shaped intersections forming the highly visible civic centers and nodes of residential suburbs.

While Canberra did not develop until after World War II, Griffin created a successful practice in Australia designing several houses and institutional buildings. His architecture was derived entirely from Wrightian sources, most particularly the latter's California houses. Griffin's 1926 Creswick Residence in Castlecrag and the ten-story office building in Melbourne, the Keith Arcade (1927), were akin to Wright's attempts at generating a distinctly Australian language based, however, more on local fauna than historical precedent.

In 1935, Griffin took the opportunity to design a library in India and left Australia. His last set of buildings, therefore, were in Lucknow, India; he unexpectedly died there in 1937. As in Australia, Griffin tried to invent a new architectural vocabulary for modern Indian architecture. He was not trying to copy Wright so much as to translate Wright into a new national style and an alternative to both the Beaux-Arts and European modernism.

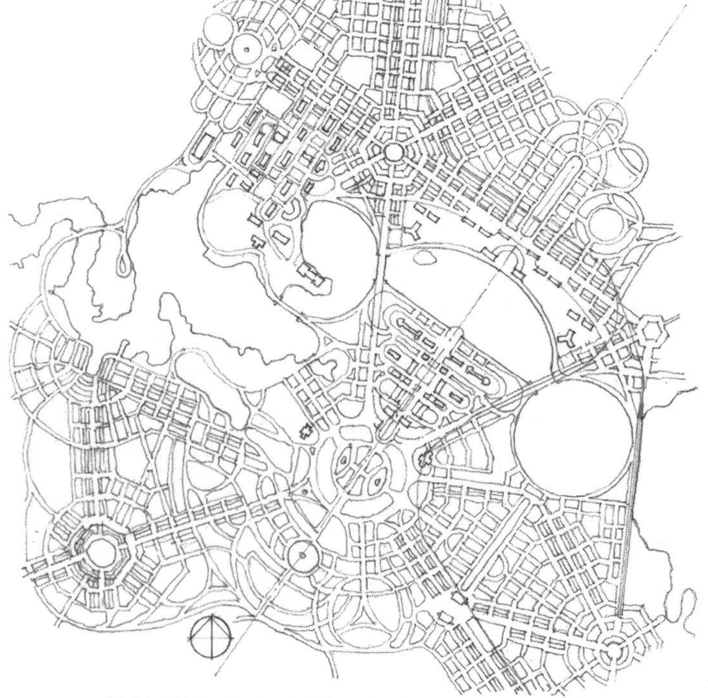

17.81 Walter Burley Griffin's plan for Canberra, Australia

**17.82 Municipal Theater, Rio de Janeiro, Brazil**

## INTERNATIONAL BEAUX-ARTS

A factor determining international trade was the U.S. economic depression of 1893, which affected the economy worldwide. With a pronounced but momentary drop in the purchase power of U.S. goods, American entrepreneurs went abroad in search of markets. The expansion of the U.S. global political reach as a result of the annexation of Hawaii in 1898 and the military victories in the Philippines and Cuba over the Spanish, helped U.S. firms for the first time focus on international possibilities. Throughout the 19th century, England and then increasingly Germany had, for example, been the world's leading exporters of iron and steel. But by World War I, it was the United States, and it was not just building materials that were exported but entire building systems and the engineers to go with them. American-engineered tall buildings, complete with Beaux-Arts cladding, went up from Buenos Aires to Shanghai. U.S.-designed bridges were soon appearing in New Zealand, Taiwan, Manchuria, Japan, Mexico, and South America, and by 1910, skyscraper components, produced in the United States and shipped abroad, were being used from east Asia to South Africa and Central America. Milken Brothers, a leading U.S. steel firm, established branch offices in London, Mexico, Havana, Cape Town, and Sydney, building office buildings, mills, and factories out of steel framing.

With the global economy centered on England and the United States, former peripheral countries underwent an economic upturn of their own as materials and products could now be advantageously exported. This modernization at the global periphery, of course, went hand in hand with the increasing disempowerment of the underclasses. In South America, the new upper class may have had factories built with U.S. steel, but on matters of culture, they more often than not bought into the latest in French fashion and urban design as visible substantiation of their policies. One of the consequences was that Beaux-Arts eclecticism, with its associations with the professional class, developed into an international movement. There were few major metropolises of the world at that time that were not touched by this phenomenon.

The combined global realities just discussed left their most dramatic imprint in Argentina and Brazil, with most of its exports of beef, wool, and wheat supported by heavy investment from England. Rio de Janeiro, during its Republican phase from the 1880s to 1910s, was significantly rebuilt under its mayor, Pereira Passos, who came to be regarded as the "Haussmann of the Tropics," with architects like Ricardo Severo (1869–1940), who was greatly influenced by Beaux-Arts academicism. The Municipal Theater (1905) by the Brazilian architect Oliveira Passos was designed to be reminiscent of the Paris Opera. One should add that the building of these structures coincided with the development of pubic hygiene and the introduction of electrical and gas services. As in Egypt, where still today debate rages as to the Egyptianness of the neo-Mamluk style, in Rio de Janeiro, a camp developed in 1910 that argued that the true national style of Brazil was the early 19th-centuy Portuguese colonial architecture. The argument was that they were built by local craftsmen, whereas the late-19th-century buildings belonged to a more alienated age. Today some ascribe the current urban difficulties to the aggressive modernization of the city under Passos. Others praise him for his foresight.

17.83 Hong Kong and Shanghai Banking Corporation Building

17.84 Kyoto National Museum, Japan

**Kyoto National Museum**

The first Asian country to modernize was Japan, but this happened only after 1854 when an American naval mission led by Commodore Matthew Perry, taking a page from the English, forced Japan to open its ports to American trade, a move that hastened the demise of the last shogunate dynasty (Tokugawa, 1603–1867). The subsequent Meiji Restoration (1868) was a period of aggressive Westernization, with the goal of transforming Japan into a modern industrial and military power. Delegations from Japan were sent to European world exhibitions to learn the latest technological developments. The Japanese also studied the Egyptian modernization program under Isma'il Pasha. In 1895 Japan invaded China and Taiwan, then parts of Russia, and it annexed Korea in 1910. The 1897 Kyoto National Museum, built in a French baroque style, was meant to cement the image of Japan on the world stage. With such a rapid introduction of Western styles, even though it was made as a way to compete with the West, came a backlash from traditionalists. Nationalists denounced Western customs and by World War II had forced the government to return to a more traditional modality, at least in outer appearance, for underneath the call for "tradition" was a policy that continued the modernization of Japan's military machine.

**Myongdong Cathedral**

Beaux-Arts eclecticism came to Korea largely through the opening of Korean ports in 1876, leading to the building of Myongdong Cathedral (1898) in the Gothic style and the Toksugung Palace (1909) in the Renaissance style. The 1910 Japanese annexation of Korea changed little as the Japanese continued to import western styles into Korea as a symbol of their own colonial power. The Bank of Korea Headquarters (1912) was built in a Renaissance style and the Seoul Anglican Church (1916) in the Romanesque. Formal education in Western architectural concepts and engineering was first introduced to Korea in 1916.

17.85 Myongdong Cathedral, Seoul, Korea

**Hong Kong and Shanghai Banking Corporation Building**

Shanghai came into existence some time in the late Song Dynasty as a small town of merchants and fishermen, but with the Treaty of Nanjing in 1842 following China's defeat in the Opium War 1841 by the British forces in Canton, its future was radically changed. The Chinese were forced to open their ports—along with other cities —to British, French, American, and other foreign occupants who brought with each of the city's expansions new buildings, roads, and management practices. By the 1920s, Shanghai was called the "Paris of the East." The earliest buildings erected by westerners in Shanghai were a hybrid of western and Chinese motifs, of which the Francisco Xavier Church in Dongjiadu (1853) is one of the few remaining examples. Others, like the Hong Kong and Shanghai Banking Corporation Building (1923), with its broad colonnaded neo-Grecian front, were more properly western. Built for the second largest banking house in the world in 1925, the building represents the apex of Shanghai's commercial prosperity. When it was built it was reported that it was the "most beautiful building from the Suez Canal to the Bering Sea." Divided vertically into three portions in classical proportions of 2:3:1, the base of the first story centers on three arches that carry above it three stories of six colonnades topped by the pediment story.

17.86 Union Buildings in Pretoria, South Africa

### COLONIAL AFRICA

In 1807 the African slave trade was made illegal by the English; it became illegal in the United States in 1808 and in Holland in 1814. Though this did not mean the immediate cessation of slave trade, it was the beginning of the end. By the end of the late 19th century, Europeans began to redefine their purpose in Africa, which was to transform its population into industrious peasants, working on cash-crop plantations, such as had been done in India and South America. Nonetheless only a small portion of the continent was under European control. This changed dramatically by the end of the 19th century, but not necessarily because of financial or commercial reasons. Driving the change was the introduction of Belgium and Germany into African colonial politics. There was little to gain per se; these colonial incursions were driven by the exigencies of political leverage in a global chess game—the English against the French, the French against the English, the Portuguese against the French and the English, and so forth. It was the cruel afterglow of colonial power.

In this way, Africa was rapidly partitioned, often in the name of the "sacred trust of civilization." Christianization, at first pursued rather haphazardly, became an increasingly important part of the European language of civilization. This was particularly the case for the areas held by the British, which witnessed the development of religious and education systems. The colonial rulers did not hesitate to use missionaries, both Catholic and Protestant, to pursue their ends. But apart from churches, roads, mines, railroads, and houses for colonial masters, the Europeans did little to improve the lot of the Africans.

The discovery of gold in South Africa in 1876, at a time when gold prices had risen, was a boon for that country's white Dutch population. But it also attracted the British, eager to control the world gold market.
In a bitter conflict, the Second Boer War (1899–1902), the British took possession of South Africa. Herbert Baker (1862–1946) came to design numerous buildings there, including cathedrals, churches, schools, universities, and the Union Buildings in Pretoria. The structure, planned as the government center of the nation, was meant as a place of reconciliation with Boers after the terrors and disasters of the war. It has a half-round shaped middle that housed the main aspects of the program, like committee chambers, with two identical blocks on the sides, representing the Boer and the English part of the population. The Africans are not represented, but it has now become the residence of the president. Later Baker was to take lessons learned in South Africa to New Delhi to partner with Sir Edwin Lutyens in the design of British-ruled India's new capital.

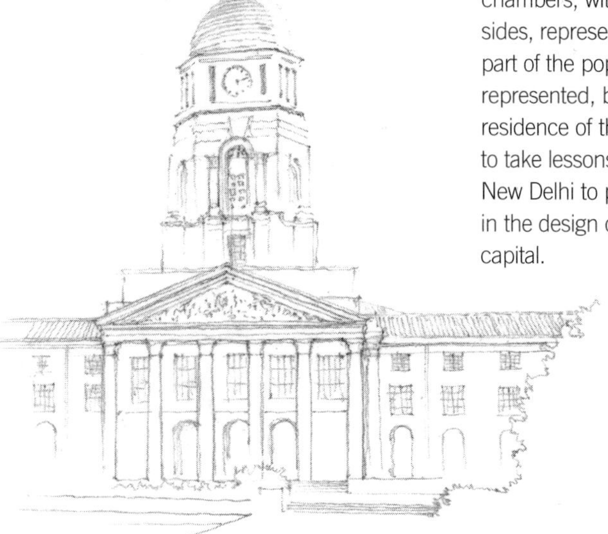

17.87 City Hall, Praetoria

17.88 AEG Pavilion, German Shipbuilding Exhibition of 1908, Berlin, Germany

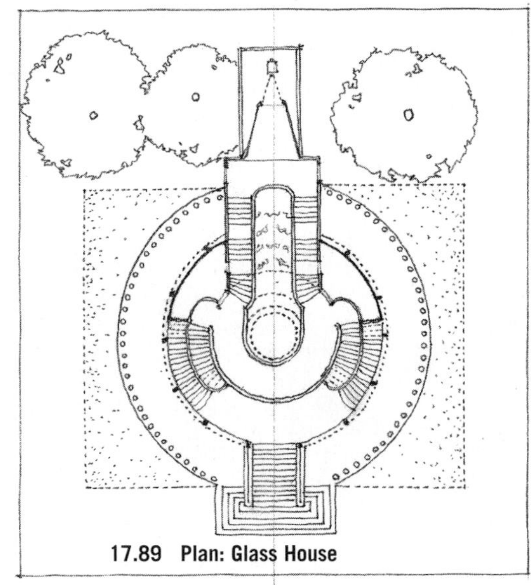

17.89 Plan: Glass House

**DEUTSCHE WERKBUND**

The transformation of Germany from an agricultural society into an industrial one and from a country with limited national and military goals to a world power on par with England occurred at an astonishing pace. Between 1894 and 1904 the value of Germany's foreign trade doubled, and by 1913 Germany overtook Great Britain in percentage of world production, and all of this without a colonial empire. Large companies like Friedrich Krupp Werke (munitions, cannons, steel, and ships), the Allgemeine Elektricitäts-Gesellschaft (AEG, maker of turbines, electric railroads, and equipment for the new German navy), and Siemens-Schukert Werke (railroad and electrical equipment) were supported by the government through lucrative military contracts and protected from international competition by tariffs. Beginning in the mid-1890s and continuing up to the outbreak of World War I, urban officials, functioning under the tight control of the imperial government and learning, belatedly, the lessons of England and France, organized special exhibitions to promote and glorify German production.

Though the architecture and architectural quality of these exhibitions varied, they were, for those who noticed, a bold showcase for innovation. German architects were not hampered by the Beaux-Arts system, which was never implemented in Germany. At the 1905 Nordwestdeutsche Kunst-Austellung in Oldenburg, one would have seen Peter Behrens' highly abstracted and formal exhibition layout with square structures, their surfaces incised with simple geometrical forms; an octagonal, domed garden pavilion; and an exhibition hall, rigorously symmetrical with a central cubical space attached at the corners to four smaller skylight boxes. At the German Shipbuilding Exhibition of 1908, Behrens built an octagonal, baptistery-like structure for the AEG. The high altar was actually a ship's deck on which stood a great searchlight, the most advanced of its kind in the world and the pride and joy of the German navy. At the 1910 exhibition of concrete manufacturers, visitors would have seen Behrens's all-concrete pavilion for Zementwahrenfabrikanten Deutschlands.

At the 1914 Werkbund Exhibition in Cologne, visitors would have seen a dramatic Glass House by Bruno Taut. It consisted of two spaces: a type of crypt below, set within a cylindrical concrete plinth, and a domed space above. The crypt contained a pool at its center with water cascading down small terraces decorated with pale yellow glass. Access to the dome above was by means of curving stairs at the top of the plinth, on which rested a 14-sided structure of concrete beams. On top of that structure, Taut set the prismatic dome with a double skin of glass, consisting of an outer protective layer of reflective glass and an inner layer of colored glass, as if in a three-dimensional explosion of light, color, and geometry. Apart from the structure, surfaces were all made of glass in keeping with its purpose, an advertising pavilion for the glass industry. Walls were made of shiny glass tiles, transparent glass bricks, and translucent colored glass. Even the steps were made of glass.

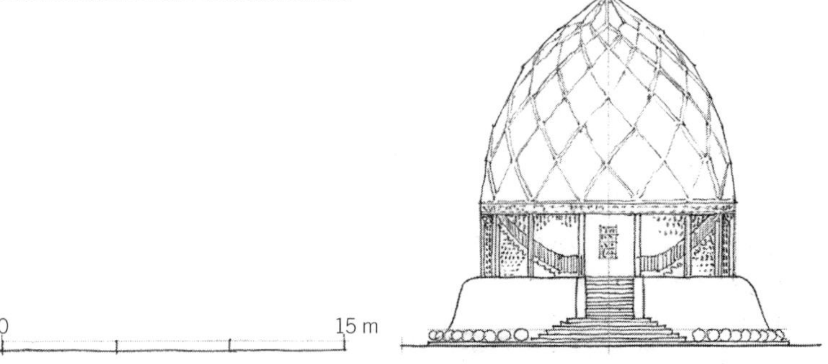


17.90 Elevation: Glass House, Werkbund Exhibtion, Cologne, Germany

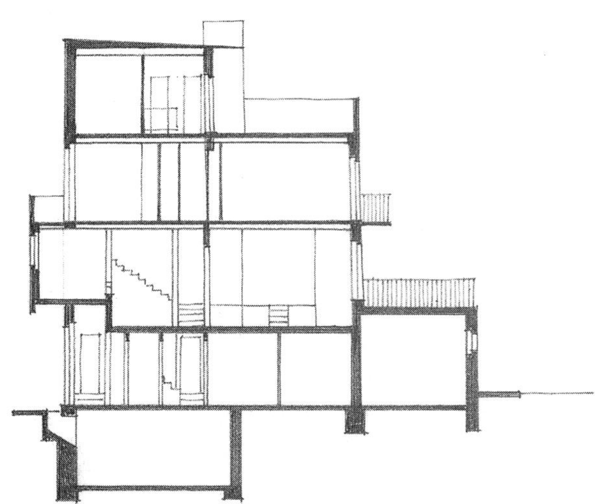

17.91 Section: Moller House, Vienna, Austria

17.92 Looshaus on Michaelerplatz, Vienna, Austria

## Adolf Loos

Adolf Loos (1870–1933) was born in Moravia and studied architecture at the Dresden Polytechnic, after which he spent three years in the United States. Eventually he settled in Vienna in 1896 and worked for a local firm before branching out on his own. He soon began writing essays on a variety of subjects having to do with Viennese art and society. Most were critical of art nouveau, which at that time was triumphant in the great cities of Europe, Vienna included. In 1908 Loos wrote a now-famous article entitled "Architecture and Ornament" in which, relying on Jean-Jacques Rousseau's critique of civilization, he railed against the use of ornament by advanced European cultures. For Loos, ornament was appropriate in tribal societies where it played an important part in social interaction; but for advanced civilization ornament was no longer a necessary form of communication. Loos was not opposed, however, to using the color and texture of natural materials for their ornamental quality. His opinions put a damper on his career, but nonetheless, he did secure a number of jobs leading up to the design for a commercial building in Vienna, now called the Looshaus (1909–10).

By the time Loos designed the Steiner House (1910), even the residual classical motifs of his earlier work were gone to leave a pure white exterior. The building, in retrospect, seems to anticipate the modernist aesthetic that would become the norm in the 1930s onward, but from Loos's perspective the stark exterior was meant to contrast with the interior. "On the outside, the building must remain dumb and reveal all its richness only on the inside," Loos wrote in 1914. The Moller House (1927–8) is paradigmatic of Loos's approach. Its facade is simple and rather forbidding, with the entrance, balcony, and windows bound together into a tight compositional unit. Despite the external symmetry, the interior is labyrinthine. The living and family rooms on the second floor are separated by steps and framed openings to create a range of areas, some more private in feel than others. The interiors of the principal rooms are richly outfitted with wood veneers. Though Loos is seen as the harbinger of the modern movement, his work maintained strong allegiance to the arts and crafts ideal of interiority and intimacy.

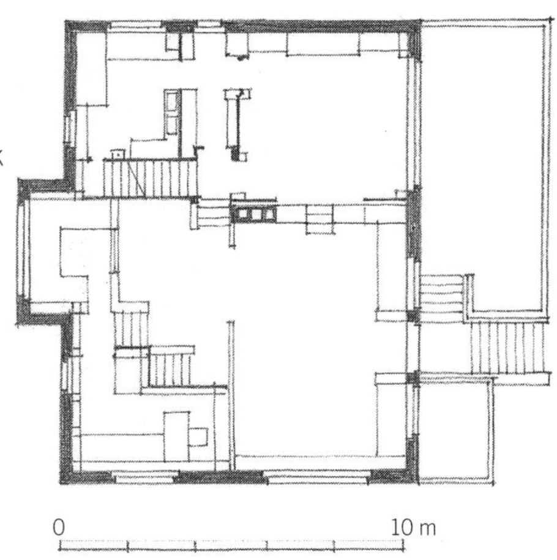


17.93 Plan: Moller House

17.94 Dodge Brothers Motor Car Company plant, Hamtramck, Michigan, USA

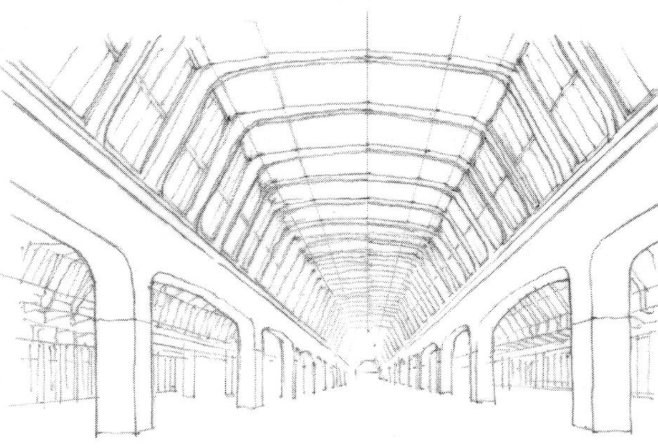

17.95 Ford Engineering Lab, Dearborn, Michigan, USA

**CONCRETE**

Portland cement was named after the tiny island of Portland in Dorset, England, where a desirable limestone used in its manufacture was found. But, by 1900, U.S. manufacturers were outproducing the English as well as perfecting new ways to integrate it with steel. By the end of the second decade of the 20th century, the demand for cement was staggering, as manufacturers competed with each other for stronger materials. Among the earliest modern experiments with concrete were those spearheaded by the engineer François Coignet, who, during the reign of Napoleon III, was placed in charge of important civil engineering projects during the rebuilding of Paris. Coignet built a church, Le Vésinet Parish Church (1864), entirely of concrete with an iron vault. Though the concrete was not structural in that it did not support the roof, he proved that concrete could be poured into complex forms and, in this case, to mimic at a distance a medieval building. Initially, concrete was thought to be advantageous over other materials, since it was thought to not require skilled labor, and thus not a few early concrete buildings are in the English colonies, such as the Secretariat and Army Headquarters in India at Simla (1886). To build with a single material with a single technique required less specification writing, costing, and site supervision.

What eventually spurred the development of concrete was not the question of cost (for it turned out to be more expensive than one thought) but the fact that it was resistant to fire. Since a steel frame could easily buckle when heated, it had to be protected by brick, tile, or cement. Concrete, by way of contrast, was inherently fireproof. And when one takes into consideration the speed of construction, economy, ease of maintenance, and seismic stability, it is clear that a concrete frame would have some clear advantages over steel. The secret of concrete construction was that it did not need large heavy beams, as it held inside it a weaving of steel bars. The problem of how to attach the bars to each other was solved in 1884 by Ernest Leslie Ransome, superintendent of the Pacific Stone Company of San Francisco, who patented a special machine that could twist iron bars into the necessary three-dimensional steel armatures that are embedded in the concrete. The Kahn System of reinforced concrete developed by Albert Kahn had, by 1907, already been used in 1500 U.S. buildings and 90 in England and in dozens around the globe. But it was the Panama Canal (1904–14), built by U.S. engineers, that was the preeminent showcase of concrete, unifying prefabrication skills, railroad engineering, contracting ingenuity and streamlined production processes, at a scale never seen before.

At the Larkin Building (Buffalo, New York, 1911), built by the firm of Lockwood, Greene and Company, we see the full articulation of the modern column-and-slab paradigm. The Larkin Company was a large mail-order facility and needed a building for packing, handling, and shipping. The ten-story building, about 200 meters long, had two railroad tracks running inside the building along its entire length at the ground floor, allowing four trains of freight cars to load and unload at once; loading docks along the facade allowed immediate access to carts and newly developed gasoline powered trucks.

Albert Kahn developed these ideas for new large-scale manufacturing enterprises, such as the Packard Motors Company manufacturing plant in Detroit, Michigan, the Dodge Brothers Motor Car Company plant in Hamtramck, Michigan, and the Pierce Arrow plant in Buffalo, New York. He went on to build more than one thousand buildings for Ford Motor Company and hundreds for General Motors. In 1923, he built a 15-story building in Detroit for Ford Motor Company, which was at the time the largest manufacturing corporation in the world.

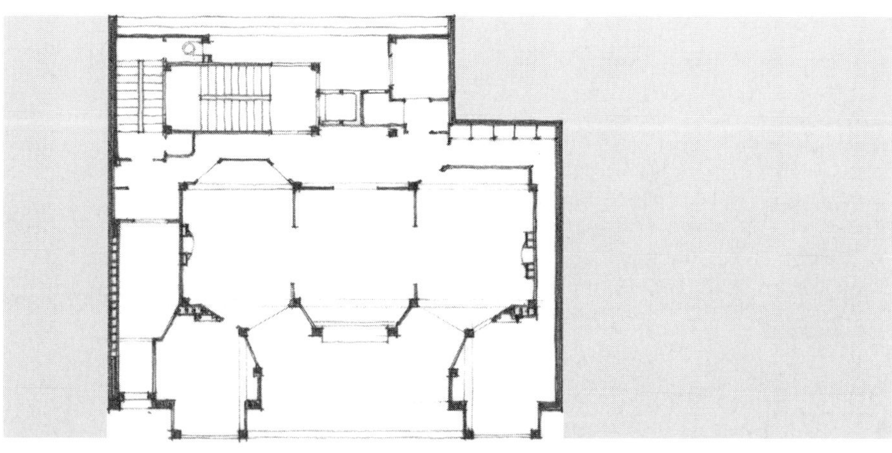

**17.96 Plan: 25b, rue Franklin, Paris, France**

**17.97 25b, rue Franklin, Paris**

In Spain, the young Antonio Gaudí was also experimenting with concrete, producing forms that today still are staggeringly fresh, as in the strange vase- and bottle-shaped skylights of the Casa Mila (1905–10) in Barcelona. But the architect who most wanted to integrate the use of concrete into the world view of the architect was Auguste Perret (1874–1954). Though by no means seeking as expressionistic a form as Gaudí, he argued that the visual properties of concrete's load-bearing capacity were just as important as its structural properties. Working in the spirit of Eugène Emmanuel Viollet-le-Duc, Perret aimed to integrate architecture and civil engineering in ways that others, like Max Berg and Gaudí, were not. Perret was thus the most "theoretical" of architects working in concrete. His 25b, rue Franklin, in Paris (1902–4), a speculative apartment building in a fashionable quarter of the city, aimed to prove that concrete could be adapted to domestic architecture in an age when most thought it suitable only for factories and warehouses.

Due to concerns about the weather-worthiness of concrete, the concrete was not visible on the outside. Smooth, colored bricks covered the concrete elements, while tiles depicting chestnut leaves were applied to the thin brick walls that filled the spaces between the columns. Each floor consisted of a six-room apartment with a bathroom, staircase, and lift at the rear. The five principal rooms were arranged symmetrically around the central salon. Despite the conventionality of the plan, the novelty of the design consisted in the allocation of all internal load bearing to slender columns.

Despite the brilliant fusion of architecture and engineering, Perret, a civil engineer and not an architect, had a deep distrust of architectural freedoms. When asked to engineer a building designed by Henry van der Velde, a theater in Paris, he complained that the building was structurally inconsistent and forced van de Velde to resign. Van de Velde had originally been a painter, and, in the course of learning to design buildings in a self-taught manner, he had come to see architecture in the terms of its creative autonomy over engineering. It was Le Corbusier, who more than anyone, understood and theorized the need to integrate the innovations of structure with those of living. The tension, however, between the requirements of engineering and those of design, which was here opened up, remains a point of theoretical contention to this day.

**17.98 Le Vésinet Parish Church, France**

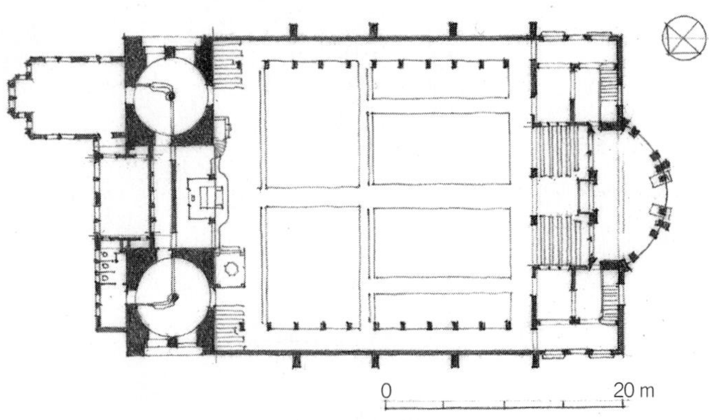


17.99 **Plan: Garnisonskirche, Ulm, Germany**

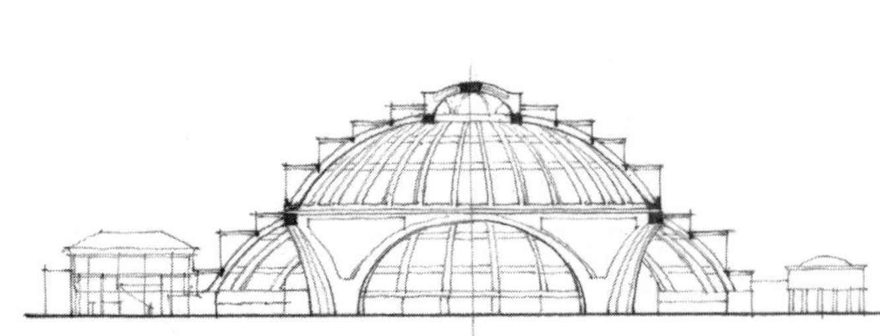

17.100 **Section: Breslau Jahrhunderthalle**

### Garnisonskirche

Even though Ransome's factories brought to fore the radical modernity of reinforced concrete from the point of view of civil engineering, the architectural question still remained an open one. The potential for concrete to take any form was already noted in the mid-19th century and was in fact one of the reasons that many designers, especially those working in accordance with the theories of John Ruskin, saw it as debasing architecture. For this reason, as well as the difficulty of working against the grain of antiquated building codes, advancement in reinforced concrete, architecturally speaking, was thwarted in England. It was France and Germany that took the leadership.

If the French contribution was in attempting to integrate concrete into the conventions of architectural practices, the Germans contributed toward its engineering. One of the earliest uses of concrete in a major public building in Germany was the Garnisonskirche in Ulm (1906–8), a Protestant church that, as its name implies, was made for a military base. It was designed by Theodor Fischer (1862–1938), a prolific architect and noted educator and one of the founders of the Werkbund. He argued for a contextual modernity and thus seems today more neomedieval than modern. The building is certainly a landmark in the history of modern architecture. The body of the church consisted of a reinforced-concrete skeleton with brick infill. The towers were huge empty silos 55 meters high, with a bell chamber suspended between them.

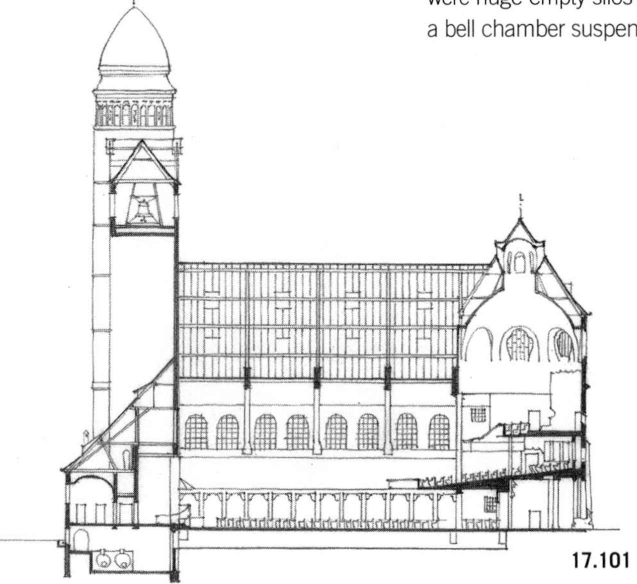

17.101 **Section: Garnisonskirche**

A second important building was the Breslau Jahrhunderthalle (1913), which showed off the virtuosity and elegance of concrete. Built to commemorate the centennial anniversary of the defeat of Napoleon's army in 1813 by the Prussian army near Breslau, Germany, the building was part of a campaign by the city to define itself as the Metropole des Ostens. It was designed by Max Berg, Frankfurt am Main's building department director, to serve as both an exhibition hall and assembly hall.

The Jahrhunderthalle was an enormous building, with an enclosed floor space of over 5600 square meters, which could hold 10,000 people. Due to the fires that had occurred at the World Exhibition in Brussels (1910), the builders decided to use concrete, even though no building on that scale had ever been erected in concrete. The structure consisted of four large curved arches that formed a continuous ring on which rested the dome. To provide a more secure environment against weather, the glazing was not laid in the interstices of the ribs. Instead, Berg designed a system of stepped glazing applied to the outside of the dome in the form of vertical windows and horizontal roofs. From the inside, the small horizontal roof planes disappear in the light that streams through the vertical apertures of glass.

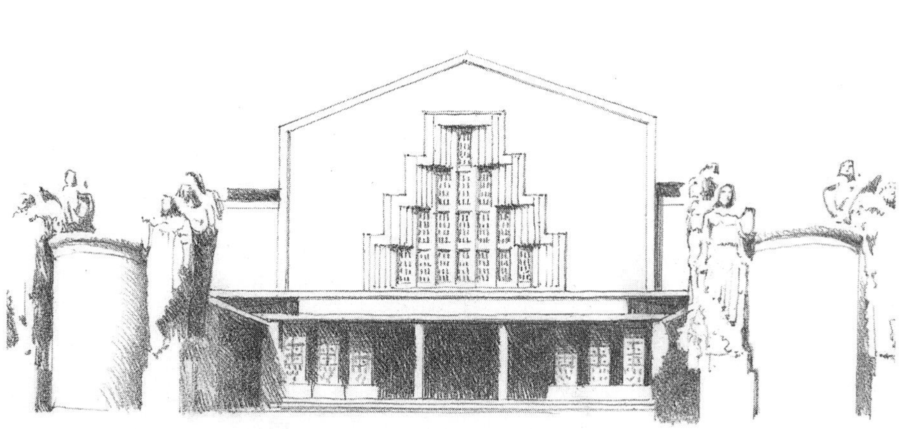

17.102 Pavilion of Commerce, 1908 Jubilee Exhibition, Prague

17.103 Pavel Janák's study for a facade

### Czech Cubists

Architecture before and after World War I was surprisingly imaginative and experimental. Expressionism, as it soon came to be known, had begun to develop before World War I in the work of Bruno Taut and a few others. Particularly influential were the writings of Paul Scheerbart, who in 1914 published a book entitled *Glass Architecture*, describing a utopian architecture of colored glass in combination with sparkling jewels and enamel. The expressionists, despite their differences, all envisioned an architecture about as far removed from classicism as could be imagined at that time. The old notion that architecture reembodied the power of the past gave way to a desire to create an architecture that spoke to the immediacy of perception and the psychology of the beholder. As one commentator, Heinrich de Fries, explained, "Buildings are in the highest degree alive ... We can only guess at the extent to which the art of spatial articulation will one day transcend the art of pictorial creation." Expressionism rejected the duality of interior and exterior, and of building and landscape. It also opened architecture to influences from the other arts, in opposition to the arts and crafts movement, which had hoped to integrate the artistic conception within the framework of craftmaking.

The movement was particularly strong in Prague between 1910 and 1914, where in the 1880s, artists, dissatisfied with the poor standards of the Prague Academy of Painting, departed en masse for Munich, a leading center for the German arts-and-crafts movement. Many went to Paris where they encountered the work of Auguste Rodin, whom many Czechs admired because of the spontaneity and expressiveness of his work. Other sources of inspiration were to be found in French cubism, which began to be exhibited beginning in 1908. But despite the pictorial innovations of Pablo Picasso and George Braque, the possibility of a "cubist" architecture was not pursued in France and certainly not in Germany where French developments were generally viewed with suspicion. The introduction of cubism into architecture in Prague was thus new ground. And to this, one has to add sources, for example, the art movement *Der Sturm*, known for vibrant colors and fractured geometries. Czech cubism was thus a synthesis of various European influences, including its own regional baroque. The result was a distinct style emerging already by 1905.

One of the leading architects among the Czech cubists was Jan Kotera (1871–1923), a professor at the Prague School of Decorative Arts since 1898 and the chair of the department of architecture at the Prague Academy of Fine Arts from 1910. He saw prismatic shapes as appropriate to the intellectual vitality of the modern age. Structure had to give way to the logic of visual dynamics. This was also true for Pavel Janák (1882–1956), whose idiosyncratic interpretation of cubism led him to shift toward tapered, slanted, and triangular forms. He argued that the orthogonal architecture reflected its dependency on matter and weight, whereas the new cubist style, with its angles, expressed the active nature of the human spirit and its ability to prevail over matter.

**17.104 Interior, Grosse Schauspielhaus, Berlin, Germany**

## EXPRESSIONISM

After World War I, with the downfall in Germany of the aristocratic regime, expressionist architecture found one of its more realistic voices in Hans Poelzig (1869–1936), whose first major commission, the Grosse Schauspielhaus (1918–9) in Berlin, had a plaster ceiling, hung from the rafters, that looked like cave stalactites. Thousands of light bulbs, variously colored in shades of yellow, green, and red, were embedded in the vault so that the whole thing resembled both a cave and, when the lights were dimmed, a starry night sky. The foyer was supported by a single column that, like a fusion between a fountain and a plant, spread successive rings of colored petals —also illuminated by recessed colored light bulbs—until it reached the vault above.

Another important figure in the expressionist camp was Hans Bernhard Scharoun (1893–1972), who rejected the crystalline shapes of some of the other expressionists in favor of soft, rubbery forms. In his design for a stock exchange building (1922), he warped and bent space around the central lobby, giving the appearance of a building that had ingested the various aspects of the program.

In Italy, expressionism took an even stronger form under the name of futurists, initially a literary movement created by Filippo Tommaso Marinetti in 1909. It was his manifesto, *Le Futurisme*, published in Paris, that coined the name of the movement. Marinetti was a keen follower of the cubist movement and even took a group of Italian painters to Paris to show them the recent work. Soon, however, the Italians developed their own distinctive style, significantly more aggressive in tone in comparison both to the French and to the quiet utopianism of Scheerbart. The futurists were enamored in particular of technology, speed, and machinery and expressed this in their painting and poetry. They saw the outbreak of World War I as positive for the Italians in that it would propel the young country, so they hoped, into the modern age. “Art,” so Marinetti stated, “can be nothing but violence, cruelty, and injustice.” The movement eventually came to include architecture, as in a 1914 manifesto by Umberto Boccioni, which proclaimed the movement’s antipathy to the classical styles. Boccioni argued instead for an architecture of “dynamic awareness.” The leading architect among the group was Antonio Sant’Elia (1888–1916), who built little, but whose influential visionary drawings portrayed highly industrialized futuristic cities.

The expressionists formed several groups, such as the Arbeitsrat für Kunst (Worker’s Council for Art) and the Novembergruppe (November Group, named after the 1917 Russian Revolution). In 1918, the November Group, in its first manifesto, called upon cubists, futurists, and expressionists to join together in the regeneration of Germany.

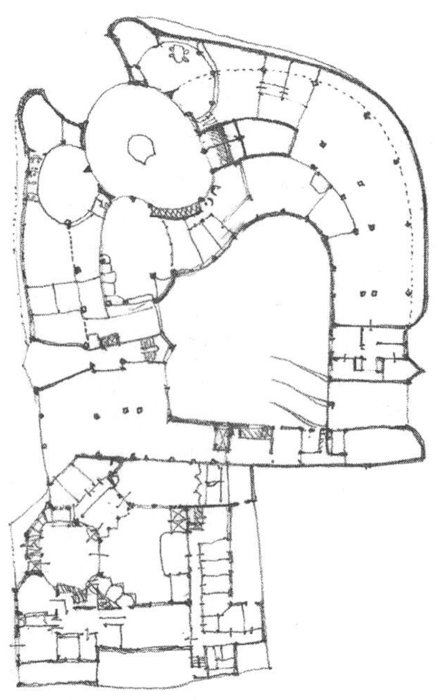

**17.105 Scharoun’s project for a stock exchange**

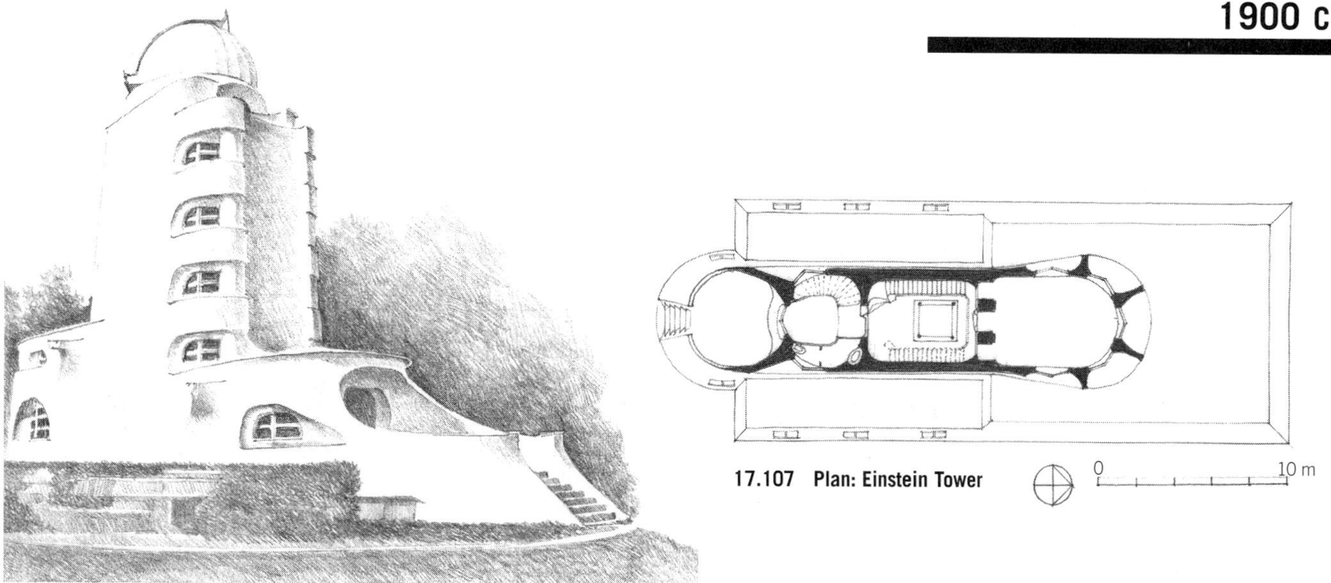


17.106 **Einstein Tower, Potsdam, Germany**

17.107 **Plan: Einstein Tower**

There was something unmistakably romantic about expressionism in its rejection of rationalism and pragmatism. But it also created an architecture designed without the requirements of historical precedents. Up until then, visionary architecture had been only at the margins of architectural practice. The English arts and crafts, for example, had certain visionary ambitions, but it never produced a successful conception of the monumental or the urban.

The architect most associated with expressionism was Eric Mendelsohn (1887–1953 ), who was as famous for his drawings as he was for his buildings. His sketches, many unrelated to any commission, emphasized the building's flowing silhouette. There are no pictorial enhancements, no landscape features, just the building without context, drawn in dark lines on a white sheet of paper. Despite his seemingly impossible and grandiose ambitions for the field of architecture, Mendelsohn was an extremely successful architect, even during the 1920s, and was, one could argue, the first professionally successful modernist architect, employing as many as 40 people in his office.

Mendelsohn was naturally drawn to concrete, but the technology at that time was still rather limited, and even though he first conceived of the Einstein Tower (Potsdam, Germany, 1917–21) as a concrete building, it was in actuality a brick structure with a concrete-stucco exterior. The tower, his first major commission, was built for the Astrophysical Institute in Potsdam and is still in use today. The building, surrounded by a forest, was sited in a clearing on a plateau at the edge of a drop off. (The site is now somewhat altered.)

In studying its exterior shape, the form in some places seems to have been carved out; at other places it seems to have been molded. In the vicinity of the windows, it seems to be a soft encasement of a mysterious, angular metallic structure within. In approaching the building, a set of steps leads to an elevated deck that opens to the entrance lobby, with one stair bringing one down and another leading up the tower. The telescope at the top of the tower transmits light to a series of mirrors down to the basement laboratory. Between the shaft and the base, to the rear of the building, there is the study and sleeping quarters for the scientists.

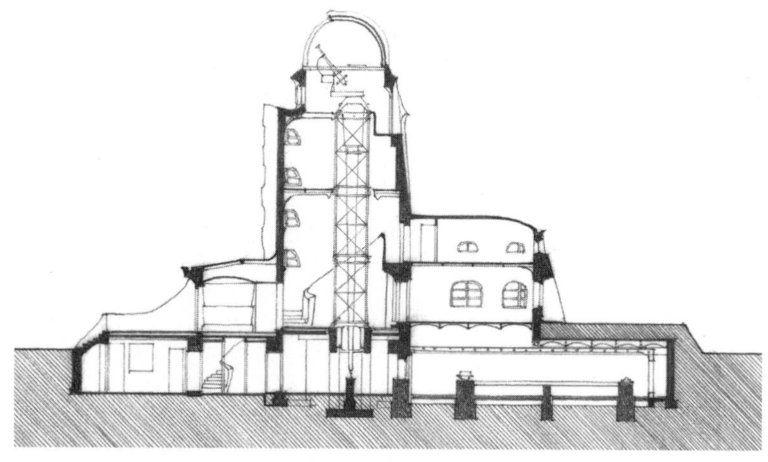

17.108 **Section: Einstein Tower**

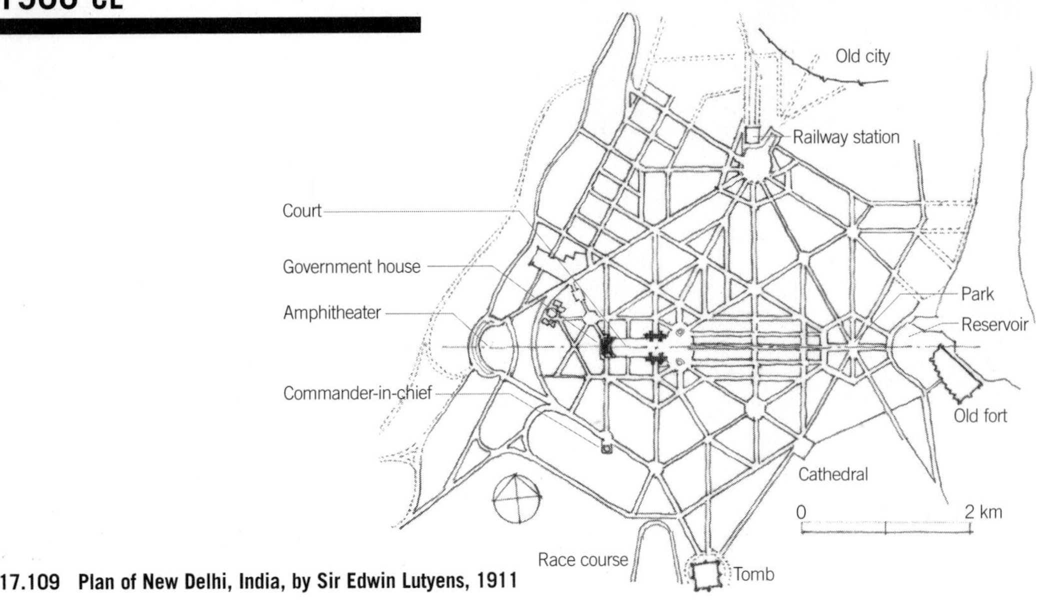


**17.109 Plan of New Delhi, India, by Sir Edwin Lutyens, 1911**

## New Delhi

In 1911, at a coronation *darbar* in Delhi, India, George V announced his decision to build a new capital for imperial India, one that could unfalteringly display the English determination to maintain British rule in India in perpetuity. Calcutta had been the seat of the colonial government, but this was only because of historical circumstances. Delhi was chosen as the site for this new capital to ensure its identification with the one-time Moghul seat of power. Immediately a debate raged over whether the architecture should acknowledge the "indigenous" idiom or reflect the conventions of colonial neoclassicism. After intense lobbying by advocates of both sides, viceroy Lord Charles Hardinge decided that a design that was "plain classic" with a "touch of Orientalism" would be best. His argument was not that different from that of a century earlier, when the classical revival had been advocated based on the eternal principles of classical architecture. With that, the colonial ideologues were back where they began, but with a "touch of Orientalism."

New Delhi's master plan and the design of its principal building, the Viceroy's Palace, was executed by Sir Edwin Lutyens. The Secretariats were designed by Herbert Baker, who had just completed the Union Buildings in Pretoria to great success. The master plan reflected Beaux-Arts academicism; a series of radial spokes were elegantly stitched together over 85 square kilometers to create an expansive vision of a capital city. Different classes of bungalows as appropriate for officers were distributed around its expanse. At its center was the grand east-west path, King's Way, with the Viceroy's Palace and Secretariat, raised on a hill, as its western terminus. The other end of King's Way was marked by a diminutive memorial to the unknown soldier, designed by Lutyens.

Overall, Lutyens's and Baker's designs (even though they had a personal falling out) harmonized well. Finished in red and yellow Rajasthan sandstone, both sets of designs stress the horizontal, utilizing the Indian *chajja*, or overhang, to cast long continuous shadows in sharp contrast in the bright Indian sun. Small *chattris*, campaniles, and the domes provide the vertical counterpoint. Baker, ever more the imperialist than Lutyens, did not hesitate to incorporate some elephants and sandstone screens to make his designs more "oriental" in tone. But the general expression of the entire viceroyal complex displays the restrained and accomplished use of a stripped neoclassical vocabulary, arguably some of Lutyens's and Baker's best work. Indeed, the greatest impact is from the distance at the terminus of King's Way (now called Raj Path), where the broad horizontal sweeps off the complex effectively emphasize the three domes and two campaniles.

**17.110 Viceroy's Palace, New Delhi**

17.111 Lister County Courthouse, Sölvesburg, Sweden

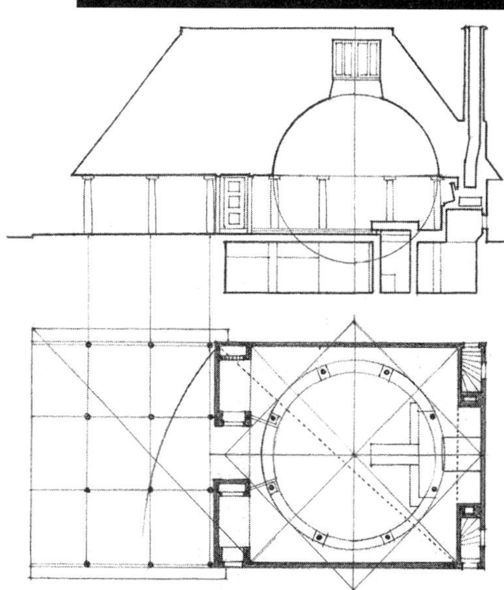

17.112 Plan and section: Woodland Cemetery Chapel, Stockholm, Sweden

## Gunnar Asplund

Sweden had been fortunate to escape the ravages of World War I and with the comparative postwar prosperity, the young Gunnar Asplund (1885–1940) was in an excellent position to make a name for himself with his design of the Woodland Cemetery (co-designed with Sigurd Lewerentz, 1917–20) in Stockholm and for the Lister County Court House (1917–21) in Sölvesborg, Sweden. The latter building is a simple rectangle with a circular courtroom embedded in the plan to the rear. In 1913–4, Asplund had taken a trip to Rome, Ravenna, and Sicily that brought him into contact with the great architectural works of the past. He was drawn less to the more famous monuments than to simple medieval churches, nestled against other buildings or silhouetted against the open sky. Though he can be considered a modernist, his interest in nonmachine aesthetic monumentality has led many to view him as a classicist, but such distinctions are not as clear-cut as one might think. One should see Asplund as a continuation of late-19th-century romanticism.

Under Asplund, Swedish national romanticism shed its overt allegiance to the middle ages and sought out an abstract formalism, as one can see, for example, in the Stockholm Public Library (1920–28), a building of absolute functional clarity. It was composed of a cylindrical reading room within a U-shaped building that contains other parts of the program, forming the impression from afar of a tower rising from the center of a square building. From the entrance, the visitor is conducted upward by a dramatic but simply designed staircase, framed by an Egyptian-styled portal. Within the reading room, above the three open tiers of books, there rises the rough surfaces of the cylindrical walls, ending in a row of windows and a flat ceiling. On the exterior, the facade is divided into two, with the base almost as tall as the upper part. Dividing the sections is an Egyptian-style frieze filled with mysterious symbols that refer to learning and the arts.

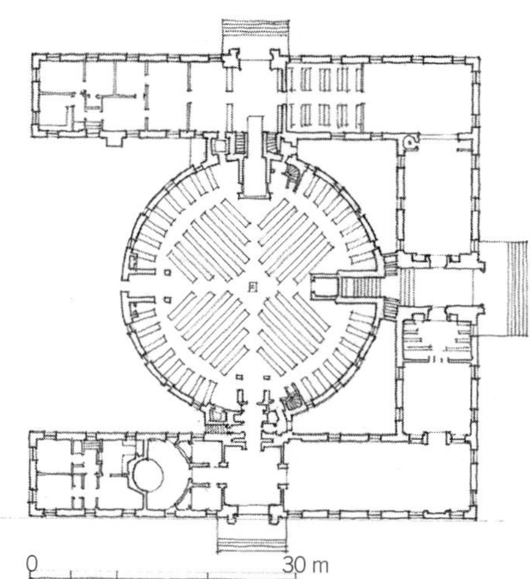


17.113 Plan: Stockholm Public Library

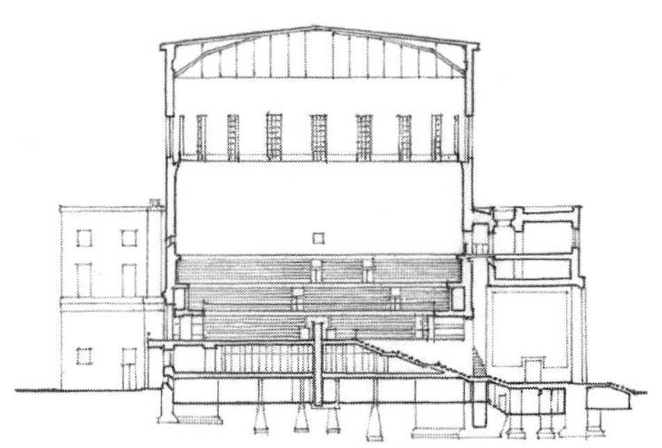

17.114 Section: Stockholm Public Library

17.115 Hollyhock House, Los Angeles, California, USA

17.116 Interior fireplace, Hollyhock House

**Hollyhock House**

Following the murder of his wife and six others by a deranged servant at Taliesin, Frank Lloyd Wright began to distance himself from the arts and crafts ideology in which he was then working. Both the Imperial Hotel in Tokyo and the Hollyhock House (1921) in Los Angeles are more monumental and scenic in compositional strategy than his earlier work. Both also drew more consciously from the local aesthetic and, one could say, "cultural" references deriving from Mayan architecture that had come to be seen in the western United States as a type of regional exotic. The Hollyhock House was also invested with strong symbolic meanings. The house was built for Aline Barnsdall, a wealthy oil heiress, and a supporter of left-wing causes in the Hollywood section of Los Angeles at the peak of excitement over that city's role in the fast-growing motion picture industry. It was located just below the Hollywood foothills, on the top of a hill; it was designed as a palace-citadel isolated from the outer world by boulevards and streets. Its style has variously been called Egyptian, Aztec, or pueblo.

The basic diagram of the house is relatively simple. A rectangle is overlaid at one end by a crossbar holding the living quarters. The carpark was at the other end. The intersection between the rectangular garden and the living quarters—marked by the axial arrangement between living room flanked by music room and library on one end and a circular pool on the other with a garden court in between—is a complex set of closed and open spaces operating on different levels, with even the roofs accessible as terraces. The building was built of stuccoed hollow tile and wood. The kitchen, dining, and servants' wing is on the north and closes the house off against the motor court. The blatant use of pre-Columbian forms stemmed from Wright's belief that the pre-Columbian architecture was a repository of strength and power. This was far different from the rustic but refined humanistic sensibility of Taliesin.

Architecture was no longer interlocked with the landscape by means of a series of gardens but rather self-consciously human-made, evoking a continuity with the abstract cosmic order of the sun, moon, and mountains. The main iconographic element of the house was the fireplace, located in a living room covered by a tentlike roof. Backlit by windows and illuminated from above by a skylight, it seems almost freestanding, even to the extent that the hearth is separated from the living room by a moat that also serves as a reflecting pool.

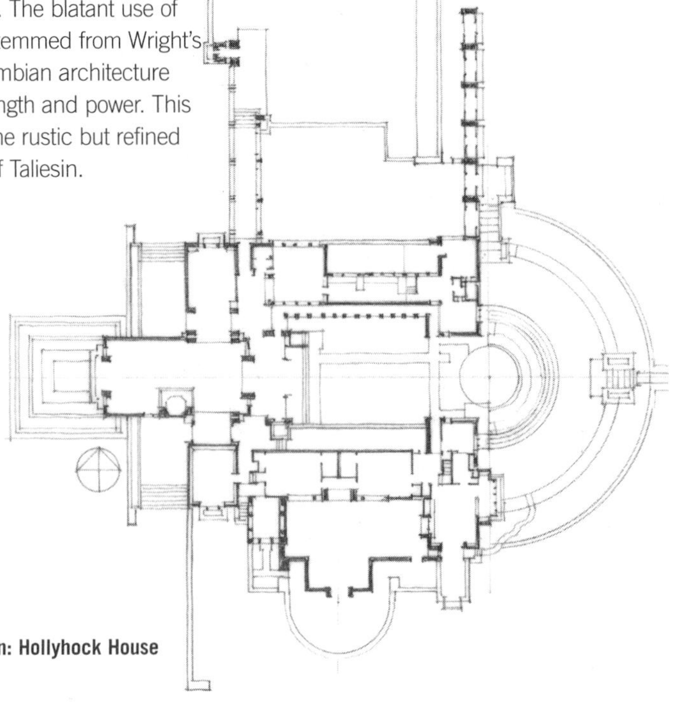

17.117 Plan: Hollyhock House

**17.118 Theo van Doesburg's color design for Amsterdam University Hall**

## DE STIJL MOVEMENT

In Holland, after World War I, expressionism gave way to a vibrant avant-gardist culture that focused on issues of abstraction and color, at the center of which were Piet Mondrian and Theo van Doesburg. The latter still had ties to the expressionist cause in that he advocated a form of three-dimensional color environment. It was a position that Walter Gropius outright rejected as did eventually van Doesburg's fellow countryman and architect, Jacobus Johannes Pieter Oud (1890-1963). They argued that architecture needed to focus on social and economic realities and that it cannot give itself over to abstract spiritual ambitions. Initially, however, among the artists of the de Stijl movement—a name that derived from the journal of the Dutch modernist movement—there was an ambition to cooperate around the need to rid architecture of its conventional subject matter in favor of only abstract vertical and horizontal elements. Though the movement remained strong until the late 1920s, by the mid-twenties, the separation between artists, like van Doesburg, and architects eager to work within realistic needs of the clients, had become unbridgeable.

Van Doesburg's designs for the cinema-dance hall (Café Aubette, Strasbourg, 1926–8) involved broad compositions of colored rectangles in relief, oriented at 45-degree angles. Van Doesburg was certainly influenced by the work of Mondrian. Mirrors were placed between the windows to reflect the ceiling and the three other walls, all treated in a manner that turned the architectural surface into a kind of plastic relief sculpture. As van Doesburg explained in several essays published in *de Stijl* between 1926–28, the essence of the countercomposition was it opposition to the orthogonal character of architecture and nature. Art demanded the addition of another dimension, one based on the oblique. This allowed art to aspire to a spiritual expression that was not possible to the arts based on weight and gravity. In that sense art was opposed to all manner of function and construction.

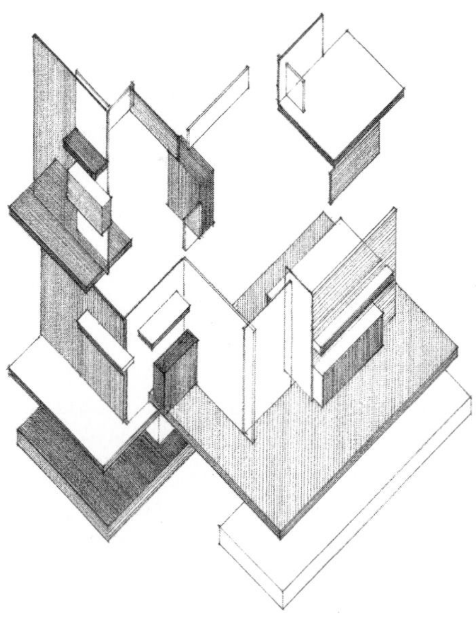

**17.119**
**Color construction by Theo van Doesburg and Cornelis van Eesteren**

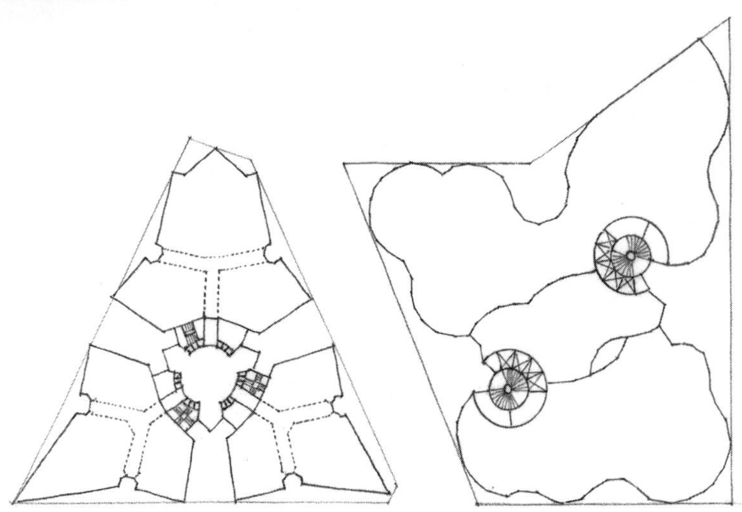

17.120 **Plans for Friedrichstrasse Office Tower and Glass Skyscraper project**

17.121 **Friedrichstrasse Office Tower project**

### Friedrichstrasse Office Tower

In 1921 a competition was held for a tall office building along the Friedrichstrasse in Berlin, and though Mies van der Rohe (1886–1969) did not win, largely because he flouted all the rules of the prospectus, his design has entered the lore of skyscraper history for its radical innovation. Mies began his training with his father as a stone mason, but his talent led him to Berlin, where he worked for a while for Bruno Paul, one of Germany's most influential art nouveau architects, and then for the more modernist-oriented Peter Behrens. The houses that Mies built during the 1920s were certainly competent but hardly imaginative. His unbuilt work, by way of contrast, was highly imaginative and a logical extension of the developing modernist aesthetic. His submittal for the office tower competition, for example, shows a building composed of three angular prismatic towers linked in the middle by a circulation core with an open cylindrical space left free all the way from bottom to top. The steel skeleton with cantilevered floor slabs was sheathed completely in glass. The design reduced the building to fundamental elements, the circulation core and office pods. Mies did not, as was conventional, see each floor as filling the site to maximum capacity. Instead, the building breaks apart the block into three separate 30-story-high towers that only at the buildings' tangents touch the outer perimeter of the site. The core that contains the stairways, elevators, and lavatories constitute a type of trunk clearly visible in the plans. Mies showed the buildings rising high above the haphazard townhouse-apartment blocks.

This project, along with his contemporary design for a Country House in Brick, placed Mies firmly within the emerging modernist movement that aimed to show a way beyond the expressionism that was still the principle post–World War I aesthetic. Mies was no expressionist, but he nonetheless joined the Novembergruppe in 1922. The original political motivation of the group by that time had been lost, but the organization remained important because of its exhibitions, and Mies soon became the director in charge of the Novembergruppe's architectural exhibitions.

In a series of blunt and terse texts, Mies laid out his ambitions: "We refuse to recognize the problem of form, but only the problems of building." To which he added: "Essentially the task is to free the practice of building from the control of aesthetic speculators and restore it to what it should exclusively be: Building." This declaration of purpose was published in a journal called *G*, which appeared in July 1923 under the editorship of Richeter, Lissitzky, and Werner Graeff and which announced its hostility toward romance and subjectivity in art. Though these skyscrapers and the Brick House had minimum investment in their structural logic, Mies, by the mid-1920s, was moving toward a position that placed structure—stripped of allusions and illusions, and the raw realities of building—into the center of architectural production.

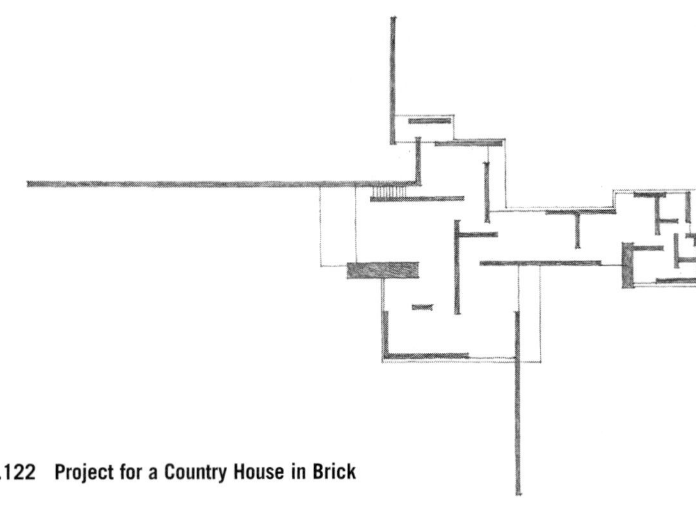

17.122 **Project for a Country House in Brick**

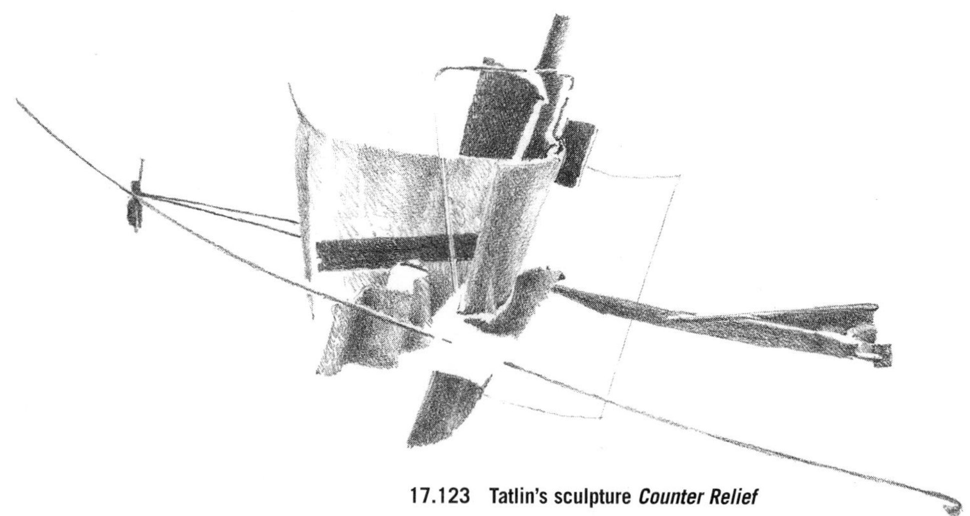

17.123 Tatlin's sculpture *Counter Relief*

**RUSSIAN CONSTRUCTIVISM**

When Karl Marx, in the 1860s, critiqued capitalist society and proposed an alternative world controlled by the proletariat, he assumed that change would take place in industrialized Europe. But when the revolution did come in 1917, it was in the underdeveloped country of Russia. It was, however, a moment of optimism and vindication for all those who were hoping to see a better life for repressed social classes. In accordance with that optimism, a new aesthetic order was conceived by the Russian avant-garde that was in many ways derived from European avant-gardist ideas, as with cubism, which began in 1908, or with *Der Sturm* movement, beginning in 1910. The Russian avant-garde perceived its historical situation not only as a confirmation of these aesthetic impulses but also as a singular opportunity for translating them into a politically purposeful reality.

Constructivism, as Russian revolutionary art came to be known, first emerged as a term at the beginning of the 1920s. For the constructivists, art-for-art's-sake was dead. Art had to reflect the newly established truth of the world. Their initial aesthetic was directly linked to a type of factory production that was no longer dominated by the bourgeois class but was the springboard for the leap into a universal human culture. Constructivism, though it was grounded in an image of labor, was not a one-to-one translation of industry into aesthetics. Rather it was the first aesthetic that admitted and in fact glorified the mass-produced object. Constructivists used the term "laboratory work" to describe their formal investigations and to emphasize their solidarity with both science and labor. Laboratory work was, however, not to be equated with the pragmatism of problem solving, for the constructivists, though they admired utilitarianism, also spoke of the need for a formal language that was imbued with an aura of heroism.

Constructivists experienced considerable success in Europe among those favorably disposed toward the social experiment underway in the Soviet Union. El Lissitzky (1890–1941) in fact spent much of the 1920s in Germany, with Russian artists like Wassily Kandinsky, who taught at the Bauhaus, and Kasimir Malevich, Naum Gabo, and others who travelled to Europe. And, in turn, architects like Bruno Taut, Hannes Meyer, Erich Mendelsohn, and Le Corbusier visited and in some cases worked in the Soviet Union. Until 1925, however, the constructivists had little to show in actual construction, given the chaotic state of the economy, but by the end of the decade the number of buildings began to multiply rapidly. There was a debate about the nature and value of aesthetic theory and its relationship to technology and function. Constructivists differentiated themselves from social functionalists as they argued that architects must work on a higher plane than that of pure function. As a result they tended to think in terms of geometric laconism and striking visual effects.

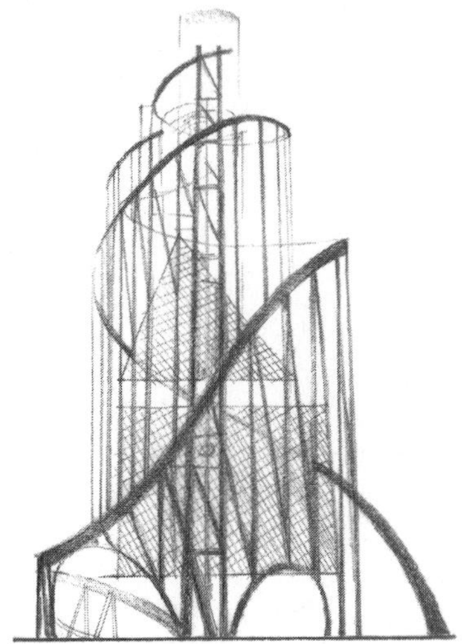

17.124 Drawing of the Monument to the Third International

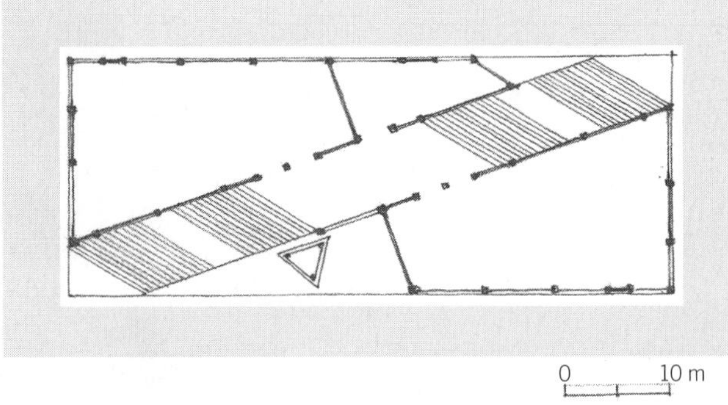


17.125 Plan: Soviet Pavilion, Paris, France

**Tatlin's Tower**

Vladimir Tatlin (1885–1953) occupies a central position in early constructivism and became, with Kazimir Malevich (1878–1935), an important catalyst in the avant-garde movement of the 1920s. He studied art in Moscow and went to Paris, where he met Picasso and other cubists. During this period, his work moved away from painting to become three-dimensional explorations into material and gravity. Some of his more interesting works were installed in the corners of a room in a type of dialogue with the walls. Tatlin defined his efforts as aiming at synthesizing the various branches of art with technology. His artistic explorations and utopian theory coalesced in his project for a huge 400-meter-high tower (designed in 1919) that was meant to straddle the Neva River in the center of Petrograd. The monument, of which a 5-meter-high model was built, consisted of three rooms of glass suspended in a vast spiral structure stiffened along its slope by a leaning truss.

The lower room, a cube, was to rotate on its axis at the speed of one revolution per year and was intended for legislative assemblies. The second room was in the form of a pyramid and was to rotate on its axis at the rate of one revolution per month. This space was for legislative assemblies. The third room, a cylinder, was to rotate at the speed of one revolution per day and was reserved for information services. It contained offices for a newspaper that issued pamphlets and manifestoes. Radio masts rose from the peak of the monument. The tower became a symbol of the new Soviet Union (or USSR), and smaller versions of it were presented at various exhibitions abroad.

One commentator, the noted artist, El Lissitzky, even wrote that it was the modern equivalent to Sargon's pyramid but created in a new material for a new context. The iron, he added, represented the will of the proletariat, whereas the glass was a sign of a clear conscience. Another commentator saw the spiral as the symbol par excellence of modern times.

Tatlin's most immediate follower was Aleksandr Rodchenko (1891–1956), who entered the Moscow avant-garde circles in 1915. He began working on combinations of material elements in three dimensions in 1918, producing complicated combinations of regular and irregular rectilinear geometrical elements placed in asymmetrical balance.

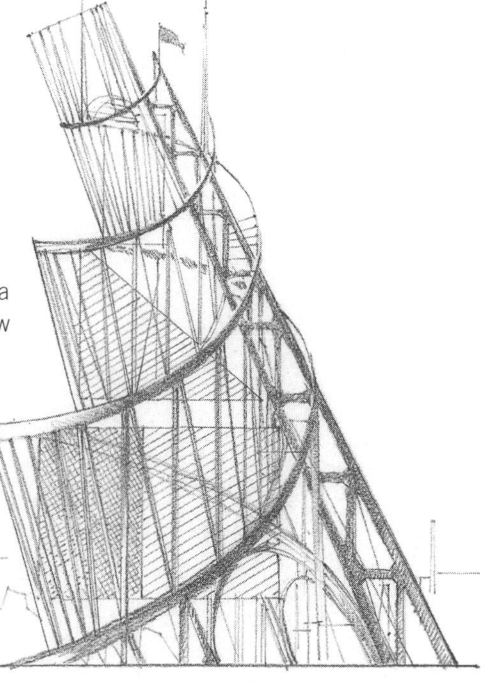

17.126 Drawing of the Monument to the Third International

17.127 **Rusakov Factory Club, Moscow, Russia**

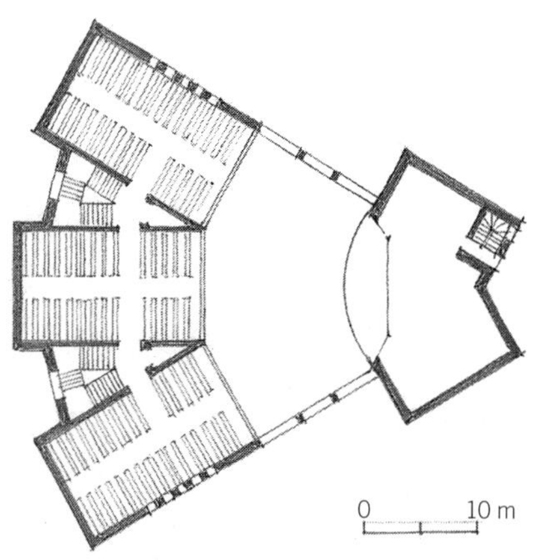


17.128 **Plan: Rusakov Factory Club, Moscow**

### Soviet Pavilion

Konstantin Stepanovich Melnikov (1890–1974) was one of the most productive of the constructivist architects. He was hailed in his own time for his work and selected by the jury of the 1933 Milan Triennale as one of the 12 great architects of the contemporary world. He built only about 20 structures; only a few survive. Like Tatlin, he began his career as a painter but changed his direction to include architecture, graduating from the Moscow School of Painting and Sculpture in 1917. He was trained in a neoclassical style, as would have been standard prior to the revolution.

One of his first major works was the Soviet Pavilion in Paris, which was built for the 1925 international exhibition of the decorative arts, with displays by Rodchenko. Melnikov, starting with a building made of pyramids and spirals in a Tatlinian manner, eventually created a startling angular composition with a staircase running diagonally up and then down the entire building. Though a relatively small building, the staircase gave to it a monumental cast. The structure was built not of steel but of wood fitted in Moscow by peasants wielding the traditional Russian axe and shipped to Paris for assembly by French carpenters. The flying roof panels were painted red, the walls gray, and the window mullions white.

There was a debate in the USSR at the time about whether the new Soviet architecture should aspire to be technologically advanced or reflect the local craft traditions. Melnikov favored the latter, but he was more than flexible when it came to larger commissions, such as the Rusakov Factory Club (1927). Workers' clubs had been created after the revolution to promote communist teachings, but by 1924 most workers had shown themselves to be less than zealous for such uplift. A new generation of workers' clubs came into being that focused more on club activities than ideology.

At a time when living space in Moscow averaged 5 square meters per capita, the clubs were one of the few places outside of the factory where workers could meet and congregate. Melnikov went even further and interpreted them as an expression of a group individuality against the backdrop of urban anonymity. Melnikov's Rusakov Factory Club is highly expressive despite the symmetry and simplicity of its plan. The lecture hall that was its main programmatic element was divided into three subunits that seemed to break through the building's exterior and to hover dangerously above the entrance. Each auditorium box seated 190 people, and each faced a large common stage. Three rooms for club functions were located in a mezzanine just below the seating.

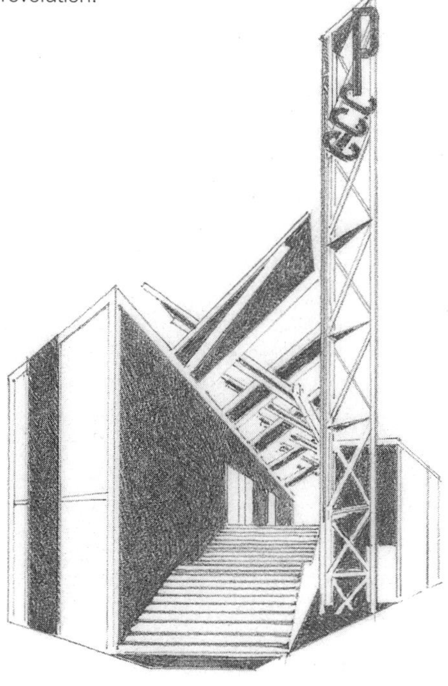

17.129 **Soviet Pavilion, Paris**

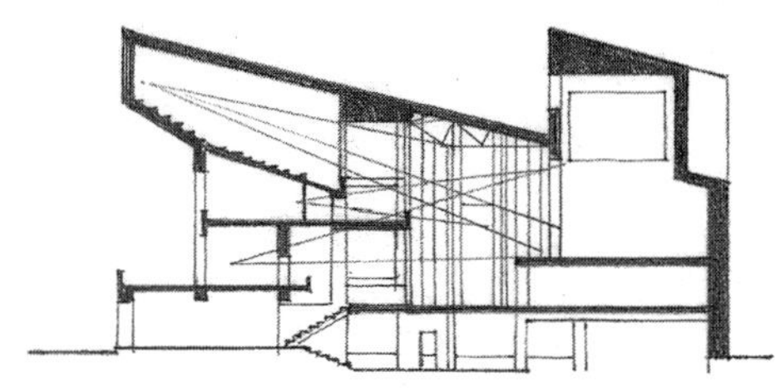

17.130 **Section: Rusakov Factory Club**

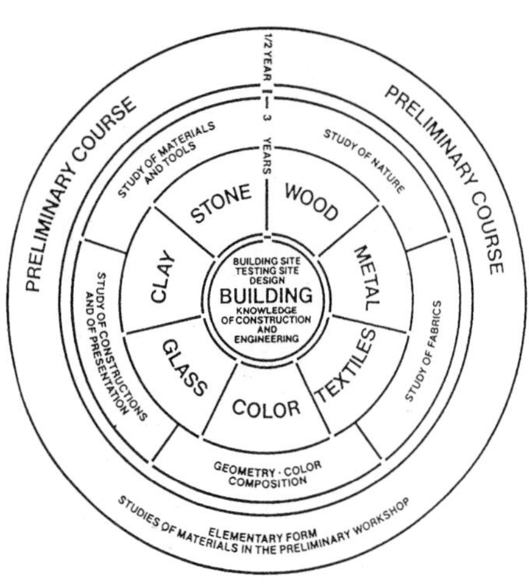


**17.131 Diagram of the Bauhaus curriculum**

**17.132 Bauhaus building, Dessau, Germany**

## BAUHAUS

Walter Gropius, who had been a member of the Werkbund and worked in Peter Behrens's office from 1908–10, had every ambition before the war of succeeding Hermann Muthesius as leader of the Werkbund. But after World War I, it was clear to Gropius that the Werkbund was too conservative in its attitude toward industry. And so, in 1919, he founded a school in Weimar, one of the prestigious cultural centers of Germany, known as the Bauhaus. The school aimed to reach out to industry, even though this took place more in theory than in reality. The school was also significantly less pragmatically oriented than the Werkbund had been, and its relationship with the local government was never particularly warm. In 1924 the reduction of funding from the city forced it to move to Dessau. The move from Weimar to Dessau brought new life to the institution, and indeed the time in Dessau was to be its most productive. The city even helped finance the campus, which was designed by Gropius and opened in 1926.

The Bauhaus, though it lasted only 14 years, until it was forced to close by the Nazis, became the lightning rod for debates, enabling the furthering of modern architecture in the brief channel in time between the early 1920s and the return of neoclassicism and nationalism in the 1930s.

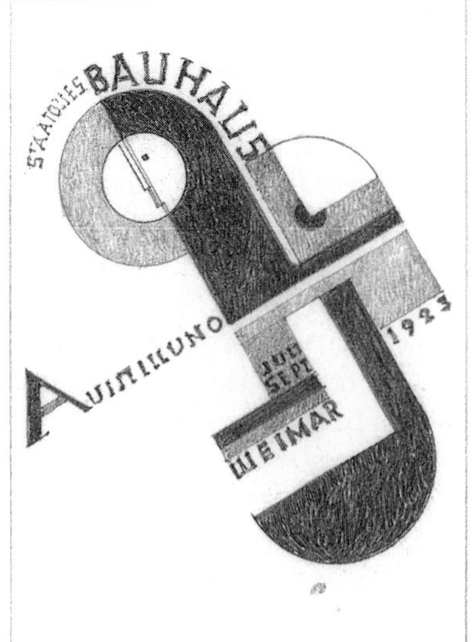


**17.133 Joost Schmidt's poster for the 1923 Bauhaus exhibition in Weimar**

Initially the Bauhaus's purpose was to produce a new "guild of craftsmen," but that does not mean that it was reactionary, for Gropius was also aiming for a school that could unify the arts and close the gap between industry and craft. In that sense, unlike William Morris, who saw craft as a bulwark against industry, or the Werkbund, which was seeking an industrialized craft, Gropius was seeking to discover the internal ethos of industrial production itself. The question was not just how to make things, but how to perceive and experience things as well. For that reason, Gropius brought in painters, including Lyonel Feininger, Paul Klee, and Johannes Itten.The celebration of painters as formmakers reflected a not-so-subtle shift away from the social, and thus from the contentious political issues of the time, toward the language of abstraction and design. Itten was placed in charge of the basic course required of all incoming students. Its purpose was to free the creative powers of the students and to guide them toward a suitable direction in their later studies. Personality conflicts led Itten to eventually leave, and he was replaced by the Russian, Wassily Kandinsky; but, as was typical for the Bauhaus, neither he nor Klee gave painting classes but rather classes on color and form, which had to be examined objectively, its use and application related to the contexts in which they were applied.

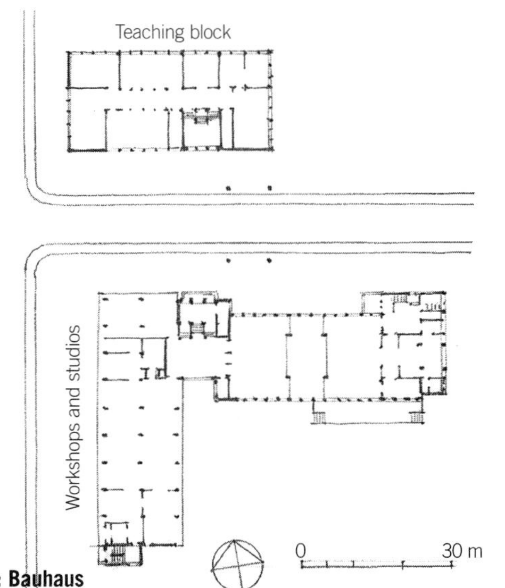


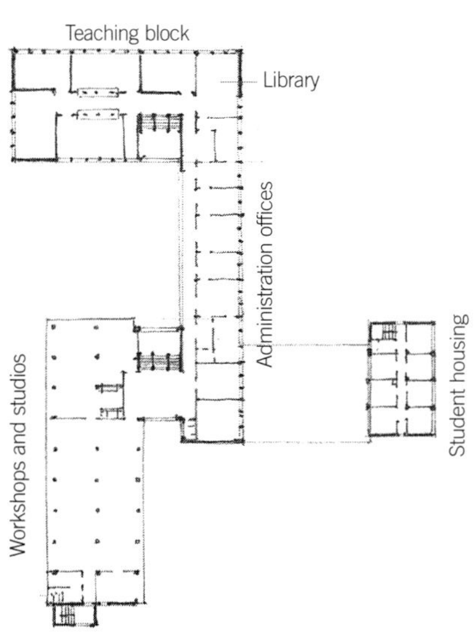


**17.134 Ground- and second-floor plans: Bauhaus**

The program of the Dessau building included workshops, administrative offices, lecture hall and stage, as well as workrooms, canteen, and student accommodations. Gropius divided the program into two large pieces separated by a road and connected by a bridge. The bridge, fittingly, was where Gropius had his office. To go from the classrooms to the studio spaces, one had to pass by Gropius' office. The pieces were not particularly unified in the classical sense, for each had its own programmatic logic. The dormitory at the east end stood awkwardly connected to the long one-story-high space that contained the lecture hall and canteen, which, in turn, was linked to the main building with two stories of studio spaces transformed into a glazed box. The L-shaped area containing offices and classrooms, on the other hand, was designed with horizontal banding of white stucco, contrasting with the windows. The only two colors in the whole composition are white and black.

Criticism of the school came not only from conservation factions but from moderns as well. Le Corbusier, though he would change his mind later, argued that modern architecture cannot be taught aesthetically as it was allied primarily with industry. In other words, for Corbusier, architecture should not emerge out of what for him was decorative design. Similarly, Theo van Doesburg, the Dutch artist, argued that the Bauhaus, in emphasizing individual creativity, had abandoned the all-important search for a relationship between artist and society. Despite these difficulties the Bauhaus remained the leading school of modernist design in Europe.

In 1928 Gropius stepped down as head of the Bauhaus and appointed Hannes Meyer (1889–1954), a Swiss architect, to take over. Meyer's socialist political allegiances led to conflict with the government, and he was forced to resign in 1930. The position then went to Mies van der Rohe, who held the school afloat until it was officially closed by the Nazis in 1933.

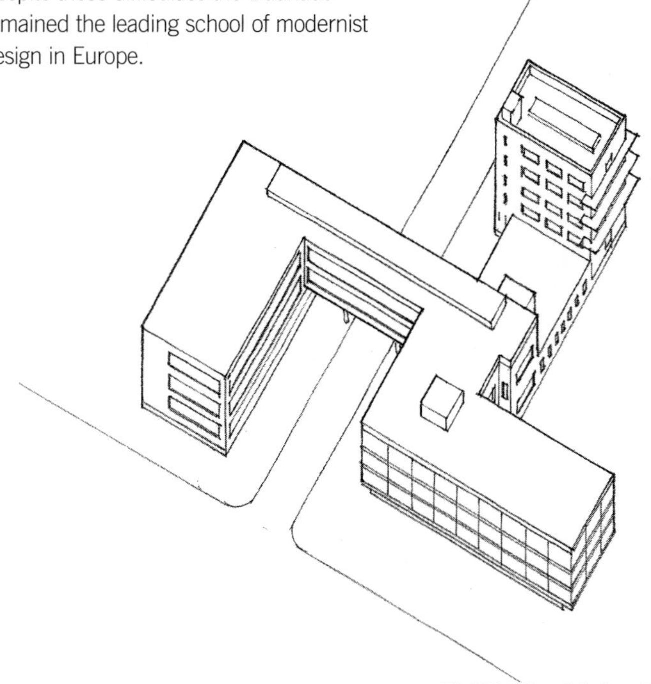

**17.135 Pictorial view: Bauhaus**

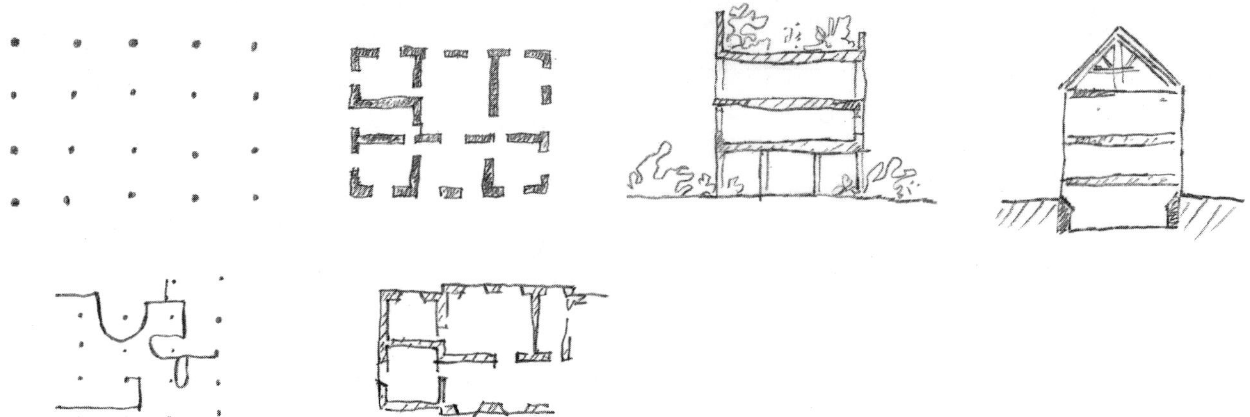

**17.136 Facsimile of sketches illustrating Le Corbusier's five points of a new architecture**

***Vers une architecture***

Due to the dominance of the Beaux-Arts system, the innovations in design that were taking place in other parts of Europe and in the United States had only minimal resonance in France. For modernism to develop it needed someone who could break its cultural isolation and provide a suitable alternative. That person was Charles Edouard Jeanneret, better known as Le Corbusier (1887–1965), a Swiss-born architect who worked briefly in the offices of Auguste Perret and Peter Behrens and then moved permanently to Paris at the age of 29 in 1916.

Building activity in Europe was at an all-time low, but it led to a good deal of thinking about the nature and substance of architecture and to a general shift toward a more pragmatic modernist aesthetic rather than to the ephemeral spiritualism of the expressionists. This is certainly discernible in his articles in *L'Esprit nouveau* and also in his epochal book, *Vers une architecture,* which established itself as the most significant summary statement of the ideals of the modernist movement to appear anywhere since the war.

Born in 1887 to a middle-class family in the Swiss Jura, Jeanneret's first modest foray into architecture was the design and construction of a few family houses at La Chaux-de-Fonds, Switzerland (1905–8). These houses, symmetrical and staid in their art-and-crafts style of composition, betray little of the direction that Jeanneret was to take. But once in Paris, and after a travel tour to Turkey, Greece, Italy, and other parts of Europe and the Mediterranean in 1911, Jeanneret allowed his unique style to develop rapidly. He was strongly influenced by the modern painters, in particular the cubists, and took up painting, working in that art form until his death.

**17.137 Illustration from *Toward a New Architecture***

He also took on the name, Le Corbusier, whose reference is somewhat obscure, but mostly likely meant "the Crow." From the outset of his career, Le Corbusier was very interested in publications as a medium for communicating his ideas before they were translated into built architecture. He published a series of articles in the progressive journal, *L'Esprit Nouveau,* which he collected and published as *Vers une architecture* in 1923. The book outlined "five points" for a new architecture: the *piloti* (stilts), the free plan, the free facade, the strip window, and the roof terrace. These features, he argued, were based on structural properties of reinforced concrete as well as the increasing availability of mass-produced architectural elements. They also allowed—or perhaps one can say, forced—the architect to work with pragmatic forms. The idea of the *piloti* was to remain with Le Corbusier throughout his career. Inspired by Rousseauesque thinking that invested undisturbed nature with an ideal of plenitude, Le Corbusier's *piloti* was meant to liberate the land from the oppression of a building that interrupted its flow. Along with the roof garden, the *piloti* was one of Le Corbusier's prescient environmental ideas that has found new currency of late.

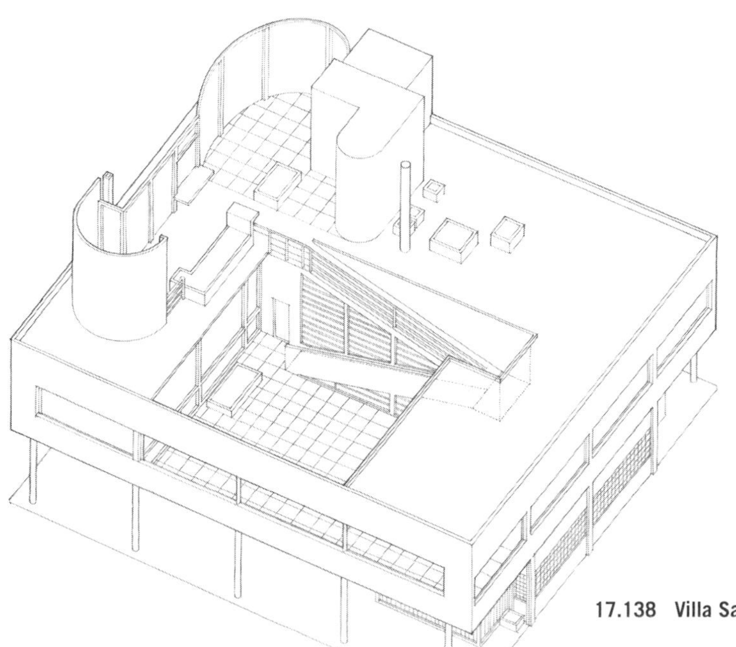

17.138 Villa Savoye, Poissy, Paris, France

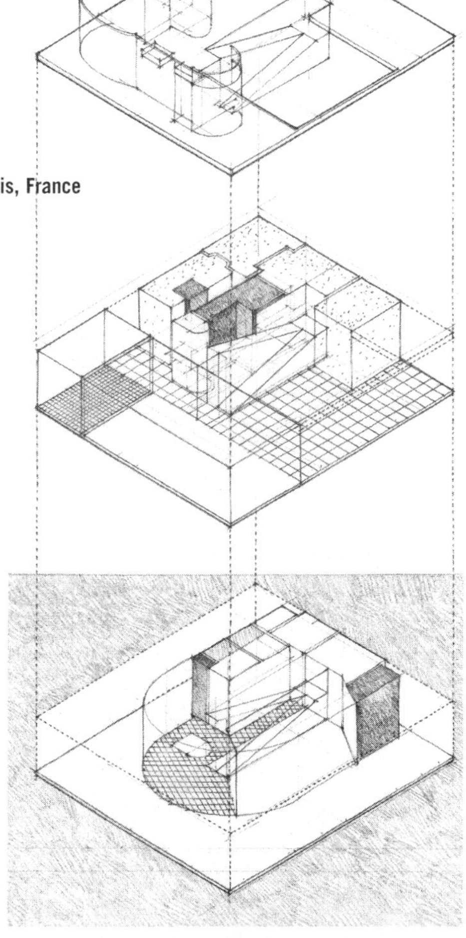

17.139 Villa Savoye: Expanded view of spaces

### Villa Savoye

In the 1920s, Le Corbusier designed a series of houses in Paris and its suburbs that explored and demonstrated the possibilities of his Five Points. The Maisons La Roche-Jeanneret (1923), which now houses the Foundation Le Corbusier, was a combined set of houses for two different clients. Le Corbusier responded to the spatial demands of the different households by designing interweaving layers of spaces, connected by a central court. The house was painted white, but on the inside, walls were painted in a variety of soft hues of red, yellow, and blue, as well as white. His most influential work from this time was the Villa Savoye (1931) at Poissy, a suburb of Paris, where the client owned a large parcel of land that swelled up to a gentle hill. At its apex, Le Corbusier placed a cubic volume, lifted on *piloti*, a column-and-slab construction in reinforced concrete. The walls were built of brick and stuccoed over. The plans on every floor were customized to their functional requirements, and a simple strip window was the centerpiece of the elevation.

The ground-floor plan was designed around the turning radius of the client's automobile, which, after dropping off his master at the entry on axis with the center, was to be parked by the chauffeur in parking slots located around the curve. In *Vers une architecture*, Le Corbusier had praised the design of the modern French automobile as an aesthetic achievement as great as the Parthenon. Inside the front door, and past the chauffeur's quarters, a carefully designed ramp rose up the middle of the villa. Living spaces were arranged around the ramp on three sides on the first floor. A terrace fills up the rest. The ramp reversed direction and ends on the roof, where a freestanding wall with a single window self-consciously frames the landscape. Although Le Corbusier celebrated the automobile, he also designed the building as a promenade with experiences unfolding at every turn. Once again, though the exterior was white, apart from the red entrance door, some of the interior walls were painted in pastel hues of beige, rose, and blue.

17.140 Villa Savoye

17.141 Le Corbusier's vision for the residential quarter of the Radiant City

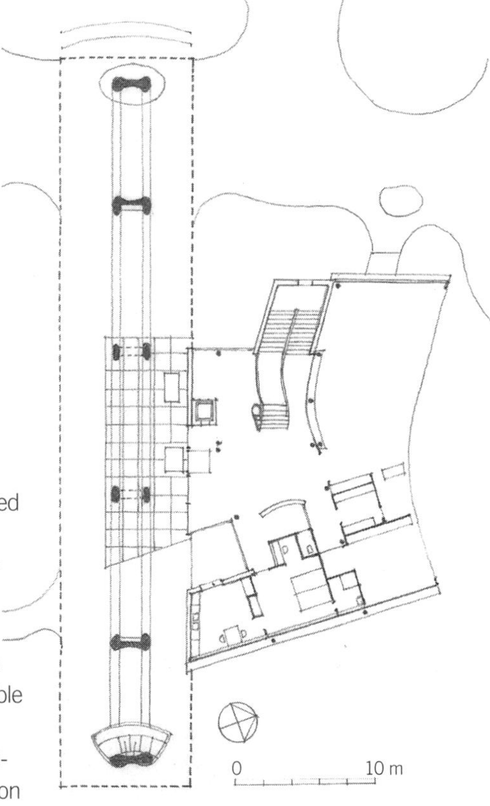


17.142 Plan: Pavilion Suisse, Paris, France

## Pavilion Suisse

Le Corbusier's houses, in his philosophical universe, were preliminary to the main focus of his ideas, which was to reinvent the industrial city. He published his ideas in the form of several utopian proposals to remake Paris, including *The Contemporary City* (1922) and *The Radiant City* (1933). Drawn from the viewpoint of a bird or a plane, these cities erased a huge swath of the existing urban fabric of Paris, leaving only some of the more respected monuments and churches in place. The new city consisted of rows of identical cruciform skyscrapers clustered around an airfield in the center. In later schemes, he showed housing organized in long multistory blocks that twisted and turned to create bounded fields between their curves. Le Corbusier also made a series of perspectives from the human-eye level that showed a continuous green landscape flowing under the skyscrapers as far as the eye could see. The audacity of Le Corbusier's proposals, particularly the impunity with which he proposed to erase the historic city (which was probably simply meant to be polemical), immediately provoked loud reactions, both of praise and horror. For his defenders, his urban designs catapulted him into the role of the messiah of a new industrial age. Le Corbusier was never able to realize any of his urban plans as he wished, even though they eventually came to influence urban planning the globe over, especially after World War II.

Le Corbusier's personal influence was based mostly on his architecture. A few Unité d'Habitations from the 1950s and a highly compromised master plan for a new city in India, Chandigarh, were all that he was able to build. However, the Pavilion Suisse (1932), a student dormitory that he was able to build at the Cité Universitaire, Paris, is from this time. Raised on robust dumbbell-shaped, exposed concrete *piloti*, the Pavilion Suisse has two rows of long and narrow rooms arrayed around the central corridor. A plywood closet separates the kitchen from the living area in each room. The toilets and baths are shared.

17.143 Pavilion Suisse, Paris

# 1950 CE

The landmarks in the early formation of the Modern Movement date from the 1920s and included Walter Gropius's new school of design, the Bauhaus (founded in 1919), Le Corbusier's book *Vers une Architecture* (Towards a New Architecture), first published in 1923, and Ludwig Mies van de Rohe's Weissenhof Siedlung Exhibition in 1927. CIAM (Congres Internationaux d'Architecture Moderne), founded in 1928, also played an important role as it quickly grew into an organization with dozens of members from around the world, all committed to the ideals of bringing functionalism and rationalism to urban planning. Modernism's appeal was, however, not universal. Germany under Hitler and the USSR under Joseph Stalin rejected Modernism in favor of a monumental neoclassical style, opening up deep rifts between modernists and traditionalists. Even in France, despite the work and efforts of Le Corbusier, there were only a handful of modernist buildings before World War II. During this period the fascists in Italy were unusual in that they readily adopted modern architecture—though still classicizing in nature—to express their nationalist ideals.

It was really only after World War II that modern architecture came into its own and began to make significant and sustained contributions to urban space: Säynätsalo Town Hall in Finland; the new capitals, Chandigarh in India and Brasília in Brazil; as well as the Prager Strasse in Dresden, Germany, and the New York State Capital in Albany. The move of Mies van der Rohe to teach at the Illinois Institute of Technology in Chicago, of Walter Gropius to Harvard University, and of George Kepes to the Massachusetts Institute of Technology (MIT), as well as the founding of a school of design at Ulm, Germany, firmly established the modernist ethos at the academic level. Corporate architecture became particularly prominent with the sleek and anonymous surfaces of the Lever House (1950–52), designed by the firm of Skidmore Owings and Merrill (SOM), and the Seagram Building (1954-5) by Mies van der Rohe, both in New York City, setting the tone. SOM soon specialized in designing corporate headquarters in the United States and abroad, and became one of the largest architectural firms of the time. The relative coherency and anonymity of post-World War II architecture was offset by prestige commissions that brought bold and exciting forms into the urban context: the Berlin Philharmonic Hall (Hans Scharoun, 1956–63), the Sydney Opera House (Jørn Utzon, 1957–73), and the Guggenheim Museum (Frank Lloyd Wright, 1956–59). By the 1960s architects began experimenting with large scales and simple forms in a style that came to be known as Brutalism, as exemplified by the Yamanashi Press and Broadcasting Center (Kenzo Tange, 1964–67) in Kofu, Japan, and the Royal National Theatre (Denys Lasdun, 1976) in London, buildings with exaggerated forms and large-scale massing. In the 1960s, however, the limitations of modern architecture's claims to universality, its anti-contextual aesthetic, and the drabness of housing projects started to come under heavy criticism. Among the first architects to chart a new path was a group from England which came to be known under the banner of the journal it founded, Archigram. Influenced by Pop Art, they promoted an architecture that was mobile, flexible, transitory, and youth-oriented. These and other critiques developed into a larger movement that in the 1970s came to be known as Postmodernism. Some architects, like Aldo Rossi in Italy, hoped for a return to history; others, like Robert Venturi and Denise Scott Brown, sought out parody and irony; whereas Peter Eisenman in the United States and Oswald Mathias Ungers in Germany aimed for a formalism more rigorous than even that of the modernists. The most enduring aspect of Postmodernism was its call for a heightened awareness to a building's context, but how context was to be defined was much debated and varied from Daniel Liebeskind's highly abstract Jewish Museum in Berlin (2001) to the claim by Prince Charles of England for a return to traditional styles. In the 1990s, in opposition to the conservative tenor of much architectural production, a group of avant-garde architects, among them Rem Koolhaas from Holland, called for a revival of modernist forms and abstractions. Advances in technology and computers also meant that architects were able to build structures that in a previous decade were unthinkable. Frank Gehry's Guggenheim Museum (1997) in Bilbao, Spain, with its curved titanium skin, and Peter Cook's and Colin Fournier's blue, bubble-shaped Kunsthaus (2003) in Graz, Austria, are noted examples.

## 1950 CE

▲ **Rockefeller Center**
1929–34

▲ **Barcelona Pavilion**
1928–9

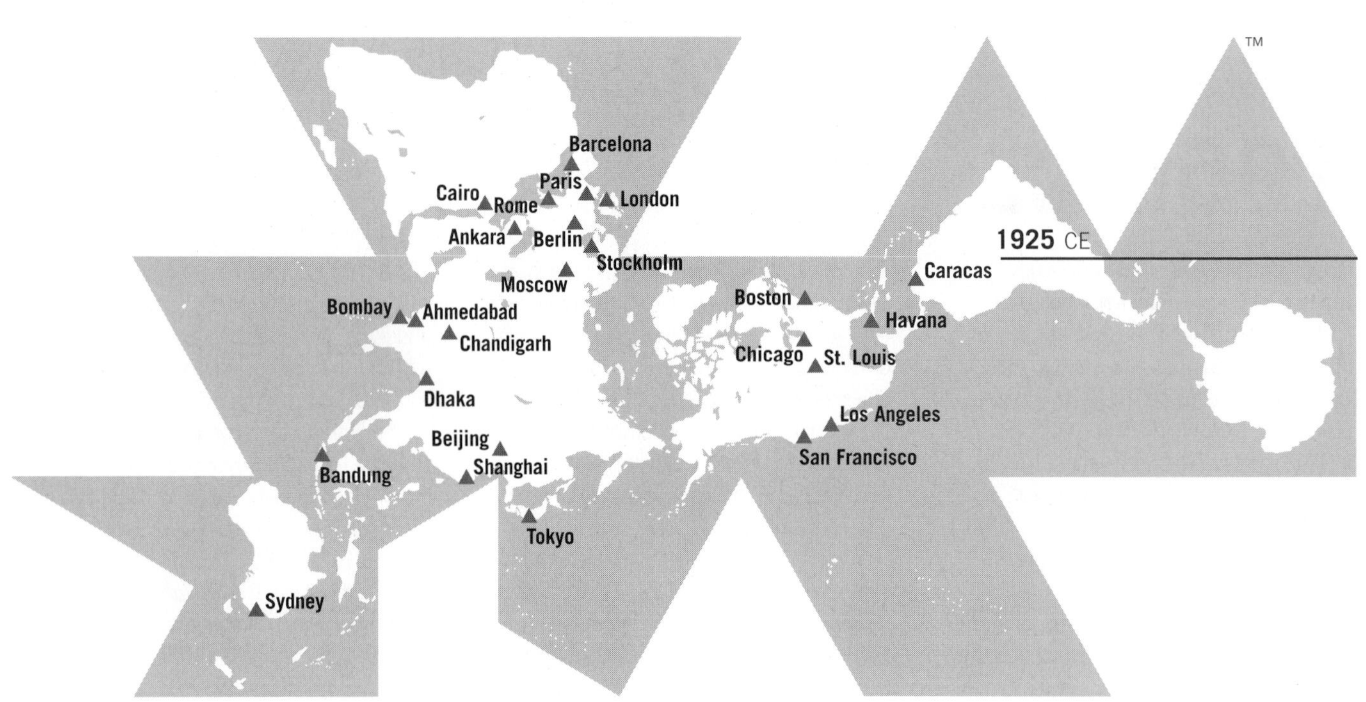


▲ **Lovell House**
1927–9

▲ **Dymaxion House**
1927

▲ **Weissenhof Siedlung**
1927

▲ Palace of the Soviets
1933

▲ Marin County Civic Center
1957

▲ Casa del Fascio
1936

▲ Brasília
1956–60

▲ Sher-e-Banglanagar
1962–7

▲ Esposizione Universale di Roma (EUR)
1937–42

▲ Zeppelinfeld
1937

▲ Säynätsalo Town Hall
1949–52

▲ National Art School, Havana
Begun 1959

▲ Bata Shoe Factory
1937

▲ Great Hall of the People
1958–59

▲ Health and Education Ministry
1936–46

▲ Olympic Stadium
1961–64

1950 CE

---

▲ Japanese Pavilion, Paris Expo
1937

▲ TWA Terminal
1965–62

▲ Kleinhans Music Hall
1938–40

▲ Sydney Opera House
1957–73

▲ Church of Christ the Worker
1958–60

▲ AT&T Building
1980–4

▲ IIT Library Building
1944–5

▲ School of Architecture, Ahmedabad
1965

▲ Millowner's Association Building
1954

▲ Berlin Science Center
1981

▲ Guggenheim Museum
1956–9

▲ Piazza d'Italia
1975–8

▲ Yale University Art Gallery
1951–3

▲ Beaubourg Museum
1972–6

▲ Pyramide du Louvre
1989

▲ Salk Institute
1959–66

▲ Farnsworth House
1951

▲ Heidi Weber House
1965

▲ Magney House
1982–84

▲ Eames House
1945–9

▲ House for Dr. Bartholomew
1961–3

▲ Fallingwater
1936–7

▲ Villa Mairea
1938–41

▲ Ronchamp
1955

▲ Light Chapel
1986

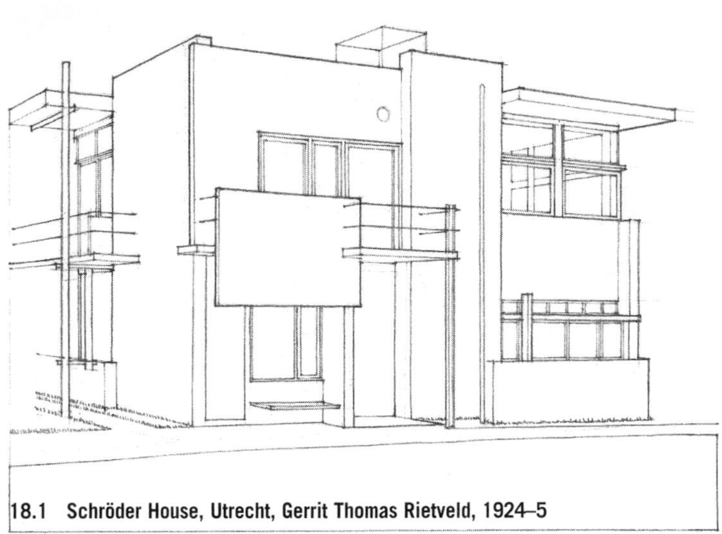

18.1 **Schröder House, Utrecht, Gerrit Thomas Rietveld, 1924–5**

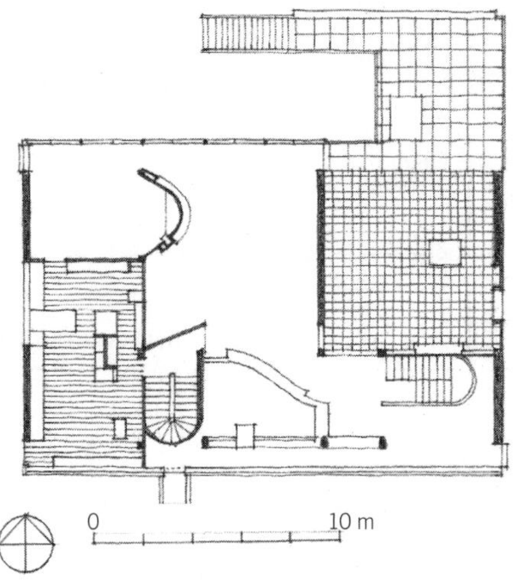


18.2 **Villa Garches, Vaucresson, Le Corbusier, 1926–7**

**MODERNISM**

An inescapable problem in discussing 20th-century architecture is the definition of such terms as modernity, modernization, and modernism. As to the word "modernism," one must be forewarned that different artistic fields have sometimes contradictory understandings of the term. In the collages of Kurt Schwitters, modernism might be used to indicate fragmentation; in James Joyce's *Finnigan's Wake*, a heightened sense of subjectivity; and in the music of Arnold Schoenberg, the desire for objectivity. In architecture, Modernism, as it came to be understood in the late 1920s, was associated with white walls, simple forms, and an attention to function, structure, and use. It positioned itself in particular in opposition to late-19th-century historicism. This definition was established with Philip Johnson's and Henry-Russell Hitchcock's book, *The International Style*, which followed an exhibition in the New York Museum of Modern Art (1932). Though many might question the oversimplifications of the exhibition, there can be no doubt that the period from 1924 to about 1933 was one of optimism.

From that time period, one can mention the following works: Gerrit Rietveld's Schröder House (Utrecht, Netherlands, 1924); Alvar Aalto's Viipuri Library (1927–35); Richard Neutra's Lovell House (Hollywood, California, 1927); Karl Ehn's Karl-Marx-Hof (Vienna, Austria, 1927–30); Jan E. Kpula's Salda's Villa (near Prague, Czechoslovakia, 1928); Clemenz Holzmeister's Grand National Assembly Hall (Ankara, Turkey, 1928); Le Corbusier's Villa Savoye (Poissy, France, 1929–31); Mies van der Rohe's German National Pavilion (1929); Johannes Duiker's Open Air School (Amsterdam, 1930; and Lúcio Costa's and Oscar Niemeyer's Ministry of Health and Education (Rio de Janeiro, Brazil, 1936–46).

From a stylistic point of view, one must take into consideration the emergence of Neue Sachlichkeit (the "new objectivity") in Germany, which developed around 1905 as a critique of the excesses of the Jugendstil and then, after World War I, as a critique of Expressionism. The term Neue Sachlichkeit was used already in 1924 by the critic G. F. Hartlaub to describe the tendency toward clean lines and matter-of-factness in design.

Though Functionalism, as it came to be known, lay at the very heart of the Modern Movement, it was hardly a unified ideal. For Mies van der Rohe, the emphasis was on clarity in a building's form and detailing; for Walter Gropius, it was on the building's massing and organization. Le Corbusier rethought the use of concrete and the free plan, as defined by his Five Points. Modernism was also more than white surfaces. Color was important, though this rarely translated in the black and white photographs of the time.

Among the places where one can find Modernism's origins are the arts-and-crafts movement in England, and in the work of William Morris, Charles Rennie Mackintosh, and others. This legacy traces itself through to the Bauhaus, with its workshops producing tea cups and saucers in accordance with the idea that the transformation of bourgeois culture is linked to the transformation of bourgeois taste. Though the Garden City Movement, which began in the late-19th century, was an extension of arts-and-crafts ideals into the realm of the city, it was not until Le Corbusier wrote the book *Urbanism* in 1924 that urban design was given a purely modern cast.

Modernism is also, of course, to be linked to the emergence of new materials, like steel, concrete, and glass, which enabled, already in the second half of the 19th century, the production of the skyscrapers, bridges, and train sheds that changed the city in both plan and silhouette. Here one can mention the work of Peter Behrens for the corporate giant AEG (Allgemeine Elektricitäts-Gesellschaft). Walter Gropius and others were particularly enamored of industrial buildings and their formal possibilities, and began to see them as potential models for design already before World War I. Mies van der Rohe was particular responsible for bringing the aesthetics of steel and glass into the modern era.

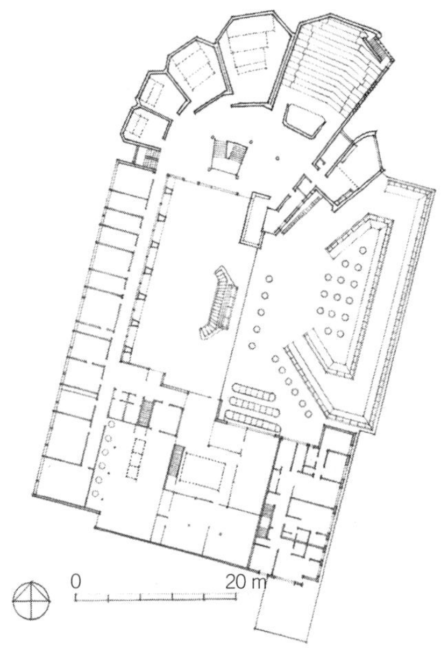

**18.3 Plan and pictorial view: Wolfsburg Cultural Center, Germany**

Though Modernism and modernization are often linked, modernization, of course, predates Modernism in that it is a phenomenon of the Industrial Revolution of the 19th century. A discussion of modernization would focus on the secularization of society, the emergence of a professional class, the shift away from an agriculturally-based economy to a factory-based one, and the rationalization of the building industries. Though England and then Germany paved the way, it was not a purely European phenomenon. Egypt sought to modernize itself in the 1880s as did, in the following decades, Japan and China. As to the politics that are associated with modernization, these have varied from totalitarianism and dictatorship to republicanism and democracy. Though many 20th-century architects attempted to bring Modernism and modernization into a tight relationship, the message was not always accepted. In the USSR under Stalin in the 1930s, and in Japan during that time period as well, the call for modernization went hand-in-hand with a neo-traditionalist ideology.

The word modernity is often used to describe the impact of modernization on the social and personal realms. But because the word points primarily to the presence of a rupture in the historical fabric, and because not all historical ruptures are a consequence of industrialization, modernity can be more broadly used to point to any number of significant revisions of norms and values.

The tightest relationship between Modernism and modernization was to be found in the days of the newly forming Soviet Union when there was a sense of excitement about the new social promise of communism. At the core of this movement were not only Russians like El Lissitzky, but also Mart Stam, a Dutch architect, as well as Max Taut and Hannes Meyer, both Germans, the latter serving as the head of the Bauhaus for a few years before moving to Moscow. For these men, and for like-minded Constructivists, factory life had to find its expression in cubist forms, open steel structures, and the absence of historical references. The fact of the matter, however, was that by the 1930s not that much had been built in the USSR, plagued as it was by economic problems and aesthetic controversies.

The events in the USSR did, however, show the possibility of integrating modernism, modernization, and nationalism, a potent synthesis that was particularly attractive to the elites of non-European countries eager to find alternatives to the Beaux-Arts. This was first tested in Turkey, founded in 1923 following the demise of the Ottoman Empire, and then in Brazil, which had been independent since 1822, but which under Getulio Vargas strove for nationalist self-articulation. It was most vigorously explored in post-WWII India, where several modernist-styled cities and capitals were built.

The work of Frank Lloyd Wright and Alvar Aalto have a somewhat unusual position in the discussions about Modernism, given that both are integral to its history and yet both were critics of the emphasis on functionalism, arguing that architecture should not be based on the principle of a rupture with the past. Both also placed a strong emphasis on landscape and siting.

The history of Modernism and modernization are integrally intertwined with various movements opposed to its aesthetics, reaching as far back as the 1880s. Some of these movements responded to the destruction of the landscape, others to the leftist agenda of some of the early Modernists, others to their distaste for new art forms. It was out of these movements that there came the call for the preservation of pre-modern architecture. Preservation had its origins in Europe in the late 19th century and to a large extent from among the supporters of the Gothic style, who were concerned about the deteriorating condition of medieval churches and what they saw as the loss of spiritual focus in modern life. By the 1950s, however, preservation had expanded to embrace many different styles and had began to draw in supporters from the political and cultural mainstream; by the 1970s, it had achieved broad institutional and governmental legitimacy. Today, entire landscapes in many parts of the world are being set aside under the protection of the United Nations Educational, Scientific and Cultural Organization (UNESCO).

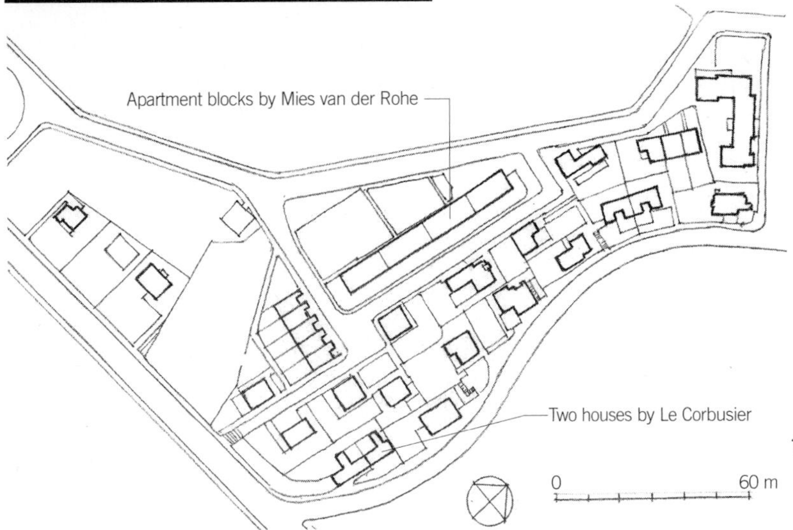


**18.4 Site plan: Weissenhof Siedlung, Weissenhof, Germany**

**18.5 Mies van der Rohe's apartment block, Weissenhof Siedlung**

### Weissenhof Siedlung

By the late 1920s, with the German economy slowly gaining steam after the inflationary crisis of 1923, housing projects sponsored by municipal and state governments and cooperative building societies had begun to be built across Germany. To support these efforts, the Deutsche Werkbund, at the time under a promodernist leadership, sponsored an exhibition of houses to be designed by architects from all over Europe, with Stuttgart chosen as the site because of the progressive politics of its regional government. Ludwig Mies van der Rohe headed the project, which opened in 1927. What was presented to the world was not just Mies van der Rohe's own vision but a map of almost the entire landscape of modernist thinking. Included in the exhibition were buildings by Le Corbusier, Walter Gropius, Adolf Loos, J. J. P. Oud, Hans Scharoun, and Bruno Taut, among others. Initially, he even hoped that Eric Mendelsohn and Henry van der Velde would come, but that did not materialize.

Instead of laying the houses out on a grid, as would have been more common, Mies organized the buildings into a loose rectangular composition above a broad S-shaped road that followed the slope of the land, with the taller buildings at the top. The only proviso was that all the architects had to employ flat roofs and white facades. Included in the exhibition were row houses, duplexes, single-family houses, and apartment buildings.

The exhibition attracted a good deal of criticism by various defenders of traditional architecture. Already in the 1890s, however, many in the bourgeois class had begun to challenge the drift toward faster trains, taller buildings, and bigger cities, seeing in these phenomena disruptions of long-established cultural and social norms. By the turn of the century, the first preservation societies were born that aimed at protecting not only major landmarks but barns and vernacular structures. Others argued for legislation to protect the landscape from urban development and industrial encroachment.

Prior to World War I, the tone of these societies was somewhat muted and even in places associated with progressive thinking, since the struggle in main was against industrialization and greed. But after World War I, when industrialization was more openly embraced by Mies and other leading architects, the conservative elements attacked modern architecture openly as yet another phenomenon of disruption. That modernism had been embraced by the Russians was seen as further proof by the conservatives of its alienation from the values of the middle class. An important figure in this critique was Paul Schultze-Naumburg (1869–1949), who began his career as a painter but who wrote and lectured widely against the modern movement.

The Weissenhof Siedlung marked a turning point in the history of modernism. Though the movement was hardly uniform, with important differences between the leading members, the exhibition gave the appearance to the public and indeed to the architects themselves of a common mission. But the exhibition also marked the emergence in Europe of an almost unbridgeable gap between the moderns and antimoderns. It remains a contested and confusing boundary to this day.

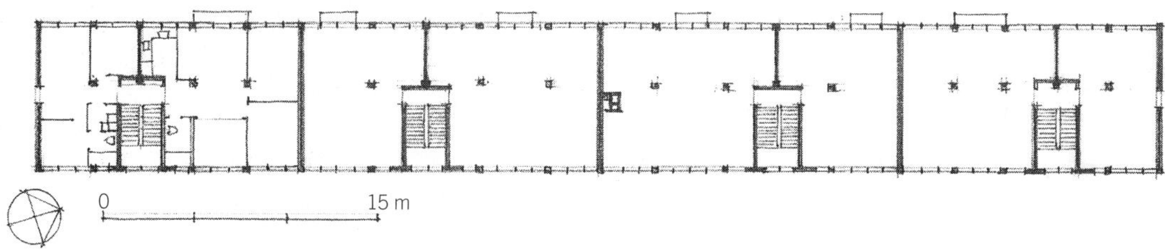


**18.6 First-floor plan: Mies van der Rohe's apartment block, Weissenhof Siedlung**

The building that Mies designed for the exhibition, an apartment block, was the earliest use of structural steel in an apartment building in Europe. The steel, of course, allowed Mies to use thin, nonload-bearing walls on the interior. But as would become typical of Mies, he combined the walls that contained the water and plumbing pipes with stairwell walls to create a "core" that repeated itself on the various floors. This "service core" is in the shape of a two-pronged fork, with the staircase between the prongs. The walls contained the plumbing and water pipes for the kitchens and bathrooms. It was a brilliant and simple expression—and unification—of structure, space, and function.

Compare this with the building by Le Corbusier, which was designed following the principles of the Five Points. It was elevated against the slope of a hill and had a roof terrace with a pergola and planters. Much as in Mies's plan, Le Corbusier's interior too is almost completely open, but in Le Corbusier's case, the partition walls do not reach the facade. There are no rooms in the conventional sense but rather a typically French enfilade organization along the facade. The kitchen, bath, and toilet are lined up against the far wall, which might seem reasonable given the need for pipes and ventilation. But the wall is suspended in space and thus the pipes had to be hidden in the floor. Both buildings speak to the image of the new man. Mies's building organizes the service elements around their functionality, separating the bodily functions, like eating and bathing, from empty space. Le Corbusier organizes the space around culturally based hierarchies, while bathing and cooking areas are whittled down and placed in marginal spaces.

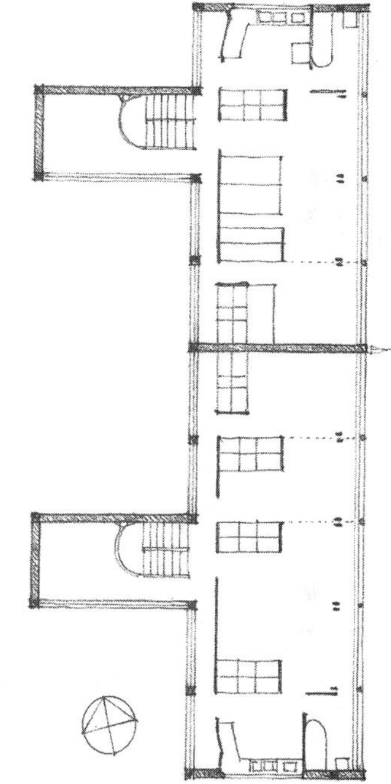

First-floor plan

Section 0 8 m

**18.8 Two houses by Le Corbusier, Weissenhof Siedlung**

**18.7 Two Houses by Le Corbusier, Weissenhof Siedlung**

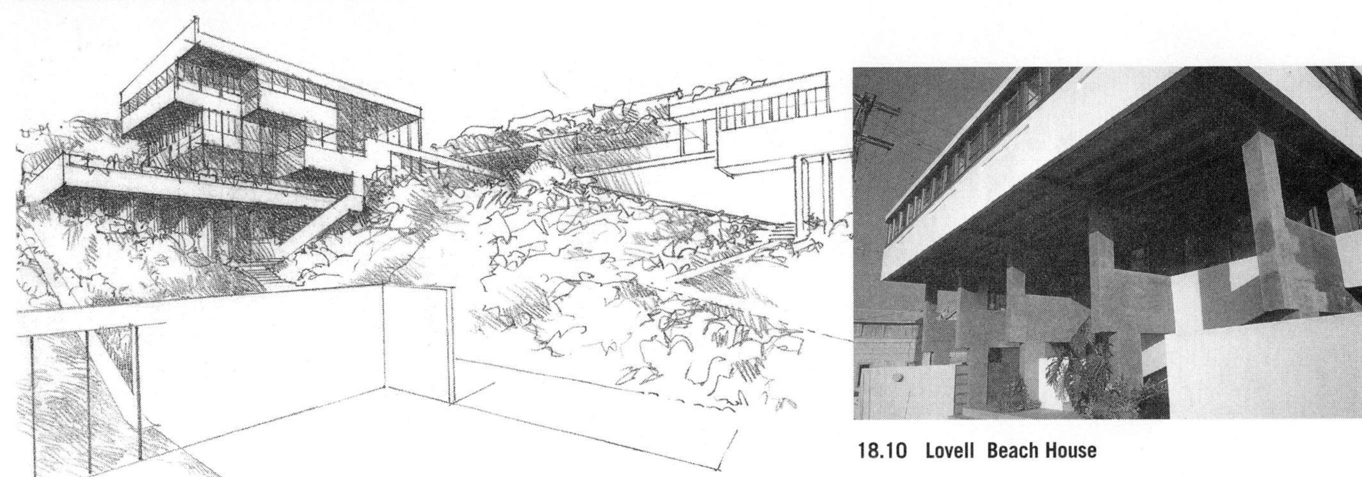

18.10 Lovell Beach House

18.9 Pictorial view: Lovell House, Los Angeles, California, USA

**Lovell House**

The same clients who commissioned Rudolf Schindler to design the Beach House also commissioned Richard Neutra (1892–1970) to design their principal residence in Hollywood Hills, Los Angeles. It was built against a steep hill with views to the city to the south. The entrance was at the top level. At that level there were also the family bedrooms and sleeping porches. A staircase, enclosed on two sides by glass and with spectacular views, leads down to the main floor and the living room, which faces south. The guest room and kitchen were to the north. It was the first completely steel-framed residence in the United States, the prefabricated elements bolted together in less than 40 hours. The house was not a box, however, but rather a complex structure with extended balconies and sleeping porches on the upper floor suspended from powerful roof beams above. The dominant interior colors were blue, gray, white, and black. Carpets and draperies were in shades of gray. The metal trim was gray and the woodwork black. Potted plants softened the hard lines. The surface of the building was either glass or white steel panels.

After a trip to Japan, China, India, and Europe and a meeting with Mies, Gropius, and others in Germany, Neutra returned to California to continue his career, building several startlingly modern houses that were to set the norm for later developments. Roofs were flat and layouts simple, and there was extensive use of glazing. There were no vertical accents as might have been seen by more romantic modernists, rather the buildings were composed of horizontal and vertical planes in an asymmetrical organization. Overhangs provided shade as did nearby trees. Neutra made extensive use of sliding glass doors that connected the living spaces to the outside gardens and patios, soon to become a mainstay of U.S. domestic design. Pools incorporated into the geometry of the plan tempered the heat and sunshine while casting reflections on the ceilings.

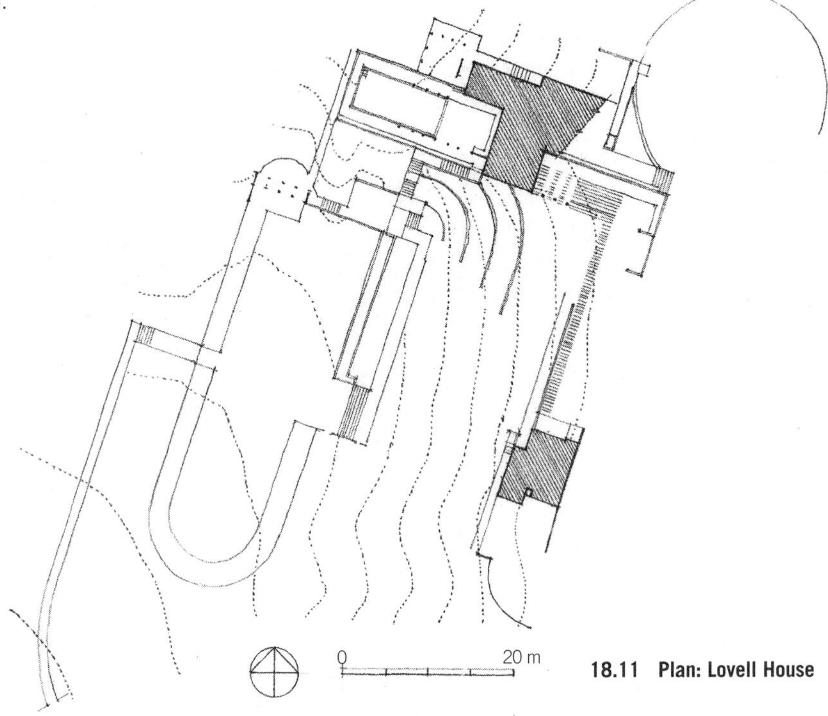

18.11 Plan: Lovell House

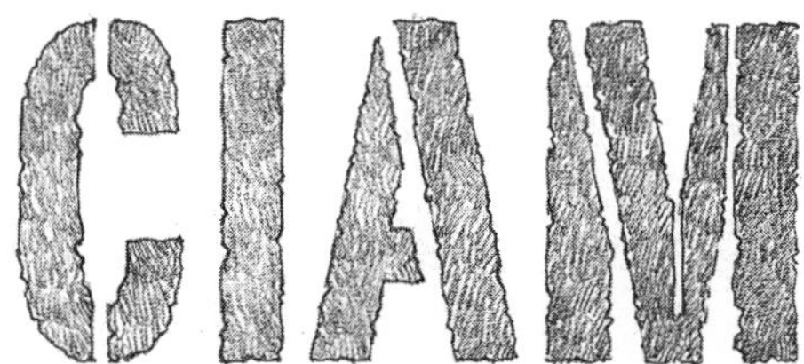


**18.12 Logo of CIAM**

**CIAM**

From the early 20th century onward, European architects banded together in various organizations to define their position and forward their cause in political and cultural matters. The Werkbund, which still exists today, was founded in 1907 and had among its members Peter Behrens, Walter Gropius, and Bruno Taut. The Novembergruppe, formed in 1918, was more short-lived and lasted only a few years, though it was more clearly promodern, seeing the postwar economy as an opportunity to rethink social relations and architectural expression. The group that had the most important impact on architectural thinking was, however, CIAM (Congres Internationaux d'Architecture Moderne, 1928–45), the first international organization dedicated to discussing and promoting modern architecture. The organization came into being as a result of the competition for the design of the Palace of the League of Nations held in Geneva, Switzerland, in 1927, a competition that turned into a contest between modernists and traditionalists, with Le Corbusier's entry rejected in favor of a Beaux-Arts project designed by P. N. Nénot. Though CIAM was constantly changing its composition and priorities, Le Corbusier played the dominant role, along with Walter Gropius and the Swiss architectural historian, Siegfried Giedion. From the earliest moments on, there were fierce arguments, but the group managed to hang together for almost two decades. Nonetheless, in the five congresses held before World War II, CIAM shifted its position from an organization that encouraged a plurality of views about modern architecture to one increasingly dominated by the ideas of Le Corbusier.

The first congress in 1928 produced a manifesto known as the Sarraz Declaration, named after the Château de la Sarraz in France, where the group met. Twenty-four architects signed the document, which attacked the academies for their sterilizing grip on the architectural profession and promoted instead an architecture based on practical, economic, and sociological considerations. The document also held that modern architecture had to aim to satisfy not only the material needs of the population but also the spiritual and intellectual demands of contemporary life. Urbanism was not to be based on arbitrary aesthetic principles but on a collective and methodological land policy. This realism was eventually replaced by a more utopian ethos emphasizing the question of whether one should adopt a sociological approach or a more formal one. The urban designers with practical experience tended to favor the former, whereas Le Corbusier favored the latter.

At CIAM 3, held in Brussels, Belgium, Le Corbusier began to gain the upper hand in determining the agenda and in promoting his Ville Radieuse (the Radiant City). At the fourth CIAM congress in 1933 the participants published their conclusions as the Athens Charter (so-called because the Congress was held on board a ship that sailed from Marseilles to Athens). It committed CIAM to rigidly functional cities, with citizens to be housed in high, widely-spaced apartment blocks, based on CIAM planning principles that called for the separation of living functions. Green belts would separate each zone of the city. Generally speaking, it was assumed, as Le Corbusier phrased it, that the positions adopted by the CIAM would be accepted by "an enlightened population that would understand, desire and demand what the specialists have envisioned for it."

18.13 **Barcelona Pavilion, Barcelona, Spain**

18.14 **Barcelona Pavilion**

**Barcelona Pavilion**

Mies van der Rohe's German National Pavilion, built for the 1929 Barcelona International Exhibition, became an icon of the modernist aesthetic almost from the beginning. It was visited by people from all over the world, showing a side of modernism that many had not expected from Mies, whom many had assumed to be a defender of harsh industrial architecture. Here, however, they saw a building molded around the visual and sensual aspects of the building's surfaces and materials. The Barcelona Pavilion, as the German National Pavilion is known today, rested on a white travertine platform and was entered from the west, from a path that led down a forested hill. The view to the immediate left—as one stood on the marble floor—was of a nude female statue, by Georg Kolbe, standing in a pool of water. This pool was framed by walls clad in dramatically veined green marble from the Greek island of Tinos. The walls extended out from under the roof to create shimmering reflections on its surfaces, the whole contrasting with the green of the forested hill above. Facing south, the wall would have received the bright Spanish sun in contrast to the cool hues of the interior surfaces.

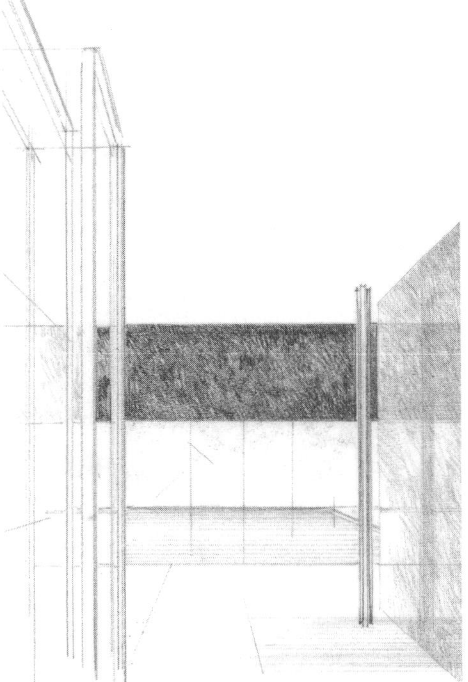

18.15 **Column detail: Barcelona Pavilion**

To the physical impression of free-flowing spaces one has to add the visual sensation created by the rich color and the opulent surfaces, as well as the dazzling play of reflections given off by the polished materials and even from the columns that were encased in highly reflective chrome sheathing. The columns form a structural rhythm of two rows of four, in syncopated relationship, within which Mies placed the walls, sometimes quite close to the columns, sometimes further, but it is impossible to understand the columns as part of a structural-rationalist system. They are, in essence, broken apart to stand in dialogue with both the walls and the viewers of the space. The minimalism of the design relies no doubt on the elementarist compositions of Kazimir Malevich and other constructivists; but Mies was no socialist, at least in the political sense. The building, in fact, one could almost say is completely cleansed of any socialist implications, for Mies has translated function into an aesthetic that is now comprehensible to an elite clientele. Mies was doing much of what Adolf Loos had done in the previous decade, unifying a language of stark modernism on the exterior with lush and sensuous materials on the interior. But unlike Loos, whose interiors were secretive, here they are open, yet mysteriously shimmering.

18.16 **Barcelona Pavilion**

Despite the openness of the plan, the building has a clearly identifiable spatial focus defined loosely by four different walls, the most important one made of a rare marble called onyx *dorée*, golden with veins that ranged from dark gold to white. It was flanked by a wall of milk glass lit from within. In front of the onyx wall was a table and a pair of metal-framed chairs set side by side with white leather cushions. Behind the chairs through a wall of green glass, one could make out the water pool.

From inside, the view through the green glass, like sunshades, darkened the Tinian marble, rising behind the pool, and accented its veining. One saw a series of conjoining and overlapping visual planes, starting with the horizontal view of the trees behind the building framed by the roof and the top of the Tinian marble wall and then descending through various layers to the floor of the building.

The floor, surfaced in white travertine, and matching to some degree the whiteness of the roof, creates for the visitor a floating sensation interrupted only in the central room where the space in front of the great onyx slab is covered by a thin black carpet. On the opposite wall, as if to shield the interior from penetrating gazes through the window, the glass is covered by drapery of scarlet silk. The central space is thus a type of stage set within the single column off to one side, standing in respectful distance to the onyx wall.

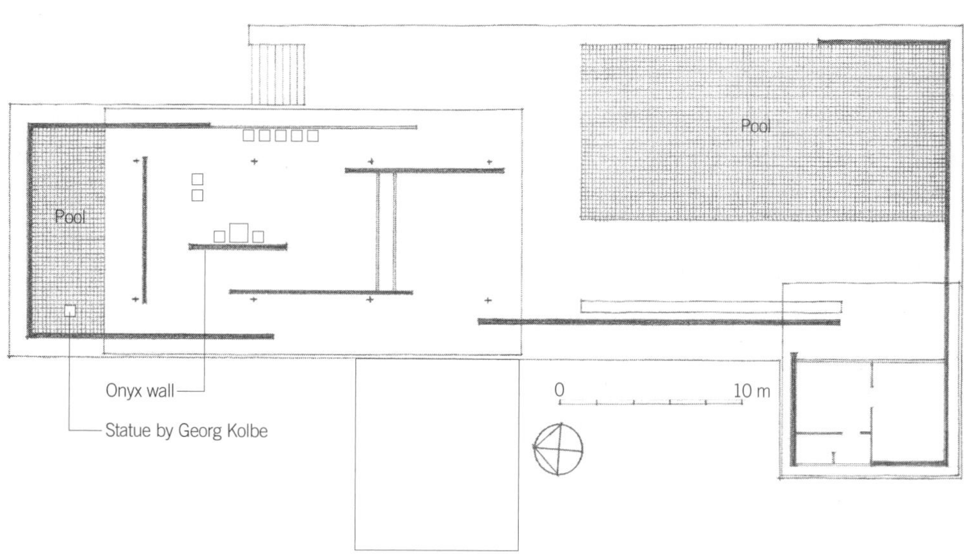


18.17 **Plan: German (Barcelona) Pavilion, Barcelona, Spain**

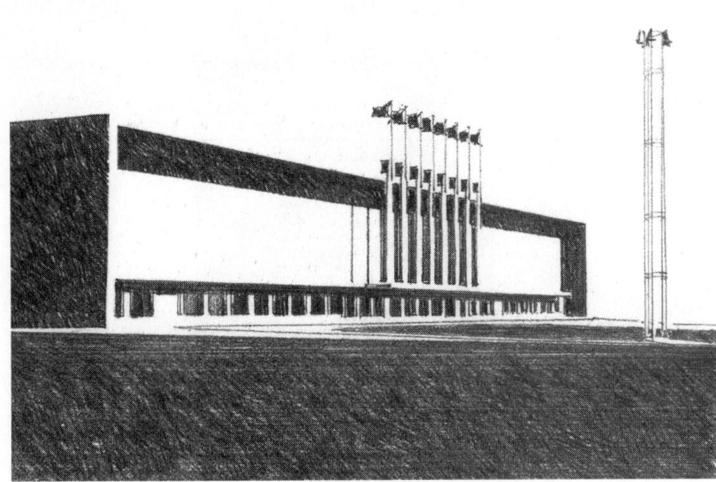

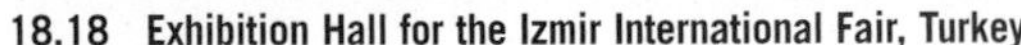

18.18 **Exhibition Hall for the Izmir International Fair, Turkey**

18.19 **Exhibition Hall in Ankara, Turkey**

### Ankara

The legitimacy of modernist architecture received a timely boost not in Europe, where it was to remain contested for decades, but from Turkey. When the Turkish Republic was founded by Mustafa Kemal (also known as Atatürk) after the nationalist War of Independence in 1923, modern architecture was implemented by the state as part of its official program. The program was that of a secular and industrialized nation based on technical and scientific progress, with institutions modeled after those of the rest of Europe. For the new capital, Atatürk chose Ankara, at that time a small town in central Anatolia, more or less in the center of the nation. Its redesign into a capital by the German planner Hermann Jansen, who won the competition in 1927, can be considered to be, along with Canberra, amongst the first in a long string of modernist capitals that would include Brasília, Chandigarh, and Islamabad. Ankara, it should be added, stands in contrast to other places where modernism was introduced as a colonial imposition. Bandung was built by the Dutch, Beirut and Casablanca by the French, and Taipei, China (now the capital of Taiwan), was largely planned by the Japanese. Ankara was an expression of a new political-aesthetical phenomenon, national modernism, and is to be differentiated from romantic nationalism, which favored historical illusions and was a product of the Victorian era.

Most of the first buildings in Ankara were designed by architects and planners from Germany and Central Europe. The Austrian architect Clemenz Holzmeister (1886–1983), for example, was commissioned with the design of the government district, including several ministries, the presidential palace, and the Grand National Assembly Hall. Different from the "white modernism" of the European avant-garde, these architects, discussed by the architectural historian Sibel Bozdogan in her book, adopted a more moderate and somewhat heavier looking modernism, with plain cubic facades, which in terms of overall organization was often indebted to classical principles and vocabulary, such as the use of symmetry, axial vistas, courtyards, and colonnades.

Buildings for education, infrastructure, industry, and public spaces popularized progressive Kemalist ideals and new architectural forms. New schools—especially for girls—people's houses, centers of popular education, places for physical education, recreation, leisure, and entertainment were among the new typologies that became emblematic of the republic's modernity. The Ismet Pasa Girls' Institute in Ankara, a vocational school, was designed by the Swiss Ernst Engli in 1930.

Modern architecture and planning was also employed for model villages, factories, and large infrastructural projects such as the Cubuk Dam outside Ankara (1936). The Exhibition Hall in Ankara designed by Turkish architect Sevki Balmumcu, was erected to showcase technological accomplishments of the Turkish Republic. The building was distinctively modern (the exhibition hall was designed by Ferruh Orel, 1939) as were the structures built for the Izmir International Fair. Comparatively few examples of modern residential architecture were carried out during the 1930s, a phenomenon that testifies to the lack of an independent middle class.

18.20 **Lower plaza, Rockefeller Center, New York City**

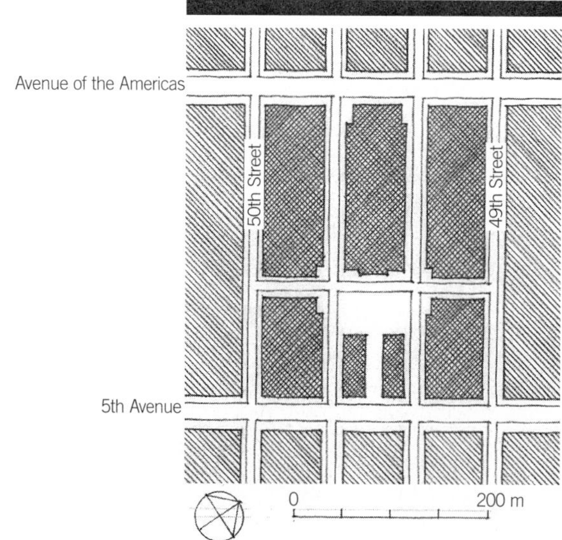


18.21 **Plan diagram: Rockefeller Center**

**Rockefeller Center**

By the late 1920s New York had risen to the level of a world metropolis. Dozens of tall buildings had been constructed, including new civic and institutional buildings. Skyscraper architects had moved away from overt historicism toward the elegant lines of art deco, as at the Chrysler Building (1928–30). The Chanin Building (1927–9) went even further with a neutral gridlike facade. Rockefeller Center, designed by Raymond Hood and Wallace K. Harrison, was nothing less than a city within a city, composed not of one building but of 14 buildings between 48th and 51st streets in New York City. At the core of the composition was the 71-story RCA Building (1931–2), facing onto a sunken plaza defined on its flanks by low-rise buildings—the British Empire Building and La Maison Française. The RCA Building was sheathed in a yellowish limestone with aluminum trim, with the windows arranged vertically in slightly recessed strips to emphasize its soaring qualities. In its complete avoidance of references to a classical past, as well as the thinness of the central tower, this building, in many respects, paved the way for the skyscraper aesthetic developed by the modernists.

Radio City Music Hall, containing the nation's largest indoor theater, was on the next block. Innovative was the introduction of a cross street, Rockefeller Plaza, that divided up the central parcel. Though rarely emulated, the building was much admired for its urban design implications. The setbacks, which were required by zoning regulations, were woven so fluidly into the design that one could hardly imagine the building without them. By contrast, one can compare it to the RCA Building, the Chanin Building, or even the Empire State Building, with its stockier base. To emphasize the tower quality, the lower buildings were designed to look more substantial, basically as stone volumes that also help frame the views of the tower.

Artists were brought in to create sculptures and murals, which are excellent examples of art deco, for placement over the entrance doors and in the lobby. These included Paul Manship, who designed a gilded statue of Prometheus recumbent. The Mexican socialist artist Diego Rivera was commissioned to create a mural for the lobby, but when it was discovered that it contained a portrait of Vladimir Lenin and other anticapitalist imagery, it was removed.

Tall buildings constructed in New York City from 1920 to 1930 include:

- Standard Oil Building (1920–8)
- Bowery Savings Bank (1921–3)
- Barclay-Vesey Building (1923–7)
- Ritz Tower (1925–7)
- Paramount Building (1926–7)
- Chanin Building (1927–9)
- Chrysler Building (1928–30)
- RCA Building (1929–31)
- McGraw Hill Building (1930–1)
- Empire State Building (1930–1).

18.22 **Rockefeller Center**

18.23 Model of 4D House

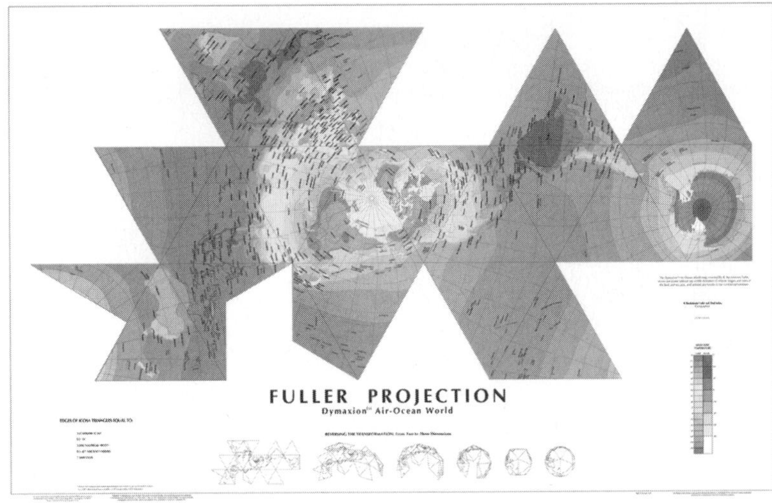


18.24 Buckminster Fuller's Dymaxion map

**Buckminster Fuller**

In the midst of the gathering storm of modernist architecture, one of the most radical rethinkings of human habitation on the earth was initiated by Buckminster Fuller (1895–1983). In 1929, at the age of 32, Fuller decided to study what he called the ecological principles of life. His goal was to analyze nature's resources and think of ways to make them available to all of humanity through an informed, efficient, flexible, and responsible attitude toward design. His key concepts were: synergetics, which is what he called the underlying coordinate system of both physical and metaphysical nature; and ephemeralization, which is, essentially, doing more with less. Unlike some European modernists, who saw housing as primarily a question of social needs allied loosely with industrial realities, Fuller saw housing as tightly interwoven with industrialization and social utopian thinking. What resulted in 1928, after a series of experiments with large-scale towers and multiple-family housing systems, was the project for a prefabricated, mass-produced 4D House.

In the 4D House, plumbing and electrical networks, as well as the appliances, were all contained in the central mast. Energywise, the house could operate independently from any utility networks, which made the house flexible enough to be located anywhere on the globe. It also made it sustainable.

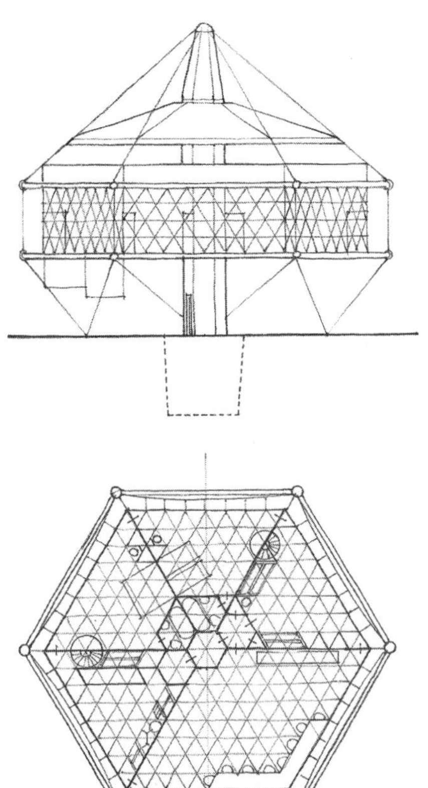

18.25 Plan and elevation: A Minimum Dymaxion House

The house was enclosed by transparent, shuttering walls made of vacuum-pane glass, which eliminated the need for windows. A specially designed ventilation system ensured that no dusting was necessary, as air drawn through the vents would be filtered and then heated or cooled as desired. An in-home laundry facility was designed to wash, dry, fold, and place clean laundry in appropriate compartments. The entire structure was to be mass-produced and flown to its site by blimps, with installation requiring only a single day. All of this, Buckminster estimated, was only slightly more than the cost of a 1928 Ford or Chevrolet automobile. The 4D house, however, was never realized.

Fuller's breakthrough discovery was the geodesic dome, which was designed to have the best possible ratio of volume to weight. Fuller determined that a network of triangular struts arranged on great circles (geodesics) would create local triangular rigidity and distribute the stress in a manner that would make it into the most efficient structure ever designed. Geodesic domes, in fact, become stronger as they increase in size. Industry and the U.S. military immediately saw the potential of geodesic domes, and they were built by the thousands around the world. The U.S. Pavilion at the 1967 Montreal Expo was a giant geodesic dome.

18.26 **Fuller projection of the earth's land mass**

18.27 **U.S. Pavilion, Montreal Expo, Montreal, Canada**

Fuller was dedicated to dismantling the historicist maps of the world and to replacing them with a map that would represent the earth accurately. This resulted in his invention of the Dymaxion Map (1941), which showed the earth as an island in one ocean, without any distortion of the relative shapes and sizes of the continents. This map, used in this book as well, showed the earth as a single planet. The map can be cut up and folded to create a cuboctahedron globe. The term "Dymaxion," was derived from a mixture of "dynamism," "maximum," and "ions."

A poet, philosopher, engineer, architect, artist, businessman, environmentalist, and visionary, Fuller is remembered not only for his originality but also for his energy and pedagogical dedication. From the advent of the Dymaxion Map to the geometries that led Richard Smalley and others to the Nobel-prize-winning discovery of carbon Bucky Balls (the most symmetrical large molecules known), Fuller influenced a whole generation of architects, scientists, and visionary thinkers. Fuller was one of the earliest advocates of renewable energy sources—solar, wind, and waves—and coined the term "Spaceship Earth" to emphasize the fact that we live on an interconnected ecological planet.

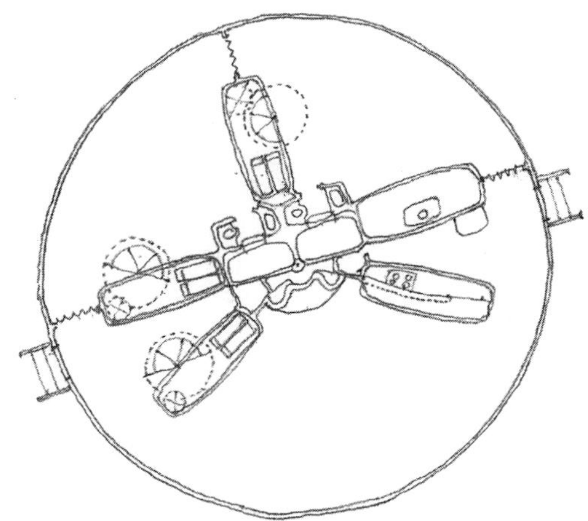

18.28 **Plan and exterior view: The Wichita House that Buckminster Fuller developed with the Beech Aircraft Company of Wichita, Kansas.**

**18.29 Boris Iofan's winning design for the Palace of the Soviets Competition, Moscow, USSR**

### Palace of the Soviets

To celebrate the new Soviet state, Joseph Stalin planned to build a huge Palace of the Soviets in Moscow, Russia. A competition was held in 1931 under the hopeful auspices of the architectural community. It was believed that Russia, as an emerging world power, would continue the trend set by constructivists. Over 160 Soviet architects and firms and 24 foreigners volunteered designs; among the latter were Le Corbusier, Walter Gropius, Hannes Meyer, Erich Mendelsohn, and August Perret. The modernists, however, were to be sorely disappointed when the top award went to Boris Iofan and Vladimir Shchuko for a design that called for a towering wedding cake concoction of enormous massing and height. It was to be topped by a huge apotheosis of Vladimir Lenin.

The edifice was much closer to contemporary icons of capitalism, like the relatively coterminous Wrigley Building (1920) in Chicago, than even to Russian Neoclassical architecture. Due to the war, it was never built, and after the war, Stalin lost interest in it. While this was a serious blow for the modernists, one should remember that Stalin may have rejected modernism, but he did not reject modernization, which he applied ruthlessly and with serious social consequences.

The Palace of the Soviets competition was carried out in four phases. The first, open only to the Soviet architects, assisted in the formulation of the exact functions of the palace and only required that the building be conceived as a People's Forum for mass demonstrations and rallies. The results of this phase, published and exhibited in Moscow, established the guidelines for the second stage of the competition, such as a large auditorium to accommodate 15,000 people and a series of spaces to serve as a theater and cinema. The stipulations for the third stage of the competition stressed "monumental quality, simplicity, integrity and elegance" and the use "both of new methods and the best employed in Classical architecture."

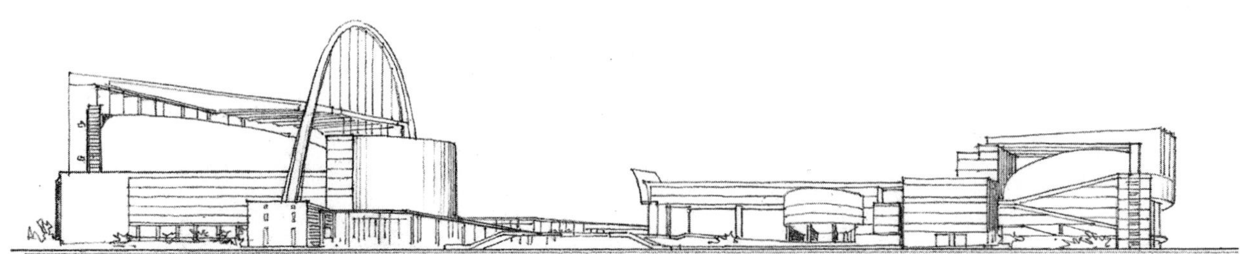

**18.30 Elevation: Le Corbusier's design for the Palace of the Soviets**

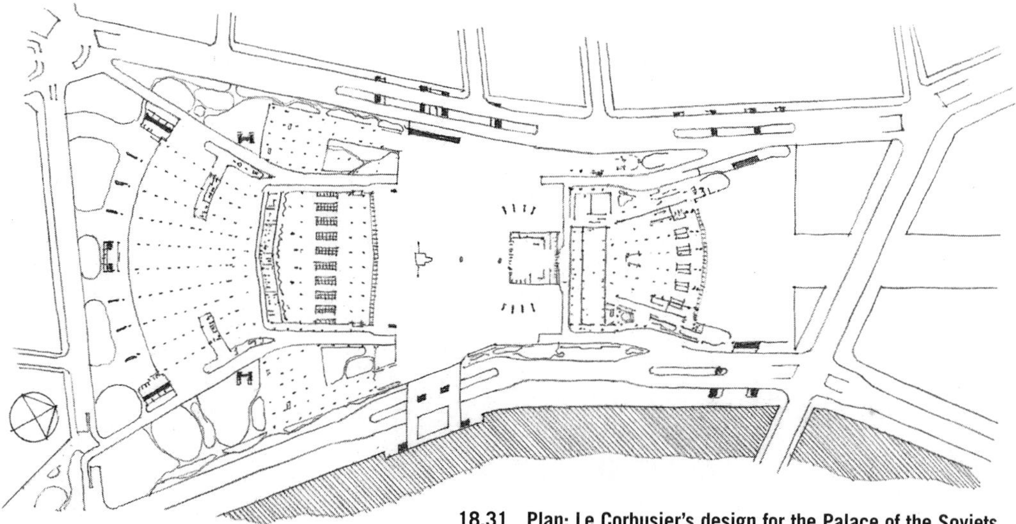

18.31 Plan: Le Corbusier's design for the Palace of the Soviets

Le Corbusier's design was conceived in the mold of a constructivist's solution in that it optimized the functional requirements of the complex, but in a manner that created a striking visual image, especially from above. Unlike most of the competition entries that tried to squeeze all the functions into a single mass, Le Corbusier distributed the functions into two main volumes. The foci of these volumes were the two wedge-shaped auditoriums, neatly fitted into the irregular site on the banks of the Moscow River. The plans of two auditoriums (designed with Gustave Lyon), were optimized not only for sightlines and acoustics, but for ease of access and egress as well.

The sculptural drama of Le Corbusier's design was provided by the roofs of the auditoriums, which were suspended from splayed girders. The girders of the larger auditorium were suspended by cables from a soaring parabolic arch. This arch, much like Eero Saarinen's post–World War II arch in St. Louis still to come, would have towered above the Moscow skyline, and would have, from certain vistas, framed the bulbous domes of the Kremlin within its curve. One can think of the arch as modernity's inscription on the skyline. It would have been the first modern building with such an ambition, apart perhaps from the Eiffel Tower, which had no particular program and was conceived as part of preparations for the World's Fair of 1889.

In preparation for the construction of Iofan's building, the Cathedral of Christ the Savior was demolished in 1931. However, water from the adjoining Moscow River began to flood the site, delaying construction. By the outbreak of World War II, the steel skeleton was almost complete, but in the course of the war, much of the steel was melted down to make tanks to fight the Nazis. Nikita Khrushchev abandoned the project after Stalin's death in 1953 and had the existing structure converted into a Moscow Metro station and a giant public swimming pool. Recently, the Cathedral of Christ the Savior has been rebuilt at the site (consecrated August 19, 2000).

18.32 Le Corbusier's design for the Palace of the Soviets

18.33 Cathedral of Christ the Savior, Moscow, Russia, rebuilt 1996

18.34 **Bata Shoe Factory, Ziln, Czech Republic**

18.35 **Bata Shoe Factory**

**Czechoslovakia**

In many places in Europe, national romanticism hindered the advancement of modernism, given that many nationalists saw modernism and its associations with industrialism and socially progressive politics as antithetical to the idyllic past that was central to romantic ideology. This explains to some extent why the first true example of modernism as a state-sponsored aesthetic flourished in Turkey and some other non-European places, where romanticism was not as firmly developed. Nonetheless, nationalism, even in Europe, began to see in modernism an expression of their country's search for autonomy and capitalist strength. One of the first places where this new equation was spelled out was in Czechoslovakia, which emerged as an independent state out of the dismembered Austro-Hungarian empire in 1918, with the small central European country inheriting both a large portion of the former empire's ethnic diversity and its economic strength. Despite its political, ethnic, and cultural diversity, Czechoslovakia became one of Europe's most politically stable and democratic systems during the restless interwar years. This stability is generally attributed to Tomas Garrigue Masaryk (1850–1937), the first president of the republic and an internationally respected scholar-statesman.

Though Czechoslovakian government officials never gave modernism state sponsorship, this did not hamper the younger generation and the educated and prosperous middle-class Czechoslovaks from seeing modernism as an articulation of Czechoslovakia's political emancipation from the old Austro-Hungarian empire. The teaching of Otto Wagner disciples like Jan Kotera and Joze Plecnik, who belonged to the same generation as Josef Hoffman and Adolf Loos, was immensely influential.

By 1937, the Czechoslovakian firm, the Bata Shoe Company, became the world market-leader in shoe production, becoming the first manufacturer in Europe to mass-produce good quality shoes at an affordable price. The company's founder, Tomas Bata invested in an extensive building program, first, in his hometown of Zlín, where he located the company headquarters, and later in factory towns that he and his successor, Jan Bata, established on three continents. Bata had factories and sales organizations in 33 countries and was at the time one of the most international companies in the world. Bata systematically hired young Czech architects and engineers with international experience. One of these young professionals was Vladimir Karfik, who had worked for Le Corbusier and Frank Lloyd Wright.

The Bata headquarters, a 17-story-high building, designed by Karfik (1937), is one of the first high-rise buildings in Europe. It was built with a structural frame of reinforced concrete on a module of 6.15 by 6.15 meters (20 by 20 feet). This so-called Bata standard was the basis for all Bata buildings, ranging from factories and retail stores to various public buildings. Contrary to traditional dispositions in skyscraper design, three service pods were located on the perimeter of the building. This created an unobstructed rectangle measuring 80 by 20 meters organized as an open-plan office in which reconfigurable office modules were the only spatial dividers. Electricity and telephone networks with plugs laid in the floor on a 3-by-3–meter grid facilitated flexibility in space organization. The most striking feature of the building is Jan Bata's office. It was envisioned as a vertically mobile office, with which Bata could dock on every floor wherever he was needed. By means of an intercom Bata was able to communicate with his employees in the building. The interior of the office elevator, designed with wood paneling and double windows, was well lit by natural light. Among the most difficult tasks Karfik faced was how to make a sink with running cold and hot water possible and how to adapt the cabin to quick temperature changes when moving in the shaft.

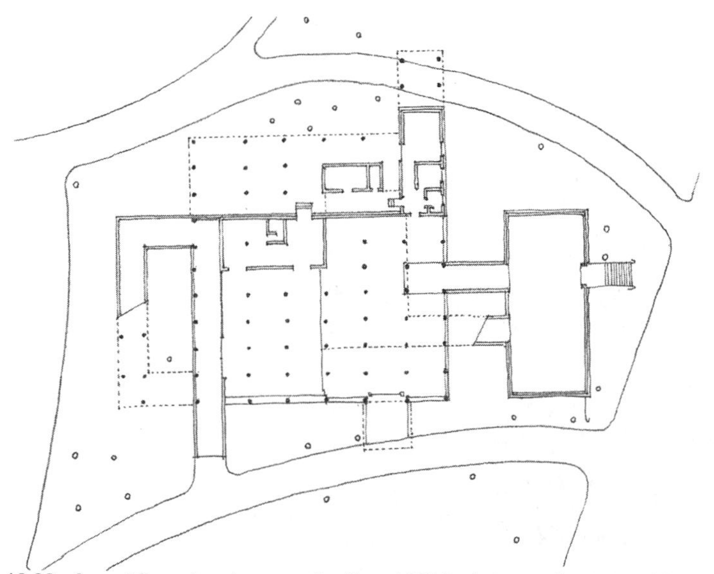

18.36 Ground-floor plan: Japanese Pavilion, 1937 Paris International Exposition

18.37 Japanese Pavilion, 1937 Paris International Exposition

**Japanese Pavilion**

The Japanese investment in industrial modernism began during the years of the Meiji period (1869–1912), after the United States warships steamed into the ports of Japan and forced Japan to open its economy to international trade. In 1869 a new constitution pledged Japan to maintain this policy. The years of the Meiji period were thus characterized by rapid industrialization and mechanization, accompanied by the complete adoption of Western clothes, habits, and manners. With this effort came the creation, for the very first time, of buildings based on European architectural styles. The French second empire style, in particular, was carefully studied and implemented; Kingo Tatsuno and Tokuma Kataya were two of the better-known names from this time period, the former the premier architect of the city and the latter the architect to the crown.

In the years leading up to World War II, European modernism began to establish a foothold amongst the country's avant-garde. Young Japanese architects traveled in Europe or took up apprenticeship with European architects, among them Mamoru Yamada. After completing the Electrical Laboratory for the Ministry of Public Works (1929), the only Japanese work to be included in Hitchcock and Johnson's International Style Exhibition of 1932, Yamada traveled to Europe, spending a considerable amount of time in Germany. His later work, Tokyo Teishin Hospital (1938), with its white tiled exterior finish, large standardized windows, and minimal ornamentation, is considered to be representative of Japanese rationalist architecture of the prewar period.

By the mid-1930s, the Japanese government repressed the further development of the modernist style and called for a return to more traditional looks. This coincided with the invasion in 1931 of Chinese Manchuria, which Japan claimed as a source of raw materials, such as coal, oil, and bauxite.

A successful example of a modernist Japanese design in Europe is the Japanese Pavilion designed for the Paris International Exposition of 1937 by Junzo Sakakura, who had trained under Le Corbusier in Paris from 1931 to 1936. Initially, he had been commissioned to oversee the construction of a traditional-style pavilion, but he surreptitiously modified that design to create a delicate structure of steel, glass, and concrete that was well integrated into its sloped and wooded site—distinctly modern, yet clearly Japanese. Rather than the literal use of a traditional Japanese architectural vocabulary, Sakakura incorporated a delicate steel frame reminiscent of wooden structures typical of Japanese residential architecture, along with subtle ornaments that evoked design features from traditional architecture.

18.38 Tokyo Teishin Hospital, Tokyo, Japan

18.39 House by Lúcio Costa

18.40 Ministry of Health and Education, Rio de Janeiro, Brazil

### Brazilian Modernism

Though Brazil became independent from Portugal in 1822, its economy remained tied to Europe. But after the economic crash of 1929, Brazil's export-oriented economy was shattered, giving rise to a powerful military that supported President Getulio Vargas (1883–1954) who, as virtual dictator (r. 1930–45), created a tightly controlled state-sponsored program of modernization. It can be called the first example of "postcolonial modernism." And, as in Kemal Atatürk's Turkey, modern architecture was to play an important part in this project.

In 1930, Lúcio Costa was appointed Director of the Escola Nacional de Belas Arts. Though Costa knew little about modern architecture, he added a "functional" component to the Beaux-Arts course that was taught at the school, but more importantly he brought in a Russian émigré, Gregori Warchavchik, who had trained in Odessa, Ukraine, and Rome before moving to São Paulo in 1923. Warchavchik (1896–1972) achieved fame through an exhibition of the "modernist house" that was opened to the public in March and April 1930. It had a white, cubic volume (though a parapet concealed a pitched tiled roof) that earned the architect a place in the 1930 CIAM congress under Le Corbusier.

Early in his career Costa had little work and spent his time instead studying books on the architecture of Walter Gropius, Ludwig Mies van de Rohe and, most of all, Le Corbusier. At this time Le Corbusier had built little, other than his "white" houses. It is important to note that Le Corbusier was very influential in Brazil, as in much of the postcolonial world, less for his built work, which was very limited, but more for his prolific publications. With the publication of manifestoes like *Vers une architecture*, *The Contemporary City*, *Precisions*, and more importantly the carefully scripted volumes documenting his built and unbuilt work, the *Oeuvres Complete*, Le Corbusier's ideas quickly became known, earning him fame and notoriety. Le Corbusier offered the most synthetic, rational, multiscale, well illustrated, and widely publicized solutions to the problem of modern living. It was this larger vision, largely unrealized in Europe and the United States, that struck a resonating chord with nationalistic aspirations of people like Lúcio Costa in Brazil, Kenzo Tange in Japan, and Jawaharlal Nehru in India.

In 1936, Gustavo Capanema, a new 33-year-old minister of education and health, took the bold step of commissioning Costa to build its official headquarter. Costa's initial design was a merger of the two halves of Le Corbusier's competition entry for the League of Nations project (1927). His final design, prepared in collaboration with Oscar Niemeyer (in consultation with Le Corbusier), was a 14-story-high tower located in the middle of a rectangular site, running the entire length of the width. Ten-meter-high *piloti* (much higher than what Le Corbusier had proposed) vehemently lift the structure clear of the ground. On the cross axis, along one length of the site there is the double-height block of the auditorium and the public spaces. Its most dramatic statement for the time was the use of a curtain wall on the south side and a system of *brise soleil* (sunshades) on the other—neither were seen at this scale anywhere in the United States, and it was the first large-scale application of *brise soleil* in the world. Internally the circulation corridor was separated from the offices by a two-meter high division with doors at regular intervals. Since the ceiling-to-ceiling height was 4 meters, the gap was designed to enable air circulation through the building. Two towering curved shapes, covered with blue tiles, functioned as vents and housing for mechanical services and water on the roof line, recalling Le Corbusier's drawings of ocean liners. There was a restaurant on the roof terrace as well.

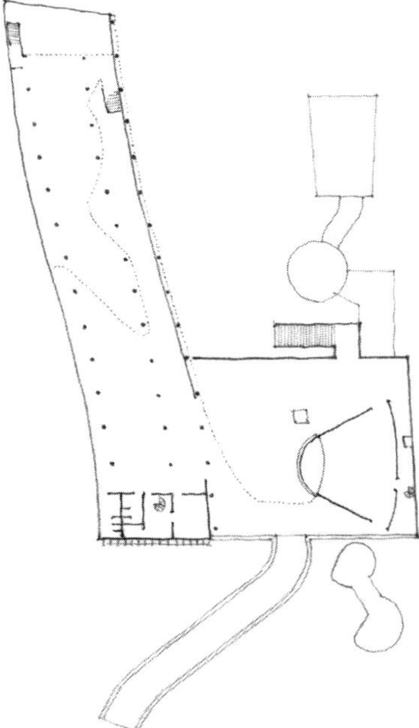

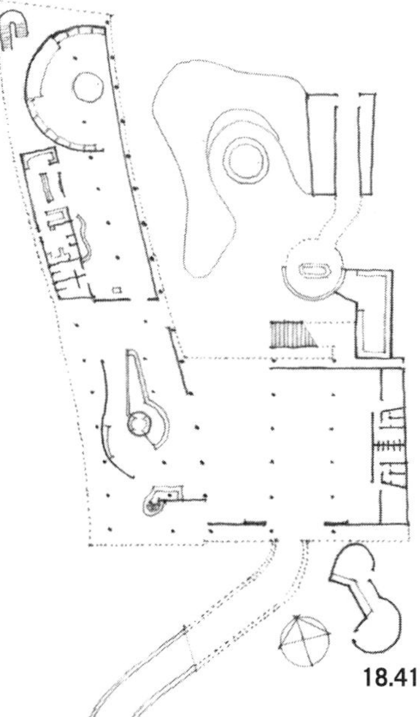

**18.41 Plans: Brazilian Pavilion, New York World's Fair, 1939**

Costa and Niemeyer also collaborated on the design of the Brazilian Pavilion for the New York World's Fair of 1939, whose slogan was "the world of tomorrow." Costa wanted a building that would stand out neither by its scale (the site was not big) nor by its luxury (Brazil was still poor) but through its inherent formal qualities. Simplicity and the suggestion of direct functionalism was its message. Costa's and Niemeyer's two-story design lifted the main volume of the Pavilion above the ground and made a statement out of its access ramp, a large sweeping curve, that forcefully wedged itself into the upper floor. The ground floor was partially enclosed and had freestanding displays for national beverages like coffee, maté, and guarana. The rear garden had a display of Brazilian flora and fauna. The upper floor, with the main auditorium, had an exhibition space with double-height steel columns that partially supported a free-plan mezzanine. Its main facade had a *brise soleil* in front, and floor-to-ceiling glazing in the back. Its side walls were blank.

With the success of the Brazilian pavilion, the uplifted two-story *brise soleil* structure, accessed by a ramp, hovering over the landscape, made from concrete and glass, and occasionally steel, became the national style of Brazilian modernism. Rio de Janeiro's architects were more aligned to Le Corbusier, while São Paolo's were more eclectic. In the late 1940s, structural innovations were added to the Brazilian "style," particularly the use of prestressed concrete and box trusses.

Not everything, however, was European modernism and structural expression. Lina Bo Bardi, for instance, designed a house made of adobe and straw, and Bernard Rudofsky, who lived in Brazil for three years (1938–41) and later wrote *Architecture Without Architects*, built a house for Joan Arnstein organized around five internal garden courtyards. The living room abutted a covered terrace and in summer, extended into the largest patio, designated in Rudofsky's floor plan as a living area as well. Similarly, the dining room extended into another patio with luxurious vegetation. The master bedroom also has a private garden and solarium. The children's bedrooms opened onto a garden with two terraces. Another small patio served as a service area and garden for the servants.

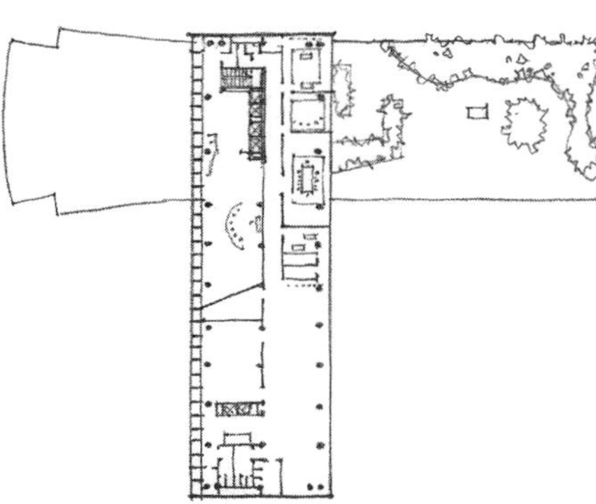

Third-floor plan

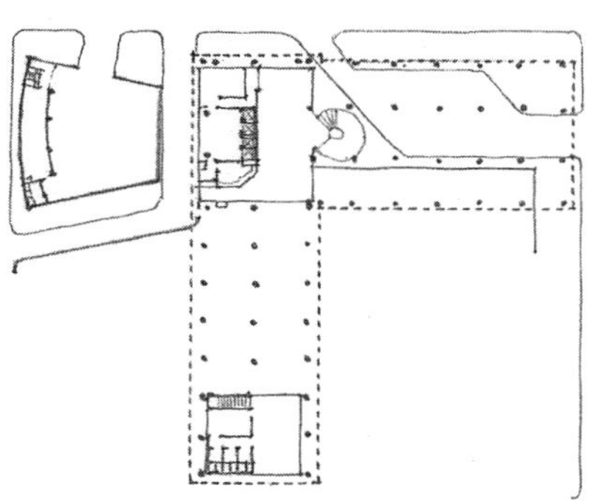

Ground-floor plan

**18.42 Plans: Ministry of Health and Education Building**

18.43 Villa Mairea, Noormarkku, Finland

18.44 Living room: Villa Mairea

**Villa Mairea**

In an age that tended to see the architect as solving the pressing social and spatial needs of the time and thus sublimating his or her ego, Alvar Aalto (1898–1976) developed a style that was more personal. A Scandinavian, Aalto came to modernism more cautiously than did the architects in Turkey and Brazil, where national interests propelled modernism forward aggressively. Aalto, like Gunnar Asplund, had an unbounded enthusiasm for Italy and in particular for the small villages, writing that the "curving, living, unpredictable line which runs in dimensions unknown to mathematicians" is the incarnation of "everything that forms a contrast in the modern world between brutal mechanicalness and religious beauty in life." His Muurame Church, near Jyväskylä (1926–9), painted completely white, is a starkly romantic and modern vision of just such a late medieval, early Renaissance integration of form and landscape.

The same vision is embodied in the Villa Mairea (Noormarkku, Finland, 1938–41). The villa's overall planning is certainly Wrightian, and early sketches show a relationship to Frank Lloyd Wright's Fallingwater. But in terms of composition, Aalto's design has a more cubist understanding of space, not obviously, as one saw in Pavel Janák's work in Czechoslovakia, but in the asymmetrical tensions that exist in the plan between solid and void and between the implied square of the garden and the house, which is clamped against one corner.

The 1930s in Europe saw a return to the rustic and to the aesthetic of austere naturalism, which had been held at bay by the modernists in the 1920s. In keeping with this trend, Aalto allowed for an overt "regional" gloss in the choice of the wood on the exterior and the use of rustic wooden rails for the balconies, which are, however, offset by the ship's railings on the balcony and the smooth bamboo railings for the interior staircase.

Though one could easily see Villa Mairea —because of its almost eclectic fusion of different motifs—as breaking the mold of modernist structures, one can also locate this building as an extension of the late-19th century modernism of Greene and Greene, Antonio Gaudí, Victor Horta, and Adolf Loos.

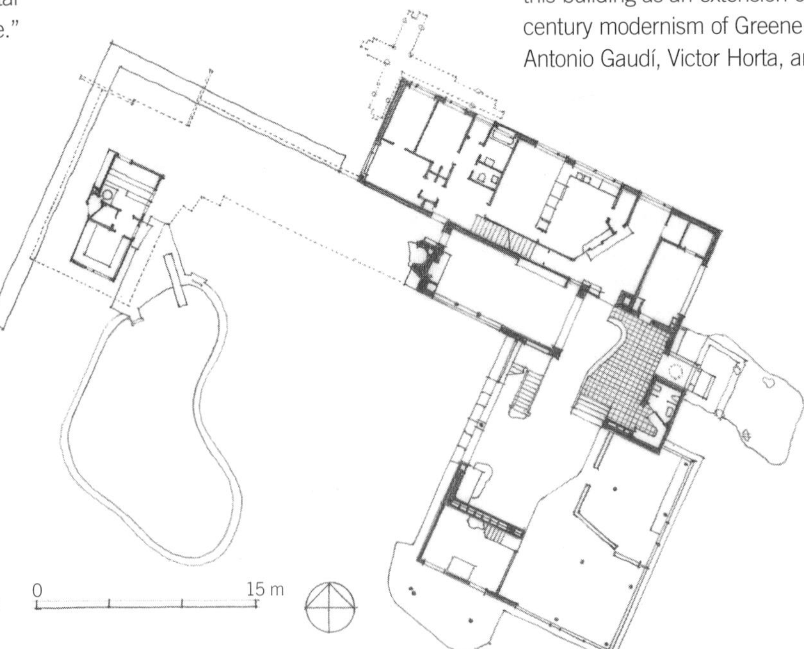


18.45 Ground-floor plan: Villa Mairea

**18.46 Hanna House, Palo Alto, California, USA**

### Usonian Houses

Through the 1930s Frank Lloyd Wright continued to critique both the Beaux-Arts and Le Corbusier's modernism. Somewhat like Aalto, he tried to infuse modernism with a national-romantic sentiment—in his case holding out the ideal of a democracy rooted in simple lives and closely associated with the land. The traditional city, which derived from Europe, he argued, would eventually be replaced by a dispersed network of habitation. Anticipating this, he designed a futuristic Broadacre City (1932) that was to cover 10 square kilometers. Though Broadacre remained a utopian project, Wright was able to realize certain aspects of it with his Usonian houses. The origin of the name Usonian is not exactly known; but it is likely derived from U.S.-onia, the name for the reformed Americana society that Wright tried to bring about for 25 years. The houses, constructed between 1936 and 1943, have very characteristic features that set the standard that would be incorporated in American housing stock after World War II and that would remain characteristic of U.S. suburbs to some extent until the 1980s. In the United States there had been a long tradition of pattern-book houses that could be constructed without an architect by local builders. Wright's Usonian houses extended that tradition, except that what was imitated was not so much the individual plans as the general idea.

The Great Depression had left thousands homeless, and Wright was eager to show that architecture was elastic enough to accommodate changing economic conditions without loss of integrity. Wright proposed a single-story house that did not require expensive excavations for basements or upper-floor framing. There was no use of expensive steel, but rather wood was used in conjunction with brick, local stone, and prefabricated blocks. The bricks were not stuccoed over and the wood was left plain, thus reducing finishing costs. The houses were sited not only to make optimal use of the site within the constrictions of the lot but also to include as much openness as possible from the living room to the garden.

Heating was incorporated into the concrete floor in the form of looped water pipes buried under the slab. The elaborate millwork needed to conceal radiators in the Prairie houses could thus be eliminated. Wright fused the dining and living rooms and in some cases made them one space, which was a radical change from his earlier houses and indeed from the centuries of tradition that mandated that the kitchen, because of noise, smells, and activities of the servants or maids be set apart from the dining room. In these houses, the owners were not expected to be wealthy enough to afford a maid. Wright also wanted to create spaces that were conducive to family conversation. The kitchen was also placed close to the carport so that the distance between the car and the kitchen for the transport of groceries was minimum.

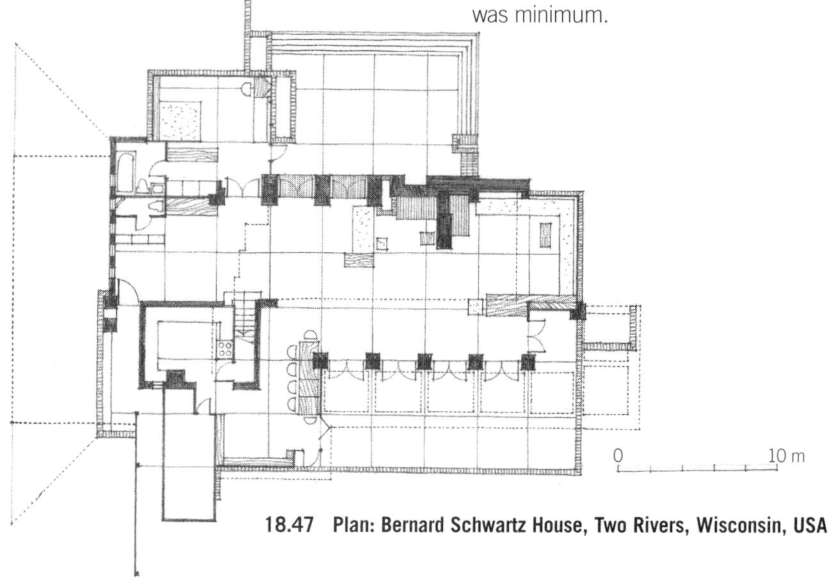


**18.47 Plan: Bernard Schwartz House, Two Rivers, Wisconsin, USA**

18.48 Fallingwater, Bear Run, Pennsylvania, USA

**Fallingwater**

Frank Lloyd Wright's Usonian houses were a long way from the iconic house of the same era that he designed in the middle of Edgar J. Kaufmann's heavily wooded estate at Bear Run in western Pennsylvania. With a fortune made on his department stores, Kaufmann, on the advice of his son who was a student at the Taliesin school, engaged Wright in 1935 to design a family retreat. Unlike the minimalist Usonian houses, Fallingwater (1936) is a dramatic statement on the possibilities of reinforced concrete expressed by a triple set of deeply overhanging cantilevered terraces. The cantilevers float over a dramatic waterfall, the Kaufmann's favorite spot on the site. Inside, the focus of the house is the stone hearth built directly onto the black slate bedrock.

The Kaufmanns had wanted a house that looked at the waterfall, but Wright, in keeping with his theme of design, built them one that was on the waterfall and became one with it. Wright's justifications for this design lay in his conceptions of "organic architecture," a decidedly subjective term but one meant to indicate a building that was integrated into its site and context in the form of a sympathetic counterpoint. The waterfall itself, for example, was not visible, but its seasonal variations could certainly be heard.

The diagonal plan and stepped section is of course a response to the contours of the site, a point particularly important to Wright and anticipated in part in earlier projects like the Freeman House (1924–5). Here the ornamenting of the building's surface has given way to rustic, horizontally coursed yellowish stones that contrast with the white stuccoed surfaces of the balconies and roof lines. Windows are hidden in the recesses with thinly mullioned glazing capturing some of the spaces in between the floor and roof to create indoor-outdoor rooms.

The house, when viewed from below the waterfall, seems to hover provocatively over the site, its straight lines contrasting with the huge boulders and the white of the balconies with the rich foliage of the forest. The stone walls that anchor the cantilevers mimic the stratified pattern of the rock ledges and rise up into the house in the form of towers that anchor the composition and seem almost like ancient ruins.

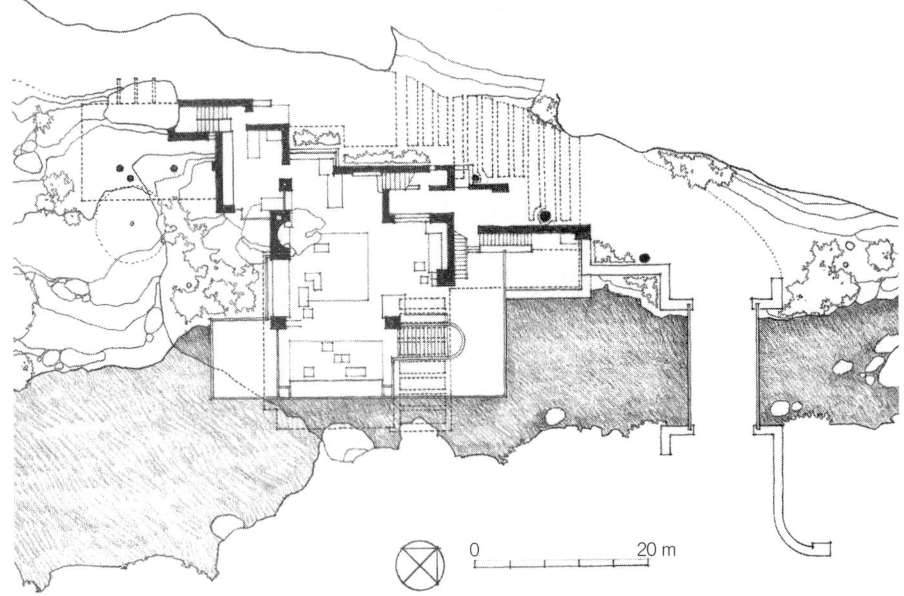


18.49 Main floor plan: Fallingwater

18.50 Cranbrook Academy of Art, Bloomfield Hills, Michigan, USA

18.51 Kleinhans Music Hall, Buffalo, New York, USA

**Kleinhans Music Hall**

While Wright held court in the Midwest from his office at Taliesin, Wisconsin, another modernist vision was being fashioned by Eliel Saarinen (1873–1950), a Finn, who, because he was somewhat older than Mies and Gropius, did not have the opportunity to influence U.S. modernism in the way that Mies and Gropius did. But his works did expand the basis for the new style in the United States where patronage of modernism was generally quite thin. Invited to the United States in 1923 to teach at the University of Michigan in Ann Arbor after receiving second prize in the international competition for the Chicago Tribune Tower, he eventually became resident master at the Cranbrook Academy of Art, Bloomfield Hills, Michigan.

Among Saarinen's first public buildings was the Kleinhans Music Hall in Buffalo, New York (1938). It has two halls, a large and small one, with the smaller appendaged to the rear of the larger one. The three symmetrically arranged volumes, the stage, the auditorium, and the small hall, defined the visible shape of the building. The external walls are of yellowish brick laid in a lightly textured way. There are no windows, and there is no ornamentation apart from the roofline, which projects over the surface of the wall just far enough to form a thin shadow line.

The rounded wall of the smaller hall is articulated by vertical panels decorated only lightly with square patterns. A broad reflecting pool surrounds the rounded hall. The entrance, which puts one between the two halls, is along the sides and is defined by a broad horizontal porch that allows one to drive up and load and unload. Apart from stepped horizontal molding over the entrance that marks off the levels of the balconies inside, the building is extraordinarily mute about its use and relies on its shape alone to convey its purpose.

In 1925 Saarinen was asked to design the campus of the Cranbrook Educational Center, which came to house the Cranbrook Academy of Art, an art and design school founded in 1932. It was based on an arts-and-crafts model, with an emphasis on master craftsmen working alongside student apprentices. Saarinen was also asked to become the first head of the school and his wife Loja the head of the school's department of weaving. The plan, loosely monastic in feel, ranges from the austere and formal to the more sensual and intimate. Though the arts-and-crafts sensibility to surface and form is apparent, the detailing is crisp and modern.

18.52 Facsimile of Saarinen's wash drawing of Kleinhans Music Hall

18.53 **Beirut Municipal Building, Lebanon**

### Lebanese Modernism

At the conclusion of World War I, the Ottoman Empire was split at the Treaty of Versailles into four mandated territories. The rest of the Ottoman territories, aside from Turkey, were assigned to monarchies, such as that of Saudi Arabia. The British controlled Palestine and Iraq, while the French controlled Lebanon and Syria under the League of Nations mandates.

Lebanon, under the French mandate, is a fascinating example of the complexities of emerging modernism. Beirut's Municipal Building (1924) is eclectic and hearkens back to the cosmopolitanism of Ottoman Beirut. Its architect, Yusuf Aftimous, had been municipal architect during the Ottoman period when municipal governance, particularly late in the 19th century, had been an important institution. Aftimous's design utilized a Beaux-Arts style plan that rationalized an ethos of modernist simplicity. Its facade, constructed of hand-carved yellow limestone that had become compulsory for all new construction in the area, was articulated by a blend of ornamental styles. A series of advancing and receding facades corresponds to the functions behind them.

Beirut's Parliament (1930–34), built after the Municipal Building, turned into a stronger display of local and regional ornamental designs in an attempt to cast the building in a decidedly Lebanese nationalist rather than a post-Ottoman mold. (Emir Fakhr ad-Din II, 1586–1635, who resisted the Ottomans, is considered to be the father of Lebanese nationalism.) Various elements were incorporated into the facade of the building, such as an arch composed of yellow-colored local brickwork and, on either side of the portal, long thin windows that terminate with two *muqarna*-like motifs.

18.54 **Beirut Parliament Building, Lebanon**

At the same time, Auguste Perret was brought in from Paris to design the St. George Hotel (1930–2) in collaboration with Antoine Tabet, a local architect, intellectual, political activist, and former disciple of Perret. The rectangular hotel building was constructed with concrete and articulated as a horizontal mass. The building's forms follow its functions, with the bottom floors housing the central reception areas and the restaurant, while the upper floors contain the hotel rooms.

18.55 Esther Cinema, Tel Aviv, Israel

### Israeli Modernism

During the British mandate in Palestine (1920–48), modern architecture became the dominant style among Jews living in the area. Initially, their search for national expression was inspired by oriental imagery and traditional Palestinian crafts. This so-called "oriental eclecticism" was, however, eventually replaced by modernist experiments, most notably by Richard Kauffmann in his rural and town planning designs, which laid the groundwork for the infrastructure of later Zionist settlement projects. Modernism in this case was associated not only with socialist-religious idealism but also with the search for a tabula rasa free from past memories of the Jewish diaspora. Modern architecture's claim to be founded not on cultural but on natural parameters, such as heat, wind, light, topography, and materials was seen as a symbolic incentive for the New Jew.

The rise of fascism in Europe sent several modernists to Palestine in the 1930s. Erich Mendelsohn, Alexander Klein, and Adolf Rading consolidated and diversified Zionist and modernist concepts. Mendelsohn's architecture—for instance, his Hadassah University Medical Center on Mount Scopus in Jerusalem (1936–9)—consists of firmly grounded plain volumes, courtyards, and carefully punched blank walls. It was invested with an abstracted, quasi-oriental imagery, in opposition to whitewashed international modernist architecture, such as Zeev Rechter's Engle House in Tel Aviv (1933).

The transition to Israeli statehood (1948) was followed by a massive modernization project, the blueprint of which was prepared by the state planning division headed by Arieh Sharon, a Bauhaus disciple of Hannes Meyer. Sharon's designs returned to a strict rational modernism, visually cleansed of oriental symbolism. This soon fell under the criticism of younger Israeli-born architects, who challenged their modernist training, seeking instead ways to reestablish communal identity and visceral ties with the past. Aligning themselves with post–World War II criticism, particularly the teaching of Team X and Louis Kahn, their modern architecture sought local expression in shaded communal spaces, hierarchical layouts, broken volumes, and local building materials as was evident in the early example of Ram Karmi's Negev Center (1960).

18.56 Hadassah University Medical Center, Mount Scopus, Jerusalem, Israel

18.57 House of German Art in Munich, Germany

18.58 The Zeppelin Tribune, Nuremberg, Germany

### Nazis

By the mid 1930s, modernist architecture had begun to develop along different tracks. Turkey and Brazil were the first to adopt it as a an extension of nationalist politics. In Europe, we encounter private sector modernism in the form of villas and houses. There are also examples from the public sector in the form of social housing but mainly in places that were controlled by left-leaning governments, as in Vienna (during the period from 1919 to 1934) and in the USSR. Though the fascist regimes in Germany and Italy were outspoken in their condemnation of communism, their take on modern architecture was neither uniform nor totally negative. The strongest attack on modern architecture came from the Nazis, even though the ground was laid well before the 1930s. In fact, it is safe to say that once modernism began to be identified with a particular set of aesthetic ideas, in the mid- to late1920s, it brought forth just as many critics as adherents.

In 1933, when the Nazis came to power, the new government began a systematic purging of academic institutions but stayed clear, at first, of dictating issues relative to style. Though no modernist architects were imprisoned, none received any commissions after 1933. Gropius eventually went to teach at Harvard University in 1937, and Mies went to Chicago to become the director of architecture at the Illinois Institute of Technology.

Despite the overwhelming ideological importance assigned to architecture by the Nazis, its architectural production proved to be inconsistent and quite varied. Adolf Hitler, who had once nursed ambitions of being a painter, took a great interest in architecture and set out guidelines on the matter, such as the need for German art to be "clear" and heroic and for buildings to be made for eternity. Yet Nazi party members held widely differing views.

One of Hitler's favorite architects was Paul Ludwig Troost (1879–1934), whose House of German Art in Munich (begun in 1933) had a blocked mass and flat surface free of ornament, save the bare necessities, to evoke a classical building. It was fronted by a long porch of columns, as if standing in sharp military order. The enormous Zeppelinfeld by Albert Speer (1905–81), designed as part of a vast party headquarters complex, maintained those ideas. It attempted to fuse the principle of modernist clarity with the proportional logic from antiquity. Speer went on, as Hitler's personal architect, not only to design the New Chancellery Wing of the government but also to make the plans for the redesigning of Berlin in a way that Hitler thought suitable for a new superpower. The plan featured a wide and long boulevard cutting through the city with an enormous vaulted hall at the apex of the composition. Only a few buildings were ever built and most were removed after World War II.

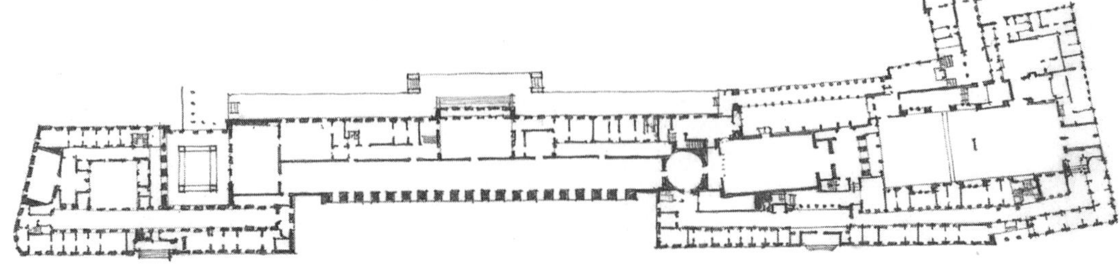

18.59 Plan: New Chancellery Wing, Berlin, Germany

**18.60 Palace of Italian Civilization, EUR, Rome**

**Italian Fascist Architecture**

With the end of the First World War, Italian architecture entered a new phase of self-awareness, especially in light of the rise of Fascism following Benito Mussolini's coup in 1922. Due to the strong nationalistic impulse at the core of Fascist ideology, Italian architects found themselves reflecting upon the role of tradition in their architecture, but this return to tradition with its links to national romanticism had a very different character in Italy than in Germany. The implementation in Italy of a vast state-sponsored building program that included the construction of post offices, train stations, civic buildings, and even small towns placed the Italian situation closer in spirit to Turkey. For many architects, the Fascist critique of passivity was translated into a legitimation of modernism. Italian Fascist architecture, therefore, did not see itself as antithetical to the clean geometries and white surfaces of modern architecture. There was, however, a fierce debate over the precise style that was to be most representative of the Fascist ethos. As a result, the avant-garde ideal of merging life and art fused in Italy with the sinister ambitions of totalitarianism, with artists and architects drawing numerous parallels between Mussolini and the condottieri of the Renaissance and beyond that to the Roman empire. Members of the Italian Movement for Rational Architecture (MIAR), founded in 1928, hoped to find inspiration in Greco-Roman classicism as well as the vernacular traditions of the Mediterranean region.

Some of the most significant examples of large-scale urban renewal requiring demolition in Rome, Milan, Turin, Bergamo, and Genoa were overseen by Mussolini's architect, Marcello Piacentini. He was also responsible for two significant new urban schemes: Città Universitaria (1932–35) and the Esposizione Universale di Roma (EUR) (1937–42), originally intended as the site of the 1942 Universal Exposition in Rome. The onset of World War II eclipsed plans for the exposition, but several pavilions were realized, including Ernesto La Padula's metaphysical and iconic Palace of Italian Civilization (1937–40). It was a glass box protected from the outside by facades that consisted of six registers of identical arched openings clad in travertine.

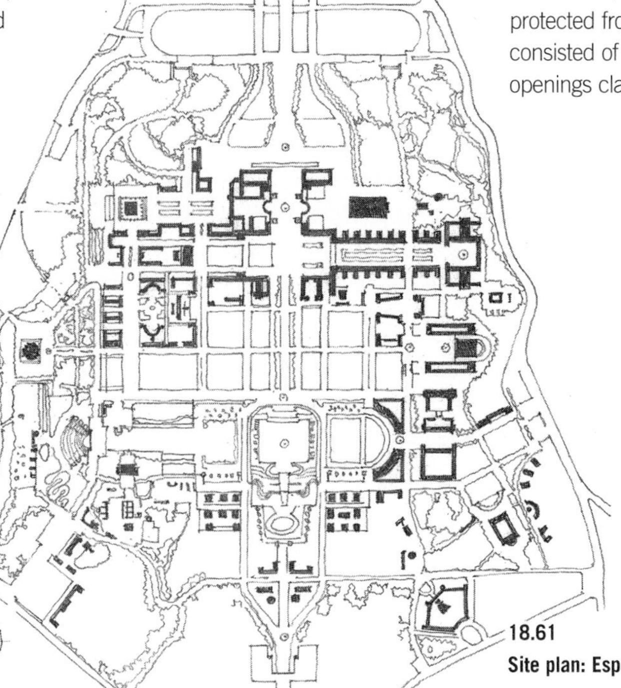

**18.61 Site plan: Esposizione Universale di Roma (EUR)**

18.62 **Casa del Fascio, Como, Italy**

Casa del Fascio

Interior-exterior mustering

Area for outside rallies

Rally area for 100,000 people

18.63 **Site plan: Casa del Fascio**

### Casa del Fascio

Among the many representatives of the modernist movement in Italy, Giuseppe Terragni (1904-43) was certainly the most prominent. He studied architecture at the Milan Polytechnic and became a member of Grupp 7, founded in 1926, which consisted of seven architects unified in their advocacy of rationalism and fascism. Terragni's Casa del Fascio (1933–6) in Como, designed as the regional headquarters of the Fascist Party, is not, despite its white boxy form, as ahistorical as it appears, for it fuses the model of the socialist meeting hall with the principle of an Italian palazzo in its courtyard plan. The building was designed as a "house of glass," which is more apparent from the inside than the outside. Some 20 percent of its surface is glass, with large windows framing various aspects of the city and its silhouette. This sense of openness was meant to be seen as a symbol of the Fascist claim that the leaders and the people were part of a single continuum. Thus the array of glass doors between the piazza and the atrium could be swung open on special occasions. The argument extended to the use of glass. The meeting room of the Directorio Federale (provincial directorate), for example, overlooks the central atrium through a glass wall.

Though today modern openness is almost expected, this was quite a novelty at the time. The spiritual core of the building was the Sacrario, located to the left of the entrance foyer, dedicated to the Fallen for the Revolution. The building, technically a meeting hall, thus had a quasi-religious function.

The organization of the building is simple. An exposed gridded balcony or loggia faces onto the large piazza, with the balcony allowing the leaders to address the crowds inside and outside at the same time. The ceiling of the entrance foyer was covered with black marble and the walls were in red granite in the form of an open *cella*. To heighten the sense of funerary religiosity, Terragni made the floor level of the Sacrario slightly lower than that of the atrium. The main hall reads like a kit of parts—with the columns holding up large concrete beams on which are placed horizontal louvres that filter in light—but with a gap in the center that brings in direct daylight.

Unlike Le Corbusier's idea of architecture, which favored column grids, thin walls, and horizontal windows, Terragni created a complexly layered geometric architecture that allowed the building to be axial in approach and entry and yet have an interior that can be defined as a series of interpenetrating asymmetries that fit together as in a puzzle.

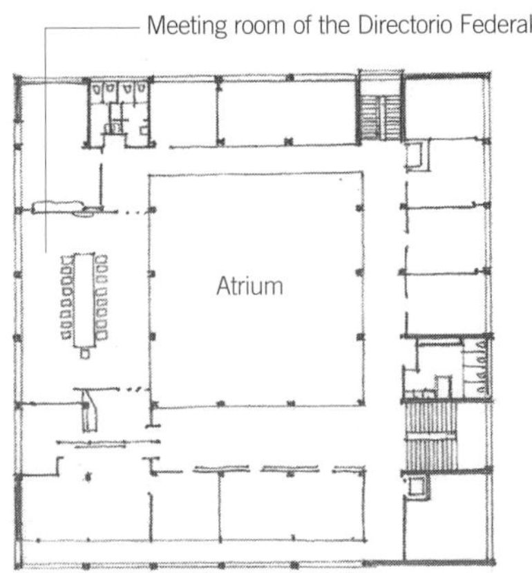


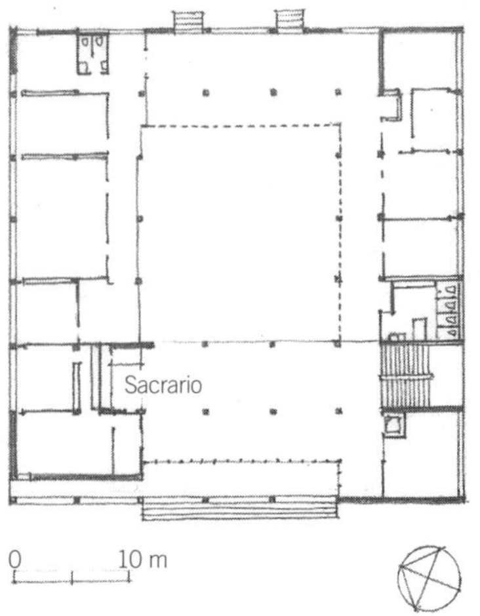


18.64 **Ground- and first-floor plans: Casa del Fascio**

18.65 **IIT Library Building, Chicago, Illinois, USA**

18.66 **Crown Hall, IIT**

### IIT Library Building

The Illinois Institute of Technology (IIT) in Chicago was created in 1944 out of two smaller institutions, one of which was the Armour Institute of Technology, a small technology school to which Ludwig Mies van der Rohe had been appointed as head of the architecture department. With limited means, Mies laid out one of the first truly modern campuses in the United States. They were all steel buildings with brick and glass infill. For Mies steel and glass represented not only the authenticity of technology but also of modern times and, indeed, following the Allied victory of World War II, the spiritual legitimation of modernity.

Mies laid out the campus on a 24-foot grid. This was the first time he used a modular system, and it was more for practical reasons than ideological. Twenty-four feet matched the dimension of the standard U.S. classroom, and modularity also made for uniform and cheaper buildings. The grid system also guaranteed that if only a part of the campus was constructed, future architectural unity could be preserved. The buildings were all rectangular and more or less of the same height but varied in shape, according to program.

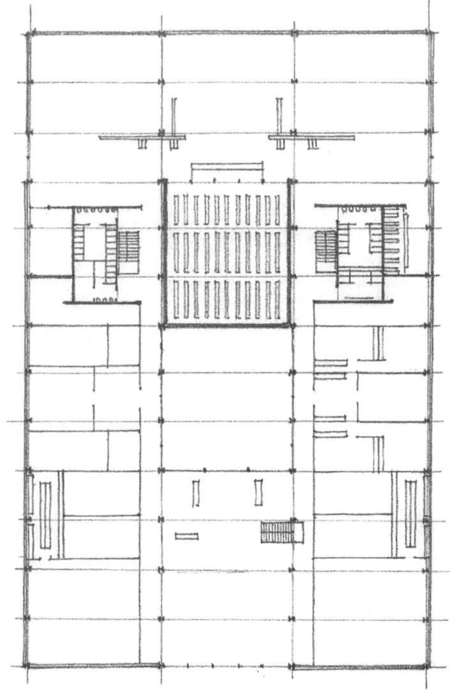

18.67 **Main-floor plan: IIT Library Building**

A new type of space became central to Mies's aesthetics. In the earlier decades, spaces flowed along walls and columns. It was compressed here, expanded there. His interest now changed to large, vacuous spaces defined by a simple symmetry of form and bounded at the perimeter by columns conceived in rigorous geometrical order.

Mies fully realized the potential of these ideas in the plans for his unbuilt Library Building (1942–3), roughly 100 by 70 meters in dimension and a lofty 8 meters high in interior elevation. Mies did not abandon his notion of a core, however, formed here by the book stacks placed in a square toward one end of the building and flanked by bathrooms and stairs. The solid mass of the stacks was contrasted by an open courtyard. In front of that, there was an interior waiting room. The plan was flexible but not "free" in the Le Corbusian sense. It was layered, thickened, and thinned as one progressed into the building. Since this could be regarded as a one-story building, the fire code permitted the use of unencased steel, allowing Mies to reveal the structural elements inside and out with maximum clarity. Mies elaborated on the theme in the Crown Hall at IIT (1950–6) and later in his career at the National Gallery in Berlin (1962–7).

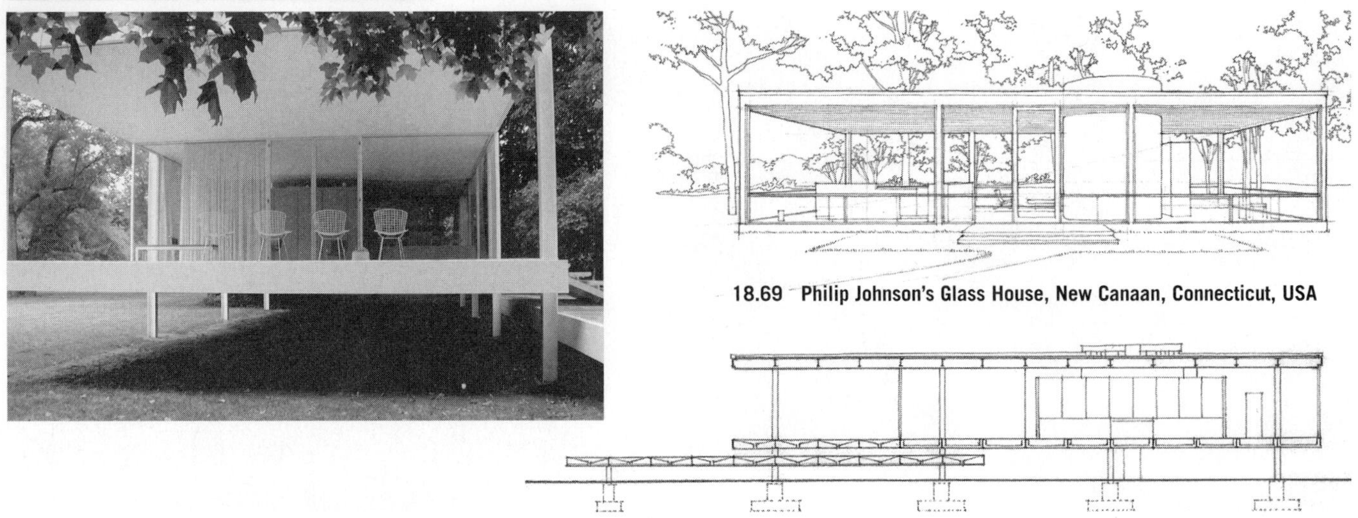

18.69 Philip Johnson's Glass House, New Canaan, Connecticut, USA

18.68 Farnsworth House, Plano, Illinois, USA

18.70 Section: Farnsworth House, Plano, Illinois

**Farnsworth House**

Of Mies van der Rohe's few commissions for private residences, the best known was the Farnsworth House (1946–51) in Illinois. Because the site, not far from a river, was prone to flooding, Mies elevated the house 2.2 meters above ground level. Entrance was gained by a broad flight of steps interrupted by a large open podium. Two sets of four columns support a roof cantilevered at both ends. There are no walls but rather sheets of glass between the columns that span from floor to ceiling. The plan, as was typical for Mies, had a core as well as perimeter glass walls, and in this case, there were neither interstitial walls nor structure apart from the exterior columns. In that sense, it lacked an important element of Mies's architecture, namely defined space itself. The house borrowed this, however, from the surrounding landscape in the form of an outdoor antespace with its own terrace. The floors are made of travertine, and the steel frame is painted white, creating a sense of grace and refinement. The curtains were of natural shantung silk and the woodwork of teak.

Despite the difficulties of living in the Farnsworth House, it became the model for several other experiments, the most notable being the private residence designed by Philip Johnson on his estate in New Canaan, Connecticut (1949). Though similar in its openness, the Johnson house was far more successful. Placed on a low plinth, its connection to the landscape was much more intimate. Furthermore, unlike Mies's steel building, Johnson used steel for the posts but the roof was of wood, which was significantly easier to construct and repair. Johnson separated the bathroom core from the kitchen, which he reduced to the level of furniture, whereas Mies included kitchen and bathroom in the core. A generation later, the Farnsworth House was also a major reference point in the minimalist houses of the Australian Glenn Murcutt.

In a sense, however, Mies's most iconic contribution was in the field of institutional architecture. His steel and glass skyscraper, as articulated in the Seagram Building in New York City (1954–8), was readily adopted as the symbol of U.S. corporate identity after World War II.

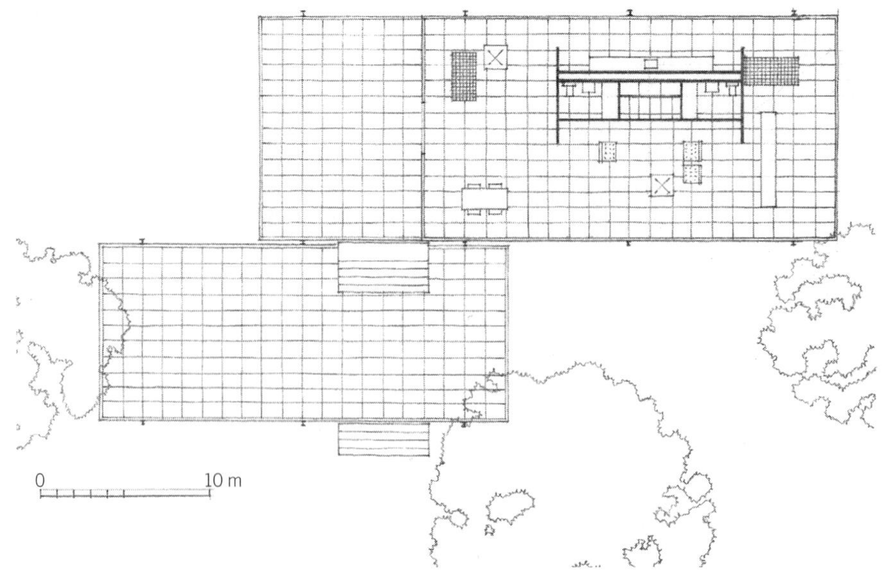


18.71 Plan: Farnsworth House

18.72 Eames House, Pacific Palisades, California, USA

18.73 Eames House

### Eames House

John Entenza (1905–84), editor of the influential Los Angeles-based *Arts and Architecture* magazine, was an important but much-overlooked sponsor of modern architecture in America, bringing the works of many artists and architects to public attention. To combat the housing shortage after World War II, he started a drive to assemble well-designed houses rapidly and cheaply, using wartime technologies and materials. To speed his project along, he invited architects in January 1945 to construct prototype houses in Los Angeles to explore the feasibility of this idea. Of the 24 houses completed by 1966, one of the most innovative was a project by Charles Eames and Ray Eames, a husband-and-wife team who designed the house as a residence for themselves. Born in St Louis and trained in architecture at Washington University, Charles had taught in Michigan where, at the Cranbrook Academy of Art, he met Eero Saarinen, with whom he entered a competition project, Organic Design in Home Furnishings, that was sponsored by the Museum of Modern Art in New York City.

For the Entenza project, the Eames initially had in mind a pristine Mies-like cube standing on two slender steel columns, cantilevered out from the slope of a hillside lot. However, in 1947, the Eames decided to build the house more to conform to their personal lifestyle. Still using the same amount of steel, they designed it to enclose more space. The new house, anchored by a retaining wall, nestles against the hillside, parallel to its contours, making it a statement as much about the site, the location, and the inhabitants, as about the deployment of prefabricated industrial materials. Their house featured extremely thin steel framing, with exposed corrugated metal roofing; the building consisted of 18 bays, 2.3 meters wide, 6 meters long, and 5 meters high, which determined the rhythm of the structure. Glazed panels—transparent, opaque, or translucent, as the situation demanded, and occasionally interrupted by painted panels in bright, primary colors—appeared to be an homage to Mondrian. The windows were operable at midlevel, and sliding doors connected to and integrated the courtyard. Grass, plants, and trees surround the building on all sides.

The Eames used the building as a backdrop for the collection of items they had accumulated from around the world. They made a film called *House after Five Years of Living*, implying that their house was not so much a designer display but an organic organism with the patina of lived-in existence that reflects the character and preferences of the inhabitants. Other than designing plans for houses, the Eames designed exhibitions, made films, and built toys and furniture. One of their earliest successes was a technique for bending plywood, which was used in World War II field hospitals for making leg splints and, later, for chair seats. They also designed a chaise lounge and ottoman manufactured by the Herman Miller Company, for which they also designed a headquarters building. Their films were experimental and conceptual; their best known film, *Powers of Ten*, attempted to show a post-Einsteinian universe.

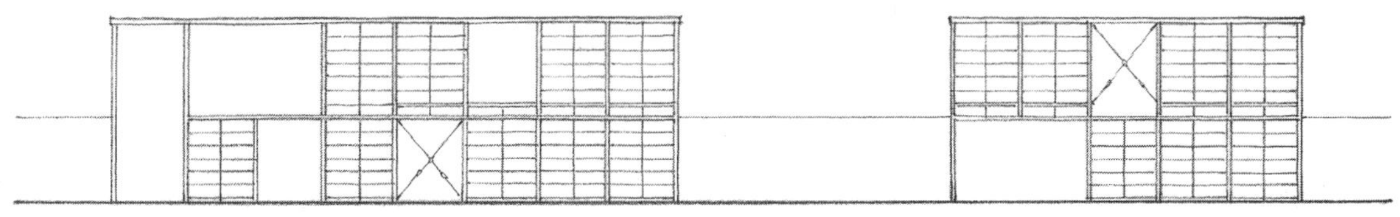

18.74 Elevation: Eames House

**18.75 Guggenheim Museum, New York City**

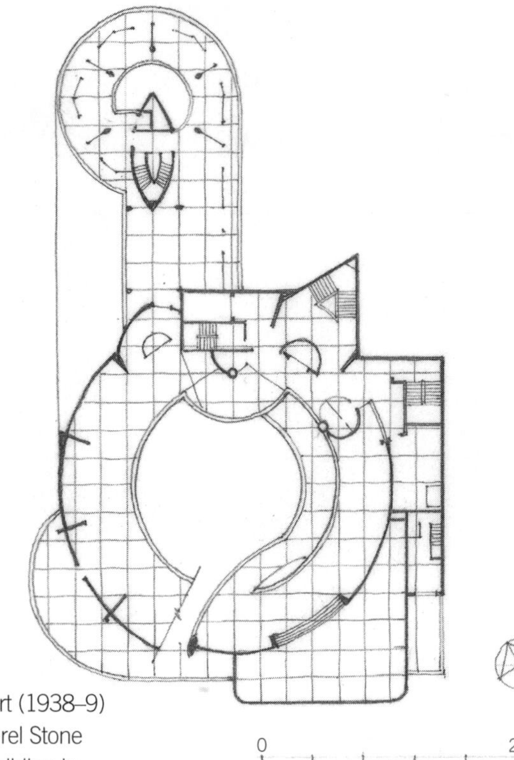


**18.76 Upper floor plan: Guggenheim Museum**

### Guggenheim Museum

After World War II, modern architecture's insistence on a rationalized functional aesthetic ran up against the more emerging need to express monumentality, particularly in large civic structures. Frank Lloyd Wright's design for the Guggenheim Museum (1956–9) in Manhattan, New York, was particularly innovative in this respect, with its large symbolic space at its center. The sides of the building are fully occupied by a gently spiraling ramp, designed to allow visitors to view art continuously without interruption. It also, of course, enabled everyone viewing the art to be seen, an idea close to the sensibility of Charles Garnier's Paris Opera House. The ramp, expanding in diameter as it ascends, generates the external profile of the Guggenheim, contrasting sharply with the rectilinear geometry of Manhattan blocks. Wright defended the spiral by arguing that abstract art no longer needed to be seen in the traditional framework of rooms and walls. But as innovative and controversial as Wright's exhibition ideas were, there is no debate about the building's impressive central space. Accessed virtually directly from the street, the space was conceived as an extension of the building's urban site. In that respect it constituted an important breakthrough in the relationship between modernism and civic space.

Though the Museum of Modern Art (1938–9) by Philip Goodwin and Edward Durel Stone was technically the first modern building in New York, the Guggenheim was the first truly modernist civic structure of the city.

The project went through several permutations. At first the building was to be a type of private gallery, showing the works of Solomon R. Guggenheim, but later in 1952 the museum expanded its definition to become something much broader, rivaling the Museum of Modern Art as an institution of experimentation and tastemaking across the whole range of modern art. The new expanded program forced Wright to make changes and concessions, but he did not change his stance that flat paintings would be well served by hanging against curving walls. The positive public reception of the building offset complaints by curators and painters.

**18.77 Section: Guggenheim Museum**

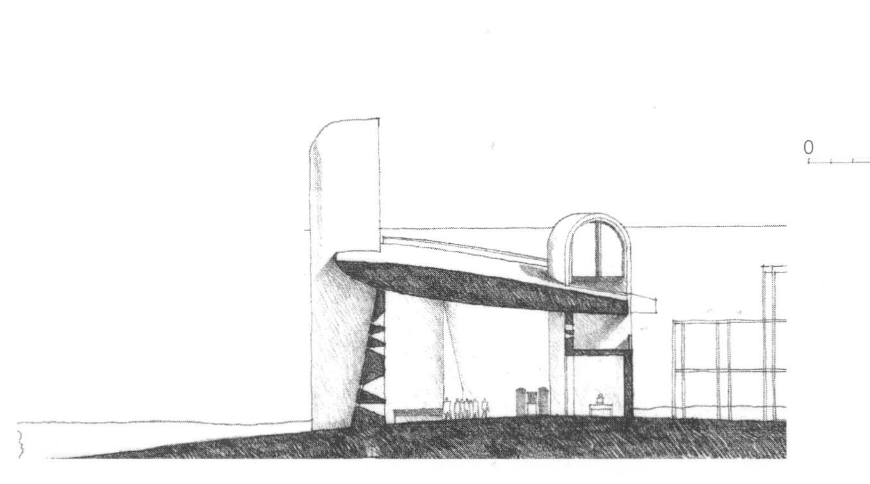

18.78 **Section: Notre Dame de Haut, Ronchamp, France**

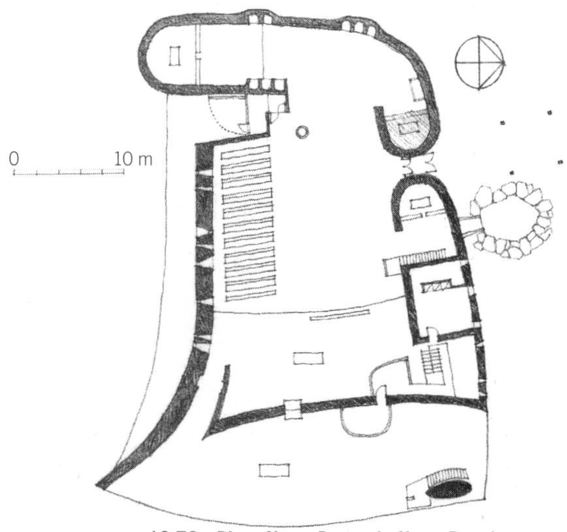


18.79 **Plan: Notre Dame de Haut, Ronchamp**

**Chapel at Ronchamp**

Le Corbusier accepted two commissions from religious institutions: one was for a chapel for Notre Dame de Haut at Ronchamp (1955), the other for a monastery at La Tourette near Lyon (1957–60), France. Although he personally was not a church-going Catholic, his work was imbued with a contemplative quality that made him a natural for these commissions. Corbusier's own work ethic was practically monastic and his office, at one end of his atelier in Paris, was frugal. Thus we find the monastery at La Tourette a stark cubic mass consisting of monk's cells, surrounding a traditional inner courtyard. The finish is raw concrete. The church on the north side of the plan, with its simple rectangular body, has an air of grandeur and mystery. Light filters into the interior by means of carefully placed conical funnels, the insides of which are painted in bright colors.

The church is better understood in light of the Ronchamp chapel. In this edifice, singular and memorable, Le Corbusier perhaps left his most expressive testament. The hilltop chapel, with its sweeping curves, brilliant white walls, and deep shadows, is a stunning object in the gently rolling landscape.

Fundamentally, the reinforced concrete chapel is a sculpture, a carefully conceived assemblage of forms. Its principal design element is the curve deployed repeatedly to form a dramatic set of intersections and trapped spaces. Three continuous walls, changing direction, thickness, and height, create a volume that defies the conventional expectations of facade and interior. Two convex curves bulge out on the north and west, creating a backside, while two concave indents to the south and east, represent the front. On top of the walls, on columns hidden in the walls, there floats a thick roof that appears like the underside of a shallow bowl. From some perspectives, it appears to be the bottom of a cushion.

18.80 **Notre Dame de Haut, Ronchamp**

Three towers, clustered together with hooded tops, rise above the roof, forming vertical counterpoints to the general horizontality and earth-boundness of the building. Light washes down into the inner space of these towers and spills into the inner sanctum. These towers serve as a chapel, a sacristy, and a baptistery. The west wall has a series of irregularly placed, punched-out windows of various sizes and depth that bring spots of intense light into the interior. Inside, the roof hangs like a cloth over the nave, while sloping gently to the south toward the altar. A statue of the Virgin Mary stands in an alcove in the eastern wall, designed so that it can be faced both outside and inside. The church is used as the backdrop to outdoor services on special occasions. Near the church, using stones from the site, Le Corbusier constructed a small stepped pyramid.

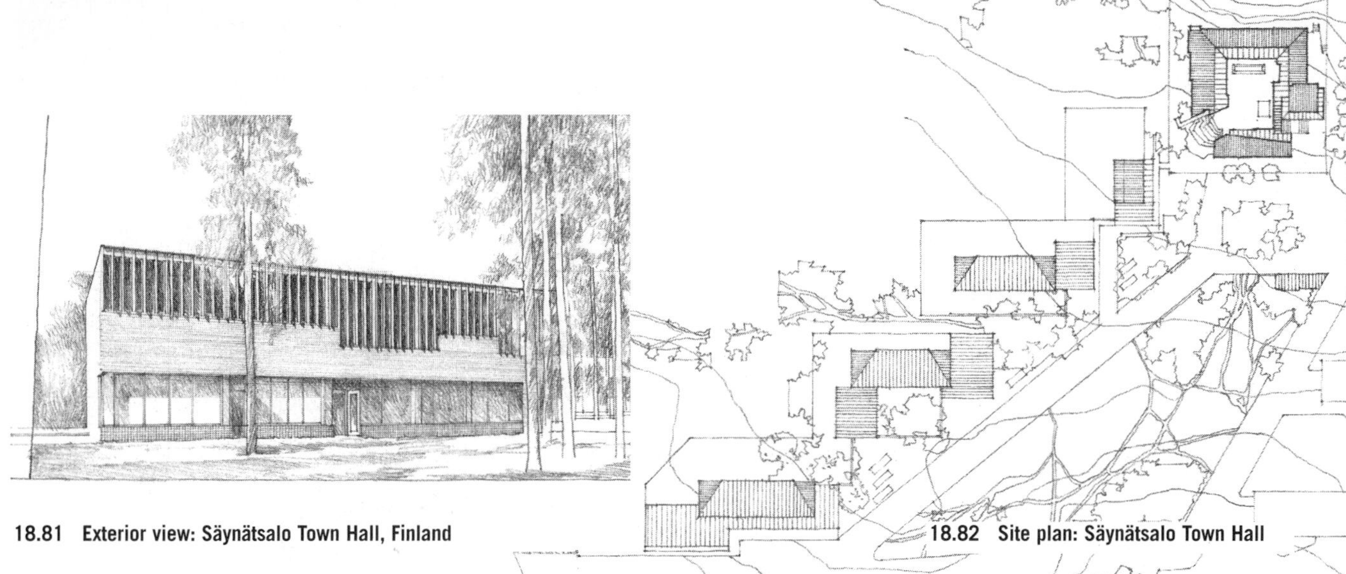

18.81 **Exterior view: Säynätsalo Town Hall, Finland**

18.82 **Site plan: Säynätsalo Town Hall**

### Säynätsalo Town Hall

By the time Alvar Aalto designed the Säynätsalo Town Hall (1949–52) in Finland, his reputation was secure and largely due to the acclaimed Finnish Pavilion at the Paris World's Fair in 1937. In this town hall he began to move away from the modernist-cubist complexity toward imageries that had fascinated him as a youth, with the courtyard a reference to both ancient Crete and medieval Italy. The space, for that reason, is less a courtyard than a civic enclave raised above the lower slope. One enters it at one corner by means of a staircase fractured to make it seem to be molded to the landscape. The council chamber is in view through the gap. Square in plan, it has a pitched roof that rises over the composition. The external surfaces are all in textured brick in Flemish bond. Aalto's design mixes attention to function with attention to the building's picturesque qualities. The staggers, angles, and shifts enhance the three-dimensional quality of the building as do the windows of different sizes and proportions. In some places, the brick, as it touches the ground, rests on black tiles that cover the foundation. In other places the brick floats effortlessly over the windows. There is no visible roof, apart from a razor thin line of dark flashing, making the volumes read more abstractly than if the roof were visible.

More modernist in flavor is the Seinäjoki Town Center (1958), which returns Aalto to the cubist play of volume and solid, and of frame and opening. The site consists of two parcels straddling a busy road. Aalto created an esplanade through the site, with the buildings defining and expanding its spatial elements.

0 10 m

18.83 **Plan: Säynätsalo Town Hall**

18.84 **Town Hall, Säynätsalo, Finland**

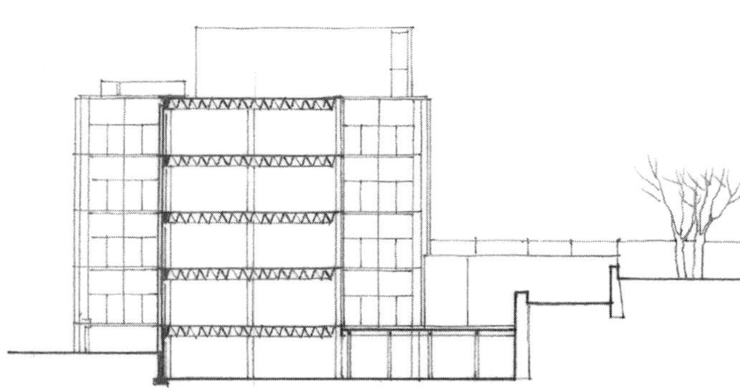

18.85 Section: Yale University Art Gallery

18.86 Yale University Art Gallery, New Haven, Connecticut

**Yale University Art Gallery**
Louis Kahn (1901–74), like Wright before him, developed an aesthetic somewhat outside of the developing norms of international modernism. But that does not mean that his work was not influenced by modernism and its drive to master abstraction. Unlike many who saw function as mainly a question of human usage, Kahn was intrigued by the interaction between humans and the technical systems that are an integral part of the architectural world. At the Yale University Art Gallery in New Haven, Connecticut (1951–4), Kahn even made a virtue out of the services. Electrical wiring, outlets, lighting fixtures, and ductwork are all open to the eye. The building's programmatic needs were organized by packaging them into cylinders and rectangles. The idea is not unlike the way Mies attempted to unify secondary program elements into a vertical spine, except that here they become almost sculptural. The uncompromising bluntness of the building foreshadows an aesthetic that came to be known as brutalism, which was to take root in the late 1960s.

Kahn went to the American Academy in Rome in 1950, followed by travels to Italy, Egypt, and Greece in 1951. His interest in Greek and Roman architecture should, therefore, not lead us to believe that he saw in that architecture the same values as historicists or that he was reactionary with respect to modernism. Rather, he saw in the ancient architecture an aesthetic of abstraction and a struggle to make the building hold its own against the overwhelming beauty of the landscape. He preferred the archaic and more stubby Temple of Paestum to the refined proportions of the Parthenon. His interest in monumentality was, therefore, not an interest in largeness but rather an awareness of the triangulated psychological space between viewer, building, and landscape. It did lead Kahn to use simple but arresting forms and even symmetries at a time when these would have been frowned upon by functionalists. This is certainly the case at the Salk Institute for Biological Studies (1959–65) in La Jolla, California, and at the National Assembly Building, Sher-e-Banglanagar, in Dacca, Bangladesh (1962–83). In both, the compacted formal unity is animated by individualized forms that seem to stand in a springlike tension with the overall design.

In Kahn's work space does not flow from one area to another, as with Eero Saarinen or Le Corbusier; it is rather assembled, like molecular units. The plan is not primarily a series of pointlike columns with thin walls defining space, but rather it is a building stamping its footprint on the earth. Kahn, however, continually downplayed entrances in his architecture, thus reinstating the need to enter and move around his buildings. There are symmetries but no axes.

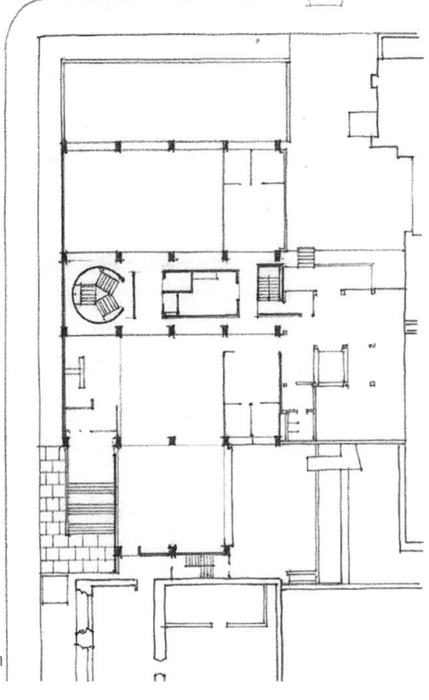


18.87 First-floor plan: Yale University Art Gallery

18.88 **Brasília, Brazil**

18.89 **Site plan: Brasília**

**Brasília**

In Brazil, modern architecture served as an expression of national identity and reached its zenith with the creation of Brasília in 1956 (inaugurated in 1960). A hinterland capital had been proposed for Brazil since the late 19th century as a way to shift focus from the coastal towns and create a geographically neutral center for the whole country. President Juscelino Kubitschek, who advocated rapid industrialization and who made the decision to go ahead with the new capital, invited the Brazilian-born-and-trained Oscar Niemeyer (1907–) to design the main buildings and, after a competition, Lúcio Costa to prepare the master plan.

Costa's plan, prepared for a city of half a million people, was based on the CIAM (Congres Internationaux d'Architecture Moderne) principles separating habitation, recreation, work, and circulation. Designed around two axes intersecting to form a cross, Brasília was an automobile city. Long high-speed roads, three multilane systems on each axis, with over and underpasses at intersections, were designed to enable rapid transportation.

A dam built across the River Paranoa created long finger lakes around the southern, eastern, and northern edges of a U-shaped plateau on which the city was located. Running east-west, bisecting the plateau was the main monumental axis of the city. On the north-south cross axis, arranged in a gentle curve to respond to the outline of the plateau, were the main residential units, the "superblocks," organized in three layers, with parking at the eastern edge. Each residential superblock, 240 by 240 meters, was conceived as a grouping of six-story apartment units, raised on *piloti*, with play space for children within. Nestled between the fingers of the lakes, in the north and south, were plots for private dwellings. Further inland to the west, the airport and the train station were located.

The functional, ceremonial, and visual focus of the city was the so-called Plaza of the Three Powers, at the eastern edge of the plateau. Approaching from the west, the eleven towers of the ministries start a grand procession, culminating in the rectangular blocks of the Foreign Ministry and the Treasury, beyond which, at the center of the axis, is the National Congress. This building is singular and unique in the history of modern architecture. It houses two major chambers, the larger one for the Chamber of Deputies and the smaller one for the Senate. The raked visitors' seating of the round Chamber of Deputies is expressed in the roofline in the form of an upward turned bowl. The senate chamber has a traditional dome over it. Together, the saucer and dome, lifted clear above the ground on a giant platform, make for a memorable skyline, self-consciously designed as the icon of Brasília. Below, in two stories, accessed by a ramp, are all the offices.

18.90 **Ministry of External Relations, Brasília**

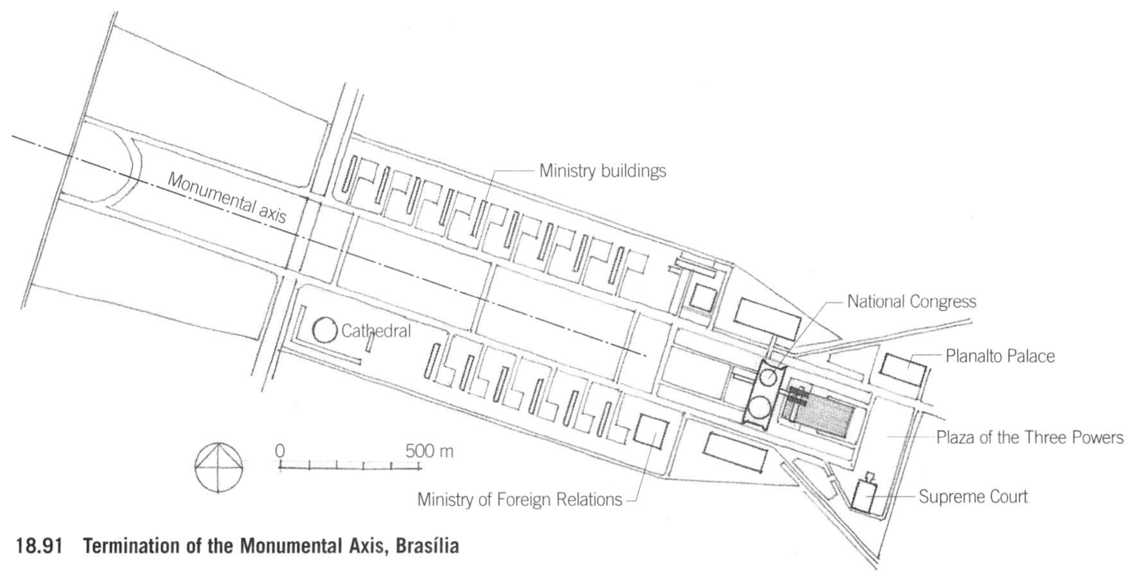


**18.91 Termination of the Monumental Axis, Brasília**

Further east, in line with the ramp, rise twin towers, linked by the walkway of the Secretariat. They sit in the middle of a rectangular reflective pool at the eastern edge of which is the climax of the whole complex, a gigantic plaza with the executive office of the president (the Planalto Palace) and the Supreme Court at either end. One of the multilane highways cuts through the Plaza, next to the Planalto Palace, connecting to the peripheral roads and the residence of the president, the Palácio da Alvorada, at the water's edge.

These three buildings together, all designed by Niemeyer, represent a monumentalization of the Brazilian national modern style. All three are concrete slab structures, glazed all around and sandwiched between deep overhanging roofs and floor slabs. In the Planalto Palace, a whole story lies below the ground slab, and in the other two buildings the ground slab lifts the main floor above the ground.

Within, the plans remind one more of Mies's precise geometries than Le Corbusier's sensuous curves. The colonnades lining the expressive edges of the buildings (always only on two opposite sides, except in the later foreign ministry building where they are on all four sides) were designed by Niemeyer as delicately wrought curvilinear forms, expressive less of their character as load-bearing members and more as tie beams stretched thin by tension, almost to the point of disappearing at their edges. (Joaquim Cardoso did the structural calculations.) In the Planalto Palace the colonnades face the plaza; in the Supreme Court, they are located toward the side; and in the Palacio da Alvorada (actually the first to be built), they are turned laterally, forming a string of inverted arches across the facade.

After World War II, Brazilian modern architecture became widely influential in the development of modern architecture around the world, though it began as derivative of European modernism. Brasília's foreign ministry building was the model for Lincoln Center in New York. Oscar Niemeyer was effectively the chief architect of the United Nations Headquarters (1947) building in New York City after Le Corbusier was removed from the project and Wallace Harrison appointed head of the United Nations Board of Design. Wallace Harrison's design of the Albany Civic Center (1962–8), one of the largest modernist-styled civic centers in the United States, was inspired by Costa's and Niemeyer's Plaza of the Three Powers in Brasília.

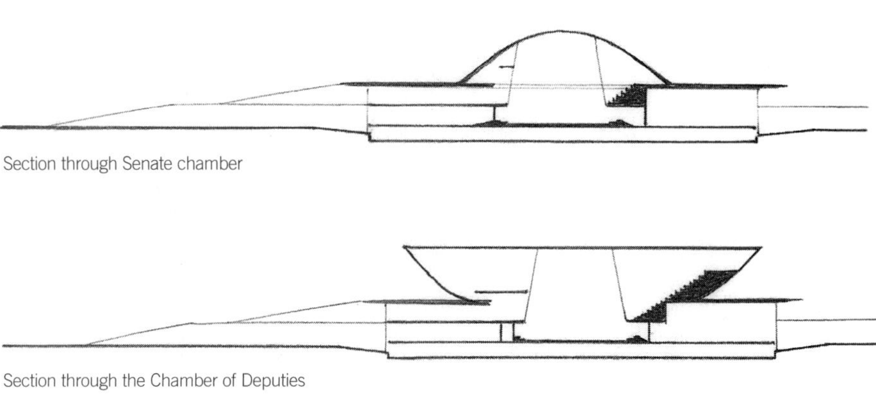


**18.92 National Congress, Brasília**

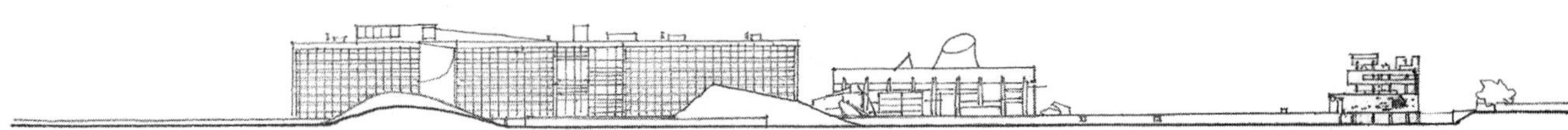

**18.93 Northwest elevation: Chandigarh, India**

## Chandigarh

When India attained independence in 1947 it was divided into two countries along religious lines, resulting in the creation of the new Islamic nation of Pakistan. In that division the Indian state of Punjab lost its capital, Lahore, to Pakistan, so Jawaharlal Nehru, the first prime minister of independent India, decided to construct a new capital, Chandigarh. Like Getulio Vargas and Juscelino Kubitschek, Nehru modeled his development plans on Franklin Delano Roosevelt's New Deal and initiated a series of state-sponsored industrialization projects. His sentiment was expressly antinostalgic. He wanted Chandigarh to be a "new city, unfettered by the traditions of the past, and a symbol of the nation's faith in the future."

When Le Corbusier joined the project in 1952, the urban plan had already been prepared by Albert Mayer, an American town planner, on the principles of the city-beautiful movement with superblocks accessed by gently curving roads. Le Corbusier shrunk the superblocks into 800 by 1200-meter rectangular neighborhood units or sectors, serviced by a diminishing hierarchy of roads and bicycle paths, according to CIAM principles.

Within these sectors, Le Corbusier wanted to design multistory residential units (perhaps like those in Brasília, or like his Unité d'Habitations, the first of which had just been constructed in Marseilles), but that idea was immediately dismissed by the officers in charge of the project who were committed to a low-rise suburban image, inspired in part by the sprawling cantonments the British had built for their officers in colonial India.

All the state housing, therefore, was done not by Le Corbusier but by his cousin, Pierre Jeanneret (who was the project architect), and the English husband-and-wife team, Maxwell Fry and Jane Drew (who had been working in Africa), assisted by a team of nine Indian architects and planners. Most of the construction was made of load-bearing exposed brick walls, accented by random rubble-stone porticoes and concrete window protectors, plastered and painted white.

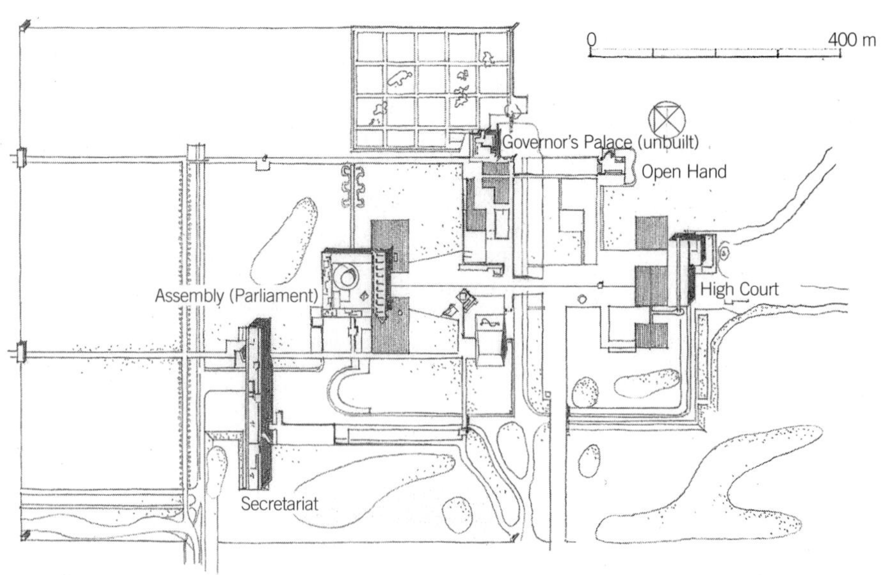


**18.94 Site plan: Chandigarh**

18.95 Secretariat, Chandigarh, India

18.96 High Court, Chandigarh

**Secretariat and High Court**

Le Corbusier invested all his energies in designing Chandigarh's Capitol Complex (1951–62), containing the High Court, Assembly, and Secretariat for the states of Punjab and Haryana, located at the northern end of the city in a vast open plain, bound visually only by the distant Himalayan foothills. The area of the plain is loosely defined by two adjoining 800-meter squares that contain within them two 400-meter squares. The vehicular roads are located somewhat below grade; the earth excavated from them was used to make the artificial hills that screen the Capitol from the rest of the city. A largely irregularly shaped pedestrian plaza, linking the Assembly and the High Court and studded with a set of symbolic follies, forms the conceptual center of the Capitol.

The High Court, first to be built, is contained within a tight frame with a second roof (with suspended arches) built above the first to provide shade. Three huge pylons create a monumental gateway. In front there are two reflecting pools that double the building. Its elevation has a vertical rhythm created by the divisions of the nine courts. The elevation, in fact, is almost the same as its plan. Indeed, with its inversion in the reflecting pools in front, the High Court's elevation conceptually spins around an imaginary axis on the ground plane. Although made of cast-in-place rough concrete, the High Court, like Neimeyer's Brasília buildings, appears lightweight and airy, particularly when reflected in the pools.

The Secretariat takes the form of a long slab, with a dramatic roofline. In the larger composition it functions as a backdrop to the Assembly. Having a long double-loaded corridor with a skillfully modulated curtain of concrete that serves as a *brise soleil* on both sides, the Secretariat was a restatement of Le Corbusier's collective living solution, the Unité d'Habitation. But while the Unité was raised on robust concrete *piloti*, the Secretariat appears firmly anchored to the ground, a manifestation of Le Corbusier's new, more engaged relationship to the ground plane.

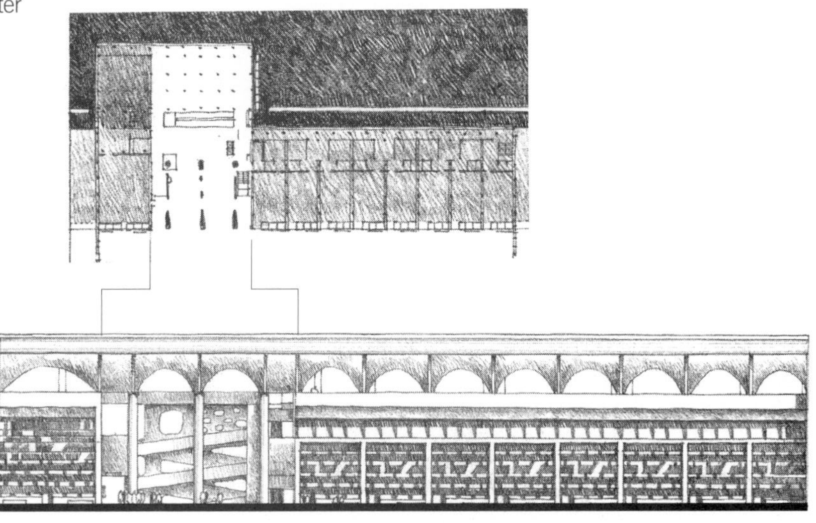

18.97 Plan diagram and elevation: High Court, Chandigarh

**18.98 Assembly Building, Chandigarh**

**Assembly Building**

Le Corbusier's design for the Assembly Building is decidedly more brutalist and primitivist inspired, no less by the innumerable sketches he made of the bulls in the Indian fields and the villages whose details he recorded studiously in his sketchbooks. On a trip to Ahmedabad in western India, Le Corbusier saw a hyperbolic paraboloid under construction for a thermal power station. Le Corbusier was mesmerized by the form and immediately decided to use it in the Assembly. At this time he was also working on several projects in France, all of which explored the sculptural possibilities of ruled surfaces, among them a temporary pavilion with the mathematician and musician Xenaxis. Le Corbusier literally dropped the hyperbolic paraboloid into the basic box he had earlier designed for the Assembly. Around it a forest of columns, rising high into a black ceiling, created the foyer. Three edges of the box were given to offices. Concrete *brise soleil* furnished the skin. On the fourth edge of the box, the side facing the plaza, Le Corbusier built a monumental portal, facing the portal of the High Court across the plaza. A row of thin pylons holds up a free-form roof that looks like the horns of a bull in outline. As built, the Assembly Building looks like a majestic bull standing firm on the vast Indian plain, quite the contrast to Neimeyer's palaces in Brasília, which barely touch the ground and seem to fly above it in defiance of gravity.

Mention must be made of the Open Hand Monument that Le Corbusier gifted to Chandigarh as its symbol. It stands in the Capitol, a 23-meter-high sculpture of burnished steel. While the aesthetic origins of the sculpture are diverse, Le Corbusier's most ambitious hope for the Open Hand was articulated by him in a letter to Nehru from 1955, when he proposed the Open Hand as a symbol of the Nonaligned Movement (NAM).

Nehru's brainchild, NAM, was an attempt to propose a third alternative to the divisive two-world theory (communist versus capitalist) of the Cold War. Although not adopted for NAM, the Open Hand as a symbol of Chandigarh, a city embodying Nehru's hopes for a modern India, still remains close to that ideal.

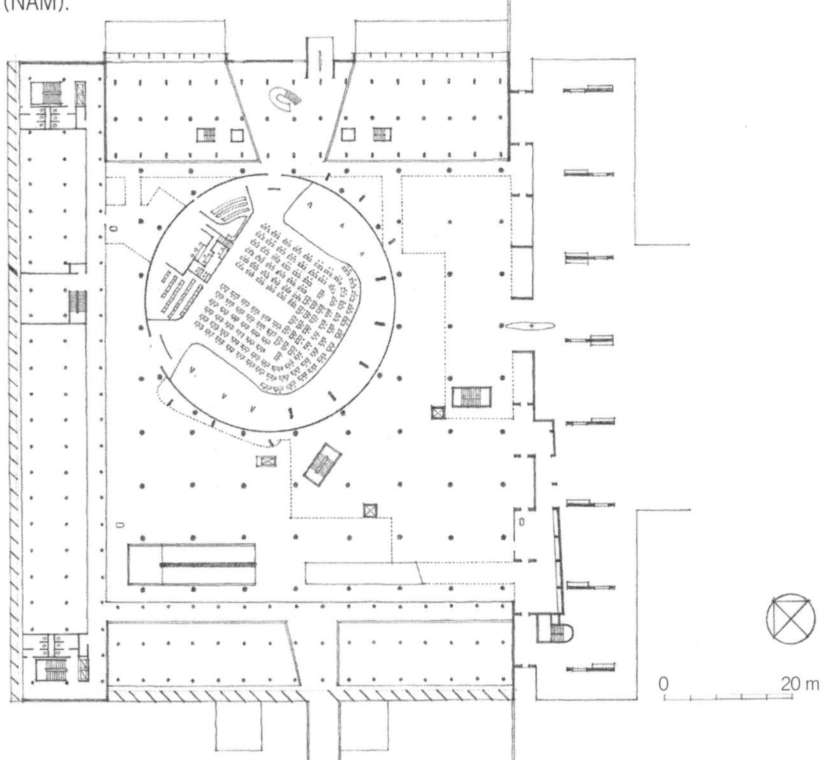


**18.99 Plan: Assembly Building, Chandigarh**

18.100 Millowner's Association Building, Ahmedabad, India

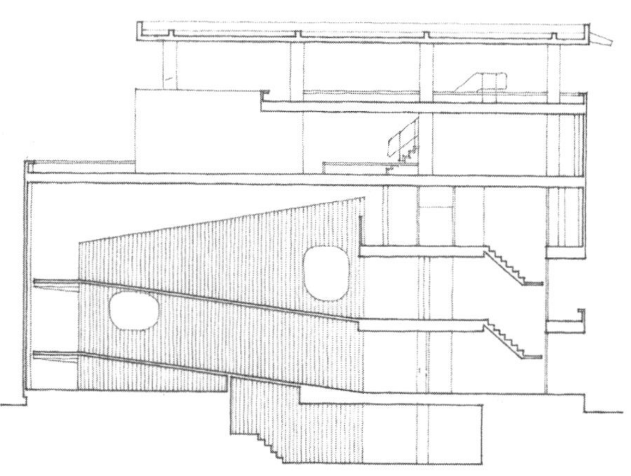

18.101 Section: Shodhan House, Ahmedabad, India

**Ahmedabad**

One of the Indian architects who admired Le Corbusier and had apprenticed in his atelier, Balkrishna Doshi, was at this time practicing in Ahmedabad, the textile capital of India. At Doshi's invitation, Le Corbusier designed the Shodhan and Sarabhai houses, a public museum, and the Millowner's Association Building in Ahmedabad. Constructed at the same time, in 1956, toward the end of Le Corbusier's life, the Shodhan and Sarabhai houses, along with the Millowner's Association Building, are skillful variations on Le Corbusier's older typologies and a succinct summary of some of his lifelong formal preoccupations. The Shodhan, Le Corbusier published, was a reinterpretation of the Villa Savoye, which makes sense in part because the Shodhan too has a central ramp around which the volumes are distributed, with an open terrace on the second floor. The Shodhan, however, transforms Villa Savoye's strip windows into muscular *brise soleil* and has a parasol roof, both of which have more in common with his solitary project in Argentina, the Maison Currutchet (1949).

By contrast, the Sarabhai House consists of parallel load-bearing brick walls with low, vaulted ceilings and a roof garden with a water slide spilling into a free-form swimming pool. Its lineage begins with Le Corbusier's 1919 Monol house, followed by a group of Mediterranean villas he designed in the late 1940s, the Roq and Rob project, the Feuter House, and the Jaoul House of 1953. In stark contrast with the upright volumes and the play of light and shade of the Shodhan, the Sarabhai House stays close to the ground and merges with the soil, especially as its roof garden has matured.

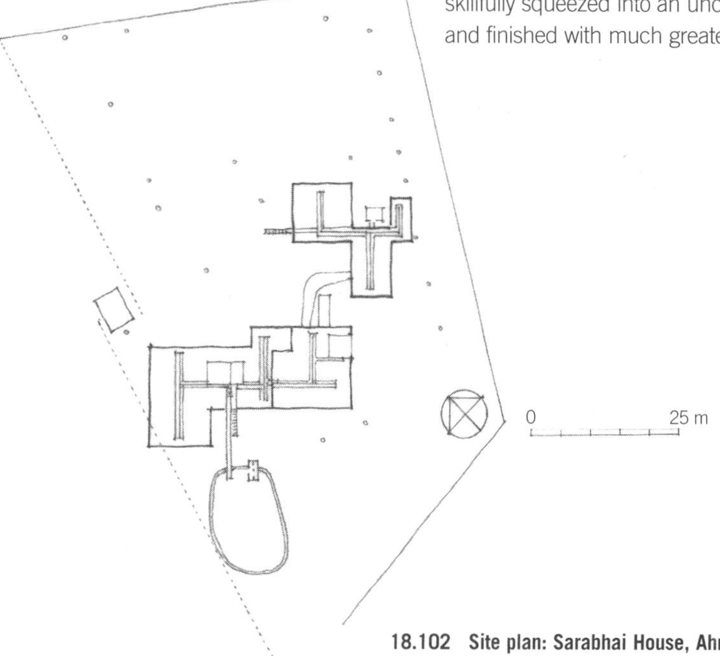


18.102 Site plan: Sarabhai House, Ahmedabad, India

Le Corbusier's Millowner's Association Building (1954) was his quintessential institutional statement, with a central ramp piercing midheight into the cubic volume of the main space. The north-south orientation made for the usual contrast between the *brise soleil* of the two sides, and within Le Corbusier unleashed a carefully orchestrated but exuberant interplay of free forms and multiple heights that produce a palpable feeling of an inhabited sculptural volume. Years later Le Corbusier was to redo the Millowner's Association Building for his solitary commission in the United States, the Carpenter Center for the Visual Arts, this time skillfully squeezed into an uncomfortable site and finished with much greater restraint.

**18.103 TWA Terminal, John F. Kennedy International Airport, New York City**

**18.104 TWA Terminal, John F. Kennedy International Airport**

**Eero Saarinen**

Born in 1910 in Finland, Eero Saarinen, Eliel Saarinen's son, injected poetry into the structural possibilities of reinforced concrete and steel construction. Eero Saarinen's career ended prematurely with his death in 1961; but in the short space of 11 years, he had already worked on nearly 30 projects in Europe and the United States, some of which would become international architectural icons and symbols of the United States' postwar identity as a technological superpower. Among these are the St. Louis Gateway Arch (1948–64), General Motors Technical Center (1948–56) in Detroit, Michigan, and TWA Terminal (1956–62) at New York's John F. Kennedy International Airport.

Eero Saarinen's competition winning entry for the Gateway Arch at St. Louis, Missouri (1947 competition; constructed 1961–66), was conceived as a huge arch located at the banks of the Mississippi River. It was designed as a symbolic gateway to the West and a way to revitalize the flagging economy of the city. Settling the West was a core element of the preindustrial American identity, and the arch, an achievement of industrial technology, was intended to commemorate the conquest of the West that began on the right bank of the Mississippi. A catenary curve, the Arch's span and rise are both 192 meters. It consists of a double skin of steel, stainless steel without and carbon steel within, reinforced where required by concrete. Each leg is an equilateral triangle, 16.5 meters to a side at the ground, that tapers off to 5 meters at the summit. The double walls are a meter apart at the base and about 20 centimeters apart above the 120-meter level. The interstitial space below the 90-meter mark is filled with reinforced concrete. Above that, steel stiffeners are used. A Museum of Westward Expansion is located at the ground level and a viewing deck at the top.

Saarinen's TWA terminal (1956–62) at New York's John F. Kennedy International Airport was conceived as a bird with wings spread and poised to take off, the two massive winglike forms soaring high to form the main terminal space. Saarinen designed the terminal almost entirely using modelling techniques and tactile interaction with the highly sculptural form, rather than drawing plans on paper. The structure is a combination of four barrel vaults, supported on four Y-shaped columns. Together they make an interior passenger terminal space 15 meters high and 96 meters long.

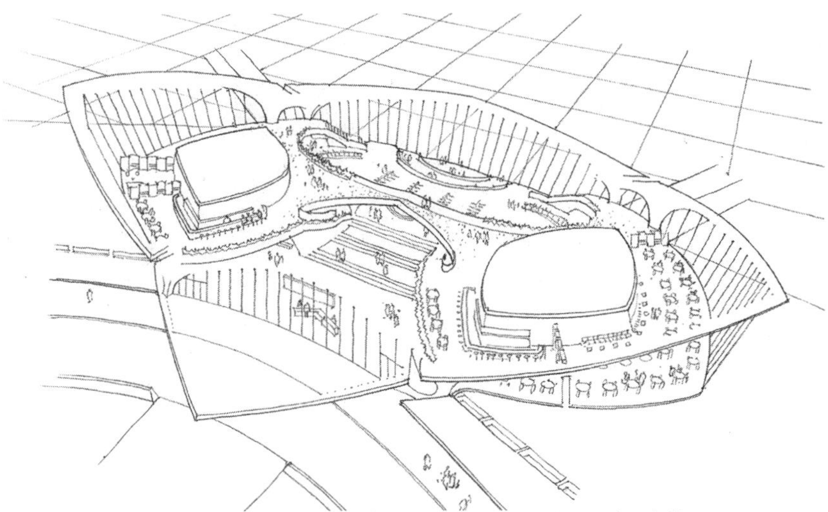

**18.105 Pictorial view: TWA Terminal, John F. Kennedy International Airport**

18.106 Sydney Opera House, Sydney, Australia

**Sydney Opera House**

European modernism was brought to Australia by Harry Seidler, who had studied with Walter Gropius at Harvard, but Seidler's seminal influence may have come from a summer he spent with Oscar Niemeyer in Brazil in 1948. The Seidler House (1947–8) was very much influenced by Brazilian-style modernism, whereas Seidler's Waks House (1949–50) was a restatement of Le Corbusier's 1920's villas.

The project that truly and dramatically catapulted Sydney into the international architectural stage was Jørn Utzon's design for the Sydney Opera House (1957–73). Located right on the water's edge, with the graceful curve of the Sydney Harbor Bridge as a backdrop, Utzon's prizewinning entry imagined a series of interlocking shells hovering above a vast stepped platform, simultaneously conjuring an image of sails and technological virtuosity.

Supported on 580 concrete piers sunk up to 25 meters below sea level, Utzon's original design conceived the project as a series of parabolas, but he later transformed them into ribs from a sphere of identical radii. The shells are sheathed in white ceramic tile and contain five performance spaces. Although Utzon never completed the project himself, it quickly became the signature project of Australia. And, indeed, it ushered in the era of expensive prestige buildings that served to enhance the image of a city or region. These buildings—and one thinks ahead to the Guggenheim Museum in Bilbao by Frank Gehry—were very much tied into the tourist economy. Prestige buildings also changed the tone of modernism and provided it a new legitimacy and purpose at the global scale.

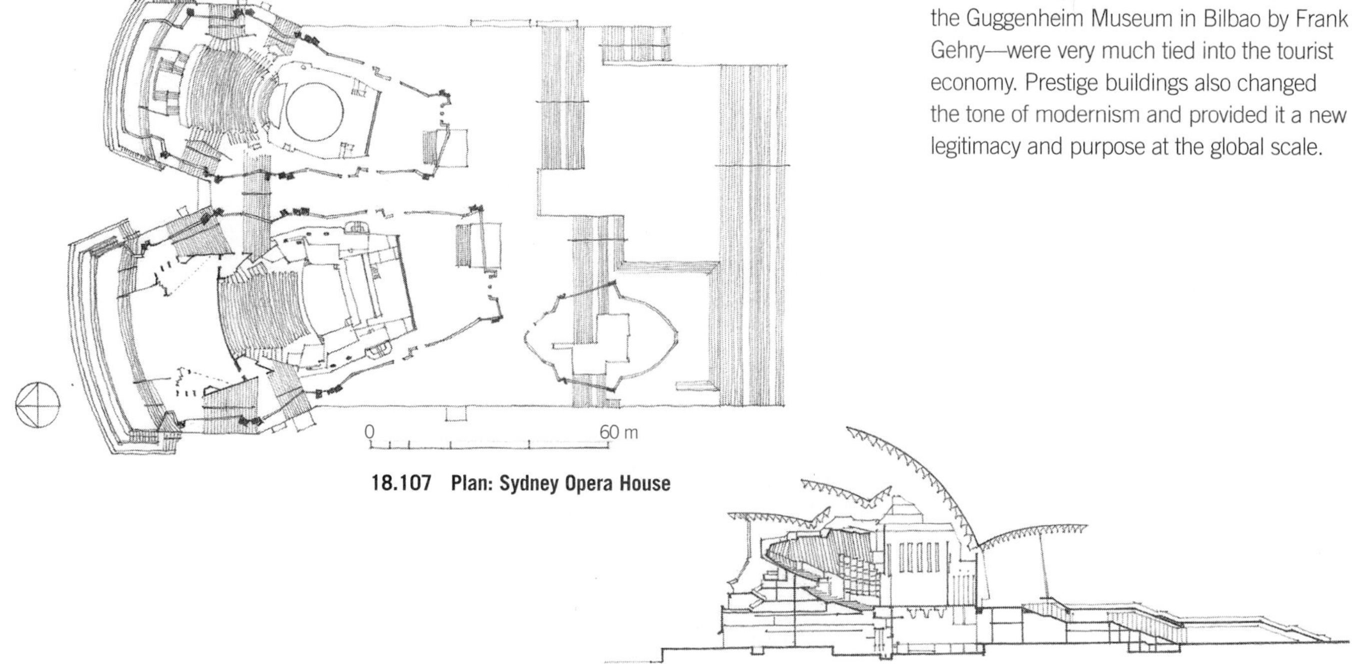


18.107 Plan: Sydney Opera House

18.108 Section: Sydney Opera House

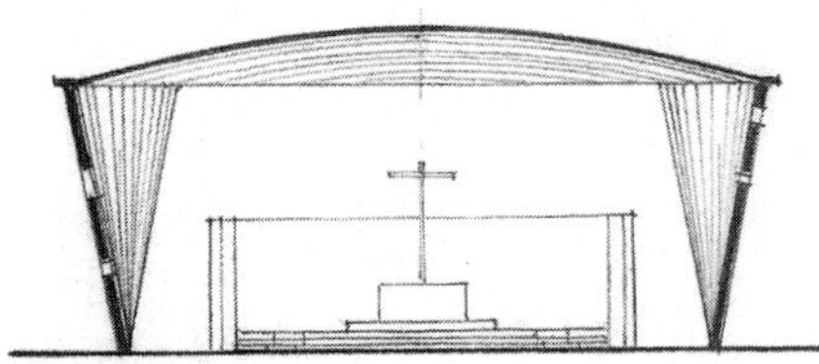

18.109 Section: Church of Christ the Worker, Atlántida, Uruguay

18.110 Church of Christ the Worker

**Uruguayan Modernism**

An instructive comparison with the high-tech structural achievements of the likes of Eero Saarinen and Utzon can be made with the work of Eladio Dieste, a Uruguayan architect practicing since the early 1960s. Uruguayan President Jorge Batlle and then the Batllistas, as his followers were known, undertook a series of socialist-oriented reforms that led to an economic expansion that was especially strong in the 1950s.

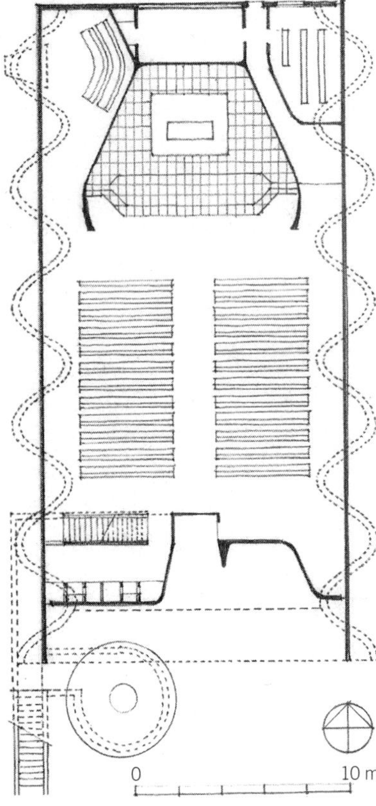


An engineer by training, Dieste made his reputation building a whole range of structures, from grain silos, factory sheds, markets, maintenance hangars, fruitpacking plants, warehouses, and bus terminals to a handful of churches of exceptional spans and beauty. In most, he uses gaussian vaults, which are self-supporting shells that stand up not only because they are light but also because they are bent or folded in such a way that they are subject to limited lateral thrusts. Dieste also perfected techniques of reinforced masonry with the objective of minimizing the use of material and maximizing the size of openings.

Dieste's Church of Christ the Worker, (1958–60) in Atlántida, Uruguay, is a simple rectangle, with side walls rising up in undulating curves to the maximum amplitude of their arcs. The undulation enables the thin walls to be self-stabilizing, much as a bent sheet of paper has greater strength than a flat one. At the top, the geometry of the wall is merged with the continuous double curvature of the ceiling (reinforced with tie-rods concealed in troughs). The beauty of the forms is then augmented by the subtle interplay with light. While small, punched rectangular openings diffuse light through the interior, a triple row of baffles above the entrance, opening in opposite directions, flood the space with indirect light. His warehouse for the fruit packing plant in Salto (1971–2) consists of a series of large discontinuous double-curvature vaults spanning approximately 150 feet. Not only do the vaults make the span seem effortless but the glazed slits light up the vaults and space to create a space of rare sensuality.

18.111
Plan and interior view:
Church of Christ the Worker

18.112 Aula Magna, La Ciudad Universitaria de Caracas, Venezuela

18.113 Diego Rivera House, Mexico City

**Caribbean Modernism**

In the Caribbean, modernism, as an expression of nationalist sentiments, was first propounded not by architects but by poets and writers, for example, Rubén Darío (Panama), José Asunción Silva (Colombia), Manuel Gutiérrez Nájera (Mexico), José Enrique Rodó (Uruguay), José Martí (Cuba), Bienvenido Nouel (Dominican Republic), and Luis Lloréns Torres (Puerto Rico). It was not until the 1940s and 50s that what is now called tropical modernism emerged as the language of autonomy and independence. Though strongly influenced by Le Corbusier, tropical modernism developed along its own regional lines, emphasizing not only clean lines but the need for shaded surfaces, wide windows, surrounding gardens, and lightweight construction.

In the Dominican Republic, the work of Guillermo González-Sánchez, in Puerto Rico in the work of various local and foreign architects, including Antonin Nechodoma and Henry Klumb, and in Mexico the work of Juan O'Gorman and Felix Candela, among others, can be singled out for its trailblazing character.

The Ciudad Universitaria de Caracas, the masterwork of the Venezuelan architect Carlos Raúl Villanueva, represents one of the highest expressions of modern architecture in Latin America. Built over three decades, from 1944 to 1970, as an autonomous urban assemblage next to Plaza Venezuela, this compendium of more than 40 buildings was developed through a period of radical economic, social, and political changes. At the center of the campus was a succession of spaces in which inside and outside merge seamlessly into one another.

Villanueva visualized a system of flows and paths, or "movements," as a fundamental design criterion behind his conception of the university's covered plaza with its large canopy of irregular shape and varying height protecting the shaded space within. Here Villanueva incorporated the work of several avant-garde artists of the time, such as Fernand Leger, Antoine Pevsner, Victor Vasarely, Jean Arp, Henri Laurens, as well as a group of Venezuelan geometric abstract artists, such as Mateo Manaure, Pascual Navarro, Oswaldo Vigas, and Armando Barrios.

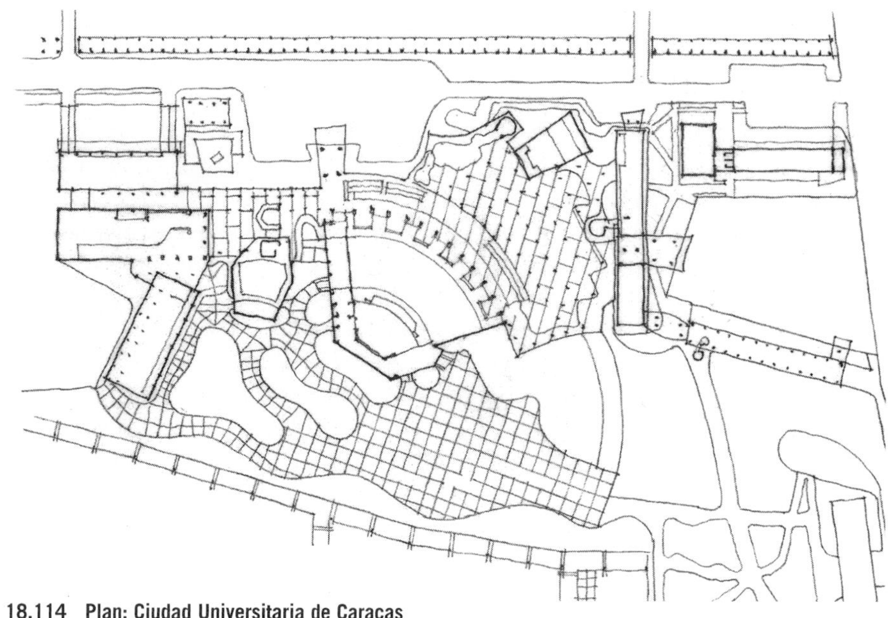

18.114 Plan: Ciudad Universitaria de Caracas

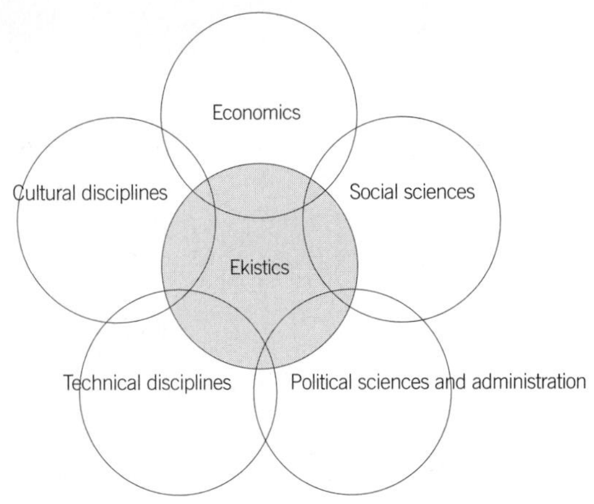


**18.115 Diagram of ekistics and the sciences contributing to it**

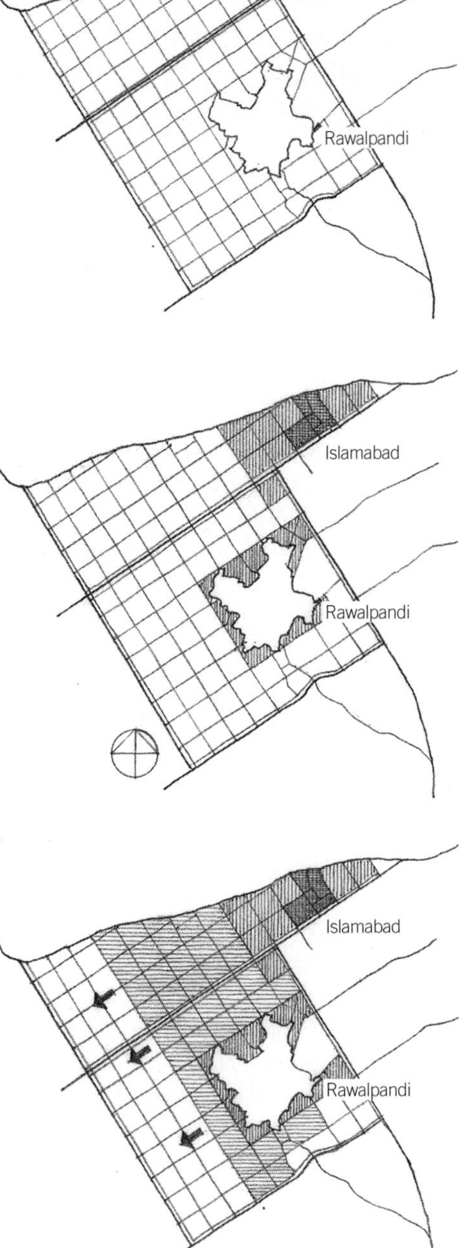


**18.116 Islamabad, Pakistan: A growing dynametropolis**

### Ekistics

Constantinos Doxiadis (1913–75), former chief town planning officer of Athens, Greece, started his own firm in 1951 and after that built in dozens of countries, including India, Bangladesh, Ethiopia, France, Ghana, Iran, Iraq, Italy, Jordan, Pakistan, and Syria. His was one of the largest international practices at the time. Doxiadis introduced issues like regional climate and geography into the discussion of modernism at a time when this was still rare. He coined the term ekistics, derived from the Greek *oikos*, meaning "house," to refer to the science of human settlements. Doxiadis aspired to expand the scientific basis of architecture, urban design, and planning in order to reject arbitrary self-expression and monotonic versions of rationalism and also to embrace extra-technological and nonfunctionalist concerns. He soon surrounded himself with an international and interdisciplinary group that included global visionaries (Buckminster Fuller and Margaret Mead, for example), architects, planners, and United Nations consultants (Jaqueline Tyrwhitt and Charles Abrams), economists and environmental thinkers (Barbara Ward and Renee Dubos)—all of whom, albeit to different degrees, supported Doxiadis' vision. His planning model was called Dynapolis, a term signifying a dynamic city that would change though time and allow the urban core to expand continually in a unidirectional manner so as to avert the congestion and do away with the permanence and monumentality of stationary city centers. The business district and residential areas would also grow along this axis, and industrial areas would be pushed to the edges. This logic of functional separation extended to the system of social ordering, so that each residential sector was broken down to smaller community scales arranged hierarchically.

The model of Dynapolis informed many plans for urban restructuring, from Baghdad, Iraq (1958), to Athens, Greece (1960), to Washington, D.C., and it became the basis for the creation of Islamabad, the new capital of Pakistan (1960). Doxiadis designed Islamabad's master plan and the prototypes of the major housing types, but the design of the individual buildings was assigned to local and foreign architects. The master plan was based on his concept of a moving core—the idea that commercial heart of the city would continue to grow as necessary, creating a linear city in its wake.

18.117 **Great Hall of the People, Beijing, China**

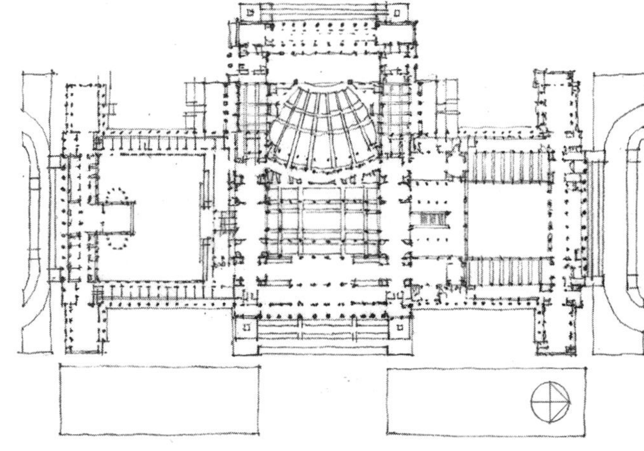

18.118 **Great Hall of the People, Beijing, China**

**Mao Tse-tung's China**

In 1949 the Communists under Mao Tse-tung liberated China from Japanese occupation and ousted the republican government of Chiang Kai-shek, which fled to the island of Taiwan. Suspicious of bright city lights, they put Shanghai, China's largest center of industry and finance and also of her intellectual and cultural life, into four decades of hibernation. The new China realized a series of land reforms between 1949 and 1953. And much of what was regarded as the worst manifestations of westernization—opium use, gambling, and prostitution—was systematically cleaned up. Infrastructural upgrades and resumption of manufacturing brought a wave of rebuilding in the postwar landscape, especially in the north. Hospital and educational buildings were erected with a stylistic divide between the traditional Chinese look with the gabled roof atop otherwise normative structures and the ethnic look of regional architecture.

A growing alliance with the Soviet Union and the Eastern bloc countries of Europe brought an influx of Soviet models of urban and architectural planning. A series of "wedding cake" exposition centers in the Soviet style were built in various cities to promote Sino-Soviet friendship. The 1952 Exhibition Center in Beijing (designed by a Russian, Sergei Andreyev, and a Chinese architect, Dai Nianci) was followed by one in Shanghai (designed by Sergei Andreyev and Chen Zhi). An iconic Russian spiral sits on top of a tower that was fronted by a plaza centered on a fountain.

In 1958–59, the civic monuments of the Great Hall of the People, the Ethnic Cultural Center, and the Main Station were designed in Beijing. The Great Hall of the People occupied the complete western edge of Tiananmen Square. It was a Soviet-style, stripped classical building whose primary expression was a relentless row of columns. A central block was pulled forward and expressed at a more monumental scale. Behind the facade a diverse array of large and small assembly halls were jammed into the rectangular mass.

The period of the Cultural Revolution 1965–76 was another time of internal turmoil for China. Minimal dwellings that often disregarded family and privacy in favor of communal living were institutionalized, while a cult of shrines to Mao proliferated. Mao's death in 1976 closed a chapter on the most turbulent time for urban dwellers. His mausoleum, with his embalmed body, was constructed in Tiananmen Square, on the main axis of the Forbidden City. The early 1980s brought a slow opening of doors to the West by Deng Xiaoping and the post-1989 period brought a paced opening of market capitalism.

18.119 **Beijing Exhibition Center**

18.120 **School of Music, National School of Art, Havana, Cuba**

18.121 **School of Ballet, National School of Art, Havana**

**National School of Art, Havana**

In 1961, two years after the Cuban Revolution, Fidel Castro and Ernesto Che Guevara decided to transform the golf course of the Havana Country Club into an experimental project that would make art available to all. The master plan for the National Art Schools complex was given to the young Cuban architect Ricardo Porro, who had just returned from exile. Porro invited his Italian colleagues Vittorio Garatti and Roberto Gottardi, in Caracas, Venezuela, to collaborate on the project. The three architects initiated a unique process that would generate its own criteria in which the design and construction of the schools occurred simultaneously with the beginning of the schools' academic activities. Porro designed the School of Plastic Arts and the School of Modern Dance; Gottardi, the School of Dramatic Arts; and Garatti, the School of Music and the School for Ballet.

Even though each has its particularities, the five schools followed three common guiding principles: first, a response to the tropical landscape that allowed for an intimate relationship between nature and architecture; second, the use of earthen materials produced on the island instead of steel and cement; and third, the use of the Bóveda Catalana, or Catalan Vault, as the primary structural system. Though this ancient and versatile technique required very little by way of resources and materials and was partially in response to the economically austere circumstances of Cuba, especially after the blockade imposed by United States in October 1960, it conferred to the architecture the sensuality and the eroticism that Porro claimed as typically Cuban.

By 1965 the schools, still unfinished, began to generate controversy, as they were accused of being examples of an "individualism" that contradicted the increasingly influential standardized models of the Soviet-functionalist style. This eventually led to the abandonment of the project. Castro's government, however, has initiated a process of restoration with Gottardi, the only one of the three architects still in Cuba, as its director.

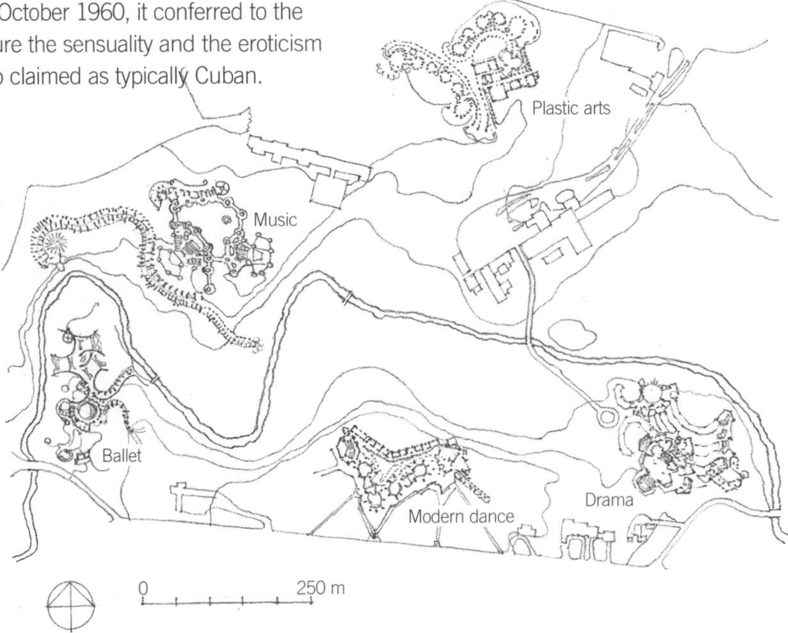


18.122 **Site plan: National School of Art, Havana**

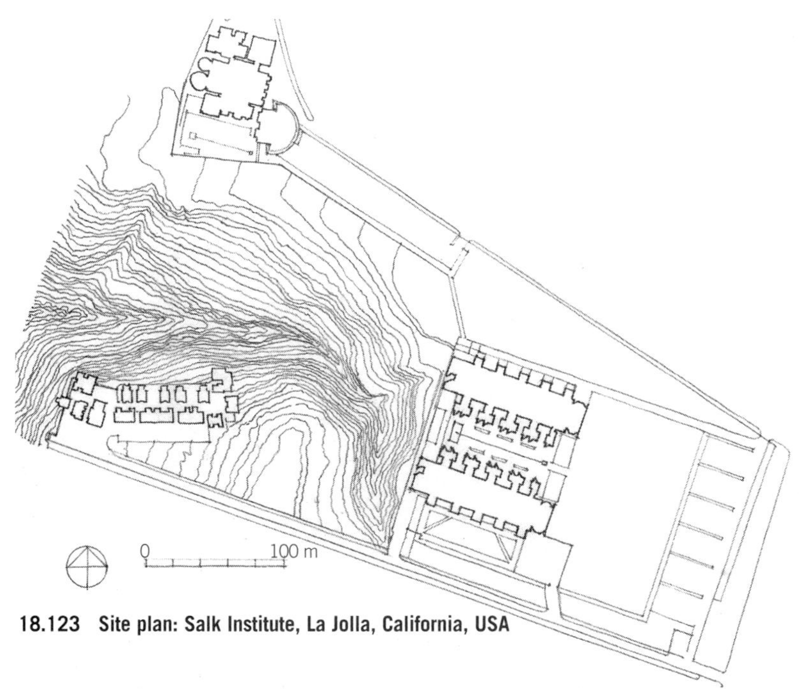


**18.123 Site plan: Salk Institute, La Jolla, California, USA**

**18.124 Salk Institute**

**Salk Institute**

For Dr. Jonas Salk, the discoverer of the polio vaccine, medical research was not entirely the domain of scientists and administrators; it belonged to the public, and in Louis Kahn, Salk found the architect who could transform that ideal into architectural form. The Salk Institute building (1965–7) is in La Jolla, near San Diego, California, close to a bluff overlooking the Pacific Ocean. Three floors of laboratories, completely open in all directions, are separated by half-floors dedicated to mechanical ducts. As was typical of Kahn, the building went through several design permutations before its final form was agreed upon. It consisted of two rectangular laboratory blocks separated by a courtyard, with towers housing the scientists' study rooms projecting from the laboratories but sitting in the courtyard space. Circulation towers were located on the other side of the laboratories, aligned to the study towers. The circulation towers were attached to the body of the laboratories, presenting to the outside an austere and windowless form, whereas the study towers were separated from the laboratories by bridges to declare a physical and psychological differentiation. The diagonal walls of the towers allow each office to have an ocean view.

The courtyard is elevated one floor above the level of the site to better capture the views. Originally, Kahn had envisioned the court as a lush garden, but in 1966, after seeing the work of Luis Barragán, Kahn invited him to see the designs, and it was Barragán who came up with the idea of an empty plaza. One enters the plaza from the east, through a quiet garden. A narrow waterway slices through the courtyard on its axis and ends in the quiet waterfall of a viewing terrace.

The building has no columns, but it is held up by concrete wall elements, with a reddish pozzolana additive placed in the concrete to give it a slightly reddish hue. The space between the elements on the piazza is left open to form a colonnade. Otherwise, Kahn used wooden infills. The concrete is meticulously poured, with Kahn emphasizing the joints by means of V-shaped grooves. The holes left by the formwork were not patched but left visible across the surface of the material. These carefully crafted surfaces contrast with the textured whiteness of the travertine used to pave the courtyard.

All of Kahn's work, but especially the Salk Institute building, aims to restore the sense of monumentality and gravitas that he felt had been lost in modern architecture. Monumentality did not mean overbearing shapes or empty rhetoric but rather the confidence that form can mediate and ennoble the spaces of human activity. In 1938 an architectural critic had written that "if it is a monument, it is not modern; if it is modern, it cannot be a monument." But by the late 1950s and 1960s, architects had begun to return to the ambition of monumentality. One can think of the Sydney Opera House, designed by Jørn Utzon and begun in 1957. Kahn, however, tried to fuse structure with architecture while not becoming subservient to the fallacy of rationalism. It was a delicate balance that Kahn aimed to achieve. In this, he is something akin in his approach to Mies van der Rohe, except that Kahn, in his admiration for Roman architecture, Scottish castles, and Greek temples, wanted to emphasize the solidity and tactility of his buildings, unlike the buildings of Mies, which tend, despite the attention to detail and materials, to be cold and impersonal.

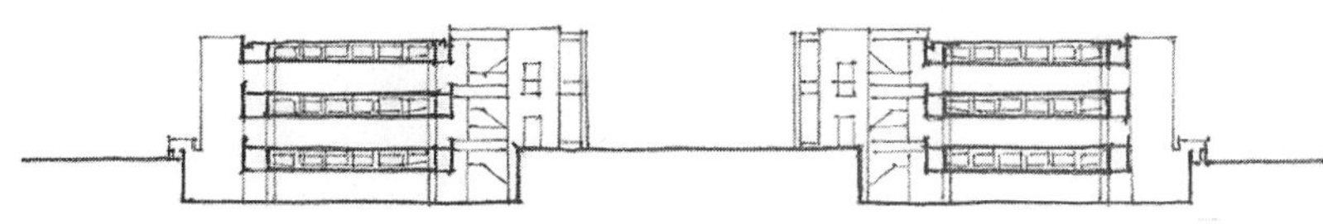

**18.125 Section through laboratory buildings: Salk Institute**

18.126 **Totsuka Country Club, Yokohama, Japan**

18.127 **Nichinan Cultural Center, Nichinan, Japan**

**Metabolism**

On the basis of the design for his internationally acclaimed Hiroshima memorial, Kenzo Tange (1913–2005) was invited to attend the 8th CIAM (Congres Internationaux d'Architecture Moderne) meeting held in England in 1951, on which occasion he met Le Corbusier, Siegfried Giedion, Walter Gropius, and Jose Luis Sert, among others. This was the CIAM that discussed the question of the "urban core," rekindling Tange's interests in urban planning. Tange became a member of Team X after the dissolution of CIAM in 1956 and presented his design for the Tokyo City Hall (1957) at their Otterlo, Netherlands, meeting in 1959. At this meeting he also brought along Kiyonori Kikutake's drawings for the reorganization of Tokyo, which envisioned tall circular residential towers on land and the factories on giant cylinders in the bay. This was the beginning of his interest in urbanization as an organic system, and this led to the development of "metabolism."

Tange presented his metabolist concepts at the World Design Conference held in Tokyo in 1958. This conference was conceived as an alternative to Team X and was attended among others by Kikutake, Kurokawa, Noboru Kawazoe, Fumihiko Maki, Peter and Alison Smithson, Jacob Bakema, Paul Rudolph, Ralph Erskine, Louis Kahn, Jean Prouve, Minoru Yamasaki, B. V. Doshi, and Raphael Soriano.

Unlike Team X, which approached urban design and planning by hoping to solve problems at the human scale, the metabolists worked at the largest scale conceivable, seeing their structures through a biological metaphor as an expression of the city's new lifeforce. Thus, despite this large scale, It was a philosophical proposition about inhabiting the earth in harmony with the forces of nature.

While Tange's urban plans bore little fruit, his architectural practice, patronized by Japan's elite, flourished. With an uncanny aesthetic sense, rivaled by few who worked with exposed concrete at such large scales, Tange built a celebrated body of work in the 1960s and 1970s. The Totsuka Country Club (1960–1) acquired its upward turning profile from Chandigarh's Assembly; the Nichinan Cultural Center (1960–2), with its forceful fins, was a beast unto itself; and finally the Olympic Stadium in Tokyo was a stellar display not only of the structural possibilities of concrete and tensile cable but of the ability of structure to generate poetic forms such as had been rivaled only by Santiago Calatrava in the recent past.

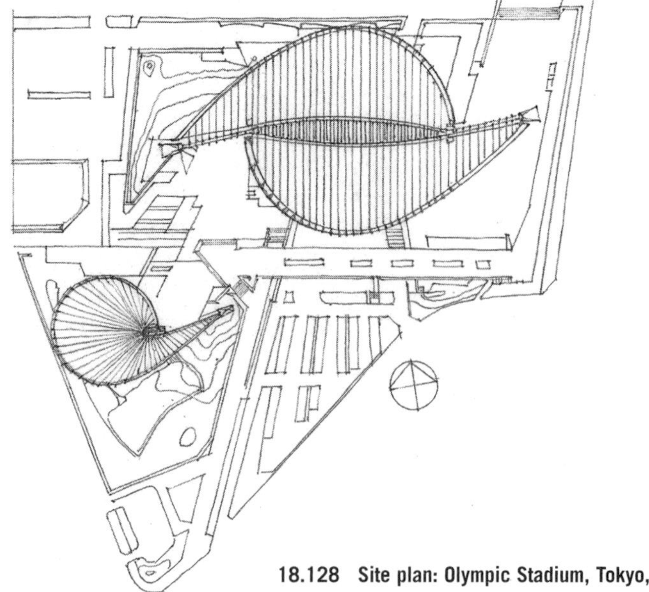

18.128 **Site plan: Olympic Stadium, Tokyo, Japan**

18.129 **University of Ibadan, Nigeria**

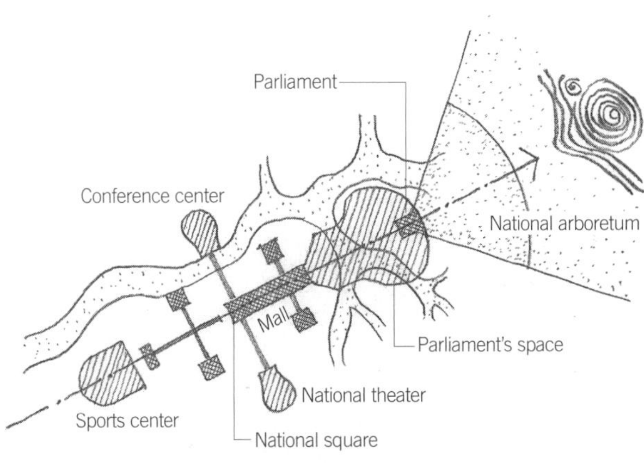


18.130 **Master plan concept for Abuja, Nigeria** (Facsimile of the original drawing by Dr. Nnamdi Elleh)

### University of Ibadan

World War II left England and France considerably weakened. By the mid-1960s, almost all of the English colonies in Africa had achieved independence, including Uganda in 1962 and Zanzibar and Kenya in 1963. Most immediately embarked on an aggressive campaign of modernization. New capitals, schools, and hospitals had to be built, but traditional architecture had also been neglected and so skilled builders and craftspeople were rare. In 1945, in all of Africa, including Egypt, there were only 26 cities with a population over 100,000. By the 1970s there were 120 such cities, but architectural development was spotty.

After Nigeria' s independence in 1960, several modernists arrived in Lagos, including the husband and wife team of Maxwell Fry and Jane Drew, who designed the University of Ibadan in the early 1960s after having worked in Chandigarh, India. The University's nucleus is a series of connected buildings consisting of a ring of residential colleges, arranged around a center, with buildings devoted to teaching and administration. Open balconies, screens, and covered passageways make use of prevailing winds. The plan can be described as loosely hierarchical, with sports and residential complexes at one end and the class and administration buildings at the other.

By 1991 new oil revenues created enough wealth and stability, and Nigeria's capital was moved to a new city, Abuja, located on the Gwanga Plains in the middle of the country. Abuja's master plan was designed by Kenzo Tange, blending Lúcio Costa's airplane plan for Brasília with the circulation pattern of Tokyo. It had the shape of a body with head, torso, arms, and tail. The head contained the three principal government buildings, the torso the main body of the city, and the arms the conference center and theater. Though it was designed as a site for a democratic government, the head can be easily barricaded in times of civil disturbances. Abuja is currently far from complete.

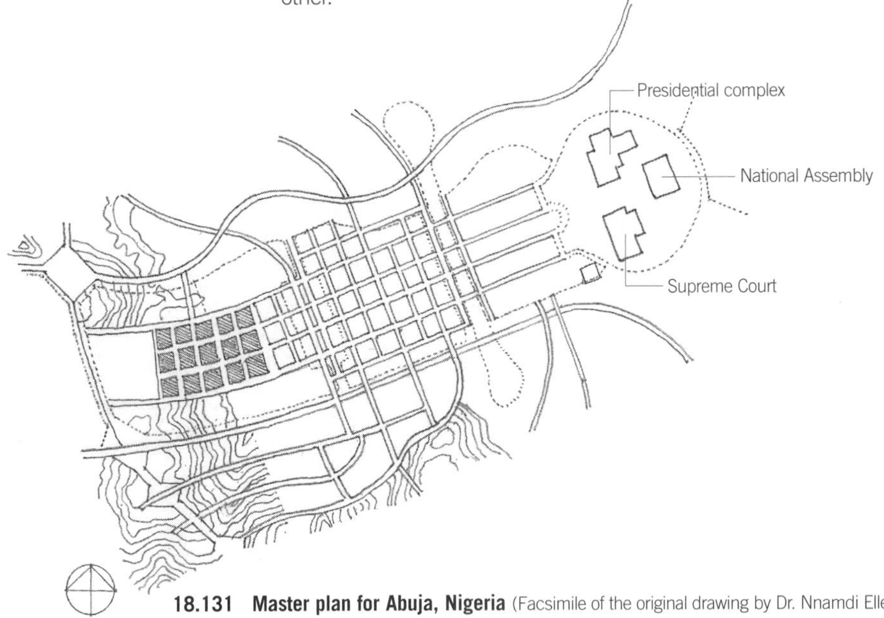


18.131 **Master plan for Abuja, Nigeria** (Facsimile of the original drawing by Dr. Nnamdi Elleh)

18.132 Business Men's Assurance Co. of America, Kansas City, Missouri, USA

18.133 Alcoa Building, San Francisco, California, USA

### SOM

By the 1970s, Skidmore, Owings and Merrill (SOM), founded in 1936, comprised about a thousand architects, engineers, and technicians who provided complete planning, designing, engineering, and construction services. It was one of the world's first multitasking architectural corporations. The firm had seven principal offices, located in New York City, Chicago, San Francisco, Portland, Oregon, Washington, D.C., Paris, and Los Angeles. Commissions ranged from presidential libraries to routine industrial buildings. Though there was diversity in aesthetic production, there can be no doubt that perfecting the Miesian paradigm and making modernism the language par excellence for corporations was an important part of the firm's reputation. This can be seen in the headquarters of the Business Men's Assurance Co. of America (Kansas City, Missouri, 1963), situated outside of the city on the edge of a park. Its frame is steel clad in white Georgian marble, with the windows set back to create a stark minimalist effect. The Alcoa Building in San Francisco (1964) took this one step further, with the exoskeletal crossbracing, rather than the floors, serving both structural and symbolic purposes.

On the one hand, their unrelenting and uncompromising abstraction seems to make them mute and faceless yet, on the other hand, the reduction of architecture to its structural logic with its rhetorical emptiness seems to reflect a modern life with the faceless corporation as its social and aesthetic center.

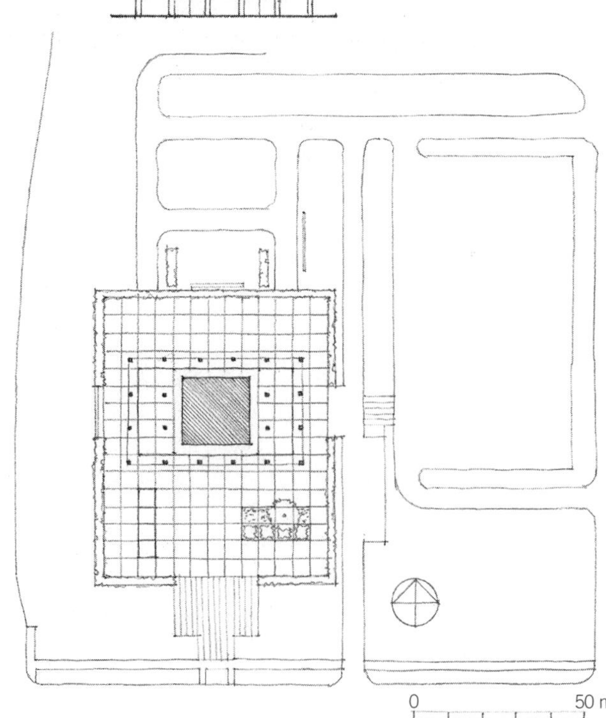


18.134 Site plan and elevation: Headquarters for the Business Men's Assurance Co. of America

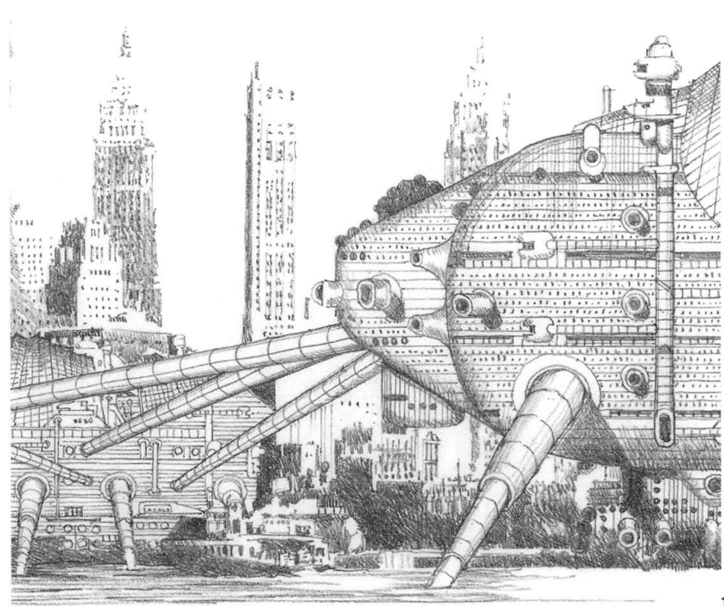

18.135 Portion of Ron Herron's Walking City

### Archigram

*Archigram* was a publication, begun in 1961, that quickly became known for its alternative ideas. Short for "Architectural Telegram," *Archigram* was produced by the young English architects Peter Cook, David Greene, Michael Webb, Ron Herron, Warren Chalk, and Dennis Crompton. The full *Archigram* group later included Colin Fournier, Ken Allison, and Tony Rickaby. Though the actual collaborations between these architects were often sporadic and difficult, the magazine's agenda called for a holistic vision of the city and its parts as a living, flowing, pulsing, and flexible organism. Challenging the grid established by Le Corbusier, *Archigram*'s texts, collages, and comic book-style designs emphasized the use of anything but 90-degree angles and thematized the curving and twisting of Le Corbusier's straight lines. Using bright colors, a nonstandard format, and an explicitly cut-and-paste style of assembly, *Archigram* delivered visions of technologically advanced cities that walked on four legs, Plug-in Cities that could be stacked and changed like cords in an outlet, and Instant Cities that could be flown in and made to sprout like spring flowers into the hands of any eager architect, critic, or admirer. Though much of the *Archigram* structures were unbuildable, Peter Cook's recently built Kunsthaus in Graz, Austria, with its amorphous blue shape set in contrast with the traditional architecture around it, gives some indication of the *Archigram* aesthetic and the excitement that it can generate.

The work of one member of the *Archigram* group, Mark Fisher, a student of Peter Cook at the Architectural Association (AA) in London, embraced the language and images of the youth culture that was blooming in England and abroad. His investigations into inflatable technology led to the Automat in 1968. It was a user-responsive pneumatic structure supported by internal bracing cables, which, attached to high pressure jacks, allowed the structure to expand and contract in response to a user's weight requirements. Fisher improved the Automat in his design of the Dynomat, the surface of which was controlled by a series of valves, again responding to user interactions. The structure could be deflated and folded to fit in the back of a car.

In 1977 Mark Fisher was asked to design inflatable stage props for the Animals tour for the rock group Pink Floyd. In the process of design Fisher created the theme of two towering pneumatic icons. For the first show Fisher also designed a bloated, inflatable "nuclear" family, including 2.5 children. The most memorable of the Animals tour inflatables were the series of pigs, which flew over the audiences' heads, snorting and ultimately exploding above and behind Pink Floyd's stage.

From his success with Pink Floyd's Animals, Mark Fisher went on to develop many of rock and roll's most memorable sets, including Pink Floyd's Wall and Division Bell sets and the Lisbon Expo '98.

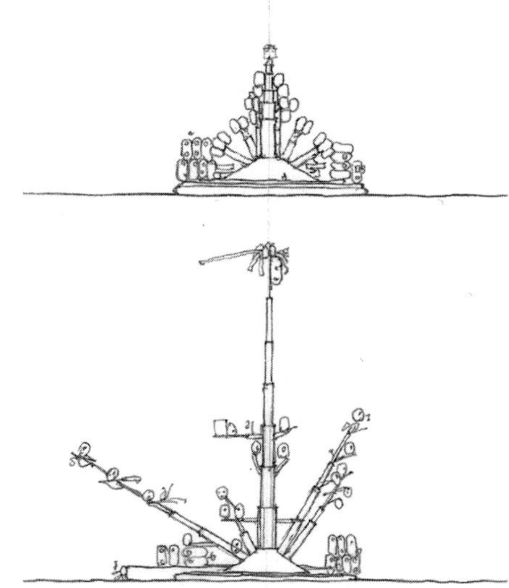

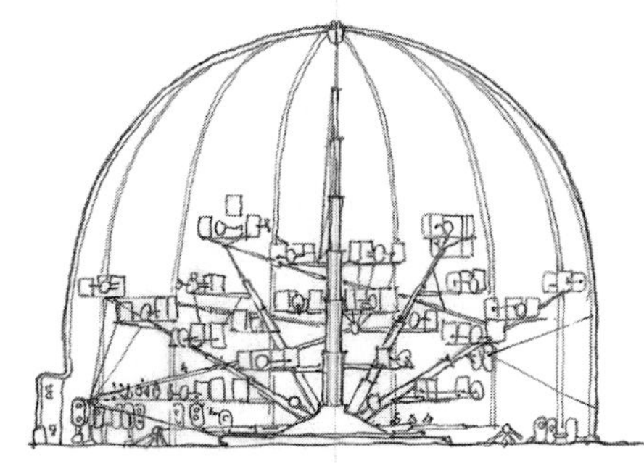

18.136 Peter Cook's Blow-out Village

18.137 Johnson Art Museum, Cornell University, Ithaca, New York, USA

18.138 Foundling Estate, London, England

## BRUTALISM

In the mid-1960s, numerous architects, with Kenzo Tange in the lead, became interested in megastructures that consisted of simple large-scale repetitive structures packed with program. Cultural contexts were meant to play only a limited role in these buildings. Instead, the buildings emphasized material simplicity and secular anonymity. They spoke of the ethos of managerial grandness. The Foundling Estate in London (1973) has long lines of housing stacked on massive piers. Though these structures were soon maligned, they brought modernism to a new pitch in their fearless acceptance of large-scale realities.

Brutalism was particularly popular among university administrators, and many campuses in the United States have at least one example of late 1960s brutalism, such as Kane Hall at the University of Washington, Seattle, designed by Walker and McGough (1969). Similarly, but much larger, is the Rand Afrikaans University in Johannesburg, Republic of South Africa (1975), designed by William Meyer, which fused the latest trends in megastructure with ideas that were seen as specifically African.

Chinese-born I. M. Pei (1917–) took the brutalist aesthetic but refined its surfaces and forms to develop a distinctive style that appealed to many city leaders during the days in which museums and cultural buildings were coming to be seen as an established aspect of a city's profile. His East Building, National Gallery (1974–8), Washington, D.C., for example, was composed of stark masses, deep recesses, sharp edges, and wide openings, but it was clad in a white sandstone that foreshadowed a new generation of elegant, modernist civic structures. His Johnson Art Museum on the campus of Cornell University (1970–3), Ithaca, New York, consisted of a set of distinct vertical concrete masses holding up the main mass of the gallery high in the air, while huge panes of glass filled in the open volumes, making the whole structure unexpectedly transparent. Pei's most famous structure, the extension of the Louvre in Paris (1989), is a fascinating study in contrast. While most of the structure is below ground, the only thing above ground is a glass pyramid in the middle of the courtyard of the Louvre.

18.139 East Building, National Gallery, Washington, D.C., USA

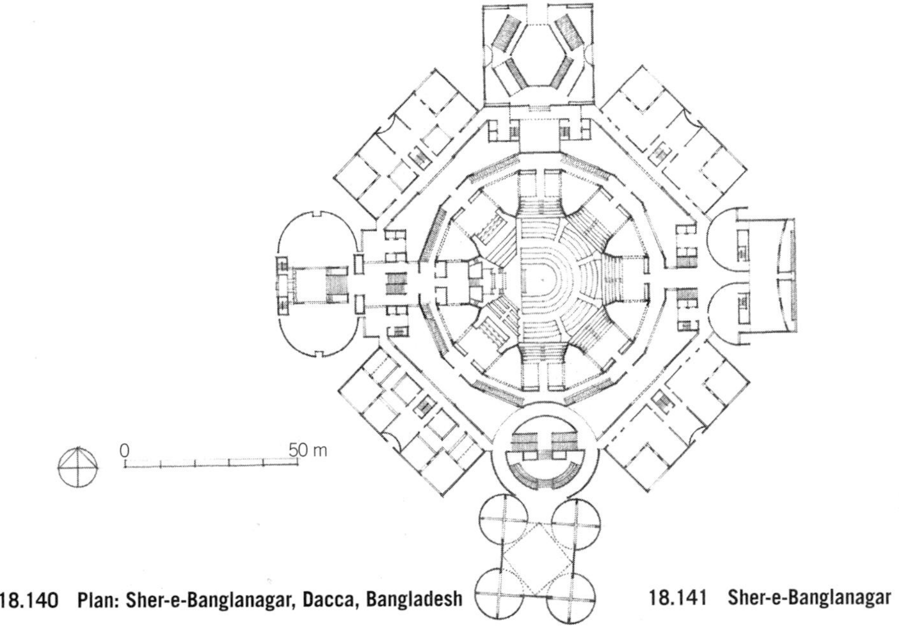


**18.140 Plan: Sher-e-Banglanagar, Dacca, Bangladesh**

**18.141 Sher-e-Banglanagar**

Louis Kahn spent more than a decade working on Sher-e-Banglanagar in Dacca (as it came to be called after Bangladesh became independent in 1971) and almost went bankrupt in the process. It was completed well after Kahn's death in 1974, but when it was finished in the late 1980s, it instantly arrested the attention of the Bangladeshi populace and was celebrated as a triumphant display of their independence. What the Bangladeshi citizens see is a closely clustered assembly of monolithic concrete towers, slashed open, with huge triangular, rectangular, and semicircular openings. Together they form the outer envelope, the serving zone, to the central chamber of the parliament, with the trusses of the gigantic roof structure just visible from a distance.

The entrance to the building is from the north, through a large square building with grand staircases. The four buildings for offices are packaged between this building and the other axially-placed elements, which are: the minister's offices to the west, lunch rooms to the east, and a mosque to the south. The mosque, preceded by a circular ablution space, is formed by four round towers clamped against a rotated square; it is tilted a few degrees from the axis because of its orientation toward Mecca.

Within, Sher-e-Banglanagar is a studied essay in the use of natural light to illuminate monumental spaces as is the Pantheon's oculus—split, spliced, and reimagined through a series of cubist transformations. From the outside, however, Sher-e-Banglanagar sits in silent dignity, with a vast swath of land cleared all around it, first to make a reflecting pool and then a giant plaza. Unlike the great plazas of Brasília and Chandigarh, Bangladesh's plaza became an instant success. Everyday thousands of people throng its vast expanse, playing, picnicking, protesting, or otherwise participating in the public affairs of civic life.

Kahn's Sher-e-Banglanagar, like Le Corbusier's Chandigarh, was his largest, and last built project, and along with the Kimball Art Museum in Fort Worth, Texas, and the Salk Institute in California, certainly the finest of his later work. Where the Kimball Art Museum is about the invention of the section and the very precise and subtle measurement of light in its galleries and where the Salk Institute is a singular and profound meditation on the framing of a view, Sher-e-Banglanagar, though of much cruder workmanship, is Kahn's most complex essay on the interplay of light and mass in a tightly controlled formal order.

**18.142 Sher-e-Banglanagar**

18.143 School of Architecture, Ahmedabad, India

18.144 Gandhi Ashram Museum, Ahmedabad, India

**Doshi and Correa**

The Brazilian government was toppled by a military coup in 1965, arresting the development of Brazilian modernism. However, in south Asia, as in other parts of the postcolonial world, a more regional modern architecture continued to flourish. The Indian team of architects that had worked with Le Corbusier in Chandigarh continued to build throughout north India. Aditya Prakash, for instance, was responsible for designing many new campuses and universities, such as those in Ludhiana and Hissar in the 1960s. Shivnath Prasad, in New Delhi, developed Le Corbusier's brutalist vocabulary at the Akbar Hotel (1965–69) and at the Sri Ram Center for Performing Arts (1966–72). Mazharul Islam, in Bangladesh, used brick and concrete at his Jahangir University Dormitory (1969). In general, building was done with load-bearing brick walls, with concrete lintels and slabs and deep overhangs as protection from the sun. Thus, unlike Brazil, where structural innovation became an integral part of the national modern style, in India, architects readily experimented with low-tech solutions for their modernist buildings, using exposed brick and concrete, constructed with simple technical skill and inexpensive finishes.

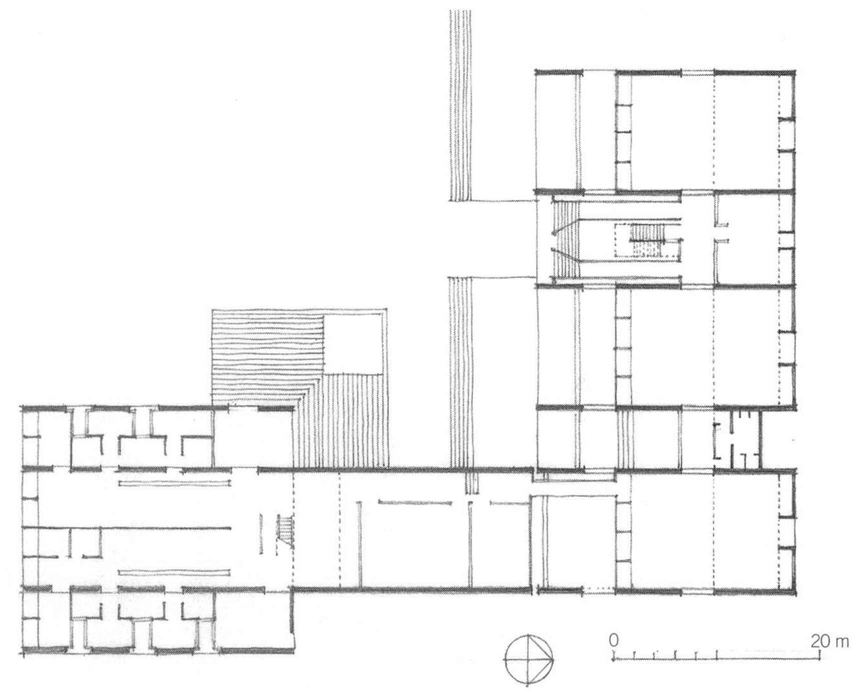


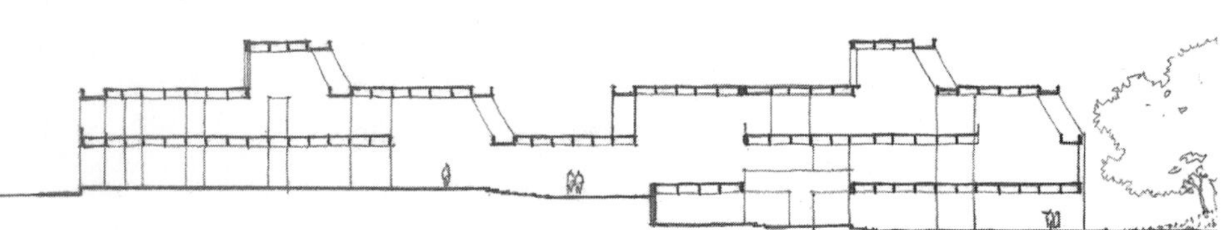

18.145 Plan and section: School of Architecture, Ahmedabad

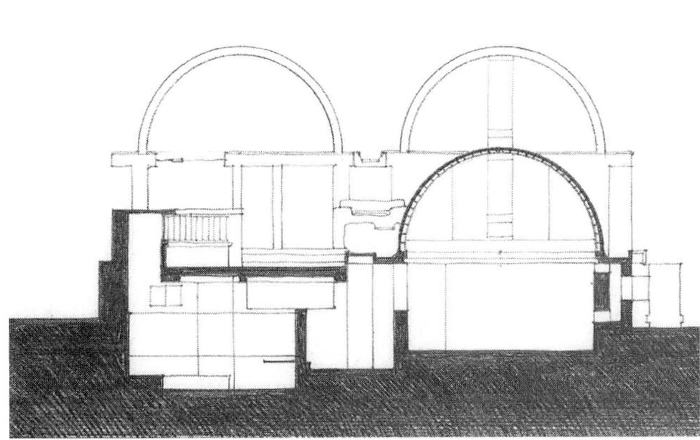

18.146 Section: Sangath, Ahmedabad, India

18.147 Sangath

Balkrishna V. Doshi (1927–) trained several of India's prominent architects in Ahmedabad, including Charles Correa, (1930–). One of Doshi's successful early projects was the School of Architecture in Ahmedabad (1965), a reworking of Le Corbusier's design for the College of Art in Chandigarh. Unlike Le Corbusier's design, which was closed off and regulated by a very strict circulation system, Doshi's school maintained the principle of the north light, but he opened the building up so that it operated as a multifunctional space. Later in life, Doshi moved more in the direction of Louis Kahn, asking more fundamental questions of materials and assembly. The design of Sangath (1979), his own office, took on the work of rethinking a climatic response from first principles. The consequence was a structure that was just as much below ground as above, with a series of vaulted roofs (covered with broken china) derived from the original shed that stood on the site.

Correa extended Le Corbusier's battle with the sun to create a series of houses made of brick and concrete that used the section as well as a pergola roof to create microclimatic conditions. His Parekh House (1967–8) in Ahmedabad, for instance, had two sections, one for the summer and the other for the winter.

The distant influence of Kahn's Trenton Bath Houses can be seen in Correa's design for the Gandhi Ashram Museum (1958–63), intended to house artifacts and an exhibition of the life of Mahatma Gandhi. Here Correa used a 6-meter grid composed of I-shaped brick piers to set up an interconnected network of open-to-the-sky, covered-but-open, and fully enclosed spaces that showed an early skill developing courtyardlike spaces to his advantage. Correa used a mud-tile roof, held up on concrete beams, that drained into channels in the concrete slabs. All the water collected in a central pond though huge concrete gargoyles, reminiscent of Le Corbusier's. Operable wooden louvers enabled air circulation in the enclosed spaces.

Correa's later work took his climatic solutions and open-to-sky propositions and transformed them into innovative solutions adapted to various sites and programs. For his residential tower in Bombay, the Kanchenjunga apartments (1970–83), for instance, he punched out double-height spaces in the corners to create an open feeling and to set up air circulation through each apartment. His Kovalam Beach Resort (1969–74) utilized the natural slope of the ocean-facing hill to create a rhythm of rooms and terraces, each open to the sky.

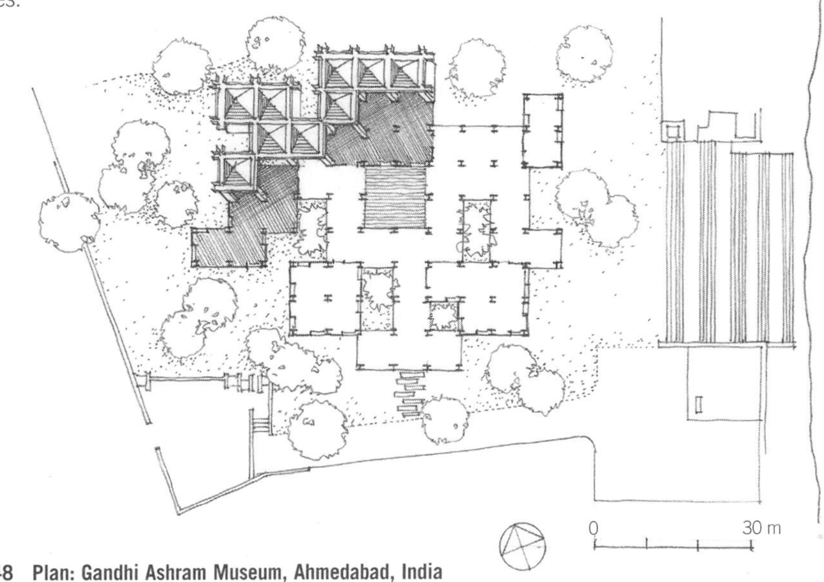


18.148 Plan: Gandhi Ashram Museum, Ahmedabad, India

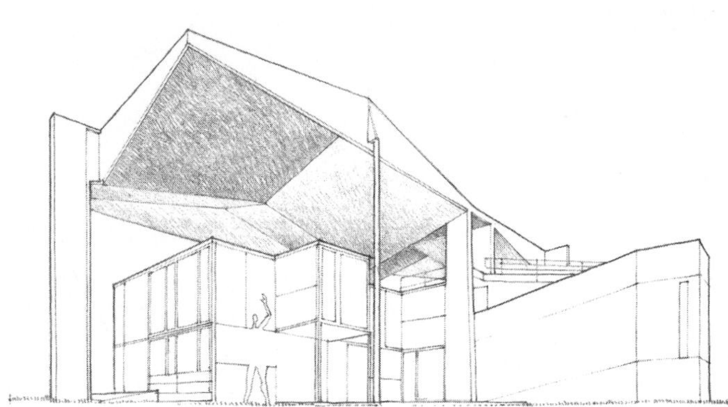

18.149 Heidi Weber House (Centre Le Corbusier), Zurich, Switzerland

18.150 Piazza d'Italia, New Orleans, Louisiana, USA

## POSTMODERNISM

The word postmodernism does not refer to a particular definable style, and in this it is very different from other designations, like Georgian or shingle style and, even for that matter, the international style, which, despite its multiple meanings and origins in architecture, by the 1950s meant a set of practices loosely defined around the ideals of CIAM. But what had seemed so promising in 1950 was by 1970 seen not only as constricting but also failing to live up to its promises. Critics more and more began to associate modernism with the worst forms of capitalism, bureaucracy, and totalitarianism. And for the Europeans, modernism after World War II meant endless rows of hastily built, drab housing blocks. There were in Europe no Brasílias, Chandigarhs, or Daccas, and few examples of successful civic modernism. In the United States, modernism was more successful. It had made significant inroads in domestic architecture, had thoroughly transformed the corporate landscape, and even had a few successful civic projects to show for itself, such as Lincoln Center (1956) in New York City and Civic Center Plaza (1965–6) in Chicago. But, as in Europe, vast housing blocks shot up that exacerbated post-World War II social and racial tensions. Thus it was that the "death of modernism" was announced with the destruction in 1972 of the Pruitt-Igoe Housing Complex (1952–5) in St. Louis, Missouri, which was built with a great deal of optimism but, because of mismanagement and changing attitudes, became the very symbol of urban blight and racial imbalance.

Beginning in the late 1960s, architects began to return to the question of context, history, traditions, and form as a way to revitalize the purpose and meaning of their profession. In the long run, the protest against modernism began in the United States and developed in Europe into a global movement that eventually dampened the spread of international modernism. Dreary housing estates for the lower classes continue, of course, to be built around the world where speed and efficiency constrain design.

Postmodernism was by no means a single or unified field of production, nor did it even mean a rejection of modernism. In fact, Le Corbusier's Heidi Weber House (1965), one of his last designs, shows that even he was able to rethink modernism's aesthetic once again. Two floating steel canopies, painted gray and held up on thin supports, shelter the house below, which is designed out of modular steel elements variously open to the interior with big sheets of glass or closed off by brightly colored panels.

The challenge was taken up by Philip Johnson (1906–2005), who was fascinated with the Russian constructivists and built a constructivist-styled office building in St. Louis. Michael Graves (1934–) was fascinated with the paintings of Le Corbusier and the architecture of Gerrit Rietveld. His buildings used color and celebrated the methodology of collage. Other architects moved in the direction of social realism, such as Robert Venturi (1925–) and Denise Scott Brown (1931–), who were influenced by Pop Art and who turned their gaze at highway architecture and most specifically to Las Vegas, Nevada. Charles Moore (1925–93) was part of a movement that sought a deeper personal commitment to architecture than that which could be provided by a standard professional practice. In his writings we see the beginnings of an interest in phenomenology, a movement that was to grow steadily in the United States and abroad and that was linked to a trend toward political conservatism in architecture.

18.151 AT&T Building, New York City

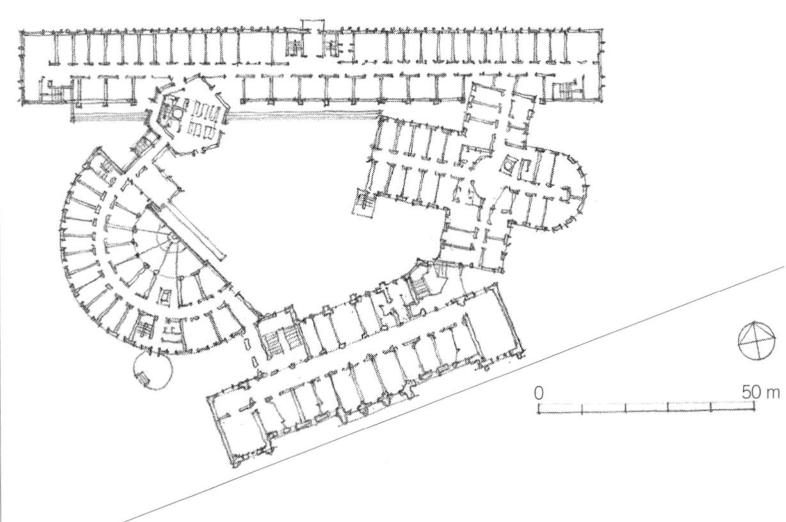


18.152 Plan: Social Science Research Center, Berlin, Germany

Moving from Philip Johnson to Charles Moore, one can recognize the inherent complexity of postmodernism, for though it heralded a release from the strictures of modernism and was thus a liberating movement, it also had conservative leanings, as was brought to the fore by the phenomenologists who, in the United States and elsewhere, began to replace the more socially oriented architects in academia. Those who wanted to take up the issue of community service often left the field of architecture for a discipline like planning. Among the early phenomenologists, Christian Norberg Schultz (1926–2000) was strongly influenced by Martin Heidegger and argued for a rationally based aesthetic, whereas Moore argued that architecture needed to integrate a sensibility to landscape with an aesthetic determined by psychology and memory. At the opposite extreme from phenomenology was psychoanalysis, which among architects, unlike artists at the time, received very little interest. Even postmodernism in architecture had its limitations.

Certainly one of the most intriguing aspects of postmodernism was its interest in irony. No architecture prior to, or even hence, has allowed the designer to experiment with cultural and historical images with as free a reign as postmodernism. Examples include: Piazza d'Italia (New Orleans, 1975–8) by Charles Moore, the AT&T building (1984) by Philip Johnson, the National Collegiate Football Hall of Fame (1967; unbuilt) by Venturi and Scott Brown, and the Animal Crackers House (1976–8) by Stanley Tigerman. Tigerman, influenced by inflated Pop forms, built an addition to a house that looks like a series of rollers that can be turned by using the ventilators on the sides as knobs. It is half industrial and half cartoonish in character. Even more provocative were the designs of the New York–based firm known as SITE (Sculpture in the Environment), which received commissions from a forward-looking supermarket chain known as Best. In one project, they peeled the brick facade from the box, and in another, they designed the facade to appear as if it were in a state of decay and ruin. The irony was not aimed at the strangeness of pop art but the strangeness of suburban architecture. They were the first to engage the question of the shopping mall in the form of critique and humor simultaneously.

Robert Stern (1939–) also interrogated the image of the American suburb in his Point West Place office building in Framingham, Massachusetts (1983–4), which in essence placed an Egyptianesque facade onto an otherwise generic office building. James Stirling's project for the Berlin Social Science Research Center (1981) begins with an existing building and appendaged behind it, in the form of a collage, an amphitheater, a castle, an octagonal baptistery, a church, and *uffizi* (religious offices). Through this historicism, which relies on precedents from the classical to the Renaissance, he pokes fun at a city that, unlike other European capitals, has no real history, since it was basically a modern city of the late 18th century. This instant Europeanization of Berlin was also meant to challenge Europe's fascination with its own past.

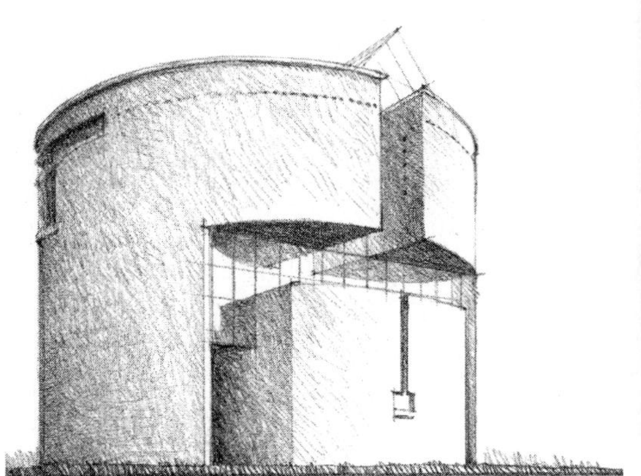

18.153 House at Stabio, Switzerland

18.154 Beaubourg Museum, Paris, France

But architecture was not all just open exploration without rules. Many postmodernists rejected humor and more particularly the openendedness of the design process in favor of authenticity and seriousness. This movement was particularly strong in Europe. The German architect and theorist, Leon Krier (1946–), a particularly strident critic of modernism, argued for a new Hellenism; in England, Prince Charles called for a return to premodern English styles. In Italy, Aldo Rossi (1937–97), though witty, argued for a typological coherence to architecture and challenged both modernists and postmodernists by staying within the brutalist aesthetic as at the Gallaratese (1969–73), a large apartment building project on the outskirts of Milan, where Rossi designed one of the blocks with a rhetoric of extreme formalist stoicism. Nonetheless, the emergence of an ethos of "regionalism" grew even though in many places, regional traits had to be significantly enhanced, purified, and dehybridized to fit the requirement that it be "not modernist." The work of the Swiss architect Mario Botta (1943–) was championed for awhile as "regionalist" in that it drew, though vaguely, on historical forms. Nonetheless, it remained modern in the organization of the plan and monumental in its volumetric massing.

Whereas many of the more conservative postmodernists attempted to orient architecture back to its temporal, contextual and historical roots, Peter Eisenman (1932–), along with John Hedjuk (1929–2000) and a few others, rejected any softening of architecture in the direction of culture. Architecture, to maintain itself as a discipline, had to remain aloof from cultural traditions and bourgeois demands. Eisenman thus created for his buildings a set of formal constraints that had nothing to do with function or program. His radical formalism lies at the opposite end of the spectrum from Robert Venturi's pop contextualism. Nonetheless, both celebrated the disjuncture of expectations in the understanding of what is architecture. Eisenman's architecture, however, maintained a focus on the design process by seeking out a self-referential language that excluded the traditional priority of client needs. He proved that function is just as flexible as form.

This is somewhat different from Rossi, who wanted functionalism to bend to the primacy of form. Postmodernism, through the influences of pop art, also began to accommodate itself to the new medium of signage and advertising. The Beaubourg Museum (1977–81) in Paris, designed by the firm Piano and Rogers, was originally to have large billboards suspended from its metal structure. Air conditioning ducts are blue, electricity conduits are yellow; elevator cables are red; staircases gray; and the structure, white. Given the emphasis on visual impact that architecture made, postmodern architects, on the subject of technology, had little to contribute, but Helmut Jahn in his office building in Chicago (1979) left elements of the structure exposed and experimented with new forms of skyscrapers that were to foreshadow the skyscraper revival of the 1990s.

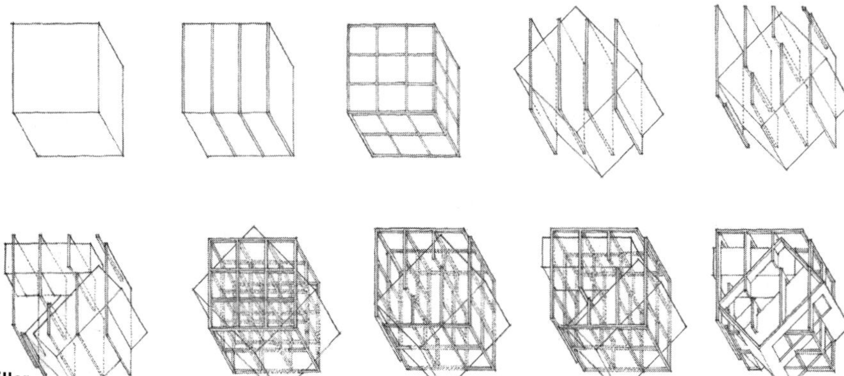

18.155 Eisenman's drawings for House III for Robert Miller

18.156 Bilbao Guggenheim Museum, Bilbao, Spain

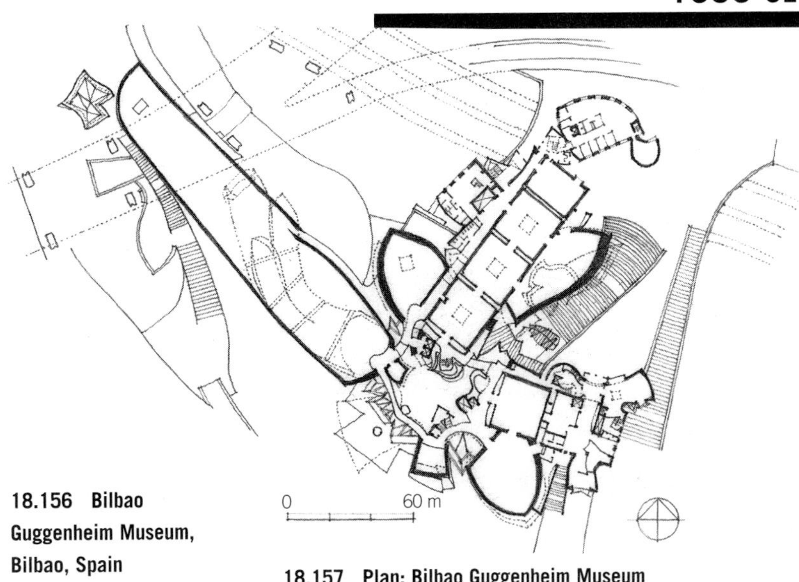


18.157 Plan: Bilbao Guggenheim Museum

**Postmodern Museum**

Throughout the 19th century and into a good part of the 20th, the museum carried with it the imprint of the Enlightenment. The ordering of space, the systematization of knowledge, and the owning of precious objects went hand in hand with the conception of history, the advances of archaeology, and the understanding of art. Museums also become symbols of national pride, as for instance the National Gallery in London (1861) and the Kyoto National Museum (1898). The imprint of neoclassicism was so strong in all these buildings, so strong, in fact, that the modern movement could do little to challenge the equation. Apart from the Museum of Modern Art in New York (1931) or Frank Lloyd Wright's Guggenheim Museum (1951), there are few well-known built examples of museums in the modern style. It was only in the 1970s that the modern museum emerged as a force within design culture. The Beaubourg Museum (1977–81) in Paris defied all the predictions of disaster to become one of the most visited sites in Paris, apart from the Eiffel Tower. But it was still more the exception than the rule.

But by the 1990s, with the boom in the global economy and a heightened competition for tourist dollars, museums soon became more than just signs of a city's cultural strength; they had become instrumental to the economies of entire regions. A blockbuster exhibition could bring in millions of dollars in secondary revenue and taxes. If there is one building type that piqued the interest of architects, planners, politicians, and the public alike, it was the museum. What the civic center or philharmonic hall had been in the 1960s, the pedestrian zone in the 1980s, the museum had become in the 1990s. The transition began with the Neue Staatsgalerie by James Stirling (1977–83) and was complete by the time of the opening of the Pyramide du Louvre by I. M. Pei in 1989.

Nonetheless, given the economic power of the museum, the architect is no longer expected to be responsible for representing conservative traditions dating back to the ancient Romans; the architect is not even responsible for representing high culture, as Mies van der Rohe and Louis Kahn had thought so many decades ago. Rather, the architect is responsible for representing the irrefutable modernity of contemporary culture itself. One hardly even needs to mention Bilbao as the museum that not only revived an entire city and district but revived the museum industry itself. It is the only museum—and for that matter piece of architecture—in history to have an economic principle named after it: the Bilbao effect.

18.158 Pyramide du Louvre, Paris, France

18.159 Light Chapel

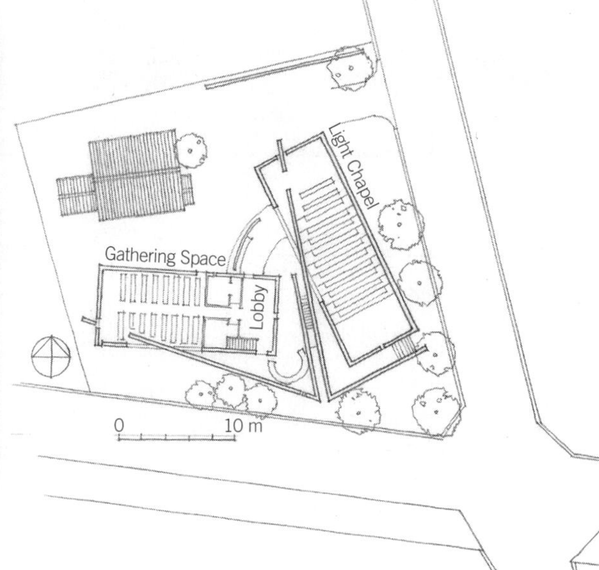


18.160 Site plan: Ibaraki Kasugaoka Kyokai Church, Osaka, Japan

18.161 Section: Light Chapel

## POSTMODERN NONWESTERN WORLD

In most of the nonwestern world, modernism was, in one way or another, tied up with nationalism and national identity. Modernism, in other words, was saturated with questions of identity well before postmodernism placed its emphasis on this theme. Modernism was laden with political meaning, regardless of its claims to the purely functional or universal. The postmodern crisis in the United States and Europe, which raised the question of identity and meaning was therefore moot in the nonwestern world. Postmodernism, nonetheless, had a profound impact on the nonwestern world primarily because it enforced an equation between modernism with the West. Modernism came to be seen as "imposed" on the nonwestern world. This denied these regions the right to claim modern architecture as a rightful part of its history and identity and hastened the search for a style that was considered more authentic or regional, even if it meant going against the grain of regional historical differentiation.

In this way, the nonwestern world in the 1980s and early 1990s found itself in the situation of reassessing its claims to modernity and nationalism and undertook a reexamination of its roots. Japanese architecture, for example, moved away from metabolic and high modern expressions. Arata Isozaki (1931–) became more literal in his references, whereas younger, self-trained architects like Tadao Ando (1941–) gravitated toward more elemental forms that stressed the interplay of light and materials in the experience of minimalist, poetic creations. His work became the hallmark of a new and highly successful Japanese aesthetic that was highly modern and yet, in being so abstract, appealed to defenders of "regional" architecture. His concrete work, the predominant material of his expression, was immaculately poured. His Chapel on the Water (Shingonshu Honpukuji, 1991) in Hokkaido, Japan, for instance, focused the experience on an indelible moment where a stair descended through a round pond with a smattering of water lilies. At his Light Chapel (Ibaraki Kasugaoka Kyokai Church, 1989), the altar wall is composed of four pieces of concrete that weightlessly hover to create a luminous cross; at the rear, in another tour de force, the slight gap between the walls allows a blinding sliver of light to penetrate the dark stillness.

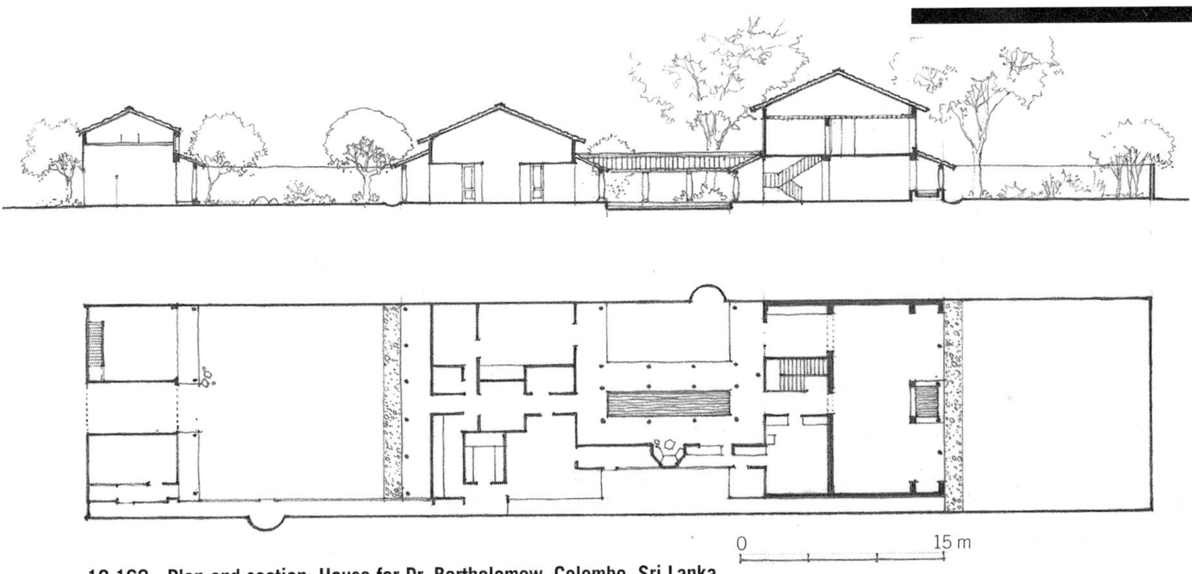


**18.162 Plan and section: House for Dr. Bartholomew, Colombo, Sri Lanka**

Though Japanese postmodernism could be seen as a highly refined form of modernism, so refined that many could see it as stripped of all except the most basic of cultural references, the rise of postmodernism in other places was significantly more messy and was often accompanied by the erosion of the secular nation-state as the common reference point for diverse communities. Postmodernism allowed alternative claims to the conventions of nationalism. Immediately, of course, what constituted "roots" became highly contested, particularly in places like south Asia, where different claims, given India's complex past, could be made upon history and its associated aesthetics. Thus for instance, right-wing Hindu nationalists demolished a mosque in northern India, sparking interfaith riots in the early 1990s on the grounds that it had been built on the foundations of a Hindu temple a millennium ago. Similarly, the Islamic world saw a resurgence of more orthodox claims to Islamic identity in cultural expression, forcing the rollback of national modernism in places such as Turkey and Egypt. Often, however, the tendency to see everything before modernism as traditional (i.e., firmly established and permanent) has left a gap in how to engage earlier aesthetic modalities in the modern world.

A long list could be made of architects of the postcolonial and nonwestern world who are searching for a way to resolve this issue without resorting to, or endorsing, regressive, nationalist politics. For the most part, such architects, deeply steeped in the sensibilities of modern architecture, have attempted to reimagine their practices by referencing easily accessible and often somewhat stereotypical claims to mandalas, and traditional construction systems. Others talk of "urban morphologies," "place-making," and even "genius loci," a term that has its origins in European Romantic philosophy of the early 19th century. More realistic was the work of Hasan Fathy (1899–1989) in Egypt. He worked to create low-cost architecture, utilizing ancient design methods and materials. He also trained local inhabitants to make their own materials and build their own buildings. Climatic conditions, public health considerations, and ancient craft skills also affected his design decisions.

Geoffrey Bawa (1919–2003), an architect from Sri Lanka, though trained at the Architectural Association in London, engaged problems of managing large land and water systems while building with masons who know nothing of modern building techniques. He drew, nonetheless, on local solutions and developed an aesthetic that is freely eclectic in its expression. His house for Dr. Bartholomew (1961–3) utilized a mixture of locally available materials, including coconut trunks, granite, and fired-earth tiles, as well as concrete for the foundation. He also introduced water pools not only for cooling but also to serve as visual beacons along the circulation path.

18.163 Simpson Lee House, Mt. Wilson, Australia

18.164 Marie Short House, Kempsey, Australia

In Mexico, Luis Barragán (1902–88), who had collaborated with Louis Kahn in the design for the plaza at the Salk Institute building, developed a design vocabulary of simple forms, their elegance brightened by the use of color. He differentiated in his own house windows that were meant for framing a view and those that just were there to admit light. One of the most consistent explorations of a localized modernism was undertaken by Australia's Glenn Murcutt. Beginning with a sensibility strongly impressed by Mies van der Rohe's minimalist architecture, Murcutt's one-man practice has taken up small projects in the manner of California's Case Study Houses. His designs minimize the use of material while maximizing their effectiveness in controlling climate. His buildings disturb the land as little as possible and are constructed as efficiently as possible. A deep-seated knowledge of the site and of local conditions is cardinal to Murcutt's ethic; by choice, he has never practiced outside of Australia, although he teaches worldwide.

Murcutt's Magney House (1982–4), located 500 meters from the southern Pacific coast of Australia, has a masonry wall 2.1 meters high to the south to buffer the building against cold ocean winds. By contrast, the northern facade is completely glazed, though protected by retractable louvers, to take in the light and views. A continuous band of glazing, about 2 meters off the ground, encircles the house to admit ambient light and to make the sky visible from inside. Above this, two asymmetrical curves built with corrugated metal sheets not only protect the glazing and collect water that is stored in subterranean tanks but also give to the house its signature roof profile as a "machine" for living. Two vents from the kitchens hover above the roof like periscopes. Taut V-shaped steel struts hold the roof overhang, calculated to keep the summer sun out and to admit the sun in winter. The plan is simple: a thin band of serving spaces to the south are separated from the northern bank of living spaces by a corridor, located exactly where the gully collecting water from the two roofs runs. Murcutt's Simpson-Lee House (1989–94) is built on the same principles but with a very different expression.

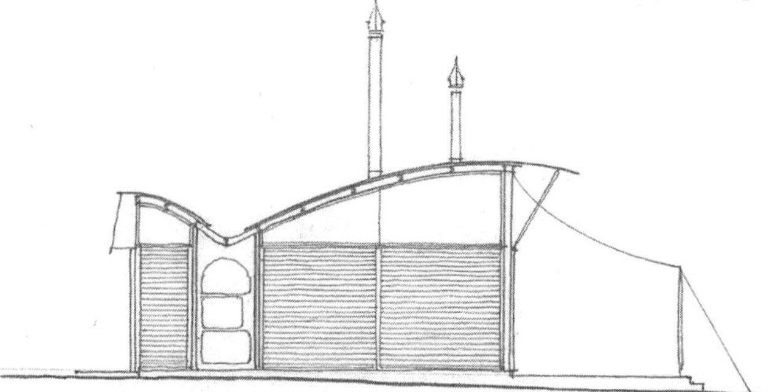

18.165 Section: Magney House, Bingie Bingie, Australia

# Globalization Takes Command

The awareness that we live in a world of global relationships is now itself global. There is, however, no singularity to this phenomenon, just as the distinction between global and local is much too narrow to be an effective tool of comprehension. In what follows, we shall map out seven different trends that can be found at the global level. Each comes to terms with the contemporary realities of globalization, to use that awkward word, differently. And even though there are many overlaps, each is governed by a set of circumstances, ideologies, and politics that differentiate it from the others.

To start, one has to understand the scale of architecture in the global economy. Construction activity for the year 2000 around the globe was worth over 3.4 trillion dollars and constituted a large portion of the global economy alongside tourism. The numbers will only increase given the economic development in Asia, Latin America, and Eastern Europe. Though a vast proportion of these construction dollars are filtered through large, anonymous real-estate corporations, there are a host of large firms that provide architectural services at this level. In this context, the word "global" refers to large international firms now working in the Asian and south Asian market.

Kohn Pedersen Fox Associates (KPF) is just such a firm. Founded in 1976 and originally working mainly in the United States and Europe, it has recently designed the Tigamas master plan (1990), Kuwait International Hotel (1991), Singapore Arts Center (1992), Tel Aviv Peninsula master plan (1996), as well as De Hoftoren-Ministry Headquarters for The Hague, Netherlands (2003), to list only a small fraction of their work. Seattle-based Callison Architecture is another firm operating at the global level. With five hundred people under a single roof, it is the retail expert of the world, designing in the Philippines (Ayala Center Greenbelt), China (Bank of China, Shangdi Center), Japan (Seibu Department Stores), India (Gardens Galleria), Qatar (Pearl of the Gulf), Dubai (Diera City Centre), and Russia (Ikea stores). HOK, Gensler, NBBJ, RTKL, and Ellerbe Beckett are some of the other large firms practicing worldwide.

China, of course is a big draw since it has opened itself up to foreign investment in a massive industrialization and capitalization program, the likes of which have never been seen before. By 2020, 15 of the world's largest 20 cities are going to be in China. At any particular moment, there are said to be more than 500 cranes at work transforming the skyline of Shanghai. The worldwide price of steel has doubled in the last two years because of the demand from China, meaning that the cost of tall buildings in the rest of the world has risen appreciably. While the material effects of this transformation are felt worldwide, another kind of competition for supremacy is being waged in Asia in the race to claim the tallest building in the world. In less than 10 years, this title has shifted from Kuala Lumpur to Shanghai, to Taipei, and soon back to Shanghai. The power of tall buildings as a global icon was verified with the destruction of Minoru Yamasaki's twin towers of the World Trade Center by terrorists. That a handful of fanatical religious zealots, planning vengeance in a remote field in the middle of Afghanistan, could focus so precisely on these skyscrapers as the embodiment of the United States, testifies to the continuing hold of architecture as an icon, as well as its perishability, in the global imagination of our world.

19.1 Skyline of modern Shanghai, China

19.2 OMA's Central Public Library, Seattle, Washington, USA

A second way to map architecture at the global level is to follow the careers of those who self-consciously infiltrate the global economy with the principles of high design. Frank Gehry is the leader in this respect, designing opera houses, museums, and institutional headquarters the world over. These buildings are meant to be high profile and are readily used in tourist brochures. This tendency began after World War II with such commissions as Jørn Utzon's Sydney Opera House (1959-73), Hans Scharoun's Berlin Philharmonic Hall (1956-63), and Philip Johnson's and John Burgee's AT&T Building (1978) in New York City. The most recent examples include the construction in Seoul of the Leeum Museum with buildings by Rem Koolhaas, Mario Botta, and Jean Nouvel. Qatar is being transformed into a world-class cultural center with completion of five new museums, the Islamic Museum by I. M. Pei and another one by Santiago Calatrava, the renowned Spanish architect-engineer. The global commodification of prestige buildings should not lead us to dismiss their potential importance in the history of architecture, for they are places where architects can experiment not only with new technologies but also with new ideas about program and function. These buildings also are for many the most accessible examples of avant-garde architectural production.

Nonetheless, these projects are not unambiguous. The Guggenheim Museum in Bilbao, Spain, has brought in millions in tourist dollars, and the advantages and disadvantages need to be continually kept in mind. But even this is not a new phenomenon. The "Bilbao effect" is today what the great international exhibitions were to the 19th century—economic engines that, on the one hand, promise an enhancement of awareness and knowledge but, on the other hand, extend the flattening process of capital. The Qatar museums are specifically aimed at tourists, whom officials hope will be lured to beach resorts and expansive desert landscapes, "all in a very safe environment." According to one official, "We expect tourism growth to more than double in the next six years, from the 400,000 visitors that presently visit Qatar, to more than one million tourists in 2010."

Among the elite designers who work at the global scale, it is only Rem Koolhaas who has an actual theory about the status and future of architecture. Nonetheless, Koolhaas, like others, has become the favored architect of the governmental and capitalist elite, or at least those who want to think fast and preferably big, whether it be the Dutch for their embassy in Berlin, the Chinese and their CCTV tower in Beijing, the European Union and its headquarters in Brussels, Samsung with its Leeum Museum in Seoul, or Prada with its elegant store in New York City. The difference between KPF and Rem Koolhaas is thus blurry, for both operate at the intersection of high capital and high design. Koolhaas, however, has a practice that seeks to articulate much more strongly than KPF the autonomy of the architect and the symbolic celebration of capital in the name of architecture. To this effect, Koolhaas in 1975 founded Office for Metropolitan Architecture (OMA), a pure design corporation that in his own words blends "contemporary architecture, urbanism and cultural analysis" and tries to address the problems associated with contemporary globalization with truly innovative and radical solutions. Besides institutional buildings in Europe, the United States, and Asia, OMA has designed urban plans for large cities, proposed a new logo for the European Union, and even prepared the digital identity for a global high-fashion retail giant.

**19.3 Interior and exterior views of Santiago Calatrava's Quadracci Pavilion, Milwaukee Art Museum, USA**

In contradistinction to this approach are the architectural practices that come from the direction of nongovernmental organizations (NGOs) that aim to solve pressing social and economic problems. NGOs are more flexible than government bureaucracies and thus often more capable of identifying problems and suggesting solutions that are acceptable to local communities. The amount of unacknowledged work done by NGOs around the world is staggering. An example is the unprecedented building effort undertaken by Abhiyan, a collection of 40 NGOs in Kutch in western India, who came together after the devastating earthquake of January 26, 2000, to find ways of building 20,000 dwellings for the affected communities of Kutch. Within a year, Abhiyan, under the leadership of Sandeep Virmani, was able to have these dwellings constructed by empowering local communities to build for themselves in a systematic manner. While rebuilding, they emphasized developing techniques for reinforcing the structures so that they would be more earthquake-resistant and more sustainable.

To do this, they did not fetishize local or traditional building techniques but freely adapted low-tech, innovative building techniques developed in other countries with seismic issues, such as Japan, with the help of local masons who also had their own ideas on how to build. In the end, it was found that by simply altering the manner in which some of the reinforcing was tied together and by introducing ferro-cement walls at strategic places, the new structures could not only be made much more seismically resistant but could be explained to the local mason quickly and coherently. Such work by "barefoot architects" around the world is the other side of the world of global capital.

A fourth type of architecture operating at the global level is produced by local architects with small firms who, despite varying design methodologies, advocate a carefully crafted and well-thought-out relationship between program and the constraints formed by climate, site conditions, and materials.

One could mention Atelier Feichang Jianzhu's Split House near Beijing, where the architect uses rammed earth not only for its natural thermal insulating properties but also because rammed earth has been a part of Chinese architecture since time immemorial. And when framed against the backdrop of the nearby cliffs, one can even see in it a Ruskinian ethos about the nature of material and geology. In Adira Broid Rojkind's F-2 House, volcanic basalt, a common local material in Mexico City, is used as a visual and tactile contrast to the cast-in-place concrete. The aesthetic is close to that of Marcel Breuer, who helped create a form of modernism that was compatible with the open landscape and the need to capture the breeze. Both these houses, therefore, are high modernist, but that should not be any reason to condemn them. Designing within the context of "the local" does not mean that one has to use or replicate ancient techniques, nor does it mean one has to aestheticize local customs, as is so often done by those who reduce the Chinese tradition of screening to working with metal screens.

**19.4 Two views of Sardarnagar, a new township near Bhuj, India, established by Hunnarshala (Sandeep Virmani, Director) after the devastating earthquake of 2001**

These projects, if one wants to critique them, are all very serious. Irony is particularly remote in today's aesthetic and will, sadly, remain so, given the penchant to appear respectful to tradition and inheritance. For that reason, we would like to point to a fifth global phenomenon, architecture produced locally but by amateurs and architects with an open sensibility to the potential in ready-mades: a house in Massachusetts made completely out of newspaper, furniture included; a house in Nevada using automobile tires; complete buildings made out cardboard tubes; squatter settlements in Mexico that make use of discarded building materials; architects who use off-the-shelf technologies to subvert expectations: and those who build houses with shipping containers. Sean Godsell's Future Shack, for instance, combines a parasol with a shipping container to design a mass-produced relocatable house. The Rural Studio, developed by the late Samuel Mockbee at Auburn University in Alabama, is exemplary in this regard. Working with the basic principle that even the poorest deserve the dignity of good architecture, Mockbee worked with his students to design and build innovative and imaginative architectural solutions. Sidings made from salvaged automobile windscreens and license plates are only some of the ways in which he has advanced the frontier of architectural practice.

A sixth category of global production revolves around the question of environment. There are several historical tracks that one can take to understand the origins of this movement. Some reach back to 19th-century efforts to reform industrialism, some to the tradition of environmentally sensitive architecture such as that of Frank Lloyd Wright's Taliesin, some to the ecology movement of the 1960s, some to the development of the Green Party in Germany, and some to the emergence of the field of environmental management in the 1970s. Since most of the issues involved law, government, and industry, architecture has only recently begun to find a role within the debates. Today some architects specialize in design-build projects, others in green-housing projects, self-sufficient houses, solar houses, eco villages, and now, so-called "health houses." The central term in this movement is the word "sustainability," used, however, by different groups in different contexts. In the context of environmental management, the issues revolve around questions of politics, government, law, planning, and banking. Architectural design, as such, is often left to the end of the process. This has begun to change as now most large firms offer a specialization in green architecture.

To establish a common standard of measurement when talking about green buildings, U.S. architects now use the LEED (Leadership in Energy and Environmental Design) Green Building Rating System. It intends to stimulate competition in designing effective green buildings and assuring that they meet certain criteria. Connections between sustainability and architectural design, can, however, range from low-cost amateur-designed architecture to high-cost, heavily researched, and technically sophisticated architecture. Among the architects who work with low budgets, one could point to Thomas Herzog in Germany, who combines conventional methods of environmental design (e.g., high spaces to reduce air-conditioning costs) with high-end technology such as specially designed types of glass and cooling systems. William McDonough has championed the ideological imperative that sustainability should have for the leading corporations of the world. His Volkswagen headquarters and his projected 65,000-square-meter plant, built on 320 acres of former rain forest in Brazil, are just two of his larger commissions. At the high-end of green architecture, one could point to Foster and Partners' design for the Commerzbank in Frankfurt, Germany, now the tallest building in Europe. Interspersed in the tower are sky gardens.

**19.5 Antioch Baptist Church, Perry County, Alabama, a project of Auburn University's Rural Studio**

**19.6 Commerzbank, Frankfurt, Germany**

A final but increasingly important global formation centers on the World Heritage List to preserve buildings and building environments, created under the auspices of UNESCO (United Nations Educational, Scientific, and Cultural Organization) in 1972. Only 30 years old, the list now consists of more than 800 properties in 134 countries. The list is continually expanded and some are hoping that even places like Chandigarh will be placed on the list. The square meters of space that is now curated, or under some form of protection, has risen globally over a hundred-thousand fold if not more, if one remembers that now entire valleys, villages, and landscape are under protection.

Preservation enhances the image of architecture, that is for sure, and places finances not in the making of new architecture but in its upkeep and maintenance. But one must suspect that it is just as much the lure of tourist dollars that drives the search for heritage as it is a need to preserve identity. The Dogon cities of Djenné were inscribed onto the list in 1988, and now a road is being planned to reach the remote location. Being "protected" will certainly be a mixed blessing. More than 400,000 people visit the remote site of Machu Picchu every year, even though it is a heritage-protected site. Global heritage is another form of global intermixing. Whether that intermixing is to be understood as a form of cultural liberation from the hegemony of "the local" or as cultural contamination by the hegemony of the global is a question that is only to be resolved politically. In 1994, a new category was created by UNESCO, "cultural landscapes." It was introduced to open the way for a broader representation of what UNESCO calls "human heritage," but what its delimitations are will become increasingly complex given that "cultural landscapes" will become increasingly entangled with politics.

# Glossary

**Abacus** The rectangular stone slab forming the top of a column capital, plain in the Doric style but molded or otherwise enriched in other styles.

**Abbey** 1. A monastery under the supervision of an abbot, or a convent under the supervision of an abess, belonging to the highest rank of such institutions. 2. The church of an abbey.

**Acanthus** A Mediterranean plant whose large, toothed leaves became a common motif in the ornamental program of Corinthian and composite capitals and friezes.

**Accouplement** The placement of two columns or pilasters very close together.

**Acropolis** 1. The fortified high area or citadel of an ancient Greek city, typically marked by an important temple. 2. The citadel of Athens and site of the Parthenon.

**Adobe** Sun-dried brick made of clay and straw, commonly used in countries with little rainfall.

**Aedicule** A small construction designed in the form of a building, as a canopied niche flanked by colonnettes or a door or window opening, framed by columns or pilasters and crowned with a pediment.

**Aggregate** From the Latin *aggregare*, to add together. Any of various hard, inert, mineral materials, as sand and gravel, added to a cement paste to make concrete or mortar.

**Agora** A marketplace or public square in an ancient Greek city, usually surrounded by public buildings and porticoes and commonly used as a place for popular or political assembly.

**Alameda** 1. A public promenade lined with shade trees. 2. In Latin America, a boulevard, park, or public garden with such a promenade.

**Alcazar** A castle or fortress of the Spanish Moors, specifically, the palace of the Moorish kings in Seville, Spain, which was later used by Spanish kings.

**Altar** 1. An elevated place or structure upon which sacrifices are offered or incense burned in worship or before which religious rites are performed. 2. The table in a Christian church upon which the Sacrament of the Eucharist is celebrated.

**Amalaka** The bulbous, ribbed stone finial of a *shikhara* in Indian architecture.

**Ambo** Either of two raised stands from which the Gospels or Epistles were read or chanted in an early Christian church.

**Ambulatory** 1. The covered walk of an atrium or cloister. 2. An aisle encircling the end of the choir or chancel of a church, originally used for processions.

**Amphitheater** 1. An oval or round building with tiers of seats around a central arena, as those used in ancient Rome for gladiatorial contests and spectacles.

**Ang** A lever arm in traditional Chinese construction, placed parallel to the rafters and raked at an angle to counterbalance the forces applied by the inner and outer purlins. The *ang* supports the outermost purlin by means of a bracket or crossbeam and is pinned at the inner end against a purlin. The *ang* first appeared in the 3rd century CE, but served purely as a decorative element after the Song dynasty.

**Annular vault** A barrel vault with a circular plan in the shape of a ring.

**Anta** In Greek temples, a rectangular pier or pilaster formed by thickening the end of a projecting wall.

**Apadana** The grand columnar audience hall in a Persian palace.

**Apse** A semicircular or polygonal projection of a building, usually vaulted and used esp. at the sanctuary or the east end of a church to define the space for an altar. Also called an exedra.

**Apteral** 1. Without a colonnade along the sides. 2. Having no aisles, as a church. 3. Revealing no aisles, as a church facade.

**Aqueduct** A conduit or artificial channel for conducting water from a remote source, usually by gravity, esp. an elevated structure constructed by the Romans to carry a water channel across a valley or over a river.

**Arabesque** A complex and ornate design that employs flowers, foliage, and sometimes animal and geometric figures to produce an intricate pattern of interlaced lines.

**Arcade** 1. A range of arches supported on piers or columns, a composition dating back to Hellenistic times and used mainly in Islamic and Christian architecture. 2. An arched, roofed gallery or passageway with shops on one or both sides.

**Arch** A curved structure for spanning an opening and designed to support a vertical load primarily by axial compression.

**Architecture parlante** "Speaking architecture," a term used in 18th-century France to describe the architecture of buildings that, in their plans or elevations, create an image that suggests their functions.

**Architrave** 1. The lowermost division of a classical entablature, resting directly on the column capitals and supporting the frieze. 2. A molded or decorative band framing a rectangular door or window opening.

**Arcuate** Curved or arched like a bow: a term used in describing the arched or vaulted structure of a Romanesque church or Gothic cathedral, as distinguished from the trabeated architecture of an Egyptian hypostyle hall or Greek Doric temple.

**Arris** A sharp edge or ridge formed by two surfaces meeting at an exterior angle, as that formed by adjoing flutes of a classical column.

**Aryaka** In Indian architecture, a line of five columns symbolizing the Five Dhiyana Buddhas.

**Asana** Throne in a Hindu temple.

**Ashlar** A squared building stone finely dressed on all faces adjacent to those of other stones so as to permit very thin mortar joints.

**Ashram** House for resting in Indian architecture.

**Atrium** 1. The main or central inner hall of an ancient Roman house, open to the sky at the center and usually having a pool for the collection of rainwater. Also called *cavaedium*. 2. The forecourt of an early Christian church, flanked or surrounded by porticoes. 3. An open, skylit court around which a house or building is built. 4. A skylit, central court in a building, esp. a large interior one having a glass roof and surrounded by several stories of galleries.

**Attic** 1. A low story or decorative wall above an entablature or the main cornice of a classical facade. 2. A room or space directly under the roof of a building, esp. a house; a garret.

**Axis** 1. The line about which a rotating body turns. 2. A line about which a three-dimensional body or figure is symmetrical. 3. Any line used as a fixed reference in conjunction with one or more other references for determining the position of a point or of a series of points forming a curve or a surface. 4. A straight line to which elements in a composition are referred for measurement or symmetry.

**Axonometric projection** The orthographic projection of a three-dimensional object inclined to the picture plane in such a way that its three principal axes are foreshortened. The resulting drawing has all lines parallel to the three principal axes drawn to scale but diagonal and curved lines distorted.

**Bagh** Garden in Indian architecture.

**Bagilu** Gateway in Indian architecture.

**Baldachin, baldacchino** 1. A canopy of fabric carried in religious processions or placed over an altar or throne. 2. An ornamental canopy of stone or marble permanently placed over the high altar in a church.

**Balloon frame** A wooden building frame with studs that rise the full height of the frame from the sill plate to the roof plate, with joists nailed to the studs and supported by sills or by ribbons let into the studs; used esp. in the United States and in Scandinavia.

**Baluster** Any of a number of closely spaced supports, often vase-shaped, for a railing. Also called banister.

**Balustrade** A series of balusters used to support a rail in a stair or balcony. Also called banister.

**Bangla** In Bengal, a hut with a curved thatched roof, the form of which was emulated in brick temples.

**Banister** See **balustrade**.

**Baoli** A stepped well in Indian architecture.

**Baptistery** A part of a church or a separate building in which the rite of baptism is administered.

**Baradari** A Moghul pavillion having triple arcades on each of its four sides, hence its translation as twelvedoored; a summer house.

**Barrel vault** A vault having a semicircular cross section.

**Base** The lowermost portion of a wall, column, pier, or other structure, usually distinctively treated and considered as an architectural unit.

**Basilica** 1. A large oblong building used as a hall of justice and public meeting place in ancient Rome, typically having a high central space lit by a clerestory and covered by timber trusses, as well as a raised dais in a semicircular apse for the tribunal. The Roman basilica served as a model for early Christian basilicas. 2. An early Christian church, characterized by a long, rectangular plan, a high colonnaded nave lit by a clerestory and covered by a timbered gable roof, two or four lower side aisles, a semicircular apse at the end, a narthex, and often other features, as an atrium, a bema, and small semicircular apses terminating the aisles.

**Bastion** A projecting part of a rampart or other fortification, typically forming an irregular pentagon attached at the base to the main work.

**Batter** A backward slope of the face of a wall as it rises.

**Bay** 1. A major spatial division, usually one of a series, marked or partitioned off by the principal vertical supports of a structure. 2. Any of a number of principal compartments or divisions of a wall, roof, or other part of a building marked off by vertical or transverse supports.

**Bazaar** A marketplace or shopping quarter where goods are exposed for sale, esp. in the Middle East, consisting either of rows of small shops or stalls in a narrow street; or of a certain section of town divided into narrow passageways.

**Beacon citadel** A component of the Qin Dynasty defense, comprising strategic places from which garrison troops could survey the surrounding area and light fires to transmit signals.

**Beacon tower** Any of the high towers built along a great wall at regular intervals from which warning signals or alarms could be sent back and forth by means of fire and smoke.

**Belvedere** A building or architectural feature of a building, designed and situated to look out upon a pleasing scene.

**Bema** 1. The sanctuary space surrounding the altar of an Eastern church. 2. A transverse open space separating the nave and the apse of an early Christian church, developing into the transept of later cruciform churches.

**Bhumi** 1. Earth in Indian architecture. 2. The horizontal relief of a *shikhara* or temple tower.

**Biyong** Jade ring moat: a ritual structure in Chinese architecture enclosing a space in the shape of the *bi*, a flat jade ceremonial disk. Originally a separate structure, the *biyong* later became part of a single ritual complex with the *mingtang*.

**Blind arcade** A series of arches simulating the pattern of the arcade on a wall surface.

**Bouleuterion** A place of assembly in ancient Greece, esp. for a public body.

**Boulevard** Originally, the flat summit of a rampart; later, any of the major tree-lined thoroughfares, which were often laid out over old fortifications.

**Bracket** A support projecting horizontally from a wall to bear the weight of a cantilever or to strengthen an angle, as along an eave or under a bay window.

**Brahmin** Any of the priests belonging to the Indian upper class.

**Brise-soleil** A screen, usually of louvers, placed on the outside of a building to shield the windows from direct sunlight.

**Broken pediment** A pediment having its raking cornices interrupted at the crown or apex, the gap often being filled with an urn, a cartouche, or other ornament.

**Bungalow** 1. In India, a one-story thatched or tiled house, usually surrounded by a veranda. The term is a corruption of a Hindustani word. 2. In the United States, a derivative of the Indian bungalow, popular esp. in the first quarter of the 20th century, usually having one story or one-and-a-half stories, a widely bracketed gable roof, a large porch, and often built of rustic materials.

**Burj** A Moghul fortified tower.

**Buttress** An external support built to stabilize a structure by opposing its outward thrusts, esp. a projecting support built into or against the outside of a masonry wall.

**Cai** One of eight grades of modular timber sections in traditional Chinese construction, based on the size and span of a building.

**Caldarium** The room in an ancient Roman bath containing a bath of hot water.

**Camber** A slight convex curvature intentionally built into a beam, girder, or truss to compensate for an anticipated deflection.

**Campanile** The Italian word for a tower, usually a bell tower near but not attached to the body of a church.

**Cantilever** A beam or other rigid structural member extending beyond a fulcrum and supported by a balancing member or a downward force behind the fulcrum.

**Capital** The distinctively treated upper end of a column, pillar, or pier that crowns the shaft and takes the weight of the entablature or architrave.

**Cardo** The main north-south route in an ancient Roman town.

**Caryatid** A sculptured female figure used as a column, esp. in ancient Greece.

**Castellated** Having turrets and battlements, like a castle.

**Castrum** An ancient Roman military camp having streets laid out in a grid pattern.

**Catacomb** 1. An underground cemetery consisting of linked galleries and chambers with recesses for coffins and tombs. 2. The subterranean complex of layered corridors with burial vaults, chambers, and niches, covered with inscribed tablets and often decorated with frescoes, built by the early Christians in and near Rome.

**Cathedral** The principal church of a diocese, containing the bishop's throne, called the cathedra.

**Causeway** 1. A road or path raised above surrounding low or wet ground. 2. A raised passageway ceremonially connecting the valley temple with an ancient Egyptian pyramid.

**Cella** Latin for *naos*, the principal chamber or enclosed part of a classical temple, where the cult image was kept.

**Cement** A calcined mixture of clay and limestone, finely pulverized and used as an ingredient in concrete and mortar.

**Cenotaph** A monument erected in memory of a deceased person whose remains are buried elsewhere, often having the form of a domed pavilion or temple replica.

**Centering** A temporary structure or framework for supporting a masonry arch or vault during construction, until the work can support itself.

**Central plan** The plan for a building organized around a large or dominant space, usually characterized by two axes crossing each other at right angles.

**Chamfer** A beveled surface, usually formed or cut at a 45-degree angle to the adjacent principal faces.

**Chancel** The space about the altar of a church for the clergy and choir, often elevated above the nave and separated from it by a railing or screen.

**Chapel** A separately dedicated part of a church for private prayer, meditation, or small religious services.

**Chattri** In Indian architecture, a roof-top kiosk or pavilion having a dome, usually supported on four columns.

**Chaumukha** A Jain sanctuary having four

entrances and four votive images placed back-to-back, each facing a cardinal point.

**Che-wu** The means by which roofs are bent in Chinese architecture.

**Chi-hsin** A type of bracket tier in Chinese architecture, the arms of which are completely closed.

**Chih** In Chinese architecture, the bronze or stone disk situated between a column's base and foot.

**Chlorite** A soft stone that hardens after exposure to air, used for intricate carving in Indian architecture.

**Choir** The part of a church set apart for clergy and the singers of a choir, usually part of the chancel.

**Chorten** A memorial mound of earth in a Tibetan Buddhist religious center.

**Chu** A column in Chinese architecture.

**Chuan-chien** A pyramidal roof in Chinese architecture.

**Ch'uan** A rafter in Chinese architecture.

**Ci** A Chinese shrine.

**Citadel** A fortress in a commanding position in or near a city, used in the control of the inhabitants and in defense during attack or siege.

**Classical** Of or pertaining to the art or architecture of ancient Greece and Rome, on which the Italian Renaissance and subsequent styles, e.g., the baroque and the classic revival, based their development.

**Clerestory** The uppermost section of a Gothic nave characterized by a series of large windows rising above adjacent rooftops to admit daylight to the interior.

**Cloister** 1. A covered walk having an arcade or colonnade on one side that opens onto a courtyard.

**Cloister vault** A compound vault formed by four coves meeting along diagonal vertical planes.

**Coffer** Any of a number of recessed, usually square or octagonal panels in a ceiling, soffit, or vault.

**Colonnade** A row of regularly spaced columns carrying an entablature and usually one side of a roof structure.

**Colonnette** A small, slender column used more often for visual effect than structural support.

**Colossal order** An order of columns more than one story in height. Also called giant order.

**Column** 1. A rigid, relatively slender structural member designed primarily to support compressive loads applied at the member ends. 2. A cylindrical support in classical architecture, consisting of a capital, shaft, and usually a base, either monolithic or built up of drums the full diameter of the shaft.

**Composite order** One of the five classical orders, popular esp. since the beginning of the Renaissance but invented by the ancient Romans, in which the Corinthian order is modified by superimposing four diagonally set Ionic volutes on a bell of acanthus leaves.

**Compression** A force that acts to press and squeeze together, resulting in a reduction in size or volume of an elastic body; many materials (e.g., masonry) are stronger in compression than in tension.

**Concrete** An artificial, stonelike building material made by mixing cement and various mineral aggregates with sufficient water to cause the cement to set and bind the entire mass. Concrete is weak in tension, but the insertion of steel bars helps reinforce concrete to withstand tensile forces.

**Congling** A Chinese temple.

**Corbel** A brick or stone projecting from within a wall, usually to support a weight.

**Corinthian order** The most ornate and least used of the five classical orders, developed by the Greeks in the 4th century BCE but used more extensively in Roman architecture; similar in most respects to the Ionic but usually of slenderer proportions and characterized esp. by a deep bell-shaped capital decorated with acanthus leaves and an abacus with concave sides.

**Cornice** 1. The uppermost member of a classical entablature, consisting typically of a *cymatium*, corona, and bed molding. 2. A continuous, molded projection that crowns a wall or other construction, divides it horizontally for compositional purposes, or conceals lighting fixtures, curtain rods, and the like.

**Corps de logis** In French architecture, a term describing the central element of a building as opposed to its subsidiary wings and pavilions.

**Crenel** Any of the open spaces alternating with the merlons of a battlement.

**Crennelation** The regular alternation of merlons and crenels, originally for defense but later used as a decorative motif.

**Cromlech** A circular arrangement of megaliths enclosing a dolmen or burial mound.

**Crossing** The intersection of the nave and transept in a Latin cross-plan church, over which a tower or dome was often built.

**Cross-in-square** A typical Byzantine church plan having nine bays, the center bay of which is a large square surmounted by a dome while the smaller, square corner bays are domed or vaulted, and the rectangular side bays barrel-vaulted.

**Crypt** An underground chamber or vault used as a burial place, esp. one beneath the main floor of a church.

**Cupola** A light structure on a dome or roof, usually crowned with a dome and serving as a belfry, lantern, or **belvedere**.

**Curtain wall** An exterior wall supported wholly by the structural frame of a building and carrying no loads other than its own weight and wind loads. Often consisting of glass panels, this modern innovation made possible other inventions like the *plan libre* or free plan.

**Cyclopean wall** A wall formed with enormous, irregular blocks of stones fitted closely together without the use of mortar. The methods of its construction were so hard to fathom that it was thought to have been erected by a race of giants—the Cyclops.

**Dado** 1. A rectangular groove cut in a member to receive the end of another. 2. The part of a pedestal between the base and the cornice or cap. 3. The lower portion of an interior wall when faced or treated differently from the upper section, as with paneling or wallpaper.

**Dargah** The tomb complex of a Muslim saint.

**Darwaza** An entrance gate in Indian architecture.

**Decorated style** The second of the three phases of English Gothic architecture from the late-13th through the late-14th centuries, characterized by rich tracery, elaborate ornamental vaulting, and refinement of stonecutting techniques.

**Dentil** Any of a series of closely spaced, small, rectangular blocks forming a molding or projecting beneath the coronas of Ionic, Corinthian, and composite cornices.

**Dharmashala** A place of rest for pilgrims of the Indian subcontinent.

**Diwan-i amm** In architecture of the Indian subcontinent, a hall for public meetings.

**Diwan-i khass** In architecture of the Indian subcontinent, a hall for private meetings.

**Dolmen** A prehistoric monument consisting of two or more large upright stones supporting a horizontal stone slab, found esp. in Britain and France and usually regarded as a tomb.

**Dome** A vaulted structure having a circular or polygonal plan and usually the form of a portion of a sphere, so constructed as to exert an equal thrust in all directions.

**Doric order** The oldest and simplest of the five classical orders, developed in Greece in the 7th century BCE and later imitated by the Romans, characterized by a fluted column having no base, a plain cushion-shaped capital supporting a square abacus, and an entablature consisting of a plain architrave, a frieze of triglyphs and metopes, and a cornice, the corona of which has *mutules* on its soffit. In the Roman Doric order, the columns are slenderer, and usually have bases, the channeling is sometimes altered or omitted, and the capital consists of a bandlike necking, an echinus, and a molded abacus.

**Dormer** A projecting structure built out from a sloping roof, usually housing a vertical window or ventilating louver.

**Dou-gong** A bracket system used in traditional Chinese construction to support roof beams, project the eaves outward, and support the interior ceiling. The absence of a triangular tied frame in Chinese architecture made it necessary to multiply the number of supports under the rafters. To reduce the number of pillars would normally require the area of support afforded by each pillar to be increased by the *dou-gong*. The main beams support the roof through intermediary queen posts and shorter upper beams, enabling the roof to have a concave curve. This distinctive curve is believed to have developed at the beginning of the Tang period, presumably to lighten the visual weight of the roof and allow more daylight into the interior.

**Drum** 1. Any of several cylindrical stones laid one above the other to form a column or pier. 2. A cylindrical or faceted construction, often pierced with windows, supporting a dome.

**Dukhang** A Tibetan Buddhist place for prayer.

**Dunbao** A beacon citadel standing apart from a wall in Chinese military architecture.

**Duomo** Italian designation for a true cathedral.

**Durbar** 1. The court of a native prince in India. 2. The audience hall in which an Indian prince or British governor gave a state reception in India.

**Durg** An Indian term for fort.

**Dvipa** An Indian lamp column.

**Echinus** 1. The prominent circular molding supporting the abacus of a Doric or Tuscan capital. 2. The circular molding under the cushion of an Ionic capital, between the volutes, usually carved with an egg-and-dart pattern.

**Eclecticism** A tendency in architecture and the decorative arts to freely mix various historical styles with the aim of combining the virtues of diverse sources or of increasing allusive content, particularly during the second half of the 19th century in Europe and the United States.

**Elevation** An orthographic projection of an object or structure on a vertical picture plane parallel to one of its sides, usually drawn to scale.

**Enfilade** An axial arrangement of doorways connecting a series of rooms so as to provide a vista down the entire length of the suite.

**Engaged column** A column built so as to be truly or seemingly bonded to the wall before which it stands.

**Entablature** The horizontal section of a classical order that rests on the columns, usually composed of a cornice, frieze, and architrave.

**Entasis** A slight convexity given to a column to correct an optical illusion of concavity if the sides were straight.

**Exedra** See **apse**.

**Facade** The front of a building or any of its sides facing a public way or space, esp. one distinguished by its architectural treatment.

**Fang** 1. A tie beam in the *dou-gung* system of traditional Chinese construction. 2. A ward or district of a Chinese city.

**Fang-ch'eng ming-lou** A Ming or Qing dynasty shrine in front of a tomb.

**Fascia** 1. One of the three horizontal bands making up the architrave in the Ionic order. 2. Any broad, flat, horizontal surface, as the outer edge of a cornice or roof.

**Fen** A modular unit in traditional Chinese construction, equal to 1/15 of the height and 1/10th of a width of a *cai*.

**Finial** A relatively small, usually foliated ornament terminating the peak of a spire or pinnacle.

**Fire-resistive construction** Building construction in which the the structural frame, floors, walls, roof, and shaft enclosures have fire-resistance ratings at least equal to those specified by the appropriate authorities.

**Flamboyant style** The final phase of French Gothic architecture from the late-14th through the middle of the 16th centuries, characterized by flamelike tracery, intricacy of detailing, and frequent complication of interior space.

**Fluting** A decorative motif consisting of a series of long, rounded, parallel grooves, as on the shaft of a classical column.

**Flying buttress** An inclined bar of masonry carried on a segmental arch and transmitting an outward and downward thrust from a roof or vault to a solid buttress that through its mass transforms the thrust into a vertical one; a characteristic feature of Gothic construction.

**Folly** A whimsical or extravagant structure built to serve as a conversation piece, lend interest to a view, or commemorate a person or event, found esp. in 18th-century England.

**Forum** The public square or marketplace of an ancient Roman city, the center of judicial and business affairs, and a place of assembly for the people, usually including a basilica and a temple.

**Frieze** 1. The horizontal part of a classical entablature between the cornice and architrave, often decorated with sculpture in low relief.
2. A decorative band, as one along the top of an interior wall, immediately below the cornice, or a sculptured one in a stringcourse on an outside wall.

**Frigidarium** The room in an ancient Roman bath containing a bath of unheated water.

**Fu-chiao lu-tou** In traditional Chinese construction, the system for supporting a corner condition with bracket supports.

**Fu-tien** A hip roof in traditional Chinese construction.

**Gable** The triangular portion of wall enclosing the end of a pitched roof from cornice or eaves to ridge.

**Gable roof** A roof sloping downward in two parts from a central ridge, so as to form a gable at each end.

**Gallery** 1. A long, relatively narrow room or hall, esp. one for public use and having architectural importance through its scale or decorative treatment. 2. An upper level passage in a medieval church above the side aisle and below the clerestory window, used for circulation, seating, and even the display of art.

**Garbh-griha** A "womb chamber," the dark, innermost sanctuary of a Hindu temple, where the statue of the deity is placed.

**Ghat** A broad flight of steps descending to a river in India, esp. a river used as a sacred Indian bathing site.

**Giant order** See **colossal order**.

**Golden section** A proportion between the two dimensions of a plane figure or the two divisions of a line, in which the ratio of the smaller to the larger is the same as the ratio of the larger to the whole: a ratio of approximately 0.618 to 1.000

**Gompa** A Tibetan Buddhist monastery.

**Gong** 1. A cantilevered bracket in traditional Chinese construction. 2. A Chinese palace. Also, see **kung**.

**Gopura** A monumental, usually ornate gateway tower to a Hindu temple enclosure, esp. in southern India.

**Greek cross** A centralized church plan having the form of a cross whose arms are identical and symmetrical about the central space.

**Groin vault** A compound vault formed by the perpendicular intersection of two vaults, forming arched diagonal arrises called groins.

**Guan** A Chinese monastery.

**Gumbad, gunbad** A pre-Moghul dome often applied to mausoleums.

**Gumpha** An Indian cave temple.

**Gurudwara** A Sikh religious site, typically including a temple and rest area.

**Hacienda** 1. A large, landed estate for farming and ranching in North and South American areas once under Spanish influence. 2. The main house on such an estate.

**Hammer beam** One of pair of short horizontal members attached to the foot of a principal rafter at the level of the wall plate, used in place of a tie beam.

**Hashira** 1. A sacred post in Shinto architecture, shaped by human hands. 2. A column, post, or pillar serving as the basic vertical member of a traditional Japanese wooden structure.

**Haweli** An Indian residential building group organized around open courtyards.

**Henge** A circular arrangement of vertically oriented wooden posts or stones.

**Hipped roof** A roof having sloping ends and sides meeting at an inclined projecting angle called a hip.

**Hippodrome** An open-air stadium with an oval track for horse and chariot races in ancient

Greece and Rome.

**Historicism** 1. The reference to a historical moment or style. 2. In architecture, a building whose form adheres to the stylistic principles of an earlier period.

**Hôtel** An 18th-century French townhouse having one or two stories oriented horizontally in a large suburban estate setting.

**Hsieh-shan** A traditional Chinese gable and hip roof.

**Hsuan-shan** A traditional Chinese overhanging gable roof.

**Hua biao** See **que**.

**Hypocaust** A system of flues in the floor or walls of ancient Roman buildings, esp. baths, that provided central heating by receiving and distributing the heat from a furnace.

**Hypostyle** Of or pertaining to a hall having many rows of columns carrying the roof or ceiling.

**Icon** A representation of a sacred Christian personage, as Christ or a saint or angel, typically painted on a wood surface and itself venerated as sacred, esp. in the tradition of the Eastern Church.

**Imam** A mosque's leader of group prayer.

**Insula** A block of buildings or space surrounded by fours streets in an ancient Roman town.

**Ionic order** A classical order that developed in the Greek colonies of Asia Minor in the 6th century BCE, characterized esp. by the spiral volutes of its capital. The fluted columns typically had molded bases and supported an entablature consisting of an architrave of three fascias, a richly ornamented frieze, and a cornice corbeled out on egg-and-dart and dentil moldings. Roman and Renaissance examples are often more elaborate, and usually set the volutes of the capitals 45 degrees to the architrave.

**Iwan** A large vaulted hall serving as an entrance portal and opening onto a courtyard: prevalent in Parthian, Sassanian, and later in Islamic architecture.

**Jami masjid** Friday mosque: A congregational mosque for public prayer, especially on Fridays.

**Jataka** The storytelling of the birth of the Buddha.

**Jian** 1. A standard unit of space in Chinese architecture, marked by adjacent frame supports. The nature and appropriate scale of a building determine the number of *jian* to be allotted: the resulting width, depth, and height of the building then determine the number of *fen* required for the cross section of each structural member. 2. The spatial unit that serves as the basis for the modular structure of a Chinese city: a number of *jian* connected become a building; several buildings arranged along the sides of a lot frame a courtyard; a number of courtyard units side by side become an alley; several alleys line up to create a small street district; a number of such districts form a rectangular ward; wards surround the palace-city and create a grid of streets.

**Jing** In Chinese architecture, a room for private prayer.

**Ka'aba** A small, cubical stone building in the courtyard of the Great Mosque at Mecca containing a sacred black stone and regarded by Muslims as the House of God, the objective of their pilgrimages and the point toward which they turn in praying.

**Kalyan mandapa** In India, a hall with columns in which the marriage of the temple deity and his consort is ritually performed.

**Ke** A Chinese pavillion of many stories.

**Ken** A linear unit for regulating column spacing in traditional Japanese construction, equal to 6 *shaku* (5.97 feet or 1.818 m) in the *inaka-ma* method, and in the *kyo-ma* method, initially set at 6.5 *shaku* (6.5 feet or 1.970 m), but later varying according to room width as determined by tatami units.

**Keystone** Voussoir at the crown of an arch, serving to lock the other voussoirs in place. Until the keystone is in place, no true arch action is incurred.

**Kondo** Golden Hall: the sanctuary where the main image of worship is kept in a Japanese Buddhist temple. The Jodo, Shinshu, and Nicheiren sects of Buddhism use the term *hondo* for this sanctuary, the Shingon and Tendai sects use *chudo*, and the Zen sect uses *butsuden*.

**Kovil** A Tamil description of a temple.

**Kuan** A Taoist monastery consisting of twin main halls connected by a covered corridor.

**Kung** 1. See **gong**. 2. In traditional Chinese architecture, buildings of no special importance within a compound, often not constructed along the central axis of the site plan.

**Kuttambalam** A hall for music and dance in a Kerala temple.

**Lacunar** A ceiling, soffit, or vault decorated with a pattern of recessed panels.

**Lan-e** A lintel in traditional Chinese construction.

**Lanzón** A column of rock portraying a Peruvian mythical being.

**Lathe-turned** Of or pertaining to a column whose cylindrical shaft is ornamented with incisions revealing its construction, during which it was laid on a lathe and then carved.

**Latin cross** A dominant church plan type in western medieval architecture, in which the church is in the shape of a cross with a nave longer than the intersecting transept.

**Lena** In Indian architecture, a cave, often used as a sanctuary.

**Lhakhang** A Tibetan Buddhist meeting hall.

**Liang** A beam for supporting purlins in traditional Chinese construction.

**Liecheng** During the Western Zhou Dynasty, the construction of forts at regular intervals along China's northern boundary without connecting walls.

**Ling** A purlin in traditional Chinese construction.

**Linga** A phallus, symbol of the god Siva in Hindu architecture.

**Lingdao** The spirit way that led from the south gate to a royal tomb of the Tang dynasty, lined with stone pillars and sculptured animal and human figures.

**Lingtai** Spirit altar: a raised astronomical observatory in Chinese architecture, usually the central, circular upper story of the *mingtang*.

**Lintel** A beam supporting the weight above a door or window opening.

**Loggia** A colonnaded or arcaded space within the body of a building but open to the air on one side for viewing into a public square or garden. Loggias may occur either on the ground or an upper floor of a building.

**Lotus** A representation of various aquatic plants in the water lily family, used as a decorative motif in ancient Egyptian and Hindu art and architecture.

**Lou** A Chinese multistoried pavilion or tower.

**Luloukong** The place where a road passes through the Great Wall of China.

**Lu-tou** In traditional Chinese construction, the base or lowest member in a set of brackets.

**Machicolation** A projecting gallery or parapet at the top of a castle wall, supported by corbeled arches and having openings in the floor through which stones, molten lead, or boiling oil could be cast upon an enemy beneath.

**Madao** A ramp built on the inside of the Great Wall of China for circulation and the delivery of supplies.

**Madrasa** A Muslim theological school arranged around a courtyard and usually attached to a mosque, found from the 11th century on in Egypt, Anatolia, and Persia.

**Maharaja** A great Indian king.

**Mahasti** A cemetery on the Indian subcontinent.

**Maidan** The large open square of a city, used as a marketplace or parade ground, esp. in the Indian subcontinent.

**Mandala** A diagram of the cosmos, often used to guide the design of Indian temple plans.

**Mandapa** A large, porchlike hall leading to the sanctuary of a Hindu or Jain temple and used for religious dancing and music.

**Mandir** A temple or palace in Indian architecture.

**Mani** A Tibetan Buddhist wall of inscribed stones.

**Mansard roof** A roof having on each of its four sides a steeper lower part and a shallower upper part.

**Manzil** A tower residence in Indian architecture.

**Martyrium** 1. A site that bore witness to important events in the life of Christ or one of his apostles. 2. A place where the relics of a martyr are kept. 3. A church erected over the tomb of a martyr or in honor of a martyr.

**Masjid** A mosque.

**Mastaba** An ancient Egyptian tomb made of mud brick, rectangular in plan with a flat roof and sloping sides, from which a shaft leads to underground burial and offering chambers.

**Matha** A Hindu or Jain monastery.

**Megalith** A very large stone used as found or roughly dressed, esp. in ancient construction work.

**Megaron** A building or semi-independent unit of a building, typically having a rectangular principal chamber with a center hearth and a porch, often of columns in antis: traditional in Greece since Mycenaean times and believed to be the ancestor of the Doric temple.

**Men** A gate in Chinese architecture.

**Menhir** A prehistoric monument consisting of an upright megalith, usually standing alone but sometimes aligned with others in parallel rows.

**Merlon** One of the solid parts between the crenels of a battlement.

**Metope** Any of the panels, either plain or decorated, between triglyphs in the Doric frieze.

**Miao** A Chinese temple. Also, known as *shi*.

**Mihrab** A niche or decorative panel in a mosque designating the *qibla*.

**Minaret** A lofty, slender tower attached to a mosque, having stairs leading up to one or more projecting balconies from which the muezzin calls the Muslim people to prayer.

**Minbar** A pulpit in a mosque, recalling the three steps from which Muhammad addressed his followers.

**Mingtang** Bright hall: a ritual structure in Chinese architecture that serves as the symbolic center of imperial power. The first is presumed to have been built under the Zhou dynasty in the first millennium BCE.

**Minster** Originally, a monastery church; later, any large or important church, as a cathedral or the principal church of a town.

**Module** A unit of measurement used for standardizing the dimensions of building materials or regulating the proportions of an architectural composition.

**Mortar** A plastic mixture of lime or cement, or a combination of both, with sand and water, used as a bonding agent in masonry construction.

**Mortuary temple** An ancient Egyptian temple for offerings and worship of a deceased person, usually a deified king. In the New Kingdom, cult and funerary temples had many features in common: an avenue of sphinxes leading to a tall portal guarded by a towering pylon; an axial plan with a colonnaded forecourt and a hypostyle hall set before a dark, narrow sanctuary in which stood a statue of the deity; and walls lavishly decorated with pictographic carvings in low or sunken relief. Many of the major temples grew by accretion due to the pious ambitions of successive pharaohs, who believed in the afterlife and were determined to create an enduring reputation through their buildings.

**Mosaic** A decorative pattern or figural image or narrative made of small, usually colored pieces of tile, enamel, or glass set in mortar.

**Mosque** A Muslim building or place of public worship.

**Mullion** 1. A vertical member between the lights of a window or the panels in wainscoting. 2. One of the radiating bars of a rose window.

**Muqarna** A system of decoration in Islamic architecture, formed by the intricate corbeling of brackets, squinches, and inverted pyramids; sometimes wrought in stone but more often in plaster.

**Muthamman baghdadi** A frequently used Moghul building plan in which the corners of a square or rectangle are chamfered, resulting in an irregular octagon.

**Nandaimon** The principal south gateway to a Japanese temple or shrine.

**Naos** See **cella**.

**Narthex** 1. The portico before the nave of an early Christian or Byzantine church, appropriate for penitents. 2. An entrance hall or vestibule leading to the nave of a church.

**Nave** The principal or central part of a church, extending from the narthex to the choir or chancel and usually flanked by aisles.

**Necropolis** A historic burial ground, esp. a large, elaborate one of an ancient city.

**Neoclassicism** The classicism prevailing in the architecture of Europe, America, and various European colonies during the late-18th and early-19th centuries, characterized by the introduction and widespread use of Greek and Roman orders and decorative motifs, the subordination of detail to simple, strongly geometric compositions, and the frequent shallowness of relief in ornamental treatment of facades.

**Niche** An ornamental recess in a wall, often semicircular in plan and surmounted by a half dome, as for a statue or other decorative object.

**Nuraghe** Any of the large, round or triangular stone towers found in Sardinia and dating from the second millennium BCE to the Roman conquest.

**Obelisk** A tall, four-sided shaft of stone that tapers as it rises to a pyramidal point, originating in ancient Egypt as a sacred symbol of the sun-god Ra and usually standing in pairs astride temple entrances.

**Oblique projection** A method of projection in which a three-dimensional object, having one principal face parallel to the picture plane, is represented by projecting parallel lines at some angle other than 90 degrees to the picture plane.

**Oculus** A circular opening, esp. one at the crown of a dome.

**Ogee** A molding having a profile of a double curve in the shape of an elongated S.

**Ogive** A rib crossing a compartment of a rib vault on a diagonal.

**Open plan** A floor plan having no fully enclosed spaces or distinct rooms.

**Opus incertum** Ancient Roman masonry formed of small rough stones set irregularly in mortar, sometimes traversed by bands of bricks or tiles. Also called *opus antiquum*.

**Opus reticulatum** An ancient Roman masonry wall faced with small pyramidal stones set diagonally with their square bases forming a netlike pattern.

**Oriel** A bay window supported from below by corbels or brackets.

**Pagoda** A Buddhist temple in the form of a square or polygonal tower with roofs projecting from each of its many stories, erected as a memorial or to hold relics. From the stupa, the Indian prototype, the pagoda gradually changed in form to resemble the traditional multistoried watch tower as it spread with Buddhism to China and Japan. Pagodas were initially of timber but from the 6th century on were more frequently of brick or stone, possibly due to Indian influence.

**Pailou** A monumental gateway in Chinese architecture, having a trabeated form of stone or wood construction with one, three, or five openings and often bold projecting roofs, erected as a memorial at the entrance to a palace, tomb, or sacred place; related to the Indian *toranas* and the Japanese *torii*.

**Palladian motif** A window or doorway in the form of a roundheaded archway flanked on either side by narrower compartments, the side compartments capped with entablatures on which the arch of the central compartment rests.

**Palmette** A stylized palm leaf shape used as a decorative element in classical art and architecture.

**Panopticon** A building, as a prison, hospital, library, or the like, so arranged that all parts of the interior are visible from a single point.

**Pantheon** 1. A temple dedicated to all the gods of a people. 2. A public building serving as the burial place of or containing the memorials to the famous dead of a nation.

**Parapet** A low, protective wall at the edge of a terrace, balcony, or roof, esp. that part of an exterior wall, fire wall, or party wall that rises above the roof.

**Pardah** A screen in Indian architecture.

**Parti** Used by the French at the École des Beaux-Arts in the 19th-century, the design idea or sketch from which an architectural project will be developed.

**Passage grave** A megalithic tomb of the Neolithic and early Bronze Ages found in the British Isles and Europe, consisting of a roofed burial chamber and narrow entrance passage, covered by a tumulus, believed to have been used for successive family or clan burials spanning a number of generations.

**Pavilion** A central or flanking projecting subdivision of a facade, usually accented by more elaborate decoration or greater height and distinction of skyline; used frequently in French Renaissance and baroque architecture.

**Pediment** 1. The low-pitched gable enclosed by the building's horizontal and raking cornices of a Greek or Roman temple. 2. A similar or derivative element used to surmount a major division of a facade or crown an opening.

**Pendentive** A spherical triangle forming the transition from the circular plan of a dome to the polygonal plan of its supporting structure.

**Pergola** A structure of parallel colonnades supporting an open roof of beams and crossing rafters or trelliswork, over which climbing plants are trained to grow.

**Peripteral** Having a single row of columns on all sides.

**Peristyle** 1. A colonnade surrounding a building or a courtyard. 2. The courtyard so enclosed.

**Perpendicular style** The final phase of English Gothic architecture, prevailing from the late 14th through the early 16th centuries, characterized by perpendicular tracery, fine intricate stonework, and elaborate fan vaults. Also called rectilinear style.

**Piano nobile** The principal story of a large building, as a palace or villa, with formal reception and dining rooms, usually one flight above the ground floor.

**Piazza** An open square or public place in a city or town, esp. in Italy.

**Picturesque** The late 18th-century term describing irregular and uncultivated landscapes and designs.

**Pida deul** The pyramidal roofed area of an Orissian temple.

**Pilaster** A shallow rectangular feature projecting from a wall, with a capital and a base and architecturally treated as a column.

**Pilier cantoné** A Gothic pier supporting the arcade, the aisle vaultings, and the responds of the nave vaults, with a massive central core to which are attached four colonettes.

**Piloti** A column of steel or reinforced concrete supporting a building above an open-ground level, thereby leaving the space available for other uses.

**Plinth** 1. The usually square slab beneath the base of a column, pier, or pedestal. 2. A continuous, usually projecting, course of stones forming the base or foundation of a wall.

**Podium** 1. A low wall serving as a base for a colonnade or dome. 2. A raised platform encircling the arena of an ancient Roman amphitheater, where the seats of privileged spectators are located.

**Pol** A gateway in Indian architecture.

**Polis** A Greek city-state.

**Portcullis** A strong grating of iron or timber hung over the gateway of a fortified place in such a way that it could be lowered quickly to prevent passage.

**Porte-cochère** 1. A porch roof projecting over a driveway at the entrance to a building and sheltering those getting in or out of vehicles. 2. A vehicular passageway leading through a building or screen wall into an interior courtyard.

**Portico** A porch or walkway with a roof supported by columns, often leading to the entrance of a building.

**Propylaea** A vestibule or gateway of architectural importance before a Greek temple precinct or other enclosure.

**Propylon** A freestanding gateway in the form of a pylon that precedes the main gateway to an ancient Egyptian temple or sacred enclosure.

**Proscenium** The front part of the stage of an ancient Greek or Roman theater upon which the actors performed.

**Pu** The distance between purlins in traditional Chinese construction.

**Puan** A roof purlin in Chinese architecture.

**Pueblo** A communal dwelling and defensive structure of the native American Indians of southwestern United States, built of adobe or stone, typically many storied and terraced, with entry through the flat roofs of the chambers by ladder. Pueblo structures were built on the desert floor, in valleys, or in the more easily defended cliff walls of mesas.

**Purlin** A longitudinal member of a roof frame for supporting common rafters between the ridge and eaves.

**Pylon** A monumental gateway to an ancient Egyptian temple, consisting either of a pair of tall truncated pyramids and a doorway between them or of one such masonry mass pierced with a doorway, often decorated with painted reliefs.

**Qibla** 1. The direction toward which Muslims face to pray, esp. the Ka'aba at Mecca. 2. The wall in a mosque in which the mihrab is set, oriented to Mecca.

**Que** A Chinese watchtower. Also, *hua biao.*

**Quoin** One of the stones forming an external angle of a wall, usually differentiated from the adjoining surfaces by material, texture, color, size, or projection.

**Radiating chapel** In a Gothic church, one of several chapels projecting radially from the curve of an ambulatory or apse.

**Raking cornice** Either of two straight, sloping cornices on a pediment, following or suggesting the slope of a roof.

**Rammed earth** A stiff mixture of clay, sand, or other aggregate and water compressed and dried within forms as a wall construction.

**Ratha** A Hindu temple cut out of solid rock to resemble a chariot.

**Rayonnant style** The middle phase of French Gothic architecture from the end of the 13th through the late-14th centuries, characterized by circular windows with radiating lines of tracery.

**Rectilinear style** See **Perpendicular style**.

**Rekha deul** The sanctuary and convexly tapered tower of an Orissian temple.

**Rib** Any of several archlike members supporting a vault at the groins, defining its distinct surfaces or dividing these surfaces into panels.

**Ribat** An Islamic fortified monasterylike building providing soldiers with an opportunity to exercise their religion.

**Rose window** A large, circular window, usually of stained glass and decorated with tracery symmetrical about the center.

**Rotunda** A round, domed building, or a large and high circular space in a building, esp. one surmounted by a dome.

**Rustication** Ashlar masonry having the visible faces of the dressed stones raised or otherwise contrasted with the horizontal and usually the vertical joints, which may be rabbeted, chamfered, or beveled.

**Sacristy** A room in a church where the sacred vessels and vestments are kept.

**Samadhi** An Indian templelike memorial containing a shrine with an image of the deceased.

**Sanctuary** 1. A sacred or holy place. 2. The most sacred part of a church in which the principal altar is placed. 3. An especially holy place in a temple. 4. A church or other sacred place where fugitives were formerly immune from arrest.

**Sangrahalaya** A place of rest for Jain pilgrims.

**Sarwandam sutun** A type of Moghul column that tapers as it nears the ground and forms a bulb at its foot.

**Scenae frons** The highly decorative wall or backdrop at the rear of the stage of a Roman theater.

**Schist** A crystalline metamorphic rock found in northwest Pakistan that has a parallel or foliated arrangement of mineral grains.

**Section** An orthographic projection of an object or structure as it would appear if cut through by an intersecting plane to show its internal configuration, usually drawn to scale.

**Sha** In Chinese architecture, the finial on top of a pagoda.

**Shaft** 1. The central part of a column or pier between the capital and the base. 2. A distinct, slender, vertical masonry feature engaged in a wall or pier and supporting or feigning to support an arch or a ribbed vault.

**Shahjahani column** A type of Moghul column with a multifaceted shaft and capital and a rotated base with four foliated faces.

**Shala** A barrel-vaulted roof shape used decoratively in India on pediments and parapets.

**Shanmen** The front entry gate of a Chinese temple.

**Shi** See ***miao***.

**Shia** A Muslim sect that believes Ali to be the successor to Muhammad.

**Shikhara** A tower of a Hindu temple, usually tapered convexly and capped by an *amalaka*.

**Shoro** A structure from which the temple bell is hung, as one of a pair of small, identical, symmetrically placed pavilions in a Japanese Buddhist temple.

**Sobo** The priests' quarters in a Japanese Buddhist temple.

**Spandrel** 1. The triangular-shaped, sometimes ornamented area between two adjoining arches or between an arch and the rectangular framework surrounding it. 2. A panellike area in a multistory frame building, between the sill of a window on one level and the head of a window immediately below.

**Sphinx** A figure of an imaginary creature having the body of a lion and the head of a man, ram, or hawk, commonly placed along avenues leading to ancient Egyptian temples or tombs.

**Spire** A tall, acutely tapering pyramidal structure surmounting a steeple or tower.

**Splay** A surface that makes an oblique angle with another, as where a window or door opening widens from the frame toward the face of the wall.

**Squinch** An arch or corbeling built across the upper inside corner of a square tower to support the side of a superimposed octagonal structure.

**Stambha** A freestanding memorial pillar in Indian architecture, bearing carved inscriptions, religious emblems, or a statue.

**Stele** An upright stone slab or pillar with a carved or inscribed surface, used as a monument or marker, or as a commemorative tablet in the face of a building.

**Stoa** An ancient Greek portico, usually detached and of considerable length, used as a promenade or meeting place around public places.

**Stucco** A coarse plaster composed of portland or masonry cement, sand, and hydrated lime, mixed with water and applied in a plastic state to form a hard covering for exterior walls.

**Stupa** A Buddhist memorial mound erected to enshrine a relic of Buddha and to commemorate some event or mark a sacred spot. Modeled on a funerary tumulus, it consists of an artificial dome-shaped mound raised on a platform, surrounded by an outer ambulatory with a stone *vedika* and four *toranas*, and crowned by a *chattri*. The name for the stupa in Ceylon is *dagoba*, and in Tibet and Nepal, *chorten*.

**Stylobate** A course of masonry forming the foundation for a row of columns, esp. the outermost colonnade of a classical temple.

**Sufi** A Muslim mystic.

**Sultan** The ruler of a Muslim country.

**Sunni** A Muslim sect that considers Abu Bakr to be the successor to Muhammad.

**Suq** The traditional market street in an Arab country.

**Synagogue** A building or place of assembly for Jewish worship and religious instruction.

**Ta** A Chinese pagoda in which a deceased high priest is buried.

**Takht** The throne or elevated platform used by royalty in a mosque.

**Tambour** A term describing a cylindrical shape, such as the drum supporting a dome, the vertical part of a cupola, or the core of a capital.

**Temenos** In ancient Greece, a piece of ground specially reserved and enclosed as a sacred place.

**Tension** A structural force that acts to stretch or pull apart a material, resulting in the elongation of an elastic body. Ductile materials like steel effectively resist tension.

**Tepidarium** A room of moderately warm temperature in an ancient Roman bath, between the *frigidarium* and the *calidarium*.

**Thermae** An elaborate public bathing establishment of the ancient Greeks or Romans, consisting of hot, warm, and cool plunges, sweat rooms, and athletic and other facilities.

**Thrust** The outward force or pressure exerted by one part of a structure against another.

**Ting** A courtyard in Chinese architecture, the site of large, often ceremonial gatherings.

**Tirtha** A place or site considered holy in Indian architecture.

**Tokonoma** Picture recess: a shallow, slightly raised alcove for the display of a *kakemono* or flower arrangement. One side of the recess borders the outside wall of the room through which light enters, while the interior side adjoins the *tana*. As the spiritual center of a traditional Japanese house, the *tokonoma* is located in its most formal room.

**Torana** An elaborately carved, ceremonial gateway in Indian Buddhist and Hindu architecture, having two or three lintels between two posts.

**Torsion** The twisting of an elastic body about its longitudinal axis caused by two equal and opposite torques, producing shearing stresses in the body.

**Tou-kung** See ***dou-gong***.

**Trabeated** Of or pertaining to a system of construction employing beams or lintels.

**Transept** 1. The major transverse part of a cruciform church, crossing the main axis at a right angle between the nave and choir. 2. Either of the projecting arms of this part, on either side of the central aisle of a church.

**Triforium** An arcaded wall corresponding to the space between the vaulting and the roof of an aisle, usually opening onto the nave between the nave arches and clerestory.

**Triglyph** One of the vertical blocks separating the metopes in a Doric frieze, typically having two vertical grooves or glyphs on its face, and two chamfers or hemiglyphs at the sides.

**Tuk** A fortification holding Jain shrines.

**Tumulus** An artificial mound of earth or stone, esp. over an ancient grave.

**Turret** A small tower forming part of a larger structure, frequently beginning some distance above the ground.

**Tympanum** 1. The recessed triangular space enclosed by the horizontal and raking cornices of a triangular pediment, often decorated with sculpture. 2. A similar space between an arch and the horizontal head of a door or window below.

**Ulu Jami** A Friday mosque having a large *sahn* for large congregations, dating from the 7th to the 11th centuries.

**Vault** An arched structure of stone, brick, or reinforced concrete, forming a ceiling or roof over a hall, room, or other wholly or partially enclosed space. Because it behaves as an arch extended in a third dimension, the longitudinal supporting walls must be buttressed to counteract the thrusts of the arching action.

**Vav** An Indian step well.

**Vedas** The oldest sacred writings of Hinduism, composed between 1500 and 800 BCE, incorporating four collections of hymns, prayers, and liturgical formulas: Rig-Veda, Yajur-Veda, Sama-Veda, and Atharva-Veda.

**Vedika** 1. A hall for reading the Vedas. 2. A railing enclosing a sacred area, as a stupa.

**Vihara** A Buddhist monastery in Indian architecture often excavated from solid rock, consisting of a central pillared chamber surrounded by a veranda onto which open small sleeping cells. Adjacent to this cloister was a courtyard containing the main stupa.

**Volute** A spiral, scroll-like ornament, as on the capitals of the Ionic, Corinthian, and composite orders.

**Voussoir** Any of the wedge-shaped units in a masonry arch or vault that has side cuts that converge at one of the arch centers.

**Wainscot** A lining of wood, usually in the form of paneling, covering the lower portion of a wall.

**Wat** A Buddhist monastery or temple in Thailand or Cambodia.

**Westwork** The monumental western front of a Romanesque church, treated as a tower or towers containing a low entrance hall below and a chapel open to the nave above.

**Xanadu** A place of idyllic beauty and contentment; S. T. Coleridge's modification of Xandu, modern Shangtu, the site of Kublai Khan's summer residence in southeastern Mongolia.

**Xuanzi painting** A lesser type of Qing painting, usually focused on dynamic floral motifs and used to decorate buildings considered to be of relatively little import.

**Yingbi** A screen wall in Chinese architecture that protects the main gate to a monastery or house against evil spirits, which were believed to only move in a straight line.

**Yingzao fashi** A compendium of Chinese architectural tradition and building methods, compiled by Li Jie and printed in 1103: it has 34 chapters devoted to technical terms, construction methods, measurements and proportions of architectural elements, labor management, building materials, and decoration.

**Yin-yang** In Chinese philosophy and religion, the interaction of two opposing and complementary principles—one that is feminine, dark, and negative (yin) and the other that is masculine, bright, and positive (yang)—that influences the destinies of creatures and things.

**Yuan qi** A Taoist description of life's vital energy.

**Zaojing** The wooden dome under which an imperial throne or statue was placed in Chinese architecture.

**Zhaobi** In Chinese architecture, the panel sitting in front of an entrance gate to emphasize the gate's import.

**Zhen** The Ming military system through which the Great Wall of China was split into nine commands and five subcommands.

**Zhi** During the Han and Jin Dynasties, a Taoist cave dwelling for the practice of asceticism and sacrificial offerings to gods.

**Ziggurat** A temple tower in Sumerian and Assyrian architecture, built in diminishing stages of mud brick with buttressed walls faced with burnt brick, culminating in a summit shrine or temple reached by a series of ramps: thought to be of Sumerian origin, dating from the end of the 3rd millennium BCE.

# Bibliography


**General Sources**

*The Kodansha Bilingual Encyclopedia of Japan.* Tokyo: Kodansha International; New York: Kodansha America, 1998.

Alfieri, Bianca Maria. *Islamic Architecture of the Indian Subcontinent.* London: Laurence King Publishers, 2000.

Barraclough, Geoffrey. *Hammond Atlas of World History.* Maplewood, NJ: Hammond, 1999.

Chihara, Daigoro. *Hindu-Buddhist Architecture in Southeast Asia.* New York: E. J. Brill, 1996.

Coaldrake, William Howard. *Architecture and Authority in Japan.* London and New York: Routledge, 1996.

Coe, Michael D., and Rex Koontz. *Mexico: From the Olmecs to the Aztecs.* London: Thames & Hudson, 2002.

Crouch, Dora P., and June G. Johnson. *Traditions in Architecture: Africa, America, Asia, and Oceania.* New York: Oxford University Press, 2001.

Evans, Susan Toby, and David L. Webster, eds. *Archaeology of Ancient Mexico and Central America: An Encyclopedia.* New York: Garland Publishers, 2001.

Ferguson, William M., and Richard E. W. Adams. *Mesoamerica's Ancient Cities: Aerial Views of Pre-Columbian Ruins in Mexico, Guatemala, Belize, and Honduras.* Albuquerque: University of New Mexico Press, 2001.

Grube, Nikolai. *Maya: Divine Kings of the Rain Forest.* Assisted by Eva Eggebrecht and Matthias Seidel. Cologne, Germany: Könemann, 2001.

Huntington, Susan L., with contributions by John C. Huntington. *The Art of Ancient India: Buddhist, Hindu, Jain.* New York: Weatherhill, 1985.

Kostof, Spiro. *A History of Architecture: Settings and Rituals.* Revisions by Greg Castillo. New York: Oxford University Press, 1995.

Kowalski, Jeff Karl, ed. *Mesoamerican Architecture as a Cultural Symbol.* New York: Oxford University Press, 1999.

Kubler, George. *The Art and Architecture of Ancient America: The Mexican, Maya, and Andean Peoples.* New Haven, CT: Yale University Press, 1990.

Loewe, Michael, and Edward L. Shaughnessy, eds. *The Cambridge History of Ancient China: From the Origins of Civilization to 221 B.C.* Cambridge, UK, and New York: Cambridge University Press, 1999.

Meister, Michael W., ed. Coordinated by M. A. Dhaky. *Encyclopedia of Indian Temple Architecture, Volumes 1 and 2.* New Delhi: American Institute of Indian Studies; Philadelphia: University of Pennsylvania Press, 1983.

Michell, George. *Architecture of the Islamic World: Its History and Social Meaning.* New York: Thames and Hudson, 1984.

Nishi, Kazuo, and Kazuo Hozumi. *What is Japanese Architecture?* Translated by H. Mack Horton. Tokyo and New York: Kodansha International, 1985.

Schmidt, Karl J. *Atlas and Survey of South Asian History: India, Pakistan, Bangladesh, Sri Lanka, Nepal, Bhutan.* New Delhi, India: Vision Books, 1999.

Sickman, Laurence, and Alexander Soper. *The Art and Architecture of China.* Harmondsworth, UK: Penguin Books, 1971.

Steinhardt, Nancy Shatzman. *Chinese Architecture.* New Haven, CT: Yale University Press: Beijing: New World Press, 2002.

Steinhardt, Nancy Shatzman. *Chinese Imperial City Planning.* Honolulu: University of Hawaii Press, 1990.

Tadgell, Christopher. *The History of Architecture in India: From the Dawn of Civilization to the End of the Raj.* London: Architecture Design and Technology Press, 1990.

Thapar, Romila. *Early India: From the Origins to AD 1300.* Berkeley and Los Angeles: University of California Press, 2002.

Trachtenberg, Marvin, and Isabelle Hyman. *Architecture, From Prehistory to Postmodernity.* New York: Harry N. Abrams, 2002.

**Online Resources**

Grove Art Online: www.groveart.com. Web access to the entire text of *The Dictionary of Art*, edited by Jane Turner (1996, 34 vols.), and *The Oxford Companion to Western Art*, edited by Hugh Brigstocke (2001).

Metropolitan Museum of Art Timeline of Art History: www.metmuseum.org/toah

Wikipedia: The Free Encyclopedia: en.wikipedia.org

Great Buildings Online: www.greatbuildings.com

Taj Mahal: http://www.tajmahalindia.net/taj-mahal-monument.html

**3500 BCE**

Arnold, Dieter. *The Encyclopedia of Ancient Egyptian Architecture.* Edited by Nigel and Helen Strudwick. Translated by Sabine H. Gardiner and Helen Strudwick. Princeton, NJ: Princeton University Press, 2003.

Burl, Aubrey. *The Stone Circles of the British Isles.* New Haven, CT: Yale University Press, 1976.

Clark, Grahame. *The Earlier Stone Age Settlement of Scandinavia.* London: Cambridge University Press, 1975.

Hawkins, Gerald S., and John B. White. *Stonehenge Decoded.* New York: Dorsett, 1965.

Jia, Lanpo. *Early Man in China.* Beijing: Foreign Languages Press, 1980.

McBurney, Charles, and Brian Montagu. *The Stone Age of Northern Africa.* Harmondsworth, UK: Penguin Books, 1960.

Mysliwiec, Karol. *The Twilight of Ancient Egypt, First Millennium BCE.* Ithaca, NY: Cornell University Press, 2000.

Nicholson, Paul T., and Ian Shaw, eds. *Ancient Egyptian Materials and Technology.* Cambridge, UK: Cambridge University Press, 2000.

Possehl, Gregory L. *Harappan Civilization: A Recent Perspective.* New Delhi, India: American Institute of Indian Studies; Columbia, MO: Oxford and IBH Pub. Co., 1993.

Shafer, Byron E., ed. *Religion in Ancient Egypt: Gods, Myths and Personal Practice.* Ithaca, NY: Cornell University Press, 1991.

Wilson, Peter J. *The Domestication of the Human Species.* New Haven, CT: Yale University Press, 1988.

**2500 BCE**

Crawford, Harriet E. W. *The Architecture of Iraq in the Third Millennium B.C.* Copenhagen, Denmark: Akademisk Forlag, 1977.

Downey, Susan B. *Mesopotamian Religious Architecture: Alexander through the Parthians.* Princeton, NJ: Princeton University Press, 1988.

Kemp, Barry J. *Ancient Egypt: Anatomy of a Civilization.* London and New York: Routledge, 1991.

Kenoyer, Jonathan M. *Ancient Cities of the Indus Valley Civilization.* Karachi, Pakistan: Oxford University Press; Islamabad: American Institute of Pakistan Studies, 1998.

Kubba, Shamil A. A. *Mesopotamian Architecture and Town Planning: From the Mesolithic to the End of the Proto-historic Period, c. 10,000-3,500 B.C.* Oxford, UK: B.A.R., 1987.

Oppenheim, A. Leo. *Ancient Mesopotamia: Portrait of a Dead Civilization.* Chicago, IL: University of Chicago Press, 1977.

Rossi, Corinna. *Architecture and Mathematics in Ancient Egypt.* Cambridge, UK, and New York: Cambridge University Press, 2004.

Shady, Ruth, and Carlos Leyva, eds. *La Ciudad Sagrada de Caral-Supe: Los Orígenes de la Civilización Andina y la Formación del Estado Prístino en el Antiguo Perú.* Lima, Peru: Instituto Nacional de Cultura: Proyecto Especial Arqueológico Caral-Supe, 2003.

# BIBLIOGRAPHY


### 1500 BCE

Byrd, Kathleen M. *The Poverty Point Culture: Local Manifestations, Subsistence Practices, and Trade Networks.* Baton Rouge, LA: Geoscience Publications, Dept. of Geography and Anthropology, Louisiana State University, 1991.

Chang, Kwang-chih. *Shang Civilization.* New Haven, CT: Yale University Press, 1980.

Clarke, Somers, and R. Engelbach. *Ancient Egyptian Construction and Architecture.* New York: Dover Publications, 1990.

Gibson, Jon L. *The Ancient Mounds of Poverty Point: Place of Rings.* Gainesville: University Press of Florida, 2000.

Moore, Jerry D. *Architecture and Power in the Ancient Andes: The Archaeology of Public Buildings.* Cambridge, UK, and New York: Cambridge University Press, 1996.

Oates, Joan. *Babylon: Ancient Peoples and Places.* London: Thames and Hudson, 1979.

### 800 BCE

Bell, Edward. *Prehellenic Architecture in the Aegean.* London: G. Bell and Sons, Ltd., 1926.

Burger, Richard L. *The Prehistoric Occupation of Chavín de Huántar, Peru.* Berkeley and Los Angeles: University of California Press, 1984.

Castleden, Rodney. *The Knossos Labyrinth, A View of the Palace of Minos at Knossos.* London: Routledge, 1990.

Coe, Michael D. *The Olmec World: Ritual and Rulership.* Princeton, NJ: Art Museum, Princeton University, and New York: In association with Harry N. Abrams, 1996.

Diehl, Richard A. *The Olmecs: America's First Civilization.* London: Thames & Hudson, 2004.

Eck, Diana L. *Banaras, City of Light.* New York: Columbia University Press, 1999.

El-Hakim, Omar M. *Nubian Architecture: The Egyptian Vernacular Experience.* Cairo: Palm Press, 1993.

Jastrow, Morris. *The Civilization of Babylonia and Assyria: Its Remains, Language, History, Religion, Commerce, Law, Art, and Literature.* Philadelphia and London: J. B. Lippincott Company, 1915.

Li, Hsüeh-ch'in. *Eastern Zhou and Qin Civilizations.* Translated by K. C. Chang. New Haven, CT: Yale University Press, 1985.

Ricke, Herbert, George R. Hughes, and Edward F. Wente. *The Beit el-Wali Temple of Ramesses II.* Chicago, IL: University of Chicago Press, 1967.

Scoufopoulos, Niki C. *Mycenaean Citadels.* Gothenburg, Sweden: P. Åström, 1971.

Willetts, Ronald F. *The Civilization of Ancient Crete.* Berkeley and Los Angeles: University of California Press, 1976.

### 400 BCE

Ball, Larry F. *The Domus Aurea and the Roman Architectural Revolution.* Cambridge, UK: Cambridge University Press, 2003.

Barletta, Barbara A. *Ionic Influence in Archaic Sicily: The Monumental Art.* Gothenburg, Sweden: Åström, 1983.

Barletta, Barbara A. *The Origins of the Greek Architectural Orders.* Cambridge, UK: Cambridge University Press, 2001.

Berve, Helmut. *Greek Temples, Theatres, and Shrines.* London: Thames and Hudson, 1963.

Camp, John M. *The Archaeology of Athens.* New Haven, CT: Yale University Press, 2001.

Clark, John E., and Mary E. Pye, eds. *Olmec Art and Archaeology in Mesoamerica.* Washington, DC: National Gallery of Art; New Haven, CT: distributed by Yale University Press, 2000.

Coulton, John James. *Ancient Greek Architects at Work: Problems of Structure and Design.* Ithaca, NY: Cornell University Press, 1977.

Detienne, Marcel. *The Cuisine of Sacrifice Among the Greeks.* With essays by Jeon-Louis Durand, Stella Georgoudi, Françoise Hartog, and Jesper Svendro. Chicago, IL: University of Chicago Press, 1989.

Dinsmoor, William Bell. *The Architecture of Ancient Greece: An Account of its Historic Development.* New York: Norton, 1975.

Frye, Richard Nelson. *The Heritage of Persia.* Cleveland, OH: World Pub. Co., 1963.

Fyfe, Theodore. *Hellenistic Architecture: An Introductory Study.* Cambridge UK: Cambridge University Press, 1936; Oakville, CT: Aarhus University Press, 1999.

Grant, Michael. *The Etruscans.* New York: Charles Scribner's, 1980.

Hurwit, Jeffrey M. *The Art and Culture of Early Greece, 1100-480 B.C.* Ithaca, NY: Cornell University Press, 1985.

Martienssen, Rex Distin. *The Idea of Space in Greek Architecture, with Special Reference to the Doric Temple and its Setting.* Johannesburg, South Africa: Witwatersrand University Press, 1956.

Scully, Vincent Joseph. *The Earth, the Temple, and the Gods: Greek Sacred Architecture.* New Haven, CT, Yale University Press, 1962.

Taylour, William Lord. *The Mycenaeans.* London: Thames and Hudson, 1964.

Thapar, Romila. *Aśoka and the Decline of the Mauryas.* New Delhi, India, and New York: Oxford University Press, 1997.

Warren, John. *Greek Mathematics and the Architects to Justinian.* London: Coach Publishing, 1976.

Winter, Frederick E. *Greek Fortifications.* Toronto, Ontario: University of Toronto Press, 1971.

### 0

Boatwright, Mary Taliaferro. *Hadrian and the City of Rome.* Princeton, NJ: Princeton University Press, 1987.

Chase, Raymond G. *Ancient Hellenistic and Roman Amphitheatres, Stadiums, and Theatres: The Way they Look Now.* Portsmouth, NH: P. E. Randall, 2002.

Dallapiccola, Anna Libera, with Stephanie Zingel-Avé Lallemant, eds. *The Stúpa: Its Religious, Historical and Architectural Significance.* Wiesbaden, Germany: Steiner, 1979.

Hansen, Richard D. *Excavations in the Tigre Complex, El Mirador, Petén, Guatemala.* Provo, Utah: New World Archaeological Foundation, Brigham Young University, 1990.

Lawton, Thomas. *Chinese Art of the Warring States Period: Change and Continuity, 480–222 B.C.* Washington, DC: published for the Freer Gallery of Art by the Smithsonian Institution Press, 1983.

MacDonald, William Lloyd. *The Architecture of the Roman Empire.* New Haven, CT: Yale University Press, 1982.

Rykwert, Joseph. *The Idea of a Town: The Anthropology of Urban Form in Rome, Italy and the Ancient World.* Princeton, NJ: Princeton University Press, 1976.

Sarkar, H. *Studies in Early Buddhist Architecture of India.* Delhi, India: Munshiram Manoharlal, 1966.

Schopen, Gregory. *Bones, Stones, and Buddhist Monks: Collected Papers on the Archaeology, Epigraphy, and Texts of Monastic Buddhism in India.* Honolulu: University of Hawaii Press, 1997.

Snodgrass, Adrian. *The Symbolism of the Stupa.* Ithaca, NY: Cornell University, 1985.

Stamper, John W. *The Architecture of Roman Temples: The Republic to the Middle Empire.* Cambridge, UK: Cambridge University Press, 2005.

Townsend, Richard F., ed. *Ancient West Mexico: Art and Archaeology of the Unknown Past.* New York: Thames and Hudson; Chicago: Art Institute of Chicago, 1998.

Ward-Perkins, John Bryan. *Roman Architecture.* Milan, Italy and London: Electa Architecture, 2003.

**200 CE**

Behrendt, Kurt A. *The Buddhist Architecture of Gandhāra.* Leiden, Netherlands, and Boston, MA: E. J. Brill, 2004.

Berrin, Kathleen, and Esther Pasztory. *Teotihuacán: Art from the City of the Gods.* New York: Thames and Hudson and Fine Arts Museums of San Francisco, 1993.

Litvinsky, B. A., ed. *History of Civilizations of Central Asia,* v.3, *The Crossroads of Civilizations, A.D. 250 to 750.* Paris, France: UNESCO, 1992.

MacDonald, William Lloyd. *The Pantheon: Design, Meaning, and Progeny.* Cambridge, MA: Harvard University Press, 1976.

MacDonald, William Lloyd, and John A. Pinto. *Hadrian's Villa and its Legacy.* New Haven, CT: Yale University Press, 1995.

Romain, William F. *Mysteries of the Hopewell: Astronomers, Geometers, and Magicians of the Eastern Woodlands.* Akron, OH: University of Akron Press, 2000.

Sanders, William T., and Joseph W. Michels, eds. *Teotihuacán and Kaminaljuyu: A Study in Prehistoric Culture Contact.* University Park, PA: Penn State University Press, 1977.

Sharma, G. R., ed. *Kusana Studies: Papers Presented to the International Conference on the Archaeology, History and Arts of the People of Central Asia in the Kusāna Period, Dushambe (Tadjikistan) U.S.S.R.,* September 25–October 4, 1968. Allahabad, India: Dept. of Ancient History, Culture and Archaeology, University of Allahabad, 1998.

Silverman, Helaine, and Donald Proulx. *The Nasca.* Oxford, UK: Blackwell, 2002.

Taylor, Rabun M. *Roman Builders: A Study in Architectural Process.* Cambridge, UK, and New York: Cambridge University Press, 2003.

Woodward, Susan L., and Jerry N. McDonald. *Indian Mounds of the Middle Ohio Valley: A Guide to Mounds and Earthworks of the Adena, Hopewell, Cole, and Fort Ancient People.* Blacksburg, VA: McDonald & Woodward Pub. Co., 2002.

Wang, Zhongshu. *Han Civilization.* Translated by K. C. Chang and collaborators, New Haven, CT: Yale University Press, 1982.

**400 CE**

Aikens, C. Melvin, and Takayasu Higuchi. *Prehistory of Japan.* New York: Academic Press, 1982.

Asher, Frederick M. *The Art of Eastern India, 300–800.* Minneapolis: University of Minnesota Press, 1980.

Bandmann, Günter. *Early Medieval Architecture as Bearer of Meaning.* Translated by Kendall Wallis. New York: Columbia University Press, 2005.

Barnes, Gina Lee. *Protohistoric Yamato: Archaeology of the First Japanese State.* Ann Arbor: University of Michigan Center for Japanese Studies, Museum of Anthropology, University of Michigan, 1988.

Beal, Samuel. *The Life of Hiuen-Tsiang by Hwui Li.* New Delhi, India: Asian Educational Services, 1998.

Blanton, Richard E. (et al.). *Ancient Oaxaca: The Monte Albán.* New York: Cambridge University Press, 1999.

Cunningham, Alexander. *Mahâbodhi, or the Great Buddhist Temple Under the Bodhi Tree at Buddha-Gaya.* London: W. H. Allen, 1892.

Freely, John. *Byzantine Monuments of Istanbul.* Cambridge, UK: Cambridge University Press, 2004.

Holloway, R. Ross. *Constantine and Rome.* New Haven, CT: Yale University Press, 2004.

Imamura, Keiji. *Prehistoric Japan: New Perspectives on Insular East Asia.* London: UCL Press, 1996.

Krautheimer, Richard. *Early Christian and Byzantine Architecture.* New York: Penguin Books, 1986.

Mitra, Debala. *Ajanta.* New Delhi: Archaeological Survey of India, 1980.

Ray, Himanshu P. *The Winds of Change: Buddhism and the Maritime Links of Early South Asia.* New Delhi, India: Oxford University Press, 1994.

Spink, Walter M. *Ajanta to Ellora.* Ann Arbor, MI: Marg Publications for the Center for South and Southeast Asian Studies, University of Michigan, 1967.

Weiner, Sheila L. *Ajanta: Its Place in Buddhist Art.* Berkeley and Los Angeles: University of California Press, 1977.

Williams, Joanna Gottfried. *The Art of Gupta India: Empire and Province.* Princeton, NJ: Princeton University Press, 1982.

**600 CE**

Adams, Cassandra. "Japan's Ise Shrine and Its Thirteen-Hundred-Year-Old Reconstruction Tradition." *Journal of Architectural Education,* 52, no. 1 (1988).

Berkson, Carmel, Wendy Doniger O'Flaherty, and George Michell. *Elephanta, The Cave of Shiva.* Princeton, NJ: Princeton University Press, 1983.

Bock, Felicia G. "The Rites of Renewal at Ise." *Monumenta Nipponica* 29, no. 1 (1974).

Davies, John Gordon. *Medieval Armenian Art and Architecture: The Church of the Holy Cross, Aght'amar.* London: Pindar, 1991.

Freely, John. *Byzantine Monuments of Istanbul.* Cambridge, UK: Cambridge University Press, 2004.

Goldstein, Paul S. *Andean Diaspora: The Tiwanaku Colonies and the Origins of South American Empire.* Gainesville: University Press of Florida, 2005.

Harrison, Peter D. *The Lords of Tikal: Rulers of an Ancient Maya City.* New York: Thames and Hudson, 1999.

Janusek, John Wayne. *Identity and Power in the Ancient Andes: Tiwanaku. Cities Through Time.* New York: Routledge, 2004.

Kidder, J. Edward. *The Lucky Seventh: Early Horyu-ji and its Time.* Tokyo, Japan: International Christian University and Hachiro Yuasa Memorial Museum, 1999.

Kramrisch, Stella. *The Presence of S´iva.* Princeton, NJ: Princeton University Press, 1992.

Krautheimer, Richard. *Rome: Profile of a City, 312–1308.* Princeton, NJ: Princeton University Press, 2000.

Malmstrom, Vincent H. *Cycles of the Sun, Mysteries of the Moon: The Calendar in Mesoamerican Civilization.* Austin: University of Texas Press, 1997.

Mathews, T. F. *Early Churches of Constantinople, Architecture and Liturgy.* University Park: Pennsylvania State University Press, 1971.

Mizuno, Seiichi. *Asuka Buddhist Art: Horyu-ji.* New York: Weatherhill, 1974.

Robert, Mark, and Ahmet Çakmak, eds. *Hagia Sophia from the Age of Justinian to the Present.* Cambridge, UK: Cambridge University Press, 1992.

Schele, Linda, and Peter Mathews. *The Code of Kings: The Language of Seven Sacred Maya Temples and Tombs.* New York: Scribner, 1998.

Suzuki, Kakichi. *Early Buddhist Architecture in Japan.* Tokyo, Japan: Kodansha International, 1980.

Tartakov, Gary M. "The Beginnings of Dravidian Temple Architecture in Stone." *Artibus Asiae* 42 (1980).

Utudjian, Edouard. *Armenian Architecture, 4th to 17th Century.* Translated by Geoffrey Capner. Paris: Editions A. Morancé, 1968.

Warren, John. *Greek Mathematics and the Architects to Justinian.* London: Coach Publishing, 1976.

Watanabe, Yasutada. *Shinto Art: Ise and Izumo Shrines.* New York: Weatherhill / Heibonsha, 1974.

Wharton, Annabel Jane. *Refiguring the Post-Classical City: Dura Europos, Jerash, Jerusalem, and Ravenna.* Cambridge, UK, and New York: Cambridge University Press, 1995.

## BIBLIOGRAPHY


### 800 CE

Atroshenko, V. I., and Judith Collins. *The Origins of the Romanesque: Near Eastern Influences on European Art, 4th–12th Centuries.* London: Lund Humphries, 1985.

Chandler, David P. *A History of Cambodia.* Boulder, CO: Westview Press, 2000.

Ettinghausen, Richard. *Islamic Art and Architecture 650–1250.* New Haven, CT: Yale University Press, 2001.

Flood, Finbarr Barry. *The Great Mosque of Damascus: Studies on the Makings of an Ummayyad Visual Culture.* Leiden, Netherlands and Boston, MA: E. J. Brill, 2001.

Frederic, Louis. *Borobodur.* New York: Abeville Press Publishers, 1996.

Hattstein, Markus, and Peter Delius, eds. *Islam: Art and Architecture.* Translated by George Ansell German. Cologne, Germany: Könemann, 2000.

Horn, Walter, and Ernest Born. *The Plan of St. Gall.* Berkeley and Los Angeles: University of California Press, 1972.

Joe, Wanne J. *Traditional Korea, A Cultural History.* Edited by Hongkyu A. Choe. Elizabeth, NJ: Hollym International, 1997.

Lassner, Jacob. *The Shaping of Abbasid Rule.* Princeton, NJ: 1980.

Michell, George. *Pattadakal.* New Delhi, India, and Oxford: Oxford University Press, 2002.

Milburn, Robert. *Early Christian Art and Architecture.* Berkeley and Los Angeles: University of California Press, 1988.

Tartakov, Gary Michael. *The Durga Temple at Aihole: A Historiographical Study.* New Delhi, India, and New York: Oxford University Press, 1997.

Xiong, Victor Cunrui. *Sui T'ang Ch'ang-an: A Study in the Urban History of Medieval China.* Ann Arbor: Center for Chinese Studies, University of Michigan, 2000.

### 1000

Asopa, Jai Narayan. *Origin of the Rajputs.* Delhi, India: Bharatiya Pub. House, 1976.

Conant, Kenneth John. *Carolingian and Romanesque Architecture, 800 to 1200.* Baltimore, MD: Penguin Books, 1959.

Desai, Devangana. *Khajuraho.* New Delhi, India, and New York: Oxford University Press, 2000.

Dehejia, Vidya. *The Sensuous and the Sacred: Chola Bronzes from South India.* New York: American Federation of Arts; Seattle: University of Washington Press, 2002.

Dehejia, Vidya. *Yogini, Cult and Temples: A Tantric Tradition.* New Delhi, India: National Museum, 1986.

Dodds, Jerrilynn D. *Architecture and Ideology in Early Medieval Spain.* University Park: Penn State University Press, 1990.

Grossmann, Peter. *Christliche Architektur in Ägypten.* Leiden, Netherlands, and Boston, MA: E. J. Brill, 2002.

Handa, Devendra. *Osian: History, Archaeology, Art and Architecture.* Delhi, India: Sundeep Prakashan, 1984.

Kowalski, Jeff Karl. *The House of the Governor: A Maya Palace at Uxmal, Yucatan, Mexico.* Norman: University of Oklahoma Press, 1987.

Michell, George. *Early Western Calukyan Temples.* London: AARP, 1975.

Miller, Barbara Stoler. *The Powers of Art: Patronage in Indian Culture.* New Delhi, India, and New York: Oxford University Press, 1992.

Necipog̃lu, Gülru. *The Topkapı Scroll: Geometry and Ornament in Islamic Architecture.* Topkapı Palace Museum Library MS H. Santa Monica, CA: Getty Center for the History of Arts and the Humanities, 1995.

Rivoira, Giovanni Teresio. *Lombardic Architecture: Its Origin, Development, and Derivatives.* New York: Hacker Art Books, 1975.

Spink, Walter M. *Ajanta to Ellora Bombay.* Ann Arbor, MI: Marg Publications for the Center for South and Southeast Asian Studies, University of Michigan, 1967.

Steinhardt, Nancy Shatzman. *Liao Architecture.* Honolulu: University of Hawaii Press, 1997.

Tartakov, Gary M. "The Beginning of Dravidian Temple Architecture in Stone." *Artibus Asiae* 42 (1980).

Young, Biloine W., and Melvin L. Fowler. *Cahokia, the Great Native American Metropolis.* Urbana, IL: University of Illinois Press, 2000.

### 1200

Bernier, Ronald M. *Temple Arts of Kerala: A South Indian Tradition.* New Delhi, India: S. Chand, 1982.

Bony, Jean. *French Gothic Architecture of the 12th and 13th Centuries.* Berkeley and Los Angeles: University of California Press, 1983.

Branner, Robert. *Burgundian Gothic Architecture.* London: A. Zwemmer, 1960.

Braunfels, Wolfgang. *Monasteries of Western Europe: The Architecture of the Orders.* Translated by Alastair Laing. London: Thames and Hudson, 1972.

Brumfield, William Craft. *A History of Russian Architecture.* Cambridge, UK: Cambridge University Press, 1993.

Buchwald, Hans Herbert. *Form, Style, and Meaning in Byzantine Church Architecture.* Brookfield, VT: Ashgate, 1999.

Cassidy-Welch, Megan. *Monastic Spaces and their Meanings: Thirteenth-Century English Cistercian Monasteries.* Turnhout, Belgium: Brepols, 2001.

Chandler, David P. *A History of Cambodia.* Boulder, CO: Westview Press, 2000

Coe, Michael D. *Angkor and the Khmer Civilization.* New York: Thames & Hudson, 2003.

Dehejia, Vidya, ed. *Royal Patrons and Great Temple Art.* Bombay, India: Marg Publications, 1988.

Diehl, Richard A. *Tula: The Toltec Capital of Ancient Mexico.* London: Thames and Hudson, 1983.

Dodds, Jerrilynn D., ed. *Al-Andalus: The Art of Islamic Spain.* New York: Metropolitan Museum of Art and Harry N. Abrams, 1992.

Duby, Georges. *The Age of the Cathedrals: Art and Society, 980–1420.* Translated by Eleanor Levieux and Barbara Thompson. Chicago, IL: University of Chicago Press, 1981.

Enzo, Carli, ed. *Il Duomo di Pisa: Il Battistero, il Campanile.* Florence, Italy: Nardini, 1989.

Erdmann, Kurt. *Das Anatolische Karavansaray des 13. Jahrhunderts.* Berlin: Verlag Gebr. Mann.

Findlay, Louis. *The Monolithic Churches of Lalibela in Ethiopia.* Le Caire, Egypt: Publications de la Socieltel d'archelologie copte, 1944.

Fukuyama, Toshio. *Heian Temples: Byodo-in and Chuson-ji.* Translated by Ronald K. Jones. New York: Weatherhill, 1976.

Grabar, Oleg. *The Alhambra.* Cambridge, MA: Harvard University Press, 1978.

Guo, Qinghua. *The Structure of Chinese Timber Architecture: Twelfth Century Design Standards and Construction Principles.* Gothenburg, Sweden: Chalmers University of Technology, School of Architecture, Department of Building Design, 1995.

Kinder, Terryl Nancy. *Cistercian Europe: Architecture of Contemplation.* Grand Rapids, MI: W.B. Eerdmans Pub. Co. and Cistercian Publications, 2002.

Kostof, Spiro. *Caves of God: The Monastic Environment of Byzantine Cappadocia.* Cambridge, MA: MIT Press, 1972.

Kraus, Henry. *Gold Was the Mortar: the Economics of Cathedral Building.* London and Boston: Routledge & Kegan Paul, 1979.

Krautheimer, Richard. *Early Christian and Byzantine Architecture.* Harmondsworth, UK, and New York: Penguin Books, 1986.

Liu, Dunzhen. *Chinese Classical Gardens of Suzhou.* Translated by Chen Lixian. Edited by Joseph C. Wang. New York: McGraw-Hill, 1993.

MacDonald, William Lloyd. *Early Christian and Byzantine Architecture: Great*

*Ages of World Architecture.* New York: G. Braziller, 1962.
Mannikka, Eleanor. *Angkor Wat: Time, Space, and Kingship.* Honolulu: University of Hawaii Press, 1996.
Moynihan, Elizabeth B. *Paradise as a Garden: In Persia and Mughal India.* New York: G. Braziller, 1979.
Nath, R. *History of Sultanate Architecture.* New Delhi, India: Abhinav Publications, 1978.
Noma, Seiroku. *The Arts of Japan.* Translated and adapted by John Rosenfield. Tokyo and New York: Kodansha International; New York: Harper & Row, 1978.
Ousterhout, Robert G. *Master Builders of Byzantium.* Princeton, NJ: Princeton University Press, 1999.
Panofsky, Erwin, ed. *Abbot Suger on the Abbey Church of St.-Denis and its Art Treasures.* Princeton, NJ: Princeton University Press, 1979.
Peroni, Adriano, ed. *Il Duomo di Pisa.* Modena, Italy: F. C. Panini, 1995.
Petruccioli, Attilio, ed. *Bukhara: The Myth and the Architecture.* Cambridge, MA: Aga Khan Program for Islamic Architecture, 1999.
Rabbat, Nasser. "Al-Azhar Mosque: An Architectural Chronicle of Cairo's History." (*Muqarnas 13*, 1996) p. 45–67.
Rowley, Trevor. *The Norman Heritage, 1055-1200.* London and Boston, MA: Routledge & Kegan Paul, 1983.
Simson, Otto Georg von. *The Gothic Cathedral: Origins of Gothic Architecture and the Medieval Concept of Order.* Princeton, NJ: Princeton University Press, 1988.
Starza, O. M. *The Jagannatha Temple at Puri: its Architecture, Art, and Culture.* Leiden, Netherlands, and New York: E. J. Brill, 1993.
Settar, S. *The Hoysala Temples.* Bangalore, India: Kala Yatra Publications, 1991-1992.
Strachan, Paul. *Imperial Pagan: Art and Architecture of Burma.* Honolulu: University of Hawaii Press, 1990.
Tobin, Stephen. *The Cistercians: Monks and Monasteries of Europe.* Woodstock, NY: Overlook Press, 1996.
Tozzer, Alfred M. *Chichén Itzá and its Cenote of Sacrifice: a Comparative Study of Contemporaneous Maya and Toltec.* Cambridge, MA: Peabody Museum, 1957.
Wang, Eugene Yuejin. *Shaping the Lotus Sutra: Buddhist Visual Culture in Medieval China.* Seattle: University of Washington Press, 2005.

**1400**

Ackerman, James S. *Palladio.* Harmondsworth, UK: Penguin, 1966.
Ballon, Hilary. *The Paris of Henri IV: Architecture and Urbanism.* Cambridge, MA: MIT Press, 1991.
Battisti, Eugenio. *Brunelleschi.* Translated by Robert Erich Wolf. Milan, Italy: Electa Architecture; London: Phaidon, 2002.
Blair, Sheila S., and Jonathan M. Bloom. *The Art and Architecture of Islam 1250–1800.* New Haven, CT: Yale University Press, 1994.
Borsi, Franco. *Leon Battista Alberti: The Complete Works.* London: Faber, 1989.
Bruschi, Arnaldo. *Bramante.* London: Thames and Hudson, 1977.
Burger, Richard L., and Lucy C. Salazar, eds. *Machu Picchu: Unveiling the Mystery of the Incas.* New Haven, CT: Yale University Press, 2004.
Chappell, Sally Anderson. *Cahokia: Mirror of the Cosmos.* Chicago, IL: University of Chicago Press, 2002.
Clarke, Georgia Roman House. *Renaissance Palaces: Inventing Antiquity in Fifteenth-Century Italy.* Cambridge, UK, and New York: Cambridge University Press, 2003.
Evans, Joan. *Monastic Architecture in France, from the Renaissance to the Revolution.* Cambridge, UK: Cambridge University Press, 1964.
Fedorov, Boris Nikolaevich. *Architecture of the Russian North, 12th–19th Centuries.* Translated by N. Johnstone. Leningrad, Russia: Aurora Art Publishers, 1976.
Goodwin, Godfrey. *A History of Ottoman Architecture.* London: Thames & Hudson, 1971.
Günay, Reha. *Sinan: The Architect and His Works.* Translated by Ali Ottoman. Istanbul, Turkey: Yapı-Endüstri Merkezi Yayınları, 1998.
Hall, John W., ed. *Japan in the Muromachi Age.* Ithaca, New York: East Asia Program, Cornell University, 2001.
Hitchcock, Henry Russell. *German Renaissance Architecture.* Princeton, NJ: Princeton University Press, 1981.
Howard, Deborah. *Jacopo Sansovino: Architecture and Patronage in Renaissance Venice.* New Haven, CT: Yale University Press, 1975.
Jarzombek, Mark. *On Leon Baptista Alberti: His Literary and Aesthetic Theories.* Cambridge, MA: MIT Press, 1989.
Kuran, Aptullah. *The Mosque in Early Ottoman Architecture.* Chicago, IL: University of Chicago Press, 1968.
Lieberman, Ralph. *The Church of Santa Maria dei Miracoli in Venice.* New York: Garland, 1986.
López Luján, Leonardo. *The Offerings of the Templo Mayor of Tenochtitlán.* Translated by Bernard R. Ortiz de Montellano and Thelma Ortiz de Montellano. Albuquerque: University of New Mexico Press, 2005.
Murray, Peter. *Renaissance Architecture.* Milan, Italy: Electa; New York: Rizzoli, 1985; 1978.
Pandya, Yatin. *Architectural Legacies of Ahmedabad.* Ahmedabad, India: Vastu-Shilpa Foundation for Studies and Research in Environmental Design, 2002.
Prinz, Wolfram Schloss. *Chambord und die Villa Rotonda in Vicenza.* Berlin: Mann, 1980.
Rabbat, Nasser O. *The Citadel of Cairo: A New Interpretation of Royal Mamluk Architecture.* Leiden, Netherlands, and New York: E. J. Brill, 1995.
Ryu, Je-Hun. *Reading the Korean Landscape.* Elizabeth, NJ: Hollym International, 2000.
Smith, Christine Hunnikin. *Architecture in the Culture of Early Humanism: Ethics, Aesthetics, and Eloquence, 1400–1470.* New York: Oxford University Press, 1992.
Sumner-Boyd, Hilary, and John Freely. *Strolling Through Istanbul: A Guide to the City.* New York: Kegan Paul, 2001; New York: Columbia University Press, 2003.
Tafuri, Manfredo. *Venice and the Renaissance.* Translated by Jessica Levine. Cambridge, MA: MIT Press, 1989.
Treib, Marc, and Ron Herman. *A Guide to the Gardens of Kyoto.* Tokyo: Shufunotomo Co., 1980.
Van der Ree, Paul, Gerrit Smienk, and Clemens Steenbergen. *Italian Villas and Gardens: A Corso di Disegno.* Munich, Germany: Prestel, 1992.
Vogt-Göknil, Ulya. *Living Architecture: Ottoman.* New York: Grosset & Dunlap, 1966.
Von Hagen, Victor Wolfgang. *The Desert Kingdoms of Peru.* New York: New American Library, 1968.
Wright, Kenneth R. *Machu Picchu: A Civil Engineering Marvel.* Reston, VA: American Society of Civil Engineers, 2000.
Zhu, Jianfei. *Chinese Spatial Strategies: Imperial Beijing, 1420–1911.* London and New York: Routledge Curzon, 2004.

**1600**

Argan, Giulio Carlo. *Michelangelo Architect.* Translated by Marion L. Grayson. London: Thames and Hudson, 1993.
Balas, Edith. *Michelangelo's Medici Chapel: A New Interpretation.* Philadelphia, PA: American Philosophical Society, 1995.
Begley, W. E., and Z. A. Desai. *Taj Mahal: The Illumined Tomb: An Anthology of Seventeenth-Century Mughal and European Documentary Sources.* Cambridge, MA: Aga Khan Program for Islamic Architecture; Seattle: University of Washington Press, 1989.

## BIBLIOGRAPHY


Blake, Stephen P. *Half the World: The Social Architecture of Safavid Isfahan, 1590–1722.* Costa Mesa, CA: Mazda Pub., 1999.

Blunt, Anthony. *Guide to Baroque Rome.* New York: Harper & Row, 1982.

Borsi, Francio. *Bernini.* Translated by Robert Erich Wolf. New York: Rizzoli, 1984.

Coaldrake, William Howard. *Gateways of Power: Edo Architecture and Tokugawa Authority, 1603-1951.* Ph.D. dissertation, Harvard University, 1983.

Coffin, David R. *The Villa in the Life of Renaissance Rome.* Princeton, NJ: Princeton University Press, 1979.

D'Amico, John F. *Renaissance Humanism in Papal Rome: Humanists and Churchmen on the Eve of the Reformation.* Baltimore, MD: Johns Hopkins University Press, 1983.

De Tolnay, Charles. *Michelangelo: Sculptor, Painter, Architect.* Princeton, NJ: Princeton University Press, 1974.

Dussel, Enrique D. *The Invention of the Americas: Eclipse of "The Other" and the Myth of Modernity.* Translated by Michael D. Barber. New York: Continuum, 1995.

Evans, Susan, and Joanne Pillsbury, eds. *Link Palaces of the Ancient New World.* A Symposium at Dumbarton Oaks, 10th and 11th October 1998. Washington, DC: Dumbarton Oaks Research Library and Collection, 2004.

Gotch, John. *Alfred Inigo Jones.* New York: B. Blom, 1968.

Guise, Anthony, ed. *The Potala of Tibet.* London and Atlantic Highlands, NJ: Stacey International, 1988.

Günay, Reha. *Sinan: The Architect and His Works.* Translated by Ali Ottoman. Istanbul, Turkey: Yapı-Endüstri Merkezi Yayınları, 1998.

Hersey, George L. *High Renaissance Art in St. Peter's and the Vatican: An Interpretive Guide.* Chicago, IL: University of Chicago Press, 1993.

Hughes, Quentin. *Malta: A Guide to the Fortifications.* Valletta, Malta: Said International, 1993.

Inaji, Toshir̄o. *The Garden as Architecture: Form and Spirit in the Gardens of Japan, China, and Korea.* Translated and adapted by Pamela Virgilio. Tokyo and New York: Kodansha International, 1998.

Ishimoto, Yasuhiro. *Katsura: Tradition and Creation in Japanese Architecture.* Text by Kenzo Tange. Photos by Yasuhiro Ishimoto. New Haven, CT: Yale University Press, 1972.

Krautheimer, Richard. *Roma Alessandrina: The Remapping of Rome under Alexander VII, 1655–1667.* Poughkeepsie, NY: Vassar College, 1982.

Lazzaro, Claudia. *The Italian Renaissance Garden: From the Conventions of Planting, Design, and Ornament to the Grand Gardens of 16th-Century Central Italy.* New Haven, CT: Yale University Press, 1990.

Lees-Milne, James. *Saint Peter's: The Story of Saint Peter's Basilica in Rome.* Boston, MA: Little, Brown, 1967; Chicago, IL: University of Chicago Press, 1986.

Lev, Evonne. *Propaganda and the Jesuit Baroque.* Berkeley and Los Angeles: University of California Press, 2004.

Meek, Harold Alan. *Guarino Guarini and his Architecture.* New Haven, CT: Yale University Press, 1988.

Michell, George. *The Vijayanagara Courtly Style: Incorporation and Synthesis in the Royal Architecture of Southern India, 15th-17th Centuries.* New Delhi and Manohar, India: American Institute of Indian Studies, 1992.

Millon, Henry A., ed. *Triumph of the Baroque: Architecture in Europe, 1600-1750.* New York: Rizzoli, 1999.

Nath, R. *Architecture of Fatehpur Sikri: Forms, Techniques & Concepts.* Jaipur, India: Historical Research Documentation Programme, 1988.

Nath, R. *History of Mughal Architecture.* New Delhi, India: Abhinav, 1982.

Necipog̃lu, Gülru. *The Age of Sinan: Architectural Culture in the Ottoman Empire.* London: Reaktion, 2005.

Paludan, Ann. *The Imperial Ming Tombs.* New Haven, CT: Yale University Press, 1981.

Partner, Peter. *Renaissance Rome, 1500–1559: A Portrait of a Society.* Berkeley and Los Angeles: University of California Press, 1976.

Rizvi, Kishwar. *Transformations in Early Safavid Architecture: The Shrine of Shaykh Safi al-din Ishaq Ardabili in Iran (1501–1629).* Ph.D. dissertation, Massachusetts Institute of Technology, 2000.

Sinding-Larsen, Amund. *The Lhasa Atlas: Traditional Tibetan Architecture and Townscape.* Boston, MA: Shambhala; New York: Random House, 2001.

Studio, Fianico. *The Medici Villas.* Florence, Italy: Libreria Editrice Fiorentina, 1980.

Summerson, Sir John Newenham. *Architecture in Britain, 1530 to 1830.* Harmondsworth, UK, and New York: Penguin Books, 1991.

Summerson, Sir John Newenham. *Inigo Jones.* New Haven, CT: Published for the Paul Mellon Centre for Studies in British Art by Yale University Press, 2000.

Thompson, Jon, and Canby, Sheila R., eds. *Hunt for Paradise: Court Arts of Safavid Iran, 1501–1576.* Milan, Italy: Skira; London: Thames & Hudson, 2003.

Walton, Guy. *Louis XIV's Versailles.* London: Viking, 1986.

Zhao, Lingyang. *Zheng He, Navigator, Discoverer and Diplomat.* Singapore: Unipress, 2001.


### 1700


Arciszewska, Barbara, and Elizabeth McKellar, eds. *Articulating British Classicism: New Approaches to Eighteenth-Century Architecture.* Hants, UK: Aldershot, 2004.

Arshi, Pardeep Singh. *The Golden Temple: History, Art, and Architecture.* New Delhi, India: Harman Pub. House, 1989.

Blunt, Anthony, ed. *Baroque and Rococo: Architecture and Decoration.* London: Elek, 1978.

Banerjea, Dhrubajyoti. *European Calcutta: Images and Recollections of a Bygone Era.* New Delhi, India: UBS Publishers' Distributors Pvt. Ltd.

Berger, Patricia Ann. *Empire of Emptiness: Buddhist Art and Political Authority in Qing China.* Honolulu: University of Hawaii Press, 2003.

Bourke, John. *Baroque Churches of Central Europe.* London: Faber and Faber, 1962.

Gollings, John. *City of Victory, Vijayanagara: The Medieval Hindu Capital of Southern India.* New York: Aperture, 1991.

Gutschow, Niels, and Erich Theophile, eds. *Patan: Architecture of a Historic Nepalese City.* Excerpts from a Proposed Research and Publication Project (1998–2000) of the Kathmandu Valley Preservation Trust. Kathmandu, Nepal: Kathmandu Valley Preservation Trust, 1998.

Erlanger, Philippe. *The Age of Courts and Kings: Manners and Morals, 1558–1715.* New York: Harper & Row, 1967.

Harman, William. *The Sacred Marriage of a Hindu Goddess.* Bloomington: Indiana University Press, 1989.

Herrmann, Wolfgang. *Laugier and Eighteenth-Century French Theory.* London: A. Zwemmer, 1962.

Herrmann, Wolfgang. *The Theory of Claude Perrault.* London: A. Zwemmer, 1973.

Metcalf, Thomas R. *Ideologies of the Raj.* Cambridge, UK, and New York: Cambridge University Press, 1994.

Otto, Christian F. *Space into Light: The Church Architecture of Balthasar Neumann.* New York: Architectural History Foundation, 1979.

Pierson, William H., Jr. *The Colonial and Neocolassical Styles.* Oxford, UK: Oxford University Press, 1970.

Roy, Ashim K. *History of the Jaipur City.* New Delhi, India: Manohar, 1978.

Sachdev, Vibhuti, and Giles Tillotson. *Building Jaipur: The Making of an Indian City.* London: Reaktion Books, 2002.

Sarkar, Jadunath. *A History of Jaipur, c. 1503–1938.* Hyderabad, India: Orient Longman, 1984.

Singh, Khushwant. *A History of the Sikhs.* New Delhi, India, and Oxford, UK:

Oxford University Press, 2004.
Sitwell, Sacheverell. *Baroque and Rococo.* London: Weidenfeld & Nicolson, 1967.
Smith, Bardwell, and Holly Baker Reynolds, eds. *The City as a Sacred Center: Essays on Six Asian Contexts.* Leiden, Netherlands, and New York: E. J. Brill, 1987.
Smith, Charles Saumarez. *The Building of Castle Howard.* London: Faber and Faber, 1990.
Smith, Woodruff D. *Consumption and the Making of Respectability, 1600–1800.* New York: Routledge, 2002.
Wittkower, Rudolf. *Palladio and Palladianism.* New York: G. Braziller, 1974.

**1800**

Aasen, Clarence T. *Architecture of Siam: A Cultural History Interpretation.* Kuala Lumpur, Malaysia, and New York: Oxford University Press, 1998.
Aldrich, Megan (et al.) *A. W. N. Pugin: Master of Gothic Revival.* Edited by Paul Atterbury. New Haven, CT: Published for the Bard Graduate Center for Studies in the Decorative Arts, New York, by Yale University Press, 1995.
Ayres, James. *Building the Georgian City.* New Haven, CT: Yale University Press, 1998.
Bastéa, Eleni. *The Creation of Modern Athens: Planning the Myth.* Cambridge, UK, and New York: Cambridge University Press, 2000.
Bergdoll, Barry. *Karl Friedrich Schinkel: An Architecture for Prussia.* New York: Rizzoli, 1994.
Brandon, James R., William P. Malm, and Donald H. Shively. *Studies in Kabuki: Its Acting, Music, and Historical Context.* Honolulu: University Press of Hawaii, 1978.
Brooks, Michael W. *John Ruskin and Victorian Architecture.* New Brunswick, NJ: Rutgers University Press, 1987.
Charlesworth, Michael, ed. *The Gothic Revival, 1720–1870: Literary Sources and Documents.* The Banks, Mountfield, UK: Helm Information, 2002.
Chattopadhyay, Swati. *Representing Calcutta: Modernity, Nationalism, and the Colonial Uncanny.* London: New York: Routledge, 2005.
Conner, Patrick. *Oriental Architecture in the West.* London: James and Hudson, 1979.
Crook, Joseph Mordaunt. *The Dilemma of Style: Architectural Ideas from the Picturesque to the Post-Modern.* London: Murray, 1987.
Drexler, Arthur, ed. *The Architecture of the École des Beaux-Arts.* New York: Museum of Modern Art; Cambridge, MA: MIT Press, 1977.
Du Prey, Pierre de la Ruffinière. *John Soane, The Making of an Architect.* Chicago, IL: University of Chicago Press, 1982.
Forêt, Philippe. *Mapping Chengde: The Qing Landscape Enterprise.* Honolulu: University of Hawaii Press, 2000.
Gosner, Pamela W. *Caribbean Georgian, the Great and Small Houses of the West Indies.* Washington, DC: Three Continents Press, 1982.
Herrmann, Wolfgang. *Gottfried Semper: In Search of Architecture.* Cambridge, MA: MIT Press, 1984.
Hitchcock, Henry Russell. *Early Victorian Architecture in Britain.* New Haven, CT: Yale University Press, 1954.
Kaufmann, Emil. *Architecture in the Age of Reason: Baroque and Postbaroque in England, Italy, and France.* New York: Dover Publications, 1968.
Leiter, Samuel L. *Kabuki Encyclopedia: An English-Language Adaptation of Kabuki Jiten.* Westport, CT: Greenwood Press, 1979.
Leiter, Samuel L., ed. *A Kabuki Reader: History and Performance.* Armonk, NY: M. E. Sharpe, 2002.
McCormick, Thomas. *Charles-Louis Clérisseau and the Genesis of Neo-Classicism.* New York: Architectural History Foundation; Cambridge, MA: MIT Press, 1990.
Metcalf, Thomas R. *An Imperial Vision: Indian Architecture and Britain's Raj.* Berkeley and Los Angeles: University of California Press, 1989.
Mitter, Partha. *Much Maligned Monsters: History of European Reactions to Indian Art.* Oxford, UK: Clarendon Press, 1977.
Moore, Elizabeth H., Philip Stott, and Suriyavudh Sukhasvasti. *Ancient Capitals of Thailand.* London: Thames and Hudson, 1996.
Port, Michael Harry. *Imperial London: Civil Government Building in London 1850–1915.* New Haven, CT: Published for the Paul Mellon Centre for Studies in British Art by Yale University Press, 1995.
Pundt, Hermann G. *Schinkel's Berlin: A Study in Environmental Planning.* Cambridge, MA: Harvard University Press, 1972.
Schumann-Bacia, Eva. *John Soane and the Bank of England.* London and New York: Longman, 1991.
Stewart, David B. *The Making of a Modern Japanese Architecture: 1868 to the Present.* Tokyo and New York: Kodansha International, 1987.
Summerson, Sir John Newenham. *Georgian London.* New York: C. Scribner's Sons, 1946.
Unrau, John. *Ruskin and St. Mark's.* London: Thames and Hudson, 1984.
Upton, Dell. *Architecture in the United States.* Oxford, UK, and New York: Oxford University Press, 1998.
Vernoit, Stephen. *Occidentalism: Islamic Art in the 19th Century.* New York: Nour Foundation in association with Azimuth Editions and Oxford University Press, 1997.
Vidler, Anthony. *The Writing of the Walls: Architectural Theory in the Late Enlightenment.* New York: Princeton Architectural Press, 1987.
Watkin, David. *German Architecture and the Classical Ideal.* Cambridge, MA: MIT Press, 1987.
Whittaker, Cynthia Hyla, ed. *Russia Engages the World, 1453–1825.* Cambridge, MA: Harvard University Press, 2003.

**1900**

Baker, Geoffrey H. *Le Corbusier: An Analysis of Form.* New York: Van Nostrand Reinhold; London: E & FN Spon, 1996.
Blau, Eve. *The Architecture of Red Vienna, 1919–1934.* Cambridge, MA: MIT Press, 1999.
Borsi, Franco. *The Monumental Era: European Architecture and Design, 1929–1939.* Translated by Pamela Marwood. New York: Rizzoli, 1987.
Bozdoğan, Sibel. *Modernism and Nation Building: Turkish Architectural Culture in the Early Republic.* Seattle: University of Washington Press, 2001.
Cody, Jeffrey W. *Exporting American Architecture, 1870–2000.* London and New York: Routledge, 2003.
Collins, Peter. *Changing Ideals in Modern Architecture, 1750–1950.* Montreal, Quebec, and Ithaca, NY: McGill-Queens University Press, 1998.
Colomina, Beatriz, ed. *Privacy and Publicity: Modern Architecture as Mass Media.* Cambridge, MA: MIT Press, 1996.
Condit, Carl W. *The Chicago School of Architecture: A History of Commercial and Public Building in the Chicago Area, 1875–1925.* Chicago, IL: University of Chicago Press, 1964.
Cunningham, Colin. *Victorian and Edwardian Town Halls.* London: Routledge & Kegan Paul, 1981.
Curtis, William J. R. *Modern Architecture since 1900.* Oxford, UK: Phaidon, 1982.
Dernie, David. *Victor Horta.* London: Academy Editions, 1995.
Dwivedi, Sharada and Rahul Mehrotra. *Bombay: The Cities Within.* Bombay, India: Eminence Designs Pvt. Ltd., 2001.
Egbert, Donald Drew and David Van Zanten, ed. *The Beaux-Arts Tradition in French Architecture.* Princeton, NJ: Princeton University Press, 1980.
Elleh, Nnambi. *African Architecture, Evolution and Transformation.* New York: McGraw-Hill, 1977.
Elleh, Nnamdi. *Architecture and Power in Africa.* Westport, CT: Praeger, 2002.
Evenson, Norma. *The Indian Metropolis: A View Toward the West.* New Haven, CT: Yale University Press, 1989.

## BIBLIOGRAPHY


Friedman, Mildred, ed. *De Stijl, 1917–1931: Visions of Utopia.* Minneapolis, MN: Walker Art Center; New York: Abbeville Press, 1982.

Golan, Romy. *Modernity and Nostalgia: Art and Politics in France between the Wars.* New Haven, CT: Yale University Press, 1995.

Guha-Thakorte, Tapati. *The Making of a New "Indian" Art: Artists, Aesthetics and Nationalism in Bengal, c. 1850–1920.* Cambridge, UK: Cambridge University Press, 1992.

Hildebrand, Grant. *The Wright Space: Pattern and Meaning in Frank Lloyd Wright's Houses.* Seattle: University of Washington Press, 1991.

Hosagrahar, Jyoti. *Indigenous Modernities: Negotiating Architecture and Urbanism.* London and New York: Routledge, 2006

Irving, Robert Grant. *Indian Summer—Lutyens, Baker, and Imperial Delhi.* New Haven, CT: Yale University Press, 1981.

Jarzombek, Mark. *Designing MIT: Bosworth's New Tech.* Boston, MA: Northeastern University Press, 2004.

Kopp, Anatole. *Constructivist Architecture in the USSR.* Translated by Sheila de Vallée. London: Academy Editions; New York: St. Martins Press, 1985.

Kruty, Paul, and Paul Sprague. *Two American Architects in India: Walter B. Griffin and Marion M. Griffin, 1935–1937.* Urbana-Champaign, IL: School of Architecture, University of Illinois, 1997.

Kultermann, Udo., ed. *Kenzo Tange, 1946–1969.* Architecture and Urban Design. Zürich, Switzerland: Verlag für Architektur Artemis, 1970.

Kultermann, Udo. *New Directions in African Architecture.* Translated by John Maass. London: Studio Vista, 1969.

Lahuerta, Juan José. *Antoni Gaudí, 1852–1926: Architecture, Ideology, and Politics.* Edited by Giovanna Crespi. Translated by Graham Thompson. Milan, Italy: Electa Architecture; London: Phaidon, 2003.

Levine, Neil. *The Architecture of Frank Lloyd Wright.* Princeton, NJ: Princeton University Press, 1996.

Lizon, Peter. *The Palace of the Soviets: The Paradigm of Architecture in the USSR.* Colorado Springs, CO: Three Continents Press, 1995.

Loyer, François. *Victor Horta: Hotel Tassel 1893–1895.* Translated by Susan Day. Brussels, Belgium: Archives d'Architecture Moderne, 1986.

Maciuika, John V. *Before the Bauhaus: Architecture, Politics, and the German State, 1890–1920.* New York: Cambridge University Press, 2005.

Markus, Thomas A., ed. *Order in Space and Society: Architectural Form and its Context in the Scottish Enlightenment.* Edinburgh, Scotland: Mainstream, 1982.

Martinell, César. *Gaudí: His Life, His Theories, His Work.* Translated by Judith Rohrer. Cambridge, MA: MIT Press, 1975.

Middleton, Robin, ed. *The Beaux-Arts and Nineteenth-Century French Architecture.* Cambridge, MA: MIT Press, 1982.

Moravánszky, Ákos. *Competing Visions: Aesthetic Invention and Social Imagination in Central European Architecture, 1867–1918.* Cambridge, MA: MIT Press, 1998.

Nitzan-Shiftan, Alona. *Isrealizing Jerusalem: The Encounter Between Architectural and National Ideologies 1967–1977.* Ph.D. dissertation, MIT, 2002.

Oechslin, Werner. *Otto Wagner, Adolf Loos, and the Road to Modern Architecture.* Translated by Lynette Widder. Cambridge, UK, and New York: Cambridge University Press, 2002.

Okoye, Ikemefuna. *"Hideous" Architecture: Feint and Resistance in Turn of the Century South-Eastern Nigerian Building.* Ph.D. dissertation, Massachusetts Institute of Technology, 1995.

Oldenburg, Veena Talwar. *The Making of Colonial Lucknow, 1856–1877.* Princeton, NJ: Princeton University Press, 1984.

Pawley, Martin. *Buckminster Fuller.* London: Trefoil Publications, 1990.

Pyla, Panayiota. *Ekistics, Architecture and Environmental Politics 1945–76: A Prehistory of Sustainable Development.* Ph.D. dissertation, Massachusetts Institute of Technology, 2002.

Rabbat, Nasser. "The Formation of the Neo-Mamluk Style in Modern Egypt" in *The Education of the Architect: Historiography, Urbanism and the Growth of Architectural Knowledge.* Edited by Martha Pollak. Cambridge, MA: MIT Press, 1997.

Rowland, Anna. *Bauhaus Source Book.* Oxford, UK: Phaidon, 1990.

Sarnitz, August. *Adolf Loos, 1870–1933: Architect, Cultural Critic, Dandy.* Köln, Germany, and Los Angeles: Taschen, 2003.

Scriver, Peter. *Rationalization, Standardization, and Control in Design: A Cognitive Historical Study of Architectural Design and Planning in the Public Works Department of British India, 1855–1901.* Delft, Netherlands: Publikatieburo Bouwkunde, Technische Universiteit Delft, 1994.

Scully, Vincent Joseph. *The Shingle Style Today: or, The Historian's Revenge.* New York: G. Braziller, 1974.

Sheaffer, M. P. A. *Otto Wagner and the New Face of Vienna.* Vienna, Austria: Compress, 1997.

Siry, Joseph. *Carson Pirie Scott: Louis Sullivan and the Chicago Department Store Chicago Architecture and Urbanism.* Chicago: University of Chicago Press, 1988.

———. *Unity Temple: Frank Lloyd Wright and Architecture for Liberal Religion.* Cambridge, UK: Cambridge University Press, 1996.

Starr, S. *Frederick Melnikov: Solo Architect in a Mass Society.* Princeton, NJ: Princeton University Press, 1978.

Steele, James. *Charles Rennie Mackintosh: Synthesis in Form.* London: Academy Editions, 1995.

Steiner, Hadas. *Bathrooms, Bubbles, and Systems: Archigram and the Landscapes of Transience.* Ph.D. dissertation, Massachusetts Institute of Technology, 2001.

Stern, Robert A. M. *New York 1930: Architecture and Urbanism between Two World Wars.* New York: Rizzoli, 1987.

Stern, Robert A. M., Gregory Gilmartin, and John Montague Massengale. *New York 1900: Metropolitan Architecture and Urbanism, 1890–1915.* New York: Rizzoli, 1983.

Stewart, Janet. *Fashioning Vienna: Adolf Loos's Cultural Criticism.* London: New York: Routledge, 2000.

Summerson, John Newenham. *The Turn of the Century: Architecture in Britain around 1900.* Glasgow, Scotland: University of Glasgow Press, 1976.

Toman, Rolf. *Vienna: Art and Architecture.* Cologne, Germany: Könemann, 1999.

Turnbull, Jeff, and Peter Y. Navaretti, eds. *The Griffins in Australia and India: The Complete Works and Projects of Walter Burley Griffin and Marion Mahony Griffin.* The Faculty of Architecture, Building and Planning, The University of Melbourne. Melbourne, Australia: Miegunyah Press, 1998

Turner, Paul Venable. *Campus: An American Planning Tradition.* New York: Architectural History Foundation: Cambridge, MA: MIT Press, 1984.

Turner, Paul Venable. *The Education of Le Corbusier.* New York: Garland Pub., 1977.

Van Zanten, David. *Designing Paris: The Architecture of Duban, Labrouste, Duc, and Vaudoyer.* Cambridge, MA: MIT Press, 1987.

Woods, Mary N. *From Craft to Profession: The Practice of Architecture in Nineteenth-Century America.* Berkeley and Los Angeles: University of California Press, 1999.

Yaha, Maha. *Unnamed Modernisms: National Ideologies and Historical Imaginaries in Beirut's Urban Architecture.* Ph.D. dissertation, Massachusetts Institute of Technology, 2004.

Zabel, Craig and Munshower, Susan Scott, eds. *American Public Architecture: European Roots and Native Expressions.* University Park, PA: Penn State University Press, 1989.

**1950**

Baljeu, Joost. *Theo van Doesburg.* London: Studio Vista, 1974.

Bettinotti, Massimo, ed. *Kenzo Tange, 1946–1996: Architecture and Urban Design.* Milan, Italy: Electa, 1996.

Cannell, Michael T. *I.M. Pei: Mandarin of Modernism.* New York: Carol Southern Books, 1995.

Cavalcanti, Lauro. *When Brazil Was Modern: Guide to Architecture, 1928–1960.* Translated by Jon Tolman. New York: Princeton Architectural Press, 2003.

Cohen, Jean-Louis. *Le Corbusier and the Mystique of the USSR: Theories and Projects for Moscow, 1928–1936.* Translated by Kenneth Hylton. Princeton, NJ: Princeton University Press, 1992.

Colquhoun, Alan. *Modernity and the Classical Tradition: Architectural Essays, 1980–1987.* Cambridge, MA: MIT Press, 1989.

Curtis, William J. R. *Balkrishna Doshi, An Architecture for India.* New York: Rizzoli, 1988.

Curtis, William J. R. *Le Corbusier: Ideas and Forms.* New York: Rizzoli, 1986.

Doxiades, Konstantinos Apostolouv. *Ecology and Ekistics.* Edited by Gerald Dix. Boulder, CO: Westview Press, 1977.

Ellin, Nan. *Postmodern Urbanism.* New York: Princeton Architectural Press, 1999.

Fromonot, Francoise. *Glenn Murcutt: Buildings + Projects 1969–2003.* London: Thames & Hudson, 2003.

Grigor, Talinn. *Cultivat(ing) Modernities: The Society for National Heritage, Political Propaganda, and Public Architecture in Twentieth-Century Iran.* Ph.D. dissertation, Massachusetts Institute of Technology, 2005.

Ghirardo, Diane Yvonne. *Architecture after Modernism.* New York: Thames and Hudson, 1996.

———. *Building New Communities: New Deal America and Fascist Italy.* Princeton, NJ: Princeton University Press, 1989.

Ibelings, Hans. *Supermodernism: Architecture in the Age of Globalization.* Translated by Robyn de Jong-Dalziel. Rotterdam, Netherlands: NAi Publishers, 2002.

Jencks, Charles. *Kings of Infinite Space: Frank Lloyd Wright & Michael Graves.* New York: St. Martin's Press, 1985.

———. *The Architecture of the Jumping Universe: A Polemic: How Complexity Science is Changing Architecture and Culture.* London: Academy Editions, 1997.

———. *The Language of Post-Modern Architecture.* New York: Rizzoli, 1991.

Khan, Hasan-Uddin. *Charles Correa.* Singapore, Malaysia: Concept Media; New York: Aperture, 1987.

Kirkham, Pat. *Charles and Ray Eames: Designers of the Twentieth Century.* Cambridge, MA: MIT Press, 1995.

Klotz, Heinrich. *The History of Postmodern Architecture.* Translated by Radka Donnell. Cambridge, MA: MIT Press, 1988.

Lodder, Christina. *Russian Constructivism.* New Haven, CT: Yale University Press, 1983.

Loomis, John A. *Revolution of Forms: Cuba's Forgotten Art Schools.* New York: Princeton Architectural Press, 1999.

Makiya, Kanan. *The Monument: Art, Vulgarity, and Responsibility in Iraq.* London: Andre Deutsch, 1991.

McCoy, Esther. *Case Study Houses, 1945–1962.* Los Angeles: Hennessey & Ingalls, 1977.

Merkel, Jayne. *Eero Saarinen.* London and New York: Phaidon, 2005.

Mumford, Eric, ed. *Modern Architecture in St. Louis: Washington University and Postwar American Architecture, 1948–1973.* St. Louis, MO: School of Architecture, Washington University; Chicago: distributed by the University of Chicago Press, 2004.

Murray, Peter. *The Saga of the Sydney Opera House: The Dramatic Story of the Design and Construction of the Icon of Modern Australia.* New York: Spon Press, 2003.

Neuhart, John. *Eames Design: The Work of the Office of Charles and Ray Eames.* New York: Harry N. Abrams, 1989.

Nilsson, Sten. *The New Capitals of India, Pakistan and Bangladesh.* Lund, Sweden: Studentlitteratur, 1973.

Pommer, Richard and Otto, Christian F. *Weissenhof 1927 and the Modern Movement in Architecture.* Chicago, IL: University of Chicago Press, 1991.

Portoghesi, Paolo. *Postmodern, the Architecture of the Postindustrial Society.* New York: Rizzoli, 1983.

Prakash, Vikramaditya. *Chandigarh's Le Corbusier: The Struggle for Modernity in Postcolonial India.* Seattle: University of Washington Press, 2002.

Robson, David. *Geoffrey Bawa: The Complete Works.* London: Thames & Hudson, 2002.

Skidmore, Owings & Merrill. *The Architecture of Skidmore, Owings & Merrill, 1950–1962.* New York: Praeger, 1962.

Smith, Elizabeth A. T. and Michael Darling. *The Architecture of R. M. Schindler.* New York: Harry N. Abrams, 2001.

Stanford Anderson, ed. *Eladio Dieste: Innovation in Structural Art.* New York: Princeton Architectural Press, 2004.

Stäubli, Willy. *Brasilia.* London: Leonard Hill Books, 1966.

Steele, James. *An Architecture for People: The Complete Works of Hassan Fathy.* New York: Whitney Library of Design, 1997.

Steele, James. *Architecture for Islamic Societies Today.* London: Academy Editions; Berlin: Ernst & Sohn; New York: St. Martin's Press, 1994.

Stewart, David B. *The Making of a Modern Japanese Architecture: 1868 to the Present.* Tokyo and New York: Kodansha International, 1987.

Svácha, Rostislav. *The Architecture of New Prague, 1895–1945.* Translated by Alexandra Büchler. Cambridge, MA: MIT Press, 1995.

Taylor, Jennifer. *Australian Architecture Since 1960.* Sydney, Australia: Law Book Co., 1986.

Underwood, David Kendrick. *Oscar Niemeyer and the Architecture of Brazil.* New York: Rizzoli, 1994.

von Vegesack, Alexander, ed. *Czech Cubism: Architecture, Furniture, and Decorative Arts, 1910–1925.* New York: Princeton Architectural Press, 1992.

Weston, Richard. *Alvar Aalto.* London: Phaidon Press, 1995.

Zukowsky John, ed. *The Many Faces of Modern Architecture: Building in Germany between the World Wars.* Munich, Germany, and New York: Prestel, 1994.

# Photo Credits

The publishers wish to thank the institutions and individuals who have kindly provided photographic materials for use in this book. In all cases, every effort has been made to contact the copyright holders, but should there be any errors or omissions the publishers would be pleased to insert the appropriate acknowledgment in any subsequent edition of this book.

1.25 Catalhöyük Research Project
1.38 Paul Drougas

2.1 CM Dixon/ HIP/The Image Works
2.5, 2.6 © J.M. Kenoyer, Courtesy Dept. of Archaeology and Museums, Govt. of Pakistan
2.9 Courtesy of the Oriental Institute of the University of Chicago
2.17, 2.19 David Friedman
2.28 Tor Eigeland/Alamy
2.40 Peter Adams/Digital Vision
2.44 © Lawrence Migdale
2.48 Photo Courtesy of Haresh Bhojwani
2.50 AAAC Ltd

3.2 Nasser Rabbat
3.9 David Friedman
3.11, 3.15 Nasser Rabbat
3.16 Robert Harding Picture Library Ltd/Alamy
3.22 Sibel Bozdogan
3.31, 3.35 David Friedman
3.38 Stanford Anderson

4.2 Gnu Free Documentation License, Version 1.2 (http://www.gnu.org/copyleft/fdl.html)
4.5 Photo Courtesy of Mag. Alfred Diem
4.10 © Ben Hewitt, 2006
4.16 The Metropolitan Museum of Art, Charlotte C. and John C. Weber Collection, Gift of Charlotte C. and John C. Weber through the Live Oak Foundation, 1988 (1988.20.4ab-.5ab) Photograph © 1989 The Metropolitan Museum of Art
4.21 Library of Congress, Prints & Photographs Division, LC-B2- 71-9[P&P]
4.25 Visual Resources Collection, CAUP © University of Washington
4.34 www.arch-imagelibrary.com
4.46 The Art Archive

5.2, 5.7 Visual Resources Collection, CAUP © University of Washington
5.8 Gnu Free Documentation License, Version 1.2 (http://www.gnu.org/copyleft/fdl.html)
5.27, 5.32, 5.34 Visual Resources Collection, CAUP © University of Washington
5.38 PhotoDisc, Inc.
5.47, 5.50 Stanford Anderson
5.58, 5.59 Nasser Rabbat
5.61 Photo Courtesy of Nikhil Karkera
5.64 John and Susan Huntington. Courtesy of the John C. and Susan L. Huntington Photographic Archive of Buddhist and Related Art, The Ohio State University.
5.70 Uniphoto/AAA Collection
5.73 Peter and Jackie Main
5.78 The Art Archive/Archaeological and Ethnological Museum Guatemala City/Dagli Orti

6.5 Visual Resources Collection, CAUP © University of Washington
6.15 Photo by Claude Dupras www.claude.dupras.com
6.19 The Art Archive/Bibliothèque des Arts Décoratifs Paris/Dagli Orti
6.26 Visual Resources Collection, CAUP © University of Washington
6.29 © Walter Bibikow/Panoramic Images
6.34 Photo taken by Philippe J. Moore
6.43 David Friedman
6.47, 6.50 Stanford Anderson
6.53 John and Susan Huntington. Courtesy of the John C. and Susan L. Huntington Photographic Archive of Buddhist and Related Art, The Ohio State University.
6.60 E. Stewart © 2003
6.62 Dinodia/Omni-Photo Communications, Inc.
6.66 John and Susan Huntington. Courtesy of the John C. and Susan L. Huntington Photographic Archive of Buddhist and Related Art, The Ohio State University.
6.67 Dinodia/Omni-Photo Communications, Inc.
6.69 Tibor Bognar/Alamy
6.79 © Wesley Shu
6.91 The Art Archive/Dagli Orti

7.2 Bryn Mawr College, Lantern Slides of Classical Antiquity.
7.5 Photo by Adrienne Bassett
7.7, 7.10 David Friedman
7.11 Gnu Free Documentation License, Version 1.2 (http://www.gnu.org/copyleft/fdl.html)
7.15 Jeffrey A. Cohen
7.16 Visual Resources Collection, CAUP © University of Washington
7.23 Sibel Bozdogan
7.38 www.arch-imagelibrary.com
7.41, 7.44 Melanie Michailidis
7.47 John and Susan Huntington. Courtesy of the John C. and Susan L. Huntington Photographic Archive of Buddhist and Related Art, The Ohio State University.
7.53 With special permission by Prof. Dr. S.-W. Breckle
7.54 Brian & Tonette Vaughn-Go
7.62 Photo taken by Eamonn Lawlor
7.67 Creative Commons Attribution ShareAlike License v. 2.5 (http://creativecommons.org/licenses/by-sa/2.5/)
7.70, 7.71, 7.74, 7.75 John Lopez

8.3 Photograph taken by A.J. Rao
8.5 www.arch-imagelibrary.com
8.6 Peter and Jackie Main
8.8, 8.12 www.arch-imagelibrary.com
8.13 Peter and Jackie Main
8.14 John and Susan Huntington. Courtesy of the John C. and Susan L. Huntington Photographic Archive of Buddhist and Related Art, The Ohio State University.
8.17 © Dr. Volker Thewalt, www.bamiyan.de
8.18 © Wesley Shu
8.19 Creative Commons Attribution ShareAlike License v. 2.5 (http://creativecommons.org/licenses/by-sa/2.5/)
8.30 Bildarchiv Monheim GmbH/Alamy
8.37, 8.44 David Friedman
8.46 Photo Courtesy of Angel Lahoz
8.48 Talinn Grigor
8.52 Dia-Store
8.53 Jeffrey Tapley © 2001
8.56 Photo Courtesy of Jolene Howard Kennedy
8.59 Nicole Galeazzi/Omni-Photo Communications, Inc.
8.61 All Rights Reserved 2005 Ken Wolf
8.63 National Land Image Information (Color Aerial Photograph), Ministry of Land, Infrastructure and Transport

9.3 Gnu Free Documentation License, Version 1.2 (http://www.gnu.org/copyleft/fdl.html)
9.5 © 1967, Spencer H. Daines
9.6 David Friedman
9.12 Jeffrey A. Cohen
9.15 Ricardo Barquín Molero/Cosmonauta.org
9.29, 9.31, 9.33 Talinn Grigor
9.34 John and Susan Huntington. Courtesy of the John C. and Susan L. Huntington Photographic Archive of Buddhist and Related Art, The Ohio State University.
9.39, 9.41, 9.43 R. D. MacDougall Collection. © Cornell University
9.45 Uniphoto/AAA Collection
9.49 Mark L. Brack

10.6, 10.11 Uniphoto/AAA Collection
10.24, 10.27 John and Susan Huntington. Courtesy of the John C. and Susan L. Huntington Photographic Archive of Buddhist and Related Art, The Ohio State University.
10.28 R. D. MacDougall Collection. © Cornell University.
10.31 Dinodia/Omni-Photo Communications
10.33 Photo by Bethany Crome
10.53 Lars Jones, 1994, Courtesy of the Aga Khan Visual Archive, MIT
10.54 Talinn Grigor. 2000, Courtesy of the Aga Khan Visual Archive, MIT
10.58 www.arch-imagelibrary.com
10.60 Walter Denny, 1984, Courtesy of the Aga Khan Visual Archive, MIT
10.61 Nasser Rabbat
10.62 Ms. Freia Lorimer; Glenn Dale, MD
10.63 Photo by Paul Walter
10.66 Prisma/AAA Collection
10.75 Holly Young
10.78 Creative Commons Attribution ShareAlike License v. 2.5 (http://creativecommons.org/licenses/by-sa/2.5/)
10.85 The Art Archive/Dagli Orti
10.87 Church of the Holy Cross (photo), Byzantine/Aktamar, Lake Van, Turkey/ Bridgeman Art Library

10.88 Paul Drougas
10.92 View of the Temple of the Cross, Maya, 7th-8th century (photo), NO_DATA/Palenque, Chiapas State, Mexico, Index/Bridgeman Art Library
10.94 E. Leduc and A. Pevehouse
10.97 Dayna Bateman © 2005

11.2 Edifice/Adrian Mayer
11.8, 11.9 www.arch-imagelibrary.com
11.22, 11.23 R. D. MacDougall Collection. © Cornell University.
11.26, 11.28 John and Susan Huntington. Courtesy of the John C. and Susan L. Huntington Photographic Archive of Buddhist and Related Art, The Ohio State University.
11.32 Copyright © 2006 Stanley Rowin
11.36 Karsten Petersen
11.42, 11.46, 11.47 Talinn Grigor. 2000, Courtesy of the Aga Khan Visual Archive, MIT
11.48 Walter Denny, 1984, Courtesy of the Aga Khan Visual Archive, MIT
11.51, 11.52 Yasser Tabbaa, 1984, Courtesy of the Aga Khan Visual Archive, MIT
11.54 Nasser Rabbat
11.57 Sheila Blair and Jonathan Bloom
11.59, 11.60 Nasser Rabbat
11.62 D/Roger-Viollet/The Image Works
11.63 Sheila Blair and Jonathan Bloom
11.68 Photograph by Sara Yeomans
11.75, 11.83 Photo by John Pile
11.87 Nasser Rabbat
11.91 Annick Filion
11.92 David Friedman
11.95, 11.96 © Scott Foy (www.flickr.com/photos/scofo76)
11.98 David Friedman
11.102 www.thu.no
11.106, 11.107, 11.108 Photograph by Jamie Kamel Fitzgerald © 2005
11.109, 11.111 Visual Resources Collection, CAUP © University of Washington

12.10 Arindam Dutta
12.11 © Photo Josef Fojtik
12.16 Poo Kuan Hoong
12.24 Alfred da Costa, 1988, Courtesy of the Aga Khan Visual Archive, MIT
12.25 Samer Ajam
12.33 John and Susan Huntington. Courtesy of the John C. and Susan L. Huntington Photographic Archive of Buddhist and Related Art, The Ohio State University.
12.34 Dinodia/Omni-Photo Communications, Inc.
12.38 Creative Commons Attribution ShareAlike v. 2.0 (http://creativecommons.org/licenses/by-sa/2.0/) License
12.41, 12.49 Jeffrey A. Cohen
12.52, 12.53 Albert Chi-Jiun Change: http://www.flickr.com/photos/skymyr/
12.60 David Friedman
12.63 Visual Resources Collection, CAUP © University of Washington
12.64 Photo by John Pile
12.67, 12.69 David Friedman
12.71 Photo by William C. Brumfield
12.73, 12.74 Walter Denny, 1984, Courtesy of the Aga Khan Visual Archive, MIT
12.80, 12.83, 12.85 John Lopez

13.6 Photo by J. Stander
13.9 Visual Resources Collection, CAUP © University of Washington
13.12, 13.13, 13.14 Jerry V. Finrow
13.15 Photo by Qlingling Zhang, qlinrong@gmail.com
13.25 Kang Young Hwan
13.26 Vernon Fowler
13.29 © 2006 by John N. Miller. All Rights Reserved.
13.34, 13.35 Melanie Michailidis
13.36 The Aga Khan Program for Islamic Architecture, MIT
13.38 Mark Gallop
13.41, 13.43 Rajagopalan Palamadai, 1981, The Aga Khan Program for Islamic Architecture, MIT
13.47, 13.48 Walter Denny, 1984, Courtesy of the Aga Khan Visual Archive, MIT
13.50 www.arch-imagelibrary.com
13.52 © 2005 Raheli Millman
13.54 Walter Denny, 1984, Courtesy of the Aga Khan Visual Archive, MIT
13.56 David Friedman
13.57 Eddie Gerald/Alamy
13.73 Photo Courtesy of Jessica L. Stewart
13.77 Natasha Sandmeier
13.81 David Friedman
13.90 Creative Commons Attribution 2.5 (http://creativecommons.org/licenses/by/2.5/) License
13.103 Mark L. Brack
13.104 David Friedman

14.8 Photo by Michael Reeve, © 2004. Gnu Free Documentation License, Version 1.2 (http://www.gnu.org/copyleft/fdl.html)
14.10 © Wesley Shu
14.14 Gauvin Bailey, 1992, The Aga Khan Program for Islamic Architecture, MIT
14.31 Shamim Javed, 1986, The Aga Khan Program for Islamic Architecture, MIT
14.34 Sheila Blair and Jonathan Bloom, 1984,The Aga Khan Program for Islamic Architecture, MIT
14.40 Archivo Digital/Maria de Lourdes Alonso
14.42 © Wesley Shu
14.54 David Friedman
14.58 Visual Resources Collection, CAUP © University of Washington
14.67 Elizabeth Jones
14.72 Copyright Dries Bessels
14.75 Visual Resources Collection, CAUP © University of Washington
14.78 Photo by John Pile
14.80, 14.86, 14.88 Visual Resources Collection, CAUP © University of Washington
14.91 Photo by Eugene Zelenko, Wikipedia
14.95 Photo by Valerio Impicciatore
14.109 ©Mary Evans Picture Library/The Image Works
14.111 Jeremy E. Meyer ©2005
14.137, 14.141 Visual Resources Collection, CAUP © University of Washington
14.147 John and Susan Huntington. Courtesy of the John C. and Susan L. Huntington Photographic Archive of Buddhist and Related Art, The Ohio State University.
14.151, 14.153, 14.154, 14.155, 14.156 Walter Denny

15.1 Kyla Tienhaara
15.6 Photo by Domenico Ribeiro © 2006
15.11, 15.13, 15.18, 15.21 Visual Resources Collection, CAUP © University of Washington
15.22 Chris Howarth/Alamy
15.39 Visual Resources Collection, CAUP © University of Washington
15.40 Photo by John Pile
15.45 K-PHOTOS/Alamy
15.46 Copyright 2006 Anne Buchanan
15.48 Michael Bordoni
15.50 Jorge Otero-Pailos
15.55, 15.56 Photo by John Pile
15.58 Bildarchiv Monheim GmbH/Alamy
15.60 Photo by Andreas Tille
15.62 © 2006 by Ragnar Schierholz, published originally on www.flickr.com/raschi/photos
15.63 Library of Congress, Prints and Photographs Division, Historic American Buildings Survey or Historic American Engineering Record, HABS VA, 97-____,4-3.
15.64 Library of Congress, Prints and Photographs Division, Historic American Buildings Survey or Historic American Engineering Record, HABS VA, 97-____,4-69.
15.66, 15.72 Visual Resources Collection, CAUP © University of Washington
15.74 Arindam Dutta
15.78 © Wesley Shu
15.84 The Art Archive/Bibliothèque des Arts Décoratifs Paris/Dagli Orti
15.97 Phil Beck
15.104 Photograph by Mo Rizwanullah, Some rights reserved, 2006
15.106 www.arch-imagelibrary.com
16.2 Mohamad Hisyam Mohamad
16.3 Christopher Esing
16.5 Gnu Free Documentation License, Version 1.2 (http://www.gnu.org/copyleft/fdl.html)
16.6 Visual Resources Collection, CAUP © University of Washington
16.10 Photo by John Pile
16.21 Visual Resources Collection, CAUP © University of Washington, Norm Johnston, 1977
16.40 Photograph by Frank W. Peters, some rights reserved.
16.43 Courtesy of Eastern State Penitentiary Historic Site, Philadelphia/Photo: Andrew J. Simcox, 1997
16.45 Courtesy, Bury St. Edmonds Past and Present Society
16.49, 16.50 JTB Photo
16.54 Photo by Jonas Kolpin, Berlin, Germany
16.59 Jon Arnold Images/Alamy

16.60 Walter Denny
16.68, 16.73 Visual Resources Collection, CAUP © University of Washington
16.74 Don Kasak
16.75 Library of Congress, Prints and Photographs Division, Historic American Buildings Survey or Historic American Engineering Record, HABS SC, 10-CHAR, 6-24.
16.77 Library of Congress, Prints and Photographs Division, Historic American Buildings Survey or Historic American Engineering Record, HABS RI ,3-NEWP, 29-4.
16.80 Mark Tecessini
16.81 Library of Congress, Prints and Photographs Division, Historic American Buildings Survey or Historic American Engineering Record, HABS SC, 10-CHAR, 41-5.
16.83 J. Bythell sJs Files, 2006
16.90 Photograph by Simon Ho

17.4 Collection Mauruszat (Berlin, Germany)
17.15 Ting Ting Cheng from Taiwan
17.16 Photograph by Brian K. Webb
17.19 Dinodia/Omni-Photo Communications, Inc.
17.22 Amanda Brown
17.30 Visual Resources Collection, CAUP © University of Washington
17.33 Gnu Free Documentation License, Version 1.2 (http://www.gnu.org/copyleft/fdl.html)
17.36 Photo by John Pile
17.39 © 2005 Richard Ridge. Reprinted with the author's permission.
17.41 Photo: Eric Harley Parker © 2006
17.45 Robert Cowherd
17.47 © Neil Paknadel
17.52 Visual Resources Collection, CAUP © University of Washington
17.59 Library of Congress, Prints and Photographs Division, Historic American Buildings Survey or Historic American Engineering Record, HABS MO, 96-SALU, 49-4.
17.62 Faisal Hasan
17.72 Mark L. Brack
17.74, 17.77, 17.78 Visual Resources Collection, CAUP © University of Washington
17.82 Attribution ShareAlike 2.5 (http://creativecommons.org/licenses/by-sa/2.5/) License
17.84 Photo taken by Manar Hussain
17.85 Creon
17.86 Erwin de Bliek
17.94 Library of Congress, Prints and Photographs Division, Historic American Buildings Survey or Historic American Engineering Record, HAER MICH, 82-HAMT, 1-8.
17.97 Photo by John Pile
17.98 Jonathan Brusby
17.110 Dinodia/Omni-Photo Communications, Inc.
17.111 Lucky Look/Omni-Photo Communications
17.127 Martin Chad Kellogg © 2006
17.132 Mark L. Brack
17.143 Ashish Nangia

18.19 Sibel Bozdogan
18.23 Courtesy, The Estate of R. Buckminster Fuller
18.24, 18.26 The Fuller Projection Map design is a trademark of the Buckminster Fuller Institute ©1938, 1967 & 1992. All rights reserved. www.bfi.org
18.27 Photo by John Pile
18.33 Creative Commons Attribution ShareAlike License v. 2.5 (http://creativecommons.org/licenses/by-sa/2.5/)
18.34, 18.35 Erik Jenkins
18.39 Edifice/Adrian Forty
18.40 Photo by John Pile
18.43 Mark L. Brack
18.50 Visual Resources Collection, CAUP © University of Washington
18.55 Daniel Modell © 2005
18.58 © CORBIS
18.60 Arindam Dutta
18.62 © Hagen Stier, ArchitekturFotografie
18.65 Samuel Barnett, 2004
18.66 Mark L. Brack
18.68 Michael Osman
18.73 © Kai Sun Luk
18.75 © Ed McCauley, 2003
18.84 Peter Cohan
18.88 Visual Resources Collection, CAUP © University of Washington; photo by Norm Johnston 1982
18.90 Bruno Kussler Marques/2005
18.103, 18.104 Photo by John Pile
18.106 Visual Resources Collection, CAUP © University of Washington
18.110, 18.111 Stanford Anderson
18.112 Alfredo Brillembourg/U-TT.com/2006
18.113 © 2006 Stephen Silverman
18.119 © Pan Bohui
18.120, 18.121 Fabiola Lopez-Duran
18.127 Osamu Murai
18.129 Source: Nnamdi Elleh, African Architecture: Evolution & Transformation
18.132 © Bradley C. Fich/f-stop.com 2002
18.133 www.arch-imagelibrary.com
18.137 Angelo O. Mercado
18.138 Jerzy Kociatkiewicz
18.144 Hassan Uddin Khan
18.151 Photo by John Pile
18.154 © Wesley Shu
18.156 Visual Resources Collection, CAUP © University of Washington
18.159 Matthew Tsui

19.1 Licensed under Creative Commons Attribution ShareAlike 1.0 (http://creativecommons.org/licenses/by-sa/1.0/) License
19.2 John Stamets
19.3 (left) Santiago Calatrava and Paolo Roselli
19.3 (right) Santiago Calatrava and Alan Karchmer
19.4 Sandeep Virmani © Hunnarshala
19.5 Jared Fulton
19.6 Licensed under Creative Commons Attribution ShareAlike 2.0 (http://creativecommons.org/licenses/by-sa/2.0/) License

C1 David Harding
C2 Olena Sullivan
C3 Maruizio Porro
C4 Flat Earth
C5 Photo Courtesy of Angel Lahoz
C7 Photo by Baabak Afshar. Creative Commons License: Attribution-NonCommercial-ShareAlike 2.0: http://creativecommons.org/licenses/by-nc-sa/2.0/
C9 Photo by Elzbieta Twitchen
C10 Susan Novak, 2006. All Rights Reserved.
C11, C12 Corbis Digital Stock
C13 Photo by Loren Picco
C14, C15 Corbis Digital Stock
C16 © Rob McMichael - www.pixelbox.net
C17 Fahad AlSharhan
C18 Photograph courtesy Alasdair Milne
C19 Walter Denny
C20 © Grant Matthews http://www.grantmatthews.com
C22 Alamy/Florian Monheim
C23 Corbis Digital Stock
C24 Photographed and Copyrighted by Justin Evans, homeinbrighton.co.uk
C25 Photograph by Simon Ho
C27 Photo by Rob Williams www.orangejack.com
C28 Visual Resources Collection, CAUP © University of Washington
C29 © Wesley Shu
C30 Alpen/Walker Images
C31 Photo by David Dennis. This photo is public and uses a CreativeCommons.org Attribution-Share Alike License.

# Index

**F**

**M**